Street by Street

LONDON

5th edition May 2007
© Automobile Association Developments Limited 2007

Original edition printed May 2001

This product includes map data licensed from Ordnance Survey® with the permission of the Controller of Her Majesty's Stationery Office. © Crown copyright 2007. All rights reserved. Licence number 100021153.

The copyright in all PAF is owned by Royal Mail Group plc.

Published by AA Publishing (a trading name of Automobile Association Developments Limited, whose registered office is Fanum House, Basing View, Basingstoke, Hampshire RG21 4EA. Registered number 1878835).

Produced by the Mapping Services Department of The Automobile Association. (A03278)

A CIP Catalogue record for this book is available from the British Library.

Printed by Oriental Press in Dubai

Key to map pages	ii-iii
Key to map symbols	iv-1
Enlarged map pages	2-19
Main map pages	20-217
Index – towns & villages	218-219
Index – streets	220-307
Index – featured places	308-329
Acknowledgements	330

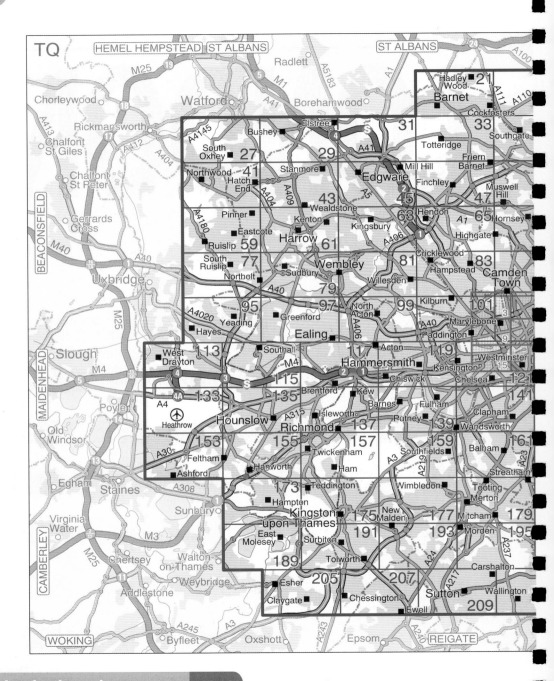

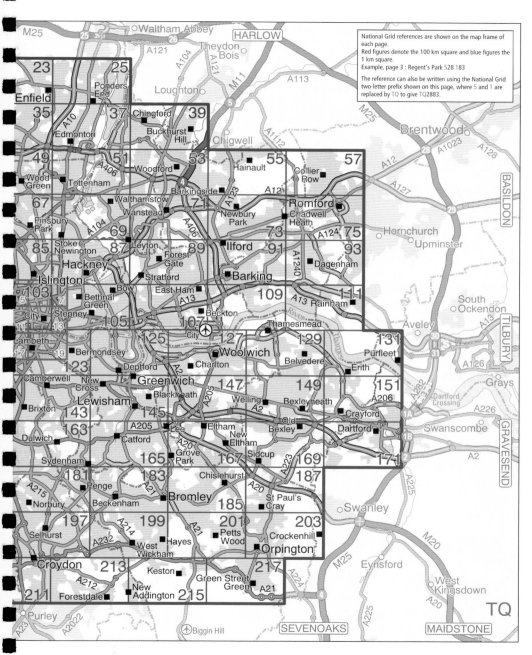

National Grid references are shown on the map frame of each page.
Red figures denote the 100 km square and blue figures the 1 km square.
Example, page 3 : Regent's Park 528 183

The reference can also be written using the National Grid two-letter prefix shown on this page, where 5 and 1 are replaced by TQ to give TQ2883.

3.6 inches to 1 mile **Scale of main map pages** 1:17,500

| 0 | 1/2 | miles | 1 |

| 0 | 1/2 | 1 | kilometres | 1 1/2 |

iv

	Motorway & junction		Level crossing

Junction 9 — Motorway & junction

Services — Motorway service area

Primary road single/dual carriageway

Services — Primary road service area

A road single/dual carriageway

B road single/dual carriageway

Other road single/dual carriageway

Minor/private road, access may be restricted

One-way street

Pedestrian area

Track or footpath

Road under construction

Road tunnel

Parking

Park & Ride

Bus/coach station

Railway & main railway station

Railway & minor railway station

Underground station

Docklands Light Railway (DLR) station

Light railway & station

LC — Level crossing

Tramway

Ferry route

Airport runway

County, administrative boundary

Congestion Charging Zone *

Charge-free routes through the Charging Zone

17 — Page continuation 1:17,500

3 — Page continuation to enlarged scale 1:10,000

River/canal, lake, pier

Aqueduct, lock, weir

Beach

Woodland

Park

Cemetery

Built-up area

Industrial / business building

Leisure building

Retail building

Other building

IKEA — IKEA store

* The AA central London Congestion Charging map is also available

City wall		Castle		

City wall

Hospital with 24-hour A&E department

Post Office

Public library

Tourist Information Centre

Seasonal Tourist Information Centre

Petrol station, 24 hour
Major suppliers only

Church/chapel

Public toilets

Toilet with disabled facilities

Public house
AA recommended

Restaurant
AA inspected

Hotel
AA inspected

Theatre or performing arts centre

Cinema

Golf course

Camping
AA inspected

Caravan site
AA inspected

Camping & caravan site
AA inspected

Theme park

Abbey, cathedral or priory

Castle

Historic house or building

National Trust property

Museum or art gallery

Roman antiquity

Ancient site, battlefield or monument

Industrial interest

Garden

Garden Centre
Garden Centre Association Member

Garden Centre
Wyevale Garden Centre

Arboretum

Farm or animal centre

Zoological or wildlife collection

Bird collection

Nature reserve

Aquarium

Visitor or heritage centre

Country park

Cave

Windmill

Distillery, brewery or vineyard

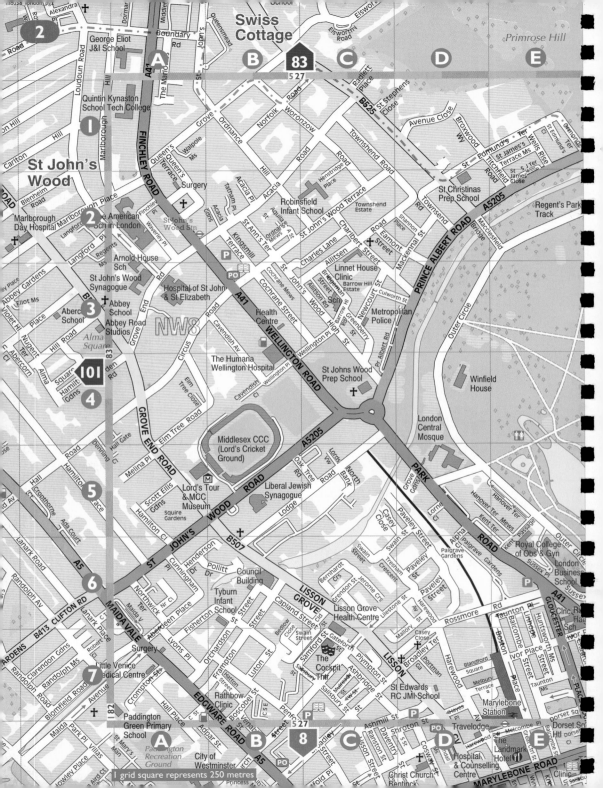

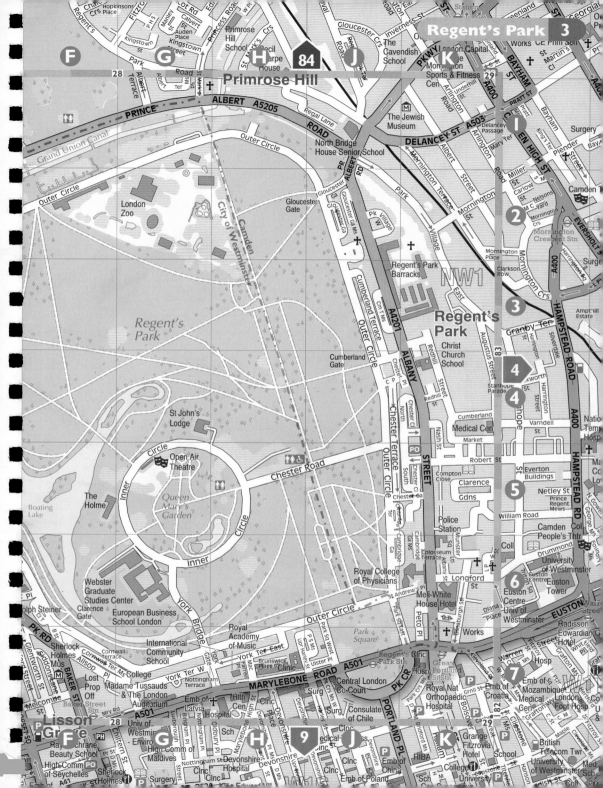

I grid square represents 250 metres

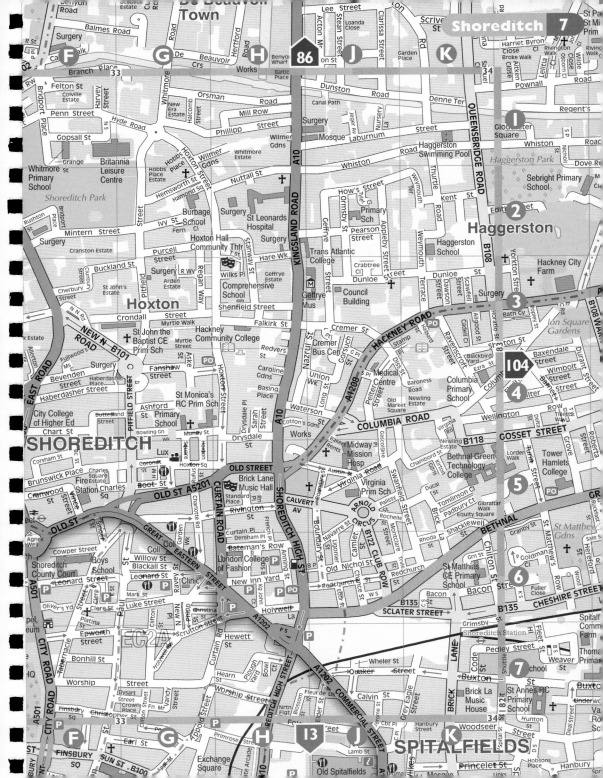

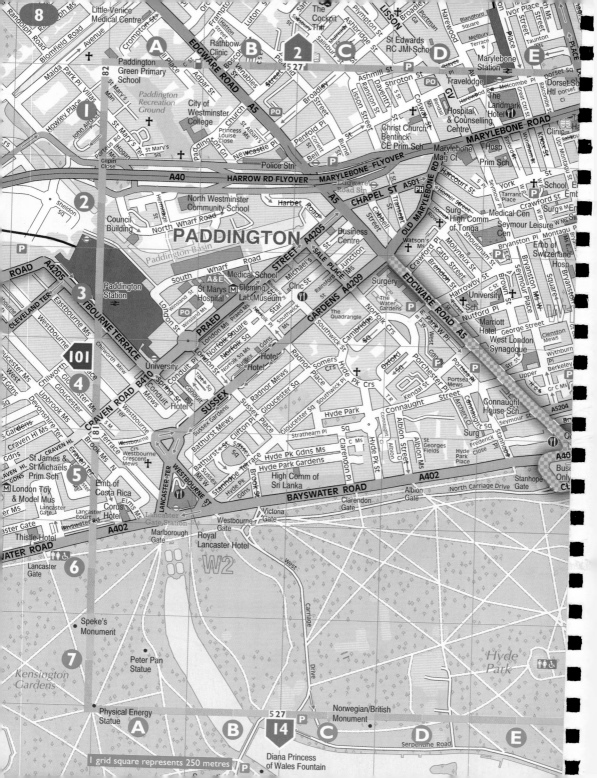

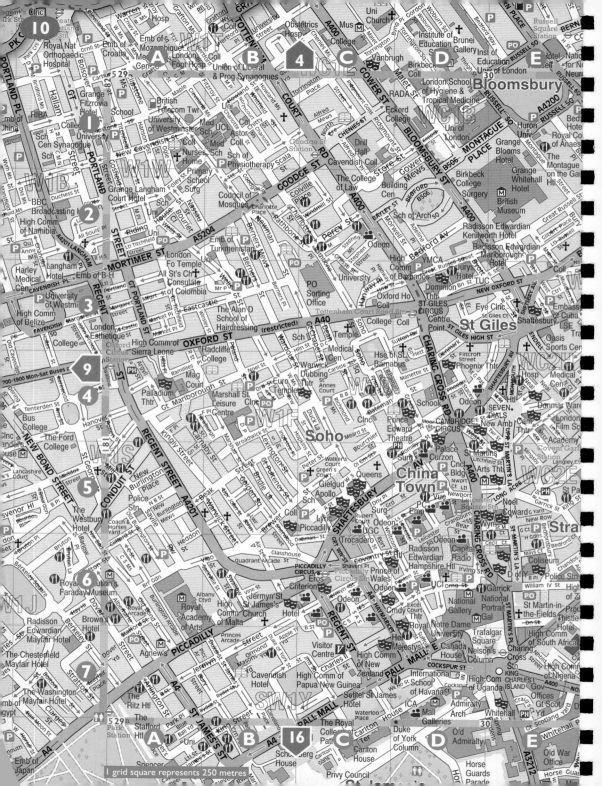

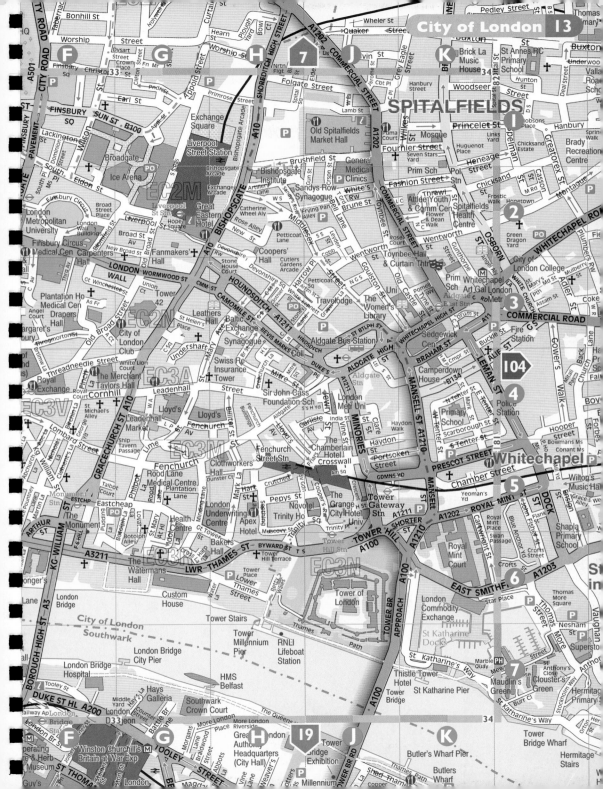

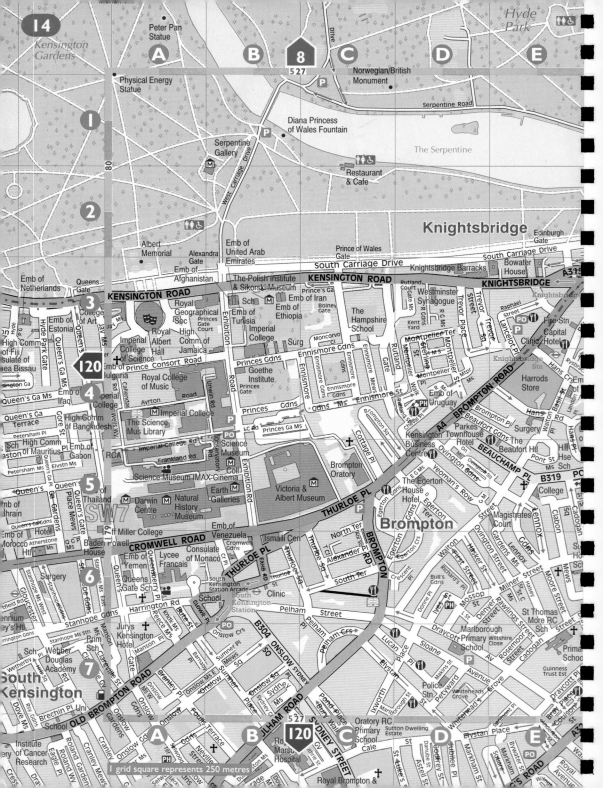

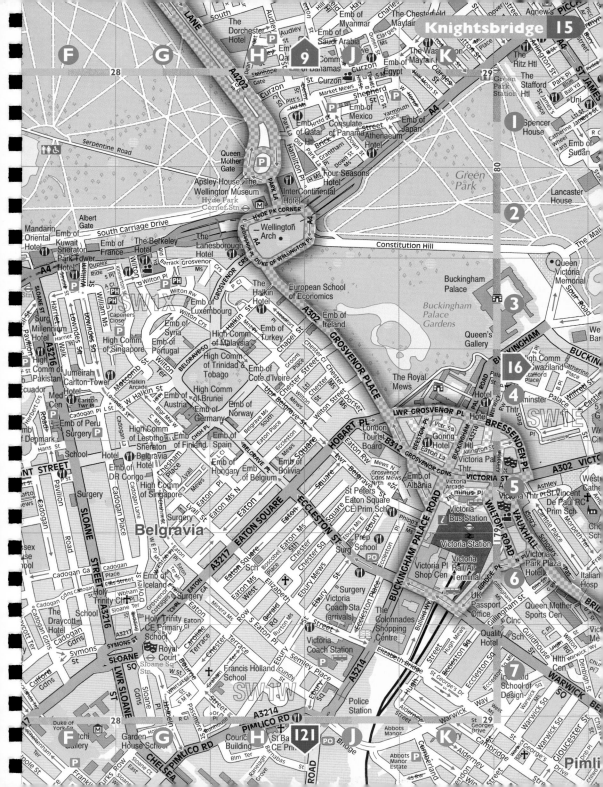

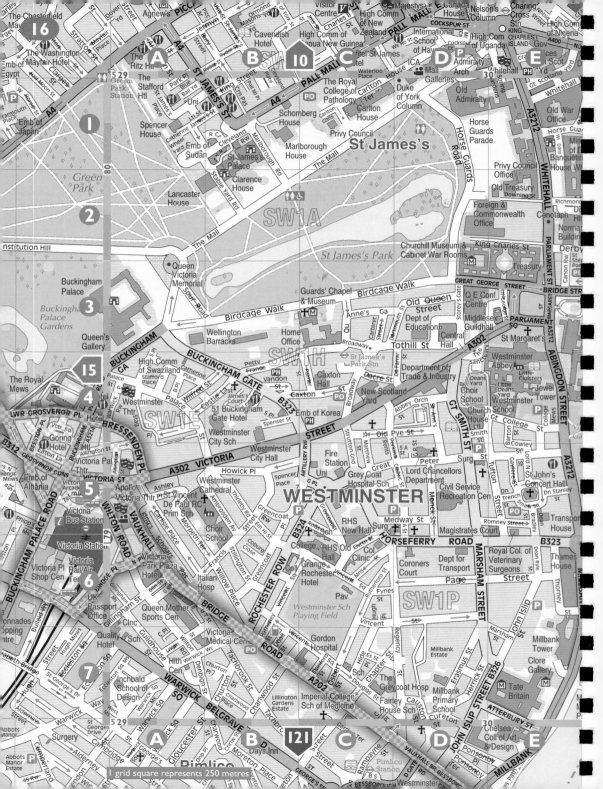

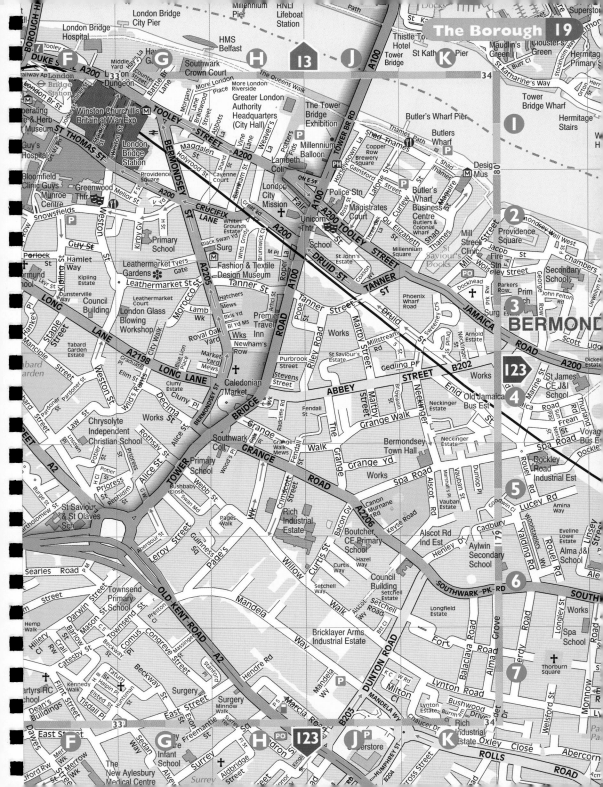

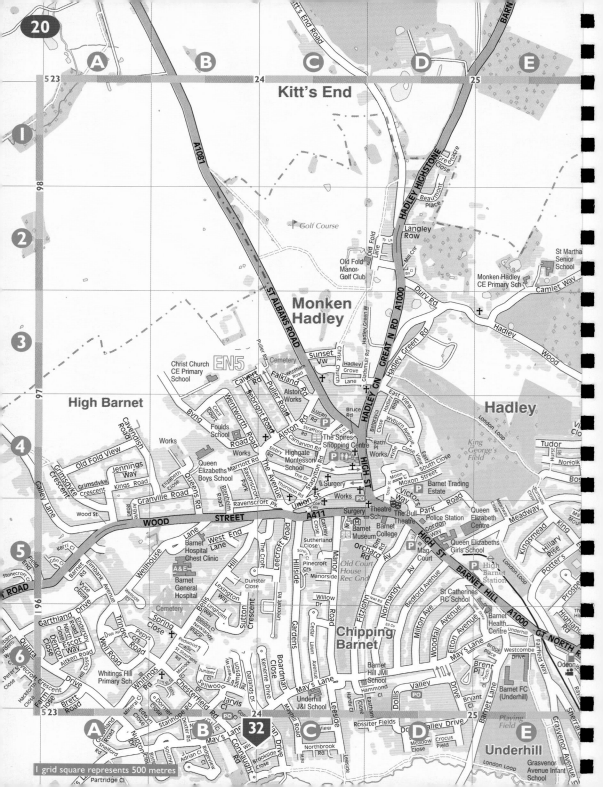

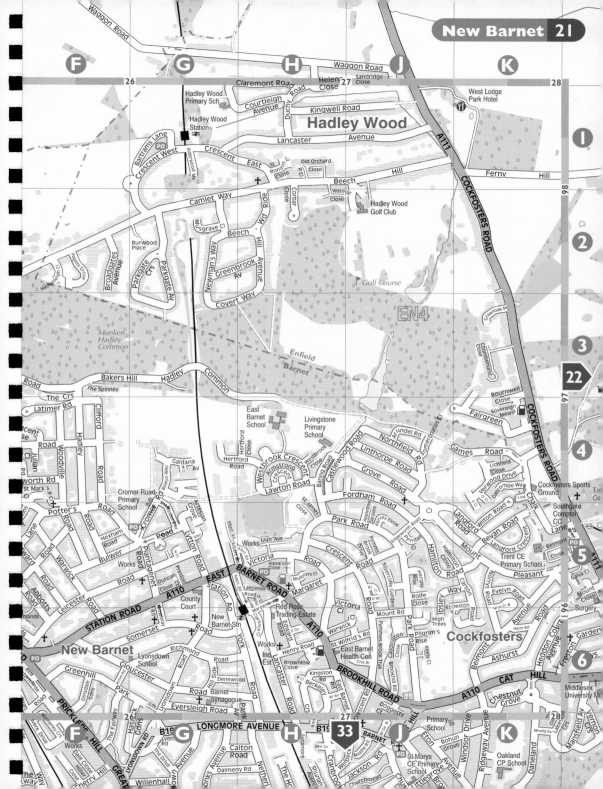

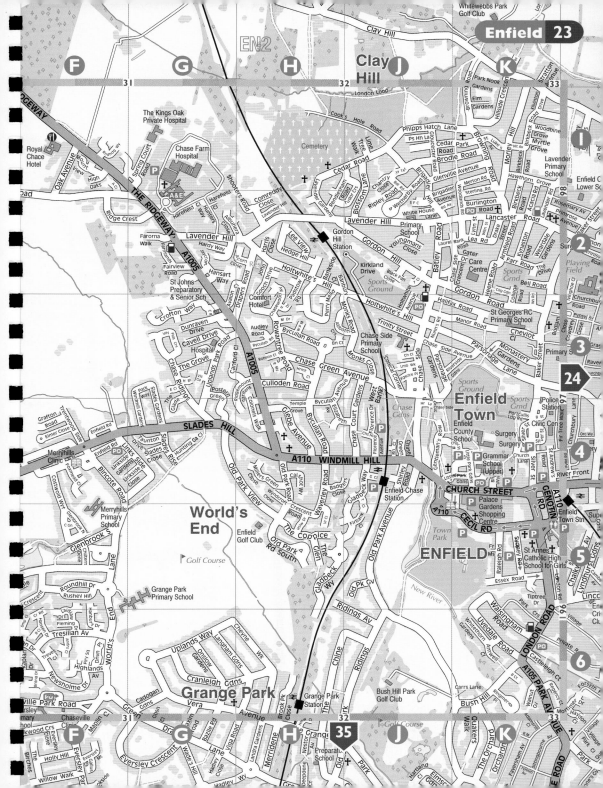

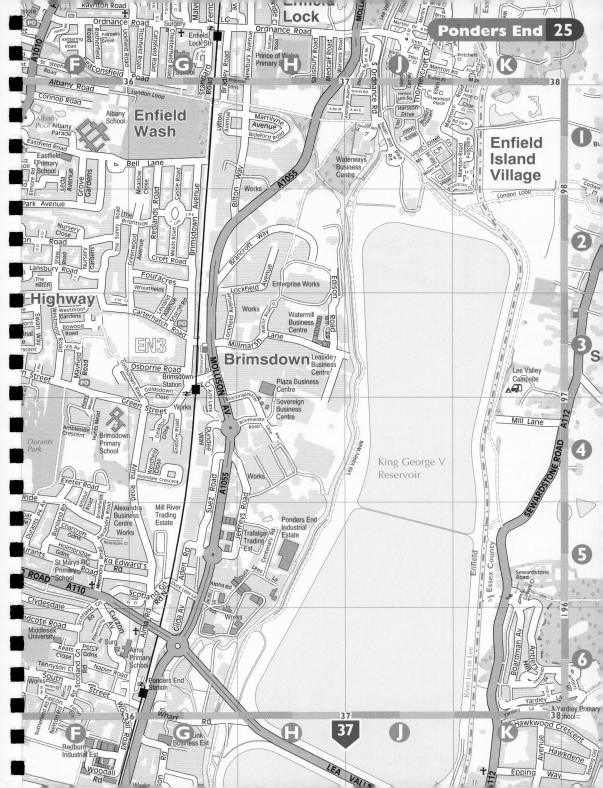

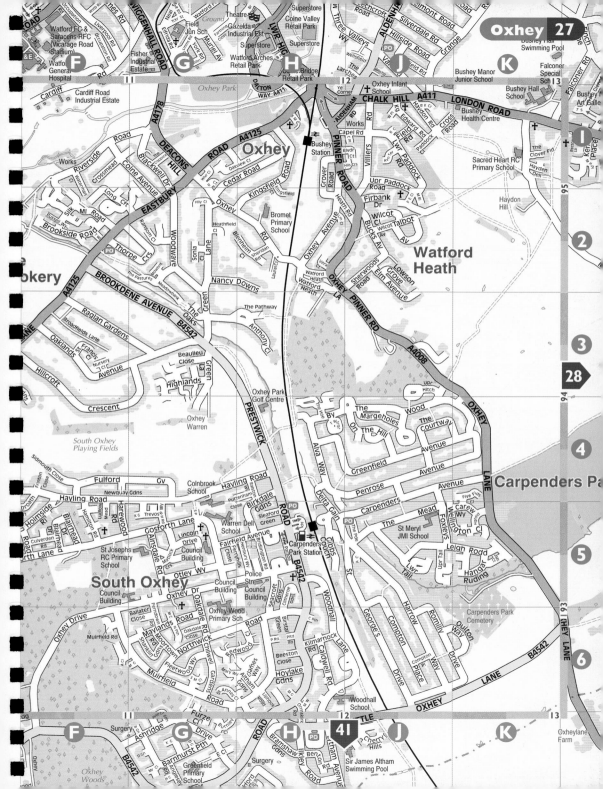

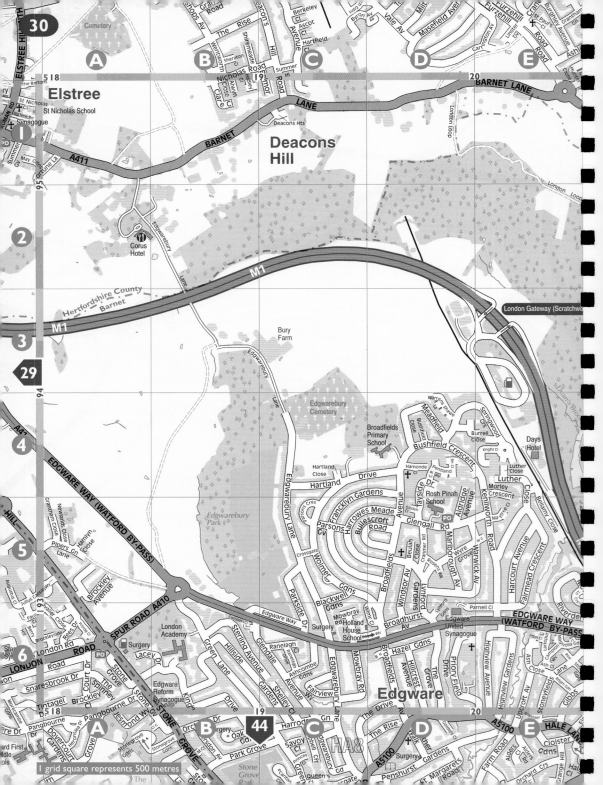

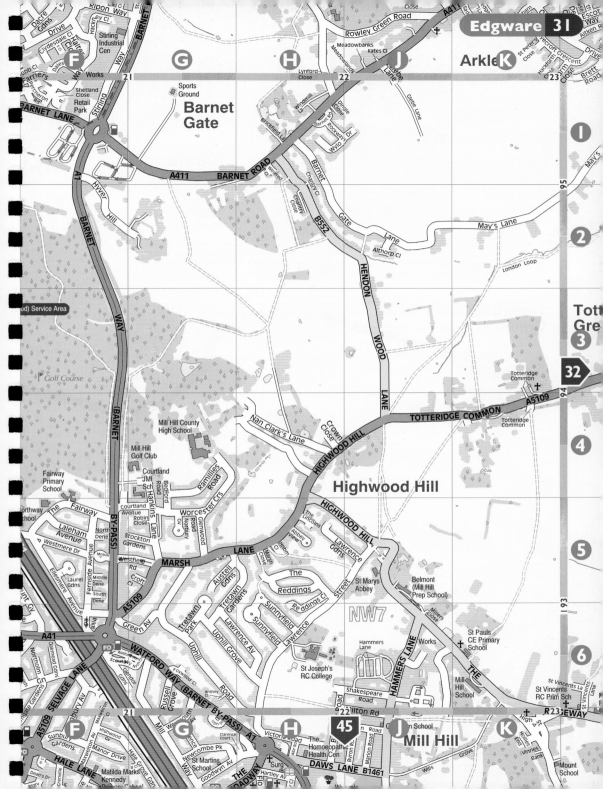

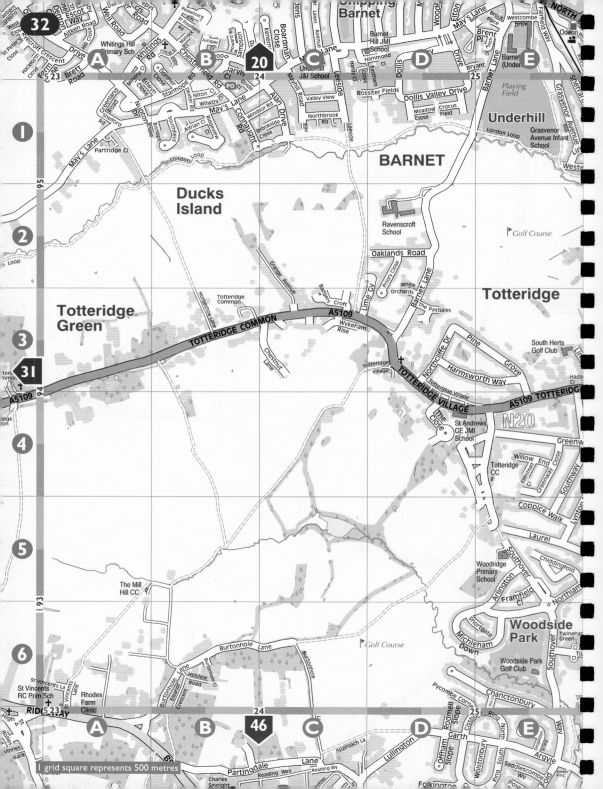

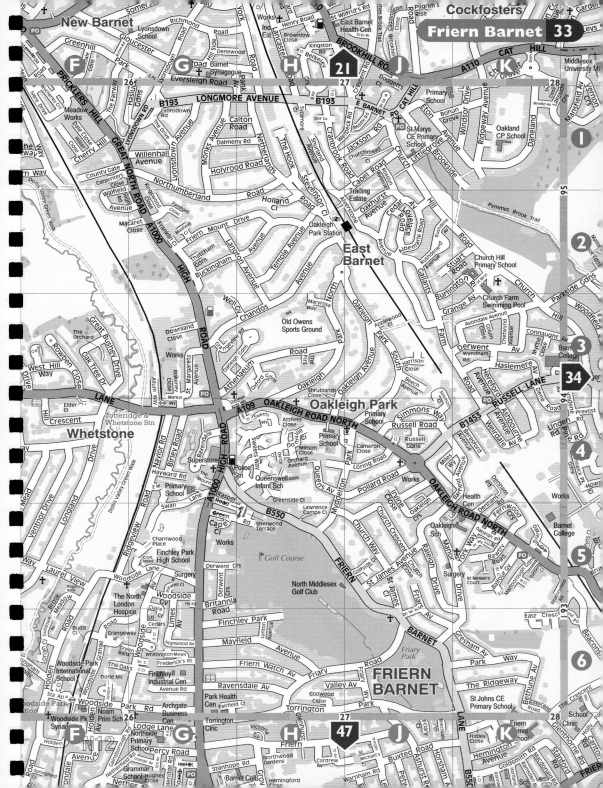

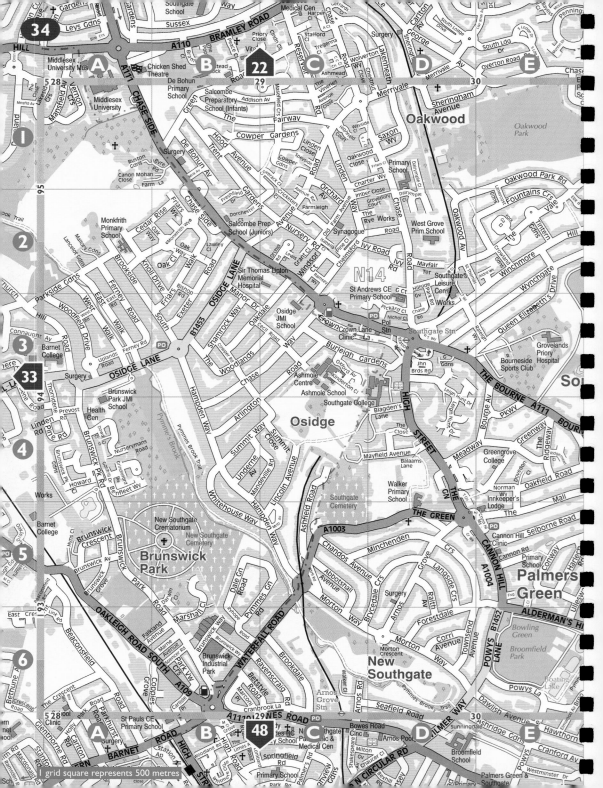

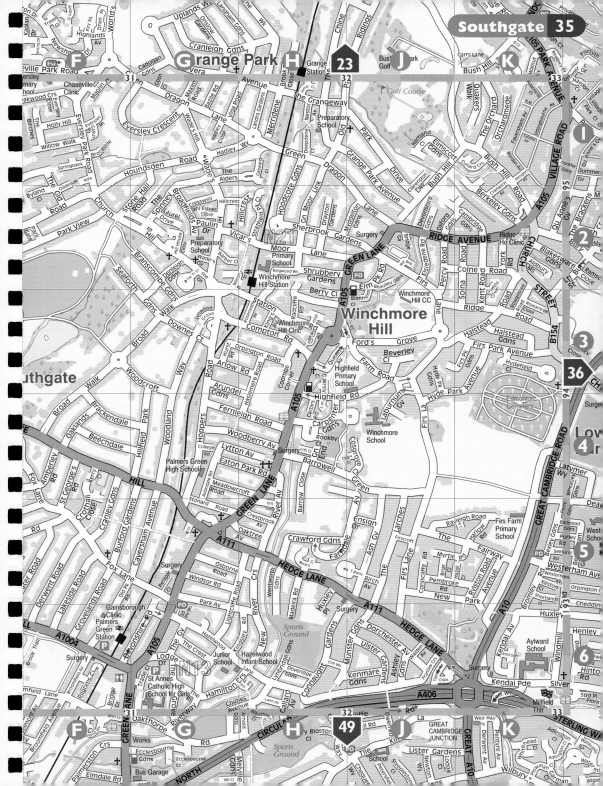

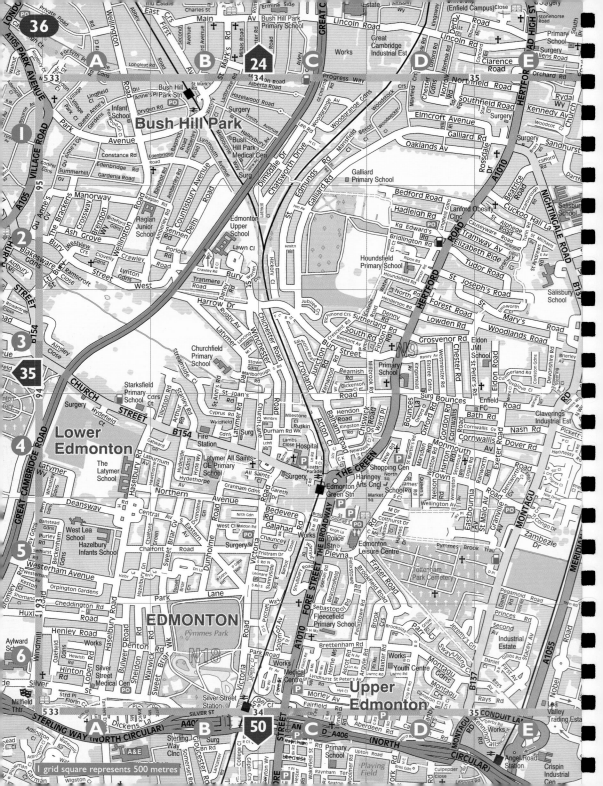

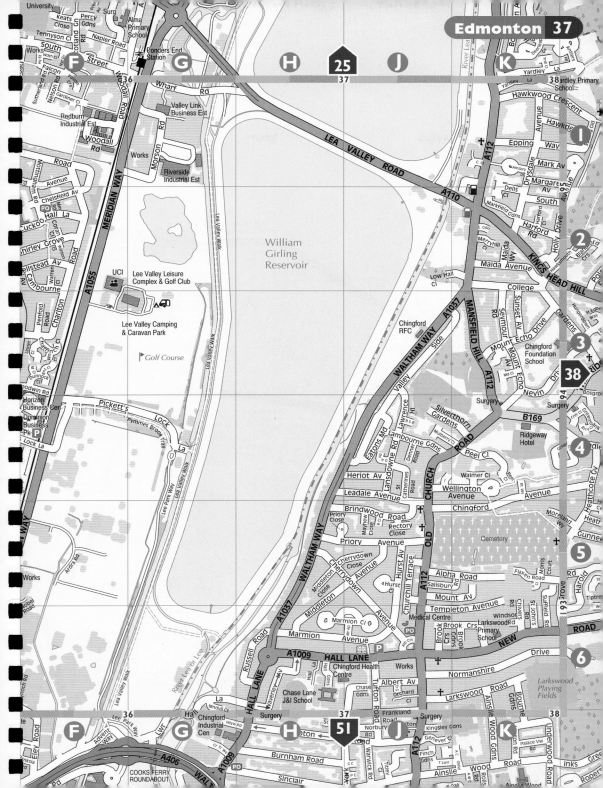

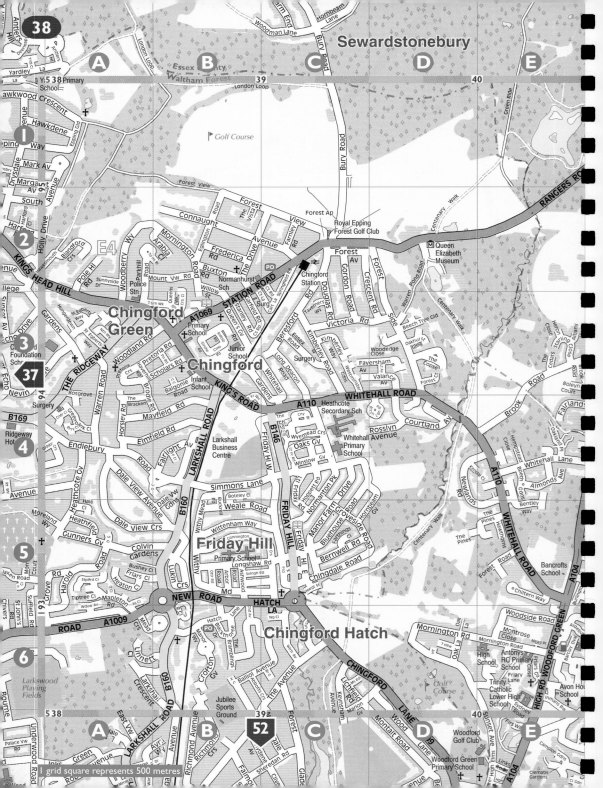

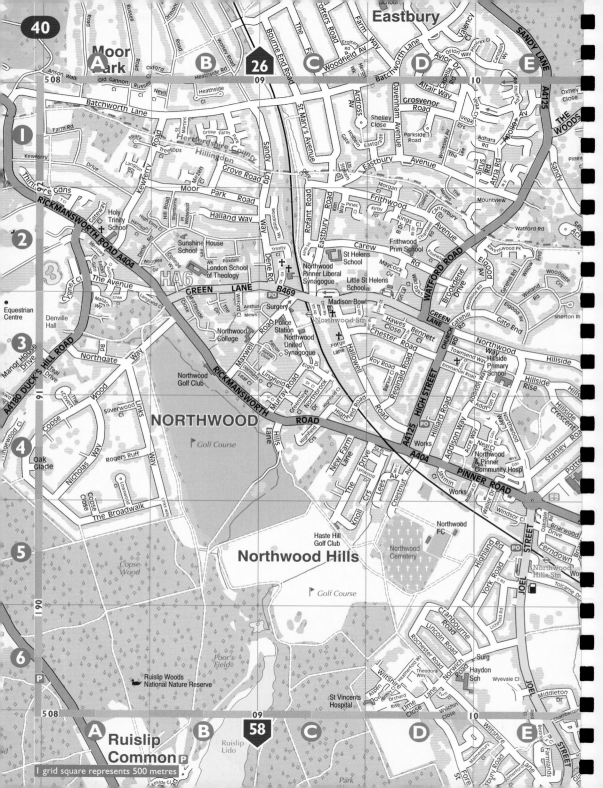

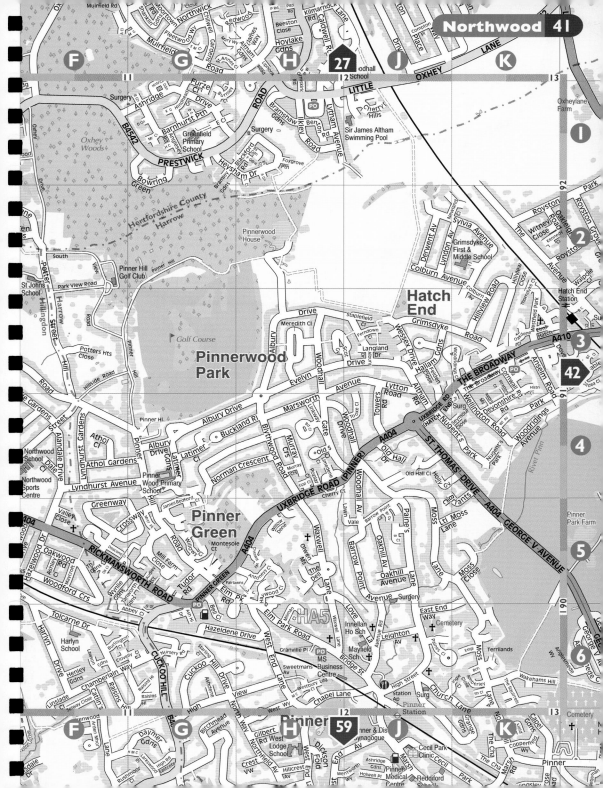

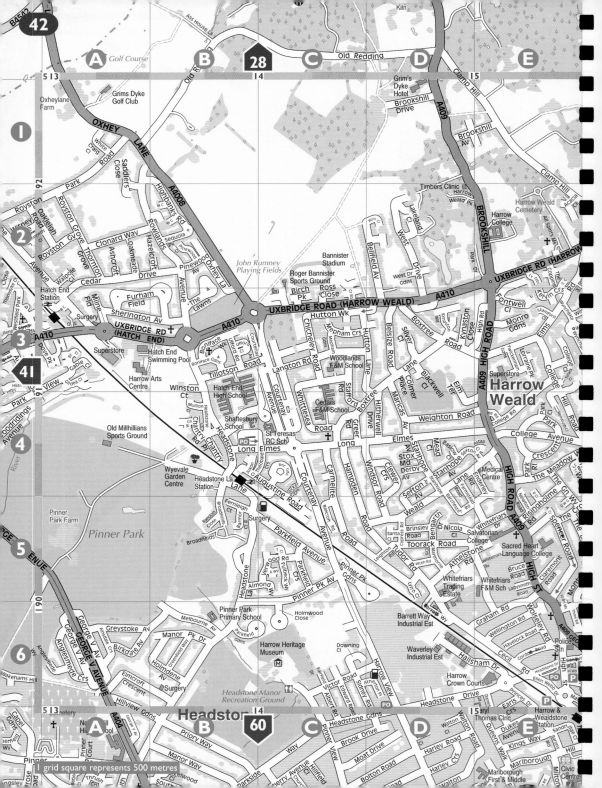

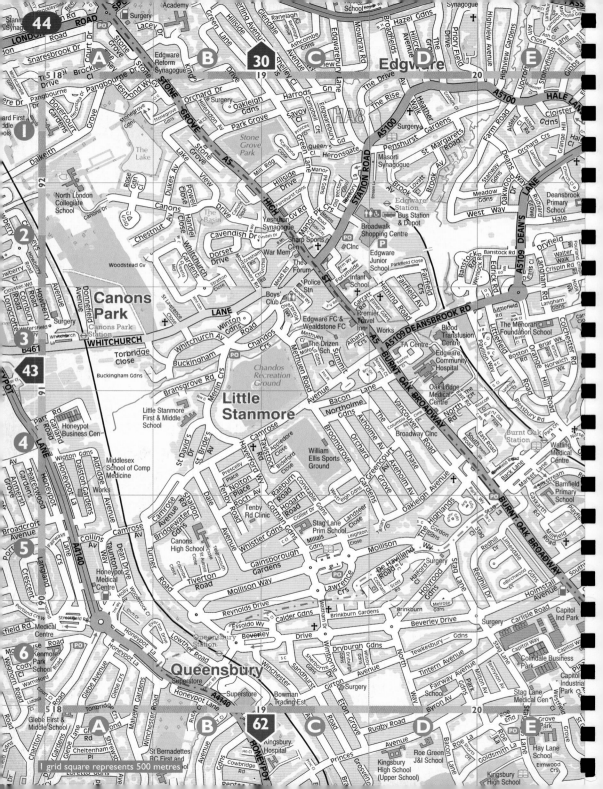

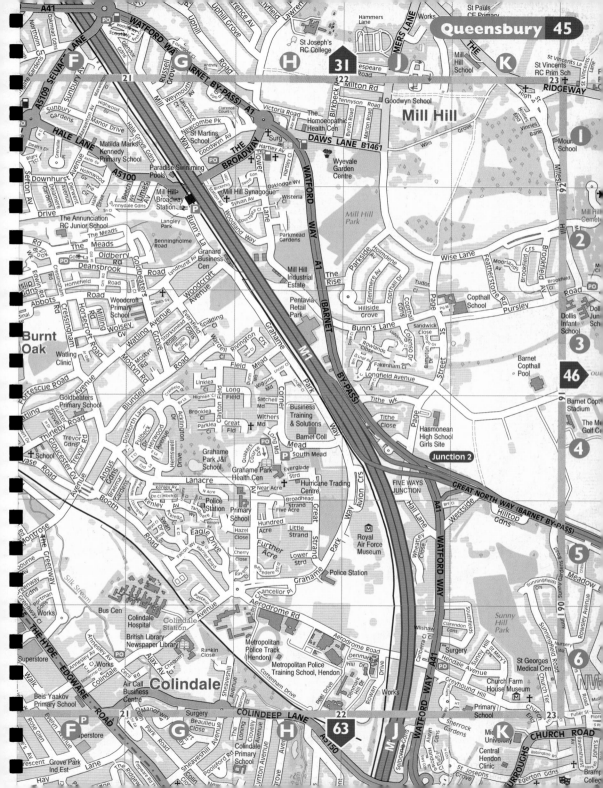

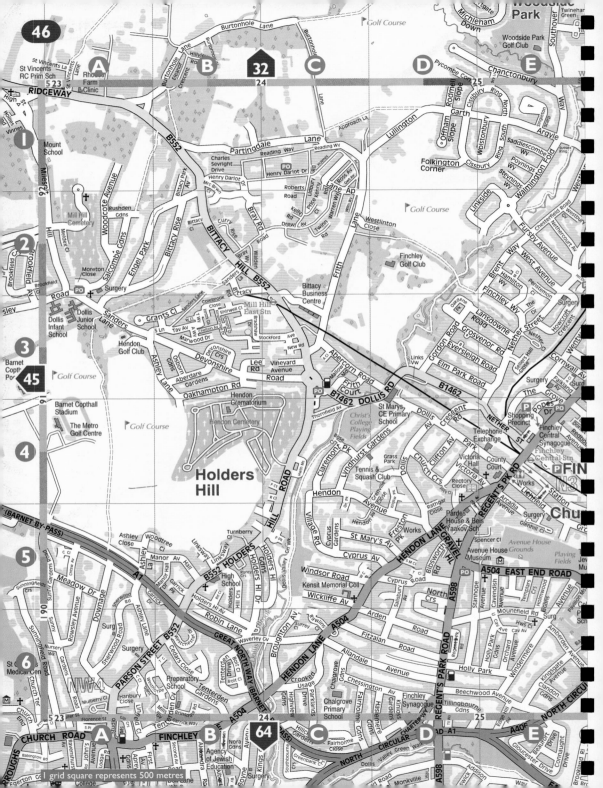

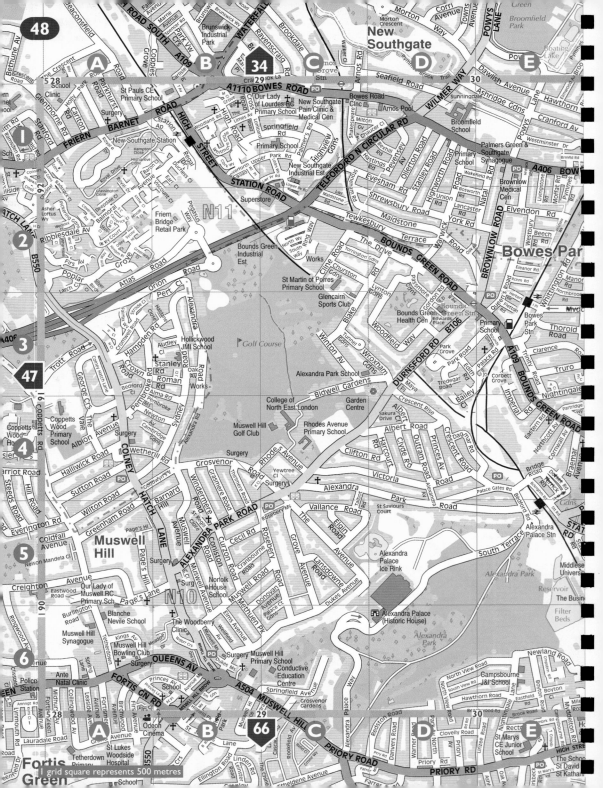

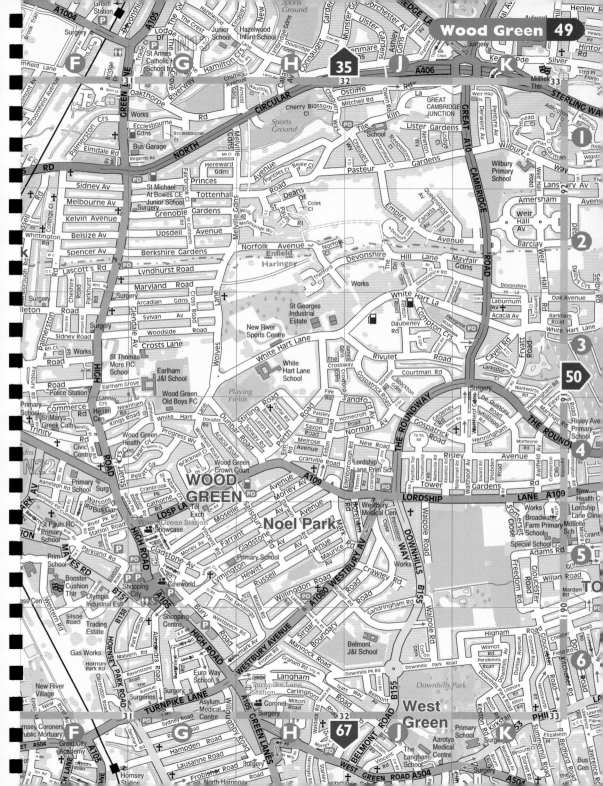

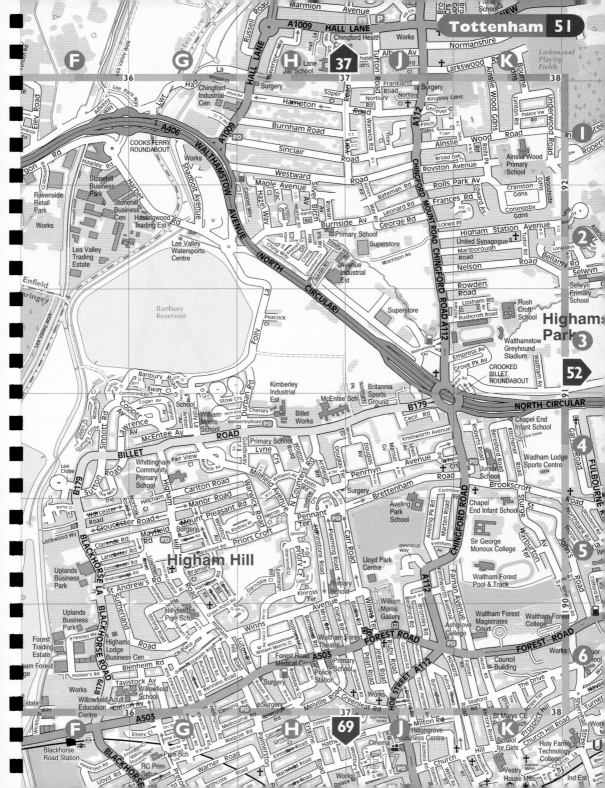

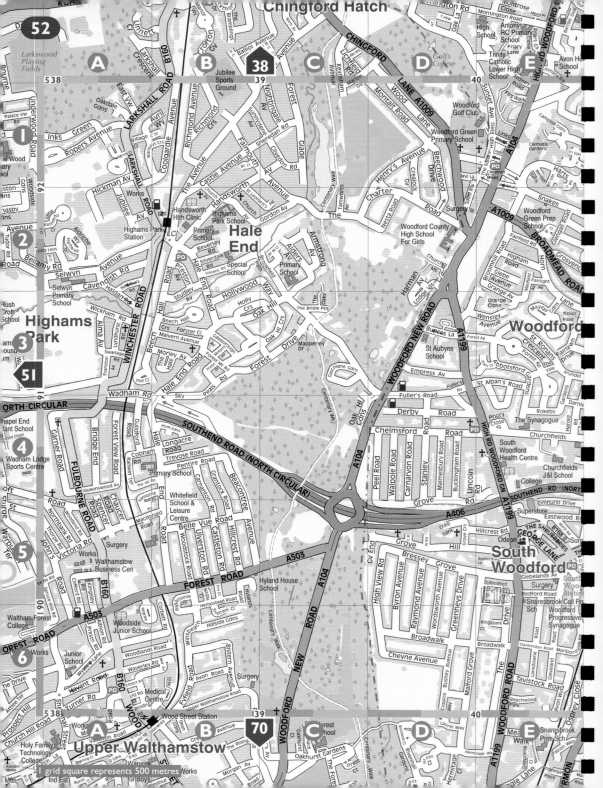

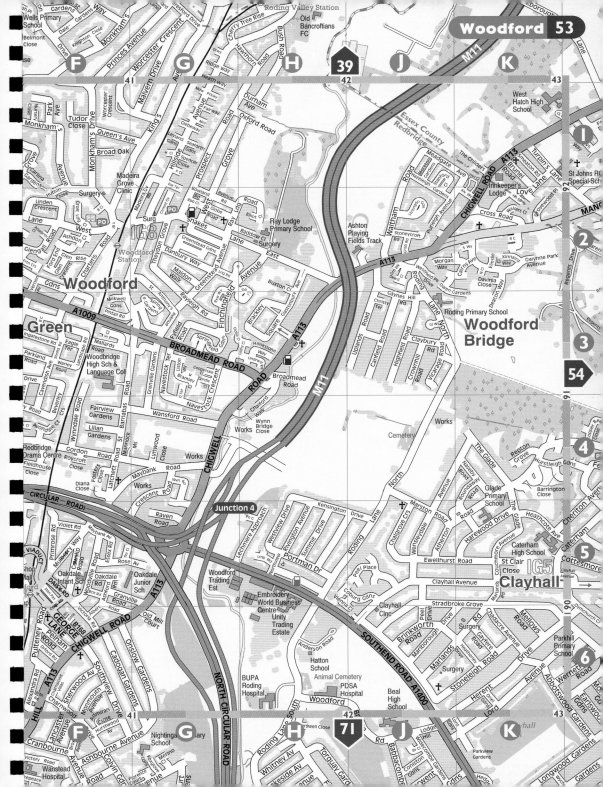

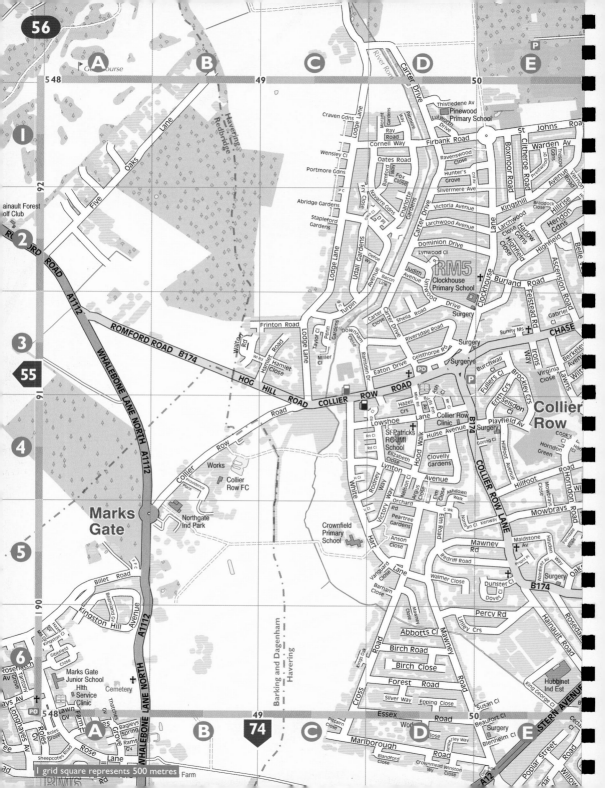

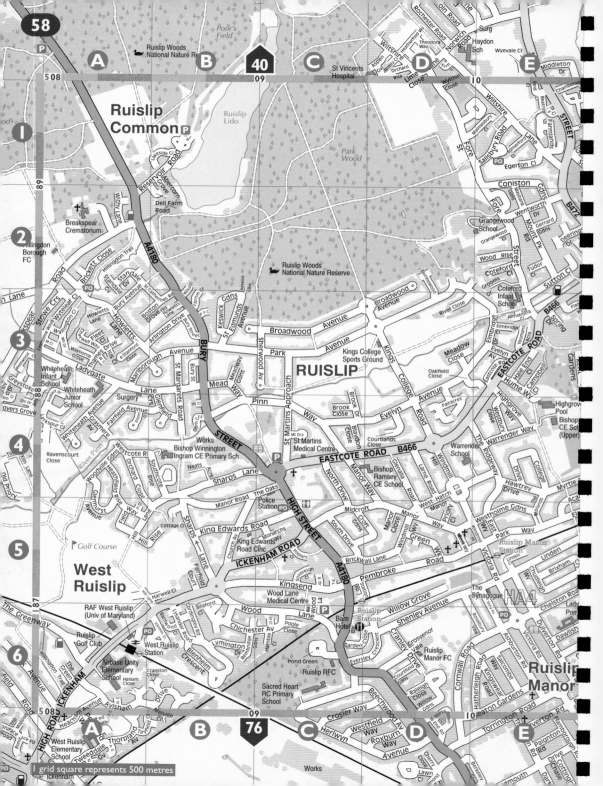

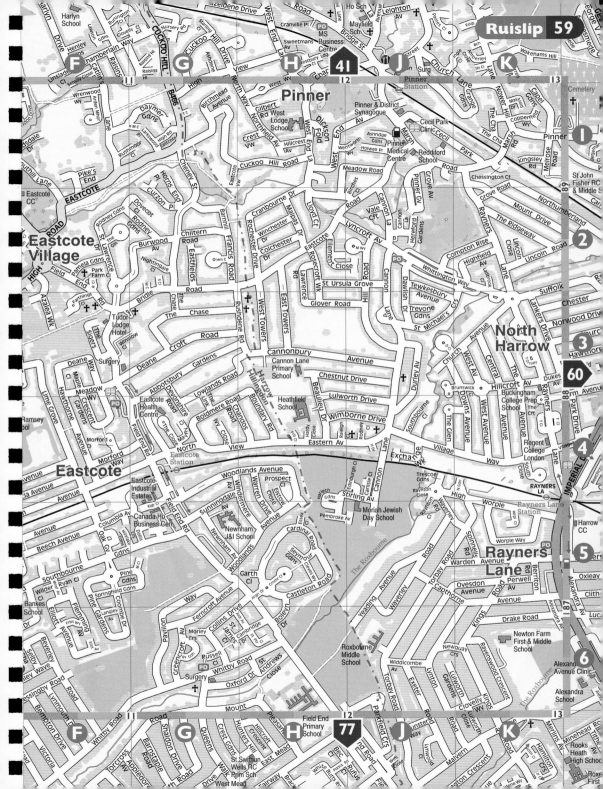

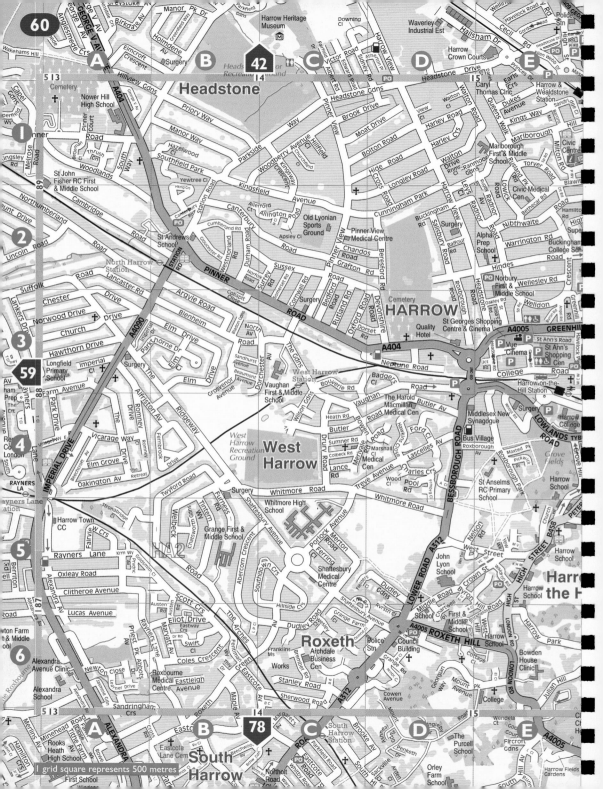

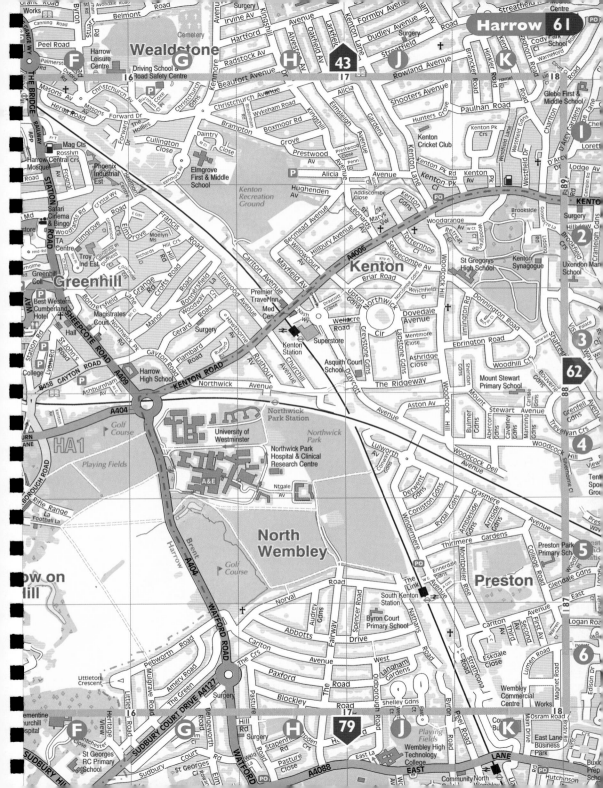

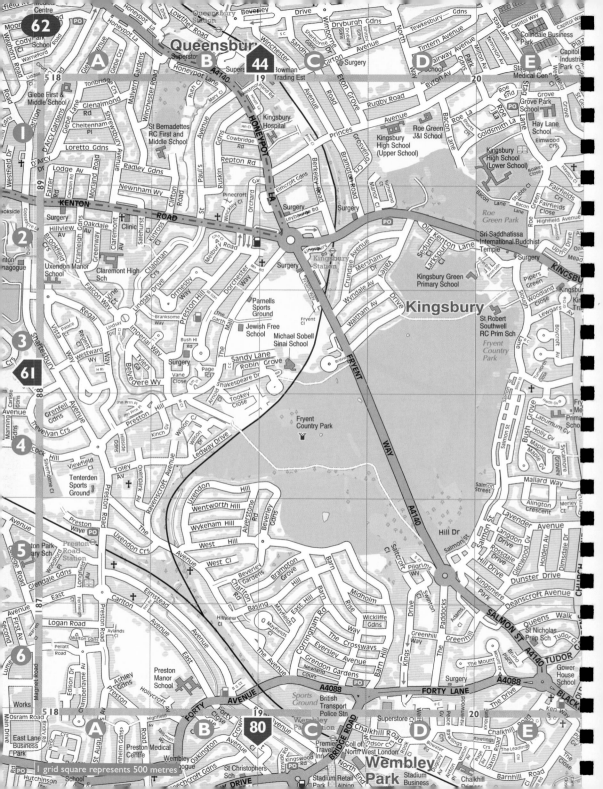

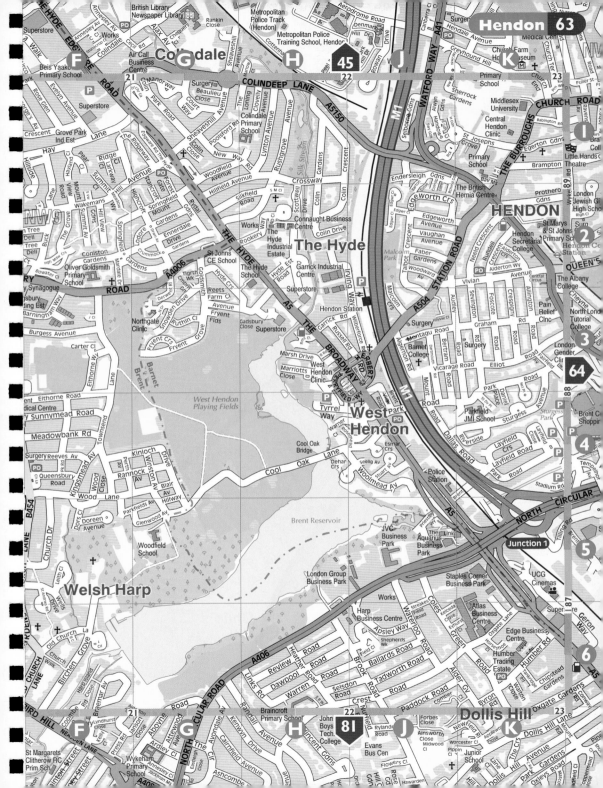

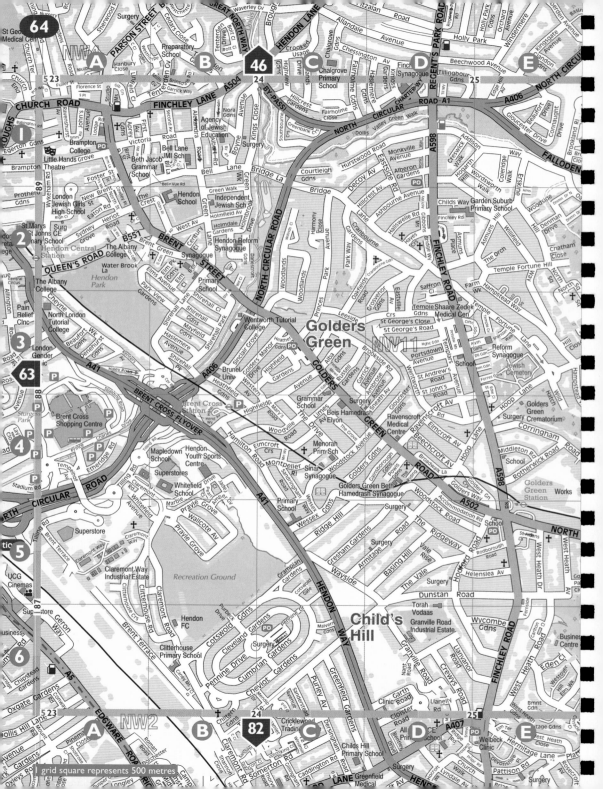

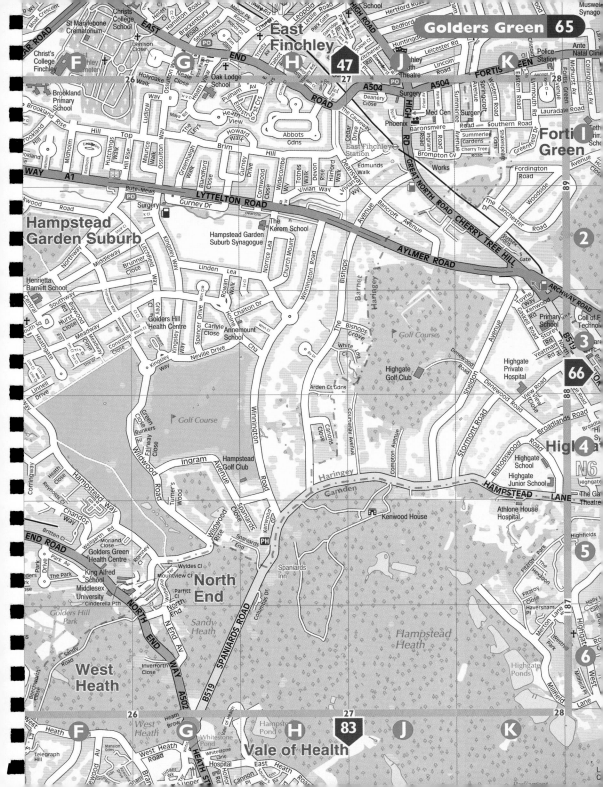

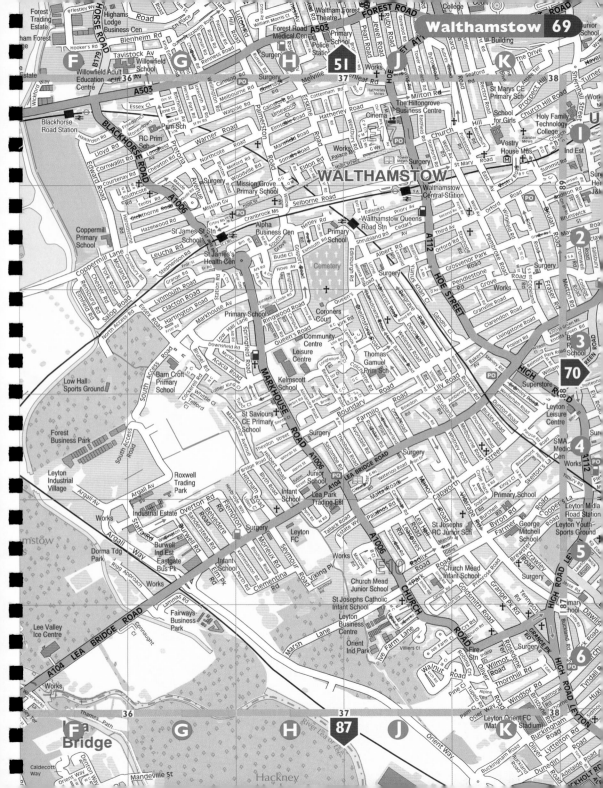

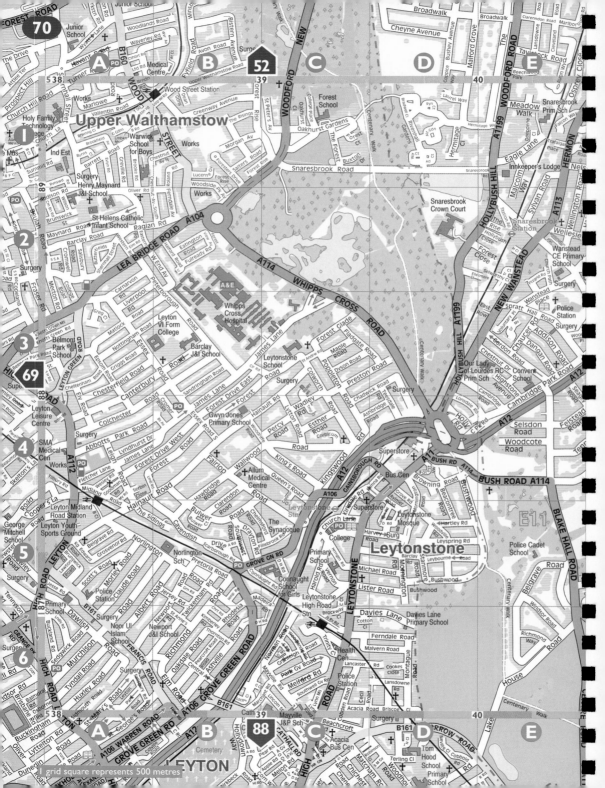

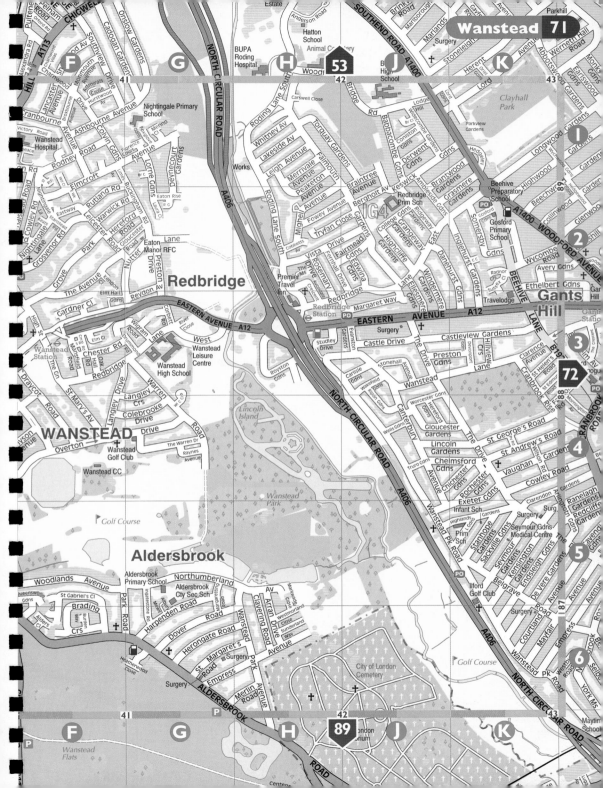

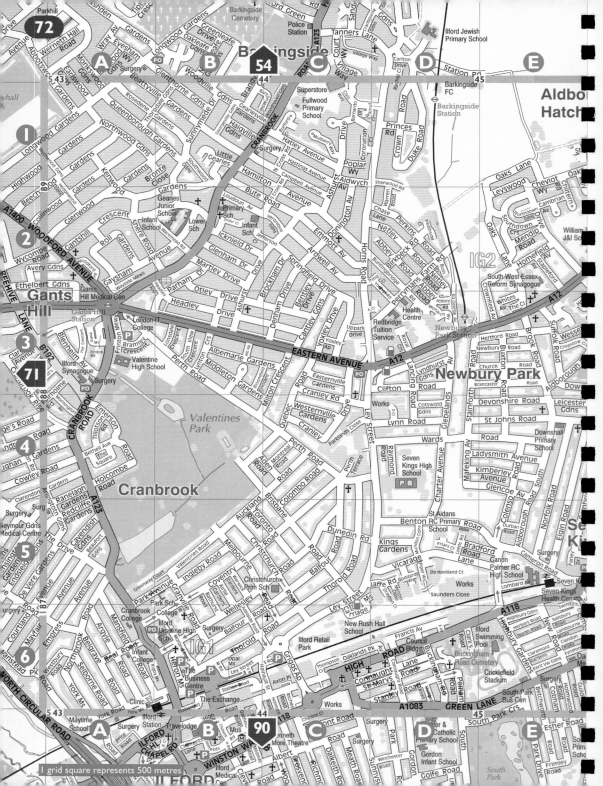

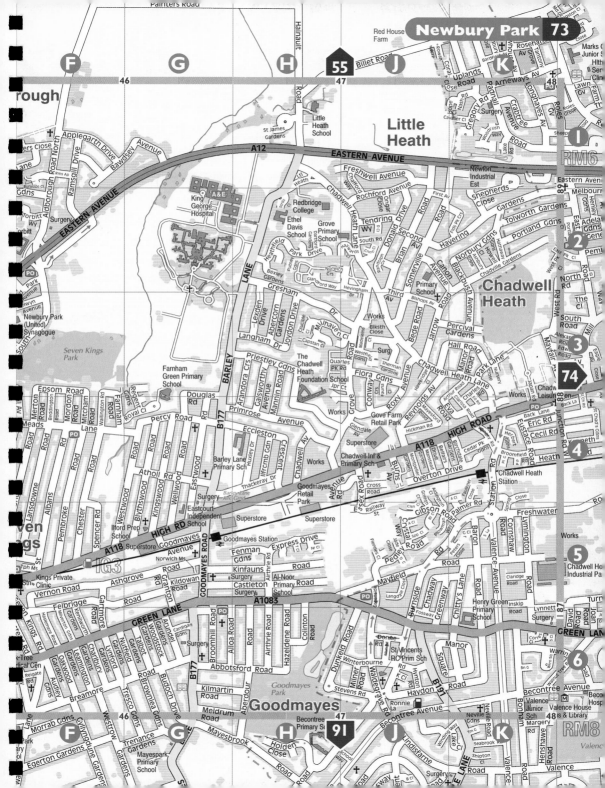

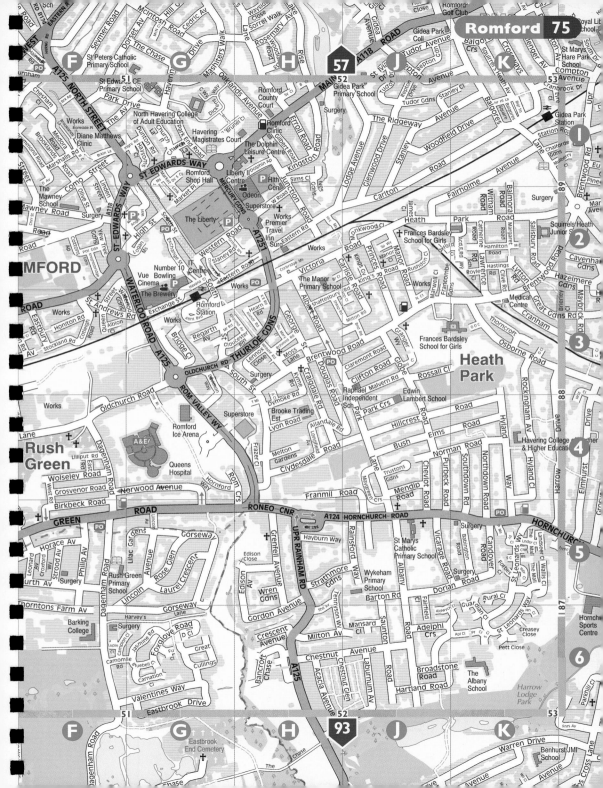

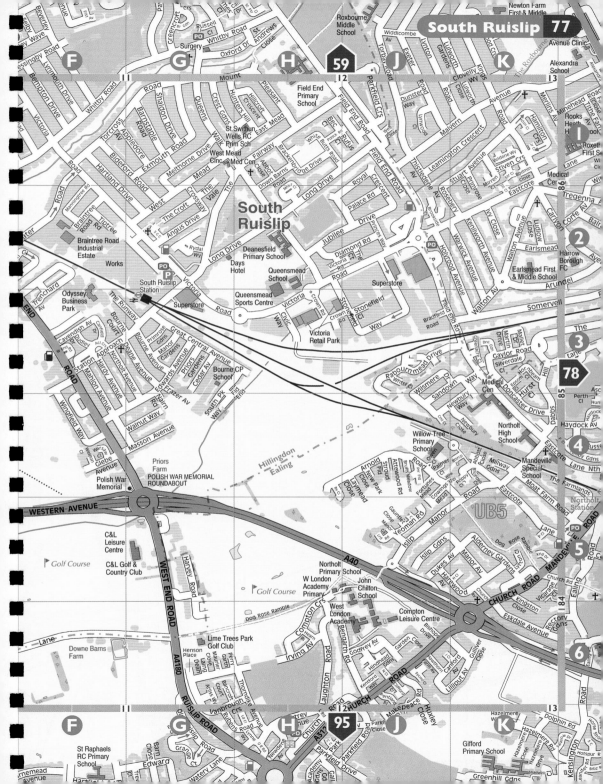

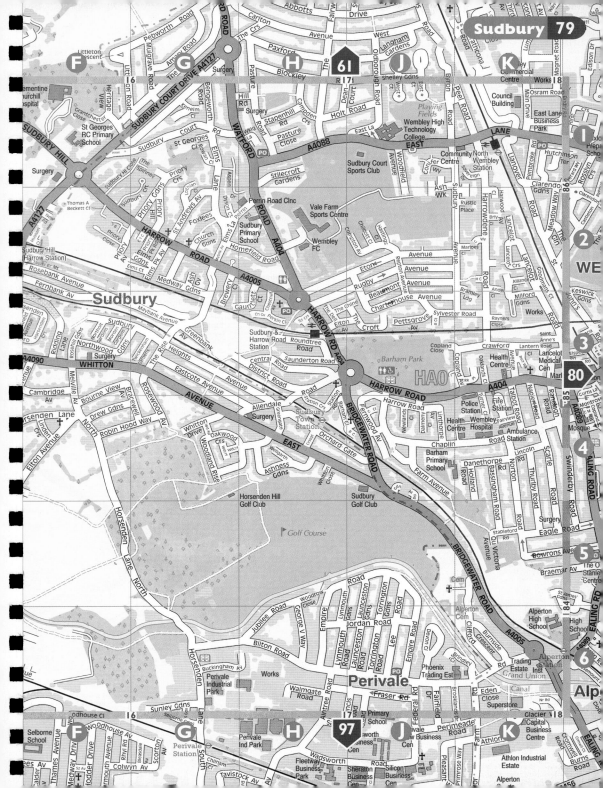

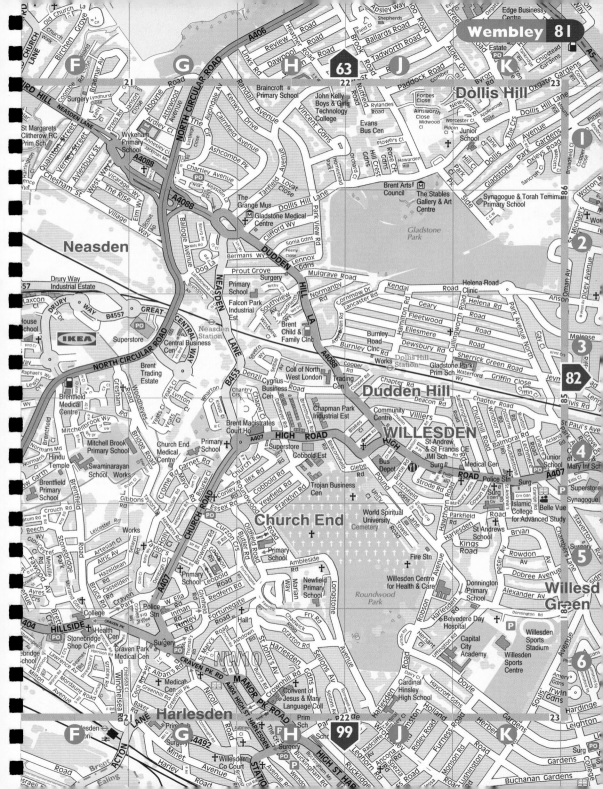

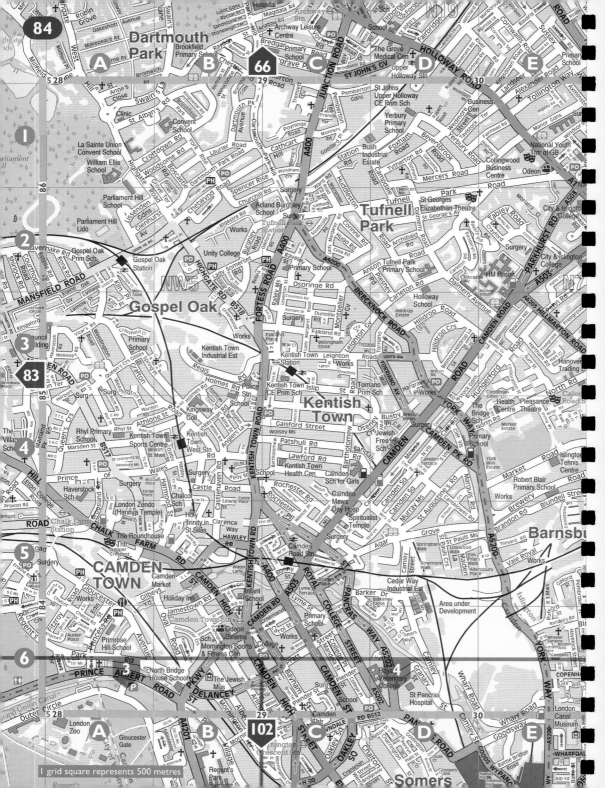

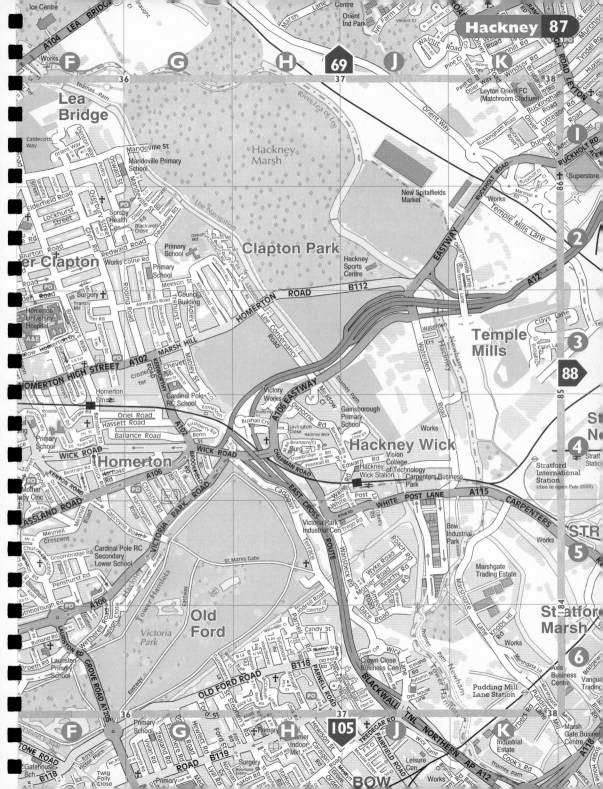

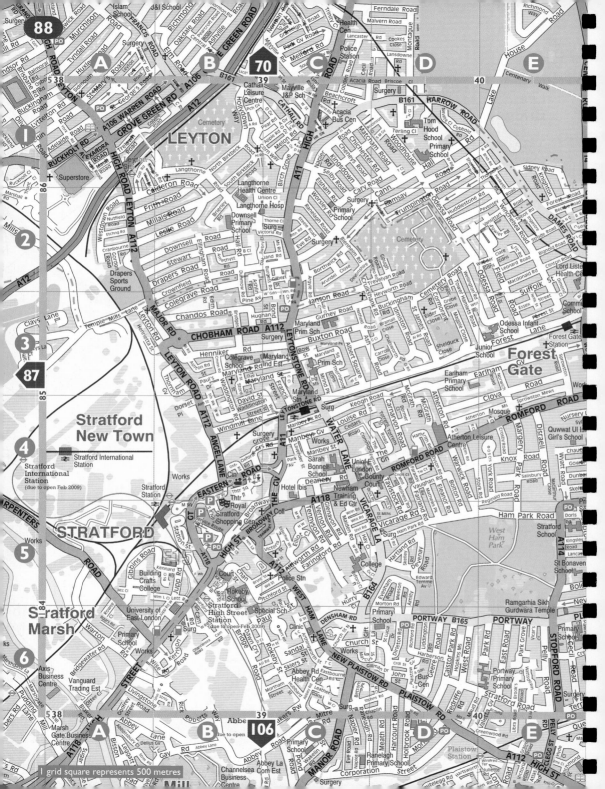

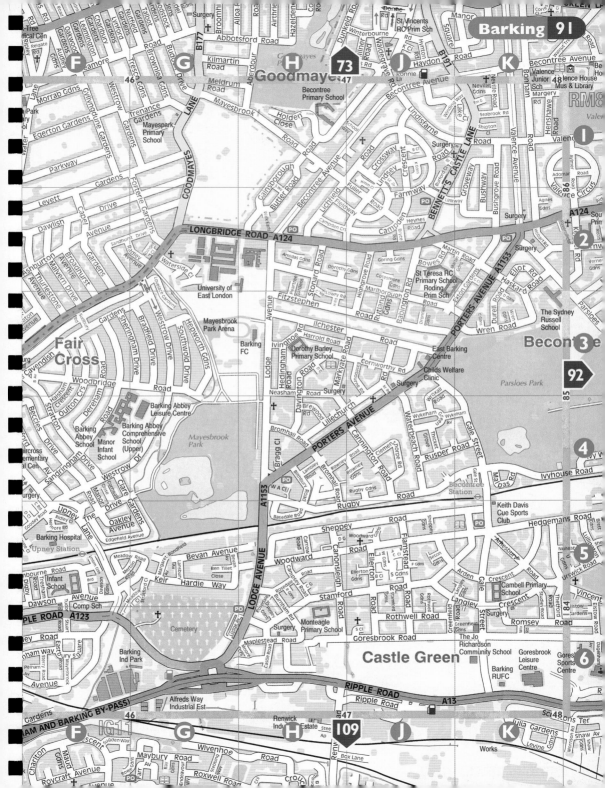

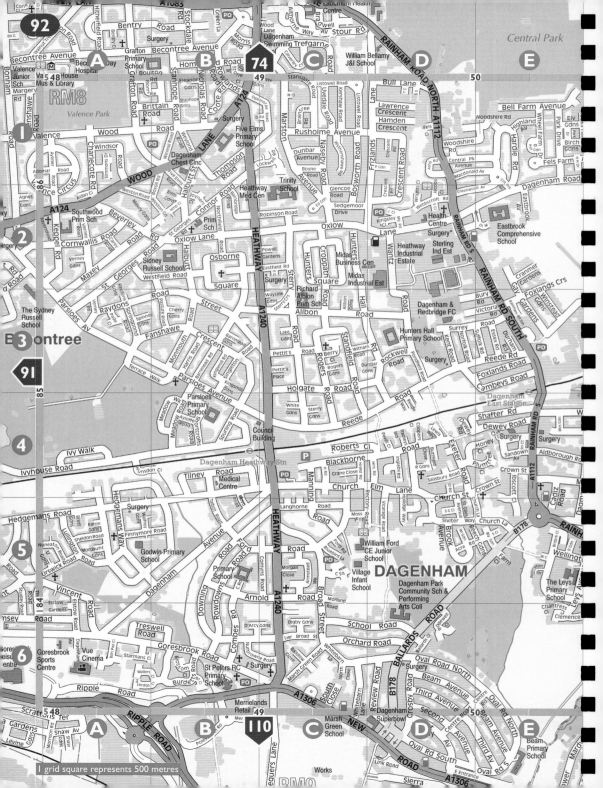

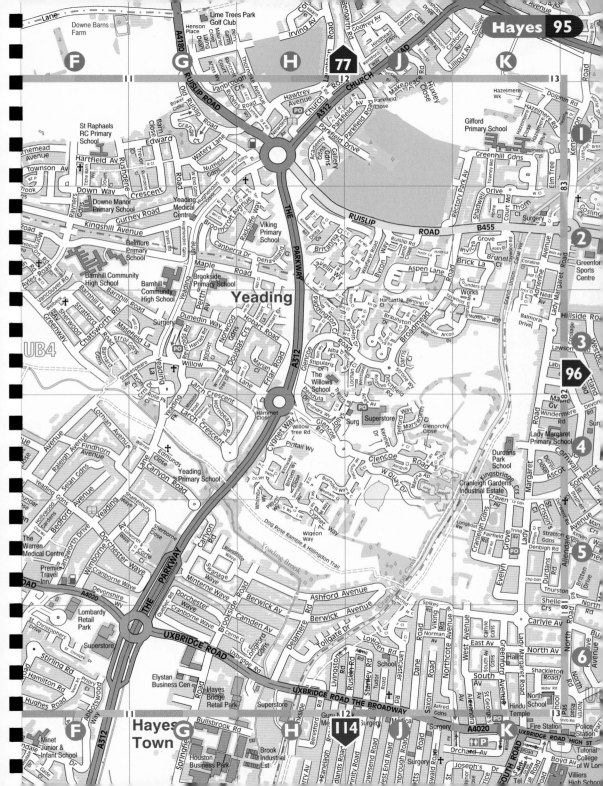

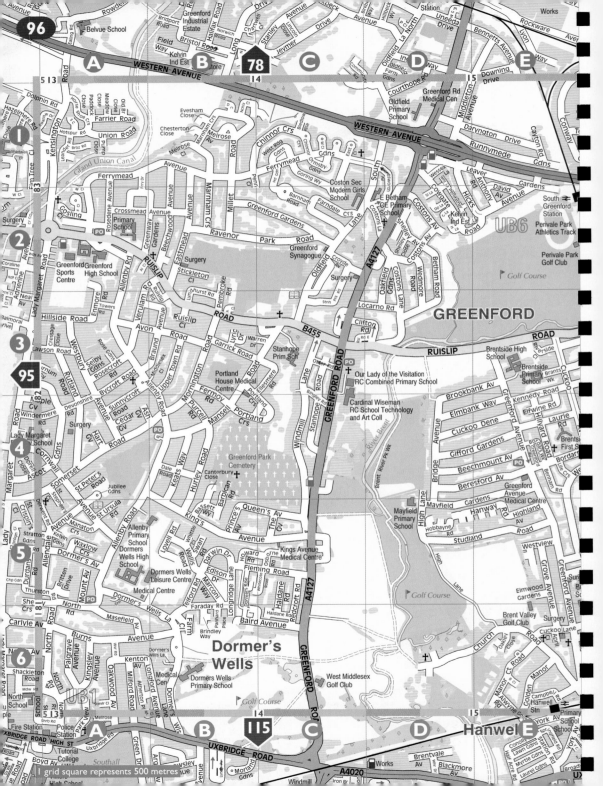

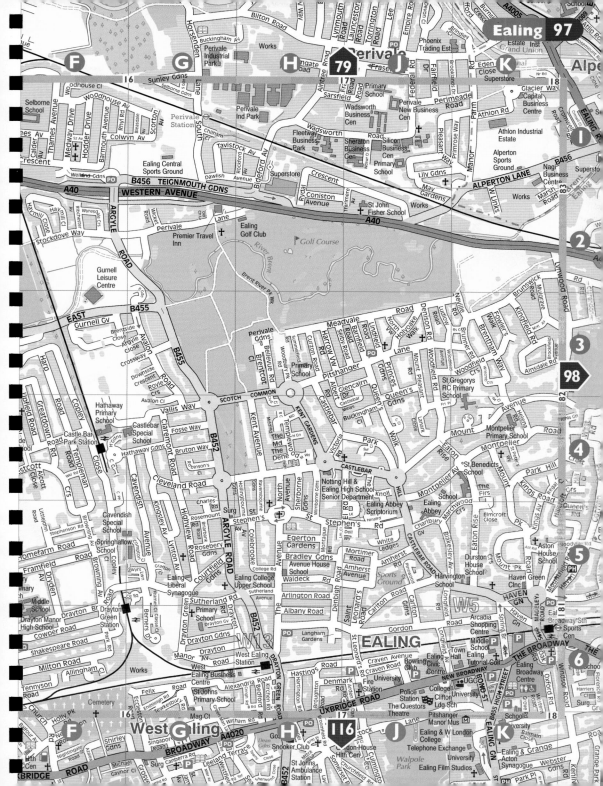

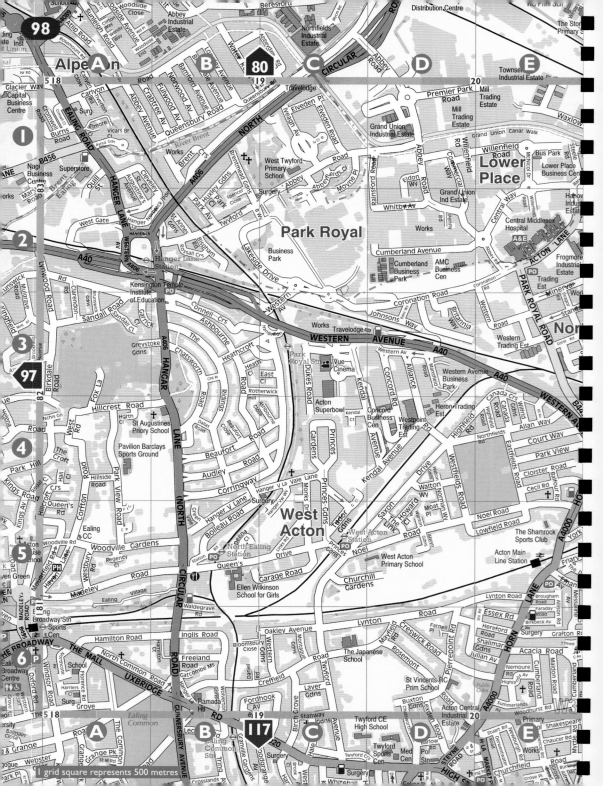

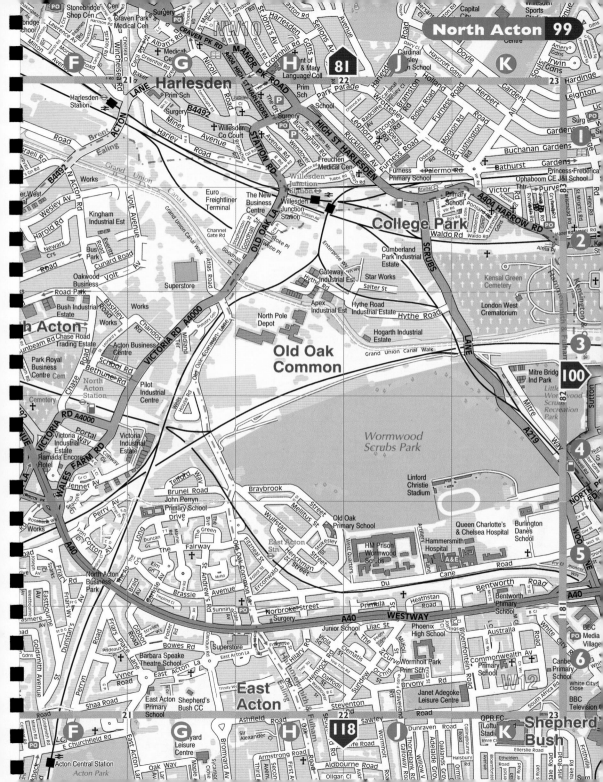

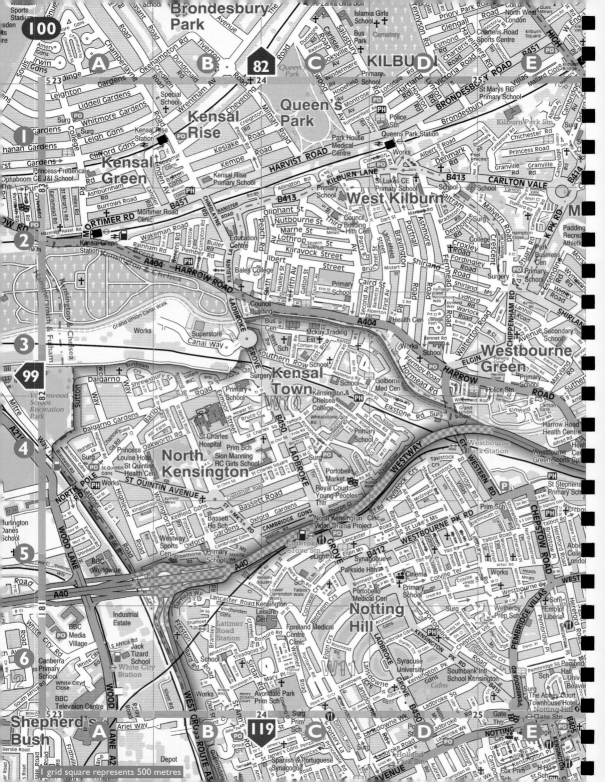

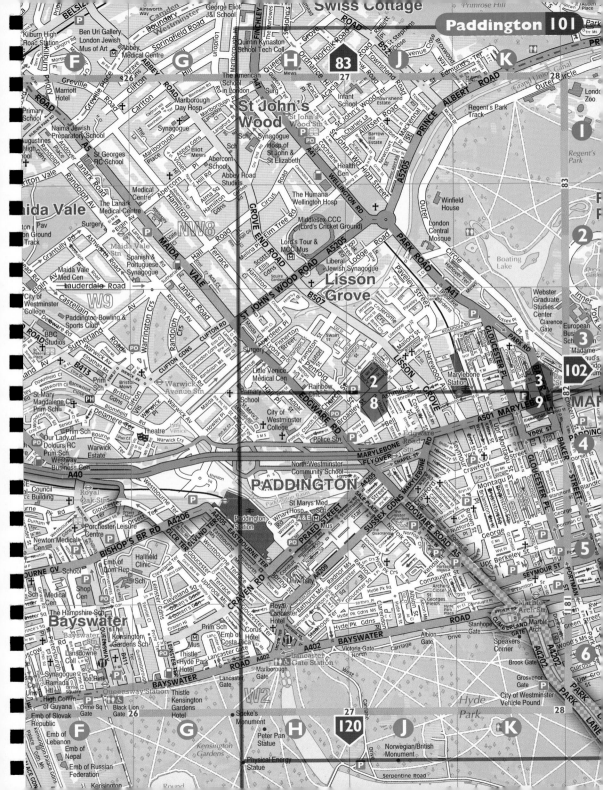

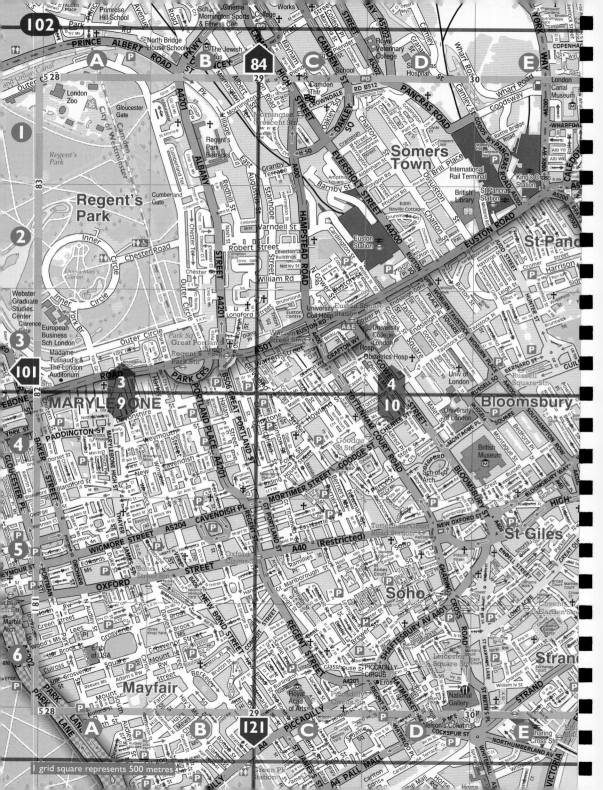

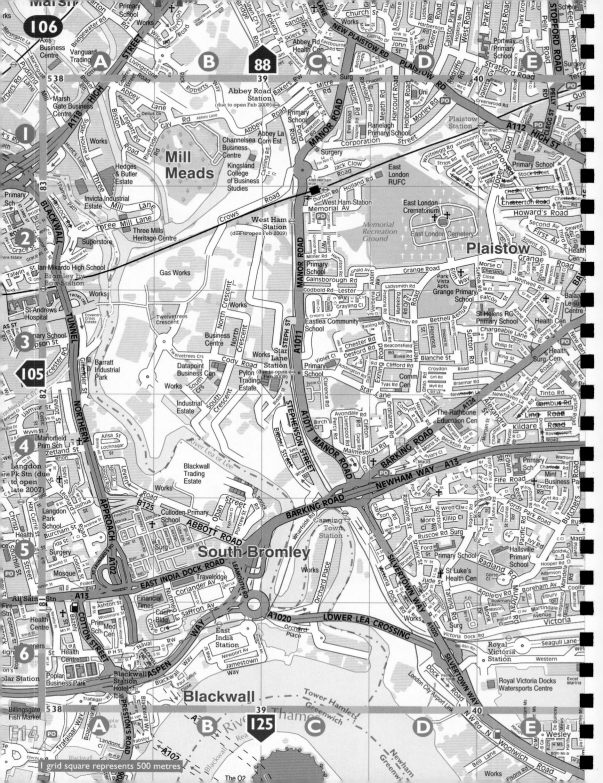

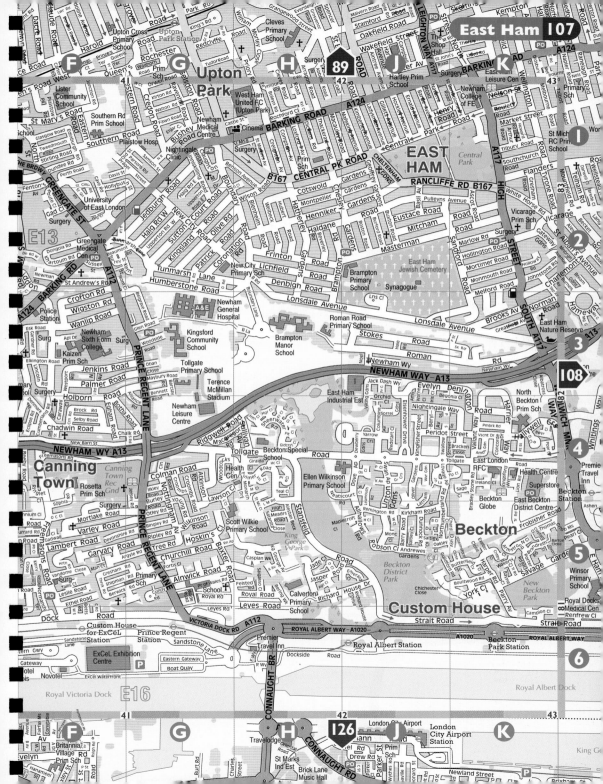

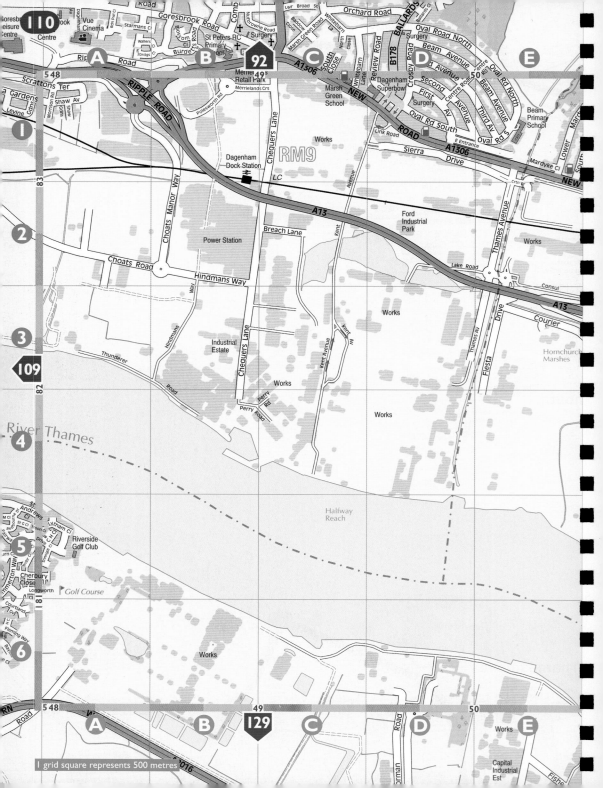

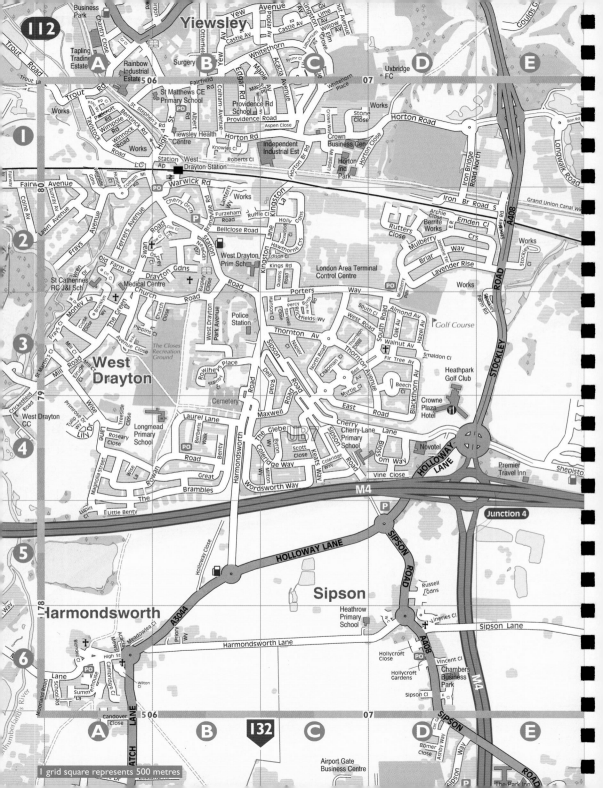

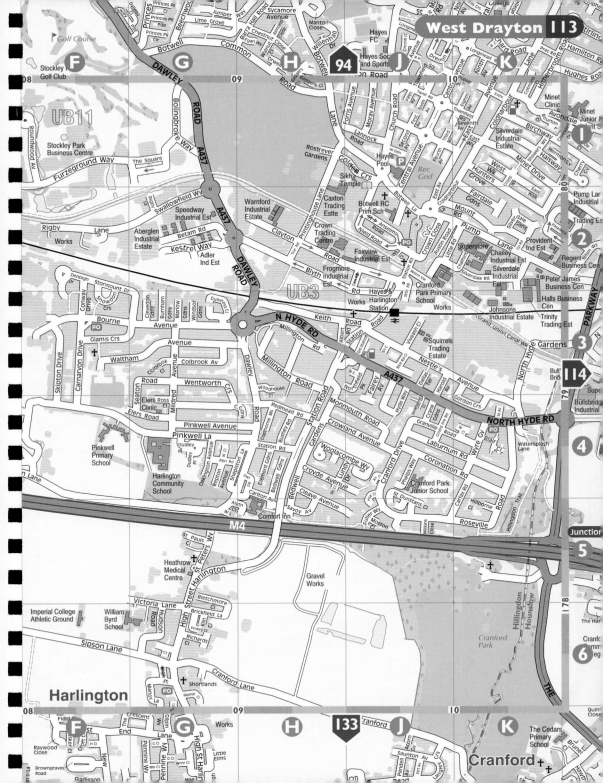

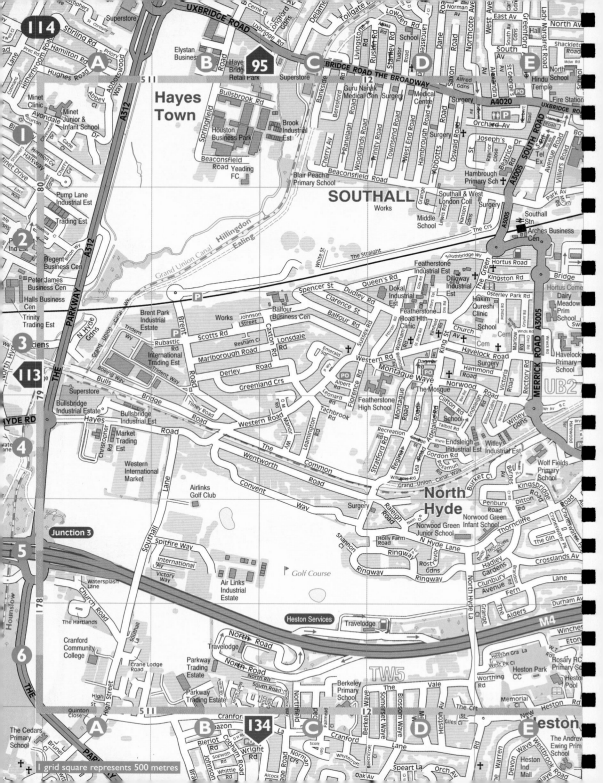

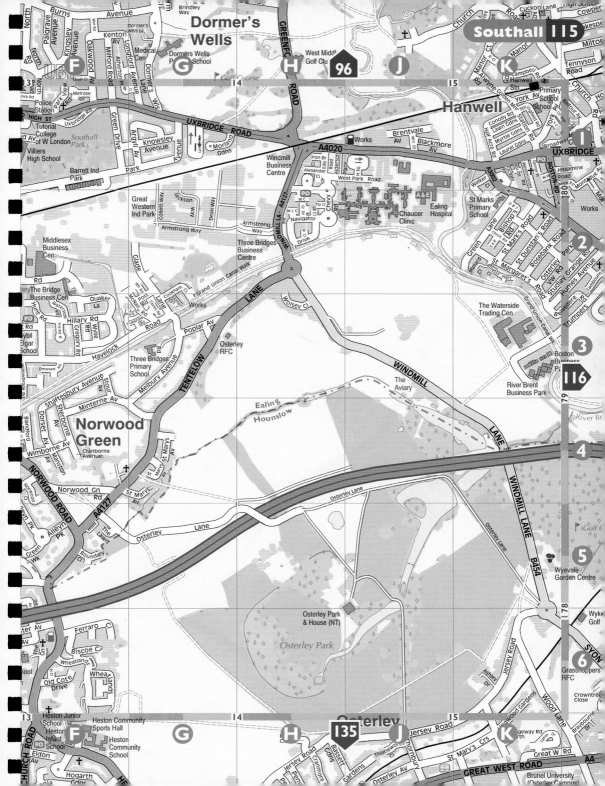

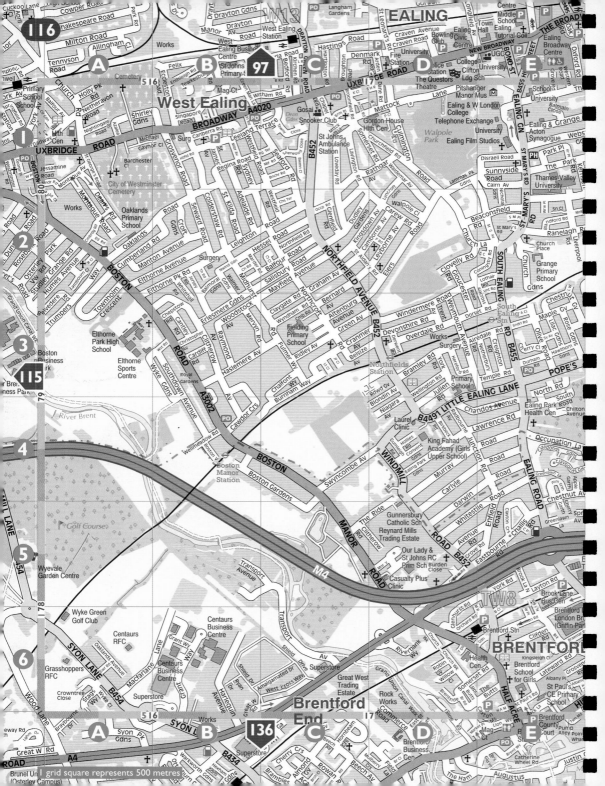

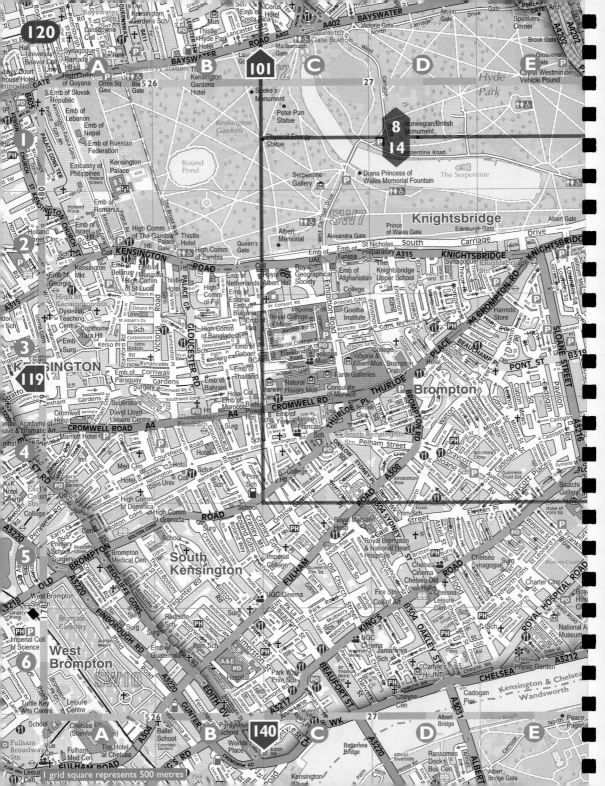

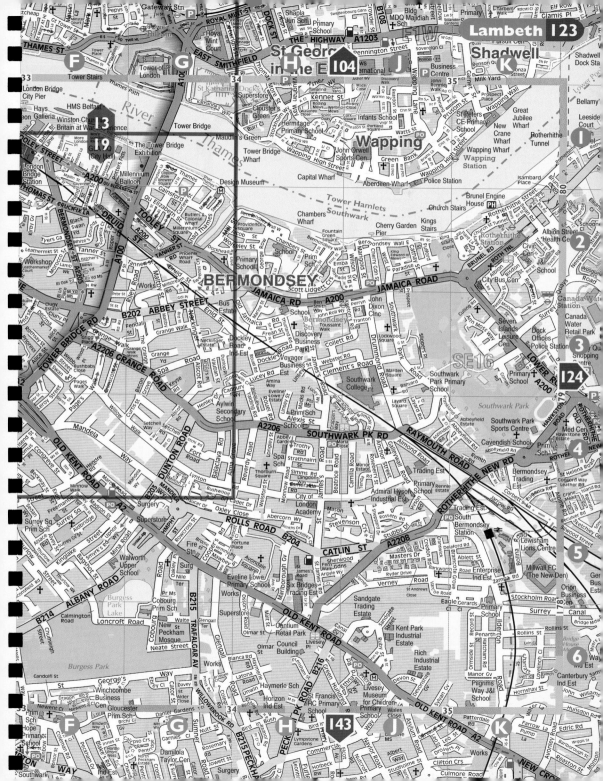

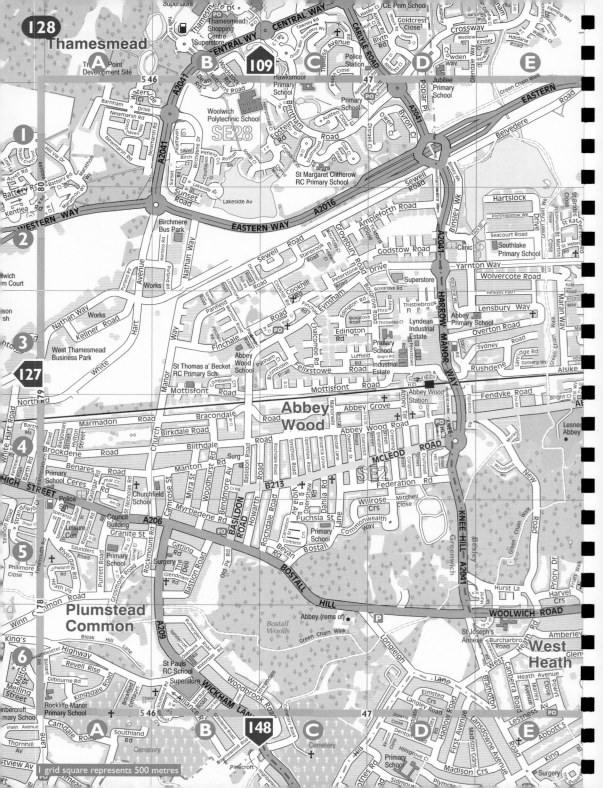

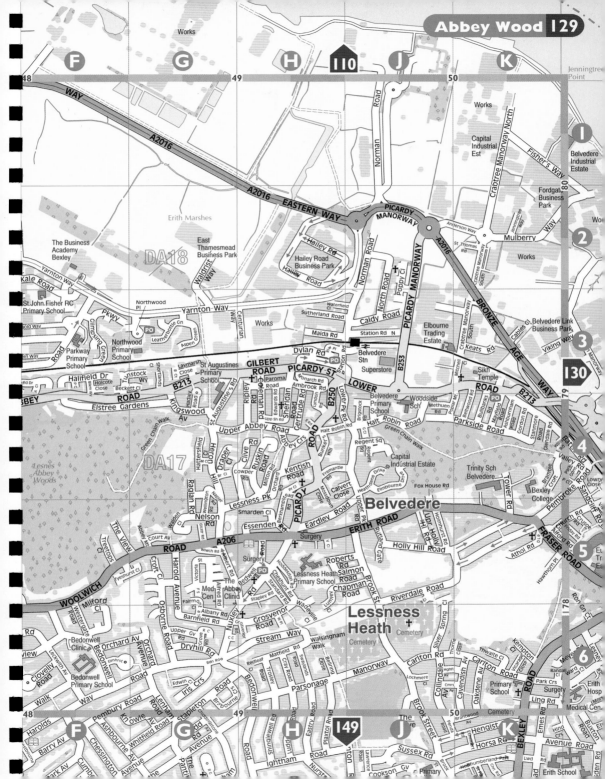

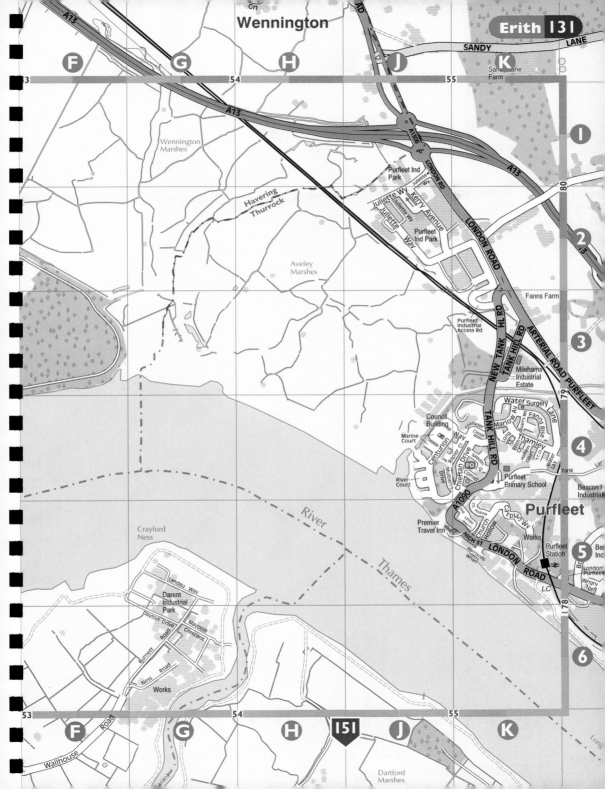

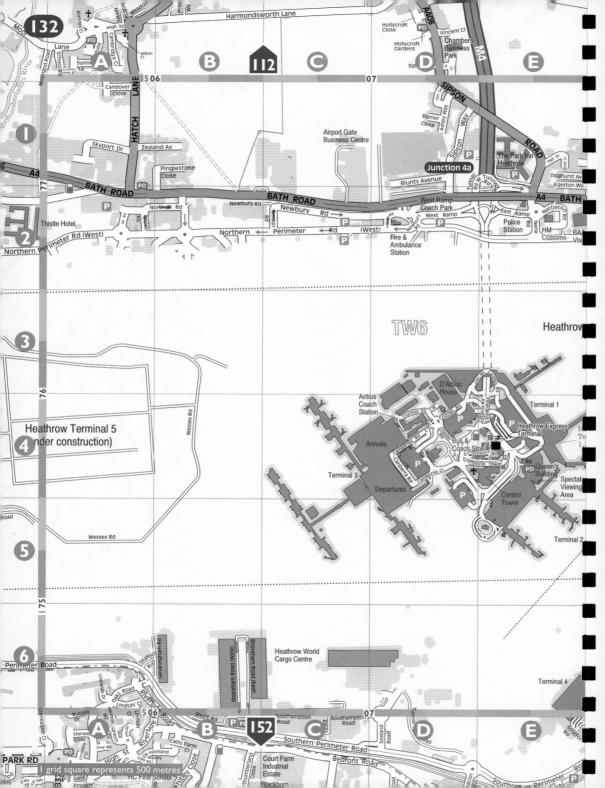

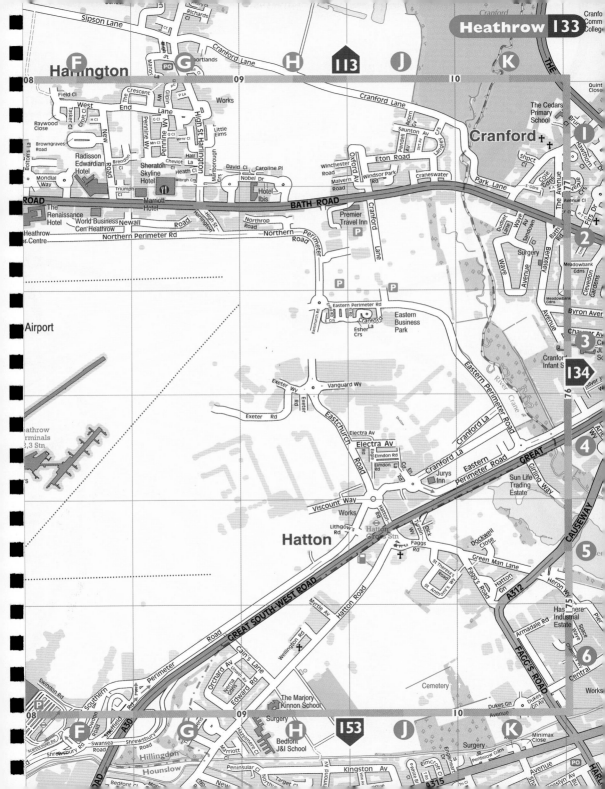

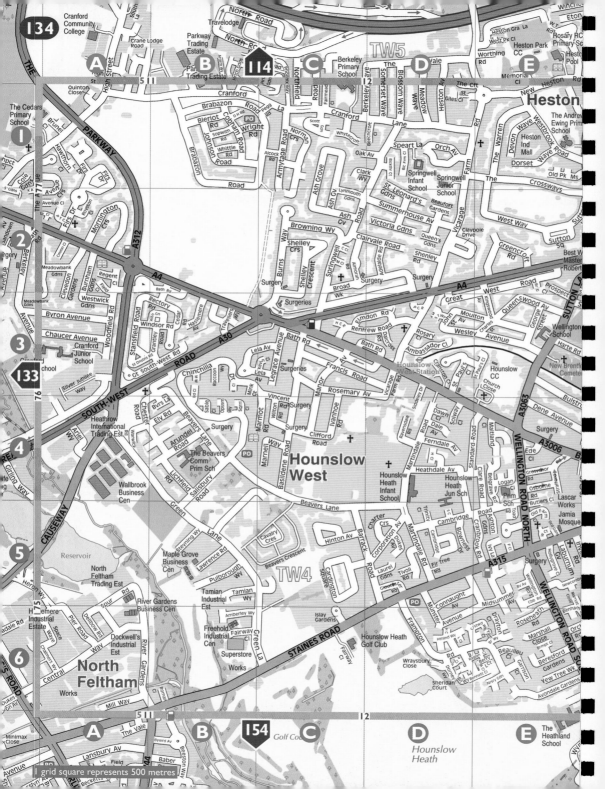

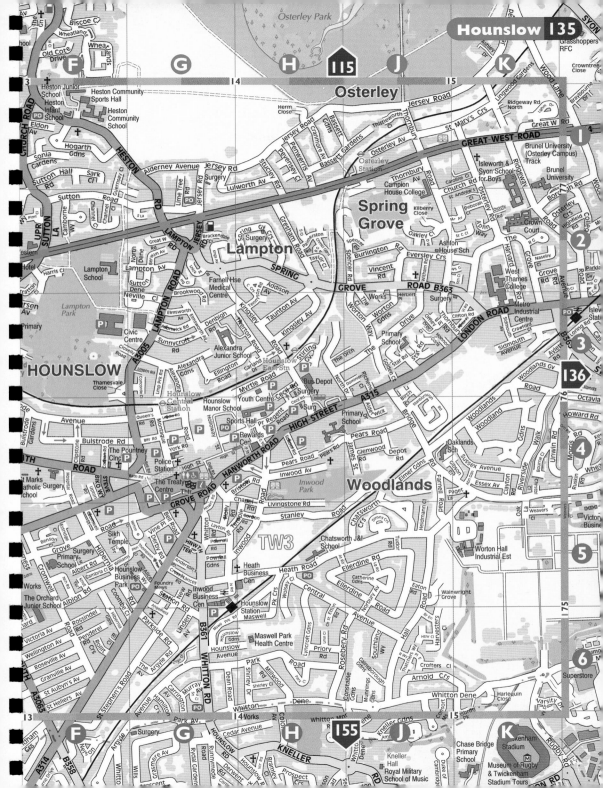

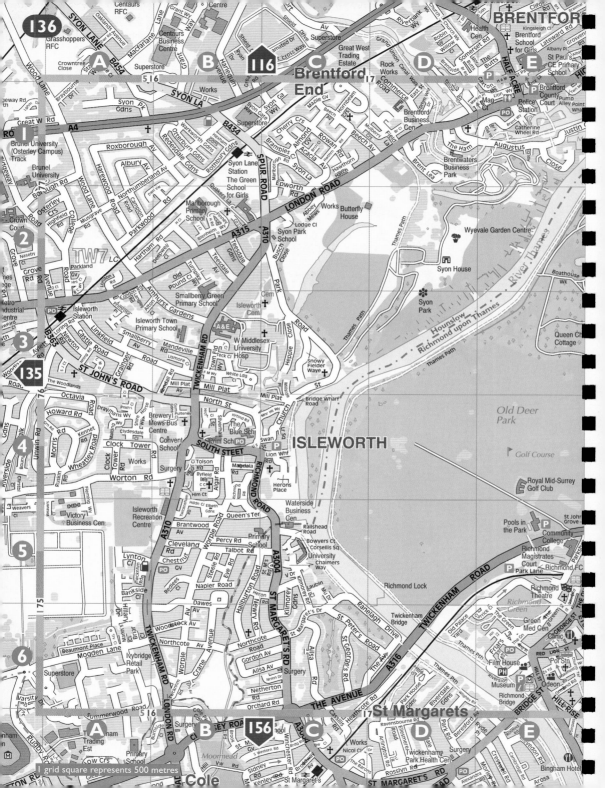

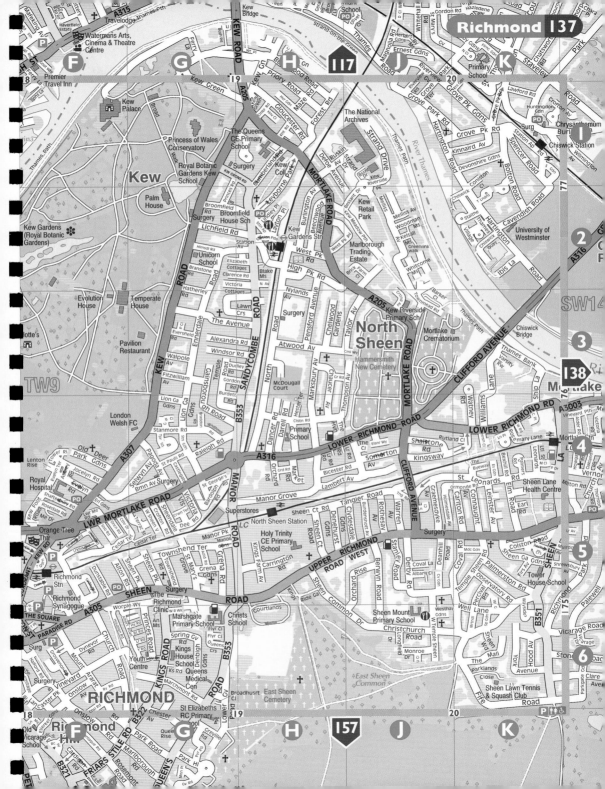

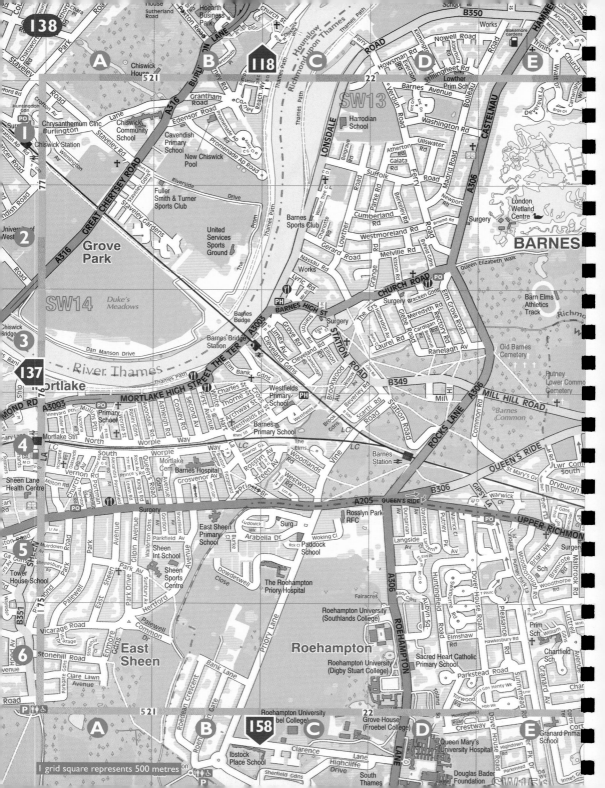

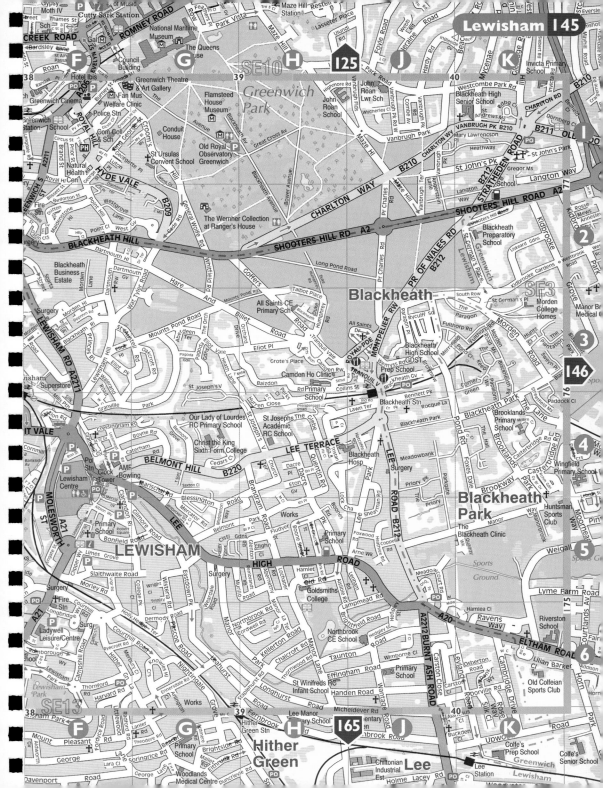

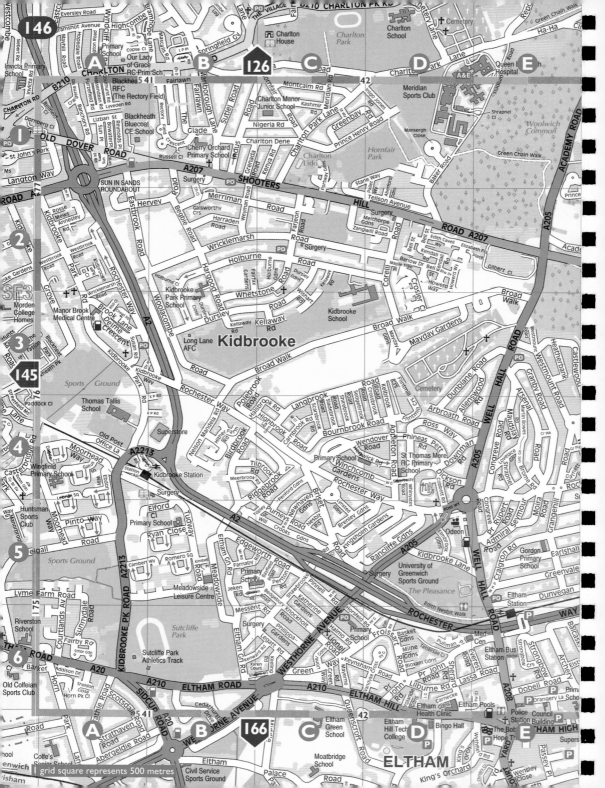

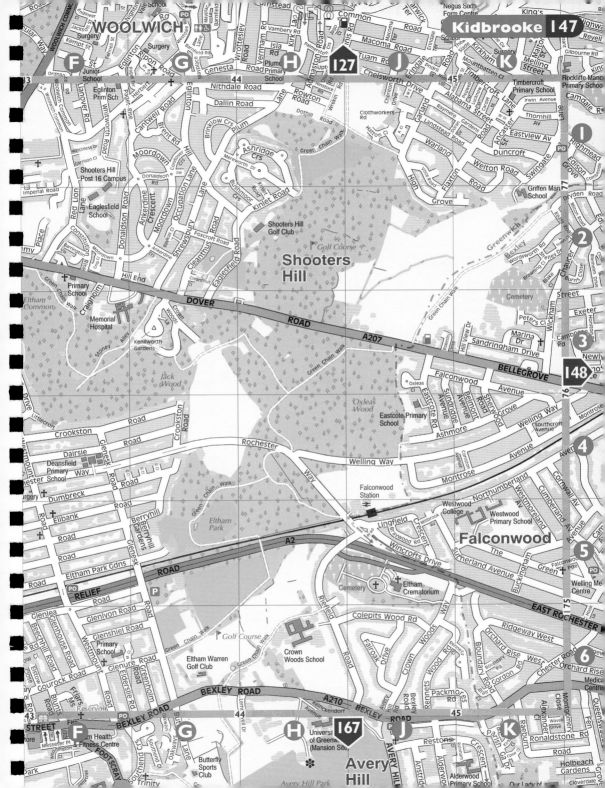

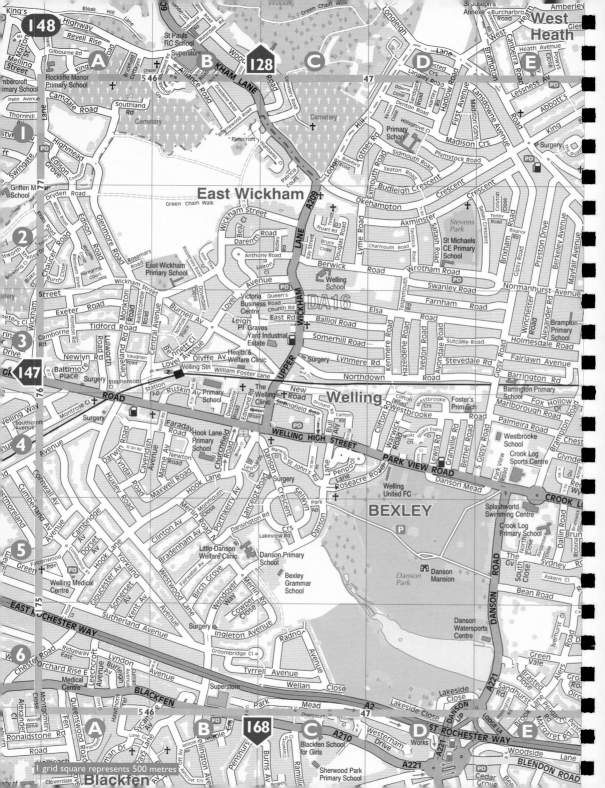

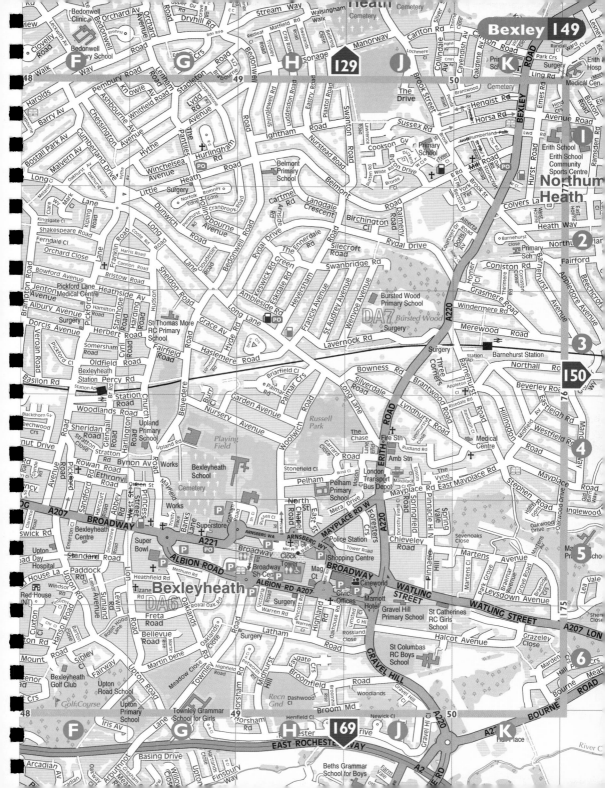

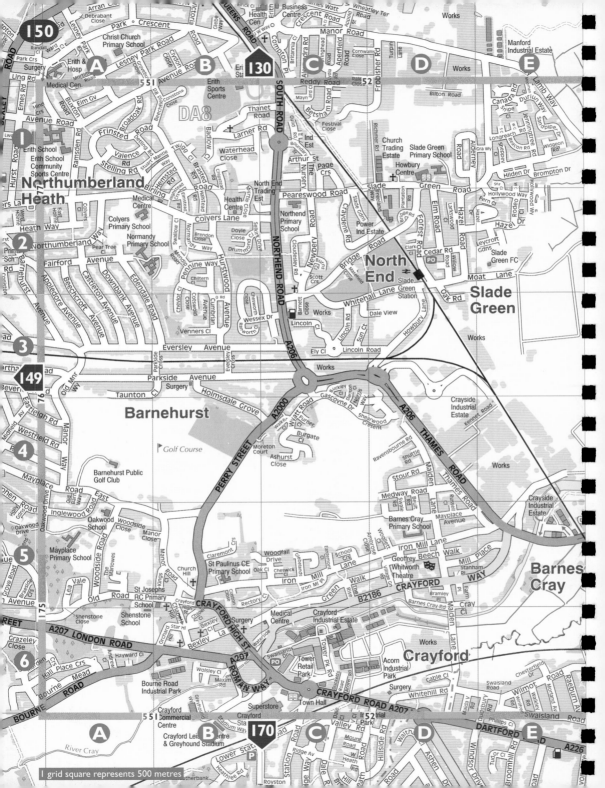

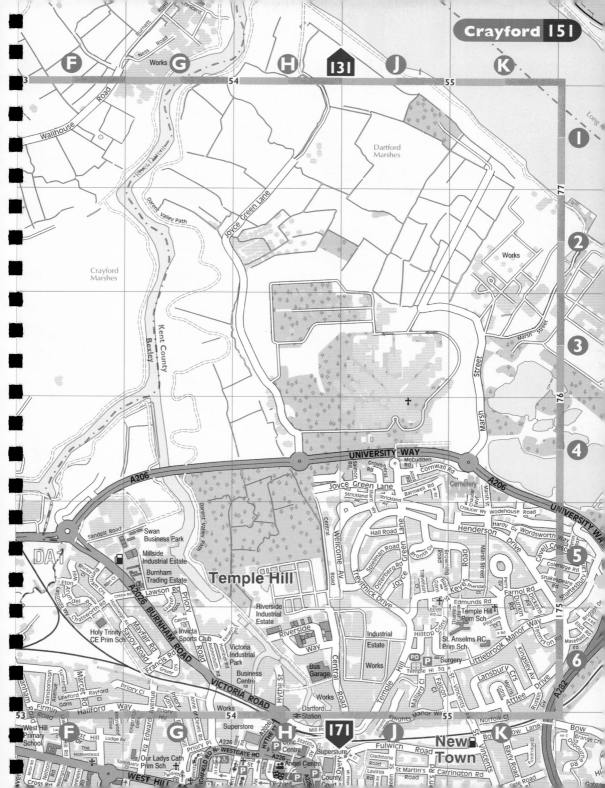

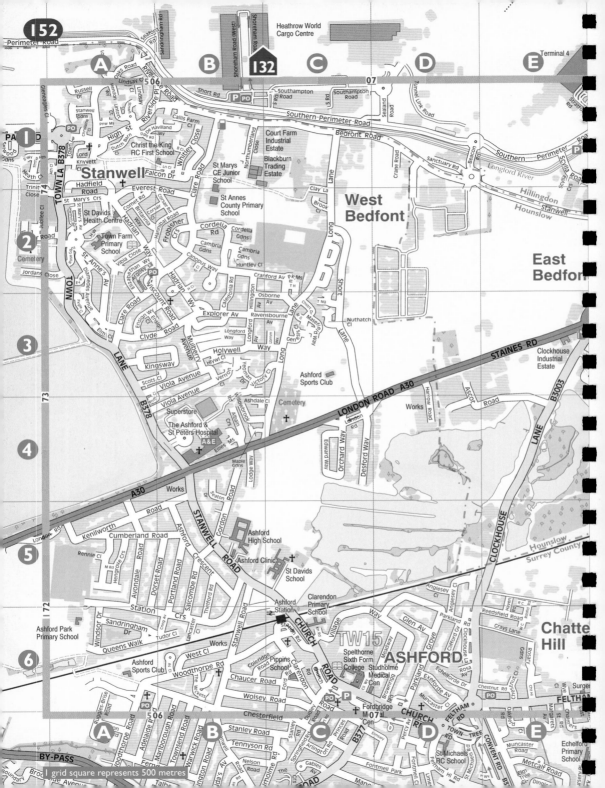

152
Perimeter Road

Heathrow World
Cargo Centre

A   B   132   C   D   E Terminal 4

Shoreham Road West
Seaford Rd
Sandringham Rd

Perimeter Road

Russell
Dr
Lindsay Dr
Lindsay Pl
Riverside Rd
Short Rd

Southampton
Road
Southampton
Road

Southern Perimeter Road

P PO

Bedfont Road

Southern   Perimeter   Road
Tunnel Link Road

Callis Farm Cl
Northumberland Cl
Crane Road
Sanctuary Rd
Beacon Rd
Longford River
Scylla Rd
P

Stanwell Gdns
High St
De Havilland Dr
pnw Ms

Court Farm Industrial
Estate

Sealand Rd

Hillingdon
Hounslow
Stanwell

PO
Lord
Knyvett
Cl
Christ the King
RC First School
Dutch Barn
Whitethorn Rd
Clare Road
St Marys
CE Junior
School
Blackburn
Trading
Estate
Clay La

Stanwell
Trinity
Close
Hadfield
Road
Falcon Dr
Everest Road
Corsair
St Annes
County Primary
School
Brook Rd
**West
Bedfont**

St Mary's Crs
Comet Rd
Britannia
Frobisher
Crs
Cordelia
Rd
Cordelia
Gdns
Long   Road
**East
Bedfon**

St Davids
Health Centre
Hadrian
Cambria
Gdns
Cambria
Gdns
Huntlui Cl
Short   Lane

2
Cemetery
Town Farm
Primary School
Vibia Close
Canopus Way
Cranford Av
Pk Ms
T H
Jordans Close
St Anne's Av
Diemedes Avenue
Viscount Road
Elizabethan Way
PO
Hillingdon
Osborne
Av
T Ng

Clare Road
Ensign Wy
Explorer Av
Ravensbourne
Nuthatch
Lane

3
Clyde Road
Longford
Way
Longford
Way
Vernon
Dr
Victory Rd
Way

LANE
Kingsway
Mulberry   Avenue
Holywell
Way
HVwll Cl
Scots Cl
Viola Avenue
Yeomans Dr
Vernon Dr
Way
Ashford
Sports Club

Viola Avenue
Albion
Willowbrook
Ashdale Cl
Cemetery
LONDON ROAD A30
London
Rd
Works

Superstore
The Ashford &
St Peters Hospital
A&E
Eliots Ms
STAINES RD
Clockhouse
Industrial
Estate

4
London Rd
A30
Works
Seaton
Rd
Maple
Gdns
Lodge Way
Orchard Way
Desford Way
Edward Way
Harrow Road
Ascot Road
Lane
B3003

5
Kenilworth   Road
Cumberland Road
Gordon Road
Ashford   Crescent
STANWELL   ROAD
Ashford
High School
Ashford Clinic
St Davids
School
Clockhouse
Hounslow
Surrey County
Rennie Cl
Hengrove Crs
Avondale Dr
Dorset Road
Portland Road
Salcombe Rd
Thetford Rd

Clarendon
Primary
School
Anglesey Av
Anglesey Ct
Reedsfield Rd
Grays Lane
**Chatte
Hill**

Station
Crs
Lancaster
Tudor Cl
Ashford
Station
CHURCH   ROAD
Village
Way
glen Av
Grove
Parkland Rd
Clifford Rd
Clockhouse La
Rosa
Rd
Echelforde Dr
Rosary
Gdns

6
Ashford Park
Primary School
Windsor Dr
Sandringham
Dr
Queens Walk
Stanwell   Road
Works
Stanwell Rd
TW15
Spelthorne
Sixth Form
College
ASHFORD
Studholme
Medical
Cen
Parkland Gr
Exeforde Av
Muncaster Rd
PO
Chestnut Rd
Wye Rd
Surger

Ashford
Sports Club
Woodthorpe Rd
West Cl
Colnbridge
Road
Chaucer Road
Wolsey   Road
Coleridge
Road
Pippins
School
Clarendon
Rd
Ford   Rd
Fordbridge
M Cen
CHURCH   RD
Browning Rd
Echelforde Dr
FELTHAM
Margarets
Rd
Ockfield

Ruggles-Brise Road
Adelaide Road
Marlborough Rd
Warrick Rd
Townsend Road
Stanley Road
Tennyson Rd
Chesterfield   Road
Princes Rd
B377
Clarendon Rd
PO
P
Dudley Rd
Convent Rd
Percy Av
TOWN   RD
TREE   RD
Felrham Hi Rd
Muncaster
Road
Metcalf Road
Echelford
Primary
School

A   B   C   D   E
BY-PASS
Nelson Rd
Ida's Av
Brocklesmere Avenue
Tennyson Rd
Springfield Rd
Arlington Av
Fontmell Park
St Michaels
RC School
Fontmell Rd
Convent Rd

1 grid square represents 500 metres

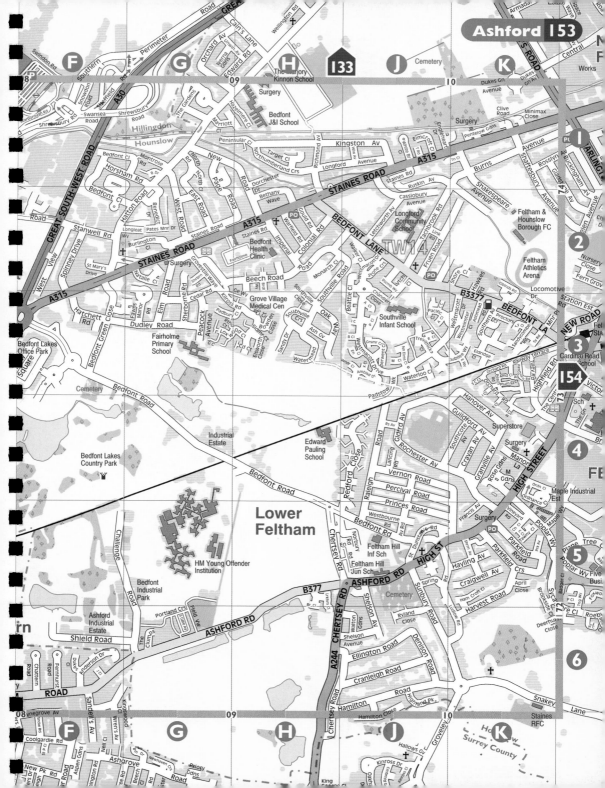

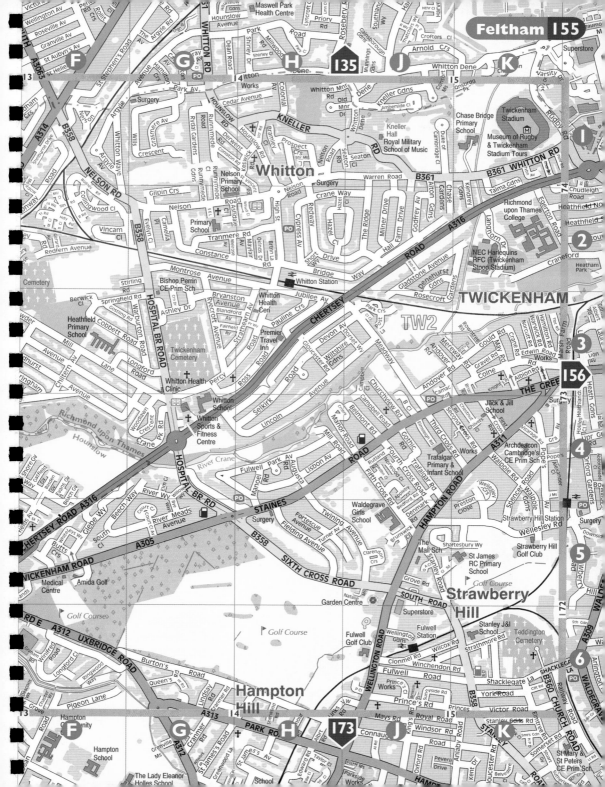

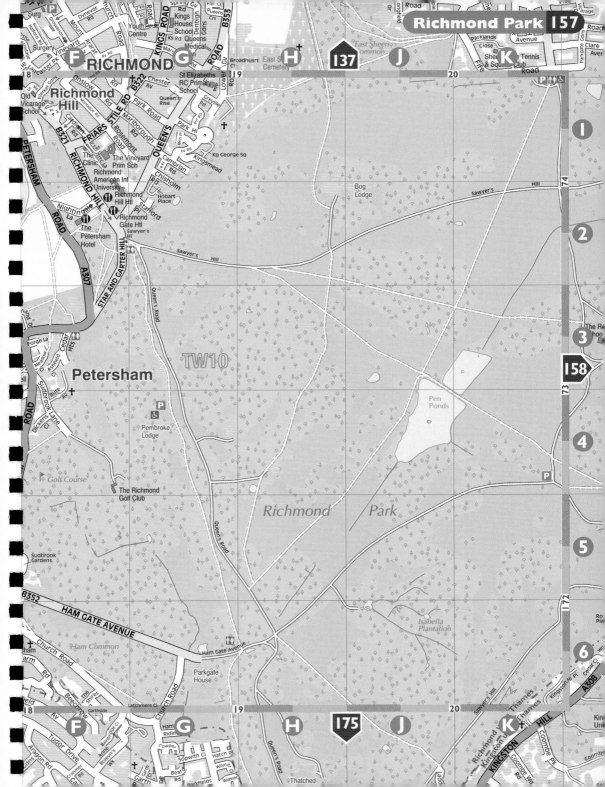

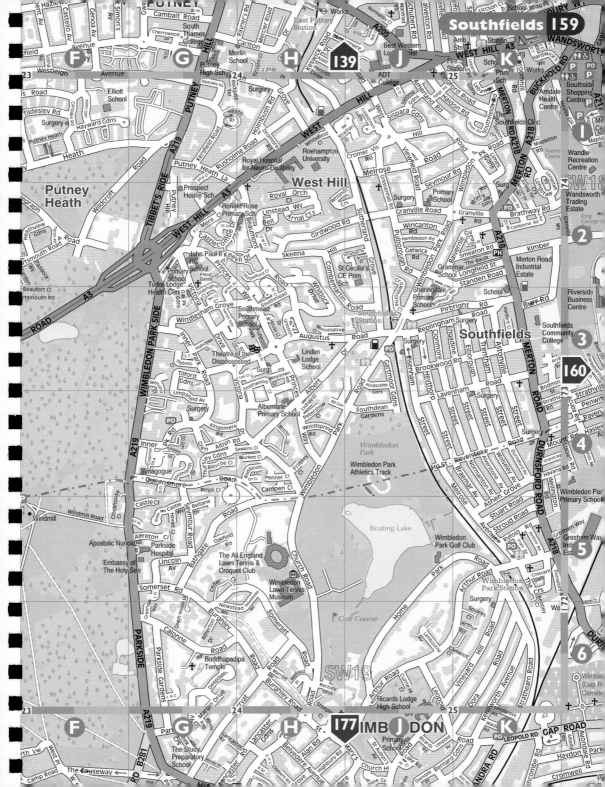

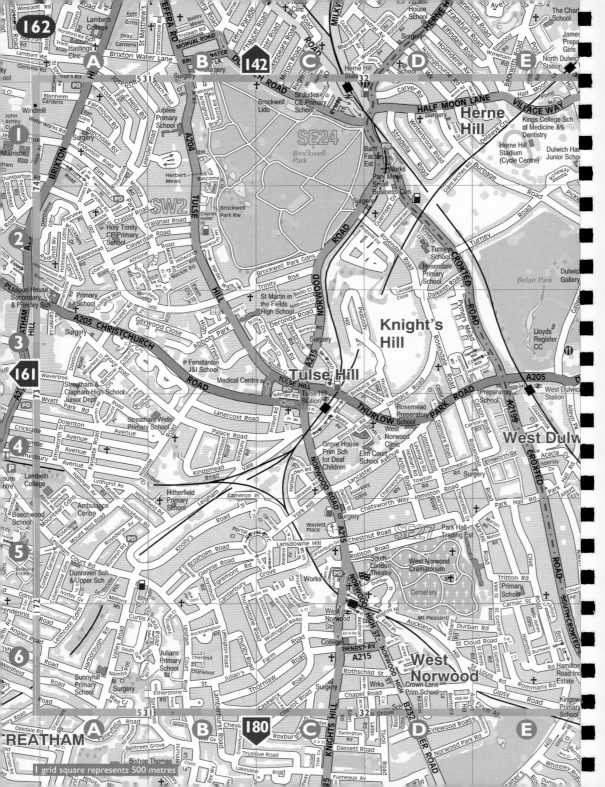

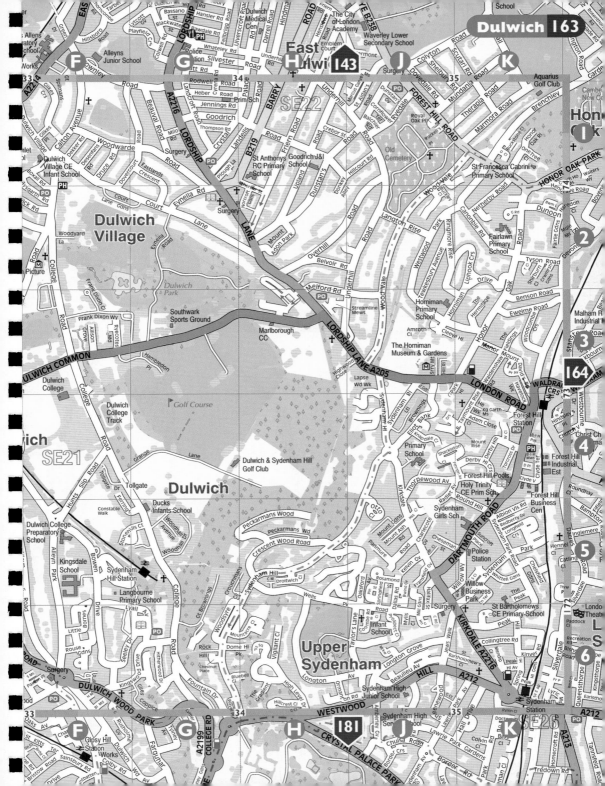

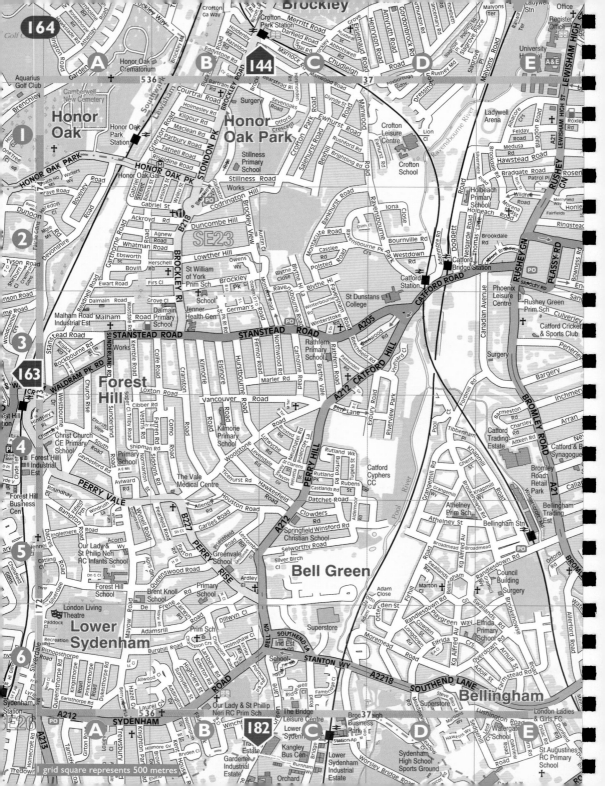

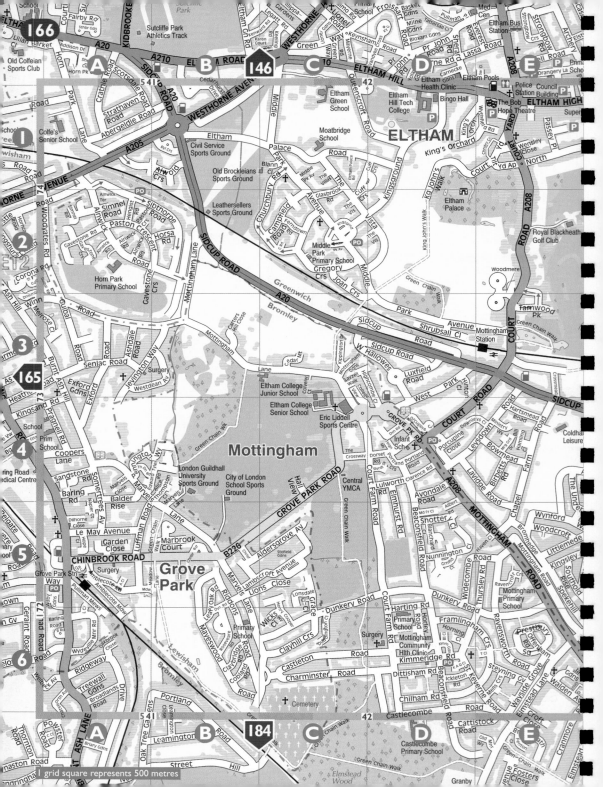

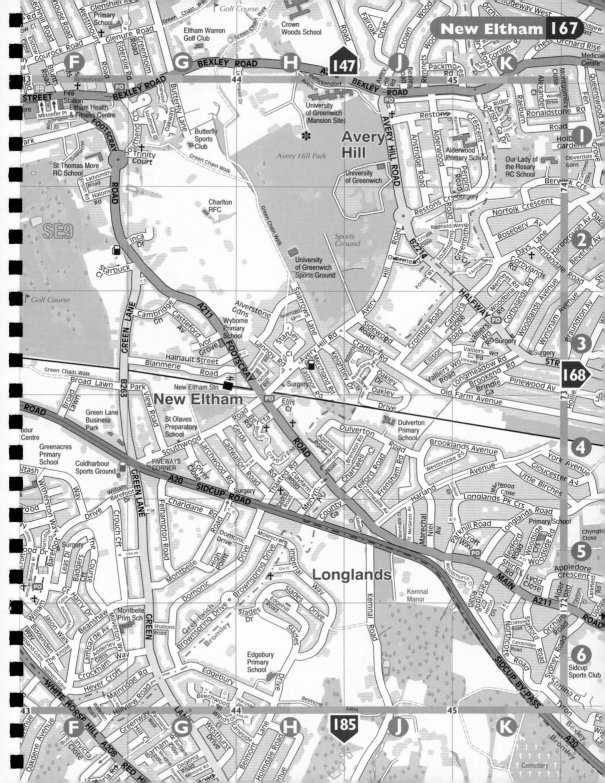

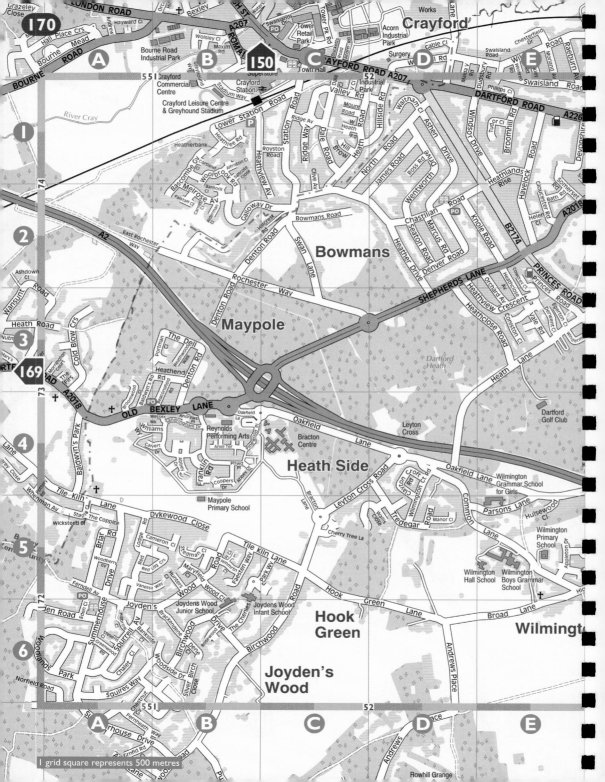

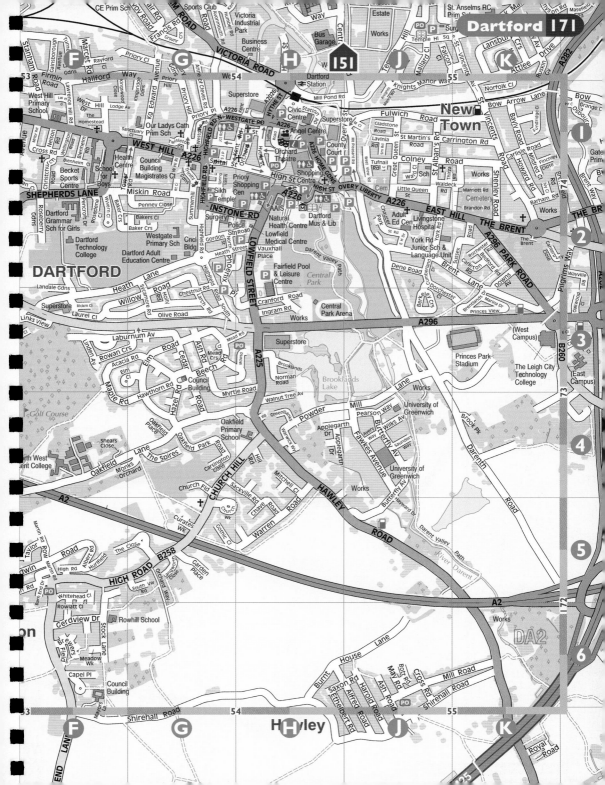

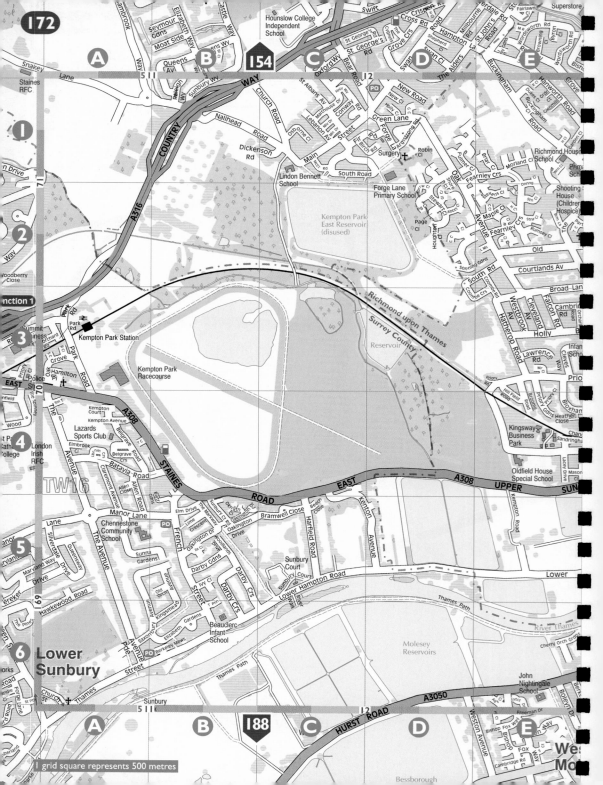

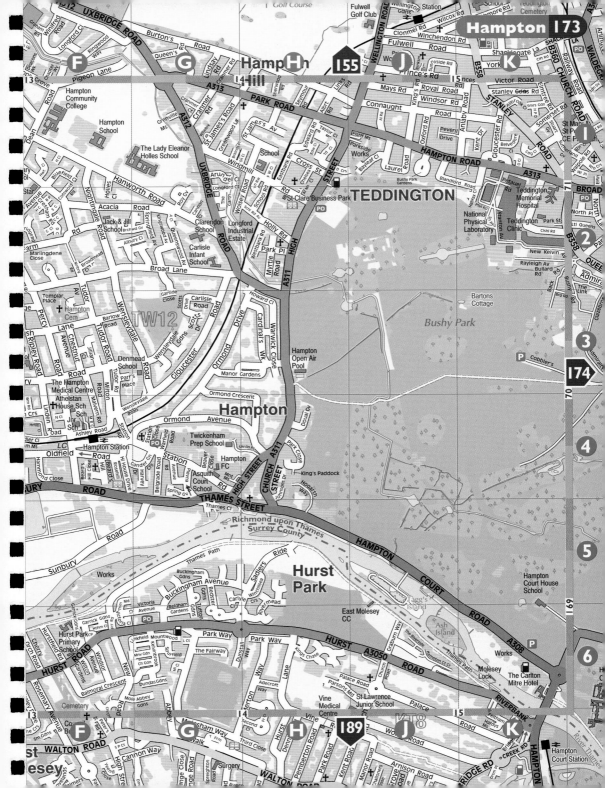

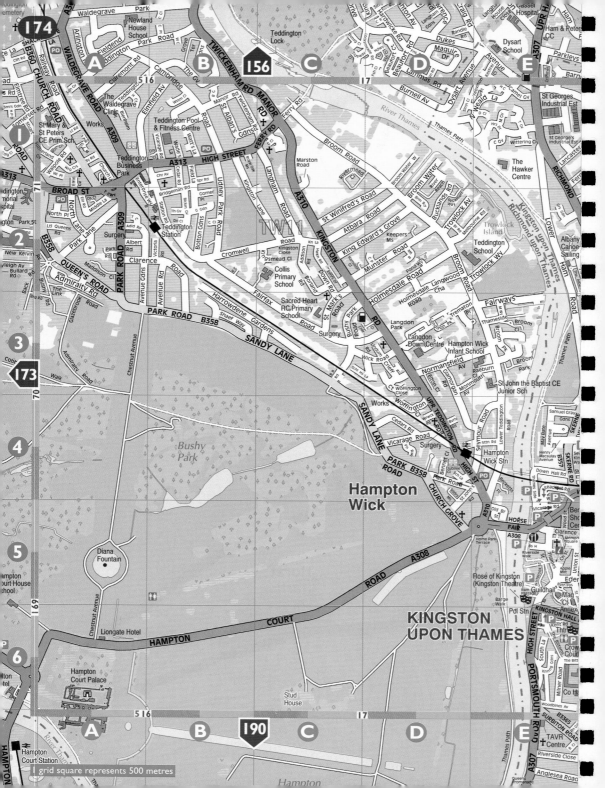

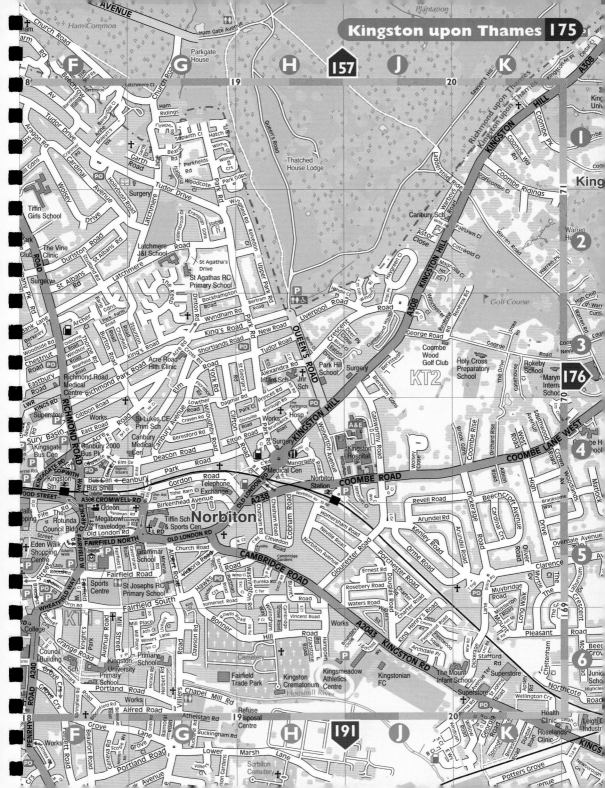

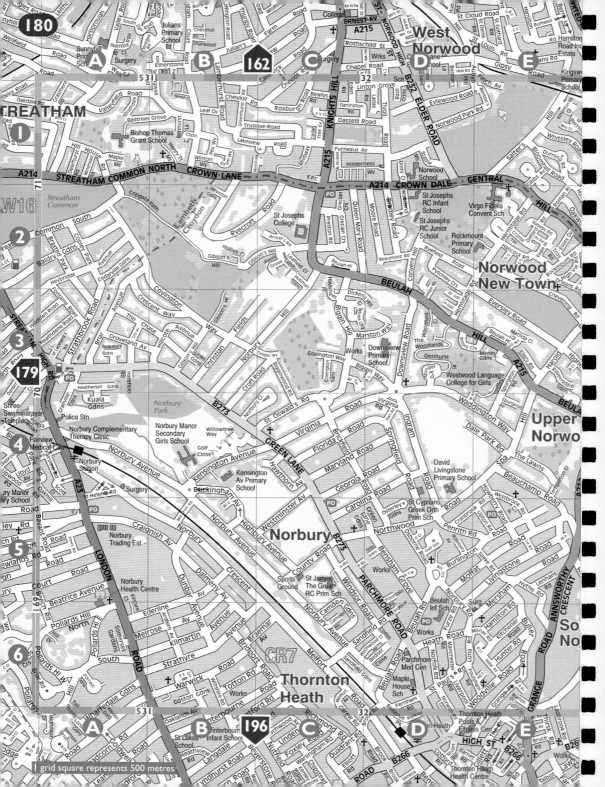

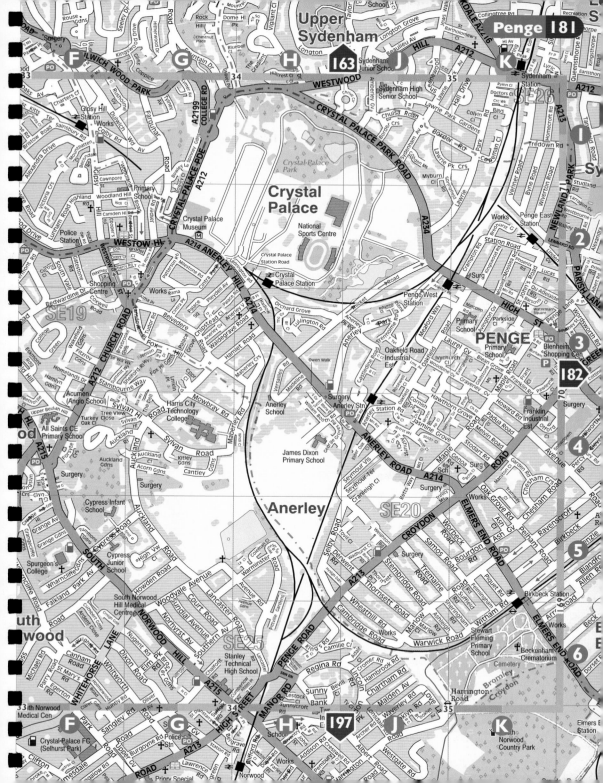

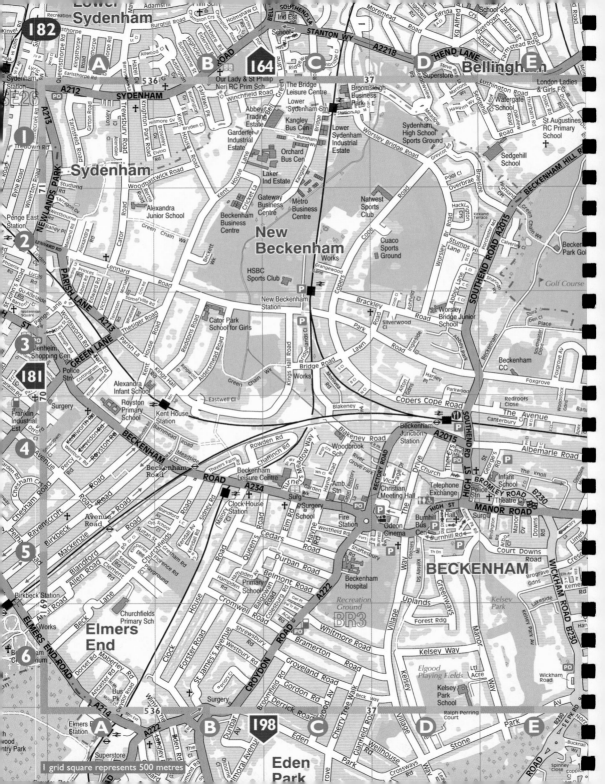

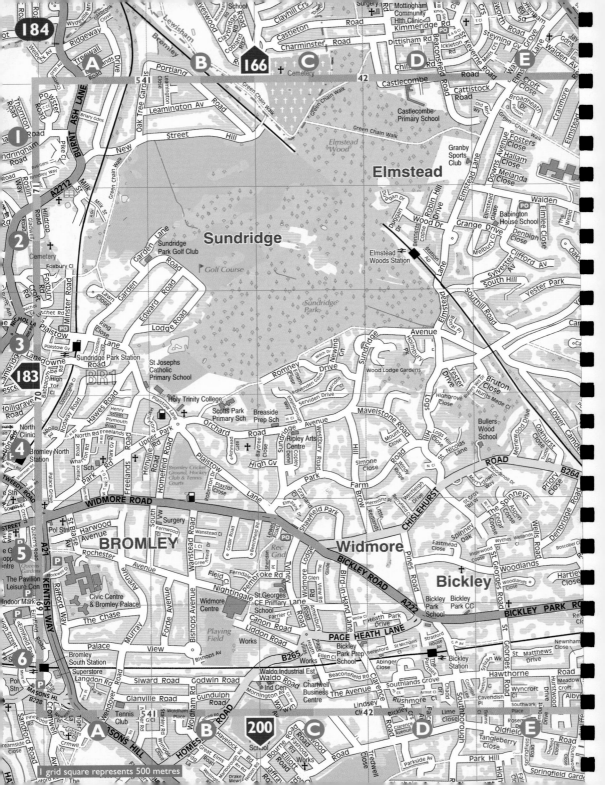

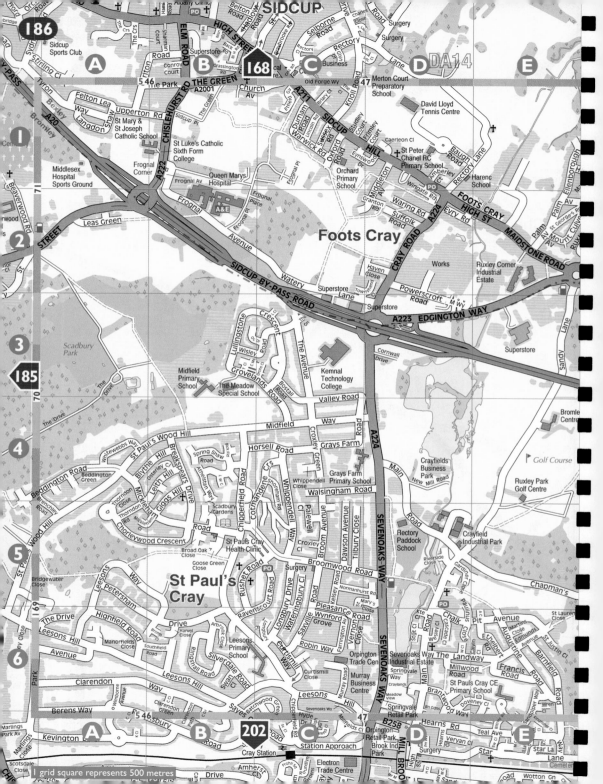

F **G** **H** **169** **J** **K**

I

2

3

4

5

6

F **G** **203** **J** **K**

Norfield Road

Gattons WI

Cemetery

Parsonage Lane

Manor Farm

The Spinney

The Grove

Way

St James

A223

NORTH CRAY ROAD

High Beeches

Bedensfield Clinic

PO

Burdett Close

Gower Close

Thursland Road

Road

Buillers Close

Vill Rd

Beds Road

N Cray Rd

Honeyden Road

Cornell Close

Barton Rd

Paddocks

Ruxley

Whitney Walk

Bexley, Kent County

Golf Course

Stonehill Green

Chalk Wood

Birchwood Park Golf Club

Bexley

Bromley

Garden Centre

MAIDSTONE ROAD

Old Maidstone Road

B2173

A20

Birchwood R

70

A20

B2173

B2173

Works

Pucknells Close

Harest Way

Setan Dr

Collier Way

Russett Way

Wisteria C

Walnut W

4

Leydenhat

y Ski

Cray Valley Golf Club

Golf Course

Cookham Road

Upper Hockenden

Kent County

Bromley

Heathwood Gdns

Lawn Ct

Crescent Gdns

Woodview Rd

Cedar Close

Ash

LONDON

A20

The Croft

Dale Ro

Sermon Drive

Brook Road

Rowan Road Way

Almon Dr

Chapman's Lane

Hockenden Lane

Hockenden

Lane

Star Lane

Laburnum Av

Bourne Way

Laven der Hill

Farm Avenue

Lynden

Cherry Avenue

Mo ello Close

Sheepcote Lane

8 49 50

48 49 50

71

2

70

3

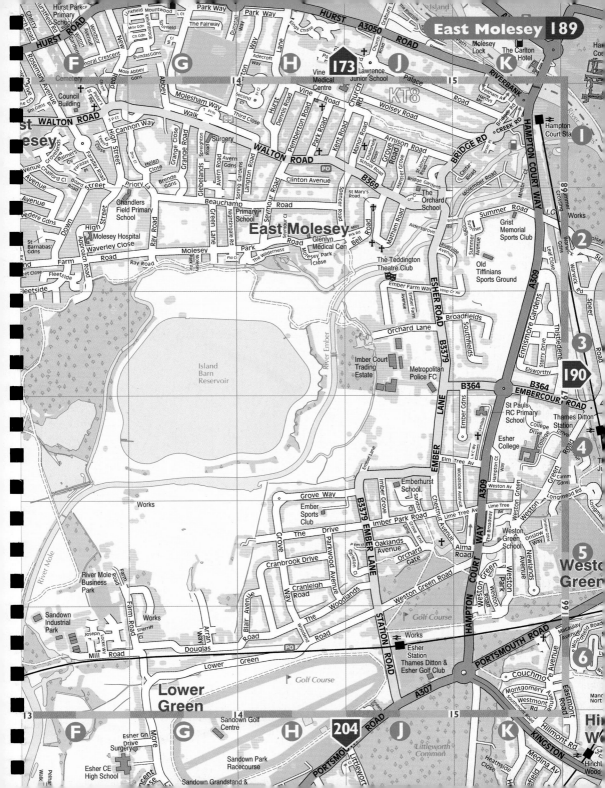

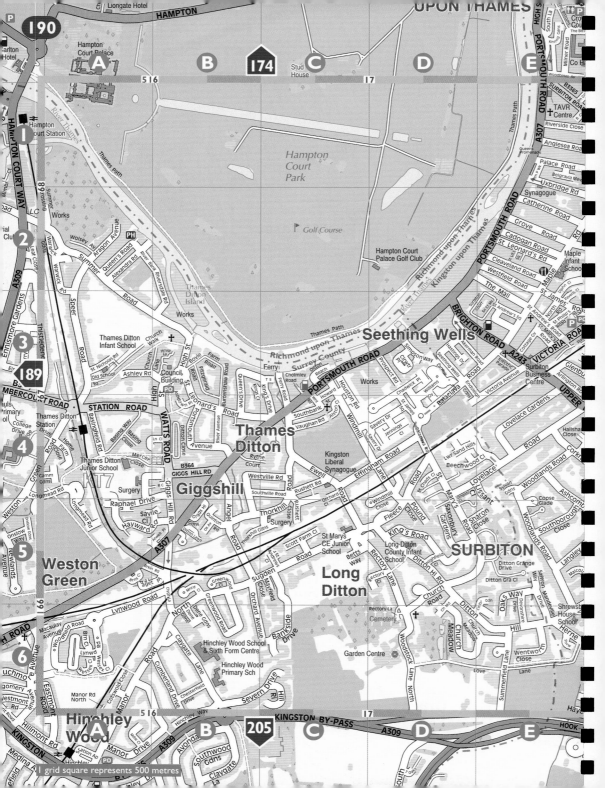

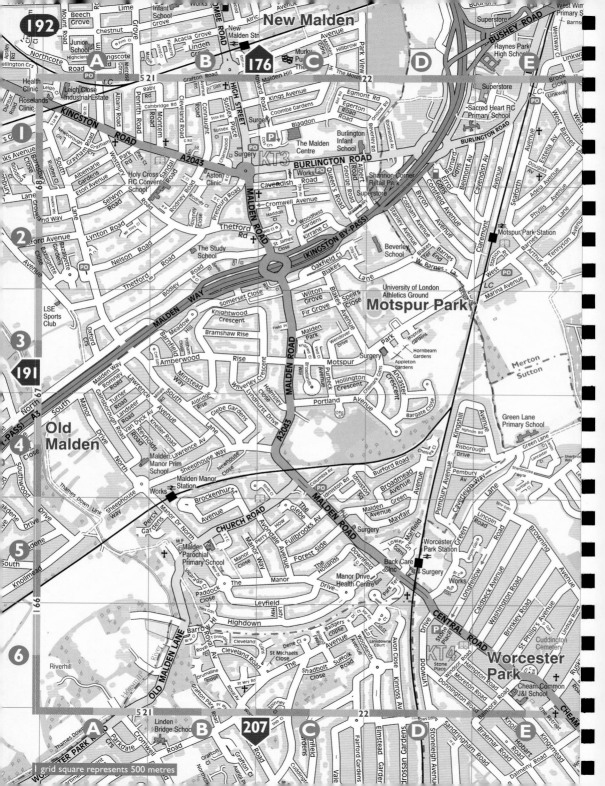

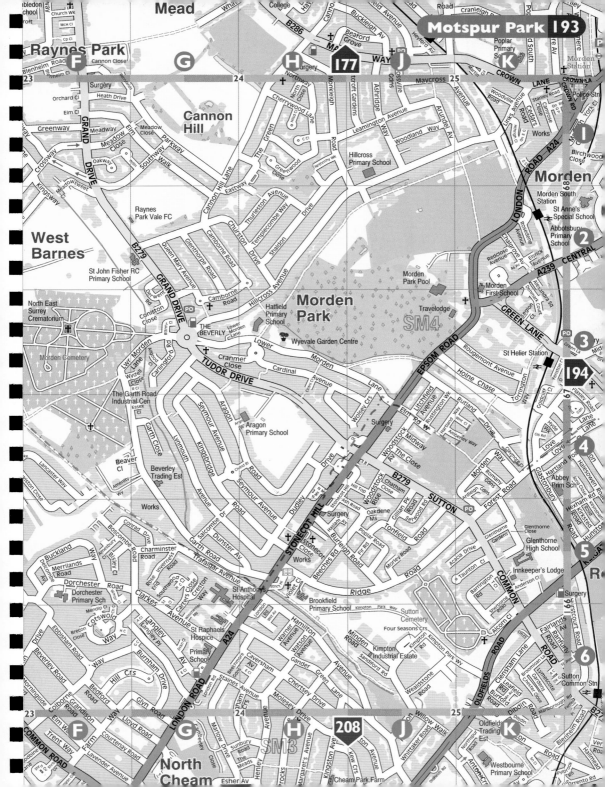

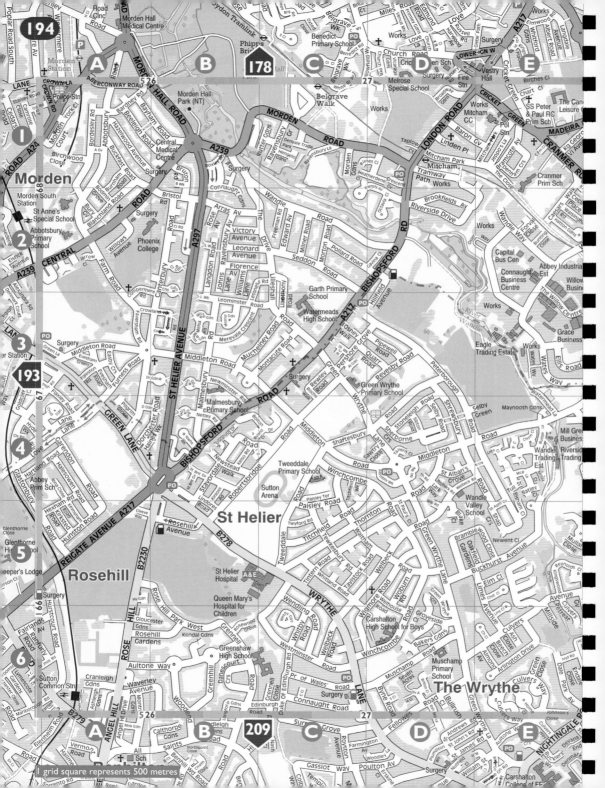

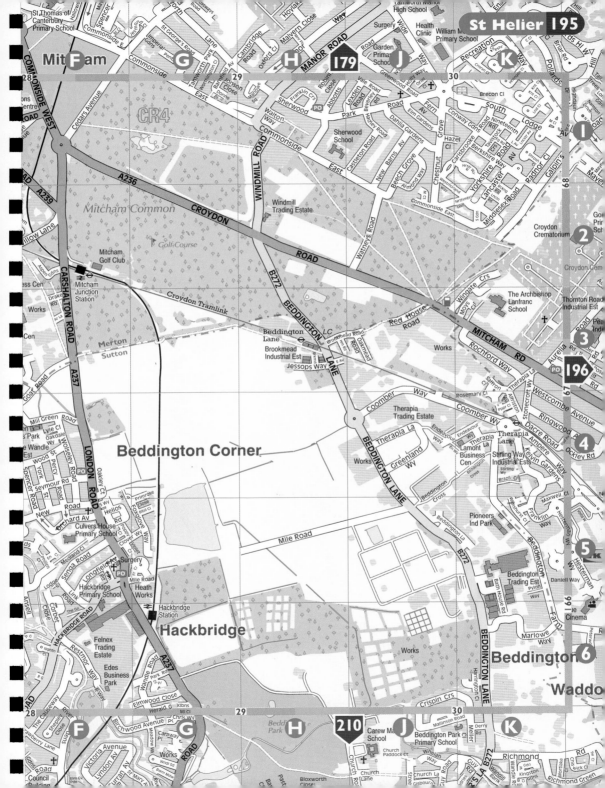

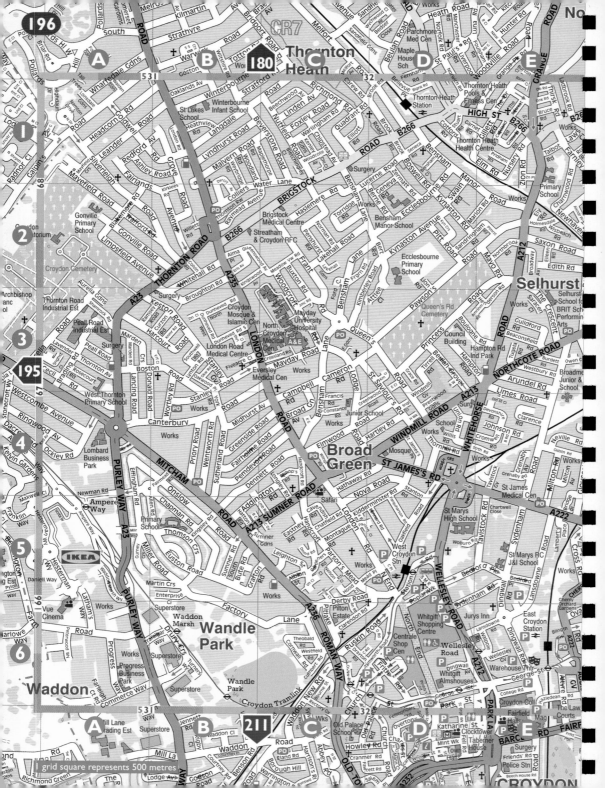

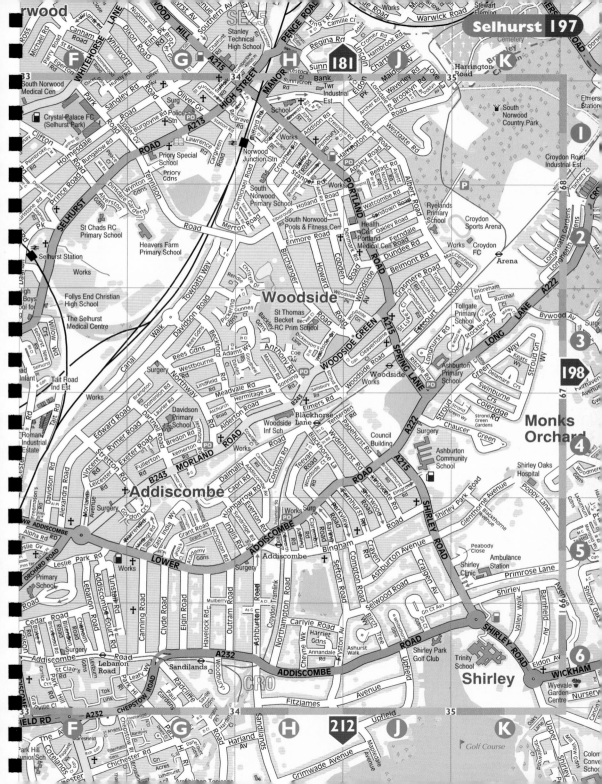

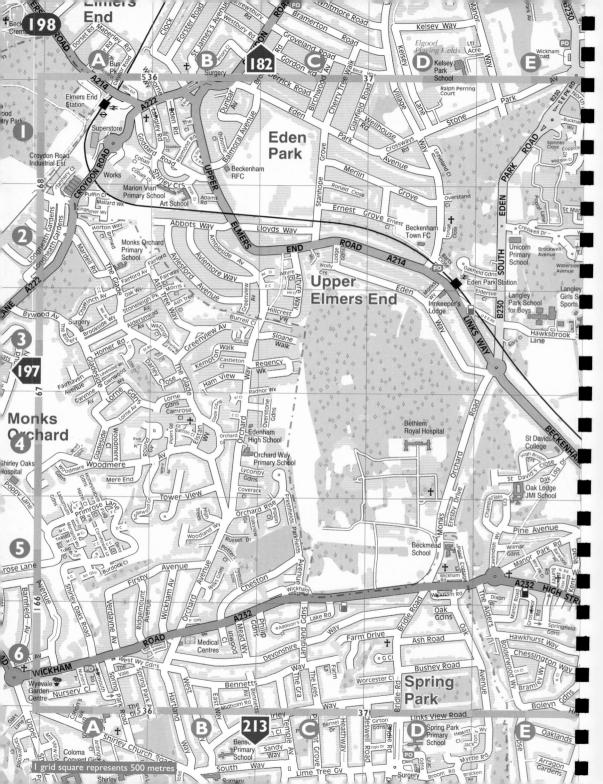

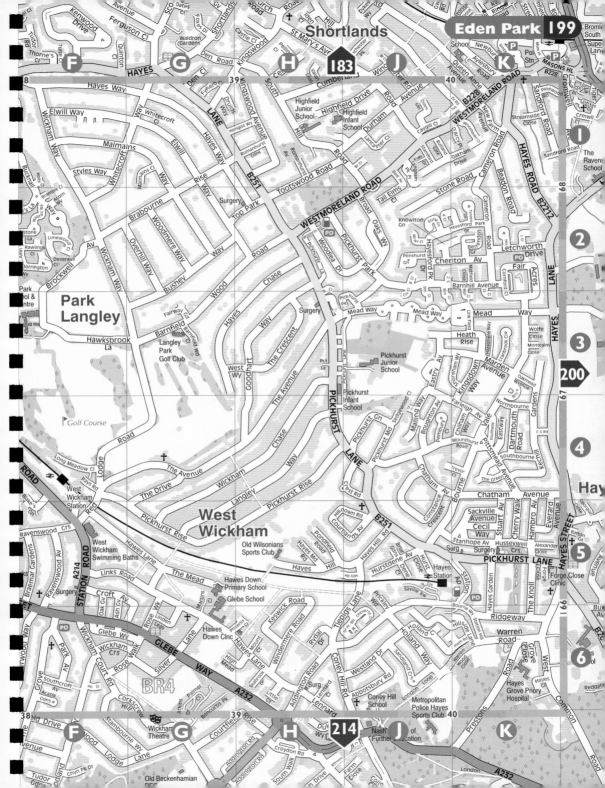

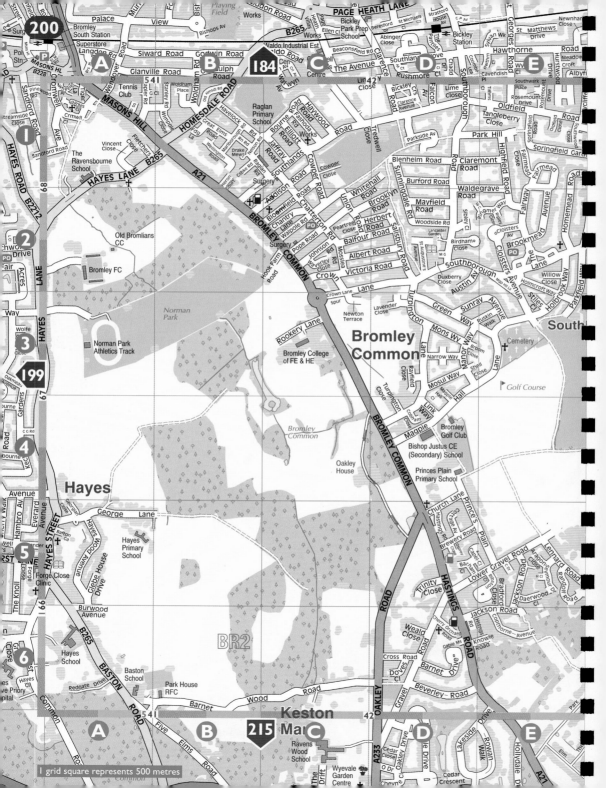

PAGE HEATH LANE

B265

184

199

215

Bromley Common

Hayes

BR2

Keston Mark

Places and roads (labels visible on map):

Bromley South Station
Superstore
Langdon Rd
Siward Road
Glanville Road
Palace View
Bishops Av
Godwin Road
Gulph Road
Tennis Club
Homesdale Road
Raglan Primary School
Masons Hill
Hayes Lane
The Ravensbourne School
Old Bromlians CC
Bromley FC
Norman Park
Norman Park Athletics Track
Bromley College of FE & HE
Rookery Lane
Bromley Common
Newton Terrace
Crown Lane
Crown Lane Spur
Lavender Close
Green Way
Sunray Avenue
Cemetery
South
Golf Course
Bromley Golf Club
Bishop Justus CE (Secondary) School
Oakley House
Princes Plain Primary School
Church Lane
George Lane
Hayes Primary School
Hayes Street
Forge Close Clinic
Burwood Avenue
Hayes School
Baston School
Park House RFC
Trinity Close
Hastings Road
Lower Gravel Road
Weald Close
Jackson Road
Cross Road
Barnet Road
Beverley Road
Barnet Wood Road
Ravens Wood School
Wyevale Garden Centre
Cedar Crescent
Hollydale

Blenheim Road
Claremont Road
Burford Road
Mayfield Road
Waldegrave Road
Park Hill
Highfield Road
Springfield Gardens
Southborough
Whitehall Road
Brooklyn Road
Herbert Road
Balfour Road
Albert Road
Victoria Road
Oldfield Road
Tangleberry Close
Rosemount
Brookmead
Willow Way

A21
A233
A2212
B228

1 grid square represents 500 metres

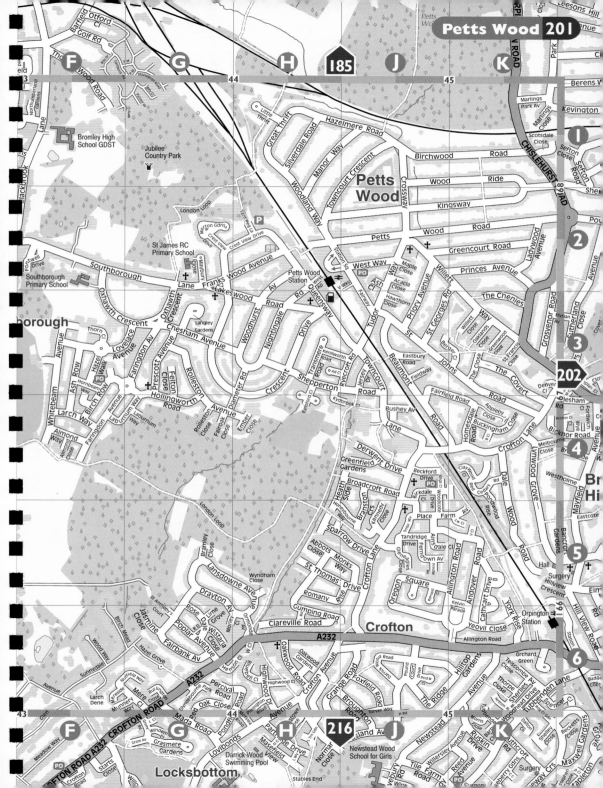

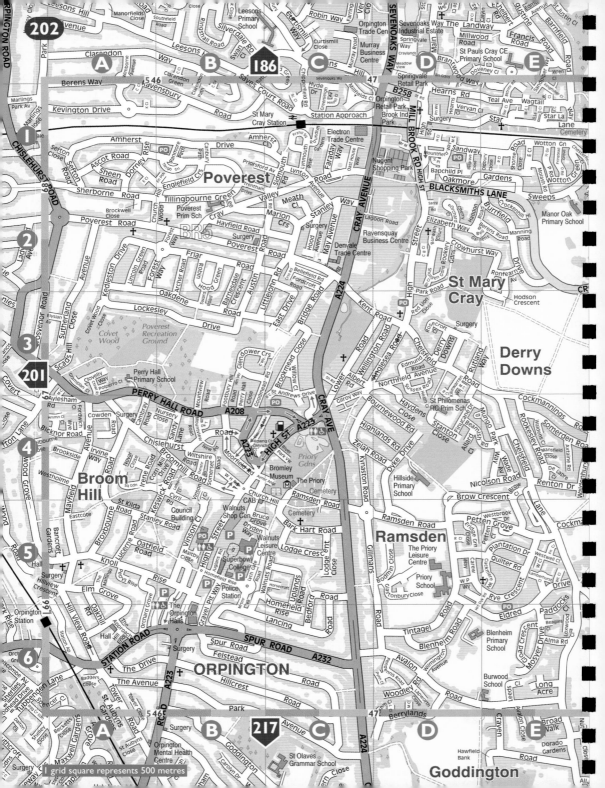

F G H 187 J K

Star Lane

Sheepcote Lane

Weeds Lane

Sheepcote Farm

Bourne Wood

Bromley London Kent County

Furness Swanley

Shawcroft School

Stones Cross Road

OCKENHILL ROAD

Kevingtown

B258

Walden's Road

Crouch Farm

Crockenhill Primary School

seven Acres

Crockenhill

GREEN COURT

Bransell Close

Broadway

CRAY ROAD B258

MAIN RD

PO

Church Road

Tudor Court

Tyler's Green Road

Old Chapel Road

Newport

East Hall Road

Lane

Darn's Hill

Woodmount

Harvest Way

Lone Barn

Gorse Road

Daltons Road

Crown Wood

Skeet Hill Lane

Kibbs Lane

F G H J K

I

2

3

4

5

6

49 50

48 49 50

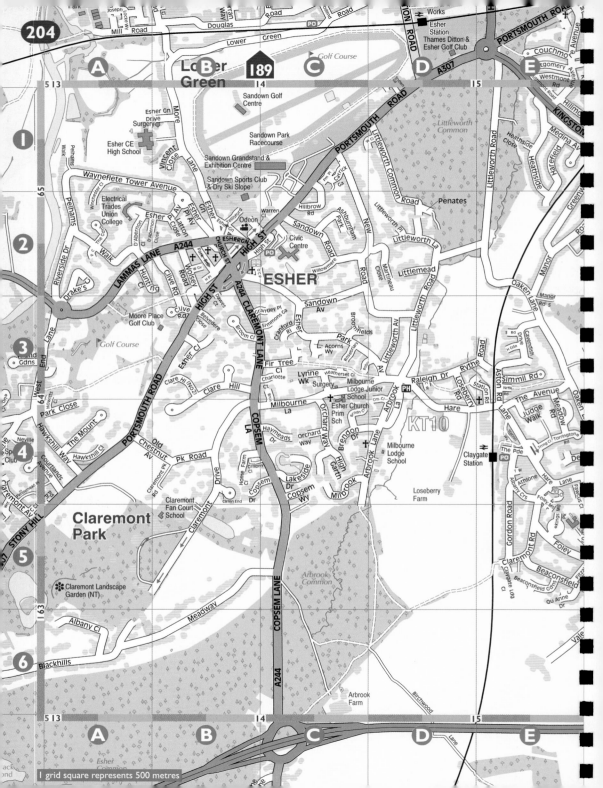

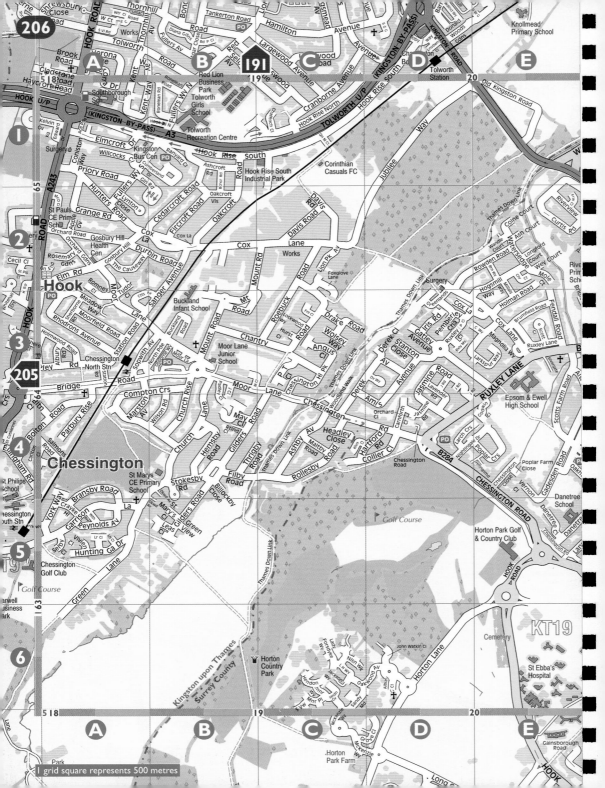

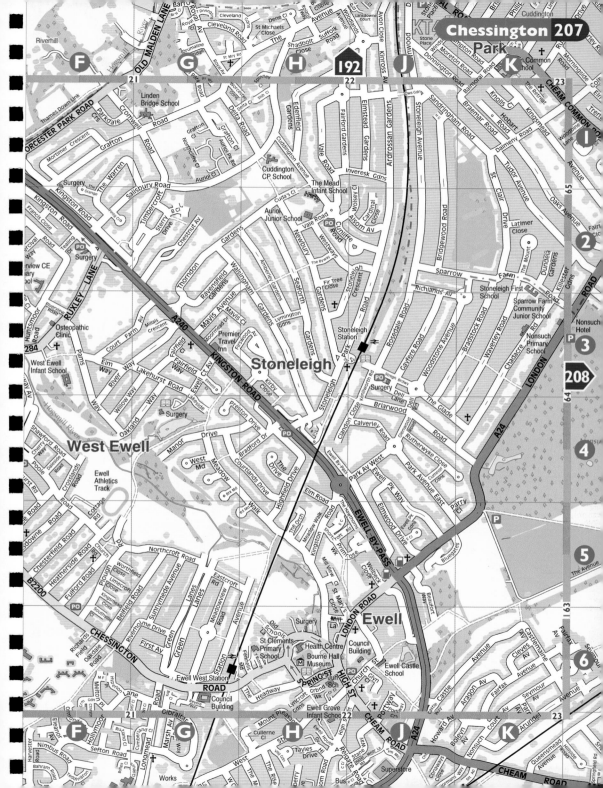

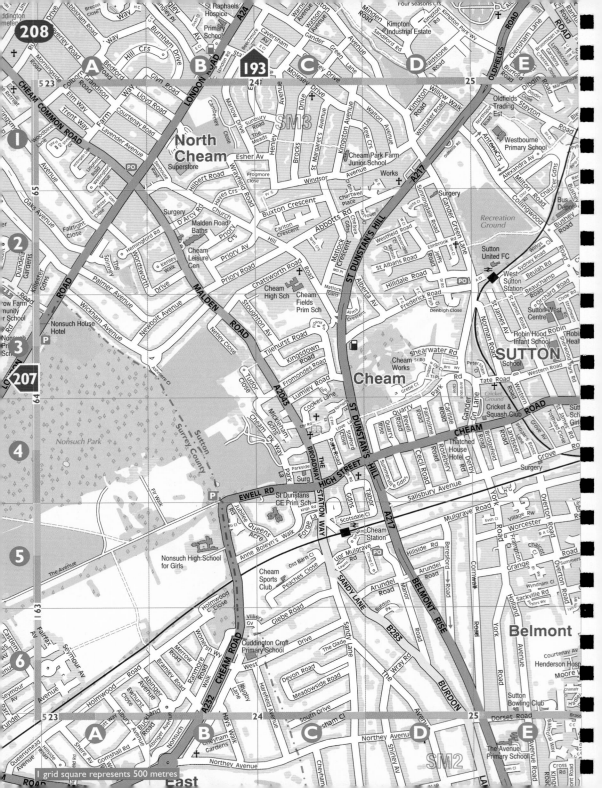

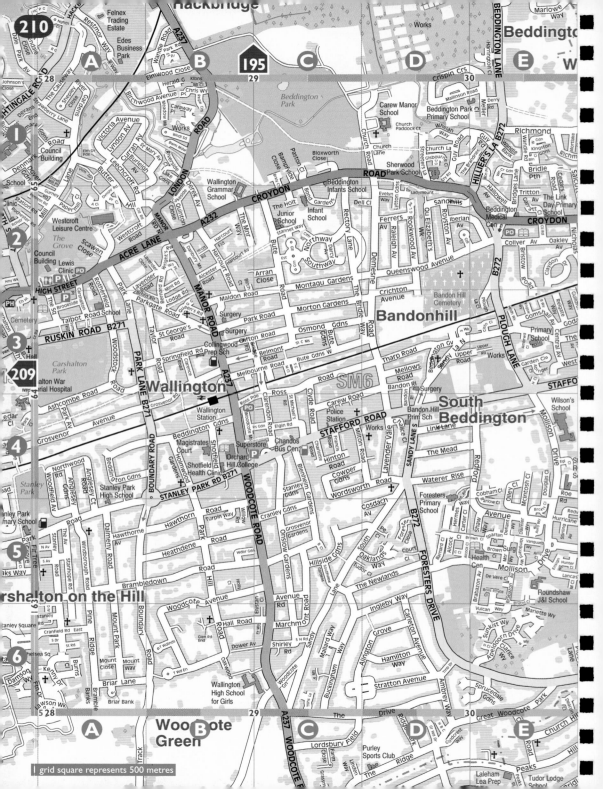

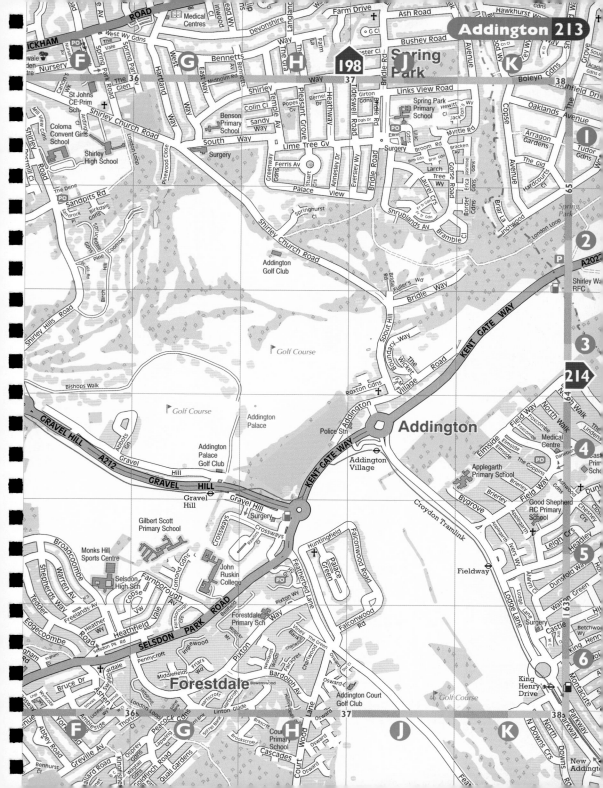

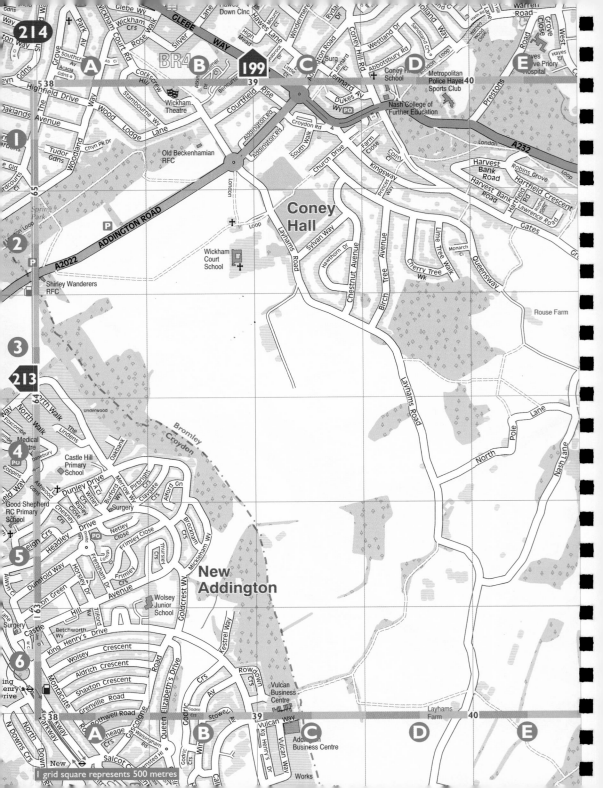

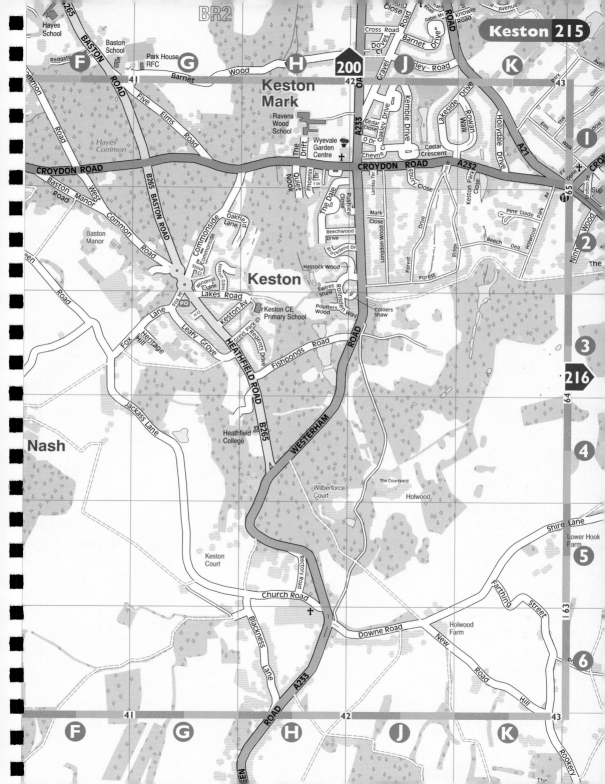

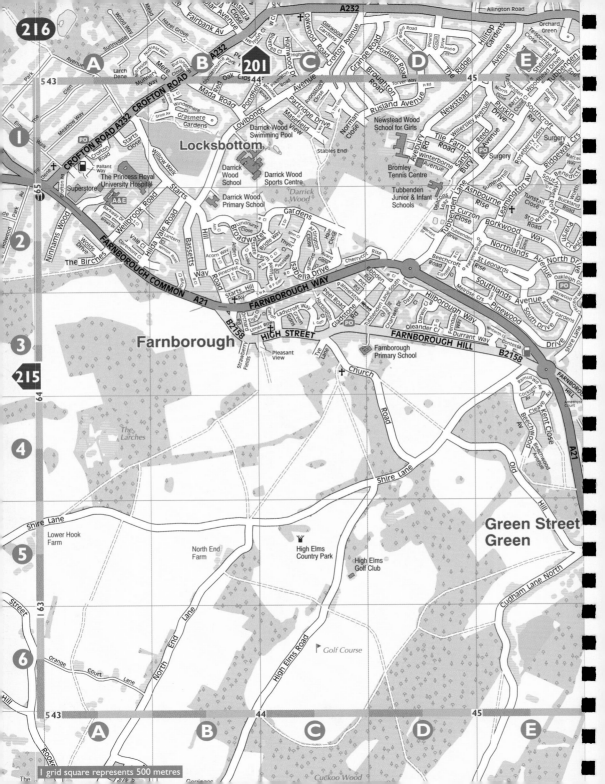

A232

Allington Road

Orchard Green

216

Sunnydale Avenue

Larch Dene

A 5 43

A232 201 44 B C D E

Wood Way
Hazel Grove
Fairbank Av
Fairbank Avenue

Oakwood Gardens
Oakwood Road
Crofton Avenue
Grange Road
Foxfield Road
The Ridge
Hilltop Gardens
Telscombe Av
Titscombe Close

Pound Court

Tubbenden

I
5 43

CROFTON ROAD A232

Mada Road

Red Oak
Pondfield
Lovibonds
Avenue

Partridge Drive
Magefield View

Norman Close
Rusland Avenue

Willersley Avenue
Newstead

Ruskin Drive
Read Avenue

Roseberry Gdns
Surgery
Ridgeway Way

Southcroft Rd

Darrick Wood
Swimming Pool

Stables End

Newstead Wood
School for Girls

Avebury

PO
Surgery

Locksbottom

Willow Walk

Grasmere Gardens

Darrick Wood
School

Darrick Wood
Sports Centre

Bromley
Tennis Centre

Winterborne
Avenue
Tile Farm Road

Sandy Bury

PO

65

The Princess Royal
University Hospital
Superstore
PO
Crofton Road

A&E

Starts Close

Darrick Wood
Primary School

Darrick Wood

Tubbenden
Junior & Infant
Schools

Summerhill

Ashbourne Rise
Curzon Close

Borkwood Way

Tunstall Close

Stowting Road

Buckland

2

Nimhams Wood
Wolds Drive
The Birches

FARNBOROUGH COMMON A21

Vale Road
Hilda Vale Road

Wellbrook Road

Hill
Bassetts

Broadwater
Gardens

Bridle Way

Thyer

Isabella Drive

Cherrycot Rise

Northlands Avenue
North Drive

Beechcroft Road
St Leonards Rise

Melrose Crs

Southlands Avenue
South Drive

Oakleigh Gdns
PO

Ashley Gardens

64

3
215
163

Farnborough

Starts Hill

FARNBOROUGH WAY

Peel Road
Gladstone Rd
Palmerston

High Street
Ladycroft Way
Tye Lane

Strawberry
Fields

Pleasant View

Farnborough
Primary School

Church

Tubbenden Lane South
Chartwell Dr

Hilborough Way

FARNBOROUGH HILL B2158
Contessa

Durrant Way
Oleander Cl
Pinewood Drive

Shire Lane

FARNBOROUGH HILL
A21

Ramus Wd
Cockett's Av
Cleave Kent Close
Beachborough Av
Beachwood Avenue

Amethyst Court

4

The Larches

Shire Lane

Old Hill

5

Shire Lane

Lower Hook
Farm

North End
Farm

High Elms
Country Park

High Elms
Golf Club

Cudham Lane North

163
Street

orange Court Lane

North End Lane

High Elms Road

Golf Course

6

Hill
The

5 43 44 45

A B C D E

**Green Street
Green**

Rooksfield

Cuckoo Wood

Goringes

1 grid square represents 500 metres

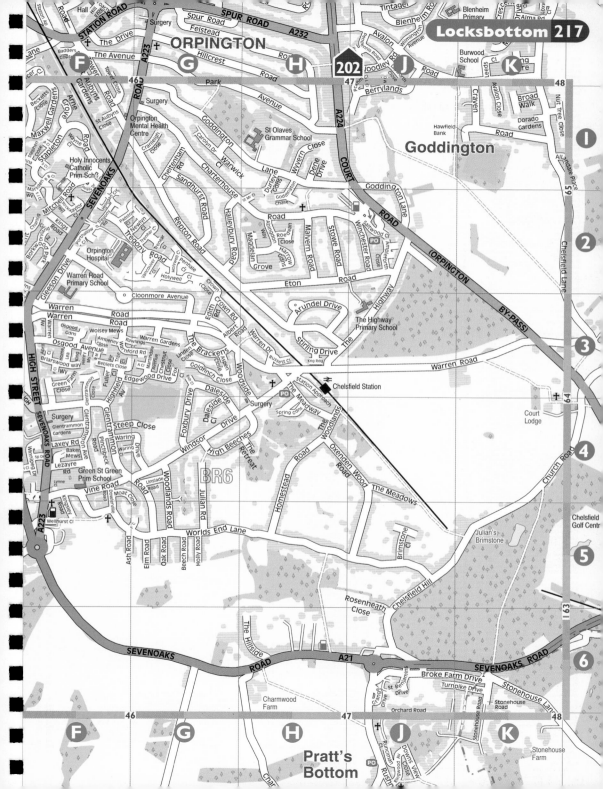

Abbey Wood 128 C4
Acton 117 K1
Acton Green 118 A4
Addington 213 J4
Addiscombe 197 G4
Aldborough Hatch 72 E1
Aldersbrook 71 G5
Alperton 80 A6
Anerley 181 H5
Ashford 152 D6
Avery Hill 167 H1
Balham 160 E2
Bandonhill 210 D3
Barking 90 D5
Barkingside 54 B6
Barnehurst 150 A4
Barnes 138 E2
Barnes Cray 150 E5
Barnet 32 D1
Barnet Gate 31 C1
Barnsbury 84 E5
Barwell 205 J5
Battersea 140 E1
Bayswater 101 F6
Beckenham 182 D5
Beckton 107 K5
Becontree 91 K3
Beddington 195 K6
Beddington Corner 195 F4
Bedford Park 118 C3
Belgravia 15 G6
Bell Green 164 C5
Bellingham 164 D6
Belmont 43 C5
Belmont 208 E6
Belvedere 129 J5
Benhilton 209 F1
Bermondsey 123 G2
Berrylands 191 G5
Bethnal Green 104 D2
Bexley 148 D1
Bexleyheath 149 G5
Bickley 184 D5
Blackfen 168 A4
Blackheath 145 J3
Blackheath Park 145 K5
Blackwall 106 B6
Bloomsbury 10 D7
Bow 105 J1
Bow Common 105 J4
Bowes Park 48 E2
Bowmans 170 C2
Brentford 116 E6
Brentford End 116 C6
Brimsdown 25 G3
Brixton 142 E3
Broad Green 196 C4
Brockley 144 C6
Bromley 105 K2
Bromley 184 A5
Bromley Common 200 C3
Bromley Park 183 H4
Brompton 14 C5
Brondesbury 82 C4
Brondesbury Park 82 B6
Brook Green 119 F3
Broom Hill 202 A4
Brunswick Park 34 A5
Buckhurst Hill 39 G5
Burnt Oak 45 F3
Bushey 28 C2
Bushey Heath 28 E2
Bushey Mead 177 G6
Bush Hill Park 35 A1
Caldecote Hill 29 F2
Camberwell 143 G2
Camden Town 84 A5
Canary Wharf 124 D1
Canning Town 107 F4
Cannon Hill 193 G1
Canonbury 85 J4
Canons Park 44 A3
Carpenders Park 27 K4
Carshalton 209 J2
Carshalton Beeches 209 J6
Carshalton on the Hill 209 K5
Castle Green 91 J6
Catford 165 F3
Chadwell Heath 73 K2
Charlton 126 C5
Chase Cross 57 G2
Chattern Hill 152 E6
Cheam 208 C3
Chelsea 121 F5
Chessington 206 A4
Child's Hill 64 C6
China Town 10 D5
Chingford 38 B3
Chingford Green 38 A3
Chingford Hatch 38 C6
Chipping Barnet 20 C6
Chislehurst 185 H3
Chislehurst West 185 F2
Chiswick 118 C4
Church End 46 E5
Church End 21 H5
City of London 12 B5
Clapham 141 G3
Clapham Park 161 J1
Clapton Park 87 H2
Claremont Park 204 A5
Claygate 205 F4
Clayhall 53 K5
Clerkenwell 5 J6
Cockfosters 21 J6
Coldblow 169 K4
Coldharbour 130 D2
Cole Park 156 B1
Colindale 45 G6
College Park 99 J2
Collier Row 57 H3
Collier's Wood 178 C3
Colney Hatch 47 K2
Coney Hall 214 C2
Coombe 176 B5
Copse Hill 176 D3
Cottenham Park 176 E4

Cranbrook 72 A4
Cranford 133 K1
Cranley Gardens 66 A1
Crayford 150 D6
Creekmouth 108 E4
Cricklewood 82 B2
Crockenhill 203 K5
Crofton 201 J6
Crooked Billet 176 E2
Crouch End 66 C3
Croydon 211 K1
Crystal Palace 181 H2
Cubitt Town 125 F4
Custom House 107 J6
Dagenham 92 D5
Dalston 86 B5
Dartford 171 F2
Dartmouth Park 66 A6
Deacons Hill 30 C1
De Beauvoir Town 86 A6
Deptford 124 C6
Derry Downs 202 E5
Dollis Hill 81 K1
Dormer's Wells 96 B6
Downham 183 G1
Ducks Island 32 B2
Dudden Hill 81 J3
Dulwich 163 G4
Dulwich Village 163 F2
Ealing 97 J6
Earl's Court 119 K5
Earlsfield 160 B3
East Acton 99 H6
East Barnet 33 H2
East Bedfont 152 E2
Eastbury 26 D6
Eastcote 59 F4
Eastcote Village 59 F2
East Dulwich 143 H6
East Finchley 47 H6
East Ham 107 J1
East Molesey 189 H2
East Sheen 138 A6
East Wickham 148 B2
Eden Park 198 C1
Edgware 30 D6
Edmonton 36 A6
Elmers End 182 A6
Elm Park 93 K3
Elmstead 184 D1
Elstree 30 A1
Eltham 166 D1
Enfield 23 J5
Enfield Highway 24 E3
Enfield Island Village 25 K1
Enfield Town 24 A3
Enfield Wash 25 G1
Erith 130 C5
Esher 204 C2
Ewell 207 J6
Fair Cross 91 F5
Fairlop 54 E4
Falconwood 147 K5
Farnborough 216 A3
Feltham 154 A4
Field Common 188 E4
Finchley 46 E4
Finsbury 5 J4
Finsbury Park 66 E6
Foots Cray 186 C2
Forestdale 213 G6
Forest Gate 88 B3
Forest Hill 164 A5
Fortis Green 65 K1
Forty Hill 24 B2
Foxbury 185 J1
Friday Hill 38 C5
Friern Barnet 33 J6
Fulham 139 G1
Fullwell Cross 54 D4
Furzedown 161 G6
Gants Hill 71 K3
Gidea Park 57 H5
Giggshill 190 B4
Globe Town 105 F2
Goddington 217 J1
Golders Green 64 C3
Goodmayes 73 H6
Gospel Oak 84 A3
Grange Hill 54 D2
Grange Park 23 G6
Greenford 96 D3
Greenhill 61 F2
Green Street Green 216 E5
Greenwich 125 G5
Grove Park 138 A2
Grove Park 166 B5
Hackbridge 195 G6
Hackney 86 E4
Hackney Wick 87 J4
Hadley 20 E4
Hadley Wood 21 H1
Haggerston 86 B1
Hainault 55 F5
Hale End 52 B2
Ham 156 E5
Hammersmith 118 E4
Hampstead 83 H2
Hampstead Garden Suburb ..65 F2
Hampton 173 G4
Hampton Hill 155 H6
Hampton Wick 174 C4
Hanwell 115 J1
Hanworth 154 C5
Harlesden 81 J6
Harmondsworth 113 F6
Haringay 67 G2
Harold Park 60 D3
Harrow 60 E5
Harrow on the Hill 60 D5
Harrow Weald 42 B4
Hatch End 41 J3
Hatton 133 H5
Hayes 200 A4
Hayes 215 H1
Hayes End 94 B3
Hayes Town 114 B1
Headstone 60 B1

Heath Park 75 K3
Heath Side 170 C4
Hendon 63 K2
Herne Hill 162 D1
Heston 134 E1
Higham Hill 51 G5
Highams Park 51 K5
High Barnet 20 A4
Higham 85 H3
Highgate 65 K4
Highwood Hill 31 H4
Hinchley Wood 205 F1
Hither Green 165 H1
Hockenden 187 J6
Holborn 11 G2
Holders Hill 46 B4
Holwell 26 C1
Homerton 87 F4
Honor Oak 164 A1
Honor Oak Park 164 B1
Hook 206 A3
Hook Green 170 C6
Hornsey 66 E1
Hornsey Vale 67 F2
Hounslow 135 F3
Hounslow West 134 C4
Hoxton 7 G3
Hurst Park 173 H5
Ilford 90 B1
Isle of Dogs 125 F4
Isleworth 136 C4
Islington 85 G6
Joyden's Wood 170 C6
Kennington 121 K6
Kensal Green 100 A1
Kensal Rise 100 B1
Kensal Town 100 C3
Kensington 119 K3
Kentish Town 84 C4
Kenton 61 J2
Keston 215 H2
Keston Mark 215 H1
Kevingtown 203 G3
Kew 137 C1
Kidbrooke 146 B3
Kilburn 82 C6
Kingsbury 62 D3
Kingsland 86 A5
Kingston upon Thames 174 D6
Kingston Vale 176 A1
Kitt's End 20 C1
Knightsbridge 14 D2
Knight's Hill 162 D3
Ladywell 144 D5
Lambeth 17 J4
Lampton 135 G2
Lea Bridge 87 F1
Lee 165 J1
Lessness Heath 129 J6
Lewisham 145 F5
Leyton 88 B1
Leytonstone 88 D3
Limehouse 105 G6
Lisson Grove 9 F1
Little Heath 73 J1
Little Ilford 90 A3
Little Stanmore 44 B4
Locksbottom 216 B1
Long Ditton 190 C5
Longlands 167 H5
Lower Clapton 86 E2
Lower Edmonton 36 A4
Lower Feltham 153 H5
Lower Green 189 G6
Lower Holloway 85 F3
Lower Place 98 E1
Lower Sydenham 164 A6
Loxford 90 C3
Maida Vale 100 E2
Maitland Park 83 K4
Manor Park 89 J2
Marks Gate 56 A5
Marylebone 9 G6
Mayfair 9 J6
Maypole 170 B3
Merry Hill 28 B3
Merton 177 K4
Merton Park 177 J5
Mile End 105 G3
Mill Hill 45 J1
Mill Meads 106 B1
Millwall 124 D3
Mitcham 179 F6
Monken Hadley 20 C3
Monks Orchard 197 K4
Moor Park 26 A6
Morden 193 K1
Morden Park 193 H5
Mortlake 137 K3
Motspur Park 192 D3
Mottingham 166 B4
Muswell Hill 48 A5
Nash 215 F4
Neasden 63 F3
New Addington 214 B5
New Barnet 21 H6
New Beckenham 182 B2
Newbury Park 72 D3
New Charlton 126 C4
New Cross 144 B5
New Cross Gate 144 B2
New Eltham 167 G4
Newington 17 K5
New Malden 176 C6
New Southgate 34 B6
New Town 171 J1
Noel Park 49 H5
Norbiton 175 G5
Norbury 180 C5
North Acton 99 G4
North Cheam 208 B1
North Cray 169 H5
North End 150 C2
North End 64 C4
North Feltham 154 A6
North Finchley 47 G2
North Harrow 59 K3

North Hyde 114 D4
North Kensington 100 B4
Northolt 78 A5
North Sheen 137 J3
Northumberland Heath 149 K1
North Wembley 61 H5
Northwood 40 A4
Northwood Hills 40 B5
North Woolwich 126 D2
Norwood Green 115 F4
Norwood New Town 180 E2
Notting Hill 100 C6
Nunhead 143 K5
Oakleigh Park 33 H4
Oakwood 34 D1
Old Bexley 169 H2
Old Ford 87 G6
Old Malden 192 A4
Old Oak Common 99 H3
Orpington 202 B6
Osidge 34 C4
Osterley 135 H1
Oxhey 27 H1
Paddington 8 A2
Palmers Green 34 E5
Park Langley 199 F3
Park Royal 98 C4
Parsons Green 139 K3
Peckham 143 J3
Penge 181 K3
Pentonville 5 H2
Perivale 97 F3
Petersham 157 F3
Petts Wood 201 J1
Pimlico 121 H5
Pinner 59 H1
Pinner Green 41 G5
Pinnerwood Park 41 G3
Plaistow 106 D2
Plaistow 183 K2
Plashet 89 H4
Plumstead 127 H5
Plumstead Common 128 A6
Ponders End 24 E6
Poplar 105 J6
Poverest 202 B1
Preston 61 K5
Primrose Hill 3 H1
Purfleet 131 K5
Putney 139 G6
Putney Heath 159 F2
Putney Vale 158 D5
Queensbury 44 B6
Queen's Park 100 C1
Rainham 111 K2
Ramsden 202 D5
Rayners Lane 59 K5
Raynes Park 177 F6
Redbridge 71 G2
Regent's Park 3 K3
Richmond 157 F6
Richmond Hill 157 F1
Rise Park 57 C4
Roehampton 138 C6
Romford 74 E2
Rosehill 194 A5
Rotherhithe 124 A3
Roundshaw 211 F4
Roxeth 60 C6
Ruislip 58 C3
Ruislip Common 58 A1
Ruislip Gardens 76 C1
Ruislip Manor 58 E6
Rush Green 75 F4
Ruxley 187 F2
Rydens 188 B6
St Paul's Cray 186 B5
St George in the East 104 C6
St Giles 10 D3
St Helier 194 B5
St James's 16 C1
St Johns 144 D3
St John's Wood 2 A2
St Luke's 6 C5
St Margarets 156 D1
St Mary Cray 202 D2
St Pancras 5 F5
Sands End 139 K1
Seething Wells 190 C3
Selhurst 196 E2
Seven Kings 72 E5
Shacklewell 86 C2
Shadwell 105 F6
Shepherd's Bush 118 E1
Shirley 197 K6
Shooters Hill 147 H2
Shoreditch 7 F5
Shortlands 183 H6
Sidcup 168 C6
Silvertown 126 D2
Sipson 112 C5
Slade Green 150 D3
Soho 10 C4
Somers Town 4 C3
Southall 114 C2
South Beddington 210 D4
Southborough 200 C5
South Bromley 106 B5
South Croydon 211 H4
Southend 165 F6
Southfields 159 K3
Southgate 34 E3
South Hackney 86 E6
South Hampstead 83 F5
South Harrow 78 B1
South Norwood 93 H6
South Kensington 120 B5
South Lambeth 141 K1
South Norwood 180 A6
South Oxhey 27 F5
South Ruislip 77 F3
South Tottenham 68 A2
South Wimbledon 178 B1
South Woodford 52 E5
Spitalfields 13 J1
Spring Grove 135 J2
Spring Park 198 D6

Stamford Hill 68 B4
Stanmore 43 H1
Stanwell 152 A1
Stepney 104 E4
Stockwell 141 K4
Stoke Newington 68 B6
Stonehill Green 187 G2
Stoneleigh 207 H3
Strand 10 G5
Stratford 88 A5
Stratford Marsh 87 K6
Stratford New Town 88 A4
Strawberry Hill 155 J5
Streatham 179 K1
Streatham Hill 161 K3
Streatham Park 161 H6
Streatham Vale 179 G3
Stroud Green 67 G3
Sudbury 79 F3
Summerstown 160 C4
Sundridge 184 B2
Surbiton 190 D5
Sutton 208 E3
Swiss Cottage 83 H6
Sydenham 182 A1
Teddington 173 J2
Temple Hills 79 G3
Temple Mills 87 K3
Thames Ditton 190 B4
Thamesmead 109 F6
The Borough 18 D3
The Hyde 63 H2
The Rookery 26 E2
The Wrythe 194 D6
Thornton Heath 180 C6
Tokyngton 80 D4
Tolworth 191 H5
Tooting 178 E1
Tooting Graveney 178 C1
Tottenham 50 A5
Tottenham Hale 50 B6
Totteridge 32 E3
Totteridge Green 32 A3
Tufnell Park 84 C2
Tulse Hill 162 C3
Twickenham 155 K5
Underhill 32 C5
Upper Clapton 68 C5
Upper Edmonton 36 C6
Upper Elmers End 198 C2
Upper Holloway 66 E2
Upper Norwood 180 D4
Upper Shirley 212 G2
Upper Sydenham 163 H6
Upper Tooting 160 D5
Upper Walthamstow 70 A1
Upton 89 G5
Upton Park 89 H2
Vale of Health 83 H1
Vauxhall 121 K5
Waddon 195 K6
Walham Green 139 K1
Wallend 90 A6
Wallington 210 A3
Walthamstow 69 H1
Walworth 122 D6
Wandle Park 196 B6
Wandsworth 139 K5
Wanstead 71 F4
Wapping 123 J1
Watford Heath 27 J2
Wealdstone 43 C6
Welling 148 C4
Welsh Harp 63 F5
Wembley 80 A2
Wembley Park 80 C1
West Acton 98 C5
West Barnes 193 F2
West Bedfont 152 C2
Westbourne Green 100 E4
West Brompton 120 A6
West Drayton 112 A3
West Dulwich 162 E4
West Ealing 116 B1
West Ewell 207 F4
West Green 49 J6
West Hampstead 64 E4
West Harrow 60 C4
West Heath 65 F6
West Heath 128 E6
West Hendon 63 J4
West Hill 159 H2
West Kensington 119 G5
West Kilburn 81 K5
Westminster 16 B5
West Molesey 188 E1
West Norwood 162 D6
Weston Green 189 K5
West Ruislip 58 A4
West Wickham 199 G5
Whetstone 33 F4
Whitechapel 13 K5
Whitton 155 H1
Widmore 184 C5
Willesden 81 J4
Willesden Green 81 K5
Wilmington 170 E6
Wimbledon 177 H1
Winchmore Hill 35 H3
Wood End 94 C5
Wood End Green 94 C3
Woodford 53 F2
Woodford Bridge 53 K3
Woodford Green 52 E3
Woodford Wells 39 F5
Wood Green 49 G4
Woodlands 135 J4
Woodside 197 H3
Woodside Park 32 E6
Woolwich 127 F6
Worcester Park 192 G6
World's End 23 G5
Yeading 95 G3

USING THE STREET INDEX

Street names are listed alphabetically. Each street name is followed by its postal town or area locality, the Postcode District, the page number, and the reference to the square in which the name is found.

Standard index entries are shown as follows:

Aaron Hill Rd *EHAM* E6 ....**108** A4

Street names and selected addresses not shown on the map due to scale restrictions are shown in the index with an asterisk:

Abbeville Ms *CLAP* SW4 * **141** J6

GENERAL ABBREVIATIONS

ACC	ACCESS
ALY	ALLEY
AP	APPROACH
AR	ARCADE
ASS	ASSOCIATION
AV	AVENUE
BCH	BEACH
BLDS	BUILDINGS
BND	BEND
BNK	BANK
BR	BRIDGE
BRK	BROOK
BTM	BOTTOM
BUS	BUSINESS
BVD	BOULEVARD
BY	BYPASS
CATH	CATHEDRAL
CEM	CEMETERY
CEN	CENTRE
CFT	CROFT
CH	CHURCH
CHA	CHASE
CHYD	CHURCHYARD
CIR	CIRCLE
CIRC	CIRCUS
CL	CLOSE
CLFS	CLIFFS
CMP	CAMP
CNR	CORNER
CO	COUNTY
COLL	COLLEGE
COM	COMMON
COMM	COMMISSION
CON	CONVENT
COT	COTTAGE
COTS	COTTAGES
CP	CAPE
CPS	COPSE
CR	CREEK
CREM	CREMATORIUM
CRS	CRESCENT
CSWY	CAUSEWAY
CT	COURT
CTRL	CENTRAL
CTS	COURTS
CTYD	COURTYARD
CUTT	CUTTINGS
CV	COVE
CYN	CANYON
DEPT	DEPARTMENT
DL	DALE
DM	DAM
DR	DRIVE
DRO	DROVE
DRY	DRIVEWAY
DWGS	DWELLINGS
E	EAST
EMB	EMBANKMENT
EMBY	EMBASSY
ESP	ESPLANADE
EST	ESTATE
EX	EXCHANGE
EXPY	EXPRESSWAY
EXT	EXTENSION
F/O	FLYOVER
FC	FOOTBALL CLUB
FK	FORK
FLD	FIELD
FLDS	FIELDS
FLS	FALLS
FM	FARM
FT	FORT
FTS	FLATS
FWY	FREEWAY
FY	FERRY
GA	GATE
GAL	GALLERY
GDN	GARDEN
GDNS	GARDENS
GLD	GLADE
GLN	GLEN
GN	GREEN
GND	GROUND
GRA	GRANGE
GRG	GARAGE
GT	GREAT
GTWY	GATEWAY
GV	GROVE
HGR	HIGHER
HL	HILL
HLS	HILLS
HO	HOUSE
HOL	HOLLOW
HOSP	HOSPITAL
HRB	HARBOUR
HTH	HEATH
HTS	HEIGHTS
HVN	HAVEN
HWY	HIGHWAY
IMP	IMPERIAL
IN	INLET
IND EST	INDUSTRIAL ESTATE
INF	INFIRMARY
INFO	INFORMATION
INT	INTERCHANGE
IS	ISLAND
JCT	JUNCTION
JTY	JETTY
KG	KING
KNL	KNOLL
L	LAKE
LA	LANE
LDG	LODGE
LGT	LIGHT
LK	LOCK
LKS	LAKES
LNDG	LANDING
LTL	LITTLE
LWR	LOWER
MAG	MAGISTRATE
MAN	MANSIONS
MD	MEAD
MDW	MEADOWS
MEM	MEMORIAL
MI	MILL
MKT	MARKET
MKTS	MARKETS
ML	MALL
MNR	MANOR
MS	MEWS
MSN	MISSION
MT	MOUNT
MTN	MOUNTAIN
MTS	MOUNTAINS
MUS	MUSEUM
MWY	MOTORWAY
N	NORTH
NE	NORTH EAST
NW	NORTH WEST
O/P	OVERPASS
OFF	OFFICE
ORCH	ORCHARD
OV	OVAL
PAL	PALACE
PAS	PASSAGE
PAV	PAVILION
PDE	PARADE
PH	PUBLIC HOUSE
PK	PARK
PKWY	PARKWAY
PL	PLACE
PLN	PLAIN
PLNS	PLAINS
PLZ	PLAZA
POL	POLICE STATION
PR	PRINCE
PREC	PRECINCT
PREP	PREPARATORY
PRIM	PRIMARY
PROM	PROMENADE
PRS	PRINCESS
PRT	PORT
PT	POINT
PTH	PATH
PZ	PIAZZA
QD	QUADRANT
QU	QUEEN
QY	QUAY
R	RIVER
RBT	ROUNDABOUT
RD	ROAD
RDG	RIDGE
REP	REPUBLIC
RES	RESERVOIR
RFC	RUGBY FOOTBALL CLUB
RI	RISE
RP	RAMP
RW	ROW
S	SOUTH
SCH	SCHOOL
SE	SOUTH EAST
SER	SERVICE AREA
SH	SHORE
SHOP	SHOPPING
SKWY	SKYWAY
SMT	SUMMIT
SOC	SOCIETY
SP	SPUR
SPR	SPRING
SQ	SQUARE
ST	STREET
STN	STATION
STR	STREAM
STRD	STRAND
SW	SOUTH WEST
TDG	TRADING
TER	TERRACE
THWY	THROUGHWAY
TNL	TUNNEL
TOLL	TOLLWAY
TPK	TURNPIKE
TR	TRACK
TRL	TRAIL
TWR	TOWER
U/P	UNDERPASS
UNI	UNIVERSITY
UPR	UPPER
V	VALE
VA	VALLEY
VIAD	VIADUCT
VIL	VILLA
VIS	VISTA
VLG	VILLAGE
VLS	VILLAS
VW	VIEW
W	WEST
WD	WOOD
WHF	WHARF
WK	WALK
WKS	WALKS
WLS	WELLS
WY	WAY
YD	YARD
YHA	YOUTH HOSTEL

POSTCODE TOWNS AND AREA ABBREVIATIONS

ABR/ST	Abridge/Stapleford Abbotts
ABYW	Abbey Wood
ACT	Acton
ALP/SUD	Alperton/Sudbury
ARCH	Archway
ASHF	Ashford (Surrey)
BAL	Balham
BANK	Bank
BAR	Barnet
BARB	Barbican
BARK	Barking
BARK/HLT	Barkingside/Hainault
BARN	Barnes
BAY/PAD	Bayswater/Paddington
BCTR	Becontree
BECK	Beckenham
BELMT	Belmont
BELV	Belvedere
BERM/RHTH	Bermondsey/Rotherhithe
BETH	Bethnal Green
BFN/LL	Blackfen/Longlands
BGVA	Belgravia
BKHH	Buckhurst Hill
BKHTH/KID	Blackheath/Kidbrooke
BLKFR	Blackfriars
BMLY	Bromley
BMSBY	Bloomsbury
BORE	Borehamwood
BOW	Bow
BROCKY	Brockley
BRXN/ST	Brixton north/Stockwell
BRXS/STRHM	Brixton south/Streatham Hill
BRYLDS	Berrylands
BTFD	Brentford
BTSEA	Battersea
BUSH	Bushey
BXLY	Bexley
BXLYHN	Bexleyheath north
BXLYHS	Bexleyheath south
CAMTN	Camden Town
CAN/RD	Canning Town/Royal Docks
CANST	Cannon Street station
CAR	Carshalton
CAT	Catford
CAVSQ/HST	Cavendish Square/Harley Street
CDALE/KGS	Colindale/Kingsbury
CEND/HSY/T	Crouch End/Hornsey/Turnpike Lane
CHARL	Charlton
CHCR	Charing Cross
CHDH	Chadwell Heath
CHEAM	Cheam
CHEL	Chelsea
CHIG	Chigwell
CHING	Chingford
CHSGTN	Chessington
CHST	Chislehurst
CHSWK	Chiswick
CITYW	City of London west
CLAP	Clapham
CLAY	Clayhall
CLKNW	Clerkenwell
CLPT	Clapton
CMBW	Camberwell
CONDST	Conduit Street
COVGDN	Covent Garden
CRICK	Cricklewood
CROY/NA	Croydon/New Addington
CRW	Collier Row
DAGE	Dagenham east
DAGW	Dagenham west
DART	Dartford
DEN/HRF	Denham/Harefield
DEPT	Deptford
DUL	Dulwich
E/WMO/HCT	East & West Molesey/Hampton Court
EA	Ealing
EBAR	East Barnet
EBED/NFELT	East Bedfont/North Feltham
ECT	Earl's Court
ED	Edmonton
EDGW	Edgware
EDUL	East Dulwich
EFNCH	East Finchley
EHAM	East Ham
ELTH/MOT	Eltham/Mottingham
EMB	Embankment
EMPK	Emerson Park
EN	Enfield
ENC/FH	Enfield Chase/Forty Hill
ERITH	Erith
ERITHM	Erith Marshes
ESH/CLAY	Esher/Claygate
EW	Ewell
FARR	Farringdon
FBAR/BDGN	Friern Barnet/Bounds Green
FELT	Feltham
FENCHST	Fenchurch Street
FITZ	Fitzrovia
FLST/FETLN	Fleet Street/Fetter Lane
FNCH	Finchley
FSBYE	Finsbury east
FSBYPK	Finsbury Park
FSBYW	Finsbury west
FSTGT	Forest Gate
FSTH	Forest Hill
FUL/PGN	Fulham/Parsons Green
GDMY/SEVK	Goodmayes/Seven Kings
GFD/PVL	Greenford/Perivale
GINN	Gray's Inn
GLDGN	Golders Green
GNTH/NBYPK	Gants Hill/Newbury Park
GNWCH	Greenwich
GPK	Gidea Park
GTPST	Great Portland Street
GWRST	Gower Street
HACK	Hackney
HAMP	Hampstead
HARH	Harold Hill
HAYES	Hayes
HBRY	Highbury
HCH	Hornchurch
HCIRC	Holborn Circus
HDN	Hendon
HDTCH	Houndsditch
HEST	Heston
HGDN/ICK	Hillingdon/Ickenham
HGT	Highgate
HHOL	High Holborn
HMSMTH	Hammersmith
HNHL	Herne Hill
HNWL	Hanwell
HOL/ALD	Holborn/Aldwych
HOLWY	Holloway
HOM	Homerton
HOR/WEW	Horton/West Ewell
HPTN	Hampton
HRW	Harrow
HSLW	Hounslow
HSLWW	Hounslow west
HTHAIR	Heathrow Airport
HYS/HAR	Hayes/Harlington
IL	Ilford
IS	Islington
ISLW	Isleworth
KENS	Kensington
KIL/WHAMP	Kilburn/West Hampstead
KTBR	Knightsbridge
KTN/HRWW/WS	Kenton/Harrow Weald/Wealdstone
KTTN	Kentish Town
KUT/HW	Kingston upon Thames/Hampton Wick
KUTN/CMB	Kingston upon Thames north/Coombe
LBTH	Lambeth
LEE/GVPK	Lee/Grove Park
LEW	Lewisham
LEY	Leyton
LINN	Lincoln's Inn
LOTH	Lothbury
LOU	Loughton
LSQ/SEVD	Leicester Square/Seven Dials
LVPST	Liverpool Street
MANHO	Mansion House
MBLAR	Marble Arch
MHST	Marylebone High Street
MLHL	Mill Hill
MNPK	Manor Park
MON	Monument
MORT/ESHN	Mortlake/East Sheen
MRDN	Morden
MTCM	Mitcham
MUSWH	Muswell Hill
MV/WKIL	Maida Vale/West Kilburn
MYFR/PICC	Mayfair/Piccadilly
MYFR/PKLN	Mayfair/Park Lane
NFNCH/WDSPK	North Finchley/Woodside Park
NKENS	North Kensington
NOXST/BSQ	New Oxford Street/Bloomsbury Square
NRWD	Norwood
NTGHL	Notting Hill
NTHLT	Northolt
NTHWD	Northwood
NWCR	New Cross
NWDGN	Norwood Green
NWMAL	New Malden
OBST	Old Broad Street
ORP	Orpington
OXHEY	Oxhey
OXSTW	Oxford Street west
PECK	Peckham
PEND	Ponders End
PGE/AN	Penge/Anerley
PIM	Pimlico
PIN	Pinner
PLMGR	Palmers Green
PLSTW	Plaistow
POP/IOD	Poplar/Isle of Dogs
PUR	Purfleet
PUR/KEN	Purley/Kenley
PUT/ROE	Putney/Roehampton
RAIN	Rainham (Gt Lon)
RCH/KEW	Richmond/Kew
RCHPK/HAM	Richmond Park/Ham
RDART	Rural Dartford
REDBR	Redbridge
REGST	Regent Street
RKW/CH/CXG	Rickmansworth/Chorleywood/Croxley Green
ROM	Romford
ROMW/RG	Romford west/Rush Green
RSEV	Rural Sevenoaks
RSLP	Ruislip
RSQ	Russell Square
RYLN/HDSTN	Rayners Lane/Headstone
RYNPK	Raynes Park
SAND/SEL	Sanderstead/Selsdon
SCUP	Sidcup
SDTCH	Shoreditch
SEVS/STOTM	Seven Sisters/South Tottenham
SHB	Shepherd's Bush
SKENS	South Kensington
SNWD	South Norwood
SOCK/AV	South Ockendon/Aveley
SOHO/CST	Soho/Carnaby Street
SOHO/SHAV	Soho/Shaftesbury Avenue
SRTFD	Stratford
STAN	Stanmore
STBT	St Bart's
STHGT/OAK	Southgate/Oakwood
STHL	Southall
STHWK	Southwark
STJS	St James's
STJSPK	St James's Park
STJWD	St John's Wood
STKPK	Stockley Park
STLK	St Luke's
STMC/STPC	St Mary Cray/St Paul's Cray

STNW/STAM .... Stoke Newington/Stamford Hill
STP........................St Paul's
STPAN....................St Pancras
STRHM/NOR............Streatham/Norbury
STWL/WRAY............Stanwell/Wraysbury
SUN........................Sunbury
SURB......................Surbiton
SUT........................Sutton
SWFD.....................South Woodford
SWLY......................Swanley

SYD........................Sydenham
TEDD......................Teddington
TDDIT.....................Thames Ditton
THHTH....................Thornton Heath
THMD......................Thamesmead
TOOT......................Tooting
TOTM......................Tottenham
TPL/STR..................Temple/Strand
TRDG/WHET.............Totteridge/Whetstone
TWK........................Twickenham
TWRH......................Tower Hill
UED........................Upper Edmonton

UX/CGN...................Uxbridge/Colham Green
VX/NE.....................Vauxhall/Nine Elms
WALTH....................Walthamstow
WALW......................Walworth
WAN........................Wanstead
WAND/EARL.............Wandsworth/Earlsfield
WAP........................Wapping
WAT........................Watford
WATW......................Watford west
WBLY......................Wembley
WBPTN....................West Brompton

WCHMH...................Winchmore Hill
WCHPL....................Whitechapel
WDGN.....................Wood Green
WDR/YW..................West Drayton/Yiewsley
WEA........................West Ealing
WELL.......................Welling
WEST......................Westminster
WESTW....................Westminster west
WFD........................Woodford
WHALL.....................Whitehall
WHTN......................Whitton
WIM/MER.................Wimbledon/Merton

WKENS....................West Kensington
WLGTN....................Wallington
WLSDN....................Willesden
WNWD......................West Norwood
WOOL/PLUM............Woolwich/Plumstead
WOT/HER.................Walton-on-Thames/Hersham
WPK........................Worcester Park
WWKM.....................West Wickham
YEAD......................Yeading

Index – streets

1

1 Av WOOL/PLUM SE18..........127 G3

A

Aaron Hill Rd EHAM E6..........108 A4
Abberley Ms BTSEA SW11..........141 G4
Abbess Cl BRXS/STRHM SW2..162 C5
Abbeville Ms CLAP SW4 *..........141 J6
Abbeville Rd CEND/HSY/T N8....66 D1
  CLAP SW4..........161 H1
Abbey Av ALP/SUD HA0..........98 A1
Abbey Cl HYS/HAR UB3..........114 A1
  NTHLT UB5..........95 K6
  PIN HA5..........41 G6
  ROM RM1..........75 H3
Abbey Crs BELV DA17..........129 H4
Abbeydale Rd ALP/SUD HA0....98 A1
Abbey Dr RDART DA2..........170 B4
  TOOT SW17..........179 F1
Abbeyfield Cl MTCM CR4..........178 D5
Abbeyfield Est
  BERM/RHTH SE16..........123 K4
Abbeyfield Rd
  BERM/RHTH SE16..........123 K4
Abbeyfields Cl WLSDN NW10....98 C3
  HMSMTH W6..........119 H6
  STHWK SE1..........123 H4
  STJWD NW8..........101 G1
Abbey Gv CHST BR7..........185 F4
Abbeyhill Rd BFN/LL DA15....168 A3
Abbey La BECK BR3..........182 D3
  SRTFD E15..........106 A1
Abbey Ms ISLW TW7..........136 C2
  WALTH E17..........69 J2
Abbey Mt BELV DA17..........129 G5
Abbey Orchard St WEST SW1P..16 B4
Abbey Pk BECK BR3..........182 D3
Abbey Pl DART DA1 *..........151 G6
Abbey Rd BARK IG11..........90 C6
  BELV DA17..........128 E4
  BXLYHN DA7..........149 F5
  CROY/NA CRO..........211 H1
  EN EN1..........24 A6
  CNTH/NBYPK IG2..........72 D3
  KIL/WHAMP NW6..........83 F6
  SRTFD E15..........106 B1
  WIM/MER SW19..........178 A3
  WLSDN NW10..........80 D6
Abbey St PLSTW E13..........106 E3
  STHWK SE1..........19 J4
Abbey Ter ABYW SE2..........128 D3
Abbey Vw MLHL NW7..........31 H4
Abbey Wk E/WMO/HCT KT8..173 G6
Abbey Wood Rd ABYW SE2....128 C4
Abbot Cl RSLP HA4..........77 H1
Abbotsbury Cl SRTFD E15....106 A1
  WKENS W14..........119 J2
Abbotsbury Gdns PIN HA5....59 G3
Abbotsbury Ms PECK SE15....143 K4
Abbotsbury Rd MRDN SM4....194 A4
  WKENS W14..........119 H2
  WWKM BR4..........199 J6
Abbots Cl STMC/STPC BR5....201 G5
Abbots Dr RYLN/HDSTN HA2..60 A6
Abbotsford Av
  SEVS/STOTM N15..........67 J1
Abbotsford Rd GDMY/SEVK IG3..91 H1
Abbots Gdns EFNCH N2..........65 H1
Abbots Gn CROY/NA CRO..........213 F4
Abbotshade Rd
  BERM/RHTH SE16 *..........124 A1
Abbotshall Av STHGT/OAK N14..34 C5
Abbotshall Rd CAT SE6..........165 G3
Abbots La STHWK SE1..........19 H1
Abbotsleigh Cl BELMT SM2....209 F5
Abbotsleigh Rd
  STRHM/NOR SW16..........161 H6
Abbots Mnr PIM SW1V *..........121 G5
Abbotsmede Cl TWK TW1....156 A4
Abbots Pk BRXS/STRHM SW2..162 B3
Abbot's Pl KIL/WHAMP NW6....83 F6
Abbots Rd EDGW HA8..........45 F3
  EHAM E6..........89 G6
Abbots Ter CEND/HSY/T N8....66 E3
Abbotstone Rd
  PUT/ROE SW15..........139 F4
Abbot St HACK E8..........86 B4
Abbots Wk KENS W8 *..........120 A3
Abbots Wy BECK BR3..........198 B2
Abbotswell Rd BROCKY SE4..144 C6
Abbotswood Cl BELV DA17....129 F3
Abbotswood Gdns CLAY IG5....53 K6
Abbotswood Rd EDUL SE22..143 F5
  STRHM/NOR SW16..........161 J5

Abbotswood Wy
  HYS/HAR UB3..........114 A1
Abbott Av RYNPK SW20..........177 G5
Abbott Cl HPTN TW12..........172 D2
  NTHLT UB5..........77 K4
Abbott Rd POP/IOD E14..........106 B5
Abbotts Cl IS N1 *..........85 J5
  ROMW/RG RM7..........56 D5
  THMD SE28..........109 J6
Abbotts Crs CHING E4..........38 B6
  ENC/FH EN2..........23 H5
Abbotts Dr ALP/SUD HA0....97 H3
Abbotts Md
  RCHPK/HAM TW10 *..........156 D6
Abbotts Park Rd LEY E10....70 A4
Abbotts Rd BAR EN5..........21 F5
  CHEAM SM3..........208 C2
  MTCM CR4..........195 H1
  STHL UB1..........114 D3
Abbott's Wk BXLYHN DA7....148 E1
Abchurch La MANHO EC4N....13 F5
Abdale Rd SHB W12..........118 E1
Aberavon Rd BOW E3..........105 G2
Abercairn Rd
  STRHM/NOR SW16..........179 H3
Aberconway Rd MRDN SM4..178 A6
Abercorn Cl MLHL NW7..........46 C3
  STJWD NW8..........101 G2
Abercorn Crs RYLN/HDSTN HA2..60 B5
Abercorn Gdns CHDH RM6....73 H3
  KTN/HRWW/WS HA3..........61 K4
Abercorn Gv RSLP HA4..........58 B1
Abercorn Ms
  RCHPK/HAM TW10 *..........137 G6
Abercorn Pl STJWD NW8....101 G2
Abercorn Rd MLHL NW7..........46 C3
  STAN HA7..........43 J5
Abercorn Wy STHWK SE1....123 H5
Abercrombie Dr EN EN1..........24 C2
Abercrombie St BTSEA SW11..140 D3
Aberdare Cl WWKM BR4..........199 F6
Aberdare Gdns
  KIL/WHAMP NW6..........83 F5
  MLHL NW7..........46 B3
Aberdare Rd PEND EN3..........24 E5
Aberdeen La HBRY N5..........85 H3
Aberdeen Pde UED N18 *....50 D1
Aberdeen Pk HBRY N5..........85 J3
Aberdeen Pk BAY/PAD W2 *....8 A1
Aberdeen Rd CROY/NA CRO..211 K2
  HBRY N5..........85 J2
  KTN/HRWW/WS HA3..........43 F6
  UED N18..........50 D1
  WLSDN NW10..........81 H3
Aberdeen Ter BKHTH/KID SE3..145 E3
Aberdour Rd GDMY/SEVK IG3..91 H1
Aberdour St STHWK SE1....19 G6
Aberfeldy St POP/IOD E14....106 A5
Aberford Gdns
  WOOL/PLUM SE18..........146 D2
Aberfoyle Rd
  STRHM/NOR SW16..........179 J3
Abergeldie Rd LEE/GVPK SE12..166 A1
Abernethy Rd LEW SE13....145 H5
Abersham Rd HACK E8..........86 B3
Abery St WOOL/PLUM SE18..127 K4
Abingdon Cl FNCH N3..........47 G6
  KENS W8..........119 K5
  STRHM/NOR SW16..........179 K4
Abingdon Rd FNCH N3..........47 G6
  KENS W8..........119 K3
Abingdon Vls KENS W8..........119 K3
Abingdon Wy ORP BR6..........217 H2
Abinger Av BELMT SM2..........208 A5
Abinger Cl BMLY BR1..........184 D6
  CROY/NA CRO..........214 A4
  GDMY/SEVK IG3..........91 G2
  WLGTN SM6..........210 E3
Abinger Dr NRWD SE19..........180 D3
Abinger Gdns ISLW TW7....135 K4
Abinger Gv DEPT SE8..........124 C6
Abinger Ms MV/WKIL W9....100 E3
Abinger Rd CHSWK W4..........118 C3
Ablett St BERM/RHTH SE16..123 K5
Abney Park Ter
  STNW/STAM N16 *..........68 B6
Aboyne Dr RYNPK SW20....176 D5
Aboyne Rd TOOT SW17..........160 C5
  WLSDN NW10..........81 F1
Abraham Cl OXHEY WD19....27 F6
Abridge Gdns CRW RM5..........56 C2
Abridge Wy BARK IG11..........109 H1
Abyssinia Cl BTSEA SW11....140 D5
Abyssinia Rd BTSEA SW11 *..140 D5
Acacia Av BTFD TW8..........136 C1
  HCH RM12..........75 H4
  HYS/HAR UB3..........94 D5
  RSLP HA4..........58 E5
  TOTM N17..........49 K3
  WBLY HA9..........80 B3
Acacia Cl DEPT SE8 *..........124 B4

  STAN HA7..........42 E2
  STMC/STPC BR5..........201 J2
Acacia Dr CHEAM SM3..........193 J5
Acacia Gdns STJWD NW8 *....2 B2
  UED N18..........199 F6
Acacia Gv DUL SE21..........162 E4
  NWMAL KT3..........176 B6
Acacia Ms WDR/YW UB7....112 A6
Acacia Pl STJWD NW8..........2 B2
Acacia Rd ACT W3..........98 E6
  BECK BR3..........182 C6
  DART DA1..........171 F5
  ENC/FH EN2..........23 K2
  HPTN TW12..........173 F2
  MTCM CR4..........179 F5
  STJWD NW8..........2 B2
  STRHM/NOR SW16..........179 K4
  WALTH E17..........70 C6
  WAN E11..........70 C6
  WDGN N22..........49 G4
The Acacias EBAR EN4 *..........21 H6
Acacia Wy BFN/LL DA15....168 A2
Academy Fields Rd GPK RM2..75 K2
Academy Gdns CROY/NA CRO..197 G5
  NTHLT UB5..........95 G2
Academy Pl WOOL/PLUM SE18..146 E2
Academy Rd
  WOOL/PLUM SE18..........146 E1
Acanthus Dr STHWK SE1....123 H5
Acanthus Rd BTSEA SW11....141 F4
Accommodation Rd
  GLDGN NW11..........64 D4
Ace Pde CHSGTN KT9..........206 A1
Acer Av YEAD UB4..........95 J3
Acfold Rd FUL/PGN SW6....140 A2
Achilles Cl STHWK SE1....123 H5
Achilles Rd KIL/WHAMP NW6..82 E3
Achilles St NWCR SE14....144 B1
Acklam Rd NKENS W10....100 D4
Acklington Dr CDALE/KGS NW9..45 G4
Ackmar Rd FUL/PGN SW6....139 K2
Ackroyd Dr BOW E3..........105 J4
Ackroyd Rd FSTH SE23....164 B2
Acland Cl WOOL/PLUM SE18..147 J1
Acland Crs CMBW SE5..........142 E5
Acland Rd CRICK NW2..........81 K4
Acle Cl BARK/HLT IG6..........54 B4
Acol Crs RSLP HA4..........77 F3
Acol Rd KIL/WHAMP NW6....83 F5
Acorn Cl CHING E4..........51 K1
  CHST BR7..........185 H1
  EN EN1..........24 A1
  HPTN TW12..........173 G2
  STAN HA7..........43 H3
Acorn Gdns ACT W3..........99 F4
  NRWD SE19..........181 G4
Acorn Gv HYS/HAR UB3....133 J1
  RSLP HA4..........58 D6
Acorn Pde PECK SE15 *....143 J1
Acorn Rd DART DA1..........150 C6
Acorns Wy ESH/CLAY KT10..204 C3
Acorn Wy BECK BR3..........199 F2
  FSTH SE23..........164 A5
  ORP BR6..........216 B2
Acre Dr EDUL SE22..........143 H5
Acre La BRXS/STRHM SW2..142 A5
  CAR SM5..........210 A2
Acre Rd DAG RM10..........92 D5
  KUTN/CMB KT2..........175 G3
  WIM/MER SW19..........178 C2
Acris St WAND/EARL SW18..140 B6
Acton Cl ED N9..........36 C4
Acton Hill Ms ACT W3 *....117 J1
Acton La ACT W3..........117 K1
  NWDGN UB2..........98 E2
  WLSDN NW10..........98 E1
Acton Ms HACK E8..........86 B6
Acton St FSBYW WC1X..........5 J4
Acworth Cl ED N9..........36 E2
Acworth Pl DART DA1..........171 F1
Ada Ct MV/WKIL W9..........101 G2
Ada Gdns POP/IOD E14....106 B5
  SRTFD E15..........88 D6
Adair Rd NKENS W10..........100 C3
Adam & Eve Ms KENS W8..119 K3
Adam Cl CAT SE6..........164 C6
  SYD SE26..........163 K4
Adam Rd CHING E4..........51 H3
Adams Cl BRYLDS KT5..........191 G5
  FNCH N3..........46 E3
  WBLY HA9..........62 D6
Adams Ms TOOT SW17 *....160 E4
  WDGN N22..........49 G3
Adamson Rd CAN/RD E16....106 E5
  HAMP NW3..........83 H5
Adamson Wy BECK BR3....199 F2
Adamsrill Cl EN EN1..........35 K1
Adamsrill Rd SYD SE26....164 A6

Adams Rd BECK BR3..........198 B2
  TOTM N17..........49 K5
Adams Rw MYFR/PKLN W1K..9 H6
Adams Sq BXLYHS DA6....149 F4
Adam St CHCR WC2N..........11 F6
Adam Wk FUL/PGN SW6....139 F1
Ada Pl BETH E2..........86 C6
Adare Wk STRHM/NOR SW16..161 K4
Ada Rd ALP/SUD HA0..........79 J1
  CMBW SE5..........143 F1
Ada St HACK E8..........86 D6
Adderley Gdns ELTH/MOT SE9..167 F6
Adderley Gv BTSEA SW11....161 F5
Adderley Rd
  KTN/HRWW/WS HA3..........43 F4
Adderley St POP/IOD E14..106 A5
Addington Dr
  NFNCH/WDSPK N12..........47 J2
Addington Gv SYD SE26....164 B6
Addington Rd BOW E3..........105 J2
  CAN/RD E16..........106 C4
  CROY/NA CRO..........196 C5
  FSBYPK N4..........67 G4
  WWKM BR4..........214 A2
Addington Sq CMBW SE5....142 D1
Addington St STHWK SE1....17 H3
Addington Village Rd
  CROY/NA CRO..........213 J4
Addis Cl PEND EN3..........25 F2
Addiscombe Av CROY/NA CRO..197 H4
Addiscombe Ct
  KTN/HRWW/WS HA3..........61 J2
Addiscombe Court Rd
  CROY/NA CRO..........197 F6
Addiscombe Gv CROY/NA CRO..196 E6
Addiscombe Rd CROY/NA CRO..197 F6
Addison Av HSLW TW3....135 H2
  NTGHL W11..........119 H1
  STHGT/OAK N14..........34 B1
Addison Bridge Pl
  WKENS W14..........119 J4
Addison Cl NTHWD HA6....40 E4
  STMC/STPC BR5..........201 G4
Addison Crs WKENS W14....119 H3
Addison Dr LEE/GVPK SE12..146 A6
Addison Gdns BRYLDS KT5..191 G3
  WKENS W14..........119 G3
Addison Gv CHSWK W4....118 B3
Addison Pl NTGHL W11....119 H1
Addison Rd BARK/HLT IG6..72 C1
  HAYES BR2..........200 C2
  PEND EN3..........24 E2
  SNWD SE25..........197 H1
  TEDD TW11..........174 C2
  WALTH E17..........70 E1
  WAN E11..........71 F3
  WKENS W14..........119 J3
Addison's Cl CROY/NA CRO..198 C6
Addison Ter CHSWK W4 *....117 K4
Addison Wy GLDGN NW11....64 D1
  HYS/HAR UB3..........94 D5
  NTHWD HA6..........40 D4
Addle Hl BLKFR EC4V..........12 B5
Addle St CITYW EC2V..........12 D3
Adecroft Wy E/WMO/HCT KT8..173 H6
Adela Av NWMAL KT3..........192 E2
Adelaide Av BROCKY SE4....144 C5
Adelaide Cl EN EN1..........24 A1
  STAN HA7..........43 G5
Adelaide Ct HNWL W7..........116 A2
Adelaide Gdns CHDH RM6..74 A2
Adelaide Gv SHB W12..........118 D1
Adelaide Rd CHST BR7....185 G1
  HAMP NW3..........83 K5
  HEST TW5..........134 D2
  IL IG1..........72 B6
  NWDGN UB2..........114 D4
  PUT/ROE SW15..........139 H6
  RCH/KEW TW9..........137 G5
  SURB KT6..........191 F2
  TEDD TW11..........174 A2
  WAN E11..........88 D1
  WEA W13..........116 C2
Adelaide St CHCR WC2N *....10 E6
Adelaide Ter BTFD TW8 *....116 E5
Adela St NKENS W10..........100 C3
Adelina Gv WCHPL E1..........104 E4
Adelina Ms BAL SW12..........161 J3
Adeline Pl RSQ WC1B..........10 D2
Adeliza Cl BARK IG11..........90 C5
Adelphi Crs HCH RM12....75 J3
  YEAD UB4..........94 D2
Adelphi Ter CHCR WC2N *....11 F6
Adelphi Wy YEAD UB4....94 D2
Adeney Cl HMSMTH W6....119 G6
Aden Gv STNW/STAM N16..85 K2
Adenmore Rd CAT SE6....164 D2
Aden Rd IL IG1..........72 B5
  PEND EN3..........25 G5
Adhara Rd NTHWD HA6....40 E1
Adie Rd HMSMTH W6....119 F3

Adine Rd PLSTW E13..........106 E3
Adler St WCHPL E1..........104 C5
Adley St CLPT E5..........87 G2
Adlington Cl UED N18..........49 K1
Admaston Rd
  WOOL/PLUM SE18..........147 H1
Admiral Cl STMC/STPC BR5..202 E1
Admiral Ms NKENS W10....100 B3
Admiral Pl BERM/RHTH SE16..124 B1
Admirals Cl SWFD E18....71 F1
Admiral Seymour Rd
  ELTH/MOT SE9..........146 E5
Admiral's Ga GNWCH SE10..144 E3
Admiral Sq WBPTN SW10 *..140 B2
Admiral St DEPT SE8..........144 D2
Admiral's Wk HAMP NW3....83 H1
Admiral's Wy POP/IOD E14..124 E2
Admiralty Cl DEPT SE8 *....144 D2
Admiralty Rd TEDD TW11..174 A3
Admiral Wk MV/WKIL W9....100 E4
Adnams Wk RAIN RM13....93 H4
Advance Rd WNWD SE27..162 D6
Advent Wy UED N18..........51 F1
Adys Lawn CRICK NW2....81 K4
Adys Rd PECK SE15..........143 G4
Aerodrome Rd
  CDALE/KGS NW9..........45 H6
Aerodrome Wy HEST TW5..114 B6
Affleck St IS N1 *..........5 H5
Afghan Rd BTSEA SW11....140 D3
Aftab Ter WCHPL E1 *....104 D3
Agamemnon Rd
  KIL/WHAMP NW6..........82 D3
Agar Cl SURB KT6..........191 G6
Agar Gv CAMTN NW1..........84 C5
Agar Pl CAMTN NW1..........84 C5
Agars Pl CHCR WC2N..........10 E6
Agate Cl CAN/RD E16....107 H5
Agate Rd HMSMTH W6....119 F3
Agatha Cl WAP E1W..........123 J1
Agaton Rd ELTH/MOT SE9..167 H4
Agave Rd CRICK NW2..........82 A2
Agdon St FSBYE EC1V..........6 A6
Agincourt Rd HAMP NW3....83 K2
Agister Rd CHIG IG7..........55 G1
Agnes Av IL IG1..........90 A2
Agnes Cl EHAM E6..........108 A6
Agnesfield Cl
  NFNCH/WDSPK N12..........47 J2
Agnes Gdns BCTR RM8....91 K3
Agnes Riley Gdns CLAP SW4 *..161 H2
Agnes Rd ACT W3..........118 C2
Agnes St POP/IOD E14....105 H5
Agnew Rd FSTH SE23....164 A2
Agricola Pl EN EN1..........24 B6
Aidan Cl BCTR RM8..........92 A2
Ailsa Av TWK TW1..........136 B6
Ailsa Rd TWK TW1..........136 B5
Ailsa St POP/IOD E14....106 A4
Ainger Rd HAMP NW3....83 K5
Ainsdale Crs PIN HA5....60 A1
Ainsdale Dr STHWK SE1....123 H5
Ainsdale Rd EA W5..........97 K3
  OXHEY WD19..........27 G5
Ainsley Av ROMW/RG RM7..74 D4
Ainsley Cl ED N9..........36 A3
Ainsley St BETH E2..........104 D2
Ainslie Wood Crs CHING E4..51 K1
Ainslie Wood Gdns CHING E4..37 K6
Ainslie Wood Rd CHING E4..51 J1
Ainsty St
  BERM/RHTH SE16 *..........123 K2
Ainsworth Cl CMBW SE5 *..143 F3
  CRICK NW2..........81 J1
Ainsworth Rd CROY/NA CRO..196 C5
  HOM E9..........86 E5
Ainsworth Wy STJWD NW8..83 G6
Aintree Av EHAM E6..........89 J6
Aintree Crs BARK/HLT IG6..54 C5
Aintree Est FUL/PGN SW6 *..139 H1
Aintree Rd GFD/PVL UB6....97 H1
Aintree St FUL/PGN SW6....139 H1
Airco Cl CDALE/KGS NW9....44 E6
Airdrie Cl IS N1 *..........85 F5
  YEAD UB4..........95 J4
Airedale Av CHSWK W4....118 C5
Airedale Av South
  CHSWK W4 *..........118 C5
Airedale Rd BAL SW12....160 E2
  EA W5..........116 D3
Airfield Wy HCH RM12....93 K4
Airlie Gdns IL IG1..........71 K5
  KENS W8..........119 K1
Air St REGST W1B..........10 B6
Airthrie Rd GDMY/SEVK IG3..73 H6
Aisgill Av WKENS W14....119 J5

Aisher Rd THMD SE28...........109 J6
Aislibie Rd LEE/GVPK SE12...145 H5
Aiten Pl HMSMTH W6..............11B D4
Aitken Cl HACK E8.....................86 C5
    MTCM CR4..........................194 E4
    CAT SE6.............................164 E4
Aitken Rd BAR EN5....................20 A5
Aitman Dr BTFD TW8 *...........117 H5
Ajax Av CDALE/KGS NW9..........45 G6
Ajax Rd KIL/WHAMP NW6..........82 D2
Akabusi Cl CROY/NA CRO........197 H5
Akehurst St PUT/ROE SW15....158 D1
Akenside Rd HAMP NW3............83 H3
Akerman Rd BRXN/ST SW9.....110 C7
                    SURB KT6.......190 D3
Alabama St WOOL/PLUM SE18...147 J1
Alacross Rd EA W5..................116 D2
Alan Cl DART DA1....................151 F5
Alandale Dr PIN HA5................41 F4
Alander Ms WALTH E17.............69 K1
Alan Dr BAR EN5.....................32 C1
Alan Gdns ROMW/RG RM7........74 C4
Alan Rd WIM/MER SW19..........177 H1
Alanthus Cl LEE/GVPK SE12....165 J1
Alaska St STHWK SE1................17 J2
Alba Cl YEAD UB4.....................95 H5
Albacore Crs LEW SE13..........164 E4
Alba Gdns GLDGN NW11............65 G4
Albain Crs ASHF TW15............152 B4
Albany Cl BUSH WD23..............28 D1
    BXLY DA5..........................168 D2
    ESH/CLAY KT10..................204 A6
    MORT/ESHN SW14..............137 J5
    SEVS/STOTM N15................67 H1
Albany Cottages HNWL W7 *...115 K1
Albany Ctyd MYFR/PICC W1J...10 B6
Albany Crs EDGW HA8..............44 C3
    ESH/CLAY KT10..................204 E4
Albany Ms BMLY BR1...............183 K2
    CMBW SE5........................122 D6
    IS N1..................................85 G5
    KUTN/CMB KT2 *................174 E2
    SUT SM1...........................208 E3
Albany Pde BTFD TW8 *...........117 F6
    PEND EN3............................25 F1
Albany Pk PEND EN3.................25 F1
Albany Park Av PEND EN3.........24 E2
Albany Park Rd
    KUTN/CMB KT2..................174 E2
Albany Pl BTFD TW8................116 E6
Albany Rd BELV DA17..............129 G6
    BTFD TW8.........................116 E6
    BXLY DA5..........................168 D2
    CHDH RM6...........................74 B3
    CHST BR7..........................185 G1
    FSBYPK N4...........................67 F5
    HCH RM12............................75 J5
    MNPK E12.............................89 H2
    NWMAL KT3........................192 A1
    RCHPK/HAM TW10 *...........137 G6
    UED N18...............................50 D1
    WALTH E17............................69 G3
    WALTH E17..........................122 E6
    WEA W13..............................97 H6
    WIM/MER SW19...................178 A1
Albany Rw EFNCH N2 *.............65 J1
Albany St CAMTN NW1................3 K4
Albany Ter
    RCHPK/HAM TW10 *...........137 G6
Albany Vw BKHH IG9..................38 D3
Alba Pl NTGHL W11.................100 D5
Albatross Cl EHAM E6..............107 K3
Albatross St
    WOOL/PLUM SE18.............147 K1
Albemarle Ap CONDST W1S......10 A6
Albemarle Av WHTN TW2.........154 E3
Albemarle Gdns
    GNTH/NBYPK IG2.................72 B3
    NWMAL KT3.......................192 A1
Albemarle Pk BECK BR3 *.......182 E4
    STAN HA7............................43 J1
Albemarle Rd BECK BR3.........182 E4
    EBAR EN4.............................33 J2
Albemarle St CONDST W1S......10 A6
Albemarle Wy FSBYE EC1V........6 A7
Alberta Av SUT SM1................208 C2
Alberta Est WALW SE17............122 C5
Alberta Rd EN EN1....................36 B1
    ERITH DA8.........................149 K2
Alberta St WALW SE17.............122 C5
Albert Av CHING E4....................37 J6
    VX/NE SW8.........................142 A1
Albert Br DRTSEA SW11..........140 D1
Albert Bridge Ga BTSEA SW11...140 E1
Albert Bridge Rd BTSEA SW11..140 E2
Albert Carr Gdns
    STRHM/NOR SW16...............179 K1
Albert Cl HOM E9.......................86 D6
    WDGN N22............................49 F4
Albert Cottages WCHPL E1 *....104 C4
Albert Crs CHING E4..................37 J6
Albert Dr WIM/MER SW19........159 H4
Albert Emb STHWK SE1............121 K5
Albert Gdns WCHPL E1.............105 F5
Albert Gv RYNPK SW20...........177 G4
Albert Ms BROCKY SE4 *..........144 C5
    FSBYPK N4 *.........................67 F5
    KENS W8.............................120 A3
    POP/IOD E14........................105 G6
Albert Pl FNCH N3......................46 E4
    KENS W8.............................120 A2
Albert Rd BCTR RM8..................74 B5
    BELV DA17.........................129 G5
    BKHH IG9..............................39 H4
    BXLY DA5..........................169 H1
    CAN/RD E16........................126 D1
    EA W5...................................97 H3
    EBAR EN4.............................21 H5
    FSTGT E7.............................89 F4
    FSBYPK N4............................67 F5
    HAYES BR2.........................200 C2
    HDN NW4..............................64 B1
    HPTN TW12.........................173 H1
    HSLW TW3..........................135 F5
    HYS/HAR UB3......................113 J3
    IL IG1....................................90 C1
    KIL/WHAMP NW6................100 D1
    KUT/HW KT1.......................175 F4
    LEY E10.................................70 A6
    MLHL NW7.............................45 H1
    MTCM CR4..........................179 J5
    NWDGN UB2.......................114 C3
    NWMAL KT3........................192 C1
    ORP BR6.............................217 G3
    PGE/AN SE20......................182 A3
    RCHPK/HAM TW10.............137 F6
    RDART DA2.........................171 F5
    ROM RM1.............................75 H1
    RYLN/HDSTN HA2................42 C6
    SEVS/STOTM N15................68 A3
    SNWD SE25.........................197 J1
    STMC/STPC BR5..................202 C3
    SUT SM1.............................209 H3
    SWFD E18.............................53 F6
    TEDD TW11.........................174 A2
    TWK TW1..............................156 B1
    WDGN N22............................48 D4
    WDR/YW UB7........................112 B1
Albert Sq SRTFD E15.................88 C3
    VX/NE SW8.........................142 A1
Albert St CAMTN NW1................3 K1
    NFNCH/WDSPK N12.............47 G1
    EA W5....................................97 H3
    WLSDN NW10 *.....................81 F6
Albert Terrace Ms CAMTN NW1...3 G1
Albert Wy PECK SE15...............143 J1
Albion Av MUSWH N10...............48 A4
    VX/NE SW8.........................141 J3
Albion Cl BAY/PAD W2.................8 D5
    ROMW/RG RM7.....................75 F3
Albion Dr HACK E8.....................86 B5
Albion Est BERM/RHTH SE16 *..123 K2
Albion Gdns HMSMTH W6.........118 E4
Albion Ga BAY/PAD W2................8 D5
Albion Gv STNW/STAM N16........86 A2
Albion Ms BAY/PAD W2................8 D5
    IS N1....................................85 G6
    HMSMTH W6 *....................118 E4
Albion Pl IFARR EC1M................12 A1
    HMSMTH W6.......................118 E4
    SNWD SE25........................181 H6
Albion Riverside BTSEA SW11...140 D6
Albion Rd BELMT SM2.............209 H4
    BXLYHS DA6........................149 G5
    HSLW TW3...........................135 F5
    HYS/HAR UB3......................113 J3
    KUTN/CMB KT2 *................175 K4
    STNW/STAM N16.................85 K3
    TOTM N17..............................52 A5
    WALTH E17............................51 H5
    WHTN TW2..........................155 K5
Albion St HACK E8.....................86 B5
Albion St BAY/PAD W2................8 D4
    BERM/RHTH SE16..............123 K2
    CROY/NA CRO.....................196 C5
Albion Ter CHING E4 *...............25 K5
    HACK E8................................86 B5
Albion Villas Rd SYD SE26........163 K5
Albion Wk IS N1...........................5 F3
Albion Wy LEW SE13...............145 F5
    STBT EC1A.............................12 C2
    WBLY HA9..............................80 C1
Albion Yd IS N1............................5 F3
Albrighton Rd EDUL SE22.........143 F4
Albuhera Cl ENC/FH EN2............23 G2
Albury Av BELMT SM2...............208 A6
    ISLW TW7............................136 A1
Albury Cl HOR/WEW KT19........206 D6
    HPTN TW12.........................173 F2
Albury Dr PIN HA5......................41 G4
Albury Ms MNPK E12..................71 G6
Albury Rd CHSGTN KT9............206 A5
Albury St DEPT SE8...................124 D6
Albyfield BMLY BR1..................184 E6
Albyn Rd DEPT SE8..................144 B3
Alcester Crs CLPT E5..................68 D7
Alcester Ms BAY/PAD W2 *......101 B2
Alcock Cl WLGTN SM6.............210 D5
Alcock Rd HEST TW5................134 C1
Aconbury Rd CLPT E5................68 C6
Alcorn Cl CHAM SM3................193 K6
Alcott Cl HNWL W7....................97 F4
Aldborough Rd DAGE RM10........92 E4
Aldborough Rd North
    GNTH/NBYPK IG2..................73 F2
Aldborough Rd South
    GDMY/SEVK IG3....................72 E3
Aldbourne Rd SHB W12............118 C1
Aldbridge St WALW SE17.........123 F5
Aldburgh Ms MHST W1U.............9 H5
Aldbury Av WBLY HA9................80 D5
Aldbury Ms MHST W1U...............9 G5
Aldebert Ter VX/NE SW8...........142 A1
Aldeburgh Pl WFD IG8................38 E6
Aldeburgh St GNWCH SE10.....125 K5
Alden Av SRTFD E15.................106 C2
Aldenham Rd OXHEY WD19........4 B3
Alden Md PIN HA5......................42 A3
Aldenley Rd HMSMTH W6.........118 E3
Alderbrook Rd BAL SW12.........161 G1
Alderbury Rd BARN SW13........118 E6
Alder Cl PECK SE15..................123 G6
Alder Gv CRICK NW2..................63 J6
Alderholt Wy PECK SE15 *........143 F1
Alderman Av BARK IG11............109 G2
Aldermanbury CITYW EC2V........12 D3
Aldermanbury Sq CITYW EC2V..12 D2
Aldermans Hl PLMGR N13...........34 E6
Alderman Judge Ml
    KUT/HW KT1........................175 F5
Alderman's Hl PLMGR N13.........34 E6
Aldermary Rd BMLY BR1...........183 K4
Alder Ms ARCH N19....................66 C1
Aldermoor Rd CAT SE6.............164 C5
Alderney Av HEST TW5.............135 G1
Alderney Gdns NTHLT UB5.........77 K5
Alderney Ms STHWK SE1............18 E4

Alderney Rd ERITH DA8............150 D1
    WCHPL E1...........................105 F3
Alderney St PIM SW1V................21 J6
Ald Rd MORT/ESHN SW14........138 A4
    SCUP DA14.........................186 A1
Aldersbrook Av EN EN1...............24 A3
Aldersbrook Dr
    KUTN/CMB KT2..................175 G2
Aldersbrook La MNPK E12..........89 K1
Aldersbrook Rd MNPK E12.........71 K6
Alders Cl EA W5.........................116 E5
    EDGW HA8............................44 E1
    WAN E11................................71 F6
Aldersey Gdns BARK IG11..........90 D5
Aldersford Cl BROCKY SE4.......144 A5
Aldersgate St STBT EC1A...........12 C1
Aldersgrove Av ELTH/MOT SE9..166 C4
Aldersgrove Av ELTH/MOT SE9..166 C4
Aldershot Rd KIL/WHAMP NW6..82 D6
Aldershot Ter
    WOOL/PLUM SE18 *............147 F1
Aldermead Av CROY/NA CRO....198 A3
Alderney Rd BECK BR3.............182 B3
Alderson Pl NWDGN UB2.........115 H1
Alderson St NKENS W10...........100 C3
Alderton Cl WLSDN NW10..........62 D2
Alderton Crs HDN NW4...............63 K2
Alderton Rd CROY/NA CRO......197 G4
    HNHL SE24.........................142 D4
Alderton Wy HDN NW4...............63 K2
Alderville Rd FUL/PGN SW6.....139 J3
Alderwood Ms EBAR EN4 *........21 G4
Alderwood Rd ELTH/MOT SE9..167 J1
Aldford St MYFR/PKLN W1K........9 G7
Aldgate FENCHST EC3M.............13 H4
Aldgate Barrs WCHPL E1 *.........13 K3
Aldgate High St TWRH EC3N.....13 J4
Aldine St SHB W12...................119 F2
Aldingham Gdns HCH RM12........93 J3
Aldington Cl BCTR RM8..............73 J4
Aldington Rd CHARL SE7..........126 C5
Aldis Ms TOOT SW17................178 D1
Aldis St TOOT SW17.................178 D1
Aldred Rd KIL/WHAMP NW6......82 E3
Aldren Rd TOOT SW17..............160 B5
Aldrich Crs CROY/NA CRO........214 A6
Aldriche Wy CHING E4.................52 A2
Aldrich Gdns CHEAM SM3........208 D1
Aldrich Ter WAND/EARL SW18..160 B4
Aldridge Av EDGW HA8..............30 D5
                    PEND EN3...........25 F1
                    RSLP HA4..............59 J1
                    STAN HA7.............44 A5
Aldridge Rd NWMAL KT3..........192 B4
Aldridge Road Vis NTGHL W11...100 D4
Aldrington Rd
    STRHM/NOR SW16..............179 H1
    KIL/WHAMP NW6..................-
    LEW SE13...............................-
Aldsworth Cl MV/WKIL W9........101 F3
Aldworth Gv ELTH/MOT SE9.....167 J5
Aldworth Rd SRTFD E15.............88 C5
Aldworth Gv LEW SE13.............165 F1
Aldwych HOL/ALD WC2B.............11 G4
Aldwych Av BARK/HLT IG6..........72 C2
Aldwych Cl HCH RM12................93 J2
Aldwyck Rd BXLYHS DA6..........148 E6
Alesia Cl WDGN N22...................48 E3
Alestan Beck Rd CAN/RD E16...107 H5
Alexander Av WLSDN NW10........81 K5
Alexander Cl BFN/LL DA15.........147 K6
    EBAR EN4.............................21 H5
    HAYES BR2.........................199 J6
    NWDGN UB2.......................115 F2
    WHTN TW2..........................155 K4
Alexander Evans Ms
    FSTH SE23..........................164 A4
Alexander Ms BAY/PAD W2......101 A4
Alexander Pl SKENS SW7.............14 C6
Alexander Rd ARCH N19..............66 E1
    BXLYHN DA7......................148 E3
    CHST BR7...........................185 G2
Alexander Sq CHEL SW3.............14 C6
Alexander St BAY/PAD W2........100 E5
Alexander Ter ABYW SE2 *........128 C5
Alexandra Av BTSEA SW11 *.....141 F2
    RYLN/HDSTN HA2................59 K5
    SUT SM1.............................208 E1
    WDGN N22............................48 E5
Alexandra Cl
    RYLN/HDSTN HA2 *...............78 A1
Alexandra Cottages
    NWCR SE14........................144 C2
Alexandra Crs STHGT/OAK N14...22 C6
Alexandra Crs BMLY BR1..........183 J2
Alexandra Dr BRYLDS KT5........191 H4
    NRWD SE19 *.....................181 F1
Alexandra Gdns CAR SM5.........210 A6
    HSLW TW3..........................135 G3
    MUSWH N10..........................66 B1
Alexandra Ga SKENS SW7 *.......14 A3
Alexandra Gv FSBYPK N4............67 H5
    NFNCH/WDSPK N12.............47 F1
Alexandra Ms EFNCH N2 *.........47 K6
Alexandra Palace Wy
    CEND/HSY/T N8....................66 C6
    WDGN N22............................48 C6
Alexandra Pde
    RYLN/HDSTN HA2 *...............78 A1
Alexandra Park Rd
    MUSWH N10..........................48 B5
Alexandra Pl CROY/NA CRO.....197 F5
    SNWD SE25........................196 E2
    STJWD NW8...........................2 B1
Alexandra Rd BTFD TW8..........116 E6
    CEND/HSY/T N8.....................49 G6
    CHDH RM6............................73 K3

CHSWK W4.............................118 A2
CROY/NA CRO.........................197 F5
EN EN1....................................24 E6
EHAM E6...............................108 A2
ERITH DA8.............................130 C6
HDN NW4.................................64 B1
HSLW TW3.............................135 G3
KUTN/CMB KT2......................175 H5
LEY E10...................................88 A1
MORT/ESHN SW14................138 A4
MTCM CR4.............................178 D3
MUSWH N10............................66 B1
PEND EN3................................25 F5
RAIN RM13...............................93 H6
RCH/KEW TW9......................137 G5
ROM RM1.................................75 H1
SEVS/STOTM N15....................68 B1
SWFD E18................................53 F6
SYD SE26..............................182 A2
THDIT KT7.............................190 A3
TWK TW1...............................156 E1
WALTH E17..............................69 G3
WIM/MER SW19.....................177 K1
Alexandra Sq MRDN SM4.........193 K2
Alexandra St CAN/RD E16........106 E4
    NWCR SE14.........................144 B1
Alexandria Rd WEA W13.............97 H6
Alexis St BERM/RHTH SE16.....123 H4
Alexis Rd CLPT E5......................86 D3
Alfearn Rd CLPT E5.....................86 E2
Alford Gn CROY/NA CRO...........214 B4
Alford Pl IS N1 *............................6 C2
Alford Rd ERITH DA8.................130 A4
Alfoxton Av SEVS/STOTM N15...67 H1
Alfreda St BTSEA SW11.............141 G2
Alfred Cl CHSWK W4 *..............118 A4
Alfred Gdns STHL UB1................95 J6
Alfred Ms GWRST WC1E.............10 C1
Alfred Pl GWRST WC1E..............10 C1
Alfred Rd ACT W3......................117 K1
    BAY/PAD W2........................100 E4
    BELV DA17..........................129 G5
    BKHH IG9...............................39 H4
    FELT TW13...........................154 C5
    KUT/HW KT1........................175 F6
    RDART DA2..........................171 J6
    SNWD SE25..........................197 H2
    SRTFD E15.............................88 D3
Alfred's Gdns BARK IG11...........108 E2
Alfred's Wy (East Ham &
    Barking By-Pass)
    EHAM E6..............................108 A7
Alfreton Cl WIM/MER SW19......159 G5
    RYLN/HDSTN HA2 *...............-
Alfriston Cl BRYLDS KT5...........191 G3
    DART DA1.............................170 B1
Alfriston Rd BTSEA SW11..........140 E6
Algar Cl ISLW TW7 *.................136 B4
    STAN HA7..............................43 F1
Algar Rd ISLW TW7 *...............136 B4
Algarve Rd WAND/EARL SW18..160 A3
Algernon Rd HDN NW4...............63 J3
    KIL/WHAMP NW6....................-
    LEW SE13.............................144 D5
Algiers Rd LEW SE13................144 D5
Alibon Gdns DAGE RM10............92 C3
Alibon Rd DAGE RM10................92 C3
Alice Gdns WHTN TW2..............155 F2
Alice La BOW E3..........................87 H6
Alice St STHWK SE1....................19 G4
Alice Thompson Cl
    LEE/GVPK SE12...................166 B4
Alice Walker Cl HNHL SE24 *....142 C5
Alice Wy HSLW TW3.................135 G5
Alicia Av KTN/HRWW/WS HA3...61 H1
Alicia Cl KTN/HRWW/WS HA3....61 J1
Alicia Gdns KTN/HRWW/WS HA3..61 H1
Alie St WCHPL E1........................13 K4
Alington Crs CDALE/KGS NW9...62 D6
Alington Gv WLGTN SM6...........210 D6
Aliston Cl CROY/NA CRO...........198 A5
    EHAM E6.................................-
Aliwal Ms BTSEA SW11............140 D5
Aliwal Rd BTSEA SW11.............140 D5
Alkerden Rd CHSWK W4...........118 B5
Alkham Rd STNW/STAM N16......68 B6
Allan Barclay Cl
    SEVS/STOTM N15..................68 B3
Allan Cl NWMAL KT3................192 A2
Allandale Av FNCH N3................46 C6
Allandale Pl ORP BR6................217 K1
Allandale Rd EMPK RM11...........75 H6
Allard Cl STMC/STPC BR5........202 E4
    PEND EN3..............................25 F4
Allard Crs BUSH WD23...............28 C3
Allardyce St CLAP SW4.............142 A5
Allbrook Cl TEDD TW11............173 K1
Allcot Cl EBED/NFELT TW14.....153 H3
Allcroft Rd KTTN NW5................84 A4
Allder Wy SAND/SEL CR2.........211 H5
Allenby Av SAND/SEL CR2........211 J6
Allenby Cl GFD/PVL UB6.............96 A2
Allenby Rd FSTH SE23..............164 B5
    STHL UB1...............................96 A4
    WOOL/PLUM SE18..............127 H3
Allen Cl MTCM CR4...................179 G4
    SUN TW16...........................172 A4
Allen Ct GFD/PVL UB6 *.............79 F3
Allendale Av STHL UB1...............96 A5
    SYD SE26...............................-
Allendale Cl CMBW SE5............142 E3
    SYD SE26.............................182 A4
Allendale Rd GFD/PVL UB6.........79 H4
Allen Edwards Dr VX/NE SW8...141 K2
Allen Rd BECK BR3...................182 A5
    BOW E3..................................87 H1
    CROY/NA CRO.....................196 A5
    STNW/STAM N16...................86 A2
Allensbury Pl CAMTN NW1.........84 D5
Allens Rd PEND EN3...................24 E6
Allen St KENS W8.....................119 K3
Allenswood Rd ELTH/MOT SE9..146 D4
Allerford Ct HRW HA1 *..............-
Allerford Rd CAT SE6................164 E6

Allerton Rd STNW/STAM N16.....67 J6
Allerton St IS N1...........................6 E4
Allestree Rd FUL/PGN SW6......139 H1
Alleyn Crs DUL SE21..................-
Alleyndale Rd BCTR RM8............73 J6
Alleyn Pk DUL SE21..................162 E4
    NWDGN UB2........................114 E5
Alleyn Rd DUL SE21.................162 E5
Allfarthing La
    WAND/EARL SW18...............160 B1
Allgood Cl MRDN SM4..............193 G3
Allgood St BETH E2.....................-
Allhallows La CANST EC4R.........12 E6
Allhallows Rd EHAM E6............107 J5
All Hallows Rd TOTM N17...........50 A4
Alliance Cl ALP/SUD HA0............79 K2
    HSLW TW4...........................134 E6
Alliance Rd ACT W3..................117 J3
    PLSTW E13...........................107 G4
    WOOL/PLUM SE18..............128 B6
Allied Wy ACT W3 *...................118 B2
Allingham Cl HNWL W7...............97 F6
Allington Av TOTM N17...............50 A2
Allington Cl GFD/PVL UB6...........78 C5
    WIM/MER SW19..................177 G1
Allington Rd HDN NW4................63 K2
    NKENS W10........................100 C2
    ORP BR6.............................201 K6
    RYLN/HDSTN HA2..................-
Allington St BGVA SW1W............15 A5
    WESTW SW1E.......................16 A5
Allison Cl GNWCH SE10............145 F2
Allison Gv DUL SE21.................163 F3
Allison Rd ACT W3.....................98 E5
    CEND/HSY/T N8.....................67 G2
Allitsen Rd STJWD NW8...............2 C3
Allitson Rd STJWD NW8...............-
Allnutt Wy CLAP SW4...............141 J6
Alloa Rd DEPT SE8....................124 A5
    GDMY/SEVK IG3....................73 H6
Allonby Gdns WBLY HA9.............61 J5
Alloway Rd BOW E3...................105 G2
Allport Ms WCHPL E1 *.............104 E4
All Saints' Cl ED N10..................-
All Saints Dr BKHTH/KID SE3...145 J3
All Saints Ms STAN HA7..............42 E2
All Saints Pas
    WAND/EARL SW18...............139 K6
All Saints' Rd ACT W3...............117 K3
    NTGHL W11........................100 D4
    SUT SM1.............................209 G1
    WIM/MER SW19..................178 B3
All Saints St IS N1........................5 G2
Alsop Pl CAMTN NW1 *................3 F7
All Souls' Av WLSDN NW10.........99 K1
All Souls' Pl REGST W1B..............9 K2
Allum Wy TRDG/WHET N20........33 G3
Allwood Cl SYD SE26................164 A6
Alma Av CHING E4.......................-
Alma Ct RYLN/HDSTN HA2 *......-
Alma Cl MUSWH N10..................48 B4
Alma Crs SUT SM1...................208 C3
Alma Gv STHWK SE1................123 H4
Alma Pl NRWD SE19.................181 G3
    THHTH CR7..........................196 B2
    WLSDN NW10........................99 K1
Alma Rd BFN/LL DA15..............168 B5
    CAR SM5..............................209 J4
    ENF EN3...............................25 H4
    ESH/CLAY KT10..................189 K3
    MUSWH N10..........................48 A3
    PEND EN3..............................25 G6
    STHL UB1...............................95 J6
    STMC/STPC BR5..................202 D2
    WAND/EARL SW18...............140 B5
Alma Sq KTN/HRWW/WS HA3 *..42 C4
Alma St KTTN NW5......................84 B4
    SRTFD E15..............................88 B4
Alma Ter BOW E3 *.....................-
    KENS W8 *...........................119 K3
    WAND/EARL SW18...............160 C2
Almeida St IS N1...........................85 H6
Almeric Rd BTSEA SW11...........140 E5
Almer Rd RYNPK SW20.............176 D3
Almington St FSBYPK N4 *..........67 F4
Almond Av CAR SM5.................194 E6
    EA W5..................................117 F3
    WDR/YW UB7.....................112 D3
Almond Cl FELT TW13...............153 K3
    HAYES BR2.........................201 F4
    HYS/HAR UB3........................94 C6
    PECK SE15...........................143 H3
    RSLP HA4...............................-
Almond Rd BERM/RHTH SE16...123 J4
    TOTM N17..............................50 C5
Almonds Av BKHH IG9................38 E4
Almond Wy HAYES BR2............201 F4
    MTCM CR4...........................195 J2
    RYLN/HDSTN HA2.................-
Almorah Rd HEST TW5..............134 C2
    IS N1.....................................85 K5
Almshouse La CHSGTN KT9......205 K6
Alnwick Gv MRDN SM4............194 A1
Alnwick Rd CAN/RD E16...........107 G5
    LEE/GVPK SE12...................166 A2
Alnwick Ter LEE/GVPK SE12.....166 A2
Alperton La GFD/PVL UB6...........97 K2
Alperton St NKENS W10.............100 C3
Alphabet Gdns CAR SM5...........194 C4
Alpha Est HYS/HAR UB3 *.........113 H2
Alpha Gv POP/IOD E14...............124 D2
Alpha Pl CHEL SW3...................120 D6
    CHING E4................................37 J5
    CROY/NA CRO.....................197 F5
    KIL/WHAMP NW6..................-
    SUT SM1.............................208 E4
    PEND EN3..............................-
    TEDD TW11..........................173 J1
    UED N18..................................-
Alpha Rd CHING E4.....................37 J6
    CROY/NA CRO.....................197 G5
    ENF EN3.................................25 G5
    PECK SE15...........................143 K3
    SURB KT6.............................191 G4
    TEDD TW11..........................173 J2
    UED N18..................................-
    WIM/MER SW19...................178 D3
Alpha St PECK SE15..................143 H3
Alphea Cl WIM/MER SW19........178 C3
Alpine Av BRYLDS KT5..............191 K6

Alpine Cl CROY/NA CRO 212 A1
Alpine Copse BMLY BR1 .....185 F5
Alpine Rd HOM E9 ....86 E5
Alpine Rd BERM/RHTH SE16 ..123 K4
Alpine Wy EHAM E6 ....69 K4
Alpine Vw CAR SM5 ....209 J3
Alpine Wk BUSH WD23 ....28 E4
Alpine Wy EHAM E6 ....108 K4
Alric Av NWMAL KT3 ....176 B6
  WLSDN NW10 ....81 F5
Alroy Rd FSBYPK N4 ....67 G4
Alsace Rd WALW SE17 ....123 F5
Alscot Rd STHWK SE1 ....19 K5
Alscot Wy STHWK SE1 ....19 J6
Alsike Rd ERITHM DA18 .....128 E3
Alsom Av WPK KT4 ....207 H2
Alston Cl SURB KT6 ....190 C4
Alston Rd BAR EN5 ....20 C4
  TOOT SW17 ....160 C6
  UED N18 ....42 E3
Altair Cl TOTM N17 ....50 C2
Altair Wy NTHWD HA6 ......40 D1
Altash Wy ELTH/MOT SE9 ...166 E4
Altenburg Av WEA W13 .....116 C3
Altenburg Gdns BTSEA SW11 .140 E5
Alt Gv WIM/MER SW19 ......177 J5
Altham Ct RYLN/HDSTN HA2 * .42 B4
Altham Gdns OXHEY WD19 ...27 H6
Altham Rd PIN HA5 ....41 J4
Althea St FUL/PGN SW6 ....140 A3
Althorne Gdns SWFD E18 ...52 D1
Althorne Wy DAGE RM10 ....74 C6
Althorp Cl BAR EN5 ....31 J2
Althorpe Rd HRW HA1 ......60 C2
Althorp Rd TOOT SW17 .....160 E3
Altmore Av EHAM E6 ....87 K5
Alton Av STAN HA7 ....43 F5
  ISLW TW7 ....136 A3
Alton Cl BXLY DA5 ....169 F3
  ISLW TW7 ....136 A3
Alton Gdns BECK BR3 ......182 D3
  WHTN TW2 ....155 J1
Alton Rd CROY/NA CRO 211 G2
  PUT/ROE SW15 ....158 D3
  RCH/KEW TW9 ....137 F5
  TOTM N17 ....49 K6
Alton St POP/IOD E14 .....105 K5
Altyre Cl BECK BR3 ....198 C2
Altyre Rd CROY/NA CRO 196 E6
Altyre Wy BECK BR3 ....198 C2
Alvanley Gdns
  KIL/WHAMP NW6 ....83 F3
Alva Wy OXHEY WD19 ....27 H4
Alverstone Av EBAR EN4 ...33 H2
  WAND/EARL SW18 ....159 K4
Alverstone Gdns
  ELTH/MOT SE9 ....167 G3
Alverstone Rd CRICK NW2 ..82 A5
  MNPK E12 ....90 A2
  NWMAL KT3 ....192 C1
  WBLY HA9 ....62 E5
Alverstone Gdns SNWD SE25 .197 F2
Alverton St DEPT SE8 .....124 C5
Alveston Av
  KTN/HRWW/WS HA3 ....43 H6
Alveston Sq SWFD E18 * ...52 E2
Alvey St WALW SE17 ....123 F5
Alvia Gdns SUT SM1 ....209 G2
Alvington Crs HACK E8 ....86 B5
Alway Av HOR/WEW KT19 ....206 E3
Alwold Crs LEE/GVPK SE12 .166 A1
Alwyn Av CHSWK W4 ....118 A5
Alwyn Cl BORE WD6 ....30 B1
  CROY/NA CRO 213 K5
Alwyne La IS N1 * 85 H5
Alwyne Rd HNWL W7 ....96 E6
  IS N1 ....85 J5
  WIM/MER SW19 ....177 J2
Alwyne Sq IS N1 ....85 J4
Alwyne Vlls IS N1 ....85 H5
Alwyn Gdns ACT W3 ....98 D5
  HDN NW4 ....63 J1
Alyn Bank CEND/HSY/T N8 * .66 D3
Alyth Gdns GLDGN NW11 ....64 D3
Amalgamated Dr BTFD TW8 ..116 A6
Amanda Cl CHIG IG7 ....54 C2
Amanda Ms ROMW/RG RM7 ....74 E2
Amar Ct WOOL/PLUM SE18 ...128 A4
Amardeep Ct
  WOOL/PLUM SE18 ....128 A5
Amazon St WCHPL E1 ....104 D5
Ambassador Cl HSLW TW3 ...134 D5
Ambassador Gdns EHAM E6 ..107 K4
Ambassador Sq POP/IOD E14 .124 E4
Amber Av WALTH E17 ....51 G4
Amberden Av FNCH N3 ......46 E6
Ambergate St WALW SE17 ...122 C5
Amber Gv CRICK NW2 ....64 B5
Amberley Cl ORP BR6 ......217 F3
  PIN HA5 ....41 K6
Amberley Ct SCUP DA14 ....186 D1
Amberley Gdns
  HOR/WEW KT19 ....207 H2
Amberley Gv CROY/NA CRO ..197 G4
  SYD SE26 ....163 J6
Amberley Rd ABYW SE2 .....128 E6
  BKHH IG9 ....39 G3
  EN1 N1 ....36 B2
  LEY E10 ....69 J4
  MV/WKIL W9 ....100 E3
  PLMGR N13 ....35 F4
Amberley Wy HSLWW TW4 ....154 A5
  MRDN SM4 ....193 K4
  ROMW/RG RM7 ....74 D1
Amberside Cl ISLW TW7 ....155 J1
Amber St SRTFD E15 * 88 B4
Amberwood Cl NWMAL KT3 ...192 B5
Amberwood Ri NWMAL KT3 ...192 B3
Amblecote Cl LEE/GVPK SE12 .166 A5
Amblecote Meadow
  LEE/GVPK SE12 ....166 A5
Amblecote Mdw
  LEE/GVPK SE12 * 166 A5
Amblecote Rd LEE/GVPK SE12 .166 A5
Ambler Rd FSBYPK N4 ......85 H1
Ambleside BMLY BR1 ....183 G2
Ambleside Av BECK BR3 ....198 B6

HCH RM12 ....93 K3
  STRHM/NOR SW16 ....161 J6
  WOT/HER KT12 ....188 B5
Ambleside Cl HOM E9 ......86 E5
  LEY E10 ....69 K4
  SEVS/STOTM N15 ....49 K6
Ambleside Crs PEND EN3 ...25 F4
Ambleside Dr
  EBED/NFELT TW14 ....153 J3
Ambleside Gdns BELMT SM2 .208 C4
  REDBR IG4 ....71 J1
  WBLY HA9 ....61 K5
Ambleside Rd BXLYHN DA7 ..149 H3
  WLSDN NW10 ....81 H5
Ambrey Wy WLCTN SM6 ......210 D6
Ambrook Rd BELV DA17 .....129 H3
Ambrosden Av WEST SW1P ...16 B5
Ambrose Av GLDGN NW11 ....64 C5
Ambrose Cl DART DA1 ......150 C5
  ORP BR6 ....217 F1
Ambrose St BERM/RHTH SE16 .123 J4
Amelia Cl ACT W3 ....117 J1
Amelia St WALW SE17 .....122 C5
Amen Cnr STP EC4M 12 B4
  TOOT SW17 ....179 F2
Amen Ct STP EC4M 12 B4
America Sq TWRH EC3N * ...13 J5
America St STHWK SE1 .....18 C1
Ameriand Rd PUT/ROE SW15 .159 J1
Amersham Av UED N18 ......49 K2
Amersham Gv NWCR SE14 ....144 C1
Amersham Rd CROY/NA CRO ..196 D3
  NWCR SE14 ....144 C2
Amery Gdns WLSDN NW10 ....81 K6
Amery Rd HRW HA1 ....61 G3
Amesbury Av
  BRXS/STRHM SW2 ....161 K4
Amesbury Cl WPK KT4 ......193 F5
Amesbury Dr CHING E4 .....37 K1
Amesbury Rd BMLY BR1 .....184 C6
  DAGW RM9 ....91 K5
  FELT TW13 ....154 D4
Ames Cottages POP/IOD E14 * .105 G4
Amethyst Ct ORP BR6 ......216 E4
Amethyst Rd SRTFD E15 ....88 B2
Amherst Av WEA W13 ....97 J5
Amherst Cl STMC/STPC BR5 .202 B1
Amherst Dr STMC/STPC BR5 .202 A1
Amherst Gdns WEA W13 * ...97 J5
Amherst Rd WEA W13 ....97 J5
Amhurst Pde
  STNW/STAM N16 * 68 B4
Amhurst Pk STNW/STAM N16 .68 A4
Amhurst Rd STNW/STAM N16 .86 C1
Amhurst Ter HACK E8 ......86 C2
Amidas Gdns BCTR RM8 .....91 H2
Amiel St WCHPL E1 ....104 E3
Amies St BTSEA SW11 ......140 E4
Amina Wy BERM/RHTH SE16 ..123 H3
Amis Av HOR/WEW KT19 .....206 C5
Amity Gv RYNPK SW20 ......177 F4
Amity Rd SRTFD E15 ....88 D5
Ammanford Gn
  CDALE/KGS NW9 * 63 G3
Amor Rd BTSEA SW11 ....161 F1
Amott Rd PECK SE15 ....143 H4
Ampere Wy CROY/NA CRO 195 K4
Ampleforth Cl ORP BR6 ....217 J2
Ampleforth Rd ABYW SE2 ...128 C2
Ampthill Est CAMTN NW1 ...4 A3
Ampthill Sq CAMTN NW1 * ..4 A3
Ampton St FSBYW WC1X 5 G5
Amroth Cl FSTH SE23 ......163 J3
Amroth Gn CDALE/KGS NW9 * .63 G3
Amsterdam Rd POP/IOD E14 .125 F3
Amwell Cl ENC/FH EN2 .....23 K6
Amwell St CLKNW EC1R 5 J4
Amyand Cottages TWK TW1 * .156 C1
Amyand Park Gdns TWK TW1 .156 C2
Amyand Park Rd TWK TW1 ...156 C2
Amy Cl WLGTN SM6 ....210 E5
Amyruth Rd BROCKY SE4 ....144 D6
Amy Warne Cl EHAM E6 .....107 J4
Anatola Rd ARCH N19 ......66 C6
Ancaster Crs NWMAL KT3 ...192 D3
Ancaster Ms BECK BR3 .....182 A6
Ancaster Rd BECK BR3 .....182 A6
Ancaster St WOOL/PLUM SE18 .147 K1
Anchorage Cl WIM/MER SW19 .177 K1
Anchor & Hope La CHARL SE7 .126 B4
Anchor Cl BARK IG11 ......109 H2
Anchor Dr RAIN RM13 ......111 K3
Anchor Ms BERM/RHTH SE16 * .147 K1
Anchor Ter WCHPL E1 * 104 E3
Anchor Yd FSBYE EC1V * ...6 D6
Ancill Cl HMSMTH W6 ......119 H6
Ancona Rd WLSDN NW10 .....99 J1
  WOOL/PLUM SE18 ....127 J5
Andace Park Gdns BMLY BR1 * .184 B4
Andalus Rd BRXN/ST SW9 ...141 K4
Ander Cl ALP/SUD HA0 .....79 K2
Anderson Cl ACT W3 ....99 F5
  CHEAM SM3 ....193 H5
  WCHMH N21 ....23 F6
Anderson Dr ASHF TW15 ....153 F6
Anderson Rd HOM E9 ....87 F4
  WFD IG8 ....53 G5
Anderson St CHEL SW3 .....120 E5
Anderson Sq IS N1 * 6 A1
Andover Av CAN/RD E16 ....107 H5
Andover Cl EBED/NFELT TW14 .153 J3
  GFD/PVL UB6 ....96 B3
Andover Pl KIL/WHAMP NW6 .101 F1
Andover Rd HOLWY N7 ......67 F6
  ORP BR6 ....201 K5
  WHTN TW2 ....155 J3
Andover Ter HMSMTH W6 * ..118 E4
Andre St HACK E8 ....86 C3
Andrew Borde St
  LSQ/SEVD WC2H * 10 D3
Andrew Cl BARK/HLT IG6 ...54 D3

DART DA1 ....150 A6
Andrewes Gdns EHAM E6 ....107 J5
Andrew Pl VX/NE SW8 ......141 J2
Andrews Cl BKHH IG9 ......39 G4
  CRICK NW2 * 81 K3
  HRW HA1 ....60 E3
  STMC/STPC BR5 ....186 E6
  WPK KT4 ....193 G6
Andrews Pl RDART DA2 .....170 B4
  RDART DA2 ....170 D6
Andrews Rd HACK E8 ....86 D1
Andrews Wk WALW SE17 .....122 C6
Andwell Cl ABYW SE2 ......128 C2
Anerley Gv NRWD SE19 .....181 G5
Anerley Hl NRWD SE19 .....181 G2
Anerley Pk PGE/AN SE20 ...181 J3
Anerley Park Rd PGE/AN SE20 .181 J3
Anerley Rd PGE/AN SE20 ...181 J3
Anerley Station Rd
  PGE/AN SE20 ....181 J4
Anerley V NRWD SE19 ......181 G3
Anfield Cl BAL SW12 ......161 H2
Angel Aly WCHPL E1 * 13 K2
Angel Cl UED N18 ....50 B1
Angel Corner Pde UED N18 * .50 C1
Angel Ct LOTH EC2R 13 F4
Angelfield HSLW TW3 ......135 G5
Angel Hl SUT SM1 ....209 F1
Angel Hill Dr SUT SM1 ....209 F1
Angelica Dr EHAM E6 ......108 A4
Angelica Gdns CROY/NA CRO .198 A5
Angel La HYS/HAR UB3 .....94 B4
  SRTFD E15 ....88 B4
Angell Park Gdns
  BRXN/ST SW9 ....142 B4
Angell Town Est
  BRXN/ST SW9 ....142 B3
Angel Ms PUT/ROE SW15 ....158 D2
Angel Pas CANST EC4R 12 E6
Angel Rd HRW HA1 ....60 E3
  THDIT KT7 ....190 B5
Angel Rd (North Circular)
  UED N18 ....50 D1
Angel Sq FSBYE EC1V * 6 A3
Angel St STBT EC1A 12 C3
Angel Wk HMSMTH W6 ....119 F4
Angel Wy ROM RM1 ....75 G2
Angerstein La BKHTH/KID SE3 .145 J1
Anglers La KTTN NW5 ......84 B4
Anglers Reach SURB KT6 * .190 E3
Anglesea Ms
  WOOL/PLUM SE18 ....127 G4
Anglesea Rd KUT/HW KT1 ...190 D5
  STMC/STPC BR5 ....202 D3
  WOOL/PLUM SE18 ....127 G4
Anglesey Cl ASHF TW15 ....152 D6
Anglesey Court Rd CAR SM5 .210 A4
Anglesey Dr RAIN RM13 ....111 J3
Anglesey Gdns CAR SM5 ....210 A4
Anglesey Rd OXHEY WD19 ...41 G1
  PEND EN3 ....24 D5
Anglesmede Crs PIN HA5 ...42 A6
Anglesmede Wy PIN HA5 ....42 A5
Angles Rd STRHM/NOR SW16 .161 K6
Anglia Cl TOTM N17 ....50 D3
Anglian Rd WAN E11 ....88 B1
Anglo Rd BOW E3 ....105 H1
Angus Cl CHSGTN KT9 ......206 C3
Angus Dr RSLP HA4 ....77 G2
Angus Gdns CDALE/KGS NW9 .45 F4
Angus Rd PLSTW E13 ....107 G2
Angus St NWCR SE14 ....144 B1
Anhalt Rd BTSEA SW11 .....140 D1
Ankerdine Crs
  WOOL/PLUM SE18 ....147 G2
Anlaby Rd TEDD TW11 ......173 K1
Anley Rd HMSMTH W6 ....119 G2
Anmersh Gv STAN HA7 ......43 K4
Annabel Cl POP/IOD E14 ...105 K5
Anna Cl HACK E8 ....86 B6
Annandale Gv HGDN/ICK UB10 .76 A1
Annandale Rd BFN/LL DA15 .167 K2
  CHSWK W4 ....118 B4
  CROY/NA CRO 197 H1
  GNWCH SE10 ....125 J6
Anna Neagle Cl FSTGT E7 ..88 E2
Annan Wy ROM RM1 ....57 F4
Anne Boleyn's Wk
  CHEAM SM3 ....208 B5
  KUTN/CMB KT2 ....175 F1
Anne Case Ms NWMAL KT3 * .176 A6
Anne Compton Ms
  LEE/GVPK SE12 ....165 J2
Anne of Cleves Rd DART DA1 .171 G1
Annesley Av CDALE/KGS NW9 .45 G2
Annesley Cl WLSDN NW10 ...81 G1
Annesley Dr CROY/NA CRO ..213 H2
Annesley Rd BKHTH/KID SE3 .146 A2
Annesmere Gdns
  BKHTH/KID SE3 ....146 C4
Anne St PLSTW E13 ....106 E3
Annette Cl KTN/HRWW/WS HA3 .42 E5
Annette Rd HOLWY N7 ......85 F2
Anne Way BARK/HLT IG6 ....54 C2
Anne Besant Cl BOW E3 ....87 H6
Anning St WCHPL E1 ....7 H6
Annington Rd EFNCH N2 ....47 K6
Annis Rd HOM E9 ....87 G4
Ann La WBPTN SW10 ....140 C1
Ann Moss Wy
  BERM/RHTH SE16 ....123 K3
Ann's Cl KTBR SW1X 15 F3
Ann St WOOL/PLUM SE18 ....127 J4
Annsworthy Av THHTH CR7 ..180 E6
Annsworthy Crs SNWD SE25 .180 E5
Ansar Gdns WALTH E17 .....69 G2
Ansdell Rd PECK SE15 .....143 K3
Ansdell St KENS W8 ....120 A3
Ansdell Ter KENS W8 * 120 A3
Ansell Gv CAR SM5 ....194 E5
Ansell Rd TOOT SW17 ......160 D5
Anselm Cl CROY/NA CRO 212 B1
Anselm Rd FUL/PGN SW6 ....119 K6
  PIN HA5 ....41 K3
Ansford Rd BMLY BR1 ......183 F1

Ansleigh Pl NTGHL W11 ....100 B6
Anson Cl ROMW/RG RM7 .....56 D5
Anson Rd ARCH N19 ....84 C2
  CRICK NW2 * 81 K3
Anson Wk NTHWD HA6 ....26 A6
Anstead Dr RAIN RM13 .....111 J1
Anstey Rd PECK SE15 ......143 H4
Anstice Cl CHSWK W4 ......138 B1
Anstridge Rd ELTH/MOT SE9 .167 J1
Antelope Rd
  WOOL/PLUM SE18 ....126 E3
Anthony Cl MLHL NW7 ......31 G6
  OXHEY WD19 ....27 H5
Anthony Rd GFD/PVL UB6 ...96 E1
  SNWD SE25 ....197 H3
  WELL DA16 ....148 B2
Anthony's Cl WAP E1W 123 H1
Anthony St WCHPL E1 ......104 D5
Anthus Ms NTHWD HA6 ......40 B3
Antill Rd BOW E3 ....105 G2
  TOTM N17 ....50 D5
Antill Ter WCHPL E1 ......105 F5
Antlers Hl CHING E4 ......25 K6
Anton Crs SUT SM1 ....208 E1
Anton Pl WBLY HA9 ....80 D1
Anton St HACK E8 ....86 C3
Antrim Gr HAMP NW3 ......83 K4
Antrobus Cl SUT SM1 .....208 D3
Antrobus Rd CHSWK W4 .....117 K4
Anvil Cl STRHM/NOR SW16 ..179 H3
Anvil Ter RDART DA2 ......170 B4
Anworth Cl WFD IG8 ....53 F2
Aostle Wy THHTH CR7 .....180 C5
Apeldoorn Dr WLGTN SM6 ...210 E6
Aperfield Rd ERITH DA8 ...130 C6
Apex Cl BECK BR3 ....182 E4
Apex Pde MLHL NW7 * 31 F3
Aplin Wy ISLW TW7 ....135 K2
Apollo Av BMLY BR1 ....184 A4
Apollo Cl HCH RM12 ......75 K6
Apollo Pl WAN E11 ....88 C1
  WBPTN SW10 ....140 C1
Apollo Wy ERITH DA8 .....150 B1
  THMD SE28 ....127 J3
Apothecary St BLKFR EC4V * .12 A4
Appach Rd BRXS/STRHM SW2 .142 B6
Apple Blossom Ct VX/NE SW8 .141 J1
Appleby Cl CHING E4 ......52 A2
  KTN/HRWW/WS HA3 ....43 F6
Appleby Rd CAN/RD E16 ....106 E5
  HACK E8 ....86 C5
Appleby St BETH E2 ....7 J2
Appledore Av BXLYHN DA7 ..149 K2
  RSLP HA4 ....77 F1
Appledore Cl EDGW HA8 ....44 D4
  HAYES BR2 ....199 J2
  TOOT SW17 ....160 E4
Appledore Crs SCUP DA14 ..167 K5
Appledore Wy MLHL NW7 ....46 B3
Appleford Rd NKENS W10 ...100 C3
Apple Garth BTFD TW8 .....116 E4
Applegarth CROY/NA CRO ...213 K5
  ESH/CLAY KT10 ....205 F3
Applegarth Dr DART DA1 ...171 H4
  GNTH/NBYPK IG2 ....73 F1
Applegarth Rd THMD SE28 ..128 C1
  WKENS W14 ....119 G3
Apple Gv CHSGTN KT9 ......206 A2
  EN1 N1 ....24 A4
Apple Ldg ALP/SUD HA0 ....79 J1
Apple Market KUT/HW KT1 ..174 E5
Apple Rd WAN E11 ....88 C1
Appleton Cl BXLYHN DA7 ...149 K3
Appleton Gdns NWMAL KT3 ..192 D3
Appleton Rd ELTH/MOT SE9 .146 D4
Appletree Cl PGE/AN SE20 .181 J4
Appletree Gdns EBAR EN4 ..21 J5
Apple Tree Yd STJS SW1Y ..10 B7
Applewood Cl CRICK NW2 ...81 K1
  TRDG/WHET N20 ....33 J3
Applewood Dr PLSTW E13 ...107 F3
Appold St ERITH DA8 ......130 D5
  SDTCH EC2A 13 G1
Apprentice Wy CLPT E5 ....86 D2
Approach La MLHL NW7 .....46 C1
Approach Rd BETH E2 ......104 E1
  E/WMO/HCT KT8 ....189 F2
  EBAR EN4 ....21 H4
  RYNPK SW20 ....177 F5
The Approach ACT W3 ......99 F5
  EN1 N1 ....24 A4
  HDN NW4 ....64 B2
Aprey Gdns HDN NW4 ....64 A1
April Cl FELT TW13 ......153 K5
  HNWL W7 ....115 K1
  ORP BR6 ....217 F3
April St HACK E8 ....86 B2
Apsley Cl RYLN/HDSTN HA2 .60 C3
Apsley Rd NWMAL KT3 ......175 K5
  SNWD SE25 ....197 J1
Apsley Wy CRICK NW2 ......81 H6
  MYFR/PICC W1J * 15 J1
Aquarius SURB KT6 * 191 H6
Aquarius Wy NTHWD HA6 ....40 E1
Aquila St STJWD NW8 ......2 B2
Aquinas St STHWK SE1 .....17 K1
Arabella Dr PUT/ROE SW15 .138 B5
Arabia Cl CHING E4 ....38 B2
Arabin Rd BROCKY SE4 .....144 B5
Aragon Av EW KT17 ....207 K6
  THDIT KT7 ....190 A2
Aragon Cl ENC/FH EN2 .....23 F1
  HAYES BR2 ....200 E5
  LOU IG10 ....39 J1
Aragon Dr BARK/HLT IG6 ...54 C3
  RSLP HA4 ....59 H5
Aragon Pl MRDN SM4 ......193 G4

Aragon Rd KUTN/CMB KT2 ...175 F1
  MRDN SM4 ....193 G4
Arandora Crs CHDH RM6 ....73 H4
Arbery Rd BOW E3 ....105 G2
Arbor Cl BECK BR3 ....182 E5
Arborfield Cl
  BRXS/STRHM SW2 ....162 A3
Arbor Ct STNW/STAM N16 ...67 K1
Arbour Rd PEND EN3 ......25 F3
Arbour Sq WCHPL E1 ......105 F5
Arbour Wy HCH RM12 ......93 K5
Arbroath Gn OXHEY WD19 ...26 E5
Arbroath Rd ELTH/MOT SE9 .146 D4
Arbrook Cl STMC/STPC BR5 .186 B6
Arbrook La ESH/CLAY KT10 .204 D4
Arbuthnot La BXLY DA5 ....169 F1
Arbuthnot Rd NWCR SE14 ...144 A3
Arbutus St HACK E8 ....86 B6
Arcade Chambers
  ELTH/MOT SE9 * 167 F1
Arcade Pde CHSGTN KT9 * ..206 A2
The Arcade ELTH/MOT SE9 * .167 F1
  LVPST EC2M * 13 G2
  WALTH E17 * 69 J1
Arcadia Av FNCH N3 ....46 E5
Arcadia Cl CAR SM5 ......210 A2
Arcadian Av BXLY DA5 .....169 F1
Arcadian Cl BXLY DA5 .....169 F1
Arcadian Gdns WDGN N22 ...49 G3
Arcadian Rd BXLY DA5 .....169 F1
Arcadia St POP/IOD E14 ...105 J5
Archangel St
  BERM/RHTH SE16 ....124 A2
Archbishop's Pl
  BRXS/STRHM SW2 ....162 A2
Archdale Ct SHB W12 * 118 E1
Archdale Pl NWMAL KT3 ....175 J6
Archdale Rd EDUL SE22 ....143 G6
Archel Rd WKENS W14 ......119 J6
Archer Cl KUTN/CMB KT2 ...175 F3
Archer Ct FELT TW13 * 153 K3
Archer Ms HPTN TW12 ......173 H2
Archer Rd SNWD SE25 ......197 J1
  STMC/STPC BR5 ....202 B5
Archers Dr PEND EN3 ......24 E3
Archer Sq NWCR SE14 ......124 B6
Archer St SOHO/SHAV W1D ..10 C5
Archery Cl BAY/PAD W2 ....8 D4
  KTN/HRWW/WS HA3 ....43 F6
Archery Rd ELTH/MOT SE9 ..146 E6
The Arches CHCR WC2N * ...11 F7
  RYLN/HDSTN HA2 ....60 B6
Archibald Ms MYFR/PKLN W1K .9 H6
Archibald Rd HOLWY N7 ....84 D2
Archibald St BOW E3 ......105 J3
Archie Cl WDR/YW UB7 .....112 D2
Arch St STHWK SE1 ....18 C5
Archway HARH RM3 ....57 K2
Archway Cl ARCH N19 * 84 C1
  NKENS W10 ....100 B4
  WIM/MER SW19 ....160 A3
  WLGTN SM6 * 210 E1
Archway Rd HGT N6 ....66 B3
Archway St BARN SW13 .....138 B4
Arcola St HACK E8 ....86 B3
Arcon Dr NTHLT UB5 ....95 J3
Arctic St KTTN NW5 ....84 B3
Arcus Rd BMLY BR1 ....183 H2
Ardbeg Rd HNHL SE24 ......162 E1
Arden Cl BUSH WD23 ......29 F2
  HRW HA1 ....78 D1
  THMD SE28 ....109 K5
Arden Court Gdns EFNCH N2 .65 H3
Arden Crs DAGW RM9 ....91 K5
  POP/IOD E14 ....124 D4
Arden Est IS N1 * 7 G3
Arden Gv ORP BR6 ....216 B2
Arden Mhor PIN HA5 ......58 E1
Arden Rd FNCH N3 ....46 D6
  WEA W13 ....97 J6
Ardent Cl SNWD SE25 .....181 F6
Ardfern Av STRHM/NOR SW16 .180 B6
Ardfillan Rd CAT SE6 .....165 G3
Ardgowan Rd CAT SE6 .....165 H3
Ardilaun Rd HBRY N5 .....85 J2
Ardingly Cl CROY/NA CRO ..213 F1
Ardleigh Gdns CHEAM SM3 ..193 K5
Ardleigh Rd IS N1 ....86 A4
  WALTH E17 ....51 H4
Ardleigh Ter WALTH E17 ...51 H4
Ardley Cl CAT SE6 ....164 B5
  WLSDN NW10 ....81 G1
Ardlui Rd WNWD SE27 ......162 D4
Ardmay Gdns SURB KT6 * ...191 F2
Ardmere Rd LEW SE13 ......165 G1
Ardmore La BKHH IG9 ......39 F2
Ardmore Pl BKHH IG9 ......39 F2
Ardoch Rd CAT SE6 ....165 G4
Ardra Rd ED N9 ....37 F5
Ardrossan Gdns WPK KT4 ...207 J1
Ardross Av NTHWD HA6 .....40 C5
Ardwell Av BARK/HLT IG6 ..72 C1
Ardwell Rd BRXS/STRHM SW2 .161 K4
Ardwick Rd CRICK NW2 * ...83 F2
Arena Est FSBYPK N4 * 67 H3
The Arena STKPK UB11 * ...113 J1
Argall Av LEY E10 ....69 G4
Argall Wy LEY E10 ....69 G5
Argenta Wy WLSDN NW10 ....80 D5
Argent St SURB KT6 * 191 H6
Argon Ms FUL/PGN SW6 .....140 A1
Argon Rd ED N9 ....51 G1
Argosy La STWL/WRAY TW19 .152 A2
Argus Cl ROMW/RG RM7 .....56 D4
Argus Wy NTHLT UB5 ....95 J2
Argyle Av HSLWW TW4 ......134 E6
Argyle Cl WEA W13 ....97 G3
Argyle Pl HMSMTH W6 ......118 E4
Argyle Rd BAR EN5 ....20 A5
  EA W5 ....98 A3
  GFD/PVL UB6 ....115 G1
  HSLW TW3 ....135 G6
  IL IG1 ....72 A6
  NFNCH/WDSPK N12 ....46 E1

RYLN/HDSTN HA2 ....60 B3
SRTFD E15 ....88 C2
TOTM N17 ....50 C4
UED N18 ....36 D6
WCHPL E1 ....105 F3
Argyle Sq STPAN WC1H * 5 F4
Argyle St STPAN WC1H * 4 E5
Argyle Wk BERM/RHTH SE16 ....123 H5
Argyll Av STHL UB1 ....115 G1
Argyll Cl BRXN/ST SW9 ....142 A4
Argyll Gdns EDGW HA8 ....44 D5
Argyll Rd KENS W8 ....119 K2
  WOOL/PLUM SE18 ....127 H5
Argyll St REGST W1B 10 A4
Arhnie St STHWK SE1 ....11 K5
Arica Rd BROCKY SE4 ....144 B5
Ariel Rd KIL/WHAMP NW6 ....82 E4
Ariel Wy HSLWW TW4 ....134 A4
  SHB W12 ....119 F1
Aristotle Rd CLAP SW4 ....141 J5
Arkell Gv NRWD SE19 ....180 C3
Arkindale Rd CAT SE6 ....165 F5
Arkley Crs WALTH E17 ....69 H2
Arklow Rd NWCR SE14 ....124 C6
Arkwright Rd HAMP NW3 ....83 G3
Arlesford Rd BRXN/ST SW9 ....141 K4
Arlingford Rd
  BRXS/STRHM SW2 ....162 B1
Arlington Av IS N1 ....6 D1
Arlington Cl BFN/LL DA15 ....167 K2
  LEW SE13 ....145 G6
  SUT SM1 ....193 K6
  TWK TW1 * 156 D1
Arlington Ct HYS/HAR UB3 ....113 G5
Arlington Dr CAR SM5 ....194 E6
  RSLP HA4 ....58 B3
Arlington Gdns CHSWK W4 ....117 K5
  IL IG1 ....71 K4
Arlington Pde
  BRXS/STRHM SW2 * 142 A5
Arlington Rd CAMTN NW1 * 3 K1
  RCHPK/HAM TW10 ....156 E4
  STHGT/OAK N14 ....34 B4
  SURB KT6 ....190 E5
  TEDD TW11 ....156 A6
  TWK TW1 * 156 D1
  WEA W13 ....97 H5
  WFD IG8 ....52 E4
Arlington Sq IS N1 ....6 D1
Arlington St MYFR/PICC W1J 10 A7
Arliss Wy NTHLT UB5 ....77 G6
Arlow Rd WCHMH N21 ....35 G3
Armadale Cl TOTM N17 ....68 D1
Armada Rd
  EBED/NFELT TW14 ....133 K6
  FUL/PGN SW6 ....139 K1
Armada St DEPT SE8 ....124 D6
Armada Wy EHAM E6 ....108 C5
Armagh Rd BOW E3 ....87 H6
Armfield Cl E/WMO/HCT KT8 ....188 E2
Armfield Rd ENC/FH EN2 ....23 J2
Arminger Rd SHB W12 ....118 E1
Armistice Gdns SNWD SE25 ....181 H6
Armitage Rd GLDGN NW11 ....64 C5
  GNWCH SE10 ....125 J4
Armour Cl HOLWY N7 ....85 F4
Armoury Rd DEPT SE8 ....144 E3
Armoury Wy
  WAND/EARL SW18 ....139 K6
Armstead Wk DAGE RM10 ....92 C5
Armstrong Av WFD IG8 ....52 C2
Armstrong Cl BCTR RM8 ....73 K4
  BMLY BR1 ....184 D6
  EHAM E6 ....107 K5
  RSLP HA4 ....58 B3
Armstrong Crs EBAR EN4 ....21 H4
Armstrong Rd ACT W3 ....118 C1
  FELT TW13 ....172 D1
  WOOL/PLUM SE18 ....127 H3
Armstrong Wy NWDGN UB2 ....115 G2
Armytage Rd HEST TW5 ....134 C1
Arnal Crs WAND/EARL SW18 ....159 H3
Arncliffe Cl FBAR/BDGN N11 ....48 A2
Arne Gv ORP BR6 ....217 F1
Arne St COVGDN WC2E 11 H2
Arnett Sq CHING E4 ....51 H2
Arne Wk LEW SE13 ....145 G4
Arneways Av CHDH RM6 ....73 K1
Arneway St WEST SW1P 16 D5
Arnewood Cl PUT/ROE SW15 ....158 D3
Arney's La MTCM CR4 ....195 F3
Arngask Rd CAT SE6 ....165 G3
Arnheim Pl POP/IOD E14 ....124 D3
Arnhem Pl POP/IOD E14 ....124 D3
Arnhem Wy DUL SE21 ....162 C3
Arnison Rd E/WMO/HCT KT8 ....189 G1
Arnold Circ BETH E2 ....7 J5
Arnold Cl KTN/HRWW/WS HA3 ....62 C4
Arnold Crs ISLW TW7 ....135 J6
Arnold Dr CHSGTN KT9 ....205 K4
Arnold Est STHWK SE1 ....19 K3
Arnold Gdns PLMGR N13 ....49 H1
Arnold Rd BOW E3 ....105 J2
  DAGW RM9 ....92 B5
  NTHLT UB5 ....77 J4
  SEVS/STOTM N15 ....50 B6
  TOOT SW17 ....178 E3
Arnold Ter STAN HA7 * 43 F1
Arnos Gv STHGT/OAK N14 ....34 D6
Arnos Rd FBAR/BDGN N11 ....48 C1
Arnott Cl CHSWK W4 ....118 A4
  THMD SE28 ....128 D1
Arnould Av CMBW SE5 ....142 E5
Arnsberg Wy BXLYHN DA7 ....149 H5
Arnside Gdns WBLY HA9 ....61 K5
Arnside Rd BXLYHN DA7 ....149 H2
Arnside St WALW SE17 ....122 D6
Arnulf St CAT SE6 ....164 E6
Arnull's Rd STRHM/NOR SW16 ....180 C2
Arodene Rd
  BRXS/STRHM SW2 ....162 A1
Arosa Rd TWK TW1 ....156 E1

Arragon Gdns
  STRHM/NOR SW16 ....179 K1
  WWKM BR4 ....213 K5
Arragon Rd EHAM E6 ....89 H6
  TWK TW1 ....156 D1
  WAND/EARL SW18 ....159 K3
Arran Cl ERITH DA8 ....130 A6
  WLGTN SM6 ....210 C2
Arran Dr MNPK E12 ....71 H5
  STAN HA7 ....29 J6
Arran Ct OXHEY WD19 * 27 H1
Arran Ms EA W5 ....117 G1
Arran Rd CAT SE6 ....164 E4
Arran Wy ESH/CLAY KT10 ....189 G6
Arras Av MRDN SM4 ....194 B2
Arrol Rd BECK BR3 ....181 K6
Arrow Rd BOW E3 ....105 K2
Arrowsmith Rd CHIG IG7 ....55 F1
  WFD IG8 ....53 F1
Arsenal Rd ELTH/MOT SE9 ....146 E3
Arsenal Wy WOOL/PLUM SE18 ....127 H4
Artemis Pl WAND/EARL SW18 ....159 J2
Arterberry Rd RYNPK SW20 ....177 F3
Arterial Rd Purfleet
  SOCK/AV RM15 ....131 K3
Artesian Cl ROM RM1 ....75 H5
  WLSDN NW10 ....81 F5
Artesian Gv BAR EN5 ....21 G5
Artesian Houses
  BAY/PAD W2 * 100 E5
Artesian Rd BAY/PAD W2 ....100 E5
Arthurdon Rd BROCKY SE4 ....144 D6
Arthur Gv WOOL/PLUM SE18 ....127 H4
Arthur Rd CHDH RM6 ....73 J4
  ED N9 ....36 B4
  EHAM E6 ....107 K1
  HOLWY N7 ....85 F1
  KUTN/CMB KT2 ....175 H3
  NWMAL KT3 ....192 E2
  WIM/MER SW19 ....159 H6
Arthur St CANST EC4R 13 G6
Artichoke Hl WAP E1W * 13 J6
Artichoke Pl CMBW SE5 * 142 E2
Artillery La SHB W12 ....99 J5
  WCHPL E1 ....13 H2
Artillery Pas WCHPL E1 * 13 H2
Artillery Rw WEST SW1P 16 B5
Artington Cl ORP BR6 ....216 C2
Artizan St WCHPL E1 ....13 H3
Artwell Cl LEY E10 ....69 K4
Arundel Av EW KT17 ....207 K6
  MRDN SM4 ....193 J1
Arundel Cl BTSEA SW11 ....140 D6
  BXLY DA5 ....169 G1
  CROY/NA CR0 ....211 H1
  HPTN TW12 ....173 G1
  SRTFD E15 ....88 C2
Arundel Dr ORP BR6 ....217 H3
  RYLN/HDSTN HA2 ....77 K2
  WFD IG8 ....52 E3
Arundel Gdns EDGW HA8 ....45 F3
  GDMY/SEVK IG3 ....73 G1
  NTGHL W11 ....100 D6
  WCHMH N21 ....35 G3
Arundel Gt TPL/STR WC2R * 11 H5
Arundel Pl HOLWY N7 ....85 F4
Arundel Rd BELMT SM2 ....208 D5
  CROY/NA CR0 ....196 E3
  DART DA1 ....151 F5
  EBAR EN4 ....21 J3
  HSLWW TW4 ....134 B4
  KUT/HW KT1 ....175 J5
Arundel Sq HOLWY N7 ....85 G4
Arundel St TPL/STR WC2R 11 H5
Arundel Ter BARN SW13 ....118 E6
Arvon Rd HBRY N5 ....85 G3
Asbaston Ter IL IG1 ....90 C4
Ascalon St VX/NE SW8 ....141 H1
Ascension Rd CRW RM5 ....56 E2
Ascham Dr CHING E4 ....51 K3
Ascham End WALTH E17 ....51 G4
Ascham St KTTN NW5 ....84 C3
Aschurch Rd CROY/NA CR0 ....197 G4
Ascot Cl BARK/HLT IG6 ....54 C4
  NTHLT UB5 ....78 A3
Ascot Gdns STHL UB1 ....95 K4
  WLGTN SM6 ....210 C6
Ascot Pde CLAP SW4 * 141 K5
Ascot Rd EBED/NFELT TW14 ....152 E3
  EHAM E6 ....107 K2
  SEVS/STOTM N15 ....67 K2
  STMC/STPC BR5 ....202 A1
  TOOT SW17 ....179 F2
  UED N18 ....36 C5
Ascott Av EA W5 ....117 F2
Ascott Ct PIN HA5 * 58 E1
Ashanti Ms WALTH E17 * 86 D4
Ashbourne Sq NTHWD HA6 ....40 C2
Ashbourne Av BXLYHN DA7 ....149 F1
  GLDGN NW11 ....64 D2
  RYLN/HDSTN HA2 ....60 D6
  SWFD E18 ....71 F1
  TRDG/WHET N20 ....33 K4
Ashbourne Cl EA W5 ....98 B4
  NFNCH/WDSPK N12 ....33 F6
Ashbourne Gv CHSWK W4 ....118 B5
  EDUL SE22 ....143 G5
  MLHL NW7 ....45 F1
Ashbourne Pde EA W5 * 98 B3
  GLDGN NW11 * 64 C1
Ashbourne Ri ORP BR6 ....216 D2
Ashbourne Rd EA W5 ....98 B3
  MTCM CR4 ....179 F2
Ashbourne Ter
  WIM/MER SW19 ....177 K3
Ashbridge Rd WAN E11 ....70 C4
Ashbridge St STJWD NW8 ....2 C7
Ashbrook Rd ARCH N19 ....66 D5
  DAGE RM10 ....92 D1
Ashburn Gdns SKENS SW7 ....120 B4
Ashburnham Av HRW HA1 ....61 F4

Ashburnham Cl EFNCH N2 ....47 H6
  OXHEY WD19 * 26 E5
Ashburnham Dr OXHEY WD19 ....26 E5
Ashburnham Gv GNWCH SE10 ....144 E1
Ashburnham Pk
  ESH/CLAY KT10 ....204 C2
Ashburnham Pl GNWCH SE10 ....144 E1
Ashburnham Retreat
  GNWCH SE10 ....144 D1
Ashburnham Rd BELV DA17 ....129 K4
  RCHPK/HAM TW10 ....156 D5
  WBPTN SW10 * 140 B1
  WLSDN NW10 ....100 A3
Ashburn Pl SKENS SW7 ....120 B4
Ashburton Av CROY/NA CR0 ....197 J5
  GDMY/SEVK IG3 ....91 F2
Ashburton Cl CROY/NA CR0 ....197 H5
Ashburton Gdns CROY/NA CR0 ....197 H6
Ashburton Rd CAN/RD E16 ....106 E5
  CROY/NA CR0 ....197 H5
  RSLP HA4 ....58 E6
Ashbury Gdns CHDH RM6 ....73 K2
Ashbury Pl WIM/MER SW19 ....178 B2
Ashbury Rd BTSEA SW11 ....140 E4
Ashby Av CHSGTN KT9 ....206 C4
Ashby Gv IS N1 ....85 J5
Ashby Ms BROCKY SE4 ....144 C3
  CLAP SW4 * 141 K2
Ashby Rd BROCKY SE4 ....144 C3
  SEVS/STOTM N15 ....68 C2
Ashby St FSBYE EC1V 6 B4
Ashby Wy WDR/YW UB7 ....132 D1
Ashchurch Gv SHB W12 ....118 D3
Ashchurch Park Vls SHB W12 ....118 D3
Ashchurch Ter SHB W12 ....118 C3
Ash Cl CAR SM5 ....194 E6
  CRW RM5 ....56 E3
  EDGW HA8 ....30 E6
  NWMAL KT3 ....176 A5
  PGE/AN SE20 ....181 K5
  SCUP DA14 ....168 C5
  STAN HA7 ....43 G2
  STMC/STPC BR5 ....201 J2
  SWLY BR8 ....187 K5
Ashcombe Av SURB KT6 ....190 D4
Ashcombe Gdns EDGW HA8 ....30 C5
Ashcombe Pk CRICK NW2 ....81 G1
Ashcombe Rd CAR SM5 ....210 A4
  WIM/MER SW19 ....177 K1
Ashcombe Sq NWMAL KT3 ....175 K6
Ashcombe St FUL/PGN SW6 ....140 A3
Ash Ct HOR/WEW KT19 ....206 E2
Ashcroft PIN HA5 ....42 A2
Ashcroft Av BFN/LL DA15 ....168 A5
Ashcroft Crs BFN/LL DA15 ....168 A5
Ashcroft Rd BOW E3 ....105 G2
  CHSGTN KT9 ....206 B1
Ashdale Cl STWL/WRAY TW19 ....152 B2
  WHTN TW2 ....155 G2
Ashdale Gv STAN HA7 ....43 F2
Ashdale Rd LEE/GVPK SE12 ....146 A6
Ashdene PIN HA5 ....41 G6
Ashdon Cl WFD IG8 ....53 F2
Ashdon Rd BUSH WD23 ....28 B1
  WLSDN NW10 ....81 H6
Ashdown Cl BECK BR3 ....182 E5
  BXLY DA5 ....169 K2
Ashdown Crs KTTN NW5 * 84 A3
Ashdown Est WAN E11 * 88 C2
Ashdown Pl THDIT KT7 ....190 B4
Ashdown Rd KUT/HW KT1 ....175 F5
  PEND EN3 ....25 F1
Ashdown Wk POP/IOD E14 ....124 D4
  ROMW/RG RM7 ....56 D4
Ashdown Wy TOOT SW17 ....161 F4
Ashen EHAM E6 ....108 A5
Ashenden Rd CLPT E5 ....87 G3
Ashen Dr DART DA1 ....170 D1
Ashen Gv WIM/MER SW19 ....159 K5
Asher Loftus Wy
  FBAR/BDGN N11 ....47 K2
Asher Wy WAP E1W 104 C6
Ashfield Av BUSH WD23 ....28 C1
  FELT TW13 ....154 A3
Ashfield Cl BECK BR3 ....182 D3
  RCHPK/HAM TW10 ....157 F3
Ashfield Ct BAL SW12 * 161 H4
Ashfield La CHST BR7 ....185 H2
Ashfield Pde STHGT/OAK N14 ....34 D3
Ashfield Rd ACT W3 ....118 C1
  FSBYPK N4 ....67 J3
  STHGT/OAK N14 ....34 C5
Ashfields LOU IG10 ....39 J1
Ashfield St WCHPL E1 ....104 D4
Ashford Av CEND/HSY/T N8 ....48 E6
  YEAD UB4 ....95 H5
Ashford Cl ASHF TW15 ....152 B5
  WALTH E17 ....69 H3
Ashford Crs ASHF TW15 ....152 B5
  PEND EN3 ....24 E4
Ashford Gn OXHEY WD19 ....27 H2
Ashford Ms TOTM N17 ....50 C4
Ashford Rd CRICK NW2 ....82 B2
  EHAM E6 ....90 A5
  FELT TW13 ....153 G6
  SWFD E18 ....53 F5
Ash Gv ALP/SUD HA0 ....79 G2
  EA W5 ....117 F2
  EBED/NFELT TW14 ....153 H2
  EN EN1 ....36 A1
  HACK E8 ....86 D6
  HEST TW5 ....134 C2
  HYS/HAR UB3 ....113 G1
  PGE/AN SE20 ....181 K5
  PLMGR N13 ....35 J5
  STHL UB1 ....96 A6
  WWKM BR4 ....199 H6
Ashgrove Rd BMLY BR1 ....183 G2
  GDMY/SEVK IG3 ....73 F1
Ash Hill Cl BUSH WD23 ....28 C3
Ash Hill Dr PIN HA5 ....41 G6
Ashingdon Cl CHING E4 ....38 A6
Ashington Rd FUL/PGN SW6 ....139 J3
Ashlake Rd STRHM/NOR SW16 ....161 K6

Ashland Pl MHST W1U 9 G1
Ashlar Pl WOOL/PLUM SE18 ....127 G4
Ashleigh Gdns SUT SM1 ....194 A6
Ashleigh Rd
  MORT/ESHN SW14 ....138 B4
  PGE/AN SE20 ....181 J6
Ashley Av BARK/HLT IG6 ....54 B5
  MRDN SM4 ....193 K1
Ashley Cl HDN NW4 ....46 A5
  PIN HA5 ....41 F5
Ashley Crs BTSEA SW11 ....141 F4
  WDGN N22 ....49 H4
Ashley Dr ISLW TW7 ....115 K6
  WHTN TW2 ....155 G3
Ashley Gdns ORP BR6 ....216 E3
  PLMGR N13 ....35 J5
  RCHPK/HAM TW10 ....156 E5
  WBLY HA9 ....62 A6
Ashley La CROY/NA CR0 ....211 H2
  HDN NW4 ....46 A5
Ashley Pl WEST SW1P 16 A5
Ashley Rd ARCH N19 ....66 E5
  CHING E4 ....51 J2
  FSTGT E7 ....89 G5
  HPTN TW12 ....175 F4
  PEND EN3 ....25 F6
  RCH/KEW TW9 ....137 F4
  THDIT KT7 ....190 A3
  THHTH CR7 ....196 A1
  TOTM N17 ....50 D3
  WALTH E17 ....69 G1
  WIM/MER SW19 ....178 A2
Ashling Rd CROY/NA CR0 ....197 H5
Ashlin Rd SRTFD E15 ....88 B2
Ashlone Rd PUT/ROE SW15 ....139 F4
Ashlyns Wy CHSGTN KT9 ....205 K4
Ashmead NFNCH/WDSPK N12 ....33 G6
Ashmead Ga BMLY BR1 ....184 C4
Ashmead Rd DEPT SE8 ....144 D3
  EBED/NFELT TW14 ....153 K3
Ashmere Av BECK BR3 ....183 G5
Ashmere Cl CHEAM SM3 ....208 B3
Ashmere Gv
  BRXS/STRHM SW2 ....141 K5
Ashmill St CAMTN NW1 ....2 C7
Ashmole Pl VX/NE SW8 ....122 A6
Ashmore Cl PECK SE15 ....143 H1
Ashmore Gv WELL DA16 ....147 J4
Ashmore Rd MV/WKIL W9 ....100 D2
Ashmount Est ARCH N19 * 66 D4
Ashmount Rd ARCH N19 ....66 C4
  SEVS/STOTM N15 ....68 A2
Ashmount Ter EA W5 * 116 E4
Ashmour Gdns ROM RM1 ....57 F5
Ashneal Gdns HRW HA1 ....78 D1
Ashness Gdns GFD/PVL UB6 ....79 H4
Ashness Rd BTSEA SW11 ....140 E6
Ashridge Cl
  KTN/HRWW/WS HA3 ....61 J3
Ashridge Crs
  WOOL/PLUM SE18 ....147 H1
Ashridge Dr OXHEY WD19 ....41 G1
Ashridge Gdns PIN HA5 ....59 J1
  PLMGR N13 ....48 E1
Ashridge Wy MRDN SM4 ....193 J4
  SUN TW16 ....172 A5
Ash Rd CHEAM SM3 ....193 H5
  CROY/NA CR0 ....213 J1
  DART DA1 ....171 G3
  ORP BR6 ....217 G5
  RDART DA2 ....171 K5
  SRTFD E15 ....88 C3
Ash Rw HAYES BR2 ....201 F5
Ashstead Rd CLPT E5 ....68 C4
Ashton Cl SUT SM1 ....208 E2
Ashton Gdns CHDH RM6 ....74 A3
  HSLWW TW4 ....134 E5
Ashton Rd SRTFD E15 ....88 B3
Ashton St POP/IOD E14 ....106 A6
Ashtree Av MTCM CR4 ....178 C5
Ash Tree Cl CROY/NA CR0 ....198 B3
  SURB KT6 ....191 F5
Ash Tree Dl CDALE/KGS NW9 ....62 E1
Ash Tree Wy CROY/NA CR0 ....198 B2
Ashurst Cl DART DA1 ....150 C4
  NTHWD HA6 ....40 B4
  PGE/AN SE20 ....181 J4
Ashurst Dr BARK/HLT IG6 ....72 C2
Ashurst Gdns
  BRXS/STRHM SW2 ....162 B3
Ashurst Rd EBAR EN4 ....21 K6
  NFNCH/WDSPK N12 ....47 J1
  OXHEY WD19 ....27 G1
Ashurst Wk CROY/NA CR0 ....197 J6
Ashvale Gdns CRW RM5 ....56 D1
  UED N18 ....50 E1
Ashvale Rd TOOT SW17 ....178 E1
Ashville Rd WAN E11 ....88 B1
Ash Wk ALP/SUD HA0 ....79 J2
Ashwater Rd LEE/GVPK SE12 ....165 K3
Ashwell Cl EHAM E6 ....107 J5
Ashwin St HACK E8 ....86 B4
Ashworth Cl CMBW SE5 ....142 E3
Ashworth Rd MV/WKIL W9 ....101 F1
Askern Cl BXLYHN DA7 ....148 E5
Aske St IS N1 ....7 G4
Askew Crs SHB W12 ....118 C2
Askew Rd NTHWD HA6 ....26 B4
  SHB W12 ....118 D1
Askham Rd SHB W12 ....118 D1
Askill Dr PUT/ROE SW15 ....139 H6
Askwith Rd RAIN RM13 ....111 F1
Asland Rd SRTFD E15 ....88 B6
Aslett St WAND/EARL SW18 ....160 A2
Asmara Rd CRICK NW2 ....82 C3
Asmuns Hl GLDGN NW11 ....64 E2
Asmuns Pl GLDGN NW11 ....64 D2
Aspen Cl EA W5 ....117 G2
  ORP BR6 ....217 G3
  WDR/YW UB7 ....112 C1
Aspen Copse BMLY BR1 ....184 E5
Aspen Ct HACK E8 * 86 C6
Aspen Dr ALP/SUD HA0 ....60 E6
Aspen Gdns MTCM CR4 ....195 F2

Aspen Gn ERITH DA18 ....129 G3
Aspen La NTHLT UB5 ....95 J2
Aspenlea Rd HMSMTH W6 ....119 G6
Aspen Wy FELT TW13 ....154 A5
  POP/IOD E14 ....106 A6
Aspern Gv HAMP NW3 ....83 J3
Aspinall Rd BROCKY SE4 ....144 A4
Aspinden Rd
  BERM/RHTH SE16 ....123 J4
Aspley Rd WAND/EARL SW18 ....140 A6
Asplins Rd TOTM N17 ....50 C4
Asplins Vls TOTM N17 * 50 C4
Asprey Ms BECK BR3 ....198 C2
Asquith Cl BCTR RM8 ....73 J5
Assam St WCHPL E1 ....104 C5
Assata Ms IS N1 ....85 H4
Assembly Pas WCHPL E1 ....104 E4
Assembly Wk CAR SM5 ....194 D4
Ass House La
  KTN/HRWW/WS HA3 ....28 B6
Astall Cl KTN/HRWW/WS HA3 ....42 E4
Astbury Rd PECK SE15 ....143 K2
Astell St CHEL SW3 ....120 D5
Asteys Rw IS N1 ....85 H5
Astle St BTSEA SW11 ....141 F3
Astley Av CRICK NW2 ....82 A4
Aston Av KTN/HRWW/WS HA3 ....61 J4
Aston Cl BUSH WD23 ....28 C1
  SCUP DA14 ....168 B5
Aston Gn HSLWW TW4 ....134 A3
Astonplace STRHM/NOR SW16 ....180 C2
Aston Rd EA W5 ....97 K5
  ESH/CLAY KT10 ....204 E3
  RYNPK SW20 ....177 F5
Aston St POP/IOD E14 ....105 G5
Aston Ter BAL SW12 * 161 G1
Astonville St
  WAND/EARL SW18 ....159 K3
Astor Av ROMW/RG RM7 ....74 E3
Astor Cl KUTN/CMB KT2 ....175 J2
Astoria Pde ASHF TW15 * 152 D6
  STRHM/NOR SW16 ....161 K5
Astoria Wk BRXN/ST SW9 ....142 B4
Astra Cl HCH RM12 ....93 K5
Astrop Ms HMSMTH W6 ....119 F3
Astrop Ter HMSMTH W6 ....119 F3
Astwood Ms SKENS SW7 ....120 A4
Asylum Rd PECK SE15 ....143 J1
Atalanta St FUL/PGN SW6 ....139 G2
Atbara Rd TEDD TW11 ....174 C2
Atcham Rd HSLW TW3 ....135 H5
Atcost Rd BARK IG11 ....109 G4
Atheldene Rd
  WAND/EARL SW18 ....160 B3
Athelney St CAT SE6 ....164 D5
Athelstane Gv BOW E3 ....105 H1
Athelstane Ms FSBYPK N4 * 67 G5
Athelstan Gdns
  KIL/WHAMP NW6 ....82 C5
Athelstan Rd KUT/HW KT1 ....191 G1
Athelstan Wy STMC/STPC BR5 ....186 B4
Athelstone Rd
  KTN/HRWW/WS HA3 ....42 D5
Athena Cl KUT/HW KT1 ....175 G6
  RYLN/HDSTN HA2 ....60 D6
Athenaeum Pl MUSWH N10 ....48 B5
Athenaeum Rd
  TRDG/WHET N20 ....33 G2
Athena Pl NTHWD HA6 ....40 D4
Athenlay Rd PECK SE15 ....144 A6
Athens Gdns MV/WKIL W9 * 100 E3
Atherden Rd CLPT E5 ....86 E2
Atherfold Rd BRXN/ST SW9 ....141 K4
Atherley Wy HSLWW TW4 ....154 E2
Atherstone Ms SKENS SW7 * 120 B4
Atherton Cl STWL/WRAY TW19 ....152 A1
Atherton Dr WIM/MER SW19 ....159 G6
Atherton Ms FSTGT E7 ....88 D5
Atherton Pl RYLN/HDSTN HA2 ....42 C6
  STHL UB1 ....96 A6
Atherton Rd BARN SW13 ....138 D1
  CLAY IG5 ....53 J5
  FSTGT E7 ....88 D5
Atherton St BTSEA SW11 ....140 D3
Athlone ESH/CLAY KT10 ....204 E4
Athlone Cl CLPT E5 ....86 D2
  RAD WD7 ....17 F1
Athlone Ct WALTH E17 ....52 B6
Athlone Rd BRXS/STRHM SW2 ....162 A2
Athlone St KTTN NW5 ....84 A4
Athol Cl PIN HA5 ....41 F4
Athol Gdns PIN HA5 ....41 F4
Atholl Rd GDMY/SEVK IG3 ....73 G4
Athol Rd ERITH DA8 ....130 A5
Athol Sq POP/IOD E14 ....106 A5
Atkins Dr WWKM BR4 ....214 B1
Atkinson Cl ORP BR6 ....217 G3
Atkinson Rd CAN/RD E16 ....107 G4
Atkins Rd BAL SW12 ....161 J2
  LEY E10 ....69 K3
Atlanta Bvd ROM RM1 ....75 G3
Atlantic Rd BRXN/ST SW9 ....142 B5
Atlantis Cl BARK IG11 ....109 H2
Atlas Gdns CHARL SE7 ....126 B4
Atlas Ms HACK E8 ....86 B4
Atlas Rd DART DA1 ....151 J4
  FBAR/BDGN N11 ....48 B2
  PLSTW E13 ....106 E1
  WBLY HA9 ....80 E2
  WLSDN NW10 ....99 G2
Atley Rd BOW E3 ....87 J6
Atlip Rd ALP/SUD HA0 ....80 A6
Atney Rd PUT/ROE SW15 ....139 H5
Atria Rd NTHWD HA6 ....26 E4
Attenborough Cl OXHEY WD19 ....27 J3
Atterbury Rd FSBYPK N4 ....67 H3
Atterbury St WEST SW1P 16 E7
Attewood Av WLSDN NW10 ....63 F6
Attewood Rd NTHLT UB5 ....77 J4
Attfield Cl TRDG/WHET N20 ....33 H4
Attlee Cl THHTH CR7 ....196 D3
  YEAD UB4 * 95 F2
Attlee Dr DART DA1 ....151 K6

Attlee Rd THMD SE28 ....109 H6
YEAD UB4 ....94 E2
Attlee Ter WALTH E17 ....69 K1
Attreeave St LEW EC1R 5 J6
Atwell Pl THDIT KT7 ....190 B5
Atwell Rd PECK SE15 * 143 H5
Atwood Av RCH/KEW TW9 ....137 H3
Atwood Rd HMSMTH W6 ....118 E4
Aubert Pk HBRY N5 ....85 H2
Aubert Rd HBRY N5 ....85 H2
Aubrey Pl STJWD NW8 ....101 G1
Aubrey Rd CEND/HSY/T N8 * 66 E2
NTGHL W11 ....119 J1
WALTH E17 ....51 J6
Auburn Cl NWCR SE14 ....144 B1
Aubyn Hl WNWD SE27 ....162 D6
Aubyn Sq PUT/ROE SW15 ....138 D6
Auckland Av RAIN RM13 ....111 H2
Auckland Cl NRWD SE19 ....181 H5
Auckland Gdns NRWD SE19 ......181 H4
Auckland Hl WNWD SE27 ....162 D6
Auckland Ri NRWD SE19 ....181 H4
Auckland Rd BTSEA SW11 ....140 D5
IL IG1 ....72 B5
KUT/HW KT1 ....191 G1
LEY E10 ....87 K1
NRWD SE19 ....181 G4
Auckland St LBTH SE11 ....122 A5
Aucuba Vls WELL DA16 * 148 C4
Audax CDALE/KGS NW9 * 45 H5
Auden Pl CAMTN NW1 ....84 A6
CHEAM SM3 * 208 A2
Audleigh Pl CHIG IG7 ....54 A2
Audley Cl BTSEA SW11 ....141 F4
MUSWH N10 ....48 B3
Audley Ct PIN HA5 ....41 G5
WAN E11 ....70 D1
Audley Dr CAN/RD E16 ....106 A1
Audley Gdns CDMY/SEVK IG3 ....73 F6
Audley Pl BELMT SM2 ....209 F5
Audley Rd EA W5 ....98 B4
ENC/FH EN2 ....23 H3
HDN NW4 ....63 J3
RCHPK/HAM TW10 ....137 G6
Audley St MYFR/PKLN W1K 9 H7
Audrey Cl BECK BR3 ....198 E3
Audrey Gdns ALP/SUD HA0 ....61 H6
Audrey Rd IL IG1 ....90 B1
Audrey St BETH E2 ....104 C1
Audric Cl KUTN/CMB KT2 ....175 H4
Augurs La PLSTW E13 ....107 F2
Augusta Cl E/WMO/HCT KT8 ....172 E6
Augusta Rd WHTN TW2 ....155 H4
Augustine Rd HMSMTH W6 ......119 G3
KTN/HRWW/WS HA3 ....42 B4
STMC/STPC BR5 ....186 E6
Augustus Cl BTFD TW8 ....136 E1
SHB W12 ....118 E1
STAN HA7 ....29 K5
Augustus Rd WIM/MER SW19 ..159 H3
Augustus St CAMTN NW1 ....5 F3
Aultone Wy CAR SM5 ....209 K1
SUT SM1 ....194 B6
Aulton Pl LBTH SE11 ....122 B5
Aurelia Gdns CROY/NA CR0 .....196 A2
Aurelia Rd CROY/NA CR0 ....195 K3
Auriel Av DAGE RM10 ....93 F4
Auriga Ms IS N1 ....85 K4
Auriol Cl WKENS W14 ....207 C1
Auriol Dr GFD/PVL UB6 ....78 D5
Auriol Park Rd WPK KT4 ....207 C1
Auriol Rd WKENS W14 ....119 H4
Austell Gdns MLHL NW7 ....31 G3
Austen Cl THMD SE28 ....128 C1
Austen Rd ERITH DA8 ....149 J1
RYLN/HDSTN HA2 ....60 B6
Austin Av HAYES BR2 ....200 D3
Austin Cl FSTH SE23 ....164 B2
TWK TW1 ....156 D6
Austin Friars OBST EC2N 13 F4
Austin Friars Sq OBST EC2N * 13 F4
Austin Rd BTSEA SW11 ....141 F2
HYS/HAR UB3 ....113 J2
STMC/STPC BR5 ....186 C2
Austins La HGDN/ICK UB10 ....76 A1
Austin St BETH E2 ....7 J3
Austral Cl BFN/LL DA15 ....168 A5
Australia Rd SHB W12 ....99 K6
Austral St LBTH SE11 ....18 A6
Austyn Gdns BRYLDS KT5 * 191 J5
Autumn Cl EN EN1 ....24 D3
WIM/MER SW19 ....178 B2
Autumn Dr BELMT SM2 ....209 F6
Autumn Gv BMLY BR1 ....184 A2
Autumn St BOW E3 ....87 J6
Avalon Cl ENC/FH EN2 ....23 G5
ORP BR6 ....202 E6
RYNPK SW20 ....177 H5
WEA W13 ....97 G4
Avalon Rd FUL/PGN SW6 ....140 A2
ORP BR6 ....202 D6
WEA W13 ....97 G3
Avard Gdns ORP BR6 ....216 C2
Avarn Rd TOOT SW17 ....178 E2
Avebury Pk SURB KT6 * 190 E5
Avebury Rd ORP BR6 ....216 D1
WAN E11 ....70 B5
WIM/MER SW19 ....177 J4
Aveley Cl IS N1 ....217 F1
Aveley Cl ERITH DA8 ....130 C6
Aveline St LBTH SE11 ....122 A5
Aveling Park Rd WALTH E17 ......51 J1
Aveling Rd RAIN RM13 ....93 J6
Ave Marie La STP EC4M 12 C4
Avenell Rd HBRY N5 ....85 H1
Avening Rd WAND/EARL SW18 ..159 K2
Avening Ter WAND/EARL SW18 .159 K1
Avenons Rd PLSTW E13 ....106 E4
Avenue Cl HEST TW5 ....34 C1
STHGT/OAK N14 ....34 C1
STJWD NW8 ....2 D1
WDR/YW UB7 ....112 A3
Avenue Crs ACT W3 ....117 J2
HEST TW5 ....134 A2

Avenue Elmers SURB KT6 ....191 F2
Avenue Gdns ACT W3 ....117 J2
HEST TW5 * 133 K1
MRDN/ESHN SW14 ....138 B4
SNWD SE25 ....181 H6
TEDD TW11 ....174 A5
Avenue Ga LOU IG10 ....39 G1
Avenue Pde SUN TW16 ....143 K1
WCHMH N21 .... 35 H2
Avenue Park Rd WNWD SE27 ..162 C4
Avenue Rd ACT W3 ....117 J2
BTFD TW8 ....116 D5
BXLYHN DA7 ....149 F4
ERITH DA6 ....75 J4
ERITH DA6 ....153 J5
FELT TW13 ....153 J5
FSTGT E7 ....89 F3
HGT N6 ....66 C4
HPTN TW12 ....173 G4
ISLW TW7 ....135 K2
KUT/HW KT1 ....175 F6
NFNCH/WDSPK N12 ....33 G4
NWMAL KT3 ....176 B6
PGE/AN SE20 ....181 K4
PIN HA5 ....41 J6
RYNPK SW20 ....176 E5
SEVS/STOTM N15 ....67 K2
SNWD SE25 ....181 H6
STHGT/OAK N14 ....34 C1
SUT SM1 ....208 D5
STJWD NW8 ....83 H6
STRHM/NOR SW16 ....179 J5
TEDD TW11 ....174 B3
WFD IG8 ....53 C2
WLGTN SM6 ....210 C5
WLSDN NW10 ....99 H1
Avenue South BRYLDS KT5 ......191 G4
Avenue Ter NWMAL KT3 ....175 K6
The Avenue BAR EN5 ....27 J1
BECK BR3 ....182 E4
BELMT SM2 ....208 D6
BMLY BR1 ....184 C6
BRYLDS KT5 ....191 G5
BXLY DA5 ....168 E2
CAR SM5 ....210 A5
CEND/HSY/T N8 ....49 G6
CHING E4 ....52 B2
CHSWK W4 ....118 B3
CLAP SW4 ....141 G6
CROY/NA CR0 ....212 A1
ESH/CLAY KT10 ....204 E4
EW KT17 ....208 A5
FBAR/BDGN N11 ....48 D1
GNWCH SE10 ....145 G1
HEST TW5 ....133 K2
HPTN TW12 ....172 E2
HSLW TW3 ....135 G6
KIL/WHAMP NW6 ....82 C3
KTN/HRWW/WS HA3 ....43 F4
LOU IG10 ....39 J1
MUSWH N10 ....48 C5
NTHWD HA6 ....40 A2
ORP BR6 ....202 A6
PIN HA5 ....59 K3
RCH/KEW TW9 ....137 G3
ROM RM1 ....75 F1
STMC/STPC BR5 ....186 C5
SUN TW16 ....172 A5
TOTM N17 ....50 B5
TWK TW1 ....156 C5
WAN E11 ....71 F3
WBLY HA9 ....63 F6
WEA W13 ....97 H6
WPK KT4 ....192 C6
WWKM BR4 ....199 G4
Averil Gv STRHM/NOR SW16 ...180 C2
Averill St HMSMTH W6 ....119 G6
Avern Gdns E/WMO/HCT KT8 ...189 G1
Avern Rd E/WMO/HCT KT8 ....189 G1
Avery Farm Rw BGVA SW1W * ...15 J7
Avery Gdns GNTH/NBYPK IG2 ....71 K2
Avery Hill Rd ELTH/MOT SE9 ....167 H3
Avery Rw MYFR/PKLN W1K 9 J5
Avery Wy DART DA1 ....171 J4
Aviary Cl CAN/RD E16 ....106 D4
Aviemore Cl BECK BR3 ....198 C2
Aviemore Wy BECK BR3 ....198 B3
Avignon Rd BROCKY SE4 ....144 A4
Avington Gv PGE/AN SE20 ....181 K3
Avington Wy PECK SE15 * 143 G1
Avion Crs CDALE/KGS NW9 ....45 J5
Avior Dr NTHWD HA6 ....26 D3
Avis Sq WCHPL E1 ....105 F5
Avoca Rd TOOT SW17 ....161 F6
Avocet Cl STHWK SE1 ....123 G5
Avocet Ms THMD SE28 ....127 J3
Avon Cl SUT SM1 ....209 G2
Avon Ct PIN HA5 ....41 G5
Avondale Av CRICK NW2 ....81 C1
EBAR EN4 ....33 K3
ESH/CLAY KT10 ....205 C1
NFNCH/WDSPK N12 ....47 F1
WPK KT4 ....192 C5
Avondale Cl LOU IG10 ....39 G2
Avondale Ct SWFD E18 ....53 F4
Avondale Crs PEND EN3 ....25 C4
REDBR IG4 ....71 J1
Avondale Dr HYS/HAR UB3 ....113 K1
LOU IG10 ....39 K1
Avondale Gdns HSLWW TW4 ....134 D4
Avondale Park Gdns
NTGHL W11 * 100 C6
Avondale Park Rd NTGHL W11 ..100 C6
Avondale Pavement
STHWK SE1 * 123 H5
Avondale Ri PECK SE15 ....143 G4
Avondale Rd ASHF TW15 ....152 A5
BMLY BR1 ....183 K1
CAN/RD E16 ....106 C4
ELTH/MOT SE9 ....166 D5
FNCH N3 ....47 G4
KTN/HRWW/WS HA3 ....43 F6

MORT/ESHN SW14 ....138 A4
PLMGR N13 ....35 G4
SAND/SEL CR2 ....211 J4
SEVS/STOTM N15 ....67 H2
STHL UB1 ....95 J4
WELL DA16 ....148 D5
WIM/MER SW19 ....178 A1
Avondale Sq STHWK SE1 ....123 H5
Avonley Rd NWCR SE14 ....143 K1
Avon Ms PIN HA5 ....41 K4
Avonmore Gdns WKENS W14 * ..119 H4
Avonmore Pl WKENS W14 ....119 H4
Avonmore Rd WKENS W14 ....119 J4
Avonmouth Rd DART DA1 ....151 G6
Avonmouth St STHWK SE1 ....18 C4
Avon Rd BROCKY SE4 ....144 D4
GFD/PVL UB6 ....96 A3
WALTH E17 ....52 B6
Avonstowe Cl ORP BR6 ....216 C1
Avon Wy SWFD E18 ....70 E1
Avonwick Rd HSLW TW3 ....135 G3
Avril Wy CHING E4 ....52 B1
Avro Wy WLGTN SM6 ....210 E6
Awberry Ct WATW WD18 * 26 B1
Awlfield Av TOTM N17 ....49 K4
Awliscombe Rd WELL DA16 ......148 A3
Axeholm Av EDGW HA8 ....44 D4
Axe St BARK IG11 ....90 C6
Axholme Av EDGW HA8 ....44 C4
Axis Ct GNWCH SE10 ....125 H6
Axminster Crs WELL DA16 ....148 D1
Axminster Rd HOLWY N7 ....84 E1
Axon Pl IL IG1 ....72 C6
Axtaine Rd STMC/STPC BR5 .....202 E4
Aybrook St MHST W1U 9 G2
Aycliff Ct KUT/HW KT1 * 175 H5
Aycliffe Rd SHB W12 ....118 C1
Aylands Cl WBLY HA9 ....62 A6
Aylesbury Cl FSTGT E7 ....88 D4
Aylesbury Rd HAYES BR2 ....183 K6
WALW SE17 ....122 E5
Aylesbury St CLKNW EC1R 6 A7
WLSDN NW10 ....81 F1
Aylesford Av BECK BR3 ....198 B2
Aylesford St PIM SW1V 121 J5
Aylesham Cl MLHL NW7 ....45 J3
Aylesham Rd ORP BR6 ....201 K4
Ayles Rd YEAD UB4 ....94 E2
Aylestone Av KIL/WHAMP NW6 ..82 B5
Aylett Rd ISLW TW7 * 135 K3
SNWD SE25 ....197 J1
Ayley Cft EN EN1 ....24 C6
Ayliffe Cl KUT/HW KT1 ....175 H5
Aylmer Cl STAN HA7 ....29 G6
Aylmer Dr STAN HA7 ....29 G6
Aylmer Pde EFNCH N2 ....65 K2
Aylmer Rd BCTR RM8 ....92 A1
EFNCH N2 ....65 J2
SHB W12 ....118 D2
WAN E11 ....70 D5
Aylsham Dr HGDN/ICK UB10 ......58 A6
Aylton Est BERM/RHTH SE16 * ..123 K2
Aylward Rd FSTH SE23 ....164 A4
RYNPK SW20 ....177 J5
Aylwards Ri STAN HA7 ....29 G6
Aylward St WCHPL E1 * 104 E5
Aynhoe Rd WKENS W14 ....119 G4
Aynscombe Angle ORP BR6 ....202 B4
Ayres Cl PLSTW E13 ....106 E2
Ayres Crs WLSDN NW10 ....81 F5
Ayres St STHWK SE1 ....18 D2
Ayr Gn ROM RM1 ....57 G4
Ayrsome Rd STNW/STAM N16 ....86 A1
Ayrton Rd SKENS SW7 ....14 A4
Ayr Wy ROM RM1 ....57 G4
Aysgarth Rd DUL SE21 ....162 E1
Aytoun Pl BRXN/ST SW9 ....142 A3
Aytoun Rd BRXN/ST SW9 ....142 A3
Azalea Cl HNWL W7 ....116 A1
IL IG1 ....90 B5
Azalea Ct WFD IG8 * 52 C3
Azalea Wk PIN HA5 ....59 F3
Azania Ms KTTN NW5 * 84 B4
Azenby Rd PECK SE15 ....143 G3
Azof St GNWCH SE10 ....125 H4

B

Baalbec Rd HBRY N5 ....85 H3
Babbacombe Cl CHSGTN KT9 ...205 K3
Babbacombe Gdns REDBR IG4 ...71 J1
Babbacombe Rd BMLY BR1 ....184 A4
Baber Bridge Pde
EBED/NFELT TW14 * 154 B1
Baber Dr EBED/NFELT TW14 .....154 B1
Babington Ri WBLY HA9 ....80 C4
Babington Rd BCTR RM8 ....91 J4
HCH NM12 ....75 K5
HDN NW4 ....63 K1
STRHM/NOR SW16 ....179 J1
Babmaes St STJS SW1Y 10 C7
Bache's St IS N1 ....7 F6
Back Church La WCHPL E1 ....104 C5
Back Hl CLKNW EC1R 5 K7
Back La BTFD TW8 ....136 E1
BXLY DA5 ....169 H2
CEND/HSY/T N8 ....66 E2
CHDH RM6 ....73 K4
EDGW HA8 ....44 E4
HAMP NW3 ....83 G2
RCHPK/HAM TW10 ....156 D5
Backley Gdns CROY/NA CR0 .....197 H3
Back Rd SCUP DA14 * 186 B6
TEDD TW11 ....173 K3
Bacon Gv STHWK SE1 ....19 J6
Bacon La CDALE/KGS NW9 ....62 E2
EDGW HA8 ....44 C4
Bacon Link CRW RM5 ....56 D2
Bacon's La HGT N6 ....66 A5
Bacon St BETH E2 ....7 K6
Bacton St BETH E2 ....104 E2
Baddow Cl DAGE RM10 ....92 C6

WFD IG8 ....53 H2
Baden Pl STHWK SE1 ....18 E2
Baden Powell Cl DAGW RM9 ....92 A6
SURB KT6 ....191 G6
Baden Rd IL IG1 ....90 A3
Bader Wy RAIN RM13 ....93 J4
Badger Cl FELT TW13 ....154 A5
HSLWW TW4 ....134 B4
Badgers Cl ENC/FH EN2 ....23 H4
HRW HA1 ....60 D3
HYS/HAR UB3 ....113 H1
WPK KT4 ....192 C6
Badgers Copse ORP BR6 ....202 A6
Badgers Cft ELTH/MOT SE9 ......167 F5
TRDG/WHET N20 ....32 C3
Badgers Wk NWMAL KT3 ....176 B5
Badlis Rd WALTH E17 ....51 J5
Badlow Cl ERITH DA8 ....150 B1
Badminton Cl HRW HA1 * 60 E1
NTHLT UB5 ....78 A4
Badminton Ms CAN/RD E16 ....125 K1
Badminton Rd BAL SW12 ....161 F1
Badsworth Rd CMBW SE5 ....142 D1
Bafton Ga HAYES BR2 ....200 A5
Bagley Cl WDR/YW UB7 ....112 B2
Bagley House
WOOL/PLUM SE18 * 146 D1
Bagleys La FUL/PGN SW6 ....140 B2
Bagleys Spring CHDH RM6 ....74 A1
Bagshot Ct
WOOL/PLUM SE18 * 147 F2
Bagshot Rd EN EN1 ....36 B2
Bagshot St WALW SE17 ....123 F5
Baildon St DEPT SE8 ....144 C1
Bailey Cl FBAR/BDGN N11 ....48 B3
THMD SE28 ....127 K1
Bailey Cottages
WOOL/PLUM SE18 * 146 D1
Bailey Crs CHSGTN KT9 ....205 K5
Bailey House
WOOL/PLUM SE18 * 146 D1
Bailey Ms BRXS/STRHM SW2 ...142 B6
CHSWK W4 ....117 J6
Bailey Pl SYD SE26 ....181 K2
Baillie Cl RAIN RM13 ....111 K3
Bainbridge Cl
RCHPK/HAM TW10 ....175 F1
Bainbridge St
NOXST/BSQ WC1A 10 D3
Bainbridge Rd DAGW RM9 ....92 B2
Baines Cl SAND/SEL CR2 ....211 K5
Baird Av STHL UB1 ....96 B6
Baird Cl BUSH WD23 ....28 B2
CDALE/KGS NW9 ....62 E3
LEY E10 ....69 J6
Baird Gdns NRWD SE19 ....163 F6
Baird Memorial Cottages
STHGT/OAK N14 * 34 D4
Baird Rd EN EN1 ....24 D5
Baird St STLK EC1Y 6 D7
Baizdon Rd BKHTH/KID SE3 ......145 H3
Baker Crs DART DA1 ....171 G2
Baker La MTCM CR4 ....179 F5
Baker Ms ORP BR6 ....217 F4
Baker Rd WLSDN NW10 ....81 G6
WOOL/PLUM SE18 ....146 D1
Bakers Av WALTH E17 ....69 K3
Bakers End RYNPK SW20 ....177 H5
Bakers Fld HOLWY N7 ....84 E2
Bakers Gdns CAR SM5 ....194 D6
Bakers Hl BAR EN5 ....21 F3
Baker's Ms MHST W1U 9 G3
Bakers Rents BETH E2 ....7 J5
Baker's Rw CLKNW EC1R 5 J7
SRTFD E15 ....106 C1
Baker St CAMTN NW1 ....3 F7
EN EN1 ....24 A4
MHST W1U 9 F1
Baker's Yd CLKNW EC1R * 5 J7
Bakery Cl BRXN/ST SW9 * 142 A1
Bakery Pl BTSEA SW11 ....140 E5
Balaams La STHGT/OAK N14 ......34 D4
Balaam St PLSTW E13 ....107 E2
Balaclava Rd STHWK SE1 * 19 K7
SURB KT6 ....190 D4
Bala Gn CDALE/KGS NW9 * 63 G3
Balantyne Cl SAND/SEL CR2 .....211 J6
Balcaskie Rd ELTH/MOT SE9 .....166 D6
Balchier Rd EDUL SE22 ....163 J1
Balcombe Cl BXLYHS DA6 ....148 E5
Balcombe St CAMTN NW1 ....8 E1
Balder Ri LEE/GVPK SE12 ....166 A4
Balderton St MYFR/PKLN W1K 9 H4
Baldock St BOW E3 ....105 K1
Baldry Gdns
STRHM/NOR SW16 ....179 K2
Baldwin Crs CMBW SE5 ....142 D2
Baldwin Gdns HSLW TW3 * 135 H2
Baldwin St FSBYE EC1V 6 E5
Baldwin Ter IS N1 ....6 C2
Baldwyn Gdns ACT W3 * 98 E6
Baldwyn's Pk BXLY DA5 ....170 A4
Baldwyn's Rd BXLY DA5 ....170 A4
Bale Rd WCHPL E1 ....105 G4
Bales Ter EFNCH N2 * 65 G1
Balfe St IS N1 ....5 G3
Balfour Av HNWL W7 ....116 A1
Balfour Gv TRDG/WHET N20 ....33 K3
Balfour Ms MYFR/PKLN W1K 9 H7
EDGW HA8 ....44 D4
Balfour Pl MYFR/PKLN W1K 9 H6
PUT/ROE SW15 ....138 E5
Balfour Rd ACT W3 ....98 E4
CAR SM5 ....209 K5
HBRY N5 ....85 J2
HNWL W7 ....116 A1
HRW HA1 ....60 D2
HSLW TW3 ....135 G4

IL IG1 ....72 B5
NWDGN UB2 ....114 C3
SNWD SE25 ....197 H1
WEA W13 ....116 C2
WIM/MER SW19 ....178 A3
Balfour St STHWK SE1 ....18 E6
Balgonie Rd CHING E4 ....38 B4
Balgores Crs GPK RM2 ....57 K6
Balgores La GPK RM2 ....57 K5
Balgores Sq GPK RM2 ....75 K1
Balgowan Cl NWMAL KT3 ....192 B1
Balgowan Rd BECK BR3 ....182 B6
BECK BR3 ....198 B1
Balgowan St
WOOL/PLUM SE18 ....128 A4
Balham Gv BAL SW12 ....161 F2
Balham High Rd BAL SW12 ....161 F3
Balham Hl BAL SW12 ....161 G1
Balham New Rd BAL SW12 ....161 G2
Balham Park Rd BAL SW12 ....160 E3
Balham Rd ED N9 ....36 C4
Balham Station Rd BAL SW12 ....161 F3
Balkan Wk WAP E1W * 104 D6
Balladier Wk POP/IOD E14 ....105 K4
Ballamore Rd BMLY BR1 ....165 K5
Ballance Rd HOM E9 ....87 F4
Ballantine St
WAND/EARL SW18 ....140 B5
Ballard Cl KUTN/CMB KT2 ....176 A3
Ballards Cl DAGE RM10 ....110 D1
Ballards Farm Rd
CROY/NA CR0 ....212 D4
Ballards La FNCH N3 ....47 F3
Ballards Ms EDGW HA8 ....44 C2
Ballards Ri SAND/SEL CR2 ....212 C4
Ballards Rd CRICK NW2 ....63 J6
DAGE RM10 ....110 D1
Ballards Wy SAND/SEL CR2 ......212 C4
Ballater Cl OXHEY WD19 ....27 G6
Ballater Rd BRXS/STRHM SW2 ..141 K5
SAND/SEL CR2 ....212 B3
Ballina St FSTH SE23 ....164 A2
Ballingdon Rd BTSEA SW11 ......161 F1
Ballinger Wy NTHLT UB5 ....95 J3
Balliol Av CHING E4 ....38 B5
Balliol Rd NKENS W10 ....100 A5
TOTM N17 ....50 A4
WELL DA16 ....148 C3
Balloch Rd CAT SE6 ....165 G3
Ballogie Av WLSDN NW10 ....81 G2
Ballow Cl CMBW SE5 ....143 F1
Ball's Pond Pl IS N1 * 85 K4
Balls Pond Rd IS N1 ....85 K4
Balmain Cl EA W5 ....116 E1
Balmer Rd BOW E3 ....105 J1
Balmes Rd IS N1 ....85 K6
Balmoral Av BECK BR3 ....198 B1
FBAR/BDGN N11 ....48 A2
Balmoral Cl PUT/ROE SW15 * 159 C1
Balmoral Ct E/WMO/HCT KT8 ....189 J1
Balmoral Dr STHL UB1 ....94 C3
YEAD UB4 ....94 C3
Balmoral Gdns BXLY DA5 ....169 G2
WEA W13 ....116 B3
Balmoral Gv HOLWY N7 ....85 F4
Balmoral Ms SHB W12 ....118 C3
Balmoral Rd CRICK NW2 ....81 K4
FSTGT E7 ....89 G2
GPK RM2 ....57 K1
KUT/HW KT1 ....191 G1
LEY E10 ....70 A4
RYLN/HDSTN HA2 ....59 J6
WPK KT4 ....207 K1
Balmore Crs EBAR EN4 ....22 A6
Balmore St ARCH N19 ....66 B6
Balmuir Gdns PUT/ROE SW15 ...139 F5
Balnacraig Av WLSDN NW10 ....81 G2
Balniel Ga PIM SW1V 121 J5
Baltic Cl WIM/MER SW19 ....178 C3
Baltic St East STLK EC1Y 6 C7
Baltic St West STLK EC1Y 6 C7
Baltimore Pl WELL DA16 ....148 A3
Balvaird Pl PIM SW1V 121 J5
Balvernie Gv
WAND/EARL SW18 ....159 J2
Bamber Rd PECK SE15 * 143 G2
Bamborough Gdns SHB W12 .....119 F2
Bamford Av ALP/SUD HA0 ....80 B6
Bamford Rd BARK IG11 ....90 C5
BMLY BR1 ....183 G1
Bamford Wy CRW RM5 ....56 D1
Bampfylde Cl WLGTN SM6 ....210 C1
Bampton Dr MLHL NW7 ....45 H3
Bampton Rd FSTH SE23 ....164 A5
Banavie Gdns BECK BR3 ....182 E4
Banbury Cl ENC/FH EN2 * 23 H2
Banbury Ct BELMT SM2 ....208 E5
COVGDN WC2E * 11 E5
Banbury Rd HOM E9 ....87 F5
WALTH E17 ....51 G3
Banbury St BTSEA SW11 * 140 D3
Banchory Rd BKHTH/KID SE3 ....146 A1
Bancroft Av EFNCH N2 ....65 J2
Bancroft Ct RSLP HA4 * 77 H6
Bancroft Ct NTHLT UB5 ....95 G6
Bancroft Gdns
KTN/HRWW/WS HA3 ....42 C4
ORP BR6 ....202 A5
Bancroft Rd
KTN/HRWW/WS HA3 ....42 C4
WCHPL E1 ....104 E3
Bandon Ri WLGTN SM6 ....210 D4
Banfield Rd PECK SE15 ....143 J5
Bangalore St PUT/ROE SW15 ....139 F3
Bangor Cl NTHLT UB5 ....78 B3
Banim St HMSMTH W6 ....118 E4
Banister Rd NKENS W10 ....100 C2
Bank Av MTCM CR4 ....178 C5
Bank Buildings CHING E4 * 52 B2
Bank End STHWK SE1 ....12 D7
Bankfoot Rd BMLY BR1 ....165 H6
Bankhurst Rd CAT SE6 ....164 C2
Bank La KUTN/CMB KT2 ....175 F3
PUT/ROE SW15 ....138 B6
Bank Ms SUT SM1 ....209 G4
Banksia Rd UED N18 ....50 E1
Bankside ENC/FH EN2 ....23 H2
SAND/SEL CR2 ....212 B4

STHL UB1 ....114 C1
STHWK SE1 ....12 C6
Bankside Av LEW SE13 .....145 F4
NTHLT UB5 ....94 K1
Bankside Cl BXLY DA5......170 A6
CAR SM5 ....209 J3
ISLW TW7 ....136 A5
Bankside Dr THDIT KT7.....190 C6
Bankside Rd IL IG1 ....90 C3
Banks La BXLYHS DA6 .....149 G5
Banks Wy MNPK E12 ....90 A2
The Bank HGT N6 ....8 B5
Bankton Rd BRXS/STRHM SW2.142 B5
Bankwell Rd LEW SE13 .....145 H5
Banner St STLK EC1Y 6 D7
Banning St GNWCH SE10...125 H5
Bannister Cl
   BRXS/STRHM SW2 ....162 B3
   GFD/PVL UB6 ....78 D3
Bannister Gdns
   STMC/STPC BR5 ....186 D6
Bannockburn Rd
   WOOL/PLUM SE18 ....127 K4
Bannow Cl HOR/WEW KT19...207 G2
Banstead Gdns ED N9 ....35 K5
Banstead Rd CAR SM5........209 J4
Banstead St PECK SE15......143 K4
Banstead Wy WLGTN SM6..210 E3
Banstock Rd EDGW HA8.......44 E2
Banting Dr WCHMH N21.......23 F6
Banton Cl EN EN1 ....24 D3
Bantry St CMBW SE5 ....142 E1
Banwell Rd BXLY DA5 ....168 E1
Banyard Rd BERM/RHTH SE16...123 J3
Bapchild Pl STMC/STPC BR5...202 D1
Baptist Gdns KTTN NW5......84 A4
Barandon Wk NTGHL W11 *...100 B6
Barbara Castle Cl
   FUL/PGN SW6 ....119 J6
Barbara Hucklesbury Cl
   WDGN N22 ....49 H5
Barbauld Rd STNW/STAM N16...86 A1
Barber Cl WCHMH N21 ....35 G2
Barbers Rd SRTFD E15 ......105 K1
Barbican Gdfd/pvl UB6........96 B5
Barb Ms HMSMTH W6 ....119 F3
Barbon Cl BMSBY WC1N 11 C1
Barbot Cl ED N19 ....36 C5
Barchard St WAND/EARL SW18...140 A6
Barchester Rd HNWL W7.....116 A1
Barchester St
   KTN/HRWW/WS HA3 ....42 D4
Barchester St POP/IOD E14...105 K4
Barclay Cl FUL/PGN SW6 *...186 B6
   WATW WD18 ....26 E1
Barclay Ov WFD IG8 ....38 E6
Barclay Rd CROY/NA CR0...211 K1
   FUL/PGN SW6....................139 K1
   PLSTW E13 ....107 G3
   UED N18 ....49 K2
   WALTH E17 ....51 H2
   WALW E17 ....70 D5
Barcombe Av
   BRXS/STRHM SW2 ....161 K4
Barcombe Cl STMC/STPC BR5...186 B6
Barden St WOOL/PLUM SE18...147 K1
Bardfield Av CHDH RM6.......55 K6
Bardney Rd MRDN SM4 ....194 A1
Bardolph Av CROY/NA CR0...213 H6
Bardolph Rd HOLWY N7......137 O5
   RCH/KEW TW9 ....137 H2
Bard Rd NKENS W10 ....100 B6
Bardsey Pl WCHPL E1.........104 E4
Bardsey Wk IS N1 * 85 J4
Bardsley Cl CROY/NA CR0...212 B1
Bardsley La GNWCH SE10...125 F6
Barfett St NKENS W10 ....100 D3
Barfield Av TRDG/WHET N20...33 K4
Barfield Rd BMLY BR1 ....185 F6
   WAN E11 *..........................70 D5
Barford Cl HDN NW4 ....45 J5
Barford St IS N1 ....6 A1
Barforth Rd PECK SE15......143 J4
Barfreston Wy PGE/AN SE20...181 J4
Bargate Cl NWMAL KT3......192 D4
   WOOL/PLUM SE18 ....128 A5
Barge House Rd CAN/RD E16...127 G2
Barge La BOW E3 ....87 H6
Bargery Rd CAT SE6 ....164 E3
Barge Wk KUT/HW KT1......174 E4
Bargrove Cl PGE/AN SE20...181 H3
Bargrove Crs CAT SE6........164 C4
Barham Cl ALP/SUD HA0 .....79 H4
   CHST DR7 ....185 G1
   HAYES BR2 ....200 D5
   ROMW/RG RM7 ....56 D5
Barham Ct ALP/SUD HA0 .....79 J4
Barham Rd CHST BR7.........185 G1
   DART DA1............................171 K2
   RYNPK SW20 ....176 D5
   SAND/SEL CR2 ....211 J2
Baring Cl LEE/GVPK SE12...165 K4
Baring Rd CROY/NA CR0....197 H5
   EBAR EN4 ....21 H4
   LEE/GVPK SE12 ....166 A4
Baring St IS N1 ....6 E1
Barker Cl NTHWD HA6 ....40 D3
   NWMAL KT3 ....191 J1
   RCH/KEW TW9 ....137 J3
Barker Dr CAMTN NW1........84 D5
Barker St WBPTN SW10......120 B6
Barker Wk STRHM/NOR SW16...161 J5
Barkham Rd TOTM N17........49 K5
Bark Hart Rd ORP BR6.......202 C5
Barking Rd EHAM E6 ....89 K5
   PLSTW E13 ....107 F3
   POP/IOD E14 ....106 C5
Bark Pl BAY/PAD W2...........101 F6
Barkston Gdns ECT SW5......14 C6
Barkway Dr ORP BR6..........216 A2
Barkwood Cl ROMW/RG RM7...74 E2
Barkworth Rd
   BERM/RHTH SE16 ....123 J5
Barlborough St NWCR SE14...144 A1
Barlby Gdns NKENS W10 ....100 B3
Barlby Rd NKENS W10 ....100 A4

Barley Cl ALP/SUD HA0........79 K2
Barley La GDMY/SEVK IG3...73 G3
Barley Mow Pas CHSWK W4...118 A5
Barlow Dr BKHTH/KID SE3...146 D2
Barlow Pl MYFR/PICC W1J......9 K6
Barlow Rd ACT W3...............117 J1
   CRICK NW2 ....82 D4
   HPTN TW12 ....173 F3
Barlow St WALW SE17...........19 F7
Barlow Wy RAIN RM13........111 F5
Barlow Wy South RAIN RM13....111 G5
Barmeston Rd CAT SE6......164 E4
Barmor Cl RYLN/HDSTN HA2...42 A3
Barmouth Av GFD/PVL UB6...97 F1
Barmouth Rd CROY/NA CR0...198 A6
   WAND/EARL SW18 ....160 B1
Barnabas Rd HOM E9...........87 F4
Barnaby Cl RYLN/HDSTN HA2...60 C6
Barnaby Pl SKENS SW7.........14 A7
Barnard Cl CHST BR7 ....185 J4
   SUN TW16 ....172 A3
   WLGTN SM6 ....210 D5
   WOOL/PLUM SE18 ....127 J4
Barnard Gdns NWMAL KT3...192 D1
   YEAD UB4 ....95 F3
Barnard Hl MUSWH N10......48 B5
Barnard Ms BTSEA SW11...140 D5
Barnardo Dr BARK/HLT IG6...72 C2
Barnardo Gdns WCHPL E1 *...105 F5
Barnard St WCHPL E1 ....105 F5
Barnard Rd BTSEA SW11....140 D5
   EN EN1 ....24 D5
   MTCM CR4 ....195 F1
Barnards Pl SAND/SEL CR2...211 H6
Barnby Sq SRTFD E15 *........88 C6
Barn Cl KTTN NW5 * 84 D5
   NTHLT UB5 ....95 G1
Barn Crs STAN HA7...............43 J2
Barnehurst Av BXLYHN DA7...149 K3
Barnehurst Cl ERITH DA8....149 K2
Barnehurst Rd BXLYHN DA7...149 K3
Barn End Dr RDART DA2.....171 F6
Barnes Av BARN SW13........138 D1
   NWDGN UB2 ....114 C4
Barnes Br CHSWK W4 ....138 B3
Barnes Cl MNPK E12.............89 H3
Barnes Cray Rd DART DA1...150 D3
Barnesdale Crs
   STMC/STPC BR5 ....202 B3
Barnes End NWMAL KT3....192 D2
Barnes High St BARN SW13...138 C3
Barnes Rd IL IG1 ....90 C3
Barnes St POP/IOD E14......105 G5
Barnes Ter DEPT SE8 ....124 C5
Barnet Dr HAYES BR2.........200 D6
Barnet Gate La BAR EN5......31 J2
Barnett Cl ERITH DA8 ....149 K2
Barnetts Ct RYLN/HDSTN HA2 *...78 B1
Barnett St WCHPL E1 ....104 D5
Barnet Wy (Barnet By-Pass)
   MLHL NW7 ....31 F2
Barnet Wood Rd HAYES BR2...200 C6
Barney Cl CHARL SE7..........126 B5
Barn Fld HAMP NW3 ....83 K3
Barnfield NWMAL KT3.........192 B3
Barnfield Av CROY/NA CR0...197 K6
   KUTN/CMB KT2 ....156 E6
   MTCM CR4 ....179 G5
Barnfield Cl FSBYPK N4........66 E4
   SWLY BR8 ....203 K4
   TOOT SW17 ....160 B5
Barnfield Gdns KUTN/CMB KT2...175 F6
   WOOL/PLUM SE18 ....127 G6
Barnfield Pl POP/IOD E14...124 D3
Barnfield Rd BELV DA17.....129 G6
   EA W5 ....97 J3
   EDGW HA8 ....44 E1
   SAND/SEL CR2 ....212 A6
   STMC/STPC BR5 ....186 E6
   WOOL/PLUM SE18 ....127 G6
Barnfield Wood Cl BECK BR3...199 G3
Barnfield Wood Rd BECK BR3...199 H2
Barnham Dr THMD SE28 ....128 A1
Barnham Rd GFD/PVL UB6...96 C2
Barnham St STHWK SE1.......19 H2
Barnhill PIN HA5..................59 G1
Barn Hill WBLY HA9.............62 C3
Barnhill Av HAYES BR2......199 K6
Barnhill La YEAD UB4 ....95 F1
Barnhill Rd WBLY HA9..........62 C3
   YEAD UB4 ....95 F1
Barnhurst Pth OXHEY WD19...41 G1
Barningham Wy
   CDALE/KGS NW9 ....62 E3
Barn Lea RICM FELT TW13...154 D4
Barnmead Gdns DAGW RM9...92 B3
Barnmead Rd BECK BR3......182 A4
   DAGW RM9 ....92 B3
Barnock Cl DART DA1 ....170 D2
Barn Ri WBLY HA9................62 D3
Barnsbury Cl NWMAL KT3...191 K1
Barnsbury Crs BRYLDS KT5...191 K5
Barnsbury Est IS N1 ....5 H1
Barnsbury Gv HOLWY N7......85 F5
Barnsbury La BRYLDS KT5...191 K6
Barnsbury Pk IS N1 ....85 G5
Barnsbury Rd IS N1 ....5 H1
Barnsbury Sq IS N1 ....85 G5
Barnsbury St IS N1 ....85 G5
Barnsbury Ter IS N1 ....85 F5
Barnscroft RYNPK SW20....176 E6
Barnsdale Av POP/IOD E14...124 E4
Barnsdale Rd MV/WKIL W9...100 D3
Barnsley St WCHPL E1 ....104 D3
Barnstaple La LEW SE13 *...145 F5
Barnstaple Rd RSLP HA4......77 G1
Barnston Wk IS N1 * 85 J5
Barn St STNW/STAM N16.....68 A6

Barn Wy WBLY HA9..............62 C5
Barnwell Rd
   BRXS/STRHM SW2 ....142 B6
   DART DA1............................151 J4
Barnwood Cl MV/WKIL W9...101 F3
   RSLP HA4 ....58 B6
Baron Cl FBAR/BDGN N11.....48 A1
Baroness Rd BETH E2............7 J3
Baronet Gv TOTM N17..........50 C4
Baronet Rd TOTM N17..........50 C4
Baron Gdns BARK/HLT IG6....54 B6
Baron Gv MTCM CR4 ....194 D7
Baron Rd BCTR RM8 ....73 K5
Barons Cl IS N1 * 5 K2
Baron's Court Rd WKENS W14...119 H5
Baronsfield Rd TWK TW1 *...156 C1
Barons Ga EBAR EN4 ....33 J1
Barons Keep WKENS W14 *...119 H5
Barons Md HRW HA1 ....61 E2
Baronsmead Rd BARN SW13...138 D2
Baronsmede EA W5.............117 G2
Baronsmere Ct BAR EN5 *....20 C5
Baronsmere Rd EFNCH N2...65 J1
Baron's Pl STHWK SE1...........17 K3
Barrett's Green Rd
   WLSDN NW10 ....98 E1
Barrett's Gv STNW/STAM N16...86 A3
Barrett St MHST W1U 9 H4
Barretts Cl ORP BR6 ....216 B2
Barrett St KTTN NW5............84 B4
Barrett Point Rd CAN/RD E16...126 D2
Barringer Sq TOOT SW17...161 F6
Barrington Cl CLAY IG5.........53 K4
   KTTN NW5 ....84 A3
Barrington Rd BRXN/ST SW9...142 C4
   BXLYHN DA7 ....148 E3
   CEND/HSY/T N8 ....66 D3
   CHEAM SM3 ....193 K5
Barrington Vls
   WOOL/PLUM SE18 ....147 F2
Barrington Wk NRWD SE19 *...181 F2
Barrow Av CAR SM5 ....209 K5
Barrowdene Cl PIN HA5........41 J5
Barrowell Gn WCHMH N21...35 H4
Barrowgate Rd CHSWK W4...117 K5
Barrow Hedges Cl CAR SM5...209 J5
Barrow Hedges Wy CAR SM5...209 J5
Barrow Hill KWD/TDW/WH KT20...192 B6
Barrow Hill Est STJWD NW8...2 C2
Barrow Point Av PIN HA5.......41 J5
Barrow Point La PIN HA5.......41 J5
Barrow Rd CROY/NA CR0...211 G3
   STRHM/NOR SW16 ....179 J2
Barrow Wk IS N1 ....5 K1
Barry Av BXLYHN DA7........149 F1
   SEVS/STOTM N15 ....68 A3
Barry Cl ORP BR6...............216 E1
Barry Pde EDUL SE22 *.......143 H5
Barry Rd EDUL SE22 ....163 H1
   EHAM E6 ....107 J2
   WLSDN NW10 ....80 E5
Barset Rd PECK SE15 ....143 K4
Barson's Cl PGE/AN SE20...181 K3
Barston Rd WNWD SE27 ....162 D5
Barstow Gdns CRW RM5 ......56 E3
Barstow Cr SHB W12 ....118 E1
Barton Cl EHAM E6.............108 A3
Bartatsworth Rd MTCM CR4...178 D4
Barton Cl BXLYHS DA6 ......149 F1
   EHAM E6 ....107 K6
   HDN NW4 ....45 J6
   PECK SE15 ....143 J4
The Bartons BORE WD6 *.....29 H1
Barton St WEST SW1P 16 E4
Bartram Rd BROCKY SE4....144 B6
Barton Av ROMW/RG RM7...74 E5
Bartrams La EBAR EN4.........21 G1
Bartrip St BECK BR9 ....198 D3
Barts Cl BECK BR3 ....198 D3
Barville Cl CHSGTN KT9.....205 J5
Barwick Rd FSTGT E7 ....89 F2
Barwood Av WWKM BR4.....199 K6
Bascome Mdw BARK/HLT IG6...72 C1
Bascome St BRXS/STRHM SW2...162 B2
Basden Gv FELT TW13........155 F4
Basedale Rd DAGW RM9......91 H5
Baseing Cl EHAM E6...........108 A1
Basevi Wy DEPT SE8...........124 D6

Bashley Rd WLSDN NW10.....99 F3
Basil Av EHAM E6................107 J2
Basildene Rd HSLWW TW4...134 C4
Basildon Av CLAY IG5 ....54 A4
Basildon Cl BELMT SM2......209 F6
   WATW WD18 ....26 D1
Basildon Rd ABYW SE2 ......128 B5
   WNWD SE27 ....180 D1
Basil Gdns CROY/NA CR0...198 A5
   WNWD SE27 ....180 D1
Basilon Rd BXLYHN DA7....149 F3
Basing Ct PECK SE15...........143 G2
Basingdon Wy CMBW SE5...142 E5
Basing Dr BXLY DA5............169 G1
Basingfield Rd THDIT KT7...190 A4
Basinghall Av CITYW EC2V...12 E3
Basinghall Gdns BELMT SM2...209 F6
Basinghall St CITYW EC2V...12 E3
Basing Hl GLDGN NW11 ....64 D5
Basing House Yd BETH E2 *...7 H4
Basing St NTGHL W11.........100 D5
Basing Wy FNCH N3..............46 E6
   THDIT KT7 ....190 A4
Basire St IS N1.......................85 K4
Baskerville Gdns WLSDN NW10...81 G2
Baskerville Rd
   WAND/EARL SW18 ....160 D2
Basket Gdns ELTH/MOT SE9...146 D5
Baslow Cl KTN/HRWW/WS HA3...42 D4
Baslow Wk CLPT E5...............87 F2
Bassano St EDUL SE22.......143 G6
Bassant Rd WOOL/PLUM SE18...128 A6
Bassein Park Rd SHB W12...118 C2
Bassett Cl BELMT SM2 ....209 F6
Bassett Gdns ISLW TW7......135 H1
Bassett Rd NKENS W10......100 B5
   ORP BR6 ....216 B2
Bassett St KTTN NW5...........84 A3
Bassetts Wy ORP BR6.........216 B2
Bassett Wy GFD/PVL UB6.....96 B5
Bassingham Rd ALP/SUD HA0...79 K4
   WAND/EARL SW18 ....160 B2
Basswood Cl PECK SE15......143 J4
Bastable Av BARK IG11.......109 G1
Bastion Rd ABYW SE2........128 B5
Baston Manor Rd WWKM BR4...215 F1
Baston Rd HAYES BR2........200 A6
Bastwick St FSBYE EC1V......6 B6
Basuto Rd FUL/PGN SW6...139 K2
Batavia Rd NWCR SE14......144 B1
   SUN TW16 ....172 A4
Batchwood Gn
   STMC/STPC BR5 ....202 B1
Batchworth La NTHWD HA6...40 A1
Bateman Rd BARK IG11........90 C4
Bateman's Bldgs SOHO/SHAV W1D...10 C4
Batemans Rw SDTCH EC2A...7 H6
Bateman St SOHO/SHAV W1D...10 D4
Bates Crs CROY/NA CR0......211 G3
   STRHM/NOR SW16 ....179 H3
Bate St POP/IOD E14...........105 H6
Bathgate Rd WIM/MER SW19...159 G5
Bath Cl PECK SE15 ....143 K2
Bath House Rd CROY/NA CR0...195 K6
Bath Pas KUT/HW KT1........174 E5
Bath Pl BAR EN5 ....20 D4
   SDTCH EC2A 7 G5
Bath Rd CHSWK W4 ....118 B4
   DART DA1............................171 G1
   ED N9 ....36 D4
   FSTGT E7 ....89 H4
   HSLW TW3 ....135 G4
   HSLWW TW4 ....133 H4
   HYS/HAR UB3 ....113 G2
   WDR/YW UB7 ....112 B2
Bath St FSBYE EC1V 6 D5
Bath Ter STHWK SE1 ....18 C5
Bathurst Av WIM/MER SW19...178 A4
Bathurst Gdns WLSDN NW10...99 K2
Bathurst Ms BAY/PAD W2......8 B5
Bathurst Rd IL IG1 ....71 K5
Bathurst St BAY/PAD W2.......8 B5
Bathurst Wk
   IVER SL0 *..........................132 B5
Bathway WOOL/PLUM SE18...127 F4
Batley Cl MTCM CR4...........194 E4
Batley Pl STNW/STAM N16...86 B1
Batley Rd ENC/FH EN2..........23 J3
   STNW/STAM N16 ....86 B1
Batman Cl SHB W12............118 E1
Batoum Gdns HMSMTH W6...119 F3
Batson St SHB W12.............118 D2
Batsworth Rd MTCM CR4...178 D6
Batten Cl EHAM E6.............107 K5
Batten Cottages
   POP/IOD E14 * 105 J4
Batten St BTSEA SW11.......140 D4
Battenburg Wk NRWD SE19 *...181 F2
Battersby Rd CAT SE6........165 G4
Battersea Br BTSEA SW11...140 C5
Battersea Bridge Rd
   BTSEA SW11 *....................140 C5
Battersea Church Rd
   BTSEA SW11 ....140 C1
Battersea High St BTSEA SW11...140 C3
Battersea Park Rd
   BTSEA SW11 ....141 F2
Battersea Ri BTSEA SW11...140 D6
Battersea Sq BTSEA SW11 *...140 C1
Battery Rd THMD SE28 ......127 K2
Battishill St IS N1 ....85 H5
Battle Bridge La STHWK SE1...19 G1
Battle Bridge Rd CAMTN NW1...4 E3
Battledean Rd HBRY N5........85 H3
Battle Rd ERITH DA8...........130 A6
   BELV DA17 ....149 K1
Batty St WCHPL E1 ....104 C5
Baudwin Rd CAT SE6..........165 H4
Baugh Rd SCUP DA14........186 D1
The Baulk WAND/EARL SW18...159 K2

Bavant Rd STRHM/NOR SW16...179 K5
Bavaria Rd ARCH N19............66 E2
Bavdene Ms HDN NW4..........63 K1
Bavent Rd CMBW SE5.........142 D3
Bawdale Rd EDUL SE22......143 G6
Bawdsey Av GNTH/NBYPK IG2...73 F1
Bawtree Rd NWCR SE14......144 B1
Bawtry Rd TRDG/WHET N20...33 K5
Baxendale TRDG/WHET N20...33 G4
Baxendale St BETH E2..........104 C2
Baxter Cl NWDGN UB2.......115 H3
Baxter Rd CAN/RD E16 ....107 G5
   IL IG1 ....90 B3
   IS N1 ....85 K4
   UED N18 ....36 D5
Bay Ct EA W5 * 117 F3
Baycroft Cl PIN HA5 ....41 G5
Bayfield Rd ELTH/MOT SE9...146 C5
Bayford Ms HACK E8 * 86 D5
Bayford Rd WLSDN NW10...100 B3
Bayford St HACK E8...............86 D5
Bayham Pl CAMTN NW1 ....4 A1
Bayham Rd CHSWK W4 ....118 A3
   MRDN SM4 ....194 A1
   WEA W13 ....97 H6
Bayham St CAMTN NW1 ....4 A1
Bayhurst Dr NTHWD HA6.....40 D2
Bayleaf Cl HPTN TW12 ......173 J1
Bayley St FITZ W1T 10 C2
Baylin Rd WAND/EARL SW18...160 A1
Baylis Rd STHWK SE1 ....17 J4
Bayliss Av THMD SE28.......109 K6
Bayliss Cl ENC/FH EN2..........22 E6
Bayly Rd DART DA1............171 K1
Baynard Cl CMBW SE5 * 143 F1
Baynard Cl CMBW SE5 *.....143 F1
Baynes Ms HAMP NW3 *.......83 H4
Baynes St CAMTN NW1........84 C5
Baynham Cl BXLY DA5.......169 G1
Bayonne Rd HMSMTH W6...119 H6
Bays Cl SYD SE26 ....181 J5
Bayshill Ri NTHLT UB5..........78 B4
Bayston Rd STNW/STAM N16...86 B1
Bayswater Rd BAY/PAD W2...101 G6
Baythorne St BOW E3.........105 H4
Baytree Cl BFN/LL DA15.....168 A1
   BMLY BR1 ....184 C4
Baytree Rd BRXS/STRHM SW2...142 A4
Bazalgette Cl NWMAL KT3...191 K2
Bazalgette Gdns NWMAL KT3...192 A2
Bazely St POP/IOD E14.......106 A6
Bazile Rd WCHMH N21..........35 G1
Beacham Cl CHARL SE7......126 C6
Beachborough Rd BMLY BR1...165 F5
Beachcroft Rd WAN E11 ......88 C1
Beachcroft Wy ARCH N19.....66 D5
Beach Gv FELT TW13 ....155 J5
Beachy Rd BOW E3...............87 J5
Beacon Ga NWCR SE14......144 A4
Beacon Hl HOLWY N7..........84 E3
Beacon Pl CROY/NA CR0....210 E2
Beacon Rd ERITH DA8........150 E1
   HTHAIR TW6 ....152 D1
   LEW SE13 ....165 G1
Beaconsfield Cl
   BKHTH/KID SE3 ....125 K6
   BMLY BR1 ....184 C6
   BXLY DA5 ....170 B4
   CAN/RD E16 ....106 D5
   CHSWK W4 ....118 A3
   CROY/NA CR0 ....196 E3
   IS N1 ....85 J6
   ED N9 ....36 C6
   ELTH/MOT SE9 ....166 D6
   ESH/CLAY KT10 ....204 E5
   FBAR/BDGN N11 ....33 K5
   LEY E10 ....69 K5
   NWMAL KT3 ....176 A6
   SEVS/STOTM N15 ....68 A1
   SURB KT6 ....191 G5
   TWK TW1 ....156 C2
   WALW SE17 ....19 F8
   WLSDN NW10 ....81 H6
   YEAD UB4 ....114 B2
Beaconsfield Terrace Rd
   WKENS W14 ....119 H3
Beaconsfield Wk
   FUL/PGN SW6...................139 J2
Beacontree Av WALTH E17...52 B4
Beacontree Rd WAN E11 ......70 D5
Beadlow Cl CAR SM5..........194 C3
Beadman Pl WNWD SE27 *...162 C6
Beadman St WNWD SE27...162 C6
Beadnell Rd FSTH SE23......164 A3
Beadon Rd HAYES BR2.......199 K1
   HMSMTH W6 ....119 F4
Beaford Gv RYNPK SW20...177 H6
Beagle Cl FELT TW13..........154 A6
Beagles Cl STMC/STPC BR5...202 E6
Beak St REGST W1B 10 B5
Beal Cl WELL DA16.............148 B2
Beale Cl PLMGR N13............49 H1
Beale Pl BOW E3...................105 H1
Beale Rd BOW E3..................87 H6
Beam Av DAGE RM10...........92 D6
Beaminster Gdns BARK/HLT IG6...54 B6
Beamish Dr BUSH WD23.......28 C3
Beamish Rd ED N9................36 C3
Beanacre Cl HOM E9.............87 H4
Bean Rd BXLYHS DA6.........148 E5
Beanshaw ELTH/MOT SE9...167 F6
Beansland Gv CHDH RM6......56 A2
Bear Cl ROMW/RG RM7........74 D4
Beardell St NRWD SE19......181 G2
Beardow Gv STHGT/OAK N14 *...34 C1
Beard Rd KUTN/CMB KT2...175 G1

Beardsfield PLSTW E13...88 E6
Beard's Hl HPTN TW12...173 F4
Beard's Hill Cl HPTN TW12...173 F4
Beardsley Wy ACT W3...118 A2
Bearfield Rd KUTN/CMB KT2...175 F5
Bear Gdns STHWK SE1...12 C7
Bear La STHWK SE1...12 B7
Bear Rd FELT TW13...154 C4
Bearstead Ri BROCKY SE4...164 C1
Bearstead Ter BECK BR3 *...182 D4
Bear St LSQ/SEVD WC2H...10 D5
Beatrice Av STRHM/NOR SW16...180 A4
  WBLY HA9...80 A3
Beatrice Cl PIN HA5...58 E1
  PLSTW E13...106 E3
Beatrice Pl KENS W8...120 A3
Beatrice Rd ED N9...36 E1
  FSBYPK N4...67 G4
  RCHPK/HAM TW10...137 G6
  STHL UB1...114 E1
  STHWK SE1...19 J5
  WALTH E17...77 J5
Beattie Cl EBED/NFELT TW14...153 J3
Beattock Ri MUSWH N10...66 B1
Beatty Rd STAN HA7...43 J2
  STNW/STAM N16...86 A2
Beatty St CAMTN NW1 *...4 G4
Beattyville Gdns CLAY IG5...54 A6
Beauchamp Pl CHEL SW3...14 D6
  E/WMO/HCT KT8...173 J1
  FSTGT E7...89 F5
  NRWD SE19...180 E4
  SUT SM1...208 E3
  TWK TW1...156 B2
Beauchamp St HCIRC EC1N...11 J2
Beauchamp Ter BARN SW13 *...138 C4
Beauclerc Rd HMSMTH W6...118 E3
Beauclerk Cl FELT TW13...154 A3
Beaufort EHAM E6...108 A4
Beaufort Av
  KTN/HRWW/WS HA3...61 G1
Beaufort Cl EA W5...98 B4
  PUT/ROE SW15...159 F3
  ROMW/RG RM7...74 E1
Beaufort Ct
  RCHPK/HAM TW10...156 C6
Beaufort Dr GLDGN NW11...64 E1
Beaufort Gdns CHEL SW3...14 D5
  HDN NW4...64 B3
  HEST TW5...134 D2
  IL IG1...72 A5
  STRHM/NOR SW16...180 A3
Beaufort Rd EA W5...98 B4
  KUT/HW KT1...175 F6
  RCHPK/HAM TW10...156 C6
  RSLP HA4...58 B6
  TWK TW1...156 D2
Beaufort St CHEL SW3...120 C6
Beaufort Wy EW KT17...207 J5
Beaufoy Rd TOTM N17...50 B5
Beaufoy Wk LBTH SE11...17 H7
Beaulieu Av CAN/RD E16...126 A1
  SYD SE26...163 J6
Beaulieu Cl CDALE/KGS NW9...63 G3
  CMBW SE5...142 E4
  HSLWW TW4...134 E6
  MTCM CR4...179 F4
  OXHEY WD19...27 G3
  TWK TW1...156 E1
Beaulieu Dr PIN HA5...59 H3
Beaulieu Gdns WCHMH N21...35 J2
Beaulieu Pl CHSWK W4...117 K3
Beauly Wy ROM RM1...57 G4
Beaumaris Gn
  CDALE/KGS NW9...63 G3
Beaumont Av ALP/SUD HA0...79 J3
  RCH/KEW TW9...137 G4
  RYLN/HDSTN HA2...60 B5
  WKENS W14...119 J5
Beaumont Cl KUTN/CMB KT2...175 H3
Beaumont Ct ALP/SUD HA0...79 J3
Beaumont Crs RAIN RM13...93 J4
  WKENS W14...119 J5
Beaumont Gdns HAMP NW3...64 E6
Beaumont Gv WCHPL E1...105 F3
Beaumont Ms MHST W1U *...9 J1
  PIN HA5...41 J6
Beaumont Pl BAR EN5...20 D2
  FITZ W1T...4 B6
  ISLW TW7...136 A6
Beaumont Ri ARCH N19...66 E5
Beaumont Rd CHSWK W4...117 K3
  LEY E10...70 A4
  NRWD SE19...180 D6
  PLSTW E13...107 G2
  STMC/STPC BR5...201 J3
  WIM/MER SW19...159 H2
Beaumont Sq WCHPL E1...105 F4
Beaumont St CAVSQ/HST W1G...9 H1
Beaumont Ter LEW SE13 *...165 H2
Beaumont Wk HAMP NW3...83 K5
Beauvais Ter NTHLT UB5...95 H2
Beauval Rd EDUL SE22...163 G1
Beaverbank Rd
  ELTH/MOT SE9...167 J3
Beaver Cl HPTN TW12...173 G4
  MRDN SM4...193 F4
  PGE/AN SE20 *...181 H3
Beaver Rd BARK/HLT IG6...55 J1
Beavers Crs HSLWW TW4...134 B4
Beavers La HSLWW TW4...134 B4
Beaverwood Rd CHST BR7...185 K1
Beavor La HMSMTH W6...118 D5
Bebbington Rd
  WOOL/PLUM SE18 *...127 K4
Beblets Cl ORP BR6...217 F3
Beccles Dr BARK IG11...91 F4
Beccles St POP/IOD E14...105 H5
Bec Cl RSLP HA4...77 H1
Beck Cl LEW SE13...145 F5
Beckenham Gdns ED N9...36 A5
Beckenham Gv HAYES BR2...183 G5
Beckenham Hill Rd BECK BR3...182 E2
Beckenham La HAYES BR2...183 H5

Beckenham Place Pk
  BECK BR3...182 E3
Beckenham Rd BECK BR3...182 A4
  BECK BR3...198 E4
Becket Av EHAM E6...108 A2
Becket Cl SNWD SE25...197 H3
  WIM/MER SW19 *...178 A4
Becket Fold HRW HA1 *...61 F2
Becket Rd UED N18...36 E6
Becket St STHWK SE1...18 E4
Beckett Cl BELV DA17...129 F3
  STRHM/NOR SW16...161 J4
  WLSDN NW10...81 F4
Becketts Cl EBED/NFELT TW14...154 A1
  ORP BR6...217 F1
Becketts Pl KUT/HW KT1...174 E5
Beckett Wk BECK BR3...182 B2
Beckford Cl WKENS W14...119 J4
Beckford Dr STMC/STPC BR5...201 J4
Beckford Pl WALW SE17 *...122 D5
Beckford Rd CROY/NA CR0 *...197 G3
Beck La BECK BR3...182 A6
Becklow Rd SHB W12...118 D2
Beck River Pk BECK BR3...182 C4
Beck Rd HACK E8...86 D6
Beckton Park Rd EHAM E6...108 A4
Beckton Rd CAN/RD E16...106 D4
Beck Wy BECK BR3...182 C6
Beckway Rd
  STRHM/NOR SW16...179 J5
Beckway St WALW SE17...19 G7
Beckwith Rd HNHL SE24...162 E1
Beclands Rd TOOT SW17...179 F2
Becmead Av
  KTN/HRWW/WS HA3...61 H2
  STRHM/NOR SW16...161 J6
Becondale Rd NRWD SE19...181 F1
Becontree Av BCTR RM8...91 H2
Bective Pl PUT/ROE SW15...139 J5
Becton Pl ERITH DA8...149 J2
Bedale Rd ENC/FH EN2...23 J1
Bedale St STHWK SE1...18 E1
Beddington Cross
  CROY/NA CR0...195 K4
Beddington Farm Rd
  CROY/NA CR0...195 K6
Beddington Gdns CAR SM5...210 A4
Beddington Gn
  STMC/STPC BR5...186 A6
Beddington Gv WLGTN SM6...210 D3
Beddington La CROY/NA CR0...195 F4
Beddington Rd GDMY/SEVK IG3...73 F4
  STMC/STPC BR5...185 K4
Beddington Ter
  CROY/NA CR0 *...196 A6
Bede Cl PIN HA5...41 H4
Bedens Rd SCUP DA14...187 F2
Bede Rd CHDH RM6...73 J3
Bedevere Rd ED N9...36 C5
Bedfont Cl
  EBED/NFELT TW14...153 J2
Bedfont Gn
  EBED/NFELT TW14...153 J3
Bedfont La
  EBED/NFELT TW14...153 J2
  STWL/WRAY TW19...152 C1
Bedford Av BAR EN5...20 D6
  RSQ WC1B...10 D2
  YEAD UB4...95 F5
Bedfordbury CHCR WC2N...10 D5
Bedford Cl CHSWK W4...138 C1
  MUSWH N10...48 A3
Bedford Cnr CHSWK W4 *...118 B4
Bedford Gdns KENS W8...119 K1
Bedford Hl BAL SW12...161 F4
Bedford Pk CROY/NA CR0...196 D5
Bedford Pl CROY/NA CR0...196 E5
  RSQ WC1B...10 E1
Bedford Rd BFN/LL DA15...167 K5
  CEND/HSY/T N8...66 E3
  CHSWK W4...118 A3
  CLAP SW4...141 K5
  DART DA1...171 K2
  ED N9...36 D2
  EFNCH N2...47 J6
  EHAM E6...108 A6
  HRW HA1...60 C3
  IL IG1...90 B1
  MLHL NW7...31 G4
  MUSWH N10...48 A3
  NTHWD HA6...26 B6
  ORP BR6...202 A6
  RSLP HA4...76 D2
  SEVS/STOTM N15...67 K1
  SWFD E18...52 E5
  WALTH E17...51 J5
  WDGN N22...48 D4
  WEA W13...116 C1
  WHTN TW2...155 J5
  WPK KT4...193 G6
Bedford Rw GINN WC1R...11 H1
Bedford Sq RSQ WC1B...10 D2
Bedford St COVGDN WC2E...10 E5
Bedford Vls KUT/HW KT1...175 G5
Bedford Wy STPAN WC1H...4 D7
Bedgebury Gdns
  WIM/MER SW19...159 H4
Bedgebury Rd ELTH/MOT SE9...146 C5
Bedivere Rd BMLY BR1...165 K5
Bedlow Wy CROY/NA CR0...211 F2
Bedonwell Rd BELV DA17...129 G6
  BXLYHN DA7...149 G2
Bedser Cl LBTH SE11...122 A6
  THHTH CR7...180 D6
Bedser Dr GFD/PVL UB6...78 D3
Bedster Gdns
  E/WMO/HCT KT8...173 G5
Bedwardine Rd NRWD SE19...181 F3
Bedwell Gdns HYS/HAR UB3...113 H5
Bedwell Rd BELV DA17...129 H5
  TOTM N17...50 A4
Beeby Rd CAN/RD E16...107 F4
Beech Av BARN SW13...138 A3
  BFN/LL DA15...168 B2
  BKHH IG9...39 F4

BTFD TW8...136 C1
  FNCH N3...59 F5
  TRDG/WHET N20...33 J1
Beech Cl CAR SM5...194 E6
  DEPT SE8...124 C6
  EBAR EN4...21 K3
  HCH RM12...93 K1
  PUT/ROE SW15...158 D2
  SUN TW16...172 C5
  WDR/YW UB7...112 D3
  WFD IG8 *...53 H2
Beech Copse BMLY BR1...184 E5
  SAND/SEL CR2...212 A5
Beech Ct ELTH/MOT SE9...166 D1
Beechcroft CHST BR7...185 F5
Beechcroft Av BXLYHN DA7...150 A1
  GLDGN NW11...64 D4
  NWMAL KT3...175 K4
  RKW/CH/CXG WD3...26 A1
  RYLN/HDSTN HA2...60 A4
  STHL UB1...114 E1
Beechcroft Cl HEST TW5...134 D1
  ORP BR6...216 D2
  STRHM/NOR SW16 *...180 A1
Beechcroft Gdns WBLY HA9...80 B1
Beechcroft Rd CHSGTN KT9...206 B2
  MORT/ESHN SW14 *...137 K4
  ORP BR6...216 D2
  TOOT SW17...160 D5
Beechdale WCHMH N21...35 F4
Beechdale Rd BRXS/STRHM SW2...162 A1
Beech Dr EFNCH N2...47 K6
  TRDG/WHET N20...33 K1
Beechengrove PIN HA5...41 K6
Beechen Pl FSTH SE23...163 K4
Beeches Av CAR SM5...209 J5
Beeches Cl PGE/AN SE20...181 K4
  SAND/SEL CR2 *...212 A5
Beeches Rd CHEAM SM3...193 H5
  TOOT SW17...160 E5
The Beeches CHING E4 *...38 B3
  HNWL W7 *...116 A2
Beeches Wk BELMT SM2...209 H6
Beechfield Cl
  ROMW/RG RM7...74 E4
Beechfield Gdns
  ROMW/RG RM7...74 E4
Beechfield Rd BMLY BR1...184 B5
  CAT SE6...164 C3
  ERITH DA8...150 B1
  FSBYPK N4...67 J3
Beech Gdns DAGE RM10...110 D1
  EA W5...117 F2
Beech Gv BARK/HLT IG6...54 E2
  MTCM CR4...195 J2
Beech Hall Crs CHING E4...52 B3
Beech Hall Rd CHING E4...52 A3
Beech Hl EBAR EN4...21 H1
Beech Hill Av EBAR EN4...21 H1
Beech Holt LEW SE13...145 G5
Beech House Rd
  CROY/NA CR0...211 K1
Beech Lawns
  NFNCH/WDSPK N12 *...47 H1
Beechmont Cl BMLY BR1...165 H6
Beechmore Gdns CHEAM SM3...193 G6
Beechmore Rd BTSEA SW11...140 E2
Beechmount Av HNWL W7...96 D4
Beecholme Av MTCM CR4...179 G4
Beecholme Est CLPT E5 *...86 E1
Beech Rd DART DA1...171 H5
  EBED/NFELT TW14...153 H2
  FBAR/BDGN N11...48 E2
  ORP BR6...217 G5
  STMC/STPC BR5...186 D6
Beechrow KUTN/CMB KT2...157 H4
Beech St ROMW/RG RM7...74 E1
Beech St (Below) BARB EC2Y...12 C1
Beech Tree Cl IS N1...85 G5
  STAN HA7...43 J1
Beech Tree Gld CHING E4...38 D3
Beech Tree Pl SUT SM1 *...209 F3
Beechvale Cl
  NFNCH/WDSPK N12...47 J1
Beech Wk DART DA1...150 D5
  MLHL NW7...45 J1
Beechway BXLY DA5...168 E1
Beech Wy WHTN TW2...155 F5
  WLSDN NW10...81 F5
Beechwood Av FNCH N3...46 D6
  GFD/PVL UB6...96 B2
  HYS/HAR UB3...113 G5
  ORP BR6...216 E4
  RCH/KEW TW9...137 H2
  RSLP HA4...58 D6
  RYLN/HDSTN HA2...78 B1
  THHTH CR7...196 C1
  WEA W13...116 C1
Beechwood Circle
  RYLN/HDSTN HA2...78 B1
Beechwood Cl
  CDALE/KGS NW9...45 F6
  SURB KT6...190 D4
Beechwood Crs BXLYHN DA7...148 E4
Beechwood Dr HAYES BR2...200 D2
  WFD IG8...52 D1
Beechwood Gdns CLAY IG5...71 K2
  RAIN RM13...111 K4
  RYLN/HDSTN HA2...78 B1
Beechwood Gv ACT W3...99 G6
  SURB KT6...190 D4
Beechwood Ms ED N9...36 C4
Beechwood Pk SWFD E18...52 E6
Beechwood Ri CHST BR7...167 G6
Beechwood Rd
  CEND/HSY/T N8...66 D1
  HACK E8...86 B4
  SAND/SEL CR2...212 A6
Beechworth Cl HAMP NW3...64 E6
Beecot La WOT/HER KT12...188 B6
Beecroft La BROCKY SE4...144 B6
Beecroft Ms BROCKY SE4...144 B6
Beecroft Rd BROCKY SE4...144 B6
Beehive Cl BORE WD6...29 K1
  HACK E8...86 B5
Beehive La REDBR IG4...71 K2
Beehive Pl BRXN/ST SW9...142 B4
Beeken Dene ORP BR6...216 C2
Beeleigh Rd MRDN SM4...194 A1
Beeston Cl HACK E8...86 C3

OXHEY WD19...27 H6
Beeston Pl BGVA SW1W...15 K5
Beeston Rd EBAR EN4...33 H1
Beeston Wy
  EBED/NFELT TW14...154 B1
Beethoven Rd BORE WD6...29 J6
Beethoven St NKENS W10...100 C2
Beeton Cl PIN HA5...42 A3
Begbie Rd BKHTH/KID SE3...146 B2
Beggar's Roost La SUT SM1...208 E4
Begonia Cl EHAM E6...107 J4
Begonia Pl HPTN TW12...173 F2
Beira St BAL SW12...161 G2
Bekesbourne St
  POP/IOD E14 *...105 G5
Belcroft Cl BMLY BR1...183 J3
Beldham Gdns
  E/WMO/HCT KT8...173 G6
Belfairs Dr CHDH RM6...73 J4
Belfairs Gn OXHEY WD19...41 H1
Belfast Rd SNWD SE25...197 J1
  STNW/STAM N16...68 B5
Belfield Rd HOR/WEW KT19...207 F6
Belfont Wk HOLWY N7...84 E2
Belford Gv WOOL/PLUM SE18...127 F4
Belfort Rd PECK SE15...143 K3
Belfry Cl BERM/RHTH SE16...123 J5
  BMLY BR1...185 F3
Belgrade Rd HPTN TW12...173 G4
  STNW/STAM N16...86 A2
Belgrave Cl ACT W3...117 J2
  MLHL NW7...45 F1
  STHGT/OAK N14...22 C6
  STMC/STPC BR5...202 D1
Belgrave Crs SUN TW16...172 A4
Belgrave Gdns STAN HA7...43 J1
  STHGT/OAK N14...14 A4
  STJWD NW8...83 G6
Belgrave Ms South KTBR SW1X...15 G4
Belgrave Ms West KTBR SW1X...15 G4
Belgrave Pl KTBR SW1X...15 H5
Belgrave Rd BARN SW13...138 C1
  HSLWW TW4...134 D3
  IL IG1...71 K5
  MTCM CR4...178 C2
  PIM SW1V...16 A7
  PLSTW E13...107 G3
  SNWD SE25...197 G1
  SUN TW16...172 A4
  WALTH E17...69 J3
Belgrave Sq KTBR SW1X...15 G4
Belgrave St WCHPL E1...105 F5
Belgrave Ter WFD IG8 *...39 E5
Belgrave Wk MTCM CR4...178 C6
Belgravia Cl BAR EN5...20 D4
Belgravia Gdns BMLY BR1...183 H3
Belgravia Ms KUT/HW KT1...190 E1
Belgrove St CAMTN NW1...4 E4
Belinda Rd BRXN/ST SW9...142 C4
Belitha Vls IS N1...85 G5
Bellamy Cl E14...124 D1
  KTN/HRWW/WS HA3...42 D2
  WDR/YW UB7...112 C3
Bellamy Dr STAN HA7...43 H4
Bellamy Rd CHING E4...51 K2
  ENC/FH EN2 *...23 K3
Bellamy St BAL SW12...161 G2
Bel La FELT TW13...154 D5
Bellarmine Cl THMD SE28...128 A1
Bellasis Av BRXS/STRHM SW2...161 K4
Bell Av HARH RM3...57 K4
  WDR/YW UB7...112 C3
Bell Cl PIN HA5...41 G6
Bellclose Rd WDR/YW UB7...112 B2
Bell Dr WAND/EARL SW18...159 H2
Bellefields Rd BRXN/ST SW9...142 A4
Bellegrove Cl WELL DA16...148 A3
Bellegrove Rd WELL DA16...147 K3
Bellenden Rd PECK SE15...143 G3
Belle Staines Pleasuance
  CHING E4...37 J4
Belleville Rd BTSEA SW11...140 E6
Belle Vue GFD/PVL UB6...78 D6
Belle Vue La BUSH WD23...28 D2
Bellevue Pk THHTH CR7...180 D6
Bellevue Pl WCHPL E1 *...104 E3
Belle Vue Rd CRW RM5...56 E2
  HDN NW4...64 B1
  WALTH E17...52 B5
Bellevue Rd BARN SW13...138 D3
  BXLYHS DA6...149 G6
  FBAR/BDGN N11...34 A6
  KUT/HW KT1...175 F6
  TOOT SW17...160 E2
  WEA W13...97 H5
Bellew St TOOT SW17...160 B5
Bell Farm Av DAGE RM10...92 E1
Bellfield CROY/NA CR0...213 G6
Bellfield Av
  KTN/HRWW/WS HA3...42 D2
Bellflower Cl EHAM E6...107 J4
Bell Gdns STMC/STPC BR5...202 D1
  WALTH E17 *...69 J1
Bellgate Ms KTTN NW5...84 B2
Bell Gn SYD SE26...164 C3
Bell Green La SYD SE26...182 C1
Bell Hill CROY/NA CR0...211 J1
Bell House Rd ROMW/RG RM7...74 E5
Bellina Ms KTTN NW5...84 B2
Bellingham Gn CAT SE6...164 D5
Bellingham Rd CAT SE6...165 F5
Bell La CAN/RD E16...125 J1
  HDN NW4...46 B6
  PEND EN3...25 F1
  TWK TW1...156 B3
  WBLY HA9 *...61 K6
  WCHPL E1...13 J2
Bell Meadow NRWD SE19...181 F4
Bello Cl HNHL SE24...162 C5
Bellot St GNWCH SE10...125 H5
Bell Pde HSLW TW3 *...135 G5
  WWKM BR4 *...199 F6
Bellring Cl BELV DA17...129 H6
Bell Rd E/WMO/HCT KT8...189 J2
  EN EN1...23 K3
  HSLW TW3...135 G5

Bells Hl BAR EN5...20 B6
Bell St BAY/PAD W2...8 C1
  WOOL/PLUM SE18...146 D2
Belltrees Gv
  STRHM/NOR SW16...180 A1
Bell Water Ga
  WOOL/PLUM SE18...127 F3
Bell Wharf La CANST EC4R...12 D6
Bellwood Rd PECK SE15...144 A5
Bell Yd LINN WC2A...11 J4
Bell Yard Ms STHWK SE1...19 H3
Belmont Av ALP/SUD HA0...80 B6
  EBAR EN4...21 K6
  ED N9...36 C3
  NWDGN UB2...114 D3
  NWMAL KT3...192 D2
  PLMGR N13...48 E1
  TOTM N17...49 J6
  WELL DA16...147 K3
Belmont Cir
  KTN/HRWW/WS HA3 *...43 H4
Belmont Cl CHING E4...52 B1
  CLAP SW4...141 H4
  EBAR EN4...21 K5
  TRDG/WHET N20...33 F3
  WFD IG8 *...39 F3
Belmont Gv CHSWK W4...118 A4
  LEW SE13...145 G4
Belmont Hl LEW SE13...145 G4
Belmont La CHST BR7...185 H1
  STAN HA7...43 J4
Belmont Pde CHST BR7 *...185 G1
  GLDGN NW11 *...64 D2
Belmont Pk LEW SE13...145 H5
Belmont Park Cl LEW SE13...145 H5
Belmont Park Rd LEY E10...69 K3
Belmont Rd BECK BR3...182 B5
  CHST BR7...185 G1
  CLAP SW4...141 H4
  ERITH DA8...149 J1
  IL IG1...90 C1
  KTN/HRWW/WS HA3...43 F6
  SEVS/STOTM N15...67 H1
  SNWD SE25...197 J2
  WHTN TW2...155 J4
  WLGTN SM6...210 C3
Belmont St CAMTN NW1...84 A5
Belmont Ter CHSWK W4...118 A4
Belmore Av YEAD UB4...95 F5
Belmore La HOLWY N7...84 D3
Belmore St VX/NE SW8...141 J2
Beloe Cl PUT/ROE SW15...138 D5
Belsham St HOM E9...86 E4
Belsize Av HAMP NW3...83 J3
  PLMGR N13...48 E3
  WEA W13...116 C3
Belsize Court Gdns HAMP NW3 *...83 H3
Belsize Crs HAMP NW3...83 H3
Belsize Gdns SUT SM1...209 F2
Belsize Gv HAMP NW3...83 J4
Belsize La HAMP NW3...83 H4
Belsize Ms HAMP NW3 *...83 H4
Belsize Pk HAMP NW3...83 H4
Belsize Park Gdns HAMP NW3...83 H4
Belsize Park Ms HAMP NW3 *...83 H4
Belsize Pl HAMP NW3 *...83 H4
Belsize Rd KIL/WHAMP NW6...83 G6
  KTN/HRWW/WS HA3...42 D3
Belsize Sq HAMP NW3...83 H4
Belsize Ter HAMP NW3...83 H4
Belson Rd WOOL/PLUM SE18...126 E4
Beltane Dr WIM/MER SW19...159 G5
Belthorn Crs BAL SW12...161 H2
Belton Rd FSTGT E7...89 F5
  SCUP DA14...168 B6
  TOTM N17...50 B6
  WAN E11...88 C1
  WLSDN NW10...81 H1
Belton Wy BOW E3...105 J4
Beltran Rd FUL/PGN SW6...140 A3
Beltwood Rd BELV DA17...129 K4
Belvedere Av BARK/HLT IG6...54 B5
  WIM/MER SW19...177 H1
Belvedere Buildings
  STHWK SE1...18 B3
Belvedere Cl ESH/CLAY KT10...204 B3
  TEDD TW11...173 K1
Belvedere Ct BELV DA17...129 G3
  OXHEY WD19 *...27 J1
Belvedere Dr WIM/MER SW19...177 H1
Belvedere Gv WIM/MER SW19...177 H1
Belvedere Ms PECK SE15...143 K4
Belvedere Pl
  BRXS/STRHM SW2...142 A5
Belvedere Rd ABYW SE2...128 E1
  BXLYHN DA7...149 G4
  HNWL W7...115 K3
  LEY E10...69 G5
  - NRWD SE19...181 G3
  STHWK SE1...17 G2
Belvedere Sq WIM/MER SW19...177 H1
Belvedere Strd
  CDALE/KGS NW9...45 H1
The Belvedere WBPTN SW10 *...140 B2
Belvedere Wy
  KTN/HRWW/WS HA3...62 A3
Belvoir Rd EDUL SE22...163 H2
Belvue Cl NTHLT UB5...78 A5
Belvue Rd NTHLT UB5...78 A5
Bembridge Cl KIL/WHAMP NW6...82 C5
Bembridge Gdns RSLP HA4...58 B6
Bemerton St IS N1...84 E1
Bemish Rd PUT/ROE SW15...139 G4
Bempton Dr RSLP HA4...77 F1
Bemsted Rd WALTH E17...51 H6
Benares Rd WOOL/PLUM SE18...128 A4
Benbow Rd HMSMTH W6...118 E3
Benbow St DEPT SE8...124 D6
Benbury Cl BMLY BR1...183 F1
Bench Fld SAND/SEL CR2...212 B4
The Bench
  RCHPK/HAM TW10 *...156 D5
Bencroft Rd
  STRHM/NOR SW16...179 H3

Bencurtis Pk WWKM BR4 214 B1
Bendall Ms CAMTN NW1 8 D1
Bendemeer Rd
PUT/ROE SW15 139 G4
Bendish Rd EHAM E6 89 J5
Bendmore Av ABYW SE2 128 B5
Bendon Va WAND/EARL SW18 160 A2
Benedict Cl ORP BR6 216 E1
Benedict Dr
EBED/NFELT TW14 153 G2
Benedict Rd BRXN/ST SW9 142 A4
MTCM CR4 178 C6
Benedict Wy EFNCH N2 * 47 G6
Benedict Whf MTCM CR4 178 D6
Benenden Gn HAYES BR2 199 K2
Benett Gdns
STRHM/NOR SW16 179 K5
Benfleet Cl SUT SM1 209 G1
Benfleet Wy FBAR/BDGN N11 34 A4
Bengal Rd IL IG1 90 B2
Bengarth Dr
KTN/HRWW/WS HA3 42 D5
Bengarth Rd NTHLT UB5 77 H6
Bengeworth Rd CMBW SE5 142 D4
HRW HA1 61 G6
Ben Hale Cl STAN HA7 43 G1
Benham Cl CHSGTN KT9 205 J4
Benham Gdns HSLWW TW4 134 E6
Benham Rd HNWL W7 96 E4
Benhill Av SUT SM1 209 G2
Benhill Rd CMBW SE5 142 E1
SUT SM1 209 H1
Benhill Wood Rd SUT SM1 209 G2
Benhilton Gdns SUT SM1 209 F1
Benhurst Av HCH RM12 93 K2
Benhurst La
STRHM/NOR SW16 180 B1
Benin St LEW SE13 165 G2
Benjafield Cl UED N18 36 D6
Benjamin Cl EMPK RM11 75 J3
HACK E8 86 C6
Benjamin Ms BAL SW12 161 H2
Benjamin St FARR EC1M 12 A1
Ben Jonson Rd WCHPL E1 105 G4
Benledi St POP/IOD E14 106 B5
Bennelong Cl SHB W12 99 K6
Bennerley Rd BTSEA SW11 140 E6
Bennet Cl KUT/HW KT1 174 D4
Bennetsfield Rd STKPK UB11 112 E1
Bennet's Hl BLKFR EC4V 12 B5
Bennett Cl HSLWW TW4 134 D6
NTHWD HA6 40 D3
WELL DA16 148 B3
Bennett Gv LEW SE13 144 E2
Bennett Pk BKHTH/KID SE3 145 J4
Bennett Rd BRXN/ST SW9 142 B3
CHDH RM6 74 A3
PLSTW E13 107 G3
Bennetts Av CROY/NA CR0 198 B6
GFD/PVL UB6 78 E6
Bennett's Castle La BCTR RM8 91 J2
Bennetts Cl MTCM CR4 179 G4
TOTM N17 50 B2
Bennetts Copse CHST BR7 184 D2
Bennett St CHSWK W4 118 B6
WHALL SW1A 10 A7
Bennetts Wy CROY/NA CR0 198 B6
Benningholme Rd EDGW HA8 45 G2
Bennington Rd TOTM N17 50 A4
WFD IG8 * 52 C3
Benn St HOM E9 87 G4
Benrek Cl BARK/HLT IG6 54 C3
Bensbury Cl PUT/ROE SW15 158 E2
Bensham Cl THHTH CR7 196 D1
Bensham Gv THHTH CR7 180 D5
Bensham La THHTH CR7 196 C1
Bensham Manor Rd
THHTH CR7 196 E2
Bensley Cl FBAR/BDGN N11 47 K1
Ben Smith Wy
BERM/RHTH SE16 123 H3
Benson Av PLSTW E13 107 G1
Benson Cl HSLW TW3 135 F5
Benson Quay WAP E1W 104 E6
Benson Rd CROY/NA CR0 211 G1
FSTH SE23 163 K3
Benthal Rd STNW/STAM N16 68 B6
Bentham Rd HOM E9 87 F4
THMD SE28 128 C1
Ben Tillet Cl BARK IG11 91 G5
CAN/RD E16 * 126 E1
Bentinck Ms MHST W1U 9 H3
Bentinck Rd WDR/YW UB7 112 A1
Bentinck St MHST W1U 9 H3
Bentley Cl WIM/MER SW19 159 K6
Bentley Dr CRICK NW2 82 D1
GNTH/NBYPK IG2 72 C3
Bentley Ms EN EN1 35 K1
Bentley Rd IS N1 86 A4
Bentley Wy STAN HA7 43 G1
WFD IG8 38 E5
Benton Rd IL IG1 72 D5
OXHEY WD19 41 H1
Benton's La WNWD SE27 162 D6
Benton's Ri WNWD SE27 180 E1
Bentry Cl BCTR RM8 74 A6
Bentry Rd BCTR RM8 74 A6
Bentworth Rd SHB W12 99 K5
Benwell Rd HOLWY N7 85 G2
Benwick Cl BERM/RHTH SE16 123 J4
Benwood Ct SUT SM1 209 G1
Benworth St BOW E3 105 H2
Benyon Rd IS N1 85 K6
Benyon Whf IS N1 86 A6
Berberis Wk WDR/YW UB7 112 B4
Berber Pde
WOOL/PLUM SE18 * 146 D1
Berber Rd BTSEA SW11 * 140 E6
Bercta Rd ELTH/MOT SE9 167 H4
Berenger Wk WBPTN SW10 * 140 C1
Berens Rd STMC/STPC BR5 202 D2
WLSDN NW10 100 B2
Berens Wy CHST BR7 202 A1
Beresford Av ALP/SUD HA0 80 C6
BRYLDS KT5 191 J5
HNWL W7 96 D4
TRDG/WHET N20 33 K4
TWK TW1 156 D1
Beresford Dr BMLY BR1 184 D6
WFD IG8 39 G6
Beresford Gdns CHDH RM6 74 A2
EN EN1 24 A5
HSLWW TW4 134 E6
Beresford Rd BELMT SM2 208 D5
CEND/HSY/T N8 67 G2
CHING E4 38 C3
EFNCH N2 47 J6
HBRY N5 85 K3
HRW HA1 60 D2
KUTN/CMB KT2 175 G4
NWMAL KT3 191 K1
STHL UB1 114 C1
WALTH E17 51 K4
Beresford Sq
WOOL/PLUM SE18 127 G4
Beresford St
WOOL/PLUM SE18 127 H3
Beresford Ter HBRY N5 85 J3
Berestede Rd HMSMTH W6 118 C5
Bere St WAP E1W 105 F6
Berger Cl STMC/STPC BR5 201 J3
Berger Rd HOM E9 87 F4
Berghem Ms WKENS W14 119 G3
Bergholt Av REDBR IG4 71 J2
Bergholt Crs STNW/STAM N16 68 A4
Bergholt Ms CAMTN NW1 84 C5
Bering Sq POP/IOD E14 124 D5
Bering Wk CAN/RD E16 107 H5
Berisford Ms
WAND/EARL SW18 160 B1
Berkeley Av BXLYHN DA7 148 E2
CLAY IG5 54 A5
CRW RM5 56 E3
GFD/PVL UB6 78 E4
HSLWW TW4 133 K2
Berkeley Cl KUTN/CMB KT2 175 F3
RSLP HA4 76 E1
STMC/STPC BR5 201 K4
Berkeley Ct WLGTN SM6 210 C1
Berkeley Crs DART DA1 171 J3
EBAR EN4 21 H6
Berkeley Dr E/WMO/HCT KT8 172 E6
Berkeley Gdns ESH/CLAY KT10 205 G5
KENS W8 119 K1
WCHMH N21 35 K2
Berkeley Ms MBLAR W1H 9 F3
SUN TW16 172 B6
Berkeley Pl WIM/MER SW19 177 G2
Berkeley Rd BARN SW13 138 D2
CDALE/KGS NW9 62 C1
CEND/HSY/T N8 66 D2
HGDN/ICK UB10 76 A5
MNPK E12 89 J3
SEVS/STOTM N15 67 K3
Berkeley Sq MYFR/PICC W1J 9 K6
The Berkeleys SNWD SE25 * 197 H1
Berkeley St MYFR/PICC W1J 9 K6
Berkeley Waye HEST TW5 134 D1
Berkhampstead Rd
BELV DA17 129 H5
Berkhamsted Av WBLY HA9 80 B4
Berkley Cl WHTN TW2 * 155 K5
Berkley Rd CAMTN NW1 83 K5
Berkshire Gdns PLMGR N13 49 G2
UED N18 50 D1
Berkshire Rd HOM E9 87 H4
Berkshire Wy MTCM CR4 195 K1
Bermans Wy WLSDN NW10 81 H2
Bermondsey St STHWK SE1 19 G1
Bermondsey Wall East
BERM/RHTH SE16 123 J2
Bermondsey Wall West
STHWK SE1 123 H2
Bernal Cl THMD SE28 109 K6
Bernard Ashley Dr CHARL SE7 126 A5
Bernard Av WEA W13 116 C3
Bernard Cassidy St
CAN/RD E16 106 D4
Bernard Gdns WIM/MER SW19 177 J1
Bernard Rd ROMW/RG RM7 74 E4
SEVS/STOTM N15 68 B2
WLGTN SM6 210 B3
Bernards Cl BARK/HLT IG6 54 C3
Bernard St BMSBY WC1N 4 E7
Bernays Cl STAN HA7 43 J2
Bernay's Gv BRXN/ST SW9 142 A5
Bernel Dr CROY/NA CR0 213 H1
Berne Rd THHTH CR7 196 C2
Berners Dr WEA W13 97 G6
Berners Ms FITZ W1T 10 B2
Berners Pl FITZ W1T 10 B3
Berners Rd IS N1 6 A2
WDGN N22 49 G4
Berners St FITZ W1T 10 B2
Berner Ter WCHPL E1 * 104 C5
Berney Rd CROY/NA CR0 196 E4
Bernhardt Crs STJWD NW8 2 C6
Bernhart Cl EDGW HA8 44 E3
Bernwell Rd CHING E4 38 C5
Berridge Gn EDGW HA8 44 C3
Berridge Ms KIL/WHAMP NW6 82 E3
Berridge Rd NRWD SE19 180 E1
Berriman Rd HOLWY N7 85 F1
Berriton Rd RYLN/HDSTN HA2 59 K5
Berrybank Cl CHING E4 38 A4
Berry Cl DAGE RM10 92 C3
WCHMH N21 35 H3
Berry Cottages POP/IOD E14 * 105 G5
Berry Ct HSLWW TW4 134 E6
Berrydale Rd YEAD UB4 95 J3
Berryfield Cl BMLY BR1 184 D4
Berry Field Cl WALTH E17 69 K1
Berryfield Rd WALW SE17 122 C5
Berryhill ELTH/MOT SE9 147 G5
Berry Hl STAN HA7 29 K6
Berryhill Gdns ELTH/MOT SE9 147 G5
Berrylands BRYLDS KT5 191 H2
ORP BR6 217 J1
RYNPK SW20 177 F6
Berrylands Rd BRYLDS KT5 191 G3
Berry La DUL SE21 162 E6
Berryman Cl BCTR RM8 91 J1
Berryman's La SYD SE26 164 A6
Berrymead Gdns ACT W3 117 K1
Berrymede Rd CHSWK W4 118 A3
Berry Pl FSBYE EC1V 6 B5
Berry St FSBYE EC1V 6 B7
Berry Wy EA W5 117 F3
Bertal Rd TOOT SW17 160 C6
Berthons Gdns WALTH E17 * 70 B2
Berthon St DEPT SE8 144 D1
Bertie Rd SYD SE26 182 A2
WLSDN NW10 81 J4
Bertram Rd EN EN1 24 C5
HDN NW4 63 J3
KUTN/CMB KT2 175 H3
Bertram St KTTN NW5 84 B1
Bertrand St LEW SE13 144 E4
Bertrand Wy THMD SE28 109 H6
Bert Rd THHTH CR7 196 D2
Bert Wy EN EN1 24 B5
Berwick Av YEAD UB4 95 H6
Berwick Cl STAN HA7 43 F2
WHTN TW2 155 F3
Berwick Crs BFN/LL DA15 167 K1
Berwick Gdns SUT SM1 209 G1
Berwick Rd CAN/RD E16 107 F5
WDGN N22 49 H4
WELL DA16 148 C2
Berwick St SOHO/CST W1F 10 B4
Berwyn Av HSLW TW3 135 G2
Berwyn Rd HNHL SE24 162 C3
RCHPK/HAM TW10 137 J5
Beryl Av EHAM E6 107 J4
Beryl Rd HMSMTH W6 119 G5
Berystede KUTN/CMB KT2 175 J3
Besant Cl CRICK NW2 * 82 C1
Besant Pl EDUL SE22 143 G5
Besant Placee EDUL SE22 143 G4
Besant Rd CRICK NW2 82 C2
Besant Wy WLSDN NW10 80 E3
Besley St STRHM/NOR SW16 179 H2
Bessant Dr RCH/KEW TW9 137 J2
Bessborough Pl PIM SW1V 121 J5
Bessborough Rd HRW HA1 60 D5
PUT/ROE SW15 158 D3
Bessborough St PIM SW1V 121 J5
Bessemer Rd CMBW SE5 142 E3
Bessie Lansbury Cl EHAM E6 108 A5
Bessingby Rd RSLP HA4 58 E6
Besson St NWCR SE14 143 K2
Bessy St BETH E2 * 104 E2
Best Ter SWLY BR8 * 203 K2
Bestwood St DEPT SE8 124 A4
Beswick Ms KIL/WHAMP NW6 83 F3
Betam Rd HYS/HAR UB3 113 G2
Betchworth Cl SUT SM1 209 H3
Betchworth Rd
GDMY/SEVK IG3 90 E1
Betchworth Wy CROY/NA CR0 214 A6
Betham Rd GFD/PVL UB6 96 D2
Bethany Waye
EBED/NFELT TW14 153 H2
Bethecar Rd HRW HA1 60 E2
Bethel Cl HDN NW4 64 B2
Bethell Av CAN/RD E16 106 D3
IL IG1 72 A4
Bethel Rd WELL DA16 148 D4
Bethersden Cl BECK BR3 182 C3
Bethnal Green Rd BETH E2 7 K6
Bethune Av FBAR/BDGN N11 33 K6
Bethune Rd STNW/STAM N16 67 K4
WLSDN NW10 99 F3
Bethwin Rd CMBW SE5 142 C1
Betjeman Cl RYLN/HDSTN HA2 60 A1
Betjeman Ct WDR/YW UB7 * 112 A1
Betony Cl CROY/NA CR0 198 A5
Betoyne Av CHING E4 38 C6
Betsham Rd ERITH DA8 150 C1
Betstyle Rd FBAR/BDGN N11 34 B6
Betterton Dr SCUP DA14 169 F4
Betterton Rd RAIN RM13 111 G1
Betterton St LSQ/SEVD WC2H 10 E4
Bettons Pk SRTFD E15 88 C6
Bettridge Rd FUL/PGN SW6 139 J3
Betts Cl BECK BR3 182 B5
Betts Ms WALTH E17 69 H3
Betts Rd CAN/RD E16 107 F5
Betts St WAP E1W 104 D6
Betts Wy PGE/AN SE20 181 J5
SURB KT6 190 C5
Beulah Av THHTH CR7 * 180 D5
Beulah Cl EDGW HA8 30 D5
Beulah Crs THHTH CR7 180 D5
Beulah Gv CROY/NA CR0 196 D3
Beulah Hl NRWD SE19 180 D2
Beulah Rd SUT SM1 208 E2
THHTH CR7 180 D6
WALTH E17 69 K2
WIM/MER SW19 177 J3
Beult Rd DART DA1 150 D4
Bevan Av BARK IG11 91 G5
Bevan Ct CROY/NA CR0 211 G3
Bevan Rd ABYW SE2 128 C5
EBAR EN4 21 K5
Bevan St IS N1 6 D1
Bev Callender Cl VX/NE SW8 141 G4
Bevenden St IS N1 7 F4
Beveridge Rd WLSDN NW10 81 G5
Beverley Av BFN/LL DA15 168 A2
HSLWW TW4 134 E5
RYNPK SW20 176 C4
Beverley Cl BARN SW13 138 D3
BTSEA SW11 140 C5
CHSGTN KT9 205 J2
WCHMH N21 35 J3
Beverley Ct BROCKY SE4 144 C4
Beverley Crs WFD IG8 53 F4
Beverley Dr EDGW HA8 44 B6
Beverley Gdns BARN SW13 138 C4
GLDGN NW11 64 C4
STAN HA7 43 G4
WBLY HA9 62 C5
WPK KT4 192 D5
Beverley La KUTN/CMB KT2 176 B3
Beverley Rd BARN SW13 138 C4
BXLYHN DA7 149 K3
CHING E4 52 B2
CHSWK W4 118 C5
DAGW RM9 92 A2
EHAM E6 107 H2
HAYES BR2 200 D6
KUT/HW KT1 174 D4
MTCM CR4 195 J1
NWDGN UB2 114 D4
NWMAL KT3 192 D1
PGE/AN SE20 181 J5
RSLP HA4 59 F6
WPK KT4 193 F6
Beverley Wy KUTN/CMB KT2 176 C4
Beverley Wy (Kingston
By-Pass) RYNPK SW20 176 C4
Beversbrook Rd ARCH N19 84 D1
Beverstone Rd
BRXS/STRHM SW2 142 A6
THHTH CR7 196 B1
Beverston Ms MBLAR W1H 8 E2
Bevill Allen Cl TOOT SW17 178 E2
Bevill Cl SNWD SE25 181 H6
Bevin Cl BERM/RHTH SE16 124 B1
Bevington Rd BECK BR3 182 E5
NKENS W10 * 100 C4
Bevington St
BERM/RHTH SE16 123 H2
Bevin Rd YEAD UB4 94 E2
Bevin Sq TOOT SW17 160 E5
Bevin Wy FSBYW WC1X 5 J3
Bevis Marks HDTCH EC3A 13 H3
Bewcastle Gdns ENC/FH EN2 22 E5
Bewdley St IS N1 85 G5
Bewick Ms PECK SE15 143 J1
Bewick St VX/NE SW8 141 G3
Bewley St WCHPL E1 104 D6
WIM/MER SW19 178 C2
Bewlys Rd WNWD SE27 180 C1
Bexhill Cl FELT TW13 154 D4
Bexhill Rd BROCKY SE4 164 C1
FBAR/BDGN N11 48 D1
MORT/ESHN SW14 137 K4
Bexley Cl DART DA1 150 B6
Bexley Gdns CHDH RM6 73 H2
ED N9 35 K5
Bexley High St BXLY DA5 169 H2
Bexley La DART DA1 150 B6
SCUP DA14 168 D4
Bexley Rd ELTH/MOT SE9 147 J6
ELTH/MOT SE9 167 F1
ERITH DA8 149 K1
Beynon Rd CAR SM5 209 K3
Bianca Rd PECK SE15 123 G6
Bibsworth Rd FNCH N3 46 D5
Bibury Cl PECK SE15 123 F6
Bicester Rd RCH/KEW TW9 137 H4
Bickenhall St MHST W1U 9 F1
Bickersteth Rd TOOT SW17 178 E2
Bickerton Rd ARCH N19 84 C1
Bickles Yd STHWK SE1 19 H3
Bickley Crs BMLY BR1 200 D1
Bickley Park Rd BMLY BR1 184 E6
Bickley Rd BMLY BR1 184 C5
LEY E10 69 K4
Bickley St TOOT SW17 178 E1
Bicknell Rd CMBW SE5 142 D4
Bicknoller Rd EN EN1 24 B2
Bicknor Rd ORP BR6 201 K4
Bidborough Cl HAYES BR2 199 J2
Bidborough St STPAN WC1H 4 E5
Biddenden Wy ELTH/MOT SE9 167 F6
Bidder St CAN/RD E16 106 C4
Biddestone Rd HOLWY N7 85 F2
Biddulph Rd MV/WKIL W9 101 F2
SAND/SEL CR2 211 J6
Bideford Av GFD/PVL UB6 97 H2
Bideford Cl EDGW HA8 44 C4
FELT TW13 154 E5
Bideford Gdns EN EN1 36 A2
Bideford Rd BMLY BR1 165 J5
PEND EN3 25 H1
RSLP HA4 77 F1
WELL DA16 148 C1
Bidwell Gdns FBAR/BDGN N11 48 C4
Bidwell St PECK SE15 * 143 J2
Biggerstaff Rd SRTFD E15 88 A6
Biggerstaff St FSBYPK N4 67 G6
Biggin Av MTCM CR4 178 E4
Biggin Hl NRWD SE19 180 C3
Biggin Wy NRWD SE19 180 C3
Bigginwood Rd
STRHM/NOR SW16 180 C3
Bigg's Rw PUT/ROE SW15 139 G4
Bigland St WCHPL E1 104 D5
Bignell Rd WOOL/PLUM SE18 127 G5
Bignold Rd FSTGT E7 88 E2
Big St CLPT E5 68 D5
Bigwood Rd GLDGN NW11 65 F3
Billet Rd CHDH RM6 55 J6
WALTH E17 51 F4
Billetts Hart Cl HNWL W7 115 K2
Bill Hamling Cl ELTH/MOT SE9 166 E4
Billingford Cl BROCKY SE4 144 A5
Billing Pl WBPTN SW10 * 140 A1
Billing Rd WBPTN SW10 140 A1
Billings Cl DAGW RM9 91 J5
Billing St WBPTN SW10 * 140 A1
Billington Hl CROY/NA CR0 196 E6
Billington Rd NWCR SE14 144 A1
Billiter Sq FENCHST EC3M * 13 H4
Billiter St FENCHST EC3M 13 H4
Bill Nicholson Wy TOTM N17 50 B3
Billockby Cl CHSGTN KT9 206 B4
Billson St POP/IOD E14 125 F4
Bilton Rd ERITH DA8 150 D1
GFD/PVL UB6 79 H6
Bilton Wy HYS/HAR UB3 114 A2
PEND EN3 25 H2
Bina Gdns ECT SW5 120 B4
Bincote Rd ENC/FH EN2 23 F4
Binden Rd SHB W12 118 C3
Binfield Rd CLAP SW4 141 K2
SAND/SEL CR2 212 B3
Bingfield St IS N1 84 E6
Bingham Ct IS N1 * 85 H5
Bingham Pl CAMTN NW1 3 G7
MHST W1U 9 G1
Bingham Rd CROY/NA CR0 197 H5
Bingham St IS N1 85 K4
Bingley Rd CAN/RD E16 107 G5
GFD/PVL UB6 96 C3
Binney St MYFR/PKLN W1K 9 H5
Binns Rd CHSWK W4 118 B5
Binsey Wk ABYW SE2 128 D2
Binstead Cl YEAD UB4 95 J4
Binyon Crs STAN HA7 43 F1
Birbetts Rd ELTH/MOT SE9 166 E4
Birchanger Rd SNWD SE25 197 H2
Birch Av PLMGR N13 35 J5
Birch Cl BKHH IG9 39 H5
BTFD TW8 136 C1
CAN/RD E16 106 C4
HSLW TW3 135 J4
ROMW/RG RM7 56 D6
TEDD TW11 174 B1
Birch Ct WLGTN SM6 210 B2
Birchdale Gdns CHDH RM6 73 K4
Birchdale Rd FSTGT E7 89 G3
Birchdene Dr THMD SE28 128 B2
Birchen Cl CDALE/KGS NW9 63 F6
Birchend Cl SAND/SEL CR2 211 K4
Birchen Gv CDALE/KGS NW9 63 F6
Birches Cl MTCM CR4 178 E6
PIN HA5 59 J2
The Birches CHARL SE7 126 A6
CMBW SE5 * 143 F4
HSLWW TW4 * 154 E2
ORP BR6 216 A2
WCHMH N21 35 F1
Birchfield St POP/IOD E14 105 J6
Birch Gdns DAGE RM10 92 E1
Birch Gv ACT W3 117 H1
LEE/GVPK SE12 165 J2
WAN E11 88 C1
WELL DA16 148 B5
Birch Hl CROY/NA CR0 213 F3
Birchington Cl BXLYHN DA7 149 J2
Birchington Rd BRYLDS KT5 191 G4
CEND/HSY/T N8 66 D3
KIL/WHAMP NW6 82 E6
Birchin La BANK EC3V 13 F4
Birchlands Av BAL SW12 160 E2
Birch Md ORP BR6 201 F6
Birchmead Av PIN HA5 59 G1
Birchmere Rw BKHTH/KID SE3 145 J3
Birchmore Wk HBRY N5 85 J1
Birch Pk KTN/HRWW/WS HA3 42 C3
Birch Rd FELT TW13 172 C1
ROMW/RG RM7 56 D6
Birch Rw HAYES BR2 201 F4
Birch Tree Av WWKM BR4 214 D3
Birch Tree Wy CROY/NA CR0 197 J6
Birch Wk MTCM CR4 179 G4
Birchway HYS/HAR UB3 113 K1
Birchwood Av BECK BR3 198 C1
MUSWH N10 48 A6
SCUP DA14 168 C5
WLGTN SM6 210 A1
Birchwood Cl MRDN SM4 194 A1
Birchwood Ct EDGW HA8 44 E5
Birchwood Dr HAMP NW3 83 F1
RDART DA2 170 B6
Birchwood Gv HPTN TW12 173 F2
Birchwood La ESH/CLAY KT10 204 D6
Birchwood Rd RDART DA2 170 B6
STMC/STPC BR5 201 J1
SWLY BR8 187 K3
TOOT SW17 179 G1
Birchwood Ter SWLY BR8 * 187 K4
Birdbrook Cl DAGE RM10 92 E5
Birdbrook Rd BKHTH/KID SE3 146 B4
Birdcage Wk WESTW SW1E 16 B3
Birdham Cl BMLY BR1 200 D2
Birdhurst Av SAND/SEL CR2 211 K2
Birdhurst Gdns SAND/SEL CR2 211 K2
Birdhurst Ri SAND/SEL CR2 212 A3
Birdhurst Rd SAND/SEL CR2 212 A3
WAND/EARL SW18 140 B6
WIM/MER SW19 178 D2
Bird in Bush Rd PECK SE15 143 H1
Bird-in-Hand La BMLY BR1 184 C5
Bird-in-Hand Ms FSTH SE23 163 K4
Bird-in-Hand Pas FSTH SE23 163 K4
Birds Farm Av CRW RM5 56 D4
Birdsfield La BOW E3 87 H6
Bird St MHST W1U 9 H4
Bird Wk WHTN TW2 154 E3
Birdwood Cl TEDD TW11 155 K6
Birkbeck Av ACT W3 98 E6
GFD/PVL UB6 78 C6
Birkbeck Gv ACT W3 118 A2
Birkbeck Hl DUL SE21 162 C4
Birkbeck Ms ACT W3 * 99 F6
HACK E8 86 B3
Birkbeck Pl DUL SE21 162 C3
Birkbeck Rd ACT W3 118 A1
BECK BR3 182 A5
CEND/HSY/T N8 66 E1
EA W5 116 D4
ENC/FH EN2 23 K2
GNTH/NBYPK IG2 72 D2
HACK E8 86 B3
MLHL NW7 45 H1
NFNCH/WDSPK N12 47 G1
ROMW/RG RM7 75 F5
SCUP DA14 168 B5
TOTM N17 50 B4
WIM/MER SW19 178 A2
Birkbeck St BETH E2 104 D2
Birkbeck Wy GFD/PVL UB6 78 D6
Birkdale Av PIN HA5 42 A6
Birkdale Cl BERM/RHTH SE16 123 J5
ORP BR6 201 J5
THMD SE28 109 J5
Birkdale Gdns CROY/NA CR0 213 F2
OXHEY WD19 27 H5
Birkdale Rd ABYW SE2 128 B4
EA W5 98 A3
Birkenhead Av KUTN/CMB KT2 175 G5
Birkenhead St CAMTN NW1 5 F4
Birkhall Rd CAT SE6 165 G3
Birkwood Cl BAL SW12 161 J2
Birley Rd TRDG/WHET N20 33 G4
Birley St BTSEA SW11 141 F3
Birling Rd ERITH DA8 150 A1
Birnam Rd FSBYPK N4 67 F6
Birse Crs WLSDN NW10 81 G2
Birstal Gn OXHEY WD19 27 H6

Birstall Rd SEVS/STOTM N15 ......68 A2
Biscay Rd HMSMTH W6.........119 G5
Biscoe CI HEST TW5.........115 F6
Biscoe Wy LEW SE13 *.......145 G5
Bisenden Rd CROY/NA CR0....197 H6
Bisham CI CAR SM5..........194 E5
Bisham Gdns HGT N6..........66 A6
Bishop Fox Wy
   E/WMO/HCT KT8...........188 E1
Bishop Ken Rd
   KTN/HRWW/WS HA3.........188 E1
Bishop Rd STHGT/OAK N14.....34 B3
Bishops Av BMLY............184 B6
   CHDH RM6................73 J3
   FUL/PGN SW6.............139 G3
   NTHWD HA6...............26 C6
   PLSTW E13...............89 F6
The Bishops Av EFNCH N2.....65 H3
Bishop's Bridge Rd
   BAY/PAD W2..............101 F5
Bishop's CI ARCH N19........84 C1
   BAR EN5.................32 B1
   CHSWK W4................117 K5
   EN EN1..................167 H4
   EN1 E17.................12 A5
   RCHPK/HAM TW10..........156 C5
   SUT SM1.................208 E1
   WALTH E17...............69 K1
Bishop's Ct STP EC4M........12 A3
Bishops Dr EBED/NFELT TW14..153 C1
   NTHLT UB5...............77 J6
Bishopsford Rd MRDN SM4....194 B4
Bishopsgate LVPST EC2M......13 H2
Bishopsgate Ar LVPST EC2M...13 G2
Bishops Gn BMLY BR1 *......184 B4
Bishops Gv EFNCH N2.........65 J3
   HPTN TW12...............154 E6
Bishop's Hall KUT/HW KT1...174 E1
Bishop Rd CMBW SE5 *.......142 D1
Bishop's Park Rd
   FUL/PGN SW6.............139 G3
   STRHM/NOR SW16..........179 K4
Bishop's PI SUT SM1........209 G3
Bishop's Rd CROY/NA CR0....196 C4
   FUL/PGN SW6.............139 J2
   HGT N6..................66 A3
   HNWL W7.................115 K2
   HYS/HAR UB3.............94 A5
Bishop's Ter LBTH SE11......17 K6
Bishopsthorpe Rd SYD SE26..165 K6
Bishop St IS N1.............85 J6
Bishops Wk CHST BR7........185 H4
   CROY/NA CR0.............213 F5
Bishop's Wy BETH E2........104 E1
Bishopswood Rd HGT N6.......65 K4
Bishop Wy WLSDN NW10........81 G5
Bisley CI WPK KT4..........193 F5
Bispham Rd WLSDN NW10.......98 B2
Bisson Rd SRTFD E15........106 A1
Bistern Av WALTH E17........52 A5
Bittacy CI MLHL NW7.........46 B2
Bittacy Hill MLHL NW7.......46 B2
Bittacy Park Av MLHL NW7....46 B2
Bittacy Rd MLHL NW7.........46 B2
Bittern CI YEAD UB4.........95 H4
Bittern PI WDGN N22 *.......49 F5
Bittern St STHWK SE1........18 C2
Bittoms Ct KUT/HW KT1......174 E6
The Bittoms KUT/HW KT1.....174 E6
Bixley CI NWDGN UB2........114 E4
Blackall St SDTCH EC2A.......7 G7
Blackberry Fld
   STMC/STPC BR5...........186 B4
Blackbird HI WBLY HA9.......62 E6
Blackbird Yd BETH E2 *.......7 K4
Blackborne La HAYES BR2....201 F2
Blackburne's Ms
   MYFR/PKLN W1K *..........9 G5
Blackburn Rd KIL/WHAMP NW6..83 F4
Blackbush CI CHDH RM6.......73 K2
Blackbush CI BELMT SM2.....209 F5
Blackdown Ter
   WOOL/PLUM SE18 *........146 G2
Blackenham Rd TOOT SW17...160 E6
Blacket St PUT/ROE SW15....139 G4
Black Fan CI ENC/FH EN2.....23 J2
Blackfen Pde BFN/LL DA15 *..168 B1
Blackfen Rd BFN/LL DA15....148 A6
Blackford CI SAND/SEL CR2..211 H6
Blackford Rd OXHEY WD19.....41 H1
Blackfriars Br STHWK SE1....12 A6
Black Friars La BLKFR EC4V..12 A5
Blackfriars Pas BLKFR EC4V..12 A5
Blackfriars Rd STHWK SE1....18 A1
Blackfriars U/P BLKFR EC4V..12 B5
Blackheath Av GNWCH SE10...145 H1
Blackheath Gv BKHTH/KID SE3..145 J3
Blackheath Hi GNWCH SE10...145 F2
Blackheath Pk BKHTH/KID SE3..145 J4
Blackheath Ri LEW SE13.....145 F3
Blackheath Rd GNWCH SE10...144 E2
Blackheath V BKHTH/KID SE3..145 H3
Black Horse Ct STHWK SE1 *..19 F5
Blackhorse La CROY/NA CR0..197 H4
   WALTH E17...............51 F6
Black Horse Pde PIN HA5 *...58 D1
Black Horse Rd SCUP DA14...168 B6
Blackhorse Rd DEPT SE8.....124 B6
   WALTH E17...............51 F6
Blacklands Dr YEAD UB4......94 A3
Blacklands Rd CAT SE6......165 F6
Blacklands Ter CHEL SW3.....15 J7
Blantyre St WBPTN SW10.....140 C1
Blantyre Wk WBPTN SW10 *...140 C1
Blashford St LEW SE13......165 G2
Blawith Rd HRW HA1..........60 E1
Blaydon CI RSLP HA4.........58 C4
   TOTM N17................50 D3
Blaydon Wk TOTM N17........50 D3
Bleak Hill La
   WOOL/PLUM SE18..........128 A6

Blackness Cottages
   HAYES BR2...............215 G5
Blackness La HAYES BR2.....215 H6
Blackpool Gdns YEAD UB4.....94 C3
Blackpool Rd PECK SE15.....143 J3
Black Prince Rd LBTH SE11...17 H7
Black Rod CI HYS/HAR UB3...113 J5
Blackshaw Rd TOOT SW17....178 C1
Blacksmith's La RAIN RM13...93 H6
   STMC/STPC BR5...........202 D2
Black's Rd HMSMTH W6.......119 F5
Blackstock Rd FSBYPK N4.....67 H6
Blackstone Est HACK E8......86 C5
Blackstone Rd CRICK NW2.....82 A2
Black Swan St STHWK SE1.....19 F5
Blackthorn Av WDR/YW UB7...112 D4
Blackthorn Dr CHING E4......38 C6
Blackthorn Dr WALTH DA7....149 F4
Blackthorn Rd IL IG1........90 D3
Blackthorne Av CROY/NA CR0..197 K5
Blackthorne Dr CHING E4.....38 B6
Blackthorne Rd BOW E3.....105 J3
Blacktree Ms BRXN/ST SW9 *..142 B4
Blackwall La GNWCH SE10....125 H5
Blackwall Tunnel Ap
   POP/IOD E14.............106 A2
Blackwall Tunnel Northern Ap
   BOW E3..................87 J6
   BOW E3..................87 G6
Blackwall Wy POP/IOD E14...106 A6
Blackwater CI FSTGT E7......88 D2
   RAIN RM13...............111 F4
Blackwater St EDUL SE22....143 G6
Blackwell CI CLPT E5........87 G2
   KTN/HRWW/WS HA3.........42 D3
Blackwell Dr OXHEY WD19.....27 G1
Blackwell Gdns EDGW HA8.....30 C6
Blackwood St WALW SE17....122 E5
Bladindon Dr BXLY DA5.....148 D2
Bladon Gdns RYLN/HDSTN HA2..60 B3
Blagden's La STHGT/OAK N14..34 D4
Blagdon Rd CAT SE6........164 E1
   NWMAL KT3...............192 C1
Blagdon Wk TEDD TW11......174 D2
Blagrove Rd NKENS W10......100 C4
Blair Av CDALE/KGS NW9......63 G4
   ESH/CLAY KT10...........189 H6
Blair CI BFN/LL DA15.......147 K6
   HYS/HAR UB3.............113 K4
   IS N1...................85 J4
Blairderry Rd
   BRXS/STRHM SW2..........161 K4
Blairhead Dr OXHEY WD19.....27 F5
Blair St POP/IOD E14.......106 A5
Blake Av BARK IG11..........90 E6
Blake CI CAR SM5...........194 D5
   NKENS W10...............100 A4
   RAIN RM13...............93 H6
   WELL DA16...............147 K1
Blakeden Dr ESH/CLAY KT10..205 F5
Blake Gdns DART DA1........151 J5
   FUL/PGN SW6.............139 K2
Blakehall Rd CAR SM5......209 K4
Blake Hall Rd WAN E11.......70 E5
Blake Ms RCH/KEW TW9......137 H2
Blakemore Gdns BARN SW13..118 E6
Blakemore Rd
   STRHM/NOR SW16..........161 K5
   THHTH CR7...............196 A2
Blakemore Wy BELV DA17....129 F3
Blakeney Av BECK BR3......182 C4
Blakeney CI CAMTN NW1........4 C2
   HACK E8.................86 C3
   TRDG/WHET N20...........33 J3
Blakeney Rd BECK BR3......182 C4
Blaker Ct CHARL SE7 *......146 B1
Blaker Rd CAN/RD E16......106 D3
   CROY/NA CR0.............197 F6
   FBAR/BDGN N11...........48 C3
   MTCM CR4................178 D6
Blaker Rd SRTFD E15.......106 A1
Blakes Av NWMAL KT3.......192 C2
Blake's Gn WWKM BR4.......199 F5
Blakes La NWMAL KT3.......192 C2
Blakesley Av EA W5.........97 J5
Blake's Rd PECK SE15......143 F1
Blakes Ter NWMAL KT3......192 D2
Blakesware Gdns ED N9......35 K2
Blakewood CI FELT TW13....154 A6
Blanchard CI ELTH/MOT SE9..166 D5
Blanchard Gv PEND EN3.......25 J1
Blanchard Wy HACK E8........86 C4
Blanch CI PECK SE15........143 K1
Blanchedowne CMBW SE5.....142 E5
Blanche St CAN/RD E16......106 D3
Blanchland Rd MRDN SM4....194 A2
Blandfield Rd BAL SW12.....161 F2
Blandford Av BECK BR3.....182 B5
   WHTN TW2................155 G3
Blandford CI CROY/NA CR0...210 E1
   EFNCH N2................65 G2
   ROMW/RG RM7.............74 D1
Blandford Crs CHING E4......38 A2
Blandford Rd BECK BR3.....182 A5
   CHSWK W4................118 B3
   EA W5...................116 E2
   NWDGN UB2...............114 E4
   TEDD TW11...............173 J1
Blandford Sq CAMTN NW1......2 D7
Blandford St MHST W1U........9 F3
Blandford Waye YEAD UB4.....95 G5
Bland St ELTH/MOT SE9.....146 C5
Blaney Crs EHAM E6.........108 B2
Blanmerle Rd ELTH/MOT SE9..167 G3
Blann CI ELTH/MOT SE9.....166 C6

Blean Gv PGE/AN SE20......181 K3
Bleasdale Av GFD/PVL UB6....97 G1
Blechynden Gdns NKENS W10..100 B6
Blechynden St NKENS W10 *..100 B6
Bledlow CI THMD SE28......109 J6
Bledlow Ri GFD/PVL UB6......96 C1
Bleeding Heart Yd
   HCIRC EC1N..............11 K2
Blegborough Rd
   STRHM/NOR SW16..........179 H2
Blendon Dr BXLY DA5.......168 E1
Blendon Rd BXLY DA5.......168 E1
Blendon Ter
   WOOL/PLUM SE18..........127 H6
Blendworth Wy PECK SE15...143 F1
Blenheim CDALE/KGS NW9 *....45 H5
Blenheim Av GNTH/NBYPK IG2..72 A3
Blenheim CI DART DA1.......171 F1
   GFD/PVL UB6.............96 D1
   OXHEY WD19..............27 H2
   ROMW/RG RM7.............74 E1
   RYNPK SW20..............177 F6
   WCHMH N21...............35 J3
   WLGTN SM6...............210 C5
Blenheim Crs NTGHL W11....100 C5
   RSLP HA4................58 B6
   SAND/SEL CR2............211 J5
Blenheim Dr WELL DA16.....148 A2
Blenheim Gdns
   BRXS/STRHM SW2..........162 A1
   CRICK NW2...............82 A3
   KUTN/CMB KT2............175 J4
   WBLY HA9................80 A1
   WLGTN SM6...............210 C4
Blenheim Gv PECK SE15.....143 H3
Blenheim Park Rd
   SAND/SEL CR2............211 J6
Blenheim Pas STJWD NW8 *....2 A2
Blenheim Ri SEVS/STOTM N15 *..68 B1
   BFN/LL DA15.............168 D3
   BMLY BR1................184 D1
   CHSWK W4................118 B3
   DART DA1................171 F1
   EHAM E6.................107 H2
   NTHLT UB5...............78 B4
   ORP BR6.................202 B6
   PGE/AN SE20.............181 K3
   RYLN/HDSTN HA2..........60 B3
   RYNPK SW20..............176 E5
   STJWD NW8...............2 A1
   SUT SM1.................209 F1
   WALTH E17...............51 F6
   WAN E11.................88 C2
Blenheim St CONDST W1S......9 J4
Blenheim Ter STJWD NW8......1 J1
Blenkarne Rd BTSEA SW11...160 E1
Bleriot Rd HEST TW5.......134 B1
Blessbury Rd EDGW HA8.......44 E4
Blessington Rd LEW SE13...145 G5
Blessing Wy BARK IG11.......91 J1
Bletchingley CI THHTH CR7..196 C1
Bletchley St IS N1..........6 D3
Bletchmore CI HYS/HAR UB3..113 G6
Bletsoe Wk IS N1...........6 D2
Blincoe CI WIM/MER SW19...159 G4
Blissett St GNWCH SE10....145 F2
Bliss Ms NKENS W10........100 C3
Blisworth CI YEAD UB4.......95 J3
Blithbury Rd DAGW RM9.......91 H4
Blithdale Rd ABYW SE2.....128 B4
Blithfield St KENS W8.....120 A3
Blockley Rd ALP/SUD HA0.....61 H6
Bloemfontein Av SHB W12...118 E1
Bloemfontein Rd SHB W12.....99 K6
Blomfield Rd MV/WKIL W9...101 H4
Blomfield St LVPST EC2M....13 F2
Blomfield Vis BAY/PAD W2..101 F4
Blomville Rd BCTR RM8.......92 A1
Blondel St BTSEA SW11.....141 F3
Blondin Av EA W5..........116 D4
Blondin St BOW E3..........105 J1
Bloomfield Crs
   GNTH/NBYPK IG2..........72 B3
Bloomfield PI MYFR/PKLN W1K..9 K5
Bloomfield Rd HAYES BR2...200 C2
   HGT N6..................66 A3
   KUT/HW KT1..............191 F1
   WOOL/PLUM SE18..........127 G5
Bloomfield Ter BGVA SW1W..121 F5
Bloom Gv WNWD SE27.......162 C5
Bloom Park Rd FUL/PGN SW6..139 J1
Bloomsbury CI EA W5........98 B6
Bloomsbury PI
   NOXST/BSQ WC1A..........11 F2
Bloomsbury Sq
   NOXST/BSQ WC1A..........11 F2
Bloomsbury St GWRST WC1E..10 D1
Bloomsbury Wy
   NOXST/BSQ WC1A..........10 E2
Blore CI VX/NE SW8........141 J2
Blossom CI DAGW RM9........92 B6
   EA W5...................117 F2
   SAND/SEL CR2............212 B3
Blossom La ENC/FH EN2......23 J2
Blossom St WCHPL E1........13 H1
Blossom Wy WDR/YW UB7.....112 D4
Blossom Waye HEST TW5.....114 D6
Blount St POP/IOD E14.....105 G5
Bloxam Gdns ELTH/MOT SE9..146 D6
Bloxhall Rd LEY E10.........69 G5
Bloxham Crs HPTN TW12.....172 E3
Bloxworth CI WLGTN SM6....210 C1
Blucher Rd CMBW SE5.......142 D1
Blue Anchor La
   BERM/RHTH SE16..........123 H4
Blue Anchor Yd WCHPL E1...104 C6
Blue Ball Yd WHALL SW1A....16 A1
Bluebell Av MNPK E12........89 J3
Bluebell CI HOM E9.........86 E6

NTHLT UB5.............77 K4
ORP BR6...............201 H6
ROMW/RG RM7...........75 G6
SYD SE26..............163 G6
WLGTN SM6.............195 G5
Bluebell Wy IL IG1.........90 B4
Blueberry CI WFD IG8.......52 E2
Bluebird La DAGE RM10.....92 C5
Bluebird Wy THMD SE28....127 J2
Bluefield CI HPTN TW12....173 F1
Bluegates EW KT17.........207 J5
Bluehouse Rd CHING E4......38 C5
Blue Lion PI STHWK SE1.....19 G4
Blue Riband Est
   CROY/NA CR0.............196 C6
Blundell CI HACK E8........86 C3
Blundell Rd EDGW HA8.......45 G5
Blundell St HOLWY N7.......84 E5
Blunden CI BCTR RM8........73 J5
Blunt Rd SAND/SEL CR2....211 K3
Blunts Av WDR/YW UB7.....132 D1
Blunts Rd ELTH/MOT SE9...147 F6
Blurton Rd CLPT E5.........87 F2
Blyth CI CAT SE6..........164 C1
   POP/IOD E14.............125 G4
Blythe CI CAT SE6.........164 C1
Blythe Hill CAT SE6.......164 C1
Blythe Hill La CAT SE6....164 C2
Blythe Hill PI FSTH SE23 *..164 B2
Blythe Ms WKENS W14 *.....119 G3
Blythe Rd WKENS W14......119 G3
Blythe St BETH E2.........104 D2
Blytheswood PI
   STRHM/NOR SW16..........164 A6
Blythe V CAT SE6..........164 C3
Blythe Wd Pas IL IG1 *.....72 D6
   HYS/HAR UB3.............113 H2
   THMD SE28...............109 J6
   WALTH E17...............52 A4
Blyth's Whf POP/IOD E14 *..105 G6
Blyton CI BTHM/RTH SE16...124 B4
Boadicea St IS N1..........5 G1
Boakes CI CDALE/KGS NW9....62 E1
Boardman Av CHING E4.......25 K5
Boardman CI BAR EN5........20 C6
Boardwalk PI POP/IOD E14..125 F1
Boar's Head Yd BTFD TW8 *..136 E1
Boathouse Wk PECK SE15...143 G1
   RCH/KEW TW9.............137 F6
Boat Lifter Wy
   BERM/RHTH SE16..........124 B4
Boat Quay CAN/RD E16 *....107 G6
Bob Anker CI PLSTW E13...106 E2
Bobbin CI CLAP SW4........141 H4
Bob Marley Wy HNHL SE24..142 B5
Bockhampton Rd
   KUTN/CMB KT2............175 G3
Bocking St HACK E8.........86 D6
Boddicott CI WIM/MER SW19..159 H4
Boddington Gdns ACT W3...117 H2
Bodiam CI EN EN1...........23 K3
Bodiam Rd STRHM/NOR SW16..179 J4
Bodley Rd NWMAL KT3......192 A3
Bodmin CI RYLN/HDSTN HA2...77 K1
Bodmin Gv MRDN SM4.......194 A2
Bodmin St WAND/EARL SW18..159 K4
Bodnant Gdns RYNPK SW20..176 D6
Bodney Rd CLPT E5.........87 F1
Boeing Wy NWDGN UB2......114 A3
Bofors House CHARL SE7 *..146 B1
Bognor Gdns OXHEY WD19 *...41 G1
Bognor Rd WELL DA16......148 E2
Bohemia PI HACK E8........86 E4
Bohn Rd WCHPL E1.........105 G4
Bohun Gv EBAR EN4.........33 J1
Boileau Rd BARN SW13.....118 E6
   EA W5...................98 B5
Bolden St DEPT SE8.......144 E3
Boldero PI STJWD NW8 *.....2 C7
Bolderwood Wy WWKM BR4...198 E6
Boldmere Rd PIN HA5.......59 G4
Boleyn Av EN EN1..........24 D2
Boleyn CI WALTH E17........69 J1
Boleyn Ct BKHH IG9.........38 E3
Boleyn Dr E/WMO/HCT KT8..172 E6
   RSLP HA4................59 H6
Boleyn Gdns DAGE RM10.....92 E6
   WWKM BR4................198 E6
Boleyn Rd EHAM E6........107 H1
   FSTGT E7................88 E5
Boleyn Wy BAR EN5.........21 F3
   BARK/HLT IG6............54 C2
Bolina Rd BERM/RHTH SE16..123 K5
Bolingbroke Gv BTSEA SW11..140 D6
Bolingbroke Rd WKENS W14..119 G3
Bolingbroke Wk BTSEA SW11 *..140 C1
Bolingbroke Wy
   HYS/HAR UB3.............113 G1
Bollo Bridge Rd ACT W3...117 K2
Bollo La ACT W3...........117 J3
Bolney Ga SKENS SW7.......14 C5
Bolney St VX/NE SW8......142 A1
Bolsover St GTPST W1W......3 K7
Bolstead Rd MTCM CR4.....179 G4
Bolt Ct FLST/FETLN EC4A....11 K4
Boltmore CI HDN NW4.......46 B6
Bolton CI CHSGTN KT9.....205 K4
Bolton Crs CMBW SE5......142 B1
Bolton Dr MRDN SM4.......194 B4
Bolton Gdns BMLY BR1.....183 J2
   ECT SW5.................120 A5
   TEDD TW11...............174 B2
   WLSDN NW10..............100 B1
Bolton Gardens Ms
   WBPTN SW10..............120 B5
Bolton PI IS N1 *..........85 H5
Bolton Rd CHSGTN KT9.....205 K4
   CHSWK W4................137 K1

HRW HA1...............60 C1
SRTFD E15.............88 D3
STJWD NW8.............83 F6
UED N18...............50 B1
WLSDN NW10............81 F6
Bolton's La HYS/HAR UB3...133 F1
Boltons Pl ECT SW5.......120 B5
The Boltons ALP/SUD HA0....79 F2
   WBPTN SW10..............120 B5
   WFD IG8 *...............38 C6
Bolton St MYFR/PICC W1J.....9 K7
Bombay St BERM/RHTH SE16..123 J4
Bomer Cl WDR/YW UB7......132 D1
Bomore Rd NTGHL W11......100 B6
Bonar PI CHST BR7........184 D3
Bonar Rd PECK SE15.......143 H1
Bonchester CI CHST BR7...185 F3
Bonchurch Rd NKENS W10...100 C4
   WEA W13.................116 C1
Bondfield Av YEAD UB4......95 G2
Bond Gdns WLGTN SM6......210 C2
Bond Rd MTCM CR4.........178 E5
   SURB KT6................191 G6
Bond St EA W5.............97 K6
   SRTFD E15...............88 C3
Bondway VX/NE SW8.........121 K6
Boneta Rd WOOL/PLUM SE18..126 D3
Bonfield Rd LEW SE13......145 F5
Bonham Gdns BCTR RM8......73 K6
Bonham Rd BCTR RM8........73 K6
   BRXS/STRHM SW2..........142 A6
Bonheur Rd CHSWK W4......118 A2
Bonhill St SDTCH EC2A......7 F7
Boniface Gdns
   KTN/HRWW/WS HA3.........42 B3
Boniface Wk
   KTN/HRWW/WS HA3.........42 B3
Bonita Ms BROCKY SE4.....144 A4
Bonner Hill Rd KUT/HW KT1..175 H6
Bonner Rd BETH E2........104 E1
Bonnersfield CI HRW HA1....61 G3
Bonnersfield La HRW HA1....61 G3
Bonner St BETH E2.........105 F2
Bonneville Gdns CLAP SW4..161 H1
Bonnington Sq VX/NE SW8 *..122 A6
Bonny St CAMTN NW1.........4 B1
Bonser Rd TWK TW1........156 A4
Bonsor St CMBW SE5.......143 F1
Bonville Gdns HDN NW4......63 J1
Bonville Rd BMLY BR1.....183 J1
Booker CI POP/IOD E14 *...105 H5
Booker Rd UED N18.........50 C1
Boones Rd LEW SE13.......145 H5
Boone St LEW SE13........145 H5
Boord St GNWCH SE10......125 H3
Boothby Rd ARCH N19.......66 D6
Booth CI HOM E9...........86 D6
   THMD SE28...............128 C1
Booth La BLKFR EC4V.......12 C5
Booth Rd CDALE/KGS NW9....45 F4
   CROY/NA CR0 *...........196 D1
Boot Pde EDGW HA8 *........44 C2
Boot St IS N1.............7 F5
Bordars Rd HNWL W7........96 E4
Bordars Wk HNWL W7........96 E4
Border Crs SYD SE26......181 J1
Border Gdns CROY/NA CR0...213 G2
Border Ga MTCM CR4.......178 D4
Border Rd SYD SE26.......181 J1
Bordesley Rd MRDN SM4....194 A1
Bordon Wk PUT/ROE SW15...158 D2
Boreas Wk IS N1 *.........6 B3
Boreham Av CAN/RD E16....106 E5
Boreham CI WAN E11........70 A5
Boreham Rd WDGN N22.......49 J5
Borehamwood
   WAND/EARL SW18..........160 A2
Borgard Rd
   WOOL/PLUM SE18..........126 E4
Borkwood Pk ORP BR6......217 F2
Borkwood Wy ORP BR6......216 E2
Borland Rd PECK SE15.....143 K5
   TEDD TW11...............174 C2
Borneo St PUT/ROE SW15...139 F4
Borough High St STHWK SE1..18 D3
Borough Hi CROY/NA CR0...211 H1
Borough Rd ISLW TW7......135 K2
   KUTN/CMB KT2............175 H4
   MTCM CR4................178 D5
   STHWK SE1...............18 A4
Borough Sq STHWK SE1 *....18 C3
Borrett CI WALW SE17.....122 D5
Borrodaile Rd
   WAND/EARL SW18..........160 A1
Borrowdale Av
   KTN/HRWW/WS HA3.........43 G5
Borthwick Ms SRTFD E15 *...88 C2
Borthwick Rd CDALE/KGS NW9..63 H3
   SRTFD E15...............88 C2
Borthwick St DEPT SE8....124 D5
Borwick Av WALTH E17......51 H6
Bosbury Rd CAT SE6.......165 F5
Boscastle Rd KTTN NW5.....84 B1
Boscobel CI BMLY BR1.....184 E5
Boscobel PI BGVA SW1W.....15 H6
Boscobel St BAY/PAD W2.....8 B1
Boscombe Av LEY E10.......70 B5
Boscombe CI CLPT E5.......87 G3
Boscombe Gdns STRHM/NOR SW16..179 K2
   TOOT SW17...............177 K4
Boscombe Rd SHB W12......118 D2
   WIM/MER SW19............177 K4
   WPK KT4.................192 E5
Bose CI FNCH N3...........46 C4
Bosgrove CHING E4.........38 A3
Boss St STHWK SE1.........19 J2
Bostall Heath ABYW SE2...128 D5
Bostall Hi ABYW SE2......128 D5
Bostall La ABYW SE2......128 C5
Bostall Manorway ABYW SE2..128 C4
Bostall Park Av BXLYHN DA7..149 F1
Bostall Rd STMC/STPC BR5..186 C5
Boston Gdns BTFD TW8......116 A4
   CHSWK W4................118 B6
Boston Manor Rd BTFD TW8..116 C3
Boston Pde HNWL W7 *......116 B4

Boston Park Rd BTFD TW8 * 116 D6
Boston Pl CAMTN NW1.................2 E7
Boston Rd CROY/NA CR0.........196 A3
  EDGW HA8.................................44 E3
  EHAM E6...................................60 D3
  HNWL W7..................................115 K1
Bostonthorpe Rd HNWL W7 *...115 K2
Boston St BMSBY WC1N..............11 F1
Boswell Cl STMC/STPC BR5.....202 D3
Boswell Ct BMSBY WC1N...........11 F1
Boswell Rd THHTH CR7..............196 D1
Boswell St BMSBY WC1N...........11 F1
Bosworth Cl WALTH E17...............51 H4
Bosworth Rd BAR EN5..................20 E4
  DAGE RM10.................................92 C2
  FBAR/BDGN N11.........................48 D2
  NKENS W10...............................100 C3
Botany Bay La CHST BR7...........185 H5
Botany Cl EBAR EN4.....................34 A1
Botany Ter PUR RM19 *..............131 K5
Boteley Cl CHING E4......................38 B4
Botham Cl EDGW HA8.................44 E3
Botha Rd PLSTW E13...................107 F4
Bothwell Cl CAN/RD E16...........106 E4
Bothwell St HMSMTH W6............119 G6
Botolph Aly MON EC3R................13 G6
Botolph La MON EC3R..................13 G6
Botsford Rd RYNPK SW20..........177 H5
Bott Rd RDART DA2....................171 J6
Bott's Ms BAY/PAD W2...............100 E5
Botwell Common Rd
  HYS/HAR UB3.............................94 C6
Botwell Crs HYS/HAR UB3...........94 C5
Botwell La HYS/HAR UB3.............94 C6
Boughton Av HAYES BR2............199 J4
Boughton Rd THMD SE28..........127 K3
Boulcott St WCHPL E1................105 F5
The Boulevard FUL/PGN SW6 *
  WFD IG8.....................................54 A3
Boulogne Rd CROY/NA CR0.......196 E5
Boulter Gdns RAIN RM13............93 K4
Boulton Rd BCTR RM8..................92 A1
Boultwood Rd EHAM E6...............107 K5
Bounces La ED N9..........................36 D4
Bounces Rd ED N9.........................36 D4
Boundaries Rd BAL SW12...........160 E2
  FELT TW13...............................154 B3
Boundary Av WALTH E17...............69 H4
Boundary Business Ct
  MTCM CR4...............................178 C6
Boundary Cl BAR EN5.................20 D2
  GDMY/SEVK IG3........................90 E2
  KUT/HW KT1............................175 H6
  NWDGN UB2.............................114 B3
Boundary La CMBW SE5.............122 D6
  PLSTW E13...............................107 H3
Boundary Ms STJWD NW8 *...........8 G6
Boundary Pass WCHPL E1.............7 H6
Boundary Rd BARK IG11.............108 C1
  BFN/LL DA15............................147 K6
  CAR SM5...................................210 A5
  ED N9...36 E1
  EFNCH N2...................................47 H4
  PIN HA5.......................................59 H3
  PLSTW E13...............................107 G1
  ROM RM1.....................................75 J3
  STJWD NW8..................................8 G6
  WALTH E17.................................69 A1
  WBLY HA9....................................80 A1
  WIM/MER SW19.........................178 C2
Boundary Rw STHWK SE1..........18 A2
Boundary St BETH E2......................7 J5
  ERITH DA8.................................150 C1
Boundfield Rd CAT SE6...............165 J4
Bounds Green Rd
  FBAR/BDGN N11........................48 E3
Bourchier Cl SOHO/SHAV W1D...10 C5
Bourdon Pl MYFR/PKLN W1K.........9 K5
Bourdon Rd PGE/AN SE20..........181 K5
Bourdon St MYFR/PKLN W1K.......9 K5
Bourke Cl CLAP SW4...................161 K1
  WLSDN NW10..............................81 G3
Bourlet Cl FITZ W1T.......................10 A2
Bourn Av EBAR EN4.......................21 H6
  SEVS/STOTM N15........................67 K1
Bournbrook Rd
  BKHTH/KID SE3........................146 C4
Bourne Av HYS/HAR UB3...........113 F3
  RSLP HA4.....................................77 G3
  STHGT/OAK N14.........................34 E4
Bourne Cl ISLW TW7...................135 K4
  THDIT KT7.................................190 A6
Bourne Ct RSLP HA4......................77 F3
Bourne Dr MTCM CR4.................178 C5
Bourne End Rd NTHWD HA6......26 C6
Bourne Est HLCRC EC1N *..........11 J1
Bourne Gdns CHING E4................37 K6
Bournehall Av BUSH WD23..........28 A1
Bournehall La BUSH WD23..........28 A1
Bournehall Rd BUSH WD23..........28 A1
Bourne Hill PLMGR N13................34 E4
Bourne Hill Cl PLMGR N13 *.......35 F4
Bourne Md BXLY DA5....................149 K5
Bournemead Av NTHLT UB5.........94 E1
Bournemead Cl NTHLT UB5..........94 E2
Bournemouth Cl PECK SE15.......143 H3
Bournemouth Rd PECK SE15.....143 H3
  WIM/MER SW19.........................177 K4
Bourne Pde BXLY DA5 *..............169 J2
Bourne Rd BXLY DA5...................169 K1
  CEND/HSY/T N8..........................66 E1
  HAYES BR2...............................200 C5
  WAN E11...................................88 B2
Bourneside Crs STHGT/OAK N14..34 D3
Bourneside Gdns CAT SE6.........183 F6
Bourneside Rd BGVA SW1W.......16 C7
  CROY/NA CR0...........................196 C6
Bourne Ter BAY/PAD W2............101 F4
The Bourne STHGT/OAK N14 *....34 E3
Bourne V HAYES BR2.................199 K5
Bournevale Rd
  STRHM/NOR SW16....................161 K6
Bourne Wy GFD/PVL UB6..............79 K4
Bourne Wy HAYES BR2................199 K6

HOR/WEW KT19........................206 E2
  SUT SM1....................................208 D3
  SWLY BR8.................................187 K6
Bournewood Rd
  STMC/STPC BR5.......................202 C4
  WOOL/PLUM SE18....................148 B3
Bournville Rd CAT SE6..............164 D2
Bournwell Cl EBAR EN4................21 K4
Bourton Cl HYS/HAR UB3...........113 K1
Bousfield Rd NWCR SE14...........144 A3
Boutflower Rd BTSEA SW11.......140 D5
Boutique Hall LEW SE13 *..........145 F5
Bouverie Gdns
  KTN/HRWW/WS HA3...................61 K3
Bouverie Ms STNW/STAM N16.....68 A1
Bouverie Pl BAY/PAD W2...............8 B3
Bouverie Rd HRW HA1.................60 A6
  STNW/STAM N16.......................68 A6
Bouverie St EMB EC4Y.................11 K4
Bouvier Rd PEND EN3...................24 E1
Boveney Rd FSTH SE23...............164 A2
Bovill Rd FSTH SE23...................164 A2
Bovingdon Av WBLY HA9..............80 C4
Bovingdon La CDALE/KGS NW9...45 G4
Bovingdon Rd FUL/PGN SW6.....140 A2
Bovington Dr ARCH N19................66 C6
Bow Arrow La DART DA1..............171 K1
Bowater Cl BRXS/STRHM SW2...161 K1
  CDALE/KGS NW9.........................63 F2
Bowater Gdns SUN TW16...........172 B4
Bowater Pl BKHTH/KID SE3.......146 B1
Bowater Rd WBLY HA9..................62 E6
  WOOL/PLUM SE18....................126 C3
Bow Bridge Est BOW E3..............105 K1
Bow Churchyard STP EC4M *......12 D4
Bow Common La BOW E3............105 H3
Bowden Cl EBED/NFELT TW14...153 H3
Bowden St LBTH SE11.................122 B5
Bowditch DEPT SE8.....................124 C5
Bowdon Rd WALTH E17..................69 J4
Bowen Dr DUL SE21...................163 F5
Bowen Rd HRW HA1......................60 C3
Bowen St POP/IOD E14...............105 K5
Bowens Wd CROY/NA CR0.........213 H6
Bowenswood CROY/NA CR0......213 H6
Bower Av GNWCH SE10..............145 H2
Bower Cl CRW RM5........................57 F3
  NTHLT UB5..................................95 G1
Bowerdean St FUL/PGN SW6....140 A3
Bowerman Av NWCR SE14.........124 B6
Bowerman Rd WCHPL E1 *...........105 F5
Bowes Cl BFN/LL DA15...............168 C1
Bowes Rd ACT W3........................99 G6
  BCTR RM8...................................91 J2
  FBAR/BDGN N11........................48 B1
  WOT/HER KT12........................188 A6
Bowfell Rd HMSMTH W6.............119 F6
Bowford Av BXLYHN DA7...........149 F2
Bowhill Cl BRXN/ST SW9............142 B1
Bowie Cl CLAP SW4....................161 J2
Bowland Rd CLAP SW4...............141 J5
  WFD IG8.....................................53 G2
Bowland Yd KTBR SW1X *.............15 F3
Bow La NFNCH/WDSPK N12.......47 G3
  STP EC4M....................................12 D4
Bowl Ct WCHPL E1...........................7 H7
Bowley Cl NRWD SE19...............181 G2
Bowley La NRWD SE19...............181 G1
Bowley Rd NRWD SE19 *...........105 H6
Bowling Green Cl
  PUT/ROE SW15........................158 E2
Bowling Green La CLKNW EC1R...5 K7
Bowling Green Pl STHWK SE1 *...18 E2
Bowling Green Rw
  WOOL/PLUM SE18....................126 E4
Bowling Green St LBTH SE11.....122 B5
Bowling Green Wk IS N1................7 G5
Bowls Cl STAN HA7........................43 H1
Bowman Av CAN/RD E16...........106 C5
Bowman Ms
  WAND/EARL SW18....................159 J3
Bowmans Cl WEA W13...............116 C1
Bowmans Lea FSTH SE23...........163 K2
Bowman's Meadow
  WLGTN SM6..............................210 B1
Bowman's Ms HOLWY N7.............84 E1
  WCHPL E1................................104 C6
Bowman's Pl HOLWY N7...............84 E1
Bowmans Rd DART DA1.............170 C2
Bowmead ELTH/MOT SE9...........166 E4
Bowmore Wk CAMTN NW1...........84 D5
Bowness Cl HACK E8 *...................86 B4
Bowness Dr HSLWW TW4...........134 D5
Bowness Rd BXLYHN DA7...........149 J3
  CAT SE6.....................................165 F2
Bowness Wy HCH RM12.................93 J5
Bowood Rd CLAP SW4.................141 J6
  PEND EN3...................................25 F3
Bowring Gn OXHEY WD19 *.........41 G1
Bow Rd BOW E3............................105 J2
Bowrons Av ALP/SUD HA0...........79 K5
Bowsley Ct FELT TW13...............153 K4
Bow St COVGDN WC2E.................11 F4
  SRTFD E15..................................88 C3
Bowyer Cl EHAM E6.....................107 K4
Bowyer Pl CMBW SE5..................142 D1
Bowyers Ct TWK TW1..................136 C5
Bowyer St CMBW SE5.................142 D1
Boxall Rd DUL SE21....................163 F1
Boxelder Cl EDGW HA8.................44 E1
Boxgrove Rd ABYW SE2..............128 D3
Box La BARK IG11.........................109 J1
Boxley Rd MRDN SM4..................194 B1
Boxley St CAN/RD E16...............126 A1
Boxmoor Rd CRW RM5..................56 E5
  KTN/HRWW/WS HA3...................61 H1
Boxoll Rd DAGW RM9....................92 B2
Boxted Cl BKHH IG9.......................39 J3
Boxtree La
  KTN/HRWW/WS HA3...................42 C4
Boxtree Rd
  KTN/HRWW/WS HA3...................42 C3
Boxwood Cl WDR/YW UB7..........112 C2

Boxworth Cl
  NFNCH/WDSPK N12...................47 H1
Boxworth Gv IS N1.........................85 K6
Boyard Rd WOOL/PLUM SE18...127 G5
Boyce Wy PLSTW E13.................106 E3
Boycroft Av CDALE/KGS NW9......62 E3
Boyd Av STHL UB1........................114 E1
Boyd Cl KUTN/CMB KT2..............175 H3
Boydell Ct STJWD NW8..................83 H6
Boyd Rd WIM/MER SW19............178 C2
Boyfield St STHWK SE1................18 B3
Boyland Rd BMLY BR1................183 J1
Boyle Av STAN HA7.......................43 G2
Boyle Farm Rd THDIT KT7..........190 B3
Boyne Av HDN NW4........................64 B1
Boyne Rd DAGE RM10...................92 C1
  LEW SE13..................................145 G4
Boyne Terrace Ms NTGHL W11...119 J1
Boyson Rd WALW SE17...............122 D6
Boyton Cl CEND/HSY/T N8...........48 E6
  WCHPL E1................................105 F3
Boyton Rd CEND/HSY/T N8..........48 E6
Brabant Rd WDGN N22..................49 F5
Brabazon Av WLGTN SM6...........210 E5
Brabazon Rd HEST TW5..............134 E1
  NTHLT UB5..................................96 A2
Brabazon St POP/IOD E14..........105 K5
Brabourne Cl NRWD SE19..........181 F1
Brabourne Crs BXLYHN DA7.......129 G6
Brabourne Hts MLHL NW7.............31 G4
Brabourne Ri BECK BR3..............199 F2
Bracewell Av GFD/PVL UB6..........79 F3
Bracewell Rd NKENS W10..........100 A4
Bracewood Gdns
  CROY/NA CR0...........................212 B1
Bracey St FSBYPK N4 *................66 E2
Bracken Av BAL SW12.................161 F1
  CROY/NA CR0...........................214 B1
Brackenbridge Dr RSLP HA4.......77 H1
Brackenbury Gdns
  HMSMTH W6..............................118 E3
Brackenbury Rd EFNCH N2.........47 G6
  HMSMTH W6..............................118 E3
Bracken Cl EHAM E6...................107 K4
  WHTN TW2................................155 G2
Brackendale WCHMH N21.............35 F4
Brackendale Cl HSLW TW3.........135 G2
Brackendene RDART DA2...........170 B6
Bracken Dr CHIG IG7.....................54 A2
Bracken End ISLW TW7................135 J6
Bracken Gdns BARN SW13.........138 D3
Brackenhill RSLP HA4....................77 J2
Bracken Hill Cl BMLY BR1..........183 J4
Bracken Hill La BMLY BR1..........183 J4
Bracken Ms ROMW/RG RM7........74 D5
The Brackens EN EN1...................36 A6
  ORP BR6.....................................217 G3
The Bracken CHING E4..................38 A4
Brackley Cl WLGTN SM6............210 E6
Brackley St BARB EC2Y................12 D1
Brackley Ter CHSWK W4.............118 B5
Bracklyn St IS N1............................6 E2
Bracknell Cl WDGN N22................49 G4
Bracknell Gdns HAMP NW3..........83 F2
Bracknell Wy HAMP NW3..............83 F2
Bracondale ESH/CLAY KT10.......204 C3
Bracondale Rd ABYW SE2...........128 B3
Bracton La RDART DA2...............170 C5
Bradbourne Rd BXLY DA5...........169 J2
Bradbourne St FUL/PGN SW6....139 K3
Bradbury Cl NWDGN UB2...........114 E4
Bradbury St STNW/STAM N16......86 A2
Braddock Cl CRW RM5................56 E2
  ISLW TW7.................................136 A4
Braddon Rd BAR EN5...................20 C4
Braddon Rd RCH/KEW TW9.......137 G3
Braddyll St GNWCH SE10...........125 H5
Bradenham Av WELL DA16..........148 B5
Bradenham Cl WALW SE17........122 E6
Bradenham Rd
  KTN/HRWW/WS HA3...................61 H1
  YEAD UB4....................................95 F2
Braden St MV/WKIL W9..............101 F3
Bradfield Dr BARK IG11...............91 G3
Bradfield Rd CAN/RD E16...........125 K2
  RSLP HA4.....................................77 J3
Bradford Cl HAYES BR2..............201 G5
  SYD SE26...................................163 J6
  TOTM N17...................................50 B3
Bradford Dr HOR/WEW KT19....207 H4
Bradford Rd ACT W3...................118 B2
  IL IG1..72 D5
Bradgate Rd CAT SE6..................164 E1
Brading Crs WAN E11.....................71 F6
Brading Rd BRXS/STRHM SW2..162 A2
  CROY/NA CR0...........................196 A3
Brading Ter SHB W12.................118 D3
Bradiston Rd MV/WKIL W9.........100 D2
Bradley Cl HOLWY N7...................84 E4
Bradley Gdns WEA W13.................97 H5
Bradley Rd NRWD SE19..............180 D2
  PEND EN3...................................25 G1
Bradley's Cl IS N1............................5 K2
Bradley Stone Rd EHAM E6........107 K5
Bradman Rw EDGW HA8..............44 E3
Bradmead VX/NE SW8 *.............141 G1
Bradmore Park Rd
  HMSMTH W6..............................118 E4
Bradshaw Cl WIM/MER SW19....177 K2
Bradshaw Cottages
  POP/IOD E14 *...........................105 G5
Bradshaw Dr MLHL NW7...............46 A3
Bradshaws Cl SNWD SE25.........181 H3
Bradstock Rd EW KT17...............207 H6
  HOM E9.......................................87 F4
Brad St STHWK SE1.......................17 K1
Bradwell Av DAGE RM10..............74 C1
Bradwell Cl HCH RM12.................93 K5
  SWFD E18....................................70 D1
Bradwell Ms UED N18....................36 C6
Bradwell Rd BKHH IG9..................39 J3

Brady Dr BMLY BR1......................185 F6
Bradymead EHAM E6..................108 A5
Brady St WCHPL E1......................104 D3
Braemar Av ALP/SUD HA0............79 K5
  BXLYHN DA7.............................149 K5
  THHTH CR7................................180 C6
  WDGN N22....................................49 F4
  WIM/MER SW19.........................159 K4
  WLSDN NW10..............................81 F1
Braemar Gdns BFN/LL DA15......167 J5
  CDALE/KGS NW9........................44 E4
  WWKM BR4................................199 F5
Braemar Rd BTFD TW8................116 E6
  PLSTW E13................................106 D3
  SEVS/STOTM N15.......................68 A3
Braeside BECK BR3.....................182 D1
Braeside Av RYNPK SW20..........177 H4
Braeside Cl PIN HA5......................42 A3
Braeside Crs BXLYHN DA7.........149 K5
Braeside Rd
  STRHM/NOR SW16....................179 H3
Braes St IS N1.................................85 H5
Braesyde Cl BELV DA17..............128 G3
Brafferton Rd CROY/NA CR0.......211 J2
Bragg Cl BCTR RM8........................91 H4
Bragg Rd TEDD TW11..................173 K3
Braham St WCHPL E1....................13 K4
Braid Av ACT W3.............................99 G5
Braid Cl FELT TW13.....................154 E4
Braidwood Rd CAT SE6...............165 G3
Braidwood St STHWK SE1...........19 G1
Brailsford Cl WIM/MER SW19.....178 D3
Brailsford Rd
  BRXS/STRHM SW2....................162 B1
Brainton Av
  EBED/NFELT TW14....................154 A2
Braintree Av REDBR IG4................71 J2
Braintree Rd DAGE RM10.............92 C1
  RSLP HA4.....................................77 F3
Braintree St BETH E2 *..............104 E2
Braithwaite Av ROMW/RG RM7...74 C4
Braithwaite Gdns STAN HA7.........43 K4
Braithwaite Rd PEND EN3.............25 H4
Bramalea Cl HGT N6......................66 A3
Bramall Cl SRTFD E15...................88 D3
Bramber Ct BTFD TW8 *.............117 F4
Bramber Rd
  NFNCH/WDSPK N12...................47 J1
  WKENS W14...............................119 J6
Bramble Acres Cl BELMT SM2....208 E5
Bramble Banks CAR SM5............210 A6
Bramblebury Rd
  WOOL/PLUM SE18....................127 J5
Bramble Cl BECK BR3.................199 F2
  CROY/NA CR0...........................213 J2
  SEVS/STOTM N15.......................68 C1
  STAN HA7....................................43 K3
Bramble Cft ERITH DA8..............129 K4
Brambledown Cl WWKM BR4......200 C2
Brambledown Rd CAR SM5.........210 A5
  SAND/SEL CR2..........................212 A6
Bramble Gdns SHB W12................99 H6
Bramble La HPTN TW12...............172 E2
Brambles Cl ISLW TW7................136 C1
The Brambles CHIG IG7 *.............54 E2
  SUT SM1...................................194 C6
  WDR/YW UB7............................112 A5
  WIM/MER SW19 *......................177 J1
Bramblewood Cl CAR SM5..........194 D5
The Bramblings CHING E4.............38 B2
Bramcote Av MTCM CR4.............194 E1
Bramcote Gv
  BERM/RHTH SE16....................123 K5
Bramcote Rd PUT/ROE SW15....138 E5
Bramdean Crs LEE/GVPK SE12...165 K3
Bramdean Gdns
  LEE/GVPK SE12........................165 K3
Bramerton Rd BECK BR3.............182 C6
Bramerton St CHEL SW3.............120 D6
Bramfield Rd BTSEA SW11.........160 D1
Bramford Rd
  WAND/EARL SW18....................140 B5
Bramham Gdns ECT SW5............120 A5
  CHSGTN KT9.............................205 K3
Bramhope La CHARL SE7............126 A6
Bramlands Cl BTSEA SW11........140 D4
Bramley Cl HYS/HAR UB3............94 E6
  ORP BR6.....................................201 G5
  PIN HA5..40 D6
  SAND/SEL CR2..........................211 J3
  STHGT/OAK N14.........................22 B6
  WALTH E17..................................51 H4
  WFD IG8.......................................53 G3
  WHTN TW2................................155 H1
Bramley Crs GNTH/NBYPK IG2....72 A3
  VX/NE SW8................................141 J1
Bramley Gdns OXHEY WD19........41 G1
Bramley Hl SAND/SEL CR2..........211 J3
Bramley Hyrst
  SAND/SEL CR2 *........................211 J3
Bramley Ldg ALP/SUD HA0..........79 K3
Bramley Pde STHGT/OAK N14......22 C2
Bramley Pl DART DA1..................150 D5
Bramley Rd BELMT SM2..............208 B6
  EA W5..116 D3
  NKENS W10...............................100 B6
  STHGT/OAK N14.........................22 B6
  SUT SM1....................................209 H3
Bramley Wy HSLWW TW4...........134 E6
  WWKM BR4................................198 E6
Brampton Cl CLPT E5 *..................68 D6
Brampton Gv HDN NW4.................63 K1
  KTN/HRWW/WS HA3...................43 G5
  WBLY HA9....................................62 C5
Brampton La HDN NW4..................64 A1
Brampton Park Rd WDGN N22......49 F6
Brampton Rd BXLYHN DA7.........148 E4
  CDALE/KGS NW9........................44 D4
  CEND/HSY/T N8..........................66 D2
  CROY/NA CR0...........................197 G4
  EHAM E6.....................................107 H3
  OXHEY WD19..............................41 H2
  SEVS/STOTM N15.......................67 J2
  WALTH E17..................................51 G4
Bramshaw Gdns OXHEY WD19....41 H1
Bramshaw Ri NWMAL KT3..........192 B3

Bramshaw Rd HOM E9...................87 F4
Bramshill Gdns KTTN NW5...........84 B1
Bramshill Rd WLSDN NW10..........99 G1
Bramshot Av CHARL SE7.............126 A6
Bramshot Wy OXHEY WD19..........26 E4
Bramston Cl BARK/HLT IG6..........55 F2
Bramston Rd MTCM CR4.............178 E5
  WLSDN NW10..............................99 J1
Bramwell Cl SUN TW16...............172 C5
Bramwell Ms IS N1.........................85 F6
Brancaster Dr MLHL NW7.............45 J3
Brancaster Rd
  GNTH/NBYPK IG2.......................72 E3
  STRHM/NOR SW16....................161 K5
Branceph Gdns BKHH IG9............38 E4
Branch Hl HAMP NW3....................83 G1
Branch Rd BARK/HLT IG6.............55 H1
  POP/IOD E14.............................105 G5
Branch St CMBW SE5..................143 F1
Brancker Rd
  KTN/HRWW/WS HA3...................43 K6
Brancroft Wy PEND EN3................25 G2
Brand Cl FSBYPK N4......................67 H5
Brandesbury Sq WFD IG8..............54 A3
Brandlehow Rd
  PUT/ROE SW15........................139 J5
Brandon Est WALW SE17.............122 C6
Brandon Ms BARB EC2Y *.............12 E1
Brandon Rd DART DA1................171 K2
  HOLWY N7...................................84 E5
  NWDGN UB2.............................114 E5
  SUT SM1...................................209 F2
  WALTH E17..................................70 A1
Brandon St WALW SE17................18 D7
Brandram Ms LEW SE13 *...........145 H5
Brandram Rd LEW SE13..............145 H4
Brandreth Ct HRW HA1 *..............61 F5
Brandreth Rd EHAM E6...............107 K5
  TOOT SW17...............................161 G4
The Brandries WLGTN SM6.........210 D1
Brandville Gdns BARK/HLT IG6....72 B2
Brandville Rd WDR/YW UB7.......112 B2
Brandy Wy BELMT SM2...............208 E5
Brangbourne Rd BMLY BR1.........183 F1
Brangton Rd LBTH SE11..............122 A5
Brangwyn Crs
  WIM/MER SW19.........................178 C5
Branksea St FUL/PGN SW6.........139 H1
Branksome Cl UED N18.................50 B2
Branksome Cl TEDD TW11..........155 J6
  WOT/HER KT12..........................188 C5
Branksome Rd
  BRXS/STRHM SW2....................141 K6
  WIM/MER SW19.........................177 K4
Branksome Wy
  KTN/HRWW/WS HA3...................62 D3
  NWMAL KT3...............................175 K5
Bransby Rd CHSGTN KT9...........206 A4
Branscombe Gdns WCHMH N21...35 G2
Branscombe St LEW SE13...........144 E4
Bransdale Cl KIL/WHAMP NW6....82 E6
Bransell Cl SWLY BR8..................203 K3
Bransgrove Rd EDGW HA8...........44 B4
Branston Crs STMC/STPC BR5...201 J3
Branston Rd RCH/KEW TW9 *....137 G2
Brants Wk HNWL W7 *...................96 E3
Brantwood Av ERITH DA8............149 K1
  ISLW TW7..................................136 B5
Brantwood Cl WALTH E17.............51 K6
Brantwood Gdns ENC/FH EN2......22 E6
  REDBR IG4...................................71 J2
Brantwood Rd BXLYHN DA7.......149 J3
  HNHL SE24................................142 D6
  SAND/SEL CR2..........................211 J6
  TOTM N17...................................50 C2
Brantwood Wy
  STMC/STPC BR5.......................186 B6
Brasenose Dr BARN SW13..........119 F6
Brasher Cl GFD/PVL UB6..............78 D3
Brassey Cl EBED/NFELT TW14 *.153 K3
Brassey Rd KIL/WHAMP NW6......82 D4
Brassey Sq BTSEA SW11............141 F4
Brassie Av ACT W3.........................99 G5
Brasted Rd ERITH DA8.................150 B1
Brathway Rd
  WAND/EARL SW18....................159 K2
Bratley St WCHPL E1...................104 C3
Braund Av GFD/PVL UB6..............96 B3
Braundton Av BFN/LL DA15........168 A3
Braunston Dr YEAD UB4................95 J3
Bravington Av MV/WKIL W9.........100 D3
Bravington Rd MV/WKIL W9.........100 C3
Bravingtons Wk IS N1 *...................5 G2
Braxfield Rd BROCKY SE4...........144 B5
Bracted Pk
  STRHM/NOR SW16....................180 A2
Brayard's Rd PECK SE15.............143 J3
Braybourne Dr ISLW TW7...........136 A1
Braybrooke Gdns NRWD SE19...181 F3
Braybourne Av OXHEY WD19 *....41 H4
Braycourt Av WOT/HER KT12......188 B4
Bray Crs BERM/RHTH SE16........124 A2
Braydon Rd STNW/STAM N16.......68 C5
Bray Dr CAN/RD E16....................106 C6
Brayfield Ter IS N1...........................85 G5
Brayford Sq WCHPL E1 *.............104 E5
Bray Pl CHEL SW3.........................120 E5
Brayton Gdns ENC/FH EN2...........22 D4
Braywood Rd ELTH/MOT SE9......147 J3
Brazil Cl CROY/NA CR0...............195 K4
Breach La DAGW RM9..................110 C2
Bread St STP EC4M........................12 D5
Breakspears
  STMC/STPC BR5.......................186 B4
Breakspears Dr BRCKY SE4........144 D3
Breakspears Rd BROCKY SE4.....144 C3
Bream Cl TOTM N17.......................68 D1
Bream Gdns EHAM E6..................108 A2
Breamore Cl PUT/ROE SW15.....158 D3
Breamore Rd GDMY/SEVK IG3......73 F6
Bream's Buildings LINN WC2A......11 J3
Bream St BOW E3............................87 J5

Breamwater Gdns
 RCHPK/HAM TW10....156 C5
Brearley Cl EDGW HA8....44 E3
Breasley Cl PUT/ROE SW15....138 E5
Breasy Pl HDN NW4 *....5 J5
Brechin Pl SKENS SW7 *....120 B5
Brecknock Rd ARCH N19....84 C2
Brecknock Road Est
 ARCH N19 *....84 D3
Brecon Cl MTCM CR4....195 K1
 WPK KT4....193 F6
Brecon Gn CDALE/KGS NW9 *....63 G3
Brecon Rd CROY/NA CRO....197 G4
 HMSMTH W6....119 H6
Brede Cl EHAM E6....108 A2
Bredgar Rd ARCH N19....66 C6
Bredhurst Cl PGE/AN SE20....181 K2
Bredon Rd CROY/NA CRO....197 G4
Breer St FUL/PGN SW6....140 A4
Breezer's Hl WAP E1W *....104 C6
Bremans Rw
 WAND/EARL SW18....160 B4
Bremer Ms WALTH E17 *....69 G3
Bremer Rd SKENS SW7 *....120 B3
Brenchley Cl CHST BR7....185 F4
 HAYES BR2....199 J2
Brenchley Gdns EDUL SE22....163 K1
Brenchley Rd STMC/STPC BR5....185 K5
Brenda Rd TOOT SW17....160 E4
Brende Gdns E/WMO/HCT KT8....189 G2
Brendon Av WLSDN NW10....81 G2
Brendon Cl ERITH DA8....150 C2
 ESH/CLAY KT10....204 C4
 HYS/HAR UB3....133 F1
Brendon Dr ESH/CLAY KT10....204 C4
Brendon Gdns
 RYLN/HDSTN HA2....78 B2
Brendon Rd EFNCH N2....47 C5
Brendon Rd BMR8....74 B5
 ELTH/MOT SE9....167 J4
Brendon St MBLAR W1H....8 D3
Brendon Vis WCHMN N21 *....35 J5
Brendon Wy EN EN1....36 A2
Brenley Cl MTCM CR4....179 F6
Brenley Gdns ELTH/MOT SE9....146 C5
Brent Cl BXLY DA5....169 F5
Brentcot Cl WEA W13....97 H3
Brent Crs WLSDN NW10....98 B1
Brent Cross F/O HDN NW4....64 A3
Brentfield WLSDN NW10....80 D5
Brentfield Cl WLSDN NW10....81 F4
Brentfield Gdns CRICK NW2 *....64 B4
Brentfield Rd DART DA1....171 K1
 WLSDN NW10....81 F4
Brentford Cl YEAD UB4....95 H5
Brent Gn HDN NW4....64 A3
Brentham Wy EA W5....97 K3
Brenthouse Rd HACK E8....86 D5
Brenthurst Rd WLSDN NW10....81 H4
Brentlands Dr DART DA1....171 K3
Brent La DART DA1....171 J3
Brent Lea BTFD TW8....136 D1
Brentmead Cl HNWL W7....96 E6
Brentmead Gdns WLSDN NW10....98 B1
Brenton St POP/IOD E14....105 G5
Brent Park Rd CDALE/KGS NW9....63 J3
Brent Pl BAR EN5....20 E6
Brent River Park Wk
 GFD/PVL UB6....97 H2
Brent Rd BTFD TW8....116 D6
 CAN/RD E16....106 E5
 NWDGN UB2....114 B3
 SAND/SEL CR2....212 D6
 WOOL/PLUM SE18....147 G1
Brentside BTFD TW8....116 D6
Brentside Cl WEA W13....97 F3
Brent Side BTFD TW8....116 D6
Brent Ter CRICK NW2....64 A6
The Brent DART DA1....171 K2
Brentvale Av ALP/SUD HA0....80 B6
 STHL UB1....115 K1
Brent View Rd CDALE/KGS NW9....63 J3
Brent Wy BTFD TW8....136 E1
 FNCH N3....47 E2
 WBLY HA9....80 D4
Brentwick Gdns BTFD TW8....117 F4
Brentwood Rd ELTH/MOT SE9....167 H3
Brentwood Rd ROM RM1....75 H3
Brereton Rd TOTM N17....50 B3
Bressenden Pl WESTW SW1E....15 K4
Bressey Av EN EN1....24 C2
Bressey Gv SWFD E18....52 D5
Brett Cl NTHLT UB5....95 H2
 STNW/STAM N16....68 A6
Brett Crs WLSDN NW10....81 F6
Brettell St WALW SE17....122 E5
Brettenham Av WALTH E17....51 J4
Brettenham Rd UED N18....36 C6
 WALTH E17....51 J5
Brett Gdns DAGW RM9....92 A5
Brett Pas HACK E8....86 D3
Brett Rd BAR EN5....32 A1
 HACK E8....86 D3
Brett Vis ACT W3 *....99 F4
Brewers Fld RDART DA2....171 F4
Brewer St REGST W1B....10 B5
Brewery Rd ALP/SUD HA0....79 C3
Brewery Rd HAYES BR2....200 D5
 HOLWY N7....85 F4
 WOOL/PLUM SE18....127 J5
Brewery Sq FSBYE EC1V....6 B7
 STHWK SE1....19 J1
Brewhouse La WAP E1W *....123 J1
Brewhouse Rd
 WOOL/PLUM SE18....126 E4
Brewhouse St PUT/ROE SW15....139 H5
Brewhouse Wk
 BERM/RHTH SE16....124 B1
Brewhouse Yd FSBYE EC1V....6 A6
Brewood Rd BCTR RM8....91 H4
Brewster Gdns NKENS W10....100 A4
Brewster Rd LEY E10....69 K5
Brian Cl HCH RM12....93 K2
Brian Rd CHDH RM6....73 J2

Briants Cl PIN HA5....41 J5
Briant St NWCR SE14....144 A2
Briar Av STRHM/NOR SW16....180 A3
Briar Bank CAR SM5....210 A6
Briarbank Rd WEA W13....97 G5
Briar Cl BKHH IG9....39 H4
 HPTN TW12....172 E1
 ISLW TW7....136 A6
 PLMGR N13....35 J5
Briar Crs NTHLT UB5....78 B4
Briardale Gdns HAMP NW3....82 E1
Briarfield Av EFNCH N2....47 F6
Briarfield Cl BXLYHN DA7....149 H3
Briar Gdns HAYES BR2....199 J5
Briar La CAR SM5....210 A6
 CROY/NA CRO....213 K2
Briar Rd BXLY DA5....170 A5
 CRICK NW2....82 A2
 KTN/HRWW/WS HA3....61 J2
 STRHM/NOR SW16....179 K6
 WHTN TW2....155 K3
Briarswood Wy ORP BR6....217 F3
Briar Wk EDGW HA8....44 E3
 NKENS W10 *....100 C3
 PUT/ROE SW15....138 E5
Briar Wy WDR/YW UB7....112 D2
Briarwood Cl
 CDALE/KGS NW9 *....62 E3
 FELT TW13....153 H5
Briarwood Ct WPK KT4 *....192 D5
Briarwood Dr NTHWD HA6....40 E5
Briarwood Rd CLAP SW4....141 J5
 EW KT17....207 J4
Briary Cl EDGW HA8....44 D5
 HAMP NW3 *....83 J5
Briary Ct SCUP DA14....186 C1
Briary La ED N9....36 A5
Brickbarn Cl WBPTN SW10 *....140 B7
Brick Ct EMB EC4Y *....11 J4
Brickett Cl RSLP HA4....58 A2
Brick Farm Cl RCH/KEW TW9....137 J2
Brickfield Cl BTFD TW8....136 D1
Brickfield Cottages
 WOOL/PLUM SE18....128 A6
Brickfield Farm Gdns
 ORP BR6....216 C2
Brickfield La BAR EN5....31 H1
 HYS/HAR UB3....113 G6
Brickfield Rd BOW E3....105 K3
 THHTH CR7....180 C4
 WIM/MER SW19....160 A6
Brickfields RYLN/HDSTN HA2....60 D6
Brickfields Wy WDR/YW UB7....112 C3
Brickfield Vis CAR SM5 *....209 J1
Brick Kiln Cl OXHEY WD19....27 J1
Brick La BETH E2....7 K5
 EN EN1....24 D4
 NTHLT UB5....95 K2
 STAN HA7....43 K3
Brick St MYFR/PKLN W1K....15 J1
Brickwall La RSLP HA4....58 C5
Brickwood Cl SYD SE26....163 J5
Brickwood Rd CROY/NA CRO....197 F6
Brideale Cl PECK SE15....123 G6
Bride Ct EMB EC4Y *....12 A4
Bride La EMB EC4Y *....12 A4
Bridel Ms FSBYE EC1V *....6 B5
Bridewain St STHWK SE1....19 J4
Bridewell Pl BLKFR EC4V *....12 A4
 WAP E1W....123 J1
Bridford Ms GTPST W1W *....9 K1
Bridge Av HMSMTH W6....119 F5
 HNWL W7....96 D4
Bridge Cl EN EN1....100 D5
 NKENS W10....100 B5
 ROMW/RG RM7....75 G3
Bridge Dr PLMGR N13....35 F6
Bridge End WALTH E17....52 A4
Bridge End Cl KUTN/CMB KT2....175 H4
Bridgefield Rd SUT SM1....208 E4
Bridge Gdns E/WMO/HCT KT8....189 G1
Bridge Ga WCHMH N21....35 J2
Bridge House Quay
 POP/IOD E14....125 F1
Bridgeland Rd CAN/RD E16....106 E6
Bridgelands Cl BECK BR3....182 C3
Bridge La BTSEA SW11....140 D2
 GLDGN NW11....64 C2
Bridgeman Rd IS N1....85 F5
 TEDD TW11....174 B2
Bridge Mdw NWCR SE14....124 A6
Bridgenhall Rd EN EN1....24 B2
Bridge Pde
 STRHM/NOR SW16....179 K1
 WCHMH N21 *....35 J2
Bridge Pk WAND/EARL SW18....139 K6
Bridge Pl CROY/NA CRO....196 E5
 PIM SW1V....15 K6
Bridgepoint Pl HGT N6....66 C6
Bridgeport Pl WAP E1W *....123 H1
Bridge Rd BECK BR3....182 C3
 BXLYHN DA7....149 F4
 CHSGTN KT9....206 A3
 E/WMO/HCT KT8....189 K1
 ED N9....36 C5
 EHAM E6....89 K6
 ERITH DA8....150 D2
 HSLW TW3....135 J3
 NWDGN UB2....114 E2
 RAIN RM13....111 J3
 SRTFD E15....88 B5
 STMC/STPC BR5....202 C3
 SUT SM1....209 F4
 TWK TW1....156 C1
 WALTH E17....69 H4
 WBLY HA9....80 C1
 WDGN N22....48 E4
 WLSDN NW10....81 G5

Bridges Road Ms
 WIM/MER SW19....178 A2
Bridge St CHSWK W4....118 A4
 TWK TW1....156 B2
 WHALL SW1A....16 E3
Bridge Ter LEW SE13 *....145 G5
 SRTFD E15....88 B5
The Bridge EA W5 *....117 C1
 KTN/HRWW/WS HA3....61 F1
Bridgetown Cl NRWD SE19....181 F1
Bridgeview HMSMTH W6....119 F5
Bridge Vis WIM/MER SW19 *....177 K1
Bridgewater Cl
 STMC/STPC BR5....185 K5
Bridgewater Gdns EDGW HA8....44 B5
Bridgewater Rd ALP/SUD HA0....79 K6
 SRTFD E15....88 A6
Bridgewater Sq BARB EC2Y *....12 C1
Bridgewater St BARB EC2Y....12 C1
Bridge Wy GLDGN NW11....64 C2
 WHTN TW2....155 H2
Bridgeway BARK IG11....91 F5
Bridgeway St CAMTN NW1....4 C3
Bridge Wharf Rd ISLW TW7....136 C4
Bridgewood Cl PGE/AN SE20....181 J3
Bridgewood Rd
 STRHM/NOR SW16....179 J3
 WPK KT4....207 J2
Bridgford St
 WAND/EARL SW18....160 B5
Bridgman Rd CHSWK W4....117 K3
Bridgwater Rd RSLP HA4....76 E2
Bridle Cl HOR/WEW KT19....206 E2
 KUT/HW KT1....190 E1
 SUN TW16....172 A5
Bridle La SOHO/CST W1F....10 C5
 TWK TW1....156 C1
Bridle Pth CROY/NA CRO....210 E1
The Bridle Pth WFD IG8....52 C3
Bridlepath Wy
 EBED/NFELT TW14....153 H2
Bridle Rd CROY/NA CRO....213 J5
 ESH/CLAY KT10....205 H4
 PIN HA5....59 C3
Bridle Wy CROY/NA CRO....213 J5
 ORP BR6....216 C2
Bridlington Rd ED N9....36 D2
 OXHEY WD19....27 H5
Bridport Av ROMW/RG RM7....74 D3
Bridport Pl IS N1....7 F2
Bridport Rd GFD/PVL UB6....78 B6
 THHTH CR7....180 B6
 UED N18....50 A1
Bridstow Pl BAY/PAD W2....100 E5
Brief St BRXN/ST SW9....142 C2
Brierley CROY/NA CRO....213 K6
Brierley Av ED N9....36 E3
Brierley Cl SNWD SE25....197 H1
Brierley Rd BAL SW12....161 H4
 WAN E11....88 B2
Brierly Gdns BETH E2 *....104 E1
Brigade Cl RYLN/HDSTN HA2....60 D6
Brigade St BKHTH/KID SE3 *....145 J3
Brigadier Av ENC/FH EN2....23 J2
Brigadier Hl ENC/FH EN2....23 J1
Briggs Cl MTCM CR4....179 G4
Bright Cl BELV DA17....128 E4
Brightfield Rd LEE/GVPK SE12....145 H6
Brightling Rd BROCKY SE4....164 C1
Brightlingsea Pl POP/IOD E14....105 H6
Brightman Rd
 WAND/EARL SW18....160 C3
Brighton Av WALTH E17....69 H2
Brighton Dr NTHLT UB5....78 A4
Brighton Rd BELMT SM2....209 G5
 EFNCH N2....47 G5
 EHAM E6....108 A2
 SAND/SEL CR2....211 J6
 STNW/STAM N16....86 A2
 SURB KT6....190 D3
Brighton Ter BRXN/ST SW9....142 A5
Brights Av RAIN RM13....111 K3
Brightside Rd LEW SE13....165 G1
Bright St POP/IOD E14....105 K5
Brightwell Cl CROY/NA CRO....196 B5
Brightwell Crs TOOT SW17....178 E1
Brig Ms DEPT SE8....124 D6
Brigstock Rd BELV DA17....129 J4
 THHTH CR7....196 C2
Brill Pl CAMTN NW1....4 D3
Brim Hl EFNCH N2....47 G3
Brimpsfield Cl ABYW SE2....128 C3
Brimsdown Av PEND EN3....25 G2
Brimstone Cl ORP BR6....217 J5
Brindle Ga BFN/LL DA15....167 K4
Brindley Cl ALP/SUD HA0....79 H6
 BXLYHN DA7....149 H4
Brindley St BROCKY SE4....144 C2
Brindley Wy BMLY BR1....183 K1
 STHL UB1....96 B6
Brindwood Rd CHING E4....37 H5
Brinkburn Cl ABYW SE2....128 B4
 EDGW HA8....44 D6
Brinkburn Gdns EDGW HA8....44 C6
Brinkley Rd WPK KT4....192 E6
Brinklow Crs
 WOOL/PLUM SE18....147 G1
Brinkworth Rd CLAY IG5....53 G1
Brinkworth Wy HOM E9....87 H4
Brinsdale Rd HDN NW4....46 B6
Brinsley Rd
 KTN/HRWW/WS HA3....42 D5
Brinsley St WCHPL E1 *....104 D5
Brinsworth Cl WHTN TW2....155 J4
Brinton Wk STHWK SE1....18 A1
Brion Pl POP/IOD E14....106 A4
Brisbane Av WIM/MER SW19....178 A4
Brisbane Rd IL IG1....72 C5
 EA W5....116 E3
 LEY E10....69 K6
Brisbane St CMBW SE5....142 E1
Briscoe Cl WAN E11....70 D6
Briscoe Rd WIM/MER SW19....178 C2

Briset Rd ELTH/MOT SE9....146 C4
Briset St FARR EC1M....12 A1
Briset Wy HOLWY N7....67 F6
Bristol Cl STWL/WRAY TW19....152 B1
 WLGTN SM6....210 E6
Bristol Gdns MV/WKIL W9....101 F3
Bristol Ms MV/WKIL W9....101 F3
Bristol Park Rd WALTH E17 *....69 G1
Bristol Rd BTFD E7....89 F4
 GFD/PVL UB6....78 B6
 MRDN SM4....194 B2
Briston Gv CEND/HSY/T N8....66 E3
Bristowe Cl BRXS/STRHM SW2....162 B1
Bristow Rd BXLYHN DA7....149 F2
 CROY/NA CRO....210 E2
 HSLW TW3....135 G4
 NRWD SE19....181 F1
Britannia Cl CLAP SW4....141 J5
 ERITH DA8....130 C6
 NTHLT UB5....95 H2
Britannia Ga CAN/RD E16....125 K1
Britannia La WHTN TW2....155 H2
Britannia Rd BRYLDS KT5....191 G4
 FUL/PGN SW6....140 A1
 IL IG1....90 B1
 NFNCH/WDSPK N12....33 G6
 POP/IOD E14....124 D4
Britannia Rw IS N1....85 J6
Britannia St FSBYW WC1X....5 G4
Britannia Wk IS N1....6 E4
Britannia Wy FUL/PGN SW6....140 A1
 STWL/WRAY TW19....152 A2
 WLSDN NW10....98 D3
British Est BOW E3....105 J2
British Gv CHSWK W4....118 C5
British Grove Pas CHSWK W4 *....118 C5
British Legion Rd CHING E4....38 D4
British St BOW E3....105 H2
Britten Cl BORE WD6....30 E1
 GLDGN NW11....65 F5
Brittenden Pde ORP BR6 *....217 F4
Britten Dr STHL UB1....96 A5
Britten St CHEL SW3....120 C5
Brittidge Rd WLSDN NW10 *....81 G5
Britton Cl CAT SE6....165 G2
Britton St FARR EC1M....6 A7
Brixham Crs RSLP HA4....58 E5
Brixham Gdns GDMY/SEVK IG3....90 E3
Brixham Rd WELL DA16....148 E2
Brixham St CAN/RD E16....127 F1
Brixton HI BRXS/STRHM SW2....162 A1
Brixton Hill Pl
 BRXS/STRHM SW2....161 K2
Brixton Ov BRXS/STRHM SW2....142 B5
Brixton Rd BRXN/ST SW9....142 B5
Brixton Station Rd
 BRXN/ST SW9....142 B4
Brixton Water La
 BRXS/STRHM SW2....142 A6
Broadbent Cl HGT N6....66 B5
Broadbent St
 MYFR/PKLN W1K....9 J5
Broadberry Ct UED N18....50 D1
Broad Bridge Cl
 BKHTH/KID SE3....145 K1
Broad Common Est
 STNW/STAM N16 *....68 C5
Broadcoombe SAND/SEL CR2....213 F5
Broad Ct COVGDN WC2E *....11 F4
Broadcroft Av STAN HA7....43 K5
Broadcroft Rd
 STMC/STPC BR5....201 J4
Broadeaves Cl SAND/SEL CR2....212 A3
Broadfield Cl CRICK NW2....82 A1
 ROM RM1....75 H2
Broadfield Ct BUSH WD23....28 E4
Broadfield La CAMTN NW1....84 E5
Broadfield Pde EDGW HA8 *....30 D5
Broadfield Rd CAT SE6....165 H3
Broadfields E/WMO/HCT KT8....189 J3
 RYLN/HDSTN HA2....42 B5
Broadfields Av EDGW HA8....30 D6
 WCHMH N21....35 G2
Broadfields Hts EDGW HA8 *....30 D6
Broadfield Sq EN EN1....24 D4
Broadfields Wy WLSDN NW10....81 H3
Broadfield Wy BKHH IG9....39 G5
Broadgate EBAR EN4....21 F2
Broadgates Rd
 WAND/EARL SW18....160 C3
Broad Green Av CROY/NA CRO....196 C4
Broadhead Strd
 CDALE/KGS NW9....45 H5
Broadhinton Rd CLAP SW4....141 G4
Broadhurst Av EDGW HA8....30 D4
 GDMY/SEVK IG3....91 F2
Broadhurst Cl
 KIL/WHAMP NW6....83 G4
 RCHPK/HAM TW10....137 G6
Broadhurst Gdns
 KIL/WHAMP NW6....83 G4
 RSLP HA4....59 G6
Broadlands FELT TW13....155 H5
Broadlands Av ENC/FH EN3....24 D4
 STRHM/NOR SW16....161 K4
 PEND EN3....24 D4
Broadlands Cl HGT N6....66 A5
 ENC/FH EN3....24 D4
 STRHM/NOR SW16....161 K4
Broadlands Rd BMLY BR1....166 A6
 HGT N6....65 K5
Broadlands Wy NWMAL KT3....192 C3
Broad La CEND/HSY/T N8....67 F2
 HPTN TW12....172 E5
 SEVS/STOTM N15....68 C2
Broad Lawn ELTH/MOT SE9....167 F4
Broadlawns Ct
 KTN/HRWW/WS HA3....43 F4
Broadley St STJWD NW8....2 B7
Broadley Ter CAMTN NW1....2 D7
Broadmead CAT SE6....164 D5
Broadmead Av WPK KT4....192 D4
Broadmead Cl HPTN TW12....173 F2
 PIN HA5....41 J3

Broadmead Rd WFD IG8....52 E2
 YEAD UB4....95 J3
Broad Oak WFD IG8....52 E1
Broad Oak Cl CHING E4....51 K1
 STMC/STPC BR5....186 B5
Broadoak Rd ERITH DA8....150 A1
Broad Oaks SURB KT6....191 J1
Broad Oaks Wy HAYES BR2....199 J3
Broadstone Pl MHST W1U....9 G2
Broadstone Rd HCH RM12....93 J6
Broad St DAGE RM10....174 A2
 TEDD TW11....174 A2
Broad Street Av LVPST EC2M....13 G2
Broad Street Pl LVPST EC2M....13 F2
Broadview CDALE/KGS NW9....62 C3
Broadview Rd
 STRHM/NOR SW16....179 J3
Broad Wk BKHTH/KID SE3....146 B3
 HEST TW5....134 C2
 ORP BR6....202 E5
 RCH/KEW TW9....137 G1
 WCHMH N21....35 F4
Broadwalk RYLN/HDSTN HA2....60 B2
The Broad Wk KENS W8....120 B2
The Broadwalk NTHWD HA6....40 A5
Broadwall STHWK SE1....11 K7
Broadwater Gdns ORP BR6....216 C2
Broadwater Rd THMD SE28....127 J3
 TOOT SW17....160 D6
 TOTM N17....50 B4
Broadway BARK IG11....90 C6
 BXLYHS DA6....148 E5
 GPK RM2....57 K1
 HNWL W7....115 K1
 RAIN RM13....111 J3
 SRTFD E15....88 B5
 STJSPK SW1H....16 C4
 SURB KT6....191 J5
 SWLY BR8....203 K3
 WEA W13....116 B1
Broadway Av CROY/NA CRO....196 E2
 TWK TW1....156 C1
Broadway Cl WFD IG8....53 F2
Broadway Ct WIM/MER SW19....177 K2
Broadway Gdns MTCM CR4....194 D1
Broadway Market HACK E8....86 D6
Broadway Market Ms
 HACK E8 *....86 C6
Broadway Ms PLMGR N13....49 C6
 STNW/STAM N16....68 A3
 WCHMH N21....35 H3
Broadway Pde CHING E4 *....52 A2
 HYS/HAR UB3 *....113 J2
 RYLN/HDSTN HA2 *....60 B2
The Broadway ACT W3 *....117 H2
 BCTR RM8....74 B6
 CDALE/KGS NW9....63 H5
 CEND/HSY/T N8....66 E3
 CHEAM SM3....208 C4
 EA W5....97 K6
 FBAR/BDGN N11 *....47 K1
 HCH RM12....93 K2
 KTN/HRWW/WS HA3....42 E5
 MLHL NW7....45 G1
 SCUP DA14....168 C5
 STAN HA7....29 J1
 SUT SM1....209 G2
 THDIT KT7....189 K5
 WFD IG8....53 F1
 WIM/MER SW19....177 J2
Broadwell Pde
 KIL/WHAMP NW6 *....83 G4
Broadwick St SOHO/CST W1F....10 B5
Broadwood Av RSLP HA4....58 C2
Broadwood Ter WKENS W14 *....119 J4
Broad Yd FARR EC1M....6 A7
Brocas Cl HAMP NW3....83 J5
Brockbenc Ct HAYES BR2....215 H2
Brockdish Av BARK IG11....91 F3
Brockenhurst
 E/WMO/HCT KT8....188 E2
Brockenhurst Av WPK KT4....192 B5
Brockenhurst Gdns IL IG1....90 C3
 MLHL NW7....45 G2
Brockenhurst Ms UED N18....36 C6
Brockenhurst Rd
 CROY/NA CRO....197 J4
Brockenhurst Wy
 STRHM/NOR SW16....179 J3
Brocket Wy CHIG IG7....54 E1
Brockham Cl WIM/MER SW19....177 H2
Brockham Crs CROY/NA CRO....214 B5
Brockham Dr
 BRXS/STRHM SW2....162 A2
 GNTH/NBYPK IG2....72 C3
Brockham St STHWK SE1....18 D4
Brockhurst Cl STAN HA7....43 F2
Brockill Crs BROCKY SE4....144 B5
Brocklebank Rd CHARL SE7....126 A4
 WIM/MER SW19....160 A2
Brocklehurst St NWCR SE14....144 A1
Brocklesby Rd SNWD SE25....197 J1
Brockley Av STAN HA7....30 A5
Brockley Cross BROCKY SE4....144 C4
Brockley Gdns BROCKY SE4....144 C3
Brockley Gv BROCKY SE4....164 C1
Brockley Hall Rd BROCKY SE4....164 B2
Brockley Hl STAN HA7....29 J2
Brockley Ms BROCKY SE4....164 B1
Brockley Pk FSTH SE23....164 B2
Brockley Ri FSTH SE23....164 B2
Brockley Rd BROCKY SE4....144 C4
 FSTH SE23....164 B1
Brockleyside STAN HA7....29 K6
Brockley Vw FSTH SE23....164 B2
Brockley Wy FSTH SE23....163 K4
Brockman Ri BMLY BR1....165 G5
Brock Pl BOW E3....105 K3
Brock Rd PLSTW E13....107 F4
Brocks Dr CHEAM SM3....208 C1

Brockshot Cl BTFD TW8 116 E6
Brock St PECK SE15 143 K4
Brockton Cl ROM RM1 75 H1
Brockway Cl WAN E11 70 C6
Brockwell Av BECK BR3 198 E2
Brockwell Cl STMC/STPC BR5 202 A2
Brockwell Park Gdns
HNHL SE24 162 C2
Brockwell Park Rw
BRXS/STRHM SW2 162 B2
Brodia Rd STNW/STAM N16 86 A1
Brodie Rd CHING E4 38 A3
ENC/FH EN2 23 J1
Brodie St STHWK SE1 123 G5
Brodlove La WAP E1W 105 F6
Brodrick Gv ABYW SE2 128 C4
Brodrick Rd TOOT SW17 160 E3
Brograve Gdns BECK BR3 182 E5
Broke Farm Dr ORP BR6 217 J6
Broken Whf BLKFR EC4V 12 C5
Brokesley St BOW E3 105 H3
Broke Wk HACK E8 * 86 C6
Bromar Rd CMBW SE5 143 F4
Bromborough Gn
OXHEY WD19 41 G1
Bromefield STAN HA7 43 K3
Bromehead St WCHPL E1 104 E5
Brome House CHARL SE7 * 146 D1
Bromell's Rd CLAP SW4 141 H5
Brome Rd ELTH/MOT SE9 146 E4
Bromfelde Rd CLAP SW4 141 J4
Bromfield St IS N1 5 K2
Bromhall Rd BCTR RM8 91 H4
Bromhedge ELTH/MOT SE9 166 E5
Bromholm Rd ABYW SE2 128 C3
Bromley Av BMLY BR1 183 H3
Bromley Common HAYES BR2 200 D4
Bromley Ct BMLY BR1 183 H3
Bromley Crs HAYES BR2 183 J6
RSLP HA4 76 D2
Bromley Gdns HAYES BR2 183 J5
Bromley Gv HAYES BR2 183 G5
Bromley Hall Rd POP/IOD E14 106 A4
Bromley High St BOW E3 105 K2
Bromley Hl BMLY BR1 183 H2
Bromley La CHST BR7 185 H3
Bromley Rd BECK BR3 182 D4
CAT SE6 164 E5
CHST BR7 185 H3
LEY E10 69 K3
TOTM N17 50 B4
UED N18 35 K6
WALTH E17 51 J6
Bromley St WCHPL E1 105 F4
Brompton Ar CHEL SW3 * 14 E3
Brompton Cl HSLWW TW4 134 E6
Brompton Cottages
WBPTN SW10 * 120 B6
Brompton Dr ERITH DA8 150 E1
Brompton Gv EFNCH N2 65 J1
Brompton Park Crs
FUL/PGN SW6 120 A6
Brompton Pl CHEL SW3 14 E4
Brompton Rd CHEL SW3 14 C6
Brompton Sq CHEL SW3 14 C4
Brompton Ter
WOOL/PLUM SE18 * 147 F2
Bromwich Av HGT N6 84 A1
Bromyard Av ACT W3 118 B1
Brondesbury Ms
KIL/WHAMP NW6 * 82 E5
Brondesbury Pk
KIL/WHAMP NW6 82 A5
Brondesbury Rd
KIL/WHAMP NW6 100 D1
Brondesbury Vls
KIL/WHAMP NW6 100 D1
Bronhill Ter TOTM N17 * 50 C4
Bronsart Rd FUL/PGN SW6 139 H1
Bronson Rd RYNPK SW20 177 G5
Bronte Cl ERITH DA8 149 J2
FSTGT E7 88 E3
GNTH/NBYPK IG2 72 A2
Bronte Gv DART DA1 151 J5
Bronti Cl WALW SE17 122 D5
Bronze Age Wy BELV DA17 129 K3
Bronze St DEPT SE8 144 D1
Brook Av DAGE RM10 92 D5
EDGW HA8 44 D2
WBLY HA9 80 B1
Brookbank Av HNWL W7 96 D4
Brookbank Rd LEW SE13 144 E4
Brook Cl ACT W3 117 H1
GPK RM2 57 H4
HOR/WEW KT19 207 G6
RSLP HA4 58 C4
RYNPK SW20 192 E1
STWL/WRAY TW19 152 C2
TOOT SW17 161 F4
Brook Ct BECK BR3 * 182 C4
Brook Crs CHING E4 37 J6
ED N9 36 D6
Brookdale FBAR/BDGN N11 34 C6
Brookdale Rd BXLY DA5 169 F1
CAT SE6 164 E2
WALTH E17 51 J6
Brookdene Av OXHEY WD19 27 F2
Brookdene Dr NTHWD HA6 40 D3
Brookdene Rd
WOOL/PLUM SE18 127 K4
Brook Dr HRW HA1 60 C1
LBTH SE11 17 K5
RSLP HA4 58 C4
Brooke Av RYLN/HDSTN HA2 78 C1
Brooke Cl BUSH WD23 28 C2
Brookehowse Rd CAT SE6 164 E5
Brookend Rd BFN/LL DA15 167 K3
Brooker Cl POP/IOD E14 105 H4
Brooke Rd STNW/STAM N16 86 C1
WALTH E17 70 A1
Brooke St HCIRC EC1N 11 J2
Brooke Wy BUSH WD23 28 C2
Brookfield Av EA W5 97 K3
MLHL NW7 45 K2
SUT SM1 209 J1
WALTH E17 70 A1
Brookfield Cl MLHL NW7 45 K2
Brookfield Crs
KTN/HRWW/WS HA3 61 K2
MLHL NW7 45 K2
Brookfield Gdns
ESH/CLAY KT10 205 F4
Brookfield Pk KTTN NW5 84 B1
Brookfield Pth WFD IG8 52 B2
Brookfield Rd CHSWK W4 118 B3
ED N9 36 C5
HOM E9 87 G4
Brookfields PEND EN3 25 F5
Brookfields Av MTCM CR4 194 D2
Brook Gdns BARN SW13 138 C4
CHING E4 37 K6
KUTN/CMB KT2 175 K4
Brook Ga MYFR/PKLN W1K 9 F6
Brook Gn HMSMTH W6 119 F3
Brookhill Cl EBAR EN4 21 J6
Brook Hill Cl
WOOL/PLUM SE18 127 G5
Brookhill Rd EBAR EN4 21 H6
WOOL/PLUM SE18 127 G5
Brookhouse Gdns CHING E4 38 C6
Brooking Cl BCTR RM8 91 J1
Brooking Rd FSTGT E7 88 E3
Brookland Cl GLDGN NW11 64 E1
Brookland Garth GLDGN NW11 64 E1
Brookland Hl GLDGN NW11 64 E1
Brookland Ri GLDGN NW11 64 E1
Brooklands DART DA1 171 H3
Brooklands Ap ROM RM1 75 F1
Brooklands Av BFN/LL DA15 167 J4
WIM/MER SW19 160 A4
Brooklands Cl ROMW/RG RM7 75 F1
Brooklands Ct
KIL/WHAMP NW6 * 82 D5
WCHMH N21 23 K6
Brooklands Dr GFD/PVL UB6 79 J6
Brooklands La ROMW/RG RM7 75 F1
Brooklands Pk BKHTH/KID SE3 145 K4
Brooklands Pl HPTN TW12 173 G1
Brooklands Rd ROMW/RG RM7 75 F1
THDIT KT7 190 A5
The Brooklands ISLW TW7 * 135 J2
Brook La BKHTH/KID SE3 146 A3
BMLY BR1 183 K2
BXLY DA5 168 E1
Brook La North BTFD TW8 116 E5
Brooklea Cl CDALE/KGS NW9 45 G4
Brooklyn Av SNWD SE25 197 J1
Brooklyn Cl CAR SM5 194 D6
Brooklyn Gv SNWD SE25 197 J1
Brooklyn Rd HAYES BR2 200 C2
SNWD SE25 197 J1
Brooklyn Wy WDR/YW UB7 112 A3
Brookmead CROY/NA CR0 195 H3
Brook Md HOR/WEW KT19 207 G4
Brookmead Av BMLY BR1 200 E2
Brookmead Cl
STMC/STPC BR5 202 C4
Brook Meadow
NFNCH/WDSPK N12 33 F6
Brook Meadow Cl WFD IG8 52 C2
Brookmead Rd CROY/NA CR0 195 H3
Brook Ms North BAY/PAD W2 101 G6
Brookmill Cl OXHEY WD19 * 27 F2
Brookmill Rd DEPT SE8 144 D2
Brook Pk DART DA1 171 K4
Brook Park Cl WCHMH N21 35 H1
Brook Pl BAR EN5 20 E6
Brook Rd BKHH IG9 38 E4
CEND/HSY/T N8 66 E1
CRICK NW2 63 J6
GNTH/NBYPK IG2 72 E3
GPK RM2 57 H5
SURB KT6 191 F6
THHTH CR7 196 D1
TWK TW1 156 B1
WDGN N22 * 49 F5
Brook Rd South BTFD TW8 116 E6
Brooks Av EHAM E6 107 K3
Brooksbank St HOM E9 * 87 F4
Brooksby Ms IS N1 85 G5
Brooksby St IS N1 85 G5
Brooksby's Wk HOM E9 87 F3
Brookscroft CROY/NA CR0 * 213 H6
Brookscroft Rd WALTH E17 51 K4
Brookshill KTN/HRWW/WS HA3 42 E2
Brookshill Av
KTN/HRWW/WS HA3 42 D1
Brookshill Dr
KTN/HRWW/WS HA3 42 D1
Brookside BARK/HLT IG6 54 C2
CAR SM5 210 A3
EBAR EN4 33 J1
ORP BR6 202 A4
WCHMH N21 35 F1
Brookside Cl BAR EN5 32 C1
FELT TW13 153 K5
KTN/HRWW/WS HA3 61 K2
RSLP HA4 77 J2
Brookside Crs WPK KT4 192 D5
Brookside Rd ARCH N19 66 C6
ED N9 36 D6
GLDGN NW11 64 C3
OXHEY WD19 27 F2
YEAD UB4 95 G6
Brookside South EBAR EN4 34 A2
Brookside Wy CROY/NA CR0 198 A3
Brooks La CHSWK W4 117 H6
Brook's Ms MYFR/PKLN W1K 9 J5
Brooks Rd CHSWK W4 117 H5
PLSTW E13 88 E6
Brook St BAY/PAD W2 8 B5
BELV DA17 129 J5
ERITH DA8 149 K1
KUT/HW KT1 175 F5
MYFR/PKLN W1K 9 H5
TOTM N17 50 B5
Brooksville Av
KIL/WHAMP NW6 82 C6
Brookview Rd
STRHM/NOR SW16 179 H1
Brookville Rd FUL/PGN SW6 139 J1
Brook Wk EDGW HA8 45 F2
EFNCH N2 47 H4
Brook Water La HDN NW4 * 64 B2
Brookway BKHTH/KID SE3 145 K4
RAIN RM13 111 K4
Brookwood Av BARN SW13 138 C4
Brookwood Cl HAYES BR2 199 J1
Brookwood Rd HSLW TW3 135 G3
WAND/EARL SW18 159 J3
Broom Av STMC/STPC BR5 186 C5
Broom Cl ESH/CLAY KT10 204 B3
HAYES BR2 200 D3
TEDD TW11 174 E3
Broomcroft Av NTHLT UB5 95 G2
Broome Rd HPTN TW12 172 E4
Broome Wy CMBW SE5 142 E1
Broomfield WALTH E17 69 H4
Broomfield Av LOU IG10 39 K1
PLMGR N13 35 F6
PLMGR N13 49 F1
Broomfield Cl CRW RM5 57 F3
Broomfield Cottages
WEA W13 * 116 C1
Broomfield La PLMGR N13 34 E6
Broomfield Pl WEA W13 116 C1
Broomfield Rd BECK BR3 198 B1
BXLYHS DA6 149 H6
CHDH RM6 73 K4
PLMGR N13 48 E1
RCH/KEW TW9 137 G2
SURB KT6 191 G5
TEDD TW11 174 D2
WEA W13 116 C1
Broomfields ESH/CLAY KT10 204 C3
Broomfield St POP/IOD E14 105 J4
Broom Gdns CROY/NA CR0 213 J1
Broomgrove Gdns EDGW HA8 44 C4
Broomgrove Rd BRXN/ST SW9 142 A3
Broomhall Rd SAND/SEL CR2 211 K6
Broomhill Ri BXLYHS DA6 149 H6
Broomhill Rd DART DA1 170 E1
GDMY/SEVK IG3 73 G6
ORP BR6 202 B4
WAND/EARL SW18 139 K6
WFD IG8 52 E2
Broomhouse La FUL/PGN SW6 139 K3
Broomhouse Rd
FUL/PGN SW6 139 K3
Broomloan La SUT SM1 193 K6
Broom Md BXLYHS DA6 169 H1
Broom Pk TEDD TW11 174 E3
Broom Rd CROY/NA CR0 213 J1
TEDD TW11 174 D2
Broomsleigh St
KIL/WHAMP NW6 * 82 E3
Broom Water TEDD TW11 174 D2
Broom Water West
TEDD TW11 174 D1
Broomwood Cl BXLY DA5 170 A4
CROY/NA CR0 198 A2
Broomwood Rd BTSEA SW11 160 E1
STMC/STPC BR5 186 C5
Broseley Gv SYD SE26 182 B1
Broster Gdns SNWD SE25 181 G6
Brougham Rd ACT W3 98 E5
HACK E8 86 C6
Brougham St BTSEA SW11 140 E3
Brough Cl KUTN/CMB KT2 * 174 E1
VX/NE SW8 141 K1
Broughton Av FNCH N3 46 C6
RCHPK/HAM TW10 156 D6
Broughton Dr BRXN/ST SW9 142 B5
Broughton Gdns HGT N6 66 C3
Broughton Rd FUL/PGN SW6 140 A3
ORP BR6 216 D1
THHTH CR7 196 B3
WEA W13 97 H6
Broughton Road Ap
FUL/PGN SW6 * 140 A3
Broughton St VX/NE SW8 141 G3
Brouncker Rd ACT W3 117 K2
Brow Cl STMC/STPC BR5 202 E4
Brow Crs STMC/STPC BR5 202 D5
Browell's La FELT TW13 154 B4
Brown Cl WLGTN SM6 210 E5
Brownfield St POP/IOD E14 106 A5
Browngraves Rd
HYS/HAR UB3 133 F1
Brown Hart Gdns
MYFR/PKLN W1K 9 H5
Brownhill Rd CAT SE6 165 F2
Browning Av HNWL W7 97 F5
SUT SM1 209 J2
WPK KT4 192 E5
Browning Cl HPTN TW12 154 E6
MV/WKIL W9 101 G3
WALTH E17 70 A1
WELL DA16 147 K5
Browning Ms CAVSQ/HST W1G * 9 H2
Browning Rd DART DA1 151 J5
ENC/FH EN2 23 K1
MNPK E12 89 K4
WAN E11 70 D4
Browning St WALW SE17 122 D5
Browning Wy HEST TW5 134 C2
Brownlea Gdns GDMY/SEVK IG3 73 G6
Brownlow Cl EBAR EN4 21 H6
Brownlow Ms BMSBY WC1N 5 H7
Brownlow Rd CROY/NA CR0 212 A2
FBAR/BDGN N11 48 E2
FNCH N3 47 F3
FSTGT E7 88 E2
HACK E8 86 C6
WEA W13 * 116 B1
WLSDN NW10 81 G5
Brownlow St GINN WC1R 11 H2
Brownrigg Rd ASHF TW15 152 D6
Brownspring Dr
ELTH/MOT SE9 167 G6
Brown's Rd BRYLDS KT5 191 G4
WALTH E17 51 J6
Brown St MBLAR W1H 8 E3
Brownswell Rd EFNCH N2 47 H5
Brownswood Rd FSBYPK N4 67 J6
Broxash Rd BTSEA SW11 161 F1
Broxbourne Av SWFD E18 71 F1
Broxbourne House BOW E3 105 K3
Broxbourne Rd FSTGT E7 88 E1
ORP BR6 202 A5
Broxholm Rd WNWD SE27 162 B5
Broxted Rd CAT SE6 164 C4
Broxwood Wy STJWD NW8 2 D1
Bruce Castle Rd TOTM N17 50 B4
Bruce Cl NKENS W10 100 B4
WELL DA16 148 C2
Bruce Dr SAND/SEL CR2 213 F6
Bruce Gdns TRDG/WHET N20 33 K5
Bruce Gv ORP BR6 202 B5
TOTM N17 50 B5
Bruce Rd BAR EN5 20 C4
BOW E3 105 K2
KTN/HRWW/WS HA3 42 E5
MTCM CR4 179 F3
SNWD SE25 196 E1
WLSDN NW10 81 F5
Bruckner St NKENS W10 100 C2
Brudenell Rd TOOT SW17 160 E5
Bruffs Meadow NTHLT UB5 77 J4
Bruford Ct DEPT SE8 124 D6
Bruges Pl CAMTN NW1 84 C5
Brumfield Rd HOR/WEW KT19 206 E3
Brunel Cl HEST TW5 134 A1
NRWD SE19 181 G2
NTHLT UB5 95 K2
ROM RM1 75 G1
Brunel Ct WLSDN NW10 99 J2
Brunel Est BAY/PAD W2 * 100 E4
Brunel House
WOOL/PLUM SE18 * 146 D1
Brunel Ms NKENS W10 100 B2
Brunel Rd ACT W3 99 G4
BERM/RHTH SE16 123 K2
WALTH E17 69 G3
WFD IG8 53 K1
Brunel St CAN/RD E16 106 D5
Brunel Wk WHTN TW2 155 F2
Brune St WCHPL E1 13 J2
Brunner Cl GLDGN NW11 65 F2
Brunner Rd EA W5 97 K3
WALTH E17 69 H2
Bruno Pl CDALE/KGS NW9 62 E6
Brunswick Av FBAR/BDGN N11 34 A5
Brunswick Cl BXLYHS DA6 148 E5
PIN HA5 59 K4
THDIT KT7 190 A5
WHTN TW2 155 J5
WOT/HER KT12 188 B6
Brunswick Ct STHWK SE1 19 H3
Brunswick Crs FBAR/BDGN N11 34 A5
Brunswick Gdns BARK/HLT IG6 54 C3
EA W5 98 A3
KENS W8 119 K1
Brunswick Gv FBAR/BDGN N11 34 A5
Brunswick Ms MBLAR W1H 9 F3
STRHM/NOR SW16 179 J2
Brunswick Pk CMBW SE5 142 E2
Brunswick Park Gdns
FBAR/BDGN N11 34 A4
Brunswick Park Rd
FBAR/BDGN N11 34 A4
Brunswick Pl CAMTN NW1 3 H7
IS N1 7 F5
NRWD SE19 181 H3
Brunswick Quay
BERM/RHTH SE16 124 B3
Brunswick Rd BXLYHS DA6 148 E5
EA W5 97 K3
KUTN/CMB KT2 175 H4
LEY E10 70 A5
PEND EN3 25 J1
SEVS/STOTM N15 68 A2
SUT SM1 209 F2
Brunswick Sq BMSBY WC1N 5 F6
TOTM N17 50 B2
Brunswick St WALTH E17 70 A2
Brunswick Vls CMBW SE5 143 F2
Brunswick Wy FBAR/BDGN N11 34 B6
Brunton Pl POP/IOD E14 105 G5
Brushfield St WCHPL E1 13 H1
Brushwood Cl POP/IOD E14 105 K4
Brussels Rd BTSEA SW11 140 C5
Bruton Cl CHST BR7 184 E3
Bruton La MYFR/PICC W1J 9 K6
Bruton Pl MYFR/PICC W1J 9 K6
Bruton Rd MRDN SM4 194 B1
Bruton St MYFR/PICC W1J 9 K6
Bruton Wy WEA W13 97 G4
Bryan Av WLSDN NW10 81 K5
Bryan Rd BERM/RHTH SE16 124 C2
Bryanston Av WHTN TW2 155 G3
Bryanston Cl NWDGN UB2 114 E4
Bryanstone Rd CEND/HSY/T N8 66 D2
Bryanston Ms East MBLAR W1H 8 E2
Bryanston Ms West MBLAR W1H 8 E2
Bryanston Pl MBLAR W1H 8 E2
Bryanston Sq MBLAR W1H 8 E3
Bryanston St MBLAR W1H 8 E4
Bryant Cl BAR EN5 20 D6
Bryant Rd NTHLT UB5 95 G2
Bryant St SRTFD E15 88 B5
Bryantwood Rd HOLWY N7 85 G3
Brycedale Crs STHGT/OAK N14 34 D6
Bryce Rd BCTR RM8 91 J2
Bryden Cl SYD SE26 182 B1
Brydges Pl CHCR WC2N 10 E6
Brydges Rd SRTFD E15 88 B3
Brydon Wk IS N1 84 E6
Bryett Rd HOLWY N7 84 E1
Brymay Cl BOW E3 105 J1
Brynmaer Rd BTSEA SW11 140 E2
Bryn-Y-Mawr Rd EN EN1 24 B5
Bryony Rd SHB W12 99 J6
Buchanan Cl WCHMH N21 23 F6
Buchanan Gdns WLSDN NW10 99 K1
Buchan Rd PECK SE15 143 K4
Bucharest Rd
WAND/EARL SW18 160 B2
Buckden Cl LEE/GVPK SE12 165 K1
Buckfast Rd MRDN SM4 194 A1
Buckfast St BETH E2 104 C2
Buckhold Rd
WAND/EARL SW18 159 K1
Buckhurst Av CAR SM5 194 D5
Buckhurst St WCHPL E1 104 D3
Buckhurst Wy BKHH IG9 39 H5
Buckingham Av
E/WMO/HCT KT8 173 G5
EBED/NFELT TW14 154 A1
GFD/PVL UB6 79 G6
THHTH CR7 180 B4
TRDG/WHET N20 33 G2
WELL DA16 147 K5
Buckingham Cl EA W5 97 J4
EN EN1 24 A3
HPTN TW12 172 E1
STMC/STPC BR5 201 K4
Buckingham Ct BELMT SM2 * 208 E6
Buckingham Dr CHST BR7 185 G1
Buckingham Gdns
E/WMO/HCT KT8 173 G5
STAN HA7 44 A3
THHTH CR7 180 B5
Buckingham Ga WESTW SW1E 16 A4
Buckingham La FSTH SE23 164 B2
Buckingham Ms IS N1 86 A4
WESTW SW1E * 16 A4
WLSDN NW10 99 H1
Buckingham Palace Rd
BGVA SW1W 15 K5
Buckingham Pde STAN HA7 * 43 J1
Buckingham Pl WESTW SW1E 16 A4
Buckingham Rd EDGW HA8 44 B3
HPTN TW12 154 E6
HRW HA1 60 D2
IL IG1 72 D6
IS N1 86 A4
KUT/HW KT1 191 G1
LEY E10 87 K1
MTCM CR4 195 K2
RCHPK/HAM TW10 156 E4
SRTFD E15 88 D3
SWFD E18 52 D4
WAN E11 71 G2
WDGN N22 48 E4
WLSDN NW10 99 H1
Buckingham St CHCR WC2N 11 F6
Buckingham Wy WLGTN SM6 210 C6
Buckland Crs HAMP NW3 83 H5
Buckland Ri PIN HA5 41 G4
Buckland Rd CHSGTN KT9 206 B3
LEY E10 70 A6
ORP BR6 216 E2
Bucklands OXHEY WD19 * 27 H5
Bucklands Rd TEDD TW11 174 D2
Buckland St IS N1 7 F3
Bucklands Whf KUT/HW KT1 * 174 E5
Buckland Wk MRDN SM4 194 B1
Buckland Wy WPK KT4 193 F5
Buck La CDALE/KGS NW9 63 F2
Buckleigh Av RYNPK SW20 177 J6
Buckleigh Rd
STRHM/NOR SW16 179 K3
Buckleigh Wy NRWD SE19 181 G4
Bucklersbury MANHO EC4N * 12 E4
Bucklers' Wy CAR SM5 209 K1
Buckle St WCHPL E1 13 K3
Buckley Cl DART DA1 150 C3
FSTH SE23 163 J2
Buckley Rd KIL/WHAMP NW6 82 D5
Buckmaster Cl BRXN/ST SW9 142 B4
Buckmaster Rd BTSEA SW11 140 D5
Bucknall St NOXST/BSQ WC1A 10 E3
Bucknall Wy BECK BR3 198 E1
Bucknell Cl BRXS/STRHM SW2 142 A5
Buckner Rd BRXS/STRHM SW2 142 A5
Buckrell Rd CHING E4 38 B4
Bucks Av OXHEY WD19 27 J2
Buckstone Cl FSTH SE23 163 K1
Buckstone Rd UED N18 50 C2
Buck St CAMTN NW1 84 B6
Buckters Rents
BERM/RHTH SE16 124 B1
Buckthorne Rd BROCKY SE4 164 B1
Budd Cl NFNCH/WDSPK N12 33 F6
Buddings Cir WBLY HA9 80 E1
Bude Cl WALTH E17 69 H2
Budge La MTCM CR4 194 E4
Budge Rw MANHO EC4N 12 E5
Budleigh Crs WELL DA16 148 D2
Budoch Dr GDMY/SEVK IG3 73 G6
Buer Rd FUL/PGN SW6 139 H3
Bugsby's Wy GNWCH SE10 125 J4
Bulganak Rd THHTH CR7 196 D1
Bulinca St WEST SW1P * 16 E7
Bullace Rw CMBW SE5 142 E2
Bull Aly WELL DA16 148 C4
Bullard Rd TEDD TW11 173 K2
Bullards Pl BETH E2 105 F2
Bullbanks Rd BELV DA17 129 K4
Bulleid Wy BGVA SW1W 15 K7
Bullen St BTSEA SW11 140 D3
Buller Cl PECK SE15 143 H1
Buller Rd BARK IG11 90 E5
THHTH CR7 180 E6
TOTM N17 50 C5
WDGN N22 49 G5
WLSDN NW10 100 B2
Bullers Cl SCUP DA14 187 F1
Bullers Wood Dr CHST BR7 184 D4
Bullescroft Rd EDGW HA8 30 D5
Bullivant St POP/IOD E14 106 A6
Bull La CHST BR7 185 J3
DAGE RM10 92 D1
UED N18 50 A1
Bull Rd SRTFD E15 106 D1
Bullrush Cl CAR SM5 194 D6
CROY/NA CR0 197 F3
Bulls Aly MORT/ESHN SW14 * 138 A4
Bull's Br NWDGN UB2 113 K3
Bulls Bridge Rd NWDGN UB2 114 A3
Bullsbrook Rd YEAD UB4 114 B1
Bull's Gdns CHEL SW3 14 D6
Bull Yd PECK SE15 143 H2
Bulmer Gdns
KTN/HRWW/WS HA3 61 K4
Bulstrode Av HSLW TW3 134 E4
Bulstrode Gdns HSLW TW3 135 F4
Bulstrode Pl MHST W1U 9 H2
Bulstrode Rd HSLW TW3 135 F4
Bulstrode St MHST W1U 9 H3
Bulwer Court Rd WAN E11 70 B5
Bulwer Gdns BAR EN5 21 G5
Bulwer Rd BAR EN5 21 F5
UED N18 36 A6

WAN E11 ....70 B5
Bulwer St *SHB* W12 ....119 F1
Bunces La *WFD* IG8 ....52 D3
Bungalow Rd *SNWD* SE25 ......197 F1
The Bungalows
  RYLN/HDSTN HA2 * 77 K1
  STRHM/NOR SW16 ....179 C3
Bunhill Rw *STLK* EC1Y 6 E6
Bunhouse Pl *BGVA* SW1W 121 F5
Bunker's HI *BELV* DA17 ....129 H4
  GLDGN NW11 ....69 C5
  SCUP DA14 ....169 G5
Bunning Wy *HOLWY* N7 * 84 E5
Bunn's La *MLHL* NW7 ....45 G2
Bunsen St *BOW* E3 ....105 G1
Buntingbridge Rd
  BARK/HLT IG6 ....72 D2
Bunting Cl *ED* N9 ....37 F3
  MTCM CR4 ....194 E1
Bunton St *WOOL/PLUM* SE18 ..127 F3
Bunyan Rd *WALTH* E17 ....51 G6
Buonaparte Ms *PIM* SW1V 121 J5
Burbage Cl *HYS/HAR* UB3 ......94 B5
  STHWK SE1 * 18 C5
Burbage Rd *HNHL* SE24 ....162 E1
Burberry Cl *NWMAL* KT3 ......176 B5
Burbridge Wy *TOTM* N17 ....50 C5
Burcham St *POP/IOD* E14 ....105 K5
Burcharbro Rd *ABYW* SE2 .....128 E6
Burchell Ct *BUSH* WD23 ....28 C2
Burchell Rd *LEY* E10 ....69 K5
  PECK SE15 ....143 J3
Burcher Gale Gv *PECK* SE15 ..143 G1
Burchwall Cl *CRW* RM5 ....56 E3
Burcote Rd *WAND/EARL* SW18 .160 C3
Burden Cl *BTFD* TW8 ....116 D5
Burdenshott Av
  RCHPK/HAM TW10 ....137 J5
Burden Wy *WAN* E11 ....71 F6
Burder Cl *IS* N1 ....86 A4
Burder Rd *IS* N1 ....86 A4
Burdett Av *RYNPK* SW20 ......176 C4
Burdett Cl *HNWL* W7 * 116 A1
  SCUP DA14 ....187 F1
Burdett Rd *BOW* E3 ....105 H3
  CROY/NA CR0 ....196 E3
  RCH/KEW TW9 ....137 G4
Burdetts Rd *DAGW* RM9 ....92 B6
Burdock Cl *CROY/NA* CR0 .....198 A5
Burdock Rd *TOTM* N17 ....50 C6
Burdon La *BELMT* SM2 ....208 D6
Burdon Pk *BELMT* SM2 ....208 D6
Burfield Cl *TOOT* SW17 ....160 B6
Burford Cl *BARK/HLT* IG6 ....72 C1
  BCTR RM8 ....91 J1
Burford Gdns *PLMGR* N13 ......35 F5
Burford Rd *BMLY* BR1 ....200 D1
  BTFD TW8 ....117 F5
  CAT SE6 ....164 C4
  EHAM E6 ....107 J2
  SRTFD E15 ....88 B5
  SUT SM1 ....193 K6
  WPK KT4 ....192 D4
Burford Wk *FUL/PGN* SW6 * 108 A6
Burford Wy *CROY/NA* CR0 .....214 A5
Burgate Cl *DART* DA1 ....150 C4
Burges Gv *BARN* SW13 ....138 E1
Burges Rd *EHAM* E6 ....90 A1
Burgess Av *CDALE/KGS* NW9 ...63 F2
Burgess Cl *FELT* TW13 ....154 D6
Burgess HI *CRICK* NW2 ....82 E2
Burgess Ms *WIM/MER* SW19 ..178 A2
Burgess Rd *SRTFD* E15 ....88 C2
  SUT SM1 ....209 F2
Burge St *STHWK* SE1 ....19 F5
Burghill Rd *SYD* SE26 ....164 A6
Burghley Av *BRXN/ST* SW9 ...142 A4
Burghley Rd
  WIM/MER SW19 * 159 H3
Burghley Pl *MTCM* CR4 ....194 E2
Burghley Rd *CEND/HSY/T* N8 ...49 G6
  KTTN NW5 ....84 B2
  WAN E11 ....70 C5
  WIM/MER SW19 ....159 H6
Burgh St *IS* N1 ....6 C2
Burgon St *BLKFR* EC4V 12 B4
Burgos Cl *CROY/NA* CR0 ....211 G4
Burgos Gv *GNWCH* SE10 ......144 E2
Burgoyne Rd *BRXN/ST* SW9 ..142 A4
  FSBYPK N4 ....67 H3
  SNWD SE25 ....197 F1
Burham Cl *PGE/AN* SE20 ......181 K3
Burhill Gv *PIN* HA5 ....41 J5
Burke Cl *PUT/ROE* SW15 ......138 B5
Burke St *CAN/RD* E16 ....106 D4
Burket Cl *NWDGN* UB2 ....114 D4
Burland Rd *BTSEA* SW11 ......140 E6
  CRW RM5 ....56 E2
Burleigh Av *BFN/LL* DA15 .....148 A6
  WLGTN SM6 ....210 A1
Burleigh Gdns *STHGT/OAK* N14 ..34 C3
Burleigh Pde *STHGT/OAK* N14 * ..34 D3
Burleigh Pl *PUT/ROE* SW15 ..139 G6
Burleigh Rd *CHEAM* SM3 ......193 H6
  EN EN1 ....24 B5
Burleigh St *COVGDN* WC2E 11 F5
Burleigh Wk *CAT* SE6 ....165 F3
Burleigh Wy *ENC/FH* EN2 ....23 K4
Burley Cl *CHING* E4 ....51 J1
  STRHM/NOR SW16 ....179 J5
Burley Rd *CAN/RD* E16 ....107 G5
Burlington Av *CONDST* W1S 10 A6
Burlington Cl *RCH/KEW* TW9 ..137 H2
  ROMW/RG RM7 ....74 D3
Burlington Cl
  EBED/NFELT TW14 ....153 G2
  EHAM E6 ....107 J5
  MV/WKIL W9 ....100 D4
  ORP BR6 ....201 G6
  PIN HA5 ....41 F6
Burlington Gdns *ACT* W3 ....118 A1
  CHDH RM6 ....74 A4
  CHSWK W4 ....117 K5
  CONDST W1S 10 A6
Burlington La *CHSWK* W4 .....137 K1
Burlington Ms *CHSWK* W4 .....117 K1

Burlington Pde *CRICK* NW2 * 82 B1
Burlington Pl *FUL/PGN* SW6 ..139 G2
  WFD IG8 ....38 E1
Burlington Ri *EBAR* EN4 ....33 J3
Burlington Rd *CHSWK* W4 .....117 K5
  ENC/FH EN2 ....23 K2
  FUL/PGN SW6 ....139 H5
  ISLW TW7 ....135 J2
  MUSWH N10 ....48 A6
  NWMAL KT3 ....192 C1
  THHTH CR7 ....180 D5
  TOTM N17 ....50 C4
Burma Rd *STNW/STAM* N16 ....85 K2
Burma Ter *NRWD* SE19 ....181 F1
Burmester Rd *TOOT* SW17 ....160 B5
Burnaby Crs *CHSWK* W4 ....117 K6
Burnaby Gdns *CHSWK* W4 ....117 J6
Burnaby St *WBPTN* SW10 .....140 B1
Burnbrae Cl
  NFNCH/WDSPK N12 ....47 F2
Burnbury Rd *BAL* SW12 ....161 H3
Burncroft Av *PEND* EN3 ....24 E3
Burndell Wy *YEAD* UB4 ....95 H4
Burne Jones Ho *WKENS* W14 ..119 H4
Burnell Av
  RCHPK/HAM TW10 ....137 H6
  WELL DA16 ....148 B3
Burnell Gdns *STAN* HA7 ....43 K5
Burnell Rd *SUT* SM1 ....209 F2
Burnell Wk *STHWK* SE1 * 123 G5
Burnels Av *EHAM* E6 ....108 A2
Burness Cl *HOLWY* N7 ....85 F4
Burne St *CAMTN* NW1 ....8 C1
Burnett Cl *HOM* E9 ....86 E4
Burnett La *BARK/HLT* IG6 ....54 B3
Burnett Rd *ERITH* DA8 ....131 G6
Burney Av *BRYLDS* KT5 ....191 G2
Burney St *GNWCH* SE10 ....145 F1
Burnfoot Av *FUL/PGN* SW6 ...139 H2
Burnham Av *HGDN/ICK* UB10 ..76 A2
Burnham Cl *EN* EN1 ....24 A1
  KTN/HRWW/WS HA3 ....61 G1
  MLHL NW7 ....45 J3
  STHWK SE1 * 19 J7
Burnham Crs *DART* DA1 ....151 F5
  WAN E11 ....71 G1
Burnham Dr *WPK* KT4 ....193 G6
Burnham Gdns *CROY/NA* CR0 ..197 G4
  HSLWW TW4 ....134 A1
  HYS/HAR UB3 ....113 G5
Burnham Rd *CHING* E4 ....51 H1
  DAGW RM9 ....91 H5
  DART DA1 ....151 G6
  MRDN SM4 ....194 A2
  ROMW/RG RM7 ....74 E1
  SCUP DA14 ....169 F5
Burnham St *BETH* E2 ....104 E2
  KUTN/CMB KT2 ....175 H4
Burnham Ter *DART* DA1 * 151 G6
Burnham Wy *SYD* SE26 ....182 C1
  WEA W13 ....116 C4
Burnhill Rd *BECK* BR3 ....182 D5
Burnley Cl *OXHEY* WD19 ....41 G1
Burnley Rd *BRXN/ST* SW9 ....142 A3
  WLSDN NW10 ....81 J3
Burnsall St *CHEL* SW3 ....120 D5
Burns Av *BFN/LL* DA15 ....168 C1
  CHDH RM6 ....73 J4
  EBED/NFELT TW14 ....153 J1
  STHL UB1 ....96 A6
Burns Cl *CAR* SM5 ....210 A6
  ERITH DA8 ....150 C2
  WALTH E17 ....70 A1
  WELL DA16 ....148 A2
  WIM/MER SW19 ....178 C2
  YEAD UB4 ....94 E4
Burnside Av *CHING* E4 ....51 H2
Burnside Cl *BAR* EN5 ....20 E4
  BERM/RHTH SE16 ....124 A1
  TWK TW1 ....156 B1
Burnside Crs *ALP/SUD* HA0 ....79 K6
Burnside Rd *BCTR* RM8 ....73 J6
Burns Rd *ALP/SUD* HA0 ....98 A1
  BTSEA SW11 ....140 E3
  PLSTW E13 ....106 E3
  WLSDN NW10 ....81 H1
Burns Wy *HEST* TW5 ....134 C2
Burnt Ash HI *LEE/GVPK* SE12 ..165 J1
Burnt Ash La *BMLY* BR1 ....183 K2
Burnt Ash Rd *LEE/GVPK* SE12 ..165 J1
Burnt House La *RDART* DA2 ...171 J6
Burnthwaite Rd *FUL/PGN* SW6 ..139 J1
Burnt Oak Broadway
  EDGW HA8 ....44 D3
Burnt Oak Flds *EDGW* HA8 .....44 E4
Burnt Oak La *BFN/LL* DA15 ...168 C2
Burntwood Cl
  WAND/EARL SW18 * 160 C3
Burntwood Grange Rd
  WAND/EARL SW18 ....160 C3
Burntwood La *TOOT* SW17 ....160 D2
Burntwood Vw *NRWD* SE19 * ..181 G1
Buross St *WCHPL* E1 ....104 D5
Burpham Cl *YEAD* UB4 ....95 H4
Burrage Gv *WOOL/PLUM* SE18 ..127 H4
Burrage Pl *WOOL/PLUM* SE18 ..127 G5
Burrage Rd *WOOL/PLUM* SE18 ..127 H6
Burrard Rd *CAN/RD* E16 ....106 E5
  KIL/WHAMP NW6 ....82 E2
Burr Bank Ter *RDART* DA2 ....171 F6
Burr Cl *BXLYHN* DA7 ....149 G4
  WAP E1W 123 H1
Burrell Cl *CROY/NA* CR0 ....198 B3
  EDGW HA8 ....30 D4
Burrell Rw *BECK* BR3 ....182 D5
Burrell St *STHWK* SE1 ....11 K7
Burrells Whf *POP/IOD* E14 ....124 E5
Burrfield Dr *STMC/STPC* BR5 ..202 E2
Burritt Rd *KUT/HW* KT1 ....175 H5
Burroughs Cottages
  POP/IOD E14 * 105 G4
Burroughs Gdns *HDN* NW4 .....63 K1
The Burroughs *HDN* NW4 ......63 K2
Burrow Gn *CHIG* IG7 ....55 F1
Burrow Rd *CHIG* IG7 ....55 G1
  EDUL SE22 ....143 F5
Burrows Ms *STHWK* SE1 ....18 A2
Burrows Rd *WLSDN* NW10 ....100 A2
Burr Rd *WAND/EARL* SW18 ...159 K3

Bursar St *STHWK* SE1 * 19 C1
Bursdon Cl *BFN/LL* DA15 .....168 A4
Bursland Rd *PEND* EN3 ....25 F1
Burslem Av *BARK/HLT* IG6 ......55 G2
Burslem St *WCHPL* E1 ....104 D5
Burstock Rd *PUT/ROE* SW15 ..139 H5
Burston Rd *PUT/ROE* SW15 ..139 G6
Burstow Rd *RYNPK* SW20 .....177 H4
Burtenshaw Rd *THDIT* KT7 ...190 B4
Burtley Cl *FSBYPK* N4 ....67 J5
Burton Bank *IS* N1 * 85 K5
Burton Cl *CHSGTN* KT9 ....205 K5
  THHTH CR7 ....180 E6
Burton Gdns *HEST* TW5 ....134 E2
Burton Gv *WALW* SE17 ....122 E5
Burtonhole Cl *MLHL* NW7 ......32 B6
Burtonhole La *MLHL* NW7 ......32 A5
  MLHL NW7 ....46 B1
Burton La *BRXN/ST* SW9 * 142 B3
Burton Ms *BGVA* SW1W 15 H7
Burton Pl *STPAN* WC1H 4 D6
Burton Rd *BRXN/ST* SW9 .....142 C5
  KIL/WHAMP NW6 ....82 D5
  KUTN/CMB KT2 ....175 F3
  SWFD E18 ....53 F1
Burton's Rd *HPTN* TW12 ....155 G6
Burton St *STPAN* WC1H 4 D6
Burt Rd *CAN/RD* E16 ....126 B1
Burtwell La *DUL* SE21 ....162 E6
Burwash Ct *STMC/STPC* BR5 ..202 D2
Burwash Rd
  WOOL/PLUM SE18 ....127 J5
Burwell Av *GFD/PVL* UB6 ....78 E4
Burwell Cl *WCHPL* E1 * 104 D5
Burwell Rd *LEY* E10 ....69 G5
Burwood Av *HAYES* BR2 ....200 A6
  PIN HA5 ....59 G2
Burwood Cl *SURB* KT6 ....191 H5
Burwood Gdns *RAIN* RM13 ...111 H3
Burwood Pl *BAY/PAD* W2 ....8 D3
Bury Av *RSLP* HA4 ....58 A3
  YEAD UB4 ....94 C1
Bury Cl *BERM/RHTH* SE16 ....124 A1
Bury Ct *HDTCH* EC3A 13 H3
Bury Gv *MRDN* SM4 ....194 A2
Bury Pl *NOXST/BSQ* WC1A 10 E2
Bury Rd *DAGE* RM10 ....92 E3
  WDGN N22 ....49 G6
Buryside Cl *GNTH/NBYPK* IG2 ..73 F2
Bury St *ED* N9 ....36 C3
  HDTCH EC3A 13 H4
  RSLP HA4 ....58 B3
  STJS SW1Y 10 B7
Bury St West *ED* N9 ....36 A2
Bury Wk *CHEL* SW3 ....14 D5
Busby Pl *KTTN* NW5 ....84 D4
Busch Cl *ISLW* TW7 ....136 C2
Bushbaby Cl *STHWK* SE1 ....19 G5
Bushberry Rd *HOM* E9 ....87 G4
Bush Cl *GNTH/NBYPK* IG2 ......72 D2
Bush Cottages
  WAND/EARL SW18 ....139 K6
Bushell Cl *BRXS/STRHM* SW2 ..162 A4
Bushell Gn *BUSH* WD23 ....28 D4
Bushell St *WAP* E1W * 123 H1
Bushey Av *STMC/STPC* BR5 ..201 J4
  SWFD E18 ....52 D6
Bushey Cl *CHING* E4 ....38 A5
Bushey Av *STMC/STPC* BR5 ..201 J4
Bushey La *SUT* SM1 ....208 E1
Bushey Lees *BFN/LL* DA15 * ..168 A1
Bushey Rd *CROY/NA* CR0 .....198 D6
  HYS/HAR UB3 ....113 H4
  PLSTW E13 ....89 G1
  RYNPK SW20 ....177 F5
  SEVS/STOTM N15 ....68 A3
  SUT SM1 ....208 E2
Bushey Wy *BECK* BR3 ....199 G3
Bushfield Cl *EDGW* HA8 ....30 D4
Bushfield Crs *EDGW* HA8 ....30 D4
Bushfields *LOU* IG10 ....39 K1
  STAN HA7 ....43 K4
Bushgrove Rd *BCTR* RM8 ....91 K2
Bush Gv *CDALE/KGS* NW9 ......62 E4
  STAN HA7 ....43 K4
Bush HI *WCHMH* N21 ....35 K2
Bush Hill Rd *KTN/HRWW/WS* HA3 ..62 B3
  WCHMH N21 ....35 K2
Bush House
  WOOL/PLUM SE18 * 146 D1
Bush La *CANST* EC4R 12 E5
Bushmead Cl
  SEVS/STOTM N15 * 68 B1
Bushmoor Crs
  WOOL/PLUM SE18 ....147 G2
Bushnell Rd *TOOT* SW17 ......161 G4
Bush Rd *BKHH* IG9 ....39 H6
  DEPT SE8 ....124 A4
  HACK E8 ....86 D6
  HPTN TW12 ....154 C6
  RCH/KEW TW9 ....99 G6
  WAN E11 ....71 F6
Bushway *BCTR* RM8 ....91 K2
Bushwood *WAN* E11 ....70 D5
Bushwood Dr *STHWK* SE1 * 19 K7
Bushwood Rd *RCH/KEW* TW9 ..137 H1
Bushy Park Gdns *HPTN* TW12 ..173 J1
Bushy Park Rd *TEDD* TW11 ...174 C5
Bushy Rd *TEDD* TW11 ....173 K2
Butcher Rw *WAP* E1W 105 F5
Butchers Rd *CAN/RD* E16 .....106 E5
Butcher Yd *WOOL/PLUM* SE18 ..127 H5
Bute Gdns *HMSMTH* W6 ....119 G4
  RCHPK/HAM TW10 ....157 F3
  WLGTN SM6 ....210 C3
Bute Gdns West *WLGTN* SM6 ..210 C3
Bute Ms *GLDGN* NW11 ....65 F2
Bute Rd *BARK/HLT* IG6 ....54 C6
  CROY/NA CR0 ....196 B5
  WLGTN SM6 ....210 C2
Bute St *SKENS* SW7 ....14 A6
Butler Av *HRW* HA1 ....60 E4
Butler Pl *WEST* SW1P 16 C4
Butler Rd *BCTR* RM8 ....91 H2

HRW HA1 ....60 C4
  WLSDN NW10 ....81 H5
Butlers Cl *HSLWW* TW4 ....134 E5
Butlers & Colonial Whf
  STHWK SE1 ....19 K2
Butler St *BETH* E2 * 105 F2
Buttercup Cl *NTHLT* UB5 ....77 K4
Buttercup Sq
  STWL/WRAY TW19 * 152 A3
Butterfield Cl
  BERM/RHTH SE16 * 123 H2
  TOTM N17 ....49 J2
  TWK TW1 ....156 A1
Butterfield House
  CHARL SE7 * 146 D1
Butterfields *WALTH* E17 ....70 A2
Butterfield Sq *EHAM* E6 ....107 K5
Butterfly Av *DART* DA1 ....171 J5
Butter HI *CAR* SM5 ....210 A1
Butterfly La *ELTH/MOT* SE9 ...167 G1
Butterfly Wk *CMBW* SE5 * 142 E2
Butteridges Cl *DAGW* RM9 .....92 B6
Butterly Av *DART* DA1 ....171 J4
Buttermere Cl
  EBED/NFELT TW14 ....153 J3
  MRDN SM4 ....193 G3
  SRTFD E15 * 69 J3
  STHWK SE1 * 19 J7
Buttermere Rd
  STMC/STPC BR5 ....202 E1
Buttermere Wk *HACK* E8 ....86 B4
Butterwick *HMSMTH* W6 ......119 F4
Butterworth Gdns *WFD* IG8 ....52 E2
Buttesland St *IS* N1 ....7 F4
Buttfield Cl *DAGE* RM10 ....92 D4
Buttmarsh Cl
  WOOL/PLUM SE18 ....127 G5
Buttsbury Rd *IL* IG1 ....90 C3
Butts Crs *FELT* TW13 ....155 F5
Buttsmead *NTHWD* HA6 ....40 A3
Butts Piece *NTHLT* UB5 * 95 F1
Butts Rd *BMLY* BR1 ....183 H1
The Butts *BTFD* TW8 ....116 E6
Buxhall Crs *HOM* E9 ....87 H4
Buxted Rd *EDUL* SE22 ....143 F5
  HACK E8 ....86 B5
  NFNCH/WDSPK N12 ....47 J1
Buxton Cl *WFD* IG8 ....53 H2
Buxton Crs *CHEAM* SM3 ......208 C2
Buxton Dr *NWMAL* KT3 ....176 A5
  WAN E11 ....53 H3
Buxton Gdns *ACT* W3 ....98 D6
Buxton Ms *CLAP* SW4 ....141 K3
Buxton Pth *OXHEY* WD19 * 27 G5
Buxton Rd *ARCH* N19 ....66 D5
  CHING E4 ....38 B2
  CRICK NW2 ....81 K4
  EHAM E6 ....107 J2
  ERITH DA8 ....150 A1
  GNTH/NBYPK IG2 ....72 E3
  MORT/ESHN SW14 ....138 B4
  SRTFD E15 ....88 C3
  THHTH CR7 ....196 C2
  WALTH E17 ....69 G1
Buxton St *WCHPL* E1 * 7 K7
Byam St *FUL/PGN* SW6 ....140 B3
Byards Cft *STRHM/NOR* SW16 ..179 J4
Bychurch End *TEDD* TW11 * ..174 A1
Bycroft Rd *STHL* UB1 ....96 A4
Bycroft St *PGE/AN* SE20 ......182 A3
Byculla Av *ENC/FH* EN2 ....23 H4
Byculla Rd *ENC/FH* EN2 ....23 H4
Byelands Cl *BERM/RHTH* SE16 ..124 A1
The Bye *ACT* W3 ....99 G5
Byeways *WATW* WD18 ....26 E1
Bye Ways *WHTN* TW2 ....155 G5
The Byeways *BRYLDS* KT5 ..191 H2
The Bye Wy
  KTN/HRWW/WS HA3 ....42 E4
The Byeway
  MORT/ESHN SW14 ....137 K4
Byfeld Gdns *BARN* SW13 ......138 D2
Byfield Cl *BERM/RHTH* SE16 ..124 B2
Byfield Rd *ISLW* TW7 ....136 B4
Byford Cl *SRTFD* E15 ....88 C5
Bygrove *CROY/NA* CR0 ....213 K4
Bygrove Rd *WIM/MER* SW19 ..178 C2
Bygrove St *POP/IOD* E14 ......105 K5
Byland Cl *ABYW* SE2 ....128 C3
  CAR SM5 ....194 C4
  STHGT/OAK N14 ....34 C2
Byne Rd *CAR* SM5 ....194 D6
  SYD SE26 ....181 K2
Bynes Rd *SAND/SEL* CR2 .....211 K5
Byng Pl *GWRST* WC1E 4 C7
Byng Rd *BAR* EN5 ....20 B4
Byng St *POP/IOD* E14 ....124 D2
Bynon Av *BXLYHN* DA7 ....149 F4
Byre Rd *STHGT/OAK* N14 ....34 B1
Byrne Rd *BAL* SW12 ....161 G3
Byron Av *CDALE/KGS* NW9 .....62 D1
  HSLWW TW4 ....134 A3
  MNPK E12 ....89 J4
  NWMAL KT3 ....192 D2
  SUT SM1 ....209 H2
  SWFD E18 ....53 E6
Byron Av East *SUT* SM1 ....209 H2
Byron Cl *HACK* E8 ....86 C6
  HPTN TW12 ....154 E6
  PGE/AN SE20 ....181 J6
  STRHM/NOR SW16 ....179 K2
  SYD SE26 * 164 B6
  THMD SE28 ....109 J6
  WOT/HER KT12 ....188 D5
Byron Ct *ENC/FH* EN2 ....23 H3
  HRW HA1 ....60 E3
Byron Dr *EFNCH* N2 ....65 H3
  ERITH DA8 ....149 H1
Byron Gdns *SUT* SM1 ....209 H2
Byron Hill Rd *RYLN/HDSTN* HA2 ..60 D6
Byron Ms *HAMP* NW3 ....83 J3
  MV/WKIL W9 ....100 E3
Byron Rd *ALP/SUD* HA0 ....79 J1
  CRICK NW2 ....81 J1
  EA W5 ....117 G1
  HRW HA1 ....60 E3

KTN/HRWW/WS HA3 ....43 F6
  LEY E10 ....69 K5
  MLHL NW7 ....45 J1
  WALTH E17 ....51 J6
Byron St *POP/IOD* E14 ....106 A5
Byron Ter *ED* N9 * 36 E2
Byron Wy *NTHLT* UB5 ....95 J2
  WDR/YW UB7 ....112 C4
  YEAD UB4 ....94 D3
Bysouth Cl *CLAY* IG5 ....54 B4
  SEVS/STOTM N15 ....67 K3
By The Wd *OXHEY* WD19 * ...27 J4
Bythorn St *BRXN/ST* SW9 ....142 A4
Byton Rd *TOOT* SW17 ....178 E2
Byward Av *EBED/NFELT* TW14 ..154 B1
Byward St *MON* EC3R 13 H6
Bywater Pl *BERM/RHTH* SE16 ..124 B1
Bywater St *CHEL* SW3 ....120 E5
The Byway *BELMT* SM2 ......209 H6
  HOR/WEW KT19 ....207 H2
Bywell Pl *GTPST* W1W * 10 A2
Bywood Av *CROY/NA* CR0 .....197 K3

C

Cabbell St *BAY/PAD* W2 ....8 C2
Cabinet Wy *CHING* E4 ....51 H2
Cables Cl *PI NWCH* SE10 ....145 F2
Cables Cl *ERITH* DA8 ....129 K3
Cable St *WCHPL* E1 ....104 D6
Cable Trade Pk *CHARL* SE7 * ..125 K5
Cabot Sq *POP/IOD* E14 ....124 D1
Cabot Wy *EHAM* E6 ....89 H6
Cabul Rd *BTSEA* SW11 ....140 D3
Cactus Cl *CMBW* SE5 * 143 F3
Cadbury Cl *ISLW* TW7 ....136 B2
Cadbury Wy *BERM/RHTH* SE16 ..19 K6
Caddington Cl *EBAR* EN4 ....21 J6
Caddington Rd *CRICK* NW2 .....82 C1
Caddis Cl *STAN* HA7 * 43 F3
Cadell Cl *BETH* E2 ....7 K3
Cade Rd *GNWCH* SE10 ....145 G2
Cader Rd *WAND/EARL* SW18 ..160 B1
Cadet Dr *STHWK* SE1 ....123 G5
Cadet Pl *GNWCH* SE10 ....125 H5
Cadiz Rd *DAGE* RM10 ....92 E5
Cadiz St *WALW* SE17 ....122 D5
Cadman Cl *BRXN/ST* SW9 ....142 C1
Cadmer Cl *NWMAL* KT3 ....192 B1
Cadmus Cl *CLAP* SW4 * 141 J3
Cadogan Cl *HOM* E9 * 87 H5
  RYLN/HDSTN HA2 ....78 B2
  TEDD TW11 ....173 K1
Cadogan Gdns *CHEL* SW3 ....15 F7
  FNCH N3 * 47 F4
  SWFD E18 ....53 F6
  WCHMH N21 ....23 G6
Cadogan Ga *KTBR* SW1X 15 G6
Cadogan La *KTBR* SW1X 15 G5
Cadogan Pl *KTBR* SW1X 15 G5
Cadogan Rd *SURB* KT6 ....190 E2
  WOOL/PLUM SE18 ....127 K6
Cadogan Sq *KTBR* SW1X 14 E5
Cadogan St *CHEL* SW3 ....15 F6
  KTBR SW1X 15 F6
Cadogan Ter *HOM* E9 ....87 H4
Cadoxton Av *SEVS/STOTM* N15 ..68 B3
Cadwallon Rd *ELTH/MOT* SE9 ..167 G4
Caedmon Rd *HOLWY* N7 ....85 F2
Caerleon Cl *ESH/CLAY* KT10 ..205 H5
  SCUP DA14 ....186 D1
Caernarvon Cl *MTCM* CR4 ....179 K6
Caernarvon Dr *CLAY* IG5 ....54 A4
Caesars Wk *MTCM* CR4 ....194 E2
Cahill St *STLK* EC1Y * 6 D7
Cahir St *POP/IOD* E14 ....124 E4
Cain's La *EBED/NFELT* TW14 ..133 G6
Caird St *NKENS* W10 ....100 C2
Cairn Av *EA* W5 ....116 E1
Cairndale Cl *BMLY* BR1 ....183 J5
Cairnfield Av *CRICK* NW2 ....81 G1
Cairngorm Cl *TEDD* TW11 * ...174 B1
Cairns Av *WFD* IG8 ....53 K2
Cairns Cl *DART* DA1 ....151 G6
Cairns Rd *BTSEA* SW11 ....140 D6
Cairn Wy *STAN* HA7 ....43 F2
Cairo New Rd *CROY/NA* CR0 ..196 C6
Cairo Rd *WALTH* E17 ....69 J1
Caister Ms *BAL* SW12 ....161 G2
Caistor Park Rd *SRTFD* E15 ....88 D6
Caistor Rd *BAL* SW12 ....161 G2
Caithness Gdns *BFN/LL* DA15 ..168 A1
Caithness Rd *MTCM* CR4 ......179 G3
  WKENS W14 ....119 G3
Calabria Rd *HBRY* N5 ....85 H4
Calais St *CMBW* SE5 ....142 C2
Calbourne Av *HCH* RM12 ....93 K3
Calbourne Rd *BAL* SW12 ....160 E2
Caldbeck Av *WPK* KT4 ....192 E6
Caldecote Gdns *BUSH* WD23 ..28 E1
Caldecote La *BUSH* WD23 ....29 F1
Caldecot Rd *CMBW* SE5 ....142 D3
Caldecott Wy *CLPT* E5 ....87 F1
Calder Av *GFD/PVL* UB6 ....97 F1
Calder Cl *EN* EN1 ....24 A4
Calder Gdns *EDGW* HA8 ....44 C5
Calderon Rd *WAN* E11 ....88 A2
Calder Rd *MRDN* SM4 ....194 B2
Caldervale Rd *CLAP* SW4 ......141 J6
Calderwood St
  WOOL/PLUM SE18 ....127 F4
Caldew St *CMBW* SE5 ....142 E1
Caldicote Gn *CDALE/KGS* NW9 * ..63 G3
Caldwell Rd *OXHEY* WD19 ....27 H1
Caldwell St *BRXN/ST* SW9 ....142 A1
Caldy Rd *BELV* DA17 ....129 J3
Caldy Wk *IS* N1 * 85 J4
Caledonian Cl
  GDMY/SEVK IG3 * 73 H5
Caledonian Rd *HOLWY* N7 ......85 F5
  IS N1 ....5 F2
Caledonian Sq *CAMTN* NW1 * ..84 D5
Caledonian Wharf Rd
  POP/IOD E14 ....125 G4

Caledonia Rd STWL/WRAY TW19 .....152 B3
Caledonia St IS N1 .....5 F3
Caledon Rd EHAM E6 .....89 K6
  WLGTN SM6 .....210 A2
Cale St CHEL SW3 .....120 D5
Calidore Cl BRXS/STRHM SW2 * 162 A1
California La BUSH WD23 .....28 D3
California Rd NWMAL KT3 .....191 K1
Callaby Ter IS N1 * 85 K4
Callaghan Cl LEW SE13 .....145 H5
Callaghan Cottages WCHPL E1 * 104 E4
Callander Rd CAT SE6 .....164 E4
The Callanders BUSH WD23 * 28 E5
Callard Av PLMGR N13 .....49 H1
Callcott Rd KIL/WHAMP NW6 .....82 D5
Callcott St KENS W8 .....119 K1
Callendar Rd SKENS SW7 .....14 A4
Callis Farm Cl STWL/WRAY TW19 .....152 B1
Callisons Pl GNWCH SE10 .....125 H5
Callis Rd WALTH E17 .....69 H5
Callow St WBPTN SW10 .....120 B6
Calmington Rd CMBW SE5 .....123 F6
Calmont Rd BMLY BR1 .....183 G2
Calne Av CLAY IG5 .....54 B4
Calonne Rd WIM/MER SW19 .....159 G6
Calshot Rd HTHAIR TW6 .....132 E5
Calshot St IS N1 .....5 C2
Calshot Wy ENC/FH EN2 .....23 H4
  HTHAIR TW6 * 132 E5
Calthorpe Gdns EDGW HA8 .....44 A1
  SUT SM1 .....209 G1
Calthorpe St FSBYW WC1X 5 H6
Calton Av DUL SE21 .....163 F1
Calton Rd BAR EN5 .....33 G1
Calverley Cl BECK BR3 .....182 E2
Calverley Crs DAGE RM10 .....74 C6
Calverley Gv ARCH N19 .....66 D5
Calverley Rd EW KT17 .....207 J4
Calvert Av BETH E2 * 7 H5
Calvert Cl BELV DA17 .....129 H4
  SCUP DA14 .....187 F2
Calvert Dr RDART DA2 .....170 B4
Calverton Rd EHAM E6 .....90 A6
Calvert Rd BAR EN5 .....20 B3
  GNWCH SE10 .....125 J5
Calvert St CAMTN NW1 .....84 A6
Calvin Cl STMC/STPC BR5 .....186 E6
Calvin St WCHPL E1 .....7 J7
Calydon Rd CHARL SE7 .....126 A5
Calypso Pk PECK SE15 .....143 F1
Calypso Wy BERM/RHTH SE16 .....124 C3
Camac Rd WHTN TW2 .....155 J4

Camarthen Gn CDALE/KGS NW9 * 63 G3
Cambalt Rd PUT/ROE SW15 .....139 G6
Camberley Av EN EN1 .....24 A5
  RYNPK SW20 .....176 E5
Camberley Cl CHEAM SM3 .....208 B1
Camberley Rd HTHAIR TW6 .....132 D4
Cambert Wy BKHTH/KID SE3 .....146 A5
Camberwell Church St CMBW SE5 .....142 E2
Camberwell Glebe CMBW SE5 .....142 E2
Camberwell Gv CMBW SE5 .....142 E2
Camberwell Gv CMBW SE5 .....142 E2
Camberwell New Rd CMBW SE5 .....142 C1
Camberwell Rd CMBW SE5 .....122 D6
Camberwell Station Rd CMBW SE5 .....142 D2
Cambeys Rd DAGE RM10 .....92 E3
Camborne Av DAGE RM10 .....92 D4
  WEA W13 .....116 C2
Camborne Cl HTHAIR TW6 .....132 D4
Camborne Crs HTHAIR TW6 .....132 D4
Camborne Ms WAND/EARL SW18 .....159 K2
Camborne Rd BELMT SM2 .....208 E5
  CROY/NA CRO 197 H4
  MRDN SM4 .....193 G3
  SCUP DA14 .....168 D5
  WAND/EARL SW18 .....159 K2
  WELL DA16 .....147 K3
Camborne Rd South CROY/NA CRO 197 H4
Camborne Wy HEST TW5 .....135 F2
Cambourne Av ED N9 .....37 F3
Cambourne Ms NTGHL W11 .....100 C5
Cambray Rd BAL SW12 .....161 H3
  ORP BR6 .....202 A4
Cambria Cl BFN/LL DA15 .....167 K3
  HSLW TW3 .....135 F5
Cambria Ct EBED/NFELT TW14 .....154 A1
Cambria Gdns STWL/WRAY TW19 .....152 B2
Cambrian Av CNTH/NBYPK IG2 .....72 E2
Cambrian Cl WNWD SE27 .....162 C5
Cambrian Gn CDALE/KGS NW9 .....63 G2
Cambrian Rd LEY E10 .....69 J3
  RCHPK/HAM TW10 .....157 G1
Cambria Rd CMBW SE5 .....142 D4
Cambria St FUL/PGN SW6 .....140 A1
Cambridge Av GFD/PVL UB6 .....79 F4
  KIL/WHAMP NW6 .....100 E1
  NWMAL KT3 .....176 C5
  WELL DA16 .....148 A5
Cambridge Barracks Rd WOOL/PLUM SE18 .....126 E4
Cambridge Circ SOHO/SHAV W1D 10 D4
Cambridge Cl HSLWW TW4 .....134 D5
  RYNPK SW20 .....176 E4
  WALTH E17 .....69 H3
  WDGN N22 .....49 G4
  WDR/YW UB7 .....112 A4
  WLSDN NW10 .....80 E1
Cambridge Cls BETH E2 .....104 D1
  TEDD TW11 * 174 C1
Cambridge Dr LEE/GVPK SE12 .....145 K5
  RSLP HA4 .....59 H6
Cambridge Gdns EN EN1 .....24 C3
  KIL/WHAMP NW6 .....100 E1
  KUT/HW KT1 .....175 H5
  MUSWH N10 .....48 A4
  NKENS W10 .....100 C5
TOTM N17 .....49 K3
  WCHMH N21 .....35 K2
Cambridge Ga CAMTN NW1 .....3 J6
Cambridge Gate Ms CAMTN NW1 .....3 J6
Cambridge Gn ELTH/MOT SE9 .....167 G3
Cambridge Gv HMSMTH W6 .....118 E4
  PGE/AN SE20 * 181 J4
Cambridge Grove Rd KUT/HW KT1 .....175 H6
Cambridge Heath Rd BETH E2 .....104 D2
Cambridge Pde EN EN1 * 24 C5
Cambridge Pk TWK TW1 .....156 E2
  WAN E11 .....70 E3
Cambridge Pk Rd WAN E11 .....70 E4
Cambridge Pas HOM E9 .....86 E5
Cambridge Pl KENS W8 .....120 A2
Cambridge Rd BARK IG11 .....90 C5
  BARN SW13 .....138 C3
  BMLY BR1 .....183 K3
  BTSEA SW11 .....140 E2
  CAR SM5 .....209 J4
  CHING E4 .....38 A3
  E/WMO/HCT KT8 .....188 E1
  GDMY/SEVK IG3 .....72 E5
  HNWL W7 .....116 A2
  HPTN TW12 .....172 E5
  HSLWW TW4 .....134 D5
  KIL/WHAMP NW6 .....100 E2
  KUT/HW KT1 .....175 H5
  MTCM CR4 .....179 H6
  NWMAL KT3 .....192 A1
  PGE/AN SE20 .....181 H6
  RCH/KEW TW9 .....137 H1
  RYLN/HDSTN HA2 .....60 A2
  RYNPK SW20 .....176 E4
  SCUP DA14 .....168 A6
  STHL UB1 .....114 E1
  TEDD TW11 .....156 B6
  TWK TW1 .....156 E1
  WALTH E17 .....70 E3
  WOT/HER KT12 .....188 A3
Cambridge Rd North CHSWK W4 .....117 J5
Cambridge Rd South CHSWK W4 .....117 J5
Cambridge Rw WOOL/PLUM SE18 .....127 G5
Cambridge Sq BAY/PAD W2 .....8 B3
Cambridge St PIM SW1V 121 G5
Cambridge Ter CAMTN NW1 .....3 J5
  ED N9 * 36 B2
Cambridge Terrace Ms CAMTN NW1 * 3 K5
Cambridge Yd HNWL W7 * 116 B2
Cambstone Cl YEAD UB4 .....95 J4
Cambus Cl YEAD UB4 .....95 J4
Cambus Rd CAN/RD E16 .....106 E4
Camdale Rd WOOL/PLUM SE18 .....148 A1
Camden Av FELT TW13 .....154 B4
  YEAD UB4 .....95 G4
Camden Cl CHST BR7 .....185 H4
Camden Gdns CAMTN NW1 * 84 B5
  SUT SM1 .....209 F4
  THHTH CR7 .....180 C6
Camden Gv CHST BR7 .....185 G2
Camden High St CAMTN NW1 .....4 A1
Camden Hill Rd NRWD SE19 .....181 F2
Camdenhurst St POP/IOD E14 .....105 G5
Camden Lock Pl CAMTN NW1 .....84 A5
Camden Ms CAMTN NW1 .....84 C4
Camden Park Rd CAMTN NW1 .....84 D4
  CHST BR7 .....184 E3
Camden Pas IS N1 .....6 A2
Camden Rd BXLY DA5 .....169 G3
  CAMTN NW1 .....84 B4
  CAR SM5 .....209 K3
  SUT SM1 .....209 F3
  WALTH E17 .....69 H3
  WAN E11 .....71 F3
Camden Rd Permanent Wy CAMTN NW1 * 4 C1
Camden Rw BKHTH/KID SE3 .....145 H3
  PIN HA5 * 41 G6
Camden Sq CAMTN NW1 .....84 D5
Camden St CAMTN NW1 .....84 B5
Camden Ter CAMTN NW1 * 84 D4
Camden Wk IS N1 .....6 A1
Camden Wy CHST BR7 .....184 E3
  THHTH CR7 .....180 C6
Camelford Wk NTGHL W11 * 100 C5
Camelford Ct NTGHL W11 * 100 C5
Camel Gv KUTN/CMB KT2 .....174 E1
Camellia Pl WHTN TW2 .....155 G2
Camellia St VX/NE SW8 .....141 K1
Camelot Cl THMD SE28 .....128 C3
  WIM/MER SW19 .....159 J6
Camel Rd CAN/RD E16 .....126 D1
Camera Pl WBPTN SW10 .....120 B6
Cameron Cl BXLY DA5 .....170 D5
  ED N9 .....33 J4
  UED N18 .....50 D1
Cameron Pl STRHM/NOR SW16 .....162 B5
Cameron Rd CAT SE6 .....164 C4
  CROY/NA CRO 196 C4
  GDMY/SEVK IG3 .....72 E5
  HAYES BR2 .....199 K1
Cameron Sq MTCM CR4 .....178 D4
Cameron Ter LEE/GVPK SE12 * 166 A5
Camerton Cl HACK E8 .....86 B4
Camilla Rd BERM/RHTH SE16 .....123 J4
Camille Cl SNWD SE25 .....181 H6
Camlan Rd BMLY BR1 .....165 J6
Camlet St BETH E2 .....7 J6
Camlet Wy EBAR EN4 .....20 E5
Camley St CAMTN NW1 .....4 D1
Camm Gdns KUT/HW KT1 * 175 G5
  THDIT KT7 .....189 K4
Camomile Av MTCM CR4 .....178 E4
Camomile Rd ROMW/RG RM7 .....75 F6
Campana Rd FUL/PGN SW6 .....139 K2
Campbell Av BARK/HLT IG6 .....72 C1
Campbell Cl ROM RM1 .....57 G3
  RSLP HA4 .....58 C3
  STRHM/NOR SW16 .....179 J1
  WOOL/PLUM SE18 .....147 F2
Campbell Cottages MTCM CR4 * 179 F5

Campbell Cft EDGW HA8 .....44 C1
Campbell Gordon Wy CRICK NW2 .....81 K2
Campbell Rd BOW E3 .....105 J2
  CROY/NA CRO 196 C4
  EHAM E6 .....89 J6
  HNWL W7 .....96 E6
  SRTFD E15 .....88 C2
  TOTM N17 .....50 B4
  WALTH E17 .....69 H1
  WHTN TW2 .....155 J4
Campbell Wk IS N1 .....84 E6
Campdale Rd HOLWY N7 .....84 D1
Campden Crs ALP/SUD HA0 .....79 H1
  BCTR RM8 .....91 J2
Campden Gdns KENS W8 * 119 K2
Campden Hill Ga KENS W8 * 119 K2
Campden Hill Pl NTGHL W11 * 119 J1
Campden Hill Rd KENS W8 .....119 K2
Campden Hill Sq KENS W8 .....119 J1
Campden House Cl KENS W8 .....119 K2
Campden House Ter KENS W8 * 119 K2
Campden Rd SAND/SEL CR2 .....212 A5
  STHGT/OAK N14 .....34 D1
Campden St KENS W8 .....119 K2
Campden Ter CHSWK W4 * 118 B5
Campden Wy BCTR RM8 .....91 J3
Camperdown St WCHPL E1 .....13 K4
Campfield Rd ELTH/MOT SE9 .....166 C2
Campion Cl CROY/NA CRO 212 A2
  EHAM E6 .....107 K6
  KTN/HRWW/WS HA3 .....62 B3
  ROMW/RG RM7 .....75 F6
Campion Ct ALP/SUD HA0 .....98 A1
Campion Gdns WFD IG8 .....52 E1
Campion Pl THMD SE28 .....128 C1
Campion Rd ISLW TW7 .....136 A2
  PUT/ROE SW15 .....139 F5
Campion Ter CRICK NW2 .....82 B1
Campus Rd WALTH E17 .....69 H3
Campus Vw WIM/MER SW19 .....176 E1
Cam Rd SRTFD E15 .....88 B6
Camrose Av ERITH DA8 .....129 K6
  FELT TW13 .....154 A6
  STAN HA7 .....44 A5
Camrose Cl CROY/NA CRO 198 B4
  MRDN SM4 .....193 K1
Camrose St WOOL/PLUM SE18 .....128 B5
Canada Av UED N18 .....49 J2
Canada Crs ACT W3 .....98 E4
Canada Park Pde EDGW HA8 * 44 D4
Canada Rd ACT W3 .....98 E4
  ERITH DA8 .....150 E1
Canada Sqaure POP/IOD E14 * 124 E1
Canada St BERM/RHTH SE16 .....124 A2
Canada Wy SHB W12 .....99 K6
Canadian Av CAT SE6 .....164 E3
Canal Ap DEPT SE8 .....124 B6
Canal Bvd KTTN NW5 .....84 D3
Canal Cl NKENS W10 .....100 B3
  WCHPL E1 .....105 G3
Canal Gv PECK SE15 .....123 J6
Canal Pth BETH E2 .....7 K3
Canal St CMBW SE5 .....122 E6
Canal Wk CROY/NA CRO 197 F3
  IS N1 .....85 K6
  WLSDN NW10 * 81 G2
Canal Wy NKENS W10 .....100 B3
Canal Whf GFD/PVL UB6 * 79 G6
Canal Yd NWDGN UB2 * 114 A4
Canberra Cl DAGE RM10 .....93 F5
  HDN NW4 .....45 J5
Canberra Dr NTHLT UB5 .....95 G2
Canberra Rd ABYW SE2 .....128 E6
  CAN/RD E16 .....107 G5
  CHARL SE7 .....126 B6
  EHAM E6 .....89 K6
  WEA W13 .....116 B1
Canbury Av KUTN/CMB KT2 .....175 G4
Canbury Ms SYD SE26 .....163 H5
Canbury Park Rd KUTN/CMB KT2 .....175 F4
Canbury Pth STMC/STPC BR5 .....202 B1
Cancell Rd BRXN/ST SW9 .....142 B2
Candahar Rd BTSEA SW11 .....140 D3
Candle Gv PECK SE15 .....143 J4
Candlefield Cl SRTFD E15 .....88 D4
Candle Ms TWK TW1 .....156 B2
Candler St SEVS/STOTM N15 * 67 K3
Candover Cl WDR/YW UB7 .....132 A1
Candover Rd HCH RM12 .....75 K5
Candover St CTPST W1W * 10 A2
Candy St BOW E3 .....87 H6
Caney Ms CRICK NW2 .....64 B6
Canfield Dr RSLP HA4 .....77 F3
Canfield Gdns KIL/WHAMP NW6 .....83 G4
Canfield Pl KIL/WHAMP NW6 .....83 G4
Canfield Rd RAIN RM13 .....93 J6
  WFD IG8 .....53 J3
Canford Av NTHLT UB5 .....77 K6
Canford Cl ENC/FH EN2 .....23 F3
Canford Gdns NWMAL KT3 .....192 B3
Canford Pl TEDD TW11 * 174 C2
Canford Rd BTSEA SW11 .....161 F5
Canham Rd CHSWK W4 .....118 B3
  SNWD SE25 .....181 F6
Canmore Gdns STRHM/NOR SW16 .....179 H3
Cann Hall Rd WAN E11 .....88 D2
Canning Crs WDGN N22 .....49 F4

Canning Cross CMBW SE5 .....143 F3
Canning Pl KENS W8 .....120 B3
Canning Place Ms KENS W8 * 120 B3
Canning Rd CROY/NA CRO 197 G6
  HBRY N5 .....85 H1
  KTN/HRWW/WS HA3 .....42 C6
  SRTFD E15 .....106 C1
  WALTH E17 .....69 G1
Cannington Rd DAGW RM9 .....91 J5
Cannizaro Rd WIM/MER SW19 .....177 F2
Cannonbury Av PIN HA5 .....59 H3
Cannon Cl HPTN TW12 .....173 G2
  RYNPK SW20 .....177 F6
Cannon Dr POP/IOD E14 .....105 J6
Cannon Hill KIL/WHAMP NW6 .....83 F3
Cannon Hill La RYNPK SW20 .....177 G6
Cannon Hill Ms STHGT/OAK N14 .....34 E5
  PIN HA5 .....59 J2
Cannon La HAMP NW3 .....83 H1
Cannon Pl CHARL SE7 .....126 D5
  HAMP NW3 .....83 H1
Cannon Rd BXLYHN DA7 .....149 G2
  STHGT/OAK N14 .....34 E5
Cannon St BLKFR EC4V 12 C4
Cannon Street Rd WCHPL E1 .....104 D5
Canon Av CHDH RM6 .....73 J2
Canon Beck Rd BERM/RHTH SE16 .....123 K2
Canonbie Rd FSTH SE23 .....163 K2
Canonbury Crs IS N1 .....85 J5
Canonbury Gv IS N1 .....85 J5
Canonbury La IS N1 .....85 H5
Canonbury Pk North IS N1 .....85 J4
Canonbury Pk South IS N1 .....85 J4
Canonbury Pl IS N1 .....85 H5
Canonbury Rd EN EN1 .....24 C1
  IS N1 .....85 H4
Canonbury Sq IS N1 .....85 H5
Canonbury St IS N1 .....85 J5
Canonbury Vls IS N1 .....85 H5
Canonbury Yd East IS N1 * 85 H4
Canon Mohan Cl STHGT/OAK N14 * 34 A1
Canon Murnane Rd STHWK SE1 .....19 J5
Canon Rd BMLY BR1 .....184 B6
Canon Rw WHALL SW1A 16 E3
Canons Cl EDGW HA8 .....44 B2
Canons Cottages EDGW HA8 * 44 B2
Canons Ct EDGW HA8 * 44 B2
Canons Dr EDGW HA8 .....44 A2
Canonsleigh Rd DAGW RM9 .....91 H5
Canon St IS N1 .....85 J6
Canon's Wk CROY/NA CRO 213 F1
Canrobert St BETH E2 .....104 D2
Cantelowes Rd CAMTN NW1 .....84 D5
Canterbury Av BFN/LL DA15 .....168 D4
  IL IG1 .....71 J4
Canterbury Cl BECK BR3 .....182 E4
  CMBW SE5 .....142 D3
  EHAM E6 .....107 K5
  GFD/PVL UB6 .....96 B5
  NTHWD HA6 .....40 D2
Canterbury Crs BRXN/ST SW9 .....142 B4
Canterbury Gv WNWD SE27 .....162 C5
Canterbury Pl WALW SE17 .....18 B7
Canterbury Rd CROY/NA CRO 196 A4
  FELT TW13 .....154 D4
  HRW HA1 .....60 C2
  KIL/WHAMP NW6 .....100 E1
  LEY E10 .....70 A4
  MRDN SM4 .....194 B3
Canterbury Ter KIL/WHAMP NW6 .....100 E1
Cantley Gdns GNTH/NBYPK IG2 .....72 C3
  NRWD SE19 .....181 G4
Cantley Rd HNWL W7 .....116 B3
Canton St POP/IOD E14 .....105 J5
Cantrell Rd BOW E3 .....105 J3
Cantwell Rd WOOL/PLUM SE18 .....147 G1
Canvey St STHWK SE1 .....12 C7
Cape Cl BARK IG11 .....90 B5
Cape Cl HAYES BR2 .....200 D5
Capel Cl HAYES BR2 .....200 D5
  TRDG/WHET N20 .....33 G5
Capel Gdns GDMY/SEVK IG3 .....91 F2
  PIN HA5 .....59 K1
Capel Pl RDART DA2 .....170 D4
Capel Rd EBAR EN4 .....33 J1
  FSTGT E7 .....89 F2
  OXHEY WD19 .....27 J1
Capener's Cl KTBR SW1X 15 G3
Capern Rd WAND/EARL SW18 .....160 B3
Cape Rd TOTM N17 * 50 C6
Cape Yd WAP E1W * 123 H1
Capital Interchange Wy BTFD TW8 .....117 H5
Capitol Wy CDALE/KGS NW9 .....44 E6
Capland St STJWD NW8 .....2 B6
Caple Pde WLSDN NW10 * 99 H1
Caple Rd WLSDN NW10 .....99 H1
Caprea Cl YEAD UB4 .....95 H4
Capstan Cl CHDH RM6 .....73 H3
Capstan Dr RAIN RM13 .....111 J4
Capstan Ride ENC/FH EN2 .....23 G3
Capstan Rd DEPT SE8 .....124 C4
Capstan Sq POP/IOD E14 .....125 F2
Capstan Wy BERM/RHTH SE16 .....124 B1
Capstone Rd BMLY BR1 .....165 J6
Capthorne Av RYLN/HDSTN HA2 .....59 J5
Capuchin Cl STAN HA7 .....43 H2
Capulet Ms CAN/RD E16 .....125 K1
Capworth St LEY E10 .....69 J5
Caractacus Cottage Vw WATW WD18 .....26 E2
Caractacus Gn WATW WD18 .....26 D2
Caradoc Cl BAY/PAD W2 .....100 E5
Caradoc Evans Cl FBAR/BDGN N11 * 48 B1

Caradoc St GNWCH SE10 .....125 H5
Caradon Cl WAN E11 .....70 C5
Caradon Wy SEVS/STOTM N15 .....67 K1
Caravel Ms DEPT SE8 * 124 D6
Caraway Cl PLSTW E13 .....107 F4
Caraway Pl WLGTN SM6 .....210 B1
Carberry Rd NRWD SE19 * 181 F2
Carbery Av ACT W3 .....117 G2
Carbis Cl CHING E4 .....38 B3
Carbis Rd POP/IOD E14 .....105 H5
Carburton St CTPST W1W 9 K1
Cardale St POP/IOD E14 .....125 F3
Carden Rd PECK SE15 .....143 J4
Cardiff Rd HNWL W7 .....116 B3
  PEND EN3 .....24 D5
  WATW WD18 .....27 F1
Cardiff St WOOL/PLUM SE18 .....147 K1
Cardigan Gdns GDMY/SEVK IG3 .....73 G2
Cardigan Pl LEW SE13 * 145 G3
Cardigan Rd BARN SW13 .....138 D3
  BOW E3 .....105 H1
  RCHPK/HAM TW10 .....157 F1
  WIM/MER SW19 .....178 B2
Cardigan St LBTH SE11 .....122 B5
Cardigan Wk IS N1 * 85 J5
Cardinal Av KUTN/CMB KT2 .....175 F1
  MRDN SM4 .....193 H3
Cardinal Bourne St STHWK SE1 * 19 F5
Cardinal Cl CHST BR7 .....185 J4
  EDGW HA8 .....44 E3
  MRDN SM4 .....193 H3
  WPK KT4 .....207 H2
Cardinal Crs NWMAL KT3 .....175 K5
Cardinal Dr BARK/HLT IG6 .....54 C2
  WOT/HER KT12 .....188 C5
Cardinal Hinsey Cl WLSDN NW10 .....99 J1
Cardinal Pl PUT/ROE SW15 .....139 G5
Cardinal Rd FELT TW13 .....154 A3
  RSLP HA4 .....59 H5
Cardinals Wk HPTN TW12 .....173 H5
Cardinals Wy ARCH N19 .....66 D5
Cardinal Wy KTN/HRWW/WS HA3 .....42 E6
Cardine Ms PECK SE15 .....143 J1
Cardington Sq HSLWW TW4 .....134 C5
Cardington St CAMTN NW1 .....4 B5
Cardozo Rd HOLWY N7 .....84 E3
Cardrew Av NFNCH/WDSPK N12 .....47 H1
Cardross St HMSMTH W6 .....118 E3
Cardwell Rd HOLWY N7 * 84 E2
Cardwell Ter HOLWY N7 * 84 E2
Carew Cl HOLWY N7 .....67 H6
Carew Rd MTCM CR4 .....179 F5
  NTHWD HA6 .....40 D1
  THHTH CR7 .....180 C6
  TOTM N17 .....50 C5
  WEA W13 .....116 D2
  WLGTN SM6 .....210 C4
Carew St CMBW SE5 .....142 D3
Carew Wy OXHEY WD19 .....27 K5
  STMC/STPC BR5 .....202 E6
Carey Gdns VX/NE SW8 .....141 H2
Carey La CITYW EC2V 12 C3
Carey Pl PIM SW1V 16 C7
Carey Rd DAGW RM9 .....92 A2
Carey St LINN WC2A 11 H4
Carey Wy WBLY HA9 .....80 E2
Carfax Pl CLAP SW4 * 141 J5
Carfax Rd HCH RM12 .....93 H2
  HYS/HAR UB3 .....113 J5
The Carfax SYD SE26 * 163 K5
Carfree Cl IS N1 .....85 G5
Cargill Rd WAND/EARL SW18 .....160 B3
Cargreen Rd SNWD SE25 .....197 G1
Carholme Rd FSTH SE23 .....164 C3
Carisbrook Cl EN EN1 .....24 B2
Carisbrooke Av BXLY DA5 .....168 E3
Carisbrooke Cl HSLWW TW4 .....154 D3
  STAN HA7 .....43 K5
Carisbrooke Cl NTHLT UB5 * 77 K6
Carisbrooke Gdns PECK SE15 .....143 G1
Carisbrooke Rd HAYES BR2 .....200 B1
  MTCM CR4 .....195 K1
  WALTH E17 .....51 F7
Carker's La KTTN NW5 .....84 B3
Carleton Av WLGTN SM6 .....210 D6
Carleton Cl ESH/CLAY KT10 .....189 J5
Carleton Gdns ARCH N19 * 84 C3
Carleton Rd DART DA1 .....171 J2
  HOLWY N7 .....84 D3
Carleton Vls KTTN NW5 * 84 C3
Carlile Cl BOW E3 .....105 H1
Carlina Gdns WFD IG8 .....53 F1
Carlingford Rd HAMP NW3 .....83 H2
  MRDN SM4 .....193 G3
  SEVS/STOTM N15 .....49 J6
Carlisle Av ACT W3 .....99 G5
  TWRH EC3N 13 J4
Carlisle Cl KUTN/CMB KT2 .....175 H4
  PIN HA5 .....59 J4
Carlisle Gdns IL IG1 .....71 J3
  KTN/HRWW/WS HA3 .....61 K4
Carlisle La STHWK SE1 .....17 H4
Carlisle Ms BAY/PAD W2 .....8 B2
  KUTN/CMB KT2 .....175 H4
Carlisle Pl FBAR/BDGN N11 .....34 B6
  WEST SW1P 16 A5
Carlisle Rd CDALE/KGS NW9 .....44 E6
  DART DA1 .....171 K1
  FSBYPK N4 .....67 G5
  HPTN TW12 .....173 G3
  KIL/WHAMP NW6 .....82 C6
  LEY E10 .....69 J5
  ROM RM1 .....75 J2
  SUT SM1 .....208 D4
Carlisle St SOHO/SHAV W1D 10 C4
Carlisle Wk HACK E8 .....86 B4
Carlisle Wy TOOT SW17 .....178 A1
Carlos Pl MYFR/PKLN W1K 9 H6
Carlow St CAMTN NW1 * 4 A2
Carlton Av EBED/NFELT TW14 .....134 B1
  HYS/HAR UB3 .....113 H4
  KTN/HRWW/WS HA3 .....43 J6
  SAND/SEL CR2 .....211 K5
  STHGT/OAK N14 .....22 D6

Carlton Av East *WBLY* HA9 ......**61** K6
Carlton Av West *ALP/SUD* HA0 ....**61** J6
Carlton CI *CHSGTN* KT9 ....**205** K4
  EDGW HA8 ....**44** C1
  HAMP NW3 ....**64** E6
Carlton Dr *CHEAM* SM3 ....**208** C2
Carlton Dene EW *KT17* * **207** J3
Carlton Dr *BARK/HLT* IG6 ....**54** D6
  PUT/ROE SW15 ....**139** G6
Carlton Gdns *EA* W5 ....**97** J5
  ST/S SW1Y ....
Carlton Ga *MV/WKIL* W9 ....**100** E4
Carlton Gdns *SCUP* DA14 * **168** A6
Carlton Gv *PECK* SE15 ....**143** J2
Carlton Hl *STJWD* NW8 ....**101** G1
Carlton House Ter *ST/S* SW1Y ...**16** C1
Carlton Ms *KIL/WHAMP* NW6 * ...**82** E3
Carlton Pde *WBLY* HA9 * **62** A5
Carlton Park Av *RYNPK* SW20 ...**177** F5
Carlton Rd *CHSWK* W4 ....**118** A2
  EA W5 ....**97** J6
  ERITH DA8 ....**129** K6
  FBAR/BDGN N11 ....**48** A1
  FSBYPK N4 ....**67** G4
  GPK RM2 ....**75** J2
  MNPK E12 ....**89** H2
  MORT/ESHN SW14 ....**137** K4
  NWMAL KT3 ....**176** B5
  SAND/SEL CR2 ....**211** K5
  SCUP DA14 ....**186** A1
  WALTH E17 ....**51** G4
  WAN E11 ....**70** D5
  WELL DA16 ....**148** C4
  WOT/HER KT12 ....**188** A4
Carlton Sq *WCHPL* E1 * **105** F3
Carlton St *ST/S* SW1Y **10** C6
Carlton Ter *SYD* SE26 ....**163** K6
  UED N18 ....**35** K6
  WAN E11 ....**70** D5
Carlton Tower PI *KTBR* SW1X **15** F4
Carlwell St *TOOT* SW17 ....**178** D1
Carlyle Av *BMLY* BR1 ....**184** C6
  STHL UB1 ....**96** A6
Carlyle CI *E/WMO/HCT* KT8 .....**173** G6
  EFNCH N2 ....**65** G3
  WLSDN NW10 ....**81** F6
Carlyle Ct *WBPTN* SW10 * **140** B2
Carlyle Gdns *STHL* UB1 ....**95** K6
Carlyle Rd *CROY/NA* CR0 ....**197** H6
  EA W5 ....**116** D5
  MNPK E12 ....**89** J2
  THMD SE28 ....**109** H6
Carlyle Sq *CHEL* SW3 ....**120** C5
Carlyon Av *RYLN/HDSTN* HA2....**77** K2
Carlyon CI *ALP/SUD* HA0 ....**80** A6
Carlyon Rd *ALP/SUD* HA0 ....**98** A1
  YEAD UB4 ....**95** G5
Carlys CI *BECK* BR3 ....**182** A5
Carmalt Gdns *PUT/ROE* SW15 ..**139** F5
Carmel Ct *KENS* W8 * **120** A2
Carmelite Rd
  KTN/HRWW/WS HA3 ....**42** C1
Carmelite St *EMB* EC4Y **11** K5
Carmel Wy *RCH/KEW* TW9 ......**137** H5
Carmen St *POP/IOD* E14 ....**105** K5
Carmichael CI *BTSEA* SW11 * ...**140** C4
  RSLP HA4 ....**76** E2
Carmichael Ms
  WAND/EARL SW18 ....**160** C2
Carmichael Rd *SNWD* SE25 .....**197** H2
Carminia Rd *TOOT* SW17 ....**161** G4
Carnaby St *SOHO/CST* W1F **10** A4
Carnac St *WNWD* SE27 ....**162** E6
Carnanton Rd *WALTH* E17 ......**52** B4
Carnarvon Av *EN* EN1 ....**24** B3
Carnarvon Dr *HYS/HAR* UB3 ....**113** G3
Carnarvon Rd *BAR* EN5 ....**20** C3
  LEY E10 ....**70** A3
  SRTFD E15 ....**88** D4
  SWFD E18 ....**52** D4
Carnation CI *ROMW/RG* RM7 ....**75** G6
Carnation St *ABYW* SE2 ....**128** C5
Carnbrook Rd *BKHTH/KID* SE3 ..**146** D4
Carnecke Gdns *ELTH/MOT* SE9 ..**146** D6
Carnegie CI *PEND* EN3 ....
  SURB KT6 ....**191** H6
Carnegie PI *WIM/MER* SW19 ....**159** G3
Carnegie St *IS* N1 ....**5** G2
Carnet CI *DART* DA1 ....**170** B2
Carnforth CI *HOR/WEW* KT19 ...**206** D4
Carnforth Gdns *HCH* RM12 ......**93** J3
Carnforth Rd
  STRHM/NOR SW16 ....**179** J3
Carnoustie Dr *IS* N1 ....**85** F5
Carnoustie CI *THMD* SE28 ....**109** K5
Carnwath Rd *FUL/PGN* SW6 ....**139** K4
Carol CI *NWK/WS* NW4 ....**64** B1
Carolina CI *SRTFD* E15 ....**88** C3
Carolina Rd *THHTH* CR7 ....**180** C5
Caroline CI *CROY/NA* CR0 ....**212** A2
  ISLW TW7 ....**135** K1
  MUSWH N10 ....**48** B5
  STRHM/NOR SW16 ....**162** A5
  WDR/YW UB7 ....**112** A2
Caroline Ct *STAN* HA7 * **43** G2
Caroline Gdns *BETH* E2 ....**7** H4
  PECK SE15 ....**143** J1
Caroline Av *BAY/PAD* W2 ......**101** H5
  BTSEA SW11 ....**141** F3
  HYS/HAR UB3 ....**133** H1
  OXHEY WD19 ....**27** J1
Caroline St *WIM/MER* SW19 ....**177** J3
Caroline St *WCHPL* E1 ....**105** F5
Caroline Ter *BGVA* SW1W **15** G7
Caroline Wk *HMSMTH* W6 .....**119** H6
Carol St *CAMTN* NW1 ....**84** C6
Carolyn Dr *ORP* BR6 ....**217** G1
Carpenders Av *OXHEY* WD19 ...**27** J1
Carpenter CI *EW* KT17 ....**207** H6
Carpenter Gdns *WCHMH* N21 ...**35** H4
Carpenters CI *BAR* EN5 ....**33** F1
Carpenters Ms *HOLWY* N7 * **84** E3
Carpenters PI *CLAP* SW4 ....**141** J5
Carpenters Rd *SRTFD* E15 ......**87** K5
Carpenter St *MYFR/PKLN* W1K ..**9** J7
Carrara Ms *HACK* E8 ....**86** C3

Carrara Whf *FUL/PGN* SW6......**139** H4
Carri CI *STAN* HA7 ....**43** G2
Carre Ms *CMBW* SE5 ....**142** C2
Carr Gv *WOOL/PLUM* SE18 ....**126** D4
Carriage Dr East *CHEL* SW3 ...**121** F5
Carriage Dr North
  BTSEA SW11 ....**140** E1
Carriage Dr South
  BTSEA SW11 ....**140** E2
Carriage Dr West *BTSEA* SW11 ..**140** E2
Carriage Ms *IL* IG1 ....**72** C6
Carrick CI *ISLW* TW7 ....**136** B4
Carrick Dr *BARK/HLT* IG6 ....**54** C4
Carrick Ga *ESH/CLAY* KT10 .....**204** C1
Carrick Ms *DEPT* SE8 ....**124** D6
Carrill Wy *BELV* DA17 ....**128** E4
Carrington CI *CROY/NA* CR0 ....**198** B4
Carrington Gdns *FSTGT* E7 * ...**88** E2
Carrington PI *ESH/CLAY* KT10 *.**204** B2
Carrington Rd *DART* DA1 ....**171** J1
  RCHPK/HAM TW10 ....**137** H5
Carrington Sq
  KTN/HRWW/WS HA3 ....**42** C3
Carroll CI *MYFR/PICC* W1J...**15** J1
Carroll CI *KTTN* NW5 ....**84** C2
Carroll CI *SRTFD* E15 ....**88** D3
Carronade PI *THMD* SE28 ......**127** H5
Carron CI *POP/IOD* E14 ....**105** K5
Carroun Rd *VX/NE* SW8 ....**142** A1
Carrowway La *GFD/PVL* UB6 ....**96** D6
Carrow Rd *DAGW* RM9 ....**91** H5
Carr Rd *NTHLT* UB5 ....**78** B5
  WALTH E17 ....**51** H5
Carrs La *WCHMH* N21 ....**23** K6
Carr St *POP/IOD* E14 ....**105** G5
Carshalton Park Rd *CAR* SM5 ...**209** K4
Carshalton Rd *MTCM* CR4 .....**195** F2
  SUT SM1 ....**209** G3
Carsington Gdns *DART* DA1 ....**171** G4
Carslake Rd *PUT/ROE* SW15 ...**159** F1
Carson Rd *CAN/RD* E16 ....**106** E4
  DUL SE21 ....**162** E4
  EBAR EN4 ....**21** K5
Carstairs Rd *CAT* SE6 ....**165** F5
Carston CI *LEE/GVPK* SE12 ....**145** J6
Carswell CI *REDBR* IG4 ....**71** H1
Carswell Rd *CAT* SE6 ....**165** F2
Carter CI *CDALE/KGS* NW9 .....**63** F3
  CRW RM5 ....**56** D3
Carteret St *STJSPK* SW1H **16** C3
Carteret Wy *DEPT* SE8 ....**124** B4
Carterhatch La *EN* EN1 ....**24** C1
Carterhatch Rd *PEND* EN3 ....**25** G3
Carter La *BLKFR* EC4V **12** B4
Carter PI *WALW* SE17 ....**122** D5
Carter Rd *PLSTW* E13 ....**89** F6
  WIM/MER SW19 ....**178** C2
Carters CI *KTTN* NW5 ....**84** D4
Carters Hill CI *ELTH/MOT* SE9 ..**166** B3
Carter's St *WALW* SE17 ....**122** D4
Carter's Yd *WAND/EARL* SW18 ..**159** K1
Carthew Rd *HMSMTH* W6 .....**118** E3
Carthew VIs *HMSMTH* W6 .....**118** E3
Carthusian St *FARR* EC1M **12** C1
Cartimg La *TPL/STR* WC2R **11** F6
Cart La *CHING* E4 ....**38** C5
Cartmel CI *TOTM* N17 ....**50** D3
Cartmel St *NTHLT* UB5 ....**77** J4
Cartmel Gdns *MRDN* SM4 .....**194** B2
Cartmel Rd *BXLYHN* DA7 ....**149** H2
Cartwright Gdns *STPAN* WC1H...**4** E5
Cartwright St *WCHPL* E1 ......**13** K5
Cartwright Wy *BARN* SW13 ....**138** E1
Carver CI *CHSWK* W4 ....**117** K3
Carver Rd *HNHL* SE24 ....**162** D1
Carville Crs *BTFD* TW8 ....**117** F5
Cary Rd *WAN* E11 ....**88** C2
Carysfort Rd *CEND/HSY/T* N8 ...**66** D1
  STNW/STAM N16 ....**85** K1
Cascade Av *MUSWH* N10 ......**66** C1
Cascade CI *STMC/STPC* BR5 ...**186** D6
Cascade Rd *BKHH* IG9 ....**39** H4
Casella Rd *NWCR* SE14 ....**144** A1
Casewick Rd *WNWD* SE27 ....**180** C1
Casey CI *STJWD* NW8 ....**2** C5
  STJWD NW8 ....
Casino Av *HNHL* SE24 ....**142** D6
Caspian CI *CMBW* SE5 ....**142** E1
Caspian Wk *CAN/RD* E16 ......**107** H5
Caspian St *CMBW* SE5 ....**142** E1
Cassandra CI *NTHLT* UB5 ......**78** D2
Casselden Rd *WLSDN* NW10 ...**81** F5
Cassidy Rd *FUL/PGN* SW6 ....**139** K1
Cassilda Rd *ABYW* SE2 ....**128** B4
Cassilis Rd *POP/IOD* E14 .....**124** D2
  TWK TW1 ....**156** C1
Cassiobury Av
  EBED/NFELT TW14 ....**153** J2
Cassiobury Rd *WALTH* E17 ....**69** F2
Cassland Rd *HOM* E9 ....**87** G4
  THHTH CR7 ....**197** F1
Casslee Rd *CAT* SE6 ....**164** C2
Casson St *WCHPL* E1 ....**104** C4
Castellain Rd *MV/WKIL* W9 ....**101** F3
Castellan Av *GPK* RM2 ....**57** K6
Castellane CI *STAN* HA7 ....**43** F3
Castello Av *PUT/ROE* SW15 ...**139** F6
Castelnau *BARN* SW13 ....**138** E1
Casterbridge Rd
  BKHTH/KID SE3 ....**145** K4
Casterton St *HACK* E8 ....**86** D4
Castile Rd *WOOL/PLUM* SE18 ..**127** F4
Castillon Rd *CAT* SE6 ....**165** H4
Castlands Rd *CAT* SE6 ....**164** C4
Castle Av *CHING* E4 ....**52** B2
  EW KT17 ....**207** J5
  RAIN RM13 ....**111** H1
Castlebar Hl *EA* W5 ....**97** J4
Castlebar Ms *EA* W5 ....**97** J4
Castlebar Pk *EA* W5 ....**97** H4

Castlebar Rd *WEA* W13 ....**97** J5
Castle Baynard St *BLKFR* EC4V ..**12** C5
Castlebrook CI *LBTH* SE11 ......**18** A6
Castle CI *ACT* W3 ....**117** J2
  BUSH WD23 ....
  HAYES BR2 ....**183** H6
  WIM/MER SW19 ....**159** G5
Castlecombe Dr
  WIM/MER SW19 ....**159** G2
Castlecombe Rd
  ELTH/MOT SE9 ....**184** D1
Castle CI *BANK* EC3V * **13** F4
  SYD SE26 ....**164** B6
Castledine Rd *PGE/AN* SE20 ...**181** J3
Castleden Dr *REDBR* IG4 ....**71** J4
Castleford Av *ELTH/MOT* SE9 ...**167** G3
Castleford CI *TOTM* N17 ....**50** B2
Castlegate *RCH/KEW* TW9 .....**137** G4
Castlehaven Rd *CAMTN* NW1 ..**84** B5
Castle Hill Av *CROY/NA* CR0 ....**213** K6
Castle Hill Pde *WEA* W13 * **97** H6
Castle La *WESTW* SW1E **16** A4
Castleleigh Ct *ENC/FH* EN2 ....**23** K5
Castlemaine Av *EW* KT17 .....**207** K6
  SAND/SEL CR2 ....**212** B5
Castle Md *CMBW* SE5 * **142** D1
Castle Ms *CAMTN* NW1 * **84** B4
  NFNCH/WDSPK N12 ....**47** G1
  TOOT SW17 ....**160** D6
Castle Pde *EW* KT17 * **207** J5
Castle PI *CAMTN* NW1 ....**84** B4
Castlereagh St *MBLAR* W1H **8** C3
Castle Rd *CAMTN* NW1 ....**84** B4
  DAGW RM9 ....**91** H6
  ISLW TW7 ....**136** A3
  NFNCH/WDSPK N12 ....**47** G1
  NTHLT UB5 ....**78** B4
  NWDGN UB2 * **114** E3
  PEND EN3 ....**25** G2
Castle Rw *CHSWK* W4 * **118** A5
Castle St *EHAM* E6 ....**107** G1
  KUT/HW KT1 * **175** F5
Castleton Av *BXLYHN* DA7 .....**150** A2
Castleton CI *CROY/NA* CR0 ....**198** E3
Castleton Gdns *WBLY* HA9 .....**80** A1
Castleton Rd *ELTH/MOT* SE9 ...**166** C6
  GDMY/SEVK IG3 ....**73** H5
  MTCM CR4 ....**195** J1
  RSLP HA4 ....**59** J5
  WALTH E17 ....**52** B5
Castletown Rd *WKENS* W14 ....**119** H5
Castleview CI *FSBYPK* N4 ......**67** J6
Castleview Gdns *IL* IG1 ....**71** J3
Castle Vils *CRICK* NW2 * **81** K5
Castle Wk *SUN* TW16 * **172** B6
Castlewood Dr *ELTH/MOT* SE9 ..**146** E3
Castle Yd *HGT* N6 ....**66** A4
  RCH/KEW TW9 ....**136** E6
Castle Yd *STHWK* SE1 ....**12** B7
Castor La *POP/IOD* E14 ....**105** K6
Catalina Rd *HTHAIR* TW6 ......**132** E4
Catalpa Ct *LEW* SE13 ....**165** G1
Caterham Av *CLAY* IG5 ....**54** A5
Caterham Rd *LEW* SE13 ......**145** G4
Catesby St *WALW* SE17 * **19** F6
Catford Broadway *CAT* SE6 ...**164** E2
Catford Hl *CAT* SE6 ....**164** C3
Catford Island *CAT* SE6 * **164** E2
Catford Rd *CAT* SE6 ....**164** D3
Cathall Rd *WAN* E11 ....**88** B1
Cathay St *BERM/RHTH* SE16 ...**123** J2
Cathcart Dr *ORP* BR6 ....**201** K6
Cathcart Hl *ARCH* N19 ....**84** C1
Cathcart Rd *WBPTN* SW10 * ..**120** A6
Cathcart St *KTTN* NW5 ....**84** B4
Catherall Rd *HBRY* N5 ....**85** J1
Catherine CI *LOU* IG10 ....**39** K1
Catherine Ct *STHGT/OAK* N14 ..**22** C6
Catherine Dr *RCH/KEW* TW9 ...**137** F5
Catherine Gdns *HSLW* TW3 ....**135** J5
Catherine Griffiths Ct
  CLKNW EC1R **5** K6
Catherine Gv *GNWCH* SE10 ...**144** E2
Catherine PI *HRW* HA1 ....**61** F2
  WESTW SW1E **16** A4
Catherines CI *WDR/YW* UB7 *..**112** A2
Catherine St *HOL/ALD* WC2B *..**11** G5
Catherine St *VX/RYNPK* SW20 *.**176** E3
Catherine Wheel Aly
  LVPST EC2M **13** H2
Catherine Wheel Rd
  BTFD TW8 ....**136** E1
Catherine Wheel Yd
  WHALL SW1A **16** A1
Cathles Rd *BAL* SW12 ....**161** G1
Cathnor Rd *SHB* W12 ....**118** E2
Catling CI *FSTH* SE23 ....**163** K5
Catlin's La *PIN* HA5 ....**41** F6
Catlin St *BERM/RHTH* SE16 ....**123** J5
  HNHL SE24 ....**162** C3
Cator La *BECK* BR3 ....**182** C5
Cato Rd *CLAP* SW4 ....**141** J4
Cator Rd *CAR* SM5 ....**209** K5
  SYD SE26 ....**182** A2
Cator St *PECK* SE15 ....**123** G6
Cato St *MBLAR* W1H **8** C2
Catsey La *BUSH* WD23 ....**28** C2
Catsey Wd *BUSH* WD23 ......**28** C2
Catterick CI *FBAR/BDGN* N11 ...**48** A2
Cattistock Rd *ELTH/MOT* SE9 ..**184** D1
Cattley CI *BAR* EN5 ....**20** C5
Catton St *RSQ* WC1R **11** G2
Caudwell Ter
  WAND/EARL SW18 * **160** C1
Caulfield Rd *EHAM* E6 ....**89** K5
  PECK SE15 ....**143** J3
Causeway *EBED/NFELT* TW14 ..**134** A5
The Causeway *BELMT* SM2 ....**209** G6

Causewayside
  CAR SM5 ....**210** A1
  CHSGTN KT9 ....**206** A2
  EFNCH N2 ....**65** H1
  ESH/CLAY KT10 ....**205** F5
  TEDD TW11 ....**174** A2
  WAND/EARL SW18 ....**140** A6
  WIM/MER SW19 ....**177** F1
Causeyware Rd *ED* N9 ....**36** C2
Cautley Av *CLAP* SW4 ....**141** H6
Cavalier CI *CHDH* RM6 ....**73** J1
Cavalier Gdns *HYS/HAR* UB3 ...**94** B5
Cavalry Crs *HSLW* TW4 ....**134** C5
Cavalry Gdns *PUT/ROE* SW15 ..**139** J6
Cavan PI *PIN* HA5 * **41** K4
Cavaye PI *WBPTN* SW10 ......**120** B5
Cavell Crs *DART* DA1 ....**151** K5
Cavell Dr *ENC/FH* EN2 ....**23** G3
Cavell Rd *TOTM* N17 ....**49** K3
Cavell St *WCHPL* E1 ....**104** D4
Cavendish Av *BFN/LL* DA15 ....**168** B2
  ERITH DA8 ....**129** K6
  FNCH N3 ....**46** E6
  HCH RM12 ....**93** H4
  HRW HA1 ....**78** D2
  NWMAL KT3 ....**192** E2
  RSLP HA4 ....**77** F5
  STJWD NW8 ....**2** A3
  WEA W13 ....**97** G4
  WELL DA16 ....**148** B4
  WFD IG8 ....**53** F5
Cavendish CI *KIL/WHAMP* NW6 ..**82** D4
  STJWD NW8 ....**2** B3
  UED N18 ....**50** D1
  YEAD UB4 ....**94** C4
Cavendish Crs *HCH* RM12 .....**93** K4
  ESH/CLAY KT10 ....**204** E3
  WAN E11 ....**70** E1
Cavendish Gdns *BARK* IG11 ....**91** F3
  CHDH RM6 ....**73** K4
  CLAP SW4 * **161** H1
  IL IG1 ....**71** K2
Cavendish Ms North *GTPST* W1W.**9** K1
Cavendish Ms South
  GTPST W1W **9** K2
Cavendish Pde *CLAP* SW4 * ...**141** H6
  HSLW TW4 ....**134** D3
Cavendish PI *BMLY* BR1 ....**184** E6
  CAVSQ/HST W1G **9** K3
  KIL/WHAMP NW6 ....**82** D5
Cavendish Rd *BAR* EN5 ....**209** G5
  CHDH RM6 ....**73** K4
  CHSWK W4 ....**137** K2
  CLAP SW4 ....**141** H6
  CROY/NA CR0 ....**196** C5
  FSBYPK N4 ....**67** H3
  KIL/WHAMP NW6 ....**82** C5
  NWMAL KT3 ....**192** C2
  UED N18 ....**50** D1
  WIM/MER SW19 ....**178** D3
Cavendish Sq *CAVSQ/HST* W1G..**9** K3
Cavendish St *IS* N1 ....**6** E3
Cavendish Ter *BOW* E3 * **105** H2
  FELT TW15 * **154** A4
Cavenham Gdns *IL* IG1 ....**90** D1
Caverleigh Wy *WPK* KT4 ....**192** D5
Caverley Gdns
  KTN/HRWW/WS HA3 ....**61** K4
Cave Rd *PLSTW* E13 ....**107** F1
  RCHPK/HAM TW10 ....**156** D6
Caversham Av *CHEAM* SM3 ...**193** H6
  PLMGR N13 ....**35** F5
Caversham Flats *CHEL* SW3 *..**120** E6
  HOM E9 * **87** F5
  TEDD TW11 * **174** A2
Caversham Rd *KTTN* NW5 .....**84** C4
  KUT/HW KT1 ....**175** G5
  SEVS/STOTM N15 ....**67** J1
Caversham St *CHEL* SW3 .....**120** E6
Caverswall St *SHB* W12 ....**100** A5
Cawdor Crs *HNWL* W7 ....**116** B4
Cawnpore St *NRWD* SE19 ....**181** F1
Caxton Gv *BOW* E3 ....**105** J2
Caxton Ms *BTFD* TW8 * **116** D6
Caxton Rd *NWDGN* UB2 ......**114** C3
  SHB W12 ....**119** G1
  WIM/MER SW19 ....**178** B1
The Caxtons *BRXN/ST* SW9 *..**142** C1
Caxton St *STJSPK* SW1H **16** C4
Caxton St North *CAN/RD* E16 ..**106** D5
Caxton Wy *ROM* RM1 ....**75** J2
  WATW WD18 ....**26** B2
Cayenne St *STHWK* SE1 ......**19** H2
Caygill CI *HAYES* BR2 ....**199** J1
Cayley Rd *NWDGN* UB2 ......**115** G3
Cayton Rd *GFD/PVL* UB6 .....**96** E1
Cayton St *FSBYE* EC1V **6** E5
Cazenove Rd *STNW/STAM* N16 ..**68** B6
  WALTH E17 ....**51** J5
Cecil Av *BARK* IG11 ....**90** D5
  EN EN1 ....**24** B5
  WBLY HA9 ....**80** B3
Cecil CI *CHSGTN* KT9 ....**205** K2
  EA W5 * **97** K4
  CHCR WC2N **10** E6
Cecil Ct *CEND/HSY/T* N6 ....**66** B4
Cecilia CI *EFNCH* N2 ....**47** G6
Cecilia Rd *HACK* E8 ....**86** B3
Cecil Pk *PIN* HA5 ....**59** K1
Cecil PI *MTCM* CR4 ....**194** E2
Cecil Rd *ACT* W3 ....**98** E4
  CDALE/KGS NW9 ....**45** F6
  CHDH RM6 ....**73** K4
  CROY/NA CR0 ....**195** K3
  ENC/FH EN2 ....**23** H5
  HSLW TW3 ....**135** H3
  HYS/HAR UB3 ....**113** J2
  IL IG1 ....**90** B1
  MUSWH N10 ....**48** B5
  WAN E11 ....**70** D1
  WELL DA16 ....**148** B3
  WLGTN SM6 ....**210** B3
Central Buildings *EA* W5 * **97** K6

Central Circ HDN NW4 * 63 K2
Central Ct CHIC IG7 ....54 E1
Central Hall Buildings
  ARCH N19 * 66 C6
Central HI NRWD SE19 ....117 H2
Central Pde ACT W3 * 117 K1
  BFN/LL DA15 * 168 B5
  E/WMO/HCT KT8 * 188 E1
  GFD/PVL UB6 * 97 G2
  HRW HA1 * 60 E2
  PEND EN3 * 24 E3
  PGE/AN SE20 * 182 A3
  STRHM/NOR SW16 * 161 K6
  SURB KT6 * 191 F3
  WALTH E17 * 69 J1
Central Park Av DAGE RM10 ....92 E2
Central Park Est
  HSLWW TW4 * 134 C5
Central Park Rd EHAM E6 ......107 J1
Central PI SNWD SE25 * 197 H1
Central Rd ALP/SUD HA0 ....79 H5
  DART DA1 ....151 H6
  MRDN SM4 ....194 A2
  WPK KT4 ....192 D6
Central Sq E/WMO/HCT KT8 ....188 E1
  GLDGN NW11 * 64 E3
Central St FSBYE EC1V 6 C5
Central Ter BECK BR3 * 182 A6
Central Wy CAR SM5 ....209 J5
  EBED/NFELT TW14 ....134 A6
  NTHWD HA6 ....40 A1
  THMD SE28 ....109 H6
  WLSDN NW10 ....98 E2
Centre Av ACT W3 ....118 C1
Centre Common Rd CHST BR7 ..185 H1
Centre Rd DAGE RM10 ....110 D1
  WAN E11 ....70 E3
Centre St BETH E2 ....104 D1
The Centre FELT TW13 ....153 K4
Centre Wy ED N9 * 36 B6
Centric CI CAMTN NW1 * 84 B6
Centurian Wy ERITHM DA18 ...129 C5
Centurion La ALP/SUD HA0 ....79 H5
Centurion Rd HOLWY N7 ....85 F5
Centurion Sq CHARL SE7 * 146 D6
Centurion Wy PUR RM19 ....131 J4
Century CI HDN NW4 ....64 B2
Century Ct WATW WD18 * 26 A3
Century Ms CLPT E5 * 86 E2
Century Rd WALTH E17 ....51 G6
Cephas Av WCHPL E1 ....104 E3
Cephas St WCHPL E1 ....104 E3
Ceres Rd WOOL/PLUM SE18 ...128 A4
Cerise Rd PECK SE15 ....143 H2
Cerne CI NDYD UB4 ....94 B4
Cerne Rd MRDN SM4 ....194 B3
Cervantes Ct BAY/PAD W2 * ..101 F5
  NTHWD HA6 ....40 D3
Ceylon Rd WKENS W14 ....119 H3
Chabot Dr PECK SE15 ....143 J4
Chadacre Av CLAY IG5 ....53 K6
Chadacre Rd EW KT17 ....207 K3
Chadbourn St POP/IOD E14 ...105 K1
Chad Crs ED N9 ....36 E5
Chadd Dr BMLY BR1 ....184 D6
Chadville Gdns CHDH RM6 ....73 K2
Chadway BCTR RM8 ....73 J6
Chadwell Av CHDH RM6 ....73 H1
Chadwell Heath La CHDH RM6 .73 H1
Chadwell St CLKNW EC1R 5 K4
Chadwick Av CHING E4 ....38 B6
  WCHMH N21 * 23 F6
  WIM/MER SW19 * 178 A2
Chadwick CI IL IG1 ....90 B1
  PECK SE15 ....143 G3
  WAN E11 ....70 C4
  WLSDN NW10 ....81 H6
Chadwick St WEST SW1P 16 C5
Chadwick Wy THMD SE28 ......109 K6
Chadwin Rd PLSTW E13 ....107 F4
Chadworth Wy
  ESH/CLAY KT10 ....204 D5
Chaffinch Av CROY/NA CR0 ...198 A3
Chaffinch CI CROY/NA CR0 ...198 A2
  ED N9 ....37 F5
  SURB KT6 ....206 C1
Chaffinch Ct ORP BR6 ....202 B4
Chaffinch Rd BECK BR3 ....182 A4
Chafford Wy CHDH RM6 ....73 J1
Chagford St CAMTN NW1 * 2 E7
Chailey Av EN EN1 ....24 B3
Chailey CI HEST TW5 ....134 C2
Chalbury Wk IS N1 * 5 H2
Chalcombe Rd ABYW SE2 .....128 C3
Chalcot CI BELMT SM2 ....208 E5
Chalcot Crs CAMTN NW1 ....83 K6
Chalcot Gdns HAMP NW3 ......83 K4
Chalcot Ms STRHM/NOR SW16 .161 K5
Chalcot Rd CAMTN NW1 ....83 K6
Chalcot Sq CAMTN NW1 ....84 A5
Chalcott Gdns SURB KT6 * 190 D5
Chalcroft Rd LEW SE13 ....145 H6
Chaldon Rd FUL/PGN SW6 ....139 H1
Chale Rd BRXS/STRHM SW2 ...161 K3
Chalet CI BXLY DA5 ....170 A6
Chalet Est MLHL NW7 * 31 H4
Chalfont Av WBLY HA9 ....80 D4
Chalfont Gn ED N9 ....36 A5
Chalfont Ms
  WAND/EARL SW18 ....159 J3
Chalfont Rd ED N9 ....36 A5
  HYS/HAR UB3 ....113 K2
  SNWD SE25 ....181 G6
Chalfont Wk PIN HA5 * 41 G5
Chalfont Wy WEA W13 ....116 C3
Chalford CI E/WMO/HCT KT8 ..189 F1
Chalforde Gdns GPK RM2 .....75 K1
Chalford Rd DUL SE21 ....162 E6
Chalford Wk WFD IG8 ....53 H4
Chalgrove Av MRDN SM4 ......193 K2
Chalgrove Crs CLAY IG5 ......53 J5

Chalgrove Gdns FNCH N3 .....46 C6
Chalgrove Rd BELMT SM2 .....209 H5
  HACK E8 ....86 E4
  TOTM N17 ....50 D4
Chalice CI WLGTN SM6 ....210 D4
Chalkenden CI PGE/AN SE20 ..181 J3
Chalk Farm Pde HAMP NW3 * .84 A5
Chalk Farm Rd CAMTN NW1 ...84 A5
Chalk Hill Rd HMSMTH W6 ...119 G4
Chalkhill Rd WBLY HA9 ....80 C1
Chalklands WBLY HA9 ....80 E1
Chalk La EBAR EN4 ....21 K4
Chalkley CI MTCM CR4 ....178 E5
Chalkmill Dr EN EN1 ....24 D4
Chalk Pit Av STMC/STPC BR5 .186 E6
Chalk Pit Wy SUT SM1 ....209 G3
Chalk Rd PLSTW E13 ....107 F4
Chalkstone CI WELL DA16 ....148 B2
Chalkwell Park Av EN EN1 ....24 A5
Chalky La CHSGTN KT9 ....205 K6
Challenge CI WLSDN NW10 ....81 G6
Challenge Rd ASHF TW15 .....153 F5
Challice Wy BRXS/STRHM SW2 .162 A3
Challis Rd BTFD TW8 ....116 E5
Challoner CI EFNCH N2 ....47 H5
Challoner Crs WKENS W14 ....119 J5
Challoners CI E/WMO/HCT KT8 .189 F1
Challoner St WKENS W14 .....119 J5
Chalmers Rd ASHF TW15 .....152 E6
Chalmers Rd East ASHF TW15 .152 E6
Chalmers Wk WALW SE17 * ...122 C6
Chalmers Wy
  EBED/NFELT TW14 ....134 A6
  TWK TW1 ....136 C5
Chalsey Rd BROCKY SE4 ......144 C5
Chalton St CAMTN NW1 ....4 C1
Chamberlain CI IL IG1 ....90 C1
Chamberlain Cottages
  CMBW SE5 * 142 E2
Chamberlain Crs WWKM BR4 ..198 E5
Chamberlain Gdns HSLW TW3 .135 H2
Chamberlain La PIN HA5 ......58 E1
Chamberlain Rd FNCH N3 * 47 G1
  WEA W13 ....116 B2
Chamberlain St CAMTN NW1 * .83 K5
Chamberlayne Rd PIN HA5 ....41 F6
  SURB KT6 ....191 F4
Chamberlayne Rd
  WLSDN NW10 ....82 A6
Chamblens Garages
  HMSMTH W6 * 118 C4
Chambers Gdns EFNCH N2 ...47 H1
Chambers La WLSDN NW10 ...81 K5
Chambers PI SAND/SEL CR2 ..211 K5
Chambers Rd HOLWY N7 ....84 E2
Chambers St
  BERM/RHTH SE16 ....123 H2
Chamber St WCHPL E1 ....13 K5
Chambord St BETH E2 ....7 K5
Champa CI TOTM N17 ....50 B5
Champion Crs SYD SE26 ......164 B6
Champion Gv CMBW SE5 .....142 E4
Champion Hill CMBW SE5 .....142 E4
Champion Pk CMBW SE5 ......142 E3
Champion Rd SYD SE26 ....164 B6
Champness CI WWKD SE27 ...162 E6
Champness Rd BARK IG11 ....91 F5
Champneys CI BELMT SM2 ...208 D5
Champneys OXHEY WD19 * ...27 J4
Chancellor Gdns
  SAND/SEL CR2 ....211 H6
Chancellor PI CDALE/KGS NW9 .45 H5
Chancellor PI HMSMTH W6 ...119 F5
Chancellors Rd HMSMTH W6 ..119 F5
Chancellors Whf HMSMTH W6 .119 F6
Chancelot Rd ABYW SE2 ......128 C4
Chancel St STHWK SE1 ....12 A7
Chancery La BECK BR3 ....182 E5
  LINN WC2A 11 H2
Chancery Ms TOOT SW17 .....160 D4
Chance St BETH E2 ....7 J6
Chanctonbury CI
  ELTH/MOT SE9 ....167 G5
Chanctonbury Gdns
  BELMT SM2 ....209 F5
Chanctonbury Wy
  NFNCH/WDSPK N12 ....32 E6
Chandler Av CAN/RD E16 .....106 E4
Chandler CI HPTN TW12 ......172 E4
Chandlers CI
  EBED/NFELT TW14 ....153 J3
Chandlers Ct LEE/GVPK SE12 * .166 A4
Chandlers Dr ERITH DA8 .....130 A4
Chandlers Ms POP/IOD E14 ..124 D2
Chandler St WAP E1W 123 J1
Chandler Wy ROM RM1 ....75 G2
Chandler Wy PECK SE15 ......143 G1
Chandos Av EA W5 ....116 D4
  STHGT/OAK N14 ....34 C5
  TRDG/WHET N20 ....33 H3
  WALTH E17 ....51 J5
Chandos CI BKHH IG9 ....39 G4
Chandos Crs EDGW HA8 ....44 C3
Chandos PI CHCR WC2N 10 E6
Chandos Rd CRICK NW2 ....82 A3
  EFNCH N2 ....47 G5
  HRW HA1 ....60 C2
  PIN HA5 ....59 G4
  SRTFD E15 ....88 B3
  TOTM N17 ....50 B5
  WLSDN NW10 ....99 G2
Chandos St CAVSQ/HST W1G ..9 K3
Chandos Wy GLDGN NW11 .....65 F5
Channel CI HEST TW5 ....135 F1
Channel Gate Rd NKENS W10 .100 C6
  WLSDN NW10 ....99 K1
Channel Islands Est IS N1 ....85 J4
Channelsea Rd SRTFD E15 ...88 B4

Chantress CI DAGE RM10 .....92 E6
Chantrey CI SCUP DA14 ......187 F1
Chantrey Rd BRXN/ST SW9 ..142 A4
Chantry CI ABYW SE2 ....128 D3
  BAR EN5 ....31 H1
  ENC/FH EN2 ....23 J2
  KTN/HRWW/WS HA3 ....42 D4
  MV/WKIL W9 ....100 D3
Chantry Crs WLSDN NW10 ....81 G5
Chantry PI KTN/HRWW/WS HA3 .42 B4
Chantry Rd CHSGTN KT9 .....206 B3
  KTN/HRWW/WS HA3 ....42 B4
Chantry Sq KENS W8 * 120 A3
Chantry St IS N1 ....6 B1
The Chantry CHING E4 ....38 A5
Chantry Wy MTCM CR4 ....178 C6
Chant Sq SRTFD E15 * 88 B5
Chant St SRTFD E15 ....88 B5
Chapel CI DART DA1 ....150 B6
  WLSDN NW10 ....81 H3
Chapel Ct EFNCH N2 * 47 J6
  STHWK SE1 ....18 E2
  WOOL/PLUM SE18 ....128 A6
Chapel Farm Rd
  ELTH/MOT SE9 ....166 C5
Chapel House St POP/IOD E14 .124 E5
Chapel La PIN HA5 ....41 H6
Chapel Market IS N1 ....5 K2
Chapel Mill Rd KUT/HW KT1 ..175 G6
Chapel Pth CAVSQ/HST W1G ...9 J4
  IS N1 ....5 K2
  TOTM N17 ....50 B3
Chapel Rd BXLYHN DA7 ....149 H5
  HNWL W7 ....115 H3
  IL IG1 ....90 B1
  TWK TW1 ....156 C2
  WEA W13 ....116 C1
  WNWD SE27 ....162 C6
Chapel Side BAY/PAD W2 .....101 F6
Chapel St BAY/PAD W2 ....8 C2
  ENC/FH EN2 ....23 J4
  KTBR SW1X 15 H4
Chapel Vw SAND/SEL CR2 ...212 A6
Chaplemount Rd WFD IG8 * ...53 K2
Chaplin CI ALP/SUD HA0 * ...79 K4
  STHWK SE1 ....17 K2
Chaplin Ms ELTH SE11 ....122 B5
Chaplin Rd ALP/SUD HA0 .....79 J4
  CRICK NW2 ....81 J4
  SRTFD E15 ....106 C1
  TOTM N17 ....50 A5
Chapman CI WDR/YW UB7 ....112 C3
Chapman Crs
  KTN/HRWW/WS HA3 ....62 A3
Chapman Rd BELV DA17 ......129 H5
  CROY/NA CR0 ....196 B5
  HOM E9 ....87 H4
Chapmans Gn WDGN N22 * ...49 G4
Chapman's La STMC/STPC BR5 .186 E5
  SWLY DA8 ....187 H5
Chapman Sq WIM/MER SW19 ..159 G4
Chapman St WCHPL E1 ....104 D6
Chapman Ter WDGN N22 * 49 H4
Chapter CI CRICK NW2 ....81 K3
  WALW SE17 ....122 C5
Chapter St WEST SW1P 16 C7
Chapter Wy HPTN TW12 ......155 F6
Chara PI CHSWK W4 ....118 A6
Charcroft Gdns PEND EN3 ...25 F5
Chardin Rd CHSWK W4 * 118 B4
Chardmore Rd
  STNW/STAM N16 ....68 C5
Charecroft Wy WKENS W14 ..119 G2
Chareford Rd CAN/RD E16 ...106 A6
Chargeable La PLSTW E13 ...106 E3
Chargeable St CAN/RD E16 ..106 D3
Chargrove CI
  BERM/RHTH SE16 ....124 A2
Charing Cross CHCR WC2N * .10 E7
Charing Cross Rd
  LSQ/SEVD WC2H 10 D5
Chariot CI BOW E3 ....87 J6
Charlbert St STJWD NW8 ......2 C2
Charlbury Av STAN HA7 ....43 K1
Charlbury Gdns
  GDMY/SEVK IG3 ....73 F6
Charlbury Gv EA W5 ....97 J5
Charlecote Gv SYD SE26 .....163 J5
Charlecote Rd BCTR RM8 ....92 A1
Charlemont Rd EHAM E6 .....107 K2
Charles Babbage CI
  CHSGTN KT9 ....205 J5
Charles Barry CI CLAP SW4 ..141 H4
Charles Cobb Gdns
  CROY/NA CR0 ....211 G3
Charles Coveney Rd
  PECK SE15 ....143 G2
Charles Dickens Ter
  PGE/AN SE20 * 181 K3
Charlesfield ELTH/MOT SE9 ..166 B5
Charles Flemwell Ms
  CAN/RD E16 * 125 K1
Charles Grinling Wk
  WOOL/PLUM SE18 ....127 F4
Charles Haller St
  BRXS/STRHM SW2 ....162 B2
Charles La STJWD NW8 ....2 C1
Charles PI CAMTN NW1 * 4 B5
Charles Rd CHDH RM6 ....73 K4
  DAGE RM10 ....93 K4
  FSTGT E7 ....89 G5
  SRTFD E15 * 106 D2
  WIM/MER SW19 ....177 K4
Charles II PI CHEL SW3 * 120 E5
Charles II St STJS SW1Y 10 C7
Charles Sevright Dr MLHL NW7 .46 B1
Charles Sq IS N1 ....7 F5
Charles Square Est IS N1 .....7 F5
Charles St BARN SW13 ....138 B4

CAN/RD E16 ....126 B1
CROY/NA CR0 ....211 J1
EN EN1 ....24 B6
WLSDN NW10 ....81 H3
MYFR/PICC W1J 9 K7
Charleston CI FELT TW13 .....153 K5
Charleston St WALW SE17 ....18 D7
Charles Whincup Rd
  CAN/RD E16 ....126 A1
Charleville Circ SYD SE26 ...181 H1
Charleville Rd WKENS W14 ..119 J5
Charleville Rd ERITH DA8 ...150 A1
Charlmont Rd TOOT SW17 ....178 D2
Charlotte CI BXLYHN DA6 ....149 F6
  ESH/CLAY KT10 ....204 C5
Charlotte Despard Av
  BTSEA SW11 ....141 G2
Charlotte Ms ESH/CLAY KT10 * .204 B2
  FITZ W1T 10 B1
  NKENS W10 ....100 B5
Charlotte Pde FSTH SE23 * ...164 B4
Charlotte Park Av BMLY BR1 .184 D6
Charlotte PI FITZ W1T 10 B2
  PIM SW1V 16 A7
Charlotte Rd BARN SW13 ....138 C2
  SDTCH EC2A 7 G6
  WLGTN SM6 ....210 C4
Charlotte Rw CLAP SW4 .....141 H4
Charlotte St FITZ W1T 10 B1
Charlotte Ter IS N1 * 5 H1
Charlow CI FUL/PGN SW6 ....140 B3
Charlton Church La
  CHARL SE7 ....126 B5
Charlton Crs BARK IG11 .....109 F1
Charlton Dene CHARL SE7 ...146 B1
Charlton King's Rd KTTN NW5 .84 D3
Charlton La CHARL SE7 ......126 B5
Charlton Park La CHARL SE7 .126 C6
Charlton Park Rd CHARL SE7 .126 C6
Charlton PI IS N1 ....6 A2
Charlton Rd BKHTH/KID SE3 .145 K1
  ED N9 ....37 F3
  KTN/HRWW/WS HA3 ....61 K1
  WBLY HA9 ....62 B5
  WLSDN NW10 ....81 G6
Charlton Wy BKHTH/KID SE3 .145 H1
Charlwood CROY/NA CR0 .....213 H6
Charlwood PI PIM SW1V 16 B7
Charlwood Rd PUT/ROE SW15 .139 G5
Charlwood St PIM SW1V 16 B7
Charlwood Ter PUT/ROE SW15 .139 G5
Charmian Av STAN HA7 ....43 K5
Charminster Av
  WIM/MER SW19 ....177 K5
Charminster Rd
  ELTH/MOT SE9 ....166 C6
  WPK KT4 ....193 G5
Charmouth Rd WELL DA16 ...148 D2
Charnock Rd CLPT E5 ....86 D1
Charnwood Av
  WIM/MER SW19 ....177 K5
Charnwood CI NWMAL KT3 ...192 B1
Charnwood Dr SWFD E18 .....53 F6
Charnwood Gdns
  POP/IOD E14 ....124 D4
Charnwood PI TRDG/WHET N20 .33 G5
Charnwood Rd SNWD SE25 ...196 E2
Charnwood St CLPT E5 * 68 C6
Charnwood Vls SWFD E18 ....53 F6
Charrington Rd CROY/NA CR0 .196 C6
Charrington St CAMTN NW1 ...4 C2
Charsley Rd CAT SE6 ....164 E4
Chart CI CROY/NA CR0 ....197 K3
  HAYES BR2 ....183 H4
  MTCM CR4 ....194 E1
Charter Av GNTH/NBYPK IG2 .72 D5
Charter Crs HSLWW TW4 .....134 D5
Charterhouse Av ALP/SUD HA0 .79 J4
Charterhouse Buildings
  FARR EC1M * 6 C7
Charterhouse Ms FARR EC1M .12 D1
Charterhouse Rd HACK E8 ...86 C3
  ORP BR6 ....217 G1
Charterhouse Sq FARR EC1M .12 C1
Charterhouse St
  HCIRC EC1N 11 K2
The Charterhouse FARR EC1M * .6 C7
Charteris Rd FSBYPK N4 ......67 F5
  KIL/WHAMP NW6 ....82 D6
  WFD IG8 ....53 F2
Charter Rd KUT/HW KT1 .....175 J5
The Charter Rd WFD IG8 ......52 C2
Charters CI NRWD SE19 .....181 F1
Charter Sq KUT/HW KT1 ......175 J5
Charter Wy FNCH N3 ....64 D1
  STHGT/OAK N14 ....34 B5
Chartfield Av PUT/ROE SW15 .138 E6
Chartfield Sq PUT/ROE SW15 * .139 G6
Chartham Gv WNWD SE27 ....162 B5
Chartham Rd SNWD SE25 ....181 J6
Chart Hills CI THMD SE28 ...110 A6
Chartley Av CRICK NW2 ....81 G1
  STAN HA7 ....43 F2
Chartley Pde CRICK NW2 * ...81 G1
Chartridge OXHEY WD19 * ...27 G6
Chartridge CI BUSH WD23 ...28 C1
Chart St IS N1 ....7 F4
Chartwell CI CROY/NA CR0 ..196 E5
  ELTH/MOT SE9 ....167 J4
  GFD/PVL UB6 ....96 C1
Chartwell Dr ORP BR6 ....216 D3
Chartwell Gdns CHEAM SM3 .208 C1
Chartwell PI CHEAM SM3 ....208 C2
  RYLN/HDSTN HA2 ....60 D6
Charville La HGDN/ICK UB10 .94 A2
Charwood STRHM/NOR SW16 .162 B6
Chase CI RYNPK SW20 ....177 H5
Chase Court Gdns ENC/FH EN2 .23 J4
Chase Cross Rd CRW RM5 ...56 E3
Chasefield Rd TOOT SW17 ...160 E6

Chase Gdns CHING E4 ....37 J6
  WHTN TW2 ....155 J1
Chase Gn ENC/FH EN2 ....23 J4
Chase Green Av ENC/FH EN2 .23 H3
Chase La BARK/HLT IG6 ....72 D2
Chaseley Ct CHSWK W4 ....117 J5
Chaseley St POP/IOD E14 * ...105 G5
Chasemore Ct MTCM CR4 ....194 E4
Chasemore Gdns
  CROY/NA CR0 ....211 G3
Chase Ridings ENC/FH EN2 ..23 G3
Chase Rd ACT W3 ....99 F5
  STHGT/OAK N14 ....34 D5
Chase Side ENC/FH EN2 ......23 J3
  STHGT/OAK N14 ....34 B2
Chase Side Av ENC/FH EN2 ..23 J3
  RYNPK SW20 ....177 H5
Chase Side Crs ENC/FH EN2 .23 J2
The Chase BMLY BR1 ....184 A6
  BXLYHN DA7 ....149 K4
  CLAP SW4 ....141 G4
  EDGW HA8 ....44 D4
  FSTGT E7 ....89 H2
  LOU IG10 ....39 H2
  PIN HA5 ....59 K1
  PIN HA5 ....59 K1
  ROM RM1 ....57 G6
  ROMW/RG RM7 ....93 F1
  STAN HA7 ....43 G2
  STRHM/NOR SW16 ....180 A3
  SUN TW16 ....172 A4
  WLGTN SM6 ....210 E3
Chaseville Pde WCHMH N21 * .23 F5
Chaseville Park Rd
  WCHMH N21 ....22 E6
Chase Wy STHGT/OAK N14 ...34 B3
Chasewood Av ENC/FH EN2 ..23 H3
Chasewood Pk HRW HA1 * ...78 E1
Chastilian Rd DART DA1 .....170 D2
Chatfield Rd BTSEA SW11 ...140 B4
  CROY/NA CR0 ....196 C5
Chatham Av HAYES BR2 ......199 K4
Chatham CI CHEAM SM3 ......193 J4
  GLDGN NW11 ....64 E2
Chatham PI HOM E9 ....86 E4
Chatham Rd BTSEA SW11 ....160 E1
  KUT/HW KT1 ....175 H5
  SWFD E18 ....52 D5
  WALTH E17 ....51 G6
Chatsworth Av BFN/LL DA15 .168 A5
  BMLY BR1 ....184 A1
  HDN NW4 ....46 A5
  RYNPK SW20 ....177 H4
  WBLY HA9 ....80 B3
Chatsworth CI CHSWK W4 * ..117 K6
  HDN NW4 ....46 A5
  WWKM BR4 ....199 J6
Chatsworth Crs HSLW TW3 ..135 J5
Chatsworth Est CLPT E5 * 87 F2
Chatsworth Gdns ACT W3 ....98 D6
  NWMAL KT3 ....192 C2
  RYLN/HDSTN HA2 ....60 C6
Chatsworth PI MTCM CR4 ....178 E6
  TEDD TW11 ....156 B6
Chatsworth Ri EA W5 ....98 B3
Chatsworth Rd CHEAM SM3 ..208 B3
  CHSWK W4 ....117 K6
  CLPT E5 ....86 E1
  CRICK NW2 ....82 B4
  CROY/NA CR0 ....211 K2
  DART DA1 ....151 H6
  EA W5 ....98 B3
  SRTFD E15 ....88 D3
  YEAD UB4 ....95 G3
Chatsworth Wy WNWD SE27 ..162 D4
Chattern HI ASHF TW15 ......152 E6
Chattern Rd ASHF TW15 .....153 F6
Chatterton Ms FSBYPK N4 * ..85 H1
Chatterton Rd FSBYPK N4 ....85 H1
  HAYES BR2 ....200 B2
Chatto Rd BTSEA SW11 ......140 E6
Chaucer Av HSLWW TW4 .....134 A3
  RCH/KEW TW9 ....137 H4
  YEAD UB4 ....94 E5
Chaucer CI FBAR/BDGN N11 .48 C1
Chaucer Dr STHWK SE1 ....19 K7
Chaucer Gdns SUT SM1 ......208 E2
Chaucer Pk DART DA1 ....171 K3
Chaucer Rd ACT W3 ....117 K1
  ASHF TW15 ....152 B6
  BFN/LL DA15 ....168 D3
  FSTGT E7 ....89 H4
  HARH RM3 ....57 K3
  HNHL SE24 ....142 C6
  SUT SM1 ....208 E2
  WALTH E17 ....52 A2
  WAN E11 ....53 H6
  WELL DA16 ....148 A2
Chaucer Wy DART DA1 ....151 K5
  WIM/MER SW19 ....178 C2
Chauncey CI ED N9 ....36 C5
Chaundrye CI ELTH/MOT SE9 .166 E6
Chauntler CI CAN/RD E16 ....107 F6
Chave Rd RDART DA2 ....171 H5
Cheam Common Rd WPK KT4 .192 E6
Cheam Man CHEAM SM3 ......208 C4
Cheam Park Wy CHEAM SM3 .208 B4
Cheam Rd BELMT SM2 ....208 C5
  EW KT17 ....207 J5
  SUT SM1 ....208 B4
Cheam St PECK SE15 * 143 J4
Cheapside CITYW EC2V 12 D4
  EFNCH N2 * 47 K6
  PLMCR N13 ....49 G2
  WDGN N22 * 49 J4
Cheddar CI FBAR/BDGN N11 .47 K2
Cheddar Waye YEAD UB4 .....95 F5
Cheddington Rd UED N18 ....36 A6
Cheeseman CI HPTN TW12 ...172 D2
Cheesemans Ter
  WKENS W14 * 119 J5

Chelford Rd BMLY BR1 183 G1
Chelmer Crs BARK IG11 109 H1
Chelmer Rd HOM E9 87 F3
Chelmsford Av CRW RM5 57 F3
Chelmsford Cl BELMT SM2 208 E6
EHAM E6 107 K5
HMSMTH W6 119 G6
Chelmsford Gdns IL IG1 71 J4
Chelmsford Rd STHGT/OAK N14 34 C2
SWFD E18 52 D4
WALTH E17 69 J3
WAN E11 70 B5
Chelmsford Sq WLSDN NW10 82 A6
Chelsea Br VX/NE SW8 121 G6
Chelsea Bridge Ga VX/NE SW8 121 F6
Chelsea Bridge Rd
BGVA SW1W 121 F5
Chelsea Cl EDGW HA8 44 C5
HPTN TW12 173 H1
WLSDN NW10 81 F6
WPK KT4 192 D4
Chelsea Crs CRICK NW2 * 82 D4
WBPTN SW10 * 140 B2
Chelsea Emb CHEL SW3 120 E6
Chelsea Gdns BGVA SW1W * 121 F5
CHEAM SM3 208 C2
WEA W13 97 F4
Chelsea Harbour Dr
WBPTN SW10 140 B2
Chelsea Manor Gdns
CHEL SW3 * 120 D6
Chelsea Manor St CHEL SW3 120 D5
Chelsea Ms EMPK RM11 75 K5
Chelsea Park Gdns CHEL SW3 120 C6
Chelsea Sq CAR SM5 209 K6
CHEL SW3 120 C5
Chelsea Towers CHEL SW3 * 120 D6
Chelsea Village
FUL/PGN SW6 * 140 A1
Chelsfield Av ED N9 37 F2
Chelsfield Gdns SYD SE26 163 K5
Chelsfield Hl ORP BR6 217 J6
Chelsfield La ORP BR6 217 K2
STMC/STPC BR5 202 E4
Chelsfield Rd STMC/STPC BR5 202 D3
Chelsham Rd CLAP SW4 141 J4
SAND/SEL CR2 211 K5
Chelston Rd RSLP HA4 58 E6
Chelsworth Dr
WOOL/PLUM SE18 127 J6
Cheltenham Av TWK TW1 156 B2
Cheltenham Cl NTHLT UB5 78 B4
NWMAL KT3 175 K6
Cheltenham Gdns EHAM E6 107 J1
LOU IG10 39 J1
Cheltenham Pl ACT W3 117 K2
KTN/HRWW/WS HA3 62 A1
Cheltenham Rd LEY E10 70 A3
ORP BR6 217 G1
PECK SE15 143 K5
Cheltenham Ter CHEL SW3 120 E5
Chelton Av MLHL NW7 46 B3
Chelverton Rd PUT/ROE SW15 139 G5
Chelwood Cl CHING E4 37 K1
NTHWD HA6 40 A3
Chelwood Gdns
RCH/KEW TW9 137 H3
Chenappa Cl PLSTW E13 106 E2
Chenduit Wy STAN HA7 43 F1
Cheney Rw WALTH E17 51 H4
Cheneys Rd WAN E11 88 C1
Cheney St PIN HA5 59 G1
Chenies Ms GWRST WC1E 4 C7
Chenies Pl CAMTN NW1 4 D2
Chenies St GWRST WC1E 10 C1
The Chenies ORP BR6 201 K3
RDART DA2 170 B6
Chenies Wy WATW WD18 26 C2
Cheniston Gdns KENS W8 * 120 A3
Chepstow Cl PUT/ROE SW15 139 H6
Chepstow Cnr BAY/PAD W2 * 100 E5
Chepstow Crs GDMY/SEVK IG3 72 E3
NTGHL W11 100 E6
Chepstow Gdns STHL UB1 95 K5
Chepstow Pl BAY/PAD W2 100 E6
Chepstow Ri CROY/NA CR0 212 B1
Chepstow Rd BAY/PAD W2 100 E5
CROY/NA CR0 212 A1
HNWL W7 116 B3
Chepstow Vls NTGHL W11 100 D6
Chequers BKHH IG9 39 F3
Chequers Cl CDALE/KGS NW9 45 G6
STMC/STPC BR5 202 A1
Chequers La DAGW RM9 110 B3
Chequers Pde PLMGR N13 * 49 J1
The Chequers PIN HA5 * 41 H6
Chequer St STLK EC1Y 6 D7
Chequers Wy PLMGR N13 49 J1
Cherbury Cl THMD SE28 109 K5
Cherbury St IS N1 7 F3
Cherimoya Gdns
E/WMO/HCT KT8 173 G6
Cherington Rd HNWL W7 * 116 A1
Cheriton Av CLAY IG5 54 A5
HAYES BR2 199 K2
Cheriton Cl EA W5 97 J4
EBAR EN4 21 K4
Cheriton Ct WOT/HER KT12 188 B5
Cheriton Dr WOOL/PLUM SE18 147 J1
Cheriton Sq TOOT SW17 161 F4
Cherry Av STHL UB1 114 C1
Cherry Blossom Cl PLMGR N13 49 H1
Cherry Cl BRXS/STRHM SW2 * 162 B2
CAR SM5 194 E6
CDALE/KGS NW9 45 H5
EA W5 116 E3
MRDN SM4 193 H1
RSLP HA4 76 D1
Cherrycot Ri ORP BR6 216 C2
Cherry Ct PIN HA5 41 H5
Cherry Crs BTFD TW8 136 C1
Cherry Croft Gdns PIN HA5 * 41 K3
Cherrydown Av CHING E4 37 H5
Cherrydown Cl CHING E4 37 J5
Cherrydown Rd SCUP DA14 168 E4
Cherrydown Wk
ROMW/RG RM7 56 D5
Cherry Gdns DAGW RM9 92 B3
NTHLT UB5 78 B5
Cherry Garden St
BERM/RHTH SE16 123 J2
Cherry Garth BTFD TW8 116 E4
Cherry Gv HYS/HAR UB3 114 A1
UX/CGN UB8 94 A4
Cherry Hl BAR EN5 33 F1
KTN/HRWW/WS HA3 42 E3
Cherry Hill Gdns CROY/NA CR0 211 F2
Cherry Hills OXHEY WD19 41 J1
Cherrylands Cl
CDALE/KGS NW9 * 62 E6
Cherry La WDR/YW UB7 112 C4
Cherry Orch CHARL SE7 126 B6
WDR/YW UB7 112 B2
Cherry Orchard Cl
STMC/STPC BR5 202 D2
Cherry Orchard Gdns
CROY/NA CR0 196 E5
E/WMO/HCT KT8 172 E6
Cherry Orchard Rd
CROY/NA CR0 196 E5
E/WMO/HCT KT8 173 F6
HAYES BR2 200 D6
Cherry Rd PEND EN3 24 E1
Cherry St ROMW/RG RM7 75 F2
Cherry Tree Cl ALP/SUD HA0 79 G2
HOM E9 86 E6
RAIN RM13 111 J1
Cherry Tree Ct CHARL SE7 * 126 B6
Cherry Tree Dr
STRHM/NOR SW16 161 K5
Cherry Tree Hl EFNCH N2 65 J2
Cherry Tree La RAIN RM13 111 H2
RDART DA2 170 C5
Cherry Tree Ri BKHH IG9 39 G6
Cherry Tree Rd EFNCH N2 65 K1
SRTFD E15 88 C3
Cherry Tree Wk BECK BR3 198 C1
STLK EC1Y 6 D7
WWKM BR4 214 D2
Cherry Tree Wy STAN HA7 43 H2
Cherry Wk HAYES BR2 199 K5
RAIN RM13 111 H1
Cherry Wy HOR/WEW KT19 207 F4
Cherrywood Cl BOW E3 105 G2
KUTN/CMB KT2 175 H3
Cherrywood Dr
PUT/ROE SW15 139 G6
Cherrywood La RYNPK SW20 193 H1
Chertsey Dr CHEAM SM3 193 H6
Chertsey Rd FELT TW13 153 J5
IL IG1 90 D2
TWK TW1 156 B1
WAN E11 70 B6
WHTN TW2 155 H3
Chertsey St TOOT SW17 179 F1
Chervil Cl FELT TW13 153 K5
Chervil Ms THMD SE28 128 C1
Cherwell Ct HOR/WEW KT19 206 E2
Cherwell Wy RSLP HA4 58 A3
Cheryls Cl FUL/PGN SW6 140 A2
Cheseman St SYD SE26 163 J5
Chesfield Rd KUTN/CMB KT2 175 F3
Chesham Av STMC/STPC BR5 201 G3
Chesham Cl KTBR SW1X * 15 G5
ROMW/RG RM7 75 F1
Chesham Crs PGE/AN SE20 181 K4
Chesham Ms KTBR SW1X 15 G4
Chesham Pl KTBR SW1X 15 G5
Chesham Rd KUT/HW KT1 175 H5
PGE/AN SE20 181 K5
WIM/MER SW19 178 C2
Chesham St KTBR SW1X 15 G5
WLSDN NW10 81 F1
Chesham Ter WEA W13 116 C2
Chesham Wy WATW WD18 26 C1
Cheshire Cl MTCM CR4 179 K6
WALTH E17 51 K4
Cheshire Gdns CHSGTN KT9 205 K4
Cheshire Rd WDGN N22 49 F3
Cheshire St BETH E2 104 C3
Chesholm Rd STNW/STAM N16 86 A1
Cheshunt Rd BELV DA17 129 H5
FSTGT E7 89 F4
Chesilton Rd FUL/PGN SW6 139 J2
Chesil Wy YEAD UB4 94 D2
Chesley Gdns EHAM E6 107 J2
Chesney Crs CROY/NA CR0 214 A5
Chesney St BTSEA SW11 141 F2
Chesnut Av North WALTH E17 70 B1
Chesnut Gv TOTM N17 50 C6
Chesnut Rd TOTM N17 50 C6
Chesnut Rw FNCH N3 * 46 E3
Chessell Cl THHTH CR7 196 C1
Chessington Av BXLYHN DA7 149 F1
FNCH N3 46 D6
Chessington Cl
HOR/WEW KT19 206 E4
Chessington Ct PIN HA5 59 K1
Chessington Hall Gdns
CHSGTN KT9 205 K5
Chessington Hill Pk
CHSGTN KT9 206 C4
Chessington Pde
CHSGTN KT9 * 205 K3
Chessington Rd CHSGTN KT9 206 C4
Chessington Wy WWKM BR4 198 E6
Chesson Rd WKENS W14 119 J6
Chesswood Wy PIN HA5 41 H5
Chester Av RCHPK/HAM TW10 157 G1
WHTN TW2 154 E3
Chester Cl BARN SW13 * 138 E4
KTBR SW1X 15 H3
SUT SM1 193 K6
Chester Cl North CAMTN NW1 3 K4
Chester Cl South CAMTN NW1 3 K5
Chester Crs HACK E8 86 B3
Chester Dr RYLN/HDSTN HA2 60 A3
Chesterfield Cl
STMC/STPC BR5 202 E1
Chesterfield Dr DART DA1 150 E6
ESH/CLAY KT10 190 B6
Chesterfield Gdns FSBYPK N4 67 H2
GNWCH SE10 * 145 G1
MYFR/PICC W1J * 9 J7
Chesterfield Gv EDUL SE22 143 G6
Chesterfield Hl MYFR/PICC W1J 9 J7
Chesterfield Ms FSBYPK N4 67 H2
Chesterfield Rd BAR EN5 20 B6
CHSWK W4 117 K6
FNCH N3 46 E2
HOR/WEW KT19 207 F5
LEY E10 70 A4
Chesterfield St MYFR/PICC W1J 9 J7
Chesterfield Wy
HYS/HAR UB3 * 113 K2
PECK SE15 143 K1
Chesterford Gdns HAMP NW3 83 F2
Chesterford Rd MNPK E12 90 A4
Chester Gdns MRDN SM4 194 B2
PEND EN3 36 D1
WEA W13 * 97 H5
Chester Ga CAMTN NW1 3 J5
Chester Ms KTBR SW1X 15 J4
Chester Pl CAMTN NW1 3 J4
NTHWD HA6 * 40 C3
Chester Rd ARCH N19 66 B6
BFN/LL DA15 147 K6
CAMTN NW1 3 H5
CAN/RD E16 106 C3
ED N9 36 D3
FSTGT E7 89 H5
GDMY/SEVK IG3 73 F5
HSLWW TW4 134 A4
HTHAIR TW6 132 D4
NTHWD HA6 40 D3
TOTM N17 49 K6
WALTH E17 69 F2
WAN E11 71 F3
WIM/MER SW19 177 F2
Chester Rw BGVA SW1W 15 G7
Chester Sq BGVA SW1W 15 H6
Chester Square Ms
BGVA SW1W * 15 J5
The Chesters NWMAL KT3 176 B4
Chester St BETH E2 86 C6
KTBR SW1X 15 H4
Chester Ter CAMTN NW1 3 J4
Chesterton Cl GFD/PVL UB6 96 B1
WAND/EARL SW18 139 K6
Chesterton Ct EA W5 * 97 K5
Chesterton Dr
STWL/WRAY TW19 152 C3
Chesterton Rd NKENS W10 100 C4
PLSTW E13 106 E2
Chesterton Sq KENS W8 119 J4
Chesterton Ter KUT/HW KT1 175 H5
PLSTW E13 106 E2
Chester Wy LBTH SE11 17 K7
Chesthunte Rd TOTM N17 49 J4
Chestnut Aly FUL/PGN SW6 * 119 J6
Chestnut Av ALP/SUD HA0 79 H3
BKHH IG9 39 H5
BTFD TW8 116 E5
CEND/HSY/T N8 66 E2
E/WMO/HCT KT8 174 A6
EDGW HA8 44 A2
ESH/CLAY KT10 189 J4
FSTGT E7 89 F2
HCH RM12 75 H6
HOR/WEW KT19 207 G2
HPTN TW12 173 F3
MORT/ESHN SW14 138 A4
NTHWD HA6 40 D5
WWKM BR4 214 C3
Chestnut Av South WALTH E17 70 A2
Chestnut Cl ASHF TW15 152 E6
BFN/LL DA15 168 B4
BKHH IG9 39 H5
CAR SM5 194 E5
CAT SE6 165 F6
HYS/HAR UB3 94 C6
HYS/HAR UB3 132 E1
NWCR SE14 144 C2
ORP BR6 217 G3
STHGT/OAK N14 22 C6
STNW/STAM N16 67 K6
STRHM/NOR SW16 162 B6
Chestnut Cottages
TRDG/WHET N20 * 32 C3
Chestnut Dr BXLYHN DA7 148 E4
KTN/HRWW/WS HA3 43 F3
PIN HA5 59 H3
WAN E11 70 E3
Chestnut Gln HCH RM12 75 H6
Chestnut Gv ALP/SUD HA0 79 H3
BAL SW12 161 F2
BARK/HLT IG6 54 E2
EA W5 116 E3
EBAR EN4 21 K6
ISLW TW7 136 B5
MTCM CR4 195 J2
NWMAL KT3 176 A6
SAND/SEL CR2 212 D5
Chestnut La TRDG/WHET N20 32 C3
Chestnut Ms WFD IG8 52 E1
Chestnut Pl NRWD SE19 163 G6
Chestnut Ri BUSH WD23 28 B2
WOOL/PLUM SE18 127 K5
Chestnut Rd ASHF TW15 152 D6
DART DA1 171 G3
KUTN/CMB KT2 175 F3
RYNPK SW20 177 G5
WHTN TW2 155 K4
WNWD SE27 162 D5
The Chestnuts BECK BR3 * 182 A6
PIN HA5 * 41 K3
Chestnut Ter SUT SM1 * 209 F2
Chestnut Wy FELT TW13 154 A5
Cheston Av CROY/NA CR0 198 B5
Cheswick Cl DART DA1 150 C5
Chesworth Cl ERITH DA8 150 B2
Chettle Cl STHWK SE1 18 E4
Chetwode Rd TOOT SW17 160 E5
Chetwynd Av EBAR EN4 33 K3
Chetwynd Rd KTTN NW5 84 B2
Chetwynd Vls KTTN NW5 * 84 B2
Chevalier Cl STAN HA7 29 K5
Cheval Pl SKENS SW7 14 D4
Cheval St POP/IOD E14 124 D3
Cheveney Wk HAYES BR2 183 K6
Chevening Rd GNWCH SE10 125 J5
KIL/WHAMP NW6 100 B1
NRWD SE19 180 E3
The Chevenings SCUP DA14 168 D5
Cheverton Rd ARCH N19 66 D5
Chevet St HOM E9 87 G3
Chevington CRICK NW2 * 82 D4
Cheviot Cl BELMT SM2 209 H6
BUSH WD23 28 C1
BXLYHN DA7 150 B3
ENC/FH EN2 23 K3
HYS/HAR UB3 133 G1
Cheviot Gdns CRICK NW2 64 B6
Cheviot Rd EMPK RM11 75 J4
WNWD SE27 180 C1
Cheviot Wy GNTH/NBYPK IG2 72 E2
Chevron Cl CAN/RD E16 106 E5
Chevy Rd NWDGN UB2 115 H2
Chewton Rd WALTH E17 69 G1
Cheyne Av SWFD E18 52 D6
WHTN TW2 154 E3
Cheyne Cl HAYES BR2 215 J1
Cheyne Gdns CHEL SW3 120 D6
Cheyne Hl BRYLDS KT5 191 G1
Cheyne Ms CHEL SW3 120 D6
Cheyne Park Dr WWKM BR4 214 A1
Cheyne Pth HNWL W7 97 F4
Cheyne Pl CHEL SW3 * 120 E6
Cheyne Rw CHEL SW3 120 D6
Cheyne Wk CHEL SW3 120 D6
CROY/NA CR0 197 H6
HDN NW4 64 A3
WBPTN SW10 140 C1
WCHMH N21 23 G6
Cheyneys Av EDGW HA8 43 K2
Chichele Gdns CROY/NA CR0 212 A2
Chichele Rd CRICK NW2 82 B3
Chicheley Rd
KTN/HRWW/WS HA3 42 C3
Chicheley St STHWK SE1 17 H2
Chichester Av RSLP HA4 58 B6
Chichester Cl BKHTH/KID SE3 146 B1
EHAM E6 107 J5
HPTN TW12 172 E2
Chichester Ct EW KT17 * 207 H6
STAN HA7 44 A6
Chichester Gdns IL IG1 71 K4
Chichester Rd BAY/PAD W2 * 101 F4
CROY/NA CR0 212 A1
ED N9 36 B3
KIL/WHAMP NW6 100 E1
WAN E11 88 C1
Chichester St PIM SW1V 121 H5
Chichester Wy
EBED/NFELT TW14 154 B2
POP/IOD E14 125 G4
Chichester Whf ERITH DA8 130 B5
Chicksand St WCHPL E1 13 K2
Chiddingfold
NFNCH/WDSPK N12 32 E5
Chiddingstone Av
BXLYHN DA7 149 G1
Chiddingstone St
FUL/PGN SW6 139 K3
Chieftan Dr PUR RM19 131 K4
Chieveley Pde BXLYHN DA7 * 149 J4
Chieveley Rd BXLYHN DA7 149 J5
Chignell Pl WEA W13 116 B1
Chigwell Hl WAP E1W 104 D6
Chigwell Rd SWFD E18 53 G5
Chilcott Cl ALP/SUD HA0 79 J2
Childebert Rd TOOT SW17 161 G4
Childeric Rd NWCR SE14 144 B1
Childerley St FUL/PGN SW6 139 H2
Childers St DEPT SE8 124 B6
The Childers WFD IG8 53 K1
Child La GNWCH SE10 125 J3
Childs Ct HYS/HAR UB3 94 E6
Childs La NRWD SE19 * 181 F2
Child's Ms ECT SW5 * 119 K4
Child's Pl ECT SW5 119 K4
Child's St ECT SW5 119 K4
Child's Wk ECT SW5 * 119 K4
Childs Wy GLDGN NW11 64 D2
Chilham Cl BXLY DA5 169 G2
GFD/PVL UB6 97 G1
Chilham Rd ELTH/MOT SE9 166 D6
Chilham Wy HAYES BR2 199 K4
Chillerton Rd TOOT SW17 179 F1
Chillington Dr BTSEA SW11 140 B5
Chillingworth Gdns
TWK TW1 * 156 A4
Chillingworth Rd HOLWY N7 85 F3
Chilmark Gdns NWMAL KT3 192 C3
Chilmark Rd
STRHM/NOR SW16 179 J5
Chiltern Av BUSH WD23 28 C1
WHTN TW2 155 F3
Chiltern Cl BUSH WD23 28 B1
BXLYHN DA7 150 B2
CROY/NA CR0 212 A1
WPK KT4 193 F6
Chiltern Dene ENC/FH EN2 23 F5
Chiltern Dr BRYLDS KT5 191 J3
Chiltern Gdns CRICK NW2 82 B1
HAYES BR2 199 J1
Chiltern Rd BOW E3 105 J3
GNTH/NBYPK IG2 72 E1
PIN HA5 59 G2
The Chilterns BELMT SM2 * 209 F6
Chiltern St MHST W1U 9 G2
Chiltern Wy WFD IG8 38 E5
Chilthorne Cl CAT SE6 164 C2
Chilton Av EA W5 116 E4
Chilton Gv DEPT SE8 124 A4
Chilton Rd EDGW HA8 44 C2
RCH/KEW TW9 137 H4
Chilton St BETH E2 7 K6
Chilvers Cl WHTN TW2 155 K4
Chilver St GNWCH SE10 125 J5
Chilwell Gdns OXHEY WD19 27 G6
Chilworth Gdns SUT SM1 209 G1
Chilworth Ms BAY/PAD W2 101 G5
Chilworth St BAY/PAD W2 101 G5
Chimes Av PLMGR N13 49 G1
China Hall Ms
BERM/RHTH SE16 123 K4
China Ms BRXS/STRHM SW2 162 A2
Chinbrook Crs LEE/GVPK SE12 166 A5
Chinbrook Rd LEE/GVPK SE12 166 B5
Chinchilla Dr HSLWW TW4 134 B3
The Chine ALP/SUD HA0 79 H3
MUSWH N10 66 C1
WCHMH N21 35 H1
Chingdale Rd CHING E4 38 C5
Chingford Av CHING E4 37 K5
Chingford La WFD IG8 52 D1
Chingford Mount Rd CHING E4 51 J1
Chingford Rd CHING E4 51 J3
Chingley Cl BMLY BR1 183 H2
Ching Wy CHING E4 51 H2
Chinnery Cl EN EN1 24 B1
Chinnor Crs GFD/PVL UB6 96 C1
Chipka St POP/IOD E14 125 F2
Chipley St NWCR SE14 124 B6
Chippendale St CLPT E5 87 F1
Chippenham Cl PIN HA5 * 58 D1
Chippenham Gdns
KIL/WHAMP NW6 100 E2
Chippenham Ms
MV/WKIL W9 * 100 E3
Chippenham Rd MV/WKIL W9 100 E3
Chipperfield Rd
STMC/STPC BR5 186 C6
Chipping Cl BAR EN5 20 C4
Chipstead Av THHTH CR7 196 C1
Chipstead Cl BELMT SM2 209 F6
NRWD SE19 181 G3
Chipstead Gdns CRICK NW2 63 K6
Chipstead Rd ERITH DA8 150 B1
HTHAIR TW6 132 D4
Chipstead St FUL/PGN SW6 139 K3
Chirk Cl YEAD UB4 95 J3
Chisenhale Rd BOW E3 105 G1
Chisholm Rd CROY/NA CR0 197 F6
RCHPK/HAM TW10 157 G1
Chislehurst Av
NFNCH/WDSPK N12 47 G3
Chislehurst High St CHST BR7 185 G2
Chislehurst Rd BMLY BR1 184 D5
ORP BR6 202 A4
RCHPK/HAM TW10 157 F1
SCUP DA14 186 B1
STMC/STPC BR5 201 K1
Chislet Cl BECK BR3 182 D3
Chisley Rd SEVS/STOTM N15 68 A3
Chiswell Sq BKHTH/KID SE3 146 A3
Chiswell St CMBW SE5 * 142 E1
STLK EC1Y 12 E1
Chiswick Br CHSWK W4 137 K3
Chiswick Cl CROY/NA CR0 211 F1
Chiswick Common Rd
CHSWK W4 118 A4
Chiswick High Rd CHSWK W4 117 H5
Chiswick House Grounds
CHSWK W4 * 118 A6
Chiswick La CHSWK W4 118 B5
Chiswick La South CHSWK W4 118 C6
Chiswick Ml CHSWK W4 118 C6
Chiswick Pk CHSWK W4 * 117 K3
Chiswick Pier CHSWK W4 * 138 C1
Chiswick Quay CHSWK W4 137 K2
Chiswick Rd CHSWK W4 117 K4
ED N9 36 D4
Chiswick Sq CHSWK W4 118 B6
Chiswick Staithe CHSWK W4 137 K2
Chiswick Village CHSWK W4 117 J6
Chiswick Whf CHSWK W4 118 C6
Chitterfield Ga WDR/YW UB7 132 D1
Chitty's La BCTR RM8 73 K6
Chitty St FITZ W1T 10 B1
Chivalry Rd BTSEA SW11 140 D6
Chivenor Gv KUTN/CMB KT2 174 E1
Chivers Rd CHING E4 37 K5
Choats Manor Wy DAGW RM9 110 B2
Choats Rd BARK IG11 109 J1
Chobham Gdns
WIM/MER SW19 159 G4
Chobham Rd SRTFD E15 88 C3
Cholmeley Cl HGT N6 * 66 B4
Cholmeley Crs HGT N6 66 B4
Cholmeley Pk HGT N6 66 B5
Cholmley Gdns
KIL/WHAMP NW6 82 E3
Cholmley Rd THDIT KT7 190 C3
Cholmley Ter THDIT KT7 * 190 C4
Cholmley Vls THDIT KT7 * 190 C4
Cholmondeley Av
WLSDN NW10 99 J1
Chopwell Cl SRTFD E15 * 88 B5
Chorleywood Crs
STMC/STPC BR5 186 A5
Choumert Gv PECK SE15 143 H3
Choumert Ms PECK SE15 143 H3
Choumert Rd PECK SE15 143 G4
Chow Sq HACK E8 86 B3
Chrislaine Cl
STWL/WRAY TW19 152 A1
Chrisp St POP/IOD E14 105 K5
Christabel Cl ISLW TW7 135 K4
Christ Church Av ERITH DA8 130 A6
Christchurch Av ALP/SUD HA0 80 A4
KIL/WHAMP NW6 82 C5
KTN/HRWW/WS HA3 61 G1
NFNCH/WDSPK N12 47 G2
RAIN RM13 111 H2
TEDD TW11 174 B1
Christchurch Cl ENC/FH EN2 23 J3
NFNCH/WDSPK N12 * 47 H3
WIM/MER SW19 178 C3
Christchurch Gdns
KTN/HRWW/WS HA3 61 G1
Christchurch Hl HAMP NW3 83 H1
Christ Church La BAR EN5 20 C3
Christchurch Ldg EBAR EN4 * 21 K5
Christchurch Pk BELMT SM2 209 G5
Christ Church Rd BECK BR3 * 182 D5
BRYLDS KT5 191 G4
CEND/HSY/T N8 66 E3
Christchurch Rd BFN/LL DA15 168 A6
BRXS/STRHM SW2 162 A3
DART DA1 171 F2
IL IG1 72 B5
MORT/ESHN SW14 137 J6
WIM/MER SW19 178 C4

Christchurch Sq HOM E9 ....86 E6
Christchurch St CHEL SW3 ......120 E6
Christchurch Ter CHEL SW3 * ...120 E6
Christchurch Wy SDTCH SE10 ...125 H5
Christian Flds
  STRHM/NOR SW16 ....180 B3
Christian St WCHPL E1 ....104 C5
Christie Dr CROY/NA CRO 197 H2
Christie Rd E9 ....87 G4
Christina Sq FSBYPK N4 ....67 H5
Christina St SDTCH EC2A 7 H3
Christine Worsley Cl
  WCHMH N21 ....35 H1
Christopher Av HNWL W7 ....116 B3
Christopher Cl
  BERM/RHTH SE16 ....124 A2
  BFN/LL DA15 ....148 A6
Christopher Gdns DAGW RM9 ...91 K3
Christopher Pl CAMTN NW1 * 4 D4
Christopher Rd NWDGN UB2 ...114 A4
Christophers Ms NTGHL W11 * ..119 H1
Christopher St SDTCH EC2A 7 F7
Christy Ter WFD IG8 ....53 J3
Chryssell Rd BRXN/ST SW9 .....142 B1
Chubworthy St NWCR SE14 ....124 B6
Chudleigh Crs GDMY/SEVK IG3 ..90 E2
Chudleigh Gdns SUT SM1 ....209 G1
Chudleigh Rd BROCKY SE4 .....144 C6
  KIL/WHAMP NW6 ....82 B5
  WHTN TW2 ....155 K1
Chudleigh St WCHPL E1 ....105 F5
Chudleigh Wy RSLP HA4 ....58 E1
Chulsa Rd SYD SE26 ....181 J1
Chumleigh Gdns CMBW SE5 * ..123 F6
Chumleigh St CMBW SE5 ......123 F6
Church Ap DUL SE21 ....162 G5
Church Av BECK BR3 ....182 D4
  CAMTN NW1 ....84 B4
  CHING E4 ....52 B2
  MORT/ESHN SW14 ....138 A5
  NTHLT UB5 ...
  NWDGN UB2 ....114 D3
  PIN HA5 ....59 J3
  RSLP HA4 ....58 B3
  SCUP DA14 ....186 B1
Churchbury Cl EN EN1 ....24 A3
Churchbury La EN EN1 ....24 A2
Churchbury Rd ELTH/MOT SE9 ..166 C2
  EN EN1 ....24 A3
Church Cl EDGW HA8 ....44 E1
  HSLW TW3 ....134 E3
  HYS/HAR UB3 ....94 B4
  KENS W8 * 120 A2
  NTHWD HA6 ....40 D5
  TRDG/WHET N20 ....33 J5
  WDR/YW UB7 ....112 B3
Church Crs FNCH N3 ....46 D4
  HOM E9 ....86 E6
  MUSWH N10 ....66 B1
  TRDG/WHET N20 ....33 J5
Churchcroft Cl BAL SW12 * 161 F2
Churchdown BMLY BR1 ....165 H6
Church Dr CDALE/KGS NW9 .....63 F3
  RYLN/HDSTN HA2 ....60 C1
  WWKM BR4 ....214 C1
Church Elm La DAGE RM10 .....92 C4
Church End HDN NW4 ....63 K1
  WALTH E17 ....69 J1
Church Farm La CHEAM SM3 ...208 C4
Church Fld RDART DA2 ....171 G4
Churchfield Av
  NFNCH/WDSPK N12 ....47 H2
Churchfield Cl HYS/HAR UB3 ...94 D6
  RYLN/HDSTN HA2 ....60 C1
Churchfield Rd ACT W3 ....117 K1
  HNWL W7 ....115 K2
  WEA W13 ....116 C1
  WELL DA16 ....148 B4
Churchfields E/WMO/HCT KT8 ..173 F6
  GNWCH SE10 ....125 F6
  SWFD E18 ....52 E5
Churchfields Av FELT TW13 ....154 E5
Churchfields Rd BECK BR3 .....182 A5
Churchfield Wy
  NFNCH/WDSPK N12 ....47 G3
Church Gdns ALP/SUD HA0 ......79 G2
  EA W5 ....116 E2
Church Garth ARCH N19 * 66 D1
Church Ga FUL/PGN SW6 ....139 H4
Church Gn BRXN/ST SW9 ......142 B3
  HYS/HAR UB3 ....94 D5
Church Gv KUT/HW KT1 ....174 D5
  LEW SE13 ....144 E5
Church HI CAR SM5 ....209 K3
  DART DA1 ....150 B5
  HRW HA1 ....60 E5
  ORP BR6 ....202 C5
  RDART DA2 ....171 G5
  WALTH E17 ....69 J1
  WCHMH N21 ....35 F2
  WIM/MER SW19 ....177 J5
  WOOL/PLUM SE18 ....126 E3
Church Hill Rd CHEAM SM3 ....208 C2
  EBAR EN4 ....33 J1
  SURB KT6 ....191 F2
  WALTH E17 ....69 J1
Church Hill Wd
  STMC/STPC BR5 ....202 B2
Church Hollow PUR RM19 ......131 K5
Church Hyde
  WOOL/PLUM SE18 ....127 K6
Churchill Av
  KTN/HRWW/WS HA3 ....61 H3
Churchill Gdns ACT W3 ....98 C5
Churchill Gardens Rd
  PIM SW1V 16 B6
Churchill Ms WFD IG8 * 52 D5
Churchill Pl POP/IOD E14 ....124 E1
Churchill Rd CAN/RD E16 ....107 G5
  CRICK NW2 ....81 K4
  EDGW HA8 ....44 B2
  KTTN NW5 ....84 B2
  SAND/SEL CR2 ....211 J6
Churchill Ter CHING E4 ....37 J2

Churchill Wk HOM E9 ....86 E3
Church Manor Wy ABYW SE2 ...128 B4
Church Manorway ERITH DA8 ..130 A3
Church Md CMBW SE5 * 142 D1
Churchmead Cl EBAR EN4 .....33 J2
Church Meadow SURB KT6 .....190 D6
Churchmead Rd WLSDN NW10 ..81 J4
Churchmore Rd
  STRHM/NOR SW16 ....179 H4
Churchpark Ct
  WLGTN SM6 ....210 D1
Church Pde ASHF TW15 * 152 C6
Church Pas BAR EN5 * 20 E5
Church Pth CHSWK W4 ....117 K3
  MTCM CR4 ....178 D6
  NFNCH/WDSPK N12 ....47 G1
  WAN E11 ....70 D1
  WIM/MER SW19 ....177 J5
Church PI EA W5 * 116 E2
  MTCM CR4 ....178 D6
Church Ri CHSGTN KT9 ....206 B4
  FSTH SE23 ....164 A3
Church Rd ACT W3 ....117 K2
  ASHF TW15 ....152 C6
  BARK IG11 ....90 C6
  BARN SW13 ....138 D3
  BKHH IG9 ....39 F3
  BXLYHN DA7 ....149 G3
  CHEAM SM3 ....208 C4
  CROY/NA CRO 211 J2
  E/WMO/HCT KT8 ....189 J1
  ERITH DA8 ....129 K5
  ESH/CLAY KT10 ....205 H4
  FELT TW13 ....172 B1
  GNTH/NBYPK IG2 ....72 E5
  HAYES BR2 ....183 H6
  HAYES BR2 ....183 K5
  HDN NW4 ....63 K1
  HEST TW5 ....114 A5
  HGT N6 ....66 A5
  HNWL W7 ....96 B6
  HOR/WEW KT19 ....207 F5
  HYS/HAR UB3 ....94 A4
  IS N1 ....85 J2
  ISLW TW7 ....135 J2
  LEY E10 ....69 K4
  MNPK E12 ....89 K3
  NRWD SE19 ....181 F5
  NTHLT UB5 ....95 J1
  NTHWD HA6 ....40 D3
  NWDGN UB2 ....114 E3
  ORP BR6 ....216 C5
  PEND EN3 ....36 E1
  RCHPK/HAM TW10 .....137 F6
  RCHPK/HAM TW10 .....157 F6
  SCUP DA14 ....168 D5
  STAN HA7 ....43 H1
  SURB KT6 ....190 D6
  TEDD TW11 ....155 K6
  TOTM N17 ....50 B3
  WALTH E17 ....51 G5
  WELL DA16 ....148 C3
  WIM/MER SW19 ....177 H1
  WLGTN SM6 ....210 C1
  WLSDN NW10 ....81 G1
Church Rw CHST BR7 ....185 H4
  FUL/PGN SW6 * 140 A1
  HAMP NW3 ....83 G2
  WAND/EARL SW18 * 139 K6
Church Row Ms CHST BR7 ....185 H4
  CHSWK W4 ....118 C6
  CROY/NA CRO 211 H1
  DAGE RM10 ....92 D5
  ED N9 ....35 K3
  ESH/CLAY KT10 ....204 B2
  EW KT17 ....207 J6
  HPTN TW12 ....173 H4
  HSLW TW3 ....135 H6
  ISLW TW7 ....135 K2
  KUT/HW KT1 ....174 E5
  SRTFD E15 ....88 C6
  SUN TW16 ....172 A4
  TW16 ....156 B3
Church Street Est STJWD NW8 ..2 B7
Church St North SRTFD E15 ....88 C6
Church Ter BKHTH/KID SE3 ....145 H4
  FUL/PGN SW6 ....140 A3
  HDN NW4 ....63 K1
  RCHPK/HAM TW10 .....136 E6
Church Vw EFNCH N2 * 47 J6
  FSTH SE23 ....163 K4
Church Vw FSTH SE23 ....164 A4

Churchview Rd WHTN TW2 .....155 J3
Church Wk BTFD TW8 ....116 D6
  BUSH WD23 ....28 A1
  CDALE/KGS NW9 ....63 F6
  CRICK NW2 ....82 D1
  HYS/HAR UB3 ....94 C5
  RDART DA2 ....171 G5
  RYNPK SW20 ....177 F6
  STNW/STAM N16 ....179 H5
  THDIT KT7 ....190 A3
Churchway CAMTN NW1 * 4 D4
Church Wy TRDG/WHET N20 ....33 J5
Churchyard Rw LBTH SE11 ....18 B6
Churston Av PLSTW E13 ......89 F6
Churston Cl
  BRXS/STRHM SW2 * 162 C3
Churston Dr MRDN SM4 ......193 G2
Churston Gdns
  FBAR/BDGN N11 ....48 C2
Churton Pl CHSWK W4 * 117 A6
Churton St PIM SW1V 16 B7
Chyngton Cl BFN/LL DA15 ....168 A5
Cibber Rd FSTH SE23 ....164 A4
Cicada Rd WAND/EARL SW18 ..160 B1
Cicely Rd PECK SE15 ....143 H2
Cinderella Pth GLDGN NW11 ...65 F5
Cinderford Wy BMLY BR1 .....165 H6
Cinema Pde EDGW HA8 * 44 C2
Cinnamon Cl CROY/NA CRO * ..195 K4
  PECK SE15 ....143 G1
Cinnamon St WAP E1W 123 J1
Cintra Pk NRWD SE19 ....181 G3
Circle Gdns WIM/MER SW19 ...177 K6
The Circle CRICK NW2 ....81 G1
  WAP E1W 123 J1
The Circuits PIN HA5 ....59 G1
Circular Rd TOTM N17 ....50 B6
Circular Wy WOOL/PLUM SE18 ..126 E6
Circus Ms MBLAR W1H * 8 D1
Circus PI LVPST EC2M * 13 F2
Circus Rd STJWD NW8 ....2 A4
Circus St GNWCH SE10 ....125 F6
Cirencester St BAY/PAD W2 ..101 F4
Cissbury Ring North
  NFNCH/WDSPK N12 ....46 D1
Cissbury Ring South
  NFNCH/WDSPK N12 ....46 D1
Cissbury Rd SEVS/STOTM N15 ..67 K2
Citadel Pl LBTH SE11 ....122 A5
Citizen Rd HOLWY N7 ....85 G2
Citron Ter PECK SE15 * 143 J4
City Barracks SHB W12 * 119 F1
City Gdn Rw FSBYE EC1V 6 B3
City Rd FSBYE EC1V 6 C4
  STLK EC1Y 13 F1
City Wk STHWK SE1 ....19 G4
Civic Wk BARK/HLT IG6 ....72 C1
Clabon Ms KTBR SW1X 14 E5
Clack St BERM/RHTH SE16 ....123 K2
Clacton Rd TOTM N17 * 50 B5
  WALTH E17 ....69 G3
Claire Ct NFNCH/WDSPK N12 ...33 G6
Claire Gdns STAN HA7 ....43 J1
Claire Pl POP/IOD E14 ....124 D3
Clairvale Rd HEST TW5 ....134 C2
Clairview Rd
  STRHM/NOR SW16 ....179 G1
Clairville Gdns HNWL W7 .....115 K1
Clamp Hi STAN HA7 ....42 B4
Clancarty Rd FUL/PGN SW6 ...139 K3
Clandon Cl ACT W3 ....117 J2
  EW KT17 ....207 H4
Clandon Gdns FNCH N3 ....46 E6
Clandon Rd GDMY/SEVK IG3 ....72 E6
Clandon St DEPT SE8 ....144 D3
Clandon Ter RYNPK SW20 * ...177 G5
Clanricarde Gdns BAY/PAD W2 ..100 E6
Clapgate Rd BUSH WD23 ......28 B1
Clapham Common North Side
  CLAP SW4 ....141 G5
Clapham Common South Side
  CLAP SW4 ....161 G1
Clapham Common West Side
  CLAP SW4 ....140 D5
Clapham Court Ter
  CLAP SW4 * 141 K4
Clapham Crs CLAP SW4 ....141 J5
Clapham High St CLAP SW4 ...141 J4
Clapham Manor St CLAP SW4 ..141 H4
Clapham Park Est CLAP SW4 * ..161 J2
Clapham Park Rd CLAP SW4 ..141 J5
Clapham Park Ter
  BRXS/STRHM SW2 * 141 K6
Clapham Rd BRXN/ST SW9 .....141 K3
Clapham Rd South IS N1 ....85 K5
Claps Gate La EHAM E6 ......108 B3
Clapton Common CLPT E5 .....68 C4
Clapton Pas CLPT E5 ....86 E2
Clapton Sq CLPT E5 ....86 E3
Clapton Ter CLPT E5 ....68 E5
Clapton Wy CLPT E5 ....86 C2
Clara Pl WOOL/PLUM SE18 ....127 F4
Clare Cl BORE WD6 ....30 B1
  EFNCH N2 ....47 G6
Clare Cnr ELTH/MOT SE9 ......167 G2
Clare Ct NTHWD HA6 ....40 D2
Claredale St BETH E2 ....104 C1
Clare Gdns BARK IG11 ....91 F4
  FSTGT E7 ....88 E2
  NTGHL W11 ....100 C5
Clare La IS N1 ....85 J5
Clare Lawn Av
  MORT/ESHN SW14 ....138 A6
Clare Ms FUL/PGN SW6 ....140 A1
Claremont Av
  KTN/HRWW/WS HA3 ......62 A2
  NWMAL KT3 ....192 D2
  SUN TW16 ....172 A4
Claremont Cl
  BRXS/STRHM SW2 * 162 A3
  CAN/RD E16 ....127 F1
  IS N1 ....5 K3

ORP BR6 ....216 A2
Claremont Crs DART DA1 .....150 B5
Claremont Dr ESH/CLAY KT10 ..204 B5
Claremont End
  ESH/CLAY KT10 ....204 B4
Claremont Gdns
  GDMY/SEVK IG3 ....72 E6
  SURB KT6 ....191 F2
Claremont Gv CHSWK W4 .....138 B1
  WFD IG8 ....53 G2
Claremont House
  WATW WD18 * 26 B1
Claremont Pk FNCH N3 ....46 C4
Claremont Park Rd
  ESH/CLAY KT10 ....204 B4
Claremont Rd BMLY BR1 ......200 D1
  CRICK NW2 ....64 A4
  CROY/NA CRO 197 H6
  EBAR EN4 ....21 G1
  EMPK RM11 ....75 J3
  ESH/CLAY KT10 ....204 B5
  FSTGT E7 ....89 F2
  HGT N6 ....66 B4
  KTN/HRWW/WS HA3 .....42 E5
  MV/WKIL W9 ....100 C1
  SURB KT6 ....191 F2
  TEDD TW11 ....156 C1
  TWK TW1 ....156 C2
  WALTH E17 ....51 F5
  WAN E11 ....88 B1
  WEA W13 ....97 G4
Claremont Sq IS N1 ....5 J3
Claremont St GNWCH SE10 ...124 E6
  UED N18 ....50 C2
Claremont Ter THDIT KT7 * ...190 C4
Claremont Vs CMBW SE5 * ...142 E1
  KUT/HW KT1 * 175 J5
Claremont Wy CRICK NW2 ....64 A5
Clarence Av BMLY BR1 ......200 D1
  CLAP SW4 ....161 J2
  IL IG1 ....71 K3
  NWMAL KT3 ....175 K5
Clarence Cl BUSH WD23 ....28 E2
  EBAR EN4 ....21 G1
Clarence Crs CLAP SW4 .....161 J1
  SCUP DA14 ....168 C5
Clarence Gdns CAMTN NW1 ....3 K5
  CHIG IG7 ....54 A2
Clarence Ga PUT/ROE SW15 ..158 C1
Clarence La PUT/ROE SW15 ..158 C1
Clarence Ms BAL SW12 ......161 J2
  CLPT E5 ....86 E3
  TOOT SW17 ....160 D5
Clarence Pas CAMTN NW1 * ...4 E3
Clarence Pl CLPT E5 ....86 E3
Clarence Rd BMLY BR1 ......184 B6
  BXLYHS DA6 ....149 F5
  CAN/RD E16 ....106 C3
  CHSWK W4 ....117 H5
  CLPT E5 ....86 C2
  CROY/NA CRO 196 E5
  DEPT SE8 ....124 B6
  ELTH/MOT SE9 ....166 D4
  KIL/WHAMP NW6 ....82 C6
  MNPK E12 ....89 G2
  PEND EN3 ....24 E6
  RCH/KEW TW9 ....137 G2
  SCUP DA14 ....168 C5
  SEVS/STOTM N15 ....67 J2
  SUT SM1 ....209 F2
  TEDD TW11 ....174 A1
  WALTH E17 ....51 F5
  WDGN N22 ....48 E4
  WIM/MER SW19 ....178 A2
  WLGTN SM6 ....210 B3
Clarence St KUT/HW KT1 .....174 E5
  KUT/HW KT1 ....175 F5
  KUTN/CMB KT2 ....175 F5
  NWDGN UB2 ....114 C3
  RCH/KEW TW9 ....137 F5
Clarence Ter CAMTN NW1 * 3 H5
  HSLW TW3 ....135 G5
Clarence Wk CLAP SW4 ......141 K3
Clarence Wy CAMTN NW1 .....84 B5
Clarendon Cl BAY/PAD W2 * 8 C5
  HOM E9 ....86 E6
  STMC/STPC BR5 ....186 B6
Clarendon Cross NTGHL W11 ..100 B6
Clarendon Dr PUT/ROE SW15 ..139 F6
Clarendon Gdns HDN NW4 .....45 H5
  IL IG1 ....71 K3
  MV/WKIL W9 ....101 G3
  WBLY HA9 ....79 K2
Clarendon Ga BAY/PAD W2 .....8 B4
Clarendon Gn STMC/STPC BR5 ..186 B6
Clarendon Gv CAMTN NW1 .....4 B4
  STMC/STPC BR5 ....202 B1
Clarendon Ms BAY/PAD W2 .....8 C4
Clarendon Pth
  STMC/STPC BR5 ....202 B1
Clarendon Pl BAY/PAD W2 .....8 C5
  BH/WHM TN16 * 145 G1
Clarendon Ri ASHF TW15 .....152 C6
  LEW SE13 ....145 F4
Clarendon Rd ASHF TW15 ....152 C6
  CROY/NA CRO 196 C6
  EA W5 ....98 A2
  HRW HA1 ....60 E3
  HYS/HAR UB3 ....113 J2
  NTGHL W11 ....100 B6
  SEVS/STOTM N15 ......67 J1
  SWFD E18 ....52 E6
  UED N18 ....50 C2
  WALTH E17 ....70 A3
  WAN E11 ....70 B5
  WDGN N22 ....48 E5
  WIM/MER SW19 ....178 A3
Clarendon St PIM SW1V 121 G5
Clarendon Ter MV/WKIL W9 ..101 G3
Clarens St CAT SE6 ....164 C4
Clare Pde GFD/PVL UB6 * 78 D4
Clare Rd GFD/PVL UB6 ....78 D4

HSLWW TW4 ....134 E4
NWCR SE14 ....144 C3
STWL/WRAY TW19 ....152 A3
WAN E11 ....70 B3
WLSDN NW10 ....81 J5
Clare St BETH E2 ....104 D1
Claret Gdns SNWD SE25 .....197 F1
Clareville Gv SKENS SW7 ....120 B4
Clareville Grove Ms
  SKENS SW7 * 120 B4
Clareville St SKENS SW7 .....120 B4
Clareville St SKENS SW7 ....120 B4
Clarewood Wy BXLYHN DA2 ..149 F2
Clarges Ms MYFR/PICC W1J 9 K7
Clarges St MYFR/PICC W1J ...9 K7
Claribel Rd BRXN/ST SW9 ....142 C3
Clarice Wy WLGTN SM6 .....210 E6
Claridge Rd BCTR RM8 ....73 K5
Clarissa Rd CHDH RM6 ....73 K5
Clarissa St HACK E8 ....86 B6
Clark Cl ERITH DA8 ....150 D2
Clarke Ms ED N9 ....36 D5
Clarke Path STNW/STAM N16 ..68 C5
Clarkes Av WPK KT4 ....193 G5
Clarkes Rd CAN/RD E16 ...
Clarks Md BUSH WD23 ....28 C2
Clarkson Rd CAN/RD E16 .....106 D5
Clarkson Rw CAMTN NW1 * 4 A3
Clarkson St BETH E2 ....104 D2
Clark's Pl OBST EC2N * 13 G3
Clark St WCHPL E1 ....104 E5
Clark Wy HEST TW5 ....134 C1
Classon Cl WDR/YW UB7 ....112 B2
Claston Cl DART DA1 ....150 H5
Claude Monet Ct EDUL SE22 * ..143 H6
Claude Rd LEY E10 ....70 A5
  PECK SE15 ....143 J5
  PLSTW E13 ....89 F6
Claude St POP/IOD E14 ......124 D4
Claudia Pl WIM/MER SW19 ...159 H3
Claudius Cl STAN HA7 ....29 K5
Claughton Rd PLSTW E13 ....107 G1
Clauson Av NTHLT UB5 ....78 B3
Clavell St GNWCH SE10 ......125 F6
Claverdale Rd
  BRXS/STRHM SW2 .....162 A2
Clavering Av BARN SW13 ....118 A6
Clavering Cl TEDD TW11 .....156 B6
Clavering Rd MNPK E12 ....71 H5
Claverley Gv FNCH N3 ....46 E4
Claverley Vls FNCH N3 ....47 F3
Claverton St PIM SW1V 121 H5
Clave St WAP E1W * 123 J1
Claxton Gv HMSMTH W6 ....119 G5
Clay Av MTCM CR4 ....179 G5
Claybank Gv LEW SE13 ......144 E4
Claybridge Rd LEE/GVPK SE12 ..166 B6
Claybrook Cl EFNCH N2 * 47 H6
Claybrook Rd HMSMTH W6 ...119 G6
Claybury BUSH WD23 ....28 B2
Claybury Rd WFD IG8 ....53 J3
Claydon Dr CROY/NA CRO ...210 E2
Claydown Ms
  WOOL/PLUM SE18 ......127 F5
Clayfarm Rd ELTH/MOT SE9 ..167 H4
Claygate Cl HCH RM12 ....93 J2
Claygate Crs CROY/NA CRO ..214 A6
Claygate La ESH/CLAY KT10 ..190 B6
Claygate Lodge Cl
  ESH/CLAY KT10 ....204 E5
Claygate Rd WEA W13 ......116 C3
Clayhall Av CLAY IG5 ....53 K5
Clayhill Crs ELTH/MOT SE9 ..166 C6
Claylands Pl VX/NE SW8 ....142 B1
Claylands Rd VX/NE SW8 ....122 A6
Clay La BUSH WD23 ....28 B2
  STWL/WRAY TW19 ......152 A2
Claymore Cl MRDN SM4 .....193 K4
Claypole Dr HEST TW5 ....134 D2
Claypole Rd SRTFD E15 ......106 A1
Clayponds Av BTFD TW8 ....116 E4
Clayponds Gdns EA W5 ......116 E4
Clayponds La BTFD TW8 ....117 F5
Clayside CHIG IG7 ....54 C2
Clays La SRTFD E15 ....87 K3
Clays Lane Cl SRTFD E15 * 87 K3
Clay St MHST W1U 9 F2
Clayton Av ALP/SUD HA0 ......80 A5
Clayton Cl EHAM E6 ....107 K5
Clayton Crs BTFD TW8 ......116 E5
  IS N1 ...
Clayton Croft Rd RDART DA2 ..170 D4
Clayton Dr DEPT SE8 ....124 B5
Clayton Fld CDALE/KGS NW9 ...45 G4
Clayton Ms GNWCH SE10 ....145 G2
Clayton Rd CHSGTN KT9 .....205 J2
  HYS/HAR UB3 ....113 H2
  ISLW TW7 ....135 K4
  PECK SE15 ....143 H5
  ROMW/RG RM7 ....56 D5
Clayton St LBTH SE11 ....122 B6
Claytonville Ter BELV DA17 * ..129 K2
Clayworth Cl BFN/LL DA15 ..168 C1
Cleanthus Cl
  WOOL/PLUM SE18 ......147 G2
Cleanthus Rd
  WOOL/PLUM SE18 ......147 G2
Clearbrook Wy WCHPL E1 ....104 E5
Clearwater Pl SURB KT6 .....190 D5
Clearwater Ter NTGHL W11 ..119 G2
Clearwell Dr MV/WKIL W9 ...101 F3
Cleave Av HYS/HAR UB3 ....113 H4
  ORP BR6 ....216 E4
Cleaveland Rd SURB KT6 ....190 E2
Cleaverholme Cl SNWD SE25 ..197 J3
Cleaver Sq LBTH SE11 ....122 B5
Cleaver St LBTH SE11 ....122 B5
Cleeve Hill FSTH SE23 ......163 H3
Cleeve Park Gdns SCUP DA14 ..168 C4
Cleeve Wy PUT/ROE SW15 ...158 C1
  SUT SM1 ....194 A5
Clegg St PLSTW E13 ....106 E1
  WAP E1W 123 J1
Clematis Cottages SHB W12 *

Clematis Gdns *WFD* IG8............52 E1
Clematis St *SHB* W12............99 H6
Clem Attlee Ct *FUL/PGN* SW6 *............1 C4
Clem Attlee Pde
  FUL/PGN SW6 *............119 J6
Clemence Rd *DAGE* RM10............92 E6
Clemence St *POP/IOD* E14............105 H4
Clement Av *CLAP* SW4............141 J5
Clement Cl *CHSWK* W4............118 A4
  KIL/WHAMP NW6............82 B5
Clement Gdns *HYS/HAR* UB3............113 H4
Clementhorpe Rd *DAGW* RM9............91 J4
Clementina Rd *LEY* E10............69 H5
Clementine Cl *WEA* W13............116 C2
Clement Rd *BECK* BR3............182 A5
  WIM/MER SW19............177 H1
Clements Av *CAN/RD* E16............106 E6
Clements Cl
  NFNCH/WDSPK N12............33 F6
Clements Inn *LINN* WC2A............11 H4
Clements La *IL* IG1............90 B1
  MANHO EC4N............13 C5
Clements Pl *BTFD* TW8............116 E5
Clement's Rd
  BERM/RHTH SE16............123 H3
  EHAM E6............89 K5
  IL IG1............90 B1
  WOT/HER KT12............188 A6
Clendon Wy
  WOOL/PLUM SE18............127 J4
Clennam St *STHWK* SE1 *............18 D2
Clensham Ct *SUT* SM1............193 K6
Clensham La *SUT* SM1............193 K6
Clenston Ms *MBLAR* W1H............9 F2
Cleopatra Pl *STAN* HA7............29 K5
Clephane Rd *IS* N1............85 J4
Clere Pl *SDTCH* EC2A............7 F6
Clere St *SDTCH* EC2A............7 F6
Clerkenwell Cl *CLKNW* EC1R............5 K7
Clerkenwell Gn *CLKNW* EC1R............6 A7
Clerkenwell Rd *CLKNW* EC1R............5 J7
Clermont Rd *HOM* E9............86 E6
Clevedon Gdns *NWDGN* UB2............114 A2
  HYS/HAR UB3............113 G3
Clevedon Rd *KUT/HW* KT1............175 H5
  PGE/AN SE20............182 A4
  TWK TW1............156 E1
Cleveland Av *CHSWK* W4............118 C4
  HPTN TW12............173 F3
Cleveland Gdns *BARN* SW13............138 C3
  BAY/PAD W2............101 G5
  CRICK NW2............64 B6
  SEVS/STOTM N15............55 J5
  WPK KT4............192 B6
Cleveland Gv *WCHPL* E1............104 E3
Cleveland Ms *FITZ* W1T............10 A6
Cleveland Park Av *WALTH* E17............69 J1
Cleveland Park Crs *WALTH* E17............69 J1
Cleveland Pl *STJS* SW1Y............10 D7
Cleveland Ri *MRDN* SM4............193 G4
Cleveland Rd *BARN* SW13............138 C3
  CHSWK W4............117 K3
  ED N9 *............36 D2
  IL IG1............90 B1
  IS N1............85 K5
  ISLW TW7............136 B5
  NWMAL KT3............192 B1
  SWFD E18............52 E6
  WEA W13............97 G4
  WELL DA16............148 A3
  WPK KT4............192 B6
Cleveland Rw *WHALL* SW1A............16 B1
Cleveland Sq *BAY/PAD* W2............101 G6
Cleveland St *CAMTN* NW1............3 K7
Cleveland Ter *BAY/PAD* W2............101 G5
Cleveland Wy *HPTN* TW12............1 C4
Cleveley Crs *EA* W5............98 A5
Cleveleys Rd *CLPT* E5............86 D1
Clevely Cl *CHARL* SE7............126 D4
Cleverly Est *SHB* W12 *............118 D1
Cleve Rd *KIL/WHAMP* NW6............82 E5
  SCUP DA14............168 E5
Cleves Av *EW* KT17............207 K6
Cleves Cl *LOU* IG10............39 J1
Cleves Rd *EHAM* E6............89 H6
  RCHPK/HAM TW10............156 D5
Cleves Wy *HPTN* TW12............172 E2
  RSLP HA4............59 H5
Clewer Crs *KTN/HRWW/WS* HA3............42 D4
Clifden Ms *CLPT* E5............87 F2
Clifden Rd *BTFD* TW8............116 E6
  CLPT E5............86 E3
  TWK TW1............156 A3
Cliffe Rd *SAND/SEL* CR2............211 K5
Clifford Av *CHST* BR7............184 E2
  CLAY IG5............54 B4
  MORT/ESHN SW14............137 K3
  WLGTN SM6............210 C2
Clifford Cl *NTHLT* UB5............77 J6
  PLSTW E13 *............107 F2
Clifford Dr *BRXN/ST* SW9............142 C5
Clifford Gdns *HYS/HAR* UB3............113 J4
  WLSDN NW10............100 A1
Clifford Gv *ASHF* TW15............152 D6
Clifford Rd *ALP/SUD* HA0............79 K6
  BAR EN5............21 F4
  CAN/RD E16............106 D3
  ED N9............36 E1
  HSLWW TW4............134 C4
  RCHPK/HAM TW10............156 C4
  SNWD SE25............197 H1
  WALTH E17............51 F4
Clifford St *CONDST* W1S............10 A6
Clifford Wy *WLSDN* NW10............81 H2
Cliff Rd *CAMTN* NW1............84 D4
Cliff Ter *DEPT* SE8............144 D3
Cliffview Rd *LEW* SE13............144 D4
Cliff Wk *CAN/RD* E16............106 D5
Clifton Av *FELT* TW13............154 D6
  FNCH N3............46 D4
  KTN/HRWW/WS HA3............43 H5
  SHB W12............118 C2
  WALTH E17............69 F1
  WBLY HA9............80 B4
Clifton Cl *ORP* BR6............216 C3

Clifton Ct *BECK* BR3 *............182 E4
Clifton Crs *PECK* SE15............143 J1
Clifton Gdns *CHSWK* W4............118 A4
  ENC/FH EN2............23 F3
  GLDGN NW11............64 D3
  MV/WKIL W9............101 G5
  SEVS/STOTM N15............56 B4
Clifton Ga *WBPTN* SW10 *............120 B6
Clifton Gv *HACK* E8............86 C4
Clifton Pde *FELT* TW13 *............154 D6
Clifton Pk Av *RYNPK* SW20............177 F5
Clifton Pl *BAY/PAD* W2............8 B5
  BERM/RHTH SE16............123 K2
  KUTN/CMB KT2 *............175 H4
  WBPTN SW10............120 B6
Clifton Ri *NWCR* SE14............144 B1
Clifton Rd *CAN/RD* E16............106 C4
  CEND/HSY/T N8............66 D3
  EMPK RM11............75 J3
  FNCH N3............47 G4
  FSTGT E7............89 J5
  GFD/PVL UB6............96 C3
  GNTH/NBYPK IG2............72 D3
  HTHAIR TW6............132 E5
  ISLW TW7............135 K3
  KTN/HRWW/WS HA3............62 B2
  KUTN/CMB KT2............175 H4
  MV/WKIL W9............101 G3
  NWDGN UB2............114 D4
  SCUP DA14............167 K6
  SNWD SE25............197 G1
  TEDD TW11............155 K6
  WDGN N22............48 C4
  WELL DA16............148 D4
  WIM/MER SW19............177 G2
  WLSDN NW10............99 J1
Clifton St *SDTCH* EC2A............13 G1
Clifton Ter *FSBYPK* N4............67 G6
Clifton Vis *MV/WKIL* W9............101 F4
Clifton Wy *ALP/SUD* HA0............80 A6
  PECK SE15............143 K1
Cline Rd *FBAR/BDGN* N11............48 C2
Clink St *STHWK* SE1............12 E7
Clinton Av *E/WMO/HCT* KT8............189 H1
  WELL DA16............148 A4
Clinton Crs *BARK/HLT* IG6............54 E2
Clinton Rd *BOW* E3............105 G2
  FSTGT E7............88 E2
  SEVS/STOTM N15............55 J3
Clinton Ter *DEPT* SE8 *............124 D6
  SUT SM1............209 G2
Clipper Cl *BERM/RHTH* SE16............124 A2
Clipper Wy *LEW* SE13............145 F5
Clippesby Cl *CHSGTN* KT9 *............206 B4
Clipstone Ms *FITZ* W1T............9 K1
Clipstone Rd *HSLW* TW3............135 F4
Clipstone St *GTPST* W1W............9 K1
Clissold Cl *EFNCH* N2............47 K6
Clissold Crs *STNW/STAM* N16............85 K2
Clissold Rd *STNW/STAM* N16............85 K1
Clitheroe Av *RYLN/HDSTN* HA2............60 A5
Clitheroe Gdns *OXHEY* WD19............27 H5
Clitheroe Rd *BRXN/ST* SW9............141 K3
  CRW RM5............56 E1
Clitherow Av *HNWL* W7............116 B3
Clitherow Rd *BTFD* TW8............116 C5
Clitterhouse Crs *CRICK* NW2............64 A5
Clitterhouse Rd *CRICK* NW2............64 A5
Clive Av *DART* DA1............170 C1
Clive Cl *WLSDN* NW10 *............81 H5
Cliveden Cl *NFNCH/WDSPK* N12............33 G6
Cliveden Pl *BGVA* SW1W............15 G7
Cliveden Rd *WIM/MER* SW19............177 J4
Clivedon Ct *WEA* W13............97 H4
Clivedon Rd *CHING* E4............52 C1
Clive Rd *BELV* DA17............129 H4
  DUL SE21............162 E5
  EBED/NFELT TW14............153 K1
  EN EN1............24 C5
  ESH/CLAY KT10............204 B2
  GPK RM2............75 K2
  TWK TW1............156 A6
  WIM/MER SW19............178 D2
Clivesdale Dr *HYS/HAR* UB3............113 K1
Clive Wy *EN* EN1............24 C5
Cloak La *CANST* EC4R............12 D5
Clockhouse Av *BARK* IG11............90 C6
Clockhouse Cl *WIM/MER* SW19............159 F5
Clockhouse La *ASHF* TW15............152 D6
  CRW RM5............56 E3
Clock House Pde *PLMGR* N13 *............49 U1
Clockhouse Pl *PUT/ROE* SW15............139 H6
Clock House Rd *BECK* BR3............182 B6
Clock Pde *ENC/FH* EN2 *............23 K6
Clock Tower Ms *IS* N1 *............6 C1
  THMD SE28............109 H6
Clock Tower Pl *HOLWY* N7............84 E4
Clock Tower Rd *ISLW* TW7............136 A4
Cloister Cl *RAIN* RM13............111 K1
  TEDD TW11............174 C1
Cloister Gdns *EDGW* HA8............44 E5
  SNWD SE25............197 J3
Cloister Rd *ACT* W3............98 E4
  CRICK NW2............64 C6
Cloisters Av *HAYES* BR2............200 D3
Clonard Wy *PIN* HA5............42 A2
Clonbrock Rd *STNW/STAM* N16............86 A2
Cloncurry St *FUL/PGN* SW6............139 G3
Clonmel Cl *RYLN/HDSTN* HA2............60 D6
  TOTM N17............49 K6
Clonmel Rd *FUL/PGN* SW6............139 J2
  TEDD TW11............155 J3
Clonmore St
  WAND/EARL SW18............159 J3
Clonmore St *WAND/EARL* SW18............159 J3
Clorane Gdns *HAMP* NW3............82 E1
Closemead Cl *NTHWD* HA6............40 A2
The Close *ALP/SUD* HA0............80 A4
  BECK BR3............198 B1
  BUSH WD23 *............28 A1
  BXLY DA5............169 H1
  CAR SM5............209 J6

CHDH RM6............74 A3
CHEAM SM3............193 J4
CHING E4............52 A3
CHSWK W4............118 A5
EBAR EN4............33 K1
GNTH/NBYPK IG2............72 E3
ISLW TW7............135 J5
MTCM CR4............194 E1
NWMAL KT3............175 K5
PIN HA5............59 G4
PIN HA5............59 K4
RCH/KEW TW9............137 J4
RDART DA2............171 F5
SCUP DA14............186 C1
SNWD SE25............197 H3
STHGT/OAK N14............34 D2
STMC/STPC BR5............201 K3
SURB KT6............191 F4
TRDG/WHET N20............33 J4
WBLY HA9............80 C1
Cloth Ct *STBT* EC1A............12 A1
Cloth Fair *STBT* EC1A............12 B2
Clothier St *HDTCH* EC3A............13 H3
Cloth St *STBT* EC1A............12 C1
Clothworkers Rd
  WOOL/PLUM SE18............147 J1
Cloudesdale Rd *TOOT* SW17............161 G4
Cloudesley Pl *IS* N1............5 K1
Cloudesley Rd *BXLYHN* DA7............149 G2
  ERITH DA8............150 C2
  IS N1............5 K2
Cloudesley St *IS* N1............5 K1
Clouston Cl *WLGTN* SM6............210 E3
Clova Rd *FSTGT* E7............88 E4
Clove Crs *POP/IOD* E14............106 A6
Clovelly Av *CDALE/KGS* NW9............63 H1
  HGDN/ICK UB10............76 A2
Clovelly Cl *HGDN/ICK* UB10............76 A2
  PIN HA5............41 G6
Clovelly Gdns *EN* EN1............36 A2
  ROMW/RG RM7............56 D4
Clovelly Rd *BXLYHN* DA7............129 F6
  CEND/HSY/T N8............66 D1
  CHSWK W4 *............118 A2
  EA W5............116 D2
  HSLW TW3............135 F5
Clovelly Wy *ORP* BR6............202 A3
  RYLN/HDSTN HA2............59 J2
  WCHPL E1............104 E5
Clover Cl *WAN* E11............70 B1
Cloverdale Gdns *BFN/LL* DA15............168 A1
The Clover Fld *BUSH* WD23............27 K1
Clover Ms *CHEL* SW3 *............120 F6
Clover Wy *WLGTN* SM6............195 G5
Clove St *PLSTW* E13............106 E3
Clowders Rd *CAT* SE6............164 C5
Clowser Cl *SUT* SM1............209 G3
Cloysters Gn *WAP* E1W *............123 H1
Cloyster Wd *EDGW* HA8............43 K3
Club Gardens Rd *HAYES* BR2............199 K4
Club Rw *BETH* E2............7 J6
The Clumps *ASHF* TW15............153 G6
Clunbury Av *NWDGN* UB2............114 E5
Clunbury St *IS* N1............7 F3
Cluny Est *STHWK* SE1............19 G4
Cluny Ms *ECT* SW5............119 K4
Cluny Pl *STHWK* SE1............19 G4
Clutton St *POP/IOD* E14............105 K4
Clydach Rd *EN* EN1............24 C5
Clyde Circ *SEVS/STOTM* N15............68 A1
Clyde Ct *CAMTN* NW1............4 D2
Clyde Flats *FUL/PGN* SW6 *............139 J1
Clyde Pl *LEY* E10............69 K4
Clyde Rd *CROY/NA* CR0............197 G6
  SEVS/STOTM N15............68 A1
  STWL/WRAY TW19............152 A3
  SUT SM1............208 E3
  WDGN N22............48 D4
  WLGTN SM6............210 C3
Clydesdale *PEND* EN3............25 F5
Clydesdale Av *STAN* HA7............43 K6
Clydesdale Cl *ISLW* TW7............136 A4
Clydesdale Gdns
  RCHPK/HAM TW10............137 J5
Clydesdale Rd *EMPK* RM11............75 H4
  NTGHL W11............100 D5
Clyde St *DEPT* SE8............124 C6
Clyde Ter *FSTH* SE23............163 K4
Clyde V *FSTH* SE23............163 K4
Clyfford Rd *RSLP* HA4............76 D2
Clymping Dene
  EBED/NFELT TW14............154 A2
Clyston Rd *WATW* WD18............26 D1
Clyston St *VX/NE* SW8............141 H3
Coach & Horses Yd
  CONDST W1S............9 K5
Coach House La *HBRY* N5............85 H2
  WIM/MER SW19............159 G6
Coach House Ms *FSTH* SE23............164 A2
  NWCR SE14 *............144 A2
Coach House Yd
  WAND/EARL SW18 *............140 A5
Coalecroft Rd *PUT/ROE* SW15............139 F5
Coal Post Cl *ORP* BR6 *............217 F5
Coates Av *WAND/EARL* SW18............160 D1
Coates Cl *THHTH* CR7............180 D6
Coates Hill Rd *BMLY* BR1............185 F5
Coates Rd *BORE* WD6............29 G1
Coate St *BETH* E2............104 C1
Cobalt Cl *BECK* BR3............198 A1
Cobbett Rd *ELTH/MOT* SE9............146 D4
  WHTN TW2............155 F3
Cobbetts Av *REDBR* IG4............71 H2
Cobbett St *VX/NE* SW8............142 A1
Cobble La *IS* N1............85 H5
Cobble Ms *HBRY* N5............85 J1
Cobbler's Wk *TEDD* TW11............173 K5
Cobblestone Pl *CROY/NA* CR0............196 D5
Cobbold Ms *SHB* W12 *............118 C2
Cobbold Rd *SHB* W12............118 C2
  WAN E11............88 C1
  WLSDN NW10............81 H4
Cobb's Rd *HSLWW* TW4............134 E5
Cobb St *WCHPL* E1............13 J2
Cobden Ms *SYD* SE26............181 J1
Cobden Rd *ORP* BR6............216 D2
  SNWD SE25............197 H2

WAN E11............88 C1
Cobham Av *NWMAL* KT5............192 D2
Cobham Cl *BFN/LL* DA15............168 C1
  BTSEA SW11............160 D1
  EDGW HA8............44 D5
  EN EN1............24 E6
  HAYES BR2............200 D4
  WLGTN SM6............210 E4
Cobham Ms *CAMTN* NW1............84 D6
Cobham Pl *BXLYHN* DA6............148 E6
Cobham Rd *GDMY/SEVK* IG3............90 E1
  HEST TW5............134 B1
  KUT/HW KT1............175 H5
  WALTH E17............52 A4
Cobland Rd *LEE/GVPK* SE12............166 B6
Coborn Rd *BOW* E3............105 H2
Coborn St *BOW* E3............105 H2
Cobourg Rd *CMBW* SE5............123 G6
Cobourg St *CAMTN* NW1............4 B5
Coburg Cl *WEST* SW1P............16 B6
Coburg Crs *BRXS/STRHM* SW2............162 A3
Coburg Dwellings *WCHPL* E1 *............104 E6
Coburg Gdns *CLAY* IG5............53 H5
Coburg Rd *WDGN* N22............49 F5
Cochrane Ms *STJWD* NW8............2 B2
Cochrane Rd *WIM/MER* SW19............177 H3
Cochrane St *STJWD* NW8............2 B2
Cockcrow Hi *SURB* KT6 *............190 E5
Cockerell Rd *WALTH* E17............69 G4
Cockfosters Pde *EBAR* EN4 *............22 A5
Cockfosters Rd *EBAR* EN4............22 A5
Cock La *STBT* EC1A............12 A2
Cockmannings La
  STMC/STPC BR5............202 E5
Cockmannings Rd
  STMC/STPC BR5............202 E5
Cocks Crs *NWMAL* KT3............192 C1
Cockpit Av *ORP* BR6............216 E4
Cockpit Yd *CWALL* SW1A............10 D7
Cockspur St *STJS* SW1Y............10 D7
Cocksure La *SCUP* DA14............169 H6
The Coda Centre
  FUL/PGN SW6 *............139 H2
Code St *WCHPL* E1............7 K7
Codling Cl *WAP* E1W............123 H1
Codling Wy *ALP/SUD* HA0............79 K2
Codrington Hi *FSTH* SE23............164 B2
Codrington Ms *NTGHL* W11............100 C5
Cody Cl *KTN/HRWW/WS* HA3............43 K6
  WLGTN SM6............210 D5
Cody Rd *CAN/RD* E16............106 B3
  SEVS/STOTM N15 *............197 H3
Coe's Alley *BAR* EN5............20 C5
Coffey St *DEPT* SE8............144 D1
Cogan Av *WALTH* E17............51 G4
Coin St *STHWK* SE1............17 K1
Coity Rd *KTTN* NW5............84 A4
Coke St *WCHPL* E1............104 C5
Cokers La *DUL* SE21............162 D3
Colas Ms *KIL/WHAMP* NW6............82 E6
Colbeck Ms *SKENS* SW7............120 A4
Colbeck Rd *HRW* HA1............60 C4
Colberg Pl *STNW/STAM* N16 *............68 A4
Colborne Wy *WPK* KT4............208 A1
Colbrook Av *HYS/HAR* UB3............113 G3
Colbrook Cl *HYS/HAR* UB3............113 G3
Colburn Av *PIN* HA5............41 K3
Colburn Wy *SUT* SM1............209 H1
Colby Rd *NRWD* SE19............181 F1
  WOT/HER KT12............188 A4
Colchester Dr *PIN* HA5............59 H2
Colchester Rd *EDGW* HA8............44 E4
  LEY E10............70 A4
  NTHWD HA6............40 E6
  WALTH E17............69 J3
Colchester St *WCHPL* E1............13 K3
Coldbath Sq *CLKNW* EC1R............5 J6
Coldbath St *LEW* SE13............144 E3
Cold Blow Crs *BXLY* DA5............170 A3
Cold Blow La *NWCR* SE14............144 A1
Coldershaw Rd *WEA* W13............116 B2
Coldfall Av *MUSWH* N10............47 K5
Coldharbour *POP/IOD* E14............125 F1
Coldharbour Crest
  ELTH/MOT SE9 *............167 F5
Coldharbour La *BRXN/ST* SW9............142 B5
  BUSH WD23............28 B1
  HYS/HAR UB3............113 K1
  RAIN RM13............130 D1
Coldharbour Pl *CMBW* SE5............142 D3
Coldharbour Rd *CROY/NA* CR0............211 G3
Coldharbour Wy
  CROY/NA CR0............211 G3
Coldstream Gdns
  WAND/EARL SW18............159 J1
Colebeck Ms *IS* N1............85 H4
Colebert Av *WCHPL* E1............104 E3
Colebrook Cl *MLHL* NW7............46 B3
  PUT/ROE SW15............159 G1
Colebrooke Dr *WAN* E11............71 G4
Colebrooke Pl *IS* N1............6 B1
Colebrooke Rw *IS* N1............6 A3
Colebrook Rd *STRHM/NOR* SW16............179 K4
Colebrook Wy *FBAR/BDGN* N11............48 B1
Coleby Pth *CMBW* SE5 *............142 E1
Cole Cl *THMD* SE28............128 C1
Coledale Dr *STAN* HA7............43 J4
Coleford Rd *WAND/EARL* SW18............140 B6
Cole Gdns *HEST* TW5............133 K2
Colegrave Rd *SRTFD* E15............88 B3
Colegrove Rd *PECK* SE15............123 G6
Coleherne Ms *WBPTN* SW10............120 A5
Coleherne Rd *WBPTN* SW10............120 A5
Colehill Gdns *FUL/PGN* SW6 *............139 H2
Colehill La *FUL/PGN* SW6............139 H1
Coleman Cl *SNWD* SE25............181 H5
Coleman Fds *IS* N1............6 C1
Coleman Rd *BELV* DA17............129 H4
  CMBW SE5............143 F1
Colemans Heath
  ELTH/MOT SE9............167 F5
Coleman St *CITYW* EC2V............12 E3
Colenso Dr *MLHL* NW7............45 J3
Colenso Rd *CLPT* E5............86 E2
  GNTH/NBYPK IG2............72 E2

Cole Park Rd *TWK* TW1............156 B2
Colepits Wood Rd
  ELTH/MOT SE9............147 J6
Coleraine Rd *BKHTH/KID* SE3............125 J6
  CEND/HSY/T N8............49 G5
  SUT SM1............209 J4
Coleridge Av *MNPK* E12............89 J4
  SUT SM1............209 K2
Coleridge Cl *VX/NE* SW8............141 G3
Coleridge Gdns
  KIL/WHAMP NW6............83 G5
  WBPTN SW10............140 B1
Coleridge Rd *ASHF* TW15............152 B6
  CEND/HSY/T N8............66 D3
  CROY/NA CR0............197 K4
  DART DA1............151 K5
  FSBYPK N4............67 G6
  HARH RM3............57 K3
  NFNCH/WDSPK N12............47 G1
  WALTH E17............69 H1
Coleridge Sq *WEA* W13............97 G5
Coleridge Wy *GLDGN* NW11............64 E1
  ORP BR6............202 B5
  WDR/YW UB7............112 C4
  YEAD UB4............94 E5
Cole Rd *TWK* TW1............156 B1
Colesburg Rd *BECK* BR3............182 C6
Coles Crs *RYLN/HDSTN* HA2............60 B6
Coles Gn *BUSH* WD23............28 C3
Coles Green Rd *CRICK* NW2............63 K5
Coleshill Rd *TEDD* TW11............173 K2
Colestown St *BTSEA* SW11............140 D3
Colet Cl *PLMGR* N13............49 H2
Colet Gdns *WKENS* W14............119 G5
Coley St *FSBYW* WC1X............5 H7
Colfe & Hatcliffe Glebe
  LEW SE13 *............144 E6
Colfe Rd *FSTH* SE23............164 B3
Colham Av *WDR/YW* UB7............112 B1
Colham Mill Rd *WDR/YW* UB7............112 A2
Colina Ms *SEVS/STOTM* N15............67 H2
Colina Rd *CEND/HSY/T* N8............67 H2
Colin Cl *CDALE/KGS* NW9............63 G1
  CROY/NA CR0............213 H1
  WWKM BR4............214 D1
Colin Crs *CDALE/KGS* NW9............63 H1
Colindale Av *CDALE/KGS* NW9............45 F6
Colindeep Gdns *HDN* NW4............63 J2
Colindeep La *CDALE/KGS* NW9............63 H1
Colin Dr *CDALE/KGS* NW9............63 H2
Colinette Rd *PUT/ROE* SW15............139 F5
Colin Gdns *CDALE/KGS* NW9............63 H2
Colin Park Rd *CDALE/KGS* NW9............63 G1
Colinton Rd *GDMY/SEVK* IG3............73 H6
Coliston Rd *WAND/EARL* SW18............159 K2
Collamore Av
  WAND/EARL SW18............160 D3
Collapit Cl *HRW* HA1............60 B3
Collard Pl *CAMTN* NW1............84 B5
College Ap *GNWCH* SE10............125 F6
College Av *KTN/HRWW/WS* HA3............42 E5
  UED N18............50 B1
  WHTN TW2............155 J3
College Cl *EA* W5............98 A6
  WBPTN SW10............140 B1
College Crs *HAMP* NW3............83 G4
  UED N18............50 B1
College Dr *RSLP* HA4............58 E4
  THDIT KT7............189 K4
College East *WCHPL* E1 *............13 K2
College Gdns *CHING* E4............37 K2
  ENC/FH EN2............23 J2
  NWMAL KT3............192 C2
  REDBR IG4............71 J3
  TOOT SW17............160 D4
  UED N18 *............50 B1
College Gn *NRWD* SE19............181 F3
College Gv *CAMTN* NW1............4 C1
College HI *CANST* EC4R............12 D5
College Hill Rd
  KTN/HRWW/WS HA3............42 E3
College La *KTTN* NW5............84 B2
College Ms *IS* N1............85 G5
  WEST SW1P............16 E4
College Pde *KIL/WHAMP* NW6 *............82 C6
College Park Cl *LEW* SE13............145 G5
College Pl *CAMTN* NW1............84 C6
  WALTH E17 *............70 C1
  WBPTN SW10 *............140 B1
College Rd *BMLY* BR1............183 K4
  CHING E4............38 A2
  DUL SE21............163 F2
  ENC/FH EN2............23 J2
  HRW HA1............60 E3
  ISLW TW7............136 A2
  KTN/HRWW/WS HA3............42 E4
  TOTM N17............50 B2
  WALTH E17............70 C1
  WBLY HA9............61 K5
  WCHMH N21............35 G4
  WEA W13............97 H5
  WIM/MER SW19............178 C2
  WLSDN NW10............100 A1
College St *CANST* EC4R............12 D5
College Ter *FNCH* N3............46 D4
College Vw *ELTH/MOT* SE9............166 C3
College Wy *ASHF* TW15............152 C6
  HYS/HAR UB3............94 E6
  NTHWD HA6............40 D5
College Yd *KIL/WHAMP* NW6 *............82 C6
  KTTN NW5............84 B3
Colless Rd *SEVS/STOTM* N15............68 B2
Collett Rd *BERM/RHTH* SE16............123 H3
Collett Wy *NWDGN* UB2............115 G2
Collier Cl *EHAM* E6............108 B6
  HOR/WEW KT19............206 C4
Collier Dr *EDGW* HA8............44 C5
Collier Row La *CRW* RM5............56 D1
Collier Row Rd *CRW* RM5............56 B4
Colliers Shaw *HAYES* BR2............215 J3
Collier St *IS* N1............5 G3
Colliers Water La *THHTH* CR7............196 C1
Collindale Av *BFN/LL* DA15............168 B3
  CDALE/KGS NW9............45 G6
  ERITH DA8............129 J6
Collingbourne Rd *SHB* W12............118 E1

Collingham Gdns *ECT* SW5 ....120 A4
Collingham Pl *ECT* SW5 ....120 A4
Collingham Rd *ECT* SW5 ....120 A4
Collings Cl *WDGN* N22 ....49 F2
Collington St *GNWCH* SE10 * 125 K6
Collingtree Rd *SYD* SE26 ....165 K6
Collingwood Av *BRYLDS* KT5 ....191 K5
  MUSWH N10 ....48 A6
Colling Wood Cl *PGE/AN* SE20....181 J4
Collingwood Cl *WHTN* TW2 ....155 F2
Collingwood Rd *MTCM* CR4 ....178 D5
  RAIN RM13 ....111 H1
  SEVS/STOTM N15 ....68 A1
  SUT SM1 ....208 E2
Collingwood St *WCHPL* E1 ....104 D3
Collins Av *STAN* HA7 ....44 A5
Collins Dr *RSLP* HA4 ....59 G6
Collins St *STHWK* SE1 ....18 C3
Collinson Wk *STHWK* SE1 ....18 C3
Collins Sq *BKHTH/KID* SE3 ....145 J3
Collins St *BKHTH/KID* SE3 ....145 H3
Collinwood Av *PEND* EN3 ....24 E4
Collinwood Gdns
  GNTH/NBYPK IG2 ....71 K2
Collyer Av *CROY/NA* CR0 ....210 D2
Collyer Pl *PECK* SE15 ....143 H2
Collyer Rd *CROY/NA* CR0 ....210 D2
Colman Pde *EN* EN1 * 24 A4
Colman Rd *CAN/RD* E16 ....107 G4
Colmar Cl *WCHPL* E1 ....105 F3
Colmer Pl *KTN/HRWW/WS* HA3 ....42 D3
Colmer Rd *STRHM/NOR* SW16 .....179 K3
Colmore Ms *PECK* SE15 ....143 J2
Colmore Rd *PEND* EN3 ....24 E5
Colnbrook St *STHWK* SE1 * 18 A5
Colne Av *OXHEY* WD19 ....27 F1
Colne Ct *HOR/WEW* KT19 ....206 E2
Colne Rd *CLPT* E5 ....87 G2
  WCHMH N21 ....35 K2
  WHTN TW2 ....155 K3
Colne St *PLSTW* E13 ....106 E2
Colney Hatch La
  FBAR/BDGN N11 ....47 K2
  MUSWH N10 ....48 A3
Coney Rd *DART* DA1 ....171 J1
Cologne Rd *BTSEA* SW11 ....140 C5
Colombo Rd *IL* IG1 ....72 C5
Colombo St *STHWK* SE1 ....18 A1
Colonels Wk *ENC/FH* EN2 ....23 H5
Colonial Av *WHTN* TW2 ....155 H1
Colonial Dr *CHSWK* W4 ....117 K4
Colonnade *BMSBY* WC1N 4 E7
Colonnade Rd *EBED/NFELT* TW14 .153 H2
Colonnade Wk *STHWK* SE1 * 6 A2
The Colonnade *DEPT* SE8 * 124 C4
Colosseum Ter *CAMTN* NW1 * 3 K6
Colson Rd *CROY/NA* CR0 ....196 E6
Colson Wy *STRHM/NOR* SW16 .....161 H6
Colsterworth Rd
  SEVS/STOTM N15 ....68 B1
Colston Av *CAR* SM5 ....209 J2
Colston Rd *FSTGT* E7 ....89 H4
  MORT/ESHN SW14 ....137 K5
Colthurst Crs *FSBYPK* N4 ....67 J6
Colthurst Dr *ED* N9 ....36 D5
Coltness Crs *ABYW* SE2 ....128 C5
Colton Gdns *TOTM* N17 ....49 J6
Colton Rd *HRW* HA1 ....60 E2
Coltsfoot Dr *WAN* E11 ....70 D5
Columbas Dr *HAMP* NW3 ....65 H6
Columbia Av *EDGW* HA8 ....44 D4
  RSLP HA4 ....41 K6
  WPK KT4 ....192 C4
Columbia Rd *BETH* E2 ....7 K4
  PLSTW E13 * 106 D3
Columbia Whf *PEND* EN3 * 25 G6
Columbine Av *EHAM* E6 ....107 J4
  SAND/SEL CR2 ....211 H5
Columbine Wy *LEW* SE13 * 145 F3
Columbus Gdns *NTHWD* HA6 ....40 E4
Colveiw Ct *ELTH/MOT* SE9 ....166 C3
Colvestone Crs *HACK* E8 ....86 B3
Colville Est *IS* N1 * 7 F1
Colville Gdns *NTGHL* W11 ....100 D5
Colville Houses *NTGHL* W11 * 100 D5
Colville Ms *NTGHL* W11 ....100 D5
Colville Pl *FITZ* W1T 10 B2
Colville Rd *ACT* W3 ....117 J3
  ED N9 ....36 D3
  NTGHL W11 ....100 D5
  WALTH E17 ....51 G5
  WAN E11 ....88 A1
Colville Sq *NTGHL* W11 ....100 D5
Colville Square Ms
  NTGHL W11 * 100 D5
Colville Ter *NTGHL* W11 ....100 D5
Colvin Cl *SYD* SE26 ....181 K1
Colvin Gdns *BARK/HLT* IG6 ....54 C3
  CHING E4 ....38 A5
  SWFD E18 ....71 F1
Colvin Rd *EHAM* E6 ....89 J5
  THHTH CR7 ....196 B3
Colwall Gdns *WFD* IG8 ....52 E1
Colwell Rd *EDUL* SE22 ....143 G6
Colwick Cl *HGT* N6 ....66 D4
Colwith Rd *HMSMTH* W6 ....119 F6
Colwood Gdns
  WIM/MER SW19 ....178 D3
Colworth Gv *WALW* SE17 * 18 D7
Colworth Rd *CROY/NA* CR0 ....197 H5
  WAN E11 ....70 C3
Colwyn Av *GFD/PVL* UB6 ....97 F1
Colwyn Cl *STRHM/NOR* SW16 ......179 H1
Colwyn Crs *HSLW* TW3 ....135 H2
Colwyn Gn *NTHLT* UB5 * 95 H1
Colwyn Rd *CRICK* NW2 ....81 K1
Colyer Cl *ELTH/MOT* SE9 ....167 G4
Colyer Cl *ERITH* DA8 ....149 K2
Colyers La *ERITH* DA8 ....149 J2
  WELL DA16 ....148 A2
Colyton Cl *ALP/SUD* HA0 ....79 J4
Colyton La *STRHM/NOR* SW16 ......180 B1
Colyton Rd *EDUL* SE22 ....143 J6
Colyton Wy *UED* N18 ....50 C1
Combe Av *BKHTH/KID* SE3 ....145 J1
Combedale Rd *GNWCH* SE10 ....125 K5

Combemartin Rd
  WAND/EARL SW18 ....159 H2
Comber Cl *CRICK* NW2 ....63 K6
Comber Gv *CMBW* SE5 ....142 D1
Combermere Rd
  BRXN/ST SW9 ....142 A4
  MRDN SM4 ....194 A1
Combe Rd *WATW* WD18 ....26 D1
Comberton Rd *CLPT* E5 ....68 D6
Combeside *WOOL/PLUM* SE18 ......148 A1
Combes Rd *DAGW* RM9 ....92 B6
Combwell Crs *ABYW* SE2 ....128 B3
Comely Bank Rd *WALTH* E17 ....70 A2
Comeragh Ms *WKENS* W14 ....119 H5
Comeragh Rd *WKENS* W14 ....119 H5
Comerford Rd *BROCKY* SE4 ....144 B5
Comet Cl *MNPK* E12 ....89 H2
  PUR RM19 ....131 K4
Comet Pl *DEPT* SE8 ....144 D1
Comet Rd *STWL/WRAY* TW19 ....152 A2
Comet St *DEPT* SE8 ....144 D1
Commerce Rd *BTFD* TW8 ....116 D6
  WDGN N22 ....49 F4
Commerce Wy *CROY/NA* CR0 ....211 F1
Commercial Rd *POP/IOD* E14 ....105 G5
  UED N18 ....50 A1
  WCHPL E1 ....104 C5
Commercial St *WCHPL* E1 ....13 J2
Commercial Wy *PECK* SE15 ....143 H1
  WLSDN NW10 ....98 D1
Commerell St *GNWCH* SE10 ....125 H5
Commerell St *GNWCH* SE10 ....125 H5
Commodore Pde
  STRHM/NOR SW16 * 180 A5
Commodore St *WCHPL* E1 ....105 G3
Commonade *PUT/ROE* SW15 ....139 F3
Common La *ESH/CLAY* KT10 ....205 G5
  RDART DA2 ....170 D4
Common Rd *BARN* SW13 ....138 D4
  ESH/CLAY KT10 ....204 B2
  STAN HA7 ....28 D5
Commonside *HAYES* BR2 ....215 G2
Commonside East *MTCM* CR4 ....179 F6
Commonside West *MTCM* CR4 ....179 F6
The Common *EA* W5 ....117 F1
  NWDGN UB2 ....114 C4
  SRTFD E15 ....88 C5
  STAN HA7 ....29 F4
Commonwealth Av
  HAYES UB3 ....94 B5
  SHB W12 ....99 K6
Commonwealth Rd *TOTM* N17 ....50 C3
Commonwealth Wy
  ABYW SE2 ....128 C5
Community Cl *HEST* TW5 ....134 A2
Community La *HOLWY* N7 ....84 D3
Community Rd *GFD/PVL* UB6 ....78 C6
  SRTFD E15 ....88 B3
Como Rd *FSTH* SE23 ....164 B4
Como St *ROMW/RG* RM7 ....75 F2
Compass Cl *EDGW* HA8 ....30 A4
Compass Hl *RCHPK/HAM* TW10 ...156 E1
Compayne Gdns
  KIL/WHAMP NW6 ....83 F4
Compton Av *ALP/SUD* HA0 ....79 F2
  EHAM E6 ....107 H1
  HGT N6 ....65 J4
  IS N1 ....85 H5
Compton Cl *CAMTN* NW1 ....3 K5
  EDGW HA8 * 44 E3
  ESH/CLAY KT10 ....204 D4
  GLDGN NW11 ....82 B1
  PECK SE15 ....143 H1
  WEA W13 ....97 G5
Compton Crs *CHSGTN* KT9 ....206 A4
  CHSWK W4 ....117 K6
  NTHLT UB5 ....77 H6
  TOTM N17 ....49 J3
Compton Pas *FSBYE* EC1V 6 B6
Compton Pl *ERITH* DA8 ....130 C6
  OXHEY WD19 ....27 J6
  STPAN WC1H 4 E6
Compton Ri *PIN* HA5 ....59 J2
Compton Rd *CROY/NA* CR0 ....197 J6
  HYS/HAR UB3 * 94 A4
  IS N1 ....85 H5
  WCHMH N21 ....35 H5
  WIM/MER SW19 ....177 H2
  WLSDN NW10 ....100 B2
Compton St *FSBYE* EC1V 6 A6
Compton Ter *IS* N1 ....85 H4
  WCHMH N21 * 35 G3
Comreddy Cl *ENC/FH* EN2 ....23 H2
Comus Pl *WALW* SE17 ....19 G7
Comyn Rd *BTSEA* SW11 ....140 D5
Comyns Cl *CAN/RD* E16 ....106 D4
Comyns Rd *DAGW* RM9 ....92 C5
The Comyns *BUSH* WD23 ....28 C3
Conant Ms *WCHPL* E1 ....104 C6
Concanon Rd
  BRXS/STRHM SW2 ....142 A5
Concert Hall Ap *STHWK* SE1 * 17 H1
Concord Cl *NTHLT* UB5 ....95 H2
Concorde Cl *HSLW* TW3 ....135 G3
Concorde Dr *EHAM* E6 ....107 K4
Concord Rd *ACT* W3 ....98 D3
  PEND EN3 ....25 F6
Concord Wy *BERM/RHTH* SE16 .....124 A4
Condell Rd *VX/NE* SW8 ....141 H2
Conder St *POP/IOD* E14 ....105 G5
Condover Crs
  WOOL/PLUM SE18 ....147 G1
Condray Pl *BTSEA* SW11 ....140 D1
Conduit Av *GNWCH* SE10 ....145 G1
Conduit La *SAND/SEL* CR2 ....212 C3
  UED N18 ....50 E1
Conduit Ms *BAY/PAD* W2 ....8 B5
  WOOL/PLUM SE18 ....127 G5
Conduit Pas *BAY/PAD* W2 ....8 A4
Conduit Pl *BAY/PAD* W2 ....8 B5
Conduit Rd *WOOL/PLUM* SE18 .....127 G5
Conduit St *CONDST* W1S 9 K5
Conduit Wy *WLSDN* NW10 ....80 E5
Conewood St *HBRY* N5 ....85 H1
Coney Burrows *CHING* E4 ....38 C4
Coney Hall Pde *WWKM* BR4 ....214 C1
Coney Hill Rd *WWKM* BR4 ....199 H6

Coney Wy *VX/NE* SW8 ....122 A6
Conference Cl *CHING* E4 ....38 A4
Conference Rd *ABYW* SE2 ....128 D4
Congleton Gv
  WOOL/PLUM SE18 ....127 H5
Congo Dr *ED* N9 ....36 E5
Congo Rd *WOOL/PLUM* SE18 ....127 J5
Congress Rd *ABYW* SE2 ....128 D4
Congreve Rd *ELTH/MOT* SE9 ....146 E4
Congreve St *WALW* SE17 ....19 G7
Conical Cnr *ENC/FH* EN2 ....23 J3
Conifer Av *CRW* RM5 ....56 D1
Conifer Cl *ORP* BR6 ....216 D2
Conifer Gdns *EN* EN1 ....35 K1
  STRHM/NOR SW16 ....162 A5
  SUT SM1 ....194 E6
Conifers Cl *TEDD* TW11 ....174 B3
Conifer Wy *ALP/SUD* HA0 ....79 J1
  HYS/HAR UB3 ....94 E6
  SWLY BR8 ....187 J6
Conigar Rd *FUL/PGN* SW6 ....139 K3
Coningham Ms *SHB* W12 ....118 D1
Coningham Rd *SHB* W12 ....118 E2
Coningsby Av *CDALE/KGS* NW9 .....45 G1
Coningsby Cottages *EA* W5 ....116 E2
Coningsby Gdns *CHING* E4 ....51 K2
Coningsby Rd *EA* W5 ....116 E2
  FSBYPK N4 ....67 H4
  SAND/SEL CR2 ....211 J6
Conington Rd *LEW* SE13 ....144 E3
Conisbee Ct *STHGT/OAK* N14 ....22 C6
Conisborough Crs *CAT* SE6 ....165 F5
Coniscliffe Cl *CHST* BR7 ....185 F4
Coniscliffe Rd *PLMGR* N13 ....35 J5
Coniston Av *BARK* IG11 ....90 E5
  GFD/PVL UB6 ....96 E2
  WELL DA16 ....147 K4
Coniston Cl *BARN* SW13 ....138 C1
  BXLYHN DA7 ....149 K2
  CHSWK W4 ....137 K3
  DART DA1 ....170 C3
  ERITH DA8 ....150 B1
  MRDN SM4 ....193 G3
Coniston Ct *BAY/PAD* W2 * 8 C4
  BXLYHN DA7 ....149 K2
  CROY/NA CR0 ....197 H4
  TOTM N17 * 50 C2
  WHTN TW2 ....155 C1
Coniston Gdns *BELMT* SM2 * 209 H4
  CDALE/KGS NW9 ....63 H2
  ED N9 ....36 E3
  PIN HA5 ....58 E1
  REDBR IG4 ....71 J1
  WBLY HA9 ....61 J5
Coniston Rd *BMLY* BR1 ....183 H2
  BXLYHN DA7 ....149 K2
  CROY/NA CR0 ....197 H4
  TOTM N17 ....50 C2
  WHTN TW2 ....155 C1
Coniston Wk *HOM* E9 ....86 E3
Coniston Wy *CHSGTN* KT9 ....206 A1
  HCH RM12 ....93 J3
Conistone Wy *HOLWY* N7 ....84 E5
Conlan St *NKENS* W10 ....100 C3
Conley Rd *WLSDN* NW10 ....81 F4
Conley St *GNWCH* SE10 ....125 H5
Connaught Av *ASHF* TW15 ....152 B6
  CHING E4 ....38 B2
  EBAR EN4 ....33 K5
  EN EN1 ....24 A3
  HSLWW TW4 ....134 D6
  MORT/ESHN SW14 ....137 K5
Connaught Br *CAN/RD* E16 ....126 C1
Connaught Cl *BAY/PAD* W2 ....8 D5
  EN EN1 ....24 A3
  LEY E10 ....69 G6
  SUT SM1 ....194 E6
  UX/CGN UB8 * 94 A4
Connaught Dr *GLDGN* NW11 ....64 E1
Connaught Gdns *MRDN* SM4 ....194 B2
  MUSWH N10 ....66 B1
  PLMGR N13 ....35 H3
Connaught La *IL* IG1 ....72 C6
Connaught Ms *FUL/PGN* SW6 * 139 J2
  HAMP NW3 * 83 J2
  WOOL/PLUM SE18 ....127 F5
Connaught Rd *BAR* EN5 ....32 B1
  CAN/RD E16 ....126 C1
  CHING E4 ....38 C2
  FSBYPK N4 ....67 G4
  IL IG1 ....72 D6
  KTN/HRWW/WS HA3 ....42 E6
  NWMAL KT3 ....192 B1
  RCHPK/HAM TW10 * 137 G6
  SUT SM1 ....194 E6
  TEDD TW11 ....173 J1
  WALTH E17 * 69 J2
  WAN E11 ....70 B5
  WEA W13 ....97 G6
  WLSDN NW10 ....99 G1
Connaught Rbt *CAN/RD* E16 ....106 E6
Connaught Sq *BAY/PAD* W2 ....8 D4
Connaught St *BAY/PAD* W2 ....8 C4
Connaught Wy *PLMGR* N13 ....35 H3
Connell Crs *EA* W5 ....98 B3
Connemara Cl *BORE* WD6 * 30 E1
Connington Crs *CHING* E4 ....38 B5
Connop Rd *PEND* EN3 ....25 F1
Connor Cl *BARK/HLT* IG6 ....54 C5
  WAN E11 ....70 C5
Connor Rd *DAGW* RM9 ....92 B3
Connor St *HOM* E9 * 87 F6
Conolly Rd *HNWL* W7 ....115 K1
Conrad Dr *WPK* KT4 ....193 F5
Conroy Ct *SCUP* DA14 ....168 A6
Consfield Av *NWMAL* KT3 ....192 D1
Consort Cl *FBAR/BDGN* N11 * 47 J2
Consort Ms *ISLW* TW7 ....135 J6
Consort Rd *PECK* SE15 ....143 J3
Cons St *STHWK* SE1 ....17 K2
Constable Av *CAN/RD* E16 ....126 A1
Constable Cl *GLDGN* NW11 ....65 F3
  YEAD UB4 ....94 A1
Constable Crs *SEVS/STOTM* N15 ...68 C2
Constable Gdns *EDGW* HA8 ....44 C4
  ISLW TW7 ....135 K6
Constable Ms *BCTR* RM8 ....91 H1
Constance Crs *HAYES* BR2 ....199 J5
Constance Rd *CROY/NA* CR0 ....196 C4

Cooper's Rd *STHWK* SE1 ....123 G5
  Coopers Rw *TWRH* EC3N 13 J5
Cooper St *CAN/RD* E16 ....106 D4
Coopers Yd *IS* N1 * 85 H5
  NRWD SE19 ....181 F2
Coote Rd *BCTR* RM8 ....74 B6
  BXLYHN DA7 ....149 G2
Copeland Rd *PECK* SE15 ....143 H3
  WALTH E17 ....69 K2
Copeman Cl *SYD* SE26 ....181 K1
Copenhagen Gdns *CHEL* SW3 ....120 C6
  CHSWK W4 ....117 K3
Copenhagen Pl *POP/IOD* E14 ....105 H5
Copenhagen St *IS* N1 ....5 F1
Cope Pl *KENS* W8 ....119 K3
Copers Cope Rd *BECK* BR3 ....182 C2
Copers Cope Rd *BECK* BR3 ....182 C2
Copford Cl *WFD* IG8 ....53 J2
Copford Wk *IS* N1 * 85 J6
Copgate Pth
  STRHM/NOR SW16 ....180 A2
Copland Av *ALP/SUD* HA0 ....79 J3
Copland Cl *ALP/SUD* HA0 ....79 J3
Copland Ms *ALP/SUD* HA0 ....80 A4
Copland Rd *ALP/SUD* HA0 ....80 A4
Copleston Rd *PECK* SE15 ....143 G4
Copley Cl *HNWL* W7 * 97 J3
  WALW SE17 ....122 C6
Copley Dene *BMLY* BR1 ....184 C4
Copley Pk *STRHM/NOR* SW16 ......180 A2
Copley Rd *STAN* HA7 ....43 J1
Coppelia Rd *BKHTH/KID* SE3 ....145 J5
Coppen Rd *BCTR* RM8 ....74 B4
Copperas St *DEPT* SE8 ....124 E6
Copper Beech Cl *CLAY* IG5 ....54 A4
  STMC/STPC BR5 ....202 D2
Copper Cl *NRWD* SE19 ....181 G5
  TOTM N17 ....50 D3
Copperdale Rd *HYS/HAR* UB3 ....113 K2
Copperfield *BARK/HLT* IG6 * 54 C4
Copperfield Dr
  SEVS/STOTM N15 ....68 B1
Copperfield Rd *BOW* E3 ....105 G3
  THMD SE28 ....109 J5
Copperfield St *STHWK* SE1 ....18 B2
Copperfield Wy *CHST* BR7 ....185 J2
  PIN HA5 ....59 K3
Coppergate Cl *BMLY* BR1 ....184 A4
Coppermead Cl *CRICK* NW2 ....82 A1
Copper Mill Dr *ISLW* TW7 ....136 A3
Copper Mill La *TOOT* SW17 ....160 B6
Coppermill La *WALTH* E17 ....68 E3
Copper Rw *STHWK* SE1 ....19 J1
Coppetts Cl *NFNCH/WDSPK* N12 ...47 K3
Coppetts Rd *MUSWH* N10 ....47 K4
Coppice Cl *BECK* BR3 ....198 E2
  RSLP HA4 * 58 A3
  RYNPK SW20 ....177 F6
  STAN HA7 ....43 F2
Coppice Dr *PUT/ROE* SW15 ....158 D1
The Coppice *BAR* EN5 * 33 F7
  BXLY DA5 ....170 A5
  ENC/FH EN2 ....23 H5
  OXHEY WD19 ....27 G1
Coppice Wk *TRDG/WHET* N20 ....32 E5
Coppies Gv *FBAR/BDGN* N11 ....34 B6
Copping Cl *CROY/NA* CR0 ....212 A2
The Coppins *CROY/NA* CR0 ....213 K4
  KTN/HRWW/WS HA3 ....42 E3
Coppock Cl *BTSEA* SW11 ....140 D3
Coppsfield *E/WMO/HCT* KT8 ....173 F5
Copse Av *WWKM* BR4 ....213 K1
Copse Cl *CHARL* SE7 ....126 A6
  NTHWD HA6 ....40 A4
  WDR/YW UB7 ....112 A3
Copse Gld *SURB* KT6 ....190 E4
Copse Hill *BELMT* SM2 ....209 F5
  RYNPK SW20 ....176 E3
The Copse *CHING* E4 ....38 D3
  EFNCH N2 * 47 K6
Copse Vw *SAND/SEL* CR2 ....213 G6
Copsewood Cl *BFN/LL* DA15 ....167 K1
Copse Wood Wy *NTHWD* HA6 ....40 A4
Coptefield Dr *BELV* DA17 ....128 E3
Copthall Av *LOTH* EC2R 13 F3
Copthall Dr *MLHL* NW7 ....45 J3
Copthall Gdns *MLHL* NW7 ....45 J3
  TWK TW1 ....156 A3
Copthorne Av *BAL* SW12 ....161 J2
  BARK/HLT IG6 ....54 E2
  HAYES BR2 ....200 E6
Copthorne Ms *HYS/HAR* UB3 ....113 H4
Coptic St *NOXST/BSQ* WC1A 10 E3
Copwood Cl
  NFNCH/WDSPK N12 ....33 H6
Coral Cl *CHDH* RM6 ....55 H6
Coraline Cl *STHL* UB1 ....95 K2
Coralline Wk *ABYW* SE2 ....128 D2
Coral Rw *BTSEA* SW11 ....140 B4
Coral St *STHWK* SE1 ....17 K3
Coram St *BMSBY* WC1N 4 E7
Coran Cl *ED* N9 ....37 F2
Corban Rd *HSLW* TW3 ....135 F4
Corbar Cl *EBAR* EN4 ....21 H3
Corbet Cl *WLGTN* SM6 ....195 F6
Corbet Gv *FBAR/BDGN* N11 ....48 C3
Corbet Pl *WCHPL* E1 ....13 J1
  WAN E11 ....71 G5
Corbett's La *BERM/RHTH* SE16 ....123 K5
Corbicum *WAN* E11 ....70 C5
Corbiere Ct *WIM/MER* SW19 ....177 G2
Corbins La *RYLN/HDSTN* HA2 ....78 B1
Corbridge Crs *BETH* E2 ....92 D1
Corbridge Ms *ROM* RM1 ....75 H2
Corby Crs *ENC/FH* EN2 ....22 E5
Corby Rd *WLSDN* NW10 ....98 E1
Cordelia Cl *HNHL* SE24 ....142 C5
Cordelia Gdns
  STWL/WRAY TW19 ....152 B2

Cordelia Rd STWL/WRAY TW19 ... 152 B2
Cordelia St POP/IOD E14 ... 105 K5
Cordingley Rd RSLP HA4 ... 58 B6
Cording St POP/IOD E14 ... 105 K4
Cordwell Rd LEW SE13 ... 145 G6
Corelli Rd BKHTH/KID SE3 ... 146 D2
Corfe Av RYLN/HDSTN HA2 ... 78 A2
Corfe Cl HSLWW TW4 ... 154 D3
YEAD UB4 ... 95 G5
Corfield Rd WCHMH N21 ... 23 F6
Corfield St BETH E2 ... 104 D3
Corfton Rd EA W5 ... 98 A5
Coriander Av POP/IOD E14 ... 106 B5
Cories Cl BCTR RM8 ... 73 K6
Corinium Cl WBLY HA9 ... 80 B2
Corinne Rd ARCH N19 ... 84 C2
Corinthian Manorway
ERITH DA8 ... 130 A4
Corinthian Rd ERITH DA8 ... 130 A4
Corkran Rd SURB KT6 ... 190 E4
Cork St Ms CONDST W1S ... 10 A6
Corkscrew Hl WWKM BR4 ... 199 F6
Cork Sq WAP E1W ... 123 H1
Cork St CONDST W1S ... 10 A6
Cork Tree Wy CHING E4 ... 51 G1
Corlett St CAMTN NW1 ... 8 C1
Cormont Rd CMBW SE5 ... 142 C2
Cormorant Cl WALTH E17 ... 51 F4
Cormorant Rd FSTGT E7 ... 88 D3
Cornbury Rd EDGW HA8 ... 43 K3
Cornelia Dr YEAD UB4 ... 95 G4
Cornelia St HOLWY N7 ... 85 F4
Cornell Cl SCUP DA14 ... 187 F2
Cornell Wy CRW RM5 ... 56 D1
Corner Fielde
BRXS/STRHM SW2 * ... 162 A3
Corner Gn BKHTH/KID SE3 ... 145 K4
Corner Md CDALE/KGS NW9 ... 45 H3
The Corner EA W5 * ... 117 F1
Corney Reach Wy CHSWK W4 ... 138 C1
Corney Rd CHSWK W4 ... 118 B6
Cornflower La CROY/NA CR0 ... 198 A5
Cornflower Ter EDUL SE22 ... 163 J1
Cornford Cl HAYES BR2 ... 199 K2
Cornford Gv BAL SW12 ... 161 G4
Cornhill BANK EC3V ... 13 F4
Cornish Ct ED N9 ... 36 D2
Cornish Gv PGE/AN SE20 ... 181 J4
Corn Mill Dr ORP BR6 ... 202 A4
Cornmill La LEW SE13 ... 144 E4
Cornmow Dr WLSDN NW10 ... 81 H3
Cornshaw Rd BCTR RM8 ... 73 K5
Cornthwaite Rd CLPT E5 ... 86 E1
Cornwall Av BETH E2 ... 104 E2
ESH/CLAY KT10 ... 205 F5
FNCH N3 ... 46 E3
STHL UB1 ... 95 K4
WDGN N22 ... 48 E4
WELL DA16 ... 147 K4
Cornwall Cl BARK IG11 ... 91 F4
Cornwall Crs NTGHL W11 ... 100 C6
Cornwall Dr STMC/STPC BR5 ... 186 D3
Cornwall Gdns SKENS SW7 ... 120 A3
SNWD SE25 * ... 197 G1
WLSDN NW10 ... 81 K4
Cornwall Gardens Wk
KENS W8 ... 120 A3
Cornwall Gv CHSWK W4 ... 118 B5
Cornwallis Av ED N9 ... 36 E4
ELTH/MOT SE9 ... 167 J4
Cornwallis Cl ERITH DA8 ... 130 C6
Cornwallis Gv ED N9 ... 36 D4
Cornwallis Rd ARCH N19 ... 66 E6
DAGW RM9 ... 92 A2
ED N9 ... 36 D4
WALTH E17 ... 69 F1
WOOL/PLUM SE18 ... 127 H4
Cornwallis Sq ARCH N19 ... 66 E6
Cornwallis Wk ELTH/MOT SE9 ... 146 E4
Cornwall Ms South
SKENS SW7 ... 120 B3
Cornwall Ms West
SKENS SW7 * ... 120 A3
Cornwall Rd BELMT SM2 ... 208 D5
CROY/NA CR0 ... 196 C6
DART DA1 ... 151 J4
FSBYPK N4 ... 67 G4
HRW HA1 ... 60 C3
PIN HA5 ... 41 K3
RSLP HA4 ... 58 D6
SEVS/STOTM N15 ... 67 K2
STHWK SE1 ... 17 J1
TWK TW1 ... 156 B2
UED N18 ... 50 C1
Cornwall Sq LBTH SE11 * ... 122 B5
Cornwall St WCHPL E1 ... 104 D6
Cornwall Ter CAMTN NW1 ... 3 F7
Cornwall Terrace Ms
CAMTN NW1 ... 3 F7
Corn Wy WAN E11 ... 88 B1
Cornwood Cl EFNCH N2 ... 65 H2
Cornwood Dr WCHPL E1 ... 104 E5
Cornworthy Rd BCTR RM8 ... 91 J3
Corona Rd LEE/GVPK SE12 ... 165 K2
Coronation Cl BARK/HLT IG6 ... 72 D1
BXLY DA5 ... 168 E1
Coronation Dr HCH RM12 ... 93 K3
Coronation Rd HYS/HAR UB3 ... 113 J4
PLSTW E13 ... 107 H2
WLSDN NW10 ... 98 D3
Coronation Vls WLSDN NW10 * ... 98 D3
Coronet Pde ALP/SUD HA0 * ... 80 A4
Coronet St IS N1 ... 7 G5
Corporation Av HSLWW TW4 ... 134 D5
Corporation Rw CLKNW EC1R ... 5 K6
Corporation St HOLWY N7 ... 84 E3
SRTFD E15 ... 106 C1
Corrance Rd
BRXS/STRHM SW2 ... 141 K5
Corri Av STHGT/OAK N14 ... 34 D6
Corrib Dr SUT SM1 ... 209 J3
Corrigan Cl HDN NW4 ... 46 A6
Corringham Rd GLDGN NW11 ... 64 E4
WBLY HA9 ... 62 C6
Corringway EA W5 ... 98 B4
GLDGN NW11 ... 65 F4
Corris Gn CDALE/KGS NW9 * ... 63 G3
Corry Dr BRXN/ST SW9 ... 142 C5
Corsair Cl STWL/WRAY TW19 ... 152 A2
Corsair Rd STWL/WRAY TW19 ... 152 B2
Corscombe Cl KUTN/CMB KT2 ... 175 K1
Corsehill St STRHM/NOR SW16 ... 179 H2
Corsellis Sq TWK TW1 ... 136 C5
Corsham St IS N1 ... 7 F5
Corsica St HBRY N5 ... 85 H4
Cortayne Rd FUL/PGN SW6 * ... 139 J3
Cortina Dr DAGW RM9 ... 110 E2
Cortis Rd PUT/ROE SW15 ... 158 E1
Cortis Ter PUT/ROE SW15 ... 138 E6
Cortland Cl DART DA1 ... 170 B1
Corunna Rd VX/NE SW8 ... 141 H2
Corunna Ter VX/NE SW8 ... 141 H2
Corwell Gdns UX/CGN UB8 ... 94 A5
Corwell La UX/CGN UB8 ... 94 A5
Coryton Pth MV/WKIL W9 ... 100 D3
Cosbycote Av HNHL SE24 ... 142 D6
Cosdach Av WLGTN SM6 ... 210 D5
Cosedge Crs CROY/NA CR0 ... 211 G3
Cosgrove Cl WCHMH N21 ... 35 J4
YEAD UB4 ... 95 H3
Cosmo Pl BMSBY WC1N ... 11 F1
Cosmur Cl SHB W12 ... 118 C3
Cossall Wk PECK SE15 ... 143 J2
Cossar Ms BRXS/STRHM SW2 ... 162 B1
Cosser St STHWK SE1 ... 17 J4
Costa St PECK SE15 ... 143 H3
Costons Av GFD/PVL UB6 ... 96 D2
Costons La GFD/PVL UB6 ... 96 D2
Cosway St CAMTN NW1 ... 8 D1
Cotall St POP/IOD E14 ... 105 J5
Coteford Cl PIN HA5 ... 58 E2
Coteford St TOOT SW17 ... 160 E6
Cotelands CROY/NA CR0 ... 212 A1
Cotesbach Rd CLPT E5 ... 86 E1
Cotesmore Gdns BCTR RM8 ... 91 J2
Cotford Rd THHTH CR7 ... 196 D1
Cotham St WALW SE17 ... 18 D7
Cotherstone HOR/WEW KT19 ... 207 F6
Cotherstone Rd
BRXS/STRHM SW2 ... 162 A3
Cotleigh Av BXLY DA5 ... 168 E4
Cotleigh Rd KIL/WHAMP NW6 ... 82 E5
ROMW/RG RM7 ... 75 F3
Cotman Cl GLDGN NW11 ... 65 G3
Cotmandene Crs
STMC/STPC BR5 ... 186 C5
Cotmans Cl HYS/HAR UB3 ... 113 K1
Coton Rd WELL DA16 ... 148 B4
Cotsford Av NWMAL KT3 ... 191 K2
Cotswold Av BUSH WD23 ... 28 C1
Cotswold Cl BXLYHN DA7 ... 150 B3
ESH/CLAY KT10 ... 190 A6
KUTN/CMB KT2 ... 175 K2
Cotswold Gdns CRICK NW2 ... 64 B6
EHAM E6 ... 107 J1
GNTH/NBYPK IG2 ... 72 D4
Cotswold Ga CRICK NW2 ... 64 C5
Cotswold Gn ENC/FH EN2 ... 23 F5
Cotswold Ms BTSEA SW11 ... 140 C2
Cotswold Ri ORP BR6 ... 202 A3
Cotswold Rd HPTN TW12 ... 173 F2
Cotswold St WNWD SE27 ... 162 C6
Cotswold Wy ENC/FH EN2 ... 23 F4
WPK KT4 ... 193 F6
Cottage Av HAYES BR2 ... 200 D5
Cottage Cl RSLP HA4 ... 58 B5
RYLN/HDSTN HA2 ... 60 D6
Cottage Field Cl SCUP DA14 ... 168 D3
Cottage Gn CMBW SE5 ... 142 E1
Cottage Gv BRXN/ST SW9 ... 141 K4
SURB KT6 ... 190 E3
Cottage Pl CHEL SW3 ... 14 C4
Cottage Rd HOLWY N7 ... 85 F3
HOR/WEW KT19 ... 207 F5
The Cottages EDGW HA8 * ... 44 D3
Cottage St POP/IOD E14 ... 105 K6
Cottenham Dr CDALE/KGS NW9 ... 45 H6
RYNPK SW20 ... 176 E3
Cottenham Park Rd
RYNPK SW20 ... 176 E4
Cottenham Pl RYNPK SW20 ... 176 E3
Cottenham Rd WALTH E17 ... 69 H1
Cotterill Rd SURB KT6 ... 191 G6
Cottesbrook St NWCR SE14 ... 144 B1
Cottesloe Ms STHWK SE1 ... 17 K4
Cottesmore Av CLAY IG5 ... 53 K5
Cottesmore Gdns KENS W8 ... 120 A3
Cottimore Av WOT/HER KT12 ... 188 A5
Cottimore Crs WOT/HER KT12 ... 188 A4
Cottimore La WOT/HER KT12 ... 188 B5
Cottimore Ter WOT/HER KT12 ... 188 A4
Cottingham Cha RSLP HA4 ... 76 E1
Cottingham Rd PGE/AN SE20 ... 182 A3
VX/NE SW8 ... 142 A1
Cottington Rd FELT TW13 ... 154 C6
Cottington St LBTH SE11 ... 122 B5
Cotton Av ACT W3 ... 99 F5
Cotton Cl DAGW RM9 ... 91 J5
WAN E11 ... 70 C6
Cotton Gardens Est LBTH SE11 ... 18 A7
Cottongrass Cl CROY/NA CR0 ... 198 A5
Cotton Hl BMLY BR1 ... 165 G6
Cotton Rw BTSEA SW11 ... 140 C4
Cottons Ap ROMW/RG RM7 ... 75 F2
Cottons Centre STHWK SE1 ... 13 G7
Cotton's Gdns BETH E2 ... 7 H4
Cotton St POP/IOD E14 ... 106 A6
Couchmore Av CLAY IG5 ... 53 K6
ESH/CLAY KT10 ... 189 K6
Coulgate St BROCKY SE4 ... 144 B4
Coulson Cl BCTR RM8 ... 73 J5
Coulson St CHEL SW3 ... 120 E5
Coulter Cl YEAD UB4 ... 95 J3
Coulter Rd HMSMTH W6 ... 118 E3
Councillor St CMBW SE5 ... 142 D1
Counter St STHWK SE1 ... 13 G7
Countess Rd KTTN NW5 ... 84 C3
Countisbury Av EN EN1 ... 36 B2
Country Wy FELT TW13 ... 172 B1
County Ga BAR EN5 ... 33 F1
ELTH/MOT SE9 ... 167 H5
County Gv CMBW SE5 ... 142 D2
County Pde BTFD TW8 * ... 136 E1
County Rd EHAM E6 ... 108 B4
THHTH CR7 ... 180 C5
County St STHWK SE1 ... 18 D5
Coupland Pl
WOOL/PLUM SE18 ... 127 H5
Courcy Rd CEND/HSY/T N8 ... 49 G6
Courier Rd DAGW RM9 ... 110 E3
Courland Gv VX/NE SW8 ... 141 J3
Courland St VX/NE SW8 ... 141 J2
The Course ELTH/MOT SE9 ... 167 F5
Courtauld Rd ARCH N19 ... 66 D5
Courtaulds Cl THMD SE28 ... 128 B1
Court Av BELV DA17 ... 129 G5
Court Cl KTN/HRWW/WS HA3 ... 43 K6
STJWD NW8 * ... 83 H5
WHTN TW2 ... 155 G5
WLGTN SM6 ... 210 D5
Court Close Av WHTN TW2 ... 155 G5
Court Crs CHSGTN KT9 ... 205 K4
Court Downs Rd BECK BR3 ... 182 E5
Court Dr CROY/NA CR0 ... 211 F2
STAN HA7 ... 30 A6
SUT SM1 ... 209 J2
Courtenay Av BELMT SM2 ... 208 E6
HGT N6 ... 65 J4
KTN/HRWW/WS HA3 ... 42 C4
Courtenay Dr BECK BR3 ... 183 G5
Courtenay Ms WALTH E17 ... 69 G2
Courtenay Pl WALTH E17 ... 69 G2
Courtenay Rd PGE/AN SE20 ... 182 A3
WALTH E17 ... 69 F2
WAN E11 * ... 88 D1
WBLY HA9 * ... 79 K1
WPK KT4 ... 208 A1
Courtenay Sq LBTH SE11 * ... 122 B5
Courtenay St LBTH SE11 ... 122 A5
Courten Ms STAN HA7 ... 43 J3
Court Farm Av
HOR/WEW KT19 ... 207 G3
Court Farm Rd ELTH/MOT SE9 ... 166 C4
NTHLT UB5 ... 78 A5
Courtfield Av HRW HA1 * ... 61 F2
Courtfield Crs HRW HA1 ... 61 F2
Courtfield Gdns ECT SW5 ... 120 A4
RSLP HA4 ... 58 D6
WEA W13 ... 97 G5
Courtfield Ms SKENS SW7 ... 120 B4
Courtfield Ri WWKM BR4 ... 214 B1
Courtfield Rd ECT SW5 ... 120 B4
Court Gdns HOLWY N7 ... 85 G4
Courtgate Cl MLHL NW7 ... 45 H2
Courthill Rd LEW SE13 ... 145 F6
Courthope Rd GFD/PVL UB6 ... 96 D1
HAMP NW3 ... 83 K2
WIM/MER SW19 ... 177 H1
Courthope Vls
WIM/MER SW19 ... 177 H3
Courthouse La
STNW/STAM N16 ... 86 B2
Court House Rd FNCH N3 ... 47 F2
Courtland Av CHING E4 ... 38 D4
IL IG1 ... 71 K6
MLHL NW7 ... 31 F5
STRHM/NOR SW16 ... 180 A3
Courtland Gv THMD SE28 ... 109 K6
Courtland Rd EHAM E6 ... 89 J6
Courtlands CHST BR7 ... 185 G3
RCHPK/HAM TW10 ... 137 H6
Courtlands Av HAYES BR2 ... 199 H5
HPTN TW12 ... 172 E2
LEE/GVPK SE12 ... 146 A6
RCH/KEW TW9 ... 137 J3
Courtlands Cl RSLP HA4 ... 58 D4
Courtlands Dr HOR/WEW KT19 ... 207 G4
Courtlands Rd BRYLDS KT5 ... 191 H4
Court La DUL SE21 ... 163 G2
Court Lane Gdns DUL SE21 ... 163 F2
Courtleet Dr BXLYHN DA7 ... 149 J2
Courtleigh Av EBAR EN4 ... 21 H1
Courtleigh Gdns GLDGN NW11 ... 64 C1
Courtman Rd TOTM N17 ... 49 J3
Court Md NTHLT UB5 ... 95 K2
Courtmead Cl HNHL SE24 ... 162 D1
Courtnell St BAY/PAD W2 ... 100 E5
Courtney Cl NRWD SE19 ... 181 F2
Courtney Crs CAR SM5 ... 209 K5
Courtney Pl CROY/NA CR0 ... 211 G1
Courtney Rd CROY/NA CR0 ... 211 G1
HOLWY N7 ... 85 G3
HTHAIR TW6 ... 132 D4
WIM/MER SW19 ... 178 D3
Courtney Wy HTHAIR TW6 ... 132 D4
Courtrai Rd FSTH SE23 ... 164 B1
Court Rd ELTH/MOT SE9 ... 166 E3
NWDGN UB2 ... 114 E4
SNWD SE25 ... 181 G5
Court Rd (Orpington By-Pass)
ORP BR6 ... 217 J2
Courtside HGT N6 ... 66 D3
SYD SE26 * ... 163 K5
The Courts STRHM/NOR SW16 ... 179 K3
Courtstreet BMLY BR1 ... 183 K5
Court St WCHPL E1 ... 104 D4
The Court MUSWH N10 * ... 66 C1
RSLP HA4 ... 77 J2
Court Vw HGT N6 * ... 66 B6
Court Wy ACT W3 ... 98 E4
BARK/HLT IG6 ... 54 C6
CDALE/KGS NW9 ... 63 G1
WHTN TW2 ... 156 A2
The Courtway OXHEY WD19 ... 27 J4
Court Yd ELTH/MOT SE9 ... 166 E1
Courtyard Ms STMC/STPC BR5 ... 186 B3
The Courtyards WATW WD18 * ... 26 B2
The Courtyard IS N1 ... 85 F5
Cousin La CANST EC4R ... 12 E6
Couthurst Rd BKHTH/KID SE3 ... 146 A1
Coutts Av CHSGTN KT9 ... 206 A3
Coutts Crs KTTN NW5 * ... 84 A1
Coval Gdns MORT/ESHN SW14 ... 137 J5
Coval La MORT/ESHN SW14 ... 137 J5
Coval Rd MORT/ESHN SW14 ... 137 K5
Covelees Wall EHAM E6 ... 108 A5
Covent Gdn COVGDN WC2E ... 11 F5
Covent Garden Piazza
COVGDN WC2E ... 11 F5
Coventry Cl EHAM E6 ... 107 K5
KIL/WHAMP NW6 ... 100 E1
Coventry Cross Est BOW E3 ... 106 A3
Coventry Rd IL IG1 ... 72 B5
SNWD SE25 ... 197 H1
WCHPL E1 ... 104 D3
Coventry St SOHO/SHAV W1D ... 10 C6
Coverack Cl CROY/NA CR0 ... 198 B5
STHGT/OAK N14 ... 34 C1
Coverdale Gdns CROY/NA CR0 ... 212 B1
Coverdale Rd CRICK NW2 ... 82 C5
FBAR/BDGN N11 ... 48 A2
SHB W12 ... 118 E1
The Coverdales BARK IG11 ... 108 D1
Coverley Cl WCHPL E1 * ... 104 C4
Coverton Rd TOOT SW17 ... 160 D6
Covert Rd BARK/HLT IG6 ... 55 F2
Coverts Rd ESH/CLAY KT10 ... 205 F5
The Covert NRWD SE19 * ... 181 G3
NTHWD HA6 ... 40 A4
ORP BR6 ... 201 K3
Covert Wy EBAR EN4 ... 21 G3
Covet Wood Cl
STMC/STPC BR5 ... 202 A3
Covey Cl WIM/MER SW19 ... 178 A5
Covington Gdns
STRHM/NOR SW16 ... 180 C3
Covington Wy
STRHM/NOR SW16 ... 180 C3
Cowbridge La BARK IG11 ... 90 B5
Cowbridge Rd
KTN/HRWW/WS HA3 ... 62 B1
Cowcross St FARR EC1M ... 12 A1
Cowdenbeath Pth IS N1 ... 84 E6
Cowden Rd ORP BR6 ... 202 A4
Cowden St CAT SE6 ... 164 D6
Cowdray Rd HGDN/ICK UB10 ... 76 A6
Cowdray Wy HCH RM12 ... 93 J2
Cowdrey Cl EN EN1 ... 24 A3
Cowdrey Ct DART DA1 ... 170 E2
Cowdrey Rd WIM/MER SW19 ... 178 A2
Cowen Av HRW HA1 ... 60 D6
Cowgate Rd GFD/PVL UB6 ... 96 D2
Cowick Rd TOOT SW17 ... 160 E6
Cowings Md NTHLT UB5 ... 77 J5
Cowland Av PEND EN3 ... 24 E5
Cow La BUSH WD23 * ... 28 A1
Cow Leaze EHAM E6 ... 108 A5
Cowleaze Rd KUTN/CMB KT2 ... 175 F4
Cowley Cl SAND/SEL CR2 ... 212 E6
Cowley Ct WAN E11 * ... 88 C1
Cowley La WAN E11 * ... 88 C1
Cowley Pl HDN NW4 ... 64 A2
Cowley Rd ACT W3 ... 118 C1
BRXN/ST SW9 ... 142 B2
HARH RM3 ... 57 K3
IL IG1 ... 71 K4
MORT/ESHN SW14 ... 138 B4
WAN E11 ... 71 F2
Cowley St WEST SW1P ... 16 E5
Cowling Cl NTGHL W11 ... 100 C6
Cowper Av EHAM E6 ... 89 J5
SUT SM1 ... 209 H2
Cowper Cl HAYES BR2 ... 200 C1
WELL DA16 ... 148 B6
Cowper Gdns STHGT/OAK N14 ... 34 C1
WLGTN SM6 ... 210 C4
Cowper Rd ACT W3 ... 118 A1
BELV DA17 ... 129 H4
HAYES BR2 ... 200 C1
HNWL W7 ... 97 F6
KUTN/CMB KT2 ... 175 G1
RAIN RM13 ... 111 J3
STHGT/OAK N14 ... 34 B3
STNW/STAM N16 ... 86 A2
UED N18 ... 50 C1
WIM/MER SW19 ... 178 B2
Cowper St STLK EC1Y ... 7 F6
Cowper Ter NKENS W10 * ... 100 B4
Cowslip Rd SWFD E18 ... 53 F6
Cowthorpe Rd VX/NE SW8 ... 141 J2
Coxe Pl KTN/HRWW/WS HA3 ... 61 G1
Cox La HOR/WEW KT19 ... 206 E3
Coxmount Rd CHARL SE7 ... 126 C5
Coxson Wy STHWK SE1 ... 19 J3
Coxwell Rd NRWD SE19 ... 181 F3
WOOL/PLUM SE18 ... 127 J5
Crabbs Croft Cl ORP BR6 * ... 216 C3
Crab Hl BECK BR3 ... 183 G3
Crabtree Av ALP/SUD HA0 ... 98 A1
CHDH RM6 ... 73 K1
Crabtree Cl BETH E2 ... 7 J3
Crabtree La FUL/PGN SW6 ... 139 G1
Crabtree Manorway North
BELV DA17 ... 129 K2
Crabtree Manorway South
BELV DA17 ... 129 K3
Craddock Rd EN EN1 ... 24 B4
Craddock St KTTN NW5 * ... 84 A4
Cradley Rd ELTH/MOT SE9 ... 167 J3
Cragie Lea MUSWH N10 * ... 48 B5
Craigdale Rd EMPK RM11 ... 75 H3
Craigen Av CROY/NA CR0 ... 197 J5
Craigerne Rd BKHTH/KID SE3 ... 146 A1
Craig Gdns SWFD E18 ... 52 D5
Craigholm WOOL/PLUM SE18 ... 147 F3
Craigmuir Pk ALP/SUD HA0 ... 80 B6
Craignair Rd
BRXS/STRHM SW2 ... 162 A2
Craignish Av
STRHM/NOR SW16 ... 180 A5
Craig Park Rd UED N18 ... 36 D6
Craig Rd RCHPK/HAM TW10 ... 156 D6
Craig's Ct WHALL SW1A ... 10 E7
Craigton Rd ELTH/MOT SE9 ... 146 E5
Craigweil Cl STAN HA7 ... 43 K1
Craigweil Dr STAN HA7 ... 43 K1
Craigwell Av FELT TW13 ... 153 K5
Crail Rw WALW SE17 ... 19 F7
Cramer St MHST W1U ... 9 H2
Crammond Cl HMSMTH W6 ... 119 H6
Cramond Ct
EBED/NFELT TW14 ... 153 H3
Crampton Rd PGE/AN SE20 ... 181 K2
Cranberry Cl NTHLT UB5 ... 95 H1
Cranberry La CAN/RD E16 ... 106 C3
Cranborne Av NWDGN UB2 ... 115 F4
SURB KT6 ... 206 C1
Cranborne Rd BARK IG11 ... 90 D6
Cranborne Waye YEAD UB4 ... 95 G6
Cranbourne Av WAN E11 ... 71 F1
Cranbourne Cl ESH/CLAY KT10 ... 204 B4
STRHM/NOR SW16 ... 179 K6
Cranbourne Dr PIN HA5 ... 59 H2
Cranbourne Gdns
BARK/HLT IG6 ... 54 D6
GLDGN NW11 ... 64 D2
Cranbourne Rd MNPK E12 ... 89 J3
MUSWH N10 ... 48 B5
NTHWD HA6 ... 40 D6
SRTFD E15 ... 88 A2
Cranbourn St LSQ/SEVD WC2H ... 10 D5
Cranbrook Cl HAYES BR2 ... 199 K3
Cranbrook Dr ESH/CLAY KT10 ... 189 H5
GPK RM2 ... 75 K1
WHTN TW2 ... 155 G3
Cranbrook La FBAR/BDGN N11 ... 34 B6
Cranbrook Ms WALTH E17 ... 69 H2
Cranbrook Pk WDGN N22 ... 49 G4
Cranbrook Ri IL IG1 ... 71 K3
Cranbrook Rd BARK/HLT IG6 ... 54 C6
BXLYHN DA7 ... 149 G2
CHSWK W4 ... 118 B5
DEPT SE8 ... 144 D3
EBAR EN4 ... 33 H1
HSLWW TW4 ... 134 E5
IL IG1 ... 72 A4
THHTH CR7 ... 180 E5
WIM/MER SW19 ... 177 H3
Cranbrook St BETH E2 ... 105 F1
Cranbury Rd FUL/PGN SW6 ... 140 A3
Crane Av ACT W3 ... 98 E6
ISLW TW7 ... 136 B6
Cranebank Ms TWK TW1 * ... 136 C6
Cranebrook WHTN TW2 ... 155 H4
Crane Cl DAGE RM10 ... 92 C4
Crane Ct FLST/FETLN EC4A ... 11 K4
MORT/ESHN SW14 * ... 137 K5
Craneford Cl WHTN TW2 ... 156 A2
Craneford Wy WHTN TW2 ... 155 K2
Crane Gdns HYS/HAR UB3 ... 113 J4
Crane Gv HOLWY N7 ... 85 G4
Crane Lodge Rd HEST TW5 ... 114 A6
Crane Md BERM/RHTH SE16 ... 124 A5
Crane Park Rd WHTN TW2 ... 155 G4
Crane Rd STWL/WRAY TW19 ... 152 D1
WHTN TW2 ... 155 K3
Cranesbill Cl CDALE/KGS NW9 ... 45 F6
Cranes Dr BRYLDS KT5 ... 191 F1
Cranes Pk BRYLDS KT5 ... 191 F1
Cranes Park Av BRYLDS KT5 ... 191 G1
Cranes Park Crs BRYLDS KT5 ... 191 G1
Crane St PECK SE15 ... 143 G2
Craneswater HYS/HAR UB3 ... 133 J1
Craneswater Pk NWDGN UB2 ... 114 E5
Crane Wy WHTN TW2 ... 155 H2
Cranfield Dr CDALE/KGS NW9 ... 45 G4
Cranfield Rd BROCKY SE4 ... 144 C4
Cranfield Rd East CAR SM5 ... 210 A6
Cranfield Rd West CAR SM5 * ... 209 K6
Cranford Av PLMGR N13 ... 48 E1
STWL/WRAY TW19 ... 152 B2
Cranford Cl RYNPK SW20 * ... 176 E4
STWL/WRAY TW19 ... 152 B2
Cranford Cottages WAP E1W * ... 105 F6
Cranford Dr HYS/HAR UB3 ... 113 J4
Cranford La HEST TW5 ... 134 C1
HYS/HAR UB3 ... 113 G6
HYS/HAR UB3 ... 133 J2
Cranford Park Rd
HYS/HAR UB3 ... 113 J4
Cranford Ri ESH/CLAY KT10 ... 204 C3
Cranford Rd DART DA1 ... 171 H3
Cranford St WAP E1W ... 105 F6
Cranford Wy CEND/HSY/T N8 ... 67 F2
Cranham Rd EMPK RM11 ... 75 K3
Cranhurst Rd CRICK NW2 ... 82 A3
Cranleigh Cl BXLY DA5 * ... 169 J1
ORP BR6 ... 217 G1
PGE/AN SE20 ... 181 J5
Cranleigh Gdns BARK IG11 ... 90 D5
KTN/HRWW/WS HA3 ... 62 A2
KUTN/CMB KT2 ... 175 G2
LOU IG10 ... 39 K1
SNWD SE25 ... 181 F6
STHL UB1 ... 95 K5
SUT SM1 ... 194 A6
WCHMH N21 ... 23 G6
Cranleigh Ms BTSEA SW11 ... 140 E3
Cranleigh Rd ESH/CLAY KT10 ... 189 H5
FELT TW13 ... 153 J6
SEVS/STOTM N15 ... 67 J2
WIM/MER SW19 ... 177 K6
Cranleigh St CAMTN NW1 ... 4 B3
Cranley Dr GNTH/NBYPK IG2 ... 72 C4
RSLP HA4 ... 58 D6
Cranley Gdns MUSWH N10 ... 66 B1
PLMGR N13 ... 35 F5
SKENS SW7 ... 120 B5
WLGTN SM6 ... 210 C5
Cranley Ms SKENS SW7 ... 120 B5
Cranley Pl SKENS SW7 ... 14 A7
Cranley Rd GNTH/NBYPK IG2 ... 72 C3
PLSTW E13 ... 107 F4
Cranley Ter HDN NW4 * ... 46 B5
Cranmer Av WEA W13 ... 116 C3
Cranmer Cl MRDN SM4 ... 193 G3
RSLP HA4 ... 59 H5
STAN HA7 ... 43 J3
Cranmer Ct HPTN TW12 ... 173 G1
KUTN/CMB KT2 ... 156 E6
Cranmer Farm Cl MTCM CR4 ... 194 E1
Cranmer Gdns DAGE RM10 ... 92 E2
Cranmer Rd BRXN/ST SW9 ... 142 B1
CROY/NA CR0 ... 211 J1
EDGW HA8 ... 30 D5
FSTGT E7 ... 89 F2
HPTN TW12 ... 173 G1
HYS/HAR UB3 ... 94 B5
KUTN/CMB KT2 ... 175 F1
MTCM CR4 ... 194 E1
Cranmer Ter TOOT SW17 ... 178 C1
Cranmore Av ISLW TW7 ... 135 H1
Cranmore Rd BMLY BR1 ... 165 H5
CHST BR7 ... 184 E1
Cranmore Wy MUSWH N10 ... 66 C1

Cranston Cl HGDN/ICK UB10........58 B6
HSLW TW3.....................................134 D3
Cranston Est IS N1.................................7 F2
Cranston Gdns CHING E4..............51 K2
Cranston Rd FSTH SE23............164 B3
Cranswick Rd
BERM/RHTH SE16...................123 J5
Crantock Rd CAT SE6..................165 F4
Cranwell Cl BOW E3.....................105 K5
Cranwich Av WCHMH N21...........35 J3
Cranwich Rd STNW/STAM N16.....68 A4
Cranwood St FSBYE EC1V..............7 F5
Cranworth Crs CHING E4................38 B3
Cranworth Gdns
BRXN/ST SW9.............................142 B2
Craster Rd BRXS/STRHM SW2....162 A2
Crathie Rd LEE/GVPK SE12.......166 A1
Cravan Av FELT TW13.................155 K4
Craven Av EA W5.............................97 J6
STHL UB1.....................................95 K5
Craven Cl STNW/STAM N16 *......68 C4
YEAD UB4.......................................94 B3
Craven Gdns BARK IG11.............108 E1
BARK/HLT IG6...............................54 D5
CRW RM5..56 E4
WIM/MER SW19...........................178 A1
Craven Hill Gdns BAY/PAD W2...101 G6
Craven Ms BTSEA SW11..............141 F4
Craven Pk WLSDN NW10..............81 G6
Craven Park Ms WLSDN NW10.....81 G6
Craven Park Rd
SEVS/STOTM N15.......................68 B3
WLSDN NW10...............................81 G6
Craven Pas CHCR WC2N...............10 E7
Craven Rd BAY/PAD W2..............101 G6
CROY/NA CRO..............................197 J5
KUTN/CMB KT2...........................175 G4
ORP BR6.......................................217 K1
WEA W13..97 J6
WLSDN NW10...............................81 G6
Craven St CHCR WC2N...................10 E7
Craven Ter BAY/PAD W2..............101 G6
Craven Wk CLPT E5.........................68 C4
Crawford Av ALP/SUD HA0............79 K3
Crawford Cl ISLW TW7................135 J3
Crawford Gdns NTHLT UB5...........95 F2
PLMGR N13....................................35 H5
Crawford Pas CLKNW EC1R............5 J7
Crawford Pl MBLAR W1H...............8 D3
Crawford Rd CMBW SE5..............142 D3
Crawford St MBLAR W1H................8 D2
MHST W1U.....................................9 F2
WLSDN NW10...............................81 F5
Crawley Rd ED N9............................36 E5
LEY E10..69 K5
WDGN N22.....................................49 E4
Crawthew Gv EDUL SE22............143 G5
Cray Av WAND/STPC BR5.............202 C2
Craybrooke Rd SCUP DA14..........168 E6
Cray Valley End FLTH/MOT SE9...167 H4
Cray Cl DART DA1..........................150 C4
Craydene Rd ERITH DA8...............150 C2
Crayford High St DART DA1........150 B6
Crayford Rd DART DA1................150 C4
HOLWY N7.....................................84 E2
Crayford Wy DART DA1.................150 C6
Crayke Hl CHSGTN KT9...............206 A5
Craylands STMC/STPC BR5.........186 D2
Crayleigh Ter SCUP DA14 *.........186 D2
Cray Rd BELV DA17......................129 H6
SCUP DA14...................................186 D4
SWLY BR8.....................................203 K3
Crays Pde STMC/STPC BR5 *.....186 M1
Cray Valley Rd
STMC/STPC BR5.......................202 B2
Crealock Gv WFD IG8....................52 D1
Crealock Rd WAND/EARL SW18...160 A1
Creasey Cl EMPK RM11..................75 K6
Crebor St EDUL SE22....................163 H1
Credenhill St HAYES BR2............200 C1
Credenhill St
STRHM/NOR SW16.................179 H2
Crediton Hl KIL/WHAMP NW6.......83 F3
Crediton Rd WLSDN NW10.............82 B6
Crediton Wy ESH/CLAY KT10.......205 G3
Credon Rd BERM/RHTH SE16.....123 K5
PLSTW E13...................................107 G1
Creechurch La HDTCH EC3A..........13 H4
Creechurch Pl HDTCH EC3A *........13 H4
Creed La BLKFR EC4V....................12 B4
Creek Cottages
E/WMO/HCT KT8 *....................189 K1
Creek Rd BARK IG11...................109 F2
DEPT SE8.....................................124 D6
E/WMO/HCT KT8........................189 K1
Creekside DEPT SE8....................144 E1
RAIN RM13...................................111 G4
Cree Wy RAIN RM13....................111 G4
Cree Wy ROM RM1........................57 G3
Crefeld Cl HMSMTH W6...............119 H6
Creffield Rd EA W5.........................98 C6
Creighton Av EFNCH N2..................47 K5
EHAM E6......................................107 H1
Creighton Cl SHB W12...................99 K6
Creighton Rd EA W5....................116 A3
KIL/WHAMP NW6.......................100 B3
TOTM N17......................................50 A3
Creigton Av EFNCH N2...................47 J6
Cremer St BETH E2..........................7 J3
Cremorne Est WBPTN SW10 *.....120 C6
Cremorne Gdns
HOR/WEW KT19.......................207 F6
Cremorne Rd WBPTN SW10.......140 B1
Crescent TWRH EC3N.....................13 J5
Crescent Ar GNWCH SE10..........125 F5
Crescent Av HCH RM12.................93 J5
Crescent Dr STMC/STPC BR5.....201 H5
Crescent East EBAR EN4................21 G1
Crescent Gdns RSLP HA4...............59 F4
SWLY BR8....................................187 K5
WIM/MER SW19..........................159 K5
Crescent Gv CLAP SW4.................141 H5
MTCM CR4....................................194 D1
Crescent La CLAP SW4.................141 J6
Crescent Pl CHEL SW3...................14 D6
Crescent Ri EBAR EN4....................21 J6

FNCH N3 *.......................................46 D4
WDGN N22......................................48 D4
Crescent Rd BECK BR3................182 E5
BFN/LL DA15................................168 A5
BMLY BR1.......................................183 K3
CEND/HSY/T N8............................66 E3
CHING E4..38 C2
DAGE RM10....................................92 D2
EBAR EN4..21 J5
ED N9..36 C3
ENC/FH EN2....................................23 J3
ERITH DA8....................................130 C6
FBAR/BDGN N11............................33 J1
FNCH N3..46 D4
KUTN/CMB KT2............................175 H3
LEY E10..69 K6
PLSTW E13......................................88 E6
RYNPK SW20................................177 G4
SEVS/STOTM N15 *......................67 G1
SWFD E18.......................................52 E5
WDGN N22......................................48 D4
WOOL/PLUM SE18......................127 G5
Crescent Rw STLK EC1Y.................6 C7
Crescent St IS N1............................85 F5
The Crescent ACT W3....................99 G5
ALP/SUD HA0................................79 K3
BAR EN5..21 F4
BARN SW13..................................138 C3
BECK BR3.....................................182 D4
BXLY DA5.......................................168 D2
CRICK NW2 *..................................81 K1
CROY/NA CRO..............................196 E3
E/WMO/HCT KT8.........................188 E1
FBAR/BDGN N11...........................33 K6
GNTH/NBYPK IG2.........................72 C3
HYS/HAR UB3..............................133 F1
LOU IG10...39 H1
NWMAL KT3.................................175 K5
RYLN/HDSTN HA2.........................60 C5
SCUP DA14...................................168 A6
STHL UB1..95 H1
SURB KT6.....................................191 F2
SUT SM1.......................................209 H4
WALTH E17 *...................................69 G2
WIM/MER SW19...........................159 J6
WWKM BR4..................................199 J6
Crescent Vw LOU IG10...................39 H1
Crescent Wy BROCKY SE4...........144 D4
ORP BR6.......................................216 E3
STRHM/NOR SW16......................180 A3
Crescentway
NFNCH/WDSPK N12....................47 J2
Crescent West EBAR EN4..............21 G1
Crescent Wood Rd SYD SE26.....163 H5
Cresford Rd FUL/PGN SW6.........140 A2
Crespigny Rd HDN NW4.................63 K3
Cressage Cl STHL UB1...................96 A3
Cresset Rd HOM E9.........................86 E4
Cresset St CLAP SW4...................141 J4
Cressida Rd ARCH N19...................66 C5
Cressingham Gv SUT SM1...........209 F3
Cressingham Rd EDGW HA8..........45 F3
LEW SE13.....................................145 F4
Cressington Cl
STNW/STAM N16........................86 A3
Cresswell Pk BKHTH/KID SE3....145 J4
Cresswell Pl WBPTN SW10.........120 D5
Cresswell Rd FELT TW13............154 D6
SNWD SE25..................................197 J1
TWK TW1......................................156 E1
Cresswell Wy WCHMH N21...........35 G2
Cressy Ct HMSMTH W6...............118 E3
WCHPL E1....................................104 E4
Cressy Houses WCHPL E1 *........104 E4
Cressy Pl WCHPL E1....................104 E4
Cressy Rd HAMP NW3...................83 K2
Cressys Cnr HSLW TW5 *.............135 G2
Crestbrook Av PLMGR N13............35 H5
Crestbrook Pl PLMGR N13 *..........35 H5
Crest Dr PEND EN3........................24 E1
Crestfield St CAMTN NW1...............5 F4
Crest Gdns RSLP HA4....................77 G1
Creston Wy WPK KT4..................193 G5
Crest Rd CRICK NW2......................81 H6
HAYES BR2...................................199 J4
SAND/SEL CR2............................212 D5
The Crest BRYLDS KT5................191 H2
HDN NW4..64 A2
HOLWY N7 *...................................84 C3
PLMGR N13....................................35 G6
Crest Vw PIN HA5.........................168 H5
Crest View Dr STMC/STPC BR5...201 G2
Crestway PUT/ROE SW15............158 D1
Crestwood Wy HSLWW TW4.......134 E6
Creswell Dr BECK BR3................198 E2
Creswick Rd ACT W3.......................98 D1
Creswick Wk GLDGN NW11 *........81 G5
Creukhorne Rd WLSDN NW10 *....81 G5
Crewdson Rd BRXN/ST SW9........142 B1
Crewe Pl WLSDN NW10..................99 H2
Crews St POP/IOD E14.................124 D4
Crewys Rd CRICK NW2..................82 C1
PECK SE15...................................143 J3
Crichton Av WLGTN SM6.............210 D3
Crichton Rd CAR SM5..................209 K5
Crichton St VX/NE SW8 *.............141 H3
Cricketers Arms Rd
ENC/FH EN2..................................23 J3
Cricketers Cl CHSGTN KT9...........29 A5
ERITH DA8....................................130 B5
STHGT/OAK N14...........................34 C2
Cricketers Ms BAL SW12 *...........161 G2
Cricketers Wk SYD SE26.............181 K1
Cricketfield Rd CLPT E5................86 D2
Cricket Gn MTCM CR4.................194 E1
Cricket Ground Rd CHST BR7.....185 G4
Cricket La BECK BR3....................182 B2
Cricket Rw EFNCH N2 *.................47 H6
Cricklade Av
BRXS/STRHM SW2....................161 K4
Cricklewood Broadway
CRICK NW2....................................82 A1
Cricklewood La CRICK NW2..........82 B2
Cridland St SRTFD E15...................88 D2
Crieff Ct TEDD TW11....................174 D3

Crieff Rd WAND/EARL SW18.......160 B1
Criffel Av BRXS/STRHM SW2.....161 J4
Crimscott St STHWK SE1...............19 H5
Crimsworth Rd VX/NE SW8..........141 J1
Crinan St IS N1.................................5 F2
Cringle St VX/NE SW8..................141 H1
Cripplegate St BARB EC2Y *.........12 C1
Crispen Rd FELT TW13.................154 D6
Crispian Cl WLSDN NW10..............81 G2
Crispin Crs CROY/NA CRO...........210 D1
Crispin Rd EDGW HA4....................44 E2
Crispin St WCHPL E1......................13 J2
Crisp Rd HMSMTH W6.................119 F5
Cristowe Rd FUL/PGN SW6 *......139 J3
Criterion Ms ARCH N19..................66 D6
Crockenhill Hl STMC/STPC BR5..202 E2
Crockenhill Rd
STMC/STPC BR5........................202 E3
Crockerton Rd TOOT SW17.........160 E4
Crockham Wy ELTH/MOT SE9.....167 F6
Crocus Cl CROY/NA CRO.............198 A5
Crocus Fld BAR EN5.......................32 D1
Croft Av WWKM BR4....................199 F5
Croft Cl ABYW SE2......................129 G5
CHST BR7....................................184 E1
HYS/HAR UB3..............................133 F1
MLHL NW7.....................................31 G5
Croft Ct RSLP HA4 *.......................58 D5
Croftdown Rd KTTN NW5..............84 A1
Crofters Cl ISLW TW7...................135 J6
Crofters Md DEPT SE8.................124 B4
Crofters Rd NTHWD HA6...............26 C6
Crofters Wy CAMTN NW1...............84 D6
Croft Gdns HNWL W7...................116 B2
RSLP HA4.......................................58 C5
Croft Lodge Cl WFD IG8.................53 F2
Croft Ms NFNCH/WDSPK N12.......33 G5
Crookston Rd ELTH/MOT SE9.....147 G4
Coombs Rd CAN/RD E16..............107 G4
Crookham Rd FUL/PGN SW6......139 J2
Crook Log BXLYHS DA6................148 E4
Croom's Hl Gv GNWCH SE10......145 F1
Crooms Hill GNWCH SE10...........145 F1
Cropley St IS N1 *..............................6 E2
Croppath Rd DAGE RM10..............92 C2
Cropthorne Ct MV/WKIL W9........101 G3
Crosby Cl FELT TW13...................154 D6
Crosby Rd DAGE RM10................110 D1
EHAM E6.......................................107 K2
Crosby Rw STHWK SE1..................18 E3
Crosby Sq HDTCH EC3A................13 H4
Crosby Wk HDTCH EC3A *.............86 B4
Crosier Cl BKHTH/KID SE3...........146 D2
Crosier Rd HGDN/ICK UB10..........76 C1
Crosier Wy RSLP HA4....................76 B6
Crosland Pl BTSEA SW11............141 F4
Crossbow Rd CHIG IG7...................55 F1
Crossbrook Rd BKHTH/KID SE3...146 D5
Cross Deep TWK TW1...................156 A4
Cross Deep Gdns TWK TW1........156 A4
Crossfield Est DEPT SE8..............144 D1
Crossfield Rd HAMP NW3...............83 H4
Crossfield St DEPT SE8................144 D1
Crossford St BRXN/ST SW9........142 A3
Crossgate EDGW HA8.....................30 C5
GFD/PVL UB6..................................79 H4
Crossland Cl EN1 *..........................36 C4
MHST W1U......................................9 G5
Cross Lances Rd HSLW TW5.......135 G5
Crossland Rd THHTH CR7............196 C3
Crosslands Av EA W5....................117 G1
Crosslands Pde NWDGN UB2 *...115 F5
Crosslands Rd HOR/WEW KT19..207 F4
Cross La BXLY DA5........................169 G2
CEND/HSY/T N8.............................67 F1
EN EN1..13 G6
Crosslet St WALW SE17................122 E4
Crosslet V GNWCH SE10..............144 E2
Crossley St HOLWY N7....................85 G4
Crossmead ELTH/MOT SE9.........166 E3
OXHEY WD19.................................27 J1
Crossmead Av GFD/PVL UB6.........96 A2
Crossness Rd BARK IG11.............109 F2
Cross Rd CHDH RM6.......................73 J2
CHING E4.......................................38 C2
CMBW SE5...................................143 F3
CROY/NA CRO.............................196 E5
DART DA1.....................................171 F1
EN EN1...23 K4
FBAR/BDGN N11............................48 B1
FELT TW13...................................154 D6
HAYES BR2...................................200 D6
HRW HA1..60 D1
KTN/HRWW/WS HA3.....................43 G5
KUTN/CMB KT2...........................175 K4
MRDN SM4...................................193 K1
RYLN/HDSTN HA2.........................59 K4
SCUP DA14...................................168 C6
STMC/STPC BR5........................202 C2
SUT SM1.......................................209 H3
WFD IG8...53 J3
WIM/MER SW19...........................177 K3
Crossway BARN SW13................138 B3
ERITH DA8....................................130 B6
HPTN TW12..................................173 H1
IS N1...86 C5
UED N18...50 C1
Crosswaite Av HNHL SE24...........142 E5
Crosswall TWRH EC3N...................13 J5
Crossway BCTR RM8.......................91 J1
CDALE/KGS NW9...........................63 H1
EN EN1...36 B5
Cross Wy HYS/HAR UB3...............113 K2
Crossway NFNCH/WDSPK N12.....47 H2
NWMAL KT3.................................193 F1
PIN HA5...41 F5
RSLP HA4.......................................77 H4
STMC/STPC BR5........................201 J1
STNW/STAM N16..........................86 A3
THMD SE28...................................109 J6
WEA W13..97 G3
WOT/HER KT12...........................188 A6
WPK KT4......................................192 C4
Crossway Pde WDGN N22 *..........48 D3
Crossways BELMT SM2................209 H6
GPK RM2...57 K5
SAND/SEL CR2............................213 H5
Crossways Rd BECK BR3.............198 D2
MTCM CR4....................................179 G6
Crossways Ter CLPT E5 *...............86 D2
The Crossways BRYLDS KT5 *....191 J5

HGT N6 *...66 B1
MORT/ESHN SW14......................137 K4
SKENS SW7....................................14 A4
Cromwell Rd ALP/SUD HA0..........97 K1
BECK BR3....................................182 B5
BRXN/ST SW9...............................14 E9
CROY/NA CRO.............................196 E4
ECT SW5.......................................120 A4
FELT TW13...................................154 A3
FNCH N3..47 G5
FSTGT E7.......................................89 F4
HSLW TW3....................................135 F5
HYS/HAR UB3..............................113 J2
MUSWH N10..................................48 B3
SKENS SW7....................................14 A6
TEDD TW11..................................174 B2
WALTH E17 *...................................70 A2
WIM/MER SW19...........................177 K1
WLGTN SM6.................................210 B4
WOT/HER KT12...........................188 A6
Cromwell St HSLW TW3..............135 F5
Cromwell Ter HSLW TW3 *..........135 F5
Crondace Rd FUL/PGN SW6.......139 K2
Crondall St IS N1 *............................7 F3
Cronin St PECK SE15....................143 G1
Crooked Billet Rbt CHING E4.........51 K3
Crooked Usage FNCH N3...............46 C6
Crooke Rd DEPT SE8...................124 B5
Crookham Rd FUL/PGN SW6......139 J2
Crookston Rd ELTH/MOT SE9.....147 G4
Croombs Rd CAN/RD E16............107 G4
Croom's Hl Gv GNWCH SE10......145 G1
Croom's Hill GNWCH SE10..........145 F1
Cropley St IS N1 *.............................7 F3
Cropthorne Ct MV/WKIL W9........101 G3
Crosby Cl FELT TW13..................154 D6
Crosby Rd DAGE RM10...............110 D1
EHAM E6......................................107 K2

HEST TW5.....................................134 E1
WBLY HA9.......................................62 C6
The Cross Wy
KTN/HRWW/WS HA3.....................42 E1
The Crossway ELTH/MOT SE9.....166 C4
WDGN N22......................................49 H5
Croston St HACK E8........................86 C6
Crosts La WDGN N22......................49 G3
Crothall Cl PLMGR N13..................35 F5
Crouch Av BARK IG11....................109 H1
Crouch Cl BECK BR3....................182 D2
Crouch Cft ELTH/MOT SE9 *........167 F5
Crouch End Hl CEND/HSY/T N8....66 D3
Crouch Hall Rd CEND/HSY/T N8...66 D3
Crouch Hl CEND/HSY/T N8............66 D3
Crouchmans Cl SYD SE26...........163 G5
Crouch Rd WLSDN NW10...............80 E5
Crowborough Pth
OXHEY WD19.................................27 H6
Crowborough Rd TOOT SW17.....179 F1
Crowden Wy THMD SE28.............109 J6
Crowder St WCHPL E1 *..............104 D6
Crowfoot Cl HOM E9 *....................87 H3
THMD SE28..................................127 K1
Crowhurst Cl BRXN/ST SW9.......142 B3
Crowhurst Wy
STMC/STPC BR5........................202 D2
Crowland Av HYS/HAR UB3........113 H4
Crowland Gdns
STHGT/OAK N14...........................34 E1
Crowland Rd SEVS/STOTM N15...68 B2
THHTH CR7...................................196 E1
Crowlands Av ROMW/RG RM7.....74 D3
Crowland Ter IS N1...........................85 K5
Crowland Wk MRDN SM4............194 A3
Crow La ROMW/RG RM7................74 B4
Crowley Crs CROY/NA CRO.........211 G3
Crowline Wk IS N1 *........................85 K4
Crown Ar KUT/HW KT1 *..............174 E5
Crownbourne Ct SUT SM1 *.........209 F2
Crown Buildings CHING E4............38 B3
Crown Cl BOW E3.............................87 J6
HYS/HAR UB3..............................113 J2
KIL/WHAMP NW6..........................83 F4
MLHL NW7......................................31 H4
ORP BR6.......................................217 G2
WOT/HER KT12...........................188 B4
Crown Ct HOL/ALD WC2B.............11 H4
Crown Dl NRWD SE19..................180 D2
Crowndale Rd CAMTN NW1.............4 B1
Crownfield Av
GNTH/NBYPK IG2.........................72 E3
Crownfield Rd SRTFD E15.............88 B3
Crownhill Rd CROY/NA CRO *......196 A3
Crownhill Rd WFD IG8....................53 J3
WLSDN NW10...............................81 H6
Crown La CHST BR7....................185 H4
HAYES BR2...................................200 C2
MRDN SM4...................................193 K1
STHGT/OAK N14...........................34 E1
STRHM/NOR SW16......................180 B1
Crown Lane Gdns
STRHM/NOR SW16 *..................180 B1
Crown Lane Sp HAYES BR2........200 C3
Crownmead Wy
ROMW/RG RM7............................74 D1
Crown Office Rw EMB EC4Y..........11 J5
Crown Pde MRDN SM4................194 A1
STHGT/OAK N14 *.........................34 C3
Crown Pth STJS SW1Y...................16 C1
Crown Pl KTTN NW5.......................84 B4
SDTCH EC2A...................................7 G7
Crown Rd BARK/HLT IG6.................72 C1
EN EN1..24 C4
KUTN/CMB KT2...........................175 K4
MRDN SM4...................................193 K1
MUSWH N10..................................48 A3
ORP BR6.......................................217 G3
RSLP HA4.......................................77 H3
SUT SM1.......................................209 F2
TWK TW1......................................156 C1
Crownstone Rd
BRXS/STRHM SW2....................142 B5
Crown St ACT W3..........................117 J1
CMBW SE5...................................142 D1
DAGE RM10...................................92 D5
RYLN/HDSTN HA2.........................60 D5
Crown Ter CRICK NW2 *................82 B2
RCH/KEW TW9............................137 G5
STHGT/OAK N14 *.........................34 C3
Crowntree Cl ISLW TW7...............116 A6
Crown Vis ACT W3 *.......................99 J2
Crown Wk WBLY HA9.....................80 B1
Crown Wdr/YW UB7......................112 C1
Crown Woods La
WOOL/PLUM SE18......................147 G3
Crown Woods Wy
ELTH/MOT SE9...........................147 J6
Crown Yd HSLW TW3...................135 H4
Crowshott Av STAN HA7................43 J5
Crows Rd BARK IG11.......................90 B4
BOW E3...87 J6
Crowther Av BTFD TW8................117 F5
Crowther Cl FUL/PGN SW6.........119 J6
Crowther Rd SNWD SE25.............197 H1
Crowthorne Cl
WAND/EARL SW18......................159 J2
Crowthorne Rd NKENS W10........100 B5
Croxden Cl EDGW HA8..................44 C6
Croxden Wk MRDN SM4..............194 B3
Croxford Gdns WDGN N22.............49 H5
Croxford Wy ROMW/RG RM7.......75 G5
Croxley Cl STMC/STPC BR5........186 C5
Croxley Gn STMC/STPC BR5.......186 C5
Croxley Rd MV/WKIL W9..............100 D2
Croxley Vw WATW WD18................26 C1
Croxted Cl DUL SE21....................162 D1
Croxted Ms HNHL SE24...............162 D2
Croxted Rd DUL SE21..................162 E4
Croyde Av GFD/PVL UB6................96 C2
HYS/HAR UB3..............................113 H4
Croyde Cl BFN/LL DA15...............167 J2
The Croydon F/O
CROY/NA CRO.............................211 H2
Croydon Gv CROY/NA CRO.........196 C5

Croydon Rd BECK BR3.....198 A2
　MTCM CR4.....195 G2
　PGE/AN SE20.....181 J5
　PLSTW E13.....106 D5
　WLSDN SM6.....197 F4
　WWKM BR4.....214 C1
　WWKM BR4.....215 F1
Croyland Rd ED N9.....36 C5
Croylands Dr SURB KT6.....191 H4
Crozier Ter HOM E9.....87 G3
Crucible CI CHDH RM6.....73 H5
Crucifix La STHWK SE1.....19 G2
Cruden St IS N1.....6 B1
Cruickshank St FSBYW WC1X.....5 J4
Cruikshank Rd SRTFD E15.....88 C2
Crummock Gdns
　CDALE/KGS NW9.....63 G2
Crumpsall St ABYW SE2.....128 D4
Crundale Av CDALE/KGS NW9.....62 C2
Crunden Rd SAND/SEL CR2.....211 K5
Crusader Ct PUR RM13.....131 K4
Crusader Gdns CROY/NA CR0.....212 A1
Crusader Wy WATW WD18.....131 H1
Crusoe Ms STNW/STAM N16.....67 K4
Crusoe Rd ERITH DA8.....150 A5
　MTCM CR4.....178 E3
Crutched Friars TWRH EC3N.....13 H5
Crutchfield La WOT/HER KT12.....188 A4
Crutchley Rd CAT SE6.....165 J4
Crystal Palace NRWD SE19 *.....181 H5
Crystal Palace Pde
　NRWD.....181 G2
Crystal Palace Park Rd
　SYD SE26.....181 J1
Crystal Palace Rd EDUL SE22.....163 H1
Crystal Palace Station Rd
　NRWD.....181 H2
Crystal Ter NRWD SE19.....180 E2
Crystal Wy BCTR RM8.....73 J5
　HRW HA1.....60 E3
Cuba Dr PEND EN3.....24 E3
Cuba St POP/IOD E14.....124 D2
Cubitt Sq STHWK SE1 *.....115 H1
Cubitt St FSBYW WC1X.....5 K4
Cubitt Ter CLAP SW4.....141 H4
Cuckmere Wy STMC/STPC BR5.....202 E5
Cuckoo Av HNWL W7.....96 E5
Cuckoo Dene HNWL W7.....96 D4
Cuckoo Hall La ED N9.....36 E2
Cuckoo Hi PIN HA5.....59 C1
Cuckoo Hill Dr PIN HA5.....41 G6
Cuckoo Hill Rd PIN HA5.....59 H1
Cuckoo La HNWL W7.....96 E6
Cuda's CI HOR/WEW KT19.....207 H1
Cuddington Av WPK KT4.....207 H1
Cudham La North ORP BR6.....216 D6
Cudham St SE6.....164 E2
Cudworth St WCHPL E1.....104 D3
Cuff Crs ELTH/MOT SE9.....146 C6
Culford Gdns CHEL SW3.....15 F7
Culford Gv IS N1.....86 A4
Culford Ms IS N1.....85 K4
Culford Rd IS N1.....86 A2
Culgaith Gdns ENC/FH EN2.....40 C2
Culham Ct NTHWD HA6 *.....40 D2
Culling Rd BERM/RHTH SE16.....123 K3
Cullington CI
　KTN/HRWW/WS HA3.....43 K6
Cullingworth Rd WLSDN NW10.....81 K3
Culloden CI BERM/RHTH SE16.....123 H5
Culloden Rd ENC/FH EN2.....23 H3
Culloden St POP/IOD E14.....106 A5
Cullum St FENCHST EC3M.....13 H5
Culmington Pde WEA W13 *.....97 H1
Culmington Rd SAND/SEL CR2.....211 J6
　WEA W13.....116 C1
Culmore Rd PECK SE15.....143 J1
Culmstock Rd BTSEA SW11.....141 F6
Culpepper CI CHIG IG7.....54 B2
　ED N9.....36 C3
Culross CI SEVS/STOTM N15.....67 J1
Culross St MYFR/PKLN W1K.....9 G6
Culsac Rd SURB KT6.....191 F6
Culverden Rd BAL SW12.....161 G5
　OXHEY WD19.....27 F5
Culver Gv STAN HA7.....43 J5
Culverhouse Gdns
　STRHM/NOR SW16.....162 A6
Culverlands CI STAN HA7.....29 H6
Culverley Rd CAT SE6.....164 E3
Culvers Av CAR SM5.....194 E6
Culvers Retreat CAR SM5.....194 E5
Culverstone CI HAYES BR2.....199 J3
Culvert PI BTSEA SW11.....141 F3
Culvert Rd BTSEA SW11.....140 E3
　SEVS/STOTM N15.....68 A2
Culworth St STJWD NW8.....2 C2
Cumberland Av WELL DA16.....147 K4
　WLSDN NW10.....98 C2
Cumberland CI BARK/HLT IG6.....54 C4
　HACK E8.....86 B4
　RYNPK SW20.....177 G3
　TWK TW1.....156 C1
Cumberland Crs WKENS W14.....119 H4
Cumberland Cresent
　WKENS W14 *.....119 H4
Cumberland Dr BXLYHN DA7.....149 F1
　CHSGTN KT9.....206 A1
　DART DA1.....171 J2
　ESH/CLAY KT10.....190 B6
Cumberland Gdns FSBYW WC1X.....5 H4
　HDN NW4.....46 B5
Cumberland Ga BAY/PAD W2.....8 E5
　CAMTN NW1.....8 E5
Cumberland House
　KUTN/CMB KT2.....175 J3
Cumberland Market
　CAMTN NW1.....3 K4
Cumberland Ms LBTH SE11.....122 B5
Cumberland Pk ACT W3.....98 E6
　CAMTN NW1 *.....3 K4
Cumberland Rd ACT W3.....98 E6
　ASHF TW15.....152 A5
　BARN SW13.....138 D2
　ED N9.....36 E3

HAYES BR2.....199 H1
　HNWL W7.....116 A2
　HRW HA1.....60 B2
　MNPK E12.....89 H2
　PLSTW E13.....89 F4
　RCH/KEW TW9.....137 H2
　SNWD SE25.....197 J3
　STAN HA7.....44 B6
　WALTH E17.....51 G5
　WDGN N22.....48 D3
Cumberland Ter PIM SW1V.....121 F5
Cumberland Terrace Ms
　CAMTN NW1 *.....3 J5
Cumberlow Av SNWD SE25.....181 H6
Cumberton Rd TOTM N17.....49 K4
Cumbrae Gdns SURB KT6.....190 E6
Cumbrian Av BXLYHN DA7.....150 B3
Cumbrian Gdns CRICK NW2.....64 B1
Cumming St IS N1.....5 H3
Cumnor CI BRXN/ST SW9 *.....142 A3
Cumnor Gdns EW KT17.....207 J4
Cumnor Rd BELMT SM2.....209 G4
Cunard Crs WCHMH N21.....35 K1
Cunard Rd WLSDN NW10.....99 F2
Cunard Rd CAN/RD E16.....107 G5
Cundy St BGVA SW1W.....15 H7
Cunliffe Rd HOR/WEW KT19.....207 H2
Cunliffe St STRHM/NOR SW16.....179 H2
Cunningham CI RMDH HA2 *.....73 J2
　WWKM BR4.....198 E6
Cunningham Pk HRW HA1.....60 D2
Cunningham Pl STJWD NW8.....2 A6
Cunningham Rd
　SEVS/STOTM N15 *.....68 C1
Cunnington St CHSWK W4.....117 K4
Cupar Rd BTSEA SW11.....141 F2
Cupola CI BMLY BR1.....184 A1
Curates Wk RDART DA2.....171 G5
Cureton St WEST SW1P *.....121 J5
Curlew CI THMD SE28.....109 K6
Curlew St STHWK SE1.....19 J2
Curlew Wy YEAD UB4.....95 H4
Curnick's La WNWD SE27.....162 D5
Curran Av MRLSL DA15.....148 A6
　WLGTN SM6.....210 A1
Currey Rd NTHLT UB5.....78 C4
Curricle St ACT W3.....118 B1
Currie Hill CI WIM/MER SW19.....159 J6
Curry Ri MLHL NW7.....46 B2
Cursitor St FLST/FETLN EC4A.....11 J3
Curtain PI SDTCH EC2A.....7 H6
Curthwaite Gdns ENC/FH EN2.....22 D5
Curtis Dr ACT W3.....99 F5
Curtis Field Rd
　STRHM/NOR SW16.....162 A6
Curtis La ALP/SUD HA0.....80 A4
Curtismill CI STMC/STPC BR5.....186 C6
Curtismill Wy
　STMC/STPC BR5.....186 C6
Curtis Rd HOR/WEW KT19.....206 E2
　HSLWW TW4.....154 E2
Curtis St STHWK SE1.....19 J6
Curtis Wy STHWK SE1.....19 J6
The Curve SHB W12.....99 J6
Curwen Av FSTGT E7.....89 F2
Curwen Rd SHB W12.....118 D2
Curzon Av PEND EN3.....25 F5
　STAN HA7.....43 G4
Curzon CI ORP BR6.....216 D2
Curzon Crs BARK IG11.....109 F2
　WLSDN NW10.....81 G5
Curzon Ga MYFR/PICC W1J.....9 H1
Curzon Rd BA W5.....97 H3
　MUSWH N10.....48 B5
　THHTH CR7.....196 B3
Curzon Sq MYFR/PICC W1J.....9 H1
Curzon St MYFR/PICC W1J.....9 H1
　MYFR/PKLN W1K.....15 H1
Cusack CI TWK TW1.....156 A5
Custom House Reach
　BERM/RHTH SE16 *.....124 C3
Cutcombe Rd CMBW SE5.....142 D3
Cuthberga CI BARK IG11.....90 C5
Cuthbert Gdns SNWD SE25.....181 F6
Cuthbert Rd CROY/NA CR0.....196 C6
　UED N18.....50 C1
　WALTH E17.....52 A6
Cutlers Gardens Ar
　LVPST EC2M.....13 H3
Cutler St HDTCH EC3A.....13 H3
The Cut STHWK SE1.....17 K2
Cuxton CI BXLYHS DA6.....149 F6
Cyclamen CI HPTN TW12.....173 F2
Cyclamen Wy HOR/WEW KT19.....206 E3
Cygnet Av EBED/NFELT TW14.....154 C2
Cygnet CI NTHWD HA6.....40 A3
　WLSDN NW10.....81 F3
The Cygnets FELT TW13.....154 D6
Cygnet St WCHPL E1.....7 K6
Cygnet Wy YEAD UB4.....95 H5
Cymbeline Ct HRW HA1 *.....61 F3
Cynthia St IS N1.....5 H3
Cypress Av WHTN TW2.....155 H2
Cypress CI CLPT E5.....68 C6
Cypress Gdns BROCKY SE4.....144 B6
Cypress Gv BARK/HLT IG6.....54 E2
Cypress Rd
　KTN/HRWW/WS HA3.....42 D5
　SNWD SE25.....181 F5
Cypress Tree CI BFN/LL DA15.....168 A3
Cyprus Av FNCH N3.....46 C5
Cyprus CI FSBYPK N4.....67 G3
Cyprus Gdns FNCH N3.....46 C5
Cyprus PI BETH E2.....104 E1
　EHAM E6.....108 A4
Cyprus Rd ED N9.....36 B4
　FNCH N3.....46 C5
Cyprus St BETH E2.....104 E1
Cyrena Rd EDUL SE22.....163 G1
Cyril Rd BXLYHN DA7.....149 F3
　ORP BR6.....202 B4
Cyrus St FSBYE EC1V.....6 B6
Czar St DEPT SE8.....124 D6

D

Dabbling CI ERITH DA8 *.....150 E1
Dabbs Hill La NTHLT UB5.....77 K4
D'Abernon CI ESH/CLAY KT10.....204 A2
Dabin Crs GNWCH SE10.....145 F2
Dacca St DEPT SE8.....124 C6
Dace Rd BOW E3.....87 J6
Dacre Av CLAY IG5.....54 A5
Dacre CI GFD/PVL UB6.....96 B1
Dacre Gdns LEW SE13.....145 H5
Dacre Pk LEE SE13.....145 H4
Dacre PL LEW SE13.....145 H4
Dacre Rd CROY/NA CR0.....195 K4
　PLSTW E13.....89 F2
　WAN E11.....70 C5
Dacres Est FSTH SE23 *.....164 A5
Dacres Rd FSTH SE23.....164 A5
Dade Wy NWDGN UB2.....114 E5
Daerwood CI HAYES BR2.....200 E5
Daffodil CI CROY/NA CR0.....198 A5
　HPTN TW12.....173 F2
Daffodil Gdns IL IG1.....90 B3
Daffodil St SHB W12.....99 H6
Dafforne Rd TOOT SW17.....160 E5
Dagenham Av DAGW RM9.....92 A6
Dagenham Rd DAGE RM10.....92 E2
　LEY E10.....69 H5
　RAIN RM13.....93 F5
　ROMW/RG RM7.....75 F4
Dagger La BORE WD6.....29 G1
Dagmar Av WBLY HA9.....80 B2
Dagmar Gdns WLSDN NW10.....100 B1
Dagmar Ms NWDGN UB2.....114 D3
Dagmar Pas IS N1.....85 H6
Dagmar Rd CMBW SE5.....143 F2
　FSBYPK N4.....67 G4
　KUTN/CMB KT2.....175 G4
　NWDGN UB2.....114 D3
　SNWD SE25.....197 F1
　WDGN N22.....48 D4
Dagmar Ter IS N1.....85 H6
Dagnall Pk SNWD SE25.....197 F2
Dagnall Rd SNWD SE25.....197 F3
Dagnall St BTSEA SW11.....140 E3
Dagonet Rd BMLY BR1.....165 K5
Dahlia Gdns IL IG1.....90 B4
　MTCM CR4.....195 J1
Dahlia Rd ABYW SE2.....128 C5
Dahomey Rd
　STRHM/NOR SW16.....179 H2
Daimler Wy WLGTN SM6.....210 E5
Daines CI MNPK E12.....71 K6
Dainford CI BMLY BR1.....183 G1
Daintry CI KTN/HRWW/WS HA3.....61 G1
Dairsie Rd ELTH/MOT SE9.....147 F2
Dairy CI BMLY BR1 *.....184 A3
　THHTH CR7.....180 D5
　WLSDN NW10.....81 J6
Dairy La WOOL/PLUM SE18.....126 E4
Dairyman CI CRICK NW2.....82 B2
Daisy CI CROY/NA CR0.....198 A5
Daisy La FUL/PGN SW6.....159 K1
Daisy Rd SWFD E18.....53 F5
Dakin PI WCHPL E1.....105 G4
Dakota CI WLGTN SM6.....211 F5
Dalberg Rd BRXS/STRHM SW2.....142 B6
Dalberg Wy ABYW SE2.....128 E3
Dalby Rd WAND/EARL SW18.....140 B5
Dalbys Crs TOTM N17.....50 A2
Dalby St KTTN NW5.....84 B4
Dalcross Rd HSLWW TW4.....134 D3
Dale Av EDGW HA8.....44 B4
　HSLWW TW4.....134 D4
Dalebury Rd TOOT SW17.....160 E4
Dale CI BAR EN5.....33 F1
　BKHTH/KID SE3.....145 K4
　DART DA1.....170 C1
Dale Dr YEAD UB4.....94 D3
Dale Gdns WFD IG8.....39 F6
Dale Green Rd FBAR/BDGN N11.....34 B5
Dale Grove NFNCH/WDSPK N12.....47 G1
Daleham Gdns HAMP NW3.....83 H4
Daleham Ms HAMP NW3.....83 H4
Dalemain Ms CAN/RD E16.....125 K1
Dale Park Av CAR SM5.....194 E6
Dale Park Rd NRWD SE19.....180 D4
Dale Rd DART DA1.....170 C1
　KTTN NW5.....84 A3
　STHL UB1.....114 C4
　SUT SM1.....208 D2
　SWLY BR8.....187 K6
　WALW SE17.....122 C6
Dale Rw NTGHL W11.....100 C5
Daleside CI ORP BR6.....217 G5
Daleside Gdns CHIG IG7.....217 G4
Daleside Rd HOR/WEW KT19.....207 F4
　STRHM/NOR SW16.....179 G1
Dalestone Ms HARH RM3.....57 J3
Dale St CHSWK W4.....118 B5
The Dale HAYES BR2.....215 H2
Dale Vw ERITH DA8.....150 D3
Dale View Crs CHING E4.....38 A4
Dale View Gdns CHING E4.....38 B4
Daleview Rd SEVS/STOTM N15.....68 A3
Dalewood Gdns WPK KT4.....192 E6
Dale Wood Rd ORP BR6.....201 K5
Daley St HOM E9.....87 F4
Daley Thompson Wy
　VX/NE SW8.....141 G4
Dalgarno Gdns NKENS W10.....100 A4
Dalgarno Wy NKENS W10.....100 A3
Dalkeith Gv STAN HA7.....43 K1
Dalkeith Rd DUL SE21.....162 D3
　IL IG1.....90 C1
Dallas Rd CHEAM SM3.....208 C4
　EA W5.....98 B4
　HDN NW4.....63 J4

SYD SE26.....163 J6
Dallas Ter HYS/HAR UB3.....113 J3
Dallega CI HYS/HAR UB3.....94 B6
Dallinger Rd LEE/GVPK SE12.....165 J1
Dalling Rd HMSMTH W6.....118 E4
Dallington Sq FSBYE EC1V.....6 B7
Dallington St FARR EC1M.....6 B7
Dallin Rd BXLYHS DA6.....149 F1
　WOOL/PLUM SE18.....147 G1
Dalmain Rd FSTH SE23.....164 A3
Dalmally Rd CROY/NA CR0.....197 G4
Dalmeny Av HOLWY N7.....84 D2
　STRHM/NOR SW16.....180 B5
Dalmeny CI ALP/SUD HA0.....79 J4
Dalmeny Crs HSLW TW3.....135 J5
Dalmeny Rd BAR EN5.....33 F3
　CAR SM5.....210 A5
　ERITH DA8.....149 J2
　HOLWY N7.....84 D2
　WPK KT4.....207 K1
Dalmeyer Rd WLSDN NW10.....81 H4
Dalmore Av ESH/CLAY KT10.....205 F4
Dalmore Rd DUL SE21.....162 D4
Dalrymple CI STHGT/OAK N14.....34 D2
Dalrymple Rd BROCKY SE4.....144 C5
Dalston Gdns STAN HA7.....44 A4
Dalston La HACK E8.....86 B4
Dalton Av MTCM CR4.....178 D5
Dalton CI ALP/SUD HA0.....79 J4
　YEAD UB4.....94 B1
Daltons Rd SWLY BR8.....203 K6
Dalton St WNWD SE27.....162 C4
Dalton Wy WAT WD17.....27 H1
Dalwood St CMBW SE5.....143 F2
Dalyell Rd BRXN/ST SW9.....142 A4
Damask Crs CAN/RD E16.....106 C3
Damer Ter WBPTN SW10.....140 B1
Dames Rd FSTGT E7.....88 E2
Dame St IS N1.....6 C2
Damien St WCHPL E1.....104 D4
Damon CI SCUP DA14.....168 C5
Damsel Ct BERM/RHTH SE16 *.....123 J2
Damson Dr HYS/HAR UB3.....94 E6
Damson Wy CAR SM5.....209 K6
Damsonwood Rd NWDGN UB2.....115 F3
Danbrook Rd
　STRHM/NOR SW16.....179 K4
Danbury CI CHDH RM6.....55 K6
Danbury Ms WLGTN SM6.....210 B2
Danbury Rd LOU IG10.....39 J1
　RAIN RM13.....93 H6
Danbury St IS N1.....6 B2
Danby St PECK SE15.....143 G4
Dancer Rd FUL/PGN SW6.....139 J2
　RCH/KEW TW9.....137 H4
Dandelion CI ROMW/RG RM7.....75 G6
Dando Crs BKHTH/KID SE3.....146 A4
Dandridge CI GNWCH SE10.....125 J5
Danebury CROY/NA CR0.....213 K4
Danebury Av PUT/ROE SW15.....158 C2
Daneby Rd CAT SE6.....165 F5
Dane CI BXLY DA5.....169 H2
　ORP BR6.....216 D3
Danecourt Gdns CROY/NA CR0.....212 A6
Danecroft Rd HNHL SE24.....142 D6
Danehurst St FUL/PGN SW6.....139 H2
Daneland EBAR EN4.....33 K1
Danemead Gv NTHLT UB5.....78 B3
Danemere St PUT/ROE SW15.....139 F4
Dane PI BOW E3.....105 H1
Dane Rd IL IG1.....90 C3
　STHL UB1.....95 J6
　WEA W13.....97 J6
　WIM/MER SW19.....178 B4
Danesbury Rd FELT TW13.....154 B4
Danescombe LEE/GVPK SE12.....165 K3
Danescourt Crs SUT SM1.....194 B6
Danescroft Av HDN NW4.....64 B2
Danescroft Gdns HDN NW4.....64 B2
Danesdale Rd HOM E9.....87 G4
Danes Ga HRW HA1.....42 E6
Danes Rd ROMW/RG RM7.....74 E5
Dane St GINN WC1R.....11 G2
Daneswood Av CAT SE6.....165 F5
Danethorpe Rd ALP/SUD HA0.....79 K4
Danetree CI HOR/WEW KT19.....206 E5
Danetree Rd HOR/WEW KT19.....206 E5
Daneville Rd CMBW SE5.....142 E2
Dangan Rd WAN E11.....70 E2
Daniel Bolt CI POP/IOD E14.....105 K4
Daniel CI HSLWW TW4.....154 D2
　TOOT SW17.....178 D2
　UED N18.....36 E6
Daniel Gdns PECK SE15.....143 G1
Daniell Wy CROY/NA CR0.....195 K5
Daniel PI HDN NW4.....63 K3
Daniel Rd EA W5.....98 B6
Daniel's Rd PECK SE15.....143 K4
Dan Leno Wk FUL/PGN SW6 *.....140 A1
Dan Manson Dr CHSWK W4.....138 A3
Dansey PI SOHO/SHAV W1D.....10 C5
Dansington Rd WELL DA16.....148 B4
Danson Crs WELL DA16.....148 C4
Danson La WELL DA16.....148 C5
Danson Md WELL DA16.....148 C4
Danson Rd BXLY DA5.....148 E6
　BXLYHS DA6.....148 E6
Danson U P BFN/LL DA15.....148 A6
Dante PI LBTH SE11.....18 A6
Dante Rd LBTH SE11.....18 B6
Danube St CHEL SW3.....15 J7
Danvers Rd CEND/HSY/T N8.....66 D1
Danvers St CHEL SW3.....120 C6
Danziger Wy BORE WD6.....24 E1

D'Arcy Rd CHEAM SM3.....208 B2
Darcy CI ISLW TW7.....136 B2
　STRHM/NOR SW16.....179 K5
Darell Rd RCH/KEW TW9.....137 H4
Darenth Rd DART DA1.....171 K4
　STNW/STAM N16.....68 B4
　WELL DA16.....148 B2
Darent Valley Pth ERITH DA8.....150 B1
Darfield Rd BROCKY SE4.....164 C5
Darfield Wy NKENS W10.....100 B6
Darfur St PUT/ROE SW15.....139 G4
Dargate CI NRWD SE19.....181 G5
Darien Rd BTSEA SW11.....140 C4
Darlands Dr BAR EN5.....20 B6
Darlan Rd FUL/PGN SW6.....139 J1
Darlaston Rd WIM/MER SW19.....177 G3
Darley CI CROY/NA CR0.....198 A3
Darley Dr NWMAL KT3.....176 A5
Darley Gdns MRDN SM4.....194 A3
Darley Rd BTSEA SW11.....160 E1
　ED N9.....36 B3
Darling Rd BROCKY SE4.....144 D4
Darling Rw WCHPL E1.....104 D3
Darlington Rd WNWD SE27.....180 C1
Darlton CI DART DA1.....150 C4
Darmaine CI SAND/SEL CR2.....211 J5
Darndale CI WALTH E17.....51 H5
　WFD IG8.....39 F4
Darnley Ter NTGHL W11.....119 G1
Darns HI SWLY BR8.....203 K4
Darrell Rd EDUL SE22.....143 H6
Darrick Wood Rd ORP BR6.....201 J6
Darris CI YEAD UB4.....95 J3
Darsley Dr VX/NE SW8.....141 J2
Dartford Av ED N9.....36 E1
Dartford Gdns CHDH RM6.....73 H2
Dartford Rd BXLY DA5.....169 K3
　DART DA1.....170 D1
Dartford St WALW SE17.....122 D6
Dartmoor Wk POP/IOD E14 *.....124 D4
Dartmouth CI NTGHL W11.....100 D5
Dartmouth Gv GNWCH SE10.....145 F2
Dartmouth HI GNWCH SE10.....145 F3
Dartmouth Park Av KTTN NW5.....84 B1
Dartmouth Park HI ARCH N19.....66 B6
　KTTN NW5.....84 B1
Dartmouth Park Rd KTTN NW5.....84 B1
Dartmouth PI CHSWK W4.....118 B6
　FSTH SE23.....163 K4
Dartmouth Rd CRICK NW2.....82 B4
　HAYES BR2.....199 K4
　HDN NW4.....63 J3
　RSLP HA4.....76 E1
　SYD SE26.....163 J6
Dartmouth Rw GNWCH SE10.....145 F3
Dartmouth St STJSPK SW1H.....16 C3
Dartmouth Ter GNWCH SE10.....145 G2
Dartnell Rd CROY/NA CR0.....197 G4
Dartrey Wk WBPTN SW10 *.....140 B1
Dart St NKENS W10.....100 C2
Darville Rd STNW/STAM N16.....68 B2
Darwell CI EHAM E6.....108 A1
Darwin CI FBAR/BDGN N11.....34 B5
　ORP BR6.....216 D3
Darwin Dr STHL UB1.....96 B5
Darwin Gdns OXHEY WD19.....41 G1
Darwin Rd EA W5.....116 C5
　WDGN N22.....49 H4
　WELL DA16.....148 A4
Darwin St WALW SE17.....19 F6
Daryngton Dr GFD/PVL UB6.....96 D1
Dashwood CI BXLYHS DA6.....149 H6
Dashwood Rd CEND/HSY/T N8.....67 F3
Dassett Rd WNWD SE27.....180 C1
Datchelor PI CMBW SE5 *.....142 E2
Datchet Rd CAT SE6.....164 C5
Date St WALW SE17.....122 E5
Daubeney Gdns TOTM N17.....49 J3
Daubeney Rd CLPT E5.....87 G2
　TOTM N17.....49 J3
Dault Rd WAND/EARL SW18.....160 B1
Davema CI CHST BR7.....185 F4
Davenant Rd ARCH N19.....66 D6
　CROY/NA CR0.....211 H2
Davenant St WCHPL E1.....104 C4
Davenham Av NTHWD HA6.....26 D3
Davenport CI TEDD TW11 *.....174 B2
Davenport Rd CAT SE6.....164 E1
　SCUP DA14.....168 E2
Daventer Dr STAN HA7.....43 F3
Daventry Av WALTH E17.....69 J3
Daventry St CAMTN NW1.....8 D1
Davern CI GNWCH SE10.....125 J4
Davey CI HOLWY N7.....85 F4
Davey Rd HOM E9.....87 J5
Davey St PECK SE15.....123 G6
David Av GFD/PVL UB6.....96 E2
David CI HYS/HAR UB3.....133 G1
Davidge St STHWK SE1.....18 B3
David Ms MHST W1U.....9 F1
Davidson Gdns VX/NE SW8.....141 K1
Davidson Rd CROY/NA CR0.....197 G4
David's Rd FSTH SE23.....163 K3
David St SRTFD E15.....88 B4
David's Wy BARK/HLT IG6.....54 E3
David Twigg CI KUTN/CMB KT2.....175 F4
Davies CI CROY/NA CR0.....197 G3
　RAIN RM13.....111 K4
Davies La WAN E11.....70 C6
Davies Ms MYFR/PKLN W1K.....9 J5
Davies St MYFR/PKLN W1K.....9 J5
Davies Wk ISLW TW7.....135 J2
Davington Gdns BCTR RM8.....91 G4
Davington Rd BCTR RM8.....91 H4
Davinia CI WFD IG8.....53 K2
Davis Rd ACT W3.....117 H1
　CHSGTN KT9.....206 C2
Davisville Rd SHB W12.....118 D2
Dawes Av ISLW TW7.....136 B6
Dawes CI ESH/CLAY KT10.....204 B3
Dawes Rd FUL/PGN SW6.....139 H1
Dawes St WALW SE17.....122 G5
Dawley Pde HYS/HAR UB3.....94 B6

Dawley Rd HYS/HAR UB3 .....94 B6
Dawlish Av GFD/PVL UB6.....97 C1
 PLMGR N13 .....34 E6
 WAND/EARL SW18.....160 A4
Dawlish Dr CDMY/SEVK IG3...91 F2
 PIN HA5.....33 J2
 RSLP HA4.....58 E6
Dawlish Rd CRICK NW2 .....82 B4
 LEY E10.....75 J1
 TOTM N17.....50 C6
Dawnay Gdns
 WAND/EARL SW18.....160 A4
Dawnay Rd WAND/EARL SW18..160 A4
Dawn Cl HSLWW TW4 .....134 D4
Dawn Crs SRTFD E15.....88 B6
Dawpool Rd CRICK NW2 .....63 H6
Daws La MLHL NW7.....45 F1
Dawson Av BARK IG11 .....91 F5
 STMC/STPC BR5.....186 C5
Dawson Cl HYS/HAR UB3 .....94 B6
 WOOL/PLUM SE18.....127 H4
Dawson Dr RAIN RM13.....93 K5
Dawson Gdns BARK IG11 .....91 F5
Dawson Pl BAY/PAD W2 .....100 E6
Dawson Rd CRICK NW2.....82 A3
 KUT/HW KT1.....175 G6
Dawson St BETH E2.....7 K5
Dawson Ter HPTN TW12 .....36 D2
Daybrook Rd WIM/MER SW19..178 A5
Daylesford Av PUT/ROE SW15..138 D5
Daymer Gdns PIN HA5 .....59 G1
Daysbrook Rd
 BRXS/STRHM SW2.....162 A3
Days La BFN/LL DA15.....167 K2
Dayton Dr ERITH DA8.....131 G6
Dayton Gv PECK SE15.....143 K2
Deacon Cl PUR/KEN CR8.....210 E6
The Deacon Est CHING E4 *....51 H2
Deacon Ms IS N1.....85 K5
Deacon Rd CRICK NW2.....81 J4
 KUT/HW KT1.....175 C4
Deacons Cl PIN HA5.....41 F5
Deacons Hts BORE WD6.....30 C1
Deacons Hl OXHEY WD19.....27 C1
Deacons Leas ORP BR6.....216 D2
Deacons Ri EFNCH N2.....65 H2
Deacons Ter IS N1 *.....85 J4
Deacons Wk HPTN TW12 .....155 F6
Deacon Wy WALW SE17.....18 D6
 WFD IG8.....53 K3
Deakin Cl WATW WD18.....26 C2
Deakins Ter ORP BR6.....202 B4
Deal Porters Wy
 BERM/RHTH SE16.....123 K3
Deal Rd TOOT SW17.....179 F2
Deals Gtwy LEW SE13.....144 E2
Deal St WCHPL E1.....104 C4
Dealtry Rd PUT/ROE SW15.....139 F5
Dean Bradley St WEST SW1P..16 E5
Dean Cl BERM/RHTH SE16.....124 A1
 HOM E9.....74 E4
Dean Ct ALP/SUD HA0.....79 H1
Deancross St WCHPL E1.....104 E5
Dean Dr STAN HA7.....44 A5
Deane Av RSLP HA4.....77 F3
Deane Cl NTHWD HA6.....40 C3
Deane Croft Rd PIN HA5.....58 E3
Deanery Cl EFNCH N2.....65 J1
Deanery Ms MYFR/PKLN W1K *..9 J1
Deanery Rd SRTFD E15.....88 C4
Deanery St MYFR/PKLN W1K..9 H7
Deane Wy RSLP HA4.....59 F3
Dean Farrar St STJSPK SW1H..16 D4
Deanfield Gdns
 CROY/NA CR0 *.....211 K3
Dean Gdns WALTH E17.....70 B1
Deanhill Ct
 MORT/ESHN SW14 *.....137 J5
Deanhill Rd MORT/ESHN SW14..137 J5
Dean Rd CRICK NW2.....82 A3
 CROY/NA CR0.....211 K2
 HPTN TW12.....155 F6
 HSLW TW3.....135 G6
 THMD SE28.....109 G6
Dean Ryle St WEST SW1P.....16 E6
Deansbrook Cl EDGW HA8.....44 E3
Deansbrook Rd EDGW HA8.....44 D3
Dean's Buildings WALW SE17..19 F7
Deans Cl CHSWK W4.....117 J6
 CROY/NA CR0.....212 B1
 EDGW HA8.....44 E2
Dean's Ct STP EC4M.....12 B4
Deanscroft Av CDALE/KGS NW9..62 E6
Dean's Dr EDGW HA8 .....45 F1
 PLMGR N13.....49 H2
Deans Gate Cl FSTH SE23.....164 A5
Dean's La EDGW HA8.....44 E2
Dean's Ms CAVSQ/HST W1G *..9 K3
Dean St HNWL W7.....116 A2
 SUT SM1.....209 F1
Dean Stanley St WEST SW1P..16 E5
Dean St FSTGT E7.....88 E3
 SOHO/SHAV W1D.....10 C3
Deansway ED N9.....36 A5
Deans Wy EDGW HA8 .....44 E1
Deansway N2.....65 H1
Deans Yd WEST SW1P.....16 D4
Dean Trench St WEST SW1P..16 E5
Dean Wy NWDGN UB2.....115 G2
Dearne Cl STAN HA7.....43 G1
De'Arn Gdns MTCM CR4.....178 D6
Dearsley Rd EN1.....24 C4
Deason St SRTFD E15 *.....88 A6
De Barowe Ms HBRY N5.....73 H3
Debden Cl CDALE/KGS NW9..45 G4
 KUT/HW KT1.....174 E1
 WFD IG8.....53 H3
De Beauvoir Crs IS N1 *.....86 A1
De Beauvoir Rd IS N1 *.....86 A1
De Beauvoir Sq IS N1.....86 A1
Debnams Rd
 BERM/RHTH SE16.....123 K4
De Bohun Av STHGT/OAK N14..34 B1
Deborah Cl ISLW TW7.....135 K2
Deborah Crs RSLP HA4.....58 B4

Debrabant Cl ERITH DA8.....130 A6
De Broome Rd FELT TW13.....154 A3
Deburgh Rd WIM/MER SW19..178 B3
Decima St STHWK SE1.....19 H4
Decimus St THHTH CR7.....196 E1
Deck Cl BERM/RHTH SE16.....124 A1
Decoy Av GLDGN NW11.....64 C2
De Crespigny Pk CMBW SE5..142 E3
Deeley Rd VX/NE SW8.....141 J2
Deepdale WIM/MER SW19.....159 G6
Deepdale Av HAYES BR2.....199 J1
Deepdale Cl FBAR/BDGN N11..48 A2
Deepdene Av CROY/NA CR0..212 B1
Deepdene Cl WAN E11.....70 E1
Deepdene Ct WCHMH N21.....35 H1
Deepdene Gdns
 BRXS/STRHM SW2.....162 A2
Deepdene Rd HNHL SE24.....142 D5
 WELL DA16.....148 B4
Deepwell Cl ISLW TW7.....136 B2
Deepwood La GFD/PVL UB6..96 D2
Deerbrook Rd HNHL SE24.....162 C3
Deerdale Rd HNHL SE24.....142 D5
Deere Av RAIN RM13.....93 J4
Deerfield Cl CDALE/KGS NW9..63 H2
Deerhurst Cl FELT TW13.....153 K6
Deerhurst Crs HPTN TW12.....173 H1
Deerhurst Rd WLHAMP NW6..82 E5
 STRHM/NOR SW16.....180 A1
Deerings Dr PIN HA5.....58 E2
Deerleap Gv CHING E4.....25 K6
Deer Park Cl KUTN/CMB KT2..175 J4
Deer Park Gdns MTCM CR4 *..194 C1
Deer Park Rd WIM/MER SW19..178 B5
Deer Park Wy WWKM BR4.....199 J6
Deeside Rd TOOT SW17.....160 C5
Dee St POP/IOD E14.....106 A5
Dee Wy ROM RM1.....57 G4
Defiant Wy WLGTN SM6.....210 E5
Defoe Av RCH/KEW TW9.....137 H1
Defoe Cl TOOT SW17.....178 D2
Defoe Pl TOOT SW17.....160 D4
Defoe Rd BERM/RHTH SE16..124 C2
 STHM/STAM N16.....68 A6
Defoe Wy CRW RM5.....56 C2
De Frene Rd SYD SE26.....164 B6
Degema Rd CHST BR7.....185 C3
Dehar Crs CDALE/KGS NW9..63 H4
De Havilland Dr
 WOOL/PLUM SE18.....127 C6
Dehavilland Cl NTHLT UB5.....95 H2
De Havilland Ct IL IG1.....72 C1
De Havilland Rd EDGW HA8..44 D5
 HEST TW5.....134 B1
De Havilland Wy
 STWL/WRAY TW19.....152 A1
Dekker Rd DUL SE21.....163 F1
Delacourt Rd BKHTH/KID SE3..146 A1
Delafield Rd CHARL SE7.....126 A5
Delaford Rd BERM/RHTH SE16..123 J5
Delaford St FUL/PGN SW6.....139 H1
Delamare Crs CROY/NA CR0..197 K3
Delamere Gdns MLHL NW7.....45 F1
Delamere Rd EA W5.....117 F2
 RYNPK SW20.....177 G4
 YEAD UB4.....95 H6
Delamere Ter BAY/PAD W2.....101 C4
Delancey Pas CAMTN NW1 *..3 K1
Delancey St CAMTN NW1.....3 K1
De Lapre Cl STMC/STPC BR5..202 E4
De Laune St LBTH SE11.....122 C6
Delaware Rd MV/WKIL W9.....101 F3
Delawyk Crs HNHL SE24.....162 E1
Delcombe Av WPK KT4.....193 F5
Delhi Rd EN EN1.....36 B2
Delhi St IS N1.....5 F1
Delia St WAND/EARL SW18..160 A2
Delisle Rd THMD SE28.....127 K2
Delius Gv SRTFD E15.....106 A1
Delia Pth CLPT E5.....86 C1
Dellbow Rd EBED/NFELT TW14..134 A6
Dell Cl SRTFD E15.....88 B6
 WFD IG8.....39 F5
 WLGTN SM6.....210 C2
Dell Farm Rd RSLP HA4.....58 B2
Dellfield Cl BECK BR3.....183 F4
Dell La EW KT17.....207 J5
Dellors Cl BAR EN5.....20 B6
Dell Rd DART DA1.....171 J2
 EW KT17.....207 J6
 PEND EN3.....25 F1
 WDR/YW UB7.....112 C3
Dells Cl CHING E4.....37 K2
 TEDD TW11.....174 A2
Dell's Ms PIM SW1V *.....16 B7
The Dell ABYW SE2.....128 B5
 ALP/SUD HA0.....79 H3
 BECK BR3 *.....182 D5
 BTFD TW8.....116 D6
 BXLY DA5.....170 B3
 EBED/NFELT TW14.....154 A3
 NRWD SE19.....181 G4
 NTHWD HA6.....26 A5
 PIN HA5.....41 H5
 WFD IG8.....39 F3
Dell Wk NWMAL KT3.....176 B5
Dell Wy WEA W13.....97 J5
Dellwood Gdns CLAY IG5.....54 A6
Delme Crs BKHTH/KID SE3..146 A3
Delmey Cl CROY/NA CR0.....212 B1
Deloraine St DEPT SE8.....144 D2
Delorme St HMSMTH W6.....119 G6
Delta Centre ALP/SUD HA0 *..80 B6
Delta Cl WPK KT4.....207 G1
Delta Est BETH E2 *.....104 C2
Delta Gain OXHEY WD19.....27 H4
Delta Gv NTHLT UB5.....95 H2
Delta Rd WPK KT4.....207 G1
Delta St BETH E2 *.....104 C2
De Luci St ERITH DA8.....129 K5
De Lucy St ABYW SE2.....128 C4

Delvers Md DAGE RM10.....92 E2
Delverton Rd WALW SE17.....122 C5
Delvino Rd FUL/PGN SW6.....139 K2
De Mandeville Ga EN EN1.....24 C5
Demesne Rd WLGTN SM6.....210 D3
Demeta Cl WBLY HA9.....80 E1
De Montfort Pde
 STRHM/NOR SW16 *.....161 K5
De Montfort Rd
 STRHM/NOR SW16.....161 K5
De Morgan Rd FUL/PGN SW6..140 A4
Dempster Cl SURB KT6.....190 D5
Dempster Rd
 WAND/EARL SW18.....160 B1
Denbar Pde ROMW/RG RM7..74 E1
Denberry Dr SCUP DA14.....168 C5
Denbigh Cl CHST BR7.....184 E2
 NTGHL W11.....100 D6
 STHL UB1.....95 J6
 SUT SM1.....208 D3
 WLSDN NW10.....81 G6
Denbigh Gdns
 RCHPK/HAM TW10.....137 G6
Denbigh Pl PIM SW1V *.....121 H5
Denbigh Rd EHAM E6.....107 H3
 HSLW TW3.....135 G3
 NTGHL W11.....100 D6
 STHL UB1.....95 J6
 WEA W13.....97 H6
Denbigh St PIM SW1V.....16 A7
Denbigh Ter NTGHL W11.....100 D6
Denbridge Rd BMLY BR1.....184 E5
Den Cl BECK BR3.....199 G1
Dendy St BAL SW12.....161 F3
Dene Av BFN/LL DA15.....168 C2
Dene Cl BROCKY SE4.....144 B4
 HAYES BR2.....199 J5
 RDART DA2.....170 B6
 WPK KT4.....192 C6
Dene Dr ORP BR6.....217 H1
Dene Gdns STAN HA7.....43 J1
 THDIT KT7.....190 B6
Denehurst Gdns ACT W3.....117 J1
 HDN NW4.....64 A3
 RCHPK/HAM TW10.....137 H5
 WFD IG8.....39 F6
 WHTN TW2.....155 G3
Dene Rd BKHH IG9.....39 J3
 DART DA1.....171 J2
 NTHWD HA6.....40 D3
 TRDG/WHET N20.....33 K3
The Dene CROY/NA CR0.....213 F2
 E/WMO/HCT KT8.....188 E2
 WBLY HA9.....80 A2
 WLGTN SM6 *.....210 C5
Denewood BAR EN5.....21 G6
Denewood Rd HGT N6.....65 K3
Dengie Wk IS N1 *.....6 A1
Denham Crs MTCM CR4.....194 E1
Denham Dr GNTH/NBYPK IG2..72 C3
Denham Rd EBED/NFELT TW14..154 B2
 TRDG/WHET N20.....33 J5
Denham Wy BARK IG11.....90 E6
Denholme Rd MV/WKIL W9..100 D2
Denholme Wk RAIN RM13.....93 H4
Denison Cl EFNCH N2.....47 G6
Denison Rd EA W5.....97 J3
 FELT TW13.....153 J6
 WIM/MER SW19.....178 C2
Denleigh Gdns THDIT KT7 *..189 K3
 WCHMH N21.....35 G3
Denman Dr ESH/CLAY KT10..205 G4
 GLDGN NW11.....64 E2
Denman Dr North
 GLDGN NW11.....64 E2
Denman Dr South
 GLDGN NW11.....64 E2
Denman Rd PECK SE15.....143 G2
Denman St SOHO/SHAV W1D..10 C6
Denmark Av WIM/MER SW19..177 H3
Denmark Ct MRDN SM4.....193 K2
Denmark Gdns CAR SM5.....209 J1
Denmark Gv IS N1.....5 J2
Denmark Hl HNHL SE24.....142 E5
Denmark Hill Dr
 CDALE/KGS NW9.....45 J6
Denmark Rd BMLY BR1.....184 A4
 CAR SM5.....209 J1
 CEND/HSY/T N8.....67 F1
 CMBW SE5.....142 D2
 KIL/WHAMP NW6.....100 D2
 KUT/HW KT1.....175 F6
 SNWD SE25.....197 J2
 WEA W13.....97 H6
 WHTN TW2.....155 H5
 WIM/MER SW19.....177 G2
Denmark St LSQ/SEVD WC2H..10 D4
 PLSTW E13.....107 F4
 TOTM N17.....50 D4
 WALTH E17.....69 J2
Denmark Ter EFNCH N2 *.....47 K6
Denmead Rd CROY/NA CR0..196 C5
Dennan Rd SURB KT6.....191 G5
Denner Rd CHING E4.....37 J4
Denne Ter HACK E8.....7 J1
Dennett Rd CROY/NA CR0..196 B4
Dennetts Gv NWCR SE14.....144 A3
Dennett's Rd NWCR SE14.....143 K2
Denning Av CROY/NA CR0..211 G3
Denning Cl HPTN TW12.....172 E1
 STJWD NW8.....101 G2
Denning Rd HAMP NW3.....83 H2
Dennington Park Rd
 KIL/WHAMP NW6.....82 E4
The Denningtons WPK KT4..192 B6
Dennis Av WBLY HA9.....80 B3
Dennis Gdns STAN HA7.....43 J1
Dennis La STAN HA7.....29 H6
Dennis Pde STHGT/OAK N14 *..34 D3
Dennis Park Crs RYNPK SW20..177 H4
Dennis Reeve Cl MTCM CR4..178 E4
Dennis Rd E/WMO/HCT KT8..189 F1
Dennis Wy CLAP SW4.....141 J4

Denny Gdns DAGW RM9.....91 H5
Denny Rd ED N9.....36 D3
Denny St LBTH SE11.....122 B5
Den Rd HAYES BR2.....183 G6
Densham Rd SRTFD E15.....88 C6
Densole Cl BECK BR3 *.....182 B4
Densworth Gv ED N9.....36 E4
Denton Cl BAR EN5.....20 A6
Denton Gv WOT/HER KT12..188 B1
Denton Rd CEND/HSY/T N8..67 F2
 DART DA1.....170 C6
 TWK TW1.....156 E1
 UED N18.....36 C6
 WELL DA16.....148 D1
Denton St WAND/EARL SW18..160 A1
Denton Ter BXLY DA5 *.....169 H4
Denton Wy CLPT E5.....87 F1
Dents Rd BTSEA SW11.....160 E1
Denvale Trade Pk MTCM CR4..194 C4
Denver Cl ORP BR6.....201 K3
Denver Rd DART DA1.....170 D6
 STNW/STAM N16.....68 A3
Denyer St CHEL SW3.....14 D6
Denzil Rd WLSDN NW10.....81 H4
Deodar Rd PUT/ROE SW15..139 H5
Deodora Cl TRDG/WHET N20..33 K5
Depot Ap CRICK NW2.....82 B2
Depot Rd HSLW TW3.....135 J4
 SHB W12.....99 K6
Depot St CMBW SE5 *.....122 E6
Deptford Br DEPT SE8.....144 D2
Deptford Broadway
 NWCR SE14.....144 D1
Deptford Church St DEPT SE8..144 D1
Deptford Gn DEPT SE8.....144 D1
Deptford High St DEPT SE8..124 D6
Deptford Whf DEPT SE8.....124 C4
De Quincey Ms CAN/RD E16..125 K1
De Quincey Rd TOTM N17.....49 K4
Derby Av HRW HA1.....42 D6
 NFNCH/WDSPK N12.....47 G1
 ROMW/RG RM7.....74 E3
Derby Ga WHALL SW1A.....16 D2
Derby Hl FSTH SE23.....163 K4
Derby Hill Crs FSTH SE23.....163 K4
Derby Rd BRYLDS KT5.....191 H5
 CROY/NA CR0.....196 C6
 EHAM E6.....89 K6
 FSTGT E7.....89 H5
 GFD/PVL UB6.....78 B6
 HOM E9.....75 F7
 HSLW TW3.....135 G5
 MORT/ESHN SW14.....137 H5
 PEND EN3.....24 D6
 SUT SM1.....208 D4
 SWFD E18.....52 D4
 UED N18.....50 E1
 WIM/MER SW19.....177 K3
Derbyshire St BETH E2.....104 C2
Derby St MYFR/PICC W1J.....15 H1
Dereham Pl CRW RM5.....56 D2
 SDTCH EC2A.....7 H5
Dereham Rd BARK IG11.....91 F4
Derek Av HOR/WEW KT19..206 C4
 WBLY HA9.....80 E5
 WLGTN SM6.....210 B3
Derek Cl HOR/WEW KT19..206 D5
Derek Walcott Cl HNHL SE24 *..142 C6
Dericote St HACK E8.....86 C6
Deri Dene Cl
 STWL/WRAY TW19 *.....152 B1
Derifall Cl EHAM E6.....107 K4
Dering Pl CROY/NA CR0.....211 J2
Dering Rd CROY/NA CR0.....211 J2
Dering St OXSTW W1C.....9 J4
Derinton Rd TOOT SW17.....161 F6
Derley Rd NWDGN UB2.....114 B3
Dermody Gdns LEW SE13.....145 G6
Dermody Rd LEW SE13.....145 G6
Deronda Rd HNHL SE24.....162 C3
Deroy Cl CAR SM5.....209 K4
Derrick Gdns CHARL SE7.....126 B3
Derrick Rd BECK BR3.....182 C6
Derry Downs STMC/STPC BR5..202 D3
Derry Rd CROY/NA CR0.....210 E2
Derry St KENS W8.....120 A2
Dersingham Av MNPK E12..90 A3
Dersingham Rd CRICK NW2..82 C1
Derwent Av CDALE/KGS NW9..63 G2
 EBAR EN4.....33 K3
 MLHL NW7.....45 F3
 PIN HA5.....41 J2
 PUT/ROE SW15.....158 B6
 UED N18.....50 A1
Derwent Cl DART DA1.....170 E3
 EBED/NFELT TW14.....153 J5
 ESH/CLAY KT10.....205 F5
Derwent Crs BXLYHN DA7..149 H3
 NFNCH/WDSPK N12.....47 G2
 STAN HA7.....43 J5
Derwent Dr PLMGR N13.....35 F6
 RYNPK SW20.....193 K3
 STMC/STPC BR5.....201 H3
 WHTN TW2.....155 F1
Derwent Gdns REDBR IG4.....71 J3
 WBLY HA9.....61 J6
Derwent Gv EDUL SE22.....143 G5
Derwent Ri CDALE/KGS NW9..63 G3
Derwent Rd EA W5.....116 D3
 EBED/NFELT TW14.....153 J5
 ESH/CLAY KT10.....204 E2
 PGE/AN SE20.....181 H5
 PLMGR N13.....35 F6
 RYNPK SW20.....193 K3
 STHL UB1.....95 J6
 WHTN TW2.....155 F1
Derwent St GNWCH SE10.....125 H5
Derwentwater Rd ACT W3.....117 K1
Derwent Wy HCH RM12.....93 K3
Desborough Cl BAY/PAD W2..101 F4
 SHPTN TW17.....188 C6
De Sails Rd HGDN/ICK UB10..94 A4
Desenfans Rd DUL SE21.....163 F1
Desford Rd CAN/RD E16.....106 C3
Desford Wy ASHF TW15.....152 C4
Desmond St NWCR SE14.....124 B6
Desmond Tutu Dr FSTH SE23..164 B3
Despard Rd ARCH N19.....66 C5
Detling Rd BMLY BR1.....165 K6
 ERITH DA8.....150 A1
Detmold Rd CLPT E5.....68 E6
Devalls Cl EHAM E6.....108 B6
Devana End CAR SM5.....209 K1

Devas Rd RYNPK SW20.....177 F4
Devas St BOW E3.....105 K3
Devenay Rd SRTFD E15.....88 D5
Devenish Rd ABYW SE2.....128 B2
De Vere Cl WLGTN SM6.....210 E5
De Vere Gdns IL IG1.....71 K5
 KENS W8.....120 B2
Deverell St STHWK SE1.....18 E5
De Vere Ms KENS W8 *.....120 B3
Devereux Ct TPL/STR WC2R..11 J5
Devereux La BARN SW13.....138 E1
Devereux Rd BTSEA SW11.....160 E1
Deveron Wy ROM RM1.....57 G4
Devey Cl KUTN/CMB KT2.....176 C3
Devizes St IS N1 *.....7 F1
Devoke Wy WOT/HER KT12..188 C6
Devon Av WHTN TW2.....155 H3
Devon Cl BKHH IG9.....39 F4
 GFD/PVL UB6.....79 J6
 TOTM N17.....50 C7
Devoncroft Gdns TWK TW1..156 B2
Devon Gdns FSBYPK N4.....67 H3
Devonhurst Pl CHSWK W4 *..118 A5
Devonia Gdns UED N18.....49 J2
Devonia Rd IS N1.....6 B1
Devon Ms
 KTN/HRWW/WS HA3 *.....61 J2
Devonport Gdns IL IG1.....71 K3
Devonport Ms SHB W12 *.....118 E1
Devonport Rd SHB W12.....118 E2
Devonport St WCHPL E1.....104 E5
Devon Ri EFNCH N2.....65 H1
Devon Rd BARK IG11.....90 E6
 BELMT SM2.....208 C6
Devons Est BOW E3.....105 K2
Devonshire Av BELMT SM2..209 G5
 DART DA1.....170 C1
Devonshire Cl CAVSQ/HST W1G..9 J2
 FSTGT E7.....89 H5
 SRTFD E15.....88 C2
Devonshire Crs MLHL NW7..46 B3
Devonshire Dr GNWCH SE10..144 E2
 SURB KT6.....190 E5
Devonshire Gdns CHSWK W4..137 K1
 TOTM N17.....49 J2
 WCHMH N21.....35 J2
Devonshire Gv PECK SE15..123 J6
Devonshire Hill La TOTM N17..49 J3
Devonshire Ms South
 CAVSQ/HST W1G.....9 J1
Devonshire Ms West
 CAVSQ/HST W1G.....9 J1
Devonshire Pl CAVSQ/HST W1G..9 J1
 CRICK NW2.....82 E1
 KENS W8.....120 A3
Devonshire Place Ms
 CAVSQ/HST W1G.....9 J1
Devonshire Rd BELMT SM2..209 G5
 BXLYHS DA6.....149 F5
 CAN/RD E16.....107 C5
 CAR SM5.....210 A2
 CHSWK W4.....118 B5
 CROY/NA CR0.....196 E4
 EA W5.....116 D3
 ED N9.....36 E3
 ELTH/MOT SE9.....166 D4
 FELT TW13.....154 C5
 FSTH SE23.....164 A2
 GNTH/NBYPK IG2.....72 D4
 HRW HA1.....60 D3
 MLHL NW7.....46 B3
 PIN HA5.....59 K1
 PIN HA5.....41 K4
 PLMGR N13.....51 G4
 STHL UB1.....96 A4
 WALTH E17.....69 J3
 WAN E11.....70 C4
 WIM/MER SW19.....178 D3
Devonshire Rw LVPST EC2M..13 H2
Devonshire Row Ms
 GTPST W1W *.....3 K7
Devonshire Sq HAYES BR2..200 A1
 LVPST EC2M.....13 H3
Devonshire St CAVSQ/HST W1G..9 J1
 CHSWK W4.....118 B6
Devonshire Ter BAY/PAD W2..101 C5
Devons Rd BOW E3.....105 K4
Devon St PECK SE15.....123 J6
Devon Wy CHSGTN KT9.....205 J3
 HOR/WEW KT19.....206 D3
Devon Waye HEST TW5.....134 E1
De Walden St CAVSQ/HST W1G..9 H2
Dewar St PECK SE15.....143 H4
Dewberry Gdns EHAM E6..107 J4
Dewberry St POP/IOD E14..106 A5
Dewey La BRXS/STRHM SW2..162 B1
Dewey Rd DAGE RM10.....92 D4
 IS N1.....5 J1
Dewey St TOOT SW17.....178 E1
Dewhurst Rd HMSMTH W6..118 C3
Dewsbury Cl PIN HA5.....59 J3
Dewsbury Gdns WPK KT4..207 J1
Dewsbury Rd WLSDN NW10..81 J3
Dexter Rd BAR EN5.....32 B1
Deyncourt Rd TOTM N17.....49 J4
D'Eynsford Rd CMBW SE5..142 E2
Diadem Ct SOHO/CST W1F *..10 C4
Diamedes Av
 STWL/WRAY TW19.....152 A2
Diameter Rd STMC/STPC BR5..201 G4
Diamond Cl BCTR RM8.....73 J5
Diamond Rd RSLP HA4.....77 H3
Diamond St PECK SE15.....143 F1
 WLSDN NW10.....81 F5
Diamond Ter GNWCH SE10..145 F2
Diana Cl DEPT SE8.....124 C6
 SCUP DA14.....168 E6
 SWFD E18.....53 F4
Diana Pl CAMTN NW1.....3 K6
Diana Rd WALTH E17.....51 H6

Dianne Wy *EBAR* EN4.................21 J5
Dianthus Cl *ABYW* SE2 *.........128 C5
Diban Av *HCH* RM12................93 K2
Dibden St *IS* N1.........................85 J6
Dibdin Rd *SUT* SM1................208 E1
Dicey Av *CRICK* NW2..................82 A3
Dickens Av *DART* DA1.............151 K5
FNCH N3.................................47 G4
Dickens Cl *ERITH* DA8...............149 J1
HYS/HAR UB3........................113 H4
RCHPK/HAM TW10...............157 F4
Dickens Est
BERM/RHTH SE16 *..............123 H3
Dickens La *UED* N18...................50 A1
Dickens Ms *FARR* EC1M...............6 A7
Dickenson Cl *ED* N9....................36 C3
Dickenson Rd *CEND/HSY/T* N8.....66 E4
FELT TW13............................172 B1
Dickenson's La *SNWD* SE25.......197 H3
Dickenson's Pl *SNWD* SE25.......197 H5
Dickens Ri *CHIG* IG7...................54 D1
Dickens Rd *EHAM* E6................107 H1
Dickens Sq *STHWK* SE1..............18 D4
Dickens St *VX/NE* SW8.............141 G3
Dickens Wood Cl *NRWD* SE19....180 C3
Dickerage La *NWMAL* KT3.........175 H6
Dickerage Rd *KUT/HW* KT1.......175 K4
Dickson Fold *PIN* HA5.................59 H1
Dickson House *CHARL* SE7 *......146 D1
Dickson Rd *ELTH/MOT* SE9.......146 D4
Dick Turpin Wy
EBED/NFELT TW14.................133 J5
Didsbury Cl *EHAM* E6..................89 K6
Digby Crs *FSBYPK* N4.................67 J6
Digby Gdns *DAGE* RM10............92 C6
Digby Pl *CROY/NA* CRO.............212 B1
Digby Rd *BARK* IG11..................91 F5
HOM E9..................................87 F3
Digby St *BETH* E2.....................104 E2
Diggon St *WCHPL* E1................105 F4
Dighton Rd *WAND/EARL* SW18..140 B6
Dignum St *IS* N1 *.......................5 J2
Digswell St *HOLWY* N7 *............85 G4
Dilhorne Cl *LEE/GVPK* SE12......166 A5
Dilke St *CHEL* SW3...................116 E5
Dillwyn Cl *SYD* SE26................164 B6
Dilston Cl *NTHLT* UB5................95 G2
Dilton Gdns *PUT/ROE* SW15.....158 D3
Dimes Pl *HMSMTH* W6.............118 E4
Dimmock Dr *GFD/PVL* UB6.........78 D3
Dimond Cl *FSTGT* E7..................88 E3
Dimsdale Dr *CDALE/KGS* NW9......62 E1
EN EN1....................................36 C2
Dimson Crs *BOW* E3.................105 J3
Dingle Cl *BAR* EN5.....................19 K6
Dingle Gdns *POP/IOD* E14 *.....105 J6
Dingley La *STRHM/NOR* SW16...161 J4
Dingley Pl *FSBYE* EC1V................6 C6
Dingley Rd *FSBYE* EC1V...............6 C5
Dingwall Av *CROY/NA* CRO.......196 D6
Dingwall Gdns *GLDGN* NW11......64 E3
Dingwall Rd *CAR* SM5...............209 K6
CROY/NA CRO.......................196 E6
WAND/EARL SW18.................160 B2
Dinmont St *BETH* E2.................104 D1
Dinsdale Gdns *BAR* EN5..............21 F6
SNWD SE25............................197 F2
Dinsdale Rd *BKHTH/KID* SE3....125 J6
Dinsmore Rd *BAL* SW12............161 G2
Dinton Rd *KUTN/CMB* KT2.......175 J1
WIM/MER SW19.....................178 C2
Diploma Av *EFNCH* N2................65 J1
Dirleton Rd *SRTFD* E15...............88 D7
Disbrowe Rd *HMSMTH* W6........119 H6
Discovery Wk *WAP* E1W *..........104 D6
Dishforth La *CDALE/KGS* NW9....45 G4
Disney Pl *STHWK* SE1.................18 D2
Disney St *STHWK* SE1.................18 D2
Dison Cl *PEND* EN3.....................25 F2
Disraeli Cl *THMD* SE28.............128 C1
Disraeli Rd *EA* W5....................116 E1
FSTGT E7................................88 E4
PUT/ROE SW15.....................139 H5
WLSDN NW10..........................98 E1
Diss St *BETH* E2..........................7 J4
Distaff La *BLKFR* EC4V................12 C5
Distillery La *HMSMTH* W6.........119 F5
Distillery Rd *HMSMTH* W6........119 F5
Distin St *LBTH* SE11....................17 J7
District Rd *ALP/SUD* HA0............79 H3
Ditchburn St *POP/IOD* E14.......106 A6
Ditchfield Rd *YEAD* UB4..............95 J3
Dittisham Rd *ELTH/MOT* SE9....166 D6
Ditton Cl *THDIT* KT7.................190 B4
Dittoncroft Cl *CROY/NA* CRO....212 A2
Ditton Grange Cl *SURB* KT6......190 E5
Ditton Grange Dr *SURB* KT6......190 E5
Ditton Hl *SURB* KT6..................190 D5
Ditton Hill Rd *SURB* KT6...........190 D5
Ditton Lawn *THDIT* KT7............190 B5
Ditton Pl *PGE/AN* SE20 *..........181 J4
Ditton Reach *THDIT* KT7............190 C3
Ditton Rd *BXLYHS* DA6.............148 E6
NWDGN UB2..........................114 C5
SURB KT6..............................191 F5
Dixey Cottages *EFNCH* N2 *.......65 J2
Dixon Cl *EHAM* E6....................107 K5
Dixon Pl *WWKM* BR4...............198 E5
Dixon Rd *NWCR* SE14...............144 B2
SNWD SE25............................181 F6
Dixon's Aly *CROY/NA* CRO *.....196 D1
Dobell Rd *ELTH/MOT* SE9.........146 E5
Dobree Av *WLSDN* NW10...........81 K5
Dobson Cl *KIL/WHAMP* NW6.......83 H5
Dockers Tanner Rd
POP/IOD E14.........................124 D4
Dockhead *STHWK* SE1................19 K3
Dock Hill Av *BERM/RHTH* SE16.124 A2
Dockland St *CAN/RD* E16.........126 E1
Dockley Rd *BERM/RHTH* SE16...123 H5
Dock Rd *BTFD* TW8 *................136 E1
CAN/RD E16...........................106 D6
Dockside Rd *CAN/RD* E16.........107 H6
Dock St *WCHPL* E1....................104 C6
Dockwell Cl *EBED/NFELT* TW14.133 K5

Doctors Cl *SYD* SE26................181 K1
Docwra's Buildings *IS* N1...........86 A4
Dodbrooke Rd *WNWD* SE27.....162 B5
Doddington Gv *WALW* SE17......122 C6
Doddington Pl *LBTH* SE11.........122 C6
Dodsley Pl *ED* N9.......................36 E5
Dodson St *STHWK* SE1...............17 K3
Dod St *POP/IOD* E14.................105 J5
Doebury Wk
WOOL/PLUM SE18.................128 B6
Doel Cl *WIM/MER* SW19...........178 B3
Doggett Rd *CAT* SE6.................164 D2
Doggetts Ct *EBAR* EN4...............21 J6
Doghurst Av *WDR/YW* UB7.......132 E1
Doghurst Dr *WDR/YW* UB7.......132 E1
Dog La *WLSDN* NW10................81 G1
Dog Rose Ramble *YEAD* UB4......76 B6
Dog Rose Ramble & Hillingdon
Trail *YEAD* UB4.......................76 B6
YEAD UB4..............................76 D6
Doherty Rd *PLSTW* E13.............106 E3
Dolben Ct *DEPT* SE8.................124 C4
Dolben St *STHWK* SE1................18 B1
Dolby Rd *FUL/PGN* SW6............139 J3
Dolland St *LBTH* SE11...............122 A5
Dollary Pde *KUT/HW* KT1 *.......175 J6
Dollis Av *FNCH* N3......................46 D4
Dollis Crs *RSLP* HA4...................59 G5
Dollis Hill Av *CRICK* NW2............81 K1
Dollis Hill La *CRICK* NW2.............81 J1
Dollis Hill La *CRICK* NW2.............81 J1
Dollis Pk *FNCH* N3.....................46 D4
Dollis Rd *MLHL* NW7..................46 C4
Dollis Valley Dr *BAR* EN5...........32 D1
Dollis Valley Green Wk
BAR EN5..................................33 F2
FNCH N3.................................64 C1
HDN NW4................................46 C5
Dollis Valley Wy *EBAR* EN4.........21 H5
Dolman Cl *FNCH* N3...................47 G5
Dolman Rd *CHSWK* W4.............118 A4
Dolman St *CLAP* SW4...............142 A5
Dolphin Ap *ROM* RM1.................75 H1
Dolphin Cl *BERM/RHTH* SE16....124 A2
SURB KT6..............................190 E3
THMD SE28............................109 K5
Dolphin La *POP/IOD* E14..........105 K6
Dolphin Rd *NTHLT* UB5..............95 K1
Dolphin Rd North *SUN* TW16 *..172 B5
Dolphin Sq *CHSWK* W4 *..........138 B1
PIM SW1V..............................121 G6
Dolphin St *KUT/HW* KT1...........175 F5
Dombey St *BMSBY* WC1N...........11 G1
Dome Buildings
RCH/KEW TW9 *....................136 E6
Dome Hill Pk *SYD* SE26............163 G4
Domett Cl *CMBW* SE5...............142 E5
Domingo St *FSBYE* EC1V..............6 C6
Dominion Cl *HSLW* TW3............135 J3
Dominion Dr *CRW* RM5...............56 D2
Dominion Pde *HRW* HA1 *...........61 F2
Dominion Rd *CROY/NA* CRO......197 G4
NWDGN UB2..........................114 D3
Dominion St *LVPST* EC2M...........13 F1
Dominion Wy *RAIN* RM13..........111 J2
Domonic Dr *ELTH/MOT* SE9.......167 G5
Domville Cl *TRDG/WHET* N20......33 H4
Donald Dr *CHDH* RM6.................73 J2
Donald Rd *CROY/NA* CRO..........196 A3
PLSTW E13..............................89 F6
Donaldson Rd
KIL/WHAMP NW6....................82 D6
WOOL/PLUM SE18.................147 F2
Donald Woods Gdns
BRYLDS KT5...........................191 H6
Doncaster Dr *NTHLT* UB5............77 K3
Doncaster Gdns *FSBYPK* N4 *....67 J3
NTHLT UB5..............................77 K3
Doncaster Gn *OXHEY* WD19......41 G1
Doncaster Rd *ED* N9...................36 D2
Donegal St *IS* N1..........................5 G4
Doneraile St *FUL/PGN* SW6.......139 G3
Dongola Rd *PLSTW* E13.............107 F2
TOTM N17................................50 A6
WCHPL E1................................105 G4
Dongola Rd West *PLSTW* E13....107 F2
Donington Av *BARK/HLT* IG6.......72 C2
Donkey Aly *EDUL* SE22.............163 H2
Donkey La *EN* EN1......................24 C3
Donnefield Av *EDGW* HA8...........44 A2
Donne Pl *CHEL* SW3....................14 D6
MTCM CR4.............................195 G1
Donne Rd *BCTR* RM8...................73 J6
Donnington Rd
KTN/HRWW/WS HA3..............61 K3
WLSDN NW10..........................81 K6
WPK KT4................................192 D6
Donnybrook Rd
STRHM/NOR SW16................179 J3
Donoghue Cottages
POP/IOD E14 *.......................105 G4
Donovan Av *MUSWH* N10...........48 B5
Donovan Pl *WCHMH* N21...........23 F5
Don Phelan Cl *CMBW* SE5.........142 E2
Don Wy *ROM* RM1......................57 G3
Doone St *TEDD* TW11................174 B2
Dorado Gdns *ORP* BR6..............217 K1
Doral Wy *CAR* SM5...................209 K3
Dorando Cl *SHB* W12 *..............99 K6
Doran Gv *WOOL/PLUM* SE18.....147 K1
Dora Rd *WIM/MER* SW19..........177 K1
Dora St *POP/IOD* E14.................105 H5
Dora Wy *BRXN/ST* SW9.............142 B3
Dorcas Ct *BXLY* DA5.................168 E5
PLMGR N13.............................35 J6
RYLN/HDSTN HA2...................60 C2
Dorchester Cl *DART* DA1...........171 J3
NTHLT UB5..............................78 B3
STMC/STPC BR5....................186 C5
Dorchester Dr
EBED/NFELT TW14................153 H1
HNHL SE24.............................142 D6

Dorchester Gdns *CHING* E4........37 J5
GLDGN NW11 *.......................64 E1
Dorchester Gv *CHSWK* W4........118 C5
Dorchester Ms *TWK* TW1..........156 D1
Dorchester Pde
STRHM/NOR SW16 *...............161 K4
Dorchester Rd *MRDN* SM4........194 B4
NTHLT UB5..............................78 B3
WPK KT4................................193 F5
Dorchester Ter *HDN* NW4 *........46 B5
Dorchester Wy
KTN/HRWW/WS HA3..............62 B3
Dorcis Av *BXLYHN* DA7............149 F3
Dordrecht Rd *ACT* W3...............118 B1
Dore Av *MNPK* E12......................90 B3
Doreen Av *CDALE/KGS* NW9......63 F5
Dore Gdns *MRDN* SM4..............194 A4
Dorell Cl *STHL* UB1.....................95 K4
Dorian Rd *HCH* RM12.................75 J5
Doria Rd *FUL/PGN* SW6............139 J3
Doric Wy *CAMTN* NW1.................4 C4
Dorie Ms *NFNCH/WDSPK* N12....33 F5
Dorien Rd *RYNPK* SW20............177 G5
Doris Av *ERITH* DA8..................149 K2
Doris Rd *FSTGT* E7.....................88 E5
Dorking Cl *DEPT* SE8.................124 C6
WPK KT4................................193 G6
Dorlcote Rd *WAND/EARL* SW18.160 D2
Dorman Pl *ED* N9........................36 C4
Dorman Wy *STJWD* NW8.............2 A1
Dorma Trad Est *LEY* E10.............69 F5
Dormans Cl *NTHWD* HA6.............40 A3
Dormay St *WAND/EARL* SW18....140 A6
Dormer Cl *BAR* EN5....................20 B6
SRTFD E15..............................88 D4
Dormers Av *STHL* UB1.................96 A5
Dormer's Ri *STHL* UB1................96 B6
Dormer's Wells La *STHL* UB1.......96 B6
Dormywood *RSLP* HA4................58 D2
Dornberg Cl *BKHTH/KID* SE3....145 K1
Dornberg Rd *BKHTH/KID* SE3 *..146 A1
Dorncliffe Rd *FUL/PGN* SW6.....139 H3
Dorney Ri *STMC/STPC* BR5.......202 A1
Dorney Wy *HSLWW* TW4...........134 D6
Dornfell St *KIL/WHAMP* NW6......82 D3
Dornton Rd *BAL* SW12..............161 G4
SAND/SEL CR2.......................212 A3
Dorothy Av *ALP/SUD* HA0...........80 A5
Dorothy Evans Cl *BCTR* RM8 *....92 D4
Dorothy Gdns *BCTR* RM8............91 H2
Dorothy Rd *BTSEA* SW11...........140 E4
Dorrell Pl *BRXN/ST* SW9...........142 B4
Dorrington St *HCIRC* EC1N..........11 J1
Dorrington Wy *BECK* BR3...........199 F2
Dorrit Ms *UED* N18......................36 B6
Dorrit St *STHWK* SE1 *...............18 D2
Dorrit Wy *CHST* BR7.................185 H2
Dors Cl *CDALE/KGS* NW9...........63 F5
Dorset Av *NWDGN* UB2.............114 D4
ROM RM1................................57 F6
YEAD UB4...............................95 F2
Dorset Buildings *EMB* EC4Y *....12 A4
Dorset Cl *CAMTN* NW1................8 E1
YEAD UB4...............................94 C2
Dorset Dr *EDGW* HA8.................44 B2
Dorset Gdns *MTCM* CR4............194 A1
Dorset Ms *FNCH* N3...................46 E4
BGVA SW1W...........................15 J4
Dorset Pl *SRTFD* E15..................88 B4
Dorset Ri *EMB* EC4Y...................12 A4
Dorset Rd *ASHF* TW15..............152 A5
BECK BR3..............................198 A6
ELTH/MOT SE9......................166 D4
FSTGT E7................................89 G1
HRW HA1................................60 C3
MTCM CR4.............................178 D5
SEVS/STOTM N15....................67 K1
VX/NE SW8............................141 H2
WDGN N22..............................48 E4
WIM/MER SW19.....................177 K4
Dorset Sq *CAMTN* NW1...............8 E1
Dorset St *MHST* W1U..................9 F2
Dorset Wy *TWK* TW2................155 H3
Dorset Waye *HEST* TW5.............134 E1
Dorton Cl *PECK* SE15................143 F1
Dorville Crs *HMSMTH* W6..........118 E3
Dorville Rd *LEE/GVPK* SE12......145 K6
Dothill Rd *WOOL/PLUM* SE18....147 H1
Douai Gv *HPTN* TW12................173 H4
Doughty Ms *BMSBY* WC1N..........5 G7
Doughty St *BMSBY* WC1N...........5 G6
Douglas Av *ALP/SUD* HA0...........80 A5
NWMAL KT3...........................192 E1
WALTH E17..............................51 J4
Douglas Cl *BARK/HLT* IG6...........54 B3
STAN HA7................................43 G1
WLGTN SM6..........................210 E4
Douglas Crs *YEAD* UB4...............95 G3
Douglas Dr *CROY/NA* CRO.........213 J1
Douglas Est *IS* N1........................85 J4
Douglas La *STWL/WRAY* TW19.152 B1
Douglas Ms *CRICK* NW2..............82 B1
Douglas Pth *POP/IOD* E14 *......125 F5
Douglas Pl *POP/IOD* E14 *........125 F5
Douglas Rd *CAN/RD* E16..........106 E4
CHING E4................................38 C2
ESH/CLAY KT10.....................189 G6
GDMY/SEVK IG3......................73 G2
HSLW TW3.............................135 G4
IS N1......................................85 J5
KIL/WHAMP NW6....................82 E6
KUT/HW KT1.........................175 H5
ROM RM1................................75 H3
STWL/WRAY TW19................152 A1
SURB KT6..............................191 G6
WDGN N22..............................49 G4
WELL DA16............................148 C2
Douglas Rd North *IS* N1...............85 J4
Douglas Rd South *IS* N1...............85 J3
Douglas St *WEST* SW1P..............16 C7
Douglas Ter *WALTH* E17 *...........51 H4
Douglas Vls *KUT/HW* KT1 *.......175 G5
Doulton Ms *KIL/WHAMP* NW6.....83 F4
Dounesforth Gdns
WAND/EARL SW18................160 A3

Douro Pl *KENS* W8....................120 A3
Douro St *BOW* E3......................105 J1
Douthwaite Sq *WAP* E1W *.......123 H1
Dove Ap *EHAM* E6.....................107 J4
Dove Cl *MLHL* NW7.....................45 H3
NTHLT UB5..............................95 F2
WLGTN SM6..........................211 F5
Dovecot Cl *PIN* HA5...................59 G2
Dove Ct *LOTH* EC2R *................12 E4
Dovedale Av *CLAY* IG5................54 A5
KTN/HRWW/WS HA3..............61 J3
Dovedale Cl *WELL* DA16............148 B2
Dovedale Ri *MTCM* CR4.............178 E3
Dovedale Rd *EDUL* SE22...........143 J6
Dovedon Cl *STHGT/OAK* N14......34 E4
Dove House Gdns *CHING* E4........37 J4
Dovehouse Md *BARK* IG11.........108 D1
Dovehouse St *CHEL* SW3...........120 D5
Dove Ms *ECT* SW5.....................120 B4
Doveney Cl *STMC/STPC* BR5.....186 D6
Dover Cl *CRICK* NW2....................64 B6
CRW RM5................................56 E5
Dovercourt Av *THHTH* CR7........196 B1
Dovercourt Est *IS* N1...................85 K4
Dovercourt Gdns *STAN* HA7........44 A1
Dovercourt La *SUT* SM1............209 G1
Dovercourt Rd *DUL* SE21..........163 F1
Doverfield Rd
BRXS/STRHM SW2.................161 K2
Dover Gdns *CAR* SM5................209 K1
Dove Pk *PIN* HA5........................41 K5
Dover Park Dr *PUT/ROE* SW15..158 E1
Dover Patrol *BKHTH/KID* SE3....146 A3
Dover Rd *ED* N9..........................36 A1
MNPK E12................................71 G6
NRWD SE19............................180 E2
WOOL/PLUM SE18.................147 G3
Dover St *CONDST* W1S................9 K6
Dover Ter *RCH/KEW* TW9 *.......137 H3
Doves Yd *IS* N1...........................85 G6
Doveton Rd *SAND/SEL* CR2......211 K3
Doveton St *WCHPL* E1................104 E3
Dowanhill Rd *CAT* SE6..............165 G3
Dowdeswell Cl
PUT/ROE SW15.....................138 D5
Dowding Pl *STAN* HA7................43 G2
Dowding Rd *HCH* RM12..............93 K5
Dowe Av *WLCTN* SM6...............210 B6
Dowgate Hl *CANST* EC4R............12 E5
Dowland St *NKENS* W10............100 C2
Dowlas St *CMBW* SE5...............143 F1
Dowlerville Rd *ORP* BR6............217 F4
Dowman Cl *WIM/MER* SW19....178 A4
Downage *HDN* NW4.....................46 A6
Downalong *BUSH* WD23.............28 D3
Downbank Av *BXLYHN* DA7.......150 A3
Down Barns Rd *RSLP* HA4...........77 H2
Down Cl *NTHLT* UB5....................95 F1
Downderry Rd *BMLY* BR1..........165 G5
Downe Cl *WELL* DA16..................148 D1
Downend *WOOL/PLUM* SE18....147 G1
Downe Rd *HAYES* BR2...............215 J6
MTCM CR4.............................178 E5
Downer's Cottages *CLAP* SW4 *141 H5
Downes Cl *TWK* TW1.................156 C1
Downes Ct *WCHMH* N21.............35 G3
Downfield *WPK* KT4...................192 C5
Downfield Cl *MV/WKIL* W9.........101 F3
Down Hall Rd *KUT/HW* KT1.......174 E4
Downham Cl *CRW* RM5...............56 C3
Downham Rd *IS* N1......................86 A5
Downham Wy *BMLY* BR1...........183 H1
Downhills Av *TOTM* N17..............49 K6
Downhills Park Rd *TOTM* N17 *...49 K6
Downhills Wy *TOTM* N17.............49 J5
Downhurst Av *MLHL* NW7...........45 F1
Downing Cl *RYLN/HDSTN* HA2....42 C6
Downing Dr *GFD/PVL* UB6...........78 E6
Downing Rd *DAGW* RM9..............92 B6
Downings *EHAM* E6...................108 A5
Downing St *WHALL* SW1A............16 E2
Downland Cl *TRDG/WHET* N20....33 G3
Downleys Cl *ELTH/MOT* SE9......166 D4
Downman Rd *ELTH/MOT* SE9....146 D4
Downs Av *CHST* BR7..................184 E1
DART DA1..............................171 K2
PIN HA5..................................59 K5
Downs Bridge Rd *BECK* BR3......183 G4
Downs Court Pde *HACK* E8 *......86 E3
Downsell Rd *SRTFD* E15..............88 B2
Downsfield Rd *WALTH* E17..........69 G3
Downshall Av *GDMY/SEVK* IG3....72 E5
Downs Hill *BECK* BR3.................183 H3
Downshire Hl *HAMP* NW3............83 H2
Downside *BECK* BR3 *...............182 D4
TWK TW1...............................156 A5
Downside Cl *WIM/MER* SW19....178 B2
Downside Crs *HAMP* NW3...........83 J3
WEA W13.................................97 G3
Downside Rd *BELMT* SM2..........209 H4
Downs La *CLPT* E5 *....................86 D2
Downs Park Rd *HACK* E8..............86 B5
Downs Rd *BECK* BR3..................182 E5
CLPT E5....................................86 C2
EN EN1....................................24 B5
THHTH CR7............................180 D3
The Downs *RYNPK* SW20...........177 G3
Downs Vw *ISLW* TW7................136 A2
Downsview Gdns *NRWD* SE19....180 D3
Downsview Rd *NRWD* SE19.......180 C3
The Downsway *BELMT* SM2.......209 G6
Downton Av
BRXS/STRHM SW2.................162 A4

Downtown Rd
BERM/RHTH SE16..................124 B2
Downway *NFNCH/WDSPK* N12....47 J3
Down Wy *NTHLT* UB5...................95 F2
Dowrey St *IS* N1..........................85 G6
Dowsett Rd *TOTM* N17................50 B5
Dowson Cl *CMBW* SE5..............142 E5
Doyce St *STHWK* SE1..................18 C2
Doyle Cl *ERITH* DA8...................150 B2
Doyle Gdns *WLSDN* NW10..........81 K6
Doyle Rd *SNWD* SE25................197 H1
D'Oyley St *BGVA* SW1W..............15 G6
Doynton St *ARCH* N19..................66 B6
Draco Ga *PUT/ROE* SW15 *.......139 F4
Draco St *WALW* SE17................122 D6
Dragonfly Cl *PLSTW* E13...........107 F2
Dragon Rd *LBTH* SE11.................17 H7
PECK SE15.............................123 F6
Dragoon Rd *DEPT* SE8...............124 C5
Dragor Rd *WLSDN* NW10............98 E3
Drake Av *CDALE/KGS* NW9.........62 C5
Drake Crs *THMD* SE28...............109 J5
Drakefell Rd *NWCR* SE14...........144 A3
Drakefield Rd *TOOT* SW17.........161 F5
Drake Ms *HAYES* BR2................200 B1
HCH RM12................................93 K5
Drake Rd *BROCKY* SE4.............144 D4
CHSGTN KT9..........................206 C3
CROY/NA CRO.......................195 K4
MTCM CR4.............................195 F5
RYLN/HDSTN HA2...................60 A6
Drake's Cl *ESH/CLAY* KT10.......204 A3
Drakes Ctyd *KIL/WHAMP* NW6....82 D5
Drake St *ENC/FH* EN2..................23 J3
FSBYW WC1X...........................11 G2
Drakewood Rd
STRHM/NOR SW16................179 J3
Draper Cl *BELV* DA17................129 G4
ISLW TW7...............................135 J3
Draper Est *STHWK* SE1 *............18 B6
Drapers Rd *ENC/FH* EN2.............23 H5
SRTFD E15..............................88 A2
TOTM N17................................50 A4
Drappers Wy
BERM/RHTH SE16..................123 H4
Draven Cl *HAYES* BR2...............199 J4
Drawell Cl *WOOL/PLUM* SE18...127 K5
Drax Av *RYNPK* SW20...............177 H2
Draxmont *WIM/MER* SW19.......177 H2
Draycot Rd *WAN* E11...................71 F3
Draycott Av *CHEL* SW3...............14 D7
KTN/HRWW/WS HA3..............61 K5
Draycott Cl *CMBW* SE5.............142 E1
CRICK NW2..............................82 B1
KTN/HRWW/WS HA3..............61 H3
Draycott Pl *CHEL* SW3................14 E7
Draycott Ter *CHEL* SW3..............15 F6
Dray Ct *ALP/SUD* HA0................79 J4
Drayford Cl *MV/WKIL* W9..........100 D3
Dray Gdns *BRXS/STRHM* SW2...142 A6
Draymans Ms *PECK* SE15 *.......143 G3
Draymans Wy *ISLW* TW7...........136 A4
Drayson Ms *KENS* W8................119 K2
Drayton Av *LOU* IG10..................39 G1
ORP BR6.................................201 G5
WEA W13.................................97 F6
Drayton Bridge Rd *HNWL* W7......97 F6
WEA W13.................................97 F6
Drayton Cl *HSLWW* TW4...........134 E6
IL IG1.......................................72 D6
Drayton Ct *WDR/YW* UB7 *.......112 C4
Drayton Court Chambers
WEA W13 *...............................97 H6
Drayton Gdns *WBPTN* SW10.....120 B5
WCHMH N21............................35 H2
WDR/YW UB7...........................97 G6
WEA W13.................................97 H6
Drayton Gn *WEA* W13.................97 H5
Drayton Green Rd *WEA* W13.......97 H6
Drayton Gv *WEA* W13..................97 H6
Drayton Pk *HBRY* N5...................85 G3
Drayton Park Ms *HOLWY* N7 *....85 G3
Drayton Rd *CROY/NA* CRO.........196 C6
TOTM N17................................50 A5
WAN E11..................................70 B5
WEA W13.................................97 H6
WLSDN NW10..........................81 H6
Dreadnought St *GNWCH* SE10..125 H5
Drenon Sq *HYS/HAR* UB3............94 D6
Dresden Cl *KIL/WHAMP* NW6......83 F4
Dresden Rd *ARCH* N19................66 D5
Dressington Av *BROCKY* SE4.....164 D1
Drew Av *MLHL* NW7....................46 D2
Drewery Ct *BKHTH/KID* SE3 *...145 H4
Drew Gdns *GFD/PVL* UB6............79 F4
Drew Rd *CAN/RD* E16................126 D1
Drews Cottages
STRHM/NOR SW16................161 J4
Drewstead Rd
STRHM/NOR SW16................161 J4
Driffield Rd *BOW* E3..................105 G1
The Drift *HAYES* BR2................215 F3
The Driftway *MTCM* CR4...........179 F4
Drinkwater Rd
RYLN/HDSTN HA2...................60 B6
Drive Ct *EDGW* HA8....................44 C1
The Drive *ACT* W3.......................98 E5
BAR EN5..................................20 D4
BARK IG11................................91 F5
BECK BR3..............................182 D5
BKHH IG9.................................38 E3
BXLY DA5...............................168 E2
CHING E4................................38 B2
CHST BR7...............................186 A6
CRW RM5................................56 D1
EBED/NFELT TW14................154 B2
EDGW HA8..............................44 C1
ENC/FH EN2.............................23 J2
ERITH DA8.............................149 J1
ESH/CLAY KT10.....................189 H5
FBAR/BDGN N11......................48 C2
FNCH N3..................................46 E6
GLDGN NW11..........................64 C3
HGT N6.....................................65 K2

HOLWY N7 85 F4
HOR/WEW KT19 207 H4
HSLW TW3 135 J3
IL IG1 71 J3
KUTN/CMB KT2 175 K3
MRDN SM4 194 B2
NTHWD HA6 40 C4
ORP BR6 202 A6
RYLN/HDSTN HA2 60 A4
RYNPK SW20 177 F3
SCUP DA14 168 C5
SURB KT6 191 F4
SWFD E18 52 E6
THHTH CR7 196 E1
WALTH E17 51 K6
WBLY HA9 62 E6
WWKM BR4 199 G4
Dr Johnson Av TOOT SW17 161 G5
Droitwich Cl SYD SE26 163 H5
Dromey Gdns
KTN/HRWW/WS HA3 43 F3
Dromore Rd PUT/ROE SW15 159 H1
Dronfield Gdns BCTR RM8 91 J3
Droop St NKENS W10 100 C3
Drovers Pl PECK SE15 143 J1
Drovers Rd SAND/SEL CR2 211 K3
Druce Rd DUL SE21 163 F1
Druid St STHWK SE1 19 J2
Druids Wy HAYES BR2 199 G1
Drumaline Rdg WPK KT4 192 B6
Drummond Av ROMW/RG RM7 75 F1
Drummond Cl ERITH DA8 150 B2
Drummond Crs CAMTN NW1 4 C4
Drummond Dr STAN HA7 43 F3
Drummond Ga PIM SW1V 121 J5
Drummond Rd
BERM/RHTH SE16 123 J3
CROY/NA CR0 196 D6
ROMW/RG RM7 74 E1
WAN E11 71 F3
Drummonds Pl RCH/KEW TW9 137 F5
Drummond St CAMTN NW1 4 A6
Drum St WCHPL E1 13 K3
Drury Crs CROY/NA CR0 196 B6
Drury La COVGDN WC2E 11 F4
HOL/ALD WC2B 10 E3
Drury Rd HRW HA1 60 C4
Drury Wy WLSDN NW10 81 F3
Dryad St PUT/ROE SW15 139 G4
Dryburgh Gdns
CDALE/KGS NW9 44 C6
Dryburgh Rd PUT/ROE SW15 138 E4
Dryden Av HNWL W7 97 F5
Dryden Cl BARK/HLT IG6 55 F2
Dryden Rd EN EN1 36 A1
KTN/HRWW/WS HA3 43 F4
WELL DA16 148 A2
WIM/MER SW19 178 B2
Dryden St COVGDN WC2E 11 F4
Dryden Wy ORP BR6 202 B5
Dryfield Cl WLSDN NW10 80 E4
Dryfield Rd EDGW HA8 44 E2
Dryhill Rd BELV DA17 129 G6
Dryland Av ORP BR6 217 F2
Drylands Rd CEND/HSY/T N8 66 E3
Drysdale Av CHING E4 37 K1
Drysdale Cl NTHWD HA6 40 C3
Drysdale Dwellings HACK E8 * 86 B3
Drysdale Pl IS N1 7 H4
Drysdale St IS N1 7 H5
Dublin Av HACK E8 86 C6
Du Burstow Ter HNWL W7 115 K2
Ducal St BETH E2 7 K5
Du Cane Cl SHB W12 * 100 A5
Du Cane Rd SHB W12 99 K5
Duchess Cl FBAR/BDGN N11 48 B1
SUT SM1 209 G2
Duchess Gv BKHH IG9 * 39 F4
Duchess Ms CAVSQ/HST W1G 9 K2
Duchess of Bedfords Wk
KENS W8 * 119 K2
Duchess St REGST W1B 9 K2
Duchy Rd EBAR EN4 21 H1
Duchy St STHWK SE1 11 K7
Ducie St CLAP SW4 141 K5
Duckett Rd FSBYPK N4 67 H3
Ducketts Rd DART DA1 150 C6
Duckett St WCHPL E1 105 F4
Ducking Stool Ct ROM RM1 75 G1
Duck La SOHO/CST W1F 10 C4
Duck Lees La PEND EN3 25 G5
Du Cros Dr STAN HA7 43 K2
Du Cros Rd ACT W3 118 B1
Dudden Hill La WLSDN NW10 81 H3
Dudden Hill Pde
WLSDN NW10 * 81 H2
Duddington Cl ELTH/MOT SE9 166 C6
Dudley Av KTN/HRWW/WS HA3 43 J6
Dudley Dr MRDN SM4 193 H5
RSLP HA4 77 F3
Dudley Gdns RYLN/HDSTN HA2 60 D5
WEA W13 116 C2
Dudley Pl HYS/HAR UB3 113 G4
Dudley Rd EBED/NFELT TW14 153 G3
FNCH N3 47 F5
IL IG1 90 B2
KIL/WHAMP NW6 100 C1
KUT/HW KT1 175 G6
NWDGN UB2 114 C2
RCH/KEW TW9 137 G3
RYLN/HDSTN HA2 60 C6
WALTH E17 51 J5
WIM/MER SW19 177 K2
Dudley St BAY/PAD W2 * 8 A2
Dudlington Rd CLPT E5 68 E6
Dudmaston Ms CHEL SW3 120 C5
Dudrich Ms EDUL SE22 143 G6
Dudsbury Rd DART DA1 170 E1
Dudset La HEST TW5 133 K2
Dufferin Av STLK EC1Y 6 E7
Dufferin St STLK EC1Y 6 D7
Duffield Cl HRW HA1 61 F2
Duffield Dr SEVS/STOTM N15 68 B1
Duff St POP/IOD E14 105 K5
Dufour's Pl SOHO/CST W1F 10 B4
Dufrey Pl CMBW SE5 * 142 E1
Dugard Wy LBTH SE11 18 A7
Duggan Dr CHST BR7 184 D2
Dugolly Av WBLY HA9 80 D1
Duke Humphrey Rd
BKHTH/KID SE3 145 H3
Duke of Cambridge Cl
WHTN TW2 155 J1
Duke of Edinburgh Rd
SUT SM1 209 H1
The Duke of Wellington Av
WOOL/PLUM SE18 127 H3
Duke of Wellington Pl
KTBR SW1X 15 H3
Duke of York Sq CHEL SW3 120 E5
Duke of York St STJS SW1Y 10 B7
Duke Rd BARK/HLT IG6 72 D1
CHSWK W4 118 A5
Duke's Av CHSWK W4 118 A5
EDGW HA8 44 B2
FNCH N3 47 F4
HRW HA1 60 E1
HSLWW TW4 134 D5
MUSWH N10 48 C6
NTHLT UB5 77 J5
NWMAL KT3 176 B6
PIN HA5 59 K3
RCHPK/HAM TW10 156 D6
Dukes Cl ASHF TW15 153 F6
HPTN TW12 172 E1
Dukes Ga CHSWK W4 * 117 K4
Dukes Green Av
EBED/NFELT TW14 133 K6
EBED/NFELT TW14 153 K1
Dukes La KENS W8 119 K2
Dukes Lane Chambers
KENS W8 * 120 A2
Dukes Lane Man KENS W8 * 120 A2
Duke's Ms MHST W1U 9 H3
MUSWH N10 48 B6
Dukes Orch BXLY DA5 169 K3
Duke's Pl HDTCH EC3A 13 J4
Dukes Point HGT N6 66 B5
Dukes Rd ACT W3 98 C3
CAMTN NW1 4 D5
EHAM E6 90 A6
Dukesthorpe Rd SYD SE26 164 A6
Duke St MHST W1U 9 H3
RCH/KEW TW9 136 E5
SUT SM1 209 H2
Duke Street Hl STHWK SE1 13 F7
Duke Street St James's
MYFR/PICC W1J 10 B7
Dukes Wy WWKM BR4 214 C1
Duke's Yd MYFR/PKLN W1K 9 H5
Dulas St FSBYPK N4 67 F5
Dulford St NTGHL W11 100 C6
Dulka Rd BTSEA SW11 140 E6
Dulverton Rd ELTH/MOT SE9 167 H4
RSLP HA4 58 E6
Dulwich Common DUL SE21 162 E3
The Dulwich Oaks DUL SE21 * 163 G5
Dulwich Rd HNHL SE24 142 B6
Dulwich Village DUL SE21 162 E1
Dulwich Wood Av NRWD SE19 181 G1
Dulwich Wood Pk NRWD SE19 163 F6
Dumbarton Rd
BRXS/STRHM SW2 161 K1
Dumbleton Cl KUT/HW KT1 175 J4
Dumbreck Rd ELTH/MOT SE9 147 F5
Dumfries Cl OXHEY WD19 26 E5
Dumont Rd STNW/STAM N16 86 A1
Dumpton Pl CAMTN NW1 84 A5
Dunbar Av BECK BR3 198 B1
DAGE RM10 92 C1
STRHM/NOR SW16 180 B5
Dunbar Cl YEAD UB4 94 E4
Dunbar Ct WOT/HER KT12 188 B6
Dunbar Gdns DAGE RM10 92 C3
Dunbar Rd FSTGT E7 88 E4
NWMAL KT3 191 K1
WDGN N22 49 G4
Dunbar St WNWD SE27 162 D5
Dunblane Rd ELTH/MOT SE9 146 D4
Dunboyne Rd HAMP NW3 83 K3
Dunbridge St BETH E2 104 C3
Duncan Cl BAR EN5 21 G5
Duncan Gv ACT W3 99 G5
Duncannon St CHCR WC2N 10 E6
Duncan Rd HACK E8 86 D6
RCH/KEW TW9 137 F5
Duncan St IS N1 6 A2
Duncan Ter IS N1 6 A3
Dunch St WCHPL E1 104 D5
Duncombe Hl FSTH SE23 164 B2
Duncombe Rd ARCH N19 66 D5
Duncrievie Rd LEW SE13 165 H1
Duncroft WOOL/PLUM SE18 147 K1
Dundalk Rd BROCKY SE4 144 B4
Dundas Gdns
E/WMO/HCT KT8 173 G6
Dundas Rd PECK SE15 143 K3
Dundee Rd PLSTW E13 107 F1
SNWD SE25 197 J2
Dundee St WAP E1W 123 J1
Dundee Wy PEND EN3 25 G4
Dundela Gdns WPK KT4 207 K2
Dundonald Cl EHAM E6 107 J5
Dundonald Rd
WIM/MER SW19 177 J3
WLSDN NW10 82 B6
Dunedin Rd IL IG1 72 C5
LEY E10 87 K1
RAIN RM13 111 H2
Dunedin Wy YEAD UB4 95 G3
Dunelm St WCHPL E1 105 F5
Dunfield Rd CAT SE6 182 E1
Dunford Rd HOLWY N7 85 F2
Dungarvan Av PUT/ROE SW15 138 D5
Dunheved Cl THHTH CR7 196 B3
Dunheved Rd North
THHTH CR7 196 B3
Dunheved Rd South
THHTH CR7 196 B3
Dunheved Rd West
THHTH CR7 196 B3
Dunholme Gn ED N9 36 B5
Dunholme La ED N9 36 B5
Dunholme Rd ED N9 36 B5
Dunkeld Rd BCTR RM8 73 H6
SNWD SE25 196 E1
Dunkery Rd ELTH/MOT SE9 166 C6
Dunkin Rd DART DA1 151 K5
Dunkirk St WNWD SE27 * 162 D6
Dunlace Rd CLPT E5 86 E3
Dunleary Cl HSLWW TW4 154 E2
Dunley Dr CROY/NA CR0 214 A4
Dunloe Av TOTM N17 49 K6
Dunloe St BETH E2 7 K3
Dunlop Pl BERM/RHTH SE16 19 K5
Dunmore Rd KIL/WHAMP NW6 82 C6
RYNPK SW20 177 F4
Dunmow Cl CHDH RM6 73 J2
FELT TW13 * 154 D6
LOU IG10 39 J1
Dunmow Dr RAIN RM13 93 H6
Dunmow Rd SRTFD E15 88 B2
Dunmow Wk IS N1 * 85 J6
Dunnage Crs
BERM/RHTH SE16 124 B4
Dunningford Cl HCH RM12 93 H3
Dunn Md CDALE/KGS NW9 45 H3
Dunnock Cl ED N9 37 F3
Dunnock Rd EHAM E6 107 J5
Dunn St HACK E8 86 B3
Dunollie Pl KTTN NW5 84 C3
Dunollie Rd KTTN NW5 84 C3
Dunoon Gdns FSTH SE23 * 164 A2
Dunoon Rd FSTH SE23 163 K2
Dunraven Dr ENC/FH EN2 23 G3
Dunraven Rd SHB W12 118 D1
Dunraven St MYFR/PKLN W1K 9 F5
Dunsany Rd HMSMTH W6 119 G3
Dunsbury Cl BELMT SM2 209 F6
Dunsfold Wy CROY/NA CR0 213 K5
Dunsford Wy PUT/ROE SW15 158 E2
Dunsmore OXHEY WD19 * 27 H4
Dunsmore Cl BUSH WD23 28 D1
YEAD UB4 95 H3
Dunsmore Rd WOT/HER KT12 188 A2
Dunsmore Wy BUSH WD23 28 D1
Dunsmure Rd STNW/STAM N16 68 A5
Dunspring La CLAY IG5 54 B5
Dunstable Ms CAVSQ/HST W1G 9 H1
Dunstable Rd
E/WMO/HCT KT8 188 E1
RCH/KEW TW9 137 F5
Dunstall Rd RYNPK SW20 176 E2
Dunstall Wy E/WMO/HCT KT8 173 H6
Dunstall Welling Est
WELL DA16 * 148 C3
Dunstan Cl EFNCH N2 * 47 G6
Dunstan Gld STMC/STPC BR5 * 201 J3
Dunstan Houses WCHPL E1 * 104 E4
Dunstan Rd GLDGN NW11 64 D5
Dunstan's Gv EDUL SE22 163 J1
Dunstan's Rd EDUL SE22 163 H2
Dunster Av MRDN SM4 193 G5
Dunster Cl BAR EN5 20 B5
CRW RM5 56 E5
Dunster Ct MON EC3R 13 G5
Dunster Dr CDALE/KGS NW9 62 E5
Dunster Gdns KIL/WHAMP NW6 82 D5
Dunsterville Wy STHWK SE1 19 F3
Dunster Wy RYLN/HDSTN HA2 77 J1
Dunston Rd BTSEA SW11 141 F3
HACK E8 7 J1
Dunston St HACK E8 86 B6
Dunton Cl SURB KT6 191 F5
Dunton Rd LEY E10 69 K4
ROM RM1 75 G1
STHWK SE1 19 J7
Duntshill Rd
WAND/EARL SW18 160 A3
Dunvegan Cl E/WMO/HCT KT8 189 G1
Dunvegan Rd ELTH/MOT SE9 146 E5
Dunwich Rd BXLYHN DA7 149 G2
Dunworth Ms NTGHL W11 100 D5
Duplex Ride KTBR SW1X 15 F3
Dupont Rd RYNPK SW20 177 G5
Duppas Av CROY/NA CR0 211 H2
Duppas Hill Rd CROY/NA CR0 211 H2
Duppas Hill Ter CROY/NA CR0 211 H1
Duppas Rd CROY/NA CR0 211 G1
Dupree Rd CHARL SE7 126 A5
Dura Den Cl BECK BR3 182 E3
Durand Gdns BRXN/ST SW9 142 A2
Durand Wy WLSDN NW10 80 E5
Durants Park Av PEND EN3 25 F5
Durants Rd PEND EN3 24 E5
Durant St BETH E2 104 C1
Durban Gdns DAGE RM10 92 E5
Durban Rd BECK BR3 182 C5
GNTH/NBYPK IG2 72 E5
SRTFD E15 106 C2
TOTM N17 50 B2
WALTH E17 51 H4
WNWD SE27 162 D6
Durbin Rd CHSGTN KT9 206 A2
Durdans Rd STHL UB1 95 K5
Durell Gdns DAGW RM9 91 K3
Durell Rd DAGW RM9 91 K3
Durfey Pl WALW SE17 142 E1
Durford Crs PUT/ROE SW15 158 E3
Durham Av HAYES BR2 199 J1
HEST TW5 114 E6
WFD IG8 53 H1
Durham Hl BMLY BR1 165 J6
Durham House St
CHCR WC2N * 11 F6
Durham Pl CHEL SW3 * 120 E5
Durham Ri WOOL/PLUM SE18 127 H5
Durham Rd CAN/RD E16 106 C3
DAGE RM10 92 E3
EA W5 116 E3
EBED/NFELT TW14 154 B2
ED N9 36 C4
EFNCH N2 47 J6
HAYES BR2 199 K1
HOLWY N7 67 F6
HRW HA1 60 B2
MNPK E12 89 H2
RYNPK SW20 176 E4
SCUP DA14 186 C1
Durham Rw WCHPL E1 105 F4
Durham St LBTH SE11 122 A5
Durham Ter BAY/PAD W2 101 F5
PGE/AN SE20 * 181 J3
Durham Wharf Dr BTFD TW8 136 D1
Durham Yd BETH E2 * 104 D2
Duriun Wy ERITH DA8 150 E1
Durley Av PIN HA5 59 J3
Durley Gdns ORP BR6 217 H2
Durley Rd STNW/STAM N16 68 A4
Durlston Rd CLPT E5 68 C6
KUTN/CMB KT2 175 F2
Durnford St SEVS/STOTM N15 68 A2
Durning Rd NRWD SE19 180 E1
Durnsford Av WIM/MER SW19 159 K4
Durnsford Rd FBAR/BDGN N11 48 D3
WIM/MER SW19 159 K5
Durrant Wy ORP BR6 216 D3
Durrell Rd FUL/PGN SW6 139 H3
Durrington Av RYNPK SW20 177 F4
Durrington Park Rd
RYNPK SW20 177 F4
Durrington Rd CLPT E5 87 G2
Dursley Cl BKHTH/KID SE3 146 B3
Dursley Gdns BKHTH/KID SE3 146 C2
Dursley Rd BKHTH/KID SE3 146 B3
Durward St WCHPL E1 104 D4
Durweston Ms MHST W1U * 9 F1
Durweston St MBLAR W1H 8 E2
Dury Rd BAR EN5 20 D2
Dutch Barn Cl
STWL/WRAY TW19 152 A1
Dutch Gdns KUTN/CMB KT2 175 J2
Dutch Yd WAND/EARL SW18 139 K6
Duthie St POP/IOD E14 106 A6
Dutton St GNWCH SE10 145 F2
Duxberry Cl HAYES BR2 200 D2
Duxford Cl HCH RM12 93 K4
Dwight Rd WATW WD18 26 B2
Dye House La BOW E3 87 J6
Dyer's Buildings
FLST/FETLN EC4A 11 J2
Dyers Hall Rd WAN E11 70 C5
Dyer's La PUT/ROE SW15 138 E4
Dyers Wy HARH RM3 57 J3
Dyke Dr STMC/STPC BR5 202 D4
Dykes Wy HAYES BR2 183 J6
Dykewood Cl BXLY DA5 170 A5
Dylan Cl BORE WD6 * 29 K2
Dylan Rd BELV DA17 129 H3
HNHL SE24 142 C5
Dylways CMBW SE5 142 E5
Dymchurch Cl CLAY IG5 54 A6
ORP BR6 216 E2
Dymock St FUL/PGN SW6 140 A4
Dymoke Rd EMPK RM11 75 H4
Dyneley Rd LEE/GVPK SE12 166 B6
Dyne Rd KIL/WHAMP NW6 82 D5
Dynevor Rd
RCHPK/HAM TW10 137 F6
STNW/STAM N16 86 A1
Dynham Rd KIL/WHAMP NW6 82 E5
Dyott St LSQ/SEVD WC2H 10 E3
Dysart Av KUTN/CMB KT2 174 D1
Dysart St SDTCH EC2A 7 F7
Dyson Ct ALP/SUD HA0 79 G2
Dyson Rd SRTFD E15 88 D4
WAN E11 70 C3
Dyson's Rd UED N18 50 D2

E

Eade Rd FSBYPK N4 67 J4
Eagans Cl EFNCH N2 * 47 H6
Eagle Av CHDH RM6 74 A3
Eagle Cl BERM/RHTH SE16 123 J6
HCH RM12 93 K4
PEND EN3 24 E5
WLGTN SM6 210 E4
Eagle Ct FARR EC1M 12 A1
Eagle Dr CDALE/KGS NW9 45 G5
Eagle Hl NRWD SE19 180 E2
Eagle House Ms CLAP SW4 141 H6
Eagle La WAN E11 70 E1
Eagle Ms IS N1 86 A4
Eagle Pl WBPTN SW10 120 B5
Eagle Rd ALP/SUD HA0 79 K5
HTHAIR TW6 133 J4
Eaglesfield Rd
WOOL/PLUM SE18 147 G2
Eagle St GINN WC1R 11 G2
Eagle Ter WFD IG8 53 F3
Eagle Wharf Rd IS N1 6 D2
Eagling Cl BOW E3 105 J2
Ealdham Sq ELTH/MOT SE9 146 B5
Ealing Golf Course
GFD/PVL UB6 * 97 G2
Ealing Gn EA W5 116 E1
Ealing Park Gdns EA W5 116 D4
Ealing Rd ALP/SUD HA0 80 A4
BOW E3 105 K2
BTFD TW8 117 F6
EA W5 116 E4
NTHLT UB5 78 A6
Ealing Village EA W5 98 A5
Eamont St STJWD NW8 2 C2
Eardemont Cl DART DA1 150 C5
Eardley Crs ECT SW5 119 K5
Eardley Rd BELV DA17 129 H5
STRHM/NOR SW16 179 H2
Earl Cl FBAR/BDGN N11 48 B1
Earldom Rd PUT/ROE SW15 139 F5
Earle Gdns KUTN/CMB KT2 175 F3
Earlham Gv FSTGT E7 88 D3
WDGN N22 49 F3
Earlham St LSQ/SEVD WC2H 10 D4
Earl Ri WOOL/PLUM SE18 127 J5
Earl Rd MORT/ESHN SW14 137 K5
Earl's Court Gdns ECT SW5 120 A4
Earl's Court Rd ECT SW5 119 K4
Earl's Court Sq ECT SW5 120 A5
Earls Crs HRW HA1 60 E1
Earlsferry Wy IS N1 84 E5
Earlsfield Rd
WAND/EARL SW18 160 B3
Earlshall Rd ELTH/MOT SE9 146 E5
Earlsmead RYLN/HDSTN HA2 77 K2
Earlsmead Rd
SEVS/STOTM N15 68 B2
WLSDN NW10 100 A2
Earls Ms WAND/EARL SW18 160 B2
Earls Ter KENS W8 * 119 K3
Earlsthorpe Ms BAL SW12 161 F1
Earlsthorpe Rd SYD SE26 164 A6
Earlstoke Est FSBYE EC1V 6 A4
Earlstoke St FSBYE EC1V 6 A4
Earlston Gv HOM E9 86 D6
Earl St SDTCH EC2A 13 G1
Earls Wk BCTR RM8 91 H2
KENS W8 119 K3
Earlswood Av THHTH CR7 196 B2
Earlswood Gdns CLAY IG5 54 A6
Earlswood St GNWCH SE10 125 H5
Early Ms CAMTN NW1 84 B6
Earnshaw St NOXST/BSQ WC1A 10 D3
Earsby St WKENS W14 119 H4
Easby Crs MRDN SM4 194 A3
Easebourne Rd BCTR RM8 91 J3
Easedale Dr HCH RM12 93 K3
Easleys Ms MHST W1U 9 H3
East Acton Ar ACT W3 * 99 H5
East Acton La ACT W3 99 G6
East Arbour St WCHPL E1 105 F5
East Av EHAM E6 89 J5
HYS/HAR UB3 113 K1
STHL UB1 95 K6
WALTH E17 69 K2
WLGTN SM6 211 F3
East Bank STNW/STAM N16 68 A4
Eastbank Rd HPTN TW12 173 H1
East Barnet Rd BAR EN5 21 G5
Eastbourne Av ACT W3 99 F5
Eastbourne Gdns
MORT/ESHN SW14 137 K4
Eastbourne Ms BAY/PAD W2 101 G5
Eastbourne Rd BTFD TW8 116 E5
CHSWK W4 117 K6
EHAM E6 108 A2
FELT TW13 154 C4
SEVS/STOTM N15 68 A3
SRTFD E15 88 C6
TOOT SW17 179 F2
Eastbourne Ter BAY/PAD W2 101 G5
Eastbournia Av ED N9 36 E5
Eastbrook Av DAGE RM10 92 E2
ED N9 36 E2
Eastbrook Dr ROMW/RG RM7 93 G1
Eastbrook Rd BKHTH/KID SE3 146 A2
Eastbury Av BARK IG11 90 E6
EN EN1 24 A2
NTHWD HA6 40 C1
Eastbury Ct OXHEY WD19 * 27 G2
Eastbury Gv CHSWK W4 118 B5
Eastbury Rd EHAM E6 108 A3
KUTN/CMB KT2 175 F3
NTHWD HA6 40 C2
OXHEY WD19 27 G2
ROMW/RG RM7 75 F3
STMC/STPC BR5 201 J3
Eastbury Sq BARK IG11 91 F6
Eastbury Ter WCHPL E1 105 F3
Eastcastle St GTPST W1W 10 A3
Eastcheap FENCHST EC3M 13 F5
East Churchfield Rd ACT W3 118 A1
Eastchurch Rd HTHAIR TW6 133 H4
East Cl EA W5 98 C3
EBAR EN4 22 A5
GFD/PVL UB6 96 C1
RAIN RM13 111 K3
Eastcombe Av CHARL SE7 126 A6
Eastcote ORP BR6 202 A5
Eastcote Av E/WMO/HCT KT8 188 E2
GFD/PVL UB6 79 G3
RYLN/HDSTN HA2 60 B6
Eastcote La NTHLT UB5 77 K4
RYLN/HDSTN HA2 77 K2
Eastcote La North NTHLT UB5 77 K4
Eastcote Rd PIN HA5 59 H2
RSLP HA4 58 C4
RYLN/HDSTN HA2 78 C1
WELL DA16 147 J3
Eastcote St BRXN/ST SW9 141 K3
Eastcote Vw PIN HA5 59 G1
East Ct ALP/SUD HA0 61 J6
East Crs EN EN1 24 A6
FBAR/BDGN N11 33 K6
Eastcroft Rd HOR/WEW KT19 207 G5
East Cross Route HOM E9 87 H5
Eastdown Pk LEW SE13 145 G5
East Dr CAR SM5 209 J6
NTHWD HA6 26 C4
STMC/STPC BR5 202 C3
East Duck Lees La PEND EN3 25 H5
East Dulwich Gv EDUL SE22 143 F6
East Dulwich Rd EDUL SE22 143 G5
East End Rd EFNCH N2 47 G6
FNCH N3 46 E5
East End Wy PIN HA5 41 J6
East Entrance DAGE RM10 110 D1
Eastern Av GNTH/NBYPK IG2 72 D3
PIN HA5 59 H4
REDBR IG4 71 H3
Eastern Av East ROM RM1 57 G5
Eastern Av West CHDH RM6 74 A1
Eastern Gtwy CAN/RD E16 107 G6
Eastern Perimeter Rd
HTHAIR TW6 133 H3
Eastern Rd BROCKY SE4 144 D5
EFNCH N2 47 K6
PLSTW E13 107 F1
ROM RM1 75 H2
WALTH E17 70 A2
WDGN N22 48 E4
Easternville Gdns
GNTH/NBYPK IG2 72 C3
Eastern Wy THMD SE28 128 B2
East Ferry Rd POP/IOD E14 124 E4
Eastfield Gdns DAGE RM10 92 C2
Eastfield Rd CEND/HSY/T N8 48 E6
DAGE RM10 92 C2
PEND EN3 25 F1
WALTH E17 69 J1
Eastfields PIN HA5 59 G2

Eastfields Av WAND/EARL SW18 139 K5
Eastfields Rd ACT W3 98 C4
MTCM CR4 179 F5
Eastfield St POP/IOD E14 105 C4
East Gdns TOOT SW17 178 D2
Eastgate Cl THMD SE28 109 K5
Eastglade NTHWD HA6 40 C1
PIN HA5 105 J6
East Hall Rd STMC/STPC BR5 203 F4
Eastham Cl BAR EN5 26 D6
East Ham Manor Wy EHAM E6 108 A5
East Harding St FLST/FETLN EC4A 11 K3
East Heath Rd HAMP NW3 83 H1
East Hi DART DA1 171 J2
WAND/EARL SW18 140 D6
WBLY HA9 62 C6
East Hill Dr DART DA1 171 J2
Eastholm GLDGN NW11 65 F1
East Holme ERITH DA8 150 A2
Eastholme HYS/HAR UB3 113 K1
East India Dock Rd POP/IOD E14 105 J6
East India Wy CROY/NA CRO 197 G5
Eastlake Rd CMBW SE5 142 C3
Eastlands Crs EDUL SE22 163 G1
East La ALP/SUD HA0 79 J1
BERM/RHTH SE16 123 H2
KUT/HW KT1 174 E6
Eastlea Ms CAN/RD E16 106 C3
Eastleigh Av RYLN/HDSTN HA2 60 B6
Eastleigh Cl BELMT SM2 209 F6
CRICK NW2 81 C1
Eastleigh Rd BXLYHN DA7 149 K3
WALTH E17 51 H5
Eastleigh Wy EBED/NFELT TW14 153 K3
Eastman Rd ACT W3 118 A2
East Md RSLP HA4 77 H1
Eastmead Av GFD/PVL UB6 96 B2
Eastmead Cl BMLY BR1 184 D5
Eastmearn Rd DUL SE21 162 D4
Eastmont Rd ESH/CLAY KT10 189 K6
Eastmoor Pl CHARL SE7 126 C3
Eastmoor St CHARL SE7 126 C3
East Mount St WCHPL E1 104 D4
Eastney Rd CROY/NA CRO 196 C5
Eastney St GNWCH SE10 125 G5
Eastnor Rd ELTH/MOT SE9 167 H3
Easton St FSBYW WC1X 5 J6
East Park Cl CHDH RM6 73 K2
East Parkside GNWCH SE10 125 H2
East Pas STBT EC1A 12 C1
East Pl WNWD SE27 162 D6
East Pole Cottages STHGT/OAK N14 * 22 D5
East Poultry Av FARR EC1M 12 A1
East Rp HHTR TW6 132 E2
East Rd CHDH RM6 74 A2
CHEL SW3 34 A4
EBAR EN4 34 A3
EBED/NFELT TW14 153 G2
EDGW HA8 44 E4
IS N1 7 F4
KUTN/CMB KT2 175 F4
PEND EN3 24 E1
ROMW/RG RM7 75 F4
SRTFD E15 88 E6
WDR/YW UB7 112 C4
WELL DA16 148 C3
WIM/MER SW19 178 B2
East Rochester Wy BFN/LL DA15 147 K6
DART DA1 170 A2
East Rw NKENS W10 100 C3
WAN E11 70 E3
Eastry Av HAYES BR2 199 J5
Eastry Rd ERITH DA8 149 H1
East Sheen Av MORT/ESHN SW14 138 A6
East Side SHB W12 99 F3
Eastside Rd GLDGN NW11 64 D1
East Smithfield WAP E1W 13 K6
East St BARK IG11 90 C5
BMLY BR1 183 K5
BTFD TW8 136 D1
BXLYHN DA7 149 H5
WALW SE17 18 C7
East Surrey Gv PECK SE15 143 G1
East Tenter St WCHPL E1 13 K4
East Ter BFN/LL DA15 167 K3
East Towers PIN HA5 59 H5
East V ACT W3 * 118 C1
East Vw BAR EN5 20 D4
CHING E4 52 A1
Eastview Av WOOL/PLUM SE18 147 K1
Eastville Av GLDGN NW11 64 D3
HYS/HAR UB3 113 K2
East Wk EBAR EN4 34 A3
Eastway HOM E9 87 J3
East Wy HAYES BR2 199 J5
HOM E9 87 J2
Eastway MRDN SM4 193 G2
East Wy RSLP HA4 58 E5
Eastway WAN E11 71 F2
Eastway Crs RYLN/HDSTN HA2 60 B6
Eastwell Cl BECK BR3 182 B4
Eastwood Cl HOLWY N7 85 G3
SWFD E18 52 E5
TOTM N17 50 E3
Eastwood Dr RAIN RM13 111 K4
Eastwood Rd GDMY/SEVK IG3 73 G4
MUSWH N10 48 A5
SWFD E18 52 E5
WDR/YW UB7 112 D2
Eastwood St STRHM/NOR SW16 179 H2
Eatington Rd LEY E10 70 B2
Eaton Cl BGVA SW1W 15 H6
STAN HA7 29 H6
Eaton Dr BRXN/ST SW9 142 C5
CRW RM5 56 D3
KUTN/CMB KT2 175 H3
Eaton Gdns DAGW RM9 92 A5
Eaton Ga BGVA SW1W 15 G6
NTHWD HA6 40 A2
Eaton La BGVA SW1W 15 K5
Eaton Ms North KTBR SW1X 15 H5
Eaton Ms South BGVA SW1W 15 H6
Eaton Ms West BGVA SW1W 15 H6
Eaton Park Rd PLMGR N13 35 G4
Eaton Ri EA W5 97 K5
WAN E11 71 G2
Eaton Rd BELMT SM2 209 H4
EN EN1 24 A4
HDN NW4 64 A2
HSLW TW3 135 J5
SCUP DA14 168 E4
Eaton Rw BGVA SW1W 15 J4
Eatons Md CHING E4 37 J4
Eaton Sq BGVA SW1W 15 H5
Eaton Ter BGVA SW1W 15 G6
NTHWD HA6 15 G6
Eaton Terrace Ms BGVA SW1W 15 G6
Eatonville Rd TOOT SW17 160 E4
Eatonville Vls TOOT SW17 160 E4
Ebbisham Dr VX/NE SW8 122 A6
Ebbisham Rd WPK KT4 193 H6
Ebbsfleet Rd CRICK NW2 82 C3
Ebdon Wy BKHTH/KID SE3 146 A4
Ebenezer Wk STRHM/NOR SW16 179 H4
Ebley Cl PECK SE15 123 G6
Ebner St WAND/EARL SW18 140 A5
Ebor St WCHPL E1 7 H6
Ebrington Rd KTN/HRWW/WS HA3 61 J5
Ebsworth St FSTH SE23 164 A2
Eburne Rd HOLWY N7 84 E1
Ebury Br BGVA SW1W 121 G5
Ebury Bridge Rd BGVA SW1W 121 G5
Ebury Cl HAYES BR2 200 E1
NTHWD HA6 40 A1
Ebury Ms BGVA SW1W 15 J6
Ebury Ms East BGVA SW1W 15 J6
Ebury Sq BGVA SW1W 15 H7
Ebury St BGVA SW1W 15 H7
Ecclesbourne Cl PLMGR N13 49 G1
Ecclesbourne Gdns PLMGR N13 49 G1
Ecclesbourne Rd IS N1 85 J5
THHTH CR7 196 D2
Eccles Rd BTSEA SW11 140 E5
Eccleston Cl EBAR EN4 21 K6
ORP BR6 201 J5
Eccleston Crs CHDH RM6 73 H4
Eccleston Ct WBLY HA9 80 A3
Eccleston Ms KTBR SW1X 15 H5
Eccleston Pl BGVA SW1W 15 J6
Eccleston Rd WEA W13 116 B1
Eccleston Sq PIM SW1V 15 K7
Eccleston Square Ms PIM SW1V 15 K7
Eccleston St BGVA SW1W 15 H5
Echelforde Dr ASHF TW15 152 D6
Echo Hts CHING E4 * 37 K3
Eckford St IS N1 5 K1
Eckstein Rd BTSEA SW11 140 E5
Eclipse Rd PLSTW E13 107 F4
Ector Rd CAT SE6 165 H4
Edans Ct SHB W12 118 C2
Edbrooke Rd MV/WKIL W9 100 E3
Eddiscombe Rd FUL/PGN SW6 139 J3
Eddy Cl ROMW/RG RM7 74 D3
Eddystone Rd BROCKY SE4 144 B6
Ede Cl HSLW TW3 134 E4
Edenbridge Cl BERM/RHTH SE16 123 J5
STMC/STPC BR5 202 E1
Edenbridge Rd EN EN1 36 A1
HOM E9 87 F5
Eden Cl ALP/SUD HA0 79 K6
BXLY DA5 170 A6
HAMP NW3 83 F2
KENS W8 119 K3
PEND EN3 25 J1
Edencourt Rd STRHM/NOR SW16 179 G2
Edendale Rd BXLYHN DA7 150 A2
Edenfield Gdns WPK KT4 207 H1
Eden Gv HOLWY N7 85 F3
WLSDN NW10 81 J6
Eden Pde BECK BR3 * 198 B1
Eden Park Av BECK BR3 198 D1
Eden Rd BECK BR3 198 B1
BXLY DA5 169 K6
CROY/NA CRO 211 K2
WALTH E17 69 K2
WNWD SE27 180 C1
Edensor Gdns CHSWK W4 138 B1
Edensor Rd CHSWK W4 138 B1
Eden St KUT/HW KT1 174 E5
Edenvale Rd MTCM CR4 179 F3
Edenvale St FUL/PGN SW6 140 A3
Eden Wk KUT/HW KT1 * 175 F5
Eden Wy BECK BR3 198 D2
BOW E3 87 H6
Ederline Av STRHM/NOR SW16 180 A6
Edgar Kail Wy CMBW SE5 143 H4
Edgarley Ter FUL/PGN SW6 * 139 H2
Edgar Rd BOW E3 105 K2
HSLWW TW4 154 E1
Edgar Wallace Cl PECK SE15 123 F6
Edgeborough Wy BMLY BR1 184 C4
Edgebury CHST BR7 167 G6
Edgecombe Cl KUTN/CMB KT2 176 A3
Edgecoombe SAND/SEL CR2 213 F6
Edgecote Cl ACT W3 117 K1
Edgefield Av BARK IG11 91 F5
Edge HI WIM/MER SW19 177 G3
WOOL/PLUM SE18 127 G6
Edge HI Av FNCH N3 46 E6
Edge HI Ct WIM/MER SW19 177 G3
Edgehill Ct WOT/HER KT12 * 188 B5
Edgehill Gdns DAGE RM10 92 C2
Edgehill Rd CHST BR7 167 H5
MTCM CR4 179 G4
WEA W13 97 J5
Edgeley La CLAP SW4 141 J4
Edgeley Rd CLAP SW4 141 H4
Edgel St WAND/EARL SW18 140 A6
Edge Point Cl STRHM/NOR SW16 180 C1
Edgepoint Cl WNWD SE27 180 C1
Edge St KENS W8 119 K1
Edgewood Dr ORP BR6 217 F3
Edgewood Gn CROY/NA CRO 198 A5
Edgeworth Av HDN NW4 63 J2
Edgeworth Cl HDN NW4 63 J2
Edgeworth Crs HDN NW4 63 J2
Edgeworth Rd EBAR EN4 21 J5
ELTH/MOT SE9 146 B5
Edgington Rd STRHM/NOR SW16 179 J2
Edgington Wy SCUP DA14 186 D5
Edgwarebury Gdns EDGW HA8 44 C1
Edgwarebury La BORE WD6 30 D2
Edgware Rd BAY/PAD W2 2 A7
CDALE/KGS NW9 45 F6
CRICK NW2 82 A1
Edgware Road Burnt Oak CDALE/KGS NW9 45 F6
Edgware Road High St EDGW HA8 44 C2
Edgware Road The Hyde CDALE/KGS NW9 63 C1
Edgware Wy (Watford By-Pass) EDGW HA8 30 A4
Edinburgh Cl BETH E2 104 E1
PIN HA5 59 J3
Edinburgh Ct KUT/HW KT1 * 175 F6
Edinburgh Ga KTBR SW1X 16 E2
Edinburgh Rd HNWL W7 116 A2
PLSTW E13 107 F1
SUT SM1 194 B6
WALTH E17 69 J2
Edington Rd ABYW SE2 128 C3
PEND EN3 24 E3
Edison Av HCH RM12 75 H5
Edison Cl HCH RM12 75 H5
WDR/YW UB7 * 112 C2
Edison Dr STHL UB1 96 B5
WBLY HA9 62 A6
Edison Gv WOOL/PLUM SE18 148 A5
Edison Rd CEND/HSY/T N8 66 D3
HAYES BR2 183 K5
PEND EN3 25 H3
WELL DA16 148 A2
Edis St CAMTN NW1 84 A1
Edith Cavell Wy WOOL/PLUM SE18 146 D2
Edith Gdns BRYLDS KT5 191 J4
Edith Gv WBPTN SW10 120 B6
Edithna St BRXN/ST SW9 141 K4
Edith Nesbit Wk ELTH/MOT SE9 146 D5
Edith Neville Cottages CAMTN NW1 4 C4
Edith Rd CHDH RM6 73 K4
EHAM E6 89 H5
FBAR/BDGN N11 48 C2
ORP BR6 217 G3
SNWD SE25 196 E2
SRTFD E15 88 B3
WEA W13 116 B2
WIM/MER SW19 178 A2
WKENS W14 119 H4
Edith Rw FUL/PGN SW6 140 A2
Edith St BETH E2 7 K2
Edith Ter WBPTN SW10 140 B1
Edith Vls WKENS W14 119 J4
Edith Yd WBPTN SW10 140 C1
Edison Cl WALTH E17 152 A3
Edmansons Cl TOTM N17 50 B5
Edmeston Cl HOM E9 87 G4
Edmund Gv FELT TW13 154 E4
Edmund Halley Wy GNWCH SE10 125 J1
Edmund Hurst Dr EHAM E6 108 B4
Edmunds Cl YEAD UB4 95 G4
Edmund St CMBW SE5 142 E1
Edmunds Wk EFNCH N2 65 J1
Edna Rd RYNPK SW20 177 G5
Edna St BTSEA SW11 140 D2
Edrick Rd EDGW HA8 44 E2
Edrick Wk EDGW HA8 44 E2
Edric Rd NWCR SE14 144 A1
Edridge Rd CROY/NA CRO 211 J1
Edward Av CHING E4 51 K2
MRDN SM4 194 C2
Edward Cl EN EN1 36 B2
HPTN TW12 173 H1
Edward Ct CAN/RD E16 106 E4
Edwardes Pl WKENS W14 119 J5
Edward Gv EBAR EN4 21 H6
Edward Mann Cl East WCHPL E1 * 105 F5
Edward Mann Cl West WCHPL E1 * 105 F5
Edward Ms CAMTN NW1 * 3 K4
Edward Pl DEPT SE8 124 C6
Edward Rd BMLY BR1 184 A3
CHDH RM6 74 A3
CHST BR7 185 G2
CROY/NA CRO 197 F4
EBAR EN4 21 H6
EBED/NFELT TW14 133 C4
HPTN TW12 173 H1
NTHLT UB5 77 G5
PGE/AN SE20 182 A3
RYLN/HDSTN HA2 42 E4
WALTH E17 69 F1
Edwards Av RSLP HA4 77 G3
Edwards Cl WPK KT4 193 G6
Edward's Cottages IS N1 * 85 H5
Edwards Dr FBAR/BDGN N11 48 D3
Edward's La STNW/STAM N16 67 K6
Edwards Ms IS N1 85 H5
MHST W1U 9 H3
Edwards Pl FBAR/BDGN N11 48 C1
Edwards Sq IS N1 5 C1
Edwards Rd BELV DA17 129 H4
Edward Temme Av SRTFD E15 88 D3
Edward Tyler Rd LEE/GVPK SE12 166 A4
Edward Wy ASHF TW15 152 C4
Edwina Gdns REDBR IG4 71 J2
Edwin Av EHAM E6 108 A2
Edwin Cl BXLYHN DA7 129 G6
RAIN RM13 111 H2
Edwin Hall Pl LEW SE13 165 G1
Edwin Pl CROY/NA CRO 196 E5
Edwin Rd EDGW HA8 45 F2
RDART DA2 171 G2
WHTN TW2 155 K3
Edwin's Md HOM E9 87 G2
Edwin St CAN/RD E16 106 E4
WCHPL E1 104 E3
Edwin Ware Ct PIN HA5 41 G5
Edwyn Cl BAR EN5 32 A1
Effie Pl FUL/PGN SW6 139 K1
Effie Rd FUL/PGN SW6 139 K1
Effingham Cl BELMT SM2 209 F5
Effingham Rd CEND/HSY/T N8 67 G2
CROY/NA CRO 196 A4
LEE/GVPK SE12 145 H6
SURB KT6 190 C4
Effort St TOOT SW17 178 D1
Effra Pde BRXS/STRHM SW2 142 B6
Effra Rd BRXS/STRHM SW2 142 B5
WIM/MER SW19 178 A2
Egan Wy HYS/HAR UB3 94 C6
Egbert St CAMTN NW1 84 A6
Egerton Cl DART DA1 58 E1
PIN HA5 58 E1
Egerton Crs CHEL SW3 14 D6
Egerton Dr GNWCH SE10 144 E2
Egerton Gdns CHEL SW3 14 D5
GDMY/SEVK IG3 91 F1
HDN NW4 63 J1
WEA W13 97 H5
WLSDN NW10 82 A6
Egerton Gardens Ms CHEL SW3 14 D5
Egerton Pl CHEL SW3 14 D5
Egerton Rd ALP/SUD HA0 80 B5
NWMAL KT3 192 C1
SNWD SE25 181 F6
STNW/STAM N16 68 B4
WHTN TW2 155 K2
Egerton Ter CHEL SW3 14 D5
Egerton Wy HYS/HAR UB3 132 E1
Egham Cl CHEAM SM3 193 H6
WIM/MER SW19 159 H4
Egham Crs CHEAM SM3 208 C1
Egham Rd PLSTW E13 107 F4
Eglantine Rd WAND/EARL SW18 140 B6
Egleston Rd MRDN SM4 194 A3
Eglington Ct CHING E4 38 B2
Eglington Rd WOOL/PLUM SE18 128 A1
Eglinton Rd WOOL/PLUM SE18 127 F6
Egliston Ms PUT/ROE SW15 139 F4
Egliston Rd PUT/ROE SW15 139 F4
Eglon Ms CAMTN NW1 83 K5
Egmont Av SURB KT6 191 G5
Egmont Rd BELMT SM2 209 G5
NWMAL KT3 192 C1
SURB KT6 191 G5
WOT/HER KT12 188 A4
Egmont St NWCR SE14 144 A1
Egremont Rd WNWD SE27 162 B5
Egret Wy YEAD UB4 95 H4
Eider Cl SRTFD E15 88 B5
Eighteenth Rd MTCM CR4 195 K1
Eighth Av HYS/HAR UB3 113 K1
MNPK E12 89 K2
Eileen Rd SNWD SE25 196 E2
Eindhoven Cl CAR SM5 195 F5
WIM/MER SW19 178 C4
Eisenhower Dr EHAM E6 107 J4
Elaine Gv KTTN NW5 84 A3
Elam Cl CMBW SE5 142 C3
Elam St CMBW SE5 142 C3
Eland Rd BTSEA SW11 140 E4
CROY/NA CRO 211 H1
Elba Pl WALW SE17 * 18 D6
Elbe St FUL/PGN SW6 140 B3
Elborough Rd SNWD SE25 197 H2
Elborough St WAND/EARL SW18 159 K3
Elbury Dr CAN/RD E16 106 E5
Elcho St BTSEA SW11 140 D1
Elcot Av PECK SE15 143 J1
Elder Av CEND/HSY/T N8 66 E2
Elderberry Cl BARK/HLT IG6 54 B3
Elderberry Gv WNWD SE27 * 162 D6
Elder Cl BFN/LL DA15 168 A3
TRDG/WHET N20 33 F4
Elder Ct BUSH WD23 28 E4
Elderfield Rd CLPT E5 87 F2
Elderfield Wk WAN E11 71 F2
Elderflower Wy SRTFD E15 88 C5
Elder Oak Cl PGE/AN SE20 181 J4
Elder Rd WNWD SE27 180 D1
Elderslie Cl BECK BR3 198 E3
Elderslie Rd ELTH/MOT SE9 147 F6
Elder St WCHPL E1 13 H1
Elderton Rd SYD SE26 164 B6
Eldertree Pl MTCM CR4 179 G4
Eldertree Wy MTCM CR4 179 G4
Elder Wk IS N1 85 H6
Eldon Av CROY/NA CRO 197 K6
HEST TW5 135 F1
Eldon Gv HAMP NW3 83 H3
Eldon Pk SNWD SE25 197 J1
Eldon Rd ED N9 36 E4
KENS W8 120 A3
TOTM N17 50 C4
WALTH E17 69 H1
WDGN N22 49 H4
Eldon Wy WLSDN NW10 98 D1
Eldred Dr STMC/STPC BR5 202 E6
Eldridge Cl EBED/NFELT TW14 153 K3
Eleanora Ter SUT SM1 * 209 G3
Eleanor Cl BERM/RHTH SE16 124 A2
SEVS/STOTM N15 68 A3
Eleanor Crs MLHL NW7 46 B1
Eleanor Gdns BAR EN5 20 B6
BCTR RM8 92 B1
Eleanor Gv BARN SW13 138 B4
Eleanor Rd FBAR/BDGN N11 48 E1
HACK E8 86 D5
SRTFD E15 88 D4
Eleanor St BOW E3 105 J2
Electra Av HTHAIR TW6 133 J4
Electric Av BRXN/ST SW9 142 B5
Electric La BRXN/ST SW9 142 B5
Electric Pde SURB KT6 190 E3
Elephant & Castle STHWK SE1 18 B6
Elephant La BERM/RHTH SE16 123 K2
Elephant Rd WALW SE17 18 C6
Elers Rd HYS/HAR UB3 113 F4
WEA W13 116 D2
Eley Rd UED N18 51 F1
Elfindale Rd HNHL SE24 142 D6
Elfin Gv TEDD TW11 174 A1
Elford Cl BKHTH/KID SE3 146 B5
Elfort Rd HBRY N5 85 G2
Elfrida Crs CAT SE6 164 D6
Elf Rw WAP E1W 104 E6
Elgal Cl ORP BR6 216 B3
Elgar Av BRYLDS KT5 191 J5
EA W5 117 F2
STRHM/NOR SW16 179 K6
Elgar Cl BKHH IG9 39 H4
BORE WD6 29 J2
DEPT SE8 144 D1
PLSTW E13 107 G1
Elgar St BERM/RHTH SE16 124 B2
Elgin Av KTN/HRWW/WS HA3 43 H5
MV/WKIL W9 100 E3
SHB W12 118 E3
Elgin Cl SHB W12 118 E2
Elgin Crs HTHAIR TW6 133 J4
NTGHL W11 * 100 D5
Elgin Dr NTHWD HA6 40 D3
Elginmeads South MV/WKIL W9 * 101 F2
Elgin Ms NTGHL W11 100 C5
Elgin Ms North MV/WKIL W9 101 F2
Elgin Rd CROY/NA CRO 197 G6
GDMY/SEVK IG3 72 E5
SUT SM1 209 G1
WDGN N22 48 E5
WLGTN SM6 210 C4
Elgood Av NTHWD HA6 40 E2
Elgood Cl NTGHL W11 100 C6
Elham Cl BMLY BR1 184 C5
Elia Ms IS N1 6 A3
Elias Pl VX/NE SW8 122 B6
Elia St IS N1 6 A3
Elibank Rd ELTH/MOT SE9 147 F5
Elim Est STHWK SE1 19 G4
Elim Wy PLSTW E13 106 C3
Eliot Bank FSTH SE23 163 J4
Eliot Gdns PUT/ROE SW15 138 D5
Eliot HI LEW SE13 145 F3
Eliot Ms STJWD NW8 2 B3
Eliot Pk LEW SE13 145 F3
Eliot Pl BKHTH/KID SE3 145 H3
Eliot Rd DAGW RM9 91 K2
Eliot V BKHTH/KID SE3 145 G3
Elizabethan Wy STWL/WRAY TW19 152 A2
Elizabeth Av ENC/FH EN2 23 H4
IL IG1 72 E2
IS N1 85 J5
Elizabeth Barnes Ct FUL/PGN SW6 * 140 A3
Elizabeth Br BGVA SW1W 15 J7
Elizabeth Cl BAR EN5 20 B4
MV/WKIL W9 101 G3
ROMW/RG RM7 56 D4
SUT SM1 208 D2
Elizabeth Clyde Cl SEVS/STOTM N15 68 A1
Elizabeth Cottages RCH/KEW TW9 137 G2
Elizabeth Fry Pl WOOL/PLUM SE18 146 D2
Elizabeth Gdns ACT W3 118 C1
ISLW TW7 136 B5
STAN HA7 43 J2
SUN TW16 172 B6
Elizabeth Ms HAMP NW3 83 J4
Elizabeth Pl SEVS/STOTM N15 67 K1
Elizabeth Ride ED N9 36 D2
Elizabeth Rd EHAM E6 89 H1
RAIN RM13 111 K4
Elizabeth Sq BERM/RHTH SE16 105 G6
Elizabeth St BGVA SW1W 15 H6
Elizabeth Wy FELT TW13 154 B6
NRWD SE19 180 E2
STMC/STPC BR5 202 B2
Elkanette Ms TRDG/WHET N20 33 G4
Elkington Rd PLSTW E13 107 F3
The Elkins ROM RM1 57 G5
Elkstone Rd NKENS W10 100 D4
Ella Ms HAMP NW3 83 K2
Ellanby Crs UED N18 50 D1
Elland Rd PECK SE15 143 K5
WOT/HER KT12 188 C6
Ella Rd CEND/HSY/T N8 66 E4
Ellement Cl PIN HA5 59 H2
Ellenborough Pl PUT/ROE SW15 138 D5
Ellenborough Rd SCUP DA14 186 E2
WDGN N22 49 J4
Ellenbridge Wy SAND/SEL CR2 212 A6
Ellen Cl BMLY BR1 184 C6
Ellen Ct ED N9 36 E4

Ellen St WCHPL E1.......104 C5
Ellen Webb Dr
  KTN/HRWW/WS HA3......42 E6
Elleray Rd TEDD TW11...174 A2
Ellerby St FUL/PGN SW6.139 G2
Ellerdale Cl HAMP NW3...83 G3
Ellerdale Rd HAMP NW3....83 G3
Ellerdale St LEW SE13....144 E5
Ellerdine Rd HSLW TW3...135 H5
Ellerker Gdns
  RCHPK/HAM TW10......157 F1
Ellerman Av WHTN TW2...154 E3
Ellerslie Rd SHB W12....118 E1
Ellerton Gdns DAGW RM9..91 J5
Ellerton Rd BARN SW13..138 D2
  DAGW RM9.............91 J5
  RYNPK SW20..........176 D3
  SURB KT6.............191 G6
  WAND/EARL SW18......160 C3
Elley Rd NRWD SE19.....180 E3
Ellery St PECK SE15.....143 J3
Ellesborough Cl OXHEY WD19..41 G1
Ellesmere Av BECK BR3..182 E5
  MLHL NW7.............31 F5
Ellesmere Cl RSLP HA4...58 A4
  WAN E11..............70 D2
Ellesmere Gdns REDBR IG4..71 J3
Ellesmere Gv BAR EN5....20 D6
Ellesmere Rd BOW E3....105 G1
  GFD/PVL UB6...........96 C5
  TWK TW1.............156 D1
  WLSDN NW10...........81 J3
Ellesmere St POP/IOD E14..105 K5
Elles Ms ASHF TW15.....152 B4
Ellingfort Rd HACK E8....86 D5
Ellingham Rd CHSGTN KT9..205 K4
  SHB W12.............118 D2
  SRTFD E15.............88 B2
Ellington Rd FELT TW13...153 J6
  HSLW TW3............135 G3
  MUSWH N10............66 B1
Ellington St HOLWY N7....85 G4
Elliot Cl SRTFD E15......88 C5
Elliot Rd HDN NW4.......63 K3
  KTN/HRWW/WS HA3 *..59 F6
Elliott Gdns HARH RM3....57 K4
Elliott Rd BRXN/ST SW9..142 C1
  CHSWK W4............118 B4
  HAYES BR2............200 C1
  THHTH CR7............196 C1
Elliott's Pl IS N1.........6 A2
Elliott's Sq HAMP NW3....83 J5
Elliott's Rw LBTH SE11....18 B6
Ellis Av RAIN RM13......111 J4
Ellis Cl EDGW HA8.......45 G2
  ELTH/MOT SE9........167 H4
  WLSDN NW10...........82 A4
Ellis Rd MTCM CR4......194 E3
  NWDGN UB2...........115 H1
Ellis St KTBR SW1X.......15 F6
Ellis Wy DART DA1 *.....171 J4
Ellsworth St BETH E2....104 D2
Elmar Rd SEVS/STOTM N15..67 K1
Elm Av EA W5...........117 F1
  OXHEY WD19...........27 J2
  RSLP HA4.............58 E5
Elmbank STHGT/OAK N14..34 E2
Elmbank Av BAR EN5......20 A5
Elmbank Dr BMLY BR1...184 C5
Elm Bank Gdns BARN SW13..138 B3
Elmbank Wy HNWL W7....96 D4
Elmbourne Dr BELV DA17..129 J4
Elmbourne Rd TOOT SW17..161 G5
Elmbridge Av BRYLDS KT5..191 K3
Elmbridge Dr RSLP HA4...58 E3
Elmbridge Rd BARK/HLT IG6..55 G2
Elmbridge Wk HACK E8....86 C5
Elmbrook Cl SUN TW16...172 A4
Elmbrook Gdns ELTH/MOT SE9..146 D5
Elmbrook Rd SUT SM1...208 D2
Elm Cl BKHH IG9.........39 H4
  BRYLDS KT5..........191 K4
  CAR SM5.............194 E5
  DART DA1............171 F3
  HDN NW4..............64 A1
  HYS/HAR UB3...........94 E5
  ROMW/RG RM7.........56 D4
  RYLN/HDSTN HA2.......60 B3
  RYNPK SW20...........193 F3
  SAND/SEL CR2........211 K4
  STWL/WRAY TW19......152 A3
  WAN E11..............71 F2
  WHTN TW2............155 G4
Elm Cottages MTCM CR4 *..178 E5
Elmcourt Rd WNWD SE27..162 D4
Elm Crs EA W5..........117 F2
  KUTN/CMB KT2........175 F4
Elmcroft CEND/HSY/T N8..67 F2
Elmcroft Av BFN/LL DA15..168 A3
  ED N9................36 D1
  GLDGN NW11...........64 D4
  WAN E11..............70 C1
Elmcroft Cl CHSGTN KT9..206 A1
  EA W5...............97 K5
  EBED/NFELT TW14.....153 J1
Elmcroft Crs GLDGN NW11..64 C4
Elmcroft Dr CHSGTN KT9..206 A1
Elmcroft Gdns CDALE/KGS NW9..62 C2
Elmcroft Rd ORP BR6....202 B4
Elmcroft St CLPT E5......86 E2
Elmdale Rd PLMGR N13....49 F1
Elmdene BRYLDS KT5......191 K5
Elmdene Cl BECK BR3....198 C2

Elmdene Rd
  WOOL/PLUM SE18......127 G5
Elmdon Rd HSLWW TW4...134 C3
  HTHAIR TW6...........133 J4
Elm Dr RYLN/HDSTN HA2...60 B3
  SUN TW16............172 B5
Elmer Cl ENC/FH EN2.....23 J5
  RAIN RM13............93 J5
Elmer Gdns EDGW HA8....44 D3
  ISLW TW7............135 J4
  RAIN RM13............93 J5
Elmer Rd CAT SE6........165 F2
Elmers Dr TEDD TW11...174 C2
Elmers End Rd BECK BR3..181 K6
Elmerside Rd BECK BR3...198 B1
Elmers Rd SNWD SE25...197 H4
Elmfield Av CEND/HSY/T N8..66 E2
  TEDD TW11...........174 A1
Elmfield Cl HRW HA1......60 E6
Elmfield Pk BMLY BR1....183 K6
Elmfield Rd BMLY BR1....183 K6
  CHING E4.............38 A4
  EFNCH N2.............47 H6
  NWDGN UB2...........114 D3
  TOOT SW17...........161 F5
  WALTH E17............69 G1
Elmfield Wy MV/WKIL W9..100 E4
  SAND/SEL CR2........212 B6
Elm Friars Wk CAMTN NW1..84 D1
Elm Gdns EFNCH N2.......47 G6
  ENC/FH EN2...........23 K1
  ESH/CLAY KT10.......205 H4
  MTCM CR4............195 J1
Elmgate Av FELT TW13...154 A5
Elmgate Gdns EDGW HA8...44 E1
Elm Gn ACT W3...........99 G5
Elmgreen Cl SRTFD E15....88 C6
Elm Gv CEND/HSY/T N8....66 E2
  CRICK NW2............82 B2
  ERITH DA8...........150 A1
  KUTN/CMB KT2........175 F4
  ORP BR6.............202 A5
  PECK SE15............143 H3
  RYLN/HDSTN HA2.......60 A1
  SUT SM1.............209 F2
  WIM/MER SW19........177 H5
Elmgrove Crs HRW HA1....61 F2
Elmgrove Gdns HRW HA1..61 G2
Elm Grove Pde CAR SM5..210 A1
Elm Grove Rd BARN SW13..138 D3
Elm Grove Rd CROY/NA CRO..197 J5
Elm Grove Rd EA W5......117 F2
Elmgrove Rd HRW HA1....61 F2
  CROY/NA CRO.........197 J5
Elm Hall Gdns WAN E11...71 F3
Elm Hatch PIN HA5.......41 K3
Elmhurst BELV DA17......129 F6
Elmhurst Av EFNCH N2 *..47 H6
  MTCM CR4............179 G4
Elmhurst Crs EFNCH N2...65 H1
Elmhurst Dr SWFD E18....52 E5
Elmhurst Rd ELTH/MOT SE9..166 D4
  FSTGT E7.............89 F5
  TOTM N17.............50 A5
Elmhurst St CLAP SW4...141 J4
Elmhurst Wy LOU IG10....39 K2
Elmington Cl BXLY DA5...169 J2
Elmington Est CMBW SE5..142 E1
Elmington Rd CMBW SE5..142 E1
Elmira St LEW SE13.....144 E4
Elm La CAT SE6.........164 C4
Elmlee Cl CHST BR7.....184 E2
Elmley Cl WOOL/PLUM SE18..127 J4
Elmore Cl ALP/SUD HA0....98 A1
Elmore Rd PEND EN3......25 F1
  WAN E11..............70 B6
Elmore St IS N1.........85 K5
Elm Pde SCUP DA14 *....168 B6
Elm Pk BRXS/STRHM SW2..162 A1
  STAN HA7.............43 H1
Elm Park Av HCH RM12...93 K2
  SEVS/STOTM N15......68 A2
Elm Park Gdns HDN NW4...64 B2
  WBPTN SW10..........120 C6
Elm Park La CHEL SW3...120 C6
Elm Park Rd CHEL SW3...120 C6
  FNCH N3.............46 D5
  LEY E10..............69 G5
  PIN HA5.............181 G6
  SNWD SE25...........181 G6
  WCHMN N21...........35 J2
Elm Pl SKENS SW7......120 C5
Elm Rd BAR EN5.........20 D5
  BECK BR3............182 C5
  CHSGTN KT9..........206 A2
  DART DA1............171 G3
  EBED/NFELT TW14.....153 G2
  ERITH DA8...........150 D2
  ESH/CLAY KT10.......205 F4
  EW KT17.............207 H4
  FSTGT E7.............88 D4
  KUTN/CMB KT2........175 G4
  MORT/ESHN SW14.....137 K4
  NWMAL KT3...........176 A6
  ORP BR6.............217 G3
  ROMW/RG RM7.........56 E6
  SCUP DA14...........168 B6
  THHTH CR7...........196 D1
  WALTH E17............69 J3
  WBLY HA9.............80 A3
  WDGN N22.............49 H4
  WLGTN SM6...........195 F5
Elm Rw HAMP NW3........83 G1
Elm Rd West MRDN SM4...193 J4
Elms Av HDN NW4.........64 B2
  MUSWH N10............48 B6
Elmscott Gdns WCHMN N21..35 J1
Elmscott Rd BMLY BR1...183 J1
Elms Ct ALP/SUD HA0....79 G2
Elms Crs CLAP SW4......161 H1
Elmsdale Rd WALTH E17...69 H1
Elms Gdns ALP/SUD HA0...79 G2
  DAGW RM9............92 A4

Elmside Rd WBLY HA9......80 C1
Elms La ALP/SUD HA0......79 G2
Elmsleigh Av
  KTN/HRWW/WS HA3....61 H1
Elmsleigh Rd WHTN TW2..155 H4
Elmslie Cl WFD IG8.......53 K2
Elms Ms BAY/PAD W2......8 B5
Elms Park Av ALP/SUD HA0..79 G2
Elms Rd CLAP SW4.......141 H6
  KTN/HRWW/WS HA3....42 E5
Elmstead Av CHST BR7...184 E1
  WBLY HA9.............62 A5
Elmstead Cl HOR/WEW KT19..207 G3
  TRDG/WHET N20........32 E4
Elmstead Gdns WPK KT4..207 J1
Elmstead Gld CHST BR7..184 D2
Elmstead La CHST BR7...184 D3
Elmstead Rd ERITH DA8..150 B2
  GDMY/SEVK IG3........72 E6
Elmsted Crs WELL DA16..128 D6
The Elms BARN SW13.....138 C4
  ESH/CLAY KT10 *.....205 F5
  NFNCH/WDSPK N12 *...47 J1
  TOOT SW17...........161 F5
  WLGTN SM6...........210 C2
Elmstone Ter
  STMC/STPC BR5 *.....202 D1
Elmstone Rd FUL/PGN SW6..139 K2
Elm St FSBYW WC1X.......5 H7
Elmsworth Av HSLW TW3..135 G3
Elm Ter CRICK NW2.......82 E1
  ELTH/MOT SE9........167 F1
  KTN/HRWW/WS HA3....42 D5
Elmton Wy CLPT E5......86 C1
Elm Tree Av ESH/CLAY KT10..189 H4
Elm Tree Cl CHARL SE7 *..126 B6
Elm Tree Rd STJWD NW8....2 A4
Elmtree Rd TEDD TW11...173 K1
Elm Vis HNWL W7 *.......96 E6
Elm Wk GPK RM2.........57 K6
  HAMP NW3.............64 E6
  ORP BR6.............215 K1
  RYNPK SW20..........193 F1
Elm Wy FBAR/BDGN N11....48 A2
  HOR/WEW KT19........207 F3
  WLSDN NW10...........81 G2
  WPK KT4.............208 A1
Elmwood Av FELT TW13...154 A5
  KTN/HRWW/WS HA3....43 G6
  PLMGR N13............48 E1
Elmwood Cl EW KT17....207 J5
  WLGTN SM6...........195 G6
Elmwood Ct ALP/SUD HA0..79 F2
Elmwood Crs CDALE/KGS NW9..62 E1
Elmwood Dr BXLY DA5....169 F2
  EW KT17.............207 J5
Elmwood Gdns HNWL W7...96 E5
Elmwood Rd CHSWK W4..117 K6
  CROY/NA CRO.........196 C4
  HNHL SE24...........142 D6
  MTCM CR4............178 E6
Elmworth Gv DUL SE21...162 E4
Elnathan Ms MV/WKIL W9..101 F3
Elphinstone Rd WALTH E17..51 H5
Elphinstone St HBRY N5...85 H2
Elrick Cl ERITH DA8.....130 B6
Elrington Rd HACK E8.....86 C4
  WFD IG8..............52 E1
Elruge Cl WDR/YW UB7...112 A2
Elsa Cottages POP/IOD E14 *..105 G4
Elsa Rd WELL DA16......148 D3
Elsa St WCHPL E1.........105 G4
Elsdale St HOM E9........86 E4
Elsden Ms BETH E2........104 E1
Elsden Rd TOTM N17......50 B4
Elsenham Rd MNPK E12....89 K3
Elsenham St
  WAND/EARL SW18......159 J3
Elsham Rd WKENS W14....119 H2
  WKENS W14...........119 H2
Elsham Ter WKENS W14 *..119 H2
Elsiedene Rd WCHMN N21..35 J3
Elsie Lane Ct BAY/PAD W2..100 E4
Elsiemaud Rd BROCKY SE4..144 C6
Elsie Rd EDUL SE22.....143 G5
Elsinore Av
  STWL/WRAY TW19......152 B2
Elsinore Gdns CRICK NW2..82 C1
Elsinore Rd FSTH SE23...164 B3
Elsinore Wy RCH/KEW TW9..137 J4
Elspeth Rd ALP/SUD HA0..80 A3
  BTSEA SW11..........140 E5
Elstan Wy CROY/NA CRO..198 B4
Elsted St WALW SE17.....19 F7
Elstow Cl ELTH/MOT SE9..59 H4
  RSLP HA4.............59 H4
Elstow Gdns DAGW RM9....92 A6
Elstow Rd DAGW RM9......92 A5
Elstree Cl HCH RM12......93 K5
Elstree Gdns BELV DA17..129 F4
  ED N9................36 C5
  IL IG1...............72 C3
Elstree HI BMLY BR1.....183 H5
Elstree HI South BORE WD6..29 J1
Elstree Pk BORE WD6.....31 F1
Elstree Rd BORE WD6......29 G1
  BUSH WD23............28 A1
Elswick Rd LEW SE13.....144 E4
Elswick St FUL/PGN SW6..140 B3
Elsworth Cl
  EBED/NFELT TW14.....153 H3
Elsworthy THDIT KT7.....189 K3
Elsworthy Rd HAMP NW3...83 J5
Elsworthy Rd HAMP NW3...83 J5
Elsworthy Ter HAMP NW3...83 J5
Elsynge Rd WAND/EARL SW18..140 D6
Eltham Gn ELTH/MOT SE9..146 B6
Eltham Green Rd
  ELTH/MOT SE9........146 B6
Eltham High St ELTH/MOT SE9..166 E1
Eltham HI ELTH/MOT SE9..166 C1
Eltham Palace Rd
  ELTH/MOT SE9........166 C1

Eltham Park Gdns
  ELTH/MOT SE9........147 F5
Eltham Rd ELTH/MOT SE9..146 B6
Elthiron Rd FUL/PGN SW6..139 K2
Elthorne Av HNWL W7...116 A2
Elthorne Park Rd HNWL W7..116 A3
  CDALE/KGS NW9.......63 F5
Elthorne Wy CDALE/KGS NW9..63 F5
Elthruda Rd LEW SE13...165 G1
Eltisley Rd IL IG1.......90 B2
Elton Av ALP/SUD HA0....79 H5
  BAR EN5..............20 C6
  GFD/PVL UB6...........79 F4
Elton Cl KUTN/CMB KT2..174 D3
Elton Pl STNW/STAM N16..86 A3
Elton Rd KUTN/CMB KT2..175 G4
Eltringham St
  WAND/EARL SW18......140 B5
Elvaston Ms SKENS SW7 *..120 B3
Elvaston Pl SKENS SW7...120 B3
Elveden Pl WLSDN NW10...98 C1
Elveden Rd WLSDN NW10...98 C1
Elvendon Rd FELT TW13..153 J5
Elverson Rd FBAR/BDGN N11..48 B2
Elver Gdns BETH E2......104 C2
Elverson Ms DEPT SE8...144 C1
Elverson Rd DEPT SE8...144 C1
Elverton St WEST SW1P...16 C7
Elvington Gn HAYES BR2..199 J1
Elvington La CDALE/KGS NW9..45 G4
Elvino Rd SYD SE26.....182 A1
Elvis Rd CRICK NW2......82 A4
Elwill Wy BECK BR3......199 G1
Elwin St BETH E2.........7 K5
Elwood St HBRY N5.......85 H1
Elwyn Gdns LEE/GVPK SE12..165 K2
Ely Cl ERITH DA8.......150 C3
  NWMAL KT3...........176 C5
Ely Cottages VX/NE SW8 *..142 A1
Ely Gdns DAGE RM10......92 E1
Elyne Rd FSBYPK N4.......67 G3
Ely Pl HCIRC EC1N.......11 K2
  WFD IG8..............54 A1
Ely Rd CROY/NA CRO......196 E3
  HSLWW TW4...........134 B4
  HTHAIR TW6...........133 J3
  LEY E10..............70 A3
Elysian Av STMC/STPC BR5..201 K3
Elysium Pl FUL/PGN SW6..139 J3
Elysium St FUL/PGN SW6..139 J3
Elystan Cl WLGTN SM6...210 C6
Elystan Pl CHEL SW3.....14 C7
Elystan St CHEL SW3......14 C6
Elystan Wk IS N1.........5 H2
Emanuel Av ACT W3........98 E5
Embankment PUT/ROE SW15..139 G4
Embankment Gdns CHEL SW3..120 E6
Embankment Pl CHCR WC2N..11 F7
The Embankment TWK TW1..156 B3
Embassy Ct SCUP DA14...168 B5
  WLGTN SM6 *.........210 B4
Emba St BERM/RHTH SE16..123 H2
Ember Cl STMC/STPC BR5..201 H4
Ember Farm Av
  E/WMO/HCT KT8........189 J3
Ember Farm Wy
  E/WMO/HCT KT8........189 J2
Ember Gdns THDIT KT7...189 K4
Ember La ESH/CLAY KT10..189 K4
Embleton Rd LEW SE13...144 E5
  OXHEY WD19...........26 E5
Embry Cl STAN HA7.......29 G6
Embry Dr STAN HA7.......43 G2
Embry Wy STAN HA7.......43 G1
Emden Cl WDR/YW UB7...112 D2
Emden St FUL/PGN SW6...140 A2
Emerald Cl CAN/RD E16..107 J5
Emerald Gdns BCTR RM8...74 B5
Emerald Sq NWDGN UB2..114 C3
Emerald St BMSBY WC1N...11 G1
Emerson Gdns
  KTN/HRWW/WS HA3....62 B3
Emerson Rd IL IG1.......72 C7
Emerson St STHWK SE1....18 C1
Emerton Cl BXLYHS DA6..149 F5
Emery Hill St WEST SW1P..16 B5
Emery St STHWK SE1......17 K4
Emes Rd ERITH DA8......149 K1
Emilia Cl PEND EN3.......24 D6
Emily Pl HOLWY N7.......85 G3
Emlyn Gdns SHB W12....118 B2
Emlyn Rd SHB W12......118 B2
Emmanuel Rd BAL SW12..161 H3
  NTHWD HA6............40 D3
Emma Rd PLSTW E13......88 E5
Emma St BETH E2........104 D1
Emmaus Wy CHIG IG7.....54 A1
Emmett Cl BORE WD6.....29 H1
Emmott Av BARK/HLT IG6..72 C2
Emmott Cl GLDGN NW11...65 G3
  WCHPL E1............105 H3
Emperor's Ga SKENS SW7..120 B3
Empire Av UED N18.......49 J2
Empire Pde UED N18 *....49 K2
  WBLY HA9.............80 C1
Empire Rd GFD/PVL UB6...79 J6
Empire Sq HGT N6........65 K3
Empire Wy WBLY HA9......80 B2
Empire Wharf Rd
  POP/IOD E14.........125 G5
Empress Av CHING E4.....51 K3
  IL IG1...............72 A6
  MNPK E12............71 G6
  WFD IG8..............52 D3
Empress Dr CHST BR7...185 G2
Empress Ms CMBW SE5 *..142 D3
Empress Pl FUL/PGN SW6..119 K5
Empress St WALW SE17...122 D6
Empson St BOW E3.......105 K4
Emsworth Cl ED N9.......36 E3
Emsworth Rd BARK/HLT IG6..54 B5
Emsworth St
  BRXS/STRHM SW2.....162 A4
Emu Rd VX/NE SW8.......141 G3

Ena Rd STRHM/NOR SW16..179 K6
Enbrook St NKENS W10...100 C2
Enclave Ct FSBYE EC1V.....6 B6
Endale Cl CAR SM5......194 E6
Endeavour Wy BARK IG11..109 G1
  CROY/NA CRO.........195 K6
  WIM/MER SW19........160 A5
Endell St LSQ/SEVD WC2H..10 E3
Enderby St GNWCH SE10..125 H5
Enderley Rd
  KTN/HRWW/WS HA3....42 D4
Endersby Rd BAR EN5.....20 A6
Endersleigh Gdns HDN NW4..63 J1
Endlebury Rd CHING E4....38 A4
Endlesham Rd BAL SW12..161 F2
Endsleigh Gdns IL IG1....71 K5
  STPAN WC1H...........4 C6
  SURB KT6............190 D3
Endsleigh Pl STPAN WC1H..4 D6
Endsleigh Rd NWDGN UB2..114 D4
  WEA W13.............97 G6
Endsleigh St STPAN WC1H..4 D6
Endway BRYLDS KT5......191 H4
Endwell Rd BROCKY SE4..144 B3
Endymion Rd
  BRXS/STRHM SW2.....162 A2
  FSBYPK N4............67 H4
Energen Cl WLSDN NW10...81 G4
Enfield Rd ACT W3......117 J2
  BTFD TW8............116 E5
  ENC/FH EN2...........23 J4
  HTHAIR TW6..........133 H5
  IS N1................86 B5
Enford St CAMTN NW1......8 E1
Engadine Cl CROY/NA CRO..212 B1
Engadine St
  WAND/EARL SW18......159 J3
Engate St LEW SE13.....145 F4
Engel Pk MLHL NW7.......46 A2
Engineer Cl WOOL/PLUM SE18..127 F6
Engleheart Dr
  EBED/NFELT TW14.....153 J1
Engleheart Rd CAT SE6..164 E2
Englewood Rd BAL SW12..161 G1
English St BOW E3......105 H3
Enid St BERM/RHTH SE16..19 K4
Enmore Av SNWD SE25...197 H2
Enmore Gdns
  MORT/ESHN SW14.....138 A6
Enmore Rd PUT/ROE SW15..139 F5
  SNWD SE25...........197 H2
  STHL UB1.............96 A3
Ennerdale Av HCH RM12...93 J3
Ennerdale Cl
  EBED/NFELT TW14.....153 J1
  SUT SM1.............208 D2
Ennerdale Dr CDALE/KGS NW9..63 F3
Ennerdale Gdns WBLY HA9..61 J5
Ennerdale Rd BXLYHN DA7..149 H2
  RCH/KEW TW9.........137 G3
Ennersdale Rd LEW SE13..145 G6
Ennismore Av CHSWK W4..118 B4
  GFD/PVL UB6...........78 E4
Ennismore Gdns SKENS SW7..14 C4
  THDIT KT7...........189 K3
Ennismore Gardens Ms
  SKENS SW7............14 C4
Ennismore Ms SKENS SW7..14 C4
Ennismore St SKENS SW7..14 C4
Ennis Rd FSBYPK N4......67 G5
  WOOL/PLUM SE18.....127 J6
Ensign Cl STWL/WRAY TW19..152 A3
Ensign Dr PLMGR N13.....35 J3
Ensign St WCHPL E1.....104 C6
Ensign Wy STWL/WRAY TW19..152 A3
  WLGTN SM6...........210 E6
Enslin Rd ELTH/MOT SE9..167 F1
Ensor Ms SKENS SW7....120 C5
Enstone Rd PEND EN3.....25 H4
  HGDN/ICK UB10.......76 A1
Enterprise Cl CROY/NA CRO..196 B6
Enterprise Rw
  SEVS/STOTM N15......68 A2
Enterprise Wy TEDD TW11..174 A1
  WAND/EARL SW18......139 K4
  WLSDN NW10...........99 H2
Enterprize Wy DEPT SE8..124 C4
Epcot Ms WLSDN NW10...100 B2
Epirus Ms FUL/PGN SW6..139 K1
Epirus Rd FUL/PGN SW6..139 J1
Epping Cl POP/IOD E14...124 D4
  ROMW/RG RM7.........56 D6
Epping Gln CHING E4......38 A1
Epping New Rd BKHH IG9..39 F2
Epping Pl IS N1..........85 G4
Epping Wy CHING E4......37 K1
Epple Rd FUL/PGN SW6...139 J2
Epsom Cl BXLYHN DA7....149 J4
  NTHLT UB5.............77 K3
Epsom Rd CROY/NA CRO..211 G2
  GDMY/SEVK IG3........73 F5
  LEY E10..............70 A3
  MRDN SM4............193 J4
Epstein Rd THMD SE28...128 C1
Epworth Rd ISLW TW7....136 C2
Epworth St SDTCH EC2A....7 F7
Equity Sq BETH E2.........7 K5
Erasmus St WEST SW1P....16 D7
Erconwald St SHB W12....99 G5
Erebus Dr THMD SE28...127 K3
Eresby Dr BECK BR3.....198 D5
Eresby Pl KIL/WHAMP NW6..82 E5
Erica Gdns CROY/NA CRO..213 K2
Erica St SHB W12.......99 J6
Eric Clarke La BARK IG11..108 C3
Ericcson Cl WAND/EARL SW18..139 K6
Eric Rd CHDH RM6........73 K4
  FSTGT E7.............88 E2
  WLSDN NW10...........81 H4
Eric St BOW E3.........105 H3

Eric Rd CHDH RM6	73	K4
FSTGT E7	88	E2
WLSDN NW10	81	H4
Eric St BOW E3	105	H3
Eridge Green Cl		
STMC/STPC BR5	202	B5
Eridge Rd CHSWK W4	118	A3
Erin Cl BMLY BR1	183	H1
Erindale WOOL/PLUM SE18	127	J6
Erindale Ter WOOL/PLUM SE18	127	J6
Erin Ms WDGN N22 *	49	H4
Erith Cr PUR RM19	131	K4
Erith Crs CRW RM5	56	E4
Erith High St ERITH DA8	130	C6
Erith Rd BELV DA17	129	J5
BXLYHN DA7	149	J4
Erlanger Rd NWCR SE14	144	A2
Erlesmere Gdns HNWL W7	116	B3
Erlich Cottages WCHPL E1 *	104	E4
Ermine Cl HSLWW TW4	134	B3
Ermine Rd LEW SE13	144	E5
SEVS/STOTM N15	68	A2
Ermine Side EN EN1	24	C6
Ermington Rd ELTH/MOT SE9	167	H4
Ernald Av EHAM E6	107	J1
Erncroft Wy TWK TW1	156	A1
Ernest Av WNWD SE27	162	C6
Ernest Cl BECK BR3	198	D2
Ernest Gdns CHSWK W4	117	J6
Ernest Gv BECK BR3	198	C2
Ernest Rd KUT/HW KT1	175	J5
Ernest St WCHPL E1	105	F4
Ernle Rd RYNPK SW20	176	E3
Ernshaw Pl PUT/ROE SW15	139	H6
Erpingham Rd PUT/ROE SW15	139	F4
Erridge Rd WIM/MER SW19	177	K5
Errington Rd MV/WKIL W9	100	D3
Errol Gdns NWMAL KT3	192	D1
YEAD UB4	95	F3
Erroll Rd ROM RM1	75	H1
Errol St STLK EC1Y	6	D7
Erskine Cl SUT SM1	209	J1
Erskine Crs TOTM N17	56	E4
Erskine Hl GLDGN NW11	64	E1
Erskine Ms HAMP NW3 *	83	K5
Erskine Rd HAMP NW3	83	K5
SUT SM1	209	H2
WALTH E17	69	H1
Erwood Rd CHARL SE7	126	D5
Esam Wy STRHM/NOR SW16	180	B1
Escot Wy BAR EN5	26	A4
Escreet Gv WOOL/PLUM SE18	127	F4
Esher Av CHEAM SM3	208	B1
ROMW/RG RM7	74	E3
WOT/HER KT12	188	A5
Esher Cl BXLY DA5	169	F3
Esher Crs HTHAIR TW6	133	J5
Esher Gn ESH/CLAY KT10	204	B2
Esher Green Dr		
ESH/CLAY KT10	204	A1
Esher Ms MTCM CR4	179	F6
Esher Park Av ESH/CLAY KT10	204	B3
Esher Place Av ESH/CLAY KT10	204	B2
Esher Rd E/WMO/HCT KT8	189	J2
CDMY/SEVK IG3	90	E1
Eskdale Av NTHLT UB5	77	K1
Eskdale Cl WBLY HA9	61	K6
Eskdale Rd BXLYHN DA7	149	H3
Eskmont Rdg NRWD SE19	181	F3
Esk Rd PLSTW E13	107	F3
Esk Wy ROM RM1	57	G3
Esmar Crs CDALE/KGS NW9	63	E4
Esmeralda Rd STHWK SE1	123	H4
Esmond Cl RAIN RM13 *	93	K5
Esmond Gdns CHSWK W4 *	118	A4
Esmond Rd CHSWK W4	118	A3
KIL/WHAMP NW6	82	D6
Esmond St PUT/ROE SW15	139	H5
Esparto St WAND/EARL SW18	160	A2
Essenden Rd BELV DA17	129	H5
SAND/SEL CR2	212	A5
Essendine Rd MV/WKIL W9	100	E2
Essex Av ISLW TW7	135	K4
Essex Cl MRDN SM4	193	G4
ROMW/RG RM7	74	D1
RSLP HA4	59	H5
Essex Ct BARN SW13	138	C3
EMB EC4Y *	11	J4
Essex Gdns FSBYPK N4	67	H3
Essex Gv NRWD SE19	180	E2
Essex Pk FNCH N3	47	F2
Essex Park Ms ACT W3	118	B1
Essex Pl CHSWK W4	117	K4
Essex Place Sq CHSWK W4 *	118	A4
Essex Rd ACT W3	98	E6
EBAR EN4	90	D5
CHDH RM6	73	J5
CHING E4	38	C3
CHSWK W4	118	A4
DAGE RM10	92	E3
DART DA1	171	G1
ENC/FH EN2	23	J4
IS N1	85	J5
LEY E10	70	A3
MNPK E12	89	J3
ROMW/RG RM7	74	D1
SWFD E18	53	F5
WALTH E17	69	G3
WLSDN NW10	81	G5
Essex Rd South WAN E11	70	B4
Essex St FSTGT E7	88	E3
TPL/STR WC2R	11	J4
Essex Vls KENS W8	119	K2
Essex Whf CLPT E5 *	69	F6
Essian St WCHPL E1	105	G4
Essoldo Wy EDGW HA8	44	B6
Estate Vy LEY E10	69	H5
Estcourt Rd FUL/PGN SW6	119	J6
SNWD SE25	197	J3
Estella Av NWMAL KT3	192	E1
Estelle Rd HAMP NW3	83	K2
Esterbrooke St WEST SW1P	16	C7
Este Rd BTSEA SW11	140	D4
Esther Cl WCHMH N21	35	H2
Esther Rd WAN E11	70	C4
Estoria Cl BRXS/STRHM SW2	162	B2
Estreham Rd		
STRHM/NOR SW16	179	J2
Estridge Cl HSLW TW3	135	F5
Estuary Cl BARK IG11	109	H2
Eswyn Rd TOOT SW17	160	E6
Etchingham Park Rd FNCH N3	47	G4
Etchingham Rd SRTFD E15	88	A2
Eternit Wk FUL/PGN SW6	139	F2
Etfield Gv SCUP DA14	186	C1
Ethelbert Cl BMLY BR1	183	K5
Ethelbert Gdns REDBR IG4	71	K2
Ethelbert Rd BMLY BR1	183	K6
ERITH DA8	149	K1
RDART DA2	171	H6
RYNPK SW20	177	G4
STMC/STPC BR5	186	E6
Ethelbert St BAL SW12	161	G3
Ethelburga St BTSEA SW11	140	D2
Etheldene Av MUSWH N10	66	C1
Ethelden Rd SHB W12	118	E1
Ethelred St LBTH SE11	17	J7
Ethel Rd CAN/RD E16	107	F6
Ethel St WALW SE17	18	D7
Etheridge Rd CRICK NW2	64	A5
Etherley Rd SEVS/STOTM N15	67	J2
Etherow St EDUL SE22	163	H2
Etherstone Rd		
STRHM/NOR SW16	162	B6
Ethnard Rd PECK SE15	123	J6
Ethronvi Rd BXLYHN DA7	149	F4
Etloe Rd LEY E10	69	J6
Eton Av ALP/SUD HA0	79	J2
EBAR EN4	33	J1
HAMP NW3	83	J5
HEST TW5	114	E6
NFNCH/WDSPK N12	47	G3
NWMAL KT3	192	A2
Eton Cl WAND/EARL SW18	160	A2
Eton College Rd HAMP NW3	83	K4
Eton Garages HAMP NW3 *	83	K4
Eton Gv CDALE/KGS NW9	44	C6
LEW SE13	145	H4
Eton Pl HAMP NW3 *	84	A5
Eton Ri HAMP NW3 *	83	K4
Eton Rd HAMP NW3	83	K5
HYS/HAR UB3	133	J1
IL IG1	90	C2
ORP BR6	217	F2
Eton St RCH/KEW TW9	136	E6
Eton Vls HAMP NW3	83	K4
Eton Wy DART DA1	151	F5
Etta St DEPT SE8	124	B6
Etton Rd HSLW TW3	135	H6
Ettrick St POP/IOD E14	106	A5
Etwell Pl BRYLDS KT5	191	G3
Euesdon Cl ED N9	36	C5
Eugenia Rd BERM/RHTH SE16	123	K5
Eureka Rd KUT/HW KT1	175	H5
Europa Pl FSBYE EC1V	6	C5
Europe Rd WOOL/PLUM SE18	126	E4
Eustace Pl WOOL/PLUM SE18	126	E4
Eustace Rd CHDH RM6	73	K4
EHAM E6	107	J2
FUL/PGN SW6	139	K1
Euston Centre CAMTN NW1 *	4	A6
Euston Rd CAMTN NW1	4	B6
CROY/NA CRO	196	B5
Euston Sq CAMTN NW1	4	C5
Euston St CAMTN NW1	4	B6
Evandale Rd BRXN/ST SW9	142	C3
Evangelist Rd KTTN NW5	84	B2
Evans Cl HACK E8	86	B4
Evans Gv FELT TW13	155	F4
Evans Rd CAT SE6	165	H4
Evanston Av CHING E4	52	A3
Evanston Gdns REDBR IG4	71	J3
Eva Rd CHDH RM6	73	J4
Evelina Rd PECK SE15	143	K4
PGE/AN SE20	181	K3
Eveline Lowe Est		
BERM/RHTH SE16	123	H3
Eveline Rd MTCM CR4	178	E4
Evelyn Av CDALE/KGS NW9	63	F1
RSLP HA4	58	C3
Evelyn Cl WHTN TW2	155	G2
Evelyn Denington Rd		
EHAM E6	107	J3
Evelyn Dr PIN HA5	41	H3
Evelyn Est DEPT SE8	124	B6
Evelyn Gdns RCH/KEW TW9	137	F5
SKENS SW7	120	C5
Evelyn Gv EA W5	117	G1
Evelyn Rd CAN/RD E16	125	K1
EA W5	21	H5
RCH/KEW TW9	137	F5
RCHPK/HAM TW10	156	D5
WALTH E17	70	A1
WIM/MER SW19	178	A1
Evelyn St DEPT SE8	124	C6
CNWCH SE10	125	F6
Evelyn Ter RCH/KEW TW9	137	F5
Evelyn Wk IS N1	6	E3
Evelyn Wy WLGTN SM6	210	D2
Evensyde WATW WD18	26	A1
Evenwood Cl PUT/ROE SW15 *	139	H6
Everard Av HAYES BR2	199	K5
Everard Wy WBLY HA9	80	A1
Everatt Cl WAND/EARL SW18 *	159	J1
Everdon Rd BARN SW13	118	D6
Everest Pl POP/IOD E14	106	A4
Everest Rd ELTH/MOT SE9	146	E6
STWL/WRAY TW19	152	A2
Everett Cl BUSH WD23	28	E3
PIN HA5	40	D6
The Everglades HSLW TW3 *	135	H4
Everglade Strd		
CDALE/KGS NW9	45	H4
Evergreen Ct		
STWL/WRAY TW19 *	152	A2
Evergreen Sq HACK E8	86	B5
Evergreen Wy HYS/HAR UB3	94	D6
STWL/WRAY TW19	152	A2
Everilda St IS N1	5	H1
Everington Rd STNW/STAM N16	86	C1
Everington St HMSMTH W6	119	G6
Everitt Rd WLSDN NW10	99	F2
Everleigh St FSBYPK N4	67	F5
Eve Rd ISLW TW7	136	B5
SRTFD E15	106	C1
TOTM N17	50	A6
WAN E11	88	C2
Eversfield Gdns EDGW HA8	45	G3
Eversfield Rd RCH/KEW TW9	137	G3
Evershed Wk CHSWK W4	117	K3
Evershot St CAMTN NW1	4	B3
Evershot Rd FSBYPK N4	67	F5
Eversleigh Rd BAR EN5	21	G6
BTSEA SW11	140	E4
EHAM E6	89	H6
FNCH N3	46	D3
Eversley Av BXLYHN DA7	150	B3
WBLY HA9	62	C6
Eversley Cl WCHMH N21	35	F1
Eversley Crescent IS N1	58	C6
RSLP HA4	58	C6
WCHMH N21	35	F1
Eversley Cross BXLYHN DA7	150	B3
Eversley Mt WCHMH N21	35	F1
Eversley Pk WIM/MER SW19	176	E1
Eversley Park Rd WCHMH N21	35	F1
Eversley Rd BRYLDS KT5	191	G1
CHARL SE7	126	A6
NRWD SE19	180	E3
Eversley Wy CROY/NA CRO	213	J2
Everthorpe Rd PECK SE15	143	G4
Everton Buildings CAMTN NW1	4	A5
Everton Dr STAN HA7	44	B6
Everton Rd CROY/NA CRO	197	H5
Evesham Av WALTH E17	51	J5
Evesham Cl BELMT SM2	208	E5
GFD/PVL UB6	96	B1
Evesham Gn MRDN SM4	194	A3
Evesham Rd FBAR/BDGN N11	48	C1
MRDN SM4	194	A3
SRTFD E15	88	D5
Evesham St NTGHL W11	100	B6
Evesham Ter SURB KT6	190	E3
Evesham Wk BRXN/ST SW9	142	B3
CMBW SE5	142	E3
Evesham Wy BTSEA SW11	141	F4
CLAY IG5	54	A6
Evry Rd SCUP DA14	186	D2
Ewald Rd FUL/PGN SW6	139	J3
Ewanrigg Ter WFD IG8	53	G1
Ewart Gv WD GN N22	49	G4
Ewart Pl BOW E3 *	105	H1
Ewart Rd FSTH SE23	164	A2
Ewe Cl HOLWY N7	84	E4
Ewell By-Pass EW KT17	207	J5
Ewell Court Av		
HOR/WEW KT19	207	G3
Ewellhurst Rd CLAY IG5	53	J5
Ewell Park Gdns EW KT17	207	J5
Ewell Park Wy EW KT17	207	J4
Ewell Rd CHEAM SM3	208	B4
SURB KT6	190	C4
SURB KT6	191	G5
Ewelme Rd FSTH SE23	163	K3
Ewen Crs BRXS/STRHM SW2	162	B2
Ewer St STHWK SE1	18	C1
Ewhurst Av SAND/SEL CR2	212	B6
Ewhurst Cl BELMT SM2	208	A6
WCHPL E1	104	E4
Ewhurst Rd BROCKY SE4	164	C6
Exbury Rd CAT SE6	164	D4
Excel Ct LSQ/SEVD WC2H	10	D6
Excel Marina CAN/RD E16	106	E6
Excelsior Cl KUT/HW KT1	175	H5
Excel Waterfront		
CAN/RD E16	107	F6
Exchange Ar LVPST EC2M	13	G2
Exchange Ct COVGDN WC2E *	11	F6
Exchange Sq SDTCH EC2A *	13	H1
Exchange St ROM RM1	75	G2
Exchange Wk PIN HA5	59	K4
Exeforde Av ASHF TW15	152	D6
Exeter Cl EHAM E6	107	K5
Exeter Gdns IL IG1	71	K5
Exeter Ms FUL/PGN SW6	139	K1
Exeter Pde CRICK NW2 *	82	C2
Exeter Rd CAN/RD E16	106	E4
CRICK NW2	82	C3
CROY/NA CRO	197	F4
DAGE RM10	92	D4
ED N9	36	E4
FELT TW13	154	E5
HTHAIR TW6	133	H4
PEND EN3	25	F4
RYLN/HDSTN HA2	59	J6
STHGT/OAK N14	34	B3
WALTH E17	69	J2
WELL DA16	148	A3
Exeter St COVGDN WC2E	11	F5
Exeter Wy HTHAIR TW6	133	H4
NWCR SE14	144	C1
Exford Gdns LEE/GVPK SE12	166	A4
Exford Rd LEE/GVPK SE12	166	A4
Exhibition Grounds		
WBLY HA9 *	80	D2
Exhibition Rd SKENS SW7	14	B5
Exit Rd EFNCH N2	47	H5
Exmoor Cl BARK/HLT IG6	54	C4
Exmoor St NKENS W10	100	B4
Exmouth Market CLKNW EC1R	5	K6
Exmouth Ms CAMTN NW1 *	4	B5
Exmouth Pl HACK E8	86	D6
Exmouth Rd RSLP HA4	77	G1
WALTH E17	69	H2
WELL DA16	148	D2
YEAD UB4	94	C2
Exmouth St WCHPL E1	104	E5
Exning Rd CAN/RD E16	106	D3
Exon St WALW SE17	19	G7
Explorer Av STWL/WRAY TW19	152	B3
Explorer Dr WATW WD18	26	D1
Express Dr GDMY/SEVK IG3	73	H5
Exton Gdns BCTR RM8	91	J3
Exton Rd WLSDN NW10	80	E5
Exton St STHWK SE1	17	J1
Eyhurst Av HCH RM12	93	J1
Eyhurst Cl CRICK NW2	63	K6
Eylewood Rd WNWD SE27	180	D1
Eynella Rd DUL SE21	163	G2
Eynham Rd SHB W12	100	A5
Eynsford Cl STMC/STPC BR5	201	H4
Eynsford Crs BXLY DA5	168	D2
Eynsford Rd CDMY/SEVK IG3	72	E6
Eynsham Dr ABYW SE2	128	C3
Eynswood Dr SCUP DA14	186	C1
Eyot Gdns HMSMTH W6	118	C5
Eyot Gn CHSWK W4	118	C5
Eyre Street HI CLKNW EC1R	5	J7
Eythorne Rd BRXN/ST SW9	142	B2
Ezra St BETH E2	7	K4

F

Faber Gdns HDN NW4	63	J2
Fabian Rd FUL/PGN SW6	139	J1
Fabian St EHAM E6	107	K3
The Facade FSTH SE23 *	163	K4
Factory La CROY/NA CRO	196	B6
TOTM N17	50	B5
Factory Pl POP/IOD E14	125	F5
Factory Rd CAN/RD E16	126	C1
Factory Yd HNWL W7 *	115	K1
Faesten Wy BXLY DA5	170	B5
Faggs Rd EBED/NFELT TW14	133	K6
Faircare ISLW TW7 *	135	J2
NWMAL KT3	176	B6
Faircares CROY/NA CRO	213	H6
Fair Acres HAYES BR2	199	K2
Faircross PUT/ROE SW15	138	C5
RSLP HA4	58	D4
Fairbank Av ORP BR6	201	G6
Fairbank Est IS N1 *	6	E3
Fairbanks Rd TOTM N17	50	C6
Fairbourne Rd TOTM N17	50	A6
Fairbridge Rd ARCH N19	66	D6
Fairbrook Cl PLMGR N13	49	G1
Fairby Rd LEE/GVPK SE12	146	A6
Fairchild Cl BTSEA SW11	140	C3
Fairchild Pl SDTCH EC2A *	7	H7
Fairchild St SDTCH EC2A	7	H7
Fair Cl BUSH WD23	28	B2
Fairclough St WCHPL E1	104	C5
Faircross Av BARK IG11	90	C4
CRW RM5	56	E4
Fairdale Gdns HYS/HAR UB3	113	K2
PUT/ROE SW15	138	E5
Fairey Av HYS/HAR UB3	113	J5
Fairey Av EW KT17	207	K6
Fairfax Cl WOT/HER KT12	188	A5
Fairfax Gdns BKHTH/KID SE3	146	B2
Fairfax Ms CAN/RD E16	126	A1
CEND/HSY/T N8 *	67	H1
PUT/ROE SW15	139	F5
Fairfax Pl KIL/WHAMP NW6	83	G5
WKENS W14	119	H3
Fairfax Rd CEND/HSY/T N8	67	G1
CHSWK W4	118	B3
KIL/WHAMP NW6	83	G5
TEDD TW11	174	B2
WKENS W14	119	H3
Fairfax Wy MUSWH N10	48	A3
Fairfield Av EDGW HA8	44	D2
HDN NW4	63	K3
OXHEY WD19	27	H1
RSLP HA4	58	A4
WHTN TW2	155	G3
Fairfield Cl BFN/LL DA15	168	A1
HCH RM12	75	J5
HOR/WEW KT19	207	G3
MTCM CR4	178	E3
NFNCH/WDSPK N12	33	G6
PEND EN3	25	F5
Fairfield Cnr KUT/HW KT1 *	175	F5
Fairfield Ct RSLP HA4	58	B5
Fairfield Crs EDGW HA8	44	D2
Fairfield Dr GFD/PVL UB6	79	J6
RYLN/HDSTN HA2	42	C6
WAND/EARL SW18	140	A6
Fairfield East KUT/HW KT1	175	F5
Fairfield Gdns CEND/HSY/T N8	66	E2
Fairfield Gv CHARL SE7	126	C6
Fairfield North		
KUTN/CMB KT2	175	F5
Fairfield Pth CROY/NA CRO	211	K1
Fairfield Rd KUT/HW KT1	175	F5
Fairfield Rd BECK BR3	182	D5
BMLY BR1	183	K3
BOW E3	105	J1
BXLYHN DA7	149	G3
CEND/HSY/T N8	66	E2
CROY/NA CRO	211	K1
IL IG1	90	B4
KUT/HW KT1	175	F5
STHL UB1	95	K4
STMC/STPC BR5	201	J3
UED N18	36	D6
WALTH E17	51	G5
WDR/YW UB7	112	B1
WFD IG8	52	E2
Fairfields CAT SE6	164	E2
Fairfields Cl CDALE/KGS NW9	62	E2
Fairfields Crs CDALE/KGS NW9	62	E1
Fairfield South KUT/HW KT1	175	F6
Fairfield St WAND/EARL SW18	140	A6
Fairfield Wy BAR EN5	20	E6
HOR/WEW KT19	207	G3
Fairfield West KUT/HW KT1	175	F5
Fairfoot Rd BOW E3 *	105	J3
Fairford Av BXLYHN DA7	149	K2
CROY/NA CRO	198	A2
Fairford Cl CROY/NA CRO	198	B2
Fairford Ct BELMT SM2 *	209	F5
Fairford Gdns WPK KT4	207	H1
Fairgreen EBAR EN4	21	K4
Fairgreen Rd THHTH CR7	196	C2
Fairhaven Av CROY/NA CRO	198	A4
Fairhaven Crs OXHEY WD19	26	E5

Exton St STHWK SE1	17	J1
Fairhazel Gdns		
KIL/WHAMP NW6	83	F4
Fairholme EBED/NFELT TW14	153	G2
Fairholme Av GPK RM2	75	J2
Fairholme Rd FNCH N3	64	C1
Fairholme Ct PIN HA5 *	42	A2
Fairholme Crs YEAD UB4	94	B3
Fairholme Gdns FNCH N3	64	C1
Fairholme Rd CROY/NA CRO	196	B4
HRW HA1	60	E2
IL IG1	72	A4
SUT SM1	208	D4
WKENS W14	119	H5
Fairholt Rd STNW/STAM N16	67	K5
Fairholt St SKENS SW7	14	D4
Fairland Rd SRTFD E15	88	D4
Fairlands Av BKHH IG9	38	E4
SUT SM1	193	K5
THHTH CR7	196	A1
Fairlawn CHARL SE7	146	B1
Fairlawn Av BXLYHN DA7	148	E3
CHSWK W4	117	K4
Fairlawn Cl CLAY IG5	54	A6
ESH/CLAY KT10	205	F4
FELT TW13	154	E6
KUTN/CMB KT2	175	K2
STHGT/OAK N14	34	C1
Fairlawn Ct CHARL SE7 *	146	B1
Fairlawn Dr WFD IG8	52	E3
Fairlawn Gdns STHL UB1 *	95	K6
Fairlawn Gv CHSWK W4	117	K4
Fairlawn Pk SYD SE26	182	B1
WLSDN NW10	98	E3
Fairlawns PIN HA5	41	J5
TWK TW1	156	D1
Fairlea Pl EA W5	97	J4
Fairlie Gdns FSTH SE23	163	K2
Fairlight Av CHING E4	38	B3
WFD IG8	52	E2
WLSDN NW10	99	G1
Fairlight Cl CHING E4	38	B3
WPK KT4	208	A2
Fairlight Rd TOOT SW17	160	C6
Fairlop Ct FNCH N3 *	93	K4
Fairlop Gdns BARK/HLT IG6	54	C5
Fairlop Rd BARK/HLT IG6	54	B5
WAN E11	70	B4
Fairmead BMLY BR1	200	E1
BRYLDS KT5	191	J5
Fairmead Cl BMLY BR1	200	E1
HEST TW5	134	C1
NWMAL KT3	176	A6
Fairmead Crs EDGW HA8	30	E5
Fairmead Gdns REDBR IG4	71	J2
Fairmead Rd ARCH N19	84	E1
CROY/NA CRO	196	A6
Fairmile Av STRHM/NOR SW16	179	J1
Fairmont Cl BELV DA17	129	G5
Fairmont Rd		
BRXS/STRHM SW2	162	A1
Fairoak Cl STMC/STPC BR5	201	G4
Fairoak Dr ELTH/MOT SE9	147	J6
Fairoak Gdns ROM RM1	57	G5
Fair Oak Pl BARK/HLT IG6	54	C5
Fairseat Cl BUSH WD23	28	E4
Fairstead Wk IS N1 *	85	J5
Fair St HSLW TW3	135	H4
Fairthorn Rd CHARL SE7	125	K5
Fairview ERITH DA8	150	C1
Fairview Av ALP/SUD HA0	79	K4
Fairview Cl SYD SE26	182	B1
Fairview Cl WALTH E17	51	G4
Fairview Ct HDN NW4	46	B5
Fairview Crs RYLN/HDSTN HA2	60	A5
Fairview Dr CHIG IG7	54	D1
ORP BR6	216	D2
Fairview Gdns WFD IG8	53	F4
Fairview Pl BRXS/STRHM SW2	162	A2
Fairview Rd CEND/HSY/T N8	66	F3
SEVS/STOTM N15	68	B2
STRHM/NOR SW16	180	A4
SUT SM1	209	H3
Fairview Vls CHING E4 *	51	J3
Fairview Wy EDGW HA8	30	C5
Fairwater Av WELL DA16	148	B4
Fairway BXLYHS DA6	149	F6
RYNPK SW20	192	E3
STMC/STPC BR5	201	J3
WFD IG8	53	G1
Fairway Av CDALE/KGS NW9	44	D6
Fairway Cl CROY/NA CRO	198	B2
GLDGN NW11	65	G4
HOR/WEW KT19	206	E2
HSLWW TW4	134	C6
Fairway Ct MLHL NW7 *	31	F5
Fairway Gdns BECK BR3	199	G3
IL IG1	90	C3
Fairways ISLW TW7 *	135	K2
STAN HA7	44	A5
TEDD TW11	174	E3
WALTH E17	70	A1
The Fairway ACT W3	99	G5
ALP/SUD HA0	61	H6
BAR EN5	33	H1
E/WMO/HCT KT8	173	F6
HAYES BR2	200	E2
HNWL W7 *	96	E5
MLHL NW7	31	F5
NTHLT UB5	78	A4
NTHWD HA6	26	C6
NWMAL KT3	176	A4
PLMGR N13	35	J3
RSLP HA4	77	F3
STHGT/OAK N14	34	B1
Fairweather Cl		
SEVS/STOTM N15	68	A1
Fairweather Rd		
STNW/STAM N16		
Fairwyn Rd SYD SE26	164	B6
Faithfield BUSH WD23 *	27	J3
Fakenham Cl MLHL NW7	45	J3
NTHLT UB5	78	A4
Fakruddin St WCHPL E1	104	C3
Falaize Av IL IG1	90	B2

Falcon Av BMLY BR1 200 D1
Falconberg Ct
SOHO/SHAV W1D * 10 C3
Falcon Cl CHSWK W4 117 J6
DART DA1 151 J6
NTHWD HA6 40 C3
STHWK SE1 12 B7
Falcon Ct IS N1 6 B3
Falcon Crs PEND EN3 25 F6
Falcon Dr STWL/WRAY TW19 152 A1
Falconer Rd BARK/HLT IG6 55 J1
BUSH WD23 28 A1
Falcon Gv BTSEA SW11 140 D4
Falcon La BTSEA SW11 140 D4
Falcon Rd BTSEA SW11 140 D4
HPTN TW12 172 E3
PEND EN3 25 F6
Falcon St PLSTW E13 106 E3
Falcon Ter BTSEA SW11 * 140 D4
Falcon Wy CDALE/KGS NW9 45 G5
KTN/HRWW/WS HA3 62 A2
POP/IOD E14 124 E4
WAN E11 70 E1
Falconwood Av WELL DA16 147 J3
Falconwood Pde WELL DA16 147 K5
Falconwood Rd CROY/NA CR0 213 J6
Falcourt Cl SUT SM1 209 F3
Falkirk Gdns OXHEY WD19 41 H1
Falkirk St IS N1 7 H3
Falkland Av FBAR/BDGN N11 34 A6
FNCH N3 46 E3
Falkland Park Av SNWD SE25 181 F6
Falkland Pl KTTN NW5 84 C3
Falkland Rd BAR EN5 20 C3
CEND/HSY/T N8 67 H1
KTTN NW5 84 C3
Falloden Wy GLDGN NW11 64 E1
Fallow Cl CHIG IG7 55 F1
Fallow Ct BERM/RHTH SE16 * 123 H5
Fallow Court Av
NFNCH/WDSPK N12 47 G3
Fallowfield STAN HA7 29 G5
Fallowfield Ct STAN HA7 29 G5
Fallow Flds LOU IG10 39 H2
Fallowfields Dr
NFNCH/WDSPK N12 47 J2
Fallows Cl EFNCH N2 47 H5
Fallsbrook Rd
STRHM/NOR SW16 179 G2
Falman Cl ED N9 36 C3
Falmer Rd EN EN1 24 A5
SEVS/STOTM N15 67 J2
WALTH E17 51 K6
Falmouth Av CHING E4 52 B1
Falmouth Cl LEE/GVPK SE12 145 J6
WDGN N22 49 F3
Falmouth Gdns REDBR IG4 71 H1
Falmouth Rd STHWK SE1 18 D5
Falmouth St SRTFD E15 88 B3
Falstaff Cl DART DA1 170 B2
Falstaff Ms HPTN TW12 173 J1
Fambridge Cl SYD SE26 164 C6
Fambridge Rd BCTR RM8 74 C5
Fane St WKENS W14 119 J6
Fanns Ri PUR RM19 131 K4
Fann St FARR EC1M 6 C7
Fanshawe Av BARK IG11 90 C4
Fanshawe Crs DAGW RM9 92 A3
Fanshawe Rd
RCHPK/HAM TW10 156 D6
Fanshaw St IS N1 7 G4
Fantail Cl THMD SE28 109 J5
Fanthorpe St PUT/ROE SW15 139 F4
Faraday Av SCUP DA14 168 C4
Faraday Cl HOLWY N7 85 F4
WATW WD18 26 B1
Faraday Pl E/WMO/HCT KT8 189 F1
Faraday Rd ACT W3 98 E6
E/WMO/HCT KT8 189 F1
NKENS W10 100 C4
SRTFD E15 88 D4
STHL UB1 96 B6
WELL DA16 148 B4
WIM/MER SW19 178 A2
Faraday Wy STMC/STPC BR5 202 C1
WOOL/PLUM SE18 126 C3
Fareham Rd
EBED/NFELT TW14 154 B2
Fareham St SOHO/CST W1F * 10 C3
Farewell Pl MTCM CR4 178 C4
Faringdon Av HAYES BR2 201 G3
Faringford Rd SRTFD E15 88 C5
Farjeon Rd BKHTH/KID SE3 146 C2
Farleigh Av HAYES BR2 199 K4
Farleigh Court Rd
CROY/NA CR0 196 A6
Farleigh Pl STNW/STAM N16 86 B2
Farleigh Rd STNW/STAM N16 86 B2
Farley Dr GDMY/SEVK IG3 72 E5
Farley Pl SNWD SE25 197 H1
Farley Rd CAT SE6 165 F2
SAND/SEL CR2 212 D5
Farlington Pl PUT/ROE SW15 158 E2
Farlow Rd PUT/ROE SW15 139 G4
Farlton Rd WAND/EARL SW18 160 A2
Farman Ter
KTN/HRWW/WS HA3 * 61 K1
Farm Av ALP/SUD HA0 79 J4
CRICK NW2 82 C1
RYLN/HDSTN HA2 60 A4
STRHM/NOR SW16 161 K6
SWLY BR8 187 K6
Farmborough Cl HRW HA1 60 D4
Farm Cl BELMT SM2 209 H5
BKHH IG9 39 G5
DAGE RM10 92 E5
FUL/PGN SW6 * 139 K1
STHL UB1 96 B6
WWKM BR4 214 D1
Farmcote Rd LEE/GVPK SE12 165 K3
Farm Cottages
E/WMO/HCT KT8 * 190 B1
Farmdale Rd CAR SM5 209 J5
CHARL SE7 125 K5
Farm Dr CROY/NA CR0 198 C6
Farmer Rd LEY E10 69 K5
Farmers Rd CMBW SE5 142 C1
Farmer St KENS W8 * 119 K1
Farmfield Rd BMLY BR1 183 H1
Farmhouse Rd
STRHM/NOR SW16 179 H3
Farmilo Rd WALTH E17 69 J4
Farmington Av SUT SM1 209 H1
Farmlands ENC/FH EN2 23 G2
PIN HA5 58 E1
The Farmlands NTHLT UB5 77 K4
Farmland Wk CHST BR7 185 G1
Farm La CROY/NA CR0 198 C6
FUL/PGN SW6 119 K6
STHGT/OAK N14 34 B1
Farmleigh STHGT/OAK N14 34 C2
Farm Pl DART DA1 150 D5
KENS W8 119 K1
Farm Rd BELMT SM2 209 H5
EDGW HA8 44 E1
ESH/CLAY KT10 189 F5
HSLWW TW4 154 D3
MRDN SM4 194 A2
NTHWD HA6 40 A1
WCHMH N21 35 J3
WLSDN NW10 81 F6
Farmstead Rd CAT SE6 164 E6
KTN/HRWW/WS HA3 42 D4
Farm St MYFR/PICC W1J 9 J6
The Farm WIM/MER SW19 * 159 G2
Farm V BXLY DA5 169 J1
Farm Wk GLDGN NW11 64 D3
Farmway BCTR RM8 91 J2
Farm Wy BKHH IG9 39 G6
HCH RM12 93 K2
NTHWD HA6 26 C6
WPK KT4 208 A1
Farnaby Rd BMLY BR1 183 H4
ELTH/MOT SE9 146 B5
Farnan Av WALTH E17 51 J5
Farnan Rd STRHM/NOR SW16 179 K1
Farnborough Av
SAND/SEL CR2 213 G5
WALTH E17 * 51 G6
Farnborough Cl WBLY HA9 62 D6
Farnborough Common
ORP BR6 216 A2
Farnborough Crs HAYES BR2 199 J5
SAND/SEL CR2 213 G6
Farnborough Hl ORP BR6 216 E3
Farnborough Wy ORP BR6 216 B3
PECK SE15 * 143 F1
Farncombe St
BERM/RHTH SE16 123 H2
Farndale Av PLMGR N13 35 H5
Farndale Crs GFD/PVL UB6 96 C2
Farnell Ms ECT SW5 120 A5
Farnell Pl ACT W3 98 D6
Farnell Rd ISLW TW7 135 J4
Farnham Cl TRDG/WHET N20 33 G2
Farnham Gdns RYNPK SW20 176 E5
Farnham Pl STHWK SE1 18 B1
Farnham Rd GDMY/SEVK IG3 73 F4
WELL DA16 148 D3
Farnham Royal LBTH SE11 122 A5
Farningham Rd TOTM N17 50 C3
Farnley Rd CHING E4 38 C2
SNWD SE25 196 E1
Farnol Rd DART DA1 151 K6
Faro Cl BMLY BR1 185 F5
Faroe Rd WKENS W14 119 G3
Farorna Wk ENC/FH EN2 23 G2
Farquhar Rd NRWD SE19 181 G1
WIM/MER SW19 159 K5
Farquharson Rd CROY/NA CR0 196 D4
Farrance Rd CHDH RM6 74 A3
Farrance St POP/IOD E14 105 J5
Farrant Av WDGN N22 49 G5
Farrant Cl ORP BR6 217 G5
Farr Av BARK IG11 109 G1
Farren Rd FSTH SE23 164 B4
Farrer Ms CEND/HSY/T N8 66 C1
Farrer Rd CEND/HSY/T N8 66 C1
KTN/HRWW/WS HA3 62 A2
Farrier Cl BMLY BR1 184 C6
Farrier Pl SUT SM1 209 F1
Farrier Rd NTHLT UB5 96 A1
Farrier St CAMTN NW1 84 B5
Farriers Wy BORE WD6 31 F1
Farrier Wk WBPTN SW10 120 B6
Farringdon La CLKNW EC1R 5 K7
Farringdon Rd CLKNW EC1R 5 J6
HCIRC EC1N 12 A2
Farringdon St
FLST/FETLN EC4A 12 A3
Farrington Av STMC/STPC BR5 186 C6
Farrington Pl CHST BR7 185 J3
Farrins Rents
BERM/RHTH SE16 124 B1
Farrow La NWCR SE14 143 K1
Farrow Pl BERM/RHTH SE16 124 B3
Farr Rd ENC/FH EN2 23 K2
Farthingale Wk SRTFD E15 88 B5
Farthing Aly STHWK SE1 * 123 H2
Farthing Flds WAP E1W 123 J1
Farthings Cl CHING E4 38 C5
PIN HA5 59 F3
The Farthings KUTN/CMB KT2 175 H4
Farthing St HAYES BR2 215 K5
Farwell Rd SCUP DA14 168 C6
Farwig La BMLY BR1 183 K4
Fashion St WCHPL E1 13 J2
Fashoda Rd HAYES BR2 200 C1
Fassett Rd HACK E8 86 C4
KUT/HW KT1 191 F1
Fassett Sq HACK E8 86 C4
Fauconberg Rd CHSWK W4 117 K6
Faulkner Cl BCTR RM8 73 K4
Faulkner St NWCR SE14 143 K2
Fauna Cl CHDH RM6 73 J3
STAN HA7 29 K6
Faunce St WALW SE17 122 C6
Favart Rd FUL/PGN SW6 139 K2
Faversham Av CHING E4 38 C3
EN EN1 35 K1
Faversham Rd BECK BR3 182 C5
CAT SE6 164 C3
MRDN SM4 194 A3
Fawcett Cl BTSEA SW11 140 C3
STRHM/NOR SW16 162 B6
Fawcett Est CLPT E5 * 68 C5
Fawcett Rd CROY/NA CR0 211 H1
WLSDN NW10 81 H5
Fawcett St WBPTN SW10 120 B6
Fawcus Cl ESH/CLAY KT10 204 E4
Fawe Park Rd PUT/ROE SW15 139 J5
Fawe St POP/IOD E14 105 K4
Fawkes Av DART DA1 171 J4
Fawley Rd KIL/WHAMP NW6 83 F3
Fawnbrake Av HNHL SE24 142 C6
Fawn Rd CHIG IG7 55 F1
PLSTW E13 107 G1
Fawns Manor Rd
EBED/NFELT TW14 153 G3
Fawood Av WLSDN NW10 81 F5
Faygate Crs BXLYHS DA6 149 H6
Faygate Rd BRXS/STRHM SW2 162 A4
Fayland Av STRHM/NOR SW16 179 H1
Fearnley Crs HPTN TW12 172 E2
Fearon St GNWCH SE10 125 K5
Featherbed La SAND/SEL CR2 213 H5
Feathers Pl GNWCH SE10 125 G6
Featherstone Av FSTH SE23 163 J4
Featherstone Rd MLHL NW7 45 K2
NWDGN UB2 114 D3
Featherstone St STLK EC1Y 6 E6
Featherstone Ter NWDGN UB2 114 D3
Featley Rd BRXN/ST SW9 142 C4
Federal Rd GFD/PVL UB6 97 J1
Federation Rd ABYW SE2 128 D4
Fee Farm Rd ESH/CLAY KT10 205 F5
Feeny Cl WLSDN NW10 81 H2
Felbridge Av STAN HA7 43 G4
Felbridge Cl BELMT SM2 209 F6
STRHM/NOR SW16 162 B6
Felbrigge Rd GDMY/SEVK IG3 73 F6
Felday Rd LEW SE13 164 E1
Felden Cl PIN HA5 41 J3
Felden St FUL/PGN SW6 139 J2
Feldman Cl STNW/STAM N16 68 C5
Felgate Ms HMSMTH W6 118 E4
Felhampton Rd
ELTH/MOT SE9 167 G5
Felix Av CEND/HSY/T N8 66 E3
Felix Pl BRXS/STRHM SW2 142 B6
Felix Rd WEA W13 97 G6
Felixstowe Rd ABYW SE2 128 D3
ED N9 36 C6
SEVS/STOTM N15 50 B6
WLSDN NW10 99 K2
Felix St BETH E2 * 104 D1
Fellbrigg Rd EDUL SE22 143 G6
Fellbrigg St WCHPL E1 104 D3
Fellbrook RCHPK/HAM TW10 156 C5
Fellmongers Yd CROY/NA CR0 211 J1
Fellowes Cl YEAD UB4 95 H3
Fellowes Rd CAR SM5 209 J1
Fellows Rd HAMP NW3 83 H5
Fell Rd CROY/NA CR0 211 J1
Felltram Wy CHARL SE7 125 K5
Felmersham Cl CLAP SW4 141 K5
Felmingham Rd PGE/AN SE20 181 K5
Felsberg Rd BRXS/STRHM SW2 161 K2
Fels Cl DAGE RM10 92 D1
Fels Farm Av DAGE RM10 92 E1
Felsham Ms PUT/ROE SW15 139 G4
Felsham Rd PUT/ROE SW15 139 F4
Felspar Cl WOOL/PLUM SE18 128 A5
Felstead Av CLAY IG5 54 A4
Felstead Rd CRW RM5 56 E2
HOM E9 87 J4
LOU IG10 39 J2
ORP BR6 202 C6
WAN E11 70 E4
Felstead St HOM E9 87 H4
Felsted Rd CAN/RD E16 107 H5
Feltham Av E/WMO/HCT KT8 189 K1
Felthambrook Wy FELT TW13 154 A6
Feltham Rd ASHF TW15 152 E6
MTCM CR4 178 E5
Felton Cl STMC/STPC BR5 201 G3
Felton Lea SCUP DA14 186 A1
Felton Rd BARK IG11 108 E1
WEA W13 116 D2
Felton St IS N1 7 F1
Fencepiece Rd BARK/HLT IG6 54 C2
Fenchurch Av FENCHST EC3M 13 G4
Fenchurch Buildings
FENCHST EC3M 13 H4
Fenchurch Pl FENCHST EC3M * 13 H5
Fenchurch St FENCHST EC3M 13 G5
Fendall Rd HOR/WEW KT19 206 E3
Fendall St STHWK SE1 19 H5
Fendt Cl CAN/RD E16 106 D5
Fendyke Rd BELV DA17 128 E4
Fenelon Pl WKENS W14 119 J4
Fen Gv BFN/LL DA15 168 A1
Fenham Rd PECK SE15 143 H1
Fenman Ct TOTM N17 50 D4
Fenman Gdns GDMY/SEVK IG3 73 H5
Fenn Cl BMLY BR1 183 K2
Fennel Cl CAN/RD E16 106 C3
CROY/NA CR0 198 A5
Fennells Md EW KT17 207 G6
Fennell St WOOL/PLUM SE18 127 F6
Fenner Cl BERM/RHTH SE16 123 J4
Fenner Sq BTSEA SW11 * 140 C4
Fenning St STHWK SE1 19 G2
Fenn St HOM E9 87 F3
Fenstanton Av
NFNCH/WDSPK N12 47 H2
Fen St CAN/RD E16 106 D6
Fentiman Rd VX/NE SW8 122 A6
Fentiman Wy RYLN/HDSTN HA2 60 B6
Fenton Cl BRXN/ST SW9 * 142 A3
CHST BR7 184 E1
HACK E8 86 B4
Fenton Rd TOTM N17 49 J3
Fenton's Av PLSTW E13 107 F2
Fenton St WCHPL E1 104 D5
Fenwick Gv PECK SE15 143 H4
Fenwick Pl BRXN/ST SW9 141 K4
SAND/SEL CR2 211 H5
Fenwick Rd PECK SE15 143 H4
Ferdinand Pl CAMTN NW1 84 A5
Ferdinand St CAMTN NW1 84 A5
Ferguson Av BRYLDS KT5 191 G2
Ferguson Cl BECK BR3 183 F6
Ferguson Dr ACT W3 99 F5
Ferguson's Cl POP/IOD E14 124 D4
Fergus Rd HBRY N5 85 H3
Ferme Park Rd CEND/HSY/T N8 66 E2
Fermor Rd FSTH SE23 164 B3
Fermoy Rd GFD/PVL UB6 96 B4
MV/WKIL W9 100 D3
Fern Av MTCM CR4 195 J1
Fernbank BKHH IG9 39 F3
Fernbank Av ALP/SUD HA0 79 F2
WOT/HER KT12 188 D4
Fernbank Ms BAL SW12 161 G1
Fernbrook Dr RYLN/HDSTN HA2 60 B4
Fernbrook Rd LEW SE13 165 H1
Ferncliff Rd HACK E8 86 C3
Fern Cl ERITH DA8 150 E2
IS N1 7 G2
Fern Ct NWCR SE14 144 A4
Ferncroft Av HAMP NW3 82 E1
NFNCH/WDSPK N12 47 J2
RSLP HA4 59 G6
Ferndale BMLY BR1 184 B5
Ferndale Av HSLWW TW4 134 D4
WALTH E17 70 B2
Ferndale Cl BXLYHN DA7 149 F2
Ferndale Rd CLAP SW4 141 K5
CRW RM5 56 E5
FSTGT E7 89 F5
SEVS/STOTM N15 68 B3
SNWD SE25 197 J2
WAN E11 70 D6
Ferndale St EHAM E6 108 B6
Ferndale Ter HRW HA1 61 F1
Ferndale Wy ORP BR6 216 D3
Ferndell Av BXLY DA5 170 A5
Fern Dene WEA W13 97 H4
Ferndene Rd HNHL SE24 142 D5
Fernden Wy ROMW/RG RM7 74 D3
Ferndown NTHWD HA6 40 E5
Ferndown Av ORP BR6 201 J5
Ferndown Cl BELMT SM2 209 H4
PIN HA5 41 J3
Ferndown Rd ELTH/MOT SE9 166 C2
OXHEY WD19 27 G6
Ferney Meade Wy ISLW TW7 136 B3
Ferney Rd EBAR EN4 34 A3
Fern Gv EBED/NFELT TW14 154 A2
Fernhall Dr REDBR IG4 71 H2
Fernham Rd THHTH CR7 196 D1
Fernhead Rd MV/WKIL W9 100 D3
Fernhill Ct WALTH E17 52 B5
Fernhill Gdns KUTN/CMB KT2 174 E1
Fernhill St CAN/RD E16 126 E1
Fernholme Rd PECK SE15 144 A6
Fernhurst Gdns EDGW HA8 44 C2
Fernhurst Rd ASHF TW15 153 F6
CROY/NA CR0 197 H4
FUL/PGN SW6 139 H2
Fern La HEST TW5 114 E5
Fernlea Rd BAL SW12 161 G3
MTCM CR4 179 F5
Fernleigh Cl CROY/NA CR0 211 G2
MV/WKIL W9 100 D2
Fernleigh Ct RYLN/HDSTN HA2 42 B5
WBLY HA9 62 A5
Fernleigh Rd WCHMH N21 35 G4
Fernley Cl PIN HA5 58 E1
Fernsbury St FSBYW WC1X 5 J5
Fernshaw Cl WBPTN SW10 * 120 B6
Fernshaw Rd WBPTN SW10 120 B6
Fernside BKHH IG9 39 F3
GLDGN NW11 64 E6
Fernside Av FELT TW13 154 A6
MLHL NW7 31 F5
Fernside Rd BAL SW12 160 E3
Ferns Rd SRTFD E15 88 C4
Fern St BOW E3 105 J3
Fernthorpe Rd
STRHM/NOR SW16 179 H2
Ferntower Rd HBRY N5 85 K3
Fern Wk BERM/RHTH SE16 123 H5
Fernways IL IG1 90 B1
Fernwood Av ALP/SUD HA0 79 J4
STRHM/NOR SW16 161 J6
Fernwood Cl BMLY BR1 184 B5
Fernwood Crs TRDG/WHET N20 33 K5
Ferny Hl EBAR EN4 21 K1
Ferranti Cl WOOL/PLUM SE18 126 C3
Ferraro Cl HEST TW5 115 F6
Ferrers Av WDR/YW UB7 112 A2
WLGTN SM6 210 D2
Ferrers Rd STRHM/NOR SW16 179 J1
Ferrestone Rd CEND/HSY/T N8 67 F1
Ferrey Ms BRXN/ST SW9 142 B3
Ferriby Cl IS N1 85 G5
Ferrier St WAND/EARL SW18 140 A5
Ferring Cl RYLN/HDSTN HA2 60 C5
Ferrings DUL SE21 163 F4
Ferris Av CROY/NA CR0 213 H1
Ferris Rd EDUL SE22 143 H5
Ferron Rd CLPT E5 * 86 D1
Ferro Rd RAIN RM13 111 J3
Ferryhills Cl OXHEY WD19 27 G5
Ferry La BARN SW13 118 C6
BTFD TW8 117 F6
RAIN RM13 111 H4
TOTM N17 68 D1
Ferrymead Av GFD/PVL UB6 96 A1
Ferrymead Dr GFD/PVL UB6 96 A2
Ferrymead Gdns GFD/PVL UB6 96 C1
Ferrymoor RCHPK/HAM TW10 156 C5
Ferry Rd BARN SW13 138 D1
E/WMO/HCT KT8 173 F6
TEDD TW11 174 C1
THDIT KT7 190 C3
TWK TW1 156 C3
Ferry Sq BTFD TW8 117 F6
Ferry St POP/IOD E14 125 F5
Festing Rd PUT/ROE SW15 139 G4
Festival Cl BXLY DA5 168 E3
ERITH DA8 150 C1
Festoon Wy CAN/RD E16 107 H6
Fetter La FLST/FETLN EC4A 11 K4
Ffinch St DEPT SE8 144 D1
Fidler Pl BUSH WD23 28 B1
Field Cl BKHH IG9 39 G5
BMLY BR1 184 B5
CHING E4 51 K2
CHSGTN KT9 205 J3
CRICK NW2 63 J6
E/WMO/HCT KT8 189 G2
HSLWW TW4 134 A2
HYS/HAR UB3 133 F1
RSLP HA4 58 A5
Fieldcommon La
WOT/HER KT12 188 D5
Field Cottages EFNCH N2 * 47 K6
FUL/PGN SW6 * 139 J3
Field Ct GINN WC1R 11 H2
Field End RSLP HA4 77 H4
Fieldend TEDD TW11 156 A6
Field End Cl OXHEY WD19 27 J2
Field End Rd PIN HA5 59 F2
RSLP HA4 77 J1
Fieldend Rd
STRHM/NOR SW16 179 H4
Fielders Cl EN EN1 24 A5
RYLN/HDSTN HA2 60 D5
Fieldfare Rd THMD SE28 109 J6
Fieldgate St WCHPL E1 104 C4
Fieldhouse Cl SWFD E18 53 F4
Fieldhouse Rd BAL SW12 161 H3
Fielding Av WHTN TW2 155 H5
Fielding La HAYES BR2 200 B1
Fielding Rd CHSWK W4 118 B3
WKENS W14 119 G3
The Fieldings FSTH SE23 163 K3
Fielding Ter EA W5 * 98 B6
Field La BTFD TW8 136 D1
TEDD TW11 174 B1
Field Md CDALE/KGS NW9 45 G3
Fieldpark Gdns CROY/NA CR0 198 B5
Field Pl NWMAL KT3 192 C3
Field Rd EBED/NFELT TW14 154 A1
FSTGT E7 88 E2
HMSMTH W6 119 H6
OXHEY WD19 27 J1
TOTM N17 49 K6
Fieldsend Rd CHEAM SM3 208 C3
Fields Est HACK E8 * 86 C5
Fieldside Cl ORP BR6 216 C2
Fieldside Cottages
TRDG/WHET N20 * 32 D2
Fieldside Rd BMLY BR1 183 G1
Fields Park Crs CHDH RM6 73 K2
Field St FSBYW WC1X 5 G4
Field Vw FELT TW13 153 G6
Fieldview WAND/EARL SW18 160 C3
Fieldview Cottages
STHGT/OAK N14 * 34 D4
Fieldway BCTR RM8 91 H2
Field Wy CROY/NA CR0 213 K5
GFD/PVL UB6 78 B6
RSLP HA4 58 A5
Fieldway STMC/STPC BR5 201 J3
Field Wy WLSDN NW10 80 E5
Fieldway Crs HBRY N5 85 G3
Fiennes Cl BCTR RM8 73 J5
Fiesta Dr RAIN RM13 110 E3
Fife Rd CAN/RD E16 106 E4
KUT/HW KT1 175 F5
MORT/ESHN SW14 137 K6
WDGN N22 49 H4
Fife Ter IS N1 5 H2
Fifield Pth FSTH SE23 164 A5
Fifth Av HYS/HAR UB3 113 J1
MNPK E12 89 K2
NKENS W10 100 C3
Fifth Cross Rd WHTN TW2 155 J4
Fifth Wy WBLY HA9 80 D2
Figge's Rd MTCM CR4 179 F3
Fig Tree Cl WLSDN NW10 81 G6
Filby Rd CHSGTN KT9 206 B4
Filey Av STNW/STAM N16 68 C5
Filey Cl BELMT SM2 209 G5
Filey Waye RSLP HA4 58 E6
Fillebrook Av EN EN1 24 A3
Fillebrook Rd WAN E11 70 B5
Filmer Chambers
FUL/PGN SW6 * 139 J2
Filmer Rd FUL/PGN SW6 139 J2
Filton Cl CDALE/KGS NW9 45 G5
Finborough Rd TOOT SW17 178 E3
WBPTN SW10 120 A6
Finchale Rd ABYW SE2 128 C3
Fincham Cl HGDN/ICK UB10 76 A1
Finch Av WNWD SE27 162 E6
Finch Cl BAR EN5 20 E6
Finch Dr EBED/NFELT TW14 154 C2
Finch Gdns CHING E4 51 J1
Finchingfield Av WFD IG8 53 G3
Finch La BANK EC3V 13 F4
Finchley Cl DART DA1 171 K1
Finchley La HDN NW4 64 B1
Finchley Pk
NFNCH/WDSPK N12 33 G6
Finchley Pl STJWD NW8 2 A2
Finchley Rd GLDGN NW11 64 D2
HAMP NW3 82 E2
STJWD NW8 2 A1
Finchley Vls
NFNCH/WDSPK N12 * 33 H6
Finchley Wy FNCH N3 46 E2
Finch Ms PECK SE15 * 143 G2
Finden Rd FSTGT E7 89 G3
Findhorn Av YEAD UB4 95 F4
Findhorn St POP/IOD E14 106 A5
Findon Cl RYLN/HDSTN HA2 * 78 B1
WAND/EARL SW18 159 K1
Findon Gdns RAIN RM13 111 J4
Findon Rd ED N9 36 D3
SHB W12 118 D2
Fingal St GNWCH SE10 125 J5
Finglesham Cl STMC/STPC BR5 202 E5
Finland Rd BROCKY SE4 144 B4
Finland St BERM/RHTH SE16 124 B3
Finlays Cl CHSGTN KT9 206 C3
Finlay St FUL/PGN SW6 139 G2
Finney La ISLW TW7 136 B2
Finnis St BETH E2 104 D2
Finnymore Rd DAGW RM9 92 A5
Finsbury Av LVPST EC2M * 13 F2

Finsbury Circ LVPST EC2M ...13 F2
Finsbury Cottages WDGN N22 ...48 E3
Finsbury Est CLKNW EC1R ...5 K5
FSBYE EC1V * ...
Finsbury Market SDTCH EC2A ...7 G7
Finsbury Park Av FSBYPK N4 ...67 J3
Finsbury Park Rd FSBYPK N4 ...85 H1
Finsbury Pavement
  LVPST EC2M ...13 F1
Finsbury Rd SDTCH EC2A ...13 F1
Finsbury St STLK EC1Y ...12 E1
Finsbury Wy BXLY DA5 ...169 G1
Finsen Rd CMBW SE5 ...142 D5
Finstock Rd NKENS W10 ...100 B5
Finucane Dr STMC/STPC BR5 ...202 D4
Finucane Gdns RAIN RM13 ...93 J4
Finucane Ri BUSH WD23 ...28 C4
Fiona Ct ENC/FH EN2 * ...23 H4
Firbank Cl CAN/RD E16 ...107 H4
  ENC/FH EN2 ...23 J5
Firbank Rd CRW RM5 ...56 D1
  PECK SE15 ...143 J3
Fircroft Gdns HRW HA1 ...78 E1
Fircroft Rd CHSGTN KT9 ...206 B2
  TOOT SW17 ...160 E5
Firdene BRYLDS KT5 ...191 K5
Fir Dene ORP BR6 ...215 K1
Fire Bell Aly SURB KT6 ...191 F5
Firebell Ms SURB KT6 ...191 F5
Firecrest Dr HAMP NW3 ...83 F1
Firefly Cl WLGTN SM6 * ...210 E5
Firefly Gdns EHAM E6 ...107 J3
Firethorn Cl EDGW HA8 ...30 E6
Fir Gv NWMAL KT3 ...192 C3
Fir Grove Rd BRXN/ST SW9 * ...142 B3
Firhill Rd CAT SE6 ...164 D5
Firle Pl WAND/EARL SW18 ...160 B2
Firmin Rd DART DA1 ...171 F1
Fir Rd CHEAM SM3 ...193 J5
  FELT TW13 ...172 C1
Firs Av FBAR/BDGN N11 ...48 A2
  MORT/ESHN SW14 ...137 K5
  MUSWH N10 ...48 A6
Firsby Av CROY/NA CR0 ...198 A5
Firsby Rd STNW/STAM N16 ...68 C5
Firs Cl ESH/CLAY KT10 ...204 E4
  FSTH SE23 ...164 A2
  MTCM CR4 ...179 G5
  MUSWH N10 ...48 A6
Firscroft PLMGR N13 ...35 J5
Firs Dr HEST TW5 ...134 A2
Firside Gv BFN/LL DA15 ...168 A3
Firs La PLMGR N13 ...35 J5
Firs Park Av WCHMH N21 ...35 K3
Firs Park Gdns WCHMH N21 ...35 K3
First Av ACT W3 ...118 C1
  BXLYHN DA7 ...148 D1
  CHDH RM6 ...73 J2
  DAGE RM10 ...110 D1
  E/WMO/HCT KT8 ...188 E1
  EN1 ...24 B6
  HDN NW4 ...64 A1
  HOR/WEW KT19 ...207 G6
  HYS/HAR UB3 ...113 J1
  MNPK E12 ...89 J2
  MORT/ESHN SW14 ...138 B3
  NKENS W10 ...100 D3
  PLSTW E13 ...106 E2
  UED N18 ...36 E6
  WALTH E17 ...69 K2
  WBLY HA9 ...61 K6
  WOT/HER KT12 ...188 A3
First Cl E/WMO/HCT KT8 ...189 H1
First Cross Rd WHTN TW2 ...155 K4
First Dr WLSDN NW10 ...80 E5
The Firs BXLY DA5 ...170 A3
  EA W5 ...97 K4
  EBED/NFELT TW14 * ...153 H1
  EDGW HA8 * ...31 F6
  TRDG/WHET N20 ...33 H1
First St CHEL SW3 ...14 D4
Firstway RYNPK SW20 ...177 F5
Firs Wk NTHWD HA6 ...40 B2
  WFD IG8 ...52 D2
Firswood Av HOR/WEW KT19 ...207 G3
Firth Gdns FUL/PGN SW6 ...139 H2
Firtree Av MTCM CR4 ...179 F5
Fir Tree Av HYS/HAR UB3 ...113 H3
Fir Tree Cl EA W5 ...97 K6
  ESH/CLAY KT10 ...204 C3
  HOR/WEW KT19 ...207 H2
  ORP BR6 ...217 G3
  ROM RM1 ...57 F6
  STRHM/NOR SW16 ...161 H6
Fir Tree Gdns CROY/NA CR0 ...213 J2
Fir Tree Gv CAR SM5 ...209 K5
Fir Tree Pl ASHF TW15 * ...152 D6
Fir Tree Rd HSLWW TW4 ...134 C4
Fir Trees Cl BERM/RHTH SE16 ...124 B1
Fir Tree Wk EN1 ...24 A4
Fir Wk CHEAM SM3 ...208 B4
Fisher Cl CROY/NA CR0 ...197 G5
  GFD/PVL UB6 ...96 A2
Fisherdene ESH/CLAY KT10 ...205 G5
Fisherman Cl
  RCHPK/HAM TW10 ...156 D6
Fishermans Dr
  BERM/RHTH SE16 ...124 A2
Fisher Rd KTN/HRWW/WS HA3 ...43 F5
Fishers Cl STRHM/NOR SW16 ...161 J5
Fishers Ct NWCR SE14 ...144 A1
Fisher's La CHSWK W4 ...118 A4
Fisher St CAN/RD E16 ...106 E4
  HHOL WC1V ...11 G2
Fisher's Wy BELV DA17 ...129 K1
Fisherton St STJWD NW8 ...2 A7
Fishguard Wy CAN/RD E16 ...127 H1
Fishponds Rd HAYES BR2 ...215 H3
  TOOT SW17 ...160 D6
Fish Street Hi MON EC3R ...13 F6
Fisons Rd CAN/RD E16 ...125 K1
Fitzalan Rd ESH/CLAY KT10 ...204 E5
  FNCH N3 ...46 C6
Fitzalan St LBTH SE11 ...17 J6

Fitzgeorge Av NWMAL KT3 ...176 A4
  WKENS W14 ...119 H4
Fitzgerald Av
  MORT/ESHN SW14 ...138 B4
Fitzgerald Rd
  MORT/ESHN SW14 ...138 A4
  THDIT KT7 ...190 B3
  WAN E11 ...70 D2
Fitzhardinge St MBLAR W1H ...9 G3
Fitzhugh Gv
  WAND/EARL SW18 ...160 C1
Fitzjames Av CROY/NA CR0 ...197 H6
  WKENS W14 ...119 H4
Fitzjohn Av BAR EN5 ...20 C6
Fitzjohn's Av HAMP NW3 ...83 H3
Fitzmaurice Pl MYFR/PICC W1J * ...9 K7
Fitzneal St SHB W12 ...99 H6
Fitzroy Cl HGT N6 ...65 K5
Fitzroy Crs CHSWK W4 * ...138 A1
Fitzroy Ms FITZ W1T ...4 A7
Fitzroy Pk HGT N6 ...65 K5
Fitzroy Rd CAMTN NW1 ...84 A6
Fitzroy Sq FITZ W1T ...4 A7
Fitzroy St FITZ W1T ...4 A7
Fitzstephen Rd BCTR RM8 ...91 H3
Fitzwilliam Av RCH/KEW TW9 ...137 G3
Fitzwilliam Ms CAN/RD E16 ...106 E6
Fitzwilliam Rd CLAP SW4 ...141 H4
Fitz Wygram Cl HPTN TW12 ...173 H1
Five Acre CDALE/KGS NW9 ...45 H5
Fiveacre Cl CROY/NA CR0 ...196 B3
Five Elms Rd DAGW RM9 ...92 B2
  HAYES BR2 ...215 G1
Five Fields Cl OXHEY WD19 ...27 K5
Five Oaks La CHIG IG7 ...55 J1
Fiveways Cnr ELTH/MOT SE9 ...167 G4
Five Ways Jct HDN NW4 ...45 J4
Fiveways Rd BRXN/ST SW9 ...142 B3
Fladbury Rd SEVS/STOTM N15 ...67 K3
Fladgate Rd WAN E11 ...70 C3
Flag La CROY/NA CR0 ...198 A5
Flag Wk PIN HA5 ...58 E2
Flambard Rd HRW HA1 ...61 G3
Flamborough Rd RSLP HA4 ...76 E1
Flamborough St POP/IOD E14 ...105 G5
Flamborough Wk
  POP/IOD E14 * ...105 G5
Flamingo Wk HCH RM12 ...93 J5
Flamstead Gdns DAGW RM9 ...91 J5
Flamstead Rd DAGW RM9 ...91 J5
Flamsteed Rd CHARL SE7 ...126 D5
Flanchford Rd SHB W12 ...118 C3
Flanders Crs TOOT SW17 ...178 E3
Flanders Rd CHSWK W4 ...118 B4
  EHAM E6 ...107 K1
Flanders Wy HOM E9 ...87 F4
Flandrian Cl PEND EN3 ...25 J1
Flank St WCHPL E1 ...104 C6
Flask Wk HAMP NW3 ...83 H2
Flather Cl STRHM/NOR SW16 ...179 H2
Flavell Ms GNWCH SE10 ...125 H5
Flaxen Cl CHING E4 ...37 K5
Flaxen Rd CHING E4 ...37 K5
Flaxley Rd MRDN SM4 ...194 A3
Flaxman Rd CMBW SE5 ...142 C3
Flaxman Ter STPAN WC1H ...4 D5
Flaxton Rd WOOL/PLUM SE18 ...147 J2
Flecker Cl STAN HA7 ...43 F1
Fleece Dr ED N9 ...36 C6
Fleece Rd SURB KT6 ...190 D5
Fleece Wk HOLWY N7 * ...84 E4
Fleeming Cl WALTH E17 ...51 H5
Fleeming Rd WALTH E17 ...51 H5
Fleet Cl E/WMO/HCT KT8 ...188 E2
  RSLP HA4 ...58 A3
Fleet Rd HAMP NW3 ...83 J3
Fleetside E/WMO/HCT KT8 ...188 E3
Fleet Sq FSBW WC1X ...5 J5
Fleet St EMB EC4Y ...11 J4
Fleet Street Hi WCHPL E1 * ...104 C3
Fleet Ter CAT SE6 * ...165 F2
Fleetwood Cl CAN/RD E16 ...107 H4
  CHSGTN KT9 ...205 K5
  CROY/NA CR0 ...212 B1
Fleetwood Rd KUT/HW KT1 ...175 J6
  WLSDN NW10 ...81 J4
Fleetwood Sq KUT/HW KT1 ...175 J6
Fleetwood St STNW/STAM N16 ...68 A6
Fleetwood Wy OXHEY WD19 ...27 G6
Fleming Cl FUL/PGN SW6 ...139 J1
  WBPTN SW10 * ...120 B6
Fleming Ct CROY/NA CR0 ...211 G3
Fleming Dr WCHMH N21 ...22 E6
Fleming Md MTCM CR4 ...178 D3
Fleming Rd STHL UB1 ...96 B5
  WALW SE17 ...122 C6
Fleming Wk CDALE/KGS NW9 * ...45 G5
Fleming Wy ISLW TW7 ...136 A4
  THMD SE28 ...109 H6
Flempton Av BAL SW12 * ...161 G3
Flempton Rd LEY E10 ...69 F6
Fletcher Cl EHAM E6 ...108 B6
Fletcher La LEY E10 ...70 A4
Fletcher Pth DEPT SE8 * ...144 D1
Fletcher Rd CHIG IG7 ...55 F1
  CHSWK W4 ...117 K3
Fletchers Cl HAYES BR2 ...200 A1
Fletcher St WCHPL E1 * ...104 C6
Fletching Rd CHARL SE7 ...126 C6
  CLPT E5 ...86 E1
Fletton Rd FBAR/BDGN N11 ...48 E3
Fleur De Lis St WCHPL E1 ...7 H7
Fleur Gates WIM/MER SW19 ...159 G2
Flexmere Rd TOTM N17 ...49 K4
Flight Ap CDALE/KGS NW9 * ...45 H4
Flimwell Cl BMLY BR1 ...183 H1
Flint Cl ORP BR6 * ...217 F4
  SRTFD E15 ...88 D4
Flint Down Cl
  STMC/STPC BR5 * ...186 B4
Flintmill Crs ELTH/MOT SE9 ...146 D4
Flinton St WALW SE17 ...123 H5

Flint St WALW SE17 ...19 F7
Flitcroft St LSQ/SEVD WC2H ...10 D4
Floathaven Cl THMD SE28 ...128 B1
Flock Mill Pl WAND/EARL SW18 ...160 A3
Flockton St BERM/RHTH SE16 ...123 H2
Flodden Rd CMBW SE5 ...142 D2
Flood La TWK TW1 * ...156 B3
Flood St CHEL SW3 ...120 D5
Flood Wk CHEL SW3 ...120 D6
Flora Cl POP/IOD E14 ...105 K5
  STAN HA7 ...29 F6
Flora Gdns CHDH RM6 ...73 J3
Floral Pl IS N1 ...85 K3
Floral St COVGDN WC2E ...11 F5
Flora St BELV DA17 ...129 G5
Florence Av ENC/FH EN2 ...23 J4
  MRDN SM4 ...194 B2
Florence Cl WOT/HER KT12 ...188 A4
Florence Ct WAN E11 ...71 F1
Florence Dr ENC/FH EN2 ...23 J4
Florence Elson Cl MNPK E12 ...90 A2
Florence Gdns CHSWK W4 ...117 K6
Florence Rd ABYW SE2 ...128 C4
  BECK BR3 ...182 A5
  BMLY BR1 ...183 K4
  CHSWK W4 ...118 A3
  EA W5 ...98 A6
  EHAM E6 ...89 G6
  FELT TW13 ...154 A3
  FSBYPK N4 ...67 G5
  KUTN/CMB KT2 ...175 G3
  NWCR SE14 ...144 C2
  NWDGN UB2 ...114 C4
  PLSTW E13 ...106 E1
  SAND/SEL CR2 ...211 K6
  WIM/MER SW19 ...178 A2
  WOT/HER KT12 ...188 A4
Florence Ter NWCR SE14 ...144 C2
Florence Vis HGT N6 * ...66 B4
Florfield Rd HACK E8 ...86 D4
Florey Sq WCHMH N21 ...23 F6
Florian Av SUT SM1 ...209 H2
Florian Rd PUT/ROE SW15 ...139 H5
Florida Cl BUSH WD23 ...28 D4
Florida Rd THHTH CR7 ...180 C4
Florida St BETH E2 ...104 D2
Florin Ct ABYW SE2 * ...128 B4
Floris Pl CLAP SW4 * ...141 H3
Floriston Av HGDN/ICK UB10 ...76 A5
Floriston Cl STAN HA7 ...43 H4
Floriston Gdns STAN HA7 ...43 H4
Floss St PUT/ROE SW15 ...139 F3
Flower & Dean Wk WCHPL E1 ...13 K2
Flower La MLHL NW7 ...45 H1
Flower Ms GLDGN NW11 ...64 C3
Flowerpot Cl SEVS/STOTM N15 ...68 B3
Flowers Cl CRICK NW2 ...81 J1
Flowers Ms ARCH N19 ...66 C5
Floyd Rd CHARL SE7 ...126 B5
Floyer Cl RCHPK/HAM TW10 ...137 G6
Fludyer St LEW SE13 ...145 H5
Foley Ms ESH/CLAY KT10 ...204 E4
Foley Rd ESH/CLAY KT10 ...204 E5
Foley St GTPST W1W ...10 A2
Folgate St WCHPL E1 ...13 H1
Foliot St SHB W12 ...99 H5
Folkestone Rd EHAM E6 ...108 A1
  UED N18 ...36 D4
  WALTH E17 ...69 K1
Folkingham La
  CDALE/KGS NW9 ...45 F4
Folkington Cnr
  NFNCH/WDSPK N12 ...46 D1
Follett St POP/IOD E14 ...106 A5
Folly La CHING E4 ...51 H3
Folly Wall POP/IOD E14 ...125 F2
Fontaine Rd
  STRHM/NOR SW16 ...180 A2
Fontarabia Rd BTSEA SW11 ...141 F5
Fontayne Av RAIN RM13 ...93 G5
  ROM RM1 ...57 G5
Fontenoy Rd BAL SW12 ...161 G4
Fonteyne Gdns WFD IG8 ...53 H5
Fonthill Ms FSBYPK N4 ...67 F6
Fonthill Rd FSBYPK N4 ...67 F5
Font Hills EFNCH N2 ...47 G5
Fontley Wy PUT/ROE SW15 ...158 D2
Fontwell Cl
  KTN/HRWW/WS HA3 ...42 E3
  NTHLT UB5 ...78 A4
Fontwell Dr HAYES BR2 ...201 F2
Football La HRW HA1 ...61 F5
Footbury Hill Rd ORP BR6 ...202 B4
The Footpath
  PUT/ROE SW15 * ...138 D6
Foots Cray High St SCUP DA14 ...186 D1
Foots Cray La SCUP DA14 ...168 D5
Footscray Rd ELTH/MOT SE9 ...167 F1
Forbes Cl CRICK NW2 ...81 J1
  HCH RM12 ...75 K5
Forbes St WCHPL E1 ...104 C5
Forbes Wy RSLP HA4 ...58 E6
Forburg Rd STNW/STAM N16 ...68 C5
Ford Cl HRW HA1 ...60 D4
  RAIN RM13 ...93 H5
  THHTH CR7 ...196 C3
Fordcroft Rd STMC/STPC BR5 ...202 C2
Forde Av BMLY BR1 ...184 B6
Fordel Rd CAT SE6 ...165 G3
Ford End WFD IG8 ...53 F2
Fordham Cl EBAR EN4 ...21 H4
Fordham St WCHPL E1 ...104 C5
Fordhook Av EA W5 ...98 B6
Fordingley Rd MV/WKIL W9 ...100 D2
Fordington Rd HGT N6 ...47 K6
Ford La RAIN RM13 ...93 H5
Fordmill Rd CAT SE6 ...164 D4
Ford Rd ASHF TW15 ...152 C6
  BOW E3 ...105 G2
  DAGE RM10 ...92 B5
Ford's Gv WCHMH N21 ...35 J3
Fords Park Rd CAN/RD E16 ...106 E5
Ford Sq WCHPL E1 ...104 D4

Ford St BOW E3 ...87 G6
  CAN/RD E16 ...106 D5
Fordwich Cl ORP BR6 ...202 A4
Fordwych Rd CRICK NW2 ...82 C5
Fordyce Rd LEW SE13 ...165 F1
Fordyke Rd BCTR RM8 ...74 A6
Foreland Ct HDN NW4 ...46 C4
Foreland St WOOL/PLUM SE18 ...127 J4
Foremark Cl BARK/HLT IG6 ...55 F2
Foreshore DEPT SE8 ...124 C5
Forest Ap CHING E4 ...52 B3
  WFD IG8 ...52 E3
Forest Ct CHST BR7 ...185 F5
  WAN E11 ...71 G2
  WFD IG8 ...39 F6
Forest Dr HAYES BR2 ...215 K2
  MNPK E12 ...89 H1
  WFD IG8 ...52 B3
Forest Dr East WAN E11 ...70 B4
Forest Dr West WAN E11 ...70 A4
Forest Edge BKHH IG9 ...39 G5
Forester Rd PECK SE15 ...143 J5
Foresters Cl BXLYHN DA7 ...149 J5
Foresters Crs BXLYHN DA7 ...149 J5
Foresters Dr WALTH E17 ...70 E1
  WLGTN SM6 ...210 E5
Forest Gdns TOTM N17 ...50 B5
Forest Ga CDALE/KGS NW9 ...63 G1
Forest Gld CHING E4 ...52 C1
  WAN E11 ...52 D1
Forest Gv HACK E8 ...86 B4
Forest Hill Rd EDUL SE22 ...163 J1
Forestholme Cl FSTH SE23 ...163 K4
  SYD SE26 * ...181 K1
Forest La CHIG IG7 ...54 A1
  FSTGT E7 ...88 E3
Forest Mount Rd WFD IG8 ...52 B3
Fore St BARB EC2Y ...12 E2
  ED N9 ...36 C4
  PIN HA5 ...58 E2
  UED N18 ...50 B1
Forest Ridge BECK BR3 ...182 D6
  HAYES BR2 ...215 J2
Forest Ri WALTH E17 ...70 B1
Forest Rd BARK/HLT IG6 ...54 E4
  CHEAM SM3 ...193 K5
  ED N9 ...36 D4
  ERITH DA8 ...150 D2
  FELT TW13 ...154 B5
  FSTGT E7 ...88 E2
  HACK E8 ...86 B4
  RCH/KEW TW9 ...137 H1
  ROMW/RG RM7 ...56 D6
  TOTM N17 ...68 A1
  WALTH E17 ...51 J6
  WAN E11 ...70 B4
  WFD IG8 ...38 E5
Forest Side BKHH IG9 ...39 G3
  CHING E4 ...38 C2
  FSTGT E7 ...89 F2
  WPK KT4 ...192 C5
Forest St FSTGT E7 ...88 E3
The Forest WAN E11 ...70 C1
Forest Vw CHING E4 ...38 B2
  WAN E11 ...70 D4
Forest View Av LEY E10 ...70 B2
Forest View Rd MNPK E12 ...89 K2
  WALTH E17 ...52 A4
Forest Wy BFN/LL DA15 ...167 J2
  STMC/STPC BR5 ...202 B2
  WFD IG8 ...39 F6
Forfar Rd BTSEA SW11 ...141 F1
  FBAR/BDGN N11 ...48 C1
  WDGN N22 ...49 H4
Forge Cl HAYES BR2 ...199 K5
Forge Cottages EA W5 * ...116 E1
Forge Dr ESH/CLAY KT10 ...205 G5
Forge La CHEAM SM3 ...208 B3
  FELT TW13 ...172 D1
  NTHWD HA6 ...40 C3
  RCHPK/HAM TW10 ...157 F3
Forge Ms CROY/NA CR0 ...213 J3
Forge Pl CAMTN NW1 * ...84 A4
Forman Pl STNW/STAM N16 ...86 B2
Formby Av
  KTN/HRWW/WS HA3 ...43 J6
Formosa St MV/WKIL W9 ...101 F3
Forres Gdns GLDGN NW11 ...64 E3
Forrester Pth SYD SE26 ...163 K6
Forrest Gdns
  STRHM/NOR SW16 ...180 A6
Forris Av HYS/HAR UB3 ...113 J1
Forset St MBLAR W1H ...8 D3
Forstal Cl HAYES BR2 ...183 K6
Forster Cl CHING E4 ...52 B3
Forster Rd BECK BR3 ...182 B6
  BRXS/STRHM SW2 ...161 K2
  TOTM N17 ...68 C3
  WALTH E17 ...69 G3
Forsters Cl CHDH RM6 ...74 B3
Forston St IS N1 ...6 E2
Forsyte Crs NRWD SE19 ...181 F4
Forsyth Gdns WALW SE17 ...122 C6
Forsythia Cl IL IG1 ...90 B3
Forsyth Pl EN EN1 ...24 A5
Forterie Gdns GDMY/SEVK IG3 ...91 G1
Fortescue Av WHTN TW2 ...155 H5
Fortescue Rd EDGW HA8 ...45 F4
  WIM/MER SW19 ...178 C3
Fortess Gv KTTN NW5 ...84 C3
Fortess Rd KTTN NW5 ...84 B2
Fortess Wk KTTN NW5 ...84 B3
Forthbridge Rd BTSEA SW11 ...141 F5
Fortis Cl CAN/RD E16 ...107 G5
Fortis Gn EFNCH N2 ...47 K6
Fortis Green Av EFNCH N2 ...48 A6
Fortis Green Rd MUSWH N10 ...48 A5
Fortismere Av MUSWH N10 ...48 A5
Fortnam Rd ARCH N19 ...66 D6
Fortnums Acre STAN HA7 ...43 F2
Fort Rd NTHLT UB5 ...78 A5
  STHWK SE1 ...19 K7
Fortrose Cl POP/IOD E14 ...106 B5

Fortrose Gdns
  BRXS/STRHM SW2 ...161 K3
Fort St CAN/RD E16 ...126 A1
  WCHPL E1 * ...13 H2
Fortuna Cl HOLWY N7 * ...85 F4
Fortunegate Rd WLSDN NW10 ...81 H5
Fortune Green Rd
  KIL/WHAMP NW6 ...82 E3
Fortune La BORE WD6 ...29 K1
Fortune Pl STHWK SE1 * ...123 G5
Fortunes Ms NTHLT UB5 ...77 J4
Fortune St STLK EC1Y ...6 E7
Fortune Wy WLSDN NW10 ...99 J2
Forty Acre La CAN/RD E16 ...106 E4
Forty Av WBLY HA9 ...80 B1
Forty Cl WBLY HA9 ...80 B1
Forty La WBLY HA9 ...62 E6
Forum Cl BOW E3 ...87 J6
Forum Magnum Sq STHWK SE1 * ...17 G2
Forumside EDGW HA8 ...44 C2
The Forum E/WMO/HCT KT8 ...189 G1
Forum Wy EDGW HA8 ...44 C2
Forval Cl MTCM CR4 ...194 E2
Forward Dr
  KTN/HRWW/WS HA3 ...61 G1
Fosbury Ms BAY/PAD W2 ...101 F6
Foscote Ms MV/WKIL W9 ...100 E4
Foscote Rd HDN NW4 ...63 K3
Foskett Rd FUL/PGN SW6 ...139 J3
Foss Av CROY/NA CR0 ...211 G3
Fossdene Rd CHARL SE7 ...126 A5
Fossdyke Cl YEAD UB4 ...95 J4
Fosse Wy WEA W13 ...97 G4
Fossil Rd LEW SE13 ...144 D4
Fossington Rd BELV DA17 ...128 D4
Foss Rd TOOT SW17 ...160 C6
Fossway BCTR RM8 ...73 J6
Foster La CITYW EC2V ...12 C3
Foster Rd ACT W3 ...99 G6
  CHSWK W4 ...118 A5
  PLSTW E13 ...106 E3
Fosters Cl CHST BR7 ...184 E1
  SWFD E18 ...53 F4
Foster St HDN NW4 ...64 A1
Fothergill Cl PLSTW E13 ...106 E1
Fothergill Dr WCHMH N21 ...22 E6
Fotheringham Rd EN EN1 ...24 B5
Foubert's Pl SOHO/CST W1F ...10 A4
Foulden Rd STNW/STAM N16 ...86 B2
Foulden Ter STNW/STAM N16 ...86 B2
Foulis Ter SKENS SW7 ...14 A7
Foulser Rd TOOT SW17 ...160 E5
Foulsham Rd THHTH CR7 ...180 D6
Foundation Pl
  ELTH/MOT SE9 * ...147 F6
Founder Cl EHAM E6 ...108 B5
Founders Cl NTHLT UB5 ...95 K2
Founders Gdns NRWD SE19 ...180 D3
Foundry Cl BERM/RHTH SE16 ...124 B1
Foundry Ms CAMTN NW1 ...4 B6
Foundry Pl
  WAND/EARL SW18 * ...160 A2
Fountain Cl UX/CGN UB8 ...94 A4
Fountain Dr CAR SM5 ...209 K6
  NRWD SE19 ...163 G6
Fountain Green Sq
  BERM/RHTH SE16 * ...123 H2
Fountain La HAMP NW3 ...83 G2
Fountain Pl BRXN/ST SW9 ...142 B2
Fountain Rd THHTH CR7 ...180 D5
  TOOT SW17 ...178 C1
Fountains Av FELT TW13 ...154 E5
Fountains Cl FELT TW13 ...154 E4
Fountains Crs STHGT/OAK N14 ...34 E2
Fountayne Rd
  SEVS/STOTM N15 ...68 C3
  STNW/STAM N16 ...68 C5
Fount St VX/NE SW8 ...141 J1
Fouracres PEND EN3 ...25 G2
Fourland Wk EDGW HA8 ...44 E2
Fournier St WCHPL E1 ...13 J1
Four Seasons Cl BOW E3 ...105 J1
Four Seasons Crs CHEAM SM3 ...193 J6
Fourth Av HYS/HAR UB3 ...113 J1
  MNPK E12 ...89 K2
  NKENS W10 ...100 C3
  ROMW/RG RM7 ...74 E5
Fourth Cross Rd WHTN TW2 ...155 J4
Fourth Wy WBLY HA9 ...80 E2
The Four Tubs BUSH WD23 ...28 D2
The Four Wents CHING E4 ...38 B4
Fowey Av REDBR IG4 ...71 J2
Fowey Cl WAP E1W ...123 J1
Fowler Cl BTSEA SW11 ...140 C4
  SCUP DA14 ...187 F4
Fowler Rd BARK/HLT IG6 ...55 J1
  FSTGT E7 ...88 E2
  IS N1 ...85 H6
Fowler's Wk EA W5 ...97 K5
Fowndes St BTSEA SW11 ...140 D4
Fox & Knot St FARR EC1M * ...12 B1
Foxberry Rd BROCKY SE4 ...144 B3
Foxborough Gdns
  BROCKY SE4 ...164 D1
Foxbourne Rd TOOT SW17 ...161 F4
Fox Burrow Rd BARK/HLT IG6 ...55 J1
Foxbury Av CHST BR7 ...185 J2
Foxbury Cl BMLY BR1 ...184 A2
  ORP BR6 ...217 G3
Foxbury Dr ORP BR6 ...217 G4
Foxbury Rd BMLY BR1 ...183 K2
Fox Cl BORE WD6 ...29 K1
  CAN/RD E16 ...106 E4
  CRW RM5 ...56 D1
  ORP BR6 ...217 G3
  WCHPL E1 ...104 E3
Foxcombe CROY/NA CR0 ...213 K4
Foxcote PECK SE15 ...123 K6
Foxcroft Rd
  WOOL/PLUM SE18 ...147 G2
Foxdell NTHWD HA6 ...40 B2
Foxearth Spur SAND/SEL CR2 ...212 B6
Foxes Dt BKHH/KID SE3 ...145 K4
  HAYES BR2 ...183 G6
Foxfield Cl NTHWD HA6 ...40 D2
Foxfield Rd ORP BR6 ...201 J6

Foxglove Cl BFN/LL DA15 ...168 B1
ED N9 ...36 E2
STHL UB1 ...95 J6
STWL/WRAY TW19 ...152 A3
Foxglove Gdns WAN E11 ...71 G1
Foxglove La CHSGTN KT9 ...206 C2
Foxglove Pth THMD SE28 ...127 K2
Foxglove Rd ROMW/RG RM7 ...75 G6
Foxglove St ACT W3 ...99 H6
Foxglove Wy WLGTN SM6 ...195 F5
Foxgrove STHGT/OAK N14 ...34 E5
Fox Gv OXHEY WD19 ...27 G2
Foxgrove Av BECK BR3 ...182 E5
Foxgrove Pth OXHEY WD19 ...41 H1
Foxgrove Rd BECK BR3 ...182 E5
Foxham Rd ARCH N19 ...84 D1
Fox Hill HAYS BR2 ...215 G5
NRWD SE19 ...181 G3
Fox Hill Gdns NRWD SE19 ...181 G3
Foxhole Rd ELTH/MOT SE9 ...146 D6
Fox Hollow Cl ...
WOOL/PLUM SE18 ...127 K5
Fox Hollow Dr BXLYHN DA7 ...148 K4
Foxholt Gdns WLSDN NW10 ...80 E6
Foxhome Cl CHST BR7 ...185 F2
Fox House Rd BELV DA17 ...129 J4
Foxlands Crs DAGE RM10 ...92 E5
Foxlands Rd DAGE RM10 ...92 E5
Fox La W5 ...98 A4
HAYES BR2 ...215 F3
PLMGR N13 ...35 H4
Foxlees ALP/SUD HA0 ...79 G2
Foxley Cl HACK E8 ...86 C3
Foxley Rd CMBW SE5 ...142 E6
THHTH CR7 ...196 C1
Foxleys OXHEY WD19 ...27 J5
Foxley Sq BRXN/ST SW9 * ...142 C1
Foxmead Cl ERIC/FH EN2 ...23 F4
Foxmore St BTSEA SW11 ...140 E2
Fox Rd CAN/RD E16 ...106 D4
Foxton Gv MITCH CR4 ...178 C5
Foxwarren ESH/CLAY KT10 ...205 F6
Foxwell St BROCKY SE4 ...144 B4
Foxwood Cl FELT TW13 ...154 A5
MLHL NW7 ...31 G6
Foxwood Green Cl EN EN1 ...36 A1
Foxwood Rd BKHTH/KID SE3 ...145 J5
Foyle Rd BKHTH/KID SE3 ...125 J6
TOTM N17 ...50 D3
Framfield Cl ...
NFNCH/WDSPK N12 ...32 E6
Framfield Rd HBRY N5 ...85 H3
HNWL W7 ...97 F5
MTCM CR4 ...179 F3
Framlingham Crs ...
ELTH/MOT SE9 ...166 D6
Frampton Cl BELMT SM2 ...208 E5
Frampton Park Rd HOM E9 ...86 E4
Frampton Rd HSLWW TW4 ...134 D6
Frampton St STJWD NW8 ...2 B7
Francemary Rd LEW SE13 ...144 D6
Frances Rd CHING E4 ...51 J2
Frances St WOOL/PLUM SE18 ...126 E4
Franche Court Rd TOOT SW17 ...160 B5
Francis Av BXLYHN DA7 ...149 H3
FELT TW13 ...153 K5
IL IG1 ...72 D1
Francis Barber Cl ...
STRHM/NOR SW16 * ...162 A4
Franciscan Rd TOOT SW17 ...161 F6
Francis Chichester Wy ...
BTSEA SW11 ...141 F2
Francis Cl HOR/WEW KT19 ...207 F2
Francis Gv WIM/MER SW19 ...177 J3
Francis Ms LEE/GVPK SE12 * ...165 J1
Francis Rd CROY/NA CRO ...196 C4
DART DA1 ...151 G1
ERITH N2 * ...65 K1
GFD/PVL UB6 ...97 J1
HRW HA1 ...61 G2
HSLWW TW4 ...134 C3
LEY E10 ...70 A6
PIN HA5 ...59 G2
STMC/STPC BR5 ...186 E6
WLGTN SM6 ...210 C4
WEST SW1P ...16 B6
Francis St SRTFD E15 ...88 C3
WEST SW1P ...16 B6
Francis Ter ARCH N19 ...84 C1
Francis Wk IS N1 ...85 F6
Francklyn Gdns EDGW HA8 ...30 C5
Francombe Gdns ROM RM1 ...75 J3
Franconia Rd CLAP SW4 ...141 H6
Frank Burton Cl CHARL SE7 ...126 A5
Frank Dixon Cl DUL SE21 ...163 F2
Frank Dixon Wy DUL SE21 ...163 F3
Frankfurt Rd HNHL SE24 ...142 D6
Frankham St DEPT SE8 ...144 D1
Frankland Cl ...
BERM/RHTH SE16 ...123 J3
WFD IG8 ...53 G1
Frankland Rd CHING E4 ...51 J4
SKENS SW7 ...14 A5
Franklin Cl KUT/HW KT1 ...175 H6
LEW SE13 ...144 E2
TRDG/WHET N20 ...33 G2
WNWD SE27 ...162 C5
Franklin Crs MTCM CR4 ...195 H1
Franklin Rd BXLYHN DA7 ...149 F1
WOT/HER KT12 ...188 A3
Franklins Rw CHEL SW3 ...15 J8
Franklin St BOW E3 ...105 K2
LEY E10 ...68 A3
Franklin Wy CROY/NA CRO ...195 K5
Franklyn Gdns BARK/HLT IG6 ...54 D2
Franklyn Rd WLSDN NW10 ...81 H5
WOT/HER KT12 ...188 A3
Franks Av NWMAL KT3 ...191 K1
Franks Wood Av ...
STMC/STPC BR5 ...201 H2
Franlaw Crs PLMGR N13 ...35 J6
Franmil Rd HCH RM12 ...75 J4
Fransfield Gv SYD SE26 ...163 J5
Franshams BUSH WD23 * ...28 A4
Frant Cl PGE/AN SE20 ...181 K3

Frant Rd THHTH CR7 ...196 C2
Fraser Cl BXLY DA5 ...169 K3
Fraser Rd ED N9 ...36 D5
ERITH DA8 ...129 K5
GFD/PVL UB6 ...79 J2
Fraser St CHSWK W4 ...118 B5
Frating Crs WFD IG8 ...52 E2
Frays Av WDR/YW UB7 ...112 A2
Frays Cl WDR/YW UB7 ...112 A3
Frazer Av RSLP HA4 ...77 G3
Frazer Cl ROM RM1 ...75 H4
Frazier St STHWK SE1 ...17 K3
Frean St BERM/RHTH SE16 ...123 H3
Freda Corbett Cl PECK SE15 ...143 H1
Frederica Rd CHING E4 ...38 B2
Frederica St HOLWY N7 * ...85 F5
Frederick Cl BAY/PAD W2 ...8 D5
SUT SM1 ...208 D3
Frederick Crs BRXN/ST SW9 ...142 C1
PEND EN3 ...24 E3
Frederick Gdns CROY/NA CRO ...196 C3
SUT SM1 ...208 D3
Frederick Pl ...
WOOL/PLUM SE18 ...127 G5
Frederick Rd RAIN RM13 ...111 F1
SUT SM1 ...208 D3
WALW SE17 ...122 C6
Frederick's Pl LOTH EC2R * ...12 E4
NFNCH/WDSPK N12 ...33 G6
Frederick Sq ...
BERM/RHTH SE16 ...105 G6
Frederick's Rw FSBYE EC1V ...6 A4
Frederick St FSBYW WC1X ...5 G5
Frederick Ter HACK E8 * ...86 B5
Frederic Ms KTBR SW1X * ...15 G3
Frederic St WALTH E17 ...69 F3
Fredora Av YEAD UB4 ...94 D3
Freeborne Gdns RAIN RM13 ...93 J4
Freedom Cl WALTH E17 ...69 F1
Freedom Rd TOTN N17 ...49 K6
Freedom St BTSEA SW11 ...140 E3
Freegrove Rd HOLWY N7 ...84 E3
Freeland Pk HDN NW4 ...46 C5
Freeland Rd EA W5 ...98 B6
Freelands Av SAND SE2 CR2 ...213 F6
Freelands Gv BMLY BR1 ...184 A4
Freelands Rd BMLY BR1 ...184 A4
Freeland Wy ERITH DA8 ...150 D2
Freeling St IS N1 ...85 F5
Freeman Cl NTHLT UB5 ...77 J5
Freeman Dr E/WMO/HCT KT8 ...188 E1
Freeman Rd MRDN SM4 ...194 C2
Freemans La HYS/HAR UB3 ...94 B6
Freemantle Av PEND EN3 ...25 F6
Freemantle St WALW SE17 ...123 F5
Freemasons Pl CROY/NA CRO * ...197 F6
CROY/NA CRO ...197 F5
Freemasons Rd CAN/RD E16 ...107 F5
CROY/NA CRO ...197 F5
Freesia Cl ORP BR6 ...217 F3
Freethorpe Cl NRWD SE19 ...181 H4
Freightmaster Est ...
RAIN RM13 * ...130 C2
Freke Rd BTSEA SW11 ...141 F4
Fremantle Rd BARK/HLT IG6 ...54 E2
BELV DA17 ...129 H4
Fremont St HOM E9 ...86 E6
French Pl SDTCH EC2A ...7 H5
French St SUN TW16 ...172 B5
Frendsbury Rd BROCKY SE4 ...144 B5
Frensham Cl STHL UB1 ...95 K3
Frensham Dr CROY/NA CRO ...214 A5
PUT/ROE SW15 ...158 D5
Frensham Rd ELTH/MOT SE9 ...167 J4
CHARL SE7 ...126 C6
Frensham St PECK SE15 ...123 H6
Frere St BTSEA SW11 ...140 D3
Freshfield Av HACK E8 ...86 B5
Freshfield Cl LEW SE13 ...145 G5
Freshfield Dr STHGT/OAK N14 ...34 B2
Freshfields CROY/NA CRO ...198 C4
Freshford St TOOT SW17 ...160 B5
Freshwater Cl TOOT SW17 ...179 F2
Freshwater Rd BCTR RM8 ...73 K5
TOOT SW17 ...179 F2
Freshwell Av CHDH RM6 ...73 J1
Fresh Wharf Rd BARK IG11 ...108 B1
Freshwood Cl BECK BR3 ...182 E4
Freshwood Wy WLGTN SM6 ...210 C6
Freston Gdns EBAR EN4 ...22 A6
Freston Rd NKENS W10 ...100 B6
Freta Rd BXLYHS DA6 ...149 G6
Frewin Rd WAND/EARL SW18 ...160 C3
Friar Ms WNWD SE27 ...162 C5
Friar Rd STMC/STPC BR5 ...202 B2
YEAD UB4 ...95 H3
Friars Av PUT/ROE SW15 ...158 C5
TRDG/WHET N20 ...33 J4
Friars Cl CHING E4 ...38 B4
IL IG1 ...72 D5
NTHLT UB5 ...95 H2
STHWK SE1 * ...12 B7
Friars Gdns ACT W3 ...99 F5
Friars Gate Cl WFD IG8 ...38 E6
Friars La RCH/KEW TW9 ...136 E6
Friars Md POP/IOD E14 ...125 F3
Friars Ms ELTH/MOT SE9 ...147 F6
Friars Pl ACT W3 ...99 F5
Friars Rd EHAM E6 ...89 H6
Friars Stile Rd ...
RCHPK/HAM TW10 ...157 F1
Friars Wk ABYW SE2 ...128 E5
STHGT/OAK N14 ...34 B1
Friars Wy ACT W3 ...99 F5
WD23 ...28 A1
Friars Wd CROY/NA CRO ...213 G6
Friary Cl NFNCH/WDSPK N12 ...47 J1
Friary Est PECK SE15 * ...143 H1
Friary La WFD IG8 ...38 E6
Friary Pk NFNCH/WDSPK N12 ...47 J6
Friary Park Ct ACT W3 * ...98 E5
Friary Rd ACT W3 ...99 F5
NFNCH/WDSPK N12 ...33 H6
PECK SE15 ...143 H1
Friary Wy NFNCH/WDSPK N12 ...33 J6
Friday HI CHING E4 ...38 C3
Friday HI East CHING E4 ...38 D3
Friday HI West CHING E4 ...38 C3

Friday Rd ERITH DA8 ...130 A5
MTCM CR4 ...178 E3
Frideswide PI KTTN NW5 ...84 C3
Friendly PI LEW SE13 ...144 D2
Friendly St DEPT SE8 ...144 D2
Friendly Street Ms DEPT SE8 ...144 D3
Friendship Wy SRTFD E15 * ...88 B6
Friends' Rd CROY/NA CRO ...211 K1
Friend St FSBYE EC1V ...6 A4
Friern Barnet La ...
TRDG/WHET N20 ...33 H5
Friern Mount Dr ...
TRDG/WHET N20 ...33 G2
Friern Pk NFNCH/WDSPK N12 ...47 H1
Friern Rd EDUL SE22 ...163 H1
Friern Watch Av ...
NFNCH/WDSPK N12 ...33 H6
Frimley Av WLGTN SW6 ...210 E3
Frimley Cl CROY/NA CRO ...214 A5
WIM/MER SW19 ...159 H4
Frimley Ct SCUP DA14 ...186 E1
Frimley Crs CROY/NA CRO ...214 A5
Frimley Gdns MITCM CR4 ...178 D6
Frimley Rd CHSGTN KT9 ...205 K3
GDMY/SEVK IG3 ...90 E1
Frimley Wy WCHPL E1 * ...105 F3
Frinstead Gv STMC/STPC BR5 ...202 E1
Frinsted Rd ERITH DA8 ...150 A1
Frinton Cl OXHEY WD19 ...27 F4
Frinton Dr WFD IG8 ...52 B3
Frinton Ms GNTH/NBYPK IG2 ...72 A3
Frinton Rd CEND/HSY/T N8 ...67 F4
EHAM E6 ...107 H2
SCUP DA14 ...169 F4
SEVS/STOTM N15 ...68 A3
TOOT SW17 ...179 F2
Friston St FUL/PGN SW6 ...140 A3
Friswell PI BXLYHN DA7 ...149 H5
Fritham Cl NWMAL KT3 ...192 B3
Frith Ct MLHL NW7 ...46 C3
Frith La MLHL NW7 ...46 C3
Frith Manor Farm Cotts ...
MLHL NW7 * ...46 A3
Frith Rd CROY/NA CRO ...196 D6
WAN E11 ...88 A1
Frith St SOHO/SHAV W1D ...10 C4
Frithville Gdns SHB W12 ...119 F1
Frithwood Av NTHWD HA6 ...40 D2
Frizlands La DAGE RM10 ...92 D1
Frobisher Cl BUSH WD23 ...28 A1
PIN HA5 ...59 H4
Frobisher Crs BARB EC2Y * ...12 D1
STWL/WRAY TW19 ...152 B2
Frobisher Gdns LEY E10 * ...69 K3
Frobisher Ms ENC/FH EN2 ...23 K4
Frobisher Rd CEND/HSY/T N8 ...67 G1
EHAM E6 ...108 A5
ERITH DA8 ...150 D1
Frogley Rd EDUL SE22 ...143 G5
Frogmore WAND/EARL SW18 ...139 K6
Frogmore Av YEAD UB4 ...94 C3
Frogmore Cl CHEAM SM3 ...208 B1
Frogmore Est HBRY N5 * ...85 J2
Frogmore Gdns CHEAM SM3 ...208 C2
YEAD UB4 ...94 D3
Frognal HAMP NW3 ...83 G3
Frognal Av HRW HA1 ...61 F1
SCUP DA14 ...186 D2
Frognal Cl HAMP NW3 ...83 G3
Frognal Gdns HAMP NW3 ...83 G2
Frognal La HAMP NW3 ...82 E3
Frognal Man HAMP NW3 * ...83 G2
Frognal Pde HAMP NW3 * ...83 G3
Frognal PI SCUP DA14 ...186 C2
Frognal Ri HAMP NW3 ...83 G1
Frognal Wy HAMP NW3 ...83 G2
Froissart Rd ELTH/MOT SE9 ...146 D6
Frome Rd SEVS/STOTM N15 ...68 A3
Frome St IS N1 ...6 C2
Fromondes Rd CHEAM SM3 ...208 B3
Fromows Cnr CHSWK W4 * ...117 K5
Frostic Wk WCHPL E1 ...13 K2
Froude St VX/NE SW8 ...141 G3
Frowyck Crs EN EN1 ...24 A3
Fruen Rd EBED/NFELT TW14 ...153 J2
Fry CI CRW RM5 ...56 C1
Fryday Grove Ms BAL SW12 * ...161 H2
Frye Ct KTN/HRWW/WS HA3 ...62 C3
Fryent Cl CDALE/KGS NW9 ...62 C3
Fryent Crs CDALE/KGS NW9 ...63 G3
Fryent Gv CDALE/KGS NW9 ...63 G3
Fryent Wy CDALE/KGS NW9 ...62 C3
Frying Pan Aly WCHPL E1 ...13 H2
Fry Rd EHAM E6 ...89 H5
WLSDN NW10 ...81 H6
Fryston Av CROY/NA CRO ...197 H6
Fuchsia Cl ROMW/RG RM7 ...75 G6
Fuchsia St ABYW SE2 ...128 C5
Fulbeck Dr CDALE/KGS NW9 ...45 G4
Fulbeck Wy RYLN/HDSTN HA2 ...42 C3
Fulbourne Rd WALTH E17 ...52 A4
Fulbourne St WCHPL E1 ...104 D4
Fulbrook Ms ARCH N19 ...84 C2
Fulbrook Rd ARCH N19 ...84 C2
Fulford Gv OXHEY WD19 ...27 F4
Fulford Rd HOR/WEW KT19 ...207 F5
Fulford St BERM/RHTH SE16 ...123 J2
Fulham Broadway ...
FUL/PGN SW6 ...139 K1
Fulham Cl HGDN/ICK UB10 ...94 A3
Fulham High St FUL/PGN SW6 ...139 H3
Fulham Palace Rd ...
FUL/PGN SW6 ...139 J3
Fulham Park Gdns ...
FUL/PGN SW6 ...139 J3
Fulham Park Rd FUL/PGN SW6 ...139 J3
Fulbourne Rd WALTH E17 ...69 H1

Fuller Rd BCTR RM8 ...91 J1
Fullers Av SURB KT6 ...191 G6
SWFD E18 ...52 E5
Fullers Cl CRW RM5 ...56 C5
Fuller's Rd SWFD E18 ...52 D4
Fuller St HDN NW4 ...64 A1
Fullers Wy North SURB KT6 ...206 B1
Fullers Wy South CHSGTN KT9 ...206 A3
Fuller's Wd CROY/NA CRO ...213 J3
Fullerton Rd CAR SM5 ...209 J6
CROY/NA CRO ...197 G4
WAND/EARL SW18 ...140 B6
Fuller Wy HYS/HAR UB3 ...113 J5
Fullwell Av CLAY IG5 ...54 A4
Fullwood PI GINN WC1R ...11 J2
Fullwood's Ms IS N1 ...7 F5
Fulmar Ct BRYLDS KT5 ...191 G5
Fulmar Rd HCH RM12 ...93 K5
Fulmead St FUL/PGN SW6 ...140 A2
Fulmer Cl HPTN TW12 ...172 D1
Fulmer Rd CAN/RD E16 ...107 H4
Fulmer Wy WEA W13 ...116 C3
Fulready Rd LEY E10 ...70 B2
Fulstone Cl HSLWW TW4 ...134 E5
Fulthorp Rd BKHTH/KID SE3 ...145 J3
Fulton Ms BAY/PAD W2 * ...101 F6
Fulton Rd WBLY HA9 ...80 C1
Fulwell Park Av WHTN TW2 ...155 F4
Fulwell Rd TEDD TW11 ...155 J6
Fulwich Rd DART DA1 ...171 J1
Fulwood Av ALP/SUD HA0 ...80 A6
Fulwood Gdns TWK TW1 ...156 A1
Fulwood Wk WIM/MER SW19 ...159 H3
Furber St HMSMTH W6 ...118 E3
Furham Fld PIN HA5 ...42 A3
Furlong Cl WLGTN SM6 ...195 F4
Furlong Rd HOLWY N7 ...85 G4
Furmage St WAND/EARL SW18 ...160 A2
Furneaux Av WNWD SE27 ...180 C1
Furner Cl DART DA1 ...150 C4
Furness Rd FUL/PGN SW6 ...140 A3
MRDN SM4 ...194 A3
RYLN/HDSTN HA2 ...60 B5
WLSDN NW10 ...99 J1
Furness Wy HCH RM12 ...93 J3
Furnival St FLST/FETLN EC4A ...11 J3
Furrow La HOM E9 ...86 E3
The Furrows WOT/HER KT12 ...188 B6
Fursby Av FNCH N3 ...46 E2
Further Acre CDALE/KGS NW9 ...45 H5
Furtherfield Cl CROY/NA CRO ...196 B3
Further Green Rd CAT SE6 ...165 H3
Furze Cl OXHEY WD19 ...41 G1
Furzedown Dr TOOT SW17 ...179 G1
Furzedown Rd ...
STRHM/NOR SW16 ...161 G6
TOOT SW17 ...179 G1
Furze Farm Cl CHDH RM6 ...56 A6
Furzefield Cl CHST BR7 ...185 G2
Furzefield Rd BKHTH/KID SE3 ...126 A6
Furzeground Wy STKPK UB11 ...113 F2
Furzeham Rd WDR/YW UB7 ...112 B2
Furzehill Sq STMC/STPC BR5 ...202 C1
Furze Rd THHTH CR7 ...180 D6
Furze St BOW E3 * ...105 J4
Fye Foot La BLKFR EC4V ...12 C5
Fyfe Wy BMLY BR1 ...183 K5
Fyfield Cl HAYS BR2 ...199 G1
Fyfield Rd BRXN/ST SW9 ...142 B4
EN EN1 ...24 B4
RAIN RM13 ...93 J6
WALTH E17 ...52 B6
WFD IG8 ...53 G3
Fynes St WEST SW1P ...16 C6

G

Gable Cl DART DA1 ...150 D6
PIN HA5 ...42 A3
Gable Ct SYD SE26 ...163 J6
Gable Ms HAYS BR2 ...200 D6
Gables Cl CMBW SE5 ...143 F2
LEE/GVPK SE12 ...165 K2
The Gables NRWD SE19 * ...181 F4
WBLY HA9 ...80 B1
Gabriel Cl CRW RM5 ...56 E3
FELT TW13 ...154 D6
Gabrielle Cl WBLY HA9 ...80 B1
Gabriel St FSTH SE23 ...164 A2
Gabriel's Whf STHWK SE1 ...11 J7
Gad Cl PLSTW E13 ...107 F2
Gaddesden Rd HOR/WEW KT19 ...206 E4
Gadsbury Cl CDALE/KGS NW9 ...63 H3
Gadwall Cl CAN/RD E16 ...107 F5
Gage Rd CAN/RD E16 ...106 C4
Gage St BMSBY WC1N ...11 F1
Gainford St IS N1 ...85 G6
Gainsborough Av DART DA1 ...151 F6
MNPK E12 ...90 B3
Gainsborough Cl BECK BR3 ...182 D3
ESH/CLAY KT10 ...189 K5
Gainsborough Ct SHB W12 ...118 E2
Gainsborough Gdns EDGW HA8 ...44 B5
GLDGN NW11 ...64 D4
HAMP NW3 ...83 H1
ISLW TW7 ...135 J6
Gainsborough Ms DUL SE21 ...162 D3
SYD SE26 ...163 J5
Gainsborough Rd BCTR RM8 ...91 H5
CHSWK W4 ...118 C4
NFNCH/WDSPK N12 ...47 F1
NWMAL KT3 ...192 A5
RAIN RM13 ...93 J6
RCH/KEW TW9 ...137 G4
SRTFD E15 ...106 C2
WAN E11 ...70 C4
WFD IG8 ...53 J2
YEAD UB4 ...94 A1
Gainsborough Sq BXLYHS DA6 ...148 E4
Gainsborough St HOM E9 ...87 H4

Gainsborough Ter ...
BELMT SM2 * ...208 D5
Gainsford Rd WALTH E17 ...69 H1
Gainsford St STHWK SE1 ...19 J1
Gairloch Rd CMBW SE5 ...143 F3
Gaisford St KTTN NW5 ...84 C4
Gaitskell Rd ELTH/MOT SE9 ...167 H3
Gaitskell Wy STHWK SE1 ...18 C2
Galahad Rd BMLY BR1 ...165 K5
ED N9 ...36 C5
Galata Rd BARN SW13 ...138 D1
Galatea Sq PECK SE15 ...143 J4
Galbraith St POP/IOD E14 ...125 F3
Galdana Av BAR EN5 ...21 G4
Galeborough Av WFD IG8 ...52 B3
Gale Cl HPTN TW12 ...172 D2
MTCM CR4 ...178 C6
Galena Rd HMSMTH W6 ...118 E4
Galen Pl NOXST/BSQ WC1A ...11 F2
Galesbury Rd ...
WAND/EARL SW18 ...160 B1
Gales Gdns BETH E2 ...104 D2
Gale St BOW E3 ...105 J4
DAGW RM9 ...91 K4
Gales Wy WFD IG8 ...53 J3
Galgate Cl WIM/MER SW19 ...159 H3
Galiants Farm Rd EBAR EN4 ...33 K3
Galleon Cl BERM/RHTH SE16 ...124 A2
ERITH DA8 ...130 A4
Galleons Dr BARK IG11 ...109 G2
The Galleries IS N1 * ...6 A2
Gallery Gdns NTHLT UB5 ...95 H1
Gallery Rd DUL SE21 ...162 E3
Galleywall Rd ...
BERM/RHTH SE16 ...123 J4
Galleywood Crs CRW RM5 ...57 F2
Galliard Rd ED N9 ...36 C2
Gallia Rd HBRY N5 ...85 H3
Gallions Cl BARK IG11 ...109 G2
Gallions Rd CAN/RD E16 ...108 C5
CHARL SE7 ...126 A4
Gallions View Rd THMD SE28 ...127 K2
Gallon Cl CHARL SE7 ...126 B4
The Gallop BELMT SM2 ...209 H6
SAND/SEL CR2 ...212 D5
Galloson Rd ...
WOOL/PLUM SE18 ...127 K4
Galloway Dr DART DA1 ...170 B2
Galloway Pth CROY/NA CRO ...211 K2
Galloway Rd SHB W12 ...118 D1
Gallus Cl WCHMH N21 ...35 F1
Gallus Sq BKHTH/KID SE3 ...146 A4
Galpin's Rd THHTH CR7 ...195 K1
Galsworthy Av CHDH RM6 ...73 H4
POP/IOD E14 ...105 G5
Galsworthy Cl THMD SE28 ...128 C1
Galsworthy Crs ...
BKHTH/KID SE3 ...146 B2
Galsworthy Rd CRICK NW2 ...82 C2
KUTN/CMB KT2 ...175 J4
Galton St NKENS W10 ...100 C2
Galva Cl EBAR EN4 ...22 A5
Galvaston Rd PUT/ROE SW15 ...139 J6
Galway Cl BERM/RHTH SE16 ...123 J5
Galway St FSBYE EC1V ...6 D5
Gambetta St VX/NE SW8 ...141 G3
Gambia St STHWK SE1 ...18 B1
Gambole Rd TOOT SW17 ...160 D6
Games Rd EBAR EN4 ...21 J4
Gamlen Rd PUT/ROE SW15 ...139 G5
Gander Green Crs HPTN TW12 ...173 F4
Gander Green La CHEAM SM3 ...193 H6
SUT SM1 ...208 D2
Gandhi Cl WALTH E17 ...69 J3
Gandolfi St PECK SE15 ...123 F6
Ganton St REGST W1B ...10 A5
Ganton Wk OXHEY WD19 * ...27 J6
Cantshill Crs GNTH/NBYPK IG2 ...72 A2
Gap Rd WIM/MER SW19 ...177 K1
Garage Rd ACT W3 ...98 C5
Garbrand Wk EW KT17 ...207 H6
Garbutt Pl MHST W1U * ...9 G1
Garbutt Rd BXLYHN DA7 ...149 G4
MTCM CR4 ...179 G3
Garden City EDGW HA8 ...44 C2
Garden Cl BAR EN5 ...20 B5
CHING E4 ...51 J1
HPTN TW12 ...172 E1
LEE/GVPK SE12 ...166 B5
NTHLT UB5 ...77 J6
PUT/ROE SW15 ...158 E2
RSLP HA4 ...58 B5
WLGTN SM6 ...210 E3
Garden Ct CHSWK W4 ...117 K3
EMB EC4Y * ...11 K5
Gardeners Rd CROY/NA CRO ...196 C5
Gardener Flats HMSMTH W6 * ...119 G6
EN EN1 ...36 A1
Garden Gv WFD IG8 ...188 B2
Garden La BMLY BR1 ...184 B2
BRXS/STRHM SW2 ...162 A3
Garden Lodge Ct EFNCH N2 * ...47 H4
Garden Pk HACK E8 ...86 B6
RDART DA2 ...171 G5
Garden Rd BMLY BR1 ...184 B1
PGE/AN SE20 ...181 K4
RCH/KEW TW9 ...137 H4
STJWD NW8 ...101 G2
WOT/HER KT12 ...188 A3
Garden Rw STHWK SE1 ...18 A4
The Gardens BECK BR3 ...183 F5
CEND/HSY/T N8 * ...66 E1
CLPT E5 ...68 B4
EBED/NFELT TW14 ...153 G1
EDUL SE22 ...143 H5
ESH/CLAY KT10 ...204 A2
HRW HA1 ...60 C3
PIN HA5 ...59 K3
Garden St WCHPL E1 ...105 F4
Garden Studios BAY/PAD W2 * ...101 G4
Garden Vls ESH/CLAY KT10 * ...205 F5
Garden Wk BECK BR3 ...182 C4
SDTCH EC2A ...7 G6

Garden Wy WLSDN NW10....80 E4
Gardiner Av CRICK NW2 *....82 A3
Gardiner Cl BCTR RM8....91 K2
  PEND EN5....37 F1
  STMC/STPC BR5....186 D5
Gardiner House CHARL SE7 *....146 D1
Gardner Cl WAN E11....71 F3
Gardner Pl EBED/NFELT TW14....154 A1
Gardner Rd PLSTW E13....107 F5
Gardners Cl FBAR/BDGN N11....34 A4
Gardners La BLKFR EC4V....12 C5
Gardnor Rd HAMP NW3....83 H2
Gard St FSBYE EC1V....6 B4
Garendon Gdns MRDN SM4....194 A4
Garendon Rd MRDN SM4....194 A4
Gareth Cl WPK KT4....193 G6
Gareth Dr ED N9....36 C5
Gareth Gv BMLY BR1....165 K6
Garfield Ms BTSEA SW11....141 G4
Garfield Rd BTSEA SW11....141 F4
  CHING E4....38 B3
  PEND EN5....24 E5
  PLSTW E13....106 D3
  WIM/MER SW19....178 B2
Garford St POP/IOD E14....105 J6
Garganey Wk THMD SE28....109 K6
Garibaldi St WOOL/PLUM SE18....127 K4
Garland Dr HSLW TW3....135 H5
Garland Rd STAN HA7....43 K4
  WOOL/PLUM SE18....147 J1
Garlick Hl BLKFR EC4V....12 D5
Garlies Rd FSTH SE23....164 B5
Garlinge Rd CRICK NW2....82 D4
Garman Cl UED N18....49 J1
Garman Rd TOTM N17....50 E5
Garnault Ms CLKNW EC1R....5 K5
Garnault Pl CLKNW EC1R....5 K5
Garnault Rd EN EN1....24 B1
Garner Cl BCTR RM8....73 K5
Garner Rd WALTH E17....52 A4
Garner St BETH E2....104 C1
Garnet Rd THHTH CR7....196 D1
  WLSDN NW10....81 G4
Garnet St WAP E1W....104 E6
Garnett Cl ELTH/MOT SE9....146 E4
Garnett Rd HAMP NW3....83 K3
Garnham St STNW/STAM N16....68 B1
Garnies Cl PECK SE15....143 G1
Garrad's Rd
  STRHM/NOR SW16....161 J3
Garrard Cl BXLYHN DA7....149 H4
  CHST BR7....185 G1
Garratt Cl CROY/NA CRO....210 E2
Garratt La WAND/EARL SW18....140 A6
Garratt Rd EDGW HA8....44 C3
Garratt Ter TOOT SW17....160 D6
Garrett Cl ACT W3....99 F4
Garrett St STLK EC1Y....6 C6
Garrick Av GLDGN NW11....64 D3
Garrick Cl EA W5....98 A3
  RCH/KEW TW9....136 D6
  WAND/EARL SW18....140 B6
Garrick Crs CROY/NA CRO....197 F6
Garrick Dr HDN NW4....46 A5
  THMD SE28....127 J3
Garrick Pk HDN NW4....46 B5
Garrick Rd CDALE/KGS NW9....63 H3
  GFD/PVL UB6....96 B3
  RCH/KEW TW9....137 H3
Garrick St COVGDN WC2E....10 E5
Garrick Wy HDN NW4....46 B3
Garrick Yd CHCR WC2N....10 E5
Garrison La CHSGTN KT9....205 K5
Garrison Rd BOW E3....87 J6
Garry Cl ROM RM1....57 G3
Garry Wy ROM RM1....57 G3
Garsdale Ter WKENS W14 *....119 J5
Garside Cl HPTN TW12....173 G2
  THMD SE28....127 H2
Garsington Ms BROCKY SE4....144 C4
Garter Wy BERM/RHTH SE16....124 A2
Garth Cl KUTN/CMB KT2....175 G1
  MRDN SM4....193 G4
  RSLP HA4....59 H5
Garth Ms EA W5 *....98 A3
Garthorne Rd FSTH SE23....164 A2
Garth Rd CHSWK W4....118 A5
  CRICK NW2....64 D6
  KUTN/CMB KT2....175 G1
  MRDN SM4....193 F4
Garthside KUTN/CMB KT2....175 F1
The Garth HPTN TW12....173 G2
  KTN/HRWW/WS HA3....62 B3
  NFNCH/WDSPK N12 *....47 J2
Garthway KTN/HRWW/WS HA3
Gartmoor Gdns
  WIM/MER SW19....159 J3
Gartmore Rd GDMY/SEVK IG3....73 F5
Garton Pl WAND/EARL SW18....160 B1
Gartons Cl PEND EN3....24 E6
Gartons Wy BTSEA SW11....140 B4
Garvary Rd CAN/RD E16....107 F5
Garway Rd BAY/PAD W2....101 F5
Gascoigne Gdns WFD IG8....52 C3
Gascoigne Pl BETH E2....7 J3
Gascoigne Rd BARK IG11....90 C6
Gascony Av KIL/WHAMP NW6....82 E5
Gascoyne Dr DART DA1....150 C4
Gascoyne Rd HOM E9....87 F5
Gaselee St POP/IOD E14....106 A6
Gaskarth Rd BAL SW12....161 G1
  EDGW HA8....44 E4
Gaskell Rd HGT N6....65 K3
Gaskell St CLAP SW4....141 K3
Gaspar Ms ECT SW5....120 A4
Gassiot Rd TOOT SW17....160 E6
Gassiot Wy SUT SM1....209 H1
Gastein Rd HMSMTH W6....119 G6
Gaston Bell Cl RCH/KEW TW9....137 G4

Gaston Rd MTCM CR4....179 F6
Gataker St BERM/RHTH SE16....123 J3
Gatcombe Ms EA W5....98 B6
Gatcombe Rd ARCH N19....84 D1
Gatcombe Wy EBAR EN4....21 K4
Gate Cottages EDGW HA8 *....30 C4
Gatehill Rd NTHWD HA6....40 E3
Gatehouse Cl KUTN/CMB KT2....175 K3
Gatehouse Sq STHWK SE1 *....12 D7
Gateley Rd BRXN/ST SW9....142 A4
Gate Ms SKENS SW7....14 D3
Gater Dr ENC/FH EN2....23 K2
Gates Ct WALW SE17 *....122 D5
Gates Green Rd WWKM BR4....214 E2
Gateside Rd TOOT SW17....160 E5
Gatestone Rd NRWD SE19....181 F2
Gate St HOL/ALD WC2B....11 G3
Gateway WALW SE17....122 D6
Gateway Ar IS N1 *....6 A2
Gateway Cl NTHWD HA6....40 A2
Gateway Gdns EHAM E6....107 K2
Gateway Ms HACK E8 *....86 B3
The Gateways
  RCH/KEW TW9....136 E5
Gatfield Gv FELT TW13....155 F4
Gathorne Rd WDGN N22....49 G5
Gathorne St BETH E2....105 F1
Gatley Av HOR/WEW KT19....206 D3
Gatliff Cl BGVA SW1W *....121 F5
Gatliff Rd BGVA SW1W....121 G6
Gatling Rd ABYW SE2....128 B5
Gatonby St PECK SE15....143 G2
Gatton Cl BELMT SM2....209 F6
Gatton Rd TOOT SW17....160 D6
Gattons Wy SCUP DA14....169 G6
Gatward Cl WCHMH N21....35 H1
Gatward Gn ED N9....36 A4
Gatwick Rd WAND/EARL SW18....159 J2
Gauden Cl CLAP SW4....141 J4
Gauden Rd CLAP SW4....141 J4
Gauntlet Cl NTHLT UB5....77 J5
Gauntlett Cl ALP/SUD HA0....79 H5
Gauntlett Rd SUT SM1....209 H3
Gaunt St STHWK SE1....18 B4
Gautrey Rd PECK SE15....143 K3
Gavel St WALW SE17 *....19 F7
Gaverick Ms POP/IOD E14....124 D4
Gavestone Crs LEE/GVPK SE12....166 B2
Gavestone Rd LEE/GVPK SE12....166 B2
Gavina Cl MRDN SM4....194 D2
Gawain Wk ED N9....36 C5
Gawber St BETH E2....104 E2
Gawsworth Cl SRTFD E15....88 C3
Gawthorne Av MLHL NW7....46 D2
Gay Cl CRICK NW2....81 K3
Gaydon La CDALE/KGS NW9....45 G4
Gayfere Rd CLAY IG5....53 K6
  EW KT17....207 J5
Gayfere St WEST SW1P....16 E5
Gayford Rd SHB W12....118 C2
Gay Gdns DAGE RM10....92 E2
Gayhurst Rd HACK E8....86 C5
Gaylor Rd NTHLT UB5....77 K3
Gaynesford Rd CAR SM5....209 K5
  FSTH SE23....164 A4
Gaynes Hill Rd WFD IG8....53 J3
Gay Rd SRTFD E15....106 B1
Gaysham Av GNTH/NBYPK IG2....72 A2
Gayton Crs HAMP NW3....83 H2
Gayton Rd HAMP NW3....83 H2
  HRW HA1....61 F2
Gayville Rd BTSEA SW11....160 E1
Gaywood Cl BRXS/STRHM SW2....162 A3
Gaywood Rd WALTH E17....51 J6
Gaza St WALW SE17....122 C5
Geariesville Gdns BARK/HLT IG6....72 B1
Gearing Cl TOOT SW17....161 G6
Geary Rd WLSDN NW10....81 J3
Geary St HOLWY N7....85 F3
Geddes Pl BXLYHS DA6....149 H5
Gedeney Rd TOTM N17....49 J4
Gedling Pl STHWK SE1....19 J4
Geere Rd SRTFD E15....88 D6
Gees Ct MHST W1U....9 H4
Gee St FSBYE EC1V....6 C6
Geffrye Est IS N1 *....7 H3
Geffrye St BETH E2....7 H2
Geldart Rd PECK SE15....143 J1
Geldeston Rd CLPT E5....68 C6
Gellatly Rd NWCR SE14....143 K3
Gelsthorpe Rd CRW RM5....56 D5
General Gordon Pl
  WOOL/PLUM SE18....127 G3
General Wolfe Rd
  GNWCH SE10....145 G2
Genesis Cl STWL/WRAY TW19....152 C3
Genesta Rd WOOL/PLUM SE18....127 G6
Geneva Dr BRXN/ST SW9....142 B5
Geneva Gdns CHDH RM6....74 A2
Geneva Rd KUT/HW KT1....191 F1
  THHTH CR7....196 D2
Genever Cl CHING E4....51 J1
Genista Rd UED N18....50 D1
Genoa Av PUT/ROE SW15....139 F6
Genoa Rd PGE/AN SE20....181 K4
Genotin Rd EN EN1....23 K4
Gentleman's Rw ENC/FH EN2....23 J4
Geoffrey Cl CMBW SE5....142 D3
Geoffrey Gdns EHAM E6....89 J1
Geoffrey Rd BROCKY SE4....144 C4
George Beard Rd DEPT SE8....124 C4
George Crs MUSWH N10....48 A3
George Downing Est
  STNW/STAM N16....68 B6
George Gange Wy
  KTN/HRWW/WS HA3....42 E6
George Groves Rd
  PGE/AN SE20....181 H4
George La HAYES BR2....200 A5
  LEW SE13....165 F1
  SWFD E18....52 E5
George Lowe Ct
  BAY/PAD W2 *....101 F4

George Mathers Rd
  LBTH SE11 *....18 A1
George Ms BRXN/ST SW9....142 B3
  CAMTN NW1 *....4 A5
George Rd CHING E4....51 J2
  KUTN/CMB KT2....175 K3
  NWMAL KT3....192 C2
George Rw BERM/RHTH SE16....123 H3
Georges Md BORE WD6....30 A1
Georges Rd HOLWY N7....85 F3
George St BARK IG11....90 C5
  CAN/RD E16....106 D5
  CROY/NA CRO....196 E6
  HNWL W7....115 K1
  HSLW TW3....134 C3
  MHST W1U....9 F3
  NWDGN UB2....114 D4
  RCH/KEW TW9....136 E6
  ROM RM1....75 H3
George Wy GFD/PVL UB6....96 A1
George Wyver Cl
  WIM/MER SW19....159 H2
George Yd BANK EC3V....13 F4
  MYFR/PKLN W1K....9 H5
Georgiana St CAMTN NW1....84 C6
Georgian Cl HAYES BR2....200 A5
  STAN HA7....43 G3
Georgian Ct WBLY HA9....80 A4
Georgian Wy HRW HA1....60 D6
Georgia Rd NWMAL KT3....191 K1
  THHTH CR7....180 C4
Georgina Gdns BETH E2 *....7 K4
Geraint Rd BMLY BR1....165 K5
Geraldine Rd CHSWK W4....117 H6
  WAND/EARL SW18....140 B6
Geraldine St LBTH SE11....18 A5
Gerald Rd BCTR RM8....74 B6
  BGVA SW1W....15 H6
  CAN/RD E16....106 D3
Gerard Av HSLWW TW4....155 F2
Gerard Gdns RAIN RM13....111 G1
Gerard Rd BARN SW13....138 C2
  HRW HA1....61 G3
Gerards Cl BERM/RHTH SE16....123 K6
Gerda Rd ELTH/MOT SE9....167 G4
Gernview Dr RDART DA2....171 H6
Germander Wy SRTFD E15....106 C2
Gernon Rd BOW E3....105 G1
Geron Wy CRICK NW2....64 A6
Gerrard Gdns PIN HA5....58 E2
Gerrard Pl SOHO/SHAV W1D *....10 D5
Gerrard Rd IS N1....6 B2
Gerrards Cl STHGT/OAK N14....22 C6
Gerrard St SOHO/SHAV W1D....10 D5
Gerridge St STHWK SE1....17 K3
Gertrude Rd BELV DA17....129 H4
Gertrude St WBPTN SW10....120 B6
Gervase Cl WBLY HA9....80 E1
Gervase Rd EDGW HA8....44 E4
Gervase St PECK SE15....143 J1
Ghent St CAT SE6....164 D4
Ghent Wy HACK E8....86 B4
Giant Arches Rd HNHL SE24....162 D2
Giant Tree Hl BUSH WD23....28 D4
Gibbfield Cl CHDH RM6....56 A6
Gibbins Rd SRTFD E15....88 A5
Gibbon Rd ACT W3....99 G6
  KUTN/CMB KT2....175 F4
  PECK SE15....143 K4
Gibbons Ms GLDGN NW11....64 D2
Gibbons Rd WLSDN NW10....81 F5
Gibbs Av NRWD SE19....180 E1
Gibbs Cl NRWD SE19....180 E2
Gibbs Couch OXHEY WD19....27 H5
Gibbs Gn EDGW HA8....30 E6
Gibbs Green Cl WKENS W14....119 J5
Gibbs Rd UED N18....36 E6
Gibbs Sq NRWD SE19....180 E1
Gibraltar Wk BETH E2....7 K5
Gibson Cl CHSGTN KT9....205 J3
  ISLW TW7....135 J3
  WCHMH N21....35 G1
  WCHPL E1....104 E3
Gibson Gdns STNW/STAM N16 *....68 B6
Gibson Rd BCTR RM8....73 J5
  LBTH SE11....17 H7
  SUT SM1....209 F3
Gibson's Hl STRHM/NOR SW16....180 B3
Gibson Sq IS N1....85 G6
Gibson St GNWCH SE10....125 H5
Gideca Cl GPK RM2....57 J6
Gideon Cl BELV DA17....129 J4
Gideon Ms EA W5 *....116 E2
Gideon Rd BTSEA SW11....141 F4
Giesbach Rd ARCH N19....66 C6
Giffard Rd UED N18....50 A2
Giffin St DEPT SE8....144 D1
Gifford Gdns HNWL W7....96 D4
Gifford St IS N1....84 E5
Gift La SRTFD E15....88 C6
Giggs Hill STMC/STPC BR5....186 C5
Giggs Hill Gdns THDIT KT7....190 B5
Giggs Hill Rd THDIT KT7....190 B5
Gilbert Cl WIM/MER SW19 *....178 A4
  WOOL/PLUM SE18....146 E2
Gilbert Gv EDGW HA8....44 E4
Gilbert Rd BELV DA17....129 H3
  BMLY BR1....183 K5
  LBTH SE11....17 K6
  PIN HA5....41 H6
  ROM RM1....75 H1
  WIM/MER SW19....178 B3
Gilbert St HSLW TW3....135 H4
  MYFR/PKLN W1K....9 H4
  SRTFD E15....70 C3
Gilbey Rd TOOT SW17....160 D6
Gilbeys Yd CAMTN NW1....84 A5
Gilbourne Rd
  WOOL/PLUM SE18....128 A6

Gilda Av PEND EN3....25 G6
Gilda Crs STNW/STAM N16....68 C5
Gildea Cl PIN HA5....42 A3
Gildea St GTPST W1W....9 K2
Gilden Crs KTTN NW5....84 A3
Gildersome St
  WOOL/PLUM SE18....127 F6
Gilders Rd CHSGTN KT9....206 B5
Giles Coppice NRWD SE19....163 G6
Gilkes Crs DUL SE21....163 F1
Gilkes Pl DUL SE21....163 F1
Gillam Wy RAIN RM13....93 J4
Gillan Gn BUSH WD23....28 C4
Gillards Ms WALTH E17....69 J1
Gillards Wy WALTH E17....69 J1
Gill Av CAN/RD E16....106 E5
Gill Cl WATW WD18....26 A1
Gillender St BOW E3....106 A3
Gillespie Rd HBRY N5....85 G1
Gillett Av EHAM E6....107 J1
Gillett Pl STNW/STAM N16 *....86 B1
Gillett Rd THHTH CR7....196 E1
Gillett St STNW/STAM N16....86 A3
Gillham Ter TOTM N17....50 C2
Gillian Park Rd CHEAM SM3....193 J5
Gillian St LEW SE13....144 E6
Gillies St KTTN NW5....84 A3
Gilling Ct HAMP NW3....83 J4
Gillingham Ms PIM SW1V....15 K6
Gillingham Rd CRICK NW2....82 C1
Gillingham Rw PIM SW1V....16 A6
Gillingham St PIM SW1V....15 K7
Gillison Wk
  BERM/RHTH SE16....123 H3
Gillman Dr SRTFD E15....88 C6
Gillmans Rd STMC/STPC BR5....202 C5
Gill St POP/IOD E14....105 H5
Gillum Cl EBAR EN4....33 K3
Gilmore Rd LEW SE13....145 G5
Gilpin Av MORT/ESHN SW14....138 A5
Gilpin Cl BAY/PAD W2....8 B1
  MTCM CR4....178 D5
Gilpin Crs UED N18....50 B1
  WHTN TW2....155 G2
Gilpin Rd CLPT E5....87 G2
Gilpin Wy HYS/HAR UB3....133 G1
Gilroy Cl RAIN RM13....93 H4
Gilroy Wy STMC/STPC BR5....202 C4
Gilsland Rd THHTH CR7....196 E1
Gilstead Rd FUL/PGN SW6....140 A3
Gilston Rd WBPTN SW10....120 B5
Gilton Rd CAT SE6....165 H5
Gippswyck Cl PIN HA5....41 H4
Gipsy La BARN SW13....138 C1
  PUT/ROE SW15....138 C6
Gipsy Rd WELL DA16....148 E3
  WNWD SE27....162 E6
Gipsy Road Gdns WNWD SE27....162 D6
Giralda Cl CAN/RD E16....107 H4
Giraud St POP/IOD E14....105 K5
Girdlers Rd HMSMTH W6....119 G4
Girdwood Rd
  WAND/EARL SW18....159 H2
Girling Wy EBED/NFELT TW14....133 K4
Gironde Rd FUL/PGN SW6....139 J1
Girton Av CDALE/KGS NW9....44 C6
Girton Cl NTHLT UB5....78 C4
Girton Gdns CROY/NA CRO....213 J1
Girton Rd NTHLT UB5....78 C4
  SYD SE26....182 A1
Gisborne Cl WLGTN SM6....210 D1
Gisburn Rd CEND/HSY/T N8....67 F1
Gissing Wk IS N1 *....85 G5
Gittens Cl BMLY BR1....165 J6
Glacier Wy ALP/SUD HA0....97 K1
Gladbeck Wy ENC/FH EN2....23 H5
Gladding Rd MNPK E12....89 H2
Glade Cl SURB KT6 *....190 E6
Glade Gdns CROY/NA CRO....198 B4
Glade La NWDGN UB2....115 G2
Gladeside CROY/NA CRO....198 A4
  WCHMH N21....35 F2
Gladesmore Rd
  SEVS/STOTM N15....68 B3
The Glade BELMT SM2....208 C6
  BMLY BR1....184 C5
  CHARL SE7 *....146 B6
  CLAY IG5....53 K5
  CROY/NA CRO....198 A4
  ENC/FH EN2....23 G4
  EW KT17....207 J4
  HACK E8 *....86 B5
  NFNCH/WDSPK N12 *....33 H6
  SHB W12....118 E2
  WCHMH N21....35 F1
  WWKM BR4....214 A2
Gladiator St FSTH SE23....164 B1
Glading Ter STNW/STAM N16....86 B1
Gladioli Cl HPTN TW12....173 F2
Gladsdale Dr PIN HA5....58 E1
Gladsmuir Cl WOT/HER KT12....188 B6
Gladsmuir Rd ARCH N19....66 C5
  BAR EN5....20 C3
Gladstone Av
  EBED/NFELT TW14....153 K1
  MNPK E12....89 J5
  WDGN N22....49 H5
  WHTN TW2....155 J2
Gladstone Ms KIL/WHAMP NW6 *....82 D4
  WDGN N22....49 G5
Gladstone Pde CRICK NW2 *....82 A1
Gladstone Park Gdns
  CRICK NW2....81 K1
Gladstone Pl BAR EN5....20 B5
  E/WMO/HCT KT8 *....189 K2
Gladstone Rd BKHH IG9....39 G3
  CHSWK W4....118 A3
  CROY/NA CRO....196 E4
  DART DA1....171 J1
  KUT/HW KT1....175 H6
  NWDGN UB2....114 D4
  ORP BR6....216 C3
  SURB KT6....190 E6

  WIM/MER SW19....177 K3
Gladstone St STHWK SE1....18 A4
Gladstone Ter VX/NE SW8....141 G2
  WNWD SE27 *....162 D6
Gladstone Wy
  KTN/HRWW/WS HA3....42 E6
Gladwell Rd BMLY BR1....183 K2
  CEND/HSY/T N8....67 F3
Gladwyn Rd PUT/ROE SW15....139 G4
Gladys Rd KIL/WHAMP NW6....82 E5
Glaisher St DEPT SE8....124 D6
Glamis Crs HYS/HAR UB3....113 F5
Glamis Pl WAP E1W....104 E6
Glamis Rd WAP E1W....104 E6
Glamis Wy NTHLT UB5....78 C4
Glamorgan Cl MTCM CR4....179 K6
Glamorgan Rd KUT/HW KT1....174 D5
Glandford Wy CHDH RM6....73 H2
Glanfield Rd BECK BR3....198 C1
Glanleam Rd STAN HA7....29 K6
Glanville Ms STAN HA7....43 F5
Glanville Rd BRXS/STRHM SW2....141 K6
  HAYES BR2....184 A5
Glasbrook Av WHTN TW2....154 E3
Glasbrook Rd ELTH/MOT SE9....166 C2
Glaserton Rd STNW/STAM N16....68 A4
Glasford St TOOT SW17....178 E2
Glasgow Rd PLSTW E13....107 F1
  UED N18....50 D1
Glasgow Ter PIM SW1V....121 H5
Glasse Cl WEA W13....97 G6
Glasshill St STHWK SE1....18 B2
Glasshouse Flds WAP E1W....105 F6
Glasshouse St REGST W1B....10 B6
Glasshouse Wk LBTH SE11....17 F7
Glasshouse Yd FARR EC1M....6 C7
Glasslyn Rd CEND/HSY/T N8....66 D2
Glassmill La HAYES BR2....183 J6
Glass St BETH E2 *....104 D3
Glass Yd WOOL/PLUM SE18....127 F3
Glastonbury Av WFD IG8....53 H3
Glastonbury Ct
  STMC/STPC BR5....202 D5
Glastonbury Pl WCHPL E1 *....104 E5
Glastonbury Rd ED N9....36 C3
  MRDN SM4....193 K4
Glastonbury St
  KIL/WHAMP NW6....82 D3
Glaston Ct EA W5 *....116 E1
Glaucus St BOW E3....105 K4
Glazbury Rd WKENS W14....119 H4
Glazebrook Cl DUL SE21....162 E4
Glazebrook Rd TEDD TW11....174 A3
Glebe Av ENC/FH EN2....23 H4
  HGDN/ICK UB10....76 A2
  KTN/HRWW/WS HA3....44 A6
  MTCM CR4....178 D5
  RSLP HA4....77 F4
  WFD IG8....52 E2
Glebe Cl CHSWK W4....118 B5
  HGDN/ICK UB10....76 A2
Glebe Ct BKHTH/KID SE3 *....145 H4
  EA W5 *....116 E1
  STAN HA7....43 J1
Glebe Crs HDN NW4....46 A1
  KTN/HRWW/WS HA3....44 A6
Glebe Gdns NWMAL KT3....192 B4
Glebe House Dr HAYES BR2....200 A5
Glebelands DART DA1....150 C5
  E/WMO/HCT KT8....189 K2
  ESH/CLAY KT10....205 G6
Glebelands Av GNTH/NBYPK IG2....72 D4
  SWFD E18....52 E5
Glebelands Cl CMBW SE5....143 F4
  NFNCH/WDSPK N12 *....47 H4
Glebelands Rd
  EBED/NFELT TW14....153 K2
Glebe La BAR EN5....31 J1
  KTN/HRWW/WS HA3....62 A1
Glebe Pth MTCM CR4....178 E6
Glebe Pl CHEL SW3....120 D6
Glebe Rd BARN SW13....138 D3
  BELMT SM2....208 C5
  BMLY BR1....183 K4
  CAR SM5....209 K4
  CEND/HSY/T N8....67 F2
  DAGE RM10....92 D4
  FNCH N3....47 G4
  HACK E8....86 B5
  RAIN RM13....111 J2
  STAN HA7....43 J1
  WLSDN NW10....81 H4
Glebe Side TWK TW1....156 A1
Glebe Sq MTCM CR4....178 E6
Glebe St CHSWK W4....118 B5
The Glebe BKHTH/KID SE3....145 H4
  CHST BR7....185 H4
  STRHM/NOR SW16 *....161 J6
  WDR/YW UB7....112 B4
  WPK KT4....192 C6
Glebe Wy ERITH DA8....130 B6
  FELT TW13....155 F5
  WWKM BR4....199 G6
Glebeway WFD IG8....53 G1
Gledhow Gdns ECT SW5....120 B4
Gledstanes Rd WKENS W14....119 H5
Gledwood Av YEAD UB4....94 D4
Gledwood Crs YEAD UB4....94 D4
Gledwood Dr YEAD UB4....94 D4
Gledwood Gdns YEAD UB4....94 E4
Gleed Av BUSH WD23....28 D4
Gleeson Dr ORP BR6....217 F3
Glegg Pl PUT/ROE SW15....139 G5
Glenaffric Av POP/IOD E14....125 G4
Glen Albyn Rd
  WIM/MER SW19....159 G4
Glenalla Rd RSLP HA4....58 D4
Glenalmond Rd
  KTN/HRWW/WS HA3....62 A1
Glenavon Cl ESH/CLAY KT10....205 G4
Glenavon Rd SRTFD E15....88 C5

Glenbarr Cl ELTH/MOT SE9 147 G4
Glenbow Rd BMLY BR1 183 H2
Glenbrook North ENC/FH EN2 23 F5
Glenbrook Rd KIL/WHAMP NW6 82 E3
Glenbrook South ENC/FH EN2 23 F5
Glenbuck Rd SURB KT6 190 E3
Glenburnie Rd TOOT SW17 160 E5
Glencairn Dr EA W5 97 J4
Glencairne Cl CAN/RD E16 107 H4
Glencairn Rd
STRHM/NOR SW16 179 K3
Glencoe Av GNTH/NBYPK IG2 72 E4
Glencoe Rd BUSH WD23 28 A1
DAGE RM10 92 C2
YEAD UB4 95 J4
Glencorse Gn OXHEY WD19 * 27 H6
Glen Crs WFD IG8 53 F2
Glendale Av CHDH RM6 73 J4
EDGW HA8 30 B6
WDGN N22 49 G3
Glendale Cl ELTH/MOT SE9 147 F4
Glendale Dr WIM/MER SW19 177 J1
Glendale Gdns WBLY HA9 61 K5
Glendale Ms BECK BR3 182 E4
Glendale Rd ERITH DA8 129 K4
Glendale Wy THMD SE28 128 D1
Glendall St BRXN/ST SW9 142 A4
Glendarvon St PUT/ROE SW15 139 G4
Glendevon Cl EDGW HA8 30 D5
Glendish Rd TOTM N17 50 C4
Glendor Gdns MLHL NW7 31 F6
Glendower Crs ORP BR6 202 B3
Glendower Gdns
MORT/ESHN SW14 138 A4
Glendower Pl SKENS SW7 14 A6
Glendower Rd CHING E4 38 B3
MORT/ESHN SW14 138 A4
Glendown Rd ABYW SE2 128 B5
Glendun Rd ACT W3 99 G6
Gleneagle Ms
STRHM/NOR SW16 179 J1
Gleneagle Rd
STRHM/NOR SW16 179 J1
Gleneagles STAN HA7 43 H2
Gleneagles Cl
BERM/RHTH SE16 123 J5
ORP BR6 201 J5
OXHEY WD19 * 41 H1
Gleneldon Ms
STRHM/NOR SW16 179 K1
Gleneldon Rd
STRHM/NOR SW16 161 K6
Glenelg Rd BRXS/STRHM SW2 141 K6
Glenesk Rd ELTH/MOT SE9 147 F5
Glenfarg Rd CAT SE6 165 G3
Glenfield Crs RSLP HA4 58 B4
Glenfield Rd BAL SW12 161 H3
WEA W13 116 C2
Glenfinlas Wy CMBW SE5 142 C1
Glenforth St GNWCH SE10 125 J4
Glengall Br POP/IOD E14 124 E3
Glengall Gv POP/IOD E14 124 E3
Glengall Rd BXLYHN DA7 149 F4
EDGW HA8 30 D5
KIL/WHAMP NW6 82 D6
PECK SE15 123 G6
WFD IG8 52 E2
Glengall Ter PECK SE15 123 G6
Glen Gdns CROY/NA CR0 211 G1
Glengarnock Av POP/IOD E14 125 F4
Glengarry Rd EDUL SE22 143 F5
Glenham Dr GNTH/NBYPK IG2 72 B2
Glenhead Cl ELTH/MOT SE9 147 G4
Glenhill Cl FNCH N3 46 E5
Glenhouse Rd ELTH/MOT SE9 147 F6
Glenhurst Av BXLY DA5 169 G3
KTTN NW5 84 A2
RSLP HA4 58 A5
Glenhurst Ri NRWD SE19 180 D3
Glenhurst Rd BTFD TW8 116 D6
NFNCH/WDSPK N12 47 H1
Glenilla Rd HAMP NW3 83 J4
Glenister Park Rd
STRHM/NOR SW16 179 J3
Glenister Rd GNWCH SE10 125 J5
Glenlea Rd ELTH/MOT SE9 147 F6
Glenloch Rd HAMP NW3 83 J4
PEND EN3 24 E3
Glenluce Rd BKHTH/KID SE3 146 A4
Glenluge Rd BKHTH/KID SE3 125 K6
Glenlyon Rd ELTH/MOT SE9 147 F6
Glenmere Av MLHL NW7 45 J3
Glenmill HPTN TW12 172 E1
Glenmore Lawns WEA W13 * 97 G5
Glenmore Pde ALP/SUD HA0 * 80 A6
Glenmore Rd HAMP NW3 83 J4
WELL DA16 148 A2
Glenmore Wy BARK IG11 109 G2
Glennie Rd WNWD SE27 162 B5
Glenny Rd BARK IG11 90 C4
Glenorchy Cl YEAD UB4 95 J4
Glenparke Rd FSTGT E7 89 F5
Glen Ri WFD IG8 53 F2
Glen Rd CHSGTN KT9 206 A1
PLSTW E13 107 G3
WALTH E17 69 H2
Glen Road End WLGTN SM6 210 B6
Glenrosa St FUL/PGN SW6 140 B3
Glenroy St SHB W12 100 A5
Glensdale Rd BROCKY SE4 144 C4
Glenshiel Rd ELTH/MOT SE9 147 F6
Glenside CHIG IG7 54 B2
Glentanner Wy TOOT SW17 160 C5
Glentham Cottages
BARN SW13 * 118 D6
Glentham Gdns BARN SW13 118 E6
Glentham Rd BARN SW13 118 D6
The Glen BELMT SM2 * 209 G4
CROY/NA CR0 213 F1
ENC/FH EN2 23 H5
HAYES BR2 183 H5
NTHWD HA6 40 B3
NWDGN UB2 114 E5
ORP BR6 215 K1
PIN HA5 59 F2
PIN HA5 59 J4
WBLY HA9 79 K2
Glenthorne Av CROY/NA CR0 197 K5
Glenthorne Cl CHEAM SM3 193 K5
Glenthorne Gdns BARK/HLT IG6 54 A6
CHEAM SM3 193 K5
Glenthorne Rd FBAR/BDGN N11 47 K1
HMSMTH W6 118 E4
KUT/HW KT1 191 G1
WALTH E17 69 G2
Glenthorpe Rd MRDN SM4 193 G2
Glenton Cl ROM RM1 57 G3
Glenton Rd LEW SE13 145 H5
Glenton Wy ROM RM1 57 G3
Glentrammon Av ORP BR6 217 F4
Glentrammon Cl ORP BR6 217 F4
Glentrammon Gdns ORP BR6 217 F4
Glentrammon Rd ORP BR6 217 F4
Glentworth St CAMTN NW1 3 F7
Glenure Rd ELTH/MOT SE9 147 F6
Glenview ABYW SE2 128 E6
Glen View Rd BMLY BR1 184 C5
Glenville Av ENC/FH EN2 23 J1
Glenville Gv DEPT SE8 144 C1
Glenville Ms WAND/EARL SW18 160 A2
Glenville Rd KUTN/CMB KT2 175 H5
Glenwood Av CDALE/KGS NW9 63 G5
RAIN RM13 111 J3
Glenwood Cl HRW HA1 61 F2
Glenwood Dr GPK RM2 75 J2
Glenwood Gdns
GNTH/NBYPK IG2 72 A2
Glenwood Gv CDALE/KGS NW9 62 E5
Glenwood Rd CAT SE6 164 D3
EW KT17 207 J4
HSLW TW3 135 J4
MLHL NW7 31 G5
SEVS/STOTM N15 67 H2
Glenwood Rw NRWD SE19 * 181 G4
Glenwood Wy CROY/NA CR0 198 A3
Glenworth Av POP/IOD E14 125 G4
Gliddon Dr CLPT E5 86 D2
Gliddon Rd WKENS W14 119 H4
Glimpsing Gn ERITHM DA18 129 F3
Gload Crs STMC/STPC BR5 202 E6
Globe Pond Rd
BERM/RHTH SE16 124 B1
Globe Rd EMPK RM11 75 J3
SRTFD E15 88 D3
WCHPL E1 104 E2
WFD IG8 53 G2
Globe St STHWK SE1 18 E3
Globe Ter BETH E2 104 E2
Glossop Rd SAND/SEL CR2 211 K6
Gloster Rd NWMAL KT3 192 B1
Gloucester Av BFN/LL DA15 167 K4
CAMTN NW1 84 A5
WELL DA16 148 A6
Gloucester Circ GNWCH SE10 145 F1
Gloucester Cl THDIT KT7 * 190 B5
WLSDN NW10 81 F5
Gloucester Ct MTCM CR4 * 195 K2
RCH/KEW TW9 * 137 H1
Gloucester Crs CAMTN NW1 84 B6
Gloucester Dr FSBYPK N4 67 H6
GLDGN NW11 64 E1
Gloucester Gdns
BAY/PAD W2 * 101 G5
EBAR EN4 22 A5
GLDGN NW11 64 D4
IL IG1 71 J4
SUT SM1 194 A6
Gloucester Ga CAMTN NW1 3 J2
Gloucester Gate Ms CAMTN NW1 3 J2
Gloucester Gv EDGW HA8 45 F4
Gloucester Ms BAY/PAD W2 101 G5
LEY E10 69 J4
Gloucester Ms West
BAY/PAD W2 101 G5
Gloucester Pde BFN/LL DA15 * 148 B6
HYS/HAR UB3 * 113 F3
Gloucester Pl CAMTN NW1 2 E6
MHST W1U 9 F2
Gloucester Place Ms
MBLAR W1H 9 F2
Gloucester Rd ACT W3 117 K2
BAR EN5 21 F6
BELV DA17 129 G5
CROY/NA CR0 196 E4
DART DA1 170 E1
EA W5 116 D2
ENC/FH EN2 23 J1
FELT TW13 154 B3
HPTN TW12 173 G3
HRW HA1 60 B2
HSLWW TW4 134 D5
KUT/HW KT1 175 H5
LEY E10 69 J4
MNPK E12 89 K1
RCH/KEW TW9 137 H1
ROM RM1 75 H3
SKENS SW7 120 B4
TEDD TW11 173 K1
TOTM N17 49 K6
UED N18 50 B1
WALTH E17 51 F6
WAN E11 71 G2
WHTN TW2 155 H3
Gloucester Sq BAY/PAD W2 8 B5
BETH E2 86 C6
Gloucester St PIM SW1V 121 H5
Gloucester Ter BAY/PAD W2 101 G5
STHGT/OAK N14 * 34 D3
Gloucester Wk KENS W8 * 119 K2
Gloucester Wy CLKNW EC1R 5 K5
Glover Cl ABYW SE2 128 D4
Glover Dr UED N18 50 E2
Glover Rd PIN HA5 59 H3
Glycena Rd BTSEA SW11 140 E4
Glyn Av EBAR EN4 21 H5
Glyn Cl EW KT17 207 J6
SNWD SE25 181 F5
Glyn Ct STAN HA7 43 H2
Glyndebourne Pk ORP BR6 216 B1
Glynde Ms CHEL SW3 14 D5
Glynde Rd BXLYHN DA7 148 E4
Glynde St BROCKY SE4 164 C1
Glyndon Rd WOOL/PLUM SE18 127 H4
Glyn Dr SCUP DA14 168 C6
Glynfield Rd WLSDN NW10 81 G5
Glynne Rd WDGN N22 49 G5
Glyn Rd CLPT E5 87 F2
PEND EN3 24 E5
WPK KT4 193 G6
Glyn St LBTH SE11 122 A5
Goat La EN EN1 24 B1
Goat Rd MTCM CR4 195 F4
Goat Whf BTFD TW8 117 F6
Gobions Av CRW RM5 57 F3
Godalming Av WLGTN SM6 210 E3
Godalming Rd POP/IOD E14 105 K4
Godbold Rd SRTFD E15 106 C3
Goddard Pl ARCH N19 84 C1
Goddard Rd BECK BR3 198 B1
Goddards Wy IL IG1 72 D5
Goddington Cha ORP BR6 217 H2
Goddington La ORP BR6 217 G1
Godfrey Av NTHLT UB5 77 J6
WHTN TW2 155 J2
Godfrey Hl WOOL/PLUM SE18 126 D4
Godfrey Rd WOOL/PLUM SE18 126 E4
Godfrey St CHEL SW3 120 D5
SRTFD E15 106 A1
Godfrey Wy HSLWW TW4 154 D2
Goding St LBTH SE11 121 K5
Godley Rd WAND/EARL SW18 160 C3
Godliman St BLKFR EC4V 12 B4
Godman Rd PECK SE15 * 143 J3
Godolphin Cl PLMGR N13 49 H2
Godolphin Pl ACT W3 99 F6
Godolphin Rd SHB W12 118 E2
Godric Crs CROY/NA CR0 214 B6
Godson Rd CROY/NA CR0 211 G1
Godson St IS N1 5 J2
Godstone Rd SUT SM1 209 G2
TWK TW1 156 C1
Godstow Rd ABYW SE2 128 D2
Godwin Cl HOR/WEW KT19 206 E4
IS N1 6 D2
Godwin Rd FSTGT E7 89 F2
HAYES BR2 184 B6
Goffers Rd BKHTH/KID SE3 145 H3
Goidel Cl WLGTN SM6 210 D2
Golborne Gdns NKENS W10 * 100 C3
Golborne Ms NKENS W10 100 C4
Golborne Rd NKENS W10 100 C4
Golda Cl BAR EN5 32 B1
Goldbeaters Gv EDGW HA8 45 G3
Goldcliff Cl MRDN SM4 193 K4
Goldcrest Cl CAN/RD E16 107 H4
THMD SE28 109 J6
Goldcrest Ms EA W5 * 97 K4
Goldcrest Wy BUSH WD23 28 C3
CROY/NA CR0 214 B6
Golden Ct HSLW TW3 135 J3
Golden Crs HYS/HAR UB3 113 J1
Golden Cross Ms NTGHL W11 * 100 D5
Golden Hind Pl DEPT SE8 * 124 C4
Golden Jubilee Br STHWK SE1 11 G7
Golden La STLK EC1Y 6 C6
Golden Lane Est STLK EC1Y 6 C7
Golden Mnr HNWL W7 96 E6
Golden Pde WALTH E17 * 52 A6
Golden Plover Cl CAN/RD E16 106 E5
Golden Sq SOHO/CST W1F 10 B5
Golden Yd HAMP NW3 83 G2
Golders Cl EDGW HA8 44 D1
Golders Gdns GLDGN NW11 64 C4
Golders Green Crs
GLDGN NW11 64 D4
Golders Green Rd GLDGN NW11 64 C3
Golders Hl HAMP NW3 * 65 F6
Goldersiea GLDGN NW11 * 64 E5
Golders Manor Dr GLDGN NW11 64 B3
Golders Park Cl GLDGN NW11 64 E5
Golders Ri HDN NW4 64 B2
Golders Wy GLDGN NW11 64 D4
Goldfinch Cl ORP BR6 217 G3
Goldfinch Rd THMD SE28 127 J3
Goldhawk Ms SHB W12 118 E2
Goldhawk Rd HMSMTH W6 118 C4
Goldhaze Cl WFD IG8 53 H3
Gold Hl EDGW HA8 45 F2
Goldhurst Ter KIL/WHAMP NW6 83 G4
Golding St WCHPL E1 104 C5
Goldington Crs CAMTN NW1 4 C2
Goldington St CAMTN NW1 4 C2
Gold La EDGW HA8 45 F2
Goldman Cl BETH E2 104 C3
Goldney Rd MV/WKIL W9 100 E3
Goldrill Dr FBAR/BDGN N11 34 A4
Goldsboro Rd VX/NE SW8 141 J2
Goldsborough Crs CHING E4 37 K4
Goldsdown Cl PEND EN3 25 G4
Goldsdown Rd PEND EN3 25 F3
Goldsmid St WOOL/PLUM SE18 127 K5
Goldsmith Av ACT W3 99 F6
CDALE/KGS NW9 63 G2
MNPK E12 89 J4
ROMW/RG RM7 74 C4
Goldsmith Cl RYLN/HDSTN HA2 60 A5
Goldsmith La CDALE/KGS NW9 62 E1
Goldsmith Pl
KIL/WHAMP NW6 * 83 F6
Goldsmith Rd ACT W3 118 A1
FBAR/BDGN N11 47 K1
LEY E10 69 K5
PECK SE15 143 H2
WALTH E17 51 F5
Goldsmiths Cl ACT W3 * 118 A1
Goldsmith's Rw BETH E2 86 C6
Goldsmith St CITYW EC2V 12 D3
Goldwell Rd THHTH CR7 196 A1
Goldwing Cl CAN/RD E16 106 E5
Golf Cl STAN HA7 43 J3
THHTH CR7 180 B4
Golf Club Dr KUTN/CMB KT2 176 A3
Golfe Rd IL IG1 90 D1
Golf Rd BMLY BR1 185 F6
EA W5 * 98 B5
Golf Side WHTN TW2 155 J5
Golf Side Cl NWMAL KT3 176 B5
Golfside Cl TRDG/WHET N20 33 J5
Gollogly Ter CHARL SE7 126 B5
Gomer Gdns TEDD TW11 174 B2
Gomer Pl TEDD TW11 174 B2
Gomm Rd BERM/RHTH SE16 123 K3
Gomshall Av WLGTN SM6 210 E3
Gondar Gdns CRICK NW2 82 D3
Gonson St DEPT SE8 124 E6
Gonston Cl WIM/MER SW19 159 H4
Gonville Crs NTHLT UB5 78 B4
Gonville Rd THHTH CR7 196 A2
Gonville St FUL/PGN SW6 139 H4
Goodall Rd WAN E11 88 A1
Gooden Ct HRW HA1 78 E1
Goodenough Rd
WIM/MER SW19 177 J3
Goodey Rd BARK IG11 91 F5
Goodge Pl FITZ W1T 10 B2
Goodge St FITZ W1T 10 B2
Goodhall Cl STAN HA7 43 H2
Goodhall St WLSDN NW10 99 H2
Goodhart Wy WWKM BR4 199 H3
Goodhew Rd CROY/NA CR0 197 H3
Gooding Cl NWMAL KT3 191 K1
Goodinge Cl HOLWY N7 84 E4
Goodinge Rd HOLWY N7 84 E4
Goodman Ct ALP/SUD HA0 * 79 K2
Goodman Crs
BRXS/STRHM SW2 161 K4
Goodman Rd LEY E10 70 A4
Goodmans Ct ALP/SUD HA0 79 K2
Goodman's Yd TWRH EC3N 13 J5
Goodmayes Av GDMY/SEVK IG3 73 G5
Goodmayes La GDMY/SEVK IG3 91 G2
Goodmayes Rd GDMY/SEVK IG3 73 G5
Goodmead Rd ORP BR6 202 C3
Goodrich Rd EDUL SE22 163 G1
Goodson Rd WLSDN NW10 81 G5
Goods Wy CAMTN NW1 4 E2
Goodway Gdns POP/IOD E14 106 B5
Goodwin Cl BERM/RHTH SE16 19 K5
MTCM CR4 178 C6
Goodwin Dr SCUP DA14 168 E4
Goodwin Gdns CROY/NA CR0 211 H4
Goodwin Rd CROY/NA CR0 211 H3
ED N9 36 E3
SHB W12 118 D2
Goodwins Ct CHCR WC2N 10 E5
Goodwin St FSBYPK N4 67 G6
Goodwood Cl MRDN SM4 193 K1
Goodwood Dr NTHLT UB5 78 A4
Goodwood Pde BECK BR3 * 198 B1
Goodwood Rd NWCR SE14 144 B1
Goodwyn Av MLHL NW7 45 G1
Goodwyn's V MUSWH N10 48 A4
Goodyers Gdns HDN NW4 64 B2
Goosander Wy THMD SE28 127 J3
Gooseacre La
KTN/HRWW/WS HA3 61 K2
Goose Green Cl
STMC/STPC BR5 186 B5
Gooseley La EHAM E6 108 A2
Goossens Cl SUT SM1 209 G3
Gophir La CANST EC4R * 12 E5
Gopsall St IS N1 7 F1
Gordon Av CHING E4 52 C2
HCH RM12 75 H6
MORT/ESHN SW14 138 B5
STAN HA7 43 F2
TWK TW1 136 B6
Gordonbrock Rd BROCKY SE4 144 D6
Gordon Cl WALTH E17 69 J3
Gordon Cottages KENS W8 * 119 K2
Gordon Crs CROY/NA CR0 197 F5
HYS/HAR UB3 113 K4
Gordondale Rd
WIM/MER SW19 159 K4
Gordon Gdns EDGW HA8 44 D5
Gordon Gv CMBW SE5 142 C3
Gordon Hl ENC/FH EN2 23 J2
Gordon House Rd KTTN NW5 84 A2
Gordon Pl KENS W8 119 K2
Gordon Rd ASHF TW15 152 B5
BARK IG11 90 E6
BECK BR3 182 C6
BELV DA17 129 K4
BFN/LL DA15 147 K6
BRYLDS KT5 191 G4
CAR SM5 209 K4
CHDH RM6 74 B3
CHING E4 38 C2
CHSWK W4 117 J6
DART DA1 171 H2
EA W5 97 J6
ED N9 36 D4
ENC/FH EN2 23 K2
ESH/CLAY KT10 204 E5
FBAR/BDGN N11 48 D3
FNCH N3 46 D3
HSLW TW3 135 H5
IL IG1 90 D1
KTN/HRWW/WS HA3 42 E6
KUTN/CMB KT2 175 G4
NWDGN UB2 114 D4
PECK SE15 143 J3
RCH/KEW TW9 137 G3
SRTFD E15 88 A2
SWFD E18 53 F4
WAN E11 70 E3
Gordon Sq STPAN WC1H 4 D7
Gordon St PLSTW E13 106 E2
STPAN WC1H 4 C6
Gordon Wy BAR EN5 20 D5
BMLY BR1 183 K4
Gorefield Pl KIL/WHAMP NW6 100 E1
Gore Rd HOM E9 86 E6
RYNPK SW20 177 F5
Goresbrook Rd DAGW RM9 91 J6
Gore St SKENS SW7 120 B3
Gorham Pl NTGHL W11 100 C6
Goring Cl CRW RM5 56 E4
Goring Gdns BCTR RM8 91 J2
Goring Rd DAGE RM10 93 F4
FBAR/BDGN N11 * 48 E2
Goring St HDTCH EC3A 13 H3
Goring Wy GFD/PVL UB6 96 E1
Gorleston Rd SEVS/STOTM N15 67 K2
Gorleston St WKENS W14 119 H4
Gorman Rd WOOL/PLUM SE18 126 E4
Gorringe Park Av MTCM CR4 178 E3
Gorse Cl CAN/RD E16 106 E5
Gorse Ri TOOT SW17 179 F1
Gorse Rd CROY/NA CR0 213 J1
STMC/STPC BR5 203 H6
Gorseway ROMW/RG RM7 75 G6
Gorst Rd BTSEA SW11 160 E1
WLSDN NW10 98 E3
Gorsuch Pl BETH E2 7 J4
Gorsuch St BETH E2 7 J4
Gosberton Rd BAL SW12 160 E3
Gosbury Hl CHSGTN KT9 206 A2
Gosfield Rd BCTR RM8 74 C5
Gosfield St GTPST W1W 9 K1
Gosford Gdns REDBR IG4 71 K2
Gosforth La OXHEY WD19 26 E5
Gosforth Pth OXHEY WD19 26 E5
Goshawk Gdns YEAD UB4 94 C2
Goslett Yd SOHO/SHAV W1D 10 D4
Gosling Cl GFD/PVL UB6 96 A2
Gosling Wy BRXN/ST SW9 142 B2
Gospatrick Rd TOTM N17 49 J4
Gosport Rd WALTH E17 69 H2
Gosport Wy PECK SE15 143 G1
Gossage Rd WOOL/PLUM SE18 127 J5
Gosset St BETH E2 104 C2
Gosshill Rd BMLY BR1 185 F5
Gossington Cl CHST BR7 167 G6
Gosterwood St DEPT SE8 124 B6
Gostling Rd WHTN TW2 155 F3
Goston Gdns THHTH CR7 180 B6
Goswell Pl FSBYE EC1V 6 B5
Goswell Rd FSBYE EC1V 6 B4
Gothic Cl DART DA1 171 G5
Gothic Ct HYS/HAR UB3 113 G6
Gothic Rd WHTN TW2 155 J4
Gottfried Ms KTTN NW5 84 C2
Goudhurst Rd BMLY BR1 183 J1
Gough Rd EN EN1 24 D3
SRTFD E15 88 D2
Gough Sq FLST/FETLN EC4A 11 K3
Gough St FSBYW WC1X 5 H6
Goulding Gdns THHTH CR7 180 D5
Gould Rd EBED/NFELT TW14 153 H2
WHTN TW2 155 K3
Gould Ter HACK E8 86 D3
Goulston St WCHPL E1 13 J3
Goulton Rd CLPT E5 86 E2
Gourley Pl SEVS/STOTM N15 68 A2
Gourley St SEVS/STOTM N15 68 A2
Gourock Rd ELTH/MOT SE9 147 F6
Govan St BETH E2 86 C6
Govier Cl SRTFD E15 88 C5
Gowan Av FUL/PGN SW6 139 H2
Gowan Rd WLSDN NW10 81 K5
Gower Cl CLAP SW4 161 H1
Gower Ms GWRST WC1E 10 D2
Gower Pl GWRST WC1E 4 B6
Gower Rd FSTGT E7 88 E4
ISLW TW7 116 A6
Gower St GWRST WC1E 4 C7
Gower's Wk WCHPL E1 104 C5
Gowland Pl BECK BR3 182 C5
Gowlett Rd PECK SE15 143 H4
Gowlland Cl CROY/NA CR0 197 H4
Gowrie Rd BTSEA SW11 141 F4
Graburn Wy E/WMO/HCT KT8 173 J6
Grace Av BXLYHN DA7 149 G3
Gracechurch St BANK EC3V 13 F5
Grace Cl BARK/HLT IG6 55 F2
EDGW HA8 44 E3
ELTH/MOT SE9 166 C5
Gracedale Rd
STRHM/NOR SW16 179 G1
Gracefield Gdns
STRHM/NOR SW16 161 K5
Grace Jones Cl HACK E8 86 B4
Grace Pl BOW E3 105 K2
Grace Rd CROY/NA CR0 196 D3
Graces Aly WCHPL E1 * 104 C6
Graces Ms CMBW SE5 142 E3
STJWD NW8 * 101 G1
Grace's Rd CMBW SE5 143 F3
Grace St BOW E3 105 K2
The Gradient SYD SE26 163 H6
Graduate Pl STHWK SE1 19 G4
Graeme Rd EN EN1 24 A3
Graemesdyke Av
MORT/ESHN SW14 137 J4
Grafton Cl HSLWW TW4 154 D3
WEA W13 97 G5
WPK KT4 207 G1
Grafton Ct EBED/NFELT TW14 153 G3
Grafton Crs CAMTN NW1 84 B4
Grafton Gdns BCTR RM8 74 A6
FSBYPK N4 67 J3
Grafton Ms FITZ W1T 4 A7
Grafton Park Rd WPK KT4 192 B6
Grafton Pl CAMTN NW1 4 D5
Grafton Rd ACT W3 98 E6
BCTR RM8 74 A6
CROY/NA CR0 196 C5
ENC/FH EN2 23 F4
HRW HA1 60 C2
KTTN NW5 84 A3
NWMAL KT3 192 B1
WPK KT4 207 F1
Grafton Sq CLAP SW4 141 H5
Grafton St CONDST W1S 9 K6
Grafton Ter HAMP NW3 83 K3
Grafton Wy E/WMO/HCT KT8 188 E1
FITZ W1T 10 A1
Grafton Yd KTTN NW5 84 B4
Graham Av MTCM CR4 179 F4
WEA W13 116 C2
Graham Cl CROY/NA CR0 198 D6
Grahame Park Wy MLHL NW7 45 H3
Graham Gdns SURB KT6 191 F5
Graham Rd BXLYHS DA6 149 H5
CHSWK W4 118 A3
HACK E8 86 C4
HDN NW4 63 K3
HPTN TW12 155 F6
KTN/HRWW/WS HA3 42 E6
MTCM CR4 179 F4
PLSTW E13 106 E3
SEVS/STOTM N15 49 H6
WIM/MER SW19 177 J3
Graham St IS N1 6 B3

Graham Ter BFN/LL DA15 * 168 C1
BCVA SW1W 15 H7
Grainger Cl NTHLT UB5 ....78 C3
Grainger Rd ISLW TW7 ....136 A3
WDGN N22 ....49 J4
Gramer Cl WAN E11 ....70 B6
Grampian Cl BELMT SM2 ....209 G5
HYS/HAR UB3 ....133 G1
ORP BR6 ....202 A3
Grampian Gdns CRICK NW2 ....64 C5
Gramsci Wy CAT SE6 ....164 E5
Granada St TOOT SW17 ....178 E1
Granard Av PUT/ROE SW15 ....138 E6
Granard Rd BTSEA SW11 ....160 E2
Granary Cl ED N9 ....36 E2
Granary Rd WCHPL E1 ....104 D3
Granary Sq IS N1 ....85 G4
Granary St CAMTN NW1 ....4 C1
Granby Rd ELTH/MOT SE9 ....146 E3
WOOL/PLUM SE18 ....127 G3
Granby St BETH E2 ....7 K6
Granby Ter CAMTN NW1 ....4 A3
Grand Av BRYLDS KT5 ....191 J3
FARR EC1M 12 B1
MUSWH N10 ....66 A1
WBLY HA9 ....80 C3
Grand Av East WBLY HA9 ....80 D3
Grand Depot Rd
WOOL/PLUM SE18 ....127 G4
Grand Dr NWDGN UB2 ....115 H2
RYNPK SW20 ....177 F6
RYNPK SW20 ....193 G2
Granden Rd
STRHM/NOR SW16 * 179 K5
Grandison Rd BTSEA SW11 ....140 E6
WPK KT4 ....193 F6
Grand Junction Whf IS N1 * 6 C3
Grand Pde FSBYPK N4 * 67 H3
MORT/ESHN SW14 * 137 K5
SURB KT6 * 191 H5
WBLY HA9 * 62 D6
Grand Union Canal Wk
BTFD TW8 ....116 D6
HNWL W7 ....115 K3
HYS/HAR UB3 ....113 K3
MV/WKIL W9 * 100 E4
NWDGN UB2 ....114 A3
NWDGN UB2 ....114 D4
RKW/CH/CXG WD3 ....26 A1
STHL UB1 ....95 K3
WDR/YW UB7 ....112 E2
WLSDN NW10 ....99 G2
Grand Union Cl MV/WKIL W9 ....100 D4
Grand Union Crs HACK E8 * 86 C6
Grand Union Wk CAMTN NW1 * 84 B5
Grand Wk WCHPL E1 * 105 G3
Granfield St BTSEA SW11 * 140 C2
Grange Av EBAR EN4 ....33 J3
KTN/HRWW/WS HA3 ....43 H5
NFNCH/WDSPK N12 ....47 G1
SNWD SE25 ....181 F5
TRDG/WHET N20 ....32 C2
WFD IG8 ....52 E2
WHTN TW2 ....155 K4
Grangecliffe Gdns SNWD SE25 ....181 F5
Grange Cl BFN/LL DA15 ....168 B5
E/WMO/HCT KT8 ....189 G1
HEST TW5 ....114 E6
HYS/HAR UB3 ....94 C4
WFD IG8 ....52 E3
Grange Ct ALP/SUD HA0 * 79 J3
BELMT SM2 * 209 F5
HRW HA1 * 79 F1
NTHLT UB5 ....95 G1
PIN HA5 * 41 J6
WLGTN SM6 * 210 B1
Grangecourt Rd
STNW/STAM N16 ....68 A5
Grange Crs CHIG IG7 ....54 D1
THMD SE28 ....109 J5
Grangedale Cl NTHWD HA6 ....40 C4
Grange Dr CHST BR7 ....184 D2
ORP BR6 ....217 J6
Grange Farm Cl
RYLN/HDSTN HA2 ....60 C6
Grange Gdns HAMP NW3 ....83 F1
PIN HA5 ....59 K1
SNWD SE25 ....181 F5
STHGT/OAK N14 ....34 D3
Grange Gv IS N1 ....85 J4
Grange Hl EDGW HA8 ....44 E1
SNWD SE25 ....181 F5
Grangehill Pl ELTH/MOT SE9 ....146 E4
Grangehill Rd ELTH/MOT SE9 ....146 E5
Grange Houses HBRY N5 * 85 J2
Grange La DUL SE21 ....163 G4
Grange Ms FELT TW13 * 153 G5
Grangemill Rd CAT SE6 ....164 D5
Grangemill Wy CAT SE6 ....164 D4
Grange Pk EA W5 ....117 F1
Grange Park Av WCHMH N21 ....35 J2
Grange Park Pl RYNPK SW20 ....176 E3
Grange Park Rd LEY E10 ....69 K6
THHTH CR7 ....180 E6
Grange Pl KIL/WHAMP NW6 ....82 E5
Grange Rd BARN SW13 ....138 D2
BELMT SM2 ....208 E5
CHSGTN KT9 ....206 A2
CHSWK W4 ....117 J5
E/WMO/HCT KT8 ....189 G1
EA W5 ....116 E1
EDGW HA8 ....45 F2
HARH RM3 ....57 K2
HGT N6 ....66 A3
HRW HA1 ....61 G3
HYS/HAR UB3 ....94 C5
IL IG1 ....90 C2
KUT/HW KT1 ....175 F6
LEY E10 ....69 J5
ORP BR6 ....201 H6
PLSTW E13 ....106 D2
RYLN/HDSTN HA2 ....60 D6
SNWD SE25 ....196 E1
STHL UB1 ....114 D2
STHWK SE1 ....19 H5
TOTM N17 ....50 C2
WALTH E17 ....69 G2
WLSDN NW10 ....81 K4
Granger Wy EMPK RM11 ....75 J3
Grange St IS N1 ....7 F1
The Grange ALP/SUD HA0 ....80 C5
CROY/NA CR0 ....198 C6
NWMAL KT3 * 192 D2
STHWK SE1 ....19 J4
WIM/MER SW19 ....177 G2
WKENS W14 * 119 J4
WOT/HER KT12 ....188 A6
WPK KT4 ....207 F2
Grange V BELMT SM2 ....209 F5
Grangeview Rd
TRDG/WHET N20 ....33 G3
Grange Wk STHWK SE1 ....19 J5
Grange Walk Ms STHWK SE1 ....19 H5
Grange Wy ERITH DA8 ....150 E1
Grangeway KIL/WHAMP NW6 ....82 E5
NFNCH/WDSPK N12 ....33 F6
WFD IG8 ....39 G6
Grangeway Gdns REDBR IG4 ....71 J2
The Grangeway WCHMH N21 ....35 H1
Grangewood BXLY DA5 ....169 G3
Grangewood Cl PIN HA5 ....58 E2
Grangewood La BECK BR3 ....182 C2
Grangewood St EHAM E6 ....89 H6
Grange Yd STHWK SE1 ....19 J5
Granham Gdns ED N9 ....36 B4
Granite St WOOL/PLUM SE18 ....128 A5
Granleigh Rd WAN E11 ....70 C6
Gransden Av HACK E8 ....86 D5
Gransden Rd SHB W12 ....118 C2
Grantbridge St IS N1 ....6 B2
Grantchester KUT/HW KT1 * 175 H5
Grantchester Cl HRW HA1 ....79 F1
Grant Cl STHGT/OAK N14 ....34 C2
TOTM N17 ....50 A5
Grantham Cl EDGW HA8 ....30 A5
Grantham Gdns CHDH RM6 ....74 B3
Grantham Pl MYFR/PKLN W1K 15 J1
Grantham Rd BRXN/ST SW9 ....141 K4
CHSWK W4 ....138 B1
MNPK E12 ....90 A1
Grantley Pl ESH/CLAY KT10 ....204 B3
Grantley Rd HSLWW TW4 ....134 B3
Grantley St WCHPL E1 ....105 F2
Grantock Rd WALTH E17 ....52 B4
Granton Rd GDMY/SEVK IG3 ....73 G5
SCUP DA14 ....186 D2
STRHM/NOR SW16 ....179 H4
Grant Pl CROY/NA CR0 ....197 G5
Grant Rd BTSEA SW11 ....140 D4
CROY/NA CR0 ....197 G5
KTN/HRWW/WS HA3 ....42 E6
Grants Cl MLHL NW7 ....46 A3
Grant St IS N1 ....5 J2
PLSTW E13 ....106 E2
Grant Ter STNW/STAM N16 * 68 C4
Grantully Rd MV/WKIL W9 ....101 F2
Grant Wy ISLW TW7 ....116 B6
Granville Ar BRXN/ST SW9 * 142 B5
Granville Av ED N9 ....36 E5
FELT TW13 ....153 K4
HSLW TW3 ....135 F6
Granville Cl CROY/NA CR0 ....197 F6
Granville Gdns EA W5 ....117 G1
STRHM/NOR SW16 ....180 A4
Granville Gv LEW SE13 ....145 F4
Granville Ms SCUP DA14 ....168 B6
Granville Pk LEW SE13 ....145 F4
Granville Pl FUL/PGN SW6 * 140 A1
MBLAR W1H 9 G4
NFNCH/WDSPK N12 * 47 G3
PIN HA5 ....41 H6
Granville Rd BAR EN5 ....20 A5
CEND/HSY/T N8 ....67 F3
CRICK NW2 ....64 D6
HYS/HAR UB3 ....113 J4
IL IG1 ....72 B5
KIL/WHAMP NW6 ....100 E1
NFNCH/WDSPK N12 ....47 G3
PLMGR N13 ....49 F2
SCUP DA14 ....168 B6
SWFD E18 ....53 F5
WALTH E17 ....69 K3
WAND/EARL SW18 ....159 J2
WDGN N22 ....49 H4
WELL DA16 ....148 D4
WIM/MER SW19 ....177 K3
Granville Sq PECK SE15 * 143 F1
Granville St FSBYW WC1X 5 H5
Grape St LSQ/SEVD WC2H 10 E3
Graphite Sq LBTH SE11 * 122 A5
Grapsome Cl CHSGTN KT9 ....205 J5
Grasdene Rd
WOOL/PLUM SE18 ....148 B1
Grasmere Av ACT W3 ....99 F6
HSLW TW3 ....155 G1
ORP BR6 ....216 B1
PUT/ROE SW15 ....158 A6
RSLP HA4 ....58 A4
WBLY HA9 ....61 K4
WIM/MER SW19 ....177 K6
Grasmere Cl
EBED/NFELT TW14 ....153 J3
Grasmere Ct WDGN N22 ....49 F2
Grasmere Gdns
KTN/HRWW/WS HA3 ....43 G5
ORP BR6 ....216 B1
REDBR IG4 ....71 J2
Grasmere Rd BMLY BR1 ....183 J4
BXLYHN DA7 ....149 K2
MUSWH N10 ....48 B4
ORP BR6 ....216 B1
PLSTW E13 ....106 E1
SNWD SE25 ....197 J3
STRHM/NOR SW16 ....180 A1
TOTM N17 ....50 C2
Grasshaven Wy THMD SE28 ....128 A1
Grassington Cl FBAR/BDGN N11 ....48 A2
Grassington Rd SCUP DA14 ....168 B6
Grassmount FSTH SE23 ....163 J4
Grass Pk FNCH N3 ....46 D4
Grassway WLGTN SM6 ....210 C2
Grasvenor Av BAR EN5 ....32 E1
Grately Wy PECK SE15 * 143 F1
Gratton Rd WKENS W14 ....119 H3
Gratton Ter CRICK NW2 ....82 B1
Gravel Hl BXLYHS DA6 ....149 J6
CROY/NA CR0 ....213 G4
FNCH N3 ....46 D5
Gravel Hill Cl BXLYHS DA6 ....169 J1
Gravel La WCHPL E1 ....13 J3
Gravel Pit Wy ORP BR6 ....202 B6
Gravel Rd HAYES BR2 ....200 D6
WHTN TW2 ....155 K3
Gravelwood Cl CHST BR7 ....167 H5
Gravenel Gdns TOOT SW17 * 178 D1
Graveney Gv PGE/AN SE20 ....181 K3
Graveney Rd TOOT SW17 ....160 D6
Gravesend Rd SHB W12 ....99 J6
Gray Av BCTR RM8 ....74 B5
Gray Gdns RAIN RM13 ....93 J4
Grayham Crs NWMAL KT3 ....192 A1
Grayham Rd NWMAL KT3 ....192 A1
Grayland Cl BMLY BR1 ....184 C4
Grayling Cl CAN/RD E16 ....106 C3
Grayling Ct EA W5 * 116 E1
Grayling Rd STNW/STAM N16 ....67 K6
Grayling Sq BETH E2 * 104 C2
Grays Cottages
STMC/STPC BR5 * 186 D4
Grayscroft Rd
STRHM/NOR SW16 ....179 J3
Grays Farm Rd
STMC/STPC BR5 ....186 C4
Grayshott Rd BTSEA SW11 ....141 F4
Gray's Inn Rd FSBYW WC1X 5 F4
Gray's Inn Sq GINN WC1R 11 J1
Grays La ASHF TW15 ....152 E6
Grayswood Gdns RYNPK SW20 ....176 E5
Gray's Yd MHST W1U * 9 H4
Graywood Ct
NFNCH/WDSPK N12 ....47 G3
Grazebrook Rd
STNW/STAM N16 ....67 K6
Grazeley Cl BXLYHS DA6 ....149 K6
Great Benty WDR/YW UB7 ....112 B4
Great Brownings DUL SE21 ....163 G6
Great Bushey Dr
TRDG/WHET N20 ....33 F3
Great Cambridge Jct
PLMGR N13 ....49 J1
Great Cambridge Rd EN EN1 ....24 C2
UED N18 ....49 K1
Great Castle St REGST W1B 10 A3
Great Central Av RSLP HA4 ....77 G3
Great Central St CAMTN NW1 ....8 E1
Great Central Wy WBLY HA9 ....80 E3
WLSDN NW10 ....81 G3
Great Chapel St
SOHO/SHAV W1D 10 C3
Great Chart St BTSEA SW11 ....140 B4
Great Chertsey Rd CHSWK W4 ....138 A2
FELT TW13 ....154 E5
Great Church La HMSMTH W6 ....119 G5
Great College St WEST SW1P 16 E4
Great Cross Av GNWCH SE10 ....145 H1
Great Cullings ROMW/RG RM7 ....75 G6
Great Cumberland Ms
MBLAR W1H 8 E4
Great Cumberland Pl
MBLAR W1H 8 E3
Great Dover St STHWK SE1 ....18 E4
Greatdown Rd HNWL W7 ....97 F4
Great Eastern Rd SRTFD E15 ....88 B5
Great Eastern St SDTCH EC2A 7 G6
Great Eastern Whf
BTSEA SW11 ....140 D1
Great Elms Rd HAYES BR2 ....200 B1
Great Fld CDALE/KGS NW9 ....45 G4
Greatfield Av EHAM E6 ....107 K3
Greatfield Cl ARCH N19 ....84 C2
BROCKY SE4 ....144 D5
Greatfields Rd BARK IG11 ....90 D6
Great Galley Cl BARK IG11 ....109 H2
Great Gardens Rd EMPK RM11 ....75 K3
Great Gatton Cl CROY/NA CR0 ....198 B4
Great George St STJSPK SW1H 16 D3
Great Guildford St STHWK SE1 ....18 C1
Great Harry Dr ELTH/MOT SE9 ....167 F6
Great James St BMSBY WC1N 11 H1
Great Marlborough St
REGST W1B 10 A4
Great Maze Pond STHWK SE1 ....19 F1
Great New St
FLST/FETLN EC4A * 11 K3
Great North Leisure Pk
NFNCH/WDSPK N12 * 47 H3
Great North Rd BAR EN5 ....20 D3
BAR EN5 ....33 F1
EFNCH N2 ....65 J2
Great North Wy (Barnet
By-Pass) HDN NW4 ....45 K4
Greatorex St WCHPL E1 ....104 C4
Great Ormond St BMSBY WC1N 11 F1
Great Percy St FSBYW WC1X 5 J4
Great Peter St WEST SW1P 16 D5
Great Portland St GTPST W1W 9 K1
Great Pulteney St
SOHO/CST W1F 10 B5
Great Queen St DART DA1 ....171 J1
HOL/ALD WC2B 11 F3
Great Russell St
NOXST/BSQ WC1A 10 E2
Great St Thomas Apostle
BLKFR EC4V 12 D5
Great Scotland Yd
WHALL SW1A 16 E1
Great Smith St WEST SW1P 16 D4
Great South-west Rd
EBED/NFELT TW14 ....133 K4
HSLWW TW4 ....134 A3
Great Spilmans EDUL SE22 ....143 F6
Great Strd CDALE/KGS NW9 ....45 H5
Great Suffolk St STHWK SE1 ....18 B2
Great Sutton St FSBYE EC1V 6 B7
Great Swan Aly LOTH EC2R 12 E3
Great Thrift STMC/STPC BR5 ....201 H1
Great Titchfield St GTPST W1W 9 K1
Great Tower St MON EC3R 13 G6
Great Trinity La BLKFR EC4V 12 D5
Great Turnstile HHOL WC1V * 11 H2
Great Western Rd NTGHL W11 ....100 D4
Great West Rd BTFD TW8 ....116 D5
HEST TW5 ....134 D3
HEST TW5 ....135 G2
HMSMTH W6 ....118 E5
ISLW TW7 ....135 K1
Great West Road Chiswick
CHSWK W4 ....118 C6
Great West Road Ellesmere Rd
CHSWK W4 ....117 K6
Great West Road Hogarth La
CHSWK W4 ....118 A6
Great Winchester St
OBST EC2N 13 F3
Great Windmill St
SOHO/SHAV W1D 10 C6
Greatwood CHST BR7 ....185 F3
Great Yd STHWK SE1 ....19 H2
Greaves Cl BARK IG11 ....90 E5
Greaves Cottages
POP/IOD E14 * 105 G4
Greaves Pl TOOT SW17 ....160 D6
Grebe Av YEAD UB4 ....95 H5
Grebe Cl BARK IG11 ....109 G3
FSTGT E7 ....88 D3
WALTH E17 ....51 G3
Grebe Ct SUT SM1 ....208 D3
Grebe Ter KUT/HW KT1 * 175 F6
Grecian Crs NRWD SE19 ....180 C2
Greek St SOHO/SHAV W1D 10 D4
Greenacre Cl BAR EN5 ....20 D1
NTHLT UB5 ....77 K3
Greenacre Gdns WALTH E17 ....70 A1
Greenacre Pl WLGTN SM6 ....195 G6
Green Acres CROY/NA CR0 ....212 B1
SCUP DA14 * 168 A6
Greenacres BUSH WD23 ....28 D4
ELTH/MOT SE9 ....167 F1
Greenacres Cl ORP BR6 ....216 C2
Greenacres Dr STAN HA7 ....43 H3
Greenacre Sq
BERM/RHTH SE16 * 124 A2
Greenacre Wk STHGT/OAK N14 ....34 D5
Green Arbour Ct STBT EC1A * 12 A3
Green Av MLHL NW7 ....31 F6
WEA W13 ....116 C3
Greenaway Av UED N18 * 51 F1
Greenaway Gdns HAMP NW3 ....83 F2
Green Bank
NFNCH/WDSPK N12 ....33 F6
WAP E1W 123 J1
Greenbank Av ALP/SUD HA0 ....79 G3
Greenbank Cl CHING E4 ....38 A4
Greenbank Crs HDN NW4 ....64 C1
Greenbanks DART DA1 ....171 H4
Greenbay Rd CHARL SE7 ....146 C1
Greenberry St STJWD NW8 ....2 C3
Greenbrook Av EBAR EN4 ....21 G2
Green Chain Wk BMLY BR1 ....183 G1
BMLY BR1 ....183 H3
CHARL SE7 ....126 C4
ELTH/MOT SE9 ....147 G6
ELTH/MOT SE9 ....184 C1
HAYES BR2 ....183 G3
SYD SE26 ....182 A2
THMD SE28 ....128 E1
WOOL/PLUM SE18 ....126 E6
Green Cl CAR SM5 ....194 E6
CDALE/KGS NW9 ....62 E3
FELT TW13 ....172 D1
GLDGN NW11 ....65 G4
HAYES BR2 ....183 H6
Greencoat Pl WEST SW1P 16 B6
Greencoat Rw WEST SW1P 16 B5
Green Court Av CROY/NA CR0 ....197 J6
Greencourt Av EDGW HA8 ....44 D4
Green Court Gdns
CROY/NA CR0 ....197 J6
Greencourt Rd
STMC/STPC BR5 ....201 K2
Greencroft EDGW HA8 ....44 E1
Greencroft Av RSLP HA4 ....59 G6
Greencroft Gdns EN EN1 ....24 A4
KIL/WHAMP NW6 ....83 F5
Greencroft Rd HEST TW5 ....134 E2
Green Dl EDUL SE22 ....143 F6
Green Dragon La BTFD TW8 ....117 F5
WCHMH N21 ....23 F6
Green Dragon Yd WCHPL E1 ....104 C4
Green Dr STHL UB1 ....115 F1
Green End CHSGTN KT9 ....205 K2
WCHMH N21 ....35 H4
Greenend Rd CHSWK W4 ....118 B2
Green Farm Cl ORP BR6 ....217 F3
Greenfell Man DEPT SE8 * 124 C5
Greenfield Av BRYLDS KT5 ....191 K3
OXHEY WD19 ....27 J4
Greenfield Ct ELTH/MOT SE9 ....166 D5
Greenfield Dr BMLY BR1 ....184 B5
EFNCH N2 ....65 K1
Greenfield Gdns CRICK NW2 ....64 C6
DAGW RM9 ....91 J6
STMC/STPC BR5 ....201 H4
Greenfield Rd DAGW RM9 ....91 K6
SEVS/STOTM N15 ....68 A2
WCHPL E1 ....104 C5
Greenfields STHL UB1 ....96 A6
Greenfield Wy
RYLN/HDSTN HA2 ....42 B6
Greenford Av HNWL W7 ....96 E4
STHL UB1 ....95 K6
Greenford Gdns GFD/PVL UB6 ....96 B2
Greenford Rd GFD/PVL UB6 ....78 E5
STHL UB1 ....96 C6
SUT SM1 ....209 F2
Green Gdns ORP BR6 ....216 C3
Greengate GFD/PVL UB6 ....79 H4
Greengate St PLSTW E13 ....107 F1
Greenhalgh Wk EFNCH N2 ....65 G1
Greenham Cl STHWK SE1 ....17 J3
Greenham Crs CHING E4 ....51 H2
Greenham Rd MUSWH N10 ....48 A5
Greenhaven Dr THMD SE28 ....109 J5
Greenheys Cl NTHWD HA6 ....40 C4
Greenheys Dr SWFD E18 ....52 D6
Greenhill BKHH IG9 ....39 G3
HAMP NW3 ....83 H2
SUT SM1 ....194 B6
WBLY HA9 ....62 D6
Green Hl WOOL/PLUM SE18 ....126 E5
Greenhill Ct BAR EN5 * 21 F6
Greenhill Crs WATW WD18 ....26 C1
Greenhill Gdns NTHLT UB5 ....95 K1
Greenhill Gv MNPK E12 ....89 J2
Greenhill Pde BAR EN5 * 21 F6
Greenhill Pk BAR EN5 ....21 G6
WLSDN NW10 ....81 G6
Greenhill Rd HRW HA1 ....60 E3
WLSDN NW10 ....81 G6
Greenhill's Rents FARR EC1M * 12 A1
Greenhills Ter IS N1 ....85 K4
Greenhill Ter NTHLT UB5 * 95 K1
WOOL/PLUM SE18 ....126 E5
Greenhill Wy HRW HA1 ....60 E3
WBLY HA9 ....62 D6
Greenhithe Cl BFN/LL DA15 ....167 K2
Greenholm Rd ELTH/MOT SE9 ....147 G6
Green Hundred Rd PECK SE15 ....123 H6
Greenhurst Rd WNWD SE27 ....180 B1
Greening St ABYW SE2 ....128 D4
Greenland Crs NWDGN UB2 ....114 B3
Greenland Ms DEPT SE8 ....124 A5
Greenland Pl CAMTN NW1 * 84 B6
Greenland Quay
BERM/RHTH SE16 ....124 B4
Greenland Rd BAR EN5 ....32 A1
CAMTN NW1 ....84 C6
Greenlands HOR/WEW KT19 ....206 D3
Greenland St CAMTN NW1 * 84 B6
Greenland Wy CROY/NA CR0 ....195 J4
Green La BCTR RM8 ....74 B6
CHSGTN KT9 ....206 A4
E/WMO/HCT KT8 ....189 G2
EDGW HA8 ....30 B6
ELTH/MOT SE9 ....167 G4
FELT TW13 ....172 D1
HDN NW4 ....64 B2
HNWL W7 ....115 K2
HSLWW TW4 ....134 B6
IL IG1 ....72 D6
MRDN SM4 ....194 A4
NTHWD HA6 ....40 B3
NWMAL KT3 ....191 K2
OXHEY WD19 ....27 G3
PGE/AN SE20 ....182 A3
STAN HA7 ....29 H6
THHTH CR7 ....180 C4
UX/CGN UB8 ....94 A4
WPK KT4 ....192 E4
Green Lane Cottages
STAN HA7 * 29 H6
Green Lane Gdns THHTH CR7 ....180 D5
Green Lanes HOR/WEW KT19 ....207 G6
PLMGR N13 ....49 F1
SEVS/STOTM N15 ....49 H6
WCHMH N21 ....35 J3
Greenlaw Ct EA W5 * 97 K5
Greenlaw Gdns NWMAL KT3 ....192 C4
Greenlawn La BTFD TW8 ....116 E5
Green Lawns
NFNCH/WDSPK N12 * 47 F2
RSLP HA4 * 59 G5
Greenlaw St
WOOL/PLUM SE18 ....127 F3
Green Leaf Av WLGTN SM6 ....210 D2
Greenleaf Cl
BRXS/STRHM SW2 * 162 B2
Greenleafe Dr BARK/HLT IG6 ....54 B6
Greenleaf Rd EHAM E6 ....89 G6
WALTH E17 ....51 H6
Greenlea Pk WIM/MER SW19 * 178 D4
Greenleigh Av STMC/STPC BR5 ....202 C1
Greenlink Wk RCH/KEW TW9 ....137 J2
Green Man La
EBED/NFELT TW14 ....133 K5
WEA W13 ....97 G6
Greenman St IS N1 ....85 J5
Greenmead Cl SNWD SE25 ....197 H2
Green Moor Link WCHMH N21 ....35 H2
Greenmoor Rd PEND EN3 ....24 E3
Greenoak Pl EBAR EN4 ....21 K3
Green Oaks NWDGN UB2 * 114 C4
Greenoak Wy WIM/MER SW19 ....159 G6
Greenock Rd ACT W3 ....117 J3
STRHM/NOR SW16 ....179 J4
Greenock Wy ROM RM1 ....57 G3
Green Pde HSLW TW3 * 155 G1
Greenpark Wy GFD/PVL UB6 ....78 E6
Green Pond Cl WALTH E17 ....51 H6
Green Pond Rd WALTH E17 ....51 G6
Green Ride CHING E4 ....38 E1
Green Rd STHGT/OAK N14 ....34 B1
TRDG/WHET N20 ....33 G5
Greenroof Wy GNWCH SE10 ....125 J3
Greens Ct NTGHL W11 * 119 J1
SOHO/CST W1F 10 C5
Greens End WOOL/PLUM SE18 ....127 G4
Greenshank Cl WALTH E17 ....51 G3
Greenside BCTR RM8 ....73 J6
BXLY DA5 ....169 F3
Greenside Cl CAT SE6 ....165 G4
TRDG/WHET N20 ....33 H4
Greenside Rd CROY/NA CR0 ....196 B4
SHB W12 ....118 D3
Greenslade Rd BARK IG11 ....90 E5
Greenstead Av WFD IG8 ....53 G2
Greenstead Gdns
PUT/ROE SW15 ....138 D6
WFD IG8 ....53 G2
Greensted Rd LOU IG10 ....39 K2
Greenstone Ms WAN E11 ....70 E3
Green St FSTGT E7 ....89 F3
MYFR/PKLN W1K 9 F5
PEND EN3 ....25 F4
Greenstreet Hl NWCR SE14 * 144 A4
Greensward BUSH WD23 ....28 B1
Green Ter CLKNW EC1R 5 K5
The Green ACT W3 ....99 G5
BKHH IG9 * 39 F3
BXLYHN DA7 ....149 H2
CAR SM5 * 210 A2
CROY/NA CR0 ....213 H6
ED N9 ....36 C4
FELT TW13 ....154 A4
HAYES BR2 ....199 K4

HEST TW5 ....115 F6
Grenfell Av HCH RM12 ....75 H5
Grenfell Ct MLHL NW7 * 45 K2
Grenfell Gdns
 KTN/HRWW/WS HA3 ....62 A4
Grenfell Rd NTGHL W11 ....100 B6
 TOOT SW17 ....178 E2
Grennell Cl SUT SM1 ....194 C6
Grennell Rd SUT SM1 ....194 D6
Grenoble Gdns PLMGR N13 ....49 G2
Grenville Cl BRYLDS KT5 ....191 K5
 FNCH N3 ....47 F4
Grenville Gdns WFD IG8 ....53 C3
Grenville Ms ARCH N19 ....66 E5
 HPTN TW12 ....173 C1
Grenville Pl MLHL NW7 ....45 F1
 SKENS SW7 * 120 B5
Grenville Rd ARCH N19 ....66 E5
 BMSBY WC1N 5 F7
Gresham Av TRDG/WHET N20 ....33 K6
Gresham Cl BXLY DA5 ....169 F1
 ENC/FH EN2 ....23 J4
Gresham Dr CHDH RM6 ....73 H2
Gresham Gdns GLDGN NW11 ....64 C5
Gresham Rd BECK BR3 ....182 B5
 BRXN/ST SW9 ....142 B4
 CAN/RD E16 ....107 F5
 EDGW HA8 ....44 B2
 EHAM E6 ....107 K1
 HPTN TW12 ....173 H2
 HSLW TW3 ....135 H2
 SNWD SE25 ....197 H1
 WLSDN NW10 ....81 F3
Gresham St CITYW EC2V 12 C5
Gresham Wy WIM/MER SW19 ...159 K5
Gresley Cl SEVS/STOTM N15 * ...67 K1
 WALTH E17 ....69 G3
Gresley Rd ARCH N19 ....66 C5
Gressenhall Rd
 WAND/EARL SW18 ....159 J1
Gresse St FITZ W1T 10 C2
Gresswell Cl SCUP DA14 ....168 B5
Gresswell St FUL/PGN SW6 .....139 G2
Gretton Rd TOTM N17 ....50 A3
Greville Cl TWK TW1 ....156 C2
Greville Ms KIL/WHAMP NW6 ....83 F6
Greville Rd KIL/WHAMP NW6 ...101 F1
 RCHPK/HAM TW10 ....157 G1
 WALTH E17 ....70 A1
Greville St HCIRC EC1N 11 K2
Grey Cl GLDGN NW11 ....65 G3
Greycoat Pl WEST SW1P 16 C5
Greycoat St WEST SW1P 16 C5
Greycot Rd BECK BR3 ....182 D1
Grey Eagle St WCHPL E1 ....13 K1
Greyfell Cl STAN HA7 ....43 H1
Greyhound Hl HDN NW4 ....45 J6
Greyhound La
 STRHM/NOR SW16 ....179 J2
Greyhound Rd DART DA1 ....150 B6
Greyladies Gdns
 GNWCH SE10 * 145 F3
Greys Park Cl HAYES BR2 ....215 G3
Greystead Rd FSTH SE23 ....163 K2
Greystoke Av PIN HA5 ....42 A6
Greystoke Cottages EA W5 * 98 A3
Greystoke Gdns EA W5 * 98 A5
 ENC/FH EN2 ....23 J2
Greystoke Pk EA W5 * 98 A5
Greystone Gdns BARK/HLT IG6 ..54 C5
 KTN/HRWW/WS HA3 ....61 J3
Greystone Dr
 STRHM/NOR SW16 ....179 G2
Grierson Rd FSTH SE23 ....164 B1
Griffin Centre
 EBED/NFELT TW14 * 154 A1
Griffin Cl WLSDN NW10 ....81 K3
Griffin Manor Wy THMD SE28 ...127 J3
Griffin Rd TOTM N17 ....50 A5
 WOOL/PLUM SE18 ....127 J5
Griffins Cl WCHMH N21 ....35 K3
Griffin Wy THMD SE28 ....127 K5
Griffith Cl BCTR RM8 ....73 J4
Griffiths Rd WIM/MER SW19 ....177 K3
Griggs Ap IL IG1 ....72 C6
Grigg's Pl STHWK SE1 ....19 H5
Grigg's Rd LEY E10 ....70 A3
Grimsby St CAN/RD E16 ....127 C2
Grimsby St BETH E2 ....7 K6
Grimsdyke Crs BAR EN5 ....20 A4
Grimsdyke Rd PIN HA5 ....41 J3
Grimsel Pth CMBW SE5 ....142 C1
Grimshaw Cl HGT N6 ....66 A4
Grimshaw Wy ROM RM1 * 75 H4
Grimston Rd FUL/PGN SW6 .....139 J3
Grimwade Av CROY/NA CR0 ....212 C1
Grimwade Cl PECK SE15 ....143 K4
Grimwood Rd TWK TW1 ....156 A2
Grindall Cl CROY/NA CR0 ....211 H2
Grindal St STHWK SE1 ....17 K3
Grindleford Av
 FBAR/BDGN N11 ....34 A4
Grindley Gdns CROY/NA CR0 * ..197 G3
Grinling Pl DEPT SE8 ....124 D6
Grinstead Rd DEPT SE8 ....124 B5
Grisle Cl ED N9 ....36 D5
Grittleton Av WBLY HA9 ....80 D4
Grittleton Rd MV/WKIL W9 ......100 E3
Grocers' Hall Ct LOTH EC2R * ...12 E4
Groombridge Cl WELL DA16 .....148 B6
Groombridge Rd HOM E9 ....87 F5
Groom Cl HAYES BR2 ....200 A1
Groom Crs WAND/EARL SW18 ..160 C2
Groomfield Cl TOOT SW17 ......161 F1
Grooms Dr PIN HA5 ....58 E2
Grosmont Rd
 WOOL/PLUM SE18 ....128 A5
Grosse Wy PUT/ROE SW15 ....158 E1
Grosvenor Av CAR SM5 ....209 K4
 HBRY N5 ....85 K3

MORT/ESHN SW14 ....138 B4
RYLN/HDSTN HA2 ....60 B4
 YEAD UB4 ....94 D1
Grosvenor Br VX/NE SW8 ....121 C6
Grosvenor Cottages
 BGVA SW1W * 15 G6
Grosvenor Crs CDALE/KGS NW9 ..62 C1
 DART DA1 ....151 G6
 KTBR SW1X 15 H4
Grosvenor Crescent Ms
 KTBR SW1X 15 H5
Grosvenor Gdns BGVA SW1W ...15 H5
 CRICK NW2 ....82 A4
 GLDGN NW11 ....64 D3
 KUTN/CMB KT2 ....174 E2
 MORT/ESHN SW14 ....138 B4
 MUSWH N10 ....48 C6
 STHGT/OAK N14 ....22 D6
 WFD IG8 ....52 E3
 WLGTN SM6 ....210 C5
Grosvenor Gardens Ms East
 BGVA SW1W 15 K4
Grosvenor Gardens Ms North
 BGVA SW1W 15 J4
Grosvenor Ga MYFR/PKLN W1K ..9 F6
Grosvenor Hl MYFR/PKLN W1K ...9 J5
 WIM/MER SW19 ....177 G5
Grosvenor Pde EA W5 * 117 H1
Grosvenor Pk CMBW SE5 ....142 D1
Grosvenor Park Rd WALTH E17 ..69 J2
Grosvenor Pl KTBR SW1X 15 H3
Grosvenor Ri East WALTH E17 ...69 K2
Grosvenor Rd BCTR RM8 ....74 B5
 BELV DA17 ....129 H6
 BTFD TW8 ....116 E6
 BXLYHS DA6 ....148 E6
 CHSWK W4 ....117 K5
 ED N9 ....36 D3
 FNCH N3 ....47 F3
 FSTGT E7 ....89 F4
 HNWL W7 ....116 B1
 HSLWW TW4 ....134 E4
 IL IG1 ....90 C1
 LEY E10 ....70 A5
 MUSWH N10 ....48 B4
 NWDGN UB2 ....114 E3
 PIM SW1V 121 H6
 RCHPK/HAM TW10 ....137 F6
 ROMW/RG RM7 ....75 F4
 SNWD SE25 ....197 H1
 STMC/STPC BR5 ....202 B2
 TWK TW1 ....156 B2
 WAN E11 ....71 G2
 WLGTN SM6 ....210 B4
 WIM/MER SW19 ....178 B3
Grosvenor Sq MYFR/PKLN W1K ...9 H5
Grosvenor St MYFR/PKLN W1K ...9 J5
Grosvenor Ter CMBW SE5 ....142 D1
Grosvenor V RSLP HA4 ....58 D6
Grosvenor Wy CLPT E5 ....68 E6
Grosvenor Wharf Rd
 POP/IOD E14 ....125 G3
Grote's Buildings
 BKHTH/KID SE3 ....145 H3
Grote's Pl BKHTH/KID SE3 ....145 H3
Groton Rd WAND/EARL SW18 ...160 A4
Grotto Pas MHST W1U 9 G1
Grotto Rd TWK TW1 ....156 A4
Grove Av HNWL W7 ....96 E5
 MUSWH N10 ....48 C4
 PIN HA5 ....59 J1
 SUT SM1 ....208 E4
 TWK TW1 ....156 A3
Grove Bank OXHEY WD19 * 27 H1
Grovebury Cl ERITH DA8 ....130 A6
Grovebury Ct STHGT/OAK N14 ...34 C2
Grovebury Rd ABYW SE2 ....128 C2
Grove Cl FSTH SE23 ....164 A3
 HAYES BR2 ....199 K6
 KUT/HW KT1 ....91 G5
 STHGT/OAK N14 * 34 B2
Grove Cottages CHEL SW3 ......120 D6
 CHSWK W4 * 118 B6
Grove Ct E/WMO/HCT KT8 ....189 J2
 EA W5 * 117 F1
Grove Crs CDALE/KGS NW9 ....44 E4
 FELT TW13 ....154 D6
 KUT/HW KT1 ....175 F6
 SWFD E18 ....52 D5
 WOT/HER KT12 ....188 A4
Grove Crescent Rd SRTFD E15 ...88 C4
Grovedale Rd ARCH N19 ....66 D6
Grove Dwellings WCHPL E1 * ...104 E4
Grove End KTTN NW5 ....84 B2
 SWFD E18 ....52 D5
Grove End La ESH/CLAY KT10 ..189 J5
Grove End Rd STJWD NW8 ....2 C4
Grove Farm Pk NTHWD HA6 ......40 B1
Grove Footpath BRYLDS KT5 ...191 F1
Grove Gdns HDN NW4 ....63 J2
 PEND EN3 ....25 F2
 STJWD NW8 ....2 E4
 TEDD TW11 ....156 B6
Grove Green Rd WAN E11 ....88 A1
Groveherst Rd DART DA1 ....151 J4
Grove Hl HRW HA1 ....60 C4
Grove Hill Rd CMBW SE5 ....143 F4
 HRW HA1 ....61 F4

Grove Market Pl
 ELTH/MOT SE9 * 166 E1
Grove Ms HMSMTH W6 ....119 F3
Grove Mill Pl CAR SM5 ....210 A1
Grove Pk CDALE/KGS NW9 ....62 D1
 CMBW SE5 ....143 F3
 SWFD E18 ....71 F2
Grove Park Av CHING E4 ....51 K3
Grove Park Br CHSWK W4 ....137 K1
Grove Park Gdns CHSWK W4 ....137 K1
Grove Park Ms CHSWK W4 ......137 K1
Grove Park Rd ELTH/MOT SE9 ..166 D4
 RAIN RM13 ....93 J6
 SEVS/STOTM N15 ....50 B3
Grove Park Ter CHSWK W4 ......137 K1
Grove Pl ACT W3 ....117 K1
 BAL SW12 ....161 G1
 HAMP NW3 ....83 H1
Grove Rd ACT W3 ....117 K1
 BARN SW13 ....138 C3
 BELV DA17 ....129 G6
 BOW E3 ....105 G2
 BTFD TW8 ....116 D5
 BXLYHN DA7 ....149 K5
 CHDH RM6 ....73 J4
 CHING E4 ....38 A5
 CRICK NW2 ....82 A3
 E/WMO/HCT KT8 ....189 J1
 EA W5 ....97 K6
 EBAR EN4 ....21 J4
 FBAR/BDGN N11 ....48 B1
 HOM E9 ....87 F6
 HSLW TW3 ....135 G5
 ISLW TW7 ....135 K2
 MITCM CR4 ....179 G5
 NFNCH/WDSPK N12 ....47 H1
 NTHWD HA6 ....40 B1
 PIN HA5 ....59 J2
 RCHPK/HAM TW10 ....157 G1
 SEVS/STOTM N15 ....68 A2
 SURB KT6 ....190 E2
 SUT SM1 ....208 E4
 SWFD E18 ....52 D5
 THHTH CR7 ....196 B1
 WALTH E17 ....69 K2
 WAN E11 ....71 F4
 WHTN TW2 ....155 J5
 WIM/MER SW19 ....178 B3
Grover Rd OXHEY WD19 ....27 H1
Grovesde Cl ACT W3 ....98 C5
 CAR SM5 ....194 D6
Groveside Rd CHING E4 ....38 C5
Grovestile Waye
 EBED/NFELT TW14 ....153 H3
Grove St BERM/RHTH SE16 .....124 C4
 UED N18 ....50 B2
Grove Ter KTTN NW5 ....84 B2
 STHL UB1 * 96 A4
 TEDD TW11 ....156 B6
Grove Terrace Ms KTTN NW5 ....84 B1
The Grove BXLYHS DA6 ....148 E5
 CDALE/KGS NW9 ....63 F2
 CEND/HSY/T N8 ....66 D2
 EA W5 ....116 E1
 EDGW HA8 ....30 D6
 ENC/FH EN2 ....23 G5
 FNCH N3 ....46 E4
 FSBYPK N4 ....67 F4
 GFD/PVL UB6 ....96 C5
 GLDGN NW11 ....64 C5
 HGT N6 ....65 K6
 ISLW TW7 ....135 K2
 PLMGR N13 ....35 G6
 SCUP DA14 ....187 F1
 SRTFD E15 ....88 C5
 TEDD TW11 ....156 B5
 WALTH E17 ....52 A5
 WOT/HER KT12 ....188 A4
 WWKM BR4 ....214 A1
Grove V CHST BR7 ....185 F2
 EDUL SE22 ....143 F5
Groveway BCTR RM8 ....74 A3
 BRXN/ST SW9 ....142 A2
Grove Wy ESH/CLAY KT10 ....189 H5
 WBLY HA9 ....80 E3
Grovewood Pl WFD IG8 ....53 K2
Grumant Rd PECK SE15 ....143 G2
Grundy St POP/IOD E14 ....105 K5
Gruneisen Rd FNCH N3 ....47 F3
Guardian Cl EMPK RM11 ....75 K6
Gubyon Av HNHL SE24 ....142 C6
Guernsey Cl HEST TW5 ....135 F2
Guernsey Gv HNHL SE24 ....162 D2
Guernsey Rd IS N1 ....85 J4
 LEY E10 ....70 B5
Guibal Rd LEE/GVPK SE12 ....166 A3
Guildersfield Rd
 STRHM/NOR SW16 ....179 K3
Guildford Av FELT TW13 ....153 K4
Guildford Gv GNWCH SE10 ......144 E2
Guildford Rd CROY/NA CR0 ......196 E3
 EHAM E6 ....107 J5
 CEND/SEVK IG3 ....73 F3
 IS N1 ....5 H3
 WALTH E17 ....52 A5
Guildhall Buildings
 CITYW EC2V * 12 D3
Guildhall Yd CITYW EC2V 12 D3
Guildhouse St PIM SW1V 16 A7
Guildown Av
 NFNCH/WDSPK N12 ....33 F6
Guild Rd CHARL SE7 ....126 C5
 ERITH DA8 ....150 C1
Guildsway WALTH E17 ....51 H4
Guilford Av BRYLDS KT5 ....191 G2
Guilford Pl BMSBY WC1N 5 G7
Guilford St BMSBY WC1N 5 F7
Guillemot Pl WDGN N22 * 49 F5
Guisborough Ct WLSDN NW10 * ..81 J5
Guinness Cl HOM E9 ....87 G5
 HYS/HAR UB3 ....113 G3
Guinness Ct CROY/NA CR0 ....197 G6
Guinness Sq STHWK SE1 ....19 G6
Guinness Trust
 STNW/STAM N16 ....68 B3
Guinness Trust Est CHEL SW3 ...14 E7

SRTFD E15 * 88 D6
Guion Rd FUL/PGN SW6 ....139 J3
Gulland Wk IS N1 * 85 J4
Gulliver Cl NTHLT UB5 ....77 K6
Gulliver Rd BFN/LL DA15 ....167 J4
Gulliver St BERM/RHTH SE16 ...124 C3
Gumleigh Rd EA W5 ....116 D4
Gumley Gdns ISLW TW7 ....136 B4
Gumping Rd STMC/STPC BR5 ...201 H6
Gundulph Rd HAYES BR2 ....184 B6
Gunmakers La BOW E3 ....87 G5
Gunnell Ct CROY/NA CR0 ....197 H3
 SYD SE26 ....163 H6
Gunner La WOOL/PLUM SE18 ...127 F5
Gunnersbury Av ACT W3 ....117 H4
Gunnersbury Av (North
 Circular Rd) EA W5 ....98 B6
Gunnersbury Cl CHSWK W4 * ...117 H2
Gunnersbury Crs ACT W3 ....117 G2
Gunnersbury Dr EA W5 ....117 G2
Gunnersbury Gdns ACT W3 ......117 G2
Gunnersbury La ACT W3 ....117 G3
Gunnersbury Ms CHSWK W4 ....117 H2
Gunners Gv CHING E4 ....38 A5
Gunners Rd TOOT SW17 ....160 C6
Gunning St
 WOOL/PLUM SE18 ....127 K4
Gunstor Rd STNW/STAM N16 * ...86 A2
Gun St WCHPL E1 ....13 J2
Gunter Gv EDGW HA8 ....45 F4
 WBPTN SW10 ....120 B6
Gunterstone Rd WKENS W14 ...119 H5
Gunthorpe St WCHPL E1 ....13 K2
Gunton Rd CLPT E5 ....86 D1
 TOOT SW17 ....179 F2
Gunwhale Cl
 BERM/RHTH SE16 ....124 A1
Gunyard Ms
 WOOL/PLUM SE18 ....146 D6
Gurdon Rd CHARL SE7 ....125 K5
Gurnell Gv WEA W13 ....97 F3
Gurney Cl BARK IG11 ....90 C5
 SRTFD E15 ....88 C3
 WALTH E17 ....51 F4
Gurney Crs CROY/NA CR0 ....196 A5
 EHAM E6 ....65 H1
Gurney Rd CAR SM5 ....210 A2
 FUL/PGN SW6 ....140 B4
 NTHLT UB5 ....95 F2
 SRTFD E15 ....88 C3
Guthrie St CHEL SW3 ....120 D5
Gutter La CITYW EC2V 12 C3
Guyatt Gdns MTCM CR4 ....179 F5
Guy Barnett Gv
 BKHTH/KID SE3 ....145 K4
Guy Rd WLGTN SM6 ....210 E1
Guyscliff Rd LEW SE13 ....145 F6
Guysfield Cl RAIN RM13 ....93 J6
Guysfield Dr RAIN RM13 ....93 J6
Guy St STHWK SE1 ....19 F2
Gwalior Rd PUT/ROE SW15 .....139 G5
Gwendolen Av
 PUT/ROE SW15 ....139 G6
Gwendolen Av PLSTW E13 ....89 H1
Gwendwr Rd WKENS W14 ....119 H5
Gwenneth Cottages
 EDGW HA8 * 44 C2
Gwillim Cl BFN/LL DA15 ....168 B1
Gwydor Rd BECK BR3 ....198 A1
Gwydyr Rd HAYES BR2 ....183 J6
Gwyn Cl FUL/PGN SW6 ....140 B1
Gwynne Av CROY/NA CR0 ....198 A4
Gwynne Park Av WFD IG8 ....53 K2
Gwynne Rd BTSEA SW11 ....140 C3
Gwynne Whf CHSWK W4 ....118 C6
Gylcote Cl CMBW SE5 ....142 E5
Gyles Pk STAN HA7 ....43 J4
Gyllyngdune Gdns
 GDMY/SEVK IG3 ....91 F3
Gwynne Pl FSBYW WC1X 5 H5

H

Haarlem Rd WKENS W14 ....119 G3
Haberdasher Pl IS N1 ....7 F3
Haberdasher St IS N1 ....7 F4
Habington Cl CMBW SE5 * 142 E1
Habitat Cl PECK SE15 ....143 J3
Haccombe Rd WIM/MER SW19 ..178 B2
Hackbridge Park Gdns
 CAR SM5 ....194 E6
Hackbridge Rd CAR SM5 ....195 F6
Hackford Rd BRXN/ST SW9 ......142 B2
Hackford Wk BRXN/ST SW9 ......142 B2
Hackington Crs BECK BR3 ....182 D2
Hackney Av HACK E8 * 86 D4
Hackney Rd BETH E2 ....7 J4
Hackney Wick HOM E9 ....87 H4
Hadar Cl TRDG/WHET N20 ....32 E5
Hadden Rd THMD SE28 ....127 K3
Hadden Wy GFD/PVL UB6 ....78 D4
Haddington Rd BMLY BR1 ....165 G5
Haddo Ct BERM/RHTH SE16 * ...123 K2
 NWMAL KT3 ....192 C2
Haddon Gv BFN/LL DA15 ....168 B2
Haddon Rd STMC/STPC BR5 ....202 E2
 SUT SM1 ....209 F2
Haddo St GNWCH SE10 ....124 E6
Hadfield Cl STHL UB1 * 95 K2
Hadfield Rd STWL/WRAY TW19 ..152 A2
Hadleigh Cl RYNPK SW20 ....177 J5
 WCHPL E1 ....104 E3
Hadleigh Dr BELMT SM2 ....208 E6
Hadleigh Rd ED N9 ....36 D2
Hadleigh St BETH E2 ....104 E3
Hadlow Common BAR EN5 ....20 E3
Hadley Cl WCHMH N21 ....35 G1
Hadley Common BAR EN5 ....20 E2
Hadley Gdns CHSWK W4 ....118 A5
 NWDGN UB2 ....114 E4
Hadley Green Rd BAR EN5 ....20 D2
Hadley Gn West BAR EN5 ....20 D2
Hadley Gv BAR EN5 ....20 C2

Hadley Highstone BAR EN5 .....20 D2
Hadley Pde BAR EN5 * 20 C4
Hadley Rdg BAR EN5 .....20 C4
Hadley Rd BAR EN5 .....21 F5
  BELV DA17 .....129 C4
  EBAR EN4 .....22 A6
  MTCM CR4 .....195 J1
Hadley St KTTN NW5 .....84 B4
Hadley Wy WCHMH N21 .....35 G1
Hadley Wood Rd BAR EN5 .....20 E3
Hadlow Pl PLMGR SE19 .....181 H5
Hadlow Rd SCUP DA14 .....168 B6
  WELL DA16 .....148 D1
Hadrian Cl BOW E3 .....87 J6
  STWL/WRAY TW19 .....152 B2
Hadrian Est BETH E2 * 104 C1
Hadrian's Ride EN EN1 .....24 B6
Hadrian Wy GNWCH SE10 .....125 H5
Hadrian Wy STWL/WRAY TW19 ..152 B2
Haclyn Park Rd SHB W12 .....118 D2
Hafer Rd BTSEA SW11 .....140 E5
Hafton Rd CAT SE6 .....165 H5
Haggard Rd TWK TW1 .....156 C2
Hagger Ct WALTH E17 * 52 B6
Haggerston Rd HACK E8 .....86 B5
Hague St BETH E2 .....104 C2
Ha-ha Rd WOOL/PLUM SE18 ..126 E6
Haig Rd STAN HA7 .....43 J1
Haig Rd East PLSTW E13 .....107 G2
Haig Rd West PLSTW E13 .....107 G2
Haigville Gdns BARK/HLT IG6 ..72 B1
Hailes Cl WIM/MER SW19 .....178 B2
Haileybury Av EN EN1 .....36 C1
Haileybury Rd ORP BR6 .....217 G2
Hailey Rd ERITHM DA18 .....129 H2
Hailsham Av
  BRXS/STRHM SW2 .....162 A4
Hailsham Cl SURB KT6 .....190 E4
Hailsham Dr HRW HA1 .....42 D6
Hailsham Rd TOOT SW17 .....179 F2
Hailsham Ter UED N18 * 49 K1
Haimo Rd ELTH/MOT SE9 .....146 C6
Hainault Buildings LEY E10 * ..70 A5
Hainault Gore CHDH RM6 .....74 A2
Hainault Rd BARK/HLT IG6 .....55 H3
  CHDH RM6 .....55 K4
  CHDH RM6 .....74 B3
  CRW RM5 .....56 E6
  WAN E11 .....70 A5
Hainault St ELTH/MOT SE9 .....167 G3
  IL IG1 .....72 B6
Haines Wk MRDN SM4 .....194 A4
Hainford Cl PECK SE15 .....144 A5
Haining Cl CHSWK W4 .....117 H5
Hainthorpe Rd WNWD SE27 ..162 C5
Hainton Cl WCHPL E1 .....104 D5
Halberd Ms CLPT E5 .....68 D6
Halbutt St DAGW RM9 .....92 B2
Halcomb St IS N1 .....7 G1
Halcot Av BXLYHS DA6 .....149 J6
Halcrow St WCHPL E1 .....104 D4
Haldane Cl MUSWH N10 .....48 B3
  PEND EN3 .....25 K1
Haldane Pl WAND/EARL SW18 ..160 A3
Haldane Rd EHAM E6 .....107 H2
  FUL/PGN SW6 .....139 J1
  STHL UB1 .....96 C6
  THMD SE28 .....109 K6
Haldan Rd CHING E4 .....52 A2
Haldon Rd WAND/EARL SW18 ..159 J1
Hale Cl CHING E4 .....38 B4
  EDGW HA8 .....44 E1
  ORP BR6 .....216 C2
Hale End CHING E4 * 38 B4
Hale End Rd HARH RM3 .....57 K2
Hale End Cl RSLP HA4 .....58 E4
Hale End Rd WDGN N22 .....52 B2
Halefield Rd TOTM N17 .....50 C4
Hale Gdns ACT W3 .....117 H1
  SEVS/STOTM N15 .....68 C1
  TOTM N17 .....50 C6
Hale Grove Gdns MLHL NW7 ..45 F1
Hale House
  WOOL/PLUM SE18 * 146 D1
Hale La EDGW HA8 .....44 E1
  MLHL NW7 .....45 F1
Hale Rd EHAM E6 .....107 J3
  TOTM N17 .....50 C6
Halesowen Rd MRDN SM4 .....194 A4
Hales St DEPT SE8 .....144 D1
Hale St POP/IOD E14 .....105 K6
Halesworth Rd LEW SE13 .....144 E4
The Hale CHING E4 .....52 B3
Haley Rd HDN NW4 .....64 A3
Half Acre BTFD TW8 .....136 E1
Half Acre Ms BTFD TW8 .....136 E1
Half Acre Rd HNWL W7 .....115 K1
Half Moon Crs IS N1 .....5 H2
Half Moon Pas WCHPL E1 .....13 K4
Halfmoon Pas WCHPL E1 * 13 K4
Half Moon St MYFR/PICC W1J ..9 K7
Halford Cl EDGW HA8 .....44 D5
Halford Rd FUL/PGN SW6 .....119 K6
  LEY E10 .....70 B2
  RCHPK/HAM TW10 .....137 F6
Halfway Pl PUR RM19 .....131 K4
Halfway St BFN/LL DA15 .....167 K3
Haliburton Rd TWK TW1 .....136 B6
Haliday Wk IS N1 .....85 K4
Halidon Cl CLPT E5 * 68 D6
Halifax Cl TEDD TW11 .....173 K2
Halifax Rd ENC/FH EN2 .....23 J3
  GFD/PVL UB6 .....78 B6
Halifax St SYD SE26 .....163 J6
Halifield Dr BELV DA17 .....129 F3
Haling Park Gdns
  SAND/SEL CR2 .....211 H4
Haling Park Rd SAND/SEL CR2 211 J4
Haling Rd SAND/SEL CR2 .....211 K5
Halkin Ar KTBR SW1X * 15 G4
Halkin Ms KTBR SW1X * 15 G4
Halkin Pl KTBR SW1X 15 G4
Halkin St KTBR SW1X 15 H3
Hallam Cl CHST BR7 .....184 E1

Hallam Gdns PIN HA5 .....41 J3
Hallam Ms GTPST W1W 9 K1
Hallam Rd BARN SW13 .....138 E4
  SEVS/STOTM N15 .....67 H1
Hallam St GTPST W1W 9 K1
Halland Wy NTHWD HA6 .....40 B2
Hall Cl EA W5 .....98 A4
Hall Ct TEDD TW11 .....174 A1
Hall Dr SYD SE26 .....181 K1
Halley Gdns LEW SE13 .....145 G5
Halley Rd FSTGT E7 .....89 H4
Halley St POP/IOD E14 .....105 G4
Hall Farm Cl STAN HA7 .....29 H6
Hall Farm Dr WHTN TW2 .....155 J2
Hallfield Est BAY/PAD W2 * ..101 G5
Hallford Wy DART DA1 .....171 F1
Hall Gdns CHING E4 .....37 H6
Halliday Sq NWDGN UB2 .....115 J1
Halliford St IS N1 .....85 J5
Halliwell Rd BRXS/STRHM SW2 162 A1
Halliwick Court Pde
  NFNCH/WDSPK N12 * 47 K1
Hallowick Rd MUSWH N10 .....48 A4
Hall La CHING E4 .....51 H1
  HDN NW4 .....45 J5
  HYS/HAR UB3 .....133 G1
Halmead Rd SUT SM1 .....209 F1
Hall Oak Wk KIL/WHAMP NW6 ..82 D4
Hallowell Av CROY/NA CR0 .....210 E2
Hallowell Cl MTCM CR4 .....179 F6
Hallowell Rd NTHWD HA6 .....40 C3
Hallowes Crs OXHEY WD19 .....26 E5
Hallowfield Wy MTCM CR4 .....178 D6
Hall Pl BAY/PAD W2 .....2 A7
Hall Place Crs BXLY DA5 .....149 K6
Hall Rd CHDH RM6 .....73 J5
  DART DA1 .....151 J5
  EHAM E6 .....89 K6
  GPK RM2 .....57 K6
  ISLW TW7 .....135 J6
  SRTFD E15 .....88 B2
  WLGTN SM6 .....210 B6
Hallside Rd EN EN1 .....24 B1
Hall St FSBYE EC1V 6 B4
Hallsville Rd CAN/RD E16 .....106 D5
Hallswelle Pde GLDGN NW11 * ..64 D2
Hallswelle Rd GLDGN NW11 .....64 D2
The Hall BKHTH/KID SE3 .....145 K4
Hall Vw ELTH/MOT SE9 .....166 C4
Hallywell Crs EHAM E6 .....107 K4
Halons Rd ELTH/MOT SE9 .....167 F1
Halpin Pl WALW SE17 .....19 F7
Halsbrook Rd BKHTH/KID SE3 146 B4
Halsbury Cl STAN HA7 .....43 J1
Halsbury Rd SHB W12 .....118 E1
Halsbury Rd East NTHLT UB5 ..78 C2
Halsbury Rd West NTHLT UB5 ..78 B3
Halsend HYS/HAR UB3 .....114 A1
Halsey St CHEL SW3 .....14 E6
Halsham Crs BARK IG11 .....91 F4
Halsmere Rd CMBW SE5 .....142 C2
Halstead Cl CROY/NA CR0 .....211 J1
Halstead Gdns WCHMH N21 ..35 K3
Halstead Rd EN EN1 .....24 B6
  ERITH DA8 .....150 B2
  WAN E11 .....71 F2
  WCHMH N21 .....35 K3
Halston Cl BTSEA SW11 .....160 E1
Halstow Rd GNWCH SE10 .....125 K5
  WLSDN NW10 .....100 B2
Halsway HYS/HAR UB3 .....113 K1
Halton Cl FBAR/BDGN N11 .....47 K2
Halton Cross St IS N1 .....85 H6
Halton Rd IS N1 .....85 H5
Halt Pde CDALE/KGS NW9 * 63 F1
Halt Robin Rd BELV DA17 .....129 J4
Hambalt Rd CLAP SW4 .....141 H6
Hamble St RSLP HA4 .....58 C6
Hambledon WALW SE17 * 122 E6
Hambledon Gdns SNWD SE25 ..181 G6
Hambledon Pl DUL SE21 .....163 G3
Hambledon Rd
  WAND/EARL SW18 .....159 J2
Hambledown Rd
  BFN/LL DA15 * 167 J2
Hamble St FUL/PGN SW6 .....140 A4
Hambleton Cl WPK KT4 .....193 F6
Hambro Av HAYES BR2 .....199 K5
Hambrook Rd SNWD SE25 .....181 J6
Hambro Rd STRHM/NOR SW16 ..179 J2
Hambrough Rd STHL UB1 .....114 D1
Ham Common
  RCHPK/HAM TW10 .....156 E5
Ham Croft Cl FELT TW13 .....153 K5
Hamden Crs DAGE RM10 .....92 D1
Hamel Cl KTN/HRWW/WS HA3 ..43 K1
Hameway EHAM E6 .....108 A3
Ham Farm Rd
  RCHPK/HAM TW10 .....156 E6
Hamilton Av BARK/HLT IG6 .....72 D1
  CHEAM SM3 .....193 H6
  ED N9 .....36 C2
  ROM RM1 .....57 H6
  SURB KT6 .....191 H6
Hamilton Cl BERM/RHTH SE16 124 B2
  EBAR EN4 .....21 J5
  SNWD NW8 .....2 B3
  TEDD TW11 .....174 C2
  TOTM N17 .....50 B6
Hamilton Crs HSLW TW3 .....135 G6
  PLMGR N13 .....35 G6
  RYLN/HDSTN HA2 .....77 K1
Hamilton Gdns STJWD NW8 .....101 G2
Hamilton La HBRY N5 .....85 H2
Hamilton Ms MYFR/PICC W1J ..15 J2
Hamilton Pk HBRY N5 .....85 H2
Hamilton Pk West HBRY N5 .....85 H2
Hamilton Pl MYFR/PKLN W1K ..15 H1
  SUN TW16 .....172 A3

Hamilton Rd BTFD TW8 .....116 E6
  BXLYHN DA7 .....149 F3
  CHSWK W4 .....118 B3
  EA W5 .....98 A6
  EBAR EN4 .....21 J5
  ED N9 .....36 C2
  EFNCH N2 .....47 G6
  GLDGN NW11 .....64 B4
  GPK RM2 .....75 F2
  HRW HA1 .....60 E2
  HYS/HAR UB3 .....95 F6
  IL IG1 .....90 B2
  OXHEY WD19 .....27 G1
  SCUP DA14 .....168 B6
  SRTFD E15 .....106 C2
  STHL UB1 .....114 E1
  THHTH CR7 .....180 E6
  WALTH E17 .....51 G5
  WHTN TW2 .....155 K3
  WIM/MER SW19 .....178 A3
  WLSDN NW10 .....81 J3
  WNWD SE27 .....162 E6
Hamilton Road Ms
  WIM/MER SW19 * 178 A3
Hamilton Sq
  NFNCH/WDSPK N12 * 47 G2
Hamilton St DEPT SE8 .....124 D6
Hamilton Ter STJWD NW8 .....101 G2
Hamilton Wy FNCH N3 .....46 E2
  PLMGR N13 .....35 H6
  WLGTN SM6 .....210 D6
Hamlea Cl LEE/GVPK SE12 .....145 K6
Hamlet Cl CRW RM5 .....56 C3
  LEW SE13 .....145 H5
Hamlet Gdns HMSMTH W6 .....118 D4
Hamlet Rd CRW RM5 .....56 C3
  NRWD SE19 .....181 G3
Hamlet Sq CRICK NW2 .....82 C1
Hamlets Wy BOW E3 .....105 H3
The Hamlet CMBW SE5 .....142 E4
Hamlin Crs PIN HA5 .....59 G2
Hamlyn Cl EDGW HA8 .....30 A5
Hamlyn Gdns NRWD SE19 .....181 F3
Hammelton Br BMLY BR1 .....183 K5
Hammers La MLHL NW7 .....31 J6
Hammersmith Br
  HMSMTH W6 .....118 E5
  BARN SW13 .....118 E6
Hammersmith Bridge Rd
  HMSMTH W6 .....118 E5
Hammersmith Broadway
  HMSMTH W6 .....119 F4
Hammersmith Emb
  HMSMTH W6 * 119 F6
Hammersmith F/O
  HMSMTH W6 .....119 F5
Hammersmith Gv
  HMSMTH W6 .....119 F5
Hammersmith Rd
  HMSMTH W6 .....119 G4
Hammersmith Ter
  HMSMTH W6 .....118 D5
Hammerton Cl BXLY DA5 .....170 B5
Hammet Cl YEAD UB4 .....95 H4
Hammet St TWRH EC3N 13 J5
Hammond Av MTCM CR4 .....179 G5
Hammond Cl BAR EN5 .....20 C6
  GFD/PVL UB6 .....78 D3
  HPTN TW12 .....173 F4
Hammond Rd EN EN1 .....24 D4
  NWDGN UB2 .....114 D3
Hammonds Cl BCTR RM8 .....91 J1
Hammond St KTTN NW5 .....84 C4
Hamonde Cl EDGW HA8 .....30 D4
Ham Park Rd FSTGT E7 .....88 E5
Hampden Av BECK BR3 .....182 B5
Hampden Cl CAMTN NW1 .....4 D3
Hampden Gurney St
  MBLAR W1H * 8 E4
Hampden La TOTM N17 .....50 C4
Hampden Rd ARCH N19 .....66 D2
  BECK BR3 .....182 B5
  CEND/HSY/T N8 .....67 G1
  KTN/HRWW/WS HA3 .....42 C4
  KUT/HW KT1 .....175 G6
  MUSWH N10 .....48 A3
  TOTM N17 .....50 C4
Hampden Sq
  NFNCH/WDSPK N12 * 47 F1
Hampden Wy STHGT/OAK N14 ..34 B3
Hampermill La OXHEY WD19 ..26 E3
Hampshire Cl UED N18 .....50 D1
Hampshire Hog La
  HMSMTH W6 * 118 E4
Hampshire Rd WDGN N22 .....49 F3
Hampshire St KTTN NW5 * 84 D4
Hampson Wy VX/NE SW8 .....142 A2
Hampstead Av WFD IG8 .....54 A3
Hampstead Cl THMD SE28 .....128 C1
Hampstead Gdns GLDGN NW11 64 E3
  CHDH RM6 .....73 H2
Hampstead Gn HAMP NW3 .....83 J3
Hampstead Gv HAMP NW3 .....83 G2
Hampstead Hill Gdns
  HAMP NW3 .....83 J2
Hampstead La HGT N6 .....65 K4
Hampstead Rd CAMTN NW1 * ..4 A4
Hampstead Sq HAMP NW3 .....83 G1
Hampstead Wy GLDGN NW11 ..64 E2
Hampton Cl FBAR/BDGN N11 ..48 A1
  KIL/WHAMP NW6 .....100 E2
  RYNPK SW20 .....177 F5
Hampton Court Av
  E/WMO/HCT KT8 .....189 J3
Hampton Court Crs
  E/WMO/HCT KT8 .....173 J6
Hampton Court Cresent
  E/WMO/HCT KT8 .....173 J6
Hampton Court Est
  THDIT KT7 * 189 K7
Hampton Court Rd
  E/WMO/HCT KT8 .....173 K6
  E/WMO/HCT KT8 .....173 K6
Hampton Court Wy
  E/WMO/HCT KT8 .....189 K1

Hampton La FELT TW13 .....154 D6
Hampton Ri
  KTN/HRWW/WS HA3 .....62 A3
Hampton Rd CHING E4 .....51 H1
  CROY/NA CR0 .....196 D3
  FSTGT E7 .....89 F3
  IL IG1 .....90 C2
  TEDD TW11 .....173 J1
  WAN E11 .....70 B5
  WHTN TW2 .....155 J5
  WPK KT4 .....192 D6
Hampton Rd East FELT TW13 ..154 E6
Hampton Rd West FELT TW13 ..154 D4
Hampton St WALW SE17 .....18 B7
Ham Ridings
  RCHPK/HAM TW10 .....175 G5
Ham Shades Cl BFN/LL DA15 ..168 A5
Ham St RCHPK/HAM TW10 .....156 D4
The Ham BTFD TW8 .....136 D1
Ham Vw CROY/NA CR0 .....198 B3
Ham Yd SOHO/SHAV W1D * 10 C5
Hanameel St CAN/RD E16 .....125 K1
Hanbury Cl HDN NW4 .....46 A6
Hanbury Dr WCHMH N21 .....23 F5
Hanbury Ms IS N1 .....6 E1
Hanbury Rd ACT W3 .....117 H2
  TOTM N17 .....50 D5
Hanbury St WCHPL E1 .....13 K1
Hancock Rd BOW E3 .....106 A2
  NRWD SE19 .....180 E2
Handa Wk IS N1 .....85 K4
Hand Ct HHOL WC1V 11 H2
Handcroft Rd CROY/NA CR0 .....196 C5
Handel Cl EDGW HA8 .....44 B2
Handel Pde EDGW HA8 * 44 C2
Handel Pl WLSDN NW10 .....81 F4
Handel St BMSBY WC1N 5 F5
Handen Rd LEE/GVPK SE12 .....145 H6
Handforth Rd BRXN/ST SW9 ..142 B1
  IL IG1 .....90 B2
Handley Gv CRICK NW2 .....82 B1
Handley Page Rd WLGTN SM6 ..211 F5
Handley Rd HOM E9 .....86 E6
Handowe Cl HDN NW4 .....63 J1
Handside Cl WPK KT4 .....193 G5
Hands Wk CAN/RD E16 .....106 E5
Handsworth Av CHING E4 .....38 B6
Handsworth Cl OXHEY WD19 ..26 E5
Handsworth Rd TOTM N17 .....49 K6
Handtrough Wy BARK IG11 ..108 B1
Hanford Cl WAND/EARL SW18 159 K3
Hangar La (North Circular Rd)
  EA W5 .....98 A3
Hangar Ruding OXHEY WD19 ..27 K5
Hanger Gn EA W5 .....98 C3
Hanger La EA W5 .....98 B6
Hanger La (North Circular
Road) EA W5 .....98 A2
Hanger Vale La EA W5 .....98 A5
Hanger View Wy ACT W3 .....98 C5
Hankins La MLHL NW7 .....31 F3
Hanley Gdns FSBYPK N4 .....66 E5
Hanley Pl BECK BR3 .....182 D3
Hanley Rd FSBYPK N4 .....66 E5
Hanmer Wk HOLWY N7 .....67 F3
Hannah Cl BECK BR3 .....182 E6
  WLSDN NW10 .....80 D2
Hannah Mary Wy
  STHWK SE1 * 123 H4
Hannards Wy BARK/HLT IG6 ..55 H4
Hannay La ARCH N19 .....66 D4
Hannell Rd FUL/PGN SW6 .....139 H1
Hannen Rd WNWD SE27 * 162 C5
Hannibal Rd STWL/WRAY TW19 152 C2
  WCHPL E1 .....104 E4
Hannibal Wy CROY/NA CR0 .....211 F3
Hannington Rd CLAP SW4 .....141 G4
Hanover Av CAN/RD E16 .....125 K1
  FELT TW13 .....153 K3
Hanover Cir HYS/HAR UB3 .....94 A5
Hanover Cl CHEAM SM3 .....208 C2
  RCH/KEW TW9 .....137 H1
Hanover Dr CHST BR7 .....185 H1
Hanover Gdns BARK/HLT IG6 ..54 C3
  LBTH SE11 .....122 B6
Hanover Pk PECK SE15 .....143 H2
Hanover Rd SEVS/STOTM N15 ..68 B1
  WIM/MER SW19 .....178 A3
  WLSDN NW10 .....82 A5
Hanover Sq CONDST W1S 9 K4
Hanover Steps BAY/PAD W2 * ..8 D4
Hanover St CONDST W1S 9 K4
  CROY/NA CR0 .....211 H1
Hanover Ter CAMTN NW1 * 2 E5
Hanover Terrace Ms
  CAMTN NW1 * 2 E5
Hanover Wy BXLYHS DA6 .....148 E4
Hansard Ms WKENS W14 .....119 G2
Hans Crs KTBR SW1X 14 E4
Hanselin Cl STAN HA7 .....43 F1
Hansen Dr WCHMH N21 .....23 F5
Hanshaw Dr EDGW HA8 .....45 F4
Hansler Gv E/WMO/HCT KT8 ..189 J2
Hansler Rd EDUL SE22 .....143 G6
Hansol Rd BXLYHS DA6 .....149 F6
Hansom Ter BMLY BR1 * 184 A4
Hanson Cl BAL SW12 .....161 G2
  BECK BR3 .....182 E2
  MORT/ESHN SW14 .....137 K4
  WDR/YW UB7 .....112 C3
Hanson Gdns STHL UB1 .....114 D2
Hanson St GTPST W1W 10 A1
Hans Pl KTBR SW1X 14 E4
Hans Rd CHEL SW3 .....14 E5
Hanway Pl FITZ W1T 10 C2
Hanway Rd HNWL W7 .....96 D5
Hanway St FITZ W1T 10 C3
Hanworth Rd HPTN TW12 .....154 E6
  HSLW TW3 .....135 G5
  HSLWW TW4 .....154 D2
Hanworth Ter HSLW TW3 .....135 G5

Hapgood Cl GFD/PVL UB6 .....78 D3
Harben Pde HAMP NW3 * 83 H5
Harben Rd KIL/WHAMP NW6 ..83 G5
Harberson Rd BAL SW12 .....161 G3
  SRTFD E15 .....88 D6
Harberton Rd ARCH N19 .....66 C5
Harbet Rd BAY/PAD W2 .....8 B2
  UED N18 .....51 F1
Harbex Cl BXLY DA5 .....169 J2
Harbinger Rd POP/IOD E14 .....124 E4
Harbledown Pl
  STMC/STPC BR5 * 202 D1
Harbledown Rd FUL/PGN SW6 139 K2
  SAND/SEL CR2 .....212 E3
Harbord Cl CMBW SE5 .....142 E3
Harbord St FUL/PGN SW6 .....139 G2
Harborne Cl OXHEY WD19 .....41 G1
Harborough Av BFN/LL DA15 ..167 K2
Harborough Rd
  STRHM/NOR SW16 .....162 A6
Harbour Av WBPTN SW10 .....140 B2
Harbourer Rd BARK/HLT IG6 ..55 H1
Harbour Exchange Sq
  POP/IOD E14 .....124 E2
Harbour Rd CMBW SE5 .....142 D4
Harbour Yd WBPTN SW10 * 140 B2
Harbridge Av PUT/ROE SW15 ..158 D2
Harbury Rd CAR SM5 .....209 J6
Harbut Rd BTSEA SW11 .....140 C5
Harcastle Cl YEAD UB4 .....95 H3
Harcombe Rd STNW/STAM N16..86 A1
Harcourt Av BFN/LL DA15 .....168 D1
  EDGW HA8 .....30 E5
  MNPK E12 .....89 K2
  WLGTN SM6 .....210 B2
Harcourt Buildings EMB EC4Y *..11 J5
Harcourt Cl ISLW TW7 .....136 B4
Harcourt Fld WLGTN SM6 .....210 B2
Harcourt Ms GPK RM2 .....75 K1
Harcourt Rd BROCKY SE4 .....144 C5
  BXLYHS DA6 .....149 F5
  SRTFD E15 .....106 D1
  THHTH CR7 .....196 A3
  WDGN N22 .....48 D4
  WIM/MER SW19 .....177 K3
  WLGTN SM6 .....210 B2
Harcourt St MBLAR W1H 8 D2
Harcourt Ter WBPTN SW10 .....120 A5
Hardcastle Cl CROY/NA CR0 .....197 H3
Hardcourts Cl WWKM BR4 .....213 K2
Hardel Ri BRXS/STRHM SW2 ..162 C3
Hardel Wk BRXS/STRHM SW2 162 B2
Hardens Manorway
  WOOL/PLUM SE18 .....126 C3
Harders Rd PECK SE15 .....143 J3
Hardess St HNHL SE24 .....142 D4
Hardie Cl WLSDN NW10 .....81 F3
Hardie Rd DAGE RM10 .....92 E1
Harding Cl CROY/NA CR0 .....212 B1
  KUTN/CMB KT2 .....175 F2
  WALW SE17 .....122 D6
Harding Rd BXLYHN DA7 .....149 G3
Hardinge Crs
  WOOL/PLUM SE18 .....127 G3
Hardinge Rd PGE/AN SE20 * ..182 A4
Hardinge St WCHPL E1 .....104 E5
Hardman Rd CHARL SE7 .....126 A5
  KUTN/CMB KT2 .....175 F5
Hardres Ter STMC/STPC BR5 ..202 C1
Hardwick Cl STAN HA7 .....43 J1
Hardwicke Av HEST TW5 .....135 F2
Hardwicke Ms FSBYW WC1X *..5 H5
Hardwicke Rd CHSWK W4 .....118 A4
  PLMGR N13 .....48 E1
  RCHPK/HAM TW10 .....156 D6
Hardwick Gn WEA W13 .....97 H3
Hardwick Pl
  STRHM/NOR SW16 .....179 H3
Hardwicks Wy
  WAND/EARL SW18 .....139 K6
Hardwidge St STHWK SE1 .....19 G2
Hardy Av CAN/RD E16 .....125 K1
  RSLP HA4 .....77 F3
Hardy Cl BAR EN5 .....20 C6
  BERM/RHTH SE16 .....124 A2
  PIN HA5 .....59 H4
Hardy Cottages
  GNWCH SE10 * 125 G6
Hardy Gv DART DA1 .....151 K5
Hardy Pas WDGN N22 .....49 F4
Hardy Rd BKHTH/KID SE3 .....125 J6
  CHING E4 .....51 J3
  WIM/MER SW19 .....178 A3
Hardys Ms E/WMO/HCT KT8 ..189 K1
Hardy Wy ENC/FH EN2 .....23 F1
Hare & Billet Rd
  BKHTH/KID SE3 .....145 G2
Harebell Dr EHAM E6 .....108 A4
Hare Ct EMB EC4Y * 11 J4
Harecourt Rd IS N1 .....85 J4
Haredale Rd HNHL SE24 .....142 D5
Haredon Cl FSTH SE23 .....164 A2
Harefield ESH/CLAY KT10 .....204 E1
Harefield Av BELMT SM2 .....208 C6
Harefield Cl ENC/FH EN2 .....23 F1
Harefield Ms BROCKY SE4 .....144 C4
Harefield Rd BROCKY SE4 .....144 C4
  CEND/HSY/T N8 .....66 D2
  SCUP DA14 .....168 D2
  STRHM/NOR SW16 .....180 A3
Hare Hall La GPK RM2 .....75 K1
Hare La ESH/CLAY KT10 .....204 C4
Hare Marsh BETH E2 .....104 C3
Hare Rw BETH E2 .....104 D1
Haresfield Rd DAGE RM10 .....92 C4
Hare St WOOL/PLUM SE18 .....127 F3
Harewood Av MRYLBN NW1 ..2 D7
  NTHLT UB5 .....77 J5
Harewood Cl NTHLT UB5 .....77 K5
Harewood Dr CLAY IG5 .....53 K5
Harewood Pl CONDST W1S 9 K4
Harewood Rd ISLW TW7 .....136 A1
  OXHEY WD19 .....27 F5

SAND/SEL CR2 ... 212 A4
WIM/MER SW19 ... 178 D2
Harewood Rw CAMTN NW1 ... 8 D1
Harewood Ter NWDGN UB2 ... 114 E4
Harfield Gdns CMBW SE5 * ... 143 F4
Harfield Rd SUN TW16 ... 172 C5
Harford Cl CHING E4 ... 37 K2
Harford Rd CHING E4 ... 37 K2
Harford St WCHPL E1 ... 105 G3
Harford Wk EFNCH N2 ... 65 H1
Harfst Wy SWLY BR8 ... 187 K4
Harglaze Ter CDALE/KGS NW9 * ... 45 G6
Hargood Cl
KTN/HRWW/WS HA3 ... 62 A3
Hargood Rd BKHTH/KID SE3 ... 146 B2
Hargrave Pk ARCH N19 ... 66 C6
Hargrave Pl KTTN NW5 ... 84 D3
Hargrave Rd ARCH N19 ... 66 C6
Hargwyne St BRXN/ST SW9 ... 142 A4
Haringey Pk CEND/HSY/T N8 ... 66 E3
Haringey Rd CEND/HSY/T N8 ... 66 E1
Harington Ter UED N18 * ... 35 K6
Harkett Cl KTN/HRWW/WS HA3 ... 43 F5
Harland Av BFN/LL DA15 ... 167 J5
CROY/NA CR0 ... 212 C1
Harland Cl WIM/MER SW19 ... 178 A6
Harland Rd LEE/GVPK SE12 ... 165 K3
Harlands Gv ORP BR6 ... 216 B2
Harlech Gdns HEST TW5 ... 114 C6
PIN HA5 ... 59 H4
Harlech Rd STHGT/OAK N14 ... 34 E5
Harlequin Av BTFD TW8 ... 116 B6
Harlequin Cl ISLW TW7 ... 135 K6
YEAD UB4 ... 95 H4
Harlequin Ct EA W5 * ... 97 J6
Harlequin Rd TEDD TW11 * ... 174 C3
Harlescott Rd PECK SE15 ... 144 A5
Harlesden Gdns WLSDN NW10 ... 81 H6
Harlesden Rd WLSDN NW10 ... 81 K6
Harley Cl ALP/SUD HA0 * ... 79 K4
Harley Crs HRW HA1 ... 60 D1
Harleyford BMLY BR1 ... 184 B4
Harleyford Rd LBTH SE11 ... 122 A6
Harleyford St LBTH SE11 ... 122 A6
Harley Gdns ORP BR6 ... 216 E2
WBPTN SW10 ... 120 B5
Harley Gv BOW E3 ... 105 H2
Harley Pl CAVSQ/HST W1G ... 9 J2
Harley Rd HAMP NW3 ... 83 H5
HRW HA1 ... 60 D1
WLSDN NW10 ... 99 G1
Harley St CAVSQ/HST W1G ... 9 J1
Harley Vls WLSDN NW10 * ... 99 G1
Harlinger St WOOL/PLUM SE18 ... 126 D3
Harlington Cl HYS/HAR UB3 ... 133 F1
Harlington Rd BXLYHN DA7 ... 149 G4
Harlington Rd East
EBED/NFELT TW14 ... 154 A2
Harlington Rd West
EBED/NFELT TW14 ... 154 A1
Harlow Gdns CRW RM5 ... 56 E2
Harlow Rd PLMGR N13 ... 35 K5
RAIN RM13 ... 93 H6
Harlyn Dr PIN HA5 ... 41 F6
Harman Av WFD IG8 ... 52 D3
Harman Cl CHING E4 ... 38 B6
CRICK NW2 ... 82 C1
STHWK SE1 * ... 123 H5
Harman Dr BFN/LL DA15 ... 168 A1
CRICK NW2 ... 82 C1
Harman Rd EN EN1 ... 24 B6
Harmondsworth La
WDR/YW UB7 ... 112 B6
Harmondsworth Rd
WDR/YW UB7 ... 112 B4
Harmony Cl GLDGN NW11 ... 64 C2
WLGTN SM6 ... 210 E6
Harmony Pl STHWK SE1 ... 123 G5
Harmony Wy BMLY BR1 ... 183 K5
HDN NW4 ... 64 A1
Harmood Gv CAMTN NW1 ... 84 B5
Harmood St CAMTN NW1 ... 84 B4
Harmsworth Ms STHWK SE1 ... 17 K5
Harmsworth St LBTH SE11 ... 122 C6
Harmsworth Wy
TRDG/WHET N20 ... 32 D3
Harness Rd THMD SE28 ... 128 B2
Harold Av BELV DA17 ... 129 G5
HYS/HAR UB3 ... 113 J3
Harold Rd CEND/HSY/T N8 ... 67 F2
CHING E4 ... 38 A5
NRWD SE19 ... 180 E3
PLSTW E13 ... 89 F6
RDART DA2 ... 171 J6
SEVS/STOTM N15 ... 68 B2
SUT SM1 ... 209 H2
WAN E11 ... 70 C5
WFD IG8 ... 52 E4
WLSDN NW10 ... 99 F2
Haroldstone Rd WALTH E17 ... 69 F2
Harpenden Rd MNPK E12 ... 71 G6
WNWD SE27 ... 162 C4
Harper Cl STHGT/OAK N14 ... 22 C6
Harper Rd EHAM E6 ... 107 K5
STHWK SE1 ... 18 D4
Harpers Yd ISLW TW7 * ... 136 A3
TOTM N17 ... 50 B4
Harp Island Cl WLSDN NW10 ... 63 F6
Harp La MON EC3R ... 13 G6
Harpley Sq WCHPL E1 ... 104 E3
Harpour Rd BARK IG11 ... 90 C4
Harp Rd HNWL W7 ... 97 F3
Harpsden St BTSEA SW11 ... 141 F2
Harpur Ms BMSBY WC1N ... 11 G1
Harpur St BMSBY WC1N ... 11 G1
Harraden Rd BKHTH/KID SE3 ... 146 B2
Harrier Cl HCH RM12 ... 93 K4
Harrier Ms THMD SE28 ... 127 J2
Harrier Rd CDALE/KGS NW9 ... 45 G5
Harriers Cl EA W5 ... 98 A6
Harrier Wy EHAM E6 ... 107 K4
Harries Rd YEAD UB4 ... 95 G3
Harriet Cl HACK E8 ... 86 C6
Harriet Gdns CROY/NA CR0 ... 197 H6
Harriet St KTBR SW1X ... 15 F3
Harriet Tubman Cl
BRXS/STRHM SW2 ... 162 B2
Harriet Wk KTBR SW1X ... 15 F3
Harriet Wy BUSH WD23 ... 28 D2
Harringay Gdns
CEND/HSY/T N8 ... 67 H2
Harringay Rd SEVS/STOTM N15 ... 67 H2
Harrington Cl CROY/NA CR0 ... 195 K6
WLSDN NW10 ... 81 F1
Harrington Ct NKENS W10 * ... 100 D2
Harrington Gdns SKENS SW7 ... 120 A4
Harrington Hl CLPT E5 ... 68 D5
Harrington Rd SKENS SW7 ... 14 A6
SNWD SE25 ... 197 H1
WAN E11 ... 70 C5
Harrington Sq CAMTN NW1 ... 4 A2
Harrington St CAMTN NW1 ... 4 A4
Harrington Wy
WOOL/PLUM SE18 ... 126 C3
Harriott Cl GNWCH SE10 ... 125 J4
Harris Cl ENC/FH EN2 ... 23 H2
HSLW TW3 ... 135 F2
Harrison Cl NTHWD HA6 ... 40 A2
TRDG/WHET N20 ... 33 J3
Harrison Rd DAGE RM10 ... 92 D4
WLSDN NW10 ... 81 F6
Harrison's Ri CROY/NA CR0 ... 211 H1
Harrison St STPAN WC1H ... 5 F5
Harrisons Whf PUR RM19 ... 131 K5
Harris Rd BXLYHN DA7 ... 149 F2
DAGW RM9 ... 92 B3
Harris St CMBW SE5 ... 142 E1
WALTH E17 ... 69 H4
Harrods Gn EDGW HA8 ... 44 C1
Harrogate Rd OXHEY WD19 ... 27 G5
Harrold Rd BCTR RM8 ... 91 H3
Harrow Av EN EN1 ... 36 B1
Harroway Rd BTSEA SW11 ... 140 C3
Harrowby St MBLAR W1H ... 8 E3
Harrow Cl CHSGTN KT9 ... 205 K5
Harrow Crs HARH RM3 ... 57 K3
Harrowdene Cl ALP/SUD HA0 ... 79 K2
Harrowdene Gdns TEDD TW11 ... 174 B3
Harrowdene Rd ALP/SUD HA0 ... 79 K2
Harrow Dr ED N9 ... 36 B3
Harrowes Meade EDGW HA8 ... 30 C5
Harrow Fields Gdns HRW HA1 ... 78 E1
Harrow Gdns ORP BR6 ... 217 H2
Harrowgate Rd HOM E9 ... 87 G5
Harrow Gn WAN E11 ... 88 C1
Harrow La POP/IOD E14 ... 106 A6
Harrow Manor Wy ABYW SE2 ... 128 D1
Harrow Pk HRW HA1 ... 60 E6
Harrow Pl WCHPL E1 ... 13 H3
Harrow Rd ALP/SUD HA0 ... 79 C2
BARK IG11 ... 90 E6
CAR SM5 ... 209 J4
EBED/NFELT TW14 ... 152 D4
IL IG1 ... 90 C2
MV/WKIL W9 ... 100 E3
WAN E11 ... 88 D1
WBLY HA9 ... 80 B3
WLSDN NW10 ... 99 K2
Harrow Road F/O BAY/PAD W2 ... 8 B2
Harrow St CAMTN NW1 * ... 8 D1
Harrow Vw HGDN/ICK UB10 ... 94 A2
HYS/HAR UB3 ... 94 E6
RYLN/HDSTN HA2 ... 42 D6
Harrow View Rd EA W5 ... 97 H3
Harrow Wy OXHEY WD19 ... 27 J5
Harrow Weald Pk
KTN/HRWW/WS HA3 ... 42 D2
Harston Dr PEND EN3 ... 25 J1
Hartcliff Ct HNWL W7 * ... 116 A2
Hart Crs CHIG IG7 ... 55 F1
Hart Dyke Rd
STMC/STPC BR5 ... 202 D6
Harte Rd HSLW TW3 ... 134 E3
Hartfield Av NTHLT UB5 ... 95 F1
Hartfield Crs WIM/MER SW19 ... 177 J3
WWKM BR4 ... 214 E1
Hartfield Gv PGE/AN SE20 ... 181 J4
Hartfield Rd CHSGTN KT9 ... 205 K3
WIM/MER SW19 ... 177 J3
WWKM BR4 ... 214 E2
Hartfield Ter BOW E3 ... 105 J1
Hartford Av
KTN/HRWW/WS HA3 ... 43 G6
Hartford Rd BXLY DA5 ... 169 H1
HOR/WEW KT19 ... 206 D4
Hart Gv EA W5 ... 117 H1
STHL UB1 ... 96 A4
Hartham Cl HOLWY N7 ... 84 E3
ISLW TW7 ... 136 B2
Hartham Rd HOLWY N7 ... 84 E3
ISLW TW7 ... 136 A2
TOTM N17 ... 50 B5
Harting Rd ELTH/MOT SE9 ... 166 D6
Hartington Cl HRW HA1 ... 78 E2
ORP BR6 ... 216 C3
Hartington Rd CAN/RD E16 ... 107 F5
CHSWK W4 ... 137 K2
NWDGN UB2 * ... 114 D3
TWK TW1 ... 156 C2
VX/NE SW8 ... 141 K2
WALTH E17 ... 69 G3
WEA W13 ... 97 H6
Hartismere Rd FUL/PGN SW6 ... 139 J1
Hartlake Rd HOM E9 ... 87 F4
Hartland Cl EDGW HA8 ... 30 C4
WCHMH N21 ... 35 J1
Hartland Dr EDGW HA8 ... 30 C4
RSLP HA4 ... 77 F1
Hartland Rd CAMTN NW1 * ... 84 B5
FBAR/BDGN N11 ... 47 K1
HCH RM12 ... 75 J6
HPTN TW12 ... 155 G6
ISLW TW7 ... 136 B4
KIL/WHAMP NW6 ... 100 D1
MRDN SM4 ... 193 K4
SRTFD E15 ... 88 D5
Hartland Road Arches
CAMTN NW1 * ... 84 A5
Hartlands Cl BXLY DA5 ... 169 G1
The Hartlands HEST TW5 ... 114 A6
Hartland Wy CROY/NA CR0 ... 198 B6
MRDN SM4 ... 193 K4
Hartley Av EHAM E6 ... 89 J6
MLHL NW7 ... 45 H1
Hartley Cl BMLY BR1 ... 184 E5
MLHL NW7 ... 45 H1
Hartley Rd CROY/NA CR0 ... 196 D4
WAN E11 ... 70 D5
WELL DA16 ... 148 D1
Hartley St BETH E2 ... 104 E2
Hartmann Rd CAN/RD E16 ... 126 C1
Hartnoll St HOLWY N7 ... 85 F3
Harton Cl BMLY BR1 ... 184 C4
Harton Rd ED N9 ... 36 D4
Harton St DEPT SE8 ... 144 D2
Hartsbourne Av BUSH WD23 ... 28 C4
Hartsbourne Cl BUSH WD23 ... 28 D4
Hartsbourne Rd BUSH WD23 ... 28 D4
Hartscroft CROY/NA CR0 ... 213 G6
Harts Gv WFD IG8 ... 52 E1
Hartshorn Gdns EHAM E6 ... 108 A3
Harts La BARK IG11 ... 90 B5
NWCR SE14 ... 144 B1
Hartslock Dr ABYW SE2 ... 128 E2
Hartsmead Rd ELTH/MOT SE9 ... 166 E4
Hart Sq MRDN SM4 * ... 194 A2
Hart St MON EC3R ... 13 H5
Hartsway PEND EN3 ... 24 D5
Hartswood Gdns SHB W12 * ... 118 C3
Hartswood Gn BUSH WD23 ... 28 D4
Hartswood Rd SHB W12 ... 118 C3
Hartsworth Cl PLSTW E13 ... 106 D1
Hartville Rd WOOL/PLUM SE18 ... 127 K4
Hartwell Dr CHING E4 ... 52 A2
Hartwell St HACK E8 ... 86 B4
Harvard Hl CHSWK W4 ... 117 J5
Harvard Rd CHSWK W4 ... 117 J5
ISLW TW7 ... 135 K2
LEW SE13 ... 145 F6
Harvel Cl CHST BR7 ... 186 B6
Harvel Crs ABYW SE2 ... 128 E5
Harvest Bank Rd WWKM BR4 ... 214 E1
Harvesters Cl ISLW TW7 ... 135 J6
Harvest La LOU IG10 ... 39 H2
THDIT KT7 ... 190 B3
Harvest Rd FELT TW13 ... 153 K6
Harvest Wy SWLY BR8 ... 203 K4
Harvey Dr HPTN TW12 ... 173 G4
Harvey Gdns CHARL SE7 ... 126 B5
Harvey Rd CEND/HSY/T N8 ... 67 F2
CMBW SE5 ... 142 E2
HSLWW TW4 ... 154 E2
IL IG1 ... 90 B3
NTHLT UB5 ... 77 G5
WAN E11 ... 70 C5
Harvey's La ROMW/RG RM7 ... 75 G6
Harvey St IS N1 ... 7 F1
Harvill Rd SCUP DA14 ... 186 E1
Harvington Wk HACK E8 * ... 86 C5
Harvist Rd KIL/WHAMP NW6 ... 100 C1
Harwell Cl RSLP HA4 ... 58 B5
Harwood Av BMLY BR1 ... 184 A5
MTCM CR4 ... 178 D6
Harwood Cl ALP/SUD HA0 ... 79 K2
NFNCH/WDSPK N12 ... 47 J2
Harwood Ms FUL/PGN SW6 * ... 140 A1
Harwood Rd FUL/PGN SW6 ... 139 K1
Harwood Ter FUL/PGN SW6 ... 140 A2
Hascombe Ter CMBW SE5 * ... 142 E3
Haselbury Rd ED N9 ... 36 A5
Haseley End FSTH SE23 * ... 163 K2
Haselrigge Rd CLAP SW4 ... 141 J5
Haseltine Rd SYD SE26 ... 164 C6
Haselwood Dr ENC/FH EN2 ... 23 H5
Haskard Rd DAGW RM9 ... 91 K2
Hasker St CHEL SW3 ... 14 D6
Haslam Av CHEAM SM3 ... 193 H5
Haslam Cl HGDN/ICK UB10 ... 58 A6
IS N1 ... 85 G5
Haslam St PECK SE15 ... 143 G2
Haslemere Av EBAR EN4 ... 33 K3
HDN NW4 ... 64 B3
HEST TW5 ... 134 B3
HNWL W7 ... 116 B3
MTCM CR4 ... 178 C5
WAND/EARL SW18 ... 160 A4
Haslemere Cl HPTN TW12 ... 172 E1
WLGTN SM6 ... 210 E3
Haslemere Gdns FNCH N3 ... 64 C1
Haslemere Heathrow Est
HSLWW TW4 * ... 134 A3
Haslemere Rd BXLYHN DA7 ... 149 G3
CEND/HSY/T N8 ... 66 E4
GDMY/SEVK IG3 ... 73 F6
THHTH CR7 ... 196 C2
WCHMH N21 ... 35 H4
Hasler Cl THMD SE28 ... 109 J6
Hasluck Gdns BAR EN5 ... 33 G1
Hassard St BETH E2 ... 7 K3
Hassendean Rd
BKHTH/KID SE3 ... 126 A6
Hassett Rd HOM E9 ... 87 F4
Hassocks Cl SYD SE26 ... 163 J5
Hassocks Rd
STRHM/NOR SW16 ... 179 J4
Hassock Wd HAYES BR2 ... 215 H2
Hassop Rd CRICK NW2 ... 82 B2
Hasted Rd CHARL SE7 ... 126 C5
Hastings Av BARK/HLT IG6 ... 72 C1
Hastings Cl ALP/SUD HA0 ... 79 J2
BAR EN5 ... 21 G5
PECK SE15 * ... 143 H1
Hastings Dr SURB KT6 ... 190 D3
Hastings Pl CROY/NA CR0 ... 197 G5
Hastings Rd CROY/NA CR0 ... 197 G5
FBAR/BDGN N11 ... 48 C1
GPK RM2 ... 75 K2
HAYES BR2 ... 200 D6
TOTM N17 * ... 49 K6
WEA W13 ... 97 H6
Hastings St STPAN WC1H ... 4 E5
Hastings Ter
SEVS/STOTM N15 * ... 67 J2
Hastings St WOOL/PLUM SE18 ... 127 H3
Hastoe Cl YEAD UB4 ... 95 J3
Hatcham Park Ms NWCR SE14 ... 144 A2
Hatcham Park Rd NWCR SE14 ... 144 A2
Hatcham Rd PECK SE15 ... 123 K6
Hatchard Rd ARCH N19 ... 66 D6
Hatchcroft HDN NW4 ... 45 K6
Hatchers Ms STHWK SE1 ... 19 H3
Hatchett Rd
EBED/NFELT TW14 ... 153 F3
Hatch Gv CHDH RM6 ... 74 A1
Hatch La CHING E4 ... 38 C6
WDR/YW UB7 ... 132 A1
Hatch Pl KUTN/CMB KT2 ... 175 G1
Hatch Rd STRHM/NOR SW16 ... 179 K5
Hatch Side CHIG IG7 ... 54 A1
The Hatch PEND EN3 ... 25 F2
Hatchwoods WFD IG8 ... 38 D6
Hatcliffe Cl BKHTH/KID SE3 ... 145 J4
Hatcliffe St GNWCH SE10 ... 125 J5
Hatfield Cl BARK/HLT IG6 ... 54 B6
BELMT SM2 ... 208 E6
MTCM CR4 * ... 194 C1
Hatfield Ct BKHTH/KID SE3 * ... 145 K1
Hatfield Rd CHSWK W4 ... 118 A2
HNWL W7 ... 116 B1
SRTFD E15 ... 88 C3
Hatfields STHWK SE1 ... 11 K7
Hathaway Cl BARK/HLT IG6 ... 54 B2
HAYES BR2 ... 200 E5
RSLP HA4 ... 76 D2
STAN HA7 ... 43 G1
Hathaway Crs MNPK E12 ... 90 A4
Hathaway Gdns CHDH RM6 ... 73 K2
WEA W13 ... 97 G4
Hathaway Rd CROY/NA CR0 ... 196 C4
Hatherleigh Cl CHSGTN KT9 ... 205 K3
EBAR EN4 ... 21 F2
MRDN SM4 ... 193 K1
Hatherleigh Rd RSLP HA4 ... 58 E6
Hatherley Crs BFN/LL DA15 ... 168 B4
Hatherley Gdns
CEND/HSY/T N8 ... 66 E3
EHAM E6 ... 107 H2
Hatherley Gv BAY/PAD W2 ... 101 F5
Hatherley Ms WALTH E17 ... 69 J1
Hatherley Rd RCH/KEW TW9 ... 137 G2
SCUP DA14 ... 168 B5
WALTH E17 ... 69 H1
Hatherley St WEST SW1P ... 16 B7
Hathern Gdns ELTH/MOT SE9 ... 167 F6
Hatherop Rd HPTN TW12 ... 172 E3
Hathorne Cl PECK SE15 ... 143 J3
Hathorne Ter ARCH N19 * ... 66 D5
Hathway St PECK SE15 ... 143 K3
Hatley Av BARK/HLT IG6 ... 72 C1
Hatley Cl FBAR/BDGN N11 ... 47 K1
Hatley Rd FSBYPK N4 ... 67 F6
Hat & Mitre Ct FARR EC1M ... 6 B7
Hatteraick St
BERM/RHTH SE16 ... 123 K2
Hattersfield Cl BELV DA17 ... 129 G4
Hatters La WATW WD18 ... 26 B1
Hatton Cl WOOL/PLUM SE18 ... 147 J1
Hatton Cross Est
HTHAIR TW6 * ... 133 J5
Hatton Gdn HCIRC EC1N ... 11 K1
Hatton Gdns MTCM CR4 ... 194 E2
Hatton Gn EBED/NFELT TW14 ... 133 K5
Hatton Gv WDR/YW UB7 * ... 112 A2
Hatton Pl HCIRC EC1N ... 5 K7
Hatton Rd CROY/NA CR0 ... 196 B5
EBED/NFELT TW14 ... 153 F2
HTHAIR TW6 ... 133 J5
Hatton Rw STJWD NW8 * ... 2 B7
Hatton St STJWD NW8 ... 2 B7
Hatton Wall HCIRC EC1N ... 11 J1
Haunch of Venison Yd
OXSTW W1C * ... 9 J4
Havana Cl ROM RM1 ... 75 G2
Havana Rd WIM/MER SW19 ... 159 K4
Havannah St POP/IOD E14 ... 124 D2
Havant Rd WALTH E17 ... 52 A6
Havelock Cl SHB W12 * ... 99 K6
Havelock Pl HRW HA1 ... 60 E3
Havelock Rd BELV DA17 * ... 129 G4
CROY/NA CR0 ... 197 G6
DART DA1 ... 170 E2
HAYES BR2 ... 200 B1
KTN/HRWW/WS HA3 ... 42 E6
NWDGN UB2 ... 114 D3
TOTM N17 ... 50 C5
WIM/MER SW19 ... 178 B1
Havelock St IS N1 ... 84 E6
Havelock Ter VX/NE SW8 ... 141 G1
Havelock Wk FSTH SE23 ... 163 K3
Haven Cl ELTH/MOT SE9 ... 166 E5
SCUP DA14 ... 186 D2
WIM/MER SW19 ... 159 G5
YEAD UB4 ... 94 C4
Haven Ct BRYLDS KT5 * ... 191 G3
Haven Gn EA W5 ... 97 K6
Havenhurst Ri ENC/FH EN2 ... 23 G3
Haven La EA W5 ... 98 A5
Haven Rd ASHF TW15 ... 152 E6
Havens Ms BOW E3 ... 105 H4
Haven St CAMTN NW1 ... 84 B5
Havenswood Ct
KUTN/CMB KT2 ... 175 J2
The Haven RCH/KEW TW9 ... 137 H4
Havenwood WBLY HA9 ... 80 D1
Haverfield Est BTFD TW8 ... 117 F6
Haverfield Gdns
RCH/KEW TW9 ... 137 H1
Haverfield Rd BOW E3 ... 105 F2
Haverford Wy EDGW HA8 ... 44 B4
Havergal Vls
SEVS/STOTM N15 * ... 67 H1
Haverhill Rd BAL SW12 ... 161 H3
CHING E4 ... 38 A3
Havering Dr ROM RM1 ... 75 G1
Havering Gdns CHDH RM6 ... 73 J2
Havering Rd ROM RM1 ... 57 F1
Havering St WCHPL E1 ... 105 F5
Havering Wy BARK IG11 ... 109 H2
Haversham Cl TWK TW1 ... 156 E2
Haversham Pl HGT N6 ... 65 K6
Haverstock Hl HAMP NW3 ... 83 J4
Haverstock Pl FSBYE EC1V ... 5 K3
Haverstock Rd KTTN NW5 ... 84 A3
Haverstock St IS N1 ... 6 B3
Haverthwaite Rd ORP BR6 ... 216 D1
Havil St CMBW SE5 ... 143 F2
Havisham Pl NRWD SE19 ... 180 C2
Hawarden Gv HNHL SE24 ... 162 D2
Hawarden Hl CRICK NW2 ... 81 J1
Hawarden Rd WALTH E17 ... 69 F1
Hawbridge Rd WAN E11 ... 70 B5
Hawes Cl NTHWD HA6 ... 40 D3
Hawes La WWKM BR4 ... 199 G6
Hawes Rd BMLY BR1 ... 184 A4
UED N18 ... 50 D2
Hawes St IS N1 ... 85 H5
Hawfield Bank ORP BR6 ... 217 J1
Hawgood St BOW E3 ... 105 J4
Hawkdene CHING E4 ... 37 K1
Hawke Park Rd WDGN N22 ... 49 H6
Hawke Pl BERM/RHTH SE16 * ... 124 A2
Hawke Rd NRWD SE19 ... 180 E2
Hawker Rd CROY/NA CR0 ... 211 G4
Hawkesbury Rd
PUT/ROE SW15 ... 138 E6
Hawkesfield Rd FSTH SE23 ... 164 C4
Hawkesley Cl TWK TW1 ... 156 B6
Hawkes Rd EBED/NFELT TW14 ... 153 K2
MTCM CR4 ... 178 D4
Hawkesworth Cl NTHWD HA6 ... 40 C3
Hawkhurst Gdns CRW RM5 ... 57 F2
Hawkhurst Rd
STRHM/NOR SW16 ... 179 J4
Hawkhurst Wy NWMAL KT3 ... 192 A2
WWKM BR4 ... 198 E6
Hawkins Cl EDGW HA8 ... 45 F1
HRW HA1 ... 60 D4
Hawkins Rd TEDD TW11 ... 174 C2
WLSDN NW10 ... 81 G5
Hawkins Ter CHARL SE7 ... 126 D5
Hawkins Wy CAT SE6 ... 182 D1
Hawkley Gdns WNWD SE27 ... 162 C5
Hawkridge Cl CHDH RM6 ... 73 J3
Hawksbrook La BECK BR3 ... 198 E3
Hawkshaw Cl
BRXS/STRHM SW2 ... 161 K2
Hawkshead Cl BMLY BR1 ... 183 H3
Hawkshead Rd CHSWK W4 ... 118 B3
WLSDN NW10 * ... 81 H5
Hawkshill Cl ESH/CLAY KT10 ... 204 A4
Hawkshill Pl ESH/CLAY KT10 * ... 204 A4
Hawkslade Rd PECK SE15 ... 144 A6
Hawksley Rd STNW/STAM N16 ... 85 K1
Hawks Ms GNWCH SE10 * ... 145 F1
Hawksmoor Cl EHAM E6 ... 107 J5
WOOL/PLUM SE18 ... 127 K5
Hawksmoor Ms WCHPL E1 ... 104 D6
Hawksmoor St HMSMTH W6 ... 119 G6
Hawksmouth CHING E4 ... 37 K2
Hawks Rd KUT/HW KT1 ... 175 G5
Hawkstone Est
BERM/RHTH SE16 ... 123 K4
Hawkstone Rd
BERM/RHTH SE16 ... 123 K4
Hawkwell Wk IS N1 * ... 85 J6
Hawkwood Crs CHING E4 ... 37 K1
Hawkwood La CHST BR7 ... 185 H4
Hawkwood Mt CLPT E5 ... 68 D5
Hawlands Dr PIN HA5 ... 59 J4
Hawley Cl HPTN TW12 ... 172 E2
Hawley Crs CAMTN NW1 ... 84 B5
Hawley Ms CAMTN NW1 ... 84 B5
Hawley Rd CAMTN NW1 ... 84 B5
DART DA1 ... 171 H4
UED N18 ... 51 F1
Hawley Ter RDART DA2 * ... 171 K6
Hawstead Rd CAT SE6 ... 164 E1
Hawsted BKHH IG9 ... 39 F2
Hawthorn Av PLMGR N13 ... 48 E1
RAIN RM13 ... 111 K3
THHTH CR7 ... 180 C4
Hawthorn Centre HRW HA1 ... 61 F1
Hawthorn Cl HEST TW5 ... 134 A1
HPTN TW12 ... 173 F1
STMC/STPC BR5 ... 201 J3
Hawthorn Crs TOOT SW17 ... 179 F1
Hawthornden Cl
NFNCH/WDSPK N12 ... 47 J2
Hawthorndene Cl
HAYES BR2 * ... 199 J6
Hawthorndene Rd HAYES BR2 ... 199 K6
Hawthorn Dr RYLN/HDSTN HA2 ... 60 A3
WWKM BR4 ... 214 C2
Hawthorne Av BOW E3 ... 87 H6
CAR SM5 ... 210 A5
HRW HA1 ... 61 G3
MTCM CR4 ... 178 C5
RSLP HA4 ... 59 F3
Hawthorne Cl BMLY BR1 ... 184 E6
IS N1 ... 86 A4
Hawthorne Ct
STWL/WRAY TW19 * ... 152 A2
Hawthorne Crs WDR/YW UB7 ... 112 C2
Hawthorne Gv CDALE/KGS NW9 ... 62 E4
Hawthorne Rd BMLY BR1 ... 184 E6
UED N18 ... 50 B2
WALTH E17 ... 51 J6
Hawthorne Wy ED N9 ... 36 B4
STWL/WRAY TW19 ... 152 A2
Hawthorn Farm Av NTHLT UB5 ... 77 J6
Hawthorn Gdns EA W5 ... 116 E3
Hawthorn Gv ENC/FH EN2 ... 23 K1
PGE/AN SE20 ... 181 J4
Hawthorn Hatch BTFD TW8 ... 136 C1
Hawthorn Ms MLHL NW7 ... 46 C4
Hawthorn Pl ERITH DA8 ... 129 K5
HYS/HAR UB3 * ... 94 D6
Hawthorn Rd BTFD TW8 ... 136 C1
BXLYHS DA6 * ... 149 G5
CEND/HSY/T N8 ... 48 D6
DART DA1 ... 171 G4
FELT TW13 ... 153 K3
SUT SM1 ... 209 H3
WFD IG8 ... 39 G6
WLGTN SM6 ... 210 B5
WLSDN NW10 ... 81 J5
Hawthorns WFD IG8 ... 38 E5
The Hawthorns EW KT17 ... 207 H4
Hawthorn Ter BFN/LL DA15 ... 168 A1
Hawthorn Wk NKENS W10 ... 100 C3
Hawtrey Av NTHLT UB5 ... 95 H1
Hawtrey Dr RSLP HA4 ... 58 E4
Hawtrey Rd HAMP NW3 ... 83 J5
Haxted Rd BMLY BR1 ... 184 A4
Hayburn Wy HCH RM12 ... 75 H5

Hay Cl SRTFD E15 88 C5
Haycroft Gdns WLSDN NW10 81 J6
Haycroft Rd
BRXS/STRHM SW2 141 K6
SURB KT6 190 E6
Hay Currie St POP/IOD E14 105 K5
Hayday Rd CAN/RD E16 106 E4
Hayden Dell BUSH WD23 27 K1
Haydens Cl STMC/STPC BR5 202 D4
Hayden's Pl NTGHL W11 100 D5
Hayden Wy CRW RM5 56 E5
Haydock Av NTHLT UB5 78 A4
Haydock Gn NTHLT UB5 78 A4
Haydon Cl CDALE/KGS NW9 62 E1
EN EN1 36 A1
HARH RM3 57 K3
Haydon Dell Farm
BUSH WD23 * 27 K2
Haydon Dr PIN HA5 58 E1
Haydon Park Rd
WIM/MER SW19 177 K1
Haydon Rd BCTR RM8 73 J6
OXHEY WD19 27 J1
Haydon's Rd WIM/MER SW19 178 A1
Haydon St TWRH EC3N 13 J5
Haydon Wk WCHPL E1 13 J4
Haydon Wy WAND/EARL SW18 140 B5
Hayes Cha WWKM BR4 199 G3
Hayes Cl HAYES BR2 199 K6
Hayes Crs CHEAM SM3 208 B2
GLDGN NW11 64 D2
Hayes Dr RAIN RM13 93 K5
Hayes End Dr YEAD UB4 94 B4
Hayes End Rd YEAD UB4 94 B4
Hayesford Park Dr HAYES BR2 199 J2
Hayes Gdn HAYES BR2 199 K6
Hayes Gv EDUL SE22 143 G5
Hayes Hl HAYES BR2 199 H5
Hayes Hill Rd HAYES BR2 199 J5
Hayes La BECK BR3 183 G6
HAYES BR2 200 A1
Hayes Mead Rd HAYES BR2 199 H5
Hayes Pl CAMTN NW1 8 D1
Hayes Rd HAYES BR2 199 K1
NWDGN UB2 114 B4
Hayes St HAYES BR2 200 A5
Hayes Wy BECK BR3 199 F1
Hayes Wood Av HAYES BR2 200 A5
Hayfield Pas WCHPL E1 104 E3
Hayfield Rd STMC/STPC BR5 202 B2
Haygarth Pl WIM/MER SW19 177 G1
Haygreen Cl KUTN/CMB KT2 175 J2
Hay Hl MYFR/PICC W1J 9 K6
Hayland Cl CDALE/KGS NW9 63 F1
Hay La CDALE/KGS NW9 63 F1
Hayles St LBTH SE11 18 A6
Haylett Gdns KUT/HW KT1 * 190 E1
Hayling Av FELT TW13 153 K5
Hayling Cl STNW/STAM N16 86 A3
Hayling Rd OXHEY WD19 26 D5
Hayman Crs YEAD UB4 94 B1
Haymarket STJS SW1Y 10 C6
Haymeads Dr ESH/CLAY KT10 204 C4
Haymer Gdns WPK KT4 207 J1
Haymerle Rd PECK SE15 123 H6
Haymill Cl GFD/PVL UB6 97 F2
Hayne Rd BECK BR3 182 C5
Haynes Cl BKHTH/KID SE3 145 H4
FBAR/BDGN N11 34 A5
TOTM N17 50 D3
Haynes Dr ED N9 36 D5
Haynes La NRWD SE19 181 F2
Haynes Rd ALP/SUD HA0 80 A5
Hayne St STBT EC1A 12 B1
Haynt Wk RYNPK SW20 177 H6
Hay Pl SWLY BR8 * 203 K3
Hay's La STHWK SE1 13 G7
Haysleigh Gdns PGE/AN SE20 181 H5
Hay's Ms MYFR/PICC W1J 9 J7
Haysoms Cl ROM RM1 75 G1
Haystall Cl YEAD UB4 94 C1
Hay St BETH E2 86 C6
Hayter Rd BRXS/STRHM SW2 141 K6
Hayton Cl HACK E8 86 B4
Hayward Cl DART DA1 150 A6
WIM/MER SW19 178 A3
Hayward Dr DART DA1 171 J5
Hayward Gdns PUT/ROE SW15 159 F1
Hayward Rd THDIT KT7 190 A5
TRDG/WHET N20 33 G4
Haywards Cl CHDH RM6 73 J2
Hayward's Pl CLKNW EC1R * 6 A7
Haywood Cl PIN HA5 41 H5
Haywood Ri ORP BR6 216 E3
Haywood Rd HAYES BR2 200 C1
Hazel Av WDR/YW UB7 112 D3
Hazelbank BRYLDS KT5 191 K5
Hazelbank Rd CAT SE6 165 G4
Hazelbourne Rd BAL SW12 161 G1
Hazelbrouck Gdns
BARK/HLT IG6 54 D3
Hazelbury Cl WIM/MER SW19 177 K5
Hazelbury Gn ED N9 36 A5
Hazelbury La ED N9 36 A5
Hazel Cl BTFD TW8 * 136 C1
CDALE/KGS NW9 45 H5
CROY/NA CR0 198 A4
HCH RM12 93 K1
MTCM CR4 195 J1
PLMGR N13 35 K5
WHTN TW2 155 J2
Hazelcroft PIN HA5 42 A2
Hazeldean Rd WLSDN NW10 81 F5
Hazeldene Dr PIN HA5 41 G6
Hazeldene Gdns
HGDN/ICK UB10 76 A6
Hazeldene Rd GDMY/SEVK IG3 73 H6
WELL DA16 148 D3
Hazeldon Rd BROCKY SE4 144 B6
Hazel Dr ERITH DA8 150 E2
Hazeleigh Gdns WFD IG8 53 J2
Hazel Gdns EDGW HA8 30 D6
Hazelgreen Cl WCHMH N21 35 H3
Hazel Gv ALP/SUD HA0 80 A6
CHDH RM6 56 A6
EN EN1 * 36 C1
ORP BR6 201 G6
SYD SE26 164 A6
Hazelhurst BECK BR3 183 G4
Hazelhurst Rd TOOT SW17 160 C6
Hazel La BARK/HLT IG6 54 B3
Hazell Crs CRW RM5 56 D4
Hazellville Rd ARCH N19 66 D4
Hazelmere Cl
EBED/NFELT TW14 153 G1
NTHLT UB5 95 K1
Hazelmere Dr NTHLT UB5 95 K1
Hazelmere Gdns EMPK RM11 75 K2
Hazelmere Rd
KIL/WHAMP NW6 82 D6
NTHLT UB5 95 K1
STMC/STPC BR5 201 H1
Hazelmere Wk NTHLT UB5 95 K1
Hazelmere Wy HAYES BR2 199 K3
Hazel Rd DART DA1 171 G4
ERITH DA8 150 D2
SRTFD E15 * 88 C3
WLSDN NW10 99 K2
Hazel Rw NFNCH/WDSPK N12 * 47 H1
Hazeltree La NTHLT UB5 95 J2
Hazel Wk HAYES BR2 201 F3
Hazel Wy CHING E4 51 H2
STHWK SE1 19 J6
Hazelwood Av MRDN SM4 194 A1
Hazelwood Cl CLPT E5 87 G1
EA W5 117 F2
RYLN/HDSTN HA2 60 B1
Hazelwood Ct SURB KT6 191 F3
Hazelwood Dr PIN HA5 41 F5
Hazelwood La PLMGR N13 35 G6
Hazelwood Park Cl CHIG IG7 54 E1
Hazelwood Rd EN EN1 36 B1
RKW/CH/CXG WD3 26 A1
WALTH E17 69 G2
Hazlebury Rd FUL/PGN SW6 140 A3
Hazledean Rd CROY/NA CR0 196 E6
Hazledene Rd CHSWK W4 117 K6
Hazlemere Gdns WPK KT4 192 D5
Hazlewell Rd PUT/ROE SW15 139 F6
Hazlewood Crs NKENS W10 100 C3
Hazlitt Cl FELT TW13 154 D6
Hazlitt Ms WKENS W14 * 119 H3
Hazlitt Rd WKENS W14 119 H3
Heacham Av HGDN/ICK UB10 76 A1
Headcorn Rd BMLY BR1 183 J1
THHTH CR7 196 A1
TOTM N17 50 B3
Headfort Pl KTBR SW1X 15 H3
Headington Rd
WAND/EARL SW18 160 B3
Headlam Rd CLAP SW4 161 J2
Headlam St WCHPL E1 104 D3
Headley Ap GNTH/NBYPK IG2 72 A2
Headley Av WLGTN SM6 211 F3
Headley Cl CHSGTN KT9 206 C4
Headley Dr CROY/NA CR0 214 A5
GNTH/NBYPK IG2 72 B3
Heads Ms NTGHL W11 100 E5
Headstone Dr HRW HA1 42 E6
Headstone Gdns
RYLN/HDSTN HA2 60 C1
Headstone La
KTN/HRWW/WS HA3 42 B4
Headstone Pde HRW HA1 * 60 D1
Headstone Rd HRW HA1 60 E3
Head St WCHPL E1 105 F5
Headway Cl
RCHPK/HAM TW10 156 D6
The Headway EW KT17 207 H6
Heald St NWCR SE14 144 C2
Healey Rd WATW WD18 26 D1
Healey St CAMTN NW1 * 84 B4
Healy Dr ORP BR6 217 F2
Hearne Rd CHSWK W4 117 H5
Hearn Ri NTHLT UB5 77 H6
Hearn Rd ROM RM1 75 H3
Hearn's Buildings WALW SE17 19 F7
Hearns Cl STMC/STPC BR5 202 D1
Hearnshaw St POP/IOD E14 105 G5
Hearns Rd STMC/STPC BR5 202 D1
Hearn St SDTCH EC2A 7 H7
Hearnville Rd BAL SW12 161 F3
Heatham Pk WHTN TW2 156 A2
Heath Av BXLYHN DA7 128 E6
Heathbourne Rd BUSH WD23 28 E4
Heath Brow HAMP NW3 83 G1
Heath Cl EA W5 98 B3
GLDGN NW11 65 F4
GPK RM2 57 J6
HYS/HAR UB3 133 G1
SAND/SEL CR2 211 H4
STMC/STPC BR5 202 D3
Heathclose Av DART DA1 170 E2
Heathclose Rd DART DA1 170 D3
Heathcote Av CLAY IG5 53 K5
Heathcote Gv CHING E4 38 A5
Heathcote Rd TWK TW1 156 C1
Heathcote St BMSBY WC1N 5 G6
Heathcote Wy WDR/YW UB7 112 A1
Heathcroft EA W5 98 B3
Heathcroft Gdns WALTH E17 52 B4
Heathdale Av HSLWW TW4 134 D4
Heathdene Dr BELV DA17 129 J4
Heathdene Rd
STRHM/NOR SW16 180 A3
WLGTN SM6 210 B5
Heath Dr BELMT SM2 209 G6
GPK RM2 57 J4
HAMP NW3 83 F2
RYNPK SW20 193 F1
Heathedge SYD SE26 * 163 J4
Heathend Rd BXLY DA5 170 B3
Heather Av ROM RM1 57 F5
Heatherbank CHST BR7 185 F5
ELTH/MOT SE9 146 E3
Heatherbank Cl DART DA1 170 B1
Heather Cl EHAM E6 108 B5
HPTN TW12 172 E4
ISLW TW7 135 J6
LEW SE13 165 G1
ROM RM1 57 F4
VX/NE SW8 141 G4
Heatherdale Cl KUTN/CMB KT2 175 H2
Heatherdene Cl MTCM CR4 194 C1
NFNCH/WDSPK N12 47 G4
Heather Dr DART DA1 170 D2
ENC/FH EN2 23 H3
ROM RM1 57 F5
Heatherfold Wy PIN HA5 40 D6
Heather Gdns BELMT SM2 208 E4
GLDGN NW11 64 C3
ROM RM1 57 F5
Heather Gln ROM RM1 57 F5
Heatherley Dr CLAY IG5 53 K6
Heather Park Dr ALP/SUD HA0 80 C6
Heather Park Pde
ALP/SUD HA0 * 80 B5
Heather Pl ESH/CLAY KT10 204 B2
Heather Rd CHING E4 51 H2
CRICK NW2 63 H6
LEE/GVPK SE12 165 K4
Heatherset Cl ESH/CLAY KT10 204 C3
Heatherset Gdns
STRHM/NOR SW16 180 A3
Heatherside Rd
HOR/WEW KT19 207 F5
SCUP DA14 168 D5
The Heathers
STWL/WRAY TW19 152 C2
Heather Wk EDGW HA8 44 D1
NKENS W10 100 C3
Heather Wy ROM RM1 57 F4
SAND/SEL CR2 213 F6
STAN HA7 43 F2
Heatherwood Cl MNPK E12 71 F6
Heatherwood Dr YEAD UB4 94 B1
Heathfield CHING E4 38 A5
CHST BR7 185 H2
HRW HA1 * 61 F4
Heathfield Av
WAND/EARL SW18 160 C2
Heathfield Cl CAN/RD E16 107 H4
HAYES BR2 215 G3
OXHEY WD19 27 G2
Heathfield Dr MTCM CR4 178 D4
Heathfield Gdns CHSWK W4 117 K5
CROY/NA CR0 * 211 J2
GLDGN NW11 64 B3
WAND/EARL SW18 160 C1
Heathfield La CHST BR7 185 H2
Heathfield North WHTN TW2 155 K2
Heathfield Pk CRICK NW2 82 A4
Heathfield Park Dr CHDH RM6 73 H2
Heathfield Ri RSLP HA4 58 A4
Heathfield Rd ACT W3 117 J2
BMLY BR1 183 J3
BXLYHS DA6 149 G5
HAYES BR2 215 G3
SAND/SEL CR2 211 K3
WAND/EARL SW18 160 B1
Heathfield South WHTN TW2 156 A2
Heathfield Sq
WAND/EARL SW18 160 C2
Heathfield Ter CHSWK W4 117 K5
WOOL/PLUM SE18 127 K6
Heathfield V SAND/SEL CR2 213 F6
Heath Gdns DART DA1 * 171 F3
TWK TW1 156 A3
Heathgate GLDGN NW11 65 F3
Heathgate Pl HAMP NW3 83 K2
Heath Gv PGE/AN SE20 181 K3
Heath Hurst Rd HAMP NW3 83 J2
Heathhurst Rd SAND/SEL CR2 212 A6
Heathland Rd STNW/STAM N16 68 A5
Heathlands Cl TWK TW1 156 A4
Heathlands Ct HSLWW TW4 134 D6
Heathlands Ri DART DA1 170 E2
Heathlands Wy HSLWW TW4 134 D6
Heath La BKHTH/KID SE3 145 G3
DART DA1 170 E3
Heathlee Rd BKHTH/KID SE3 145 J5
DART DA1 170 B1
Heathley End CHST BR7 185 H2
Heath Ldg BUSH WD23 * 28 D3
Heathman's Rd FUL/PGN SW6 139 J2
Heath Md WIM/MER SW19 159 G5
Heath Park Dr BMLY BR1 184 D6
Heath Park Rd GPK RM2 75 J2
Heath Ri HAYES BR2 199 K3
PUT/ROE SW15 159 G1
Heath Rd BXLY DA5 169 K3
CHDH RM6 73 K4
DART DA1 170 C1
HGDN/ICK UB10 94 A3
HRW HA1 60 C4
HSLW TW3 135 H5
OXHEY WD19 27 H2
THHTH CR7 180 D6
TWK TW1 156 A3
VX/NE SW8 141 G3
Heath's Cl EN EN1 23 K3
Heathside ESH/CLAY KT10 204 E1
HAMP NW3 83 H2
HSLWW TW4 154 E2
Heath Side STMC/STPC BR5 201 J5
Heathside Av BXLYHN DA7 149 F3
Heathside Cl ESH/CLAY KT10 204 E1
GNTH/NBYPK IG2 72 D2
NTHWD HA6 40 B1
Heathside Rd NTHWD HA6 26 B6
Heathstan Rd SHB W12 99 J6
Heath St DART DA1 171 G2
HAMP NW3 83 G1
The Heath HNWL W7 * 115 K2
Heath Vw EFNCH N2 65 G1
Heathview Av DART DA1 170 B1
Heath View Cl EFNCH N2 65 G1
Heathview Crs DART DA1 170 D2
Heath View Dr ABYW SE2 128 E6
Heathview Gdns
PUT/ROE SW15 159 F2
Heathview Rd THHTH CR7 196 B1
Heath Vls WAND/EARL SW18 * 160 B3
WOOL/PLUM SE18 128 A5
Heathville Rd ARCH N19 66 E4
Heathwall St BTSEA SW11 140 E4
Heathway BKHTH/KID SE3 145 K1
CROY/NA CR0 213 H1
DAGW RM9 92 B3
Heath Wy ERITH DA8 149 K2
Heathway NWDGN UB2 * 114 C4
WFD IG8 39 G6
Heathwood Gdns CHARL SE7 126 D4
SWLY BR8 187 K5
Heathwood Pde SWLY BR8 * 187 K5
Heathwood Wk BXLY DA5 170 B3
Heaton Av HARH RM3 57 K3
Heaton Cl CHING E4 38 A5
Heaton Grange Rd GPK RM2 57 H4
Heaton Rd MTCM CR4 179 F3
PECK SE15 143 J4
Heaven Tree Cl IS N1 85 K3
Heaver Rd BTSEA SW11 * 140 C4
Heavitree Cl
WOOL/PLUM SE18 127 J5
Heavitree Rd
WOOL/PLUM SE18 127 J5
Hebden Ter TOTM N17 50 A2
Hebdon Rd TOOT SW17 160 D5
Heber Rd CRICK NW2 82 B3
EDUL SE22 163 G1
Hebron Rd HMSMTH W6 118 E3
Hecham Cl WALTH E17 51 G5
Heckfield Pl FUL/PGN SW6 139 K1
Heckford Cl WATW WD18 26 A1
Heckford St WAP E1W 105 F6
Hector St WOOL/PLUM SE18 * 127 K4
Heddington Gv HOLWY N7 85 F3
Heddon Cl ISLW TW7 136 B5
Heddon Court Av EBAR EN4 21 K6
Heddon Court Pde EBAR EN4 * 22 A6
Heddon Rd EBAR EN4 21 K6
Heddon St CONDST W1S 10 A6
Hedge Hl ENC/FH EN2 23 H2
Hedge La PLMGR N13 35 J6
Hedgeley REDBR IG4 71 K1
Hedgemans Rd DAGW RM9 91 K5
Hedgemans Wy DAGW RM9 92 A4
Hedgerley Gdns GFD/PVL UB6 96 C1
Hedger's Gv HOM E9 * 87 G4
Hedger St LBTH SE11 18 A6
Hedgewood Gdns CLAY IG5 72 A2
Hedgley St LEE/GVPK SE12 145 J6
Hedingham Cl IS N1 85 J5
Hedingham Rd BCTR RM8 91 H3
Hedley Rd WHTN TW2 155 F2
Hedley Rw HBRY N5 85 K3
Heenan Cl BARK IG11 90 C4
Heene Rd ENC/FH EN2 23 K3
Heidegger Crs BARN SW13 138 E1
Heigham Rd EHAM E6 89 J5
Heighton Gdns CROY/NA CR0 211 H3
Heights Cl RYNPK SW20 176 E3
The Heights BECK BR3 * 183 F3
CHARL SE7 126 B5
NTHLT UB5 78 A3
Heiron St WALW SE17 122 C6
Helby Rd CLAP SW4 161 J1
Helder Gv LEE/GVPK SE12 165 J2
Helder St SAND/SEL CR2 211 K4
Heldmann Cl HSLW TW3 135 J5
Helegan Cl ORP BR6 217 F2
Helena Pl HACK E8 86 D6
Helena Rd EA W5 97 K4
PLSTW E13 106 D1
WALTH E17 69 J2
WLSDN NW10 81 K3
Helena Sq BERM/RHTH SE16 105 G6
Helen Av EBED/NFELT TW14 154 A2
Helen Cl DART DA1 170 E2
E/WMO/HCT KT8 189 G1
EFNCH N2 47 G6
Helenslea Av GLDGN NW11 64 D5
Helen's Pl BETH E2 104 E2
Helen St WOOL/PLUM SE18 * 127 G4
Helford Cl RSLP HA4 58 C6
Helios Rd WLGTN SM6 195 F5
Helix Gdns BRXS/STRHM SW2 162 A1
Helix Rd BRXS/STRHM SW2 162 A1
Hellings St WAP E1W 123 H1
Helme Cl WIM/MER SW19 177 J1
Helmet Rw FSBYE EC1V 6 D6
Helmore Rd BARK IG11 91 F5
Helmsdale Cl ROM RM1 57 G3
YEAD UB4 * 95 J3
Helmsdale Rd ROM RM1 57 G3
STRHM/NOR SW16 179 H4
Helmsley Pl HACK E8 86 D5
Helmsley St HACK E8 86 D6
Helperby Rd WLSDN NW10 81 G5
Helsinki Sq BERM/RHTH SE16 124 C3
Helston Cl PIN HA5 41 K3
Helvetia St CAT SE6 164 C4
Hemans St VX/NE SW8 141 J1
Hemery Rd GFD/PVL UB6 78 D3
Hemingford Cl
NFNCH/WDSPK N12 47 H1
Hemingford Rd CHEAM SM3 208 A2
IS N1 85 F6
Heming Rd EDGW HA8 44 D2
Hemington Av FBAR/BDGN N11 47 K1
Hemlock Rd SHB W12 99 H6
Hemmen La HYS/HAR UB3 94 D6
Hemming Cl HPTN TW12 173 F4
Hemmings Cl SCUP DA14 168 C4
Hemmingsmead
HOR/WEW KT19 206 E4
Hemming St WCHPL E1 104 C3
Hemmingway Cl KTTN NW5 84 A2
Hempstead Cl BKHH IG9 38 E4
Hempstead Rd WALTH E17 52 B6
Hemp Wk WALW SE17 19 F6
Hemsby Rd CHSGTN KT9 206 B4
Hemstal Rd KIL/WHAMP NW6 82 E5
Hemsted Rd ERITH DA8 150 B2
Hemswell Dr CDALE/KGS NW9 45 G4
Hemsworth St IS N1 7 G2
Henbury Wy OXHEY WD19 27 H5
Henchman St SHB W12 99 H5
Hendale Av HDN NW4 45 J6
Henderson Cl EMPK RM11 75 K6
WLSDN NW10 80 E4
Henderson Dr DART DA1 151 K5
STJWD NW8 2 A6
Henderson Rd CROY/NA CR0 196 E3
ED N9 36 D3
FSTGT E7 89 G4
WAND/EARL SW18 160 D2
YEAD UB4 94 E2
Hendham Rd TOOT SW17 160 D4
Hendon Av FNCH N3 46 C5
Hendon Gdns CRW RM5 56 E2
Hendon Gv HOR/WEW KT19 206 C6
Hendon Hall Ct HDN NW4 * 46 B6
Hendon La FNCH N3 46 D5
Hendon Park Rw
GLDGN NW11 * 64 D3
Hendon Rd ED N9 36 C4
Hendon Wy HDN NW4 64 A3
STWL/WRAY TW19 152 A1
Hendon Wood La MLHL NW7 31 J3
Hendren Cl GFD/PVL UB6 78 D3
Hendre Rd STHWK SE1 19 H7
Hendrick Av BAL SW12 160 E1
Heneage La HDTCH EC3A 13 H4
Heneage St WCHPL E1 13 K1
Henfield Cl ARCH N19 66 C5
BXLY DA5 169 H1
Henfield Rd WIM/MER SW19 177 J4
Hengelo Gdns MTCM CR4 194 C1
Hengist Rd ERITH DA8 149 K1
LEE/GVPK SE12 166 A2
Hengist Wy HAYES BR2 199 G1
Hengrave Rd FSTH SE23 163 K2
Hengrove Ct BXLY DA5 169 F3
Hengrove Crs ASHF TW15 152 A5
Henley Av CHEAM SM3 208 C1
Henley Cl BERM/RHTH SE16 * 123 K2
GFD/PVL UB6 * 96 C1
ISLW TW7 136 A2
Henley Dr KUTN/CMB KT2 176 C3
STHWK SE1 19 K6
Henley Gdns CHDH RM6 74 A2
PIN HA5 41 F6
Henley Rd CAN/RD E16 126 E2
IL IG1 90 C2
UED N18 36 A6
WLSDN NW10 82 A6
Henley St BTSEA SW11 141 F3
Henley Wy FELT TW13 172 C1
Hennel Cl FSTH SE23 163 K5
Hennessy Rd ED N9 36 E4
Henniker Gdns EHAM E6 107 H2
Henniker Ms CHEL SW3 120 C6
Henniker Rd SRTFD E15 88 B3
Henningham Rd TOTM N17 49 K4
Henning St BTSEA SW11 140 D2
Henrietta Cl DEPT SE8 124 D6
Henrietta Ms BMSBY WC1N 5 F6
Henrietta Pl CAVSQ/HST W1G 9 J4
Henrietta St COVGDN WC2E 11 F5
SRTFD E15 88 A3
Henriques St WCHPL E1 104 C5
Henry Addlington Cl EHAM E6 108 B4
Henry Cl ENC/FH EN2 24 A1
Henry Cooper Wy
ELTH/MOT SE9 166 C5
Henry Darlot Dr MLHL NW7 46 C1
Henry Dent Cl CMBW SE5 142 E4
Henry Dickens Ct NTGHL W11 100 B6
Henry Doulton Dr TOOT SW17 161 F6
Henry Jackson Rd
PUT/ROE SW15 139 G4
Henry Macaulay Av
KUTN/CMB KT2 174 E4
Henry Peters Dr TEDD TW11 173 K1
Henry Rd EBAR EN4 21 H6
EHAM E6 107 J1
FSBYPK N4 67 J5
Henry's Av WFD IG8 52 D1
Henryson Rd BROCKY SE4 144 D6
Henry St BMLY BR1 184 A4
Henry Tate Ms
STRHM/NOR SW16 180 B1
Hensford Gdns SYD SE26 163 J6
Henshall St IS N1 85 K4
Henshawe Rd BCTR RM8 91 K1
Henshaw St WALW SE17 18 E6
Henslowe Rd EDUL SE22 143 H6
Henson Av CRICK NW2 82 A3
Henson Cl ORP BR6 201 G6
Henson Pl NTHLT UB5 77 G6
Henstridge Pl STJWD NW8 2 C2
Henty Cl BTSEA SW11 140 D1
Henty Wk PUT/ROE SW15 138 E6
Henville Rd BMLY BR1 184 B4
Henwick Rd ELTH/MOT SE9 146 C4
Henwood Side WFD IG8 53 K2
Hepburn Gdns HAYES BR2 199 J5
Hepple Cl ISLW TW7 136 C3
Hepscott Rd HOM E9 87 J4
Hepworth Gdns BARK IG11 91 G3
Hepworth Rd
STRHM/NOR SW16 179 K3
Herald Gdns WLGTN SM6 210 B1
Heralds Pl LBTH SE11 18 A6
Herald St BETH E2 104 D3
Herbal Hl CLKNW EC1R 5 K7
Herbert Crs KTBR SW1X 15 F4
Herbert Gdns CHDH RM6 73 K4
CHSWK W4 117 J6
WLSDN NW10 99 K1
Herbert Ms BRXS/STRHM SW2 162 B1
Herbert Pl ISLW TW7 135 J3
WOOL/PLUM SE18 127 G6
Herbert Rd BXLYHN DA7 149 F3
CDALE/KGS NW9 63 J3
FBAR/BDGN N11 48 E3
GDMY/SEVK IG3 72 E6
HAYES BR2 200 C2
KUT/HW KT1 175 G6
MNPK E12 89 J2
SEVS/STOTM N15 68 B2
STHL UB1 114 E1
WALTH E17 69 H4
WIM/MER SW19 177 J3
WOOL/PLUM SE18 147 G1
Herbert St KTTN NW5 84 A4
PLSTW E13 106 E1
Herbrand St BMSBY WC1N 4 E7
Hercules Pl HOLWY N7 84 E1
Hercules Rd STHWK SE1 17 H5
Hercules St HOLWY N7 84 E1
Hereford Av EBAR EN4 33 K3
Hereford Gdns IL IG1 71 J4

PIN HA5 ....59 J2
WHTN TW2 * 155 H5
Hereford Ms BAY/PAD W2 * 100 E5
Hereford Rd NWCR SE14 ....144 C1
Hereford Retreat PECK SE15...143 H1
Hereford Rd ACT W3 ....98 E6
　BAY/PAD W2 ....100 E5
　BOW E3 ....105 H1
　EA W5 ....116 D3
　WLSDN NW10 ....81 J6
　WAN E11 ....71 F2
Hereford Sq SKENS SW7 ....128 C3
Hereford St BETH E2 ....104 C3
Hereford Wy CHSCTN KT9 .....205 J3
Herent Dr CLAY IG5 ....53 K6
Heretage CI BRXN/ST SW9 ....142 C4
Hereward Gdns PLMGR N13....49 G1
Hereward Rd TOOT SW17 ....160 E6
Herga Rd KTN/HRWW/WS HA3...61 F1
Heriot Av CHING E4 ....37 J4
Heriot Rd HDN NW4 ....64 A1
Heriots CI STAN HA7 ....37 G4
Heritage HI HAYES BR2 ....215 G3
Heritage PI
　WAND/EARL SW18 * 160 C1
Heritage Vw HRW HA1 ....79 F1
Herkomer CI BUSH WD23........28 B1
Herlwyn Av RSLP HA4 ....76 C1
Herlwyn Gdns TOOT SW17....160 E6
Herm CI ISLW TW7 ....135 H1
Herm Rd MV/WKIL W9 ....100 E3
Hermes St IS N1 * 5 J3
Hermes Wy WLGTN SM6 ....210 D5
Hermiston Av CEND/HSY/T N8...66 E2
Hermit PI ABYW SE2 * 23 D5
　ENC/FH EN2 ....23 J5
　ESH/CLAY KT10 ....205 G4
　RCHPK/HAM TW10 ....136 E6
　SWFD E18 ....70 D1
Hermitage Cottages
　STAN HA7 * 42 E1
Hermitage Gdns CRICK NW2....82 E1
　NRWD SE19 ....180 D3
Hermitage La CRICK NW2 ....82 E1
　CROY/NA CRO 197 G4
　STRHM/NOR SW16 ....180 A3
　UED N18 ....49 K1
Hermitage Rd FSBYPK N4 ......67 J4
　NRWD SE19 ....180 E2
Hermitage Rw HACK E8 * 86 C5
Hermitage St BAY/PAD W2......8 A2
The Hermitage BARN SW13 ...138 C2
　FELT TW13 ....153 H3
　FSTH SE23 ....163 K3
　KUT/HW KT1 * 190 E1
　LEW SE13 ....145 F3
　RCHPK/HAM TW10 ....136 E6
Hermitage Wk SWFD E18.......70 D1
Hermitage Wall WAP E1W 123 H1
Hermitage Wy STAN HA7 ....43 G4
Hermit PI KIL/WHAMP NW6....82 E6
Hermit Rd CAN/RD E16 ....106 D4
Hermit St FSBYE EC1V 6 A4
Hermon Gv HYS/HAR UB3.....113 K1
Hermon HI WAN E11 ....70 E1
Herndon Rd
　WAND/EARL SW18 ....140 B6
Herne CI BUSH WD23 * 28 C5
Herne HI HNHL SE24 ....142 D5
Herne Hill Rd HNHL SE24 .....142 D5
Herne Ms UED N18 ....36 C6
Herne PI HNHL SE24 ....162 C1
Herne Rd BUSH WD23 ....28 B1
　SURB KT6 ....190 E6
Heron CI BKHH IG9 ....38 E3
　WALTH E17 ....51 H5
　WLSDN NW10 ....81 G4
Heron Ct HAYES BR2 ....200 B1
　KUT/HW KT1 * 175 F6
Heron Crs SCUP DA14 ....167 K6
Herondale SAND/SEL CR2 ....213 F6
Herondale Av
　WAND/EARL SW18 ....160 C1
Heron Dr FSBYPK N4 ....67 J6
Heron Flight Av HCH RM12 .....93 J5
Herongate Rd MNPK E12 ....71 H1
Heron HI BELV DA17 ....129 G4
Heron Md PEND EN3 ....25 J1
Heron Ms IL IG1 ....72 B6
Heron Quays POP/IOD E14....124 D1
Heron Rd CROY/NA CRO * 197 G5
　HNHL SE24 ....142 D5
　TWK TW1 ....136 C5
Heronsforde WEA W13 ....97 J5
Heronsgate EDGW HA8............44 C1
Herons Lea HGT N6 ....65 K3
Heronsl ea Dr STAN HA7..........44 A1
Herons PI ISLW TW7 * 136 C4
Herons Ri EBAR EN4 ....21 J5
Heron Wk NTHWD HA6 ....26 C6
Heron Wy EBED/NFELT TW14...133 K3
Herrick Rd HBRY N5 ....85 J1
Herrick St WEST SW1P 16 D7
Herries St NKENS W10 ....100 C1
Herringham Rd CHARL SE7....126 B3
Hersant CI WLSDN NW10.........81 J6
Herschell Rd FSTH SE23 ....164 A2
Hersham CI PUT/ROE SW15...158 D2
Hersham Rd WOT/HER KT12...188 A4
Hershell Ct
　MORT/ESHN SW14 * 137 J5
Hertford Av
　MORT/ESHN SW14 ....138 A6
Hertford CI EBAR EN4 ....21 H4
Hertford Ct STAN HA7 * 43 K5
Hertford End Ct NTHWD HA6...40 C1
Hertford PI FITZ W1T * 4 A6
Hertford Rd BARK IG11 ....90 A5
　EBAR EN4 ....21 G4
　ED N10 ....36 C1
　EFNCH N2 ....47 J6
　GNTH/NBYPK IG2 ....72 E3
　IS N1 ....86 A6
　PEND EN3 ....24 E2

Hertford Road High St
　PEND EN3 ....24 E2
Hertford St MYFR/PICC W1J...15 J1
Hertford Wy MTCM CR4 ....195 K1
Hertslet Rd HOLWY N7 ....85 F1
Hertsmere Rd POP/IOD E14..124 D1
Hertswood Ct BAR EN5 * 20 C5
Hervey CI FNCH N3 ....46 E4
Hervey Park Rd WALTH E17.....69 G1
Hesa Rd HYS/HAR UB3 ....94 E5
Hesewall CI CLAP SW4 ....141 H5
Hesketh PI NTGHL W11 ....100 C6
Hesketh Rd FSTGT E7 ....88 E1
Heslop Rd BAL SW12 ....160 E3
Hesper Ms ECT SW5 ....120 A5
Hesperus Crs POP/IOD E14 ..124 E4
Hessel Rd WEA W13 ....116 B2
Hessel St WCHPL E1 ....104 D5
Hesselyn Dr RAIN RM13...........93 K5

Hestercombe Av
　FUL/PGN SW6 ....139 H3
Hesterman Wy CROY/NA CRO...195 K5
Hester Rd BTSEA SW11 ....140 D1
　UED N18 ....50 C1
Hester Ter RCH/KEW TW9 .....137 H1
Heston Av HEST TW5 ....134 D1
Heston Grange La HEST TW5..114 E6
Heston Rd HEST TW5 ....135 F1
Heston St DEPT SE8 ....124 E6
Heswell Gn OXHEY WD19 * 26 E5
Hetherington Rd CLAP SW4...141 K5
Hetley Gdns NRWD SE19 * 181 G3
Hetley Rd SHB W12 ....118 E1
Heton Gdns HDN NW4.............63 J1
Hevelius CI GNWCH SE10 .....125 J5
Hever Ct ELTH/MOT SE9........167 F6
Hever Gdns BMLY BR1 ....185 F1
Heverham Rd
　WOOL/PLUM SE18 ....127 K4
Heversham Rd BXLYHN DA7..149 H3
Hevingham Dr CHDH RM6........73 J3
Hewens Rd HGDN/ICK UB10....94 A2
Hewer St NKENS W10 ....100 C4
Hewett CI STAN HA7 ....29 H6
Hewett Rd BCTR RM8 ....91 K3
Hewetts Quay BARK IG11 ....90 B6
Hewett St SDTCH EC2A 7 H7
Hewish Rd UED N18 ....50 A4
Hewison St BOW E3 ....105 H1
Hewitt Av WDGN N22 ....49 H5
Hewitt CI CROY/NA CRO 213 H1
Hewitt Rd CEND/HSY/T N8 ......67 G2
Hewlett Rd BOW E3 ....105 G1
Hexagon HGT N6 ....65 K5
Hexal Rd CAT SE6 ....165 H5
Hexham Gdns ISLW TW7 ......116 B1
Hexham Rd BAR EN5 ....20 E5
　MRDN SM4 ....194 A5
　WNWD SE27 ....162 D4
Heybourne Rd TOTM N17.........50 D3

Heybridge Av
　STRHM/NOR SW16 ....180 A2
Heybridge Dr BARK/HLT IG6.....54 D6
Heybridge Wy LEY E10 ....69 G4
Heyford Av RYNPK SW20 ....177 J6
　VX/NE SW8 ....141 K1
Heyford Rd MTCM CR4 ....178 D5
Heyford Ter VX/NE SW8 * 141 K1
Heygate St WALW SE17 ....18 C6
Heygate St WALW SE17 ....18 C7
Heynes Rd BCTR RM8 ....91 J2
Heysham Dr OXHEY WD19 * 41 G1
Heysham La HAMP NW3 ....83 F1
Heysham Rd SEVS/STOTM N15...67 K3
Heythorp St
　WAND/EARL SW18 ....159 J4
Heywood Av CDALE/KGS NW9...45 G1
Heyworth Rd CLPT E5 ....86 D1
BRTFRD E15 ....88 D3
Hibbert Rd
　KTN/HRWW/WS HA3..........61 H2
　WALTH E17 ....69 H4
Hibbert St BTSEA SW11 ....140 B4
Hibernia Gdns HSLW TW3 .....135 F6
Hibernia Rd HSLW TW3 ....135 F5
Hichisson Rd PECK SE15.......144 A6
Hickin CI CHARL SE7 ....126 C4
Hickin St POP/IOD E14 ....124 E3
Hickling Rd IL IG1 ....90 B3
Hickman Av CHING E4..............52 A2
Hickman CI CAN/RD E16 ....107 H4
Hickman Rd CHDH RM6 ....73 J4
Hickory CI ED N9 ....36 C2
Hicks Av GFD/PVL UB6 ....96 D2
Hicks CI BTSEA SW11 ....140 D4
Hicks St DEPT SE8 ....124 B5
Hidcote Gdns RYNPK SW20 ...176 E6
Hide PI WEST SW1P.................16 C7
Hide Rd HRW HA1 ....60 D1
Higham Hill Rd WALTH E17 .....51 G4
Higham Ms NRTHLT UB5 ....95 K3
Higham PI WALTH E17 ....51 G6
Higham Rd TOTM N17 ....49 K6
　WFD IG8 ....52 E2
Higham Station Av CHING E4 ...51 K2
The Highams WALTH E17 * 52 A4
Higham St WALTH E17 ....51 G6

Highbank PI
　WAND/EARL SW18 * 160 A3
Highbanks CI WELL DA16 ....148 B1
Highbanks Rd PIN HA5 ....42 B2
Highbank Wy CEND/HSY/T N8...67 G3
Highbarrow Rd CROY/NA CRO...197 G5
High Beech SAND/SEL CR2 ...212 A5
High Beeches ORP BR6..........217 F1
Highbridge Rd BARK IG11 ....90 B6
Highbrook Rd BKHTH/KID SE3...146 C4
Highbury Av THHTH CR7 ....180 B5
Highbury CI NWMAL KT3 ....191 K1
Highbury Cnr HBRY N5 ....85 H4
Highbury Crs HBRY N5 ....85 G4
Highbury Est HBRY N5 ....85 J3
Highbury Gdns GDMY/SEVK IG3...72 E6
Highbury Gra HBRY N5 ....85 H3
Highbury Gv HBRY N5 ....85 H4
Highbury HI HBRY N5 ....85 G2

Highbury New Pk HBRY N5......85 J4
Highbury Pl HBRY N5 ....85 H4
Highbury PI HBRY N5 ....85 H4
Highbury Od HBRY N5 ....85 H1
Highbury Qd HBRY N5 ....85 H2
Highbury Rd WIM/MER SW19..177 H5
Highbury Station Pde
　HBRY N5 * 85 H4
Highbury Station Rd IS N1 * 85 G4
Highbury Ter HBRY N5 ....85 H4
Highbury Terrace Ms HBRY N5...85 H3
High Cedar Dr RYNPK SW20...176 E3
Highclere Rd NWMAL KT3......176 A6
Highclere St SYD SE26 ....164 B6
Highcliffe Dr PUT/ROE SW15..158 C1
Highcliffe Gdns REDBR IG4......71 J2
Highcombe CHARL SE7 ....126 A6
Highcombe CI ELTH/MOT SE9...166 C2
High Coombe PI
　KUTN/CMB KT2 ....176 A3
Highcroft CDALE/KGS NW9.....63 G2
Highcroft Av ALP/SUD HA0 ......80 B5
Highcroft Gdns GLDGN NW11...64 D3
Highcroft Rd ARCH N19 ....66 E4
High Cross Rd TOTM N17.........50 C6
Highcross Wy PUT/ROE SW15...158 D3

Highdaun Dr
　STRHM/NOR SW16 ....196 A1
Highdown WPK KT4 ....192 B6
Highdown Rd PUT/ROE SW15...158 E1
High Dr NWMAL KT3 ....175 K4
High Elms WFD IG8 ....52 E1
High Elms CI NTHWD HA6 ....40 A2
High Elms Rd ORP BR6 ....216 C6
Highfield OXHEY WD19 ....27 K5
Highfield Av CDALE/KGS NW9...62 E2
　ERITH DA8 ....129 K6
　GFD/PVL UB6 ....78 E3
　GLDGN NW11 ....64 B4
　ORP BR6 ....217 F4
　PIN HA5 ....59 K2
　WBLY HA9 ....80 A1
Highfield CI CDALE/KGS NW9...63 G2
　CRW RM5 ....56 E2
　LEW SE13 ....165 G2
　NTHWD HA6 ....40 C3
　SURB KT6 ....190 D5
　WDGN N22 ....49 G4
Highfield Ct STHGT/OAK N14....34 C1
Highfield Crs NTHWD HA6 ....40 C3
Highfield Dr HAYES BR2 ....199 H1
　HOR/WEW KT19 ....207 H5
　WWKM BR4 ....213 K1
Highfield Gdns GLDGN NW11...64 C3
Highfield HI NRWD SE19 ....180 E3
Highfield Link CRW RM5 ....56 E2
Highfield Rd ACT W3 ....98 E4
　BMLY BR1 ....200 E1
　BRYLDS KT5 ....191 K4
　BXLYHS DA6 ....149 G6
　CHST BR7 ....186 A6
　DART DA1 ....171 G5
　FELT TW13 ....153 K3
　GLDGN NW11 * 64 C3
　ISLW TW7 ....136 A2
　NTHWD HA6 ....40 C4
　ORP BR6 ....217 F4
　SUT SM1 ....209 J3
　WCHMH N21 ....35 H4
　WFD IG8 ....53 J3
Highfield Rd North DART DA1..171 G4
Highfield Rd South DART DA1..171 G5
Highfields Gv HGT N6 ....65 K5
High Foleys ESH/CLAY KT10 ..205 H5
High Garth ESH/CLAY KT10 ...204 E4
Highgate Av HGT N6 ....66 B4
Highgate CI HGT N6 ....66 A4
Highgate Edge EFNCH N2 * 65 J2
Highgate HI ARCH N19 ....66 D5
Highgate Rd KTTN NW5 ....84 A1
Highgate Spinney
　CEND/HSY/T N8 * 66 D3
Highgate West HI HGT N6 ....66 A6
High Gv BMLY BR1 ....184 B4
　WOOL/PLUM SE18 ....147 J1
Highgrove CI CHST BR7 * 184 D4
　FBAR/BDGN N11 ....48 A1
Highgrove Ms CAR SM5 ....209 K1
Highgrove Wy RSLP HA4 ....58 E3
High Hill Ferry CLPT E5 ....68 D5
Highland Av DAGE RM10 ....92 E1
　HNWL W7 ....96 E5
　LOU IG10 ....39 G1
High Hill Ferry CLPT E5 ....68 D5
Highland Cottages
　WLGTN SM6 * 210 B2
Highland Cft BECK BR3 ....182 E2
Highland Dr BUSH WD23 ....28 B1
Highland Pk FELT TW13..........153 J6
Highland Rd BMLY BR1 ....183 J4
　BXLYHS DA6 ....149 H6
　NRWD SE19 ....181 G1
　NTHWD HA6 ....40 E5
Highlands OXHEY WD19 ....27 G3
Highlands Av ACT W3 ....98 E6
　WCHMH N21 ....23 F6
Highlands CI HSLW TW3 ....135 G2
Highlands Gdns IL IG1 ....71 K5
Highlands Rd BAR EN5 ....20 E6
　ORP BR6 ....202 C4
The Highlands BAR
　EDGW HA8 * 44 D5
Highland Ter LEW SE13 * 144 E4
High La HNWL W7 ....96 D5
Highlea CI CDALE/KGS NW9....45 G4
High Level Dr SYD SE26 ....163 H6
Highlever Rd NKENS W10 ....100 A4
High Limes NRWD SE19 * 181 F2
High Md HRW HA1 ....61 F3
Highmead WOOL/PLUM SE18...148 A1
High Md WWKM BR4 ....199 H5
Highmead Crs ALP/SUD HA0....80 B5
High Meadow CI PIN HA5 ....59 F1
High Meadow Crs
　CDALE/KGS NW9 ....63 F2

High Mdw CHIG IG7 ....54 D1
High Meads Rd CAN/RD E16...107 H5
Highmore Rd BKTH/KID SE3...145 H1
High Mt HDN NW4 ....63 J5
High Oaks ENC/FH EN2 ....23 F1
The High Pde
　STRHM/NOR SW16 * 161 K5
High Park Rd RCH/KEW TW9..137 H2
High Pth WIM/MER SW19 ....178 A3
High Point ELTH/MOT SE9 .....167 G5
High Rdg MUSWH N10 ....48 B4
Highridge PI ENC/FH EN2 * 23 H2
High Rd BKHH IG9 ....39 F4
　BUSH WD23 ....28 B1
　CHDH RM6 ....73 J3
　FBAR/BDGN N11 ....48 B1
　GDMY/SEVK IG3 ....72 E4
　KTN/HRWW/WS HA3..........42 E4
　LEY E10 ....69 K6
　NFNCH/WDSPK N12 ....33 G3
High Rd Eastcote PIN HA5 ....59 G3
High Rd Ickenham
　HGDN/ICK UB10 ....76 A1
High Rd Leyton LEY E10 ....69 K6
　LEY E10 ....69 K6
High Rd Leytonstone WAN E11...88 C1
High Rd Woodford Gn WFD IG8...52 E1
Highshore Rd PECK SE15 ......143 G3
Highstead Crs ERITH DA8......150 B2
Highstone Av WAN E11 ....71 F3
High St ACT W3 ....117 K1
　BAR EN5 ....20 C5
　BARK/HLT IG6 ....54 B5
　BMLY BR1 ....183 K6
　BORE WD6 ....29 K1
　BTFD TW8 ....116 E6
　BUSH WD23 ....28 C1
　CAR SM5 ....209 K3
　CEND/HSY/T N8 * 66 E2
　CHEAM SM3 ....208 C4
　CROY/NA CRO 211 J1
　DART DA1 ....171 H2
　E/WMO/HCT KT8 ....189 H2
　EA W5 ....97 K6
　ECT SW5 * 120 A5
　ELTH/MOT SE9 ....166 E1
　ESH/CLAY KT10 ....204 B3
　ESH/CLAY KT10 ....205 F4
　EW KT17 ....207 H6
　FBAR/BDGN N11 ....48 B1
　FELT TW15 ....153 K4
　HEST TW5 ....114 A6
　HEST TW5 ....135 F1
　HPTN TW12 ....173 G4
　HRW HA1 ....61 F3
　HSLW TW3 ....135 F4
　HYS/HAR UB3 ....113 G3
　KTN/HRWW/WS HA3..........61 H2
　KUT/HW KT1 ....174 E6
　MLHL NW7 ....31 J6
　NWMAL KT3 ....192 B1
　ORP BR6 ....202 C4
　PGE/AN SE20 ....181 K3
　PIN HA5 ....41 J6
　PLSTW E13 ....106 E1
　PUR RM19 ....131 K5
　RSLP HA4 ....58 B6
　SCUP DA14 ....168 B6
　SNWD SE25 ....197 G1
　SRTFD E15 ....88 B5
　STHGT/OAK N14 ....34 D3
　STMC/STPC BR5 ....202 D1
　STWL/WRAY TW19 ....152 A1
　SUT SM1 ....209 F2
　SUT SM1 ....209 F4
　TEDD TW11 ....174 B1
　THDIT KT7 ....190 B4
　THHTH CR7 ....196 D1
　WALTH E17 ....51 J4
　WAN E11 ....71 F3
　WBLY HA9 ....80 B2
　WDR/YW UB7 ....112 A6
　WDR/YW UB7 ....112 D1
　WHTN TW2 ....155 J2
　WIM/MER SW19 ....177 H2
　WIM/MER SW19 ....178 A3
High St Collier's Wd
　WIM/MER SW19 * 178 C3
High St Harlesden
　WLSDN NW10 ....99 H1
High St Harlington
　HTHAIR TW6 ....133 G2
High Street Ms
　WIM/MER SW19 ....177 H1
High St North MNPK E12 ....89 J4
High St South EHAM E6 ....107 K2
High Timber St BLKFR EC4V....12 C5
High Tor CI BMLY BR1 * 184 A5
High Trees BRXS/STRHM SW2...162 B3
　CROY/NA CRO 198 A6
　EBAR EN4 ....21 J6
High View PIN HA5 ....59 F2
High Vw BLFR HA9 * 80 B2
Highview Av EDGW HA8 ....30 E6
High View Av WLGTN SM6 .....211 F3
High View CI NRWD SE19 ......181 G5
Highview Gdns EDGW HA8.......30 E6
　FBAR/BDGN N11 ....48 C2
　FNCH N3 ....46 C6
High View Rd SCUP DA14 .....168 C6
High Vw Rd WEA W13 ....116 B1
Highview Rd SCUP DA14 ....168 C6
Highview Ter DART DA1 * 151 G6
The Highway BELMT SM2 ....209 H6
　ORP BR6 ....217 J3

STAN HA7 ....43 F4
WCHPL E1 ....104 C6
Highwood Av
　NFNCH/WDSPK N12 ....33 G6
Highwood CI FSTH SE23 ....163 H3
　ORP BR6 ....201 H6
Highwood Dr ORP BR6 ....201 H6
Highwood Gdns CLAY IG5 ....71 K2
Highwood Gv MLHL NW7 ....31 F5
Highwood HI MLHL NW7 ....31 H5
Highwood Rd ARCH N19 ....85 F1
High Worple RYLN/HDSTN HA2...59 H3
Highworth Rd FBAR/BDGN N11...48 D2
Highworth St CAMTN NW1 * 8 D1
Hilary Av MTCM CR4 ....179 F6
Hilary CI ERITH DA8 ....83 J6
　FUL/PGN SW6 * 140 A1
Hilary Rd SHB W12 ....99 H6
Hilberry Ct BUSH WD23 * 28 B2
Hilbert Rd CHEAM SM3 ....208 B2
Hilborough CI WIM/MER SW19...178 B3
Hilborough Rd HACK E8 * 86 B4
Hilborough Wy ORP BR6 ....216 D3
Hilda Lockert Wk
　BRXN/ST SW9 * 142 C3
Hilda Rd CAN/RD E16 ....106 C3
　EHAM E6 ....89 H5
Hilda Ter BRXN/ST SW9 ....142 B3
Hilda Vale Rd ORP BR6 ....216 A2
Hildenborough Gdns
　BMLY BR1 ....183 H3
Hilden Dr ERITH DA8 ....150 E1
Hildenlea PI HAYES BR2 ....183 H5
Hildreth St BAL SW12 ....161 G3
Hildyard Rd FUL/PGN SW6 ....119 K6
Hiley Rd WLSDN NW10 ....99 K3
Hilgrove Rd KIL/WHAMP NW6...83 F6
Hiliary Gdns STAN HA7 ....43 J5
Hiliary Crs WDGN N22 * 67 K5
Hiliary Dr ISLW TW7 * 136 A5
Hiliary Rd BAR EN5 ....21 J5
Hiliary Rd WLSDN NW10 * 115 F3
Hillbeck CI PECK SE15 ....143 K1
Hillbeck Wy GFD/PVL UB6 ......78 D6
Hillboro Ct WFD/HAR UB3......113 K5
Hillborough CI
　WIM/MER SW19 * 178 B3
Hillbrook Rd TOOT SW17 ......160 E5
Hill Brow BMLY BR1 ....184 C4
　DART DA1 ....170 C1
Hillbrow NWMAL KT3 ....176 B6
Hillbrow CI BXLY DA5 ....170 A6
Hillbrow Rd BMLY BR1 ....183 H4
　ESH/CLAY KT10 ....204 B3
Hillbury Av
　KTN/HRWW/WS HA3..........61 H2
Hillbury Rd TOOT SW17 ....161 G5
Hillcote Av STRHM/NOR SW16...180 B1
Hillcourt Av
　NFNCH/WDSPK N12 ....47 F2
Hillcourt Rd EDUL SE22 ....163 J1
Hillcrest BRYLDS KT5 ....191 G2
　BXLY DA5 ....169 K3
　HRW HA1 ....61 G2
　TRDG/WHET N20 ....33 F4
　WRK KT4 ....193 G6
Hill Crest BFN/LL DA15 ....168 B2
　HNHL SE24 ....142 E6
Hillcrest HGT N6 ....66 A4
　SEVS/STOTM N15 ....67 K2
Hillcrest Av GLDGN NW11 ....64 C2
　PIN HA5 ....59 H2
Hillcrest CI BECK BR3 ....198 C3
　SYD SE26 ....163 G6
Hill Crest Gdns CRICK NW2 ....81 J3
Hillcrest Gdns ESH/CLAY KT10...205 F2
　FNCH N3 ....46 C6
Hillcrest Rd ACT W3 ....117 H1
　BMLY BR1 ....183 K6
　DART DA1 ....170 C2
　EA W5 ....98 A4
　EMPK RM11 ....75 J4
　LOU IG10 ....39 H1
　ORP BR6 ....202 B6
　WALTH E17 ....52 B5
Hillcrest Vw BECK BR3 ....198 C3
Hillcroft Crs EA W5 ....97 K5
Hillcroft Crs EA W5 ....97 K5
　OXHEY WD19 ....27 F3
　RSLP HA4 ....59 G2
　WBLY HA9 ....80 B2
Hillcroft Rd EHAM E6 ....108 A4
Hillcroome Rd BELMT SM2 ....209 H4
Hilldale Rd SUT SM1 ....208 C2
Hilldown Rd HAYES BR2 ....199 H5
　STRHM/NOR SW16 ....179 K3
Hill Dr STRHM/NOR SW16 .....180 A6
　WBLY HA9 ....62 D5
Hilldrop Crs HOLWY N7 ....84 D3
Hilldrop La HOLWY N7 * 84 D3
Hilldrop Rd BMLY BR1 ....184 A2
　HOLWY N7 ....84 D3
Hiller Gdns CROY/NA CRO * ...211 F2
Hillersdon Av BARN SW13 .....138 D3
　EDGW HA8 ....30 B6
Hillery CI WALW SE17 ....19 F7
Hill Farm Rd NKENS W10 ....100 A4
Hillfield Av ALP/SUD HA0 ....80 C2
　CDALE/KGS NW9 ....63 G2
　CEND/HSY/T N8 ....66 E3
　MRDN SM4 ....194 D3
Hillfield CI RYLN/HDSTN HA2...60 C1
Hillfield La South BUSH WD23...28 E3
Hillfield Ms CEND/HSY/T N8.....67 F1
Hillfield Pde MRDN SM4 * 194 C3
Hillfield Pk MUSWH N10 ....66 B1

WCHMH N21......................35 G4
Hillfield Park Ms MUSWH N10....66 B1
Hill Field Rd HPTN TW12........172 E3
Hillfield Rd KIL/WHAMP NW6....82 D3
Hillfoot Av CRW RM5............56 E4
Hillfoot Rd CRW RM5............56 E4
Hillgate Pl BAL SW12..........161 C1
KENS W8.......................119 K1
Hillgate St KENS W8...........119 K1
Hill Gv FELT TW13.............154 E4
ROM RM1........................57 C6
Hill House Av STAN HA7.........43 F5
Hill House Cl WCHMH N21........35 G2
Hill House Dr HPTN TW12.......173 F4
Hill House Rd
   STRHM/NOR SW16.............180 A1
Hilliard Rd KIL/WHAMP HA6......40 D4
Hilliard's Ct WAP E1W.........123 K1
Hillier Cl BAR EN5.............33 F1
Hillier Gdns CROY/NA CRO......211 G3
Hillier Pl CHSGTN KT9.........205 K4
Hillier Rd BTSEA SW11.........160 E1
Hillier's La CROY/NA CRO......210 E1
Hillingdon Av
   STWL/WRAY TW19.............152 B3
Hillingdon Rd BXLYHN DA7......149 K4
Hillingdon St WALW SE17.......122 C6
Hillingdon Trail HYS/HAR UB3..113 K5
Hill La RSLP HA4...............58 A5
Hillman Dr NKENS W10..........100 A3
Hillman St HACK E8.............86 D4
Hillmarton Rd HOLWY N7.........84 E3
Hillmead Dr BRXN/ST SW9......142 C5
Hillmont Rd ESH/CLAY KT10....204 E3
Hillmore Gv SYD SE26..........182 B1
Hillreach WOOL/PLUM SE18......126 E5
Hill Ri ED N9..................36 D1
   ESH/CLAY KT10..............190 C6
   FSTH SE23..................163 J3
   GFD/PVL UB6.................78 C5
   GLDGN NW11..................64 E3
   RCHPK/HAM TW10.............136 E6
   RSLP HA4....................58 A5
Hillrise Rd ARCH N19...........66 E4
   CRW RM5.....................56 E4
Hill Rd ALP/SUD HA0............79 H1
   CAR SM5...................209 J4
   HRW HA1.....................61 C2
   MTCM CR4...................179 G4
   MUSWH N10...................48 A5
   NTHWD HA6...................40 B2
   PIN HA5.....................59 J3
   RDART DA2..................171 H4
   STJWD NW8..................101 C1
   SUT SM1....................209 C3
Hillsboro Rd EDUL SE22........143 F6
Hillsborough Gn OXHEY WD19.....26 E3
Hillsgrove Cl WELL DA16.......148 D1
Hill Side BAR EN5..............21 G6
Hillside CDALE/KGS NW9.........63 F2
   ESH/CLAY KT10..............204 B3
   WIM/MER SW19...............177 C2
   WLSDN NW10..................81 F6
Hillside Av FBAR/BDGN N11......47 K2
   WBLY HA9....................80 B2
   WFD IG8.....................45 G5
Hillside Cl MRDN SM4..........193 H1
   STJWD NW8..................101 F1
   WFD IG8.....................53 C1
Hillside Crs ENC/FH EN2........23 J1
   NTHWD HA6...................40 E4
   OXHEY WD19..................27 H1
   RYLN/HDSTN HA2..............60 C6
Hillside Dr EDGW HA8...........44 C2
Hillside Gdns BAR EN5..........20 C4
   BRXS/STRHM SW2.............162 B4
   EDGW HA8....................30 B6
   FBAR/BDGN N11...............48 C2
   HGT N6......................66 B3
   KTN/HRWW/WS HA3.............62 A4
   NTHWD HA6...................41 F5
   WALTH E17...................52 B6
   WLGTN SM6..................210 C5
Hillside Gv MLHL NW7...........45 J3
   STHGT/OAK N14...............34 D2
Hillside La HAYES BR2.........199 K6
Hillside Ri NTHWD HA6..........40 E4
Hillside Rd BELMT SM2.........208 D5
   BRXS/STRHM SW2.............162 A4
   CROY/NA CR0................211 H3
   DART DA1...................170 D1
   EA W5.......................98 A4
   HAYES BR2..................183 J6
   NTHWD HA6...................40 E3
   PIN HA5.....................41 F3
   SEVS/STOTM N15.............68 A1
   STHL UB1....................96 A3
The Hillside ORP BR6..........217 H6
Hills La NTHWD HA6.............40 D4
Hillsleigh Rd KENS W8.........119 J1
Hills Ms EA W5.................98 A6
Hills Pl SOHO/SHAV W1D........10 A4
Hill's Rd BKHH IG9.............39 F3
Hillstowe St CLPT E5...........68 E6
Hill St MYFR/PICC W1J..........9 J7
   MAYFR/PICC W1J.............136 E6
Hill Top CHEAM SM3............193 J4
   GLDGN NW11..................64 E3
Hilltop WALTH E17..............51 K6
Hilltop Av WLSDN NW10..........80 E5
Hilltop Cottages SYD SE26....163 J6
Hilltop Gdns DART DA1.........151 J6
   HDN NW4.....................46 B6
   ORP BR6....................201 K6
Hilltop Rd KIL/WHAMP NW6.......82 E5
Hill Top Vw WFD IG8............53 K2
Hilltop Wy STAN HA7............29 G5
Hillview RYNPK SW20...........176 E4
Hillview Av
   KTN/HRWW/WS HA3.............62 A2
Hillview Cl PIN HA5............41 K2
   WBLY HA9....................80 B1
Hillview Crs IL IG1............71 K5
   ORP BR6....................201 K5
Hill View Dr THMD SE28........127 K1
   WELL DA16..................147 K3

Hill View Gdns CDALE/KGS NW9...63 F2
Hillview Gdns HDN NW4..........64 B1
   RYLN/HDSTN HA2..............42 A6
Hill View Rd ESH/CLAY KT10....205 G5
   ORP BR6....................202 A5
   TWK TW1....................156 B1
Hillview Rd CHST BR7..........185 F1
   MLHL NW7....................32 B6
   PIN HA5.....................41 K3
   SUT SM1....................209 G1
Hillway CDALE/KGS NW9..........63 F2
   HGT N6......................66 A6
Hillworth BECK BR3............182 E5
Hillworth Rd
   BRXS/STRHM SW2.............162 B2
Hillyard Rd HNWL W7............96 E4
Hillyard St BRXN/ST SW9......142 B2
Hillyfield WALTH E17...........51 G5
Hillyfield Cl HOM E9...........87 G3
Hilly Fields Crs BROCKY SE4..144 D4
Hilsea St CLPT E5..............86 E2
Hilton Av NFNCH/WDSPK N12.....47 H1
Himalayan Wy WATW WD18........26 D1
Himley Rd TOOT SW17...........178 D1
Hinchley Cl ESH/CLAY KT10....205 F3
Hinchley Dr ESH/CLAY KT10....205 F3
Hinchley Wy ESH/CLAY KT10....205 G3
Hinckley Rd EDUL SE22........143 H5
Hind Cl CHIG IG7...............55 F1
Hind Ct FLST/FETLN EC4A.......11 K4
Hind Crs ERITH DA8............149 K1
Hinde Ms MHST W1U..............9 H3
Hindes Rd HRW HA1.............60 E2
Hinde St MHST W1U..............9 H3
Hindhead Gdns NTHLT UB5.......77 J6
Hindhead Gn OXHEY WD19.........41 C1
Hindhead Wy WLGTN SM6........210 E3
Hindmans Rd EDUL SE22........143 H6
Hindmans Wy DAGW RM9.........110 B5
Hindmarsh Cl WCHPL E1 *......104 C6
Hindrey Rd CLPT E5.............86 D3
Hindsley's Pl FSTH SE23......163 K4
Hinkler Rd KTN/HRWW/WS HA3....43 K6
Hinksey Pth ABYW SE2..........128 E3
Hinstock Rd
   WOOL/PLUM SE18.............147 H1
Hinton Av HSLWW TW4..........134 C5
Hinton Cl ELTH/MOT SE9.......166 D3
Hinton Rd BRXN/ST SW9........142 B5
   UED N18.....................36 A6
   WLGTN SM6..................210 C4
Hippodrome Pl NTGHL W11......100 C6
Hirst Crs WBLY HA9.............80 A1
Hitcham Rd WALTH E17...........69 H4
Hithermoor Rd
   HYS/HAR UB3................113 K1
Hither Farm Rd
   BKHTH/KID SE3..............146 B4
Hitherfield Rd BCTR RM8........74 A1
   STRHM/NOR SW16.............162 A4
Hither Green La LEW SE13.....165 C1
Hitherwell Dr
   KTN/HRWW/WS HA3.............42 D4
Hitherwood Dr NRWD SE19......163 G6
Hive Cl BUSH WD23..............28 D4
Hive Rd BUSH WD23..............28 D4
Hoadly Rd STRHM/NOR SW16.....161 J5
Hobart Cl TRDG/WHET N20........33 J4
Hobart Dr YEAD UB4.............95 H3
Hobart Gdns THHTH CR7.........180 E6
Hobart La YEAD UB4.............95 H3
Hobart Pl BCVA SW1W............15 J5
   RCHPK/HAM TW10.............157 F2
Hobart Rd BARK/HLT IG6.........54 C5
   DAGW RM9....................91 K2
   WPK KT4....................207 K1
   YEAD UB4....................95 H3
Hobbayne Rd HNWL W7............96 D5
Hobbes Wk PUT/ROE SW15.......138 E6
Hobbs Gn EFNCH N2..............47 G6
Hobbs Pl IS N1.................7 G2
Hobbs Place Est IS N1..........7 G2
Hobbs Rd WNWD SE27...........162 D6
Hobby St PEND EN3..............25 F5
Hobday St POP/IOD E14.........105 K5
Hobsons End CHST BR7..........185 K2
Hobsons Pl WCHPL E1 *.........104 C4
Hobury St WBPTN SW10.........120 B6
Hockenden La SWLY BR8.........187 H6
Hocker St BETH E2..............7 J5
Hockley Av EHAM E6............107 J1
Hockley Dr GPK RM2.............57 K5
Hockley Ms BARK IG11..........108 E1
Hocroft Av CRICK NW2...........82 D1
Hocroft Rd CRICK NW2...........82 D1
Hocroft Wk CRICK NW2...........82 D1
Hodder Dr GFD/PVL UB6..........97 F1
Hoddesdon Rd BELV DA17.......129 H5
Hodes Rw HAMP NW3.............83 K2
Hodford Rd GLDGN NW11..........64 D5
Hodges Wy WATW WD18............26 E1
Hodgkins Cl THMD SE28........109 K6
Hodgkins Ms STAN HA7...........43 H1
Hodister Cl CMBW SE5.........142 D1
Hodson Cl RYLN/HDSTN HA2......59 J1
Hodson Crs STMC/STPC BR5....202 E3
Hodson Pl PEND EN3.............25 J1
Hoe La EN EN1..................24 D1
Hoe St WALTH E17...............69 J2
The Hoe OXHEY WD19.............27 H4
Hoffmann Gdns
   SAND/SEL CR2...............212 C4
Hoffman Sq IS N1 *.............7 F4
Hofland Rd WKENS W14.........119 H3
Hogan Ms BAY/PAD W2............8 A2
Hogarth Cl CAN/RD E16........107 H4
   EA W5.......................98 A4
Hogarth Crs CROY/NA CR0......196 D4
   WIM/MER SW19...............178 C4
Hogarth Gdns HEST TW5.......135 F1
Hogarth Hl GLDGN NW11..........64 D1
Hogarth Pl ECT SW5 *.........120 A4
Hogarth Rd BCTR RM8............91 H3
   ECT SW5....................120 A4

EDGW HA8......................44 C5
Hogarth Wy HPTN TW12.........173 H4
Hog Hill Rd CRW RM5............56 B3
Hogshead Pas WAP E1W *.......104 D6
Hogsmill Wy HOR/WEW KT19....206 E3
Holbeach Cl CDALE/KGS NW9.....45 G4
Holbeck Rw PECK SE15.........143 H1
Holbeach Rd CAT SE6..........164 E2
Holbein Ga NTHWD HA6..........40 A4
Holbein Ms BCVA SW1W..........121 F5
Holbein Pl BCVA SW1W..........15 G2
Holborn HCIRC EC1N.............11 J2
Holborn Circ HCIRC EC1N.......11 K2
Holborn Pl HHOL WC1V..........11 G2
Holborn Rd PLSTW E15.........107 F4
Holborn Viad STBT EC1A........12 A3
Holbrook Cl EN EN1.............24 B2
Holbrooke Ct HOLWY N7.........84 E1
Holbrook La CHST BR7.........185 J3
Holbrook Rd SRTFD E15.........106 D1
Holburne Cl
   BKHTH/KID SE3..............146 B2
Holburne Gdns
   BKHTH/KID SE3..............146 B2
Holburne Rd BKHTH/KID SE3....146 B2
Holcombe Hl MLHL NW7..........31 J5
Holcombe Rd IL IG1.............72 A4
   TOTM N17....................50 B6
Holcombe St HMSMTH W6........118 E5
Holcote Cl BELV DA17..........129 F3
Holcroft Rd HOM E9............86 E4
Holden Av CDALE/KGS NW9.......62 E5
   NFNCH/WDSPK N12............47 F1
Holdenby Rd BROCKY SE4......144 B6
Holden Cl BCTR RM8............91 H1
Holdenhurst Av FNCH N3........47 G2
Holden Rd NFNCH/WDSPK N12.....33 E6
Holden St BTSEA SW11.........141 F3
Holdernesse Rd ISLW TW7.....136 B2
   TOOT SW17..................160 E5
Holderness Wy WNWD SE27.....180 J1
Holders Hill Av HDN NW4.......46 B5
Holders Hill Crs HDN NW4......46 B5
Holders Hill Dr HDN NW4.......46 B5
Holders Hill Pde MLHL NW7 *...46 C5
Holders Hill Rd HDN NW4.......46 C5
Holford Ms FSBYW WC1X *........5 C4
Holford Rd HAMP NW3...........83 G1
Holford St FSBYW WC1X..........5 J4
Holford Yd FSBYW WC1X *........5 J3
Holgate Av BTSEA SW11........140 C4
Holgate Gdns DAGE RM10.......92 C5
Holgate St CHARL SE7.........126 C3
Holland Av BELMT SM2.........208 E5
   RYNPK SW20.................176 D5
Holland Cl HAYES BR2.........199 J6
   ROMW/RG RM7.................74 E2
   STAN HA7....................43 H1
   TRDG/WHET N20...............33 H2
Holland Dr FSTH SE23.........164 B5
Holland Gdns BTFD TW8........117 C5
   WKENS W14..................119 H3
Holland Pk BRXN/ST SW9......142 B1
   NTGHL W11..................119 J1
Holland Park Av
   NTGHL W11..................119 H1
Holland Park Gdns
   NTGHL W11..................119 H1
Holland Park Ms NTCHL W11....119 J1
Holland Park Rd WKENS W14....119 J3
Holland Park Ter NTGHL W11...119 H1
Holland Pas IS N1..............85 J6
Holland Pl KENS W8............120 A2
Holland Pl Chambers
   KENS W8 *..................120 A2
Holland Rd ALP/SUD HA0........79 K4
   EHAM E6....................90 A5
   SNWD SE25..................197 H2
   WKENS W14..................119 G2
   WLSDN NW10..................99 J1
The Hollands WPK KT4.........192 C5
Holland St KENS W8............119 K2
   STHWK SE1...................12 B7
Holland Villas Rd WKENS W14..119 H2
Holland Wk STAN HA7............43 G1
Holland Wy HAYES BR2.........199 J6
Hollar Rd STNW/STAM N16.......86 B1
Hollen St SOHO/CST W1F........10 B4
Holles Cl HPTN TW12..........173 F2
Holles St CAVSQ/HST W1G........9 K3
Holley Rd ACT W3.............118 B2
Hollickwood Av
   NFNCH/WDSPK N12............47 K2
Holliday Sq BTSEA SW11 *.....140 C4
Hollidge Wy DAGE RM10.........92 D5
Hollies Av BFN/LL DA15.......167 K3
Hollies Cl STRHM/NOR SW16....180 B2
   TWK TW1....................156 A4
Hollies End MLHL NW7...........45 K1
Hollies Rd EA W5..............116 D4
The Hollies
   KTN/HRWW/WS HA3.............61 C1
Hollies Wy BAL SW12 *........161 F2
Holligrave Rd BMLY BR1.......183 K4
Hollingbourne Av
   BXLYHN DA7.................149 G6
Hollingbourne Gdns WEA W13....97 H4
Hollingbourne Rd HNHL SE24...162 D1
Hollingsworth Rd
   CROY/NA CR0................212 D4
Hollington Crs NWMAL KT3.....192 C3
Hollington Rd EHAM E6........107 K2
   TOTM N17....................50 C5
Hollingworth Cl
   E/WMO/HCT KT8..............188 E1
Hollingworth Rd
   STMC/STPC BR5..............201 C4
Hollman Gdns
   STRHM/NOR SW16.............180 C2

Holloway Cl WDR/YW UB7.......112 B5
Holloway La WDR/YW UB7.......112 C4
Holloway Rd ARCH N19..........66 D6
   EHAM E6....................107 K2
   HOLWY N7....................85 F2
   WAN E11.....................88 D1
Holloway St HSLW TW3.........135 G4
The Hollow WFD IG8.............38 D6
Holly Av BAR EN5..............21 K2
   STAN HA7....................44 A5
   WOT/HER KT12...............188 C5
Holly Bank MUSWH N10..........66 C1
Hollybank Cl HPTN TW12.......173 F1
Hollybrake Cl CHST BR7.......185 J3
Hollybush Cl
   KTN/HRWW/WS HA3.............42 E4
   OXHEY WD19..................27 C2
   WAN E11.....................70 E1
Hollybush Gdns BETH E2.......104 D2
Hollybush Hl WAN E11..........70 D4
Holly Bush La HPTN TW12......172 E5
Hollybush Pl BETH E2.........104 D2
Hollybush Rd KUTN/CMB KT2....175 F2
Hollybush St PLSTW E15.......107 F2
Hollybush Ter NRWD SE19 *....181 F2
Holly Bush V HAMP NW3.........83 G2
Holly Cl BECK BR3............199 F1
   BKHH IG9....................39 H5
   FELT TW13..................172 D1
   WLGTN SM6..................210 B5
   WLSDN NW10..................81 G5
Holly Crs BECK BR3...........198 C3
   WFD IG8.....................52 B3
Hollycroft Av HAMP NW3........82 E1
   WBLY HA9....................62 A6
Hollycroft Cl SAND/SEL CR2...212 A3
   WDR/YW UB7.................112 D1
Hollycroft Gdns WDR/YW UB7...112 D6
Hollydale Cl NTHLT UB5........78 B3
Hollydale Dr HAYES BR2.......215 K1
Hollydale Rd PECK SE15.......143 K2
Hollydene BRXN/ST SW9........142 C2
   PECK SE15..................143 K1
Holly Dr BKHH IG9..............39 H1
   CHING E4....................37 K2
Holly Farm Rd NWDGN UB2......114 D5
Hollyfield Av FBAR/BDGN N11...47 K1
Hollyfield Rd BRYLDS KT5.....191 G4
Holly Gdns BXLYHN DA7........149 K5
   WDR/YW UB7.................112 C2
Hollygrove BUSH WD23..........28 D2
Holly Gv CDALE/KGS NW9........62 E4
   PECK SE15..................143 C3
   PIN HA5.....................41 J4
Hollygrove Cl HSLW TW3.......134 E5
Holly Hedge Ter LEW SE13.....145 G6
Holly Hl HAMP NW3.............83 G1
   WCHMH N21...................35 F1
Holly Hill Rd BELV DA17......129 J5
Holly Lodge Gdns HGT N6.......66 A6
Hollymead CAR SM5............209 K1
Holly Ms WBPTN SW10..........120 B5
Holly Mt HAMP NW3 *...........83 G2
Holly Park Est FSBYPK N4......67 F4
Holly Park Gdns FNCH N3.......46 E6
Holly Park Rd FBAR/BDGN N11...34 A6
   HNWL W7.....................96 A6
Holly Pk FNCH N3..............46 D6
   FSBYPK N4...................67 F4
Holly Rd CHSWK W4 *..........118 A4
   DART DA1...................171 G3
   HPTN TW12..................173 H2
   HSLW TW3...................135 G5
   ORP BR6....................217 J5
   TWK TW1....................156 B3
   WAN E11.....................70 D4
Holly St HACK E8...............86 B5
Hollytree Cl WIM/MER SW19....159 G3
Hollytree Pde SCUP DA14 *....186 D1
Hollyview Cl HDN NW4..........63 J3
Holly Vls HMSMTH W6..........118 E3
Holly Wk HAMP NW3.............83 G2
Holly Wy MTCM CR4............195 K1
Hollywood Gdns YEAD UB4.......95 H5
Hollywood Ms WBPTN SW10 *....120 B6
Hollywood Rd CHING E4.........51 G1
   WBPTN SW10.................120 B6
Hollywoods CROY/NA CR0......213 H6
Hollywood Wy ERITH DA8.......150 E2
   WFD IG8.....................51 J1
Holman Ct EW KT17 *..........207 J6
Holman Rd BTSEA SW11.........140 C3
   HOR/WEW KT19...............206 E3
Holmbridge Gdns PEND EN3......25 F5
Holmbrook Dr HDN NW4..........64 B2
Holmbury Ct RYNPK SW20.......176 A4
Holmbury Gv CROY/NA CR0......213 H5
Holmbury Pk BMLY BR1.........184 C2
Holmbury Vw CLPT E5...........68 D5
Holmbush Rd PUT/ROE SW15....139 H1
Holmcote Gdns HBRY N5.........85 J3
Holmcroft Wy HAYES BR2......200 E2
Holmdale Rd CHST BR7.........185 H1
   KIL/WHAMP NW6...............82 E5
Holmdale Ter SEVS/STOTM N15...68 A3
Holmdene Av HNHL SE24.......142 D6
   MLHL NW7....................45 H1
   RYLN/HDSTN HA2.............42 B6
Holmdene Cl BECK BR3.........183 F5
Holmdene Ct BMLY BR1.........184 D6
Holmead Rd FUL/PGN SW6......140 A1
Holme Cl CHSHNT EN8...........31 K1
Holme Ct ISLW TW7............136 B4
Holme Lacey Rd
   LEE/GVPK SE12..............165 J1
Holme Rd EHAM E6.............107 J6
   WALTH E17...................51 H6
Holmes Cl EDUL SE22..........143 H5
Holmesdale Av
   MORT/ESHN SW14.............137 J4
Holmesdale Cl SNWD SE25.....181 G6
Holmesdale Rd BXLYHN DA7....148 E3
   HGT N6......................66 B4
   RCH/KEW TW9................137 G2
   SNWD SE25..................196 E2

TEDD TW11.....................174 D5
Holmesley Rd FSTH SE23.......164 B1
Holmes Rd KTTN NW5.............84 B4
   TWK TW1....................156 A4
   WIM/MER SW19...............178 B5
Holmes Ter STHWK SE1...........17 J2
Holme Wy STAN HA7.............43 F2
Holmewood Gdns
   BRXS/STRHM SW2.............162 A2
Holmewood Rd
   BRXS/STRHM SW2.............161 K2
   SNWD SE25..................181 F6
Holmfield Av HDN NW4..........64 B2
Holmhurst Rd BELV DA17.......129 J5
Holmleigh Rd STNW/STAM N16....68 A5
   WIM Oak Cl PUT/ROE SW15...159 J1
Holmsdale Gv BXLYHN DA7.....150 B3
Holmshaw Cl SYD SE26.........164 C5
Holmside Ri OXHEY WD19........27 F5
Holmside Rd BAL SW12.........161 F1
Holmsley Cl NWMAL KT3.......192 C5
Holmstall Av CDALE/KGS NW9....44 E6
Holmstall Pde EDGW HA8 *......44 E6
Holmwood Cl BELMT SM2.......208 B6
   NTHLT UB5...................78 B4
   RYLN/HDSTN HA2.............42 C6
Holmwood Gdns FNCH N3.........46 E5
   WLGTN SM6..................210 B4
Holmwood Gv MLHL NW7..........45 F1
Holmwood Rd BELMT SM2 *.....208 A5
   CHSGTN KT9.................205 K3
   GDMY/SEVK IG3...............73 F5
Holne Cha EFNCH N2...........65 G1
   MRDN SM4...................193 K3
Holness Rd SRTFD E15..........88 D4
Holroyd Rd ESH/CLAY KT10....205 H6
   PUT/ROE SW15...............139 F5
Holstein Wy ERITH DA18.......128 E3
Holstock Rd IL IG1.............72 C6
Holsworth Cl RYLN/HDSTN HA2...60 B3
Holsworthy Sq FSBYW WC1X......5 H7
Holsworthy Wy CHSGTN KT9....205 J3
Holt Cl CHIG IG7...............55 F1
   MUSWH N10...................65 K1
Holton St WCHPL E1...........105 F3
Holt Rd ALP/SUD HA0...........79 H1
   CAN/RD E16.................126 C2
The Holt BARK/HLT IG6.........54 C2
   MRDN SM4...................193 K1
   WLGTN SM6..................210 C2
Holt Wy CHIG IG7...............55 F1
Holtwhite Av ENC/FH EN2.......23 J3
Holtwhite's Hl ENC/FH EN2.....23 J3
Holwell Pl PIN HA5.............59 J1
Holwood Cl WOT/HER KT12......188 B6
Holwood Park Av ORP BR6.....215 G2
Holwood Pl CLAP SW4..........141 J5
Holybourne Av
   PUT/ROE SW15...............158 D2
Holyhead Cl BOW E3...........105 J2
Holyoake Ct BERM/RHTH SE16...124 B2
Holyoake Wk EA W5.............97 J5
   EFNCH N2....................47 G6
Holyport Rd FUL/PGN SW6.....139 F1
Holyrood Gdns EDGW HA8........44 D5
Holyrood Ms CAN/RD E16.......125 K3
Holyrood Rd BAR EN5...........33 F1
Holyrood St STHWK SE1..........19 G2
Holywell Cl BERM/RHTH SE16...123 J5
   BKHTH/KID SE3..............145 K5
   ORP BR6....................217 G2
Holywell La SDTCH EC2A.........7 H5
   STWL/WRAY TW19.............152 B3
Holywell Rw SDTCH EC2A.........7 G6
Holywell Wy
   STWL/WRAY TW19.............152 B3
Home Cl CAR SM5..............194 E6
   NTHLT UB5...................95 K2
Home Ct FELT TW13 *..........153 K3
   SURB KT6...................190 E2
Homecroft Rd SYD SE26........181 K1
   WDGN N22....................49 H4
Home Farm Cl ESH/CLAY KT10..204 B4
   THDIT KT7..................190 A4
Home Farm Rd
   WOT/HER KT12...............188 C6
Homefarm Rd HNWL W7...........96 E5
Homefield Av GNTH/NBYPK IG2...72 D2
Homefield Cl STMC/STPC BR5..202 C1
   WLSDN NW10..................80 E4
   YEAD UB4....................95 H3
Homefield Gdns EFNCH N2.......47 H6
   WIM/MER SW19...............177 J1
Homefield Pk SUT SM1.........209 F3
Homefield Ri ORP BR6.........202 C4
Homefield Rd ALP/SUD HA0......79 G3
   BMLY BR1...................184 B4
   CHSWK W4...................118 C4
   EDGW HA8....................45 F2
   WIM/MER SW19...............177 H2
   WOT/HER KT12...............188 C4
Homefield St IS N1 *...........7 C3
The Homefield MRDN SM4 *.....177 J5
Home Gdns DAGE RM10...........92 E1
   DART DA1...................171 H1
Homeland Dr BELMT SM2.......209 F6
Homelands Dr NRWD SE19......181 F3
Home Lea ORP BR6.............217 F3
Homeleigh Rd PECK SE15.......143 K5
Home Md STAN HA7..............43 J4
Homemead CROY/NA CR0........195 H3
   HAYES BR2..................200 D2
Home Park Rd
   WIM/MER SW19...............159 K5
Home Park Ter KUT/HW KT1....174 E5
Home Park Wk KUT/HW KT1.....190 E1
Homer Cl BXLYHN DA7.........150 A2
Homer Dr POP/IOD E14........124 D4
Homer Rd CROY/NA CR0........198 A3
   HOM E9......................87 G4

Homer Rw CAMTN NW1 8 D2
Homersham Rd KUT/HW KT1 175 H5
Homer St MBLAR W1H 8 D2
Homerton Gv HOM E9 87 F3
Homerton High St HOM E9 87 F3
Homerton Rd HOM E9 87 H3
Homerton Rw HOM E9 86 E3
Homerton Ter HOM E9 86 E4
Homesdale Cl WAN E11 70 E2
Homesdale Rd HAYES BR2 200 B1
ORP BR6 201 K4
Homesfield GLDGN NW11 64 E2
Homestall Rd EDUL SE22 143 K6
Homestead Gdns
ESH/CLAY KT10 204 E3
Homestead Paddock
STHGT/OAK N14 22 B6
Homestead Pk CRICK NW2 81 H1
Homestead Rd BCTR RM8 74 B6
FUL/PGN SW6 139 J1
ORP BR6 217 H5
The Homestead DART DA1 171 F1
Homewillow Cl WCHMH N21 35 H1
Homewood Cl HPTN TW12 172 E2
Homewood Crs CHST BR7 185 K2
Homewood Gdns
SNWD SE25 * 197 F2
Honduras St FSBYE EC1V 6 C6
Honeybourne Rd
KIL/WHAMP NW6 83 F3
Honeybourne Wy
STMC/STPC BR5 201 H5
Honeybrook Rd BAL SW12 161 H2
Honey Cl DAGE RM10 92 E4
Honeyden Rd SCUP DA14 187 F2
Honeyman Cl CRICK NW2 82 B5
Honeypot Cl CDALE/KGS NW9 62 B1
Honeypot La CDALE/KGS NW9 62 B1
KTN/HRWW/WS HA3 44 B6
STAN HA7 44 A4
Honeysett Rd TOTM N17 50 B5
Honeysuckle Cl STHL UB1 95 J6
Honeysuckle Gdns
CROY/NA CR0 198 A4
Honeywell Rd BTSEA SW11 160 D1
Honeywood Rd ISLW TW7 * 136 B5
WLSDN NW10 99 H1
Honeywood Wk CAR SM5 209 K2
Honister Cl STAN HA7 43 H4
Honister Gdns STAN HA7 43 H3
Honister Pl STAN HA7 43 H4
Honiton Gdns MLHL NW7 46 B3
PECK SE15 * 143 K3
Honiton Rd KIL/WHAMP NW6 100 D1
ROMW/RG RM7 75 F3
WELL DA16 148 A3
Honley Rd CAT SE6 164 E2
Honnor Gdns ISLW TW7 135 J3
Honor Oak Pk FSTH SE23 163 K2
Honor Oak Ri FSTH SE23 163 K1
Honor Oak Rd FSTH SE23 163 K3
Hood Av MORT/ESHN SW14 137 K6
STHGT/OAK N14 34 B1
STMC/STPC BR5 202 C2
Hood Cl CROY/NA CR0 196 C5
Hoodcote Gdns WCHMH N21 35 H2
Hood Rd RAIN RM13 93 G6
RYNPK SW20 176 C3
Hood Wk ROMW/RG RM7 56 D4
Hooker's Rd WALTH E17 51 F6
Hook Farm Rd HAYES BR2 200 C2
Hook Green La RDART DA2 170 C6
Hooking Gn RYLN/HDSTN HA2 60 B2
Hook La WELL DA16 148 A6
Hook Ri North SURB KT6 206 C1
Hook Ri South CHSGTN KT9 206 B1
Hook Rd CHSGTN KT9 205 K3
HOR/WEW KT19 206 E5
SURB KT6 191 F6
Hooks Hall Dr DAGE RM10 92 E1
Hookstone Wy WFD IG8 53 H3
The Hook BAR EN5 33 H1
Hook U/P (Kingston By-Pass)
CHSGTN KT9 205 K1
Hook Wk EDGW HA8 44 E2
Hooper Rd CAN/RD E16 106 E5
Hooper's Ms ACT W3 117 K1
BUSH WD23 28 B3
Hooper St WCHPL E1 104 C6
Hoop La GLDGN NW11 64 D4
Hop Ct ALP/SUD HA0 * 79 J4
Hope Cl BTFD TW8 117 F5
CHDH RM6 73 K1
IS N1 85 J4
LEE/GVPK SE12 166 A5
SUT SM1 209 G3
Hopedale Rd CHARL SE7 126 A6
Hopefield Av
KIL/WHAMP NW6 100 C1
Hope Gdns ACT W3 117 J2
Hope La ELTH/MOT SE9 167 G5
Hope Pk BMLY BR1 183 J3
Hopes Cl HEST TW5 115 F6
Hope Sq LVPST EC2M 13 G2
Hope St BTSEA SW11 140 C5
Hopetown St WCHPL E1 * 13 K2
Hopewell St CMBW SE5 142 E1
Hopewell Yd CMBW SE5 142 E1
Hop Gdns CHCR WC2N 10 E6
Hopgood St SHB W12 119 F1
Hopkins Cl MUSWH N10 48 A3
Hopkins Ms SRTFD E15 88 D6
Hopkinsons Pl CAMTN NW1 * 83 K6
Hopkins Rd LEY E10 69 K4
Hopkins St SOHO/CST W1F 10 B4
Hoppers Rd WCHMH N21 35 G4
Hoppett Rd CHING E4 38 C5
Hopping La IS N1 * 85 H4
Hoppingwood Av NWMAL KT3 176 B6
Hoppner Rd YEAD UB4 94 B1
Hop St GNWCH SE10 125 J4
Hopton Gdns NWMAL KT3 192 D3
Hopton Pde
STRHM/NOR SW16 * 179 K1
Hopton Rd
STRHM/NOR SW16 179 K1
WOOL/PLUM SE18 127 G3
Hoptons Gdns STHWK SE1 * 12 B7
Hopton St STHWK SE1 12 B7
Hoptree Cl
NFNCH/WDSPK N12 * 33 F6
Hopwood Cl TOOT SW17 160 B5
Hopwood Rd WALW SE17 122 E6
Hopwood Wk HACK E8 * 86 C5
Horace Av ROMW/RG RM7 75 F5
Horace Rd BARK/HLT IG6 54 C6
FSTGT E7 89 F2
KUT/HW KT1 175 G6
Horatio Pl POP/IOD E14 125 F2
Horatio St BETH E2 7 K3
Horatius Wy CROY/NA CR0 211 F4
Horbury Crs NTGHL W11 100 E6
Horbury Ms NTGHL W11 100 D6
Horder Rd FUL/PGN SW6 139 H2
Hordle Prom East PECK SE15 143 G1
Hordle Prom North PECK SE15 143 G1
Hordle Prom West PECK SE15 143 F1
Horley Cl BXLYHS DA6 149 H6
Horley Rd ELTH/MOT SE9 166 D6
Hormead Rd MV/WKIL W9 100 D3
Hornbeam Cl IL IG1 90 D3
LBTH SE11 17 J6
MLHL NW7 31 H5
NTHLT UB5 77 K3
Hornbeam Crs BTFD TW8 136 C1
Hornbeam Gdns NWMAL KT3 192 D3
Hornbeam Gv CHING E4 38 D5
Hornbeam Rd BKHH IG9 39 H5
YEAD UB4 95 G4
Hornbeam Sq BOW E3 87 H6
Hornbeams Ri FBAR/BDGN N11 48 A2
Hornbeam Wy HAYES BR2 201 F3
Hornbuckle Cl
RYLN/HDSTN HA2 60 D6
Hornby Cl HAMP NW3 83 H5
Horncastle Cl LEE/GVPK SE12 165 K2
Horncastle Rd LEE/GVPK SE12 165 K2
Hornchurch Cl KUTN/CMB KT2 174 E1
Hornchurch Rd HCH RM12 75 H5
Horndean Cl PUT/ROE SW15 158 D3
Horndon Cl CRW RM5 56 E4
Horndon Gn CRW RM5 56 E4
Horndon Rd CRW RM5 56 E4
Horne House CHARL SE7 * 146 D1
Horner La MTCM CR4 178 C5
Horne Wy PUT/ROE SW15 139 F3
Hornfair Rd CHARL SE7 146 C1
Hornford Wy ROMW/RG RM7 75 G4
Horniman Dr FSTH SE23 163 J3
Horniman Gdns FSTH SE23 * 163 J3
Horning Cl ELTH/MOT SE9 166 D6
Horn La ACT W3 117 K1
GNWCH SE10 125 K4
WFD IG8 52 E2
Horn Link Wy GNWCH SE10 125 K4
Horn Park Cl LEE/GVPK SE12 146 A6
Horn Park La LEE/GVPK SE12 146 A6
Horns Cft BARK IG11 90 E5
Horns End Pl PIN HA5 59 G2
Hornsey Chambers CLPT E5 * 68 D6
Hornsey La HGT N6 66 C4
Hornsey Lane Est ARCH N19 66 D4
Hornsey Lane Gdns HGT N6 66 C4
Hornsey Park Rd
CEND/HSY/T N8 49 F6
Hornsey Ri ARCH N19 66 D4
Hornsey Rise Gdns ARCH N19 66 D4
Hornsey Rd ARCH N19 66 E5
Hornsey St HOLWY N7 85 F3
Hornshay St PECK SE15 123 K6
Horns Rd BARK/HLT IG6 72 C2
Hornton Pl KENS W8 119 K2
Hornton St KENS W8 119 K2
Horsa Rd ERITH DA8 149 K1
LEE/GVPK SE12 166 B2
Horsebridges Cl DAGW RM9 92 A6
Horsecroft Cl ORP BR6 202 C5
Horsecroft Rd EDGW HA8 45 F3
Horse Fair KUT/HW KT1 174 E5
Horseferry Pl GNWCH SE10 125 F6
Horseferry Rd POP/IOD E14 105 G6
WEST SW1P 16 C5
Horse Guards Av WHALL SW1A 16 E1
Horse Guards Rd WHALL SW1A 16 D1
Horse Leaze EHAM E6 108 B5
Horsell Rd HBRY N5 85 G3
STMC/STPC BR5 186 B4
Horselydown La STHWK SE1 19 J2
Horsenden Av GFD/PVL UB6 78 E3
Horsenden Crs GFD/PVL UB6 79 F3
Horsenden La North
GFD/PVL UB6 78 E4
Horsenden La South
GFD/PVL UB6 79 G6
Horseshoe Cl CRICK NW2 63 K6
POP/IOD E14 125 F5
Horse Shoe Crs NTHLT UB5 96 A1
Horseshoe La ENC/FH EN2 23 J4
TRDG/WHET N20 32 B3
Horseshoe Ms
BRXS/STRHM SW2 141 K5
Horse Yd IS N1 85 H6
Horsfeld Gdns ELTH/MOT SE9 146 D6
Horsfeld Rd ELTH/MOT SE9 146 C6
Horsford Rd
BRXS/STRHM SW2 142 A6
Horsham Av
NFNCH/WDSPK N12 47 J1
Horsham Rd BXLYHS DA6 169 H1
EBED/NFELT TW14 153 F1
Horsley Dr CROY/NA CR0 214 A5
KUTN/CMB KT2 174 E1
Horsley Rd BMLY BR1 184 A4
CHING E4 38 A4
Horsley St WALW SE17 122 E6
Horsmans Pl DART DA1 * 171 H2
Horsman St CMBW SE5 122 D6
Horsmonden Cl ORP BR6 201 K4
Horsmonden Rd BROCKY SE4 144 C6
Hortensia Rd WBPTN SW10 140 B1
Horticultural Pl CHSWK W4 118 A5
Horton Av CRICK NW2 82 C2
Horton Bridge Rd
WDR/YW UB7 112 C1
Horton Cl WDR/YW UB7 112 C1
Horton Pde WDR/YW UB7 * 112 B1
Horton Rd HACK E8 86 D4
WDR/YW UB7 112 B1
Horton St LEW SE13 144 E4
Horton Wy CROY/NA CR0 198 A2
Hortus Rd NWDGN UB2 114 E2
Hosack Rd TOOT SW17 161 F4
Hoser Av LEE/GVPK SE12 165 K4
Hosier La STBT EC1A 12 B2
Hoskin's Cl CAN/RD E16 107 G5
HYS/HAR UB3 113 J5
Hoskins St GNWCH SE10 125 G5
Hospital Bridge Rd WHTN TW2 155 G3
Hospital Rd HSLW TW3 135 F4
Hospital Wy LEW SE13 165 G1
Hotham Cl E/WMO/HCT KT8 173 F6
Hotham Rd PUT/ROE SW15 139 F4
Hotham Road Ms
WIM/MER SW19 178 B3
Hotham St SRTFD E15 88 C6
Hothfield Pl BERM/RHTH SE16 123 K3
Hotspur Rd NTHLT UB5 96 A1
Hotspur St LBTH SE11 122 B5
Houblon Rd
RCHPK/HAM TW10 137 F6
Houghton Cl HACK E8 * 86 B4
HPTN TW12 172 D2
Houghton Rd SEVS/STOTM N15 68 B1
Houghton St LINN WC2A * 11 H4
Houlder Crs CROY/NA CR0 211 H4
Houndsden Rd WCHMH N21 35 F1
Houndsditch HDTCH EC3A 13 H3
Houndsfield Rd ED N9 36 D2
Hounslow Av HSLW TW3 135 G6
Hounslow Gdns HSLW TW3 135 G6
Hounslow Rd
EBED/NFELT TW14 154 A2
FELT TW13 154 C6
WHTN TW2 155 H1
Houseman Wy CMBW SE5 142 E1
Houston Rd FSTH SE23 164 B4
SURB KT6 190 C3
Hove Av WALTH E17 69 H2
Hoveden Rd CRICK NW2 82 B3
Hove Gdns SUT SM1 194 A5
Hoveton Rd THMD SE28 109 J5
Howard Av BXLY DA5 168 D3
Howard Cl ACT W3 98 D5
BUSH WD23 28 E2
CRICK NW2 * 82 C2
FBAR/BDGN N11 34 A4
HPTN TW12 173 H3
LOU IG10 39 J1
Howard Rd BARK IG11 90 D6
BMLY BR1 183 K3
CRICK NW2 82 B2
DART DA1 171 K1
EHAM E6 107 K1
IL IG1 90 B2
ISLW TW7 136 A4
NWMAL KT3 176 B6
PGE/AN SE20 181 K4
SEVS/STOTM N15 68 A3
SNWD SE25 197 H2
STHL UB1 96 B5
STNW/STAM N16 85 K2
SURB KT6 191 G3
WALTH E17 51 J6
WAN E11 88 C1
Howards Cl PIN HA5 * 41 F5
Howards Crest Cl BECK BR3 183 F5
Howard's La PUT/ROE SW15 139 F5
Howard's Rd PLSTW E13 106 E2
Howard St THDIT KT7 190 C4
Howards Yd
WAND/EARL SW18 160 A2
Howard Wk EFNCH N2 65 G1
Howard Wy BAR EN5 20 B6
Howarth Rd ABYW SE2 128 B5
Howberry Cl EDGW HA8 43 K2
Howberry Rd EDGW HA8 43 K3
THHTH CR7 180 E4
Howbury La ERITH DA8 150 D3
Howbury Rd PECK SE15 143 K4
Howcroft Crs FNCH N3 46 E3
Howcroft La GFD/PVL UB6 96 D2
Howden Cl THMD SE28 109 K6
Howden Rd SNWD SE25 181 G5
Howden St PECK SE15 143 H4
Howe Cl ROMW/RG RM7 56 C4
Howell Cl CHDH RM6 73 K2
Howell Wk STHWK SE1 18 B7
Howerd Wy BKHTH/KID SE3 146 D2
Howes Cl FNCH N3 46 E6
Howfield Pl TOTM N17 * 50 B6
Howgate Rd
MORT/ESHN SW14 138 A4
Howick Pl WESTW SW1E 16 B5
Howie St BTSEA SW11 140 D1
Howitt Cl HAMP NW3 83 J4
Howitt Rd HAMP NW3 83 J4
Howitts Cl ESH/CLAY KT10 204 A4
Howland Ct PIN HA5 * 42 A2
Howland Ms East FITZ W1T 10 B1
Howland St FITZ W1T 10 B1
Howland Wy
BERM/RHTH SE16 124 B2
Howletts La RSLP HA4 58 A3
Howletts Rd HNHL SE24 162 D1
Howley Pl BAY/PAD W2 101 G4
Howley Rd CROY/NA CR0 211 H1
Howsman Rd BARN SW13 118 D6
Howson Rd BROCKY SE4 144 B5
Howson Ter
RCHPK/HAM TW10 * 157 F1
How's St BETH E2 7 J2
Howton Pl BUSH WD23 28 D3
Hoxton Market IS N1 7 G5
Hoxton Sq IS N1 7 G5
Hoxton St IS N1 7 G1
Hoylake Gdns MTCM CR4 179 H6
OXHEY WD19 27 H6
RSLP HA4 59 F5
Hoylake Rd ACT W3 99 G5
Hoyland Cl PECK SE15 * 143 J1
Hoyle Rd TOOT SW17 178 D1
Hoy St CAN/RD E16 106 D5
Hubbard Dr CHSGTN KT9 205 J4
Hubbard Rd WNWD SE27 162 D6
Hubbard St SRTFD E15 88 C6
Hubert Cl WIM/MER SW19 * 178 B4
Hubert Gv BRXN/ST SW9 141 K4
Hubert Rd EHAM E6 107 H2
RAIN RM13 111 H2
Huddart St BOW E3 105 H4
Huddleston Cl BETH E2 * 104 E1
Huddlestone Rd CRICK NW2 81 K4
FSTGT E7 88 E2
Huddleston Rd HOLWY N7 84 C1
Hudson Cl SHB W12 * 99 K6
Hudson Pl WOOL/PLUM SE18 127 H5
Hudson Rd BXLYHN DA7 149 G3
HYS/HAR UB3 113 G6
Huggin Hl BLKFR EC4V 12 D5
Huggins Pl BRXS/STRHM SW2 162 A3
Hughan Rd SRTFD E15 88 B3
Hugh Dalton Av FUL/PGN SW6 119 J6
Hughenden Av
KTN/HRWW/WS HA3 61 H2
Hughenden Gdns NTHLT UB5 95 G2
Hughenden Rd WPK KT4 192 D4
Hughes Cl NFNCH/WDSPK N12 47 G1
Hughes Rd HYS/HAR UB3 95 F6
Hughes Ter CAN/RD E16 * 106 D4
Hughes Wk CROY/NA CR0 196 D4
Hugh Gaitskell Cl
FUL/PGN SW6 * 119 J6
Hugh Ms PIM SW1V 15 K7
Hugh Pl WEST SW1P 16 C6
Hugh St PIM SW1V 15 K7
Hugo Gdns RAIN RM13 93 H4
Hugon Rd FUL/PGN SW6 140 A4
Hugo Rd ARCH N19 84 C2
Huguenot Pl
WAND/EARL SW18 140 B6
WCHPL E1 13 K1
Huitt Sq BTSEA SW11 140 C4
Hullbridge Ms IS N1 85 K6
Hull Cl BERM/RHTH SE16 * 124 A1
Hull St FSBYE EC1V 6 C5
Hulme Pl STHWK SE1 18 D3
Hulse Av BARK IG11 90 D4
ROMW/RG RM7 56 D4
Hulsewood Cl RDART DA2 170 E5
Hulverston Cl BELMT SM2 209 F6
Humber Cl WDR/YW UB7 112 A1
Humber Dr NKENS W10 100 B3
Humber Rd BKHTH/KID SE3 125 K6
CRICK NW2 63 K6
DART DA1 151 G6
Humberstone Rd PLSTW E13 107 G2
Humbolt Rd HMSMTH W6 119 H6
Humes Av HNWL W7 116 A3
Hume Wy RSLP HA4 58 E3
Humphrey Cl CLAY IG5 * 53 K4
Humphrey St STHWK SE1 123 G5
Humphries Cl DAGW RM9 92 B2
Hundred Acre
CDALE/KGS NW9 45 H5
Hungerdown CHING E4 38 A3
Hungerford Rd HOLWY N7 84 E3
Hungerford St WCHPL E1 * 104 D5
Hunsdon Cl DAGW RM9 92 B4
Hunsdon Rd NWCR SE14 144 A1
Hunslett St BETH E2 * 104 E1
Hunston Rd MRDN SM4 194 A5
Hunt Cl BKHTH/KID SE3 * 145 K3
NTGHL W11 119 G1
Hunter Cl STHWK SE1 19 F5
TOOT SW17 161 F3
WLGTN SM6 210 E5
Hunter Ct CMBW SE5 * 142 E5
Huntercrombe Gdns
OXHEY WD19 41 G1
Hunter Rd RYNPK SW20 177 F4
THHTH CR7 180 E6
Hunters Cl BXLY DA5 170 B5
Hunters Ct RCH/KEW TW9 136 E6
Hunter's Gv CRW RM5 56 D1
HYS/HAR UB3 113 K1
KTN/HRWW/WS HA3 61 J1
ORP BR6 216 C2
Hunters Hall Rd DAGE RM10 92 D3
Hunters Hl RSLP HA4 77 G1
Hunters Meadow NRWD SE19 163 F6
Hunters Rd CHSGTN KT9 206 A1
IL IG1 90 B3
Hunters Sq DAGE RM10 92 C2
Hunter St BMSBY WC1N 5 F6
Hunters Wy CROY/NA CR0 212 A2
ENC/FH EN2 23 G2
Hunting Cl ESH/CLAY KT10 204 A2
Huntingdon Cl MTCM CR4 195 K1
NTHLT UB5 78 A4
Huntingdon Gdns CHSWK W4 137 K1
WPK KT4 208 A1
Huntingdon Rd ED N9 36 E3
EFNCH N2 47 J6
Huntingdon St CAN/RD E16 106 D5
IS N1 85 F5
Huntingfield CROY/NA CR0 213 H5
Huntingfield Rd
PUT/ROE SW15 138 D5
Hunting Gate Cl ENC/FH EN2 23 G4
Hunting Gate Dr CHSGTN KT9 206 A5
Hunting Gate Ms WHTN TW2 * 155 K3
Huntings Rd DAGE RM10 92 C4
Huntland Cl RAIN RM13 111 K4
Huntley Cl STWL/WRAY TW19 152 B2
Huntley St GWRST WC1E 10 C1
Huntley Wy RYNPK SW20 * 176 D5
Huntly Dr FNCH N3 46 E2
Huntly Rd SNWD SE25 197 F1
Hunton St WCHPL E1 104 C4
Hunt Rd NWDGN UB2 115 F3
Hunts Cl BKHTH/KID SE3 145 K3
Hunt's La SRTFD E15 106 A1
Huntsman Cl FELT TW13 154 A6
Huntsman Rd BARK/HLT IG6 55 H2
Huntsman St WALW SE17 19 G7
Hunts Md PEND EN3 25 F4
Hunts Medde Cl CHST BR7 184 D3
Hunts Mede Cl CHST BR7 184 E3
Huntsmoor Rd
HOR/WEW KT19 207 F3
Huntspill St TOOT SW17 160 B5
Hunts Slip Rd DUL SE21 163 F5
Huntsworth Ms CAMTN NW1 2 E6
Hurdwick Pl CAMTN NW1 * 4 A2
Hurley Cl WOT/HER KT12 188 A6
Hurley Crs BERM/RHTH SE16 124 A1
Hurley Rd GFD/PVL UB6 96 B4
Hurlfield RDART DA2 171 F5
Hurlingham Gdns
FUL/PGN SW6 139 J4
Hurlingham Pk
FUL/PGN SW6 * 139 J4
Hurlingham Rd BXLYHN DA7 149 G1
FUL/PGN SW6 139 J3
Hurlingham Sq
FUL/PGN SW6 * 139 K4
Hurlock St HBRY N5 85 H1
Hurlstone Rd SNWD SE25 196 E2
Hurn Court Rd HSLWW TW4 134 C3
Huron Cl ORP BR6 216 E4
Huron Rd TOOT SW17 161 F4
Hurren Cl BKHTH/KID SE3 145 H4
Hurricane House
WOOL/PLUM SE18 * 146 D1
Hurricane Rd WLGTN SM6 210 E5
Hurry Cl SRTFD E15 88 C6
Hursley Rd CHIG IG7 55 F1
Hurst Av CHING E4 37 J5
HGT N6 66 C3
Hurstbourne ESH/CLAY KT10 205 F4
Hurstbourne Gdns BARK IG11 90 D4
Hurstbourne Rd FSTH SE23 164 B3
Hurst Cl CHING E4 37 J5
CHSGTN KT9 206 C3
GLDGN NW11 65 F3
HAYES BR2 199 J5
NTHLT UB5 77 K4
Hurstcourt Rd SUT SM1 194 A5
Hurstdene Av HAYES BR2 199 J5
Hurstdene Gdns
SEVS/STOTM N15 68 A4
Hurstfield HAYES BR2 199 K2
Hurstfield Crs YEAD UB4 94 C4
Hurstfield Rd E/WMO/HCT KT8 173 F6
Hurst La ABYW SE2 128 E5
E/WMO/HCT KT8 189 H1
Hurstleigh Gdns CLAY IG5 53 K4
Hurst Pl ABYW SE2 128 D5
DART DA1 * 171 F1
Hurst Ri BAR EN5 20 E4
Hurst Rd BFN/LL DA15 168 C4
BKHH IG9 39 H3
BXLY DA5 169 F3
CROY/NA CR0 211 K3
E/WMO/HCT KT8 173 H6
ERITH DA8 149 K1
WALTH E17 51 K6
WCHMH N21 35 G3
WOT/HER KT12 188 C1
Hurst Springs BXLY DA5 169 F3
Hurst St HNHL SE24 162 C1
Hurst View Rd SAND/SEL CR2 212 A5
Hurst Wy SAND/SEL CR2 212 A4
Hurstway Rd NTGHL W11 * 100 B6
Hurstway Wk NTGHL W11 * 100 B6
Hurstwood Av BXLY DA5 169 F3
ERITH DA8 150 B2
SWFD E18 71 F1
Hurstwood Dr BMLY BR1 184 E6
Hurstwood Rd GLDGN NW11 64 C1
Hurtwood Rd WOT/HER KT12 188 E4
Huson Cl HAMP NW3 * 83 J5
Hussain Cl HRW HA1 79 F2
Hussars Cl HSLWW TW4 134 D4
Husseywell Crs HAYES BR2 199 K5
Hutching's St POP/IOD E14 124 D2
Hutchings Wk GLDGN NW11 65 F1
Hutchins Cl SRTFD E15 88 A5
Hutchinson Ter WBLY HA9 79 K1
Hutchins Rd THMD SE28 109 G6
Hutton Cl GFD/PVL UB6 78 D3
WFD IG8 53 F2
Hutton Gv NFNCH/WDSPK N12 47 F2
Hutton La KTN/HRWW/WS HA3 42 C3
Hutton Rw EDGW HA8 44 E3
Hutton St EMB EC4Y 11 K4
Hutton Wk
KTN/HRWW/WS HA3 42 C3
Huxbear St BROCKY SE4 144 C6
Huxley UED N18 * 49 K1
Huxley Cl NTHLT UB5 95 J1
Huxley Dr CHDH RM6 73 H4
Huxley Gdns WLSDN NW10 98 B2
Huxley Pde UED N18 * 49 K1
Huxley Pl PLMGR N13 35 H6
Huxley Rd LEY E10 70 A6
UED N18 35 K6
WELL DA16 148 A4
Huxley Sayze UED N18 * 49 K1
Huxley St NKENS W10 100 C2
Hyacinth Cl HPTN TW12 173 F2
IL IG1 90 B4
Hyacinth Rd PUT/ROE SW15 158 D3
Hyde Cl BAR EN5 20 D4
PLSTW E13 106 E1
Hyde Crs CDALE/KGS NW9 63 G2
Hyde Dr STMC/STPC BR5 202 C1
Hyde Estate Rd
CDALE/KGS NW9 63 H2
Hyde Farm Ms BAL SW12 161 J3
Hydefield Cl WCHMH N21 35 K3
Hydefield Ct ED N9 36 A4
Hyde La BTSEA SW11 140 D2
Hyde Park Av WCHMH N21 35 K3
Hyde Park Cnr MYFR/PICC W1J 15 H2
Hyde Park Crs BAY/PAD W2 8 C4
Hyde Park Gdns BAY/PAD W2 8 B5
WCHMH N21 35 J3
Hyde Park Gardens Ms
BAY/PAD W2 8 B5
Hyde Park Ga SKENS SW7 120 B3
Hyde Park Gate Ms
SKENS SW7 * 120 B2
Hyde Park Pl BAY/PAD W2 8 D5
Hyde Park Sq BAY/PAD W2 8 C4

Hyde Park St BAY/PAD W2 8 C5
Hyderabad Wy SRTFD E15 88 C5
Hyde Rd BXLYHN DA7 149 G3
IS N1 7 F1
RCHPK/HAM TW10 137 G6
Hydeside Gdns ED N9 36 B4
Hyde's Pl IS N1 85 H5
Hyde St DEPT SE8 124 D6
The Hyde CDALE/KGS NW9 45 F6
CDALE/KGS NW9 63 G2
Hydethorpe Av ED N9 36 B4
Hydethorpe Rd BAL SW12 161 H3
Hyde V GNWCH SE10 145 F1
Hyde Wk MRDN SM4 193 K4
Hyde Wy ED N9 36 B4
HYS/HAR UB3 113 J4
Hyland Cl EMPK RM11 75 K4
Hylands Rd WALTH E17 52 B5
Hyland Wy EMPK RM11 75 K4
Hylton St WOOL/PLUM SE18 128 A4
Hyndewood FSTH SE23 164 A5
Hyndman St PECK SE15 123 J6
Hynton Rd BCTR RM8 73 J6
Hyperion Pl HOR/WEW KT19 207 F6
Hyrstdene SAND/SEL CR2 211 H2
Hyson Rd BERM/RHTH SE16 123 J5
Hythe Av BXLYHN DA7 149 G1
Hythe Cl STMC/STPC BR5 202 D1
UED N18 36 C6
Hythe Rd THHTH CR7 180 E5
WLSDN NW10 99 H2
Hythe St DART DA1 171 H1
Hyver Hl BAR EN5 31 F1

I

Ibbotson Av CAN/RD E16 106 D5
Ibbott St WCHPL E1 104 E3
Iberian Av WLGTN SM6 210 D2
Ibis La CHSWK W4 137 K2
Ibis Wy YEAD UB4 95 H5
Ibscott Cl DAGE RM10 92 E4
Ibsley Gdns PUT/ROE SW15 158 D3
Ibsley Wy EBAR EN4 21 J6
Iceland Rd BOW E3 87 J6
Ickburgh Est CLPT E5 * 68 D6
Ickburgh Rd CLPT E5 86 D1
Ickenham Cl RSLP HA4 58 B6
Ickenham Rd RSLP HA4 58 B5
Ickleton Rd ELTH/MOT SE9 166 D6
Icknield Dr GNTH/NBYPK IG2 72 B2
Ickworth Park Rd WALTH E17 69 G1
Ida Rd SEVS/STOTM N15 67 K2
Ida St POP/IOD E14 106 A5
Iden Cl HAYES BR2 183 H6
Idlecombe Rd TOOT SW17 179 F2
Idmiston Rd SRTFD E15 88 D3
WNWD SE27 162 D5
WPK KT4 192 C4
Idmiston Sq WPK KT4 192 C4
Idol La MON EC3R 13 G6
Idonia St DEPT SE8 144 C1
Iffley Rd HMSMTH W6 118 E3
Ifield Rd WBPTN SW10 120 A6
Ightham Rd ERITH DA8 149 H1
Ilbert St NKENS W10 100 C2
Ilchester Pl WKENS W14 119 J3
Ilchester Rd BCTR RM8 91 H3
Ildersly Gv DUL SE21 162 E4
Ilderton Rd BERM/RHTH SE16 123 K5
Ilex Cl SUN TW16 172 B5
Ilex Rd WLSDN NW10 81 H4
Ilex Wy STRHM/NOR SW16 180 B1
Ilford Hl IL IG1 90 A1
MNPK E12 89 K2
Ilford La IL IG1 90 B2
Ilfracombe Gdns CHDH RM6 73 H4
Ilfracombe Rd BMLY BR1 165 J5
Iliffe St WALW SE17 122 C5
Iliffe Yd WALW SE17 122 C5
Ilkley Cl NRWD SE19 * 180 E2
Ilkley Ct FBAR/BDGN N11 48 A2
Ilkley Rd CAN/RD E16 107 G4
OXHEY WD19 41 H1
Illingworth Wy EN EN1 24 A6
Ilmington Rd
KTN/HRWW/WS HA3 61 K3
Ilminster Gdns BTSEA SW11 140 D5
Imber Cl STHGT/OAK N14 34 C2
Imber Cross THDIT KT7 * 190 A4
Imber Gv ESH/CLAY KT10 189 J4
Imber Park Rd ESH/CLAY KT10 189 J5
Imber St IS N1 6 E1
Imperial Av STNW/STAM N16 * 86 A2
Imperial Cl RYLN/HDSTN HA2 60 A3
Imperial College Rd
SKENS SW7 14 B4
Imperial Crs FUL/PGN SW6 140 B3
Imperial Dr RYLN/HDSTN HA2 60 B3
Imperial Gdns MTCM CR4 179 G6
Imperial Ms EHAM E6 107 H1
Imperial Pl CHST BR7 185 F4
Imperial Rd EBED/NFELT TW14 153 H2
FUL/PGN SW6 140 A2
WDGN N22 48 E3
Imperial Sq FUL/PGN SW6 140 A2
Imperial St BOW E3 106 A2
Imperial Wy CHST BR7 167 H5
CROY/NA CR0 211 G4
KTN/HRWW/WS HA3 62 A3
Imre Cl SHB W12 118 E1
Inca Dr ELTH/MOT SE9 167 G2
Inchmery Rd CAT SE6 164 E4
Inchwood CROY/NA CR0 213 K2
Independent Pl HACK E8 86 B3
Independents Rd
BKHTH/KID SE3 145 J4
Inderwick Rd CEND/HSY/T N8 67 F3
Indescon Ct POP/IOD E14 124 E2
India St TWRH EC3N 13 J4
India Wy SHB W12 99 K6
Indigo Ms POP/IOD E14 * 106 A6
STNW/STAM N16 85 K1
Indus Rd CHARL SE7 146 B1
Infant House
WOOL/PLUM SE18 * 146 D1
Ingal Rd PLSTW E13 106 E3
Ingate Pl VX/NE SW8 141 G3
Ingatestone Rd MNPK E12 71 G5
SNWD SE25 197 J2
WFD IG8 53 F3
Ingelow Rd VX/NE SW8 141 G3
Ingersoll Rd PEND EN3 24 E1
SHB W12 118 E1
Ingestre Pl SOHO/CST W1F 10 B4
Ingestre Rd FSTGT E7 88 E2
KTTN NW5 84 B2
Ingham Cl SAND/SEL CR2 213 F6
Ingham Rd KIL/WHAMP NW6 82 E2
SAND/SEL CR2 212 E6
Inglebert St CLKNW EC1R 5 J4
Ingleborough St
BRXN/ST SW9 142 B3
Ingleby Dr HRW HA1 78 D1
Ingleby Rd DAGE RM10 92 D4
HOLWY N7 84 E1
IL IG1 72 B5
Ingleby Wy CHST BR7 185 F1
WLGTN SM6 210 D6
Ingle Cl PIN HA5 41 K6
Ingledew Rd
WOOL/PLUM SE18 127 J5
Inglefield Sq WAP E1W * 123 J1
Inglehurst Gdns REDBR IG4 71 K2
Inglemere Rd FSTH SE23 164 A5
MTCM CR4 178 E3
Ingleside Cl BECK BR3 182 D3
Ingleside Gv BKHTH/KID SE3 125 J6
Inglethorpe St FUL/PGN SW6 139 G2
Ingleton Av WELL DA16 148 B6
Ingleton Rd CAR SM5 209 J6
UED N18 50 C2
Ingleton St BRXN/ST SW9 142 B3
Ingleway NFNCH/WDSPK N12 47 H2
Inglewood CROY/NA CR0 213 G6
Inglewood Cl BARK/HLT IG6 55 F2
POP/IOD E14 124 D4
Inglewood Copse BMLY BR1 184 D5
Inglewood Rd BXLYHN DA7 150 A5
KIL/WHAMP NW6 82 E3
Inglis Rd CROY/NA CR0 197 G5
EA W5 98 B6
Inglis St CMBW SE5 142 C2
Ingram Av GLDGN NW11 65 G4
Ingram Cl LBTH SE11 17 H6
STAN HA7 43 J1
Ingram Rd DART DA1 171 H3
EFNCH N2 65 J1
THHTH CR7 180 D4
Ingram Wy GFD/PVL UB6 78 D6
Ingrave Rd ROM RM1 75 F1
Ingrave St BTSEA SW11 140 D4
Ingrebourne Rd RAIN RM13 111 K3
Ingress St CHSWK W4 118 B5
Inigo Jones Rd CHARL SE7 146 D1
Inkerman Rd KTTN NW5 84 B4
Inks Gn CHING E4 52 A1
Inkwell Cl NFNCH/WDSPK N12 33 G5
Inman Rd WAND/EARL SW18 160 B2
WLSDN NW10 81 G6
Inmans Rw WFD IG8 38 E6
Inner Cir CAMTN NW1 3 G5
Inner Park Rd
WIM/MER SW19 159 G4
Inner Ring East HTHAIR TW6 132 E4
Innes Cl RYNPK SW20 177 H5
Innes Gdns PUT/ROE SW15 158 E1
Innes St PECK SE15 143 F1
Innes Yd CROY/NA CR0 211 J1
Inniskilling Rd PLSTW E13 107 G1
Innovation Cl ALP/SUD HA0 80 A6
Inskip Cl LEY E10 69 K6
Inskip Rd BCTR RM8 73 K5
Institute Pl HACK E8 86 D3
Instone Rd DART DA1 171 H2
Integer Gdns WAN E11 * 70 B4
International Av HEST TW5 114 B5
Inver Ct BAY/PAD W2 * 101 F5
Inveresk Gdns WPK KT4 207 J1
Inverforth Cl HAMP NW3 65 G6
Inverforth Rd FBAR/BDGN N11 48 B1
Inverine Rd CHARL SE7 126 A5
Invermore Pl
WOOL/PLUM SE18 127 H4
Inverness Av EN EN1 24 A2
Inverness Dr BARK/HLT IG6 54 E2
Inverness Gdns KENS W8 120 A1
Inverness Pl BAY/PAD W2 * 101 F6
Inverness Rd HSLW TW3 134 E5
NWDGN UB2 114 D4
UED N18 50 D1
WPK KT4 193 G5
Inverness St CAMTN NW1 84 B6
Inverness Ter BAY/PAD W2 101 F6
WDGN N22 * 49 H4
Inverton Rd PECK SE15 144 A5
Invicta Cl CHST BR7 185 F1
EBED/NFELT TW14 153 J3
Invicta Gv NTHLT UB5 95 K2
Invicta Pde SCUP DA14 * 168 C6
Invicta Plaza STHWK SE1 12 A7
Invicta Rd BKHTH/KID SE3 145 K1
Inville Rd WALW SE17 122 E5
Inwood Av HSLW TW3 135 H4
Inwood Cl CROY/NA CR0 198 B6
Inwood Rd HSLW TW3 135 H5
Inworth St BTSEA SW11 140 D3
Inworth Wk IS N1 * 85 J6
Iona Cl CAT SE6 164 D2
MRDN SM4 194 A4
Ion Sq BETH E2 * 104 C1
Ipswich Rd TOOT SW17 179 G2
Ireland Cl EHAM E6 107 K4
Ireland Pl WDGN N22 48 E3
Irene Ms HNWL W7 * 116 A1
Irene Rd FUL/PGN SW6 139 K2
ORP BR6 202 A4
Ireton Cl MUSWH N10 48 A3
Ireton St BOW E3 105 J3
Iris Av BXLY DA5 169 F1
Iris Cl CROY/NA CR0 198 A5
EHAM E6 107 J4
SURB KT6 * 191 G4
Iris Crs BXLYHN DA7 129 G6
Iris Rd HOR/WEW KT19 206 D3
Iris Wy CHING E4 51 H2
Irkdale Av EN EN1 24 B2
Iron Bridge Cl NWDGN UB2 115 H1
WLSDN NW10 81 G3
Ironbridge Rd STKPK UB11 * 112 D1
Iron Bridge Rd STKPK UB11 * 112 E1
Iron Bridge Rd North
STKPK UB11 112 D1
Iron Bridge Rd South
WDR/YW UB7 112 E2
Iron Mill La DART DA1 150 D5
Iron Mill Pl DART DA1 150 C5
WAND/EARL SW18 * 160 A1
Iron Mill Rd WAND/EARL SW18 160 A1
Ironmonger La CITYW EC2V 12 E4
Ironmonger Rw FSBYE EC1V 6 D5
Ironmongers Pl POP/IOD E14 124 D4
Ironside Cl BERM/RHTH SE16 124 A2
Irons Wy CRW RM5 56 E3
Irvine Av KTN/HRWW/WS HA3 43 G6
Irvine Cl TRDG/WHET N20 33 J4
Irvine Wy ORP BR6 202 A4
Irving Av NTHLT UB5 77 H6
Irving Gv BRXN/ST SW9 142 A3
Irving Ms IS N1 85 J4
Irving Rd WKENS W14 119 G3
Irving St LSQ/SEVD WC2H 10 D6
Irving Wy CDALE/KGS NW9 63 H2
Irwell Est BERM/RHTH SE16 * 123 K2
Irwin Av WOOL/PLUM SE18 147 K1
Irwin Gdns WLSDN NW10 81 K6
Isaac Wy STHWK SE1 18 D2
Isabella Cl STHGT/OAK N14 34 C2
Isabella Ct RCHPK/HAM TW10 157 G1
Isabella Dr ORP BR6 216 C2
Isabella Ms IS N1 * 86 A4
Isabella Pl KUTN/CMB KT2 175 G1
Isabella Rd HOM E9 * 86 E3
Isabella St STHWK SE1 18 A1
Isabel St BRXN/ST SW9 142 A2
Isambard Ms POP/IOD E14 125 F3
Isambard Pl BERM/RHTH SE16 123 K1
Isham Rd STRHM/NOR SW16 179 K5
Isis Cl PUT/ROE SW15 139 F5
RSLP HA4 58 A3
Isis St WAND/EARL SW18 160 B4
Island Centre Wy PEND EN3 25 J1
Island Farm Av
E/WMO/HCT KT8 188 E2
Island Farm Rd
E/WMO/HCT KT8 188 E2
Island Rd BERM/RHTH SE16 124 A4
MTCM CR4 178 E3
Island Rw POP/IOD E14 105 H5
Isla Rd WOOL/PLUM SE18 127 H6
Islay Gdns HSLWW TW4 134 C6
Islay Wk IS N1 * 85 J4
Islay Whf POP/IOD E14 * 106 A4
Isledon Rd HOLWY N7 85 G1
Islehurst Cl CHST BR7 185 F4
Islington Gn IS N1 6 A1
Islington High St IS N1 6 A2
Islington Park Ms IS N1 85 H5
Islington Park St IS N1 85 G5
Islington Town Hall IS N1 85 H5
Islip Gdns EDGW HA8 45 F2
NTHLT UB5 77 J5
Islip Manor Rd NTHLT UB5 77 J5
Islip St KTTN NW5 84 C3
Ismailia Rd FSTGT E7 89 F5
Isom Cl PLSTW E13 107 F2
Ivanhoe Dr
KTN/HRWW/WS HA3 43 H5
Ivanhoe Rd CMBW SE5 143 G4
HSLWW TW4 134 C4
Ivatt Pl WKENS W14 119 J5
Ivatt Wy SEVS/STOTM N15 49 H6
Iveagh Av WLSDN NW10 98 C1
Iveagh Cl HOM E9 87 F6
WLSDN NW10 98 C1
Ivedon Rd WELL DA16 148 D3
Ive Farm Cl LEY E10 69 J6
Ive Farm La LEY E10 69 J6
Iveley Rd CLAP SW4 141 H3
Ivere Dr BAR EN5 33 F1
Iverhurst Cl BXLYHS DA6 148 E6
Iverna Ct KENS W8 119 K3
Iverna Gdns
EBED/NFELT TW14 133 G6
KENS W8 119 K3
Iverson Rd KIL/WHAMP NW6 82 D4
Ivers Wy CROY/NA CR0 213 K5
Ives Gdns ROM RM1 75 H1
Ives Rd CAN/RD E16 106 C4
Ives St CHEL SW3 14 D6
Ivimey St BETH E2 * 104 C2
Ivinghoe Cl EN EN1 24 A3
Ivinghoe Rd BCTR RM8 91 H3
BUSH WD23 28 D2
Ivor Gv ELTH/MOT SE9 167 G3
Ivor Pl CAMTN NW1 2 E7
Ivor St CAMTN NW1 84 C5
Ivory Ct FELT TW13 153 K3
Ivorydown BMLY BR1 165 K6
Ivybridge Cl TWK TW1 156 B1
Ivychurch Cl PGE/AN SE20 181 J3
Ivy Church La WALW SE17 * 123 G5
Ivy Cl DART DA1 171 K1
PIN HA5 59 G4
RYLN/HDSTN HA2 77 K2
SUN TW16 172 B5
Ivy Ct BERM/RHTH SE16 * 123 H5
Ivy Crs CHSWK W4 117 K4
Ivydale Rd CAR SM5 194 E6
PECK SE15 144 A6
Ivyday Gv STRHM/NOR SW16 162 A5
Ivydene E/WMO/HCT KT8 188 E2
Ivydene Cl SUT SM1 209 G2
Ivy Gdns CEND/HSY/T N8 66 E3
MTCM CR4 179 J6
Ivyhouse Rd DAGW RM9 91 K4
Ivy La HSLWW TW4 134 E5
Ivymount Rd WNWD SE27 162 B5
Ivy Rd BROCKY SE4 144 C5
CAN/RD E16 106 E5
CRICK NW2 82 A2
HSLW TW3 135 G5
STHGT/OAK N14 34 D2
SURB KT6 * 191 H6
TOOT SW17 178 D1
WALTH E17 69 J3
Ivy St IS N1 7 G2
Ivy Wk DAGW RM9 92 A4
NTHWD HA6 * 40 C4
Ixworth Pl CHEL SW3 14 C7
Izane Rd BXLYHS DA6 149 G5

J

Jacaranda Cl NWMAL KT3 176 B6
Jacaranda Gv HACK E8 86 B5
Jackass La HAYES BR2 215 F4
Jack Clow Rd SRTFD E15 106 C1
Jack Cornwell St MNPK E12 90 A2
Jack Dash Wy EHAM E6 107 J3
Jackman Ms WLSDN NW10 81 G1
Jackman St HACK E8 86 D6
Jackson Cl HOM E9 87 F5
Jackson Rd BARK IG11 90 D6
EBAR EN4 33 J1
HAYES BR2 200 E5
HOLWY N7 85 F2
Jackson's La HGT N6 66 A4
Jackson's Pl CROY/NA CR0 196 E5
Jackson St WOOL/PLUM SE18 127 F6
Jackson's Wy CROY/NA CR0 213 J1
Jackson Wy HOR/WEW KT19 206 C6
NWDGN UB2 115 G2
Jack Walker Ct HBRY N5 85 H2
Jacobs Cl DAGE RM10 92 D2
Jacob St STHWK SE1 19 K2
Jacob's Well Ms MHST W1U 9 H3
Jacqueline Cl NTHLT UB5 77 J6
Jacqueline Creft Ter HGT N6 * 66 A3
Jacqueline Vls WALTH E17 * 70 A2
Jade Cl BCTR RM8 73 J5
CAN/RD E16 107 H5
CRICK NW2 64 B4
Jade Ter KIL/WHAMP NW6 * 83 G5
Jaffe Rd IL IG1 72 C5
Jaffray Rd HAYES BR2 200 C1
Jaggard Wy BAL SW12 160 E2
Jago Cl WOOL/PLUM SE18 127 H6
Jago Wk CMBW SE5 142 E1
Jamaica Rd BERM/RHTH SE16 123 J3
THHTH CR7 196 C3
Jamaica St WCHPL E1 104 E4
James Av BCTR RM8 74 B5
CRICK NW2 82 A3
James Bedford Cl PIN HA5 41 G5
James Cl GLDGN NW11 * 64 C3
GPK RM2 75 J2
PLSTW E13 106 E1
James Collins Cl MV/WKIL W9 100 D3
James Gdns TOTM N17 49 J3
James Joyce Wk
BRXN/ST SW9 142 C5
James Joyes Wk HNHL SE24 * 142 C5
James La WAN E11 70 A4
James Lee Sq PEND EN3 25 J1
Jameson St KENS W8 119 K1
James Pl TOTM N17 50 B4
James Rd DART DA1 170 D2
James St BARK IG11 90 C5
COVGDN WC2E 11 F5
EN EN1 24 B6
HSLW TW3 135 J4
MHST W1U 9 H4
Jamestown Rd CAMTN NW1 84 B6
Jamestown Wy POP/IOD E14 106 B6
James Watt Wy ERITH DA8 130 C6
James Wy OXHEY WD19 27 H6
James Yd CHING E4 * 52 B2
Jamuna Cl POP/IOD E14 105 G4
Jane St WCHPL E1 104 D5
Janet St POP/IOD E14 124 D3
Janeway Pl BERM/RHTH SE16 123 J2
Janeway St BERM/RHTH SE16 123 H2
Janson Cl SRTFD E15 88 C3
WLSDN NW10 81 F1
Janson Rd SRTFD E15 88 C3
Jansons Rd SEVS/STOTM N15 50 A6
Japan Crs FSBYPK N4 67 F5
Japan Rd CHDH RM6 73 K4
Jardine Rd WAP E1W 105 F6
Jarrett Cl BRXS/STRHM SW2 162 C3
Jarrow Cl MRDN SM4 194 A2
Jarrow Rd BERM/RHTH SE16 123 K4
CHDH RM6 73 J3
TOTM N17 68 D1
Jarrow Wy HOM E9 87 H2
Jarvis Cl BAR EN5 20 B6
Jarvis Rd EDUL SE22 143 F5
SAND/SEL CR2 211 K4
Jasmin Cl NTHWD HA6 40 D4
Jasmine Cl IL IG1 90 B3
ORP BR6 201 G6
STHL UB1 95 J6
Jasmine Ct LEE/GVPK SE12 165 K1
Jasmine Gdns CROY/NA CR0 213 K1
RYLN/HDSTN HA2 60 A6
Jasmine Gv PGE/AN SE20 181 J4
Jasmine Rd HOR/WEW KT19 206 D4
ROMW/RG RM7 75 G6
Jasmine Ter WDR/YW UB7 112 D2
Jasmin Rd HOR/WEW KT19 206 D4
Jason Wk ELTH/MOT SE9 167 F6
Jasper Cl PEND EN3 24 E1
Jasper Rd CAN/RD E16 107 H5
NRWD SE19 181 G2
Javelin Wy NTHLT UB5 95 H2
Jaycroft ENC/FH EN2 23 G2
Jay Gdns CHST BR7 166 E6
Jay Ms SKENS SW7 120 B2
Jean Batten Cl WLGTN SM6 211 F5
Jebb Av BRXS/STRHM SW2 161 K1
Jebb St BOW E3 105 J1
Jedburgh Rd PLSTW E13 107 G2
Jedburgh St BTSEA SW11 141 F5
Jeddo Ms SHB W12 118 C2
Jeddo Rd SHB W12 118 C2
Jefferson Cl GNTH/NBYPK IG2 72 B2
WEA W13 116 C3
Jeffrey's Pl CAMTN NW1 84 C5
Jeffreys Rd CLAP SW4 141 K3
PEND EN3 25 H5
Jeffrey's St CAMTN NW1 84 B5
Jeffs Cl HPTN TW12 * 173 G2
Jeffs Rd SUT SM1 208 D2
Jeger Av BETH E2 7 J1
Jeken Rd ELTH/MOT SE9 146 B5
Jelf Rd BRXS/STRHM SW2 142 B6
Jellicoe Gdns STAN HA7 43 G2
Jellicoe Rd TOTM N17 49 K3
WATW WD18 26 E1
Jemmett Cl KUTN/CMB KT2 175 J4
Jem Paterson Ct HRW HA1 * 78 E2
Jengar Cl SUT SM1 209 F2
Jenkins La BARK IG11 108 C2
Jenkins Rd PLSTW E13 107 F3
Jenner Av ACT W3 99 F4
Jenner Cl SCUP DA14 168 B6
Jenner Rd STNW/STAM N16 68 B6
Jenner Wy HOR/WEW KT19 206 C6
Jennett Rd CROY/NA CR0 211 G1
Jennifer Rd BMLY BR1 165 J5
Jennings Cl SURB KT6 190 D4
Jennings Rd EDUL SE22 163 G1
Jennings Wy BAR EN5 20 A4
Jenningtree Rd ERITH DA8 150 E1
Jenningtree Wy BELV DA17 129 K2
Jenny Hammond Cl WAN E11 88 D1
Jenson Wy NRWD SE19 181 G3
Jenton Av BXLYHN DA7 149 F3
Jephson Rd FSTGT E7 89 G5
Jephson St CMBW SE5 142 E2
Jephtha Rd
WAND/EARL SW18 159 K1
Jeppo's La MTCM CR4 194 E1
Jerdan Pl FUL/PGN SW6 139 K1
Jeremiah St POP/IOD E14 105 K5
Jeremy's Gn UED N18 36 D6
Jermyn St STJS SW1Y 10 A7
Jerningham Av CLAY IG5 54 B5
Jerningham Rd NWCR SE14 144 B3
Jerome Crs STJWD NW8 2 C6
Jerome St WCHPL E1 13 J1
Jerrard St LEW SE13 144 E4
Jerrold St IS N1 * 7 H3
Jersey Av KTN/HRWW/WS HA3 43 H5
Jersey Dr STMC/STPC BR5 201 J3
Jersey Rd CAN/RD E16 107 G4
HNWL W7 116 B2
HSLW TW3 135 G2
IL IG1 90 B2
IS N1 85 J4
ISLW TW7 135 H1
LEY E10 70 B5
RAIN RM13 93 J5
TOOT SW17 179 G3
Jersey St BETH E2 104 D2
Jersey Vls HNWL W7 * 115 K2
Jerusalem Pas CLKNW EC1R 6 A7
Jerviston Gdns
STRHM/NOR SW16 180 B2
Jervois House
WOOL/PLUM SE18 * 146 D1
Jesmond Av WBLY HA9 80 B4
Jesmond Cl MTCM CR4 179 G6
Jesmond Dene HAMP NW3 * 83 G4
Jesmond Rd CROY/NA CR0 197 G4
Jesmond Wy STAN HA7 44 A1
Jessam Av CLPT E5 68 D5
Jessamine Rd HNWL W7 115 K1
Jessamine Ter SWLY BR8 * 187 K4
Jesse Rd LEY E10 70 A5
Jessett Cl ERITH DA8 130 A4
Jessica Rd WAND/EARL SW18 160 B1
Jessop Av NWDGN UB2 114 E4
Jessops Wy CROY/NA CR0 195 H3
Jessup Cl WOOL/PLUM SE18 127 H4
Jetstar Wy NTHLT UB5 95 J2
Jevington Wy LEE/GVPK SE12 166 A3
Jewel Rd WALTH E17 51 J6
Jewry St TWRH EC3N 13 J4
Jews Rw WAND/EARL SW18 140 A5
Jews Wk SYD SE26 163 J6
Jeymer Av WLSDN NW10 81 K3
Jeymer Dr GFD/PVL UB6 78 C6
Jeypore Rd WAND/EARL SW18 160 B2
Jillian Cl HPTN TW12 173 F3
Jim Bradley Cl
WOOL/PLUM SE18 127 F4
Joan Crs ELTH/MOT SE9 166 C2
Joan Gdns BCTR RM8 74 A6
Joan Rd BCTR RM8 74 A6
Joan St STHWK SE1 18 A1
Jocelyn Rd RCH/KEW TW9 137 F4
Jocelyn St PECK SE15 143 H2
Jockey's Flds FSBYW WC1X 11 H1
Jodane Rd DEPT SE8 124 C4
Jodrell Cl ISLW TW7 136 B2
Jodrell Rd BOW E3 87 H6
Joel St NTHWD HA6 40 E5
Johanna St STHWK SE1 * 17 J3
John Adam St CHCR WC2N 11 F7
John Aird Ct BAY/PAD W2 101 G4
John Archer Wy
WAND/EARL SW18 160 C1
John Ashby Cl
BRXS/STRHM SW2 161 K1
John Austin Cl KUTN/CMB KT2 175 G4
John Bradshaw Rd
STHGT/OAK N14 34 D3
John Burns Dr BARK IG11 90 E6
John Campbell Rd
STNW/STAM N16 86 A3
John Carpenter St EMB EC4Y 11 K5
John Felton Rd
BERM/RHTH SE16 * 123 H2
John Fisher St WCHPL E1 104 C6
John Gooch Dr ENC/FH EN2 23 H3
John Goodchild Wy
KUT/HW KT1 175 J6

John Harrison Wy
  BERM/RHTH SE16...124 A3
  GNWCH SE10...125 J3
John Islip St WEST SW1P...16 E7
John Lamb Ct
  KTN/HRWW/WS HA3...42 E4
John Maurice Cl WALW SE17...18 E6
John McKenna Wk
  BERM/RHTH SE16 *...123 H3
John Parker Sq BTSEA SW11 *...140 C4
John Penn St LEW SE13...144 E2
John Perrin Pl
  KTN/HRWW/WS HA3...62 A4
John Prince's Wy
  CAVSQ/HST W1G...9 K3
John Rennie Wk WAP E1W...104 D6
John Roll Wy
  BERM/RHTH SE16...123 H3
John Ruskin St CMBW SE5...142 C1
John's Av HDN NW4...64 A1
John's Cl ASHF TW15...155 F6
John Silkin La DEPT SE8...124 A5
John's La MRDN SM4...194 B2
John's Ms BMSBY WC1N...5 H7
John Smith Av FUL/PGN SW6...139 J1
John Smith Ms POP/IOD E14...106 B6
John Smith St CHARL SE7...86 C6
Johnson Rd CROY/NA CR0...196 E4
  HAYES BR2...200 C2
  HEST TW5...134 B1
  ...81 F6
Johnson's Ct CAVSQ/HST W5...209 K1
Johnsons Ct FLST/FETLN EC4A...11 K3
Johnsons Dr HPTN TW12...173 H4
Johnson St NWDGN UB2...114 E3
Johnsons Pl PIM SW1V...121 H5
Johnson St NWDGN UB2...114 D3
  WCHPL E1...104 E5
Johnsons Wy WLSDN NW10...98 C3
John Spencer Sq IS N1 *...85 H4
John's Ter CROY/NA CR0...196 D4
John St BMSBY WC1N...5 H7
  ...24 B6
  HSLW TW5...134 D3
  SNWD SE25...197 H1
  SRTFD E15...88 C6
John Trundle Highwalk
  BARB EC2Y *...12 C1
John Watkin Cl
  HOR/WEW KT19...206 D6
John Williams Cl NWCR SE14...124 A6
John Wilson St
  WOOL/PLUM SE18...127 F4
John Wooley Cl LEW SE13 *...145 H5
Joiners Arms Yd CMBW SE5 *...142 E2
Joiner St STHWK SE1...19 F1
Jollys La YEAD UB4...95 J4
Jonathan St LBTH SE11...122 A5
Jones Rd PLSTW E13...106 E3
Jonson Cl MTCM CR4...195 G1
  YEAD UB4...94 E4
Jordan Cl RYLN/HDSTN HA2...77 K1
Jordan Rd GFD/PVL UB6...79 H6
Jordans Ct DAGE RM10...92 D2
Jordans Ms WHTN TW2...155 K4
Joseph Av ACT W3...99 F5
Joseph Hardcastle Cl
  NWCR SE14...144 A1
Josephine Av
  BRXS/STRHM SW2...142 A6
Joseph Locke Wy
  ESH/CLAY KT10...189 F6
Joseph Powell Cl BAL SW12...161 H1
Joseph Ray Rd WAN E11...70 C6
Joseph St BOW E3...105 H3
Joseph Trotter Cl CLKNW EC1R...5 J4
Joshua Cl MUSWH N10...48 B3
  SAND/SEL CR2...211 H5
Joshua St POP/IOD E14...106 A5
Joslings Cl SHB W12...99 J6
Joslyn Cl PEND EN3...25 J1
Joubert St BTSEA SW11...140 E3
Jowett St PECK SE15...143 G1
Joyce Av UED N18...50 B1
Joyce Green La DART DA1...131 H2
  ERITH DA8...151 H2
Joyden's Wood Rd BXLY DA5...170 B5
Joydon Dr CHDH RM6...73 H3
Joyners Cl DAGW RM9...92 B2
Jubilee Av CHING E4...52 A2
  ROMW/RG RM7...74 E2
  WHTN TW2...155 H3
Jubilee Cl CDALE/KGS NW9...63 F3
  KUT/HW KT1...174 D4
  ROMW/RG RM7...74 E2
  WLSDN NW10 *...99 G1
Jubilee Crs ED N9...36 C3
  POP/IOD E14...106 E2
Jubilee Dr RSLP HA4...77 H2
Jubilee Gdns STHL UB1...96 A6
  STHWK SE1 *...17 H1
Jubilee Market COVGDN WC2E *...11 H5
Jubilee Pl CHEL SW3...120 D5
  GFD/PVL UB6...
Jubilee St WCHPL E1...104 E5
Jubilee Ter FUL/PGN SW6 *...139 H5
The Jubilee GNWCH SE10 *...144 E1
Jubilee Vls ESH/CLAY KT10 *...189 K5
Jubilee Wy CHSGTN KT9...206 D1
  EBED/NFELT TW14...153 K3
  SCUP DA14...168 A6
  WIM/MER SW19...178 A4
Judd St STPAN WC1H...4 E5
Jude St CAN/RD E16...106 D5
Judge Heath La HYS/HAR UB3...94 A3
Judges' Wk HAMP NW3 *...83 G1
Judge Wk ESH/CLAY KT10...204 E4
Judith Av CRW RM5...56 D2
Juer St BTSEA SW11...140 D1
Juglans Rd ORP BR6...202 B5
Jules Thorn Av EN EN1...24 C4
Julia Gdns BARK IG11...109 K1
Juliana Cl EFNCH N2...47 G6

Julian Av ACT W3...98 D6
Julian Cl BAR EN5...20 E5
Julian Hl HRW HA1...60 E6
Julian Pl POP/IOD E14...124 E5
Julian Rd ORP BR6...217 G4
Julian Tayler Pth FSTH SE23 *...163 J4
Julien Rd EA W5...116 D4
Juliette Rd PLSTW E13...106 E1
Juliette Wy BARK IG11...91 G5
Julius Caesar Wy STAN HA7...29 K6
Julius Nyerere Cl IS N1...5 N1
Junction Ap BTSEA SW11...140 D4
Junction Ms BAY/PAD W2 *...8 C3
Junction Pl BAY/PAD W2 *...8 B3
Junction Rd ARCH N19...84 C1
  DART DA1...171 G1
  EA W5...116 D4
  ED N9...36 C3
  HRW HA1...60 E6
  PLSTW E13...89 F6
  ROM RM1...75 H1
  SAND/SEL CR2...211 K4
  TOTM N17...50 C6
Junction Rd East CHDH RM6 *...74 A4
Junction Rd West CHDH RM6...74 A4
Juniper Cl BAR EN5...20 B6
  CHSGTN KT9...206 B3
  WBLY HA9...80 B3
Juniper Ct CHDH RM6...73 H5
  KTN/HRWW/WS HA3 *...43 F4
Juniper Crs CAMTN NW1...84 A6
Juniper Dr WAND/EARL SW18...140 B5
Juniper Gdns MTCM CR4...179 H4
Juniper La EHAM E6...107 J4
Juniper Rd IL IG1...90 A2
Juniper St WCHPL E1 *...104 E6
Juno Wy NWCR SE14...124 A6
Jupiter Wy HOLWY N7...85 F4
Jupp Rd SRTFD E15...88 B5
Jupp Rd West SRTFD E15...88 B6
Justice Wk CHEL SW3...120 D6
Justin Cl BTFD TW8...136 E1
Justin Rd CHING E4...51 H2
Jute La PEND EN3...25 H2
Jutland Cl ARCH N19...66 E5
Jutland Rd CAT SE6...165 F2
  PLSTW E13...106 E3
Jutsums Av ROMW/RG RM7...74 D3
Jutsums La ROMW/RG RM7...74 D3
Juxon Cl KTN/HRWW/WS HA3...42 B4
Juxon St LBTH SE11...17 H6

K

Kaduna Cl PIN HA5...58 E2
Kale Rd ERITH DA18...128 E2
Kambala Rd BTSEA SW11...140 C3
Kangley Bridge Rd SYD SE26...182 C1
Kaplan Dr WCHMH N21...23 F6
Kara Wy CRICK NW2...82 B2
Karen Cl RAIN RM13...111 J3
Karen Ct BMLY BR1...183 J4
  ...146 B6
Karenza Ct WBLY HA9 *...61 J4
Karina Cl CHIG IG7...54 E1
Karma Wy RYLN/HDSTN HA2...60 A5
Kashgar Rd WOOL/PLUM SE18...128 A5
Kashmir Rd CHARL SE7...146 C1
Kassala Rd BTSEA SW11...140 E2
Katharine St CROY/NA CR0...211 J1
Katherine Cl BERM/RHTH SE16...124 A1
Katherine Gdns BARK/HLT IG6...54 C3
  ELTH/MOT SE9...146 C5
Katherine Rd EHAM E6...89 H5
Katherine Sq NTGHL W11 *...119 H1
Kathleen Av ACT W3...98 E4
  ALP/SUD HA0...80 A5
Kathleen Rd BTSEA SW11...140 E4
Kayemoor Rd BELMT SM2...209 J5
Kay Rd BRXN/ST SW9...141 K3
Kays Ter SWFD E18 *...52 D5
Kay St BETH E2...104 C1
  SRTFD E15...88 B5
  WELL DA16...148 C2
Kean St HOL/ALD WC2B...11 G4
Keatley Gn CHING E4...51 H2
Keats Av CAN/RD E16...126 A1
  HARH RM3...57 K3
Keats Cl CHIG IG7...54 C2
  PEND EN3...25 F6
  STHWK SE1...19 J7
  WAN E11 *...71 F2
  WIM/MER SW19...178 C2
Keats Est STNW/STAM N16 *...68 B6
Keats Gv HAMP NW3...83 J2
Keats Pde ED N9 *...36 C4
Keats Rd BELV DA17...129 K3
  WELL DA16...147 K2
Keats Wy CROY/NA CR0...197 K3
  GFD/PVL UB6...96 B4
  WDR/YW UB7...112 C4
Keble Cl NTHLT UB5...78 C3
  WPK KT4...192 C5
Keble Pl BARN SW13...118 E6
Keble St TOOT SW17...160 B6
Kechill Gdns HAYES BR2...199 K4
Kedleston Dr STMC/STPC BR5...202 A3
Kedleston Wk BETH E2...104 D2
Keeble Cl WOOL/PLUM SE18 *...127 G6
Keedonwood Rd BMLY BR1...183 H1
Keel Cl BARK IG11...109 J1
  BERM/RHTH SE16...124 A1
Keeley Rd CROY/NA CR0...196 D6
Keeley St HOL/ALD WC2B...11 G4
Keely Cl EBAR EN4...21 J6
Keemor Cl WOOL/PLUM SE18 *...147 F1
Keens Cl STRHM/NOR SW16...179 J1
Keen's Rd CROY/NA CR0...211 J2
Keen's Yd IS N1 *...85 H4
Keepers Ms TEDD TW11...174 D2
The Keep BKHTH/KID SE3...145 K3

KUTN/CMB KT2...175 G2
Keesey St WALW SE17 *...122 E1
Keeton's Rd BERM/RHTH SE16...123 J5
Keevil Dr WIM/MER SW19...159 G2
Keighley Cl HOLWY N7...84 E2
Keightley Dr ELTH/MOT SE9...167 H5
Keildon Rd BTSEA SW11...140 E5
Keir Hardie Est CLPT E5 *...68 D5
Keir Hardie Wy BARK IG11...91 G5
  YEAD UB4 *...95 F2
Keith Connor Cl VX/NE SW8...141 G4
Keith Gv SHB W12...118 D1
Keith Rd BARK IG11...108 D1
  HYS/HAR UB3...113 H3
  WALTH E17...51 H4
Kelbrook Rd BKHTH/KID SE3...146 D3
Kelburn Wy RAIN RM13...111 J2
Kelceda Cl CRICK NW2...63 J6
Kelf Gv HYS/HAR UB3...94 D5
Kelfield Gdns NKENS W10...100 B5
Kelfield Ms NKENS W10...100 B5
Kelland Cl CEND/HSY/T N8 *...66 D2
Kelland Rd PLSTW E13...106 E3
Kellaway Rd BKHTH/KID SE3...146 B3
Keller Crescent MNPK E12...89 H2
Kellerton Rd LEW SE13...145 H6
Kellett Rd BRXS/STRHM SW2...142 B4
Kelling Gdns CROY/NA CR0...196 C4
Kellino St TOOT SW17...160 E6
Kellner Rd THMD SE28...128 A3
Kell St STHWK SE1...18 B4
Kelly Av PECK SE15...143 G2
Kelly Cl WLSDN NW10...81 F1
Kelly Ms MV/WKIL W9 *...100 D4
Kelly Rd MLHL NW7...46 C2
Kelly St CAMTN NW1...84 B4
Kelly Wy CHDH RM6...74 A2
Kelman Cl CLAP SW4...141 J3
Kelmore Gv EDUL SE22...143 H5
Kelmscott Cl WALTH E17...51 H1
  WATW WD18...26 C1
Kelmscott Gdns SHB W12...118 D3
Kelmscott Rd BTSEA SW11...160 D1
Kelross Rd HBRY N5...85 H2
Kelsall Cl BKHTH/KID SE3...146 A3
Kelsall Ms RCH/KEW TW9...137 J2
Kelsey La BECK BR3...182 D6
Kelsey Park Av BECK BR3...182 E5
Kelsey Park Rd BECK BR3...182 D5
Kelsey Rd STMC/STPC BR5...186 C5
Kelsey Sq BECK BR3...182 D5
Kelsey St BETH E2...104 C3
Kelsey Wy BECK BR3...182 D6
Kelsie Wy BARK/HLT IG6...54 E3
Kelso Pl KENS W8...120 A3
Kelso Rd CAR SM5...194 B4
Kelston Rd BARK/HLT IG6...54 B5
Kelton Vls KUT/HW KT1 *...175 G5
Kelvedon Cl KUTN/CMB KT2...175 H2
Kelvedon Rd FUL/PGN SW6...139 J1
Kelvin Av PLMGR N13...49 F2
  TEDD TW11...173 K2
Kelvinbrook E/WMO/HCT KT8...173 G6
Kelvin Cl HOR/WEW KT19...206 C4
Kelvin Crs KTN/HRWW/WS HA3...42 E3
Kelvin Dr TWK TW1...156 C1
Kelvin Gdns CROY/NA CR0...195 K4
  STHL UB1...96 A5
Kelvin Gv CHSGTN KT9...205 K1
  SYD SE26...163 J5
Kelvington Cl CROY/NA CR0...198 B4
Kelvington Rd PECK SE15...144 A6
Kelvin Pde ORP BR6...201 K5
Kelvin Rd HBRY N5...85 H2
  WELL DA16...148 B4
Kember St IS N1 *...85 F5
Kemble Dr HAYES BR2...215 J1
Kemble Rd CROY/NA CR0...211 H1
  FSTH SE23...164 A3
  TOTM N17...50 C4
Kemble St HOL/ALD WC2B...11 G4
Kemerton Rd BECK BR3...182 E5
  CMBW SE5...142 D4
  CROY/NA CR0...197 G4
Kemey's St HOM E9...87 G3
Kemnal Rd CHST BR7...167 J5
Kempe Rd KIL/WHAMP NW6...100 B2
Kemp Gdns CROY/NA CR0...196 D3
Kemplay Rd HAMP NW3...83 H2
Kemp Pl BUSH WD23...28 A1
Kemps Dr NTHWD HA6...40 D3
  POP/IOD E14...105 J6
Kempsford Gdns ECT SW5...119 K5
Kempsford Rd LBTH SE11...17 K7
Kempshott Rd
  STRHM/NOR SW16...179 J3
Kempson Rd FUL/PGN SW6...139 K2
Kempthorne Rd DEPT SE8...124 B4
Kempton Av NTHLT UB5...78 A4
  SUN TW16...172 C4
Kempton Cl ERITH DA8...129 K6
  HGDN/ICK UB10...76 A2
Kempton Ct SUN TW16...172 C4
Kempton Pk SUN TW16 *...172 B4
Kempton Rd EHAM E6...89 K6
  HPTN TW12...172 D5
Kempton Wk CROY/NA CR0...198 B3
Kempt St WOOL/PLUM SE18...127 F6
Kemsing Cl BXLY DA5...169 F2
  THHTH CR7...196 D1
Kemsing Rd GNWCH SE10...125 K5
Kenbury Gdns CMBW SE5...142 D3
Kenchester Cl VX/NE SW8...141 K1
Kendal Av ACT W3...98 C4
  BARK IG11...90 E6
  UED N18...35 K6
Kendal Cl BRXN/ST SW9...142 C1
  EBED/NFELT TW14...153 H2
  WFD IG8...38 D4
  YEAD UB4...94 C1
Kendal Cft HCH RM12...93 J5
Kendale Rd BMLY BR1...183 H1
Kendal Gdns SUT SM1...194 B6
  UED N18...35 K6
Kendall Av BECK BR3...182 B5
  SAND/SEL CR2...211 K6
The Keep BKHTH/KID SE3...145 K3

Kendall Pl MHST W1U...9 G2
Kendall Rd BECK BR3...182 B5
  ISLW TW7...136 B3
  WOOL/PLUM SE18...146 D1
Kendal Pde UED N18...48 B4
Kendal Pl PUT/ROE SW15...139 J6
Kendal Rd WLSDN NW10...81 J2
Kendal Steps BAY/PAD W2 *...8 C4
Kendal St BAY/PAD W2...8 C4
Kendal St NWCR SE14...143 K1
Kendon Cl WAN E11...71 F2
Kendoa Rd CLAP SW4...141 J5
Kendra Hall Rd SAND/SEL CR2...211 H5
Kendrey Gdns WHTN TW2...155 K1
Kendrick Ms SKENS SW7...14 A6
Kendrick Pl SKENS SW7 *...14 A7
Kenelm Cl HRW HA1...79 G1
Kenerne Dr BAR EN5...20 C6
Keniford Rd BAL SW12...161 G2
Kenilworth Av
  RYLN/HDSTN HA2...77 K2
  WALTH E17...51 J5
  WIM/MER SW19...177 K1
Kenilworth Crs EN EN1...24 A2
Kenilworth Gdns
  GDMY/SEVK IG3...73 F6
  LOU IG10...39 K1
  OXHEY WD19...41 G1
  STHL UB1...95 K2
  WOOL/PLUM SE18...147 G5
  YEAD UB4...94 D4
Kenilworth Rd ASHF TW15...152 A5
  BOW E3...105 G1
  EDGW HA8...30 E4
  EW KT17...207 J4
  KIL/WHAMP NW6...82 D6
  PGE/AN SE20...182 A4
  STMC/STPC BR5...201 H5
Kenley Av CDALE/KGS NW9...45 G5
Kenley Cl BXLY DA5...169 H2
  CHST BR7...185 J5
  EBAR EN4...21 J5
Kenley Gdns THHTH CR7...196 C1
Kenley Rd KUT/HW KT1...175 K5
  TWK TW1...156 C1
  WIM/MER SW19...177 J6
Kenley Wk CHEAM SM3...208 B2
  NTGHL W11...119 H1
Kenlor Rd TOOT SW17...178 C1
Kenmare Dr MTCM CR4...178 E3
  TOTM N17...50 C3
Kenmare Gdns PLMGR N13...49 J1
Kenmare Rd THHTH CR7...196 B3
Kenmere Gdns ALP/SUD HA0...80 C6
Kenmere Rd WELL DA16...148 D3
Kenmont Gdns WLSDN NW10...99 K2
Kenmore Av
  KTN/HRWW/WS HA3...61 G2
Kenmore Cl RCH/KEW TW9...137 H1
Kenmore Crs EDGW HA8...44 D5
Kenmore Gdns EDGW HA8...44 D5
Kenmore Rd
  KTN/HRWW/WS HA3...43 K6
Kenmure Rd HACK E8...86 D4
Kenmure Yd HACK E8 *...86 D4
Kennacraig Cl CAN/RD E16...126 A1
Kennard Rd FBAR/BDGN N11...47 K1
  SRTFD E15...88 B5
Kennard St BTSEA SW11...141 F2
  CAN/RD E16...126 D1
Kennedy Av PEND EN3...36 E1
Kennedy Cl MTCM CR4...179 F5
  PIN HA5...41 K2
  PLSTW E13...106 E1
  STMC/STPC BR5...201 J5
Kennedy Rd BARK IG11...90 E6
  HNWL W7...96 D4
Kennedy Wk WALW SE17 *...19 F7
Kennet Cl BTSEA SW11...140 C5
Kennet Rd DART DA1...150 C5
  ISLW TW7...136 A4
  MV/WKIL W9...100 D3
Kennet Sq MTCM CR4...178 D4
Kenneth Av IL IG1...90 B2
Kenneth Crs CRICK NW2...81 K3
Kenneth Gdns STAN HA7...43 G2
Kenneth More Rd IL IG1...90 B1
Kenneth Rd BCTR RM8...91 H1
Kennet Rd DART DA1...150 C5
Kenneth Robbins Rd TOTM N17...50 D3
Kenneth Sq MTCM CR4...178 D4
Kennet St WAP E1W...123 H1
Kennett Dr HYS/HAR UB3...95 F5
Kennett Wharf La BLKFR EC4V...12 D5
  UED N18...50 E1
Kenning St BERM/RHTH SE16...123 K2
Kenning Ter IS N1...7 G1
Kennings Wy LBTH SE11...122 B5
Kennington Gv LBTH SE11...122 A6
Kennington La LBTH SE11...122 B5
Kennington Ov LBTH SE11...122 A5
Kennington Park Gdns
  LBTH SE11...122 C6
Kennington Park Pl
  LBTH SE11...122 B6
Kennington Park Rd
  LBTH SE11...122 B6
Kennington Rd LBTH SE11...17 J7
  STHWK SE1...18 A5
Kenny Dr CAR SM5...210 A6
Kennylands Rd BARK/HLT IG6...55 G2
Kenny Rd MLHL NW7...46 C1
Kenrick Pl MHST W1U...9 G2
Kensal Rd NKENS W10...100 C3
Kensal Whf NKENS W10 *...100 B3
Kensington Av MNPK E12...89 K5
  THHTH CR7...180 B4
Kensington Church Ct
  KENS W8...120 A2
Kensington Church St
  KENS W8...119 K1
Kensington Church Wk
  KENS W8...120 A2
Kensington Ct KENS W8...120 A2
Kensington Court Gdns
  KENS W8 *...120 A3

Kensington Court Ms
  KENS W8 *...120 A3
Kensington Court Pl KENS W8...120 A3
Kensington Dr WFD IG8...53 H5
Kensington Gdns IL IG1...71 K5
Kensington Gardens Sq
  BAY/PAD W2 *...101 F5
Kensington Ga KENS W8...120 B3
Kensington Hall Gdns
  WKENS W14 *...119 J5
Kensington High St
  KENS W8...120 A2
  WKENS W14...119 H4
Kensington MI KENS W8 *...119 H4
Kensington Palace Gdns KENS W8 *...120 A1
Kensington Palace Gdns
  KENS W8...120 A2
Kensington Park Gdns
  NTGHL W11...100 C6
Kensington Park Ms
  NTGHL W11...100 C5
Kensington Park Rd
  NTGHL W11...100 E6
Kensington Pl KENS W8...119 K1
Kensington Rd KENS W8...120 B1
  NTHLT UB5...96 A1
  ROMW/RG RM7...74 E3
Kensington Sq KENS W8...120 A2
Kensington Ter SAND/SEL CR2...211 K5
Kent Av DAGW RM9...110 C3
  WEA W13...97 H4
  WELL DA16...148 A6
Kent Cl MTCM CR4...195 K1
  ORP BR6...216 E4
Kent Ct CDALE/KGS NW9 *...45 G5
Kent Dr EBAR EN4...21 K5
  TEDD TW11...173 K1
Kentford Wy NTHLT UB5...77 J6
Kent Gdns RSLP HA4...58 E5
  WEA W13...97 H4
Kent Gate Wy CROY/NA CR0...213 H4
Kent House La BECK BR3...182 B2
Kent House Rd BECK BR3...182 B2
  SYD SE26...182 C3
Kentish Rd BELV DA17...129 H4
Kentish Town Rd CAMTN NW1...84 B4
Kentish Wy BMLY BR1...184 A5
Kentlea Rd THMD SE28...127 K2
Kentmere Rd
  WOOL/PLUM SE18...127 K4
Kenton Av HRW HA1...61 F3
  STHL UB1...96 A6
  SUN TW16...172 C5
Kenton Gdns
  KTN/HRWW/WS HA3...61 J1
Kenton La KTN/HRWW/WS HA3...43 J3
Kenton Park Av
  KTN/HRWW/WS HA3...61 K1
Kenton Park Cl
  KTN/HRWW/WS HA3...61 J1
Kenton Park Crs
  KTN/HRWW/WS HA3...61 K1
Kenton Park Pde
  KTN/HRWW/WS HA3 *...61 J2
Kenton Park Rd
  KTN/HRWW/WS HA3...61 J1
Kenton Rd HOM E9...87 F4
  HRW HA1...61 H1
  KTN/HRWW/WS HA3...61 J2
Kenton St STPAN WC1H...4 D7
Kenton Wy YEAD UB4 *...94 C2
Kent Pas CAMTN NW1...2 E6
Kent Rd CHSWK W4...117 K3
  DAGE RM10...92 D3
  DART DA1...171 H1
  E/WMO/HCT KT8...189 H1
  KUT/HW KT1...174 E6
  RCH/KEW TW9...137 H1
  STMC/STPC BR5...202 E3
  WCHMH N21...35 J2
  WWKM BR4...198 E5
Kent St BETH E2...7 K2
  PLSTW E13...107 F2
Kent Ter CAMTN NW1...2 D5
Kent View Gdns
  GDMY/SEVK IG3...72 E6
Kent Wy SURB KT6...206 A1
Kentwell Cl BROCKY SE4 *...144 B5
Kentwode Gn BARN SW13...138 D1
Kenver Av NFNCH/WDSPK N12...47 H2
Kenward Rd ELTH/MOT SE9...146 B6
Kenway CRW RM5...56 E5
Ken Wy WBLY HA9...62 E6
Kenway Rd ECT SW5...120 A4
Kenwood Av BKHTH/KID SE3...146 A4
Kenwood Cl HAMP NW3...65 H5
  WDR/YW UB7...112 D6
Kenwood Dr BECK BR3...183 F6
  ...112 D6
Kenwood Gdns CLAY IG5...53 K6
  SWFD E18...53 F1
Kenwood Rd ED N9...36 C4
  HGT N6...65 K3
Kenworthy Rd HOM E9...87 G4
Kenwyn Dr CRICK NW2...81 G2
Kenwyn Rd CLAP SW4...141 H5
  DART DA1...151 H4
  RYNPK SW20...177 F4
Kenya Rd CHARL SE7...146 C1
Kenyngton Pl
  KTN/HRWW/WS HA3...61 J2
Kenyon St FUL/PGN SW6...139 G2
Keogh Rd SRTFD E15...88 C4
Kepler Rd CLAP SW4...141 K5
Keppel Rd DAGW RM9...92 A2
  EHAM E6...90 A5
Keppel St GWRST WC1E...10 D1
Kerbela St BETH E2...7 K6
Kerbey St POP/IOD E14...105 K5
Kerfield Crs CMBW SE5...142 E2
Kerfield Pl CMBW SE5...142 E2
Kerri Cl BAR EN5...20 A5
Kerrison Pl EA W5...116 E1
Kerrison Rd BTSEA SW11...140 D4
  EA W5...116 E1
  SRTFD E15...88 B6
Kerry Av SOCK/AV RM15...131 K2
  STAN HA7...29 K5
Kerry Cl CAN/RD E16...107 F5

PLMGR N13 ....35 F4
Kerry Ct STAN HA7 ....29 K6
Kerry Pth NWCR SE14 ....124 C6
Kersfield Rd PUT/ROE SW15 ....139 G1
Kershaw Cl WAND/EARL SW18 ....160 C1
Kershaw Rd DAGE RM10 ....92 C1
Kersley Ms BTSEA SW11 * 140 E2
Kersley Rd STNW/STAM N16 ....86 A1
Kersley St BTSEA SW11 ....140 E3
Kerstin Cl HYS/HAR UB3 ....94 D6
Kerswell Cl SEVS/STOTM N15 ....68 A2
Kerwick Cl HOLWY N7 ....85 F5
Keslake Rd KIL/WHAMP NW6 ....100 E1
Kessock Cl TOTM N17 ....68 D2
Kesteven Cl BARK/HLT IG6 ....55 H1
Keston Av HAYES BR2 ....215 G3
Keston Cl UED N18 ....35 K5
.........WELL DA16 ....148 D1
Keston Gdns HAYES BR2 ....215 G2
Keston Park Cl HAYES BR2 ....215 K2
Keston Rd PECK SE15 ....143 H4
.........THHTH CR7 ....196 A3
.........TOTM N17 ....67 K3
Kestrel Av EHAM E6 ....107 J4
.........HNHL SE24 ....142 C6
Kestrel Cl CDALE/KGS NW9 ....45 G5
.........HCH RM12 ....93 K5
.........KUTN/CMB KT2 ....156 E6
.........WLSDN NW10 ....81 F5
Kestrel Pl NWCR SE14 * 124 B6
Kestrel Wy CROY/NA CRO 214 B6
.........HYS/HAR UB3 ....113 G2
Keswick Av PUT/ROE SW15 ....176 B1
.........WIM/MER SW19 ....177 K5
Keswick Cl SUT SM1 ....209 G2
Keswick Gdns REDBR IG4 ....71 J2
.........RSLP HA4 ....58 B3
.........WBLY HA9 ....80 A3
Keswick Ms EA W5 ....117 F1
Keswick Rd BXLYHN DA7 ....149 H1
.........ORP BR6 ....202 A5
.........PUT/ROE SW15 ....139 H6
.........WWKM BR4 ....199 H6
Kettering St
.........STRHM/NOR SW16 ....179 G2
Kett Gdns BRXS/STRHM SW2 ....142 A6
Kettlebaston Rd LEY E10 ....69 G5
Kettlewell Cl FBAR/BDGN N11 ....48 A2
Kevelioc Rd TOTM N17 ....49 J4
Kevin Cl HSLWW TW4 ....134 C1
Kevington Cl STMC/STPC BR5 ....202 A1
Kevington Dr CHST BR7 ....202 A1
Kew Br RCH/KEW TW9 ....117 H6
Kew Br Arches CHSWK W4 * 117 H6
Kew Bridge Ct BTFD TW8 ....117 H5
Kew Bridge Rd BTFD TW8 ....117 G6
Kew Crs CHEAM SM3 ....208 C1
Kewferry Dr NTHWD HA6 ....40 A2
Kewferry Rd NTHWD HA6 ....40 A2
Kew Foot Rd RCH/KEW TW9 ....137 F5
Kew Gardens Rd
.........RCH/KEW TW9 ....137 G1
Kew Gn RCH/KEW TW9 ....117 H6
Kew Meadow Pth
.........RCH/KEW TW9 ....137 H2
Kew Riverside Pk
.........RCH/KEW TW9 ....137 J3
Kew Rd RCH/KEW TW9 ....117 G6
.........RCH/KEW TW9 ....137 F5
Key Cl WCHPL E1 ....104 D3
Keyes Rd CRICK NW2 ....82 B3
.........DART DA1 ....151 K5
Keymer Rd BRXS/STRHM SW2 ....162 A4
Keynes Cl EFNCH N2 ....47 K6
Keynsham Av WFD IG8 ....38 C6
Keynsham Gdns
.........ELTH/MOT SE9 ....146 D6
Keynsham Rd ELTH/MOT SE9 ....146 D6
.........MRDN SM4 ....194 A5
Keyse Rd STHWK SE1 ....19 J5
Keysham Av HEST TW5 ....133 K2
Keystone Crs IS N1 ....5 F5
Keyworth Cl CLPT E5 ....87 G2
Keyworth St STHWK SE1 ....18 B3
Kezia St DEPT SE8 ....124 B5
Khama Rd TOOT SW17 ....160 D6
Khartoum Rd IL IG1 ....90 B3
.........PLSTW E13 ....107 F2
.........TOOT SW17 ....160 C6
Khyber Rd BTSEA SW11 ....140 D3
Kibworth St VX/NE SW8 ....142 A1
Kidbrooke Gdns
.........BKHTH/KID SE3 ....145 K3
Kidbrooke Gv BKHTH/KID SE3 ....145 K2
Kidbrooke La ELTH/MOT SE9 ....146 D5
Kidbrooke Park Cl
.........BKHTH/KID SE3 ....146 A2
Kidbrooke Park Rd
.........LEE/GVPK SE12 ....146 A6
Kidbrooke Wy BKHTH/KID SE3 ....146 A3
Kidderminster Pl
.........CROY/NA CRO 196 C5
Kidderminster Rd
.........CROY/NA CRO 196 D4
Kidderpore Av HAMP NW3 ....82 D2
Kidderpore Gdns HAMP NW3 ....82 D2
Kiddl Pl CHARL SE7 ....126 D5
Kielder Cl BARK/HLT IG6 ....55 F2
Kielder St SDTCH EC2A 7 G6
Kilberry Cl ISLW TW7 ....135 J2
Kilburn Br KIL/WHAMP NW6 ....82 E6
Kilburn High Rd
.........KIL/WHAMP NW6 ....82 E6
Kilburn La NKENS W10 ....100 B2
Kilburn Park Rd
.........KIL/WHAMP NW6 ....100 E2
Kilburn Pl KIL/WHAMP NW6 ....100 E1
Kilburn Pl KIL/WHAMP NW6 ....82 E6
Kilburn Priory STJWD NW8 ....83 H6
Kilburn Sq KIL/WHAMP NW6 ....82 E6
Kilburn V KIL/WHAMP NW6 ....82 E6
Kildare Cl RSLP HA4 ....59 G5
Kildare Rd CAN/RD E16 ....106 E4
Kildare Ter BAY/PAD W2 ....100 E5
Kildoran Rd CLAP SW4 ....141 K6

Kildowan Rd GDMY/SEVK IG3 ....73 G5
Kilgour Rd FSTH SE23 ....164 B1
Kilkie St FUL/PGN SW6 ....140 B3
Kilkarney Rd
.........WAND/EARL SW18 ....160 B1
Kilburns Mill Cl WLGTN SM6 ....195 G6
Killearn Rd CAT SE6 ....165 G3
Killester Gdns WPK KT4 ....207 K2
Killewarren Wy
.........STMC/STPC BR5 ....202 D4
Killick St IS N1 ....5 G2
Killieser Av BRXS/STRHM SW2 ....161 K4
Killip Cl CAN/RD E16 ....106 D5
Killowen Av NTHLT UB5 ....78 C3
Killowen Rd HOM E9 ....87 F4
Killyon Rd VX/NE SW8 ....141 H3
Kilmaine Rd FUL/PGN SW6 ....139 H1
Kilmarnock Rd OXHEY WD19 ....27 H1
Kilmarsh Rd HMSMTH W6 ....119 F4
Kilmartin Av
.........STRHM/NOR SW16 ....180 B6
Kilmartin Rd GDMY/SEVK IG3 ....73 G5
Kilmartin Wy HCH RM12 ....93 K3
Kilmington Rd BARN SW13 ....118 D6
Kilmorey Gdns TWK TW1 ....156 C6
Kilmorey Rd TWK TW1 ....136 C5
Kilmorie Rd FSTH SE23 ....164 B3
Kilmuir Cl STHGT/OAK N14 * 113 J3
Kiln Ms TOOT SW17 ....178 C1
Kiln Pl KTTN NW5 ....84 A2
Kilnside ESH/CLAY KT10 ....205 G5
Kiln Wy NTHWD HA6 ....40 C2
Kiln Wood La ABR/ST RM4 ....57 F1
Kilpatrick Wy YEAD UB4 ....95 J4
Kilravock St NKENS W10 ....100 C2
Kilross Rd EBED/NFELT TW14 ....153 G3
Kilsha Rd WOT/HER KT12 ....188 A3
Kilvinton Dr ENC/FH EN2 ....23 K1
Kimbell Gdns FUL/PGN SW6 ....139 H2
Kimbell Pl BKHTH/KID SE3 ....146 B5
Kimberley Av EHAM E6 ....107 J1
.........GNTH/NBYPK IG2 ....72 E4
.........PECK SE15 ....143 K4
.........ROMW/RG RM7 ....74 E1
Kimberley Ct KIL/WHAMP NW6 ....82 C5
Kimberley Dr SCUP DA14 ....168 E4
Kimberley Gdns EN EN1 ....24 B4
.........FSBYPK N4 ....67 H2
Kimberley Rd BECK BR3 ....182 A5
.........BRXN/ST SW9 ....141 K3
.........CAN/RD E16 ....106 D3
.........CLPT E5 ....86 C2
.........CROY/NA CRO 196 C5
.........KIL/WHAMP NW6 ....100 C1
.........TOTM N17 ....50 C5
.........UED N18 ....50 D2
.........WALTH E17 ....51 G4
.........WAN E11 ....70 C6
Kimberley Wy CHING E4 ....38 C3
Kimber Rd WAND/EARL SW18 ....159 K2
Kimble Cl WATW WD18 * 26 C1
Kimble Crs BUSH WD23 ....28 C2
Kimble Rd WIM/MER SW19 ....178 C2
Kimbolton Cl LEE/GVPK SE12 ....165 J2
Kimbolton Gdns
.........ELTH/MOT SE9 ....166 D6
Kimmeridge Rd
.........ELTH/MOT SE9 ....166 D6
Kimpton Park Wy CHEAM SM3 ....193 J6
Kimpton Rd CHEAM SM3 ....208 D1
.........CMBW SE5 ....142 E2
Kinburn St BERM/RHTH SE16 * 124 A2
Kincaid Rd PECK SE15 ....143 J1
Kincardine Gdns
.........MV/WKIL W9 * 100 E3
Kinch Gv WBLY HA9 ....62 B4
Kinder Cl THMD SE28 ....109 K6
Kinder St WCHPL E1 ....104 D5
Kinderton Cl STHGT/OAK N14 ....34 C3
Kinfauns Rd
.........BRXS/STRHM SW2 ....162 B4
.........GDMY/SEVK IG3 ....73 H5
Kingaby Gdns RAIN RM13 ....93 J5
King Alfred Av CAT SE6 ....164 D6
King & Queen Cl
.........ELTH/MOT SE9 ....166 D6
King & Queen St WALW SE17 ....122 D5
King Arthur Cl PECK SE15 ....143 K1
King Charles Crs BRYLDS KT5 ....191 G4
King Charles I Island
.........WHALL SW1A 10 E7
King Charles' Rd WHALL SW1A 16 D2
King Charles Wk
.........WIM/MER SW19 * 159 H3
Kingcup Cl CROY/NA CRO 198 A5
King David La WCHPL E1 ....104 E6
Kingdon Rd KIL/WHAMP NW6 ....82 E4
King Edward Dr CHSGTN KT9 ....206 A1
King Edward Rd BAR EN5 ....20 E5
.........LEY E10 ....70 A5
.........ROM RM1 ....75 H3
.........WALTH E17 ....51 G6
King Edward III Ms
.........BERM/RHTH SE16 * 123 J2
King Edward Wk STHWK SE1 ....17 K4
Kingfield Rd EA W5 ....97 K3
Kingfield St POP/IOD E14 ....125 F4
Kingfisher Dr
.........KTN/HRWW/WS HA3 ....43 F3
.........STMC/STPC BR5 ....202 E1
.........THMD SE28 ....109 J3
Kingfisher Dr
.........RCHPK/HAM TW10 ....156 D6

Kingfisher Ms LEW SE13 ....144 E6
Kingfisher Pl WDGN N22 * 49 F5
Kingfisher St EHAM E6 ....107 J4
Kingfisher Wy BECK BR3 ....198 A2
.........WLSDN NW10 * 81 F4
King Gdns CROY/NA CRO 211 H3
King Garth Ms FSTH SE23 ....163 K4
King George Av BUSH WD23 ....28 B1
.........CAN/RD E16 ....107 H5
.........GNTH/NBYPK IG2 ....72 D5
.........WOT/HER KT12 ....188 C5
King George Sq
.........RCHPK/HAM TW10 ....157 G1
King George St GNWCH SE10 ....145 F1
King George Vi Av MTCM CR4 ....194 E1
Kingham Cl NTGHL W11 ....119 H2
.........WAND/EARL SW18 ....160 B2
King Harolds Wy BXLYHN DA7 ....148 E1
King Henry Ms HRW HA1 * 60 E5
.........ORP BR6 ....217 F5
King Henry's Dr CROY/NA CRO 214 A6
King Henry's Reach
.........HMSMTH W6 ....119 F6
King Henry's Rd HAMP NW3 ....83 K5
.........KUT/HW KT1 ....191 F1
King Henry Ter WAP E1W * 104 D6
Kinghorn St STBT EC1A 12 C2
King James Ct STHWK SE1 * 18 B3
King James St STHWK SE1 ....18 B3
King John Ct SDTCH EC2A 7 H6
King John St WCHPL E1 ....105 F4
King John's Wk ELTH/MOT SE9 ....166 D2
Kinglake Est WALW SE17 * 123 F5
Kinglake St WALW SE17 ....123 F5
Kinglet Cl FSTGT E7 ....88 E4
Kingly Ct REGST W1B * 10 B5
Kingly St REGST W1B 10 A4
King & Queen Cl
.........ELTH/MOT SE9 ....166 D6
King & Queen Whf
.........BERM/RHTH SE16 * 124 A1
Kingsand Rd LEE/GVPK SE12 ....165 K4
King's Arms Yd LOTH EC2R 12 E3
Kingsash Dr YEAD UB4 ....95 J3
Kings Av BAL SW12 ....161 J3
.........BMLY BR1 ....183 J2
.........CAR SM5 ....209 K6
.........CHDH RM6 ....74 B3
.........EA W5 ....97 K5
.........GFD/PVL UB6 ....96 B5
.........HSLW TW3 ....135 H4
.........MUSWH N10 ....48 A6
.........NWMAL KT3 ....192 C1
.........WCHMH N21 ....35 H5
.........WFD IG8 ....53 G1
King's Bench St STHWK SE1 ....18 B2
King's Bench Wk EMB EC4Y * 11 K5
Kingsbridge Av ACT W3 ....117 G2
Kingsbridge Ct POP/IOD E14 ....124 D4
Kingsbridge Crs STHL UB1 ....95 K4
Kingsbridge Dr MLHL NW7 ....46 B3
Kingsbridge Rd BARK IG11 ....108 D1
.........MRDN SM4 ....193 G4
.........NKENS W10 ....100 A5
.........WOT/HER KT12 ....188 A4
Kingsbury Gn
.........CDALE/KGS NW9 * 62 D2
Kingsbury Rd CDALE/KGS NW9 ....62 C2
.........IS N1 ....86 A4
Kingsbury Ter IS N1 ....86 A4
Kings Cha E/WMO/HCT KT8 ....173 H6
Kingsclere Cl PUT/ROE SW15 ....158 D2
Kingsclere Pl ENC/FH EN2 ....23 J3
Kingscliffe Gdns
.........WIM/MER SW19 ....159 J4
Kings Cl DART DA1 ....150 B5
.........HDN NW4 ....64 B1
.........LEY E10 ....69 K4
.........NTHWD HA6 ....40 D2
.........THDIT KT7 ....190 B3
.........WOT/HER KT12 ....188 A4
King's College Rd HAMP NW3 * 83 H5
.........RSLP HA4 ....58 D3
Kingscote Rd CHSWK W4 ....118 A3
.........CROY/NA CRO 197 J4
.........NWMAL KT3 ....176 A6
Kingscote St BLKFR EC4V 12 A5
Kings Ct PLSTW E13 ....89 F6
.........STHWK SE1 ....18 A1
Kingscourt Rd
.........STRHM/NOR SW16 ....161 K5
King's Crs FSBYPK N4 ....85 J2
Kingscroft Rd CRICK NW2 ....82 D4
King's Cross Br IS N1 * 5 F4
King's Cross Rd FSBYW WC1X 5 H5
Kingsdale Gdns NTGHL W11 ....119 G1
Kingsdale Rd PGE/AN SE20 ....182 A4
.........WOOL/PLUM SE18 ....128 A6
Kingsdown Av ACT W3 ....99 G6
.........SAND/SEL CR2 ....211 J6
.........WEA W13 ....116 C2

.........OXHEY WD19 ....27 H2
Kingsdown Cl DART DA1 * 171 G1
Kingsford St KTTN NW5 ....83 K5
Kingsford Wy EHAM E6 ....107 K4
Kings Gdns IL IG1 ....72 D5
.........KIL/WHAMP NW6 ....82 E6
Kingsgate WBLY HA9 ....80 E1
Kingsgate Av FNCH N3 ....46 E6
Kingsgate Cl BXLYHN DA7 ....149 F2
.........STMC/STPC BR5 ....186 D6
Kingsgate Est IS N1 * 86 A4
Kingsgate Pl KIL/WHAMP NW6 ....82 E5
Kingsgate Rd KIL/WHAMP NW6 ....82 E5
.........KUTN/CMB KT2 ....175 F4
Kings Gv PECK SE15 ....143 J2
.........ROM RM1 ....75 J2
Kings Hall Ms LEW SE13 * 145 F4
Kings Hall Rd BECK BR3 ....182 A3
Kings Head HI CHING E4 ....37 K2
King's Hwy WOOL/PLUM SE18 ....127 K5
Kingshill Av CRW WA5 ....56 E2
.........KTN/HRWW/WS HA3 ....61 H1
.........NTHLT UB5 ....95 F2
.........WPK KT4 ....192 D4
.........YEAD UB4 ....95 F2
Kingshill Cl YEAD UB4 * 94 E2
Kingshill Dr
.........KTN/HRWW/WS HA3 ....43 H6
Kingshold Rd HOM E9 ....86 E5
Kingsholm Gdns
.........ELTH/MOT SE9 ....146 C5
Kingshurst Rd LEE/GVPK SE12 ....165 K2
Kings Keep HAYES BR2 * 183 H6
.........KUT/HW KT1 * 191 F1
Kingsland Gn STNW/STAM N16 ....86 A4
Kingsland High St HACK E8 ....86 B4
Kingsland Pas HACK E8 * 86 A4
Kingsland Rd BETH E2 ....7 H3
.........HACK E8 ....86 B5
.........PLSTW E13 ....107 G2
King's La SUT SM1 ....209 H3
Kingslawn Cl PUT/ROE SW15 ....138 E6
Kingsleigh Cl BTFD TW8 ....116 E6
Kingsleigh Pl MTCM CR4 ....178 E6
Kingsleigh Wk HAYES BR2 ....199 J1
Kingsley Av DART DA1 ....151 K6
.........HSLW TW3 ....135 H3
.........STHL UB1 ....96 A6
.........SUT SM1 ....209 H2
.........WEA W13 ....97 G5
Kingsley Cl DAGE RM10 ....92 D2
.........EDGW HA8 * 30 D4
Kingsley Ct EDGW HA8 * 30 D4
.........GPK RM2 ....57 J3
Kingsley Dr WPK KT4 ....192 C6
Kingsley Gdns CHING E4 ....51 J1
Kingsley Ms CHST BR7 ....185 G2
.........IL IG1 ....72 B6
.........KENS W8 * 120 A4
.........WAP E1W * 104 D6
Kingsley Pl HGT N6 ....66 B4
Kingsley Rd BARK/HLT IG6 ....54 C4
.........CROY/NA CRO 196 B5
.........FSTGT E7 ....88 E5
.........HSLW TW3 ....135 H3
.........KIL/WHAMP NW6 ....82 D6
.........ORP BR6 ....217 H5
.........PIN HA5 ....59 K1
.........PLMGR N13 ....35 H6
.........RYLN/HDSTN HA2 ....59 J6
.........WALTH E17 ....52 A5
.........WIM/MER SW19 ....159 J4
Kingsley St BTSEA SW11 ....140 E4
Kingsley Wood Dr
.........ELTH/MOT SE9 ....167 F5
Kingslyn Crs NRWD SE19 ....181 F5
Kings MI HMSMTH W6 * 119 F4
Kingsman St
.........WOOL/PLUM SE18 ....126 E4
Kingsmead BAR EN5 ....20 E5
.........RCHPK/HAM TW10 ....157 G1
Kingsmead Av CDALE/KGS NW9 ....63 F4
.........MTCM CR4 ....179 H6
.........ROM RM1 ....75 G3
.........SUN TW16 ....172 B6
.........SURB KT6 ....191 H6
.........WPK KT4 ....207 K1
Kingsmead Cl BFN/LL DA15 ....168 B4
.........HOR/WEW KT19 ....207 F5
.........TEDD TW11 ....174 C2
Kingsmead Dr NTHLT UB5 ....77 K5
Kings Mead Pk ESH/CLAY KT10 ....204 E5
Kingsmead Rd
.........BRXS/STRHM SW2 ....162 B4
Kingsmere Cl PUT/ROE SW15 ....139 G4
Kingsmere Pk CDALE/KGS NW9 ....62 D5
Kingsmere Pl
.........STNW/STAM N16 * 67 K5
Kingsmere Rd
.........WIM/MER SW19 ....159 G4
Kings Ms BMSBY WC1N 5 H7
.........CLAP SW4 ....141 K6
Kingsmill Gdns DAGW RM9 ....92 B3
Kingsmill Rd DAGW RM9 ....92 B3
Kingsmill Ter STJWD NW8 ....2 B2
Kingsnympton Pk
.........KUTN/CMB KT2 ....175 J3
Kings Oak ROMW/RG RM7 ....56 C6
Kings Orch ELTH/MOT SE9 ....166 D1
King's Paddock HPTN TW12 ....173 H4
Kings Pde CAR SM5 * 209 J1
.........WLSDN NW10 * 99 K2
Kingspark Ct WFD IG8 ....52 E3
Kings Pas WAN E11 ....70 C4
Kings Pl CHSWK W4 ....117 K5
.........LOU IG10 ....39 H2
.........STHWK SE1 ....18 C1
King Sq FSBYE EC1V 6 C5

Kings Reach EMB EC4Y * 11 K5
.........WHALL SW1A 17 F1
Kings Ride Ga
.........RCHPK/HAM TW10 ....137 H5
Kingsridge Gdns DART DA1 ....171 G1
Kings Rd BAR EN5 ....20 B5
.........BARK IG11 ....90 C5
.........CHEL SW3 ....120 C6
.........CHING E4 ....38 A3
.........EA W5 ....97 K4
.........FELT TW13 ....154 C3
.........FUL/PGN SW6 ....140 B1
.........KUTN/CMB KT2 ....175 G3
.........MORT/ESHN SW14 ....138 A4
.........MTCM CR4 ....179 F6
.........ORP BR6 ....217 F2
.........PLSTW E13 ....89 F6
.........RCHPK/HAM TW10 ....137 G6
.........ROM RM1 ....75 H3
.........RYLN/HDSTN HA2 ....59 K6
.........SNWD SE25 ....181 H6
.........SURB KT6 ....190 D5
.........TEDD TW11 ....173 J1
.........TOTM N17 ....50 C4
.........TWK TW1 ....156 C1
.........UED N18 ....50 C1
.........WAN E11 ....70 C4
.........WDGN N22 ....49 F4
.........WDR/YW UB7 ....112 C3
.........WIM/MER SW19 ....177 K2
.........WLSDN NW10 ....81 K5
.........WLSDN NW10 * 188 A6
King's Scholars' Pas PIM SW1V 16 A6
King Stairs Cl
.........BERM/RHTH SE16 ....123 J2
Kingsthorpe Rd SYD SE26 ....164 A6
Kingston Av CHEAM SM3 ....208 C1
.........EBED/NFELT TW14 ....133 H1
Kingston By-Pass
.........ESH/CLAY KT10 ....204 E1
.........RYNPK SW20 ....176 C2
Kingston Cl CHDH RM6 ....56 A6
.........NTHLT UB5 ....77 K5
.........TEDD TW11 ....174 C3
Kingston Crs BECK BR3 ....182 C4
Kingston Gdns CROY/NA CRO 210 E1
Kingston Hall Rd KUT/HW KT1 ....174 E6
Kingston HI KUT/HW KT2 ....175 H4
Kingston Hill Av CHDH RM6 ....56 A6
Kingston Hill Pl
.........KUTN/CMB KT2 ....158 A6
Kingston House Est
.........SURB KT6 * 190 C3
Kingston La TEDD TW11 ....174 C3
.........WDR/YW UB7 ....112 C2
Kingston Lodge NWMAL KT3 * 192 B1
Kingston Pl
.........KTN/HRWW/WS HA3 ....43 F3
Kingston Rd BRYLDS KT5 ....191 J6
.........EBAR EN4 ....33 J1
.........ED N9 ....36 B4
.........HOR/WEW KT19 ....207 G3
.........IL IG1 ....90 C2
.........KUT/HW KT1 ....175 J6
.........NWDGN UB2 ....114 E4
.........NWMAL KT3 ....192 A1
.........PUT/ROE SW15 ....158 E3
.........ROM RM1 ....75 H1
.........RYNPK SW20 ....177 H5
.........TEDD TW11 ....174 C2
.........WIM/MER SW19 ....177 K3
Kingston Sq NRWD SE19 ....180 E1
Kingston V PUT/ROE SW15 ....158 A6
Kingstown St CAMTN NW1 ....3 K6
King St ACT W3 ....117 K1
.........CITYW EC2V 12 D4
.........COVGDN WC2E 11 F5
.........EFNCH N2 ....47 H6
.........HMSMTH W6 ....118 D4
.........NWDGN UB2 ....114 D3
.........PLSTW E13 ....106 E3
.........RCH/KEW TW9 ....136 E6
.........TOTM N17 ....50 B4
.........TWK TW1 ....156 B3
.........WHALL SW1A 10 C7
King Street Cloisters
.........HMSMTH W6 * 118 E4
King Street Pde TWK TW1 * 156 B3
Kingswater Pl BTSEA SW11 * 140 D1
Kings Wy CROY/NA CRO 211 F3
Kingsway HOL/ALD WC2B 11 G4
Kingsway KTN/HRWW/WS HA3 ....42 B4
.........MORT/ESHN SW14 ....137 J4
.........NFNCH/WDSPK N12 ....47 H2
.........NWMAL KT3 ....193 F1
.........PEND EN3 ....24 E6
.........STMC/STPC BR5 ....201 J2
.........STWL/WRAY TW19 ....152 A3
.........WBLY HA9 ....80 A2
.........WWKM BR4 ....214 D1
Kingsway Av SAND/SEL CR2 ....212 E6
Kingsway Crs RYLN/HDSTN HA2 ....60 C1
Kingsway Pde
.........STNW/STAM N16 * 85 K1
Kingsway Pl CLKNW EC1R * 5 K5
Kingsway Rd CHEAM SM3 ....208 C5
Kingswear Rd KTTN NW5 ....84 B1
.........RSLP HA4 ....58 C2
Kingswood Av BELV DA17 ....129 G4
.........HAYES BR2 ....183 H6
.........HPTN TW12 ....173 G2
.........HSLW TW3 ....134 E2
.........KIL/WHAMP NW6 ....100 B1
.........THHTH CR7 ....196 B2
Kingswood Cl ASHF TW15 ....153 F6
.........BAR EN5 ....20 B5
.........DART DA1 ....171 F3
.........EN EN1 ....24 A6
.........NWMAL KT3 ....192 C3
.........STMC/STPC BR5 ....201 J4
.........SURB KT6 ....191 F5
.........VX/NE SW8 ....141 K1
Kingswood Ct LEW SE13 * 145 F6
Kingswood Dr BELMT SM2 ....209 F6
.........CAR SM5 ....194 E5

DUL SE21 163 F6
Kingswood Pk FNCH N3 46 D5
Kingswood Pl LEW SE13 145 H5
Kingswood Rd
BRXS/STRHM SW2 161 K1
CHSWK W4 117 K3
GDMY/SEVK IG3 73 G5
HAYES BR2 183 H6
PGE/AN SE20 181 K2
WAN E11 70 C4
WBLY HA9 80 C1
WIM/MER SW19 177 J4
Kingswood Ter CHSWK W4 117 K3
Kingswood Wy WLGTN SM6 210 E5
Kingsworth Cl BECK BR3 198 B2
Kingsworthy Cl KUT/HW KT1 175 G6
Kings Yd PUT/ROE SW15 * 139 G5
SRTFD E15 * 87 J4
Kingthorpe Rd WLSDN NW10 81 F5
Kingthorpe Ter WLSDN NW10 * 81 F5
Kingwell Rd EBAR EN4 21 H1
Kingweston Cl CRICK NW2 82 C1
King William La GNWCH SE10 125 H5
King William St CANST EC4R 13 F6
King William Wk GNWCH SE10 125 F6
Kingwood Rd FUL/PGN SW6 139 H1
Kinlet Rd WOOL/PLUM SE18 147 H2
Kinloch Dr CDALE/KGS NW9 63 G4
Kinloch St HOLWY N7 85 F1
Kinloss Gdns FNCH N3 46 D6
Kinloss Rd CAR SM5 194 B4
Kinnaird Av BMLY BR1 183 J2
CHSWK W4 137 K1
Kinnaird Cl BMLY BR1 183 J2
Kinnaird Wy WFD IG8 53 K2
Kinnear Rd SHB W12 118 C2
Kinnerton Pl North
KTBR SW1X * 15 F3
Kinnerton Pl South
KTBR SW1X * 15 F3
Kinnerton St KTBR SW1X 15 G3
Kinnerton Yd KTBR SW1X * 15 G3
Kinnoul Rd HMSMTH W6 119 H6
Kinross Av WPK KT4 192 D6
Kinross Cl KTN/HRWW/WS HA3 62 B2
Kinross Ter WALTH E17 51 H5
Kinsale Rd PECK SE15 143 H4
Kinsella Gdns WIM/MER SW19 176 E2
Kintyre Cl STRHM/NOR SW16 180 A5
Kinveachy Gdns CHARL SE7 126 D5
Kinver Rd SYD SE26 163 K6
Kipling Dr WIM/MER SW19 178 C2
Kipling Est STHWK SE1 19 F3
Kipling Rd BXLYHN DA7 149 F2
Kipling St STHWK SE1 19 F3
Kipling Ter ED N9 * 35 K5
Kippington Dr ELTH/MOT SE9 166 C3
Kirby Cl BARK/HLT IG6 54 E2
HOR/WEW KT19 207 H3
LOU IG10 39 J2
NTHWD HA6 40 D3
Kirby Est BERM/RHTH SE16 * 123 J3
Kirby Gv STHWK SE1 19 G2
Kirby St HCIRC EC1N 11 K1
Kirchen Rd WEA W13 97 H6
Kirkcaldy Gn OXHEY WD19 27 G5
Kirkdale SYD SE26 163 J4
Kirkdale Cnr SYD SE26 * 163 K6
Kirkdale Rd WAN E11 70 C5
Kirkfield Cl WEA W13 116 C1
Kirkham Rd EHAM E6 107 J5
Kirkham St WOOL/PLUM SE18 127 K6
Kirkland Av CLAY IG5 54 A5
Kirkland Cl BFN/LL DA15 167 K1
Kirkland Dr ENC/FH EN2 23 J2
Kirkland Ter BECK BR3 182 D2
Kirkland Wk HACK E8 86 B4
Kirk La WOOL/PLUM SE18 127 H6
Kirkleas Rd SURB KT6 191 F5
Kirklees Rd BCTR RM8 91 J3
THHTH CR7 196 B2
Kirkley Rd WIM/MER SW19 177 K4
Kirkly Cl SAND/SEL CR2 212 A6
Kirkmichael Rd POP/IOD E14 106 A5
Kirk Rd WALTH E17 69 J3
Kirkside Rd BKHTH/KID SE3 125 K6
Kirkstall Av SEVS/STOTM N15 67 K1
Kirkstall Gdns
BRXS/STRHM SW2 161 J3
Kirkstall Rd BRXS/STRHM SW2 161 K3
Kirksted Rd MRDN SM4 194 A5
Kirkstone Wy BMLY BR1 183 H3
Kirkton Rd SEVS/STOTM N15 68 A1
Kirkwall Pl BETH E2 * 104 E2
Kirkwood Rd PECK SE15 143 J3
Kirn Rd WEA W13 97 H6
Kirrane Cl NWMAL KT3 192 C2
Kirtley Rd SYD SE26 164 B6
Kirtling St VX/NE SW8 141 H1
Kirton Cl CHSWK W4 118 A4
Kirton Gdns BETH E2 7 K5
Kirton Ldg WAND/EARL SW18 * 160 A1
Kirton Rd PLSTW E13 107 G1
Kirton Wk EDGW HA8 44 E3
Kirwyn Wy CMBW SE5 142 D1
Kitcat Ter BOW E3 105 J2
Kitchener Rd EFNCH N2 47 J6
FSTGT E7 89 F4
THHTH CR7 180 E6
TOTM N17 50 A6
WALTH E17 51 K4
Kite Pl BETH E2 * 104 C2
Kite Yd BTSEA SW11 * 140 E2
Kitley Gdns NRWD SE19 181 G4
Kitson Rd BARN SW13 138 D2
CMBW SE5 142 D1
Kittiwake Rd NTHLT UB5 95 H2
Kittiwake Wy YEAD UB4 95 H4
Kitto Rd NWCR SE14 144 A3
Kiver Rd ARCH N19 66 E6
Kiwi Ter EHAM E6 108 A2
Klea Av CLAP SW4 161 H1
Knapdale Cl FSTH SE23 163 J4
Knapmill Rd CAT SE6 164 D4
Knapmill Wy CAT SE6 164 D4
Knapp Cl WLSDN NW10 81 G4
Knapp Rd ASHF TW15 152 C6
BOW E3 105 J3
Knapton Ms TOOT SW17 179 F2
Knaresborough Dr
WAND/EARL SW18 160 A3
Knaresborough Pl ECT SW5 120 A4
Knatchbull Rd CMBW SE5 142 D2
WLSDN NW10 81 F6
Knebworth Av WALTH E17 51 J4
Knebworth Rd
STNW/STAM N16 * 86 A2
Knee Hl ABYW SE2 128 D5
Knee Hill Crs ABYW SE2 128 D4
Kneller Gdns ISLW TW7 155 J1
Kneller Rd BROCKY SE4 144 B5
NWMAL KT3 192 B4
WHTN TW2 155 H1
Knevett Ter HSLW TW3 135 F5
Knight Cl BCTR RM8 73 J6
Knighten St WAP E1W 123 J1
Knighthead Point
POP/IOD E14 * 124 D2
Knightland Rd CLPT E5 68 D6
Knighton Cl ROMW/RG RM7 75 F3
SAND/SEL CR2 211 H6
WFD IG8 39 F6
Knighton Dr WFD IG8 39 F6
Knighton La BKHH IG9 39 F4
Knighton Park Rd SYD SE26 182 A1
Knighton Rd FSTGT E7 88 E1
ROMW/RG RM7 74 E3
Knightrider Ct BLKFR EC4V * 12 B5
Knightrider St BLKFR EC4V 12 C5
Knight's Av EA W5 117 F2
Knightsbridge SKENS SW7 14 D3
Knightsbridge Gdns
ROMW/RG RM7 75 F2
Knightsbridge Gn KTBR SW1X * 14 E3
Knights Chambers ED N9 * 36 C5
Knights Cl E/WMO/HCT KT8 188 E2
Knights Hl WNWD SE27 180 C1
Knight's Hill Sq WNWD SE27 162 C6
Knight's La ED N9 36 C5
Knights Manor Wy DART DA1 171 J1
Knight's Pk KUT/HW KT1 175 F6
Knight's Pl WHTN TW2 155 K3
Knights Rdg ORP BR6 217 H3
Knights Rd CAN/RD E16 125 K1
STAN HA7 29 J6
Knights Wk LBTH SE11 18 A7
Knights Wy BARK/HLT IG6 54 C2
Knightswood Cl EDGW HA8 30 E4
Knightswood Rd RAIN RM13 111 H1
Knightwood Crs NWMAL KT3 192 B3
Knivet Rd FUL/PGN SW6 119 K6
Knobs Hill Rd SRTFD E15 87 K6
Knockholt Rd ELTH/MOT SE9 146 C6
Knole Cl CROY/NA CR0 * 197 K3
Knole Rd DART DA1 170 D2
The Knole ELTH/MOT SE9 167 F6
Knoll Crs NTHWD HA6 40 D5
Knoll Dr STHGT/OAK N14 34 A2
Knollmead BRYLDS KT5 191 K5
Knoll Ri ORP BR6 202 A5
Knoll Rd BXLY DA5 169 H2
SCUP DA14 186 C1
WAND/EARL SW18 140 A6
Knolls Cl WPK KT4 207 K1
The Knoll BECK BR3 182 E4
EA W5 97 J4
HAYES BR2 199 K6
PIN HA5 * 41 H5
Knollys Cl STRHM/NOR SW16 162 C5
Knolly's Rd STRHM/NOR SW16 162 B5
Knottisford St BETH E2 105 F2
Knotts Green Ms LEY E10 69 K3
Knotts Green Rd LEY E10 69 K3
Knowle Av BXLYHN DA7 149 F1
Knowle Cl BRXN/ST SW9 142 B4
Knowle Rd HAYES BR2 200 D6
WHTN TW2 155 K3
Knowles Cl WDR/YW UB7 112 B1
Knowles Hill Crs LEW SE13 145 G6
Knowlton Gn HAYES BR2 199 J2
Knowsley Av STHL UB1 115 G1
Knowsley Rd BTSEA SW11 140 E3
Knox Rd FSTGT E7 88 E4
Knox St CAMTN NW1 8 E1
Knoyle St NWCR SE14 124 B6
Kohat Rd WIM/MER SW19 178 B1
Koh-i-noor Av BUSH WD23 28 A1
Kossuth St GNWCH SE10 125 H5
Kramer Ms ECT SW5 * 119 K5
Kreedman Wk HACK E8 * 86 C3
Kuala Gdns STRHM/NOR SW16 180 A4
Kydbrook Cl STMC/STPC BR5 201 H4
Kylemore Cl EHAM E6 107 H1
Kylemore Rd KIL/WHAMP NW6 82 E5
Kymberley Rd HRW HA1 * 60 E3
Kyme Rd ROM RM1 75 H3
Kynance Gdns STAN HA7 43 J4
Kynance Ms SKENS SW7 120 B3
Kynance Pl KENS W8 120 B3
Kynaston Av THHTH CR7 196 D2
Kynaston Cl
KTN/HRWW/WS HA3 42 D3
Kynaston Crs THHTH CR7 196 D2
Kynaston Rd BMLY BR1 183 K1
ENC/FH EN2 23 K2
STMC/STPC BR5 202 C4
STNW/STAM N16 86 A1
THHTH CR7 196 D2
Kynaston Wd
KTN/HRWW/WS HA3 42 D3
Kynersley Cl CAR SM5 209 K1
Kynoch Rd UED N18 37 F6
Kyrle Rd BTSEA SW11 161 F1
Kyverdale Rd STNW/STAM N16 68 B4

L

Laburnum Av DART DA1 171 F3
ED N9 36 A4
HCH RM12 75 J6
SUT SM1 209 J1
TOTM N17 49 K3
Laburnum Cl ALP/SUD HA0 80 C6
CHING E4 51 H2
PECK SE15 143 K1
Laburnum Ct STAN HA7 29 J6
Laburnum Crs SUN TW16 172 A4
Laburnum Gdns CROY/NA CR0 198 A4
Laburnum Gv CDALE/KGS NW9 62 E4
HSLW TW3 134 E5
NWMAL KT3 176 A5
RSLP HA4 58 B3
STHL UB1 95 K3
WCHMH N21 35 J4
Laburnum Pl ELTH/MOT SE9 * 147 F6
Laburnum Rd HYS/HAR UB3 113 J4
MTCM CR4 179 F5
WIM/MER SW19 178 B3
Laburnum St BETH E2 7 J1
Laburnum Wy HAYES BR2 201 G4
STWL/WRAY TW19 152 C3
Lacebark Cl BFN/LL DA15 168 A2
Lacewing Cl PLSTW E13 106 E2
Lacey Cl ED N9 36 C4
Lacey Dr BCTR RM8 91 J1
EDGW HA8 30 A6
HPTN TW12 172 E4
Lackington St SDTCH EC2A 13 F1
Lacock Cl WIM/MER SW19 178 B2
Lacon Rd EDUL SE22 143 H5
Lacrosse Wy
STRHM/NOR SW16 179 J4
Lacy Rd PUT/ROE SW15 139 G5
Ladas Rd WNWD SE27 180 D1
Ladbroke Crs NTGHL W11 100 C5
Ladbroke Gdns NTGHL W11 100 D6
Ladbroke Gv NKENS W10 100 B3
Ladbroke Ms NTGHL W11 119 H1
Ladbroke Rd EN EN1 36 B1
NTGHL W11 119 J1
Ladbroke Sq NTGHL W11 100 D6
Ladbroke Ter NTGHL W11 100 D6
Ladbroke Wk NTGHL W11 119 J1
Ladbrook Cl PIN HA5 59 K2
Ladbrooke Crs SCUP DA14 168 E5
Ladbrook Rd SNWD SE25 196 E1
Ladderstile Ride
KUTN/CMB KT2 175 J1
Ladderswood Wy
FBAR/BDGN N11 48 C1
Lady Alesford Av STAN HA7 43 H1
Lady Booth Rd KUT/HW KT1 175 F5
Ladycroft Gdns ORP BR6 216 C3
Ladycroft Rd LEW SE13 144 E4
Ladycroft Wk STAN HA7 43 K4
Ladycroft Wy ORP BR6 216 C3
Lady Forsdyke Wy
HOR/WEW KT19 206 C6
Ladygate La RSLP HA4 58 A3
Ladygrove CROY/NA CR0 213 G6
Lady Harewood Wy
HOR/WEW KT19 206 C6
Lady Hay WPK KT4 192 C6
Lady Margaret Rd ARCH N19 84 C2
STHL UB1 95 K3
STHL UB1 95 K6
Ladymount WLGTN SM6 210 D2
Ladyship Ter EDUL SE22 * 163 J2
Ladysmith Av EHAM E6 107 J1
GNTH/NBYPK IG2 72 D4
Ladysmith Cl MLHL NW7 45 J3
Ladysmith Rd CAN/RD E16 106 D2
ELTH/MOT SE9 167 F1
EN EN1 24 B3
KTN/HRWW/WS HA3 42 E5
TOTM N17 50 C5
UED N18 50 D1
Lady Somerset Rd KTTN NW5 84 B2
Ladywell Cl BROCKY SE4 144 D6
Ladywell Rd LEW SE13 144 D6
Ladywell St SRTFD E15 88 D6
Ladywell Water Tower
BROCKY SE4 * 144 C4
Ladywood Av STMC/STPC BR5 201 K2
Ladywood Rd SURB KT6 191 H6
Lafone Av FELT TW13 154 B3
Lafone St STHWK SE1 19 J2
Lagado Ms BERM/RHTH SE16 124 A1
Lagonda Av BARK/HLT IG6 55 F2
Lagonda Wy DART DA1 151 F5
Lagoon Rd STMC/STPC BR5 202 C2
Laidlaw Dr WCHMH N21 23 F6
Laing Cl BARK/HLT IG6 54 D2
Laing Dean NTHLT UB5 77 G6
Laings Av MTCM CR4 178 E5
Lainlock Pl HSLW TW3 135 G2
Lainson St WAND/EARL SW18 159 K2
Lairdale Cl DUL SE21 162 D3
Lairs Cl HOLWY N7 * 84 E4
Laitwood Rd BAL SW12 161 G3
Lake Av BMLY BR1 183 K2
Lake Cl BCTR RM8 91 K1
Lakedale Rd
WOOL/PLUM SE18 127 K5
Lake Dr BUSH WD23 28 C4
Lakefield Rd WDGN N22 49 H5
Lake Gdns DAGE RM10 92 C3
RCHPK/HAM TW10 156 C5
WLGTN SM6 210 B1
Lakehall Gdns THHTH CR7 196 C2
Lakehall Rd THHTH CR7 196 C2
Lake House Rd WAN E11 88 E1
Lakehurst Rd HOR/WEW KT19 207 G3
Lakeland Cl
KTN/HRWW/WS HA3 42 D2
Lakenheath STHGT/OAK N14 22 D6
Lake Ri ROM RM1 57 H6
Lake Rd CHDH RM6 73 K1
CROY/NA CR0 198 C6
DAGW RM9 110 D2
LEY E10 69 K4
WIM/MER SW19 177 J1
Lakeside BECK BR3 182 E6
ENC/FH EN2 22 D5
HOR/WEW KT19 207 G4
WEA W13 97 J5
WLGTN SM6 210 B2
Lakeside Av REDBR IG4 71 H1
THMD SE28 128 B2
Lakeside Cl BFN/LL DA15 148 D6
RSLP HA4 58 B1
SNWD SE25 181 H5
Lakeside Crs EBAR EN4 33 K1
Lakeside Dr ESH/CLAY KT10 204 C4
HAYES BR2 215 J1
WLSDN NW10 98 B2
Lakeside Rd PLMGR N13 35 F6
WKENS W14 119 G3
Lakeside Wy WBLY HA9 80 C2
Lakes Rd HAYES BR2 215 G3
Lakeswood Rd
STMC/STPC BR5 201 G3
The Lake BUSH WD23 28 D3
Lake Vw EDGW HA8 44 B1
Lake View Est BOW E3 * 105 F1
Lakeview Rd WELL DA16 148 C5
WNWD SE27 180 C1
Lake View Ter UED N18 * 36 B6
Lakis Cl HAMP NW3 83 G2
Laleham Av MLHL NW7 31 F5
Laleham Ct SUT SM1 * 209 G3
Laleham Rd CAT SE6 165 F2
Lalor St FUL/PGN SW6 139 H3
Lambarde Av ELTH/MOT SE9 167 F6
Lamb Cl NTHLT UB5 95 J2
Lamberhurst Cl
STMC/STPC BR5 202 E5
Lamberhurst Rd BCTR RM8 74 B5
WNWD SE27 162 B6
Lambert Av RCH/KEW TW9 137 H4
Lambert Jones Ms BARB EC2Y * 12 C1
Lambert Rd BRXS/STRHM SW2 141 K6
CAN/RD E16 107 F5
NFNCH/WDSPK N12 47 H1
Lambert's Pl CROY/NA CR0 196 E5
Lambert's Rd BRYLDS KT5 191 G2
Lambert St IS N1 85 G5
Lambert Wy
NFNCH/WDSPK N12 47 G1
Lambeth Br WEST SW1P 17 F6
Lambeth High St LBTH SE11 17 G6
Lambeth Hl BLKFR EC4V 12 C5
Lambeth Palace Rd STHWK SE1 17 G5
Lambeth Rd CROY/NA CR0 196 B5
STHWK SE1 17 J5
Lambeth Wk LBTH SE11 17 H6
PECK SE15 143 G3
Lambkins Ms WALTH E17 70 A1
Lamb La HACK E8 86 D5
Lamble St KTTN NW5 84 A3
Lambley Rd DAGW RM9 91 H4
Lambolle Pl HAMP NW3 83 J4
Lambolle Rd HAMP NW3 83 J4
Lambourn Cl HNWL W7 116 A2
KTTN NW5 * 84 C2
SAND/SEL CR2 211 H6
Lambourne Av
WIM/MER SW19 159 J6
Lambourne Gdns BARK IG11 91 F5
CHING E4 37 J4
EN EN1 24 B3
Lambourne Gv
BERM/RHTH SE16 124 A5
KUT/HW KT1 175 J5
Lambourne Pl BKHTH/KID SE3 146 A2
Lambourne Rd BARK IG11 90 E5
GDMY/SEVK IG3 72 E6
WAN E11 70 A4
Lambourn Rd CLAP SW4 141 G4
Lambrook Ter FUL/PGN SW6 139 H2
Lambs Cl ED N9 36 C4
Lamb's Conduit Pas
FSBYW WC1X 11 G1
Lamb's Conduit St BMSBY WC1N 5 G7
Lambscroft Av ELTH/MOT SE9 166 B5
Lambs Gv BARK IG11 90 E5
Lambs Meadow WFD IG8 53 H5
Lambs Ms IS N1 6 A1
Lamb's Pas STLK EC1Y 6 E7
Lambs Ter ED N9 * 35 K4
Lamb St WCHPL E1 13 J1
Lambs Wk ENC/FH EN2 23 J3
Lambton Pl NTGHL W11 * 100 D6
Lambton Rd ARCH N19 66 E5
RYNPK SW20 177 F5
Lamb Wk STHWK SE1 19 G3
Lamerock Rd BMLY BR1 165 J6
Lamerton Rd BARK/HLT IG6 54 C6
Lamerton St DEPT SE8 124 D6
Lamford Cl TOTM N17 49 K3
Lamington St HMSMTH W6 118 E4
Lamlash St LBTH SE11 18 A6
Lammas Av MTCM CR4 179 F5
Lammas La ESH/CLAY KT10 204 A2
Lammas Park Gdns EA W5 116 D1
Lammas Rd HOM E9 87 F5
LEY E10 69 G6
RCHPK/HAM TW10 156 D6
Lammermoor Rd BAL SW12 * 161 G2
Lamont Rd WBPTN SW10 120 C6
Lamont Road Pas
WBPTN SW10 * 120 C6
Lamorbey Cl BFN/LL DA15 168 A4
Lamorbey Pk BFN/LL DA15 * 168 C3
Lamorna Cl ORP BR6 202 B4
WALTH E17 52 B5
Lamorna Gv STAN HA7 43 K5
Lampard Gv STNW/STAM N16 68 B5
Lampern Sq BETH E2 * 104 C2
Lampeter Sq HMSMTH W6 119 H6
Lamplighter Cl WCHPL E1 104 E3
Lamplighters Cl DART DA1 171 J1
Lampmead Rd LEE/GVPK SE12 145 H6
Lamport Cl WOOL/PLUM SE18 126 E4
Lampton Av HSLW TW3 135 F2
Lampton House Cl
WIM/MER SW19 159 G6
Lampton Park Rd HSLW TW3 135 G3
Lampton Rd HEST TW5 135 G2
Lamson Rd RAIN RM13 111 H4
Lanacre Av CDALE/KGS NW9 45 G4
Lanark Cl EA W5 97 J4
Lanark Pl MV/WKIL W9 101 G3
Lanark Rd KIL/WHAMP NW6 101 F1
Lanbury Rd PECK SE15 144 A5
Lancashire Ct MYFR/PKLN W1K 9 J5
Lancaster Av BARK IG11 90 E5
EBAR EN4 21 H1
MTCM CR4 195 K2
WAN E11 71 F1
WIM/MER SW19 177 G1
WNWD SE27 162 C4
Lancaster Cl ASHF TW15 152 B6
CDALE/KGS NW9 45 H3
HAYES BR2 199 J1
STWL/WRAY TW19 152 B1
TOTM N17 * 50 C3
WPK KT4 192 E4
Lancaster Ct WOT/HER KT12 188 A4
Lancaster Dr HAMP NW3 83 J4
HCH RM12 93 K3
POP/IOD E14 125 F1
Lancaster Garde BMLY BR1 200 D2
Lancaster Gdn KUTN/CMB KT2 174 E1
Lancaster Gdns
KUTN/CMB KT2 175 F1
WIM/MER SW19 177 H1
Lancaster Ga BAY/PAD W2 101 G6
Lancaster Gv HAMP NW3 83 J4
Lancaster House
WOOL/PLUM SE18 * 146 D1
Lancaster Ms BAY/PAD W2 * 101 G6
RCHPK/HAM TW10 157 F1
WAND/EARL SW18 * 140 A6
Lancaster Pk
RCHPK/HAM TW10 137 F6
Lancaster Pl COVGDN WC2E 11 G6
TWK TW1 156 B2
WIM/MER SW19 177 G1
Lancaster Rd EBAR EN4 21 H6
ENC/FH EN2 23 K2
FBAR/BDGN N11 48 D2
FSBYPK N4 67 G4
FSTGT E7 88 E5
NKENS W10 100 B5
NTHLT UB5 78 C4
RYLN/HDSTN HA2 60 A2
SNWD SE25 181 H6
STHL UB1 95 J6
UED N18 50 B1
WALTH E17 51 F5
WAN E11 70 C6
WIM/MER SW19 177 G1
WLSDN NW10 81 H3
Lancaster Stables HAMP NW3 * 83 J4
Lancaster St STHWK SE1 18 A3
Lancaster Ter BAY/PAD W2 8 A5
Lancaster Wk HYS/HAR UB3 94 A5
Lancaster Wy WPK KT4 193 F4
Lancaster West NTGHL W11 * 100 C5
Lancastrian Rd WLGTN SM6 210 E5
Lancefield St NKENS W10 100 D2
Lancell St STNW/STAM N16 68 A6
Lancelot Av ALP/SUD HA0 79 K2
Lancelot Crs ALP/SUD HA0 79 K2
Lancelot Gdns EBAR EN4 34 A2
Lancelot Pde ALP/SUD HA0 * 80 A3
Lancelot Pl SKENS SW7 14 E4
Lancelot Rd ALP/SUD HA0 79 K2
BARK/HLT IG6 54 E2
WELL DA16 148 B5
Lance Rd HRW HA1 60 C4
Lancer Sq KENS W8 * 120 A2
Lancey Cl CHARL SE7 126 C4
Lanchester Rd HGT N6 65 K2
Lancing Gdns ED N9 36 B3
Lancing Rd CROY/NA CR0 196 A3
FELT TW13 153 J4
GNTH/NBYPK IG2 72 D3
ORP BR6 202 C6
WEA W13 97 H6
Lancing St CAMTN NW1 4 C5
Landale Gdns DART DA1 171 F3
Landau Ter HAYES BR2 215 J2
Landau Wy ERITH DA8 131 G5
Landcroft Rd EDUL SE22 163 G1
Landells Rd EDUL SE22 163 G1
Landford Rd PUT/ROE SW15 139 F4
Landgrove Rd
WIM/MER SW19 177 K1
Landleys Flds HOLWY N7 * 84 D3
Landmann Wy NWCR SE14 124 A6
Landon Pl KTBR SW1X 14 E4
Landons Cl POP/IOD E14 125 F1
Landor Rd BRXN/ST SW9 141 K4
Landor Wk SHB W12 118 D2
Landra Gdns WCHMH N21 35 H1
Landridge Dr EN EN1 24 D1
Landridge Rd FUL/PGN SW6 139 H3
Landrock Rd CEND/HSY/T N8 66 E3
Landscape Rd WFD IG8 53 F3
Landseer Av MNPK E12 90 A3
Landseer Cl EDGW HA8 44 C5
EMPK RM11 75 K5
WIM/MER SW19 178 B4
Landseer Rd ARCH N19 84 E1
EN EN1 24 C6
NWMAL KT3 192 A4
SUT SM1 208 E4
Lands' End BORE WD6 29 K1
Landstead Rd
WOOL/PLUM SE18 147 J1
The Landway STMC/STPC BR5 186 D6
Lane Ap MLHL NW7 46 C1
Lane Cl CRICK NW2 81 K1
Lane End BXLYHN DA7 149 J4
Lane Gdns BUSH WD23 28 E3
ESH/CLAY KT10 205 F5
Lane Ms MNPK E12 89 K1
Lanercost Gdns
STHGT/OAK N14 34 E2
Lanercost Rd
BRXS/STRHM SW2 162 B4
Laneside CHST BR7 185 G1
EDGW HA8 44 E1
Laneside Av BCTR RM8 74 B4
The Lane BKHTH/KID SE3 145 K4
STJWD NW8 101 G1
Laneway PUT/ROE SW15 138 E6
Lanfranc Rd BOW E3 105 G1
Lanfrey Pl WKENS W14 119 J5
Langbourne Av HGT N6 66 A6

Langbourne Wy
ESH/CLAY KT10 205 C4
Langbrook Rd BKHTH/KID SE3 146 C4
Langcroft Cl CAR SM5 209 K1
Langdale Av MTCM CR4 178 E6
Langdale Cl BCTR RM8 73 J5
MORT/ESHN SW14 137 J5
ORP BR6 216 B1
Langdale Crs BXLYHN DA7 149 H2
Langdale Dr YEAD UB4 94 C1
Langdale Gdns HCH RM12 93 J3
Langdale Pde MTCM CR4 * 178 E5
Langdale Rd GNWCH SE10 145 F1
THHTH CR7 196 B1
Langdale St WCHPL E1 * 104 D5
Langdon Ct WLSDN NW10 81 G6
Langdon Crs EHAM E6 108 A1
Langdon Dr CDALE/KGS NW9 62 E5
Langdon House
WOOL/PLUM SE18 * 146 D1
Langdon Pk TEDD TW11 174 D3
Langdon Park Rd HGT N6 66 B4
Langdon Pl MORT/ESHN SW14 137 K4
Langdon Rd EHAM E6 90 A6
HAYES BR2 184 A6
MRDN SM4 194 B2
Langdon Shaw SCUP DA14 186 A1
Langdon Wk MRDN SM4 194 B2
Langdon Wy STHWK SE1 123 H4
Langford Cl HACK E8 86 C3
SEVS/STOTM N15 68 A3
STJWD NW8 101 G1
Langford Crs EBAR EN4 21 K5
Langford Gn CMBW SE5 143 F4
Langford Pl SCUP DA14 168 B5
STJWD NW8 101 G1
Langford Rd EBAR EN4 21 K5
FUL/PGN SW6 140 A3
WFD IG8 53 G2
Langfords BKHH IG9 39 H4
Langham Ct RSLP HA4 * 77 F3
Langham Dr GDMY/SEVK IG3 73 H3
Langham Gdns ALP/SUD HA0 61 J6
EDGW HA8 44 E3
RCHPK/HAM TW10 156 D6
WCHMH N21 23 G6
WEA W13 97 H6
Langham House Cl
RCHPK/HAM TW10 156 E6
Langham Pde
SEVS/STOTM N15 * 49 H6
Langham Park Pl HAYES BR2 199 J1
Langham Pl CHSWK W4 118 B6
REGST W1B 9 K3
SEVS/STOTM N15 49 H6
Langham Rd EDGW HA8 44 E2
RYNPK SW20 177 F4
SEVS/STOTM N15 67 J1
TEDD TW11 174 C1
Langham St GTPST W1W 10 A2
REGST W1B 9 K2
Langhedge Cl UED N18 50 B2
Langhedge La UED N18 50 B2
Langholm Cl BAL SW12 161 J2
Langholme BUSH WD23 28 C3
Langhorn Dr WHTN TW2 155 K2
Langhorne Rd DAGE RM10 92 C5
Langland Ct NTHWD HA6 40 A3
Langland Crs STAN HA7 43 K5
Langland Dr PIN HA5 41 J3
Langland Gdns CROY/NA CR0 198 C6
HAMP NW3 83 F3
Langler Rd WLSDN NW10 100 A2
Langley Av RSLP HA4 59 F6
SURB KT6 190 E5
WPK KT4 193 G6
Langley Ct BECK BR3 * 198 E1
COVGDN WC2E 10 E5
Langley Crs DAGW RM9 91 J5
EDGW HA8 30 E5
HYS/HAR UB3 133 J1
WAN E11 71 G4
Langley Dr ACT W3 117 J2
WAN E11 71 F4
Langley Gdns DAGW RM9 91 K5
STMC/STPC BR5 201 G3
Langley Gv NWMAL KT3 176 A5
Langley La VX/NE SW8 121 K6
Langley Pk MLHL NW7 45 G2
Langley Park Rd BELMT SM2 209 H5
Langley Pl WPK KT4 193 G6
Langley Rd BECK BR3 198 A1
ISLW TW7 136 A3
SAND/SEL CR2 213 F6
SURB KT6 191 F4
WELL DA16 128 D6
WIM/MER SW19 177 J4
Langley Rw BAR EN5 20 D2
Langley St LSQ/SEVD WC2H 10 E4
Langley Wy WWKM BR4 199 G5
Langley Wd BECK BR3 * 199 H2
Langmead Dr BUSH WD23 28 D3
Langmead St WNWD SE27 162 C6
Langport Ct WOT/HER KT12 188 B5
Langridge Ms HPTN TW12 172 E2
Langroyd Rd TOOT SW17 160 E4
Langside Av PUT/ROE SW15 138 D5
Langside Crs STHGT/OAK N14 34 D5
Langston Hughes Cl
HNHL SE24 * 142 C5
Lang St WCHPL E1 104 E3
Langthorn Ct LOTH EC2R * 13 F3
Langthorne Rd WAN E11 88 B1
Langthorne St FUL/PGN SW6 139 G2
Langton Av EHAM E6 108 A2
TRDG/WHET N20 33 G2
Langton Cl FSBYW WC1X 5 H5
Langton Gv NTHWD HA6 40 A1
Langton Ri EDUL SE22 163 J2
Langton Rd BRXN/ST SW9 142 C2
CRICK NW2 82 A1
E/WMO/HCT KT8 189 H2
KTN/HRWW/WS HA3 42 C3
Langton St WBPTN SW10 120 B6
Langton Vls TOTM N17 * 50 C4
Langton Wy BKHTH/KID SE3 145 K2
CROY/NA CR0 212 B2
Langtry Pl FUL/PGN SW6 119 K6
Langtry Rd NTHLT UB5 95 H1
STJWD NW8 83 F6
Langtry Wk STJWD NW8 83 G6
Langwood Cha TEDD TW11 174 D2
Langworth Cl RDART DA2 171 G5
Langworth Dr YEAD UB4 95 F5
Lanhill Rd MV/WKIL W9 100 E3
Lanier Rd LEW SE13 165 G1
Lanigan Dr HSLW TW3 135 G6
Lankaster Gdns EFNCH N2 47 H4
Lankers Dr RYLN/HDSTN HA2 59 K3
Lankton Cl BECK BR3 183 F4
Lannock Rd HYS/HAR UB3 113 J1
Lannoy Rd ELTH/MOT SE9 167 H3
Lanrick Rd POP/IOD E14 106 B5
Lanridge Rd ABYW SE2 128 E3
Lansbury Av BARK IG11 91 G5
CHDH RM6 74 A2
EBED/NFELT TW14 154 A1
UED N18 49 K1
Lansbury Cl WLSDN NW10 80 E3
Lansbury Crs DART DA1 151 K6
Lansbury Dr YEAD UB4 94 D2
Lansbury Gdns POP/IOD E14 * 106 B5
Lansbury Rd PEND EN3 25 F2
Lansbury Wy UED N18 50 A1
Lanscombe Wk VX/NE SW8 * 141 K1
Lansdell Rd MTCM CR4 179 F5
Lansdown Cl WOT/HER KT12 188 B5
Lansdowne Av BXLYHN DA7 148 D1
ORP BR6 201 G5
Lansdowne Cl BRYLDS KT5 191 J6
TWK TW1 156 A3
Lansdowne Copse WPK KT4 * 192 D6
Lansdowne Ct WPK KT4 192 D6
Lansdowne Crs NTGHL W11 100 C6
Lansdowne Dr HACK E8 86 D6
Lansdowne Gdns VX/NE SW8 141 K2
Lansdowne Gn VX/NE SW8 141 K1
Lansdowne Gv WLSDN NW10 81 G2
Lansdowne Hl WNWD SE27 162 C5
Lansdowne La CHARL SE7 126 C5
Lansdowne Ms CHARL SE7 126 C5
NTGHL W11 119 J1
Lansdowne Pl NRWD SE19 181 G3
STHWK SE1 19 F4
Lansdowne Ri NTGHL W11 100 C6
Lansdowne Rd BMLY BR1 183 K3
CHING E4 37 J4
CROY/NA CR0 196 E6
FNCH N3 46 D3
GDMY/SEVK IG3 73 F5
HACK E8 86 C4
HOR/WEW KT19 206 E5
HSLW TW3 135 G4
MUSWH N10 48 B4
NTGHL W11 100 C6
RYNPK SW20 177 F3
STAN HA7 43 J2
SWFD E18 52 E6
TOTM N17 50 C4
WALTH E17 69 J3
WAN E11 70 D6
Lansdowne Ter BMSBY WC1N 5 F7
Lansdowne Wk NTGHL W11 119 H1
Lansdowne Wy VX/NE SW8 141 K2
Lansdowne Wood Cl
WNWD SE27 162 C5
Lansdown Rd FSTGT E7 89 G5
SCUP DA14 168 C5
Lansfield Av UED N18 36 C6
Lantern Cl ALP/SUD HA0 79 K3
ORP BR6 216 B2
PUT/ROE SW15 138 D5
Lanterns Ct POP/IOD E14 124 E3
Lantern Wy WDR/YW UB7 112 B2
Lant St STHWK SE1 18 C2
Lanvanor Rd PECK SE15 143 K3
Lapford Cl MV/WKIL W9 * 100 D3
Lapse Wood Wk FSTH SE23 163 J3
Lapstone Gdns
KTN/HRWW/WS HA3 61 J3
Lapwing Cl ERITH DA8 * 150 E1
Lapwing Ter FSTGT E7 89 H3
Lapwing Wy YEAD UB4 95 H5
Lapworth Cl ORP BR6 202 D6
Lapworth Ct BAY/PAD W2 101 F4
Lara Cl CHSGTN KT9 206 A5
LEW SE13 165 F1
Larbert Rd STRHM/NOR SW16 179 H4
Larch Av ACT W3 118 B1
Larch Cl BAL SW12 161 G4
DEPT SE8 124 C6
FBAR/BDGN N11 48 A3
Larch Crs HOR/WEW KT19 206 D4
YEAD UB4 95 G4
Larch Dene ORP BR6 201 F6
Larch Dr CHSWK W4 * 117 H5
Larches Av MORT/ESHN SW14 138 A5
The Larches PLMGR N13 35 J5
Larch Gv BFN/LL DA15 168 A3
Larch Rd CRICK NW2 82 A2
DART DA1 171 G3
LEY E10 69 J6
Larch Tree Wy CROY/NA CR0 213 J1
Larch Wy HAYES BR2 201 F4
Larchwood Av CRW RM5 56 D2
Larchwood Cl CRW RM5 56 E2
Larchwood Rd ELTH/MOT SE9 167 G4
Larcombe Cl CROY/NA CR0 212 B2
Larcom St WALW SE17 18 D7
Larden Rd ACT W3 118 B2
Largewood Av SURB KT6 191 H6
Larissa St WALW SE17 * 19 F7
Larkbere Rd SYD SE26 164 B6
Larken Cl BUSH WD23 28 C3
Larken Dr BUSH WD23 28 C3
Larkfield Av
KTN/HRWW/WS HA3 43 H6
Larkfield Rd RCH/KEW TW9 137 F5
SCUP DA14 168 A5
Larkhall La CLAP SW4 141 J3
Larkhall Ri CLAP SW4 141 H4
Larkham Cl FELT TW13 153 H5
Larkhill Ter
WOOL/PLUM SE18 * 147 F1
Lark Rw BETH E2 86 E6
Larksfield Gv EN EN1 24 D2
Larkshall Crs CHING E4 38 A6
Larkshall Rd CHING E4 52 B2
Larkspur Cl CDALE/KGS NW9 62 B3
ORP BR6 202 D6
TOTM N17 49 K3
Larkspur Gv EDGW HA8 30 E6
Larkspur Wy HOR/WEW KT19 206 E3
Larkswood Cl ERITH DA8 150 D2
Larkswood Ri PIN HA5 59 G1
Larkswood Rd CHING E4 37 J6
Lark Wy CAR SM5 194 D4
Larkway Cl CDALE/KGS NW9 63 F2
Larnach Rd HMSMTH W6 119 G6
Larne Rd RSLP HA4 58 D4
Larner Rd ERITH DA8 150 B1
Larpent Av PUT/ROE SW15 139 F6
Larwood Cl GFD/PVL UB6 78 D3
Lascelles Av HRW HA1 60 D4
Lascelles Cl WAN E11 70 B6
Lascott's Rd WDGN N22 49 F2
Lassa Rd ELTH/MOT SE9 146 D6
Lassell St GNWCH SE10 125 G5
Lasseter Pl BKHTH/KID SE3 125 H6
Latchett Rd SWFD E18 53 F4
Latchingdon Gdns WFD IG8 53 J2
Latchmere Cl
RCHPK/HAM TW10 175 F1
Latchmere La KUTN/CMB KT2 175 G2
Latchmere Rd BTSEA SW11 140 E3
KUTN/CMB KT2 175 F2
Latchmere St BTSEA SW11 140 E3
Lateward Rd BTFD TW8 116 E6
Latham Cl EHAM E6 107 J5
Latham Rd BXLYHS DA6 149 H6
TWK TW1 156 A2
Latham's Wy CROY/NA CR0 196 A6
Lathkill Cl EN EN1 36 C2
Lathom Rd EHAM E6 89 K5
Latimer Av EHAM E6 89 K6
Latimer Cl PIN HA5 41 G4
WATW WD18 26 C2
WPK KT4 207 K2
Latimer Gdns PIN HA5 41 G4
Latimer Pl NKENS W10 100 A5
Latimer Rd BAR EN5 21 F4
CROY/NA CR0 * 211 H1
FSTGT E7 89 F2
NKENS W10 100 A4
SEVS/STOTM N15 68 A3
TEDD TW11 174 A1
WIM/MER SW19 178 A2
Latona Rd PECK SE15 123 H6
La Tourne Gdns ORP BR6 216 C1
Lattimer Pl CHSWK W4 138 B1
Latton Cl ESH/CLAY KT10 204 B2
WOT/HER KT12 188 E4
Latymer Gdns FNCH N3 * 46 C5
Latymer Rd ED N9 36 B4
Latymer Wy ED N9 35 K4
Laubin Cl TWK TW1 136 C5
Lauder Cl NTHLT UB5 95 H1
Lauderdale Dr
RCHPK/HAM TW10 156 E5
Lauderdale Pde
MV/WKIL W9 * 101 F2
Lauderdale Pl BARB EC2Y * 12 D2
Lauderdale Rd MV/WKIL W9 101 F2
Laud St CROY/NA CR0 211 J1
LBTH SE11 122 A5
Laughton Rd NTHLT UB5 95 H1
Launcelot Rd BMLY BR1 165 K6
Launcelot St STHWK SE1 17 J3
Launceston Gdns GFD/PVL UB6 79 J6
Launceston Pl KENS W8 120 B3
Launceston Rd GFD/PVL UB6 79 J6
Launch St POP/IOD E14 125 F3
Launders Ga ACT W3 * 117 J2
Laundress La STNW/STAM N16 86 C1
Laundry Rd HMSMTH W6 119 H6
Laura Cl EN EN1 24 A6
WAN E11 71 G2
Lauradale Rd EFNCH N2 65 K1
Laura Pl CLPT E5 86 E2
Laura Ter FSBYPK N4 * 67 H6
Laurel Av TWK TW1 156 A3
Laurel Bank
NFNCH/WDSPK N12 * 33 G6
Laurel Bank Gdns
FUL/PGN SW6 139 J3
Laurel Bank Rd ENC/FH EN2 23 J2
Laurel Cl BARK/HLT IG6 54 C2
BFN/LL DA15 168 B5
DART DA1 171 F3
OXHEY WD19 27 H2
TOOT SW17 178 D1
Laurel Crs CROY/NA CR0 213 J1
ROMW/RG RM7 75 G5
Laurel Dr WCHMH N21 35 G2
Laurel Gdns CHING E4 37 K2
HNWL W7 115 K1
HSLWW TW4 134 D5
MLHL NW7 31 F5
Laurel Gv PGE/AN SE20 181 K3
SYD SE26 182 A1
Laurel La WDR/YW UB7 112 B4
Laurel Pk KTN/HRWW/WS HA3 43 F3
Laurel Rd BARN SW13 138 D3
HPTN TW12 173 J1
RYNPK SW20 176 E4
The Laurels BRXN/ST SW9 * 142 C1
BUSH WD23 * 28 E4
RDART DA2 * 171 F5
Laurel St HACK E8 86 B4
Laurel Vw NFNCH/WDSPK N12 33 F5
Laurel Vls HNWL W7 * 115 K2
Laurel Wy SWFD E18 70 D1
TRDG/WHET N20 32 E5
Laurence Ms SHB W12 118 D2
Laurence Pountney Hl
CANST EC4R 12 E5
Laurence Pountney La
CANST EC4R 12 E5
MANHO EC4N 13 F5
Laurie Gv NWCR SE14 144 B2
Laurie Rd HNWL W7 96 E4
Laurier Rd CROY/NA CR0 197 G4
KTTN NW5 84 B1
Laurimel Cl STAN HA7 43 H2
Laurino Pl BUSH WD23 28 C4
Lauriston Rd HOM E9 87 F6
WIM/MER SW19 177 G2
Lausanne Rd CEND/HSY/T N8 67 G1
PECK SE15 143 K3
Lavender Av CDALE/KGS NW9 62 E5
MTCM CR4 178 D4
WPK KT4 208 A1
Lavender Cl CAR SM5 210 A2
CHEL SW3 120 C6
HAYES BR2 200 D3
Lavender Ct E/WMO/HCT KT8 173 G6
Lavender Gdns BTSEA SW11 140 E4
ENC/FH EN2 23 H1
KTN/HRWW/WS HA3 42 E2
Lavender Gv HACK E8 86 C5
MTCM CR4 178 D4
Lavender Hl BTSEA SW11 140 E4
ENC/FH EN2 23 H2
Lavender Pl IL IG1 90 B3
Lavender Ri WDR/YW UB7 112 D2
Lavender Rd
BERM/RHTH SE16 124 B1
BTSEA SW11 140 C4
CROY/NA CR0 196 A3
ENC/FH EN2 23 K2
HOR/WEW KT19 206 D4
SUT SM1 209 H2
WLGTN SM6 210 A3
Lavender St SRTFD E15 88 C4
Lavender Sweep BTSEA SW11 140 E5
Lavender Ter BTSEA SW11 * 140 D4
Lavender V WLGTN SM6 210 D4
Lavender Wk BTSEA SW11 140 E5
Lavender Wy CROY/NA CR0 198 A3
Lavengro Rd WNWD SE27 162 D4
Lavenham Rd
WAND/EARL SW18 159 J4
Lavernock Rd BXLYHN DA7 149 H3
Lavers Rd STNW/STAM N16 86 A1
Laverstoke Gdns
PUT/ROE SW15 158 C2
Laverton Ms ECT SW5 120 A4
Laverton Pl ECT SW5 120 A4
Lavidge Rd ELTH/MOT SE9 166 D4
Lavina Gv IS N1 5 G2
Lavington Cl HOM E9 87 H4
Lavington Rd CROY/NA CR0 211 F1
WEA W13 116 C1
Lavington St STHWK SE1 18 B1
Lavinia Rd DART DA1 171 J1
Lawdon Gdns CROY/NA CR0 211 H2
Lawford Gdns DART DA1 151 F6
Lawford Rd CHSWK W4 137 K1
IS N1 86 A5
KTTN NW5 84 C4
Lawless St POP/IOD E14 * 105 K6
Lawley Rd STHGT/OAK N14 34 B2
Lawley St CLPT E5 86 E2
Lawn Cl BMLY BR1 184 A3
EN EN1 36 B2
NWMAL KT3 176 B5
RSLP HA4 76 D1
SWLY BR8 187 K5
Lawn Crs RCH/KEW TW9 137 H3
Lawn Farm Gv CHDH RM6 74 A1
Lawn Gdns HNWL W7 115 K1
Lawn House Cl POP/IOD E14 125 F2
Lawn La VX/NE SW8 121 K6
Lawn Rd BECK BR3 182 D3
HAMP NW3 83 K3
Lawns Ct WBLY HA9 * 62 C6
The Lawns BELMT SM2 208 C5
BKHTH/KID SE3 * 145 J4
CHING E4 51 J1
NRWD SE19 180 E4
PIN HA5 42 B3
SCUP DA14 168 C6
Lawns Wy CRW RM5 56 E3
Lawnswood BAR EN5 * 20 C6
Lawn Ter BKHTH/KID SE3 145 J4
The Lawn NWDGN UB2 115 F5
Lawn V PIN HA5 41 J5
Lawrence Av MLHL NW7 31 G6
MNPK E12 90 A2
NWMAL KT3 192 B4
PLMGR N13 35 H6
WALTH E17 51 G4
WLSDN NW10 81 F6
Lawrence Buildings
STNW/STAM N16 86 B1
Lawrence Campe Cl
TRDG/WHET N20 33 H5
Lawrence Cl SEVS/STOTM N15 68 A1
SHB W12 99 K6
Lawrence Ct MLHL NW7 45 G1
OXHEY WD19 * 27 H5
Lawrence Crs DAGE RM10 92 D1
EDGW HA8 44 C5
Lawrence Dr HGDN/ICK UB10 76 A2
Lawrence Gdns MLHL NW7 31 H5
Lawrence Hl CHING E4 37 J4
Lawrence Hill Gdns DART DA1 171 F1
Lawrence Hill Rd DART DA1 171 F1
Lawrence La CITYW EC2V 12 D4
Lawrence Pde ISLW TW7 * 136 C4
Lawrence Pl IS N1 * 84 E6
Lawrence Rd EA W5 116 D4
EHAM E6 89 J6
ERITH DA8 149 J1
GPK RM2 75 K2
HPTN TW12 172 E3
HSLWW TW4 134 B5
PIN HA5 59 H2
PLSTW E13 89 F6
RCHPK/HAM TW10 156 D6
SEVS/STOTM N15 68 A1
SNWD SE25 197 G1
UED N18 36 D6
WWKM BR4 214 E2
YEAD UB4 94 A1
Lawrence St CAN/RD E16 106 D4
CHEL SW3 120 D6
MLHL NW7 31 H6
Lawrence Wy WLSDN NW10 80 E1
Lawrence Yd
SEVS/STOTM N15 68 A1
Lawrie Park Av SYD SE26 181 J1
Lawrie Park Crs SYD SE26 181 K1
Lawrie Park Gdns SYD SE26 181 J1
Lawrie Park Rd SYD SE26 181 K2
Laws Cl SNWD SE25 196 E1
Lawson Cl CAN/RD E16 107 G5
IL IG1 90 D3
WIM/MER SW19 159 G5
Lawson Gdns DART DA1 151 G6
PIN HA5 41 F6
Lawson Rd DART DA1 151 G5
PEND EN3 24 E2
STHL UB1 95 K3
Law St STHWK SE1 19 F4
Lawton Rd BOW E3 105 G2
EBAR EN4 21 H4
LEY E10 70 A5
Laxcon Cl WLSDN NW10 81 F3
Laxey Rd ORP BR6 217 F4
Laxley Cl CMBW SE5 142 C1
Laxton Pl CAMTN NW1 3 K6
Layard Rd BERM/RHTH SE16 123 J4
EN EN1 24 B2
THHTH CR7 180 E5
Layard Sq BERM/RHTH SE16 123 J4
Laycock St IS N1 85 G4
Layer Gdns ACT W3 98 C6
Layfield Cl HDN NW4 63 K4
Layfield Crs HDN NW4 63 K4
Layfield Rd HDN NW4 63 K4
Layhams Rd WWKM BR4 214 C2
Laymarsh Cl BELV DA17 129 G3
Laymead Cl NTHLT UB5 77 J4
Laystall St FSBYW WC1X 5 J7
Layton Crs CROY/NA CR0 211 G3
Layton Pl RCH/KEW TW9 137 H2
Layton Rd BTFD TW8 116 E5
HSLW TW3 135 G5
Layzell Wk ELTH/MOT SE9 166 C3
Lazenby Ct COVGDN WC2E * 10 E5
Leabank Cl HRW HA1 78 E1
Leabank Sq HOM E9 87 J4
Leabank Vw SEVS/STOTM N15 68 C3
Leabourne Rd STNW/STAM N16 68 C3
Lea Bridge Rd LEY E10 69 F6
WALTH E17 70 A2
Lea Cl WHTN TW2 154 E2
Lea Cottages MTCM CR4 * 179 F5
Lea Crs RSLP HA4 76 D2
Leacroft Av BAL SW12 160 E2
Leacroft Cl WCHMH N21 35 H4
Leadale Av CHING E4 37 J4
Leadale Rd STNW/STAM N16 68 C3
Leadbeaters Cl
FBAR/BDGN N11 47 K1
Leadenhall Pl BANK EC3V 13 G4
Leadenhall St BANK EC3V 13 G4
Leader Av MNPK E12 90 A3
The Leadings WBLY HA9 80 E1
Leaf Cl NTHWD HA6 40 B3
THDIT KT7 189 K2
Leaf Gv WNWD SE27 180 B1
Leafield Cl STRHM/NOR SW16 180 C2
Leafield La SCUP DA14 169 G6
Leafield Rd RYNPK SW20 177 J6
SUT SM1 193 K6
Leafy Gv HAYES BR2 215 G3
Leafy Oak Rd LEE/GVPK SE12 166 B6
Leafy Wy CROY/NA CR0 197 G6
Lea Gdns WBLY HA9 80 B3
Leagrave St CLPT E5 86 E1
Lea Hall Gdns LEY E10 * 69 J5
Lea Hall Rd LEY E10 69 J5
Leahurst Rd LEW SE13 * 165 H1
Leake St STHWK SE1 17 H2
Lealand Rd SEVS/STOTM N15 68 B3
Leaming Cl MNPK E12 89 J3
Leamington Av BMLY BR1 184 B1
MRDN SM4 193 J1
ORP BR6 216 E2
WALTH E17 69 J2
Leamington Cl BMLY BR1 166 B6
HSLW TW3 135 H6
Leamington Crs
RYLN/HDSTN HA2 77 J1
Leamington Gdns
GDMY/SEVK IG3 73 F6
Leamington Pk ACT W3 99 F4
Leamington Pl YEAD UB4 94 D3
Leamington Rd NWDGN UB2 114 C4
Leamington Road Vls
NTGHL W11 100 D4
Leamore St HMSMTH W6 118 E4
Leamouth Rd EHAM E6 107 J5
POP/IOD E14 106 B5
Leander Rd BRXS/STRHM SW2 162 A1
NTHLT UB5 96 A1
THHTH CR7 196 A1
Learner Dr RYLN/HDSTN HA2 60 A6
Lea Rd BECK BR3 182 D5
ENC/FH EN2 23 K2
NWDGN UB2 114 D4
Learoyd Gdns EHAM E6 108 A6
Leas Cl CHSGTN KT9 206 B5
Leas Dl ELTH/MOT SE9 167 F5
Leas Gn CHST BR7 186 A2
Leaside Av MUSWH N10 48 A6
Leaside Rd CLPT E5 68 E5
Leasowes Rd LEY E10 69 J5
Leathart Cl HCH RM12 93 K5
Leatherbottle Gn
ERITHM DA18 129 G3
Leather Cl MTCM CR4 179 F5
Leatherdale St WCHPL E1 * 105 F2
Leather Gdns SRTFD E15 88 C6
Leatherhead Cl
STNW/STAM N16 68 A5
Leatherhead Rd CHSGTN KT9 205 K5
Leather La CLKNW EC1R 5 J7
HCIRC EC1N 11 J1
Leathermarket Ct STHWK SE1 19 G3
Leathermarket St STHWK SE1 19 G3
Leather Rd BERM/RHTH SE16 124 A4
Leathersellers Cl BAR EN5 * 20 C4

Leather St WAP E1W 105 F6
Leathsale Rd RYLN/HDSTN HA2...78 D4
Leathwaite Rd BTSEA SW11...140 E5
Leathwell Rd DEPT SE8............118 A5
Lea V DART DA1..................................150 A5
Lea Valley CI CHING E4..................37 J2
Lea Valley Wk CLPT E5...................68 D4
TOTM N17...50 D5
Leaveland CI BECK BR3.................198 D1
Leaver Gdns GFD/PVL UB6..........96 D1
Leavesden Rd STAN HA7................43 F2
Leaway CLPT E5 *...............................68 E5
Lebanon Av WELL DA16................148 C5
Lebanon Gdns
   WAND/EARL SW18...................159 K1
Lebanon Pk TWK TW1...................156 C3
Lebanon Rd CROY/NA CRO...........197 J5
   WAND/EARL SW18...................139 K6
Lebrun Sq BKHTH/KID SE3......146 A5
Lechmere Ap WFD IG8.....................52 C5
Lechmere Rd CRICK NW2...............81 K4
Leckford Rd
   WAND/EARL SW18...................160 B4
Leckhampton PI
   BRXS/STRHM SW2.................162 B2
Leckwith Av ABYW SE2..................129 F6
Lecky St SKENS SW7......................120 C5
Leconfield Av BARN SW13............138 C4
Leconfield Rd HBRY N5....................85 K3
Leda Av PEND EN3.............................25 F2
Leda Rd WOOL/PLUM SE18.........126 E3
Ledbury Ms North
   NTGHL W11 *.................................100 E6
Ledbury Ms West NTGHL W11....100 E6
Ledbury Rd CROY/NA CRO...........211 K2
   NTGHL W11....................................100 D5
Ledbury St PECK SE15...................143 H1
Ledrington Rd NRWD SE19...........181 G2
Ledway Dr WBLY HA9.......................62 B6
Lee Av CHDH RM6..............................74 A3
Leechcroft Av BFN/LL DA15.......148 A6
Leechcroft Rd WLGTN SM6.........210 A1
Lee Church St LEW SE13..............145 H5
Lee CI WALTH E17...............................51 F4
Lee Conservancy Rd HOM E9......87 H3
Leecroft Rd BAR EN5........................20 C6
Leeds CI ORP BR6............................202 E6
Leeds Rd IL IG1....................................72 D5
Leeds St UED N18...............................50 C1
Lee Gn STMC/STPC BR5...............202 B3
Lee High Rd LEW SE13..................145 H5
Leeke St FSBYW WC1X.......................5 G4
Leeland Rd WEA W13......................116 B1
Leeland Ter WEA W13....................116 B1
Leeland Wy WLSDN NW10...............81 G2
Leemount CI HDN NW4 *................46 B2
Lee Pk BKHTH/KID SE3................145 J5
Lee Park Wy ED N9............................37 G5
   UED N18...37 H1
Lee Rd BKHTH/KID SE3................145 J4
   EN EN1...36 C1
   GFD/PVL UB6..................................79 J6
   MLHL NW7 *....................................46 B3
   WIM/MER SW19.............................178 A4
Lees Av NTHWD HA6.........................40 D4
Leeside BAR EN5................................32 C1
Leeside Crs GLDGN NW11...............64 C3
Leeside Rd TOTM N17.......................50 E3
Leeson Rd HNHL SE24 *................142 B6
Leesons HI CHST BR7....................185 K6
Leesons Wy STMC/STPC BR5....186 A5
The Lees CROY/NA CRO................198 C6
Lee St HACK E8...................................86 C6
Lee Ter BKHTH/KID SE3..............145 H4
The Lee NTHWD HA6.........................40 D4
Lee Vw ENC/FH EN2..........................23 H2

Leeward Gdns
   WIM/MER SW19..........................177 J2
Leeway DEPT SE8............................124 C5
The Leeways CHEAM SM3 *.........208 C4
Leewood CI LEE/GVPK SE12......165 J1
Lefevre Wk BOW E3 *.....................105 J6
Leffern Rd SHB W12........................118 D2
Lefroy Rd SHB W12.........................118 C2
Left Side STHGT/OAK N14 *..........34 D3
Legard Rd ELTH/MOT SE9.............46 B1
Legatt Rd ELTH/MOT SE9............166 C1
Legge St LEW SE13..........................145 F6
Leghorn Rd WLSDN NW10...............99 J1
   WOOL/PLUM SE18......................127 J5
Legion CI IS N1....................................85 G4
Legion Rd GFD/PVL UB6...............193 K3
Legion Ter BOW E3 *.........................87 H6
Legon Av ROMW/RG RM7................74 E3
Legrace Av HSLWW TW4...............134 C3
Leicester Av MTCM CR4................195 K1
Leicester CI WPK KT4.....................208 A2
Leicester Gdns GDMY/SEVK IG3...72 E4
Leicester Rd BAR EN5.....................20 E5
   CROY/NA CRO...............................197 F4
   EFNCH N2...47 J6
   WAN E11..71 F5
   WLSDN NW10.................................81 F5
Leicester Sq LSQ/SEVD WC2H *...10 D6
Leicester St LSQ/SEVD WC2H....10 D5
Leigham Av
   STRHM/NOR SW16.....................161 K5
Leigham CI
   STRHM/NOR SW16.....................161 K5
Leigham Court Rd
   STRHM/NOR SW16.....................162 A5
Leigham Dr ISLW TW7....................135 K2
Leigham Hall Pde
   STRHM/NOR SW16 *...................161 K5
Leigham V STRHM/NOR SW16....162 B5
Leigh Av REDBR IG4...........................71 H1
Leigh CI NWMAL KT3......................192 A1
Leigh Ct BAR EN5 *............................21 H4
Leigh Crs CROY/NA CRO...............213 K5
Leigh Gdns WLSDN NW10.............100 A1
Leigh Orchard CI
   STRHM/NOR SW16.....................162 A5

Leigh PI FELT TW15.........................154 B3
   WELL DA16......................................148 B3
Leigh Rd EHAM E6..............................90 A1
   HBRY N5..85 H2
   HSLW TW3......................................135 J5
Leigh Rodd OXHEY WD19.................27 J5
Leigh Sq STPAN WC1H......................4 E4
Leigh Ter STMC/STPC BR5 *........186 C6
Leighton Av MNPK E12....................90 A3
   PIN HA5..41 J6
Leighton CI EDGW HA8....................44 C5
Leighton Crs KTTN NW5...................84 C4
Leighton Gdns WLSDN NW10........100 A1
Leighton Gv KTTN NW5....................84 C4
Leighton PI KTTN NW5.....................84 C4
Leighton Rd EN EN1..........................36 C1
   KTN/HRWW/WS HA3...................42 D5
   KTTN NW5..84 C4
   WEA W13...116 B2
Leighton St CROY/NA CRO...........196 C5
Leila Pannell PI CHARL SE7........126 B6
Leinster Gdns BAY/PAD W2..........101 G5
Leinster Ms BAY/PAD W2 *...........137 K4
Leinster PI BAY/PAD W2................101 G5
Leinster Rd MUSWH N10..................66 B1
Leinster Sq BAY/PAD W2...............100 E5
Leinster Ter BAY/PAD W2..............101 G6
Leisure Wy NFNCH/WDSPK N12...47 H3
Leith CI CDALE/KGS NW9.................63 F2
Leithcote Gdns
   STRHM/NOR SW16.....................162 A6
Leithcote Pth
   STRHM/NOR SW16.....................162 A5
Leith HI STMC/STPC BR5.............186 B4
Leith Rd WDGN N22...........................49 H4
Leith Towers BELMT SM2 *.........209 F5
Leith Yd KIL/WHAMP NW6 *...........82 E6
Lela Av HSLWW TW4......................134 B3
Lelitia CI HACK E8..............................86 C6
Leman St WCHPL E1..........................13 K4
Lemark CI STAN HA7..........................43 J2
Le May Av LEE/GVPK SE12..........166 A5
Lemmon Rd GNWCH SE10.............125 H6
Lemna Rd WAN E11............................70 C4
Lemonwell Dr ELTH/MOT SE9....147 G6
Lemsford Ct SEVS/STOTM N15 *..68 B2
Lena Gdns HMSMTH W6................119 F3
Lena Kennedy CI CHING E4............52 A1
Lendal Ter CLAP SW4.....................141 J4
Lenelby Rd SURB KT6.....................191 H5
Lenham CI BXLYHS DA6 *.............149 F3
   SUT SM1...209 F2
   THHTH CR7 *....................................180 E5
Lennard Av WWKM BR4................199 H6
Lennard CI WWKM BR4................199 H6
Lennard Rd CROY/NA CRO...........196 C5
   HAYES BR2.....................................200 E5
   PGE/AN SE20..................................182 A2
   SYD SE26...182 A2
Lennon Rd CRICK NW2.....................82 A3
Lennox CI ROM RM1..........................75 H3
Lennox Gdns CROY/NA CRO.........211 H2
   IL IG1...71 K5
   KTBR SW1X..14 E6
   WLSDN NW10..................................81 H2
Lennox Gardens Ms CHEL SW3....14 E6
Lennox Rd FSBYPK N4.....................67 F6
   WALTH E17.......................................69 H3
Lenor CI BXLYHS DA6....................149 F5
Lensbury Wy ABYW SE2...............128 D3
Lens Rd FSTGT E7..............................89 G5
Lenthall Av GDST SE22 *.................86 B5
Lenthall Rd HACK E8..........................86 C6
Lenthorp Rd GNWCH SE10 *.......125 J4
Lentmead Rd BMLY BR1...............165 J6
Lenton Ri RCH/KEW TW9..............137 F4
Lenton St WOOL/PLUM SE18......127 J4
Lentons La CAT SE6.........................165 F6
Leof Crs CAT SE6..............................183 J2
Leominster Rd MRDN SM4............194 B3
Leominster Wk MRDN SM4...........194 B3
Leonard Av MRDN SM4..................194 B2
   ROMW/RG RM7..............................75 F5
Leonard Ct KENS W8..........................119 J3
Leonard PI HAYES BR2 *...............215 J1
   STNW/STAM N16............................86 A3
Leonard Rd CHING E4........................51 J2
   ED N9..36 B5
   FSTGT E7...88 E2
   NWDGN UB2..................................114 C4
   STRHM/NOR SW16.....................179 J2
Leonard St CAN/RD E16..................126 D1
   SDTCH EC2A.......................................7 F5
Leontine CI PECK SE15..................143 H1
Leopold Av WIM/MER SW19........177 J1
Leopold Ms HOM E9...........................86 E6
Leopold Rd EA W5............................117 G1
   EFNCH N2..47 J6
   UED N18..50 C3
   WALTH E17..69 J2
   WIM/MER SW19...............................159 J5
   WLSDN NW10.....................................81 G5
Leopold St BOW E3..........................105 H4
Leo St PECK SE15............................143 K1
Leppoc Rd CLAP SW4....................141 J6
Lerry CI WKENS W14.......................119 J6
Lerwick Ct EN EN1..............................24 A6
Lescombe CI CAT SE6.....................164 B5
Lescombe Rd FSTH SE23...............164 B5
Lesley CI BXLY DA5.........................169 J2
Leslie Gdns BELMT SM2................208 E5
Leslie Grove PI CROY/NA CRO....197 F5
Leslie Park Rd CROY/NA CRO......196 E5
Leslie Rd CAN/RD E16....................107 F5
   EFNCH N2...47 H4
   WAN E11..88 B2
Lesney Pk ERITH DA8.....................149 K1
Lesney Park Rd ERITH DA8..........149 K1
Lessar Av CLAP SW4......................141 H6
Lessingham Av TOOT SW17.........160 E6
Lessing St FSTH SE23....................164 B2

Lessington Av ROMW/RG RM7.....74 E3
Lessness Av BXLYHN DA7............148 E1
Lessness Pk BELV DA17................129 G5
Lessness Rd MRDN SM4...............194 B3
Lester Av CAN/RD E16...................106 C5
Lestock CI SNWD SE25...................181 H6
Leston CI RAIN RM13......................111 K2
Leswin PI STNW/STAM N16...........86 B1
Leswin Rd STNW/STAM N16..........86 B1
Letchford Gdns WLSDN NW10........99 J2
Letchford Ms WLSDN NW10 *........99 J2
Letchford Ter
   KTN/HRWW/WS HA3 *..................42 B4
Letchworth Av
   EBED/NFELT TW14......................153 J2
Letchworth CI HAYES BR2............199 K2
   OXHEY WD19......................................27 H1
Letchworth Dr HAYES BR2...........199 K2
Letchworth St TOOT SW17...........160 E6
Letterstone Rd FUL/PGN SW6....139 J1
Lettice St FUL/PGN SW6...............139 J2
Lett Rd SRTFD E15.............................88 B5
Leucha Rd WALTH E17.......................69 G2
Levana CI WIM/MER SW19...........159 H3
Levehurst Wy CLAP SW4..............141 K3
Leven CI OXHEY WD19 *..................41 H1
Levendale Rd FSTH SE23..............164 B4
Leven Rd POP/IOD E14....................106 A4
Leven Wy HYS/HAR UB3..................94 C5
Leveret CI CROY/NA CRO..............214 A6
Leverett St CHEL SW3......................14 D6
Leverholme Gdns
   ELTH/MOT SE9.............................167 F6
Leveson St
   STRHM/NOR SW16.....................179 H2
Leverson St STRHM/NOR SW16..179 H2
Lever St FSBYE EC1V........................6 C5
Leverton PI KTTN NW5......................84 C3
Leverton St KTTN NW5......................84 C3
Levett Gdns GDMY/SEVK IG3........91 F3
Levett Rd BARK IG11..........................90 E5
Levine Gdns BARK IG11..................109 K1
Levison Wy ARCH N19........................66 D6
Lewes CI NTHLT UB5.........................78 A4
Lewesdon CI WIM/MER SW19.....159 G3
Lewes Rd BMLY BR1........................184 C5
   NFNCH/WDSPK N12.......................47 J1
Lewey Ho BOW E3 *.........................105 H3
Lewgars Av CDALE/KGS NW9........62 E3
Lewing CI ORP BR6..........................201 K5
Lewin Rd BXLYHS DA6...................149 F5
   MORT/ESHN SW14......................138 A4
   STRHM/NOR SW16.....................179 J2
Lewis Av WALTH E17..........................51 J4
Lewis CI STHGT/OAK N14................34 C2
Lewis Crs WLSDN NW10...................81 F3
Lewis Gdns EFNCH N2.......................47 H5
Lewis Gv LEW SE13.........................145 F4
Lewisham High St LEW SE13.......144 E4
Lewisham Hl LEW SE13..................145 F3
Lewisham Pk LEW SE13.................145 F5
Lewisham Rd LEW SE13.................144 E2
Lewisham Wy BROCKY SE4............144 C3
Lewis Rd BXLYHN DA7...................149 H2
   MTCM CR4......................................178 D5
   RCH/KEW TW9 *...........................136 E6
   SCUP DA14......................................168 D5
   STHL UB1...114 D2
   SUT SM1...209 F2
   WELL DA16......................................148 D4
Lewis St CAMTN NW1........................84 B5
Lewiston CI WPK KT4......................192 E4
Lewis Wy DAGE RM10........................92 D4
Lexden Dr CHDH RM6........................73 H5
Lexden Rd ACT W3............................117 J1
   MTCM CR4......................................195 J1
Lexham Gdns ECT SW5..................120 A4
   KENS W8..119 K4
Lexham Ms KENS W8......................119 K4
Lexington St SOHO/CST W1F.......10 B4
Lexington Wy BAR EN5.....................20 B5
Lexton Gdns BAL SW12..................161 J3
Leybourne Av WEA W13..................116 B1
Leybourne CI HAYES BR2..............199 K3
   NWCR SE14......................................144 A2
Leybourne Pk RCH/KEW TW9.......137 H2
Leybourne Rd CAMTN NW1 *..........84 B6
   CDALE/KGS NW9............................62 C2
   HGDN/ICK UB10................................94 A6
   WAN E11..70 D5
Leybourne St CAMTN NW1...............84 B6
Leyburn CI WALTH E17....................70 A1
Leyburn Gdns CROY/NA CRO.......197 F6
Leyburn Gv UED N18.........................50 C2
Leyburn House CHARL SE7 *........146 D1
Leyburn Rd UED N18.........................50 C2
Leycroft Gdns ERITH DA8.............150 E2
Leyden St WCHPL E1.........................13 J2
Leydon CI BERM/RHTH SE16........124 A1
Leyes Rd CAN/RD E16....................107 G5
Leyfield WPK KT4...............................192 B6
Leyland Av PEND EN3........................25 G3
Leyland Gdns WFD IG8......................53 G1
Leyland Rd LEE/GVPK SE12.........144 K4
Leys Av DAGE RM10..........................92 E6
Leys CI DAGE RM10...........................92 E5
   HRW HA1..60 D2
Leysdown Av BXLYHN DA7...........149 K5
Leysdown Rd ELTH/MOT SE9.......166 D4
Leysfield Rd SHB W12....................118 D2
Leys Gdns EBAR EN4.........................22 A6
Leyspring Rd WAN E11......................70 D5
Leys Rd East PEND EN3....................25 G2
The Leys EFNCH N2............................65 G1
   KTN/HRWW/WS HA3.....................61 J3
Leyswood Dr GNTH/NBYPK IG2...72 E2
Leythe Rd ACT W3............................117 J2
Leyton Cross Rd RDART DA2.......170 C6
Leyton Gra LEY E10............................69 K5
Leyton Green Rd LEY E10.................70 A3
Leyton Park Rd LEY E10....................88 A1
Leyton Rd SRTFD E15........................88 B3
   WIM/MER SW19..............................178 A3
Leytonstone Rd SRTFD E15............88 C3
Leywick St SRTFD E15....................106 C1
Lezayre Rd ORP BR6.......................217 F4
Liardet St NWCR SE14....................124 B6
Liberia Rd HBRY N5............................85 H4

Liberty Av WIM/MER SW19...........178 C4
Liberty CI UED N18..............................36 B6
Liberty Ms WDGN N22 *.....................49 H4
Liberty St BRXN/ST SW9...............142 A2
Libra Rd BOW E3.................................105 H1
   PLSTW E13...106 E1
Library Ct SEVS/STOTM N15...........50 B6
Library Pde WLSDN NW10 *.............81 G6
Library St STHWK SE1........................18 B3
Lichfield CI EBAR EN4........................21 K3
Lichfield Gdns
   RCH/KEW TW9 *...........................137 F6
Lichfield Gv FNCH N3.........................46 E4
Lichfield Rd BCTR RM8.....................91 H2
   BOW E3...105 G2
   CRICK NW2...82 C2
   ED N9..36 B4
   EHAM E6...107 H2
   HSLWW TW4...................................134 B4
   NTHWD HA6...40 E6
   RCH/KEW TW9...............................137 G1
Lichfield Ter RCH/KEW TW9 *......137 F6
Lidbury Rd MLHL NW7.......................46 C2
Lidcote Gdns BRXN/ST SW9........142 B3
Liddall Wy WDR/YW UB7................112 C1
Liddell CI KTN/HRWW/WS HA3......43 K5
Liddell Gdns WLSDN NW10............100 A1
Liddell Rd KIL/WHAMP NW6...........82 E4
Lidding Rd KTN/HRWW/WS HA3....61 J2
Liddington Rd SRTFD E15.................88 D6
Liddon Rd BMLY BR1......................184 B6
   PLSTW E13...106 E2
Liden CI LEY E10..................................87 K3
Lidfield Rd STNW/STAM N16...........85 K3
Lidgate Rd CMBW SE5 *.................142 C1
Lidiard Rd WAND/EARL SW18......160 B4
Lidlington PI CAMTN NW1 *..............4 B1
Lido Sq TOTM N17...............................50 A5
Lidyard Rd ARCH N19.........................66 C5
Liffler Rd WOOL/PLUM SE18.......127 K5
Lifford St PUT/ROE SW15.............139 G5
Lightcliffe Rd PLMGR N13................35 G6
Lighter CI BERM/RHTH SE16........124 B3
Lighterman Ms WCHPL E1.............105 F5
Lighterman's Rd POP/IOD E14.......124 D2
Lightfoot Rd CEND/HSY/T N8..........66 E2
Ligonier St BETH E2.............................7 H5
Lilac CI CHING E4.................................51 H2
Lilac Gdns CROY/NA CRO..............213 J1
   EA W5..116 E3
   HYS/HAR UB3....................................94 C5
   ROMW/RG RM7................................75 F5
Lilac PI LBTH SE11...............................17 G7
Lilac St SHB W12.................................99 J6
Lilah Ms HAYES BR2........................183 G5
Lilburne Gdns ELTH/MOT SE9......146 D6
Lilburne Rd ELTH/MOT SE9..........146 D6
Lile Crs HNWL W7...............................96 E4
Lilestone Rd STJWD NW8.................2 B7
Liliford Rd CMBW SE5....................142 C3
Lilian Barker CI
   LEE/GVPK SE12...........................145 K6
Lilian Board Wy GFD/PVL UB6......78 D3
Lilian CI STNW/STAM N16................86 A1
Lilian Gdns WFD IG8...........................53 F4
Lilian Rd STRHM/NOR SW16.......179 H2
Lilburn House CHARL SE7 *...........146 D1
Lilleshall Rd MRDN SM4................194 C3
Lilley CI WAP E1W *..........................123 H1
Lilley La MLHL NW7.............................45 F1
Lillian Av ACT W3..............................117 H2
Lillian Rd BARN SW13.....................118 D6
Lillie Rd FUL/PGN SW6...................119 H6
   WDR/YW UB7..................................112 B4
Lillieshall Rd CLAP SW4.................141 G4
Lillie Yd FUL/PGN SW6...................119 K6
Lillington Gardens Est
   PIM SW1V..16 B7
Lilliput Av NTHLT UB5.......................77 K1
Lilliput Rd ROMW/RG RM7...............75 H4
Lily CI WKENS W14..........................119 H4
Lily Dr WDR/YW UB7.......................112 A4
Lily Gdns ALP/SUD HA0....................97 J1
Lily PI FARR EC1M *............................11 K1
Lily Rd WALTH E17..............................69 J3
Lilyville Rd FUL/PGN SW6.............139 J2
Limbourne Av BCTR RM8.................74 B4
Limeburner La STP EC4M.................12 A3
Lime CI BKHH IG9................................39 H5
   BMLY BR1..200 D1
   KTN/HRWW/WS HA3......................43 G5
   OXHEY WD19....................................27 H2
   PIN HA5..40 D6
   ROMW/RG RM7................................75 H2
   WAP E1W..123 H1
Lime Crs SUN TW16 *......................172 B5
Lime Kiln Dr CHARL SE7...............126 A6
Limedene CI PIN HA5.........................41 H4
Lime Gv BARK/HLT IG6......................55 G1
   BFN/LL DA15..................................168 A1
   CHING E4..51 H2
   HYS/HAR UB3....................................94 B6
   NWMAL KT3....................................176 A6
   RSLP HA4...58 E5
   SHB W12...119 F2
   TRDG/WHET N20...............................32 C3
   TWK TW1..156 A1
Limeharbour POP/IOD E14.............124 E3
Limehouse Cswy POP/IOD E14....105 H6
Limehouse Link POP/IOD E14......105 H6
Limehouse Link (Tunnel)
   POP/IOD E14...................................105 G6
Limekiln Dr CHARL SE7 *...............126 A6
Lime St FENCHST EC3M...................13 G4
   WALTH E17..69 G1
Lime Street Pas BANK EC3V *.........13 G4
Limes Av BARN SW13.....................138 C3
   CAR SM5..194 E5
   CHIG IG7..54 C1
   CROY/NA CRO.................................211 G2
   GLDGN NW11....................................64 C4
   MLHL NW7..45 J3
   NFNCH/WDSPK N12........................33 G6
   PGE/AN SE20...................................181 J2
   WALTH E17..69 J1
   WAN E11..71 F1

The Limes Av FBAR/BDGN N11.....48 B1
Limes CI CAR SM5.............................194 E5
   FBAR/BDGN N11 *............................48 C1
Limesdale Gdns EDGW HA8............44 E5
Limes Field Rd
   MORT/ESHN SW14.......................138 B4
Limesford Rd PECK SE15...............144 A5
Limes Gdns WAND/EARL SW18...159 K1
Limes Gv LEW SE13........................145 F5
Limes Rd BECK BR3........................182 E5
   CROY/NA CRO.................................196 E3
Limes Rw ORP BR6..........................216 B3
The Limes CMBW SE5 *....................142 E4
   PUR RM19..131 K5
   WAND/EARL SW18 *.....................159 K1
Limestone Wk ERITH DA18............128 D2
Lime St FENCHST EC3M...................13 G4
   WALTH E17..69 G1
Lime Tree Av ESH/CLAY KT10......189 J5
Lime Tree CI PIN HA5.........................42 A3
Lime Tree Gv CROY/NA CRO.........213 H1
Lime Tree PI MTCM CR4..................195 G2
Lime Tree Rd HEST TW5.................135 G2
Lime Tree Ter CAT SE6...................164 C3
Lime Tree Wk BUSH WD23..............28 C1
   ENC/FH EN2.......................................23 J1
   WWKM BR4.....................................214 D2
Lime Wk SRTFD E15 *........................88 C5
Limewood CI BECK BR3..................199 F2
   WALTH E17..69 H1
   WEA W13...97 H5
Limewood Rd ERITH DA8...............149 K1
Limpsfield Av THHTH CR7.............196 A2
   WIM/MER SW19...............................159 G4
Linacre CI PECK SE15......................143 J4
Linacre Rd CRICK NW2......................81 K4
Linchmere Rd LEE/GVPK SE12....165 J2
Lincoln Av ROMW/RG RM7.............57 J3
   STHGT/OAK N14...............................34 C5
   WHTN TW2.......................................155 H4
   WIM/MER SW19...............................159 G5
Lincoln CI ERITH DA8......................150 C3
   GFD/PVL UB6.....................................78 C6
   RYLN/HDSTN HA2............................59 K2
Lincoln Crs EN EN1............................24 A6
Lincoln Dr OXHEY WD19..................27 G5
Lincoln Gdns IL IG1...........................71 J4
Lincoln Green Rd
   STMC/STPC BR5...........................202 A2
Lincoln Ms KIL/WHAMP NW6 *......82 D6
   SEVS/STOTM N15.............................67 J1
Lincoln Pde EFNCH N2 *...................47 J6
   EFNCH N2...24 A5
   ERITH DA8..150 C3
   FELT TW13..154 D4
   FSTGT E7...89 H4
   MTCM CR4.......................................195 K1
   NTHWD HA6.....................................175 K6
   PLSTW E13.......................................107 F3
   RYLN/HDSTN HA2............................60 B1
   SCUP DA14.......................................186 A2
   SNWD SE25......................................181 J6
   SWFD E18..53 F4
   WPK KT4..192 E5
Lincoln's Inn Flds LINN WC2A.........11 H3
The Lincolns MLHL NW7....................31 H5
Lincoln St CHEL SW3..........................14 E7
   WAN E11..70 C6
Lincoln Ter BELMT SM2 *...............208 E5
Lincombe Rd BMLY BR1................165 J6
Lindal Crs ENC/FH EN2......................22 E6
Lindales TOTM N17............................50 C2
Lindal Rd BROCKY SE4...................144 C6
Linden Av DART DA1........................171 F3
   EN EN1..36 C1
   HSLW TW3.......................................135 G6
   RSLP HA4..58 E5
   THHTH CR7.......................................196 C1
   WBLY HA9...80 A3
   WLSDN NW10...................................100 B3
Linden CI ORP BR6...........................217 G3
   RSLP HA4..58 E5
   STAN HA7..43 H1
   STHGT/OAK N14................................34 C1
   THDIT KT7...190 B4
Linden Cottages
   WIM/MER SW19 *...........................177 H2
Linden Crs GFD/PVL UB6.................79 F4
   KUT/HW KT1....................................175 G5
   WFD IG8...53 F2
Lindenfield CHST BR7.....................185 G5
Linden Gdns BAY/PAD W2.............100 E6
   CHSWK W4.......................................118 A5
   EA W5...116 E2
   ENC/FH EN2.......................................23 K2
Linden Gv NWMAL KT3...................176 B6
   PECK SE15.......................................143 J4
   PGE/AN SE20....................................181 K2
   TEDD TW11.......................................174 A1
Linden Lea EFNCH N2.........................65 G2
   PIN HA5...41 H3
Linden Leas WWKM BR4................199 G6
Linden Ms BAY/PAD W2 *..............100 E6
   IS N1..85 K4
Linden Pde MTCM CR4....................194 D1
   FBAR/BDGN N11 *..........................173 F4
Linden PI HPTN TW12........................172 E4
   MUSWH N10..66 B1
   SEVS/STOTM N15.............................67 J1
The Lindens CHSWK W4...................137 K2
   CROY/NA CRO.................................214 A4
   NFNCH/WDSPK N12 *......................47 G1
   WALTH E17..69 K1
Linden St ROMW/RG RM7................75 F1
Linden Wy STHGT/OAK N14............34 C1
Lindeth CI STAN HA7..........................43 J2
Lindfield Gdns HAMP NW3...............83 F3
Lindfield Rd CROY/NA CRO............197 G3
   EA W5...97 J3

Lindfield St POP/IOD E14..........105 J5
Lindhill CI PEND EN3...............25 F5
Lindisfarne Md HOM E9.............87 C2
Lindisfarne Rd BCTR RM8............91 J1
RYNPK SW20........................176 D3
Lindley Est PECK SE15.............143 H1
Lindley PI RCH/KEW TW9............137 H2
Lindley Rd LEY E10.................70 A6
Lindley St WCHPL E1...............104 E4
Lindore Rd BTSEA SW11.............140 E5
Lindores Rd CAR SM5...............194 B5
Lindo St PECK SE15................143 K3
Lind Rd SUT SM1...................209 G3
Lindrop St FUL/PGN SW6............140 B3
Lindsay CI CHSGTN KT9.............206 A5
STWL/WRAY TW19....................152 A1
Lindsay Dr KTN/HRWW/WS HA3....62 A5
Lindsay Rd HPTN TW12.............155 G6
WPK KT4..........................192 E6
Lindsay Sq PIM SW1V..............121 J5
Lindsell St GNWCH SE10...........145 F2
Lindsey CI BMLY BR1...............184 C6
MTCM CR4.........................195 K1
Lindsey Gdns
EBED/NFELT TW14 *................153 G2
Lindsey Ms IS N1...................85 J5
Lindsey Rd BCTR RM8................91 J1
Lindsey St FARR EC1M...............12 B1
Lind St DEPT SE8.................144 E3
Lindum Rd TEDD TW11..............174 D3
Lindway WAND SE27................180 C1
Linfield CI HDN NW4................46 A6
Linford Md WALTH E17...............52 A6
Linford St VX/NE SW8..............141 H2
Lingards Rd LEW SE13.............145 F5
Lingey CI BFN/LL DA15............168 A4
Lingfield CI EN EN1................36 A1
Lingfield Ct
Lingfield Ct ELTH/MOT SE9 *.......86 C1
Lingfield Crs ELTH/MOT SE9.......147 J5
Lingfield Gdns ED N9...............36 E2
Lingfield Rd WIM/MER SW19.......177 G2
WPK KT4..........................208 A1
Lingham St BRXN/ST SW9...........141 K3
Lingholm Wy BAR EN5...............26 A4
Ling Rd CAN/RD E16................106 E4
ERITH DA8........................129 K6
Lingwell Rd TOOT SW17............160 D5
Lingwood Gdns ISLW TW7...........135 K1
Linhope St CAMTN NW1...............2 E6
Linkfield E/WMO/HCT KT8..........173 F6
Link Fld HAYES BR2................199 J5
Linkfield Rd ISLW TW7............136 A3
Link La WLGTN SM6................210 D4
Linklea CI CDALE/KGS NW9...........45 G3
Links Av GPK RM2...................57 K5
MRDN SM4.........................193 K1
Links Dr TRDG/WHET N20............32 E2
Links Gdns STRHM/NOR SW16........180 B3
NFNCH/WDSPK N12...................46 D2
NWMAL KT3........................175 B5
Linkside EN EN1/EN EN2.............23 F4
Linkside Gdns ENC/FH EN2..........23 F4
Links Rd ACT W3....................98 C5
CRICK NW2.........................63 H6
TOOT SW17........................179 F2
WFD IG8...........................52 E1
WWKM BR4.........................199 F5
Links Side ENC/FH EN2..............23 F4
The Links WALTH E17................69 G1
Link St HOM E9.....................86 E4
Links Vw HART DA1................171 F3
FNCH N3...........................46 C3
Links View CI STAN HA7.............43 G2
Linksview Ct HPTN TW12 *.........156 C4
Links View Rd CROY/NA CR0........213 J1
HPTN TW12........................173 H1
Links Wy BECK BR3................198 D3
NTHWD HA6.........................40 A4
TOOT SW17........................178 E2
Linksway HDN NW4...................46 B5
NTHWD HA6.........................40 B4
Links Yd WCHPL E1..................13 K1
The Link ACT W3....................80 J6
ALP/SUD HA0.......................61 J5
CRICK NW2.........................63 J5
NTHLT UB5.........................77 K3
PEND EN3..........................25 J5
PIN HA5...........................59 G5
TEDD TW11........................174 A3
Link Wy HAYES BR2................200 D4
RCHPK/HAM TW10..................156 C4
Linkway BCTR RM8...................91 J2
FSBYPK N4.........................67 K3
NWMAL KT3........................192 E1
PIN HA5...........................41 H4
RYNPK SW20.......................176 E6
The Linkway BAR EN5...............32 E1
BELMT SM2........................209 F6
Linkwood Wk CAMTN NW1............84 D5
Linley Crs ROMW/RG RM7............56 D6
Linley Rd TOTM N17.................50 A5
Linnell CI GLDGN NW11..............65 F3
Linnell Dr GLDGN NW11..............65 F3
Linnell Rd ED N9...................36 D4
UED N18...........................50 C1
Linnet CI BUSH WD23................28 C3
ED N9.............................37 F3
THMD SE28........................109 J6
Linnet Ms BAL SW12................161 F2
Linom Rd CLAP SW4................141 K5
Linscott Rd CLPT E5................86 E2
Linsdell Rd BARK IG11..............90 C6
Linsey St BERM/RHTH SE16.........123 H4
Linslade CI HSLWW TW4............134 D6
PIN HA5...........................40 E5
Linslade Rd ORP BR6...............217 G4
Linstead St KIL/WHAMP NW6.........82 E5
Linstead Wy
WAND/EARL SW18...................159 H2

Lintaine CI HMSMTH W6 *.........119 H6
Linthorpe Av ALP/SUD HA0..........79 J4
Linthorpe Rd EBAR EN4..............21 J4
STNW/STAM N16.....................68 A4
Linton CI CAR SM5................194 E4
CHARL SE7.........................126 B5
WELL DA16........................148 C2
Linton Gdns EHAM E6...............107 J5
Linton Gv WNWD SE27.............180 C1
Linton Rd BARK IG11...............90 C5
Linton St IS N1....................6 D1
Lintott Ct STWL/WRAY TW19.......152 A1
Linver Rd FUL/PGN SW6.............139 J3
Linwood CI CMBW SE5..............143 G3
Linwood Crs EN EN1.................24 C2
Linzee Rd CEND/HSY/T N8...........66 E1
Lion CI BROCKY SE4................164 D1
Lionel Gdns ELTH/MOT SE9.........146 C6
Lionel Ms NKENS W10 *............100 C4
Lionel Rd ELTH/MOT SE9...........146 C6
Lionel Rd North BTFD TW8.........117 F3
Lionel Rd South BTFD TW8.........117 G5
Lion Gate Gdns RCH/KEW TW9......137 G4
Lion Gate Ms
WAND/EARL SW18...................159 K2
Lion Mills BETH E2 *..............104 C1
Lion Park Av CHSGTN KT9..........206 C2
Lion Rd BXLYHS DA6...............149 F5
CROY/NA CR0......................196 D2
ED N9.............................36 C4
EHAM E6..........................107 K5
TWK TW1..........................156 A3
Lions CI LEE/GVPK SE12...........166 B5
Lion Wy BTFD TW8.................136 E1
Lion Wharf Rd ISLW TW7...........136 C4
Liphook Crs FSTH SE23..............163 K2
Liphook Rd OXHEY WD19.............27 H2
Lipton Rd WCHPL E1...............105 F5
Lisbon Av WHTN TW2...............155 H4
Lisbon CI WALTH E17................51 H5
Lisburne Rd HAMP NW3...............83 K2
Lisford St PECK SE15.............143 H2
Lisgar Ter WKENS W14.............119 J4
Liskeard CI CHST BR7.............185 H2
Liskeard Gdns BKHTH/KID SE3......145 K1
Lisle CI TOOT SW17................161 G6
Lisle St LSQ/SEVD WC2H.............10 C5
Lismore WIM/MER SW19 *...........177 J1
Lismore Circ KTTN NW5..............83 K3
Lismore CI ISLW TW7..............136 B3
Lismore Rd SAND/SEL CR2..........212 A4
TOTM N17..........................49 K6
Lismore Wk IS N1...................85 J4
Lisselton CI SURB KT6.............190 D4
Lissenden Gdns KTTN NW5...........84 A2
Lisson Gv CAMTN NW1................8 C1
Lisson St CAMTN NW1................8 C1
Lister CI ACT W3...................99 F4
MTCM CR4.........................178 D4
Lister Gdns UED N18................49 J1
Lister Rd WAN E11..................70 C5
Liston Rd CLAP SW4..............141 H4
TOTM N17..........................50 C4
Liston Wy WFD IG8..................53 G3
Listowel CI BRXN/ST SW9..........142 B1
Listowel Rd DAGE RM10.............92 C1
Listria Pk STNW/STAM N16..........68 A5
Litchfield Gdns WLSDN NW10.........81 J4
Litchfield Rd SUT SM1............209 G2
Litchfield St LSQ/SEVD WC2H.......10 D5
Litchfield Wy GLDGN NW11..........65 G2
Lithgow's Rd HTHAIR TW6..........133 H5
Lithos Rd HAMP NW3................83 H4
Little Acre BECK BR3.............182 D6
Little Albany St CAMTN NW1.........3 K5
Little Argyll St REGST W1B.........10 A4
Little Benty WDR/YW UB7..........112 A5
Little Birches BFN/LL DA15.......167 K4
The Little Boltons
WBPTN SW10.......................120 A5
Little Bornes DUL SE21...........163 F6
Little Britain STBT EC1A..........12 C3
Littlebrook CI CROY/NA CR0......198 A3
Littlebrook Manor Wy
DART DA1.........................151 K6
Little Brownings FSTH SE23.......163 J4
Littlebury Rd CLAP SW4..........141 J4
Little Bury St ED N9...............36 A3
Little Bushey La BUSH WD23........28 D1
Little Cedars
NFNCH/WDSPK N12 *................33 G5
Little Chester St KTBR SW1X.......15 J4
Little Cloisters WEST SW1P........16 E4
Littlecombe CI
GNWCH SE10 *.....................144 E1
Little CI WWKM BR4...............199 H6
Littlecroft ELTH/MOT SE9.........147 F4
Littledale ABYW SE2..............128 B6
Little Deans Yd WEST SW1P.........16 E4
Little Dimocks BAL SW12..........161 G4
Little Dorrit Ct STHWK SE1.........18 D2
Little Ealing La EA W5..........116 D4
Little Edward St CAMTN NW1 *......3 K4
Little Elms HYS/HAR UB3..........133 G1
Little Essex St TPL/STR WC2R *....11 J5
Little Ferry Rd TWK TW1 *........156 C3
Littlefield CI ARCH N19...........84 C2
KUT/HW KT1........................175 F5
Little Friday Rd CHING E4..........38 C4
Little Gearies BARK/HLT IG6.......72 B1
Little George St WEST SW1P.........16 E3
Little Green St KTTN NW5 *........84 B2
Littlegrove EBAR EN4..............33 J1
Little Heath CHARL SE7...........126 D6
CHDH RM6..........................73 H1
Little Heath Rd BXLYHN DA7.......149 G2

Littleheath Rd SAND/SEL CR2......212 D6
Little Ilford La MNPK E12..........89 K2
Littlejohn Rd HNWL W7 *............97 F5
STMC/STPC BR5....................202 B3
Little Marlborough St
REGST W1B *......................10 A4
Littlemead ESH/CLAY KT10.........204 D2
Littlemede ELTH/MOT SE9..........166 E5
Littlemoor Rd IL IG1...............90 D1
Littlemore Rd ABYW SE2..........128 B2
Little Newport St
LSO/SEVD WC2H.....................10 D5
Little New St FLST/FETLN EC4A.....11 K3
Little Orchard CI PIN HA5..........41 J5
Little Oxhey La OXHEY WD19........41 J1
Little Park Dr FELT TW13.........154 C4
Little Park Gdns ENC/FH EN2.......23 K4
Little Pluckett's Wy BKHH IG9.....39 H3
Little Portland St REGST W1B.......9 K3
Little Potters BUSH WD23..........28 D2
Little Queens Rd TEDD TW11......174 A2
Little Queen St DART DA1.........171 H1
Little Redlands BMLY BR1.........184 D5
Little Rd HYS/HAR UB3...........113 J2
Littlers CI WIM/MER SW19.........178 C4
Little Russell St
NOXST/BSQ WC1A....................10 E2
Little St James's St
WHALL SW1A........................16 A1
Little St Leonards
MORT/ESHN SW14...................137 K4
Little Smith St WEST SW1P.........16 D4
Little Somerset St TWRH EC3N.....13 J4
Littlestone CI BECK BR3..........182 D2
Little Strd CDALE/KGS NW9..........45 H5
Little Stream CI NTHWD HA6........40 C1
Little Thrift STMC/STPC BR5......201 H1
Little Titchfield St GTPST W1W....9 K2
Littleton Av CHING E4..............38 D3
Littleton Crs HRW HA1..............61 F6
Littleton Rd HRW HA1...............61 F6
Littleton St WAND/EARL SW18......160 B4
Little Trinity La BLKFR EC4V......12 D5
Little Turnstile HHOL WC1V........11 G2
Littlewood LEW SE13..............145 F6
Little Wood CI STMC/STPC BR5.....186 B4
Littlewood CI WEA W13............116 C3
Littleworth Av ESH/CLAY KT10.....204 D4
Littleworth Common Rd
ESH/CLAY KT10....................204 D2
Littleworth La ESH/CLAY KT10.....204 D3
Littleworth PI ESH/CLAY KT10.....204 D3
Littleworth Rd ESH/CLAY KT10.....204 D3
Livermere Rd HACK E8..............86 B6
Liverpool Gv WALW SE17..........122 E5
Liverpool Rd CAN/RD E16.........106 C4
EA W5............................116 E1
HOLWY N7.........................85 G4
KUTN/CMB KT2.....................175 H3
LEY E10...........................69 G4
THHTH CR7........................180 D6
Livesey CI KUT/HW KT1...........175 G6
Livesey PI STHWK SE1............123 H6
Livingstone Rd BTSEA SW11.......140 C4
HSLW TW3.........................135 H5
PLMGR N13.........................48 E2
SRTFD E15.........................88 A6
STHL UB1..........................95 H6
THHTH CR7........................180 E5
WALTH E17.........................69 K3
Lizard St FSBYE EC1V...............6 E5
Lizban St BKHTH/KID SE3..........146 A1
Llanelly Rd CRICK NW2..............82 D1
Llanover Rd WBLY HA9...............79 K1
WOOL/PLUM SE18...................127 F6
Llanthony Rd MRDN SM4...........194 C3
Llanvanor Rd CRICK NW2............64 D6
Llewellyn St BERM/RHTH SE16.....123 H2
Lloyd Av STRHM/NOR SW16.........179 K4
Lloyd Baker St FSBYW WC1X..........5 J5
Lloyd Ct PIN HA5...................59 H2
Lloyd Ms PEND EN3..................25 J1
Lloyd Park Av CROY/NA CR0.......212 B2
Lloyd Rd DAGW RM9.................92 B4
EHAM E6...........................89 K6
WALTH E17.........................69 F1
WPK KT4..........................208 A1
Lloyd's Av FENCHST EC3M...........13 H4
Lloyd's PI BKHTH/KID SE3 *.......145 K3
Lloyd Sq FSBYW WC1X................5 J5
Lloyd's Rw CLKNW EC1R..............5 K5
Lloyd St FSBYW WC1X................5 J5
Lloyds Wy BECK BR3..............198 B2
Lloyd Thomas Ct WDGN N22 *......49 F3
Lloyd Vls BROCKY SE4.............144 D3
Loampit HI LEW SE13..............144 E3
Loampit V LEW SE13..............144 E4
Loanda CI HACK E8..................86 B6
Loats Rd BRXS/STRHM SW2.........161 K1
Locarno Rd ACT W3................117 K1
GFD/PVL UB6......................96 C5
Lochaber Rd LEW SE13............145 H5
Lochaline St HMSMTH W6..........119 F6
Lochan CI YEAD UB4................95 J3
Lochinvar St BAL SW12...........161 G2
Lochmere CI ERITH DA8............129 J6
Lochnagar St POP/IOD E14.........106 A4
Lock Cha BKHTH/KID SE3..........145 H4
Lock CI NWDGN UB2................115 H2
Locke CI RAIN RM13................93 H5
Lockesley Dr STMC/STPC BR5......202 A3
Lockesley Sq SURB KT6 *.........190 E3
Locket Rd KTN/HRWW/WS HA3.......43 F5
Locket Road Ms
KTN/HRWW/WS HA3..................42 E5
Lockfield Av PEND EN3.............25 G3
Lockgate CI HOM E9................87 H3
Lockhart CI HOLWY N7 *............85 F4
PEND EN3..........................24 D6
Lockhart St BOW E3...............105 H3
Lockhurst St CLPT E5...............87 F2
Lockington Rd VX/NE SW8.........141 G2
Lock Keepers Cottages
TOTM N17 *........................68 D1

Lockmead Rd LEW SE13.............145 F4
SEVS/STOTM N15....................68 C3
Lock Rd RCHPK/HAM TW10..........156 D6
Lock's La MTCM CR4...............179 F4
Locksley Est POP/IOD E14........105 H5
Locksley St POP/IOD E14.........105 H4
Locksmeade Rd
RCHPK/HAM TW10..................156 C6
Lockton St NTGHL W11 *..........100 B6
Lockwell Rd DAGE RM10............92 C1
Lockwood CI CHING E4..............51 J2
Lockwood Rd
BERM/RHTH SE16 *................123 J5
Lockwood Sq
BERM/RHTH SE16...................123 J3
Lockwood Wy CHSGTN KT9.........206 C3
WALTH E17.........................51 F5
Lockyer CI PEND EN3...............25 K1
Lockyer St STHWK SE1..............19 F3
Locomotive Dr
EBED/NFELT TW14..................153 J2
Locton Gn BOW E3 *................87 H6
Loddiges Rd HOM E9................86 E5
Loder CI YEAD UB4.................95 J2
Loder St PECK SE15...............143 K1
Lodge Av CROY/NA CR0...........211 G1
DAGW RM9.........................91 H6
DART DA1.........................171 F1
GPK RM2...........................75 J2
KTN/HRWW/WS HA3..................61 K1
Lodge CI EDGW HA8.................44 B2
ISLW TW7.........................136 C2
ORP BR6..........................202 C5
UED N18...........................49 J1
WLGTN SM6........................195 F5
Lodge Ct ALP/SUD HA0..............80 A5
Lodge Crs ORP BR6...............202 C5
Lodge Dr PLMGR N13................35 G6
Lodge Gdns BECK BR3.............198 C2
Lodge HI REDBR IG4.................71 J1
WELL DA16........................148 C1
Lodgehill Park CI
RYLN/HDSTN HA2....................60 B6
Lodge La BXLY DA5................168 E1
CROX/NA CR0.....................213 K5
CRW RM5...........................56 C1
NFNCH/WDSPK N12...................47 G1
Lodge Mansions Pde
PLMGR N13 *.......................35 G6
Lodge Ms HBRY N5 *.................85 J2
Lodge PI SUT SM1................209 F3
Lodge Rd BMLY BR1...............184 B3
CROY/NA CR0......................196 C5
HDN NW4...........................46 A2
SUT SM1..........................209 F3
WLGTN SM6........................210 B3
The Lodge SHB W12 *..............119 G2
Lodge Vls WFD IG8..................52 D3
Lodore Gdns CDALE/KGS NW9........63 G2
Lodore St POP/IOD E14............106 A5
Lofthouse PI CHSGTN KT9.........205 J5
Loftie St BERM/RHTH SE16........123 H2
Lofting Rd IS N1...................85 G5
Loftus Rd BARK IG11...............90 C4
SHB W12..........................118 E1
Loftus Vls SHB W12 *............118 E1
Logan CI HSLWW TW4..............134 E4
PEND EN3..........................25 J1
Logan Ms ECT SW5................119 K4
ROM RM1...........................75 G2
Logan PI ECT SW5................119 K4
Logan Rd ED N9....................36 D4
WBLY HA9..........................62 A6
The Logans BAR EN5 *..............20 A4
Logs Hi CHST BR7................184 D4
Logs Hill CI CHST BR7...........184 D4
Lolesworth CI WCHPL E1............13 K2
Lollard St LBTH SE11...............17 H6
Loman St STHWK SE1................18 B2
Lomas CI CROY/NA CR0...........214 A5
Lomas St WCHPL E1.................13 H2
Lombard Av GDMY/SEVK IG3.........72 E5
PEND EN3..........................24 E2
Lombard La EMB EC4Y...............11 K4
Lombard Rd BTSEA SW11...........140 C3
FBAR/BDGN N11 *...................48 B1
WIM/MER SW19....................178 A5
Lombard St BANK EC3V..............13 F4
FBAR/BDGN N11 *...................48 B1
Lombard Wall CHARL SE7..........126 A3
Lombardy CI WFD IG8...............54 B3
Lombardy PI BAY/PAD W2 *........101 F6
Lomond CI ALP/SUD HA0.............80 B5
Lomond Gdns SAND/SEL CR2........213 G5
Lomond Gv CMBW SE5..............142 E1
Loncroft Rd CMBW SE5...........123 F6
Londesborough Rd
STNW/STAM N16....................86 A2
London Br CANST EC4R..............13 F6
London Bridge St STHWK SE1.......19 F1
London Bridge Wk
STHWK SE1 *.......................13 F7
London City Airport Link
CAN/RD E16.......................106 D3
Londonderry Pde ERITH DA8 *.....150 A1
London Flds HACK E8 *.............86 D5
London Fields East Side
HACK E8...........................86 D5
London Fields West Side
HACK E8...........................86 C5
London La BMLY BR1..............183 K5
HACK E8...........................86 D5
London Loop BORE WD6..............30 E2
CROY/NA CR0......................213 F1
ORP BR6..........................203 F3
SAND/SEL CR2....................213 F6
WWKM BR4........................214 D2
WWKM BR4........................214 E1
London Ms BAY/PAD W2...............8 B4
London Rd SOCK/AV RM15..........131 K2
ASHF TW15........................152 D4
BARK IG11.........................90 B5
BMLY BR1.........................183 J5
BUSH WD23.........................28 B1
CHEAM SM3........................208 B1
CROY/NA CR0......................196 C5

DART DA1.........................150 A6
ENC/FH EN2........................23 K3
EW KT17..........................207 K3
FSTH SE23........................163 K3
HRW HA1...........................61 E6
ISLW TW7.........................135 K3
KUTN/CMB KT2.....................175 G5
MRDN SM4.........................194 D1
MTCM CR4.........................194 D1
MTCM CR4.........................178 D3
PLSTW E13.........................106 E1
ROM RM7..........................74 C3
SOCK/AV RM15....................131 J1
STAN HA7..........................29 K6
STAN HA7..........................44 E2
STHWK SE1.........................17 K6
STRHM/NOR SW16..................180 A5
SWLY BR8.........................187 K5
THHTH CR7........................196 B1
TWK TW1..........................156 B2
WBLY HA9..........................80 A3
WLGTN SM6........................210 B2
London Stile CHSWK W4 *.........117 H5
London St BAY/PAD W2...............8 B4
FENCHST EC3M......................13 H5
London Ter BETH E2...............104 C1
London Wall CITYW EC2V............12 D2
LVPST EC2M.......................13 F3
London Wall Buildings
LVPST EC2M........................13 F2
Lonesome Wy MTCM CR4...........179 G1
Long Acre COVGDN WC2E...........10 E4
ORP BR6..........................202 E6
Long Acre Ct WEA W13 *...........97 G4
Longacre PI CAR SM5.............210 A4
Longacre Rd WALTH E17.............52 B4
Longbeach Rd BTSEA SW11.........140 E4
Longboat Rw STHL UB1..............95 K5
Longbridge Rd BARK IG11...........90 D4
BCTR RM8..........................91 G2
Longbridge Wy LEW SE13..........145 F6
Longbury CI STMC/STPC BR5.......186 C6
Longbury Dr STMC/STPC BR5......186 C6
Longcliffe Pth OXHEY WD19........26 E5
Long Ct PUR RM19.................131 K4
Long Cft OXHEY WD19................27 F2
Longcroft Rd EDGW HA8.............43 J3
Long Deacon Rd CHING E4...........38 C3
Longdon Wd HAYES BR2.............215 J2
Longdown Rd CAT SE6.............164 D6
Long Dr ACT W3....................99 F5
GFD/PVL UB6.......................78 B6
RSLP HA4..........................77 H2
WDR/YW UB7........................112 A1
Long Elmes
KTN/HRWW/WS HA3...................42 C4
Longfellow Rd WALTH E17...........69 H3
WCHPL E1.........................105 G2
WPK KT4..........................192 D5
Longfellow Wy STHWK SE1 *........19 J4
Longfield BMLY BR1...............183 J4
Long Fld CDALE/KGS NW9............45 G4
Longfield Av EA W5................97 J6
EMPK RM11.........................75 H4
MLHL NW7..........................31 F5
WALTH E17.........................69 G4
WBLY HA9..........................62 A3
WLGTN SM6........................195 F5
Longfield Crs SYD SE26..........163 K5
Longfield Dr
MORT/ESHN SW14...................137 J6
MTCM CR4.........................178 D4
Longfield Est STHWK SE1 *........19 K6
Longfield St
WAND/EARL SW18...................159 K2
Longford Av
EBED/NFELT TW14..................153 J1
STHL UB1..........................96 A6
STWL/WRAY TW19..................152 B5
Longford CI FELT TW13...........154 D5
HPTN TW12........................155 G2
YEAD UB4..........................96 B6
Longford Ct HOR/WEB KT19.......206 E3
HPTN TW12........................173 G2
Longford Gdns SUT SM1...........209 G1
YEAD UB4..........................96 B6
Longford Rd WHTN TW2............155 G3
Longford St CAMTN NW1..............3 K6
Longford Wy
STWL/WRAY TW19..................152 B3
Longhayes Av CHDH RM6............55 K6
Longheath Gdns
CROY/NA CR0......................197 K2
Longhedge St BTSEA SW11.........141 F3
Longhill Rd CAT SE6..............165 G4
Longhook Gdns NTHLT UB5..........94 E2
Longhurst Rd CROY/NA CR0........197 J3
LEW SE13.........................145 H6
Longland Dr TRDG/WHET N20........33 F5
Longlands Ct
BFN/LL DA15 *....................167 K5
La LBXLYHN DA7....................149 H4
CROY/NA CR0......................197 K3
FNCH N3...........................47 F4
STBT EC1A.........................12 B1
STNW/STAM N16 *...................68 A6
STWL/WRAY TW19..................152 C3
Longleat Rd EN EN1................24 A6
Longleat Wy
EBED/NFELT TW14..................153 F2
Longley Av ALP/SUD HA0............80 B6
Longley Rd CROY/NA CR0.........196 C4
HRW HA1...........................60 C3
TOOT SW17........................178 D2
Long Leys CHING E4.................51 K2
Longley St STHWK SE1 *...........19 K6
Longley Wy CRICK NW2..............82 A1
Longmans CI WATW WD18.............26 A1
Long Mark Rd CAN/RD E16.........107 H5
Longmarsh La THMD SE28..........128 A1
Long Md CDALE/KGS NW9............45 H4
Longmead CHST BR7..............185 F5

Longmead Dr *SCUP* DA14..........168 E4
Long Meadow *KTTN* NW5 *..........84 D4
Long Meadow Cl *WWKM* BR4 ....199 F4
Longmeadow Rd
BFN/LL DA15 ....167 K3
Longmead Rd *HYS/HAR* UB3..........94 E6
THDIT KT7 ....189 K4
TOOT SW17..................................178 E1
Longmoore St *PIM* SW1V..............16 A7
Longmore Av *BAR* EN5 ....33 G1
Longnor Rd *WCHPL* E1................105 F2
Long Pond Rd *BKHTH/KID* SE3...145 H2
Longport Cl *BARK/HLT* IG6............55 G2
Long Reach Rd *BARK* IG11 ....109 F3
Longreach Rd *ERITH* DA8 ....150 E1
Longridge La *STHL* UB1.................96 B6
Longridge Rd *ECT* SW5.................119 K4
Long Rd *CLAP* SW4......................141 H5
Longshaw Rd *CHING* E4................38 B5
Longshore *DEPT* SE8....................124 C4
Longstaff Crs
WAND/EARL SW18 ....159 K2
Longstaff Rd
WAND/EARL SW18 ....159 K1
Longstone Av *WLSDN* NW10 ....81 H5
Longstone Rd *TOOT* SW17...........179 G1
Long St *BETH* E2..............................7 J4
Longthornton Rd
STRHM/NOR SW16.......................179 H5
Longton Av *SYD* SE26...................163 H6
Longton Gv *SYD* SE26...................163 J6
Longview Wy *CRW* RM5.................57 F4
Longville Rd *LBTH* SE11.................18 A6
Long Wk *NWMAL* KT3...................175 K6
STHWK SE1 ....19 H4
Longwalk Rd *STKPK* UB11 ....112 E2
Longwood Ct *WPK* KT4.................192 D6
Longwood Dr *PUT/ROE* SW15.......158 E2
Longwood Gdns *CLAY* IG5 ....71 K1
Longworth Cl *THMD* SE28 ....109 K5
Long Yd *BMSBY* WC1N.....................5 G7
The Loning *CDALE/KGS* NW9.........63 H1
PEND EN3 ....24 E1
Lonsdale Av *EHAM* E6 ....107 H3
ROMW/RG RM7..............................74 E3
WBLY HA9 ....80 A3
Lonsdale Cl *EHAM* E6..................107 J3
ELTH/MOT SE9 ....166 C5
UX/CGN UB8....................................94 A5
Lonsdale Crs *GNTH/NBYPK* IG2 ...72 B3
Lonsdale Dr *ENC/FH* EN2 ....22 E6
Lonsdale Dr North *ENC/FH* EN2 ..22 E6
Lonsdale Gdns *THHTH* CR7...........196 A1
Lonsdale Ms *NTGHL* W11.............100 D5
RCH/KEW TW9 *..............................137 H2
Lonsdale Pl *IS* N1 ....85 G5
Lonsdale Rd *BARN* SW13.............138 C1
BXLYHN DA7 ....149 G3
CHSWK W4.....................................118 C4
KIL/WHAMP NW6...........................100 D1
NTGHL W11....................................100 D5
NWDGN UB2..................................114 C3
SNWD SE25 ....197 J1
WAN E11 ....70 D4
Lonsdale Sq *IS* N1 *.......................85 G5
Loobert Rd *SEVS/STOTM* N15 ....50 A6
Looe Gdns *BARK/HLT* IG6 ....54 B6
Loop Rd *CHST* BR7 ....185 H2
Lopen Rd *UED* N18 ....36 A6
Loraine Cl *PEND* EN3 ....24 E6
Loraine Cottages *HOLWY* N7 *.....85 F2
Loraine Rd *CHSWK* W4 ....117 J6
HOLWY N7 ....85 F2
Lord Av *CLAY* IG5 ....71 K1
Lord Chancellor Wk
KUTN/CMB KT2 ....175 K4
Lord Gdns *CLAY* IG5........................71 J1
Lord Hills Rd *BAY/PAD* W2 ....101 F4
Lord Holland La
BRXN/ST SW9 * 142 B3
Lord Knyvett Cl
STWL/WRAY TW19 ....152 A1
Lord Knyvetts Ct
STWL/WRAY TW19 *.......................152 B1
Lord Napier Pl *HMSMTH* W6 ....118 D5
Lord North St *WEST* SW1P..............16 E5
Lord Roberts Ms
FUL/PGN SW6 *..............................140 A1
Lords Cl *DUL* SE21 ....162 D4
FELT TW13.......................................154 D4
Lordship Gv *STNW/STAM* N16.......67 K6
Lordship La *EDUL* SE22.................163 G1
WDGN N22.......................................49 H4
Lordship Pk *STNW/STAM* N16.......67 K6
Lordship Park Ms
STNW/STAM N16...............................67 J6
Lordship Pl *CHEL* SW3 ....120 D6
Lordship Rd *NTHLT* UB5 ....77 J5
STNW/STAM N16...............................67 K6
Lordship Ter *STNW/STAM* N16 .....67 K6
Lordsmead Rd *TOTM* N17...............50 A4
Lord St *CAN/RD* E16......................126 D1
Lords Vw *STJWD* NW8 ....2 C5
Lord Warwick St
WOOL/PLUM SE18 ....126 E3
Lorenzo St *FSBYW* WC1X 5 G4
Loretto Gdns
KTN/HRWW/WS HA3 ....62 A1
Lorian Cl *NFNCH/WDSPK* N12 ....33 F6
Loring Rd *ISLW* TW7 ....136 A3
TRDG/WHET N20 ....33 J4
Loris Rd *HMSMTH* W6.....................119 F3
Lorn Ct *BRXN/ST* SW9....................142 B3
Lorne Av *CROY/NA* CR0.................198 A4
Lorne Cl *STJWD* NW8 ....2 D5
Lorne Gdns *CROY/NA* CR0............198 B4
NTGHL W11 ....119 G2
WAN E11 ....71 G1
Lorne Rd *FSBYPK* N4 ....67 F5
FSTGT E7 ....89 F2
KTN/HRWW/WS HA3 ....43 F5
RCHPK/HAM TW10 ....137 G6
WALTH E17 ....69 J2
Lorne Ter *FNCH* N3 *......................46 D5
Lorn Rd *BRXN/ST* SW9..................142 A3
Lorraine Pk
KTN/HRWW/WS HA3 ....42 E3
Lorrimore Rd *WALW* SE17 ....122 C6
Lorrimore Sq *WALW* SE17 ....122 C6
Loseberry Rd *ESH/CLAY* KT10.......204 D3
Lothair Rd *EA* W5...........................116 E2
Lothair Rd North *FSBYPK* N4 ....67 H3
Lothair Rd South *FSBYPK* N4.........67 G4
Lothbury *LOTH* EC2R........................12 E3
Lothian Av *YEAD* UB4 ....95 F4
Lothian Cl *ALP/SUD* HA0 ....79 G2
Lothian Rd *BRXN/ST* SW9 ....142 C2
Lothrop St *NKENS* W10 ....100 C2
Lots Rd *WBPTN* SW10....................140 B1
Loubet St *TOOT* SW17....................178 E2
Loudoun Av *BARK/HLT* IG6 ....72 B2
Loudoun Rd *STJWD* NW8 ....83 G6
Loughborough Pk
BRXN/ST SW9 ....142 C5
Loughborough Rd
BRXN/ST SW9 ....142 C3
Loughborough St *LBTH* SE11.....122 A5
Lough Rd *HOLWY* N7 ....85 F4
Loughton Wy *BKHH* IG9...................39 H3
Louisa Cl *HOM* E9 ....86 E5
Louisa St *WCHPL* E1......................105 F4
Louis Cl *CHST* BR7 ....166 E6
Louise Bennett Cl *HNHL* SE24 *..142 C5
Louise Gdns *RAIN* RM13 ....111 G2
Louise Rd *SRTFD* E15.......................88 C4
Louisville Rd *TOOT* SW17..............161 F5
Louvaine Rd *BTSEA* SW11 ....140 C5
Lovage Ap *EHAM* E6 ....107 J4
Lovat Cl *CRICK* NW2 ....81 H1
Lovat La *FENCHST* EC3M 13 G5
Lovatt Cl *EDGW* HA8 ....44 D2
Loveday Rd *WEA* W13 ....116 C1
Lovegrove St *STHWK* SE1 ....123 H5
Lovegrove Wk *POP/IOD* E14.........125 F1
Lovekyn Cl *KUTN/CMB* KT2...........175 G5
Lovelace Av *HAYES* BR2 ....201 F3
Lovelace Gdns *BARK* IG11 ....91 G3
SURB KT6 ....190 E4
Lovelace Gn *ELTH/MOT* SE9.........146 E4
Lovelace Rd *DUL* SE21 ....162 D4
EBAR EN4 ....33 J2
SURB KT6 ....190 D4
Lovelace Vls *THDIT* KT7 * 190 C4
Love La *BXLY* DA5..........................169 H1
CHEAM SM3 ....208 C4
CITYW EC2V 12 D3
MRDN SM4......................................193 K4
MTCM CR4 ....178 D6
PIN HA5 ....41 J6
SNWD SE25.....................................181 J6
SURB KT6..190 E6
TOTM N17 ....50 B3
WFD IG8 ....53 K2
WOOL/PLUM SE18 ....127 F4
Lovel Av *WELL* DA16 ....148 B3
Lovelinch Cl *PECK* SE15.................123 K6
Lovell Pl *BERM/RHTH* SE16............124 B3
Lovell Rd *RCHPK/HAM* TW10 ....156 D5
STHL UB1 ....96 B5
Lovell Wk *RAIN* RM13......................93 J4
Loveridge Ms *KIL/WHAMP* NW6....82 D4
Loveridge Rd *KIL/WHAMP* NW6....82 D4
Lovett Dr *CAR* SM5 ....194 B4
Lovetts Pl *WAND/EARL* SW18 ....140 B6
Lovett Wy *WLSDN* NW10.................80 E3
Love Wk *CMBW* SE5........................142 E3
Lovibonds Av *ORP* BR6 ....216 B1
Lowbrook Rd *IL* IG1 ....90 B2
Lowden Rd *ED* N9.............................36 D3
HNHL SE24 ....142 C5
STHL UB1 ....95 J6
Lowe Av *CAN/RD* E16....................106 E4
Lowe Cl *CHIG* IG7 ....55 G1
Lowell St *POP/IOD* E14..................105 G5
Lowen Rd *RAIN* RM13 ....111 F1
Lower Addiscombe Rd
CROY/NA CR0 ....196 E5
Lower Addison Gdns
WKENS W14 ....119 H2
Lower Bedfords Rd *ROM* RM1.......57 J2
Lower Belgrave St *BGVA* SW1W....15 J5
Lower Boston Rd *HNWL* W7 ....115 K1
Lower Broad St *DAGE* RM10...........92 C6
Lower Camden *CHST* BR7..............184 E4
Lower Church St
CROY/NA CR0 * 196 C6
Lower Clapton Rd *CLPT* E5 ....86 D2
Lower Clarendon Wk
NTGHL W11 ....100 C5
Lower Common South
PUT/ROE SW15 ....138 E4
Lower Coombe St
CROY/NA CR0 ....211 J2
Lower Downs Rd *RYNPK* SW20..177 G4
Lower Gravel Rd *HAYES* BR2 ....200 D5
Lower Green Gdns *WPK* KT4 ....192 D5
Lower Green Rd
ESH/CLAY KT10 ....189 H6
Lower Gn West *MTCM* CR4...........178 E6
Lower Grosvenor Pl
BGVA SW1W 15 J4
Lower Grove Rd
RCHPK/HAM TW10..........................157 G1
Lower Hall La *CHING* E4 ....51 G1
Lower Hampton Rd *SUN* TW16..172 C5
Lower Ham Rd
KUTN/CMB KT2 ....174 E2
Lower James St
SOHO/CST W1F * 10 B5
Lower John St
SOHO/CST W1F 10 B5
Lower Kenwood Av
ENC/FH EN2 ....22 E6
Lower Kings Rd
KUTN/CMB KT2 ....175 F4
Lower Lea Crossing
POP/IOD E14 ....106 C6
Lower Maidstone Rd
FBAR/BDGN N11 ....48 C2
Lower Mardyke Av *RAIN* RM13..110 E1
Lower Marsh *STHWK* SE1..............17 J3
Lower Marsh La *BRYLDS* KT5 ....191 G1
Lower Merton Ri *HAMP* NW3.........83 J5
Lower Morden La *MRDN* SM4....193 F3
Lower Mortlake Rd
RCH/KEW TW9..................................137 F5
Lower Paddock Rd
OXHEY WD19 ....27 J1
Lower Park Rd *BELV* DA17............129 H4
FBAR/BDGN N11 ....48 C1
Lower Queen's Rd *BKHH* IG9..........39 J4
Lower Richmond Rd
PUT/ROE SW15 ....139 F4
RCH/KEW TW9...................................137 J4
Lower Rd *BELV* DA17 ....129 K3
BERM/RHTH SE16..............................123 K3
ERITH DA8...130 A4
RYLN/HDSTN HA2 ....60 D6
STMC/STPC BR5................................202 C3
SUT SM1 ....209 H3
Lower Sand Hills *SURB* KT6 ....190 D4
Lower Sloane St *BGVA* SW1W.......15 F7
Lower Sq *ISLW* TW7 ....136 C4
Lower Station Rd *DART* DA1.........170 B1
Lower Strd *CDALE/KGS* NW9 ....45 H5
Lower Sunbury Rd
E/WMO/HCT KT8...............................172 E5
HPTN TW12 ....173 F5
Lower Tail *OXHEY* WD19..................27 J5
Lower Teddington Rd
KUT/HW KT1 ....174 E4
Lower Ter *HAMP* NW3......................83 G1
Lower Thames St *MON* EC3R 13 G6
Lower Tub *BUSH* WD23 ....28 D2
Lower Wood Rd
ESH/CLAY KT10 ....205 H4
Loweswater Cl *WBLY* HA9 ....61 K6
The Lowe *CHIG* IG7 ....55 G1
Lowfield Rd *ACT* W3 ....98 E5
KIL/WHAMP NW6 ....82 E5
Lowfield St *DART* DA1 ....171 H2
Low Hall Cl *CHING* E4 ....37 J2
Low Hall La *WALTH* E17 ....69 G3
Lowick Rd *HRW* HA1 ....60 E1
Lowland Gdns *ROMW/RG* RM7 .....74 D3
Lowlands Dr
STWL/WRAY TW19 ....132 A6
Lowlands Rd *HRW* HA1 ....60 E4
PIN HA5 ....59 G4
Lowman Rd *HOLWY* N7 ....85 F2
Lowndes Cl *KTBR* SW1X 15 H5
Lowndes Ct *SOHO/CST* W1F * 10 A4
Lowndes Pl *KTBR* SW1X *.................15 G5
Lowndes Sq *KTBR* SW1X..................15 F3
Lowndes St *KTBR* SW1X 15 G4
Lowood St *WCHPL* E1 ....104 D6
Lowry Cl *ERITH* DA8.......................130 A4
Lowry Crs *MTCM* CR4.....................178 D5
Lowry Rd *BCTR* RM8.........................91 H3
Lowshoe La *CRW* RM5......................56 D4
Lowson Gv *OXHEY* WD19 ....27 J2
Lowswood Cl *NTHWD* HA6 ....40 A4
Lowther Dr *ENC/FH* EN2 ....22 E5
Lowther Hl *FSTH* SE23....................164 B2
Lowther Man *BARN* SW13 *.............138 D2
Lowther Rd *BARN* SW13..................138 C2
HOLWY N7 * 85 G3
KUTN/CMB KT2..................................175 G4
STAN HA7..44 B6
WALTH E17 ....51 G5
Lowth Rd *CMBW* SE5.......................142 D3
Loxford Av *EHAM* E6 ....107 H1
Loxford La *IL* IG1 ....90 C3
Loxford Rd *BARK* IG11 ....90 B4
Loxham Rd *CHING* E4 ....51 K3
Loxham St *STPAN* WC1H *..................5 F5
Loxley Cl *SYD* SE26..........................182 A1
Loxley Rd *HPTN* TW12 ....154 E6
WAND/EARL SW18 ....160 C3
Loxton Rd *FSTH* SE23 ....164 A3
Loxwood Cl *EBED/NFELT* TW14..153 G3
STMC/STPC BR5................................202 E6
Loxwood Rd *SEVS/STOTM* N15.......50 A6
Lubbock Rd *CHST* BR7....................185 F4
Lubbock St *NWCR* SE14..................143 K1
Lucan Pl *CHEL* SW3 ....14 C7
Lucan Rd *BAR* EN5 ....20 C4
Lucas Av *PLSTW* E13 ....89 F6
RYLN/HDSTN HA2 ....60 A6
Lucas Gdns *EFNCH* N2 ....47 G5
Lucas Rd *PGE/AN* SE20...................181 K2
Lucas Sq *GLDGN* NW11 ....64 E3
Lucas St *BROCKY* SE4.....................144 D3
Lucerne Cl *PLMGR* N13 ....34 E5
Lucerne Gv *WALTH* E17 ....70 B1
Lucerne Rd *HBRY* N5 ....85 H2
ORP BR6...202 A5
THHTH CR7 ....196 C2
Lucey Rd *BERM/RHTH* SE16 ....123 H3
Lucey Wy *BERM/RHTH* SE16 ....123 H3
Lucien Rd *TOOT* SW17.....................161 F6
WIM/MER SW19..................................160 A4
Lucknow St *WOOL/PLUM* SE18..147 K1
Lucorn Cl *LEE/GVPK* SE12.............165 J1
Luctons Av *BKHH* IG9.......................39 G3
Luddesdon Rd *ERITH* DA8..............149 H1
Ludford Cl *CROY/NA* CR0..............211 H2
Ludgate Broadway
BLKFR EC4V *.......................................12 B4
Ludgate Circ *STP* EC4M 12 A4
Ludgate Hl *STP* EC4M 12 A4
Ludgate Sq *STP* EC4M * 12 B4
Ludham Cl *BARK/HLT* IG6 ....54 C4
THMD SE28 ....109 J5
Ludlow Cl *HAYES* BR2 *..................183 K6
RYLN/HDSTN HA2 ....77 K2
Ludlow Md *OXHEY* WD19...................27 F5
Ludlow Rd *EA* W5..............................97 J3
FELT TW13..153 K5
Ludlow St *FSBYE* EC1V * 6 C6
Ludlow Wy *EFNCH* N2 ....65 G1
Ludovick Wk *PUT/ROE* SW15........138 B5
Luffield Rd *ABYW* SE2.....................128 C3
Luffman Rd *LEE/GVPK* SE12 ....166 A5
Lugard Rd *PECK* SE15.....................143 J3
Lugg Ap *MNPK* E12 ....90 A1
Luke St *SDTCH* EC2A 7 G6
Lukin Crs *CHING* E4 ....38 B5
Lukin St *WCHPL* E1 ....104 E6
Lullingstone Cl
STMC/STPC BR5................................186 C3
Lullingstone Crs
STMC/STPC BR5................................186 B3
Lullingstone La *LEW* SE13...............165 G1
Lullingstone Rd *BELV* DA17 ....129 G6
Lullington Garth *BMLY* BR1...........183 H3
NFNCH/WDSPK N12 ....46 D1
Lullington Rd *DAGW* RM9 ....92 A5
PGE/AN SE20 ....181 H3
Lulot Gdns *ARCH* N19 ....66 B6
Lulworth Av *HEST* TW5 ....135 G2
WBLY HA9 ....61 J4
Lulworth Cl *RYLN/HDSTN* HA2 .....77 K1
Lulworth Crs *MTCM* CR4................178 D5
Lulworth Dr *CRW* RM5 ....56 D1
PIN HA5...59 H4
Lulworth Gdns
RYLN/HDSTN HA2 ....59 J6
Lulworth Rd *ELTH/MOT* SE9...........166 D4
PECK SE15 *.......................................143 J3
WELL DA16..148 A3
Lulworth Waye *YEAD* UB4...............95 F5
Lumen Rd *WBLY* HA9........................61 K6
Lumley Cl *BELV* DA17 ....129 H6
Lumley Flats *BGVA* SW1W 121 F5
Lumley Gdns *CHEAM* SM3.............208 C3
Lumley Rd *CHEAM* SM3..................208 C4
Lumley St *OXSTW* W1C 9 H4
Luna Rd *THHTH* CR7.......................180 D6
Lundin Wk *OXHEY* WD19 * 27 H6
Lundy Dr *HYS/HAR* UB3..................113 J4
Lundy Wk *IS* N1 * 85 J4
Lunham Rd *NRWD* SE19.................181 F2
Lupin Cl *BRXS/STRHM* SW2...........162 C4
CROY/NA CR0 ....198 A5
ROMW/RG RM7 ....75 F6
WDR/YW UB7 ....112 A5
Lupton Cl *LEE/GVPK* SE12 ....166 A6
Lupton St *KTTN* NW5 ....84 C2
Lupus St *PIM* SW1V........................121 G5
Lurgan Av *HMSMTH* W6..................119 G6
Lurline Gdns *BTSEA* SW11.............141 F2
Luscombe Wy *VX/NE* SW8..............141 K1
Lushington Rd *CAT* SE6.................182 E1
WLSDN NW10 ....99 K1
Lushington Ter *HACK* E8 *...............86 C3
Luther Cl *EDGW* HA8 ....30 E4
Luther King Cl *WALTH* E17...............69 H3
Luther Ms *TEDD* TW11 ....174 A1
Luther Rd *TEDD* TW11 ....174 A1
Luton Pl *GNWCH* SE10 ....145 F1
Luton Rd *PLSTW* E13 ....106 E3
SCUP DA14.......................................168 D5
WALTH E17 ....51 G6
Luton St *STJWD* NW8...........................2 B7
Luttrell Av *PUT/ROE* SW15............138 E6
Lutwyche Rd *FSTH* SE23 ....164 C4
Luxborough La *CHIG* IG7..................39 K6
Luxborough St *CAMTN* NW1 ....3 G7
MHST W1U 9 G1
Luxemborough Ms *SRTFD* E15........88 C3
Luxemburg Gdns
HMSMTH W6 ....119 G4
Luxfield Rd *ELTH/MOT* SE9...........166 D3
Luxford St *BERM/RHTH* SE16........124 A4
Luxmore St *BROCKY* SE4 ....144 C2
Luxor St *CMBW* SE5 ....142 D4
Lyall Av *DUL* SE21 ....163 F6
Lyall Ms *KTBR* SW1X 15 G5
Lyall Ms West *KTBR* SW1X *.............15 G5
Lyall St *KTBR* SW1X..........................15 G5
Lyal Rd *BOW* E3 ....105 G1
Lycett Pl *SHB* W12 ....118 D2
Lych Gate Rd *ORP* BR6...................202 B5
Lych Gate Wk *HYS/HAR* UB3 ....94 D6
Lyconby Gdns *CROY/NA* CR0.........198 B4
Lydd Cl *BFN/LL* DA15......................167 K5
Lydden Gv *WAND/EARL* SW18.......160 A2
Lydden Rd *WAND/EARL* SW18 ....160 A2
Lydd Rd *BXLYHN* DA7 ....149 G1
Lydeard Rd *EHAM* E6 ....89 K5
Lydford Cl *STNW/STAM* N16 ....86 A3
Lydford Rd *CRICK* NW2 ....82 B4
MV/WKIL W9 ....100 D3
SEVS/STOTM N15 ....67 K2
Lydhurst Av *BRXS/STRHM* SW2..162 A4
Lydia Rd *ERITH* DA8 ....130 C6
Lydney Cl *WIM/MER* SW19.............159 H4
Lydon Rd *CLAP* SW4 ....141 H4
Lydstep Rd *CHST* BR7 ....167 F6
Lyford Rd *WAND/EARL* SW18.........160 C2
Lyford St *WOOL/PLUM* SE18..........126 D4
Lygon Pl *BGVA* SW1W *.....................15 J5
Lyham Cl *BRXS/STRHM* SW2..........161 K1
Lyham Rd *BRXS/STRHM* SW2 ....141 K6
Lyle Cl *MTCM* CR4 ....195 F4
Lyme Farm Rd *LEE/GVPK* SE12 ...145 K5
Lyme Gv *HOM* E9 ....86 E5
Lymer Av *NRWD* SE19.....................181 G1
Lyme Rd *WELL* DA16........................148 C2
Lymescote Gdns *SUT* SM1 ....193 K6
Lyme St *CAMTN* NW1 ....84 C5
Lyme Ter *CAMTN* NW1 ....84 C5
Lyminge Cl *SCUP* DA14...................168 A6
Lyminge Gdns
WAND/EARL SW18 ....160 D3
Lymington Av *WDGN* N22................49 G5
Lymington Cl
STRHM/NOR SW16.............................179 J5
Lymington Dr *RSLP* HA4 ....58 B6
Lymington Gdns
HOR/WEW KT19 ....207 H3
Lymington Rd *BCTR* RM8..................73 K5
KIL/WHAMP NW6 * 83 F4
Lyminster Cl *YEAD* UB4 ....95 J4
Lympstone Gdns *PECK* SE15..........143 H1
Lynbridge Gdns *PLMGR* N13 ....35 H6
Lynbrook Cl *RAIN* RM13..................111 F1
Lynbrook Gv *PECK* SE15.................143 F1
Lynchen Cl *HEST* TW5 ....133 K2
Lyncourt *BKHTH/KID* SE3 * 145 G3
Lyncroft Av *PIN* HA5.........................59 H2
Lyncroft Gdns *EW* KT17..................207 H6
HSLW TW3 ....135 H6
KIL/WHAMP NW6.................................82 E3
WEA W13 ....116 D2
Lyndale *CRICK* NW2............................82 D1
THDIT KT7 ....189 K4
Lyndale Av *CRICK* NW2 ....82 D1
Lyndale Cl *BKHTH/KID* SE3............125 J6
Lyndale Hampton Court Wy
ESH/CLAY KT10.................................189 K4
Lynden Wy *SWLY* BR8 ....187 K6
Lyndhurst Av *BRYLDS* KT5 ....191 J5
MLHL NW7...45 G2
NFNCH/WDSPK N12 ....47 K2
PIN HA5...41 F4
STHL UB1 ....115 G1
STRHM/NOR SW16.............................179 J5
WHTN TW2...154 E3
Lyndhurst Cl *BXLYHN* DA7..............149 J4
CROY/NA CR0....................................212 B1
ORP BR6..216 B2
WLSDN NW10 ....81 F1
Lyndhurst Ct *BELMT* SM2 *............208 E5
Lyndhurst Dr *LEY* E10......................70 A4
NWMAL KT3 ....192 B3
Lyndhurst Gdns *BARK* IG11.............90 E4
EN EN1 ....24 A5
FNCH N3 ....46 C4
GNTH/NBYPK IG2 ....72 D3
HAMP NW3 ....83 H3
PIN HA5...41 F4
Lyndhurst Gv *CMBW* SE5 ....143 F3
Lyndhurst Leys *HAYES* BR2 *.........183 G5
Lyndhurst Prior *SNWD* SE25 *........181 F6
Lyndhurst Rd *BXLYHN* DA7.............149 J4
CHING E4 ....52 A3
GFD/PVL UB6 ....96 B3
HAMP NW3 ....83 H3
THHTH CR7 ....196 B1
UED N18 ....36 C6
WDGN N22 ....49 G2
Lyndhurst Sq *PECK* SE15 ....143 G2
Lyndhurst Ter *HAMP* NW3................83 H3
Lyndhurst Wy *BELMT* SM2.............208 E6
PECK SE15 ....143 G2
Lyndon Av *BFN/LL* DA15.................148 A6
PIN HA5 ....41 J2
WLGTN SM6 ....210 A1
Lyndon Rd *BELV* DA17 ....129 H4
Lyndon Yd *TOOT* SW17 ....160 A6
Lyne Crs *WALTH* E17 ....51 H4
Lyneham Wk *CLPT* E5 * 87 G3
Lynette Av *CLAP* SW4......................161 G1
Lynford Cl *EDGW* HA8 ....44 E4
Lynford Gdns *EDGW* HA8 ....30 D6
GDMY/SEVK IG3 ....73 F6
Lynford Ter *ED* N9 * 36 B3
Lynhurst Crs *HGDN/ICK* UB10........76 A5
Lynhurst Rd *HGDN/ICK* UB10..........76 A5
Lynmere Rd *WELL* DA16 ....148 C3
Lyn Ms *STNW/STAM* N16 *.................86 B2
Lynmouth Av *EN* EN1........................36 B1
MRDN SM4...193 G4
Lynmouth Dr *RSLP* HA4 ....59 F6
Lynmouth Gdns *GFD/PVL* UB6......79 H6
HEST TW5 ....134 C2
Lynmouth Ri *STMC/STPC* BR5 ....202 C1
Lynmouth Rd *EFNCH* N2 ....65 K1
GFD/PVL UB6 ....79 H6
STNW/STAM N16..................................68 B5
WALTH E17 ....69 G3
Lynn Cl *KTN/HRWW/WS* HA3 ....42 D5
Lynne Cl *ORP* BR6 ....217 F4
Lynnett Rd *BCTR* RM8.......................73 K6
Lynne Wk *ESH/CLAY* KT10 ....204 C3
Lynne Wy *NTHLT* UB5 ....95 H1
Lynn Ms *WAN* E11 ....70 C6
Lynn Rd *BAL* SW12 ....161 G2
GNTH/NBYPK IG2 ....72 D4
WAN E11 ....70 C6
Lynn St *ENC/FH* EN2 ....23 K2
Lynscott Wy *SAND/SEL* CR2 ....211 H6
Lynstead Cl *BMLY* BR1....................184 B5
Lynsted Cl *BXLYHS* DA6 ....149 J6
Lynsted Ct *BECK* BR3 ....182 B5
Lynsted Gdns *ELTH/MOT* SE9........146 C5
Lynton Av *CDALE/KGS* NW9 ....63 H1
NFNCH/WDSPK N12 ....33 H6
ROMW/RG RM7 ....56 D4
STMC/STPC BR5 ....202 C1
WEA W13 ....97 G5
Lynton Cl *CHSGTN* KT9 ....206 A2
ISLW TW7 ....136 A5
WLSDN NW10 ....81 G4
Lynton Crs *GNTH/NBYPK* IG2 ....72 B3
Lynton Est *STHWK* SE1 ....19 K7
Lynton Gdns *EN* EN1 ....36 A2
FBAR/BDGN N11 ....48 D2
Lynton Md *TRDG/WHET* N20 ....32 E5
Lynton Rd *ACT* W3 ....98 C6
CEND/HSY/T N8 ....66 D2
CHING E4..51 K1
CROY/NA CR0 ....196 B3
KIL/WHAMP NW6................................100 D1
NWMAL KT3..192 A2
RYLN/HDSTN HA2 ....59 J6
STHWK SE1 ....19 K7
Lynton Ter *ACT* W3 * 98 E5
Lynwood Cl *CRW* RM5 ....56 D2
RYLN/HDSTN HA2 ....77 J1
SWFD E18 ....53 G4
Lynwood Dr *CRW* RM5 ....56 D2
NTHWD HA6...40 C4
WPK KT4...192 D6
Lynwood Gdns *CROY/NA* CR0 .....211 F2
STHL UB1 ....95 K5
Lynwood Gv *ORP* BR6 ....201 K4
WCHMH N21...35 G3
Lynwood Rd *EA* W5 ....97 K2
THDIT KT7 ....190 A6
TOOT SW17 ....160 E5
Lynwood Ter
WIM/MER SW19 * 177 J4
Lyon Meade *STAN* HA7 ....43 J4
Lyon Park Av *ALP/SUD* HA0 ....80 B5
Lyon Rd *HRW* HA1 ....61 F3
ROM RM1 ....75 H4
WIM/MER SW19..................................178 B4
WOT/HER KT12 ....188 D6
Lyonsdown Av *BAR* EN5 ....33 G1
Lyonsdown Rd *BAR* EN5 ....33 G1
Lyons Pl *STJWD* NW8 ....2 A7
Lyon St *IS* N1 ....85 F5

Lyons Wk WKENS W14 119 H4
Lyon Wy GFD/PVL UB6 78 E6
Lyoth Rd STMC/STPC BR5 201 H6
Lyric Dr GFD/PVL UB6 96 B3
Lyric Ms SYD SE26 163 K6
Lyric Rd BARN SW13 138 C2
Lysander CDALE/KGS NW9 * 45 H4
Lysander Gdns SURB KT6 191 G3
Lysander Gv ARCH N19 66 D5
Lysander Ms ARCH N19 * 66 E5
Lysander Rd CROY/NA CR0 211 F4
RSLP HA4 58 B6
Lysander Wy ORP BR6 216 C1
Lysias Rd BAL SW12 161 F1
Lysia St FUL/PGN SW6 139 G1
Lysons Wk PUT/ROE SW15 * 138 D6
Lytchet Rd BMLY BR1 183 K3
Lytchet Wy PEND EN3 24 E2
Lytchgate Cl SAND/SEL CR2 212 A5
Lytcott Dr E/WMO/HCT KT8 172 E6
Lytcott Gv EDUL SE22 143 G6
Lytham Av OXHEY WD19 41 H1
Lytham Cl THMD SE28 110 A5
Lytham St WALW SE17 122 E6
Lyttelton Rd EFNCH N2 65 G2
LEY E10 87 K1
Lyttleton Cl HAMP NW3 83 J5
Lyttleton Rd CEND/HSY/T N8 * 49 G6
Lytton Av PEND EN3 25 G1
PLMGR N13 35 G4
Lytton Cl EFNCH N2 65 H2
NTHLT UB5 77 K5
Lytton Gdns WLGTN SM6 210 D2
Lytton Gv PUT/ROE SW15 139 G6
Lytton Rd BAR EN5 21 G5
GPK RM2 75 K2
PIN HA5 41 J3
WAN E11 70 C4
Lyveden Rd BKHTH/KID SE3 146 A1
TOOT SW17 178 D2

M

Maberley Crs NRWD SE19 181 H3
Maberley Rd BECK BR3 182 A6
BMLY BR1 183 J4
NRWD SE19 181 G4
Mabledon Pl CAMTN NW1 4 D5
Mablethorpe Rd
FUL/PGN SW6 139 H1
Mabley St HOM E9 87 G3
Macaret Cl TRDG/WHET N20 33 F2
Macarthur Cl FSTGT E7 88 E4
WBLY HA9 80 D4
Macarthur Ter CHARL SE7 * 126 C6
Macaulay Av ESH/CLAY KT10 189 K6
Macaulay Rd CLAP SW4 141 G4
EHAM E6 107 H1
Macbean St WOOL/PLUM SE18 127 F3
Macbeth St HMSMTH W6 118 E5
Macclesfield Br STJWD NW8 2 D2
Macclesfield Rd FSBYE EC1V 6 C4
SNWD SE25 197 K2
Macclesfield St
SOHO/SHAV W1D * 10 D5
Macdonald Av DAGE RM10 92 D1
Macdonald Rd ARCH N19 66 C6
FBAR/BDGN N11 47 K1
FSTGT E7 88 E2
WALTH E17 52 A5
Macduff Rd BTSEA SW11 141 F2
Mace Cl WAP E1W 123 J1
Mace St BETH E2 105 F1
Macfarlane La ISLW TW7 116 A6
Macfarlane Rd SHB W12 119 F1
Mac Farren Pl CAMTN NW1 3 H7
Macgregor Rd CAN/RD E16 107 G4
Machell Rd PECK SE15 143 K4
Mackay Rd VX/NE SW8 141 G4
Mackennal St STJWD NW8 2 D3
Mackenzie Cl SHB W12 99 K6
Mackenzie Rd BECK BR3 182 B4
HOLWY N7 85 F4
Mackeson Rd HAMP NW3 * 83 K3
Mackie Rd BRXS/STRHM SW2 162 B2
Mackintosh La HOM E9 87 F3
Macklin St HOL/ALD WC2B * 11 F3
Macks Rd BERM/RHTH SE16 123 H4
Mackworth St CAMTN NW1 4 A4
Maclean Rd FSTH SE23 164 B1
Macleod House CHARL SE7 * 146 D1
Macleod Rd WCHMH N21 22 E6
Macleod St WALW SE17 122 D5
Maclise Rd WKENS W14 119 H3
Macmillan Wy TOOT SW17 161 G6
Macoma Rd WOOL/PLUM SE18 127 J6
Macoma Ter
WOOL/PLUM SE18 127 J6
Maconochies Rd
POP/IOD E14 * 124 E5
Macquarie Wy POP/IOD E14 124 E4
Macroom Rd MV/WKIL W9 100 D2
Mada Rd ORP BR6 216 B1
Madams St BOW E3 105 K3
Maddison Cl EFNCH N2 47 G5
TEDD TW11 174 A2
Maddocks Cl SCUP DA14 186 E2
Maddock Wy WALW SE17 122 C6
Maddox St CONDST W1S 9 K5
Madeira Av BMLY BR1 183 H4
Madeira Gv WFD IG8 53 G2
Madeira Rd MTCM CR4 194 E1
PLMGR N13 35 H6
STRHM/NOR SW16 179 K1
WAN E11 70 B6
Madeleine Cl CHDH RM6 73 J3
Madeley Rd EA W5 97 K6
Madeline Gv IL IG1 90 D3
Madeline Rd PGE/AN SE20 181 H3
Madge Gill Wy EHAM E6 89 J6
Madge Hl HNWL W7 * 96 E6
Madinah Rd HACK E8 86 C3
Madison Crs BXLYHN DA7 148 D1
Madison Gdns BXLYHN DA7 148 D1
Madras Pl HOLWY N7 85 G4
Madras Rd IL IG1 90 B2
Madrid Rd BARN SW13 138 D2
Madron St WALW SE17 123 F5
Mafeking Av BTFD TW8 117 F6
EHAM E6 107 H1
GNTH/NBYPK IG2 72 D4
Mafeking Rd CAN/RD E16 106 D3
EN EN1 24 B4
TOTM N17 50 C5
Magazine Ga BAY/PAD W2 * 8 D7
Magdala Av ARCH N19 66 C6
Magdala Rd ISLW TW7 136 B4
SAND/SEL CR2 211 K5
Magdalene Gdns EHAM E6 108 A3
Magdalen Rd
WAND/EARL SW18 160 B3
Magdalen St STHWK SE1 19 G1
Magdelan Gv ORP BR6 217 H2
Magee St LBTH SE11 122 B6
Magellan Pl POP/IOD E14 124 D5
Magnaville Rd BUSH WD23 28 E2
Magnet Rd WBLY HA9 61 K6
Magnin Cl HACK E8 86 C6
Magnolia Cl KUTN/CMB KT2 175 J2
LEY E10 69 J6
Magnolia Ct
KTN/HRWW/WS HA3 62 B4
Magnolia Gdns EDGW HA8 30 E6
Magnolia Pl CLAP SW4 * 141 K6
EA W5 * 97 K4
Magnolia Rd CHSWK W4 117 J6
Magnolia St WDR/YW UB7 112 A4
Magnolia Wy HOR/WEW KT19 206 E3
Magnolia Whf CHSWK W4 * 117 J6
Magpie Cl CDALE/KGS NW9 45 G5
EN EN1 24 C2
FSTGT E7 88 D3
Magpie Hall Cl HAYES BR2 200 D3
Magpie Hall La HAYES BR2 200 E3
Magpie Hall Rd STAN HA7 28 E4
Magpie Pl NWCR SE14 * 124 B6
Magri Wk WCHPL E1 104 E4
Maguire Dr RCHPK/HAM TW10 156 D6
Maguire St STHWK SE1 19 K2
Mahlon Av RSLP HA4 77 F3
Mahogany Cl
BERM/RHTH SE16 124 B1
Mahon Cl EN EN1 24 B2
Maida Av BAY/PAD W2 101 G4
CHING E4 37 K2
Maida Rd BELV DA17 129 H3
Maida V MV/WKIL W9 101 G2
STJWD NW8 2 A6
Maida Vale Rd DART DA1 170 D1
Maida Wy CHING E4 37 K2
Maiden Erlegh Av BXLY DA5 169 F3
Maiden La CAMTN NW1 84 D5
COVGDN WC2E 11 F6
DART DA1 150 D5
STHWK SE1 18 D1
Maiden Rd SRTFD E15 88 C5
Maidenstone Hl GNWCH SE10 145 F2
Maidstone Av CRW RM5 56 E5
Maidstone Buildings Ms
STHWK SE1 18 D1
Maidstone Rd FBAR/BDGN N11 48 D2
SCUP DA14 186 E2
Main Av EN EN1 24 B6
NTHWD HA6 26 B4
Main Barracks
WOOL/PLUM SE18 * 126 E5
Main Dr GFD/PVL UB6 * 97 G2
WBLY HA9 79 K1
Mainridge Rd CHST BR7 167 F6
Main Rd ORP BR6 * 217 J6
ROM RM1 75 H1
SCUP DA14 167 K5
STMC/STPC BR5 186 D4
SWLY BR8 203 K3
Main St FELT TW13 172 C1
Maise Webster Cl
STWL/WRAY TW19 * 152 A2
Maismore St PECK SE15 123 H6
The Maisonettes SUT SM1 * 208 D3
Maitland Cl GNWCH SE10 144 E1
HSLWW TW4 134 E4
WOT/HER KT12 188 D6
Maitland Park Rd HAMP NW3 83 K4
Maitland Park Vls HAMP NW3 83 K4
Maitland Rd PGE/AN SE20 182 A2
SRTFD E15 88 D4
Majendie Rd
WOOL/PLUM SE18 127 J5
Major Cl BRXN/ST SW9 142 C4
Major Rd BERM/RHTH SE16 * 123 H3
SRTFD E15 88 B3
Makepeace Av HGT N6 66 A6
Makepeace Rd NTHLT UB5 95 J1
WAN E11 70 E1
Makins St CHEL SW3 14 D7
Malabar St POP/IOD E14 124 D2
Malam Gdns POP/IOD E14 105 K6
Malan Sq RAIN RM13 93 K4
Malbrook Rd PUT/ROE SW15 138 E5
Malcolm Cl PGE/AN SE20 * 181 K3
Malcolm Ct STAN HA7 43 J1
Malcolm Crs HDN NW4 63 J3
Malcolm Dr SURB KT6 190 E5
Malcolm Pl BETH E2 104 E3
Malcolm Rd PGE/AN SE20 181 K3
SNWD SE25 197 H3
WCHPL E1 104 E3
WIM/MER SW19 177 H2
Malcolms Wy STHGT/OAK N14 * 22 C6
Malcolm Wy WAN E11 70 E2
Malden Av GFD/PVL UB6 78 E4
SNWD SE25 197 J1
Malden Green Av WPK KT4 192 D5
Malden Hl NWMAL KT3 192 C1
Malden Hill Gdns NWMAL KT3 176 C6
Malden Pk NWMAL KT3 192 C3
Malden Pl KTTN NW5 84 A3
Malden Rd CHEAM SM3 208 B2
KTTN NW5 83 K3
NWMAL KT3 192 C4
Malden Wy NWMAL KT3 192 A3
Maldon Cl CMBW SE5 * 143 F4
IS N1 85 J6
Maldon Rd ACT W3 98 E6
ED N9 36 B5
ROMW/RG RM7 74 E4
WLGTN SM6 210 B3
Maldon Wk WFD IG8 53 G2
Malet St GWRST WC1E 4 C7
Maley Av WNWD SE27 162 C4
Malford Gv SWFD E18 52 D6
Malfort Rd CMBW SE5 143 F4
Malham Cl FBAR/BDGN N11 48 A2
Malham Rd FSTH SE23 164 A3
Malham Ter UED N18 * 50 D2
Mallams Ms BRXN/ST SW9 142 B4
Mallard Cl BAR EN5 * 33 H1
DART DA1 151 J6
HNWL W7 115 K2
KIL/WHAMP NW6 100 E1
WHTN TW2 155 F2
Mallard Ct WALTH E17 * 52 A4
Mallard Pl TWK TW1 156 B5
WDGN N22 49 F5
Mallards Ct OXHEY WD19 27 K5
Mallards Rd BARK IG11 109 G3
WFD IG8 53 F3
Mallard Wk BECK BR3 198 A2
Mallard Wy CDALE/KGS NW9 62 E4
NTHWD HA6 40 A3
WLGTN SM6 210 C6
Mall Chambers KENS W8 * 119 K1
Mallet Dr NTHLT UB5 77 K3
Mallet Rd LEW SE13 165 G1
Malling Cl CROY/NA CR0 * 197 K3
Malling Gdns MRDN SM4 194 B3
Malling Wy HAYES BR2 199 J4
Mallinson Rd BTSEA SW11 140 D6
CROY/NA CR0 210 D1
Mallord St CHEL SW3 120 C6
Mallory Cl BROCKY SE4 144 B5
Mallory Gdns EBAR EN4 34 A2
Mallory St STJWD NW8 2 D7
Mallow Cl CROY/NA CR0 198 A5
Mallow Md MLHL NW7 46 C3
Mallow St FSBYE EC1V 6 E6
Mall Rd HMSMTH W6 118 E5
The Mall EA W5 98 A6
EMPK RM11 75 K5
KTN/HRWW/WS HA3 62 B3
MORT/ESHN SW14 137 K6
STHGT/OAK N14 34 E5
SURB KT6 190 E2
WHALL SW1A 16 C2
Mall Vls HMSMTH W6 * 118 E5
Malmains Cl BECK BR3 199 G2
Malmains Wy BECK BR3 199 F1
Malmesbury Cl PIN HA5 58 E1
Malmesbury Rd BOW E3 105 H2
CAN/RD E16 106 D4
MRDN SM4 194 B4
SWFD E18 52 D4
Malmesbury Ter CAN/RD E16 106 D4
Malmesbury West Est BOW E3 105 H2
Malory Cl BECK BR3 182 B5
Malpas Dr PIN HA5 59 H2
Malpas Rd BROCKY SE4 144 C3
DAGW RM9 91 K4
HACK E8 86 D4
Malta Rd LEY E10 69 J5
Malta St FSBYE EC1V 6 A6
Maltby Cl ORP BR6 202 B5
Maltby Dr EN EN1 24 D1
Maltby Rd CHSGTN KT9 206 C4
Maltby St STHWK SE1 19 J4
Malthouse Dr CHSWK W4 118 C6
FELT TW13 172 C1
Maltings Pl FUL/PGN SW6 140 A2
STHWK SE1 19 H2
The Maltings ORP BR6 202 A5
ROM RM1 75 H4
SNWD SE25 * 181 F6
Malting Wy ISLW TW7 136 A4
Malton Ms NKENS W10 * 100 C5
WOOL/PLUM SE18 127 K6
Malton Rd NKENS W10 100 C5
Malton St WOOL/PLUM SE18 127 K6
Maltravers St TPL/STR WC2R 11 H5
Malt St STHWK SE1 123 H6
Malva Cl WAND/EARL SW18 140 A6
Malvern Av BXLYHN DA7 149 F1
CHING E4 52 B3
RYLN/HDSTN HA2 77 J1
Malvern Cl BUSH WD23 28 C1
MTCM CR4 179 H6
NKENS W10 100 D4
SURB KT6 191 F5
Malvern Dr FELT TW13 172 C1
GDMY/SEVK IG3 91 F2
WFD IG8 53 G1
Malvern Gdns CRICK NW2 64 C6
KTN/HRWW/WS HA3 62 A1
LOU IG10 39 K1
Malvern Ms KIL/WHAMP NW6 100 E2
Malvern Pl MV/WKIL W9 * 100 D2
Malvern Rd CEND/HSY/T N8 49 G6
ALP/SUD HA0 97 K1
EHAM E6 89 J6
EMPK RM11 75 J3
HACK E8 86 C5
HPTN TW12 173 F4
HYS/HAR UB3 133 H1
KIL/WHAMP NW6 100 E2
ORP BR6 217 H2
SURB KT6 191 F6
THHTH CR7 196 B1
TOTM N17 50 C6
WAN E11 70 C6
Malvern Ter ED N9 36 B3
IS N1 85 G6
Malvern Wy WEA W13 97 H4
Malwood Rd BAL SW12 161 G1
Malyons Rd LEW SE13 144 E6
Malyons Ter LEW SE13 144 E6
Managers St POP/IOD E14 * 125 F1
Manaton Cl PECK SE15 143 J4
Manaton Crs STHL UB1 96 A5
Manbey Gv SRTFD E15 88 C4
Manbey Park Rd SRTFD E15 88 C4
Manbey Rd SRTFD E15 * 88 C4
Manbey St SRTFD E15 88 C4
Manbre Rd HMSMTH W6 119 F6
Manbrough Av EHAM E6 108 A2
Manchester Ct CAN/RD E16 107 F5
Manchester Dr NKENS W10 * 100 C3
Manchester Gv POP/IOD E14 125 F5
Manchester Ms MHST W1U 9 G2
Manchester Rd POP/IOD E14 125 F5
SEVS/STOTM N15 67 K3
THHTH CR7 180 D6
Manchester Sq MBLAR W1H 9 G3
Manchester St MHST W1U 9 G2
Manchester Wy DAGE RM10 * 92 D2
Manchuria Rd BTSEA SW11 161 F1
Manciple St STHWK SE1 19 F3
Mandalay Rd CLAP SW4 141 H6
Mandarin Wy YEAD UB4 95 H5
Mandela Cl WLSDN NW10 80 E5
Mandela Rd CAN/RD E16 106 E5
Mandela St BRXN/ST SW9 142 B1
CAMTN NW1 84 C6
Mandela Wy STHWK SE1 19 J7
Mandeville Cl WIM/MER SW19 177 H2
Mandeville Ct CHING E4 37 G6
Mandeville Dr SURB KT6 190 E5
Mandeville Pl MHST W1U 9 H3
Mandeville Rd ISLW TW7 136 B3
NTHLT UB5 78 A4
STHGT/OAK N14 34 B4
Mandeville St CLPT E5 87 G1
Mandrake Rd TOOT SW17 160 E5
Mandrake Wy SRTFD E15 * 88 C5
Mandrell Rd
BRXS/STRHM SW2 141 K6
Manette St LSQ/SEVD WC2H 10 D4
Manford Cross CHIG IG7 55 G1
Manford Wy CHIG IG7 54 E1
CHIG IG7 55 G1
Manfred Rd PUT/ROE SW15 139 J6
Manger Rd HOLWY N7 84 E4
Mangold Wy ERITHM DA18 128 E3
Manilla St POP/IOD E14 124 D2
Manister Rd ABYW SE2 128 B3
Manley Ct STNW/STAM N16 86 B1
Manley St CAMTN NW1 84 A6
Mann Cl CROY/NA CR0 211 J1
Manningford Cl FSBYE EC1V * 6 A4
Manning Gdns
KTN/HRWW/WS HA3 61 K4
Manning Pl RCHPK/HAM TW10 157 G1
Manning Rd DAGE RM10 92 C5
STMC/STPC BR5 202 E4
WALTH E17 69 G1
Manningtree Cl
WIM/MER SW19 159 H3
Manningtree Rd RSLP HA4 77 F2
Manningtree St WCHPL E1 104 C5
Mannin Rd CHDH RM6 73 H4
Mannock Ms SWFD E18 53 G4
Mannock Rd DART DA1 151 J4
WDGN N22 49 H6
Mann's Cl ISLW TW7 136 A6
Manns Rd EDGW HA8 44 C2
Manoel Rd WHTN TW2 155 H4
Manor Av BROCKY SE4 144 C3
HSLWW TW4 134 C4
NTHLT UB5 77 K5
Manorbrook BKHTH/KID SE3 145 K5
Manor Cl BAR EN5 20 C5
CDALE/KGS NW9 62 D2
DAGE RM10 93 F4
DART DA1 150 A5
MLHL NW7 * 45 F1
RDART DA2 170 D5
ROM RM1 75 J2
RSLP HA4 58 D5
THMD SE28 109 J5
WPK KT4 192 B5
Manor Cottages NTHWD HA6 40 D4
Manor Cottages Ap EFNCH N2 47 G5
Manor Ct ACT W3 * 117 H4
E/WMO/HCT KT8 * 189 F1
HRW HA1 * 61 F3
KUTN/CMB KT2 * 175 H4
WBLY HA9 80 B2
Manor Court Rd HNWL W7 96 E6
Manor Crs BRYLDS KT5 191 H3
Manor Cft EDGW HA8 * 44 C2
Manordene Cl THDIT KT7 190 B5
Manordene Rd THMD SE28 109 J5
Manor Dr BRYLDS KT5 191 H3
ESH/CLAY KT10 205 F1
FELT TW13 172 C1
HOR/WEW KT19 207 G4
MLHL NW7 45 F1
STHGT/OAK N14 34 B2
TRDG/WHET N20 33 J5
WBLY HA9 80 B2
Manor Dr North NWMAL KT3 192 A4
The Manor Dr WPK KT4 192 C5
Manor Est BERM/RHTH SE16 123 J4
Manor Farm Cl WPK KT4 192 B5
Manor Farm Dr CHING E4 38 C5
Manor Farm Rd ALP/SUD HA0 97 K1
STRHM/NOR SW16 180 B5
Manorfield Cl ARCH N19 84 C2
Manorfields Cl CHST BR7 186 A6
Manor Gdns ACT W3 117 H4
CLAP SW4 * 141 H3
HOLWY N7 84 E1
HPTN TW12 173 G3
RCH/KEW TW9 137 G5
RSLP HA4 77 G3
RYNPK SW20 177 J5
SAND/SEL CR2 212 B4
Manor Ga NTHLT UB5 77 J5
Manorgate Rd KUTN/CMB KT2 175 H4
Manor Gv BECK BR3 182 E5
PECK SE15 123 K6
RCH/KEW TW9 137 H5
Manor Hall Av HDN NW4 46 B5
Manor Hall Dr HDN NW4 46 B5
Manor Hall Gdns LEY E10 69 J5
Manor House Dr
KIL/WHAMP NW6 82 B5
Manor House Wy ISLW TW7 136 C4
Manor La FELT TW13 153 K4
HYS/HAR UB3 113 G6
LEW SE13 145 H6
SUN TW16 172 A5
SUT SM1 209 G3
Manor Lane Ter LEW SE13 145 H6
Manor Ms KIL/WHAMP NW6 100 E1
Manor Mt FSTH SE23 163 K3
Manor Pde HRW HA1 * 61 F3
STNW/STAM N16 * 68 B6
Manor Pk CHST BR7 185 J5
LEW SE13 145 G6
RCH/KEW TW9 137 G5
Manor Park Cl WWKM BR4 198 E5
Manor Park Crs EDGW HA8 44 C2
Manor Park Dr
RYLN/HDSTN HA2 42 B6
Manor Park Gdns EDGW HA8 44 C1
Manor Park Rd CHST BR7 185 H4
EFNCH N2 47 G6
MNPK E12 89 H2
SUT SM1 209 G3
WLSDN NW10 81 H6
WWKM BR4 198 E5
Manor Pl CHST BR7 185 J5
EBED/NFELT TW14 153 K3
MTCM CR4 179 H6
SUT SM1 209 F3
WALW SE17 122 D5
Manor Rd BAR EN5 20 C5
BARK IG11 91 F4
BECK BR3 182 D5
BELMT SM2 208 D5
BFN/LL DA15 168 A5
BXLY DA5 169 J3
CAN/RD E16 106 C4
CHDH RM6 73 K3
CHIG IG7 54 A2
DAGE RM10 92 E4
DART DA1 150 B5
E/WMO/HCT KT8 189 J1
ENC/FH EN2 23 K3
ERITH DA8 130 C6
HRW HA1 61 G3
HYS/HAR UB3 94 E5
LEY E10 69 J4
LOU IG10 39 F1
MTCM CR4 179 H6
RCH/KEW TW9 137 G4
ROM RM1 75 J2
RSLP HA4 58 B5
RYNPK SW20 177 J5
SNWD SE25 197 H1
STNW/STAM N16 68 A5
TEDD TW11 174 B1
TOTM N17 50 C4
WALTH E17 51 G5
WDGN N22 48 E2
WEA W13 97 G6
WHTN TW2 155 H4
WLGTN SM6 210 B2
WWKM BR4 198 E6
Manor Rd North
ESH/CLAY KT10 190 A6
ESH/CLAY KT10 205 F1
WLGTN SM6 210 B2
Manor Rd South
ESH/CLAY KT10 204 E3
Manorside BAR EN5 20 C5
Manor Sq BCTR RM8 73 J6
Manor V BTFD TW8 116 D5
Manor Vw FNCH N3 47 F5
Manor Wy BECK BR3 182 D6
BKHTH/KID SE3 145 K5
BXLY DA5 169 H3
BXLYHN DA7 150 A4
CDALE/KGS NW9 63 G1
CHING E4 38 B6
Manorway EN EN1 36 A2
Manor Wy HAYES BR2 200 D3
MTCM CR4 179 H6
NWDGN UB2 114 C4
RAIN RM13 111 G3
RSLP HA4 58 D5
RYLN/HDSTN HA2 60 B1
SAND/SEL CR2 212 A4
STMC/STPC BR5 201 H1
Manorway WFD IG8 53 G1
Manor Wy WPK KT4 192 B5
The Manor Wy WLGTN SM6 210 B2
Manresa Rd CHEL SW3 120 C5
Mansard Beeches TOOT SW17 179 F1
Mansard Cl HCH RM12 75 J6
PIN HA5 41 H6
Manse Cl HYS/HAR UB3 113 G6
Mansel Gv WALTH E17 51 J4
Mansell Rd ACT W3 118 A1
GFD/PVL UB6 96 B4
Mansell St WCHPL E1 13 K4
Mansel Rd WIM/MER SW19 177 H2
Mansergh Cl CHARL SE7 146 D1
Manse Rd STNW/STAM N16 86 B1
Manser Rd RAIN RM13 111 G2
Mansfield Av EBAR EN4 33 K1
RSLP HA4 59 F5
SEVS/STOTM N15 67 K1
Mansfield Cl ED N9 36 C1
STMC/STPC BR5 202 E4
Mansfield Dr YEAD UB4 94 C3
Mansfield Hl CHING E4 37 K3
Mansfield Ms CAVSQ/HST W1G 9 J2
Mansfield Rd ACT W3 98 D3
CHSGTN KT9 205 J3
HAMP NW3 83 K3
IL IG1 72 A6
SAND/SEL CR2 211 K4
WALTH E17 69 H1
WAN E11 71 F3
Mansfield St CAVSQ/HST W1G 9 J2
Mansford St BETH E2 104 D2
Manship Rd MTCM CR4 179 F4
Mansion Cl BRXN/ST SW9 142 B2
Mansion Gdns HAMP NW3 83 F1
Mansion House Pl
MANHO EC4N * 12 E4
The Mansions ECT SW5 * 120 A5
Manson Ms SKENS SW7 * 120 B4

Manson Pl SKENS SW7 14 A7
Manstead Gdns CHDH RM6 73 J4
RAIN RM13 111 K5
Manston Av NWDGN UB2 115 F4
Manston Cl PGE/AN SE20 181 K4
Manstone Rd CRICK NW2 82 C3
Manston Gv KUTN/CMB KT2 174 E1
Manston Wy HCH RM12 93 K4
Manthorpe Rd
WOOL/PLUM SE18 127 H5
Mantilla Rd TOOT SW17 161 F6
Mantle Rd BROCKY SE4 144 B4
Mantlet Cl STRHM/NOR SW16 179 H3
Mantle Wy SRTFD E15 88 C5
Manton Av HNWL W7 116 A2
Manton Cl HYS/HAR UB3 94 C6
Manton Rd ABYW SE2 128 B4
PEND EN3 25 K1
Mantua St BTSEA SW11 140 C4
Mantus Cl WCHPL E1 104 E3
Mantus Rd WCHPL E1 104 E3
Manus Wy TRDG/WHET N20 33 G4
Manville Gdns TOOT SW17 161 G5
Manville Rd TOOT SW17 161 F4
Manwood Rd BROCKY SE4 164 C1
Manwood St CAN/RD E16 126 E1
Many Gates BAL SW12 161 G4
Mapesbury Ms CDALE/KGS NW9 63 J5
Mapesbury Rd CRICK NW2 82 C4
Mapeshill Pl CRICK NW2 82 A4
Mape St BETH E2 104 D3
Maple Av ACT W3 118 B1
CHING E4 51 H2
RYLN/HDSTN HA2 60 B6
Maple Cl BARK/HLT IG6 54 E2
BKHH IG9 39 H5
CLAP SW4 161 J1
FNCH N3 46 E2
HCH RM12 93 K1
HPTN TW12 172 E2
MTCM CR4 179 G4
RSLP HA4 59 F3
STMC/STPC BR5 201 J2
STNW/STAM N16 68 C3
YEAD UB4 95 H2
Maple Ct HACK E8 * 86 C4
NWMAL KT3 176 A6
Maple Crs BFN/LL DA15 168 B1
Maplecroft Cl EHAM E6 107 H5
Mapledale Av CROY/NA CR0 212 D1
Mapledene Est HACK E8 * 86 C5
Mapledene Rd HACK E8 86 B5
Maple Gdns ASHF TW15 152 B4
EDGW HA8 45 G3
Maple Gv BTFD TW8 136 C1
CDALE/KGS NW9 62 E4
EA W5 116 E3
STHL UB1 95 K4
Maplehurst Cl KUT/HW KT1 191 F1
Maple Leaf Dr BFN/LL DA15 168 A3
Mapleleaf Gdns BARK/HLT IG6 54 B6
Maple Leaf Sq
BERM/RHTH SE16 * 124 A2
Maple Ms KIL/WHAMP NW6 * 101 F1
STRHM/NOR SW16 180 A1
Maple Pl FITZ W1T 10 B1
TOTM N17 50 C3
WDR/YW UB7 112 C1
Maple Rd DART DA1 171 F3
PGE/AN SE20 181 K3
SURB KT6 190 E2
WAN E11 70 C3
YEAD UB4 95 G2
Maples Pl WCHPL E1 * 104 D4
Maplestead Rd
BRXS/STRHM SW2 162 A2
DAGW RM9 91 H6
The Maples ESH/CLAY KT10 * 205 G5
KUT/HW KT1 * 174 D5
Maple St BETH E2 104 C1
FITZ W1T 10 A1
ROMW/RG RM7 74 E1
Maplethorpe Rd THHTH CR7 196 B1
Mapleton Cl HAYES BR2 199 K2
Mapleton Crs PEND EN3 24 E1
WAND/EARL SW18 160 A1
Mapleton Rd CHING E4 38 A6
EN EN1 24 D3
WAND/EARL SW18 159 K1
Maple Tree Pl BKHTH/KID SE3 146 D4
Maple Wk NKENS W10 * 100 B3
Maple Wy FELT TW13 153 K5
Maplin Cl WCHMH N21 35 F1
Maplin Rd CAN/RD E16 106 E5
Maplin St BOW E3 105 H2
Mapperley Dr WFD IG8 52 C3
Marabou Cl MNPK E12 89 J3
Maran Wy ERITHM DA18 128 E3
Marathon Wy THMD SE28 128 A2
Marban Rd MV/WKIL W9 100 D2
Marble Cl ACT W3 117 J1
Marble Dr CRICK NW2 64 B5
Marble Hill Cl TWK TW1 156 C2
Marble Hill Gdns TWK TW1 156 C2
Marble Quay WAP E1W 13 K7
Marbrook Ct LEE/GVPK SE12 166 B5
Marcella Rd BRXN/ST SW9 142 B3
Marcellina Wy ORP BR6 216 E1
Marcet Rd DART DA1 151 F6
Marchant Rd WAN E11 70 B6
Marchant St NWCR SE14 124 B6
Marchbank Rd WKENS W14 119 J6
Marchmont Rd
RCHPK/HAM TW10 137 G6
WLGTN SM6 210 C6
Marchmont St BMSBY WC1N 4 E6
March Rd TWK TW1 156 A2
Marchside Cl HEST TW5 134 C2
Marchwood Cl CMBW SE5 143 F1
Marchwood Crs EA W5 97 K5
Marcia Rd STHWK SE1 19 H7
Marcilly Rd WAND/EARL SW18 140 C6
Marconi Pl FBAR/BDGN N11 34 B6
Marconi Rd LEY E10 69 J5
Marconi Wy STHL UB1 96 B5
Marcon Pl HACK E8 86 D4
Marco Rd HMSMTH W6 118 E3
Marcus Garvey Ms EDUL SE22 163 J1
Marcus Garvey Wy HNHL SE24 142 B5
Marcus Rd DART DA1 170 D2
Marcus St SRTFD E15 88 C6
WAND/EARL SW18 160 A1
Marcus Ter WAND/EARL SW18 160 A1
Mardale Dr CDALE/KGS NW9 63 F2
Mardell Rd CROY/NA CR0 198 A2
Marden Av HAYES BR2 199 K3
Marden Crs BXLY DA5 149 K6
CROY/NA CR0 196 A3
Marden Rd CROY/NA CR0 196 A3
ROM RM1 75 G3
TOTM N17 50 A5
Marden Sq BERM/RHTH SE16 123 J3
Marder Rd WEA W13 116 B2
Mardyke Cl RAIN RM13 110 E1
Marechal Niel Av BFN/LL DA15 167 J5
Marechal Niel Pde
SCUP DA14 * 167 J5
Maresfield CROY/NA CR0 212 A1
Maresfield Gdns HAMP NW3 83 G3
Mare St HACK E8 86 D4
Marfield Cl WPK KT4 192 D5
Marfleet Cl CAR SM5 194 D6
Margaret Av CHING E4 37 K2
Margaret Bondfield Av
BARK IG11 91 G5
Margaret Cl GPK RM2 75 K2
Margaret Gardner Dr
ELTH/MOT SE9 166 E4
Margaret Ingram Cl
FUL/PGN SW6 * 119 J6
Margaret Lockwood Cl
KUT/HW KT1 * 191 G1
Margaret Rd BXLY DA5 168 E1
EBAR EN4 21 H6
GPK RM2 75 K2
STNW/STAM N16 * 68 B5
Margaret St CAVSQ/HST W1G 9 K3
GTPST W1W 10 A3
Margaretta Ter CHEL SW3 120 D6
Margaretting Rd MNPK E12 71 G6
Margaret Wy REDBR IG4 71 J3
Margate Rd BRXS/STRHM SW2 141 K6
Margeholes OXHEY WD19 27 J4
Margery Park Rd FSTGT E7 88 E4
Margery Rd BCTR RM8 91 K1
Margery St CLKNW EC1R 5 J5
Margin Dr WIM/MER SW19 177 G1
Margravine Gdns
HMSMTH W6 119 G5
Margravine Rd HMSMTH W6 119 G6
Marguerite Vls RYNPK SW20 * 176 E3
Marham Gdns MRDN SM4 194 B3
WAND/EARL SW18 160 D3
Maria Cl STHWK SE1 123 H4
Marian Cl YEAD UB4 95 H3
Marian Pl BETH E2 104 D1
Marian Rd STRHM/NOR SW16 179 H4
Marian Sq BETH E2 104 D1
Marian St BETH E2 * 104 D1
Marian Wy WLSDN NW10 81 H5
Maria Ter WCHPL E1 105 F4
Maria Theresa Cl NWMAL KT3 192 A2
Maricas Av KTN/HRWW/WS HA3 42 D4
Marie Curie CMBW SE5 * 143 F2
Marie Lloyd Wk HACK E8 * 86 C4
Mariette Wy WLGTN SM6 210 E6
Marigold Aly STHWK SE1 12 A6
Marigold Cl STHL UB1 95 J6
Marigold Rd TOTM N17 50 E4
Marigold St BERM/RHTH SE16 123 J2
Marigold Wy CROY/NA CR0 198 A5
Marina Ap YEAD UB4 95 J4
Marina Av NWMAL KT3 192 E3
Marina Dr DART DA1 171 K3
WELL DA16 147 K3
Marina Gdns ROMW/RG RM7 74 D2
Marina Wy TEDD TW11 174 E3
Marine Ct PUR RM19 131 J4
Marine Dr BARK IG11 109 H2
WOOL/PLUM SE18 126 E4
Marinefield Rd FUL/PGN SW6 140 A3
Mariner Gdns
RCHPK/HAM TW10 156 C5
Mariner Rd MNPK E12 90 A2
Mariners Ms POP/IOD E14 125 G4
Marine St BERM/RHTH SE16 123 H3
Marion Cl BARK/HLT IG6 54 D3
Marion Crs STMC/STPC BR5 202 C2
Marion Gv WFD IG8 52 C1
Marion Ms DUL SE21 162 E5
Marion Rd MLHL NW7 45 J1
THHTH CR7 196 D2
Marischal Rd LEW SE13 145 G4
Maritime Quay POP/IOD E14 124 D5
Maritime St BOW E3 105 H3
Marius Rd TOOT SW17 161 F4
Marjorie Gv BTSEA SW11 140 E5
Mark Av CHING E4 37 K1
Mark Cl BXLYHN DA7 149 F2
HAYES BR2 215 J2
STHL UB1 115 F1
Markeston Gn OXHEY WD19 27 H6
Market Chambers
ENC/FH EN2 * 23 K4
Market Est HOLWY N7 84 E4
Market La EDGW HA8 44 E4
Market Link ROM RM1 75 G2
Market Meadow
STMC/STPC BR5 202 D1
Market Ms MYFR/PICC W1J 15 J1
Market Pde BMLY BR1 * 183 K4
ED N9 * 36 C4
EW KT17 * 207 H6
FELT TW13 * 154 D4
LEY E10 * 69 K3
SCUP DA14 * 168 B6
SNWD SE25 * 197 H1
STNW/STAM N16 * 68 C5
WALTH E17 * 51 H6
Market Pl ACT W3 117 K1
BERM/RHTH SE16 * 123 H4
BTFD TW8 136 D1
BXLYHS DA6 149 H5
DART DA1 171 H2
EFNCH N2 47 J6
GTPST W1W 10 A3
KUT/HW KT1 * 174 E5
ROM RM1 75 G2
Market Rd HOLWY N7 84 E4
RCH/KEW TW9 137 H4
Market Sq ED N9 36 D4
Market St EHAM E6 107 K1
WOOL/PLUM SE18 127 F4
Market Ter BTFD TW8 * 117 F6
The Market CAR SM5 * 194 B5
COVGDN WC2E 11 F5
Market Yard Ms STHWK SE1 19 G4
Markfield Gdns CHING E4 37 K2
Markfield Rd SEVS/STOTM N15 68 C1
Markham Pl CHEL SW3 120 E5
Markham Sq CHEL SW3 120 E5
Markham St CHEL SW3 120 D5
Markhole Cl HPTN TW12 172 E3
Markhouse Av WALTH E17 69 G3
Markhouse Rd WALTH E17 69 H3
Mark La MON EC3R 13 H5
Markmanor Av WALTH E17 69 G4
Mark Rd WDGN N22 49 H5
Marksbury Av RCH/KEW TW9 137 H4
Marks Rd ROMW/RG RM7 74 E2
Markstone Ter ORP BR6 * 202 B4
Mark St SDTCH EC2A 7 G6
SRTFD E15 88 C5
Mark Ter RYNPK SW20 * 177 F3
Markwade Cl MNPK E12 71 H5
The Markway SUN TW16 172 B5
Markwell Cl SYD SE26 163 J6
Markyate Rd BCTR RM8 91 J3
Marlands Rd CLAY IG5 53 K6
Marlborogh Rd ISLW TW7 136 C1
Marlborough Av EDGW HA8 30 D5
HACK E8 86 C6
RSLP HA4 58 A3
STHGT/OAK N14 34 C5
Marlborough Cl ORP BR6 202 A4
TRDG/WHET N20 33 K5
WALW SE17 18 B7
WIM/MER SW19 178 D2
Marlborough Ct REGST W1B * 10 A5
Marlborough Crs CHSWK W4 118 B3
HYS/HAR UB3 133 G1
Marlborough Dr CLAY IG5 53 J6
Marlborough Gdns
TRDG/WHET N20 33 K5
Marlborough Ga BAY/PAD W2 8 A6
Marlborough Gv STHWK SE1 123 H5
Marlborough Hl HRW HA1 60 E1
STJWD NW8 83 G6
Marlborough La CHARL SE7 126 B6
Marlborough Ms
BRXS/STRHM SW2 142 A5
Marlborough Pde FSBYPK N4 * 67 J5
Marlborough Park Av
BFN/LL DA15 168 B3
Marlborough Pl STJWD NW8 101 G1
Marlborough Rd ARCH N19 66 E6
BCTR RM8 91 J2
CHING E4 51 K2
CHSWK W4 117 K5
DART DA1 171 F1
EA W5 116 E2
ED N9 36 B3
FELT TW13 154 C4
FSTGT E7 89 G5
HAYES BR2 200 B1
HPTN TW12 173 F2
NWDGN UB2 114 B3
RCHPK/HAM TW10 157 G1
ROMW/RG RM7 74 C1
SAND/SEL CR2 211 J5
SRTFD E15 * 88 C2
SUT SM1 208 E1
SWFD E18 52 E6
WDGN N22 49 F3
WELL DA16 148 E4
WHALL SW1A 16 B2
WIM/MER SW19 178 D2
WOOL/PLUM SE18 127 G3
Marlborough St CHEL SW3 14 C7
Marlborough Yd ARCH N19 66 D6
Marler Rd FSTH SE23 164 C3
Marley Av BXLYHN DA7 128 E6
Marley Cl GFD/PVL UB6 96 A2
SEVS/STOTM N15 67 H1
Marley Rd BERM/RHTH SE16 * 124 A4
Marlingdene Cl HPTN TW12 173 F2
Marlings Cl CHST BR7 201 K1
Marlings Park Av CHST BR7 201 K1
Marlins Cl SUT SM1 * 209 G3
Marlins Meadow WATW WD18 26 B1
The Marlins NTHWD HA6 40 D2
Marloes Cl ALP/SUD HA0 79 K2
Marloes Rd KENS W8 120 A3
Marlow Av PUR RM19 131 K4
Marlow Cl PGE/AN SE20 181 J6
Marlow Ct CDALE/KGS NW9 45 H6
Marlow Crs TWK TW1 156 A1
Marlow Dr CHEAM SM3 208 B1
Marlowe Cl BARK/HLT IG6 54 C4
CHST BR7 185 J3
Marlowe Rd WALTH E17 70 A1
Marlowe Sq MTCM CR4 195 H1
The Marlowes DART DA1 150 A5
STJWD NW8 83 H6
Marlowe Wy CROY/NA CR0 195 K6
Marlow Gdns HYS/HAR UB3 113 G3
Marlow Rd EHAM E6 107 K2
NWDGN UB2 114 E3
PGE/AN SE20 181 J6
Marlow Wy BERM/RHTH SE16 124 A2
Marl Rd WAND/EARL SW18 140 A5
Marlton St GNWCH SE10 125 J5
Marlwood Cl BFN/LL DA15 167 K4
Marlyon Rd BARK/HLT IG6 55 H1
Marmadon Rd
WOOL/PLUM SE18 128 A4
Marmion Ap CHING E4 37 J6
Marmion Av CHING E4 37 H6
Marmion Cl CHING E4 37 H6
Marmion Ms BTSEA SW11 * 141 F4
Marmion Rd BTSEA SW11 141 F5
Marmont Rd PECK SE15 143 H2
Marmora Rd EDUL SE22 163 K1
Marmot Rd HSLWW TW4 134 C4
Marne Av FBAR/BDGN N11 34 B6
WELL DA16 148 B4
Marnell Wy HSLWW TW4 134 C4
Marne St NKENS W10 100 C2
Marney Rd BTSEA SW11 141 F5
Marnfield Crs
BRXS/STRHM SW2 162 A3
Marnham Av CRICK NW2 82 C2
Marnham Crs GFD/PVL UB6 96 B1
Marnham Cresent
GFD/PVL UB6 96 B1
Marnock Rd BROCKY SE4 144 C6
Maroon St POP/IOD E14 105 G4
Maroons Wy CAT SE6 182 D1
Marquess Rd IS N1 85 K4
Marquess Rd North IS N1 85 J4
Marquess Rd South IS N1 * 85 J4
Marquis Cl ALP/SUD HA0 80 B5
Marquis Rd CAMTN NW1 84 D4
FSBYPK N4 67 F5
WDGN N22 49 F2
Marrabon Cl BFN/LL DA15 168 B3
Marrick Cl PUT/ROE SW15 138 D5
Married Quarters EDGW HA8 * 44 D3
Marrilyne Av PEND EN3 25 H1
Marriner Ct HYS/HAR UB3 * 94 C6
Marriot Rd MUSWH N10 47 K4
Marriott Cl EBED/NFELT TW14 153 G1
Marriott Rd BAR EN5 20 B4
DART DA1 171 K2
FSBYPK N4 67 F5
SRTFD E15 88 C6
Marriotts Cl CDALE/KGS NW9 63 H3
Marriotts Yd BAR EN5 * 20 B4
Marryat Cl HSLWW TW4 134 E5
Marryat Pl WIM/MER SW19 159 H6
Marryat Rd WIM/MER SW19 177 G1
Marsala Rd LEW SE13 144 E5
Marsden Rd ED N9 36 D4
PECK SE15 143 G4
Marsden St KTTN NW5 84 A4
Marsden Wy ORP BR6 217 F2
Marshall Cl FBAR/BDGN N11 34 B6
HRW HA1 60 D4
HSLWW TW4 134 E6
WAND/EARL SW18 160 B1
Marshall Dr YEAD UB4 94 D4
Marshall Est MLHL NW7 * 31 J6
Marshall Rd LEY E10 87 K2
TOTM N17 49 K4
Marshalls Dr ROM RM1 57 G6
Marshalls Gv
WOOL/PLUM SE18 126 D4
Marshall's Pl BERM/RHTH SE16 19 K5
Marshalls Rd ROMW/RG RM7 75 F1
SUT SM1 209 F2
Marshall St SOHO/CST W1F 10 B4
Marshalsea Rd STHWK SE1 18 D2
Marsham Cl CHST BR7 * 185 G1
Marsham St WEST SW1P 16 E7
Marsh Av MTCM CR4 178 E5
Marshbrook Cl BKHTH/KID SE3 146 C4
Marsh Cl MLHL NW7 31 H5
Marsh Dr CDALE/KGS NW9 63 H3
Marsh Farm Rd WHTN TW2 156 A3
Marshfield St POP/IOD E14 125 F3
Marshgate La SRTFD E15 87 K6
Marsh Green Rd DAGE RM10 92 C6
Marsh Hl HOM E9 87 G3
Marsh La LEY E10 69 H6
MLHL NW7 31 G5
STAN HA7 43 K2
TOTM N17 50 D3
Marsh Rd ALP/SUD HA0 97 K2
PIN HA5 59 K1
Marshside Cl ED N9 36 E4
Marsh St DART DA1 151 K3
POP/IOD E14 * 124 E4
Marsh Ter STMC/STPC BR5 * 202 E1
Marsh Wall POP/IOD E14 124 D2
Marsh Wy RAIN RM13 111 F2
RAIN RM13 111 F5
Marsland Cl WALW SE17 122 D5
Marston Av CHSGTN KT9 206 A4
DAGE RM10 92 C1
Marston Cl DAGE RM10 92 C1
KIL/WHAMP NW6 83 G5
Marston Ct WOT/HER KT12 * 188 B5
Marston Rd CLAY IG5 53 J5
TEDD TW11 174 C1
Marston Wy NRWD SE19 180 C3
Marsworth Av PIN HA5 41 H4
Marsworth Cl WATW WD18 * 26 C1
YEAD UB4 95 J4
Martaban Rd STNW/STAM N16 68 A6
Martara Ms WALW SE17 122 D5
Martello St HACK E8 86 D5
Martell Rd DUL SE21 162 E5
Martel Pl HACK E8 86 B4
Marten Rd WALTH E17 51 J5
Martens Av BXLYHN DA7 149 K5
Martens Cl BXLYHN DA7 149 K5
Martham Cl BARK/HLT IG6 54 B4
THMD SE28 109 K6
Martha Rd SRTFD E15 88 D4
Martha's Buildings FSBYE EC1V 6 E6
Martha St WCHPL E1 104 E5
Marthorne Crs
KTN/HRWW/WS HA3 42 D5
Martin Bowes Rd
ELTH/MOT SE9 146 E4
Martin Cl ED N9 37 F3
Martin Crs CROY/NA CR0 196 A5
Martindale MORT/ESHN SW14 137 K6
Martindale Av CAN/RD E16 106 E6
ORP BR6 217 G3
Martindale Rd BAL SW12 161 G2
HSLWW TW4 134 D5
Martin Dene BXLYHS DA6 149 G6
Martin Dr NTHLT UB5 77 K3
RAIN RM13 111 K3
Martineau Cl ESH/CLAY KT10 204 D2
Martineau Dr TWK TW1 136 C5
Martineau Rd HBRY N5 85 H2
Martineau St WCHPL E1 104 E6
Martingales Cl
RCHPK/HAM TW10 156 E5
Martin Gdns BCTR RM8 91 J2
Martin Gv MRDN SM4 177 K6
Martin La CANST EC4R 13 F5
Martin Ri BXLYHS DA6 149 G6
Martin Rd BCTR RM8 91 J2
RDART DA2 171 F5
Martins Cl STMC/STPC BR5 186 E6
WWKM BR4 199 G6
Martins Mt BAR EN5 20 E5
Martins Pl THMD SE28 127 K1
Martin's Rd HAYES BR2 183 H5
The Martins SYD SE26 181 J1
WBLY HA9 * 80 B1
Martin St THMD SE28 127 K1
Martins Wk MUSWH N10 * 48 A4
THMD SE28 127 K1
Martin Wy MRDN SM4 177 H6
Martlet Gv NTHLT UB5 95 H2
Martlett Ct HOL/ALD WC2B 11 F4
Martley Dr GNTH/NBYPK IG2 72 B2
Martock Cl KTN/HRWW/WS HA3 61 G1
Martock Gdns FBAR/BDGN N11 47 K1
Marton Cl CAT SE6 164 D5
Marton Rd STNW/STAM N16 * 68 A6
Martys Yd HAMP NW3 * 83 H2
Marvell Av YEAD UB4 94 E4
Marvels Cl LEE/GVPK SE12 166 A4
Marvels La LEE/GVPK SE12 166 B5
Marville Rd FUL/PGN SW6 139 J1
Marvin St HACK E8 * 86 D4
Marwell Cl ROM RM1 75 J3
WWKM BR4 199 J6
Marwood Cl WELL DA16 148 C4
Marwood Dr MLHL NW7 46 B3
Mary Adelaide Cl
PUT/ROE SW15 158 B6
Mary Ann Buildings DEPT SE8 124 D6
Maryat Sq FUL/PGN SW6 139 H2
Maryatt Av RYLN/HDSTN HA2 60 B6
Marybank WOOL/PLUM SE18 126 E4
Mary Cl KTN/HRWW/WS HA3 62 B1
Mary Datchelor Cl CMBW SE5 142 E2
Maryfield Cl BXLY DA5 170 B5
Mary Gn STJWD NW8 * 83 F6
Maryland Pk SRTFD E15 88 C3
Maryland Rd MV/WKIL W9 100 E3
SRTFD E15 88 B3
THHTH CR7 180 C4
WDGN N22 49 G2
Maryland Sq SRTFD E15 88 C3
Marylands Rd MV/WKIL W9 100 E3
Maryland St SRTFD E15 88 B3
Maryland Wk IS N1 * 85 J6
Mary Lawrencson Pl
BKHTH/KID SE3 145 J1
Marylebone F/O BAY/PAD W2 8 C2
Marylebone High St
CAVSQ/HST W1G 9 H2
Marylebone La MHST W1U 9 H3
Marylebone Ms CAVSQ/HST W1G 9 H2
Marylebone Pas GTPST W1W 10 B3
Marylebone Rd CAMTN NW1 8 D1
Marylebone St CAVSQ/HST W1G 9 H2
Marylee Wy LBTH SE11 17 H7
Maryon Gv CHARL SE7 126 D4
Maryon Ms HAMP NW3 83 J2
Maryon Rd CHARL SE7 126 D4
Mary Peters Dr GFD/PVL UB6 78 D3
Mary Pl NTGHL W11 100 C6
Mary Rose Cl HPTN TW12 173 F4
Maryrose Wy TRDG/WHET N20 33 H3
Mary Seacole Cl HACK E8 86 B6
Mary's Ter TWK TW1 156 B2
Mary St CAN/RD E16 106 D4
IS N1 6 D1
Mary Ter CAMTN NW1 3 K1
Mary Wy OXHEY WD19 27 G6
Masbro' Rd WKENS W14 119 G3
Mascalls Rd CHARL SE7 126 B6
Mascotts Cl CRICK NW2 81 K1
Masefield Av STAN HA7 43 F1
STHL UB1 96 A6
Masefield Cl ERITH DA8 150 C2
HARH RM3 57 K4
Masefield Crs STHGT/OAK N14 22 C6
Masefield Gdns EHAM E6 108 A3
Masefield La YEAD UB4 95 F3
Masefield Rd HPTN TW12 154 E6
Masefield Vw ORP BR6 216 C1
Masefield Wy
STWL/WRAY TW19 152 C3
Mashie Rd ACT W3 99 G5
Mashiters Hl ROM RM1 57 F4
Mashiters Wk ROM RM1 57 G6
Maskall Cl BRXS/STRHM SW2 * 162 B3
Maskell Rd TOOT SW17 160 B5
Maskelyne Cl BTSEA SW11 140 D2
Mason Cl BERM/RHTH SE16 123 H5
BXLYHN DA7 149 J4
CAN/RD E16 106 E6
HPTN TW12 172 E4
RYNPK SW20 177 G4
Mason Ct WBLY HA9 * 62 C6
Mason Rd SUT SM1 209 F3
WFD IG8 38 C6
Mason's Arms Ms CONDST W1S * 9 K4
Mason's Av CITYW EC2V 12 E3
CROY/NA CR0 211 J2
HRW HA1 61 F2
KTN/HRWW/WS HA3 42 E6
Masons Ct EW KT17 * 207 J6
Masons Hl HAYES BR2 183 K6
WOOL/PLUM SE18 127 G4
Mason's Pl FSBYE EC1V 6 B4
MTCM CR4 178 E4
Mason St WALW SE17 19 F7
Masons Yd FSBYE EC1V 6 C5
STJS SW1Y 10 B7
Massey Cl FBAR/BDGN N11 48 B1
Massie Rd HACK E8 86 C4
Massingberd Wy TOOT SW17 161 G6
Massinger St WALW SE17 19 G7
Massingham St WCHPL E1 105 F3
Masson Av RSLP HA4 77 G4
Masterman Rd EHAM E6 107 J2

Masters CI STRHM/NOR SW16....179 H2
Masters Dr BERM/RHTH SE16....123 J1
Master's St WCHPL E1 ....105 F4
Mast House Ter
  POP/IOD E14 ....124 D4
Masthouse Ter POP/IOD E14....124 D4
Mastmaker Rd POP/IOD E14.....124 D2
Mast Quay WOOL/PLUM SE18....126 E3
Maswell Park Crs HSLW TW5....135 H6
Maswell Park Rd HSLW TW5.....135 G6
Matcham Rd WAN E11 ....88 C1
Matchless Dr
  WOOL/PLUM SE18 ....147 F1
Matfield CI HAYES BR2 ....199 E3
Matfield Rd BELV DA17 ....129 H6
Matham Gv EDUL SE22.........143 G5
Matham Rd E/WMO/HCT KT8.....189 J2
Matheson Rd WKENS W14.......119 J4
Mathews Av EHAM E6 ....108 A1
Mathews Park Av SRTFD E15....88 D4
Mathews Yd LSQ/SEVD WC2H *...10 E5
Mathieson Ct NRWD SE19......180 E3
Matilda St IS N1 ....85 F6
Matlock CI BAR EN5 ....20 B6
  HNHL SE24 ....142 D5
Matlock Crs CHEAM SM3.......208 C2
  OXHEY WD19 ....27 G5
Matlock Gdns CHEAM SM3......208 C2
Matlock PI CHEAM SM3........208 C2
Matlock Rd LEY E10...........70 A3
Matlock St POP/IOD E14......105 G5
Matlock Wy NWMAL KT3........176 A4
Matthew CI NKENS W10 *......100 B3
Matthew Ct MTCM CR4.........195 J2
Matthew Rd GFD/PVL UB6......78 D3
Matthews St BTSEA SW11 *....140 E3
Matthias Rd STNW/STAM N16...85 K5
Mattingly Wy PECK SE15......143 G1
Mattison Rd FSBYPK N4........67 G3
Mattock La WEA W13..........116 D1
Maud Cashmore Wy
  WOOL/PLUM SE18 ....126 E3
Maude Rd CMBW SE5...........143 F5
  WALTH E17.................69 G2
Maudesville Cottages
  WALTH W7 ....115 K1
Maude Ter WALTH E17..........69 G2
Maud Gdns BARK IG11.........109 F1
  PLSTW E13 ....106 D1
Maudlins Gn WAP E1W *.......123 H1
Maud Rd LEY E10..............88 A1
  PLSTW E13.................106 C1
Maudslay Rd ELTH/MOT SE9....146 E3
Maud St CAN/RD E16...........106 D4
Maud Wilkes CI KTTN NW5.....84 C3
Mauleverer Rd
  BRXS/STRHM SW2............141 K6
Maundeby Wk WLSDN NW10 *....81 G5
Maunder Rd HNWL W7.........115 K1
Maunsel St WEST SW1P.........16 C6
Maurice Av WDGN N22..........49 F6
Maurice Brown CI MLHL NW7 *..46 B1
Maurice Browne CI MLHL NW7...46 B1
Maurice St SHB W12...........99 K5
Mauritius Rd GNWCH SE10.....125 H4
Maury Rd STNW/STAM N16......68 C6
Mauveine Gdns HSLW TW5.....135 F5
Mavelstone Rd BMLY BR1.....184 C4
Maverton Rd BOW E3 *.........87 J6
Mavis Av HOR/WEW KT19......207 G5
Mavis CI HOR/WEW KT19......207 G5
Mawbey PI STHWK SE1.........123 G5
Mawbey Rd STHWK SE1........123 G5
Mawbey St VX/NE SW8........141 K1
Mawney CI ROMW/RG RM7......56 D6
Mawney Rd ROMW/RG RM7......56 D6
Mawson CI RAYNES PK SW20....177 H5
Mawson La CHSWK W4.........118 C6
Maxey Gdns DAGW RM9.........92 A2
Maxey Rd DAGW RM9..........92 A2
  WOOL/PLUM SE18 ....127 G4
Maxfield CI TRDG/WHET N20...33 G2
Maxilla Wk NKENS W10........100 B5
Maximfeldt Rd ERITH DA8.....130 B5
Maxim Rd DART DA1..........150 B6
  ERITH DA8.................130 B5
  WCHMH N21................35 G1
Maxted Pk HRW HA1 ....61 E3
Maxted Rd PECK SE15........143 H4
  HYS/HAR UB3...............94 E6
Maxwell CI CROY/NA CR0......195 K5
  HYS/HAR UB3 ....94 B6
Maxwell Gdns ORP BR6.......217 F1
Maxwell Ri OXHEY WD19 ....27 J2
Maxwell Rd FUL/PGN SW6.....140 A1
  NTHWD...................40 B3
  WDR/YW UB7 ....112 B4
  WELL DA16 ....148 B5
Maxwelton Av MLHL NW7.......45 F1
Maxwelton CI MLHL NW7.......45 F1
Maya CI PECK SE15..........143 J3
Mayall CI PEND EN3 ....25 J1
  STHWK SE1 ....18 D1
Mayall Rd HNHL SE24.........142 C6
Maya PI FBAR/BDGN N11.......48 D5
Maya Rd EFNCH N2............65 G1
May Av STMC/STPC BR5........202 C2
Maybank Av ALP/SUD HA0......79 G3
  HCH RM12.................92 C3
  SWFD E18.................53 F5
Maybank Gdns PIN HA5........58 E1
Maybank Rd SWFD E18........53 F4
May Bate Av KUTN/CMB KT2...174 E4
Mayberry PI BRYLDS KT5......191 H4
Maybourne CI SYD SE26......181 J2
Maybury CI EN EN1...........24 D1
  STMC/STPC BR5............201 G2
Maybury Gdns WLSDN NW10....81 J5
Maybury Ms HGT N6 ....66 C4
Maybury Rd BARK IG11 ....109 G1
  PLSTW E13.................107 G3
Maybury St TOOT SW17........178 D1
Maychurch CI STAN HA7........43 K4
May CI CHSGTN KT9...........206 B4
Maycock Gv NTHWD HA6........40 D2

Maycroft PIN HA5.............41 F5
Maycross Av MRDN SM4.......193 J1
Mayday Gdns BKHTH/KID SE3..146 D3
Mayday Rd THHTH CR7 ....196 A4
Mayfield Rd THHTH CR7 ....196 A1
Mayerne Rd ELTH/MOT SE9....146 C6
Mayesbrook Rd BARK IG11.....91 F6
  GDMY/SEVK IG3 ....91 G1
Mayesford Rd CHDH RM6.......73 J4
Mayeswood Rd
  LEE/GVPK SE12............165 G6
Mayfair Av BXLYHN DA7......148 E2
  CHDH RM6.................73 K5
  IL IG1...................71 K6
  WHTN TW2.................155 H2
Mayfair CI BECK BR3.........182 E4
  SURB KT6.................191 F5
Mayfair Gdns TOTM N17.......49 K2
  WFD IG8..................52 E3
Mayfair Ms CAMTN NW1 *......83 K5
Mayfair Rd DART DA1.........151 G6
Mayfair Ter STHGT/OAK N14...34 D2
Mayfield BXLYHN DA7........149 G4
Mayfield Av CHSWK W4.......118 B4
  KTN/HRWW/WS HA3 ....61 K1
  NFNCH/WDSPK N12 ....33 G6
  ORP BR6..................202 A5
  STHGT/OAK N14............34 C4
  WEA W13..................116 C3
  WFD IG8..................52 E2
Mayfield CI CLAP SW4 *......141 J6
  HACK E8..................86 B5
  PGE/AN SE20 ....181 J5
  THDIT KT7.................190 C5
  WOT/HER KT12.............188 A6
Mayfield Crs ED N9..........36 A3
  THHTH CR7.................196 A1
Mayfield Dr PIN HA5..........59 K1
Mayfield Gdns HDN NW4.......64 B3
  HNWL W7 ....96 D5
Mayfield Rd ACT W3..........98 B6
  BCTR RM8.................73 J5
  BELMT SM2................209 H4
  BELV DA17.................129 K4
  BMLY BR1.................200 D2
  CEND/HSY/T N8............66 E3
  CHING E4..................38 A4
  HACK E8..................86 B5
  PEND EN3.................25 F3
  PLSTW E13.................106 D3
  SAND/SEL CR2.............211 K6
  SHB W12..................118 B2
  WALTH E17.................51 G5
  WIM/MER SW19.............177 J4
Mayfields WBLY HA9..........62 C6
Mayfields CI WBLY HA9.......62 C6
Mayfield Vls SCUP DA14 *....186 D2
Mayflower CI
  BERM/RHTH SE16...........124 A4
  RSLP HA4..................58 A3
Mayflower Rd BRXN/ST SW9....141 K4
Mayflower St
  BERM/RHTH SE16...........123 K2
Mayfly CI PIN HA5...........59 G4
  STMC/STPC BR5............202 E1
Mayford CI BAL SW12.........160 E2
  BECK BR3.................182 A6
Mayford Rd BAL SW12.........160 E2
May Gdns ALP/SUD HA0.........97 J2
  BORE WD6.................29 K1
Maygood St IS N1 ....5 G2
Maygreen Crs EMPK RM11......75 J4
Maygrove Rd KIL/WHAMP NW6..82 D4
Mayhew CI CHING E4...........37 J5
Mayhill Rd BAR EN5...........32 C1
  CHARL SE7 ....126 A6
Maylands Av HCH RM12........93 K2
Maylands Dr SCUP DA14......168 E5
Maylands Rd OXHEY WD19......27 G6
Maynard CI ERITH DA8.......150 C1
  FUL/PGN SW6 *.............140 A1
  SEVS/STOTM N15............68 A2
Maynard Rd WALTH E17.........70 A2
Maynards Quay WAP E1W *.....104 E6
Maynooth Gdns CAR SM5......194 E4
Mayola Rd CLPT E5...........86 E2
Mayo Rd CROY/NA CR0........196 E2
  WLSDN NW10................81 G4
Mayow Rd SYD SE26..........164 A6
Mayplace Av DART DA1........150 D5
Mayplace CI BXLYHN DA7......149 J4
Mayplace La
  WOOL/PLUM SE18...........127 G6
Mayplace Rd East
  BXLYHN DA7...............149 K4
Mayplace Rd West
  BXLYHN DA7...............149 H5
Maypole Crs BARK/HLT IG6....54 D3
  ERITH DA8.................131 G6
May Rd CHING E4.............51 J2
  PLSTW E13.................106 E2
  RDART DA2 ....171 J6
  WHTN TW2.................155 K3
Mayroyd Av SURB KT6........191 H6
May's Buildings Ms
  GNWCH SE10 ....145 G1
Mays CI CHCR WC2N..........10 E6
Mays Hill Rd HAYES BR2.....183 H6
May's La BAR EN5.............31 K2
Maysoule Rd BTSEA SW11.....140 C5
Mays Rd TEDD TW11..........173 J1
Mayswood Gdns DAGE RM10.....92 E4
Maythorne Cottages
  LEW SE13.................165 G1
Mayton St HOLWY N7...........85 F1
Maytree Ct EDGW HA8.........30 E5
  RAIN RM13.................111 G1
Maytree La STAN HA7..........43 F5
Maytree Wk
  BRXS/STRHM SW2 *.........162 B4
Mayville Est STNW/STAM N16 *..86 A3

Mayville Rd IL IG1...........90 B3
  WAN E11..................88 B3
Maywood CI BECK BR3 *.......182 C5
Maze Hi BKHTH/KID SE3.......145 J1
Maze Rd RCH/KEW TW9........137 H1
McAdam Dr ENC/FH EN2........23 H5
McAuley CI ELTH/MOT SE9.....147 F6
  STHWK SE1.................17 J4
McCall CI CLAP SW4..........141 K3
McCall Crs CHARL SE7........126 D5
McCarthy Rd FELT TW13.......172 C1
McCoid Wy STHWK SE1.........18 C3
McCrone Ms HAMP NW3.........83 J5
McCudden Rd DART DA1.......151 J4
McCullum Rd BOW E3..........87 H6
McDermott CI BTSEA SW11....140 D5
McDermott Rd PECK SE15.....143 H4
McDonough CI CHSGTN KT9....206 A2
McDougall Ct RCH/KEW TW9...137 H3
McDowall CI CAN/RD E16......106 E4
McDowall Rd CMBW SE5.......142 D2
McEntee Av WALTH E17.........51 G4
McEwan Wy SRTFD E15 *.......88 B6
McGrath Rd SRTFD E15........88 D4
McGregor Rd NTGHL W11......100 D5
McIntosh CI ROM RM1..........57 G6
  WLGTN SM6................210 E5
McIntosh Rd ROM RM1.........57 G6
McKay Rd RYNPK SW20........176 E4
Mc Kellar CI BUSH WD23.......28 C4
McKerrell Rd PECK SE15......143 H2
McKillop Wy SCUP DA14......186 D5
McLeod Rd ABYW SE2........128 C4
McNair Rd NWDGN UB2........115 F3
McNeil Rd CMBW SE5.........143 F3
McNicol Dr WLSDN NW10......98 E1
McRae La MTCM CR4..........194 E4
Mead CI CAMTN NW1...........84 A5
  GPK RM2..................75 J1
  KTN/HRWW/WS HA3 ....42 D4
Mead Ct CDALE/KGS NW9.......62 E2
Mead Crs CHING E4...........38 A6
  DART DA1.................171 G3
  SUT SM1..................209 J2
Meadcroft Rd LBTH SE11.....122 B6
Meade CI CHSWK W4..........117 H6
Meadfield EDGW HA8..........30 D4
Mead PI RYLN/HDSTN HA2 *....77 K1
Meadfoot Rd
  STRHM/NOR SW16...........179 H4
Meadgate Av WFD IG8.........53 J1
Mead Gv CHDH RM6............55 K6
Mead House La HAP UB4........94 B3
Meadlands Dr
  RCHPK/HAM TW10...........156 E4
Meadow Av CROY/NA CR0......198 A3
Meadowbank BKHTH/KID SE3...145 J4
  BRYLDS KT5...............191 G3
  HAMP NW3.................83 K5
  OXHEY WD19...............27 H3
  WCHMH N21................35 F1
Meadowbank CI FUL/PGN SW6..139 F1
Meadowbank Gdns HEST TW5...133 K2
Meadowbank Rd
  CDALE/KGS NW9............63 F4
  WLSDN NW10...............81 H6
Meadow CI BAR EN5...........32 C1
  BARK IG11................91 G5
  BXLYHS DA6...............149 G6
  CAT SE6..................182 D1
  CHING E4..................38 A3
  CHST BR7.................185 G1
  ESH/CLAY KT10............205 F1
  HOM E9...................87 H4
  HSLWW TW4................155 F2
  PEND EN3.................25 G2
  RCHPK/HAM TW10...........157 F3
  RSLP HA4.................58 D3
  RYNPK SW20...............193 F1
Meadowcourt Rd
  BKHTH/KID SE3............145 J5
Meadow Cft BMLY BR1........184 E6
Meadowcroft BUSH WD23.......28 B1
Meadowcroft Rd PLMGR N13 *...35 H4
Meadowcroft Rd PLMGR N13....35 G4
Meadow Dr HDN NW4...........46 B6
  MUSWH N10................48 B6
Meadowford CI THMD SE28....109 G6
Meadow Gdns EDGW HA8........44 E2
Meadow Garth WLSDN NW10.....80 E4
Meadow La LEE/GVPK SE12....166 B5
Meadowlea CI WDR/YW UB7....112 B6
Meadow Ms VX/NE SW8........142 A1
Meadow PI CHSWK W4 *.......138 B1
  VX/NE SW8................141 K1
Meadow Rd BARK IG11........91 G5
  DAGW RM9.................92 B4
  ESH/CLAY KT10............204 E4
  FELT TW13.................154 D4
  HAYES BR2................183 H4
  PIN HA5..................41 H6
  ROMW/RG RM7..............74 E5
  STHL UB1..................95 K6
  SUT SM1..................209 J2
  VX/NE SW8................142 A1
  WIM/MER SW19.............178 A3
Meadow Rw STHWK SE1.........18 C5
Meadows CI LEY E10...........69 J6
Meadowside BKHTH/KID SE3...146 B5
  DART DA1.................171 H3
  TWK TW1..................156 B5
  WOT/HER KT12.............188 A6
Meadowside Rd BELMT SM2....208 C6
The Meadows ORP BR6........217 J4
Meadow Stile CROY/NA CR0....211 J1
Meadowsweet CI
  EHAM E6..................107 H4
  NWMAL KT3................193 F2
The Meadow CHST BR7........185 H2
Meadow Vw BFN/LL DA15......168 C3
  HRW HA1..................60 E5
  STMC/STPC BR5............186 D6

Meadowview Rd BXLY DA5.....169 F1
  CAT SE6..................164 D6
Meadow View Rd THHTH CR7...196 C2
  YEAD UB4.................95 G3
Meadow Wk DAGW RM9..........92 B4
  EW KT17..................207 H5
  RDART DA2 ....170 D1
  SWFD E18.................70 E1
  WLGTN SM6................210 B1
Meadow Wy CDALE/KGS NW9.....63 F2
  CHSGTN KT9...............206 A3
  ORP BR6..................216 A1
  RSLP HA4.................58 E3
  WBLY HA9.................80 B3
Meadow Waye HEST TW5.......134 D1
The Meadow Wy
  KTN/HRWW/WS HA3..........42 E4
  HOM E9...................86 E4
Mead Plat WLSDN NW10........80 E4
Mead Rd CHST BR7...........185 H2
  DART DA1.................171 G3
  EDGW HA8.................44 C2
  RCHPK/HAM TW10...........156 D5
Mead Rw STHWK SE1...........17 J4
Meadside CI BECK BR3........182 B4
Meads La GDMY/SEVK IG3......73 F4
Meads Rd PEND EN3...........25 G6
  WDGN N22.................49 H5
Meads Ter THHTH CR7 *.......180 D6
The Meads CHEAM SM3........208 B1
  EDGW HA8.................45 F2
  MRDN SM4.................194 D2
The Mead BECK BR3..........183 F5
  EFNCH N2.................47 G5
  OXHEY WD19...............27 J5
  WEA W13..................97 H4
  WLGTN SM6................210 D4
Meadvale Rd CROY/NA CR0....197 G4
  EA W5....................97 H3
Mead Wy CROY/NA CR0.........198 B6
  HAYES BR2................199 K3
  RSLP HA4.................58 E4
Meadway ASHF TW15..........152 D6
  BAR EN5..................20 E5
  BECK BR3.................183 F4
  BRYLDS KT5...............191 K5
  CDALE/KGS NW9............45 G5
  GDMY/SEVK IG3 ....90 E2
  GLDGN NW11...............65 E4
  GPK RM2..................57 J1
  RYNPK SW20...............193 F1
  THNGT/OAK N14............34 D3
  WFD IG8..................53 G1
  WHTN TW2.................155 J3
Meadway CI BAR EN5..........20 E4
  GLDGN NW11...............65 E4
  PIN HA5..................42 B2
Meadway Ct WBLY HA9 *.......62 E4
Meadway Gdns RSLP HA4.......58 B3
The Meadway BKHH IG9........39 H3
  BKHTH/KID SE3............145 G3
  ORP BR6..................217 H3
Meaford Wy PGE/AN SE20.....181 J3
Meanley Rd MNPK E12.........89 J3
Meard St SOHO/CST W1F........10 C4
Meath CI STMC/STPC BR5.....202 C2
Meath Rd IL IG1.............90 C2
  SRTFD E15................106 D1
Meath St BTSEA SW11........141 G2
Mecklenburgh PI BMSBY WC1N...5 G6
Mecklenburgh Sq BMSBY WC1N...5 G6
Mecklenburgh St BMSBY WC1N...5 G6
Medburn St CAMTN NW1.........4 C2
Medcroft Gdns
  MORT/ESHN SW14...........137 K5
Medebourne CI
  BKHTH/KID SE3............145 K4
Medesenge Wy PLMGR N13......49 H2
Medfield St PUT/ROE SW15...158 D2
Medhurst CI BOW E3 *........105 G1
Median Rd CLPT E5...........86 E3
Medina Av ESH/CLAY KT10.....204 E1
Medina Gv HOLWY N7...........67 J3
Medland CI WLGTN SM6.......195 F5
Medlar CI NTHLT UB5.........95 H1
Medlar St CMBW SE5.........142 D2
Medley Rd KIL/WHAMP NW6.....82 E4
Medora Rd BRXS/STRHM SW2...162 A2
  ROMW/RG RM7..............75 F1
Medusa Rd CAT SE6..........164 E1
Medway CI CROY/NA CR0......197 K3
  IL IG1...................90 C3
Medway Dr GFD/PVL UB6.......97 F1
Medway Gdns ALP/SUD HA0.....79 G2
Medway Pde GFD/PVL UB6 *....97 F1
Medway Rd BOW E3...........105 G1
  DART DA1.................150 D4
Medway St WEST SW1P.........16 D5
Medwin St CLAP SW4.........142 A5
Meerbrook Rd BKHTH/KID SE3.146 B4
Meeson Rd SRTFD E15.........88 D6
Meeson St CLPT E5...........87 G1
Meesons Whf SRTFD E15 *....106 A1
Meeting House Aly
  WAP E1W *................123 J1
Meeting House La PECK SE15..143 J2
Mehetabel Rd HOM E9.........86 E4
Meister CI IL IG1...........72 C6
Melancholy Walk... [no — line below]
Melanda CI CHST BR7........184 E1
Melanie CI BXLYHN DA7......149 F2
Melbourne Av PIN HA5........60 B1
  WDGN N22.................49 F5
  WEA W13..................116 B1
Melbourne CI ORP BR6.......201 K4
  WLGTN SM6................210 C3
Melbourne Gdns CHDH RM6.....74 A2
Melbourne Gv EDUL SE22.....143 G5
Melbourne Ms BRXN/ST SW9...142 B2
  CAT SE6..................165 F2
Melbourne PI HOL/ALD WC2B...11 H4
Melbourne Rd BUSH WD23......28 B1
  EHAM E6..................107 K1
  IL IG1...................72 B6
  LEY E10..................69 K5

  TEDD TW11................174 D2
  WALTH E17................69 H1
  WIM/MER SW19.............177 K4
  WLGTN SM6................210 B3
Melbourne Sq BRXN/ST SW9 *..142 B2
  FUL/PGN SW6 *.............140 A1
Melbourne Wy EN EN1 ....36 B1
Melbury Av NWDGN UB2........115 G3
Melbury CI CHST BR7.........184 A3
  ESH/CLAY KT10............205 H4
Melbury Ct KENS W8.........119 K3
Melbury Dr CMBW SE5.........143 F1
Melbury Gdns RYNPK SW20....176 E6
Melbury Rd
  KTN/HRWW/WS HA3..........62 B2
  WKENS W14................119 J3
Melbury Ter CAMTN NW1........2 D7
Melcombe Gdns
  KTN/HRWW/WS HA3..........62 B3
Melcombe PI CAMTN NW1........8 E1
Melcombe St CAMTN NW1........3 F7
Meldex CI MLHL NW7..........46 B3
Meldon CI FUL/PGN SW6 *.....140 A2
Meldone CI BRYLDS KT5......191 J3
Meldrum Rd STMC/STPC BR5...202 D3
Meldrum Rd GDMY/SEVK IG3....73 G6
Melfield Gdns CAT SE6......164 E6
Melford Av BARK IG11........90 E5
Melford CI CHSGTN KT9......206 B3
Melford Rd EDUL SE22.......163 H3
  EHAM E6..................107 K3
  IL IG1...................72 D6
  WALTH E17................69 G1
  WAN E11..................70 C6
Melfort Av THHTH CR7.......180 C6
Melfort Rd THHTH CR7.......180 C6
Melgund Rd HBRY N5...........85 G3
Melina CI HYS/HAR UB3.......94 A5
Melina PI STJWD NW8 *........2 A5
Melina Rd SHB W12..........118 E2
Melior PI STHWK SE1..........19 G2
Melior St STHWK SE1..........19 F2
Meliot Rd CAT SE6..........165 G4
Melksham CI CROY/NA CR0.....24 C2
Melling Dr EN EN1............24 C2
Melling St WOOL/PLUM SE18..127 K6
Mellish CI BARK IG11.........91 G6
Mellish St POP/IOD E14.....124 D3
Mellison Rd TOOT SW17......178 D1
Melliss Av RCH/KEW TW9.....137 J2
Mellitus St SHB W12..........99 H5
Mellor CI WOT/HER KT12.....188 E4
Mellow La East HGDN/ICK UB10..94 A3
Mellows Rd CLAY IG5..........53 K5
  WLGTN SM6................210 D4
Mells Crs ELTH/MOT SE9.....166 E6
Melody La HBRY N5...........85 H4
Melody Rd WAND/EARL SW18..160 B1
Melon PI KENS W8...........119 K2
Melon Rd PECK SE15.........143 H2
  WAN E11..................88 C1
Melrose Av BORE WD6.........30 A1
  DART DA1.................170 B2
  GFD/PVL UB6..............96 B1
  MTCM CR4.................179 F2
  STRHM/NOR SW16...........180 A6
  WDGN N22.................49 G4
  WHTN TW2.................155 H3
  WIM/MER SW19.............159 J4
Melrose CI GFD/PVL UB6......96 B1
  LEE/GVPK SE12............165 K3
  YEAD UB4.................95 F3
Melrose Crs ORP BR6........216 D2
Melrose Dr STHL UB1........115 F1
Melrose Gdns EDGW HA8.......44 D6
  HMSMTH W6................119 F3
  NWMAL KT3................176 A6
Melrose Rd BARN SW13.......138 C3
  PIN HA5..................59 K1
  WAND/EARL SW18...........159 J1
  WIM/MER SW19.............177 K5
Melrose Ter HMSMTH W6......119 F2
Melrose Vls BECK BR3 *.....182 D5
Melthorne Dr RSLP HA4.......77 G1
Melthorpe Gdns
  BKHTH/KID SE3............146 C2
Melton CI RSLP HA4...........59 G5
Melton Flds HOR/WEW KT19...207 F6
Melton Gdns ROM RM1.........75 G4
Melton PI HOR/WEW KT19.....207 F6
Melton St CAMTN NW1..........4 B5
Melville Av GFD/PVL UB6.....79 F3
  RYNPK SW20...............176 D3
  SAND/SEL CR2.............212 B3
Melville CI HGDN/ICK UB10....76 B3
Melville Ct DEPT SE8 *.....124 A4
Melville Gdns PLMGR N13.....49 H1
Melville PI IS N1...........85 J5
Melville Rd BARN SW13......138 D2
  CRW RM5..................56 D3
  RAIN RM13................111 G3
  SCUP DA14................168 D4
  WALTH E17................51 H1
  WLSDN NW10...............81 F5
Melville Villas Rd ACT W3 *..118 A1
Melvin Rd PGE/AN SE20......181 K4
Memel Ct STLK EC1Y..........6 C7
Memel St STLK EC1Y..........6 C7
Memorial Av SRTFD E15......106 C2
Memorial CI HEST TW5.......114 E6
Memorial Sq KUT/HW KT1.....174 E5
Mendip CI HYS/HAR UB3......133 G1
  SYD SE26.................163 K6
  WPK KT4..................193 F5
Mendip Dr CRICK NW2.........64 B6
Mendip Houses BETH E2 *.....104 E2
Mendip Rd BTSEA SW11........140 B4
  BUSH WD23................28 C1
  ERITH DA8................150 D2
  GDMY/SEVK IG3 ....73 F2
  CNTH/NBYPK IG2...........72 E3
Mendora Rd FUL/PGN SW6......139 H1
Menelik Rd CRICK NW2........82 C2
Menlo Gdns NRWD SE19.......180 D3
Menon Dr ED N9..............36 D5

Menotti St *BETH* E2 * 104 C3
Mentmore CI
  KTN/HRWW/WS HA3 ....61 J3
Mentmore Ter *HACK* E8 ......86 D5
Meon Rd *ACT* W3 ....117 K2
Meopham Rd *MTCM* CR4 ...179 H4
Mepham Crs
  KTN/HRWW/WS HA3 ....42 C3
Mepham Gdns
  KTN/HRWW/WS HA3
Mepham St *STHWK* SE1 ......17 J1
Mera Dr *BXLYHN* DA7 ....149 J5
Merantum Wy
  WIM/MER SW19 ....178 B4
Merbury CI *LEW* SE13 ....145 F6
  THMD SE28 ....127 J1
Merbury Rd *THMD* SE28 ....127 J1
Mercator PI *POP/IOD* E14 ..124 D5
Mercator Rd *LEW* SE13 ......145 G5
Mercer CI *THDIT* KT7 ....190 A4
Merceron Houses *BETH* E2 * ...104 D5
Merceron St *WCHPL* E1 ....104 D5
Mercer PI *PIN* HA5 ....41 G5
Mercers CI *GNWCH* SE10 ....125 J4
Mercers Cottages *STHWK* E1 * ..105 G5
Mercers PI *HMSMTH* W6 .....119 F4
Mercers Rd *ARCH* N19 ....84 D1
Mercer St *LSQ/SEVD* WC2H ..10 D4
Merchants CI *SNWD* SE25 ...197 H1
Merchant St *BOW* E3 * 105 H2
Merchiston Rd *CAT* SE6 .....165 G4
Merchland Rd *ELTH/MOT* SE9 ..167 H5
Mercia Gv *LEW* SE13 ....145 F5
Mercier Rd *PUT/ROE* SW15 ..139 H6
Mercury Gdns *ROM* RM1 ......75 H2
Mercury House
  HYS/HAR UB3 * 113 J2
Mercury Rd *BTFD* TW8 ....116 D5
Mercury Wy *NWCR* SE14 ....144 A6
Mercy Ter *LEW* SE13 ....144 E6
Mereboank La *WLGTN* SM6 ...211 F5
Mere CI *ORP* BR6 ....201 G6
Meredith Av *CRICK* NW2 ......82 A3
Meredith Ms *BROCKY* SE4 * ..144 C5
Meredith St *CLKNW* EC1R 6 A5
  PLSTW E13 ....106 E2
Meredyth Rd *BARN* SW13 ....138 D3
Mere End *CROY/NA* CR0 .....198 A4
Mereside Pk *ASHF* TW15 * ..153 F6
Meretone CI *BROCKY* SE4 * ..144 B5
Merevale Crs *MRDN* SM4 .....194 B3
Mereway Rd *WHTN* TW2 .....155 J3
Merewood CI *BMLY* BR1 .....185 F5
Merewood Gdns
  CROY/NA CR0 ....198 A4
Merewood Rd *BXLYHN* DA7 ..149 K4
Mereworth CI *HAYES* BR2 ..199 J2
Mereworth Dr
  WOOL/PLUM SE18 ....147 G1
Meriden CI *BARK/HLT* IG6 ....54 C4
  BMLY BR1 ....184 C3
Meridian Rd *CHARL* SE7 ....146 C1
Meridian Sq *SRTFD* E15 ......88 B5
Meridian St *ED* N9 ....27 J
  UED N18 ....50 E2
Merifield Rd *ELTH/MOT* SE9 ..146 B5
Merino CI *WAN* E11 ....71 G1
Merivale Rd *HRW* HA1 ....60 D4
  PUT/ROE SW15 ....139 H5
Merlewood Dr *CHST* BR7 ....184 E4
Merley Ct *CDALE/KGS* NW9 ..62 E1
Merlin CI *CROY/NA* CR0 .....212 A2
  CRW RM5 ....57 F2
  MTCM CR4 ....178 D6
  WLGTN SM6 ....211 F4
Merlin Crs *EDGW* HA8 ....44 B4
Merlin Gdns *CHSGTN* KT9 ..205 K3
  CRW RM5 ....57 F2
  BECK BR3 ....198 C1
Merlin Rd *CRW* RM5 ....57 F2
  WELL DA16 ....148 B5
Merlin Rd North *WELL* DA16 ..148 B5
Merlins Av *RYLN/HDSTN* HA2 ..77 J1
Merlin St *FSBYW* WC1X 5 J5
Mermagen Dr *RAIN* RM13 .....93 K5
Mermaid Ct *STHWK* SE1 ......18 E2

Merredene St
  BRXS/STRHM SW2 ....162 A1
Merriam Av *HOM* E9 ....87 H4
Merriam CI *CHING* E4 ....52 A1
Merrick Rd *NWDGN* UB2 ....114 C4
Merrick Sq *STHWK* SE1 ....18 C4
Merridene *WCHMH* N21 ....35 H1
Merrielands Crs *DAGW* RM9 ..110 C1
Merrilands Rd *WPK* KT4 ....193 F5
Merrilees Rd *BFN/LL* DA15 ..167 K2
Merrilyn CI *ESH/CLAY* KT10 ..205 G4
Merriman Rd *BKHTH/KID* SE3 ..146 B2
Merrington Rd *FUL/PGN* SW6 ..119 K6
Merrion Av *STAN* HA7 ....43 K1
Merritt Gdns *CHSGTN* KT9 ..205 K4
Merritt Rd *BROCKY* SE4 .....144 C6
Merrivale *STHGT/OAK* N14 ..34 D1
Merrivale Av *REDBR* IG4 ......71 H1
Merrivale Ms *WDR/YW* UB7 * ..112 A1
Merrow Rd *BELMT* SM2 ....208 B6
Merrows CI *NTHWD* HA6 ......40 A2
Merrow St *WALW* SE17 ......122 E5
Merrow Wk *WALW* SE17 ......122 E5
Merrow Wy *CROY/NA* CR0 ..214 A4
Merrydown Wy *CHST* BR7 ..184 E4
Merryfield *BKHTH/KID* SE3 ..145 J3
Merryfield Gdns *STAN* HA7 ..43 J1
Merryfield Wy *CAT* SE6 ....164 D2
Merryhill CI *CHING* E4 ....37 K2
Merryhill Mt *BUSH* WD23 ....28 B3
Merryhills Dr *ENC/FH* EN2 ....22 E5
Merryweather CI *DART* DA1 ..171 J1

Merryweather Ct *NWMAL* KT3 ..192 B2
Mersey Rd *WALTH* E17 ....51 H6
Mersham Dr *CDALE/KGS* NW9 ..62 D2
Mersham PI *PGE/AN* SE20 ...181 J4
  THHTH CR7 ....180 E5
Mersham Rd *THHTH* CR7 ....180 E5
Merthyr Ter *BARN* SW13 ....118 E6
Merton Av *CHSWK* W4 ....118 C4
  NTHLT UB5 ....78 C3
Merton CI *STMC/STPC* BR5 ..201 G2
Merton Hall Gdns
  RYNPK SW20 ....177 H4
Merton Hall Rd
  WIM/MER SW19 ....177 J4
Merton High St
  WIM/MER SW19 ....178 B3
Merton La *HGT* N6 ....65 K6
Merton PI *WIM/MER* SW19 * ..178 B4
Merton Ri *HAMP* NW3 ....83 J5
Merton Rd *BARK* IG11 ....91 F5
  ENC/FH EN2 ....23 K1
  GDMY/SEVK IG3 ....73 F4
  RYLN/HDSTN HA2 ....59 K6
  SNWD SE25 ....197 G2
  WALTH E17 ....70 A2
  WAND/EARL SW18 ....159 K2
  WIM/MER SW19 ....178 A3
Merton Wy *E/WMO/HCT* KT8 ..189 H1
Mertoun Ter *MBLAR* W1H * 8 E3
Merttins Rd *PECK* SE15 ....144 A5
Meru CI *KTTN* NW5 ....84 A3
Mervan Rd *BRXS/STRHM* SW2 ..142 B5
Mervyn Av *ELTH/MOT* SE9 ..167 H5
Mervyn Rd *WEA* W13 ....116 B3
Messaline Av *ACT* W3 ....98 K6
Messent Rd *ELTH/MOT* SE9 ..146 B6
Messeter PI *ELTH/MOT* SE9 ..167 F6
Messina Av *KIL/WHAMP* NW6 ..82 E6
Meteor St *BTSEA* SW11 ......141 F5
Meteor Wy *WLGTN* SM6 ....210 E5
Metford Crs *PEND* EN3 ....25 J1
Methley St *LBTH* SE11 ....122 B5
Methuen CI *EDGW* HA8 ....44 C3
Methuen Pk *MUSWH* N10 .....48 B5
Methuen Rd *BELV* DA17 .....129 J4
  BXLYHS DA6 ....149 G5
  EDGW HA8 ....44 C3
Methwold Rd *NKENS* W10 ..100 B4

Metro Centre
  STMC/STPC BR5 * 202 C3
Metropolitan CI *POP/IOD* E14 ..105 J4
Metropolitan Whf *WAP* E1W * ..123 K1
Mews North *BCVA* SW1W ...15 J5
Mews PI *WFD* IG8 ....38 E6
Mews South *WAP* SW1V 121 H5
Mews St *WAP* E1W 13 K7
The Mews *BECK* BR3 ....182 D4
  CEND/HSY/T N8 ....67 G1
  NFNCH/WDSPK N12 * 47 F1
  REDBR IG4 ....71 H2
  ROM RM1 ....75 G1
  SEVS/STOTM N15 * 68 A1
  STRHM/NOR SW16 * 180 A1
  TWK TW1 * 156 C1
Mexfield Rd *PUT/ROE* SW15 ..139 J6
Meyer Gn *EN* EN1 ....24 C1
Meyer Rd *ERITH* DA8 ....129 K6
Meymott St *STHWK* SE1 ......18 A1
Meynell Crs *HOM* E9 ....87 F5
Meynell Gdns *HOM* E9 ....87 F5
Meynell Rd *HARH* RM3 ....57 K3
  HOM E9 ....87 F5
Meyrick Rd *BTSEA* SW11 ...140 C4
  WLSDN NW10 ....81 J4
Mezen CI *NTHWD* HA6 ....40 B1
Miah Ter *WAP* E1W * 123 H1
Micawber St *IS* N1 ....6 D4
Michael Gaynor Dr *HNWL* W7 ..116 A1
Michaelmas CI *RYNPK* SW20 ..177 F6
Michael Rd *FUL/PGN* SW6 ..140 A2
  SNWD SE25 ....181 F6
  WAN E11 ....70 C5
Michaels CI *LEW* SE13 ....145 H4
Micheldever Rd
  LEE/GVPK SE12 ....165 H1
Michelham Gdns *TWK* TW1 ..156 A5
Michelsdale Dr *RCH/KEW* TW9 ..137 F5
Michel Wk *WOOL/PLUM* SE18 ..127 G5
Michigan Av *MNPK* E12 ....89 K2
Michleham Down
  NFNCH/WDSPK N12 ....32 D6
Micklefield Wy *STMC/STPC* BR5 ..186 A4
Mickleham Gdns *CHEAM* SM3 ..208 C4
Mickleham Rd
  STMC/STPC BR5 ....186 C1
Mickleham Wy *CROY/NA* CR0 ..214 B5
Micklethwaite Rd
  FUL/PGN SW6 ....119 K6
Midcroft *RSLP* HA4 ....58 C5
Middle Dartrey Wk
  WBPTN SW10 * 140 B1
Middle Dene NW7 * 31 F5
Middlefield *STJWD* NW8 ....2 B1
Middlefielde *WEA* W13 ....97 H4
Middle Green *BRYLDS* KT5 ..191 G6
Middleham Gdns *UED* N18 ....50 C2
Middleham Rd *UED* N18 ....50 C2
Middle La *CEND/HSY/T* N8 ..66 E2
  TEDD TW11 ....174 A2
Middle Lane Ms
  CEND/HSY/T N8 ....66 E2
Middle Park Av *ELTH/MOT* SE9 ..146 C6
Middle Rd *EBAR* EN4 ....33 J1
  PLSTW E13 ....106 E2
  RYLN/HDSTN HA2 ....60 A6
  STRHM/NOR SW16 ....179 H5
Middle Rw *NKENS* W10 ....100 C3
Middlesborough Rd *UED* N18 ..50 C2
Middlesex Rd *MTCM* CR4 ...195 K2
Middle St *CROY/NA* CR0 .....196 D6
  STBT EC1A 12 C1

Middle Temple La *EMB* EC4Y ..11 J4
Middleton Av *CHING* E4 ....37 H6
  GFD/PVL UB6 ....96 D1
  SCUP DA14 ....186 D2
Middleton CI *CHING* E4 ....37 H6
Middleton Dr
  BERM/RHTH SE16 ....124 A2
  PIN HA5 ....40 E6
Middleton Gdns
  GNTH/NBYPK IG2 ....72 B3
Middleton Gv *HOLWY* N7 .....84 E3
Middleton Ms *HOLWY* N7 .....84 E3
Middleton PI *GTPST* W1W 10 A2
Middleton Rd *GLDGN* NW11 ..64 E4
  HACK E8 ....86 B5
  HYS/HAR UB3 ....94 E3
  MRDN SM4 ....194 B3
  NWMAL KT3 ....175 K6
Middleton St *BETH* E2 ....104 D2
Middleton Wy *LEW* SE13 ....145 G5
Middleway *GLDGN* NW11 .....65 F3
Middle Wy *STRHM/NOR* SW16 ..179 J5
The Middle Wy
  KTN/HRWW/WS HA3 ....43 F5
Middle Yd *STHWK* SE1 ....13 F7
Midfield Av *BXLYHN* DA7 ....150 A4
Midfield Wy *STMC/STPC* BR5 ..186 C4
Midford PI *FITZ* W1T * 4 B7
Midholm *GLDGN* NW11 ....65 F1
Midholm CI *GLDGN* NW11 ....65 F1
Midholm Rd *CROY/NA* CR0 ..213 G5
Midhope St *STPAN* WC1H 5 F5
Midhurst Av *CROY/NA* CR0 ..196 B4
  MUSWH N10 ....48 A6
Midhurst Ct *HNHL* SE24 ....93 J2
Midhurst Gdns *HGDN/ICK* UB10 ..76 A3
Midhurst HI *BXLYHS* DA6 ....149 H6
Midhurst Pde *MUSWH* N10 * ..48 A6
Midhurst Rd *WEA* W13 ....116 B2
Midhurst Wy *CLPT* E5 ....86 C2
Midland Arches *CRICK* NW2 * ..63 K6
Midland Crs *HAMP* NW3 ....83 G4
Midland Rd *CAMTN* NW1 ....4 D3
  LEY E10 ....70 A5
Midland Ter *CRICK* NW2 ....82 B1
  WLSDN NW10 ....99 G3
Midlothian Rd *BOW* E3 ....105 H3
Midmoor Rd *BAL* SW12 ......161 H3
  WIM/MER SW19 ....177 G4
Midship CI *BERM/RHTH* SE16 ..124 A1
Midship Point *POP/IOD* E14 * ..124 D2
Midstrath Rd *WLSDN* NW10 ..81 G2
Midsummer Av *HSLWW* TW4 ..134 E5
Midway *CHEAM* SM3 ....193 J4
  WOT/HER KT12 ....188 A6
Midwinter CI *WELL* DA16 ....148 A4
Midwood CI *CRICK* NW2 ....81 J1
Mighell Av *REDBR* IG4 ....71 H2
Milan Rd *STHL* UB1 ....114 E2
Milborne Gv *WBPTN* SW10 ..120 B5
Milborne St *HOM* E9 ....86 E4
Milborough Crs
  LEE/GVPK SE12 ....165 H2
Milbourne La *ESH/CLAY* KT10 ..204 C4
Milbrook *ESH/CLAY* KT10 ....204 A4
Milcote St *STHWK* SE1 ....18 A3
Mildenhall Rd *CLPT* E5 ....86 E2
Mildmay Av *IS* N1 ....85 K4
Mildmay Gv North *IS* N1 ....85 K3
Mildmay Gv South *IS* N1 ....85 K3
Mildmay Pk *IS* N1 ....85 K3
Mildmay PI *STNW/STAM* N16 * ..86 A2
Mildmay Rd *IL* IG1 ....90 B1
  IS N1 ....85 K3
  ROMW/RG RM7 ....74 E2
Mildmay St *IS* N1 ....85 K4
Mildred Av *HYS/HAR* UB3 ...113 G4
  NTHLT UB5 ....78 B3
Mildred CI *DART* DA1 ....171 K1
Mildred Rd *ERITH* DA8 ....130 B5
Mile End PI *WCHPL* E1 ....105 F3
Mile End Rd *BOW* E3 ....104 E2
The Mile End *WALTH* E17 ....51 H4
Mile Rd *WLGTN* SM6 ....195 H6
Miles PI *BRYLDS* KT5 ....191 G1
Miles Rd *CEND/HSY/T* N8 ....66 E6
  MTCM CR4 ....194 D1
Miles St *VX/NE* SW8 ....121 K6
Milespit HI *MLHL* NW7 ....31 K4
Milestone CI *BELMT* SM2 ....209 H6
  ED N9 ....36 C4
Milestone Rd *NRWD* SE19 ..181 F2
Milfoil St *SHB* W12 ....99 J6
Milford CI *ABYW* SE2 ....129 F5
Milford Gdns *ALP/SUD* HA0 ..79 K3
  CROY/NA CR0 ....197 K2
  EDGW HA8 ....44 C3
Milford Gv *SUT* SM1 ....209 G2
Milford La *TPL/STR* WC2R ...11 J5
Milford Ms *STRHM/NOR* SW16 ..162 A4
Milford Rd *STHL* UB1 ....96 A6
  WEA W13 ....116 C1
Milk St *BMLY* BR1 ....184 A2
  CAN/RD E16 ....107 H6
  CITYW EC2V 12 D3
Milkwell Gdns *WFD* IG8 ....53 F3
Milkwell Yd *CMBW* SE5 ......142 D2
Milkwood Rd *HNHL* SE24 ....142 C6
Milk Yd *WAP* E1W 105 F6
Millais Av *MNPK* E12 ....90 A3
Millais Crs *HOR/WEW* KT19 ..207 G3
Millais Gdns *EDGW* HA8 ......44 C5
Millais Rd *EN* EN1 ....24 B6
  NWMAL KT3 ....192 B4
  WAN E11 ....88 A2
Millais Wy *HOR/WEW* KT19 ..206 E2
Milland Ct *BORE* WD6 ....30 E1
Millard CI *STNW/STAM* N16 * ..86 A3
Millard Ter *DAGE* RM10 * 92 C4
Millais Meadow
  BKHTH/KID SE3 146
Millbank *WEST* SW1P 16 E5
Millbank Est *WEST* SW1P * ...16 E6
Millbank Wy *LEE/GVPK* SE12 ..145 K6
Millbourne Rd *FELT* TW13 ..154 D6

Mill Br *BAR* EN5 ....20 D6
Millbrook Av *ELTH/MOT* SE9 ..147 G5
Millbrook Gdns *CHDH* RM6 ..74 A4
  GPK RM2 ....57 J5
Millbrook Rd *BRXN/ST* SW9 ..142 C4
  ED N9 ....36 D4
Mill Brook Rd *STMC/STPC* BR5 ..202 D1
Mill Cnr *BAR* EN5 ....20 D2
Mill Ct *CAR* SM5 * 195 F6
  WDR/YW UB7 ....112 A3
Mill CI *CAR* SM5 ....195 F6
Millennium Br *STHWK* SE1 ..12 C6
Millennium CI *CAN/RD* E16 ..107 F6
Millennium Dr *POP/IOD* E14 ..125 G3
Millennium PI *BETH* E2 * 104 D1
Millennium Sq *STHWK* SE1 * ..19 J2
Millennium Wy *GNWCH* SE10 ..125 J1
Millennium Whf *POP/IOD* E14 ..125 G4
Miller Av *PEND* EN3 ....25 J1
Miller CI *BMLY* BR1 ....183 K1
  CRW RM5 ....57 F2
  MTCM CR4 ....194 E4
Miller Rd *CROY/NA* CR0 .....196 A5
  WIM/MER SW19 ....178 C2
Miller's Av *HACK* E8 ....86 B3
Millers Ct *CHSWK* W4 * 118 C5
Millers Gn *ENC/FH* EN2 ....23 H4
Millers Green CI *ENC/FH* EN2 ..23 H4
Miller's Ter *HACK* E8 ....86 B3
Miller St *CAMTN* NW1 ....4 A2
Millers Wy *HMSMTH* W6 .....119 F2
Millers Yd *FNCH* N3 ....47 F4
Miller Wk *STHWK* SE1 ....17 K1
Millet Rd *GFD/PVL* UB6 ....96 B2
Mill Farm CI *PIN* HA5 ....41 G5
Mill Farm Crs *HSLWW* TW4 ..154 D5
Millfield Av *WALTH* E17 ....51 H4
Millfield La *HGT* N6 ....66 A6
  HGT N6 ....65 J6
Millfield PI *HGT* N6 ....66 A6
Millfield Rd *EDGW* HA8 ....44 E5
  HSLWW TW4 ....154 D5
Millfields CI *STMC/STPC* BR5 ..202 C1
Millfields Rd *CLPT* E5 ....86 E2
Mill Gdns *SYD* SE26 ....163 J6
Mill Gn *MTCM* CR4 ....195 F6
Mill Green Rd *MTCM* CR4 ...194 E4
Millgrove St *BTSEA* SW11 ..141 F2
Millharbour *POP/IOD* E14 ...124 E3
Millhaven CI *CHDH* RM6 ....73 H5
Mill HI *BARN* SW13 ....117 J3
Mill Hill Gv *ACT* W3 ....117 J2
  BARN SW13 ....138 K4
Mill Hill Ter *ACT* W3 ....117 J1
Millhouse PI *WNWD* SE27 ..162 C6
Milligan St *POP/IOD* E14 ....105 H6
Millington Rd *HYS/HAR* UB3 ..113 H3
Mill La *CAR* SM5 ....210 A2
  CHDH RM6 ....74 A3
  CHING E4 ....25 K5
  CRICK NW2 ....82 C2
  CROY/NA CR0 ....211 G1
  EW KT17 ....207 H6
  WFD IG8 ....52 D1
  WOOL/PLUM SE18 ....127 F5
Millman Ms *BMSBY* WC1N 5 G7
Millman PI *BMSBY* WC1N * 5 H7
Millman St *BMSBY* WC1N 5 G7
Millmark Gv *NWCR* SE14 ....144 B3
Millmarsh La *PEND* EN3 ....25 G3
Mill Mead Rd *TOTM* N17 ......50 D6
Mill PI *CHST* BR7 ....185 F4
  DART DA1 ....150 E6
  KUT/HW KT1 ....175 G6
  POP/IOD E14 ....105 G5
Mill Plat *ISLW* TW7 ....136 B4
Mill Plat Av *ISLW* TW7 ....136 B3
Mill Pond CI *VX/NE* SW8 ....141 J1
Millpond Est
  BERM/RHTH SE16 * 123 J2
Mill Pond Rd *DART* DA1 ......171 H1
Mill Rd *CAN/RD* E16 ....126 A1
  ERITH DA8 ....129 K7
  ESH/CLAY KT10 ....189 F6
  IL IG1 ....90 A1
  RDART DA2 ....171 J6
  WDR/YW UB7 ....112 A3
  WIM/MER SW19 ....178 B3
Mill Rw *BXLY* DA5 * 169 J2
  IS N1 ....7 H1
Mill's Gv *POP/IOD* E14 * 106 A5
Millshott CI *FUL/PGN* SW6 ..139 F2
Millside *CAR* SM5 ....194 E6
Millside PI *ISLW* TW7 ....136 C3
Mills Rw *CHSWK* W4 * 118 A4
Millstream Rd *PLMGR* N13 * ..19 J3
Mill St *CONDST* W1S 9 K5
  KUT/HW KT1 ....175 F5
  STHWK SE1 ....19 K3
Mills Yd *WCHPL* E1 ....104 C5
Mill Vale *BMLY* BR1 ....183 K5
Mill View CI *EW* KT17 ....207 H5
Mill View Gdns *CROY/NA* CR0 ..213 F1
Millwall Dock Rd *POP/IOD* E14 ..124 D3
Millway *NFNCH/WDSPK* N12 ..31 F4
Mill Wy *FELT* TW13 ....134 A6
  RKW/CH/CXG WD3 ....26 A1
Millway Gdns *NTHLT* UB5 ....77 K4
Millwood Rd *HSLW* TW3 ....135 H6
Millwood St *NKENS* W10 ....100 C4
Mill Yd *WCHPL* E1 ....104 C6
Milman CI *PIN* HA5 ....41 H6
Milman Rd *KIL/WHAMP* NW6 ..100 B1
Milman's St *WBPTN* SW10 ..140 C1
Milmead Ind Cen *TOTM* N17 ..50 D5
Milne Feild *PIN* HA5 ....42 A3
Milne Gdns *ELTH/MOT* SE9 ..146 D6
Milner Ct *BUSH* WD23 ....28 D1
Milner Dr *WHTN* TW2 ....155 J2
Milner PI *IS* N1 ....85 H1

Milner Rd *BCTR* RM8 ....73 J6
  KUT/HW KT1 ....174 E6
  MRDN SM4 ....194 C2
  SRTFD E15 ....106 C2
  THHTH CR7 ....180 D6
  WIM/MER SW19 ....178 A4
Milner Sq *IS* N1 ....85 G5
Milner St *CHEL* SW3 ....14 E6
Milnthorpe Rd *CHSWK* W4 ..118 A6
Milo Rd *EDUL* SE22 ....163 G1
Milroy Wk *STHWK* SE1 * 11 K7
Milton Av *BAR* EN5 ....20 D6
  CDALE/KGS NW9 ....44 D6
  CROY/NA CR0 ....196 E4
  EHAM E6 ....89 H6
  HCH RM12 ....75 H6
  HGT N6 ....66 C4
  SUT SM1 ....209 H1
  WLSDN NW10 ....81 F6
Milton CI *EFNCH* N2 ....65 G3
  STHWK SE1 ....19 J7
  SUT SM1 ....209 H1
  YEAD UB4 ....94 E5
Milton Court Rd *NWCR* SE14 ..144 B1
Milton Ct *BARB* EC2Y 12 D1
Milton Ct *STHWK* SE1 18
Milton Dr *BORE* WD6 ....30 C1
Milton Gdns *GNTH/NBYPK* IG2 ..72 C4
  STWL/WRAY TW19 ....152 C3
Milton Gv *FBAR/BDGN* N11 ..48 C1
  STNW/STAM N16 ....85 K2
Milton Pk *HGT* N6 ....66 C4
Milton Rd *ACT* W3 ....118 A1
  BELV DA17 ....129 H4
  CDALE/KGS NW9 ....63 J4
  CROY/NA CR0 ....196 E4
  HCH RM16
  HNHL SE24 ....142 C6
  HNWL W7 ....97 F6
  HRW HA1 ....60 E1
  MLHL NW7 ....45 J1
  MORT/ESHN SW14 ....138 A4
  MTCM CR4 ....179 F3
  ROM RM1 ....75 J3
  WALTH E17 ....69 J1
  WELL DA16 ....148 A2
  WIM/MER SW19 ....178 B2
  WLGTN SM6 ....210 C4
Milton St *BARB* EC2Y 12 E1
Milton Wy *WDR/YW* UB7 ...112 C4
Milverton Dr *HGDN/ICK* UB10 ..76 A1
Milverton Gdns *CDMY/SEVK* IG3 ..73 F6
Milverton Rd *KIL/WHAMP* NW6 ..82 A5
Milverton St *LBTH* SE11 .....122 B5
Milverton Wy *ELTH/MOT* SE9 ..167 F5
Milward St *WCHPL* E1 ....104 D4
Mimosa CI *ORP* BR6 ....202 D6
Mimosa Rd *HYS/HAR* UB3 ..95 J6
Mimosa St *FUL/PGN* SW6 ...139 J2
Minard Rd *CAT* SE6 ....165 H2
Mina Rd *STHWK* SE1 ....123 F5
  WIM/MER SW19 ....177 K4
Minchenden Crs
  STHGT/OAK N14 ....34 C5
Mincing La *MON* EC3R 13 G5
Minden Rd *CHEAM* SM3 ......193 H6
  PGE/AN SE20 ....181 J4
Minehead Rd *RYLN/HDSTN* HA2 ..78 A1
  STRHM/NOR SW16 ....180 A1
Mineral CI *BAR* EN5 ....32 A1
Mineral St *WOOL/PLUM* SE18 ..127 K4
Minera Ms *BCVA* SW1W 15 H5
Minerva CI *BRXN/ST* SW9 ...142 B1
  SCUP DA14 ....167 K6
Minerva Rd *CHING* E4 ....51 K3
  KUT/HW KT1 ....175 G5
  WLSDN NW10 ....98 E3
Minerva St *BETH* E2 ....104 D1
Minet Av *WLSDN* NW10 ....99 G1
Minet Dr *HYS/HAR* UB3 ......113 K1
  WLSDN NW10 ....99 G1
Minet Rd *BRXN/ST* SW9 .....142 C3
Minford Gdns *WKENS* W14 ..119 G2
Ming St *POP/IOD* E14 ....105 J6
Minimax CI *EBED/NFELT* TW14 ..153 K1
Ministry Wy *ELTH/MOT* SE9 ..166 E4
Mink Ct *HSLWW* TW4 ....134 B3
Minniedale *BRYLDS* KT5 ....191 G2
Minnow Wk *WALW* SE17 * ..19 H7
Minories *TWCH* EC3N 13 J4
Minshull PI *BECK* BR3 * 182 D3
Minshull St *VX/NE* SW8 * 141 J2
Minson Rd *HOM* E9 ....87 F1
Minstead Gdns *PUT/ROE* SW15 ..158 C2
Minstead Wy *NWMAL* KT3 ..192 B3
Minster Av *SUT* SM1 ....193 K6
Minster Ct *MON* EC3R * 13 G5
Minster Dr *CROY/NA* CR0 ...212 A2
Minster Gdns *E/WMO/HCT* KT8 ..188 E2
  CRICK NW2 ....82 C3
Minster Rd *BMLY* BR1 ....184 A2
Minstrel Gdns *BRYLDS* KT5 ..191 G1
Mintern CI *PLMGR* N13 ....35 H5
Minterne Av *NWDGN* UB2 ..115 F4
Minterne Rd
  KTN/HRWW/WS HA3 ....62 B2
Minterne Waye *YEAD* UB4 ....95 G5
Mint Gdns *DART* DA1
Minton Ms *KIL/WHAMP* NW6 ..83 F4
Mint Rd *WLGTN* SM6 ....210 B3
Mint St *STHWK* SE1 ....18 C2
Mint Wk *CROY/NA* CR0 ....211 J1
Mirabel Rd *FUL/PGN* SW6 ..119 J6
Miranda CI *WCHPL* E1 ....104 E4
Miranda Rd *ARCH* N19 ....66 C5
Mirfield St *CHARL* SE7 ....126 C4
Miriam Rd *WOOL/PLUM* SE18 ..127 K5
Miskin Rd *DART* DA1 ....171 F2
Missenden CI
  EBED/NFELT TW14 ....153 J3
Missenden Gdns *MRDN* SM4 ..194 B3
Mission Gv *WALTH* E17 ....69 H2

Mission Pl PECK SE15 143 H2
Mistletoe Cl CROY/NA CR0 198 A5
Misty's Fld WOT/HER KT12 188 B5
Mitali Pas WCHPL E1 104 C5
Mitcham La STRHM/NOR SW16 179 H1
Mitcham Pk MTCM CR4 194 E1
Mitcham Rd CROY/NA CR0 195 K3
  EHAM E6 107 J2
  GDMY/SEVK IG3 73 F4
  TOOT SW17 178 E1
Mitchellbrook Wy
  WLSDN NW10 81 F4
Mitchell Cl ABYW SE2 128 D5
  BELV DA17 129 K5
  DART DA1 171 H4
Mitchell Rd ORP BR6 217 F2
  PLMGR N13 49 H1
Mitchell St FSBYE EC1V 6 C6
Mitchison Rd IS N1 85 K4
Mitchley Rd TOTM N17 50 D5
Mitford Rd ARCH N19 66 E6
Mitre Cl BELMT SM2 209 G5
Mitre Rd SRTFD E15 106 C1
  STHWK SE1 17 H1
The Mitre POP/IOD E14 105 H6
Moat Cl ORP BR6 217 F4
Moat Crs FNCH N3 47 F6
Moat Cft DART DA16 148 D4
Moat Dr HRW HA1 60 C1
  PLSTW E13 107 G1
  RSLP HA4 58 C4
Moat Farm La NTHLT UB5 77 K4
Moat La ERITH DA8 150 D2
Moat Pl ACT W3 98 D5
  BRXN/ST SW9 142 A4
Moat Side FELT TW13 154 B6
  PEND EN3 24 E5
The Moat NWMAL KT3 176 B4
Moberly Rd CLAP SW4 161 J2
Modbury Gdns KTTN NW5 84 A4
Model Cottages WEA W13 * 116 C2
Model Farm Cl ELTH/MOT SE9 166 D5
Moelyn Ms HRW HA1 61 G2
Moffat Rd PLMGR N13 48 E2
  THHTH CR7 180 D5
  TOOT SW17 160 D6
Mogden La ISLW TW7 136 A6
Mohmmad Khan Rd WAN E11 * 70 D5
Moiety Rd POP/IOD E14 124 D3
Moira Cl TOTM N17 50 A5
Moira Rd ELTH/MOT SE9 146 E5
Moir Cl SAND/SEL CR2 212 C6
Molash Rd STMC/STPC BR5 202 E1
Mole Abbey Gdns
  E/WMO/HCT KT8 173 G6
Mole Ct HOR/WEW KT19 206 E2
Molember Ct E/WMO/HCT KT8 189 K2
Molember Rd
  E/WMO/HCT KT8 189 K2
Molescroft ELTH/MOT SE9 167 H5
Molesey Av E/WMO/HCT KT8 188 C2
Molesey Dr CHEAM SM3 193 H6
Molesey Park Av
  E/WMO/HCT KT8 189 G2
Molesey Park Cl
  E/WMO/HCT KT8 189 G2
Molesey Park Rd
  E/WMO/HCT KT8 189 G2
Molesford Rd FUL/PGN SW6 139 K2
Molesham Cl E/WMO/HCT KT8 173 G5
Molesham Wy
  E/WMO/HCT KT8 189 G1
Molesworth St LEW SE13 145 F5
Mollison Av PEND EN5 25 J6
Mollison Dr WLGTN SM6 210 E5
Mollison Wy EDGW HA8 44 C5
Molly Huggins Cl BAL SW12 161 H2
Molyneux Dr TOOT SW17 161 G6
Molyneux St MBLAR W1H 8 D2
Monarch Cl EBED/NFELT TW14 153 H2
  RAIN RM13 111 J1
  WWKM BR4 214 D2
Monarch Dr CAN/RD E16 107 H4
Monarch Ms
  STRHM/NOR SW16 180 B1
Monarch Pde MTCM CR4 * 178 E5
Monarch Rd BELV DA17 129 G3
Monarchs Wy RSLP HA4 58 C5
Monarch Wy GNTH/NBYPK IG2 72 D3
Mona Rd PECK SE15 143 K3
Monastery Gdns ENC/FH EN2 23 K2
Mona St CAN/RD E16 106 D4
Monaveen Gdns
  E/WMO/HCT KT8 173 G6
Monck's Rw
  WAND/EARL SW18 * 159 J1
Monck St WEST SW1P 16 D5
Monclar Rd CMBW SE5 142 E5
Moncorvo Cl SKENS SW7 14 C3
Moncrieff Cl EHAM E6 107 J5
Moncrieff St PECK SE15 143 H3
Monday Aly STNW/STAM N16 86 E1
Mondial Wy HYS/HAR UB3 133 F1
Money La WDR/YW UB7 112 A3
Monier Rd BOW E3 87 J5
Monivea Rd BECK BR3 182 C3
Monk Dr CAN/RD E16 106 E6
Monkfrith Av STHGT/OAK N14 34 B1
Monkfrith Wy STHGT/OAK N14 34 B2
Monkham's Av WFD IG8 53 F1
Monkham's La WFD IG8 39 F6
Monkleigh Rd MRDN SM4 177 H6
Monks Av BAR EN5 33 F1
  E/WMO/HCT KT8 188 E2
Monks Cl ABYW SE2 128 E4
  ENC/FH EN2 23 J3
  RSLP HA4 77 H2

RYLN/HDSTN HA2 * 60 A6
Monks Crs WOT/HER KT12 188 A5
Monksdene Gdns SUT SM1 209 F1
Monks Dr ACT W3 98 C4
Monks Orch DART DA1 171 F4
Monks Orchard Rd BECK BR3 198 D5
Monks Pk WBLY HA9 80 E4
Monks Park Gdns WBLY HA9 80 D5
Monks Rd ENC/FH EN2 23 H5
Monks St WOOL/PLUM SE18 127 F4
Monks Wy BECK BR3 198 D3
  GLDGN NW11 64 D1
  STMC/STPC BR5 201 H5
Monkswood Gdns CLAY IG5 54 A6
Monk Ter FSTH SE23 164 C4
Monkton Rd WELL DA16 148 A3
Monkton St LBTH SE11 17 K6
Monkville Av GLDGN NW11 64 D1
Monkville Pde GLDGN NW11 * 64 D1
Monkwell Sq BARB EC2Y 12 D2
Monkwood Cl ROM RM1 75 J2
Monmouth Av KUT/HW KT1 174 D3
  SWFD E18 71 F1
Monmouth Cl CHSWK W4 118 A3
  MTCM CR4 195 K1
  WELL DA16 148 B5
Monmouth Gv BTFD TW8 117 F4
Monmouth Pl BAY/PAD W2 100 E5
Monmouth Rd BAY/PAD W2 100 E5
  DAGW RM9 92 B3
  ED N9 36 D4
  EHAM E6 107 K2
  HYS/HAR UB3 113 H4
Monmouth St LSQ/SEVD WC2H 10 E4
Monnery Rd ARCH N19 84 C1
Monnow Rd STHWK SE1 123 H5
Mono La FELT TW13 154 A4
Monoux Gv WALTH E17 51 J4
Monroe Crs EN EN1 24 D2
Monroe Dr MORT/ESHN SW14 137 J6
Monro Gdns
  KTN/HRWW/WS HA3 42 E5
Monro Pl HOR/WEW KT19 206 C6
Monsell Rd FSBYPK N4 85 H1
Monson Rd NWCR SE14 144 A1
  WLSDN NW10 99 J1
Mons Wy HAYES BR2 200 D3
Montacute Rd BUSH WD23 28 E2
  CAT SE6 164 C2
  CROY/NA CR0 214 A6
  MRDN SM4 194 C3
Montagu Crs UED N18 36 D6
Montague Av BROCKY SE4 144 C5
  HNWL W7 116 A1
Montague Cl BAR EN5 20 C5
  WOT/HER KT12 188 A4
Montague Gdns ACT W3 98 C6
Montague Hall Pl BUSH WD23 28 A1
Montague Pl GWRST WC1E 10 D1
Montague Rd CEND/HSY/T N8 67 F2
  CROY/NA CR0 196 C5
  HACK E8 86 C3
  HNWL W7 116 A2
  HSLW TW3 135 G4
  RCHPK/HAM TW10 157 F1
  SEVS/STOTM N15 * 68 C1
  WAN E11 70 D6
  WEA W13 97 H5
  WIM/MER SW19 178 A3
Montague Sq PECK SE15 143 K1
Montague St RSQ WC1B 10 E1
  STBT EC1A 12 C2
Montague Ter HAYES BR2 199 K1
Montague Wave NWDGN UB2 114 D3
Montagu Gdns UED N18 36 D6
  WLGTN SM6 210 C2
Montagu Man MBLAR W1H 9 F1
Montagu Ms North MBLAR W1H 9 F1
Montagu Ms South MBLAR W1H 9 F2
Montagu Ms West MBLAR W1H 8 E2
Montagu Pl MBLAR W1H 8 E2
Montagu Rd HDN NW4 63 J3
  UED N18 50 D1
Montagu Rw MHST W1U 9 F2
Montagu Sq MBLAR W1H 9 F1
Montagu St MBLAR W1H 9 F2
Montana Gdns SUT SM1 52 D1
  SYD SE26 182 C1
Montana Rd RYNPK SW20 177 F4
  TOOT SW17 161 G5
Montbretia Cl
  STMC/STPC BR5 202 D1
Montcalm Cl HAYES BR2 199 K3
  YEAD UB4 95 F3
Montcalm Rd CHARL SE7 146 C1
Montclare St BETH E2 7 J5
Monteagle Av BARK IG11 90 C4
Monteagle Wy PECK SE15 143 K4
Montefiore St VX/NE SW8 141 G3
Montem Rd FSTH SE23 164 C2
  NWMAL KT3 192 B1
Montem St FSBYPK N4 67 F5
Montenotte Rd
  CEND/HSY/T N8 66 C2
Monterey Cl BXLY DA5 169 K4
Montesole Ct PIN HA5 41 G5
Montesquieu Ter
  CAN/RD E16 * 106 D5
Montford Pl LBTH SE11 122 B5
Montfort Gdns BARK/HLT IG6 54 C2
Montfort Pl WIM/MER SW19 159 G3
Montgomerie Ms FSTH SE23 163 K2
Montgomery Av
  ESH/CLAY KT10 189 K6
Montgomery Cl BFN/LL DA15 147 K6
  MTCM CR4 195 K1
Montgomery Gdns
  BELMT SM2 209 H5
Montgomery Rd CHSWK W4 117 K4
  EDGW HA8 44 B2
Montholme Rd BTSEA SW11 160 E1
Monthorpe Rd WCHPL E1 104 C4
Montolieu Gdns
  PUT/ROE SW15 138 E6

Montpelier Av BXLY DA5 168 E2
  EA W5 97 J4
Montpelier Gdns CHDH RM6 73 J4
  EHAM E6 107 J2
Montpelier Gv KTTN NW5 84 C3
Montpelier Ms SKENS SW7 14 C4
Montpelier Pl SKENS SW7 14 C4
  WCHPL E1 104 E5
Montpelier Ri GLDGN NW11 64 C4
  WBLY HA9 61 K5
Montpelier Rd EA W5 97 K4
  FNCH N3 47 G4
  PECK SE15 143 J2
  SUT SM1 209 G2
Montpelier Rw
  BKHTH/KID SE3 145 J3
  TWK TW1 156 D2
Montpelier Sq SKENS SW7 14 D3
Montpelier St SKENS SW7 14 D3
Montpelier Ter SKENS SW7 14 D3
Montpelier V BKHTH/KID SE3 * 145 J3
Montpelier Wk SKENS SW7 14 D3
Montpelier Wy GLDGN NW11 64 C4
Montrave Rd PGE/AN SE20 181 K2
Montreal Pl HOL/ALD WC2B 11 G5
Montreal Rd IL IG1 72 C4
Montrell Rd BRXS/STRHM SW2 161 K5
Montrose Av BFN/LL DA15 168 B2
  EDGW HA8 44 E5
  KIL/WHAMP NW6 100 C1
  WELL DA16 147 J4
  WHTN TW2 155 G2
Montrose Cl WELL DA16 148 A4
  WFD IG8 38 E6
Montrose Ct ALP/SUD HA0 80 A4
  NFNCH/WDSPK N12 47 F2
Montrose Gdns MTCM CR4 178 E6
  SUT SM1 194 A6
Montrose Pl KTBR SW1X 15 H3
Montrose Rd
  EBED/NFELT TW14 153 G1
  KTN/HRWW/WS HA3 42 E5
Montrose Vls HMSMTH W6 * 118 D5
Montrose Wy FSTH SE23 164 A3
Montserrat Av WFD IG8 52 B3
Montserrat Cl NRWD SE19 180 E1
Montserrat Rd PUT/ROE SW15 139 H5
Monument Wy TOTM N17 68 B3
Monza St WAP E1W 104 F6
Moodkee St BERM/RHTH SE16 123 K3
Moody St WCHPL E1 105 F2
Moon Ct LEE/GVPK SE12 * 145 K5
Moon La BAR EN5 20 D4
Moon St IS N1 85 H6
Moorcroft EDGW HA8 * 44 D4
Moorcroft Gdns HAYES BR2 200 D2
Moorcroft Rd
  STRHM/NOR SW16 161 K5
Moorcroft Wy PIN HA5 59 J2
Moore Cl MORD/VLM SE18 * 137 K4
  MTCM CR4 * 179 G5
Moore Crs DAGW RM9 91 H6
Moorefield Rd TOTM N17 50 B6
Mooreland Rd BMLY BR1 165 J3
Moore Park Rd FUL/PGN SW6 140 A1
Moore Rd NRWD SE19 180 D2
Moore St CHEL SW3 14 E6
Moore Wy BELMT SM2 208 E6
Moorey Cl SRTFD E15 106 D1
Moorfield Av EA W5 97 K3
Moorfield Rd CHSGTN KT9 206 A3
  ORP BR6 202 B4
  PEND EN3 24 E2
Moorfields LVFST EC2M 12 E2
Moorfields Highwalk
  BARB EC2Y 12 E1
Moorgate LOTH EC2R 12 E3
Moorgate Pl LOTH EC2R * 12 E3
Moorhead Wy BKHTH/KID SE3 146 A4
Moorhen Cl ERITH DA8 150 E1
Moorhouse Rd BAY/PAD W2 100 E5
  KTN/HRWW/WS HA3 43 K6
The Moorings CHSWK W4 * 117 H6
Moorland Cl CRW RM5 56 D4
  WHTN TW2 155 F2
Moorland Rd BRXN/ST SW9 142 C5
Moorlands Av MLHL NW7 45 K2
Moor La BARB EC2Y 12 E2
  CHSGTN KT9 206 B3
Moormead Dr HOR/WEW KT19 207 G3
Moor Mead Rd TWK TW1 156 B1
Moor Park Gdns
  KUTN/CMB KT2 176 B3
Moor Park Rd NTHWD HA6 40 B2
Moorside Rd BMLY BR1 165 H6
Moortown Rd OXHEY WD19 27 G6
Moot Wy WATW WD18 26 B1
Morant Gdns CRW RM5 56 D1
Morant St POP/IOD E14 105 J6
Mora Rd CRICK NW2 82 A2
Mora St FSBYE EC1V 6 C5
Moravian Pl WBPTN SW10 120 C6
Moravian St BETH E2 104 E1
Moray Av HYS/HAR UB3 113 J1
Moray Cl EDGW HA8 30 D4
  ROM RM1 57 J1
Moray Ms HOLWY N7 67 F6
Moray Rd HOLWY N7 67 F6
Moray Wy ROM RM1 57 J3
Morcambe St WALW SE17 18 D7
Mordaunt Gdns DAGW RM9 92 A5
Mordaunt Rd WLSDN NW10 81 F6
Mordaunt St BRXN/ST SW9 142 A4
Morden Ct MRDN SM4 194 A1
Morden Court Pde
  MRDN SM4 * 178 A6
Morden Gdns GFD/PVL UB6 79 F3
  MTCM CR4 194 C1
Morden Hall Rd MRDN SM4 178 A6
Morden Hl LEW SE13 145 F3
Morden La LEW SE13 145 F2

Morden Rd BKHTH/KID SE3 145 K3
  CHDH RM6 74 A4
  MTCM CR4 178 A5
  WIM/MER SW19 178 A5
Morden Road Ms
  BKHTH/KID SE3 145 K3
Morden St LEW SE13 144 E3
Morden Wy CHEAM SM3 193 K4
Morden Wharf Rd
  GNWCH SE10 125 H3
Mordon Rd GDMY/SEVK IG3 73 F4
Mordred Rd CAT SE6 165 H4
Morecambe Cl WCHPL E1 105 G4
Morecambe Gdns STAN HA7 29 K6
Morecambe St WALW SE17 18 D7
Morecambe Ter UED N18 * 35 K6
More Cl CAN/RD E16 106 D5
  WKENS W14 119 G4
Morecoombe Cl
  KUTN/CMB KT2 175 J3
Moree Wy UED N18 36 C4
Moreland Cottages BOW E3 * 105 J1
Moreland St FSBYE EC1V 6 B4
Moreland Wy CHING E4 37 K5
More La ESH/CLAY KT10 204 B1
Morella Rd BAL SW12 160 E2
More London Pl STHWK SE1 19 H1
More London Riverside
  STHWK SE1 19 H1
Moremead Rd CAT SE6 164 C6
Morena St CAT SE6 164 E6
Moresby Av BRYLDS KT5 191 J4
Moresby Rd CLPT E5 68 D5
Moreton Av ISLW TW7 135 J2
Moreton Cl CLPT E5 68 D5
  MLHL NW7 46 A2
  SEVS/STOTM N15 67 K3
Moreton Ct DART DA1 150 B4
Moreton Gdns WFD IG8 53 J1
Moreton Pl PIM SW1V 121 H5
  WPK KT4 192 C5
Moreton Rd SAND/SEL CR2 211 K5
  WPK KT4 192 D6
Moreton St PIM SW1V 121 J5
Moreton Ter PIM SW1V 121 H5
Moreton Terrace Ms North
  PIM SW1V 121 H5
Moreton Terrace Ms South
  PIM SW1V 121 H5
Morford Cl RSLP HA4 59 F4
Morford Wy RSLP HA4 59 F4
Morgan Av WALTH E17 70 B1
Morgan Cl DAGE RM10 92 C5
Morgan Rd BMLY BR1 183 K3
  HOLWY N7 85 G4
  NKENS W10 100 D4
Morgan's La HYS/HAR UB3 94 B4
  STHWK SE1 19 G1
Morgan St BOW E3 105 H2
  CAN/RD E16 106 C4
Morgan Wy WFD IG8 53 J2
Moriarty Cl BMLY BR1 201 G1
Moriarty Rd HOLWY N7 84 E2
Morie St WAND/EARL SW18 140 A5
Morieux Rd LEY E10 69 H5
Moring Rd TOOT SW17 161 F6
Morkyns Wk DUL SE21 * 163 F5
Morland Av CROY/NA CR0 197 G4
  DART DA1 150 B6
Morland Cl GLDGN NW11 65 F5
  HPTN TW12 172 E1
  MTCM CR4 178 D6
Morland Est HACK E8 86 C5
Morland Gdns STHL UB1 115 G1
  WLSDN NW10 81 F5
Morland Ms IS N1 85 G5
  IL IG1 72 B6
Morland Rd CROY/NA CR0 197 G4
  DAGE RM10 92 C5
  IL IG1 71 K6
  KTN/HRWW/WS HA3 62 A2
  PGE/AN SE20 182 A2
  SUT SM1 209 G4
  WALTH E17 69 F2
  WDGN N22 49 H4
Morley Av CHING E4 52 B3
  UED N18 36 C6
  WDGN N22 49 H5
Morley Cl ORP BR6 216 B1
Morley Crs EDGW HA8 30 E4
  RSLP HA4 59 G6
Morley Crs East STAN HA7 43 J6
Morley Crs West STAN HA7 43 J6
Morley Hl ENC/FH EN2 23 J1
Morley Rd BARK IG11 90 D6
  CHEAM SM3 193 J6
  CHST BR7 185 H4
  LEW SE13 145 G5
  LEY E10 70 A5
  SRTFD E15 106 D1
  TWK TW1 156 E1
Morley St STHWK SE1 17 K3
Morna Rd CMBW SE5 142 D3
Morning La HOM E9 86 E4
Morningside Rd WPK KT4 192 E6
Mornington Av HAYES BR2 184 B6
  IL IG1 72 A4
  WKENS W14 119 J4
Mornington Crs CAMTN NW1 4 A2
Mornington Gv BOW E3 105 J2
Mornington Ms CMBW SE5 142 D2
Mornington Pl CAMTN NW1 3 K2
Mornington Rd CHING E4 38 B2
  GFD/PVL UB6 96 B4
  NWCR SE14 144 B2
  WAN E11 71 F3
Mornington St CAMTN NW1 3 K1
Mornington Ter CAMTN NW1 3 K1
Mornington Wk
  RCHPK/HAM TW10 156 D6
Morocco St STHWK SE1 19 G3

Morpeth Gv HOM E9 87 F6
Morpeth Rd HOM E9 87 F6
Morpeth St BETH E2 105 F2
Morpeth Ter WEST SW1P 16 A5
Morpeth Wk TOTM N17 * 50 D3
Morrab Gdns GDMY/SEVK IG3 91 F1
Morrel Cl BAR EN5 21 G4
Morrells Yd LBTH SE11 122 B5
Morris Av MNPK E12 89 K3
Morris Bishop Ter HGT N6 * 66 A3
Morris Cl CROY/NA CR0 198 B5
  ORP BR6 216 E1
Morris Ct CHING E4 37 K6
Morris Gdns DART DA1 151 K6
  WAND/EARL SW18 159 K2
Morris Pl FSBYPK N4 85 G1
Morris Rd BCTR RM8 74 B6
  HARH RM3 57 K3
  ISLW TW7 135 K4
  POP/IOD E14 105 K4
  SRTFD E15 88 C4
Morris St WCHPL E1 104 D5
Morriston Cl OXHEY WD19 41 G5
Morrish Rd BRXS/STRHM SW2 161 J1
Morrison Av TOTM N17 49 J2
  YEAD UB4 95 F2
Morrison Pl FSBYPK N4 67 C6
Morse Cl PLSTW E13 106 E2
Morshead Rd MV/WKIL W9 100 E3
Morson Rd PEND EN3 37 G1
Morteyne Rd TOTM N17 49 K4
Mortham St SRTFD E15 88 C6
Mortimer Cl BUSH WD23 28 B1
  CRICK NW2 82 C1
  STRHM/NOR SW16 161 J4
Mortimer Crs KIL/WHAMP NW6 83 F1
  WPK KT4 207 F1
Mortimer Dr EN EN1 23 K6
Mortimer Est KIL/WHAMP NW6 83 F1
Mortimer Pl KIL/WHAMP NW6 83 F1
Mortimer Rd EHAM E6 107 K2
  ERITH DA8 150 A5
  IS N1 86 A5
  MTCM CR4 178 E4
  NKENS W10 100 C6
  ORP BR6 202 B3
  WEA W13 97 J5
Mortimer Sq NTGHL W11 100 B6
Mortimer St GTPST W1W 9 K5
Mortimer Ter KTTN NW5 * 84 B2
Mortlake Cl CROY/NA CR0 210 E1
Mortlake Dr MTCM CR4 178 D4
Mortlake High St
  MORT/ESHN SW14 138 B4
Mortlake Rd CAN/RD E16 107 F5
  IL IG1 90 C2
  RCH/KEW TW9 137 H1
Morton Cl CLAP SW4 141 J5
Morton Gdns WLGTN SM6 210 C3
Morton Ms ECT SW5 * 120 A4
Morton Pl STHWK SE1 17 J5
Morton Rd IS N1 85 J5
  MRDN SM4 194 C2
  SRTFD E15 88 D5
Morton Wy STHGT/OAK N14 34 C3
Morval Rd BRXS/STRHM SW2 142 B6
Morvale Cl BELV DA17 129 G4
Morven Rd TOOT SW17 160 E5
Morville St BOW E3 105 J1
Morwell St NOXST/BSQ WC1A 10 C2
Moscow Pl BAY/PAD W2 101 F6
Moscow Rd BAY/PAD W2 100 E6
Moselle Av WDGN N22 49 G5
Moselle Cl CEND/HSY/T N8 49 F6
Moselle Pl TOTM N17 50 B3
Moselle St TOTM N17 50 B3
Mossborough Cl
  NFNCH/WDSPK N12 47 F2
Mossbury Rd BTSEA SW11 140 D4
Moss Cl PIN HA5 41 K5
  WCHPL E1 104 C4
Mossdown Cl BELV DA17 129 H4
Mossford Gn BARK/HLT IG6 54 B6
Mossford La BARK/HLT IG6 54 C5
Mossford St BOW E3 105 J3
Moss Gdns FELT TW13 153 K4
  SAND/SEL CR2 213 F5
Moss Hall Crs
  NFNCH/WDSPK N12 47 F2
Moss Hall Gv
  NFNCH/WDSPK N12 47 F2
Moss La PIN HA5 41 K5
  ROM RM1 75 H5
Mosslea Rd HAYES BR2 200 C1
  ORP BR6 216 D2
  PGE/AN SE20 181 K3
Mossop St CHEL SW3 14 D6
Mossville Gdns MRDN SM4 177 J6
Moston Cl HYS/HAR UB3 113 J5
Mostyn Av WBLY HA9 80 B3
Mostyn Gdns WLSDN NW10 100 B2
Mostyn Gv BOW E3 105 J1
Mostyn Rd BRXN/ST SW9 142 B2
  EDGW HA8 45 F6
  WIM/MER SW19 177 J6
Mosul Wy HAYES BR2 200 D3
Mosyer Dr STMC/STPC BR5 202 E6
Moth Cl WLGTN SM6 210 E5
Motcomb St KTBR SW1X 15 F4
The Mothers Sq CLPT E5 * 86 D2
Moth House
  WOOL/PLUM SE18 * 146 D1
Motley Av SDTCH EC2A 7 G6
Motley St VX/NE SW8 141 H3
Motspur Pk NWMAL KT3 192 D3
Mottingham Gdns
  ELTH/MOT SE9 166 C3
Mottingham La
  LEE/GVPK SE12 166 B3
Mottingham Rd ED N9 37 F2
  ELTH/MOT SE9 166 D3
Mottisfont Rd ABYW SE2 128 C3
Moulins Rd HOM E9 86 E5
Moulton Av HSLW TW3 134 D3

Moundfield Rd
  STNW/STAM N16..............68 C3
Moundacre Cl SYD SE26......163 H6
Mount Adon Pk EDUL SE22....163 H2
Montague Pl POP/IOD E14....106 A6
Mount Angelus Rd
  RCHPK/HAM TW10............137 F6
Mount Ararat Rd
  RCHPK/HAM TW10............137 G6
Mount Ash Rd SYD SE26......163 H6
Mount Av CHING E4...........37 J5
  EA W5.....................97 K4
  STHL UB1..................96 A5
Mountbatten Cl NRWD SE19...181 F1
Mountbatten Ct BKHH IG9.....39 H4
Mountbel Rd STAN HA7........43 C5
Mount Cl BMLY BR1..........184 D4
  CAR SM5..................210 A6
  EA W5.....................97 J4
  EBAR EN4..................22 A5
Mountearl Gdns
  STRHM/NOR SW16...........162 A5
Mount Echo Av CHING E4......37 K3
Mount Echo Dr CHING E4......37 K3
Mount Ephraim La
  STRHM/NOR SW16...........161 J5
Mount Ephraim Rd
  STRHM/NOR SW16...........161 J5
Mountfield Cl CAT SE6......165 G2
Mountfield Rd EA W5.........97 K4
  FNCH N3...................46 E6
Mountfield Ter CAT SE6.....165 G2
Mountfield Wy
  STMC/STPC BR5............202 D1
Mountfort Crs IS N1.........85 C5
Mountfort Ter IS N1.........85 C5
Mount Gdns SYD SE26........163 J5
Mount Gv EDGW HA8...........30 E5
Mountgrove Rd HBRY N5.......85 J1
Mounthurst Rd HAYES BR2....199 K4
Mountington Park Cl
  KTN/HRWW/WS HA3...........61 K3
Mountjoy Cl ABYW SE2.......128 C2
Mount Ms HPTN TW12.........173 G4
Mount Mills FSBYE EC1V.......6 B5
Mount Nod Rd
  STRHM/NOR SW16...........162 A5
Mount Pde EBAR EN4 *........21 J5
Mount Pk CAR SM5...........210 A6
Mount Park Av HRW HA1.......60 C4
  SAND/SEL CR2.............211 H6
Mount Park Crs EA W5........97 K5
Mount Park Rd EA W5.........97 K5
  HRW HA1...................78 D1
  PIN HA5...................58 E2
Mount Pl ACT W3............117 J1
Mount Pleasant ALP/SUD HA0..80 A6
  EBAR EN4..................21 K5
  FSBYW WC1X.................5 H7
  HRW HA1...................60 E6
  RSLP HA4..................59 G6
  WWWD SE27................162 D6
Mount Pleasant Crs
  FSBYPK N4 *...............67 F4
Mount Pleasant Hl CLPT E5...68 D5
Mount Pleasant La CLPT E5...68 D5
Mount Pleasant Pl
  WOOL/PLUM SE18...........127 K4
Mount Pleasant Rd CRW RM5...57 F2
  DART DA1.................171 J1
  EA W5.....................97 J3
  LEW SE13.................145 F4
  NWMAL KT3................175 K6
  TOTM N17..................50 A6
  WALTH E17.................69 J3
  WLSDN NW10................82 A5
Mount Pleasant Vls FSBYPK N4.67 F4
Mount Rd BCTR RM8...........74 B5
  BXLYHS DA6...............149 F6
  CHSGTN KT9...............206 A3
  CRICK NW2.................81 K1
  DART DA1.................170 C1
  EBAR EN4..................21 J6
  FELT TW13................141 J3
  HDN NW4...................63 J4
  HYS/HAR UB3..............113 K2
  IL IG1....................90 B3
  MTCM CR4.................178 C5
  NRWD SE19 *..............180 E2
  NWMAL KT3................176 A5
  WIM/MER SW19.............159 K4
Mount Rw MYFR/PKLN W1K.......9 J6
Mountside KTN/HRWW/WS HA3...61 K4
Mounts Pond Rd
  BKHTH/KID SE3............145 H3
The Mount Sq HAMP NW3 *.....83 G1
Mount Stewart Av
  KTN/HRWW/WS HA3...........61 K4
Mount St WBPTN SW10..........9 J6
Mount Ter WCHPL E1.........104 D4
The Mount BMLY BR1 *.......184 D4
  BXLYHS DA6...............149 J6
  CLPT E5...................68 D6
  ESH/CLAY KT10............204 A4
  EW KT17..................207 K2
  HAMP NW3..................83 G1
  NTHLT UB5 *...............78 B5
  NWMAL KT3................176 A6
  TRDG/WHET N20.............33 C4
  WBLY HA9..................62 D6
Mount Vw ENC/FH EN2.........22 E1
Mountview MLHL NW7..........31 F5
  NTHWD HA6.................40 E2
Mount View NWDGN UB2.......114 C4
Mountview HAMP NW3..........83 C5
Mount View Rd
  CDALE/KGS NW9.............63 F1
  CHING E4..................38 B2

  ESH/CLAY KT10............205 H5
  FSBYPK N4.................67 F4
Mountview Rd ORP BR6.......202 B4
Mount Vs WNWD SE27.........162 C5
Mount Wy CAR SM5...........210 A6
Mountwood E/WMO/HCT KT8....173 C6
Movers La BARK IG11.........90 D6
Mowat Cl ARCH N19...........66 D5
Mowbray Gdns NTHLT UB5 *....78 A6
Mowbray Rd BAR EN5..........20 E5
  EDGW HA8..................30 C6
  KIL/WHAMP NW6.............82 C5
  NRWD SE19................181 G4
  RCHPK/HAM TW10...........156 C4
Mowbrays Cl CRW RM5.........56 E4
Mowbrays Rd CRW RM5.........56 E4
Mowlem St BETH E2..........104 D1
Mowll St BRXN/ST SW9.......142 B1
Moxon Cl PLSTW E13.........106 D1
Moxon St BAR EN5............20 D4
  MHST W1U...................9 G2
Moye Cl BETH E2 *..........104 C1
Moyers Rd LEY E10...........70 A5
Moylan Rd HMSMTH W6........119 H6
Moyne Pl WLSDN NW10.........98 C2
Moynihan Dr WCHMH N21.......22 E6
Moys Cl CROY/NA CR0........195 K3
Moyser Rd STRHM/NOR SW16...179 H1
Mozart St NKENS W10........100 D2
Muchelney Rd MRDN SM4......194 B3
Muggeridge Cl SAND/SEL CR2.211 K3
Muggeridge Rd DAGE RM10.....92 D2
Muirdown Av
  MORT/ESHN SW14...........137 K5
Muir Dr WAND/EARL SW18.....160 C1
Muirfield ACT W3............99 C5
Muirfield Cl BERM/RHTH SE16.123 J5
  OXHEY WD19................41 C1
Muirfield Crs POP/IOD E14..124 E3
Muirfield Gn OXHEY WD19.....27 C6
Muirfield Rd OXHEY WD19.....27 C6
Muirkirk Rd CAT SE6........165 F3
Muir Rd CLPT E5.............86 C1
Mulberry Av STWL/WRAY TW19.152 B3
Mulberry Cl CEND/HSY/T N8...66 E1
  CHEL SW3 *...............120 D5
  CHING E4..................37 J4
  EBAR EN4..................21 H5
  GPK RM2...................75 K1
  HDN NW4...................45 K5
  NTHLT UB5 *...............95 J1
  STRHM/NOR SW16...........161 H6
Mulberry Crs BTFD TW8......136 C1
  WDR/YW UB7...............112 D2
Mulberry Dr PUR RM19.......131 J4
Mulberry La CROY/NA CR0....197 G5
Mulberry Ms NWCR SE14......144 C2
Mulberry Pde WDR/YW UB7....112 D3
Mulberry Pl ELTH/MOT SE9...146 A4
  HMSMTH W6................118 D5
Mulberry Rd HACK E8.........86 B5
Mulberry St WCHPL E1.......104 C5
Mulberry Wk CHEL SW3.......120 C6
Mulberry Wy BARK/HLT IG6....72 C1
  BELV DA17................129 K2
  SWFD E18..................53 F5
Mulgrave Rd BELMT SM2......208 D5
  CROY/NA CR0..............211 K2
  EA W5.....................97 K2
  HRW HA1...................61 G6
  WKENS W14................119 H6
  WLSDN NW10................81 H2
Mulholland Cl MTCM CR4.....179 G5
Mulkern Rd ARCH N19.........66 D5
Mullards Cl MTCM CR4.......194 E5
Mullet Gdns BETH E2........104 C2
Mullins Pth MORT/ESHN SW14.138 A4
Mullion Cl KTN/HRWW/WS HA3..42 B4
Mullion Wk OXHEY WD19.......27 H6
Mull Wk IS N1...............85 J4
Mulready St STJWD NW8........2 C7
Multi Wy ACT W3............118 B2
Mutton Rd WAND/EARL SW18...160 C2
Mumford Mills GNWCH SE10...144 D1
Mumford Rd HNHL SE24.......142 C6
Muncaster Cl ASHF TW15.....152 D6
Muncaster Rd CLAP SW4......140 E5
Muncies Ms CAT SE6.........165 F4
Mundania Rd EDUL SE22......163 J1
Munday Rd CAN/RD E16.......106 E6
Munden St WKENS W14........119 H4
Mundesly Cl OXHEY WD19......27 G6
Mundford Rd CLPT E5.........68 E6
Mundon Gdns IL IG1..........72 D5
Mund St WKENS W14..........119 J5
Mundy St IS N1...............7 G4
Mungo-park Cl BUSH WD23 *...28 C4
Mungo Park Rd RAIN RM13.....93 J5
Mungo Park Wy
  STMC/STPC BR5............202 E4
Munnery Wy ORP BR6.........216 B1
Munnings Gdns ISLW TW7.....155 J5
Munro Dr FBAR/BDGN N11 *....48 C2
Munroe Ter WBPTN SW10......140 C1
Munro Ms NKENS W10.........100 C4
Munro Wy CLPT E5............87 H1
Munster Av HSLWW TW4.......134 D5
Munster Ct FUL/PGN SW6.....139 J3
Munster Gdns PLMGR N13......35 J6
Munster Ms FUL/PGN SW6 *...139 J1
  TEDD TW11................174 D2
Munster Sq CAMTN NW1 *.......3 K6
Munton Rd WALW SE17.........18 D6
Murchison Av BXLY DA5......168 E3
Murchison Rd LEY E10........70 A6
Murdock Cl CAN/RD E16......106 D5
Murdock St PECK SE15.......123 J6
Murfett Cl WIM/MER SW19....159 H4
Muriel St IS N1..............5 H2
Murillo Rd LEW SE13........145 G5
Murphy St STHWK SE1.........17 J3

Murray Av BMLY BR1.........184 A6
  HSLW TW3.................135 G6
Murray Cl THMD SE28........127 K1
Murray Crs PIN HA5..........41 H4
Murray Gv IS N1..............7 E3
Murray House
  WOOL/PLUM SE18 *.........146 D1
Murray Ms CAMTN NW1.........84 D5
Murray Rd EA W5............116 D4
  NTHWD HA6.................40 C4
  RCHPK/HAM TW10...........156 C4
  STMC/STPC BR5............186 C6
  WIM/MER SW19.............177 G2
Murray Sq CAN/RD E16.......106 E6
Murray St CAMTN NW1.........84 D5
Murray Ter HAMP NW3.........83 G2
Murtwell Dr CHIG IG7........54 C2
Musard Rd HMSMTH W6........119 H6
Musbury St WCHPL E1........104 E5
Muscatel Pl CMBW SE5 *.....143 F2
Muschamp Rd CAR SM5........194 D6
  PECK SE15................143 G4
Muscovy St MON EC3R.........13 H6
Museum St NOXST/BSQ WC1A...10 E3
Musgrave Cl EBAR EN4........21 G2
Musgrave Crs FUL/PGN SW6...139 K1
Musgrave Rd ISLW TW7.......136 A2
Musgrove Rd NWCR SE14......144 A2
Musjid Rd BTSEA SW11 *.....140 C3
Musquash Wy HSLWW TW4......134 B3
Muston Rd CLPT E5...........68 D6
Muswell Av MUSWH N10........48 B5
Muswell Hill MUSWH N10......48 B6
Muswell Hill Broadway
  MUSWH N10................66 B1
Muswell Hill Pl MUSWH N10...66 B1
Muswell Hill Rd MUSWH N10...66 A1
Muswell Ms MUSWH N10........48 B6
Muswell Rd MUSWH N10........48 B5
Mutrix Rd KIL/WHAMP NW6.....82 E6
Mutter Rd CLAP SW4.........141 J1
Mutton Pl CAMTN NW1.........84 A4
Muybridge Rd NWMAL KT3.....175 K5
Myatt Rd BRXN/ST SW9.......142 C2
Mycenae Rd BKHTH/KID SE3...125 K6
Myddelton Av EN EN1.........24 A1
Myddelton Cl EN EN1.........24 B2
Myddelton Pk TRDG/WHET N20..33 H5
Myddelton Pas CLKNW EC1R.....5 K4
Myddelton Rd CEND/HSY/T N8..48 E4
Myddelton Sq CLKNW EC1R......5 K5
Myddelton St CLKNW EC1R......5 K5
Myddleton Av FSBYPK N4......67 H6
Myddleton Rd WDGN N22.......49 F3
Myers La NWCR SE14.........124 A6
Mylis Cl SYD SE26..........163 J6
Myln Cl HMSMTH W6..........118 D5
Mylne Cl HMSMTH W6.........118 D5
Mylne St CLKNW EC1R..........5 J4
Myra St ABYW SE2...........128 B5
Myrdle St WCHPL E1.........104 C5
Myrna Cl WIM/MER SW19......178 D3
Myron Pl LEW SE13..........145 F4
Myrtle Av EBED/NFELT TW14..133 H6
  RSLP HA4..................58 E4
Myrtleberry Cl HACK E8 *....86 B4
Myrtle Cl EBAR EN4..........33 K4
  ERITH DA8................150 B1
  WDR/YW UB7...............112 C4
Myrtledene Rd ABYW SE2.....128 B5
Myrtle Gdns HNWL W7........115 K1
Myrtle Gv ENC/FH EN2........23 K1
  NWMAL KT3................159 K6
Myrtle Rd ACT W3...........117 K1
  CROY/NA CR0..............213 J1
  DART DA1.................171 J4
  EHAM E6...................89 J6
  HPTN TW12................173 H2
  HSLW TW3.................135 H3
  IL IG1....................72 B6
  PLMGR N13.................35 H5
  SUT SM1..................209 G3
  WALTH E17.................51 G5
Myrtleside Cl NTHWD HA6.....40 B3
Myrtle St IS N1..............7 G3
Myrtle Wk IS N1..............7 G3
Mysore Rd BTSEA SW11.......140 E5
Myton Rd DUL SE21..........162 E5

N

Nadine St CHARL SE7........126 B5
Nagle Cl WALTH E17..........52 B5
Nag's Head La WELL DA16....148 C4
Nags Head Rd PEND EN3.......24 E5
Nairne Gv HNHL SE24........142 E6
Nairn Rd RSLP HA4...........77 G4
Nairn St POP/IOD E14.......106 A4
Nalhead Rd FELT TW13.......172 B1
Namba Roy Cl
  STRHM/NOR SW16...........162 A6
Namton Dr THHTH CR7........196 A1
Nan Clark's La MLHL NW7.....31 H4
Nancy Downs OXHEY WD19......27 G2
Nankin St POP/IOD E14......105 J5
Nansen Rd BTSEA SW11.......141 F5
Nansen Village
  NFNCH/WDSPK N12 *.........33 F6
Nantes Cl WAND/EARL SW18...140 B4
Nant Rd CRICK NW2...........64 D6
Nant St BETH E2............104 D2
Naoroji St FSBYW WC1X........5 J5
Napier Av FUL/PGN SW6......139 J4
  POP/IOD E14..............124 D5
Napier Cl DEPT SE8.........144 C1
  EMPK RM11................75 K4
  WDR/YW UB7...............112 D3
  WKENS W14 *..............119 J3
Napier Ct FUL/PGN SW6 *....139 J4
Napier Gv IS N1..............7 E3
Napier Pl WKENS W14........119 J3
Napier Rd ALP/SUD HA0.......79 K6
  BELV DA17................129 G4
  EHAM E6...................90 A6

  HAYES BR2................184 A6
  ISLW TW7.................136 B5
  PEND EN3..................25 F6
  SAND/SEL CR2.............211 K5
  SNWD SE25................197 J1
  SRTFD E15................106 C1
  TOTM N17..................50 A6
  WAN E11...................88 C1
  WDR/YW UB7...............112 B3
  WKENS W14................119 J3
  WLSDN NW10................99 K2
Napoleon Rd CLPT E5.........86 D1
  TWK TW1..................156 C2
Narbonne Av CLAP SW4.......141 H6
Narborough Cl HGDN/ICK UB10.58 B4
Narborough St FUL/PGN SW6..140 A3
Narcissus Rd KIL/WHAMP NW6..82 E3
Narford Rd CLPT E5..........68 C1
Narrow Boat Cl THMD SE28...127 J2
Narrow St ACT W3...........117 J1
  POP/IOD E14..............105 G6
Narrow Wy HAYES BR2........200 B5
Nascot St SHB W12..........100 A5
Naseby Cl ISLW TW7.........135 K2
  KIL/WHAMP NW6 *...........83 G5
Naseby Ct WOT/HER KT12 *...188 B6
Naseby Rd CLAY IG5..........53 K6
  DAGE RM10.................92 C1
  NRWD SE19................180 D2
Nash Cl SUT SM1............209 H1
Nash Gn BMLY BR1...........183 K2
Nash La HAYES BR2..........214 E6
Nash Rd BROCKY SE4.........144 B5
  CHDH RM6..................73 K1
  ED N9.....................36 E4
Nash St CAMTN NW1............3 K4
Nash Wy KTN/HRWW/WS HA3.....61 H3
Nasmyth St HMSMTH W6.......118 E3
Nassau Rd BARN SW13........138 C2
Nassau St GTPST W1W.........10 A2
Nassington Rd HAMP NW3......83 J2
Natalie Cl EBED/NFELT TW14.153 C2
Natalie Ms WHTN TW2........155 J5
Natal Rd FBAR/BDGN N11......48 E2
  IL IG1....................90 A2
  STRHM/NOR SW16...........179 J2
  THHTH CR7................180 E6
Nathaniel Cl WCHPL E1 *.....13 K2
Nathans Rd ALP/SUD HA0......61 J1
National Ter
  BERM/RHTH SE16 *.........123 J2
Nation Wy CHING E4..........38 A3
Naval Rw POP/IOD E14.......106 A6
Navarino Gv HACK E8.........86 C4
Navarino Rd HACK E8.........86 C4
Navarre Gdns CRW RM5........56 C2
Navarre St BETH E2...........7 J6
Navestock Cl CHING E4 *.....38 A5
Navestock Crs WFD IG8.......53 C5
Navestock Ter WFD IG8.......53 C5
Navigator Dr NWDGN UB2.....115 H2
Navy St CLAP SW4...........141 J4
Nayim Pl HACK E8............86 D4
Naylor Gv PEND EN3..........25 F6
Naylor Rd PECK SE15........143 J1
  TRDG/WHET N20.............33 G6
Nazareth Cl PECK SE15......143 J3
Nazrul St BETH E2............7 J5
Neal Av STHL UB1............95 K3
Neal Cl NTHWD HA6...........40 E4
Nealden St BRXN/ST SW9.....142 A4
Neale Cl EFNCH N2...........47 G6
Neal Ter FSTH SE23 *.......164 A3
Neal Yd LSQ/SEVD WC2H......10 E4
Near Acre CDALE/KGS NW9.....45 H4
Neasden Cl WLSDN NW10.......81 C3
Neasden La WLSDN NW10.......81 G5
Neasden La North
  WLSDN NW10................81 G1
Neasham Rd BCTR RM8.........91 G3
Neate St CMBW SE5..........123 G6
Neath Gdns MRDN SM4........194 B3
Neathouse Pl PIM SW1V.......16 A6
Neats Acre RSLP HA4.........58 B4
Neatscourt Rd EHAM E6......107 H5
Neckinger BERM/RHTH SE16....19 K4
Neckinger Est
  BERM/RHTH SE16...........19 K4
Neckinger St STHWK SE1......19 J3
Needham Rd BAY/PAD W2......100 E5
Needleman St
  BERM/RHTH SE16...........124 A2
Neela Cl HGDN/ICK UB10......76 A1
Neeld Crs HDN NW4...........63 K2
  WBLY HA9..................80 C3
Neil James Gdns
  WNWD SE27 *..............162 E6
Nelson Cl CROY/NA CR0......196 C5
  EBED/NFELT TW14 *........153 J2
  KIL/WHAMP NW6............100 D1
  ROMW/RG RM7...............56 D5
  WOT/HER KT12.............188 A5
Nelson Gdns BETH E2........104 C2
  HSLW TW3.................155 F1
Nelson Grove Rd
  WIM/MER SW19.............178 A4
Nelson Mandela Cl
  MUSWH N10................47 K5
Nelson Mandela Rd
  BKHTH/KID SE3............146 B4
Nelson Pas FSBYE EC1V........6 D5
Nelson Rd BELV DA17........129 G5
  CEND/HSY/T N8.............67 F2
  CHING E4..................51 K2
  DART DA1.................171 J5
  ED N9.....................36 D5
  GNWCH SE10...............125 F6

  HAYES BR2................200 B1
  HRW HA1...................60 E5
  HTHAIR TW6...............132 C2
  NWMAL KT3................192 A2
  PEND EN3..................25 F5
  RAIN RM13................111 H1
  SCUP DA14................168 B6
  SEVS/STOTM N15............67 J1
  STAN HA7..................43 J2
  WAN E11...................70 E1
  WHTN TW2.................155 F1
  WIM/MER SW19.............178 A3
Nelson Sq STHWK SE1.........18 A2
Nelsons Rw CLAP SW4........141 J5
Nelson St CAN/RD E16.......106 D6
  EHAM E6..................107 K1
  WCHPL E1.................104 D5
Nelsons Yd CAMTN NW1 *.......4 A2
Nelson Ter FSBYE EC1V........6 B4
Nelson Wk HOR/WEW KT19.....206 C6
Nemoure Rd ACT W3...........98 E6
Nene Gdns FELT TW13........154 E4
Nene Rd HTHAIR TW6.........132 E2
Nepaul Rd BTSEA SW11.......140 D3
Nepean St PUT/ROE SW15.....158 D2
Neptune Cl RAIN RM13.......111 H1
Neptune Rd HRW HA1..........60 D3
  HTHAIR TW6...............133 G2
Nesbit Cl BKHTH/KID SE3....145 H3
Nesbit Rd ELTH/MOT SE9.....146 C4
Nesbitt Sq NRWD SE19 *.....181 F3
Nesham St WAP E1W..........123 H1
Ness Rd ERITH DA8..........151 H1
Ness St BERM/RHTH SE16.....123 H3
Nesta Rd WFD IG8............52 D2
Nestle's Av HYS/HAR UB3....113 J3
Nestor Av WCHMH N21.........35 H1
Netheravon Rd CHSWK W4.....118 C4
  HNWL W7..................116 A1
Netheravon Rd South
  CHSWK W4.................118 C6
Netherbury Rd EA W5........116 D3
Netherby Gdns ENC/FH EN2....22 E5
Netherby Rd FSTH SE23......163 K2
Nether Cl FNCH N3...........46 E3
Nether Ct MLHL NW7..........46 E3
Nethercourt Av FNCH N3......46 E2
Netherfield Gdns BARK IG11..90 D5
Netherfield Rd
  NFNCH/WDSPK N12..........47 F1
  TOOT SW17................161 F5
Netherford Rd CLAP SW4.....141 H3
Netherhall Gdns HAMP NW3....83 G3
Netherhall Wy HAMP NW3......83 G3
Netherlands Rd BAR EN5......33 H1
Netherleigh Cl HGT N6.......66 B6
Netherpark Dr GPK RM2.......57 H5
Nether St FNCH N3...........46 E4
  NFNCH/WDSPK N12..........33 F6
Netherton Gv WBPTN SW10....120 B6
Netherton Rd SEVS/STOTM N15.67 K3
  TWK TW1..................136 B6
Netherwood Pl HMSMTH W6 *...119 G3
Netherwood Rd WKENS W14....119 G3
Netherwood St
  KIL/WHAMP NW6.............82 D5
Netley Cl CHEAM SM3........208 B4
  CROY/NA CR0..............214 A5
Netley Dr WOT/HER KT12.....188 E4
Netley Gdns MRDN SM4.......194 B4
Netley Rd BTFD TW8.........117 F6
  GNTH/NBYPK IG2............72 D2
  MRDN SM4.................194 B4
  WALTH E17.................69 H2
Netley St CAMTN NW1 *........4 A5
Nettlecombe Cl BELMT SM2...209 F6
Nettleden Av WBLY HA9.......80 C4
Nettlefold Pl WNWD SE27....162 C5
Nettlestead Cl BECK BR3....182 C5
Nettleton Rd HTHAIR TW6....132 E2
  NWCR SE14................144 A2

Neville Av NWMAL KT3.......176 A4
  HSLW TW3.................135 G3
  KIL/WHAMP NW6.............82 C2
  PECK SE15................143 H1
  SCUP DA14................168 A6
  WAN E11...................88 D1
Neville Cl ACT W3..........117 K2
  BAR EN5...................20 E5
  CAMTN NW1..................4 A4
  CROY/NA CR0..............196 E4
  EA W5.....................97 K1
  FSTGT E7..................88 E5
  KIL/WHAMP NW6............100 D1
  KUT/HW KT1...............175 F5
  PECK SE15................143 H1
  RCHPK/HAM TW10...........137 G5
  SCUP DA14................168 A5
  WAN E11...................88 D1
Neville Dr EFNCH N2.........65 G3
Neville Gdns BCTR RM8.......91 K1
Neville Gill Cl
  WAND/EARL SW18...........159 K1
Neville Pl WDGN N22.........49 F4
Neville Rd BARK/HLT IG6.....54 C4
  BCTR RM8..................73 K6
  CROY/NA CR0..............196 E4
  EA W5.....................97 K2
  FSTGT E7..................88 E5
  KIL/WHAMP NW6............100 D1
  KUT/HW KT1...............175 H5
  RCHPK/HAM TW10...........156 C5
Neville St SKENS SW7.......120 C5
Neville Ter SKENS SW7......120 C5
Neville Wk CAR SM5.........194 D4
Nevill Rd STNW/STAM N16.....86 A2
Nevill Wy LOU IG10..........39 H1
Nevin Dr CHING E4...........37 K3
Nevinson Cl WAND/EARL SW18.160 C1
Nevis Cl ROMW/RG RM7........56 E1
Nevis Rd TOOT SW17.........161 F4
New Acres Rd THMD SE28.....127 K2
Newall Rd HTHAIR TW6.......133 F2
Newark Cl WOT/HER KT12.....188 B5
Newark Crs WLSDN NW10.......99 F2
Newark Knok EHAM E6........108 A5

Newark Rd *SAND/SEL* CR2....211 K4
Newark St *WCHPL* E1...........104 D4
New Ash Cl *EFNCH* N2............65 J1
New Barn Rd *WLGTN* SM6.......211 F4
New Barns Av *MTCM* CR4.......195 J1
New Barn Cl *CAN/RD* E16.......107 F4
PLSTW E15..........................106 E5
Newbery Rd *ERITH* DA8.......150 C2
Newbiggin Pth *OXHEY* WD19....27 G6
Newbold Cottages
  WCHPL E1..........................104 E5
Newbolt Av *CHEAM* SM5........208 A3
Newbolt Rd *STAN* HA7.............43 F2
New Bond St *CONDST* W1S........9 G4
Newborough Gn *NWMAL* KT3....192 A1
New Brent St *HDN* NW4............64 B3
New Bridge St *EMB* EC4Y........12 A4
New Broad St *LVPST* EC2M.......13 F2
New Broadway Av *EA* W5..........97 J6
Newburgh Rd *ACT* W3............117 K1
New Burlington Ms
  CONDST W1S........................10 A5
New Burlington Pl
  CONDST W1S........................10 A5
New Burlington St
  CONDST W1S........................10 A5
Newbury Gdns
  HOR/WEW KT19..................207 H2
Newbury Ms *KTTN* NW5...........84 A4
Newbury Rd *CHING* E4.............52 A3
GNTH/NBYPK IG2....................73 J2
HAYES BR2...........................183 K6
HTHAIR TW6.........................132 B2
Newbury St *STBT* EC1A...........12 C2
Newbury Wy *WLSD* UB5...........77 K4
New Butt La *DEPT* SE8...........144 D1
Newby Cl *EN* N1.....................24 A3
Newby Pl *POP/IOD* E14...........106 A6
Newby St *VX/NE* SW8.............141 F4
Newcastle Av *BARK/HLT* IG6....55 G2
Newcastle Cl *FLST/FETLN* EC4A...12 A3
Newcastle Pl *BAY/PAD* W2.........8 B2
Newcastle Rw *CLKNW* EC1R.......5 K7
New Cavendish St
  CAVSQ/HST W1..........................9 H2
New Change *STP* EC4M..............12 C4
New Charles St *FSBYE* EC1V........6 B4
New Church Rd *CMBW* SE5.......142 D1
New City Rd *PLSTW* E13..........107 G2
New Cl *FELT* TW13.................172 D1
WIM/MER SW19....................178 B6
New College Ms *IS* N1 *...........85 G5
New College Pde *HAMP* NW3 *....83 J5
Newcombe Gdns *HSLWW* TW4...134 E4
Newcombe Pk *ALP/SUD* HA0......80 B6
MLHL NW7............................45 K1
Newcombe St *KENS* W8 *.........119 K1
Newcome Gdns
  STRHM/NOR SW16..............161 K6
Newcomen Rd *BTSEA* SW11.....140 D4
WAN E11...............................88 D1
Newcomen St *STHWK* SE1 *......18 D2
New Compton St
  LSQ/SEVD WC2H *.................10 D2
New Ct *EMB* EC4Y *.................11 J5
NTHLT UB5............................78 B3
Newcourt St *STJWD* NW8............2 C2
New Crane Pl *WAP* E1W *.........123 K1
New Crescent Yd
  WLSDN NW10 *....................99 H1
New Cross Rd *NWCR* SE14......144 C1
Newdales Cl *ED* N9..................36 C4
Newdene Av *NTHLT* UB5...........95 H1
Newdigate
  STRHM/NOR SW16 *..............162 B6
Newell St *POP/IOD* E14...........105 H6
New End *HAMP* NW3.................83 G2
New End Sq *HAMP* NW3............83 H2
Newent Cl *CAR* SM5.................194 E5
PECK SE15.............................15 J6
New Era Est *IS* N1 *...................7 G1
New Farm Av *HAYES* BR2.........199 K1
New Farm La *NTHWD* HA6.........40 C4
New Ferry Ap
  WOOL/PLUM SE18..............127 G3
New Fetter La
  FLST/FETLN EC4A.................11 K3
Newfield Cl *HPTN* TW12..........173 F4
Newfield Ri *CRICK* NW2...........81 J1
New Forest La *CHIG* IG7...........54 A2
Newgate Gdns *EDGW* HA8 *.....144 A4
New Garden Dr *WDR/YW* UB7 *.112 B2
Newgate Cl *FELT* TW13...........154 E4
STBT EC1A.............................12 B2
Newgate St *CHING* E4..............38 C5
STBT EC1A.............................12 B3
New Globe Wk *STHWK* SE1.......12 C7
New Goulston St *WCHPL* E1.......13 J3
New Green Pl
  BRXS/STRHM SW2................162 B2
NRWD SE19 *.........................181 F1
Newhall Gdns *WOT/HER* KT12...188 B6
Newham's Rw *STHWK* SE1.......19 H5
Newham Wy *CAN/RD* E16.......106 D4
EHAM E6...............................107 K3
Newhaven Cl *HYS/HAR* UB3.....113 H4
Newhaven Gdns
  ELTH/MOT SE9....................146 C5
Newhaven La *CAN/RD* E16......106 D4
Newhaven Rd *SNWD* SE25......196 E2
New Heston Rd *HEST* TW5......134 E1
Newhouse Av *CHDH* RM6.........55 K6
Newhouse Cl *NWMAL* KT3......192 B4
Newhouse Wk *MRDN* SM4......194 B4
Newick Cl *BXLY* DA5..............169 J1
Newick Rd *CLPT* E5.................86 D1
New Inn Bdy *IS* N1 *................184 C3
Newington Barrow Wy
  HOLWY N7...........................85 F1
Newington Butts *WALW* SE17...18 B6
Newington Cswy *STHWK* SE1...18 B4
Newington Gn *IS* N1.................85 K3
Newington Green Rd *IS* N1.......85 K3

New Inn Broadway
  SDTCH EC2A *.........................7 H6
New Inn Sq *SDTCH* EC2A *.........7 H6
New Inn St *SDTCH* EC2A *..........7 H6
New Inn Yd *SDTCH* EC2A...........7 H6
New Kelvin Av *TEDD* TW11.......173 K2
New Kent Rd *WALW* SE17.........18 D6
New King's Rd *FUL/PGN* SW6....139 K2
New King St *DEPT* SE8............124 D6
Newland Cl *PIN* HA5.................27 K2
Newland Ct *WBLY* HA9.............62 C6
Newland Dr *EN* EN1..................24 D2
Newland Gdns *EA* W13............116 B2
Newland Rd *CEND/HSY/T* N8.....48 E5
Newlands Av *THDIT* KT7..........189 K5
Newlands Cl *ALP/SUD* HA0.......79 J4
  EDGW HA8..............................30 A5
  NWDGN UB2.........................114 D5
Newlands Pk *SYD* SE26...........181 K2
Newlands Quay *WAP* E1W.......104 E6
Newlands Rd
  STRHM/NOR SW16................179 K5
  WFD IG8................................38 D4
The Newlands *WLGTN* SM6......210 C5
Newland St *CAN/RD* E16.........126 D1
Newlands Wy *CHSGTN* KT9.....205 J3
Newlands Woods
  CROY/NA CR0......................213 H6
Newling Cl *EHAM* E6...............107 K5
Newling Est *BETH* E2..................7 J5
New London St *MON* EC3R *.......13 H5
New Lydenburg St *CHARL* SE7...126 B3
Newlyn Cl *ORP* BR6................217 G2
Newlyn Gdns *RYLN/HDSTN* HA2.59 K4
Newlyn Rd *BAR* EN5.................20 D5
  TOTM N17..............................50 B4
  WELL DA16...........................148 A3
Newman Ms *WDGN* N22...........49 G3
  CROY/NA CR0.........................196 A4
  HYS/HAR UB3...........................95 F6
  PLSTW E13............................107 F2
Newman's La *SURB* KT6..........190 E5
Newman's Rw *LINN* WC2A........11 H2
Newman St *FITZ* W1T...............10 B2
Newman's Wy *EBAR* EN4...........21 G3
Newmarket Av *NTHLT* UB5.........78 B3
Newmarsh Rd *THMD* SE28......128 A1
New Mill Rd *STMC/STPC* BR5...186 D4
Newminster Ct *ENC/FH* EN2 *....23 H5
Newminster Rd *MRDN* SM4......194 B4
New Mount St *SRTFD* E15.........88 B5
Newnham Av *RSLP* HA4............59 G5
Newnham Cl *LOU* IG10..............39 H1
  NTHLT UB5..............................78 C4
  THHTH CR7...........................180 D5
Newnham Gdns *NTHLT* UB5......78 C4
Newnham Gn *WDGN* N22 *.........49 F4
Newnhams Cl *BMLY* BR1..........184 E1
Newnham Ter *STHWK* SE1.........17 J4
Newnham Wy
  KTN/HRWW/WS HA3..............62 A2
New North Pl *SDTCH* EC2A..........7 G5
New North Rd *BARK/HLT* IG6......54 D5
  IS N1.......................................7 F1
New North St *BMSBY* WC1N.......11 G1
New Oak Rd *EFNCH* N2.............47 H5
New Oxford St
  NOXST/BSQ WC1A..................10 D3
New Pde *ASHF* TW15 *............152 C6
  WDR/YW UB7 *.......................112 B1
New Park Av *PLMGR* N13..........35 K5
New Park Ct *NTHLT* UB5............77 J4
New Park Est *UED* N18...............50 E1
New Park Rd
  BRXS/STRHM SW2................161 K2
New Place Sq
  BERM/RHTH SE16 *..............123 J3
New Plaistow Rd *SRTFD* E15.......88 C6
New Pond Pde *RSLP* HA4 *.........76 E1
Newport Av *PLSTW* E13...........107 F3
  POP/IOD E14.........................106 B6
Newport Ct *LSQ/SEVD* WC2H *...10 D5
Newport Md *OXHEY* WD19 *.......27 G6
Newport Pl *SOHO/SHAV* W1D *...10 D5
Newport Rd *BARN* SW13.........138 D2
  HTHAIR TW6.........................132 D2
  LEY E10..................................70 B6
  WALTH E17.............................69 G1
  YEAD UB4................................94 B4
New Quebec St *MBLAR* W1H.......9 F4
Newquay Crs *RYLN/HDSTN* HA2.59 J6
Newquay Gdns *OXHEY* WD19 *...27 F2
Newquay Rd *CAT* SE6..............164 E4
New Quebec St *LBTH* SE11.........17 G6
Newquay Rd *CAT* SE6..............164 E4
Newry Rd *TWK* TW1.................136 B5
New Rd *SEVS/STOTM* N15.........67 K2
Newsholme Dr *WCHMN* N21.......23 F6
New Spring Gardens Wk
  STHWK SE1 *......................121 K5
New Sq *EBED/NFELT* TW14......153 F5
  LINN WC2A..............................11 H3
Newstead Av *ORP* BR6............216 D1
Newstead Cl
  NFNCH/WDSPK N12 *............47 J2
Newstead Rd *LEE/GVPK* SE12...165 J2
Newstead Wk *CAR* SM5...........194 B4
Newstead Wy *WIM/MER* SW19.159 G6
New St *LVPST* EC2M................13 H2
New Street Hi *BMLY* BR1.........184 B1
New Street Sq
  FLST/FETLN EC4A..................11 K3
New Tank Hill Rd *PUR* RM19....131 K3
Newton Av *ACT* W3.................117 K2
  MUSWH N10............................48 A4
Newton Cl *RYLN/HDSTN* HA2....60 A6
  WALTH E17.............................69 H3
Newton Gv *CHSWK* W4............118 B4
Newton Pl *POP/IOD* E14..........124 D4
Newton Rd *ALP/SUD* HA0.........80 B5
  BAY/PAD W2...........................101 F5
  CRICK NW2...............................82 A2
  ISLW TW7..............................136 A3
  KTN/HRWW/WS HA3..................42 E5
  SEVS/STOTM N15......................68 B2
  WELL DA16...........................148 B4
  WIM/MER SW19.....................177 H3
Newton's Yd
  WAND/EARL SW18.................139 K6
Newton Ter *HAYES* BR2..........200 C3
Newton Wk *EDGW* HA8.............44 D4
Newton Wy *UED* N18.................49 J1
New Tower Buildings
  WAP E1W *.........................123 J1
Newtown St *BTSEA* SW11........141 G2
New Trinity Rd *EFNCH* N2...........47 H6
New Union Cl *POP/IOD* E14.......125 F3
New Union St *BARB* EC2Y..........12 E2
New Vis *TOTM* N17 *..................50 C4
New Wanstead *WAN* E11............70 E3
New Way Rd *CDALE/KGS* NW9....63 H1
New Wharf Rd *IS* N1...................5 F1
New Zealand Wy *RAIN* RM13.....111 H2
Niagara Av *EA* W5....................116 D4
Niagara Cl *IS* N1 *......................6 D1
Nibthwaite Rd *HRW* HA1............60 E2
Nicholas Cl *GFD/PVL* UB6.........96 B1
Nicholas Gdns *W5* W5..............116 E1
Nicholas La *MANHO* EC4N..........13 F5
Nicholas Ms *NTHWD* HA6 *.........40 A4
Nicholas Rd *ARCH* N19..............66 D5
Nichol Cl *STHGT/OAK* N14.........34 D3
Nicholes Rd *HSLW* TW3...........135 F5
Nichol La *BMLY* BR1................165 K3
Nicholfield *WK* HOLWY N7 *........84 E5
Nicholl St *BETH* E2....................86 C6
Nichols Cl *FSBYPK* N4...............67 G5
Nichols Gn *EA* W5....................98 A4
Nicholson Dr *BUSH* WD23...........28 C3
Nicholson House *CHARL* SE7 *..146 D1
Nicholson Ms *KUT/HW* KT1 *......191 F1
Nicholson Rd *CROY/NA* CR0......197 G5
Nicholson St *STHWK* SE1...........18 A1
Nickleby Cl *THMD* SE28...........109 J5
Nickols Wk *WAND/EARL* SW18...140 A5
Nicola Cl *KTN/HRWW/WS* HA3....42 D5
  SAND/SEL CR2.......................211 J4
Nicola Ms *BARK/HLT* IG6...........54 B3
Nicoll Pl *HDN* NW4....................63 K3
Nicoll Rd *WLSDN* NW10.............81 G6
Nicolson Rd *STMC/STPC* BR5...202 D4
Nicosia Rd *WAND/EARL* SW18...160 D2
Niederwald Rd *SYD* SE26.........164 B6
Nield Rd *HYS/HAR* UB3............113 J2
Nigel Cl *NTHLT* UB5...................77 J6
Nigel Fisher Wy *CHSGTN* KT9...205 K5
Nigel Ms *IL* IG1........................90 B2
Nigel Playfair Av *HMSMTH* W6...118 E5
Nigel Rd *PECK* SE15................143 H4
  FSTGT E7..............................88 E3
Nigeria Rd *CHARL* SE7............146 B1
Nightingale Av *CHING* E4............52 C1
Nightingale Cl *CAR* SM5...........195 F6
  CHSWK W4............................117 K6
  PIN HA5.................................41 H5
Nightingale Cnr
  STMC/STPC BR5 *................202 E1
Nightingale Ct *SUT* SM1..........209 G3
Nightingale Dr
  HOR/WEW KT19.................206 D4
Nightingale Est *CLPT* E5............86 C1
Nightingale La *BAL* SW12.........161 F1
  BMLY BR1.............................184 B5
  CEND/HSY/T N8......................48 C5
  RCHPK/HAM TW10.................157 F2
  WAN E11..................................71 F2
Nightingale Ms *KUT/HW* KT1 *....174 E6
  LBTH SE11 *..............................17 K6
Nightingale Pl *WBPTN* SW10...120 B6
  WOOL/PLUM SE18..................127 F6
Nightingale Rd *CAR* SM5..........209 K1
  CLPT E5..................................86 D2
  E/WMO/HCT KT8...................189 G2
  ED N9.....................................36 E2
  HNWL W7..............................116 A1

HPTN TW12...........................173 F2
STMC/STPC BR5....................201 H3
WDGN N22.............................49 J4
WLSDN NW10..........................99 H1
WOT/HER KT12......................188 B4
Nightingale Sq *BAL* SW12.......161 F2
The Nightingales
  STWL/WRAY TW19................153 C3
Nightingale V
  WOOL/PLUM SE18................127 G6
Nightingale Sq *BAL* SW12.......161 F2
Nile Cl *STNW/STAM* N16...........86 B1
Nile Dr *ED* N9...........................36 E4
Nile Rd *PLSTW* E13..................107 G1
Nile St *IS* N1..............................6 E4
Nile Ter *PECK* SE15.................123 G5
Nimmo Dr *BUSH* WD23.............28 D2
Nimrod Cl *NTHLT* UB5................95 H2
Nimrod Pas *IS* N1......................86 A4
Nimrod Rd *STRHM/NOR* SW16...179 G2
Nina Mackay Cl *SRTFD* E15 *......88 C6
Nine Acres Cl *MNPK* E12............89 J3
Nine Elms Cl
  EBED/NFELT TW14................153 J3
Nine Elms La *VX/NE* SW8.........141 H1
Ninham Wd *ORP* BR6...............216 A2
Ninth Av *HYS/HAR* UB3..............94 E6
Nisbett Wk *SCUP* DA14............168 B6
Nithdale Rd *WOOL/PLUM* SE18.147 G1
Nithsdale Gv *HGDN/ICK* UB10....76 A1
Niton Cl *BAR* EN5......................32 B1
Niton Rd *RCH/KEW* TW9..........137 H4
Niton St *FUL/PGN* SW6............139 G1
No1 St *WOOL/PLUM* SE18.......127 G3
No2 St *WOOL/PLUM* SE18.......127 G3
Noak Hill Rd *ABR/ST* RM4..........57 K1
Nobel Dr *HYS/HAR* UB3............133 H1
Nobel Rd *UED* N18......................36 E6
Noble Cnr *HEST* TW5 *.............135 F2
Noble St *CITYW* EC2V...............12 C3
Noel Rd *ACT* W3........................98 B1
  EHAM E6..................................107 J5
  IS N1.......................................6 B1
Noel St *SOHO/CST* W1F.............10 B4
Nolton Pl *EDGW* HA8.................44 B4
Nonsuch Cl *CHIG* IG7.................54 B2
Nonsuch Ct *CHEAM* SM3 *........208 B5
Nora Gdns *HDN* NW4.................64 B1
Norbiton Av *KUT/HW* KT1.........175 H5
Norbiton Common Rd
  KUT/HW KT1.......................175 J6
Norbiton Rd *POP/IOD* E14........105 H5
Norbreck Pde *EA* W5 *...............98 A2
Norbroke St *SHB* W12.................99 C6
Norbury Av *HSLW* TW3............135 J6
  STRHM/NOR SW16.................180 A4
Norbury Cl *STRHM/NOR* SW16..180 B4
Norbury Court Rd
  STRHM/NOR SW16................179 K5
Norbury Crs
  STRHM/NOR SW16................180 B5
Norbury Cross
  STRHM/NOR SW16................179 K6
Norbury Gdns *CHDH* RM6..........73 K2
Norbury Gv *MLHL* NW7...............31 G5
Norbury Hill *STRHM/NOR* SW16.180 B3
Norbury Ri *STRHM/NOR* SW16..179 K6
Norbury Rd *CHING* E4................51 J1
  FELT TW13............................153 K3
  THHTH CR7...........................180 D5
Norbury Vls *KUT/HW* KT1........175 G5
Norcombe Gdns
  KTN/HRWW/WS HA3..............61 J3
Norcott Cl *YEAD* UB4.................95 G5
Norcott Rd *STNW/STAM* N16.....68 C6
Norcroft Gdns *EDUL* SE22........163 H2
Norcutt Rd *WHTN* TW2............155 K3
Nordenfeldt Rd *ERITH* DA8.......130 A5
Norfield Rd *RDART* DA2............170 E5
Norfolk Av *PLMGR* N13..............49 H2
  SEVS/STOTM N15....................68 B3
Norfolk Cl *DART* DA1...............171 K1
  EBAR EN4................................22 A5
  EFNCH N2................................47 J6
  TWK TW1 *.............................156 C1
Norfolk Ct *BAR* EN5...................20 C5
  CRS BAY/PAD W2 *....................8 C3
  BFN/LL DA15.........................167 K2
Norfolk Crs *BAY/PAD* W2............8 C3
Norfolk Gdns *BORE* WD6...........30 D1
  BXLYHN DA7.........................149 G2
Norfolk House *STRHM/NOR* SW16.161 J1
Norfolk Ms *NKENS* W10............100 C4
Norfolk Pl *BAY/PAD* W2...............8 B3
  WELL DA16...........................148 B3
Norfolk Rd *BAR* EN5...................20 E4
  BARK IG11...............................90 E5
  DAGE RM10............................92 D3
  EHAM E6.................................89 K6
  FELT TW13............................154 B3
  GDMY/SEVK IG3.......................72 E5
  HRW HA1.................................60 B1
  PEND EN3................................36 D1
  ROMW/RG RM7........................74 E2
  STJWD NW8.............................2 B2
  THHTH CR7...........................180 D6
  WALTH E17.............................51 F4
  WIM/MER SW19.....................178 D3
  WLSDN NW10..........................81 G5
Norfolk Rw *STHWK* SE1 *...........17 J6
Norfolk Sq *BAY/PAD* W2 *...........8 B4
Norfolk Square Ms *BAY/PAD* W2...8 B4
Norfolk St *FSTGT* E7..................88 E3
Norgrove St *BAL* SW12............161 F3
Norhyrst Av *SNWD* SE25..........181 G6
Norland Pl *NTGHL* W11............119 H1
Norland Rd *NTGHL* W11............119 G1
Norlands Crs *CHST* BR7............185 G4
Norlands Ga *CHST* BR7............185 G4
Norland Sq *NTGHL* W11............119 H1
Norley V *PUT/ROE* SW15.........158 D3

Norlington Rd *LEY* E10..............70 A5
Norman Av *FELT* TW13............154 D4
  STHL UB1.................................95 J6
  TWK TW1...............................156 C2
  WDGN N22.............................49 J4
Normanby Cl *PUT/ROE* SW15...139 J6
Normanby Rd *WLSDN* NW10......81 H5
Norman Cl *ORP* BR6................216 D2
  ROMW/RG RM7........................56 C5
Norman Crs *HEST* TW5............134 C1
  PIN HA5..................................41 G4
Normand Gdns *WKENS* W14 *....119 H6
Normand Ms *WKENS* W14.........119 H6
Normand Rd *WKENS* W14.........119 J6
Normandy Av *BAR* EN5..............20 D6
Normandy Cl *SYD* SE26...........164 B5
Normandy Dr *HYS/HAR* UB3......94 A3
Normandy Rd *BRXN/ST* SW9.....142 B2
Normandy Ter *CAN/RD* E16......107 F5
Normandy Wy *ERITH* DA8.........150 B2
Norman Gv *BOW* E3.................105 G1
Normanhurst Av *WELL* DA16...148 E2
Normanhurst Dr *TWK* TW1 *.....156 B4
Normanhurst Rd
  BRXS/STRHM SW2................162 A4
  STMC/STPC BR5.....................186 C6
  WOT/HER KT12......................188 C6
Norman Pde *SCUP* DA14 *.........168 F5
Norman Rd *BELV* DA17............129 J2
  DART DA1..............................171 H3
  EHAM E6................................107 K3
  EMPK RM11.............................75 J4
  GNWCH SE10........................145 E6
  IL IG1.....................................90 B3
  SEVS/STOTM N15.....................68 B2
  SUT SM1................................208 E3
  THHTH CR7............................196 C2
  WALTH E17.............................69 J3
  WIM/MER SW19.....................178 B3
Normans Cl *WDGN* N22 *..........49 J4
  WLSDN NW10..........................81 F4
Normansfield Av *KUT/HW* KT1...174 D3
Normanshire Av *CHING* E4..........37 J6
Normanshire Dr *CHING* E4..........51 H1
Norman St *FSBYE* EC1V..............6 C5
Norman Ter *KIL/WHAMP* NW6 *...82 D3
Normanton Av
  WAND/EARL SW18................159 K4
Normanton Pk *CHING* E4............38 C5
Normanton Rd *SAND/SEL* CR2..212 A4
Normanton St *FSTH* SE23.........164 A4
Norman Wy *ACT* W3...................98 D4
  STHGT/OAK N14......................34 E4
Normington Cl
  STRHM/NOR SW16................180 B1
Norrice Lea *EFNCH* N2...............65 H2
Norris St *STJS* SW1Y.................10 C5
Norris Wy *DART* DA1................150 C4
Norroy Rd *PUT/ROE* SW15......139 G5
Norrys Cl *EBAR* EN4..................21 K6
Norrys Rd *EBAR* EN4.................21 K5
Norseman Cl *GDMY/SEVK* IG3...73 H5
Norseman Wy *GFD/PVL* UB6......78 B6
Norstead Pl *PUT/ROE* SW15....158 D4
North Access Rd *WALTH* E17......69 G3
North Acre *CDALE/KGS* NW9......45 G4
North Acton Rd *WLSDN* NW10....99 F1
Northall Rd *BXLYHN* DA7...........150 A3
Northampton Gv *IS* N1...............85 K3
Northampton Pk *IS* N1................85 J4
Northampton Rd *CLKNW* EC1R....5 K6
  CROY/NA CR0........................197 J2
  PEND EN3................................25 J2
Northampton Rw *CLKNW* EC1R *..5 K6
Northampton Sq *FSBYE* EC1V.....5 K5
Northampton St *IS* N1.................85 J5
Northanger Rd
  STRHM/NOR SW16................179 K2
North Ap *NTHWD* HA6................26 A4
North Audley St
  MYFR/PKLN W1K....................9 G5
North Av *CAR* SM5..................210 A5
  HYS/HAR UB3...........................94 C5
  RCH/KEW TW9.......................137 H2
  RYLN/HDSTN HA2....................60 B3
  STHL UB1.................................95 K6
  UED N18..................................36 C6
  WEA W13................................97 H5
North Bank *STJWD* NW8.............2 C3
Northbank Rd *WALTH* E17..........52 A5
North Birkbeck Rd *WAN* E11.......88 B1
Northborough Rd
  STRHM/NOR SW16................179 K5
Northbourne *HAYES* BR2..........199 K4
Northbourne Rd *CLAP* SW4......141 J6
Northbrook Dr *NTHWD* HA6........40 C4
Northbrook Rd *BAR* EN5.............32 C1
  CROY/NA CR0.........................196 E2
  IL IG1.....................................90 A1
  LEW SE13..............................145 H6
  WDGN N22...............................48 E3
Northburgh St *FSBYE* EC1V........6 B7
North Carriage Dr *BAY/PAD* W2...8 D5
Northchurch Rd *IS* N1..................85 J5
  WBLY HA9................................80 C4
Northchurch Ter *IS* N1................86 A5
North Circular *PLMGR* N13.........49 H1
  WALTH E17.............................51 K4
North Circular Rd *BARK* IG11......90 A5
  CHING E4 *..............................51 G2
  CRICK NW2.............................81 J3
  FNCH N3..................................46 B6
  GLDGN NW11..........................64 C6
  REDBR IG4...............................53 G6
North Cliffe Dr *WPK* KT4...........207 G1
Northcliffe Dr *TRDG/WHET* N20...32 E1
North Cl *BAR* EN5.......................20 A6
  BXLYHS DA6............................148 E5
  CHIG IG7.................................54 E2
  DAGE RM10............................92 C6
  EBED/NFELT TW14................153 H1
  MRDN SM4............................193 H1
The North Colonnade
  POP/IOD E14......................124 D1
North Common Rd *EA* W5...........98 A6

Northcote Av BRYLDS KT5 191 H4
EA W5 98 A6
ISLW TW7 136 B6
STHL UB1 95 J6
Northcote Rd BTSEA SW11 140 D5
CROY/NA CR0 196 E3
NWMAL KT3 175 K6
SCUP DA14 167 K6
TWK TW1 136 B6
WALTH E17 69 G1
WLSDN NW10 81 G5
Northcott Av WDGN N22 48 E4
North Countess Rd WALTH E17 51 H5
Northcourt FITZ W1T 10 B1
North Cray Rd SCUP DA14 187 F2
North Crs CAN/RD E16 106 B3
FNCH N3 46 D5
GWRST WC1E 10 C1
Northcroft Rd HOR/WEW KT19 207 G5
WEA W13 116 C2
North Cross Rd BARK/HLT IG6 72 C1
EDUL SE22 143 G6
Northdene CHIG IG7 54 D1
North Dene HSLW TW3 135 G2
MLHL NW7 31 F5
Northdene Gdns
SEVS/STOTM N15 68 B3
Northdown Cl RSLP HA4 76 D1
Northdown Gdns
GNTH/NBYPK IG2 72 E2
Northdown Rd EMPK RM11 75 K4
WELL DA16 148 C3
Northdown St IS N1 5 G3
North Dr BECK BR3 198 E1
HSLW TW3 135 H3
ORP BR6 216 E2
RSLP HA4 58 C4
STRHM/NOR SW16 161 H6
North End BKHH IG9 39 G2
CROY/NA CR0 196 D6
HAMP NW3 65 G6
North End Av HAMP NW3 65 G6
North End Crs WKENS W14 119 J4
North End La ORP BR6 216 B6
Northend Rd ERITH DA8 150 C2
North End Rd FUL/PGN SW6 139 K1
GLDGN NW11 64 E5
WBLY HA9 80 D1
WKENS W14 119 J4
North End Wy HAMP NW3 65 G6
Northern Av ED N9 36 B4
Northernhay Wk MRDN SM4 193 H1
Northern Perimeter Rd
HTHAIR TW6 133 F2
Northern Perimeter Rd (West)
HTHAIR TW6 132 B2
Northern Relief Rd BARK IG11 90 C5
North Eyot Gdns
HMSMTH W6 * 118 C5
Northey St POP/IOD E14 105 G6
North Farm LOU IG10 39 G1
Northfield Av PIN HA5 59 H1
STMC/STPC BR5 202 D3
WEA W13 116 C2
Northfield Cl BMLY BR1 184 D4
HYS/HAR UB3 113 J3
Northfield Crs CHEAM SM3 208 C2
Northfield Pde
HYS/HAR UB3 * 113 J3
Northfield Pk HYS/HAR UB3 113 J3
Northfield Rd DAGW RM9 92 B2
EBAR EN4 21 J4
ED N9 * 24 D6
EHAM E6 89 K4
HEST TW5 134 C1
PEND EN3 36 D1
STNW/STAM N16 68 A4
WEA W13 116 C2
Northfields WAND/EARL SW18 139 K5
Northfields Rd ACT W3 98 E4
North Gdns WIM/MER SW19 178 C3
Northgate NTHWD HA6 40 A3
Northgate Dr CDALE/KGS NW9 63 G3
North Gower St CAMTN NW1 4 A5
North Gv HGT N6 66 A4
SEVS/STOTM N15 67 K2
North Hl HGT N6 65 K3
North Hill Av HGT N6 65 K3
North Hyde Gdns
HYS/HAR UB3 113 K3
NWDGN UB2 114 A3
North Hyde La NWDGN UB2 114 D5
North Hyde Rd HYS/HAR UB3 113 H3
North Hyde Whf
NWDGN UB2 * 114 B4
Northiam NFNCH/WDSPK N12 32 E6
Northiam St HACK E8 86 D6
Northington St BMSBY WC1N 11 G1
Northlands Av ORP BR6 216 E2
Northlands St CMBW SE5 142 D3
North La TEDD TW11 174 A2
North Lodge Cl
PUT/ROE SW15 * 139 G6
North Ms BMSBY WC1N 5 H7
North Mt TRDG/WHET N20 * 33 G4
Northolm EDGW HA8 31 F6
Northolme Gdns EDGW HA8 44 C4
Northolme Ri ORP BR6 201 K6
Northolme Rd HBRY N5 85 J2
Northolt Av RSLP HA4 77 F3
Northolt Gdns GFD/PVL UB6 79 F3
Northolt Rd RYLN/HDSTN HA2 78 B2
WDR/YW UB7 132 A2
Northover BMLY BR1 165 J6
North Pde CHSGTN KT9 206 B3
EDGW HA8 * 44 C5
STHL UB1 * 96 A5
North Pk ELTH/MOT SE9 166 E1
North Pas WAND/EARL SW18 139 K6
North Peckham Est
PECK SE15 143 G1
North Pl MTCM CR4 178 E3
TEDD TW11 174 A2
Northpoint Cl SUT SM1 209 G1
North Pole La HAYES BR2 214 E4
North Pole Rd SHB W12 100 A5
Northport St IS N1 7 F1
North Ri BAY/PAD W2 * 8 D4
North Rd BELV DA17 129 J3
BMLY BR1 184 A4
BTFD TW8 117 F6
CHDH RM6 74 A2
DART DA1 170 C1
EA W5 116 E3
EBED/NFELT TW14 153 G1
ED N9 36 D3
EDGW HA8 44 D4
GDMY/SEVK IG3 72 E6
HEST TW5 114 B6
HGT N6 66 A4
HOLWY N7 84 E4
HYS/HAR UB3 94 B4
RCH/KEW TW9 137 H3
STHL UB1 96 A6
SURB KT6 190 E3
WDR/YW UB7 112 C3
WIM/MER SW19 178 C2
WOOL/PLUM SE18 127 K4
WWKM BR4 198 E5
Northrop Rd HTHAIR TW6 133 H2
North Rw MYFR/PKLN W1K 9 F5
North Several
BKHTH/KID SE3 * 145 G3
Northside Rd BMLY BR1 183 K4
North Side Wandsworth
Common WAND/EARL SW18 140 B6
Northspur Rd SUT SM1 208 E1
North Sq ED N9 36 D4
GLDGN NW11 64 E3
Northstead Rd
BRXS/STRHM SW2 162 B4
North St BARK IG11 90 C5
BMLY BR1 183 K4
BXLYHN DA7 149 H5
CAR SM5 209 K2
CLAP SW4 141 G4
DART DA1 171 G2
HDN NW4 64 A2
ISLW TW7 136 B4
PLSTW E13 107 F1
ROM RM1 75 F1
North Tenter St WCHPL E1 13 K4
North Ter CHEL SW3 14 C5
Northumberland Aly
FENCHST EC3M * 13 H4
Northumberland Av
CHCR WC2N 10 E7
EN EN1 24 D1
ISLW TW7 136 A2
MNPK E12 71 G5
WELL DA16 147 K5
Northumberland Cl ERITH DA8 149 K1
STWL/WRAY TW19 152 B1
Northumberland Crs
EBED/NFELT TW14 153 H1
Northumberland Gdns
BMLY BR1 201 F1
ED N9 36 B5
MTCM CR4 195 K2
Northumberland Gv TOTM N17 50 D3
Northumberland Pk
ERITH DA8 149 K1
TOTM N17 50 C3
Northumberland Pl
BAY/PAD W2 100 E5
Northumberland Rd BAR EN5 33 G1
EHAM E6 107 J5
RYLN/HDSTN HA2 59 K2
WALTH E17 69 J4
Northumberland St
CHCR WC2N 10 E7
Northumberland Wy
ERITH DA8 149 K2
Northumbria St POP/IOD E14 105 J5
North Verbena Gdns
HMSMTH W6 * 118 D5
North Vw EA W5 97 J3
PIN HA5 59 G4
WIM/MER SW19 176 E1
Northview Crs WLSDN NW10 81 H2
Northview Dr WFD IG8 53 H5
Northview Pde HOLWY N7 * 84 E1
North View Rd
CEND/HSY/T N8 48 D6
North Vls CAMTN NW1 84 D4
North Wk CROY/NA CR0 213 K4
North Wy CDALE/KGS NW9 44 D6
ED N9 36 E4
FBAR/BDGN N11 48 C2
Northway GLDGN NW11 65 F2
MRDN SM4 177 H6
North Wy PIN HA5 41 G6
Northway WLGTN SM6 210 C2
Northway Crs MLHL NW7 31 G6
Northway Rd CMBW SE5 142 D4
CROY/NA CR0 197 G3
Northways Pde HAMP NW3 * 83 H5
North Weald Cl HCH RM12 93 K5
North Weald La
KUTN/CMB KT2 174 E1
North Wharf Rd BAY/PAD W2 8 A2
Northwick Av
KTN/HRWW/WS HA3 61 G3
Northwick Cir
KTN/HRWW/WS HA3 61 J3
Northwick Cl STJWD NW8 2 A6
Northwick Park Rd HRW HA1 61 F3
Northwick Rd ALP/SUD HA0 79 K6
OXHEY WD19 27 G6
Northwick Ter STJWD NW8 2 A6
Northwold Dr PIN HA5 41 G6
Northwold Rd
STNW/STAM N16 68 B6
Northwood Av HCH RM12 93 J2
Northwood Gdns CLAY IG5 72 A1
GFD/PVL UB6 79 F3
NFNCH/WDSPK N12 47 H1
Northwood Pl ERITHM DA18 129 G3
Northwood Rd CAR SM5 210 A4
FSTH SE23 164 C3
HGT N6 66 C4
HTHAIR TW6 132 A2
THHTH CR7 180 D5
Northwood Wy NTHWD HA6 40 E4
North Woolwich Rd
CAN/RD E16 125 K1
North Worple Wy
MORT/ESHN SW14 138 A4
Norton Av BRYLDS KT5 191 J4
Norton Cl CHING E4 51 J1
Norton Folgate WCHPL E1 7 H7
Norton Gdns
STRHM/NOR SW16 179 K5
Norton Rd ALP/SUD HA0 79 K4
DAGE RM10 93 F4
LEY E10 69 H5
Norval Gn BRXN/ST SW9 * 142 B3
Norval Rd ALP/SUD HA0 61 H6
Norway Ga BERM/RHTH SE16 124 B3
Norway Pl POP/IOD E14 105 H5
Norway St GNWCH SE10 124 E6
Norwich Crs CHDH RM6 73 H2
Norwich Ms GDMY/SEVK IG3 73 G5
Norwich Rd FSTGT E7 88 E3
GFD/PVL UB6 78 B6
NTHWD HA6 40 D6
THHTH CR7 180 D6
Norwich St FLST/FETLN EC4A 11 J3
Norwich Wk EDGW HA8 44 E3
Norwood Av ALP/SUD HA0 80 B6
ROMW/RG RM7 75 F4
Norwood Cl CRICK NW2 82 C1
NWDGN UB2 115 F4
WHTN TW2 155 J4
Norwood Dr RYLN/HDSTN HA2 59 K3
Norwood Gdns NWDGN UB2 114 E4
YEAD UB4 95 G3
Norwood Green Rd
NWDGN UB2 115 F4
Norwood High St WNWD SE27 162 D6
Norwood Park Rd
WNWD SE27 180 D1
Norwood Rd HNHL SE24 162 C3
NWDGN UB2 114 D3
Notley St CMBW SE5 142 E1
Notson Rd SNWD SE25 197 J1
Notting Barn Rd NKENS W10 100 B3
Nottingdale Sq NTGHL W11 * 119 H1
Nottingham Av CAN/RD E16 107 G4
Nottingham Ct
LSQ/SEVD WC2H 10 E4
Nottingham Pl CAMTN NW1 3 G7
Nottingham Rd ISLW TW7 136 A3
LEY E10 70 A3
SAND/SEL CR2 211 J3
TOOT SW17 160 E3
Nottingham St MHST W1U 9 G1
Nottingham Ter CAMTN NW1 3 G7
Notting Hill Ga KENS W8 119 K1
Nova Ms CHEAM SM3 193 H4
Novar Cl ORP BR6 202 A4
Nova Rd CROY/NA CR0 196 C5
Novar Rd ELTH/MOT SE9 167 H3
Novello St FUL/PGN SW6 139 K2
Nowell Rd BARN SW13 118 D6
Nower Hl PIN HA5 59 K1
Noyna Rd TOOT SW17 160 E5
Nubia Wy BMLY BR1 165 H6
Nuding Cl LEW SE13 144 D4
Nugent Rd ARCH N19 66 E5
SNWD SE25 181 G6
Nugents Ct PIN HA5 * 41 J4
Nugent's Pk PIN HA5 41 K4
Nugent Ter STJWD NW8 101 G1
Nuneaton Rd DAGW RM9 91 K5
Nunhead Crs PECK SE15 143 J4
Nunhead Gv PECK SE15 143 K4
Nunhead La PECK SE15 143 J4
Nunnington Cl ELTH/MOT SE9 166 D5
Nunn's Rd ENC/FH EN2 23 J3
Nupton Dr BAR EN5 32 A1
Nurse Cl EDGW HA8 44 E4
Nursery Av BXLYHN DA7 149 G4
CROY/NA CR0 198 A6
FNCH N3 47 F5
Nursery Cl BROCKY SE4 144 C3
CHDH RM6 73 K3
CROY/NA CR0 198 A6
EBED/NFELT TW14 154 A2
ORP BR6 202 A4
OXHEY WD19 27 F3
PEND EN3 25 F2
PUT/ROE SW15 139 G6
SWLY BR8 187 K5
WFD IG8 53 F1
Nursery Gdns CHST BR7 185 G2
HPTN TW12 154 E6
HSLWW TW4 134 E6
PEND EN3 25 F2
Nursery La BETH E2 7 J1
FSTGT E7 88 E4
NKENS W10 100 A4
Nurserymans Rd
FBAR/BDGN N11 34 A4
Nursery Rd BRXN/ST SW9 142 A5
EFNCH N2 47 H4
HACK E8 86 E4
MTCM CR4 178 D6
PIN HA5 41 G6
STHGT/OAK N14 34 C2
SUT SM1 209 G2
THHTH CR7 196 E1
WIM/MER SW19 177 H3
WIM/MER SW19 178 A5
Nursery Rw BAR EN5 * 20 C4
WALW SE17 18 E7
Nursery St TOTM N17 50 B3
The Nursery ERITH DA8 150 C1
Nursery Wk HDN NW4 45 K6
Nurstead Rd ERITH DA8 149 H1
Nutbourne St NKENS W10 100 C2
Nutbrook St PECK SE15 143 G4
Nutbrowne Rd DAGW RM9 92 B6
Nutcroft Rd PECK SE15 143 J1
Nutfield Cl CAR SM5 209 J1
UED N18 50 C2
Nutfield Gdns GDMY/SEVK IG3 73 F6
NTHLT UB5 95 G1
Nutfield Rd CRICK NW2 81 J1
EDUL SE22 143 G6
SRTFD E15 88 A2
THHTH CR7 196 C1
Nutfield Wy ORP BR6 201 F6
Nutford Pl MBLAR W1H 8 D3
Nuthatch Cl STWL/WRAY TW19 152 C3
Nuthatch Gdns THMD SE28 127 J2
Nuthurst Av
BRXS/STRHM SW2 162 A4
Nutley Ter HAMP NW3 83 H4
Nutmead Cl BXLY DA5 169 K3
Nutmeg Cl CAN/RD E16 106 C3
Nutmeg La POP/IOD E14 106 B5
Nuttall St IS N1 7 H2
Nutter La WAN E11 71 G2
Nutt Gv EDGW HA8 29 K4
Nut Tree Cl ORP BR6 217 K1
Nutt St PECK SE15 143 G1
Nutwell St TOOT SW17 178 D1
Nuxley Rd BELV DA17 129 G6
Nyanza St WOOL/PLUM SE18 147 J1
Nylands Av RCH/KEW TW9 137 H3
Nymans Gdns RYNPK SW20 176 E6
Nynehead St NWCR SE14 144 B1
Nyon Gv CAT SE6 164 C4
Nyssa Cl WFD IG8 53 K2
Nyton Cl ARCH N19 66 E5

O

Oak Av CEND/HSY/T N8 66 E1
CROY/NA CR0 198 D6
ENC/FH EN2 23 F2
HEST TW5 134 C1
HPTN TW12 172 D1
MUSWH N10 48 B3
TOTM N17 49 K3
WDR/YW UB7 112 D3
Oakbank CROY/NA CR0 214 A4
Oakbank Av WOT/HER KT12 188 E4
Oakbank Gv HNHL SE24 142 D5
Oakbrook Cl BMLY BR1 166 A6
Oakbury Rd FUL/PGN SW6 140 A3
Oak Cl DART DA1 150 B5
STHGT/OAK N14 34 B2
Oakcombe Cl NWMAL KT3 176 B4
Oak Cottage Cl CAT SE6 165 H3
Oak Cottages HNWL W7 * 115 K2
Oak Crs CAN/RD E16 106 C4
Oakcroft Cl PIN HA5 41 F5
Oakcroft Rd CHSGTN KT9 206 B2
LEW SE13 145 G3
Oakcroft Vls CHSGTN KT9 206 B2
Oakdale STHGT/OAK N14 34 B3
Oakdale Av
KTN/HRWW/WS HA3 62 A2
NTHWD HA6 40 E5
Oakdale Cl OXHEY WD19 27 G6
Oakdale Gdns CHING E4 52 A1
Oakdale Rd FSBYPK N4 67 J3
FSTGT E7 89 F5
HOR/WEW KT19 207 F6
OXHEY WD19 27 G5
PECK SE15 144 A4
STRHM/NOR SW16 179 K1
SWFD E18 53 F5
WAN E11 70 B6
Oakdale Wy MTCM CR4 195 F4
Oakdene WEA W13 97 H4
Oakdene Av CHST BR7 185 F1
ERITH DA8 129 K6
THDIT KT7 190 B5
Oak Dene Cl EMPK RM11 75 K3
Oakdene Cl PIN HA5 41 K3
Oakdene Dr BRYLDS KT5 191 K5
Oakdene Ms CHEAM SM3 193 J5
Oakdene Pk FNCH N3 46 D3
Oakdene Rd STMC/STPC BR5 202 B3
Oakden St LBTH SE11 17 K6
Oaken Dr ESH/CLAY KT10 205 F4
Oaken La ESH/CLAY KT10 204 E2
Oakenshaw Cl SURB KT6 191 F4
Oakeshott Av HGT N6 66 A6
Oakey La STHWK SE1 17 J4
Oakfield CHING E4 51 K1
Oakfield Av
KTN/HRWW/WS HA3 43 H6
Oakfield Cl NWMAL KT3 192 C2
RSLP HA4 58 E3
Oakfield Gdns BECK BR3 198 E2
CAR SM5 194 D5
GFD/PVL UB6 96 D3
UED N18 36 A6
Oakfield La DART DA1 171 G4
HAYES BR2 215 G2
RDART DA2 170 D4
Oakfield Park Rd DART DA1 171 G4
Oakfield Pl DART DA1 171 G4
Oakfield Rd ASHF TW15 152 E6
CROY/NA CR0 196 D5
EHAM E6 89 J6
FNCH N3 47 F4
FSBYPK N4 67 G3
IL IG1 90 B1
PGE/AN SE20 181 J4
STHGT/OAK N14 34 E4
WALTH E17 51 G5
WIM/MER SW19 159 G5
Oakfields Rd GLDGN NW11 64 C3
Oakfield St WBPTN SW10 120 B6
Oakford Rd KTTN NW5 84 C2
Oak Gdns CROY/NA CR0 198 D6
EDGW HA8 44 E5
Oak Gv CRICK NW2 82 B2
RSLP HA4 59 F5
SUN TW16 172 A3
WWKM BR4 199 F6
Oak Grove Rd PGE/AN SE20 181 K4
Oak Hall Rd WAN E11 71 F3
Oakham Cl CAT SE6 * 164 C4
Oakham Dr HAYES BR2 199 K1
Oakhampton Rd MLHL NW7 46 B4
Oakhill ESH/CLAY KT10 205 G4
Oak Hl SURB KT6 191 F4
WFD IG8 52 B3
Oakhill Av HAMP NW3 83 F2
PIN HA5 41 J5
Oak Hill Crs SURB KT6 191 F4
WFD IG8 52 C3
Oak Hill Gdns WFD IG8 52 C4
Oak Hill Gv SURB KT6 191 F3
Oak Hill Pk HAMP NW3 83 F2
Oak Hill Park Ms HAMP NW3 83 G2
Oakhill Pl PUT/ROE SW15 139 K6
Oakhill Rd BECK BR3 183 F5
ORP BR6 202 A6
PUT/ROE SW15 139 J6
STRHM/NOR SW16 179 K4
Oak Hill Rd SURB KT6 * 191 F3
Oakhill Rd SUT SM1 209 F1
Oak Hill Wy HAMP NW3 83 G2
Oakhouse Rd BXLYHS DA6 149 H6
Oakhurst Av BXLYHN DA7 149 F1
EBAR EN4 33 J2
Oakhurst Cl BARK/HLT IG6 54 C4
CHST BR7 184 E4
TEDD TW11 173 K1
WALTH E17 70 C1
Oakhurst Gdns BXLYHN DA7 149 F1
CHING E4 38 D3
WALTH E17 70 C1
Oakhurst Gv EDUL SE22 143 H5
Oakhurst Rd HOR/WEW KT19 206 E4
Oakington Av HYS/HAR UB3 113 G4
RYLN/HDSTN HA2 60 A4
WBLY HA9 80 B1
Oakington Cl SUN TW16 172 B5
Oakington Dr SUN TW16 172 B5
Oakington Manor Dr WBLY HA9 80 C3
Oakington Rd MV/WKIL W9 * 100 E3
Oakington Wy CEND/HSY/T N8 66 E3
Oakland Pl BKHH IG9 38 E4
Oakland Rd SRTFD E15 88 C2
Oaklands WCHMH N21 35 F4
Oaklands Av BFN/LL DA15 168 A2
ED N9 36 D1
ESH/CLAY KT10 189 J5
ISLW TW7 116 A6
OXHEY WD19 27 F3
ROM RM1 57 G6
THHTH CR7 196 B1
WWKM BR4 213 K1
Oaklands Cl ALP/SUD HA0 79 K3
BXLYHS DA6 149 G6
CHSGTN KT9 205 J2
STMC/STPC BR5 201 K3
Oaklands Dr WHTN TW2 155 H2
Oaklands Ga NTHWD HA6 40 C2
Oaklands Gv SHB W12 118 D1
Oaklands Ms CRICK NW2 82 B2
Oaklands Park Av IL IG1 72 D6
Oaklands Pl CLAP SW4 141 J5
Oaklands Rd BMLY BR1 183 H3
BXLYHS DA6 149 G5
CRICK NW2 82 B2
HNWL W7 116 A2
MORT/ESHN SW14 138 A4
TRDG/WHET N20 32 D2
Oaklands Wy WLGTN SM6 210 D5
Oakland Wy HOR/WEW KT19 207 G4
Oak La EFNCH N2 47 H5
FBAR/BDGN N11 48 D2
ISLW TW7 135 K5
POP/IOD E14 105 H6
TWK TW1 156 B2
WFD IG8 38 D6
Oakleafe Gdns BARK/HLT IG6 54 B6
Oakleigh Av EDGW HA8 44 D5
SURB KT6 191 H5
TRDG/WHET N20 33 H3
Oakleigh Cl TRDG/WHET N20 33 K5
Oakleigh Ct EDGW HA8 * 44 E5
Oakleigh Crs TRDG/WHET N20 33 J5
Oakleigh Dr RKW/CH/CXG WD3 26 A1
Oakleigh Gdns EDGW HA8 44 B1
ORP BR6 216 E2
TRDG/WHET N20 33 G3
Oakleigh Ms TRDG/WHET N20 33 H4
Oakleigh Park Av CHST BR7 185 F5
Oakleigh Pk North
TRDG/WHET N20 33 H3
Oakleigh Pk South
TRDG/WHET N20 33 J3
Oakleigh Rd HGDN/ICK UB10 76 A5
PIN HA5 41 K2
Oakleigh Rd North
TRDG/WHET N20 33 H4
Oakleigh Rd South
FBAR/BDGN N11 34 A6
Oakleigh Wy MTCM CR4 179 G4
SURB KT6 191 H5
Oakley Av BARK IG11 91 F5
CROY/NA CR0 210 E2
EA W5 98 C6
Oakley Cl CHING E4 38 A5
EHAM E6 107 J5
HNWL W7 96 E6
ISLW TW7 135 J2
Oakley Ct MTCM CR4 195 F4
Oakley Crs FSBYE EC1V * 6 B3
Oakley Dr CAT SE6 165 G1
ELTH/MOT SE9 167 J4
HAYES BR2 215 J1
Oakley Gdns CEND/HSY/T N8 67 F2
CHEL SW3 120 D6
Oakley Pk BXLY DA5 168 D2
Oakley Pl STHWK SE1 123 G5
Oakley Rd HAYES BR2 215 J1
HRW HA1 60 E3
IS N1 85 K5
SNWD SE25 197 J2
Oakley Sq CAMTN NW1 4 B2
Oakley St CHEL SW3 120 D6
Oakley Yd BETH E2 * 7 K6
Oak Lodge Av CHIG IG7 54 D1
Oak Lodge Cl STAN HA7 43 J1
Oak Lodge Dr WWKM BR4 198 E4
Oaklodge Wy MLHL NW7 45 H2
Oakmead Av HAYES BR2 199 K3
Oakmeade PIN HA5 42 A2
Oakmead Gdns EDGW HA8 31 F6
Oakmead Pl MTCM CR4 178 D4
Oakmead Rd BAL SW12 161 G3

CROY/NA CR0 195 J3
Oakmere Rd ABYW SE2 128 B6
Oakmoor Wy CHIG IG7 54 E1
Oakmore Gdns
STMC/STPC BR5 202 E1
Oak Park Gdns
WIM/MER SW19 159 G3
Oakridge Dr EFNCH N2 47 H6
Oakridge Rd BMLY BR1 165 H6
Oak Ri BKHH IG9 39 H5
Oak Rd EA W5 97 K6
ERITH DA8 149 K1
ERITH DA8 150 D2
NWMAL KT3 176 A5
ORP BR6 217 G5
Oak Rw MTCM CR4 179 H5
Oaks Av CRW RM5 56 E5
FELT TW13 154 D4
NRWD SE19 181 F1
WPK KT4 207 K2
Oaksford Av SYD SE26 163 J5
Oaks Gv CHING E4 38 C4
Oakshade Rd BMLY BR1 165 G6
Oakshaw Rd
WAND/EARL SW18 160 A2
Oaks La CROY/NA CR0 212 E1
GNTH/NBYPK IG2 72 E2
Oaks Rd CROY/NA CR0 212 D3
STWL/WRAY TW19 132 A6
The Oaks CHSGTN KT9 205 J1
FELT TW13 * 154 D4
HAYES BR2 * 201 F3
MRDN SM4 * 193 H1
NFNCH/WDSPK N12 33 F6
OXHEY WD19 27 G3
RSLP HA4 58 B4
WFD IG8 52 C3
WOOL/PLUM SE18 127 H5
YEAD UB4 94 A1
Oak St ROMW/RG RM7 74 E2
Oaks Wy CAR SM5 209 K5
SURB KT6 190 E6
Oakthorpe Rd PLMGR N13 49 G1
Oaktree Av PLMGR N13 35 G5
Oak Tree Cl EA W5 * 97 J5
STAN HA7 43 J3
Oak Tree Ct BORE WD6 * 29 K1
Oak Tree Dell CDALE/KGS NW9 62 E2
Oak Tree Dr TRDG/WHET N20 33 F3
Oak Tree Gdns BMLY BR1 184 A1
Oaktree Gv IL IG1 90 D3
Oak Tree Rd STJWD NW8 2 B5
Oakview Cl OXHEY WD19 27 G1
Oakview Gdns EFNCH N2 65 H1
Oakview Gv CROY/NA CR0 198 B5
Oakview Rd CAT SE6 182 E1
Oak Village HAMP NW3 84 A2
Oak Vls GLDGN NW11 * 64 D3
Oak Wy ACT W3 118 B1
CROY/NA CR0 198 A3
EBED/NFELT TW14 153 H3
Oakway HAYES BR2 183 G5
RYNPK SW20 193 F1
Oak Wy STHGT/OAK N14 34 B2
Oakway Cl BXLY DA5 169 F1
Oakways ELTH/MOT SE9 167 G1
Oakwood WLGTN SM6 210 B6
Oakwood Av BECK BR3 183 F5
CHSGTN KT9 206 B5
HAYES BR2 184 A6
MTCM CR4 178 C5
STHGT/OAK N14 34 D2
STHL UB1 96 A6
Oakwood Cl CHST BR7 184 E2
LEW SE13 165 G1
STHGT/OAK N14 34 C1
WFD IG8 53 J2
Oakwood Ct WKENS W14 119 J3
Oakwood Crs GFD/PVL UB6 79 G4
WCHMH N21 34 E1
Oakwood Dr BXLYHN DA7 149 K5
EDGW HA8 44 E2
NRWD SE19 180 E2
Oakwood Gdns GDMY/SEVK IG3 73 F6
ORP BR6 201 H6
SUT SM1 193 K6
Oakwood La WKENS W14 119 J3
Oakwood Pde
STHGT/OAK N14 * 22 C6
Oakwood Park
Cottages WCHMH N21 * 35 F1
Oakwood Park Rd
STHGT/OAK N14 34 E1
Oakwood Pl CROY/NA CR0 196 B3
Oakwood Rd CROY/NA CR0 196 B3
GLDGN NW11 64 E2
ORP BR6 201 H6
PIN HA5 41 F5
RYNPK SW20 176 D4
Oakworth Rd NKENS W10 100 A4
Oarsman Pl E/WMO/HCT KT8 189 K1
Oast House Wy
STMC/STPC BR5 202 C1
Oates Cl HAYES BR2 183 G6
Oates Rd CRW RM5 56 D1
Oatfield Rd ORP BR6 202 A5
Oatland Ri WALTH E17 51 G5
Oatlands Rd PEND EN3 24 E2
Oat La CITYW EC2V 12 C3
Oban Cl PLSTW E13 107 G3
Oban Rd PLSTW E13 107 G2
THHTH CR7 196 E1
Oban St POP/IOD E14 106 B5
Oberstein Rd BTSEA SW11 140 C5
Oborne Cl HNHL SE24 142 C6
Observatory Gdns KENS W8 119 K2
Observatory Rd
MORT/ESHN SW14 137 K5
SKENS SW7 14 B5
Occupation La EA W5 116 E4
WOOL/PLUM SE18 147 G2
Occupation Rd WALW SE17 122 D5
WEA W13 116 C2
Ocean Est WCHPL E1 105 F3
Ocean St WCHPL E1 105 F4
Ockendon Ms IS N1 * 85 K4
Ockendon Rd IS N1 85 K4
Ockham Dr STMC/STPC BR5 186 B3
Ockley Rd CROY/NA CR0 196 A4
STRHM/NOR SW16 161 K6
Octagon Ar LVPST EC2M * 13 G2
Octavia Cl MTCM CR4 194 D2
Octavia Ms CRICK NW2 * 81 K4
Octavia Rd ISLW TW7 136 A4
Octavia St BTSEA SW11 140 D2
Octavius St DEPT SE8 144 D1
October Pl HDN NW4 * 46 B6
Odard Rd E/WMO/HCT KT8 189 F1
Odell Cl BARK IG11 91 F5
Odell Wk LEW SE13 144 E4
Odeon Pde ELTH/MOT SE9 * 146 D5
GFD/PVL UB6 79 H4
HOLWY N7 * 84 E1
ISLW TW7 * 135 K3
Odessa Rd FSTGT E7 88 D2
WLSDN NW10 99 J1
Odessa St BERM/RHTH SE16 124 C3
Odger St BTSEA SW11 140 E3
Odhams Wk LSQ/SEVD WC2H * 10 E4
Odsey Vls FSBYPK N4 * 67 G3
Offa's Md HOM E9 87 G2
Offenham Rd ELTH/MOT SE9 166 E6
Offerton Rd CLAP SW4 141 H4
Offham Slope
NFNCH/WDSPK N12 46 D1
The Office Village SRTFD E15 * 88 C5
Offley Pl ISLW TW7 135 J3
Offley Rd BRXN/ST SW9 142 B1
Offord Cl TOTM N17 50 C3
Offord Rd IS N1 85 F5
Offord St HOLWY N7 85 F5
Ogilby St WOOL/PLUM SE18 126 E4
Oglander Rd PECK SE15 143 G5
Ogle St GTPST W1W 10 A1
Oglethorpe Rd DAGE RM10 92 B1
Ohio Rd PLSTW E13 106 D3
Oil Mill La HMSMTH W6 118 D5
Okeburn Rd TOOT SW17 179 F1
Okehampton Crs WELL DA16 148 C2
Okehampton Rd WLSDN NW10 82 A6
Olaf St NTGHL W11 100 B6
Old Bailey STP EC4M 12 B4
Old Barn Cl BELMT SM2 208 C5
Old Barn Wy BXLYHN DA7 150 A5
Old Barrack Yd KTBR SW1X 15 G3
Old Bellgate Whf
POP/IOD E14 124 D3
Oldberry Rd EDGW HA8 45 F2
Old Bethnal Green Rd
BETH E2 104 D2
Old Bexley La BXLY DA5 170 A4
Old Bond St CONDST W1S 10 A6
Oldborough Rd ALP/SUD HA0 61 J6
Old Brewery Ms HAMP NW3 83 H2
Old Bridge Cl NTHLT UB5 96 A1
Old Bridge St KUT/HW KT1 174 E5
Old Broad St LVPST EC2M 13 G3
Old Bromley Rd BMLY BR1 183 G1
Old Brompton Rd ECT SW5 119 K5
Old Buildings LINN WC2A 11 J3
Old Burlington St CONDST W1S 10 A5
Oldbury Cl STMC/STPC BR5 202 E1
Oldbury Pl MHST W1U 9 H1
Oldbury Rd EN EN1 24 C3
Old Castle St WCHPL E1 13 K3
Old Cavendish St
CAVSQ/HST W1G 9 J3
Old Chapel Rd SWLY BR8 203 K4
Old Chestnut Av
ESH/CLAY KT10 204 A4
Old Church La CDALE/KGS NW9 62 E6
GFD/PVL UB6 97 G2
STAN HA7 43 H2
Old Church Pth
ESH/CLAY KT10 204 B2
Oldchurch Ri ROMW/RG RM7 75 G3
Old Church Rd CHING E4 37 J5
Oldchurch Rd ROMW/RG RM7 75 G3
Old Church Rd WCHPL E1 * 105 F5
Old Church St CHEL SW3 120 C6
Old Claygate La
ESH/CLAY KT10 205 G4
Old Compton St
SOHO/SHAV W1D 10 C5
Old Cote Dr HEST TW5 115 F6
Old Court Pl KENS W8 120 A2
The Old Ctyd BMLY BR1 184 A4
Old Dairy Ms BAL SW12 161 F3
KTTN NW5 * 84 B4
Old Deer Pk RCH/KEW TW9 * 137 G4
Old Deer Park Gdns
RCH/KEW TW9 137 F4
Old Devonshire Rd BAL SW12 161 G2
Old Dock Cl RCH/KEW TW9 117 H6
Old Dover Rd BKHTH/KID SE3 145 K1
Old Farm Av BFN/LL DA15 167 J3
STHGT/OAK N14 34 C2
Old Farm Cl HSLWW TW4 134 E5
Old Farm Rd EFNCH N2 47 H4
HPTN TW12 172 E2
WDR/YW UB7 112 A2
Old Farm Rd East
BFN/LL DA15 168 B4
Old Farm Rd West
BFN/LL DA15 168 A4
Oldfield Cl BMLY BR1 200 E1
GFD/PVL UB6 78 E3
STAN HA7 43 G1
Oldfield Farm Gdns
GFD/PVL UB6 78 D6
Oldfield Gv BERM/RHTH SE16 124 A4
Oldfield La North GFD/PVL UB6 78 D6
Oldfield La South GFD/PVL UB6 96 C2
Oldfield Ms HGT N6 66 C4
Oldfield Rd ACT W3 118 C2
BMLY BR1 200 E1
BXLYHN DA7 149 F3
HPTN TW12 173 F4
STNW/STAM N16 86 A1
WIM/MER SW19 177 H2
WLSDN NW10 81 H5
Oldfields Circ NTHLT UB5 78 C4
Oldfields Rd SUT SM1 208 D1
Old Fish Street Hl BLKFR EC4V * 12 C5
Old Fleet La FLST/FETLN EC4A 12 A3
Old Fold Cl BAR EN5 * 20 D2
Old Fold La BAR EN5 20 D2
Old Fold Vw BAR EN5 20 A4
Old Ford Rd BETH E2 104 E1
BOW E3 87 H6
Old Forge Cl STAN HA7 29 G6
Old Forge Rd ARCH N19 66 D6
EN EN1 24 B1
Old Forge Wy SCUP DA14 168 C6
Old Gannon Cl NTHWD HA6 26 A6
Old Gloucester St BMSBY WC1N 11 F1
Old Hall Cl PIN HA5 41 J4
Old Hall Dr PIN HA5 41 J4
Oldham Ter ACT W3 117 K2
Old Hl CHST BR7 185 F4
ORP BR6 216 E4
Oldhill St STNW/STAM N16 68 C5
Old Homesdale Rd HAYES BR2 200 B1
Old Hospital Cl BAL SW12 * 160 E3
Old House Cl WIM/MER SW19 177 H1
Old House Gdns TWK TW1 * 156 D1
Old Howletts La RSLP HA4 58 B3
Old Jamaica Rd
BERM/RHTH SE16 123 H3
Old James St PECK SE15 143 J4
Old Jewry LOTH EC2R * 12 E4
Old Kenton La CDALE/KGS NW9 62 D2
Old Kent Rd PECK SE15 123 J6
Old Kingston Rd WPK KT4 206 E1
Old Lodge Wy STAN HA7 43 G1
Old London Rd KUTN/CMB KT2 175 F5
Old Maidstone Rd SCUP DA14 187 G3
Old Malden La WPK KT4 192 B6
Old Manor Dr ISLW TW7 155 H1
Old Manor Rd NWDGN UB2 114 C4
Old Manor Wy BXLYHN DA7 150 A3
CHST BR7 184 E1
Old Manor Yd ECT SW5 * 120 A4
Old Market Sq BETH E2 7 J4
Old Marylebone Rd CAMTN NW1 8 D2
Old Mill Ct SWFD E18 53 G6
Old Mill Rd WOOL/PLUM SE18 127 J6
Old Mitre Ct EMB EC4Y * 11 K4
Old Montague St WCHPL E1 104 C4
Old Nichol St BETH E2 7 J6
Old North St FSBYW WC1X * 11 G1
Old Oak Common La
WLSDN NW10 99 G3
Old Oak La WLSDN NW10 99 H2
Old Oak Rd ACT W3 118 C1
Old Orch SUN TW16 172 B5
Old Orchard Cl EBAR EN4 21 H1
The Old Orch HAMP NW3 * 83 K2
Old Palace Rd CROY/NA CR0 211 J1
Old Palace Yd RCH/KEW TW9 136 D6
Old Paradise St LBTH SE11 17 G6
Old Park Av BAL SW12 161 F1
ENC/FH EN2 23 J5
Old Park Gv ENC/FH EN2 23 J5
Old Park La MYFR/PKLN W1K 15 J1
Old Park Ms HEST TW5 134 E1
Old Park Ridings WCHMH N21 35 J1
Old Park Rd ABYW SE2 128 B5
ENC/FH EN2 23 H4
PLMGR N13 35 F5
Old Park Rd South ENC/FH EN2 23 H5
Old Park Vw ENC/FH EN2 23 G4
Old Pearson St GNWCH SE10 * 144 E1
Old Perry St CHST BR7 185 K3
Old Post Office La
BKHTH/KID SE3 146 A4
Old Pound Cl ISLW TW7 136 B2
Old Pye St WEST SW1P 16 C4
Old Quebec St MBLAR W1H 9 F4
Old Queen St STJSPK SW1H 16 D3
Old Rectory Gdns EDGW HA8 44 C2
Old Redding
KTN/HRWW/WS HA3 42 B1
Oldridge Rd BAL SW12 161 F2
Old Rd DART DA1 150 A5
LEW SE13 145 H5
PEND EN3 24 E2
Old Royal Free Sq IS N1 5 K1
Old Ruislip Rd NTHLT UB5 95 H1
Old's Ap WATW WD18 26 A3
Old School Cl BECK BR3 182 B5
Old School Crs FSTGT E7 88 E4
Old School Pl CROY/NA CR0 211 G2
Old Schools La EW KT17 207 H6
Old School Sq THDIT KT7 190 A3
Old School Ter CHEAM SM3 * 208 B5
Old Seacoal La STP EC4M 12 A4
Old South Cl PIN HA5 41 H4
Old South Lambeth Rd
VX/NE SW8 * 141 K1
Old Sq LINN WC2A 11 H3
Old Stable Ms HBRY N5 * 85 J1
Old Station Gdns TEDD TW11 * 174 B2
Old Station Rd HYS/HAR UB3 113 J3
The Old Station Yd WALTH E17 70 A1
Oldstead Rd BMLY BR1 165 G6
Old St FSBYE EC1V 6 C6
PLSTW E13 107 F1
SDTCH EC2A 7 G5
Old Studio Cl CROY/NA CR0 196 E4
Old Swan Yd CAR SM5 209 K2
Old Town CLAP SW4 141 H4
CROY/NA CR0 211 H1
Old Tramyard
WOOL/PLUM SE18 127 K4
Old Woolwich Rd
GNWCH SE10 125 G6
Old York Rd WAND/EARL SW18 140 A6
Oleander Cl ORP BR6 216 D3
O'Leary Sq WCHPL E1 104 E4
Olga St BOW E3 105 G1
Olinda Rd STNW/STAM N16 68 B3
Oliphant St NKENS W10 100 C2
Olive Gv SEVS/STOTM N15 67 J1
Oliver Av SNWD SE25 197 G1
Oliver Cl CHSWK W4 117 J6
Oliver Gdns EHAM E6 107 J4
Oliver Gv SNWD SE25 197 G1
Oliver Ms PECK SE15 143 H3
Olive Rd CRICK NW2 82 A2
DART DA1 171 G3
EA W5 116 E3
PLSTW E13 107 G2
WIM/MER SW19 * 178 B3
Oliver Rd LEY E10 87 K1
NWMAL KT3 175 K5
RAIN RM13 93 H6
SUT SM1 209 H2
WALTH E17 70 A2
Oliver's Yd STLK EC1Y 7 F6
Olive St ROMW/RG RM7 75 F2
Ollerton Gn BOW E3 87 H6
Ollerton Rd FBAR/BDGN N11 48 D1
Olley Cl WLGTN SM6 210 E5
Ollgar Cl SHB W12 118 C1
Olliffe St POP/IOD E14 125 F3
Olmar St STHWK SE1 123 H6
Olney Rd WALW SE17 122 D6
Olron Crs BXLYHS DA6 148 E6
Olven Rd WOOL/PLUM SE18 147 H1
Olveston Wk CAR SM5 194 C3
Olwen Ms PIN HA5 41 H5
Olyffe Av WELL DA16 148 B3
Olyffe Dr BECK BR3 183 F4
Olympia Wy WKENS W14 119 H3
Olympic Wy GFD/PVL UB6 78 B6
WBLY HA9 80 C2
Olympus Gv WDGN N22 49 G4
Olympus Sq CLPT E5 86 D1
Oman Av CRICK NW2 82 A3
O'Meara St STHWK SE1 18 D1
Omega Pl IS N1 5 F3
Omega St NWCR SE14 144 C2
Ommaney Rd NWCR SE14 144 A2
Omnibus Wy WALTH E17 51 J5
Ondine Rd PECK SE15 143 G5
Onega Ga BERM/RHTH SE16 124 B3
One Tree Cl FSTH SE23 163 K1
Ongar Cl CHDH RM6 73 J2
Ongar Rd FUL/PGN SW6 119 K6
Ongar Wy RAIN RM13 93 H6
Onra Rd WALTH E17 69 J4
Onslow Av RCHPK/HAM TW10 137 F6
Onslow Cl CHING E4 38 B4
NKENS W10 100 D2
Onslow Crs CHST BR7 185 G4
SKENS SW7 14 B7
Onslow Dr SCUP DA14 168 E5
Onslow Gdns MUSWH N10 66 B2
SKENS SW7 14 A7
SWFD E18 53 F6
THDIT KT7 189 K5
WCHMH N21 23 G6
WLGTN SM6 210 C5
Onslow Ms East SKENS SW7 14 A7
Onslow Ms West SKENS SW7 14 A7
Onslow Pde STHGT/OAK N14 * 34 B3
Onslow Rd CROY/NA CR0 196 B4
NWMAL KT3 192 D1
RCHPK/HAM TW10 157 F1
Onslow Sq SKENS SW7 14 B7
Onslow St CLKNW EC1R 5 K7
Onslow Wy THDIT KT7 189 K5
Ontario St STHWK SE1 18 B5
Ontario Wy POP/IOD E14 124 D1
On The Hl OXHEY WD19 27 J4
Onyx Ms SRTFD E15 88 C4
Opal Cl CAN/RD E16 107 H5
Opal Ms IL IG1 72 B6
KIL/WHAMP NW6 82 D6
Opal St LBTH SE11 18 A7
Openshaw Rd ABYW SE2 128 C5
Openview WAND/EARL SW18 160 B3
Ophir Ter PECK SE15 143 H2
Opossum Wy HSLWW TW4 134 B4
Oppenheim Rd LEW SE13 145 F3
Oppidans Rd HAMP NW3 83 K5
Optima Pk DART DA1 * 150 D4
Orange Court La ORP BR6 216 A6
Orange Gv CHIG IG7 54 C2
WAN E11 88 C1
Orange Hill Rd EDGW HA8 44 E3
Orange Pl BERM/RHTH SE16 123 K3
Orangery La ELTH/MOT SE9 146 E6
The Orangery
RCHPK/HAM TW10 156 D4
Orange St LSQ/SEVD WC2H 10 D6
WAP E1W 123 H1
Orange Tree Hl ABR/ST RM4 57 F1
Oransay Rd IS N1 85 J4
Oratory La CHEL SW3 * 120 C5
Orbain Rd FUL/PGN SW6 139 H1
Orbel St BTSEA SW11 140 D2
Orb St WALW SE17 18 E7
Orchard Av BELV DA17 129 G6
CROY/NA CR0 198 B6
DART DA1 170 E3
EBED/NFELT TW14 133 G6
FNCH N3 46 E6
HEST TW5 134 D1
MTCM CR4 195 F5
NWMAL KT3 176 B5
STHGT/OAK N14 34 C2
STHL UB1 114 D1
THDIT KT7 190 B5
TRDG/WHET N20 33 H4
Orchard Cl ALP/SUD HA0 80 A6
BUSH WD23 28 D3
BXLYHN DA7 149 F2
CHING E4 37 J6
CRICK NW2 81 J1
EDGW HA8 44 A2
FSTH SE23 163 K1
HOR/WEW KT19 * 206 D4
IS N1 85 J5
NKENS W10 100 C4
RSLP HA4 58 A4
RYNPK SW20 193 F1
THDIT KT7 190 C5
WOT/HER KT12 188 A4
Orchard Cottages
HYS/HAR UB3 * 113 H2
KUTN/CMB KT2 * 175 H4
Orchard Ct WLGTN SM6 * 210 B3
WPK KT4 * 192 D5
Orchard Crs EDGW HA8 44 E1
EN EN1 24 B2
Orchard Dr BKHTH/KID SE3 145 H3
EDGW HA8 44 B1
Orchard Gdns CHSGTN KT9 206 A2
Orchard Ga CDALE/KGS NW9 63 G1
ESH/CLAY KT10 189 J5
GFD/PVL UB6 79 H4
Orchard Gn ORP BR6 201 K6
Orchard Gv CROY/NA CR0 198 B4
EDGW HA8 44 C4
KTN/HRWW/WS HA3 62 B2
ORP BR6 202 A6
PGE/AN SE20 181 H3
Orchard Hl DART DA1 150 B6
LEW SE13 144 E3
Orchard La E/WMO/HCT KT8 189 J3
RYNPK SW20 176 E4
WFD IG8 39 G6
Orchardleigh Av PEND EN3 24 E3
Orchardmede WCHMH N21 35 K1
Orchard Ms IS N1 85 K5
TOOT SW17 160 B5
Orchard Pl POP/IOD E14 106 C6
STMC/STPC BR5 * 186 D6
TOTM N17 50 B3
Orchard Ri CROY/NA CR0 198 B5
KUTN/CMB KT2 175 K4
PIN HA5 40 D6
RCHPK/HAM TW10 137 J5
Orchard Ri East BFN/LL DA15 147 K6
Orchard Ri West BFN/LL DA15 147 K6
Orchard Rd BAR EN5 20 C5
BELV DA17 129 H4
BMLY BR1 184 B4
BTFD TW8 116 D6
CHSGTN KT9 206 A2
DAGE RM10 92 C6
FELT TW13 153 K4
HGT N6 66 B4
HPTN TW12 172 E3
HSLWW TW4 134 E6
HYS/HAR UB3 94 E6
KUT/HW KT1 175 F5
ORP BR6 216 B3
ORP BR6 217 J6
PEND EN3 24 E6
RCH/KEW TW9 137 H4
ROMW/RG RM7 56 D5
SCUP DA14 167 K6
SUN TW16 172 A3
SUT SM1 208 E3
TWK TW1 136 B6
WELL DA16 148 C4
Orchardson St STJWD NW8 2 A7
Orchard Sq WKENS W14 * 119 J5
Orchard St DART DA1 171 H1
MBLAR W1H 9 G4
WALTH E17 69 G1
Orchard Ter EN EN1 * 36 C1
WLSDN NW10 * 81 H2
The Orchard BKHTH/KID SE3 145 G3
CHSWK W4 118 B4
EW KT17 207 H5
GLDGN NW11 64 E2
HSLW TW3 135 H3
TRDG/WHET N20 33 F3
WCHMH N21 35 K1
Orchard Vls SCUP DA14 * 186 D2
Orchard Wy ASHF TW15 152 C4
CROY/NA CR0 198 B4
EN EN1 24 A4
ESH/CLAY KT10 204 C4
RDART DA2 171 G5
SUT SM1 209 H2
Orchid Cl CHSGTN KT9 205 J5
EHAM E6 107 J4
STHL UB1 95 J5
Orchid Gdns HSLWW TW4 134 E5
Orchid Rd STHGT/OAK N14 34 C2
Orchid St SHB W12 99 J6
Orde Hall St BMSBY WC1N * 11 G1
Ordell Rd BOW E3 105 H1
Ordnance Cl FELT TW13 153 K4
Ordnance Crs GNWCH SE10 125 H2
Ordnance Hl STJWD NW8 2 B1
Ordnance Ms STJWD NW8 2 B2
Ordnance Rd CAN/RD E16 106 D4
WOOL/PLUM SE18 127 F6
Oregano Dr POP/IOD E14 106 B5
Oregon Av MNPK E12 89 K2
Oregon Cl NWMAL KT3 191 K1
Oregon Sq ORP BR6 201 J5
Orestes Ms KIL/WHAMP NW6 82 E3
Orford Gdns TWK TW1 156 A4
Orford Rd CAT SE6 164 E5
SWFD E18 53 F6
WALTH E17 69 K2
Oriel Cl MTCM CR4 195 J1
Oriel Ct HAMP NW3 83 G2
Oriel Dr BARN SW13 119 F6
Oriel Gdns CLAY IG5 53 K6
Oriel Rd HOM E9 87 F4
Oriel Wy NTHLT UB5 78 B5
Oriental Rd CAN/RD E16 126 C1
Orient St LBTH SE11 18 A6
Orient Wy CLPT E5 87 F1
LEY E10 87 J1
Oriole Wy THMD SE28 109 H6
Orion Rd MUSWH N10 48 A2
Orion Wy NTHWD HA6 26 D6
Orissa Rd WOOL/PLUM SE18 127 K5
Orkney St BTSEA SW11 141 F3
Orlando Rd CLAP SW4 141 H4
Orleans Rd NRWD SE19 180 E2
TWK TW1 156 C2
Orleston Ms HOLWY N7 85 G4
Orleston Rd HOLWY N7 85 G4
Orley Farm Rd HRW HA1 78 E2
Ormanton Rd SYD SE26 163 H6
Orme Ct BAY/PAD W2 101 F6
Ormeley Rd BAL SW12 161 G2
Orme Rd KUT/HW KT1 175 J5
SUT SM1 209 F4
Ormerod Gdns MTCM CR4 179 F5
Ormesby Cl THMD SE28 109 K6
Ormesby Wy
KTN/HRWW/WS HA3 62 B3
Orme Sq BAY/PAD W2 101 F6
Orme Square Ga BAY/PAD W2 101 F6

Ormiston Gv SHB W12 ....118 E1
Ormiston Rd GNWCH SE10......125 K5
Ormond Cl HPTN TW12 ....175 G4
Ormond Ct BBSBY WC1N..............11 F1
Ormond Dr HPTN TW12 ....173 G3
Ormonde Av HOR/WEW KT19 ....207 F6
ORP BR6 ....201 H6
Ormonde Ct STJWD NW8 * 2 C2
Ormonde Ga CHEL SW3 * 120 E5
Ormonde Pl BGVA SW1W 15 H7
Ormonde Pl R BKHH IG9 ....39 G3
Ormonde Rd
    MORT/ESHN SW14 ....137 J4
    NTHWD HA6 ....26 B6
Ormonde Ter STJWD NW8 * 66 E5
Ormond Rd ARCH N19 ....66 E5
    RCHPK/HAM TW10 ....136 E6
Ormond Yd STJS SW1Y.................10 B7
Ormsby BELMT SM2 * 209 F5
Ormsby Gdns GFD/PVL UB6 ....96 C2
Ormsby Pl STNW/STAM N16........86 B1
Ormsby St BETH E2 * 7 J2
Ormside St PECK SE15 ....123 K6
Ormskirk Rd OXHEY WD19 ....27 H6
Ornan Rd HAMP NW3 ....83 J3
Oronsay Wk IS N1 * 85 J4
Orpheus St CMBW SE5 ....142 E2
Orpington By-Pass ORP BR6 ......217 K3
Orpington Gdns UED N18..............36 A5
Orpington Rd CHST BR7 ....185 K6
    WCHMH N21............................35 C5
Orpwood Cl HPTN TW12.............173 F6
Orsett Ms BAY/PAD W2 ....101 G5
Orsett Rd LBTH SE11 ....122 A5
Orsett Ter BAY/PAD W2 ....101 G5
    WFD IG8 ....53 G4
Orsman Rd IS N1 ....7 C1
Orton Gv EN EN1 ....24 B2
Orton Rd WAP E1W 123 H1
Orville Rd BTSEA SW11 ....140 C3
Orwell Cl HYS/HAR UB3 ....94 C6
Orwell Rd PLSTW E13 ....107 G1
Osbaldeston Rd
    STNW/STAM N16 ....68 C3
Osberton Rd LEE/GVPK SE12.....145 K6
Osbert St WEST SW1P 16 C7
Osborn Cl HACK E8......................86 C6
Osborne Av STWL/WRAY TW19 ..152 C3
Osborne Cl BECK BR3 ....198 B1
    EBAR EN4 ....21 K4
    EMPK RM11 ....75 K5
    FELT TW13 * 172 C5
Osborne Ct EA W5 * 98 A4
Osborne Gdns THHTH CR7 ....180 D5
Osborne Gv WALTH E17 ....69 H1
Osborne Ms WALTH E17 ....69 J1
Osborne Rd ACT W3 ....117 J2
    BELV DA17 ....129 G5
    BKHH IG9 ....39 F3
    CRICK NW2 ....81 K4
    ESBYPK N4 ....75 K3
    FSTGT E7 ....89 F3
    HOM E9 ....87 H4
    HSLW TW3 ....134 E4
    KUTN/CMB KT2 ....175 F3
    LEY E10 ....87 K1
    PEND EN3 ....25 J3
    PLMGR N13 ....35 G5
    STHL UB1 ....114 C6
    THHTH CR7 ....180 D5
Osborne Sq DAGW RM9 ....92 B2
Osborne Ter TOOT SW17 * 179 F1
Osborn Gdns MLHL NW7 ....46 B3
Osborn Gv CHSGTN KT9 ....206 A4
Osborn La FSTH SE23 ....164 B2
Osborn St WCHPL E1 ....13 K2
Osborn Ter BKHTH/KID SE3 ....145 J3
Osborne Ct
    RYLN/HDSTN HA2 * 60 B1
Oscar Faber Pl IS N1 * 86 A5
Oscar St DEPTFORD SE8 ....144 D3
Oseney Crs KTTN NW5...................84 C4
Osgood Av ORP BR6 ....217 F3
Osgood Gdns ORP BR6...............217 F3
Osidge La STHGT/OAK N14...........34 A3
Osier Crs MUSWH N10 ....47 K4
Osiers Rd WAND/EARL SW18 ......139 K5
The Osiers WATW WD18 * 26 E1
Osier St WCHPL E1 ....104 E3
Osier Wy LEY E10.........................87 K1
    MTCM CR4 ....194 E2
Oslac Rd CAT SE6 ....182 E1
Osman Rd ED N9 ....36 C5
    HMSMTH W6 ....119 F3
Osmond Cl RYLN/HDSTN HA2......60 C6
Osmond Gdns WLGTN SM6.........210 C3
Osmund St SHB W12 * 99 H5
Osnaburgh St CAMTN NW1 ....3 K7
Osnaburgh Ter CAMTN NW1 ....3 K6
Osney Wk MRDN SM4..................194 C3
Osprey Cl EHAM E6......................107 J4
    HAYES BR2.............................200 D5
    SUT SM1 * 208 D3
    WALTH E17 ....51 C5
    WAN E11 ....70 E1
    WDR/YW UB7 ....112 A2
Osprey Est BERM/RHTH SE16.....124 A4
Osprey Ms PEND EN3 ....24 E6
Ospringe Cl PGE/AN SE20...........181 K3
Ospringe Rd KTTN NW5 ....84 C2
Osram Rd WBLY HA9 ....79 K1
Ossian Rd FSBYPK N4 ....67 F4
Ossier Ms CHSWK W4 ....118 C6
Ossington Buildings
    MHST W1U * 9 G2
Ossington Cl BAY/PAD W2 * 100 E6
Ossington St BAY/PAD W2 ....100 E6
Ossory Rd STHWK SE1 ....123 H5
Osten Ms SKENS SW7 * 120 A3
Osterberg Rd DART DA1 ....151 J5

Osterley Av ISLW TW7.................135 J1
Osterley Cl STMC/STPC BR5......186 B4
Osterley Crs ISLW TW7 * 135 K2
Osterley Gdns THHTH CR7 ....180 C5
Osterley La ISLW TW7 ....115 H4
Osterley Park Rd
    NWDGN UB2...........................114 E3
Osterley Park View Rd
    HNWL W7................................115 K2
Osterley Rd ISLW TW7 ....135 K1
    STNW/STAM N16......................86 A2
Ostliffe Rd PLMGR N13.................49 H1
Oswald Cl STHL UB1...................111 D1
Oswald Rd STHL UB1..................114 D1
Oswald's Md HOM E9 * 87 G2
Oswald St CLPT E5 ....87 F1
Osward CROY/NA CRO 213 H6
Osward Pl ED N9...........................36 C4
Osward Rd BAL SW12 ....160 E4
Oswin St LBTH SE11......................18 B6
Oswyth Rd CMBW SE5 ....143 F3
Otford Cl BMLY BR1....................185 F6
    BXLY DA5 ....150 A6
    PGE/AN SE20.........................181 K4
Otford Crs BROCKY SE4 ....164 C1
Othello Cl LBTH SE11 ....122 C5
Otis St BOW E3 ....106 A2
Otley Dr GNTH/NBYPK IG2..........72 B3
Otley Rd CAN/RD E16 ....107 C5
Otley Ter CLPT E5 ....69 F6
Otley Wy OXHEY WD19 ....27 G5
Otlinge Rd STMC/STPC BR5.......202 E1
Ottawa Gdns DAGE RM10.............93 F5
Ottaway St CLPT E5 ....86 D1
Otterbourne Rd CHING E4..............38 B5
    CROY/NA CRO 196 D6
Otterburn Gdns ISLW TW7..........136 B1
Otterburn St TOOT SW17 ....178 E2
Otter Cl SRTFD E15 ....88 A6
Otterden St CAT SE6...................164 D6
Otter Rd GFD/PVL UB6 ....96 C5
Otters Cl STMC/STPC BR5..........202 E1
Otto Cl CAT SE6...........................164 D6
    SYD SE26...............................163 J5
Otto St WALW SE17.....................122 C6
Otway Gdns BUSH WD23..............28 E2
Oulton Cl THMD SE28 ....109 J5
Oulton Crs BARK IG11 ....91 H4
Oulton Rd SEVS/STOTM N15........67 K2
Oulton Wy OXHEY WD19 ....27 K6
Ouseley Rd BAL SW12 ....160 E3
Outer Cir CAMTN NW1 ....3 F2
Outgate Rd WLSDN NW10 ....81 H5
Outram Pl IS N1 ....84 E6
Outram Rd CROY/NA CRO 197 G6
    EHAM E6 ....89 J6
    WDGN N22 ....48 D4
Outwich St HDTCH EC3A * 13 H3
Oval Ct EDGW HA8 * 44 E3
Oval Pl VX/NE SW8 * 142 A1
Oval Rd CAMTN NW1 ....84 B6
    CROY/NA CRO 196 E6
Oval Rd North DAGE RM10............92 B6
Oval Rd South DAGE RM10 ....110 B1
The Oval BETH E2 ....104 D1
    BFN/LL DA15 ....168 B2
Oval Wy LBTH SE11 ....122 A5
Overbrae BECK BR3 ....182 D2
Overbrook Wk EDGW HA8.............44 C3
Overbury Av BECK BR3 ....182 E6
Overbury Rd FSBYPK N4...............67 G4
Overbury St CLPT E5.....................87 F2
Overcliff Rd BROCKY SE4 ....164 A4
Overcourt Cl BFN/LL DA15..........168 C1
Overdale Av NWMAL KT3.............175 K5
Overdale Rd EA W5 ....116 D3
Overdown Rd CAT SE6 ....164 D6
Overhill Cottages MTCM CR4 * 179 F5
Overhill Rd EDUL SE22 ....163 H2
    PUR/KEN CR8 ....211 G6
Overhill Wy BECK BR3 ....199 G2
Overlea Rd CLPT E5 ....68 C4
Overmead ELTH/MOT SE9 ....166 E3
Overstand Cl BECK BR3 ....198 D2
Overstone Gdns CROY/NA CRO...198 D4
Overstone Rd HMSMTH W6 ....119 F4
Overton Cl ISLW TW7 ....136 A2
    WLSDN NW10 ....80 E4
Overton Dr CHDH RM6 ....73 J4
    WAN E11 ....71 F4
Overton Rd ABYW SE2 ....128 D2
    BELMT SM2 ....208 E5
    BRXN/ST SW9 ....142 B3
    LEY E10 ....69 G5
    STHGT/OAK N14 ....22 B6
Overton's Yd CROY/NA CRO 211 J6
Overy Liberty DART DA1 ....171 H2
Overy St DART DA1 ....171 J1
Ovesdon Av RYLN/HDSTN HA2....59 H5
Ovett Cl NRWD SE19 ....181 F2
Ovex Cl POP/IOD E14...................125 F3
Ovington Gdns CHEL SW3.............14 C5
Ovington Ms CHEL SW3 ....14 C5
Ovington Sq CHEL SW3.................14 C5
Ovington St CHEL SW3 ....14 C5
Owen Cl CROY/NA CRO 196 E3
    CRW RM5 ....56 C2
    NTHLT UB5 ....78 A4
    THMD SE28 ....128 D1
    YEAD UB4 * 95 F2
Owen Gdns WFD IG8 ....53 J2
Owenite St ABYW SE2 ....128 C4
Owen Rd PLMGR N13 ....49 H1
    YEAD UB4 * 95 G2
Owens Ms WAN E11 * 70 C6
Owen's Rw FSBYE EC1V 6 A4
Owen St FSBYE EC1V 6 A3
Owens Wk ED N9 * 36 C4
Owen Wy WLSDN NW10 ....80 E3
Owgan Cl CMBW SE5...................142 E1
Oxberry Av FUL/PGN SW6 ....139 H3
Oxenden Wood Rd ORP BR6.......217 H4
Oxendon St SOHO/SHAV W1D * ...10 C6
Oxenford St PECK SE15 ....143 G4
Oxenpark Av WBLY HA9................62 A4

Oxestalls Rd DEPT SE8 ....124 B5
Oxford Av HEST TW5 ....115 F5
    HYS/HAR UB3 ....133 J1
    RYNPK SW20 ....177 H5
    STHGT/OAK N14 ....34 C4
Oxford Cl ED N9 ....36 D4
    MTCM CR4 ....179 H6
    NTHWD HA6 ....40 A5
Oxford Ct MANHO EC4N 12 E5
Oxford Crs NWMAL KT3 ....192 A3
Oxford Dr RSLP HA4......................58 A5
Oxford Gdns CHSWK W4 ....117 H5
    NKENS W10 ....100 B5
    TRDG/WHET N20 ....33 H3
    WCHMH N21............................35 J2
Oxford Ga HMSMTH W6 ....119 G4
Oxford Ms BXLY DA5 ....169 H3
Oxford Rd CAR SM5 ....209 J4
    EA W5 ....97 K6
    ED N9 ....36 D4
    ESBYPK N4 ....67 H5
    HRW HA1 ....60 C5
    IL IG1 ....90 C2
    KIL/WHAMP NW6 ....100 E1
    KTN/HRWW/WS HA3 ....43 F6
    NRWD SE19 ....180 E2
    PEND EN3 ....24 D6
    PUT/ROE SW15 ....139 H5
    SCUP DA14.............................186 C1
    SRTFD E15 ....88 B4
    TEDD TW11 ....173 J1
    WFD IG8 ....53 H1
    WLGTN SM6 ....210 C3
Oxford Rd North CHSWK W4 ....117 J5
Oxford Rd South CHSWK W4 ......117 G5
Oxford Rw SUN TW16 * 172 B6
Oxford Sq BAY/PAD W2 ....8 D4
Oxford St OXSTW W1C 9 G4
Oxford Wk STHL UB1...................114 D1
Oxford Wy FELT TW13.................154 C5
Oxgate Centre CRICK NW2 * 63 K5
Oxgate Court Pde CRICK NW2 * 63 K6
Oxgate Gdns CRICK NW2 ....81 K1
Oxgate La CRICK NW2 ....63 K5
Oxhawth Crs HAYES BR2 ....201 F2
Oxhey Av OXHEY WD19 ....27 H2
Oxhey Dr NTHWD HA6 ....41 F1
Oxhey La OXHEY WD19.................27 K4
    OXHEY WD19 ....27 K4
    PIN HA5 ....42 B2
Oxhey Ridge Cl NTHWD HA6 ....40 E2
Oxhey Rd OXHEY WD19.................27 C2
Oxleas EHAM E6 ....108 B5
Oxleas Cl WELL DA16..................147 J3
Oxleay Rd RYLN/HDSTN HA2 ....60 A5
Oxleigh Cl NWMAL KT3...............192 B2
Oxley Cl STHWK SE1 ....123 G5
Oxleys Rd CRICK NW2...................63 K1
Oxlow La DAGE RM10 ....92 C2
Oxonian St EDUL SE22 ....143 G5
Oxted Cl MTCM CR4....................178 C6
Oxtoby Wy STRHM/NOR SW16 ...179 J4
Oyster Catchers Cl
    CAN/RD E16 ....107 F5
Oyster Rw WCHPL E1 * 104 E5
Ozolins Wy CAN/RD E16 ....106 D5

P

Pablo Neruda HNHL SE24 ....142 C5
Pacehaeath Cl CRW RM5 ....57 F2
Pace Pl WCHPL E1 ....104 D5
Pacific Cl EBED/NFELT TW14 ......153 J3
Pacific Rd CAN/RD E16 ....106 E5
Packham Cl ORP BR6..................217 J1
Packington Sq IS N1 ....6 C1
Packington St IS N1.......................6 B1
Packmores Rd ELTH/MOT SE9....147 J6
Padbury Cl EBED/NFELT TW14....153 G5
Padbury Ct BETH E2 ....7 K5
Padcroft Rd WDR/YW UB7 ....112 A1
Paddenswick Rd HMSMTH W6 ....118 D3
Paddington Cl YEAD UB4 ....95 H3
Paddington Gn BAY/PAD W2 ....8 A2
Paddington St MHST W1U...............9 G1
Paddock Cl BKHTH/KID SE3 ....145 K4
    NTHLT UB5 ....95 K1
    ORP BR6 ....216 B2
    OXHEY WD19 ....27 J1
    SYD SE26...............................164 A6
    WPK KT4 ....192 D5
Paddock Gdns NRWD SE19 ....181 F2
Paddock Rd BXLYHS DA6 ....149 F5
    CRICK NW2 ....81 J1
    RSLP HA4 ....77 G2
Paddocks Cl RYLN/HDSTN HA2 ....78 B2
    STMC/STPC BR5 ....202 E6
The Paddocks EA W5 * 116 B6
    EBAR EN4 ....21 K4
    MLHL NW7 * 31 K6
    WBLY HA9 ....62 D6
Paddock Wy CHST BR7 ....185 J3
    PUT/ROE SW15 ....159 F2
Padfield Rd BRXN/ST SW9 ....142 D4
Padley Cl CHSGTN KT9 ....206 B3
Padnall Rd CHDH RM6 ....74 A1
Padstow Cl ORP BR6...................217 F2
Padstow Rd ENC/FH EN2 ....23 H3
Padstow Wk
    EBED/NFELT TW14..................153 J3
Padua Rd PGE/AN SE20 ....181 K4
Pagden St VX/NE SW8.................141 G2
Pageant Crs
    BERM/RHTH SE16...................124 C1
Pageant Wk CROY/NA CRO..........212 A1
Page Av WBLY HA9 ....80 E1
Page Cl DAGW RM9 ....92 A3
    HPTN TW12 ....172 D2
    KTN/HRWW/WS HA3 ....62 B3
Page Crs CROY/NA CRO 211 H3
Page Green Rd
    SEVS/STOTM N15 * 68 C2

Page Green Ter
    SEVS/STOTM N15.....................68 B2
Page Heath La BMLY BR1............184 C6
Page Heath Vls BMLY BR1...........184 C6
Pagehurst Rd CROY/NA CRO 197 H4
Page Meadow MLHL NW7..............45 J3
Page Rd EBED/NFELT TW14........153 C1
Page's Hl MUSWH N10 ....48 A5
Page's La MUSWH N10 ....48 A5
Page St MLHL NW7 ....45 J4
    WEST SW1P 16 D6
Page's Wk STHWK SE1 ....19 H4
Pages Yd CHSWK W4 * 118 B6
Paget Cl HPTN TW12...................155 K4
Paget Gdns CHST BR7 ....185 G4
Paget La ISLW TW7......................135 J4
Paget Pl KUTN/CMB KT2 * 175 K2
    THDIT KT7 ....190 C5
Paget Ri WOOL/PLUM SE18 ....147 F5
Paget Rd HGDN/ICK UB10.............94 A3
    IL IG1 ....90 A3
    STNW/STAM N16......................67 K5
Paget St FSBYE EC1V.....................6 A4
Pagitts Gv EBAR EN4 ....21 F2
Pagnell St NWCR SE14 ....144 B1
Pagoda Av RCH/KEW TW9...........137 G4
Pagoda Gdns BKHTH/KID SE3.....145 G3
Pagoda Gv DUL SE21 ....162 E4
Paignton Rd RSLP HA4..................76 E1
    SEVS/STOTM N15.....................68 A3
Paines Cl PIN HA5..........................41 J6
Paine's La PIN HA5.........................41 J5
Pain's Cl MTCM CR4....................179 G5
Painsthorpe Rd
    STNW/STAM N16......................68 A1
Painters Ms BERM/RHTH SE16....123 H4
Painters Rd GNTH/NBYPK IG2......55 K6
Paisley Rd CAR SM5....................194 C5
    WDGN N22 ....49 H5
Paisley Ter CAR SM5...................194 C5
Pakeman St HOLWY N7..................85 F1
Pakenham Cl BAL SW12 * 161 F3
Pakenham St FSBYW WC1X..........5 H5
Palace Av KENS W8 ....120 A2
Palace Ct BAY/PAD W2 ....100 E6
    KTN/HRWW/WS HA3 ....62 A3
Palace Court Gdns
    MUSWH N10 ....48 C6
Palace Garden Ms KENS W8........120 A1
Palace Gdns BAR EN5 * 20 E5
Palace Gardens Ter KENS W8.....119 K1
Palace Ga KENS W8 ....120 B2
Palace Gates Rd WDGN N22.........48 A4
Palace Gn CROY/NA CRO 213 H5
    KENS W8 ....120 A2
Palace Gv BMLY BR1 ....184 A4
    WALTH E17 ....51 J3
Palace Ms FUL/PGN SW6 * 139 J1
    WALTH E17 ....51 J3
Palace of Westminster *
    WHALL SW1A 17 F3
Palace Pde WALTH E17 * 51 J3
Palace Pl WESTW SW1E 16 A4
Palace Rd BMLY BR1...................184 A4
    BRXS/STRHM SW2 ....162 A3
    CEND/HSY/T N8 ....66 C3
    E/WMO/HCT KT8 ....173 J6
    FBAR/BDGN N11 ....48 E2
    KUT/HW KT1 ....190 E1
    NRWD SE19 ....181 G1
    RSLP HA4 ....77 J2
Palace Sq NRWD SE19 ....181 G3
Palace St WESTW SW1E 16 A4
Palace Vw BMLY BR1 ....184 A6
    CROY/NA CRO 213 H2
    LEE/GVPK SE12 ....165 K4
Palace View Rd CHING E4..............51 K1
Palamos Rd LEY E10......................69 J5
Palatine Av STNW/STAM N16........86 A2
Palatine Rd STNW/STAM N16........86 A2
Palemead Cl FUL/PGN SW6.........139 G2
Palermo Rd WLSDN NW10 ....99 J1
Palestine Gv WIM/MER SW19.....178 C3
Palewell Cl STMC/STPC BR5.......186 C5
Palewell Common Dr
    MORT/ESHN SW14..................138 A6
Palewell Pk MORT/ESHN SW14 ..138 A6
Palfrey Pl VX/NE SW8..................142 A1
Palgrave Av STHL UB1...................96 A6
Palgrave Gdns CAMTN NW1 ....2 D6
Palgrave Rd SHB W12 ....118 C3
Palissy St BETH E2 ....7 J4
Pallant Wy ORP BR6 ....216 A1
Pallet Wy WOOL/PLUM SE18 ......146 D2
Palliser Dr RAIN RM13.................111 J4
Palliser Rd WKENS W14 ....119 H5
Pall Ml STJS SW1Y 16 C1
Pall Ml East STJS SW1Y 10 C7
Pall Ml Pl STJS SW1Y * 16 B1
Palmar Crs BXLYHN DA7 ....149 H4
Palmar Rd BXLYHN DA7 ....149 H3
Palm Av SCUP DA14....................186 E3
Palm Cl LEY E10............................87 K3
Palmeira Rd BXLYHN DA7 ....148 E4
Palmer Av BUSH WD23................208 A1
    CHEAM SM3 ....208 A3
Palmer Cl HEST TW5 ....135 F1
    NTHLT UB5 ....77 J4
    WWKM BR4.............................199 G6
Palmer Crs KUT/HW KT1 ....175 F6
Palmer Gdns BAR EN5...................20 B6
Palmer Pl HOLWY N7.....................85 G3
Palmer Rd BCTR RM8 ....74 B5
    PLSTW E13 ....107 F3
Palmers Gv E/WMO/HCT KT8 .....188 E1
Palmers La PEND EN3...................24 E1
Palmers Rd BETH E2 ....105 F1
    FBAR/BDGN N11 ....48 C1
    MORT/ESHN SW14..................137 K4
    STRHM/NOR SW16..................180 A5
Palmerston Crs PLMGR N13..........49 H1
    WOOL/PLUM SE18 ....127 H6
Palmerston Gv
    WIM/MER SW19 ....177 K3
Palmerston Rd ACT W3 ....117 K3

BKHH IG9..................................39 G4
CAR SM5 ....209 K2
CROY/NA CRO 196 E2
FSTGT E7 ....89 F3
HSLW TW3 ....135 H2
KIL/WHAMP NW6 ....84 D4
KTN/HRWW/WS HA3 ....42 E6
MORT/ESHN SW14..................137 K5
ORP BR6 ....216 C2
SUT SM1 ....209 G3
WALTH E17 ....69 H1
WDGN N22 ....49 J4
WHTN TW2 ....155 K1
WIM/MER SW19 ....177 K3
Palmerston Wy VX/NE SW8 * 141 G1
Palmer St STJSPK SW1H 16 C3
Palmers Whf KUT/HW KT1 * 174 E5
Palm Gv EA W5 ....117 F3
Palm Rd ROMW/RG RM7 ....74 E2
Pamela Ct
    NFNCH/WDSPK N12 * 47 F2
Pamela Gdns PIN HA5...................59 F2
Pams Wy HOR/WEW KT19 ....207 F3
Pandian Wy KTTN NW5 * 84 D4
Pandora Rd KIL/WHAMP NW6 ......82 E4
Panfield Ms GNTH/NBYPK IG2......72 A3
Panfield Rd ABYW SE2.................128 B3
Pangbourne Av NKENS W10 * 100 A4
Pangbourne Dr STAN HA7 ....43 K1
Pank Av BAR EN5...........................21 H6
Pankhurst Av CAN/RD E16 ....126 A1
Pankhurst Cl ISLW TW7 ....136 A4
    NWCR SE14 ....144 A1
Pankhurst Rd WOT/HER KT12.....188 A4
Pankridge OXHEY WD19 * 27 H4
Panmuir Rd RYNPK SW20...........176 E4
Panmure Cl HBRY N5.....................85 H2
Panmure Rd SYD SE26................163 J5
Pansy Gdns SHB W12.....................99 J6
Panther Dr WLSDN NW10 ....81 F3
Pantiles Cl PLMGR N13..................49 H1
The Pantiles BMLY BR1 ....184 D6
    BUSH WD23 ....28 D3
    BXLYHN DA7 ....149 C1
Panton Cl CROY/NA CRO 196 C5
Panton St STJS SW1Y....................10 C6
Paper Buildings EMB EC4Y * 11 K5
Papermill Cl CAR SM5 ....210 A2
Papillons Wk BKHTH/KID SE3.....145 K3
Papworth Gdns HOLWY N7............85 F3
Papworth Wy
    BRXS/STRHM SW2..................162 B2
Parade Ter CDALE/KGS NW9 * 62 E3
The Parade BROCKY SE4 * 144 C3
    BTSEA SW11 * 140 C5
    CAR SM5 ....209 K3
    CROY/NA CRO * 195 G6
    DART DA1 * 150 C6
    EA W5 * 97 K5
    EDUL SE22 * 143 F4
    ESH/CLAY KT10 ....204 A4
    FSBYPK N4 * 67 F4
    GFD/PVL UB6 * 79 F6
    KUT/HW KT1 * 175 F5
    OXHEY WD19 ....27 J5
    PGE/AN SE20 * 181 K4
    RCH/KEW TW9 * 137 H4
    SYD SE26 * 163 J6
    WLGTN SM6 * 211 F3
Paradise Pas HOLWY N7...............85 G3
Paradise Rd CLAP SW4 ....141 K3
    RCH/RICH TW9 ....137 F6
Paradise Rw BETH E2 * 7 H2
Paradise St BERM/RHTH SE16 ...123 J2
Paradise Wk CHEL SW3 ....120 E6
Paragon Cl CAN/RD E16 ....106 E5
Paragon Gv BRYLDS KT5............191 G3
Paragon Ms STHWK SE1 ....19 F5
Paragon Pl BKHTH/KID SE3 ....145 J3
    BRYLDS KT5 * 191 G3
Paragon Rd HACK E9.....................86 D4
The Paragon BKHTH/KID SE3 .....145 K3
Parbury Ri CHSGTN KT9..............206 A4
Parbury Rd FSTH SE23 ....164 B1
Parchmore Rd THHTH CR7 ....180 C5
Parchmore Wy THHTH CR7.........180 C5
Pardoe Rd LEY E10 ....69 K4
Pardoner St STHWK SE1 ....19 F4
Pardon St FSBYE EC1V 6 B6
Parfett St WCHPL E1....................104 C4
Parfitt Cl HAMP NW3 ....65 G5
Parfrey St HMSMTH W6 ....119 F6
Parham Dr GNTH/NBYPK IG2........72 B3
Parham Wy MUSWH N10 * 12 A7
Parish Ct SURB KT6 ....190 E3
Parish Gate Dr BFN/LL DA15 ......167 K1
Parish La PGE/AN SE20...............182 A3
Parham Whf WOOL/PLUM SE18...126 E4
Park Av BARK IG11.........................90 C4
    BMLY BR1 ....183 K2
    CAR SM5 ....210 A4
    CRICK NW2 ....82 A5
    EHAM E6 ....89 K6
    EN EN1 ....24 A6
    FNCH N3 ....47 F5
    GLDGN NW11 ....65 F5
    HSLW TW3 ....155 C1
    IL IG1 ....90 A1
    MORT/ESHN SW14..................138 A5
    ORP BR6 ....217 C2
    PLMGR N13 ....35 G5
    SRTFD E15 ....88 C3
    STHL UB1 ....114 E1
    UED N18 ....36 C6
    WDGN N22 ....48 E6
    WLSDN NW10 ....98 B2
    WWKM BR4.............................199 F6
Park Av East EW KT17 ....207 J4

Park Avenue Ms *MTCM* CR4......179 G3
Park Av North *CEND/HSY/T* N8....66 D1
  WLSDN NW10 ....81 K3
Park Av South *CEND/HSY/T* N8...66 D1
Park Av West *EW* K17............207 J4
Park Bvd *GPK* RM2..................93 H7
Park Cha *WBLY* HA9.................80 B2
Park Cl *CAR* SM5.................209 K4
  CRICK NW2........................81 J1
  HOM E9............................87 G4
  HPTN TW12......................173 H4
  HSLW TW3........................135 H4
  KTN/HRWW/WS HA3.........42 E4
  KUTN/CMB KT2................175 H4
  NFNCH/WDSPK N12 *.........33 H6
  SKENS SW7 *.....................14 B4
  WKENS W14.....................119 J3
  WLSDN NW10......................98 B2
Park Cottages *FNCH* N3.............46 D5
Park Ct *DUL* SE21 *................162 E5
  NWMAL KT3......................192 A1
  SYD SE26 *......................181 J2
  WBLY HA9.........................80 A3
Park Crs *EMPK* RM11...............75 J4
  ENC/FH EN2.......................23 K5
  ERITH DA8......................129 K6
  FNCH N3............................47 F3
  KTN/HRWW/WS HA3.........42 E4
  REGST W1B.........................3 J7
  WHTN TW2......................155 J3
Park Crescent Ms East
  GTPST W1W........................3 K7
Park Crescent Ms West
  CAVSG/HST W1G...................3 J7
Parkcroft Rd *LEE/GVPK* SE12...165 J2
Parkdale Crs *WPK* KT4.............207 F1
Parkdale Rd
  WOOL/PLUM SE18............127 K5
Park Dr *ACT* W3...................117 H5
  CHARL SE7 *....................126 D6
  DAGE RM10........................92 E1
  GLDGN NW11......................65 F5
  KTN/HRWW/WS HA3.........42 D2
  MORT/ESHN SW14.............138 A6
  ROM RM1...........................75 F1
  RYLN/HDSTN HA2...............60 A4
  WCHMH N21........................35 J1
Park End *BMLY* BR1................183 J4
Park End Rd *ROM* RM1.............75 G1
Parker Cl *CAN/RD* E16.............126 D1
  CAR SM5.........................209 K4
Parker Ms *HOL/ALD* WC2B *......11 F3
Parker Rd *BARN* SW13 *.............(??)
Parker Rd *CROY/NA* CRO..........211 J2
Parker's Rw *STHWK* SE1.............19 K3
Parker St *CAR* SM5................126 D1
  HOL/ALD WC2B 11 F3
Parker Ter *FSTH* SE23.............164 C4
Parkes Rd *CHIG* IG7.................55 F1
  PIN HA5............................59 F2
Park Farm Cl *EFNCH* N2.............47 C6
  KUTN/CMB KT2.................175 F5
Parkfield Av *FELT* TW13..........153 K5
  MORT/ESHN SW14.............138 B5
  NTHLT UB5.........................95 H1
  RYLN/HDSTN HA2...............42 C5
Parkfield Cl *EDGW* HA8.............44 D2
  NTHLT UB5.........................95 J1
Parkfield Crs *FELT* TW13.........153 K5
  RSLP HA4............................59 J6
  RYLN/HDSTN HA2...............42 C5
Parkfield Dr *NTHLT* UB5............95 H1
Parkfield Gdns
  RYLN/HDSTN HA2...............42 B6
Parkfield Pde *FELT* TW13 *......153 K5
Parkfield Rd *FELT* TW13..........153 K5
  NTHLT UB5.........................95 J1
  NWCR SE14......................144 C2
  RYLN/HDSTN HA2...............78 C1
  WLSDN NW10......................81 J5
Parkfields *CROY/NA* CRO.........198 C5
  PUT/ROE SW15.................139 F5
Parkfields Av *CDALE/KGS* NW9...63 F5
  RYNPK SW20.....................176 E4
Parkfields Cl *CAR* SM5............210 A2
Parkfields Rd *KUTN/CMB* KT2...175 C1
Parkfield St *IS* N1....................5 K2
Park Gdns *CDALE/KGS* NW9........45 J4
  ERITH DA8.......................130 A4
  KUTN/CMB KT2................175 G1
Parkgate *BKHTH/KID* SE3.........145 J4
Park Ga *EA* W5.......................97 K4
  EFNCH N2..........................47 H5
  WCHMH N21........................35 F2
Parkgate Av *EBAR* EN4...............21 J2
Parkgate Cl *KUTN/CMB* KT2.....175 J2
Park Gate Ct *HPTN* TW12 *.......173 H1
Parkgate Crs *EBAR* EN4............21 G2
Parkgate Gdns
  MORT/ESHN SW14.............138 A6
Parkgate Ms *HGT* N6.................66 C4
Parkgate Rd *BTSEA* SW11........140 D1
  WLGTN SM6.....................210 B4
Park Gates *RYLN/HDSTN* HA2 *...78 A2
Park Gv *BMLY* BR1.................184 A4
  BXLYHN DA7......................149 K5
  EDGW HA8..........................44 B1
  FBAR/BDGN N11..................48 C1
  SRTFD E15.........................88 E6
Park Grove Rd *WAN* E11...........70 C6
Park Hall Rd *DUL* SE21...........162 E5
  EFNCH N2..........................65 J1
Parkham St *BTSEA* SW11.........140 D2
Park Hill *BMLY* BR1................200 D1
  CAR SM5.........................209 K4
  CLAP SW4........................141 J6
  EA W5................................97 K4
  FSTH SE23.......................163 K4
  RCHPK/HAM TW10.............157 G1
Park Hill Cl *CAR* SM5.............209 K4
Park Hill Ri *CROY/NA* CRO.......212 B1
Parkhill Rd *BFN/LL* DA15.........167 K5

BXLY DA5..............................169 G2
CHING E4.................................38 A2
Parkhill Rd *CROY/NA* CRO.........212 A2
Parkhill Rd *HAMP* NW3..............83 K4
Park Hill Rd *HAYES* BR2..........183 H5
Park Hill Wk *HAMP* NW3 *.........83 K3
Parkholme Rd *HACK* E8.............86 C4
Park House Gdns *TWK* TW1......136 D6
Parkhouse St *CMBW* SE5.........142 E1
Parkhurst Gdns *BXLY* DA5........169 H2
Parkhurst Rd *BXLY* DA5...........169 H2
  FBAR/BDGN N11..................34 A6
  HOLWY N7..........................84 E2
  MNPK E12...........................90 A2
  SUT SM1..........................209 H2
  TOTM N17..........................50 D6
  WALTH E17 *......................69 C1
  WDGN N22........................49 F3
STHRM/NOR SW16...............179 G1
Parklands Wy *WPK* KT4............192 B6
Park La *CAR* SM5..................210 A3
  CHDH RM6.........................73 K3
  CHEAM SM3.....................208 C4
  CROY/NA CRO...................211 J2
  EMPK RM11.......................75 J4
  HCH RM12..........................93 K4
  HEST TW5........................133 K1
  MYFR/PKLN W1K................9 G6
  RCH/KEW TW9...................136 E6
  RYLN/HDSTN HA2...............78 B1
  SRTFD E15 *.......................88 A6
  STAN HA7..........................29 G5
  TEDD TW11......................174 A2
  TOTM N17..........................50 D6
  UED N18............................36 B5
  WBLY HA9..........................80 B2
  YEAD UB4...........................94 C4
Park Lane Cl *TOTM* N17............50 C5
Parklea Cl *CDALE/KGS* NW9.......45 G4
Parkleigh Rd *WIM/MER* SW19...178 A5
Parkleys *RCHPK/HAM* TW10......156 E6
Parkleys Pde
  RCHPK/HAM TW10 *...........156 E6
Park Md *BFN/LL* DA15.............168 A6
Parkmead *PUT/ROE* SW15........158 E1
Park Md *RYLN/HDSTN* HA2..........78 B1
Parkmead Gdns *MLHL* NW7.........45 G2
Park Ms *GNWCH* SE10.............125 J5
  NKENS W10 *......................(??)
  RAIN RM13.........................93 J4
  STWL/WRAY TW19.............152 C2
Park Pde *ACT* W3...................117 H3
  HYS/HAR UB3 *....................94 C5
  WLSDN NW10 ....99 H1
Park Piazza *LEW* SE13.............165 G1
Park Pl *ACT* W3....................117 H4
  BMLY BR1 *......................184 A4
  EA W5..............................116 E1
  HPTN TW12 *....................173 H2
  IS N1.................................(??)
  POP/IOD E14....................124 D1
  WBLY HA9...........................80 B2
  WHALL SW1A......................16 A1
Park Place Vls *BAY/PAD* W2.....101 G4
Park Ridings *CEND/HSY/T* N8.....49 F6
Park Ri *KTN/HRWW/WS* HA3......42 E4
Park Rise Rd *FSTH* SE23..........164 B3
Park Rd *ALP/SUD* HA0...............80 A4
  BAR EN5............................20 D5
  BECK BR3...........................182 B3
  BMLY BR1........................184 A4
  BRYLDS KT5......................191 G5
  BUSH WD23 ....28 C1
  CAMTN NW1........................3 F7
  CDALE/KGS NW9.................63 F4
  CEND/HSY/T N8..................66 E5
  CEND/HSY/T N8..................67 H1
  CHEAM SM3.....................208 C4
  CHST BR7.........................185 G2
  CHSWK W4.......................118 A6
  DART DA1........................171 K2
  E/WMO/HCT KT8................189 H1
  EBAR EN4...........................21 H5
  EFNCH N2..........................47 H6
  ESH/CLAY KT10................204 B2
  FBAR/BDGN N11..................48 C1
  FELT TW13.......................154 C6
  HDN NW4...........................63 K3
  HNWL W7............................97 F6
  HPTN TW12......................155 H6
  HSLW TW3........................135 H6
  IL IG1................................90 D1
  ISLW TW7.........................136 C4
  KUT/HW KT1.....................174 D4
  KUTN/CMB KT2................175 F3
  LEY E10.............................69 J5
  MNPK E12..........................71 F6
  MNPK E12...........................89 K2
  NWMAL KT3......................192 A1
  RCHPK/HAM TW10.............137 G1
  SNWD SE25......................197 F1
  SRTFD E15 *.......................88 A6
  STHGT/OAK N14..................34 D2
  STMC/STPC BR5.................(??)
  SUN TW16.......................172 A3
  TEDD TW11......................174 A3
  TWK TW1.........................156 D1

UED N18...............................36 B6
WALTH E17..............................69 H2
WIM/MER SW19......................178 C2
WLGTN SM6..........................195 G6
WLGTN SM6..........................210 B3
WLWGN NW10........................81 G6
YEAD UB4...............................94 C4
Park Rd East *ACT* W3.............117 K2
Park Rd North *ACT* W3............117 J2
  CHSWK W4.......................118 A6
Park Rw *GNWCH* SE10............125 C6
Park Royal Rd *WLSDN* NW10......98 B4
Parkshot *RCH/KEW* TW9..........136 E5
Parkside *BECK* BR3 *...............182 E5
Park Side *BKHH* IG9.................39 F4
Parkside *BKHTH/KID* SE3 *.......145 J1
  CHEAM SM3.....................208 C4
Park Side *CRICK* NW2...............81 J1
Parkside *FNCH* N3....................47 F4
  HPTN TW12......................173 J1
  HYS/HAR UB3 *.................113 J2
Park Side *MLHL* NW7................45 J2
  OXHEY WD19 *....................27 G1
  SCUP DA14......................168 C4
  WIM/MER SW19.................177 G1
Parkside Av *BMLY* BR1............200 D1
  BXLYHN DA7......................150 A4
  ROM RM1...........................57 F5
  WIM/MER SW19.................177 F1
Parkside Cl *PGE/AN* SE20.........181 K3
Parkside Crs *BRYLDS* KT5........191 J3
  HOLWY N7.........................(??)
Parkside Cross *BXLYHN* DA7....150 B5
Parkside Dr *EDGW* HA8.............30 C5
Parkside Est *HOM* E9 *..............87 F6
Parkside Gdns *EBAR* EN4............33 K1
  WIM/MER SW19.................159 G6
Parkside Pde *DART* DA1 *.........150 C5
Parkside Rd *BELV* DA17...........129 K4
  HSLW TW3........................135 G6
  NTHWD HA6.......................(??)
Parkside St *BTSEA* SW11.........141 F2
Parkside Ter *ORP* BR6 *...........202 E5
  UED N18 *...........................35 K6
Park Sq East *CAMTN* NW1..........3 J6
Park Square Ms *CAMTN* NW1......3 J7
Park Sq West *CAMTN* NW1 *........3 J6
Parkstead Rd *PUT/ROE* SW15...138 D6
Park Steps *BAY/PAD* W2 *............8 D5
Parkstone Av *UED* N18...............50 B1
Parkstone Rd *PECK* SE15 *.......143 H3
  WALTH E17 *......................52 A6
Park St *CROY/NA* CRO.............196 D6
  HBRY N5 *..........................85 J2
  MYFR/PKLN W1K...............(??)
  STHWK SE1 *......................12 C7
  TEDD TW11.......................173 K2
Park Ter *CAR* SM5 *...............209 J1
  PEND EN3 *........................25 G1
  WPK KT4..........................192 D5
The Park *CAR* SM5................209 K3
  EA W5..............................116 E1
  GLDGN NW11......................65 F5
  HGT N6..............................66 A4
  SCUP DA14......................186 A1
Parkthorne Cl
  RYLN/HDSTN HA2...............60 B3
Parkthorne Dr
  RYLN/HDSTN HA2...............60 A3
Parkthorne Rd *BAL* SW12........161 J2
Park Vw *ACT* W3...................117 J5
  NWMAL KT3......................176 C6
  PIN HA5.............................41 K4
  WBLY HA9..........................80 D3
  WCHMH N21........................35 F2
Park View Cr
  FBAR/BDGN N11..................34 B6
Park View Dr *MTCM* CR4.........178 C5
Park View East *HBRY* N5 *.........85 J2
Parkview Gdns *CLAY* IG5............71 K1
Park View Gdns *HDN* NW4.........64 A2
Parkview Ms *RAIN* RM13..........111 K4
Park View Rd *CRICK* NW2...........81 H2
Park View Rd *CROY/NA* CRO.....197 H5
Park View Rd *EA* W5.................98 A2
  ELTH/MOT SE9..................167 G4
  FNCH N3............................47 F4
  PIN HA5.............................41 F4
  STHL UB1.........................115 F1
  TOTM N17..........................50 C5
  WELL DA16.......................148 D4
Park Village East *CAMTN* NW1.....3 K2
Park Village West *CAMTN* NW1....3 J2
Park Vis *TOOT* SW17...............178 D1
Parkville Rd *FUL/PGN* SW6......139 J1
Park Vis *GNWCH* SE10............125 C6
Park Vista Apartments
  CAN/RD E16......................106 D2
Park Wk *WBPTN* SW10.............120 B6
Park Wy *BXLY* DA5.................170 C5
Parkway *CROY/NA* CRO............214 A6
Park Wy *E/WMO/HCT* KT8.......173 H6
  EBED/NFELT TW14.............154 A2
  EDGW HA8..........................44 D4
  ERITH DA8.........................23 C3
Parkway *ERITH* DA18..............129 F3
  GDMY/SEVK IG3.................91 F1
Park Wy *GLDGN* NW11..............(??)
Parkway *GPK* RM2....................57 H5
  RAIN RM13......................111 J3
Park Wy *RSLP* HA4...................58 B5
Parkway *RYNPK* SW20.............193 G1
  STHGT/OAK N14.................34 A3
Park Wy *TRDG/WHET* N20.........33 K6
  WFD IG8.............................53 J3
The Parkway *HEST* TW5..........113 K6
  NTHLT UB5..........................95 H2
  NWDGN UB2.....................114 A3
Park West *BAY/PAD* W2 *..........8 D3
Park West Pl *BAY/PAD* W2 *.......8 D3
Parkwood *BECK* BR3...............182 D3
Parkwood Av *ESH/CLAY* KT10...189 H5
Parkwood Ms *HGT* N6...............66 B3
Parkwood Rd *BXLY* DA5...........169 G2

ISLW TW7.............................136 A2
WIM/MER SW19.....................177 J1
Parliament Ct *WCHPL* E1 *.........13 H2
Parliament Hl *HAMP* NW3..........83 J2
Parliament Hill Flds
  KTTN NW5 *.......................84 A1
Parliament Sq *WEST* SW1P.......16 E3
Parliament St *WHALL* SW1A......16 E2
Parma Crs *BTSEA* SW11..........140 E5
Parmiter St *BETH* E2..............104 D1
Parnell Cl *EDGW* HA8...............30 D6
  SHB W12.........................118 E3
Parnell Rd *BOW* E3..................87 H6
Parnham St *POP/IOD* E14 *.......105 G5
Parolles Rd *ARCH* N19..............66 C5
Paroma Rd *BELV* DA17............129 H3
Parr Av *EW* KT17...................207 K6
Parr Cl *ED* N9.........................36 D6
Parr Rd *EHAM* E6.....................89 J1
  STAN HA7..........................43 K4
Parrs Cl *SAND/SEL* CR2...........211 K6
Parr's Pl *HPTN* TW12...............173 F5
Parr St *IS* N1............................6 E2
Parry Av *EHAM* E6..................107 K5
Parry Cl *EW* KT17.................207 K5
Parry Pl *WOOL/PLUM* SE18......127 G4
Parry Rd *NKENS* W10..............100 C2
  SNWD SE25......................181 H6
Parry St *VX/NE* SW8...............121 K6
Parsifal Rd *KIL/WHAMP* NW6......82 E3
Parsloes Av *DAGW* RM9............92 A3
Parsonage Cl *HYS/HAR* UB3.......94 D5
Parsonage Gdns *ENC/FH* EN2.....23 J3
Parsonage La *ENC/FH* EN2.........23 K3
  SCUP DA14......................169 G6
Parsonage Manorway
  BELV DA17.......................129 H6
Parsonage St *POP/IOD* E14......125 F4
Parsons Crs *EDGW* HA8.............30 C5
Parsons Gn *FUL/PGN* SW6........139 K2
Parsons Green La
  FUL/PGN SW6..................139 K2
Parsons Gv *EDGW* HA8..............30 C5
Parsons La *RDART* DA2............170 E5
Parson's Md *CROY/NA* CRO......196 C5
Parsons Rd *PLSTW* E13.............107 G1
Parson St *HDN* NW4..................46 A6
Parthenia Rd *FUL/PGN* SW6......139 K2
Partingdale La *MLHL* NW7..........46 B1
Partington Cl *ARCH* N19.............66 D5
Partridge Cl *BAR* EN5................32 A1
  BUSH WD23 *.....................28 C1
  CAN/RD E16......................107 H4
  STAN HA7..........................30 A6
Partridge Dr *ORP* BR6.............216 C1
Partridge Gn *ELTH/MOT* SE9....185 F6
Partridge Rd *HPTN* TW12.........172 E2
  SCUP DA14......................167 K3
Partridge Sq *EHAM* E6............107 J4
Partridge Wy *WDGN* N22...........48 E4
Pasadena Cl *HYS/HAR* UB3......113 K2
Pascal St *VX/NE* SW8.............141 J1
Pascoe Rd *LEW* SE13..............145 G6
Pasley Cl *WALW* SE17.............122 D5
Pasquier Rd *WALTH* E17............51 G6
Passey Pl *ELTH/MOT* SE9........166 E1
Passfield Dr *POP/IOD* E14........105 K4
Passmore Gdns
  FBAR/BDGN N11..................48 D2
Passmore St *BGVA* SW1W.........15 C7
Pasteur Cl *CDALE/KGS* NW9......45 G2
Pasteur Gdns *UED* N18..............49 F1
Paston Cl *WLGTN* SM6............210 C1
Paston Crs *LEE/GVPK* SE12......166 A1
Pastor St *LBTH* SE11................18 B6
Pasture Cl *ALP/SUD* HA0...........61 H6
  BUSH WD23 *.....................28 D1
Pasture Rd *ALP/SUD* HA0..........61 H6
  CAT SE6..........................165 J3
  DAGW RM9........................92 A2
The Pastures *OXHEY* WD19........27 F2
  TRDG/WHET N20.................32 D3
Patcham Ter *VX/NE* SW8..........141 G2
Patching Wy *YEAD* UB4.............95 J5
Paternoster Rw *STP* EC4M........12 E4
Paternoster Sq *STP* EC4M.........12 B4
Pater St *W KENS* W8...............119 K3
Pates Manor Dr
  EBED/NFELT TW14.............153 C2
Pathfield Rd
  STRHM/NOR SW16............179 J2
The Path *WIM/MER* SW19........177 J3
The Pathway *OXHEY* WD19......27 H3
Patience Rd *BTSEA* SW11.........140 D3
Patio Cl *CLAP* SW4.................161 J1
Patmore St *VX/NE* SW8...........141 H1
Patmore Wy *CRW* RM5..............56 D2
Patmos Rd *BRXN/ST* SW9.......142 C1
Paton Cl *BOW* E3...................105 J2
Patricia Ct *WELL* DA16............148 C5
Patrick Rd *PLSTW* E13.............107 G2
Patriot Sq *BETH* E2................104 D1
Patshull Pl *KTTN* NW5..............84 C4
Patshull Rd *KTTN* NW5..............84 C4
Pattenden Rd *CAT* SE6............164 C3
Patten Rd *WAND/EARL* SW18...160 D2
Patterdale Cl *BMLY* BR1...........183 H2
Patterdale Rd *PECK* SE15.........143 K1
Patterson Rd *NRWD* SE19........181 G2
Pattina Ms *BERM/RHTH* SE16....124 E1
Pattison Rd *CRICK* NW2.............82 C1
Pattison Wk *CHARL* SE7...........126 B5
Paul Cl *SRTFD* E15...................88 C5
Paulet Rd *CMBW* SE5.............142 C3
Paulet Wy *WLSDN* NW10............81 G5
Paul Gdns *CROY/NA* CRO.........197 G6
Paulhan Rd
  KTN/HRWW/WS HA3...........61 K1
Paulin Dr *WCHMH* N21.............35 G2
Pauline Crs *WHTN* TW2............155 H3
Paulinus Cl *STMC/STPC* BR5....186 D5
Paul Julius Cl *POP/IOD* E14......106 B6
Paul Robeson Cl *EHAM* E6.........90 A1
Paul St *SDTCH* EC2A..................7 G7
  SRTFD E15.........................88 C1

Paultons Sq *CHEL* SW3...........120 C6
Paultons St *CHEL* SW3...........120 C6
Pauntley St *ARCH* N19...............66 C5
Paveley Dr *BTSEA* SW11.........140 D1
Paveley St *STJWD* NW8..............2 D5
Pavement Sq *CROY/NA* CRO.....197 H5
The Pavement *CLAP* SW4.........141 H5
  EA W5 *............................117 F5
  TEDD TW11 *......................70 A5
  WAN E11 *..........................70 A5
  WIM/MER SW19 *...............177 J2
  WNWD SE27 *...................162 D6
Pavet Cl *DAGE* RM10................92 D4
Pavilion Ldg
  RYLN/HDSTN HA2...............60 D5
Pavilion Ms *FNCH* N3................46 E6
Pavilion Pde *SHB* W12 *...........100 A5
Pavilion Rd *IL* IG1.....................71 K4
  KTBR SW1X........................15 F5
Pavilion Sq *KTBR* SW1X............15 F5
The Pavilion *KTBR* SW1X *.........15 F5
Pavilion Wy *EDGW* HA8.............44 E3
  RSLP HA4...........................59 G6
Pavillion Sq *CROY/NA* CRO.......160 D5
Pavillion Ter *SHB* W12 *...........100 A5
Pawleyne Cl *PGE/AN* SE20......181 K3
Pawsons Rd *THHTH* CR7..........196 C5
Paxford Rd *ALP/SUD* HA0..........61 H4
Paxton Cl *RCH/KEW* TW9........137 G3
  WOT/HER KT12.................188 B4
Paxton Pl *WNWD* SE27...........181 K5
Paxton Rd *BMLY* BR1...............183 K3
  CHSWK W4.......................118 B6
  FSTH SE23.......................164 B5
  TOTM N17 ....50 D3
Paxton Ter *PIM* SW1V.............121 G6
Payne Cl *BARK* IG11...................90 E5
Paynell Ct *BKHTH/KID* SE3......145 H4
Payne Rd *BOW* E3...................105 K1
Paynesfield Av
  MORT/ESHN SW14.............138 A4
Paynesfield Rd *BUSH* WD23......29 F2
Payne St *DEPT* SE8.................124 C6
Paynes Wk *HMSMTH* W6..........119 H6
Payzes Gdns *WFD* IG8...............52 D2
Peabody Av *PIM* SW1V *...........121 G6
Peabody Cl *CROY/NA* CRO.......197 K5
  GNWCH SE10...................144 D2
  PIM SW1V.......................121 G6
Peabody Cottages
  HNHL SE24 *....................162 D2
Peabody Est *BTSEA* SW11.......140 D5
  CHEL SW3.......................120 C6
  CLKNW EC1R *....................5 K7
  CMBW SE5 *....................142 E2
  FUL/PGN SW6...................119 K6
  HMSMTH W6....................119 F5
  HNHL SE24......................162 D2
  NKENS W10 *....................100 A4
  STHWK SE1 *......................11 J7
  STLK EC1Y.........................12 C1
  TOTM N17 *........................50 A4
Peabody Hl *DUL* SE21.............162 C3
Peabody Sq *IS* N1 *..................85 J6
Peabody Ter *CLKNW* EC1R *.......5 K7
Peace Cl *CFD/PVL* UB6.............78 D6
  SNWD SE25......................197 J2
  STHGT/OAK N14..................22 B6
Peace Gv *WBLY* HA9.................80 D1
Peace St *WOOL/PLUM* SE18.....127 F6
Peaches Cl *BELMT* SM2...........208 C5
Peach Gv *WAN* E11...................88 B1
Peach Rd *FELT* TW13..............153 K3
  NKENS W10........................100 C2
Peachum Rd
  EBED/NFELT TW14.............153 G3
Peacock Av
  EBED/NFELT TW14.............153 G3
Peacock Cl *CHING* E4.................51 H3
Peacock St *WALW* SE17.............18 B7
Peacock Yd *WALW* SE17 *..........18 B7
Peak Hl *SYD* SE26..................163 K6
Peak Hill Av *SYD* SE26............163 K6
Peak Hill Gdns *SYD* SE26........163 K6
The Peak *SYD* SE26................163 K5
Peaketon Av *REDBR* IG4............71 H2
Peak Hl *SYD* SE26..................163 K6
Peal Gdns *WEA* W13.................97 G2
Peall Rd *CROY/NA* CRO............196 A3
Pearce Cl *MTCM* CR4..............179 F5
Pearcefield Av *FSTH* SE23........163 K3
Pear Cl *CDALE/KGS* NW9..........63 F1
  NWCR SE14......................144 B1
Pearcroft Rd *WAN* E11..............70 C6
Pearfield Rd *FSTH* SE23...........164 B5
Pearl Cl *CRICK* NW2..................64 B4
  EHAM E6...........................107 K5
Pearl St *WAP* E1W..................123 J1
Pearman St *STHWK* SE1............17 K4
Pear Pl *STHWK* SE1 *................17 J2
Pear Rd *WAN* E11......................88 B1
Pearscroft Ct *FUL/PGN* SW6....140 A2
Pearscroft Rd *FUL/PGN* SW6....140 A2
Pearse St *PECK* SE15................21 F6
Pearson Cl *BAR* EN5...................21 F4
Pearson's Av *NWCR* SE14 *......144 D2
Pearson St *BETH* E2....................7 J2
Pearson Wy *DART* DA1.............171 J4
  MTCM CR4.......................179 F4
Pears Rd *HSLW* TW3...............135 J4
Pear Tree Cl *CHING* E4..............(??)
Pear Tree Cl *CHSGTN* KT9.......206 C3
  ERITH DA8.......................150 A2
Peartree Cl *HAYES* BR2............200 A2
Pear Tree Cl *MTCM* CR4...........178 D6
Peartree Gdns *BCTR* RM8..........91 H3
  ROMW/RG RM7..................56 D5
Peartree La *WAP* E1W.............104 E6
Pear Tree Rd *EN* EN1................24 A4
Peartree St *FSBYE* EC1V.............6 B6
Peartree Wy *GNWCH* SE10.......125 K4

Pearwood Cottages
STAN HA7 *..........................29 J4
Peary Pl BETH E2...................104 E2
Pease Cl HCH RM17.................93 K5
Peasmead Ter CHING E4 *........38 A6
Peatfield Cl BFN/LL DA15.......167 K5
Pebworth Rd HRW HA1.............61 J6
Peckarmans Wd SYD SE26......163 H5
Peckett Sq HBRY N5 *.............85 J2
Peckford Pl BRXN/ST SW9......142 B4
Peckham Gv PECK SE15..........143 F1
Peckham High St PECK SE15...143 H1
Peckham Hill St PECK SE15.....143 H1
Peckham Park Rd PECK SE15...143 H1
Peckham Rd CMBW SE5...........143 F2
Peckham Rye EDUL SE22.........143 H5
Pecks Yd WCHPL E1 *..............13 J1
Peckwater St KTTN NW5..........84 C3
Pedlars Wk HOLWY N7 *...........84 E5
Pedley Rd BCTR RM8................73 J5
Pedley St WCHPL E1..................7 K7
Pedro St CLPT E5....................87 F1
Peek Crs WIM/MER SW19........177 G1
Peel Cl CHING E4......................38 A3
Peel Dr CDALE/KGS NW9..........50 H6
       CLAY IG5...........................53 J6
Peel Gv BETH E2....................104 E1
Peel Pas KENS W8...................119 K1
Peel Pl CLAY IG5......................53 J5
Peel Prec KIL/WHAMP NW6......100 D1
Peel Rd ALP/SUD HA0................79 J1
       KIL/WHAMP NW6...............100 E2
       KTN/HRWW/WS HA3...........42 E6
       ORP BR6...........................216 C2
       SWFD E18..........................52 D4
Peel St KENS W8.....................119 K1
Peerglow Est PEND EN3 *..........24 E6
Peerless St FSBYE EC1V *...........6 E5
Pegamoid Rd UED N18..............36 E5
Pegasus Cl STNW/STAM N16 *...85 K2
Pegasus Ct BTFD TW8..............117 C5
Pegasus Pl FUL/PGN SW6 *.....139 K2
       LBTH SE11 *.....................122 B6
Pegasus Rd CROY/NA CRO.......211 G4
Pegasus Wy FBAR/BDGN N11....48 B2
Pegg Rd HEST TW5..................134 C1
Pegley Gdns LEE/GVPK SE12...165 K4
Pegwell St WOOL/PLUM SE18...147 K1
Pekin St POP/IOD E14..............105 J5
Peldon Wk IS N1 *.....................85 H6
Pelham Av BARK IG11................91 F6
Pelham Cl CMBW SE5...............143 F4
Pelham Cottages BXLY DA5 *...169 J3
Pelham Crs SKENS SW7.............14 C6
Pelham Pl SKENS SW7...............14 C6
Pelham Rd BXLYHN DA7...........149 H4
       IL IG1.................................72 D6
       PGE/AN SE20......................181 K5
       SEVS/STOTM N15................68 B1
       SWFD E18............................53 F6
       WDGN N22...........................49 G5
       WIM/MER SW19...................177 K3
Pelhams Cl ESH/CLAY KT10.....204 A3
Pelham St SKENS SW7...............14 B6
Pelhams Wk ESH/CLAY KT10....204 A1
Pelier St WALTH E17................122 D6
Pelinore Rd CAT SE6...............165 H4
Pellant Rd FUL/PGN SW6.........139 H1
Pellatt Gv WDGN N22................49 G4
Pellatt Rd EDUL SE22..............143 G6
       WBLY HA9............................62 A6
Pellerin Rd STNW/STAM N16....86 A3
Pellings Cl HAYES BR2.............199 J6
Pelling St POP/IOD E14............105 H5
Pellipar Cl PLMGR N13..............35 G5
Pellipar Rd WOOL/PLUM SE18...126 E5
Pelly Rd PLSTW E13.................106 E1
       SRTFD E15...........................88 E6
Pelter St BETH E2......................7 J4
Pelton Rd GNWCH SE10...........125 H5
Pembar Av WALTH E17...............51 G1
Pemberley Cha
       HOR/WEW KT19..................206 D3
Pemberley Cl HOR/WEW KT19...206 D3
Pember Rd WLSDN NW10.........100 D2
Pemberton Av GPK RM2.............57 K6
Pemberton Gdns ARCH N19.......84 C1
       CHDH RM6...........................74 A2
       HACK E8..............................86 D5
Pemberton Rd
       E/WMO/HCT KT8.................189 H1
       FSBYPK N4..........................67 H2
Pemberton Rw
       FLST/FETLN EC4A................11 K3
Pemberton Ter ARCH N19..........84 C1
Pembridge Av WHTN TW2.........154 E3
Pembridge Crs NTGHL W11......100 D6
Pembridge Gdns
       BAY/PAD W2......................100 E6
Pembridge Ms NTGHL W11.......100 E6
Pembridge Pl BAY/PAD W2......100 E6
Pembridge Rd NTGHL W11 *.....119 K1
Pembridge Sq BAY/PAD W2.....100 E6
Pembridge Vls BAY/PAD W2.....100 E6
Pembroke Av BRYLDS KT5.......191 J2
       EN EN1................................24 D2
       IS N1..................................85 F6
       KTN/HRWW/WS HA3............43 H6
       PIN HA5..............................59 H3
Pembroke Cl ERITH DA8..........129 K4
       KTBR SW1X..........................15 H5
Pembroke Gdns DAGE RM10......92 D1
       KENS W8............................119 J3
Pembroke Ldg STAN HA7 *........43 J2
       KENS W8............................119 J4
       MUSWH N10.........................48 A4
Pembroke Pde ERITH DA8 *.....129 K5
Pembroke Pl EDGW HA8............44 C3
       ISLW TW7...........................135 K3
       KENS W8............................119 K3
Pembroke Rd BMLY BR1..........184 D5
       CEND/HSY/T N8....................66 E3
       EHAM E6.............................107 K4
       ERITH DA8..........................129 K5
       GDMY/SEVK IG3....................73 F5

GFD/PVL UB6........................96 B3
KENS W8.............................119 K4
MTCM CR4...........................179 F5
MUSWH N10..........................48 A4
NTHWD HA6..........................26 A5
PLMGR N13...........................35 J5
RSLP HA4..............................58 C5
SEVS/STOTM N15...................68 B2
SNWD SE25.........................197 F1
WALTH E17............................51 J4
WBLY HA9.............................79 K1
Pembroke Sq KENS W8............84 E6
Pembroke St IS N1..................84 E6
Pembroke Ter STJWD NW8 *......2 A1
Pembroke Vls KENS W8...........119 K4
Pembroke Wk KENS W8...........119 K4
Pembrook Ms BTSEA SW11 *...140 C5
       HAYES BR2........................199 J4
Pembury Cl CLPT E5 *...............86 D5
Pembury Ct HYS/HAR UB3.......113 G6
Pembury Crs SCUP DA14.........169 F4
Pembury Rd BXLYHN DA7.........149 F1
       CLPT E5...............................86 D5
       SNWD SE25........................197 H1
       TOTM N17............................50 B3
Pemdevon Rd CROY/NA CRO...196 B4
Pemell Cl WCHPL E1 *.............104 E3
Pemerich Cl HYS/HAR UB3 *...113 J5
Pempath Pl WBLY HA9...............61 K6
Penally Pl IS N1.......................85 K6
Penang St WAP E1W................123 J1
Penard Rd NWDGN UB2...........115 F3
Penarth St PECK SE15.............123 K6
Penates ESH/CLAY KT10..........204 D2
Penberth Rd CAT SE6..............165 F4
Penbury Rd NWDGN UB2.........114 E5
Pencraig Wy PECK SE15...........123 J6
Pencroft Dr DART DA1..............171 F2
Pendall Cl EBAR EN4.................21 J5
Penda Rd ERITH DA8...............149 J1
Pendarves Rd RYNPK SW20....177 F4
Penda's Md HOM E9...................87 G2
Pendell Av HYS/HAR UB3.........133 J1
Pendennis Rd ORP BR6...........202 D6
       STRHM/NOR SW16..............161 K6
       TOTM N17............................49 K6
Penderel Rd HSLW TW3...........135 F6
Penderry Ri CAT SE6...............165 G4
Penderyn Wy HOLWY N7............84 D3
Pendlebury House
       CHARL SE7 *......................146 D1
Pendle Rd STRHM/NOR SW16...179 G3
Pendlestone Rd WALTH E17......69 K3
Pendragon Rd BMLY BR1.........165 K5
Pendrell Rd NWCR SE14...........144 B4
Pendrell St WOOL/PLUM SE18...127 J6
Pendula Dr YEAD UB4................95 H4
Pendulum Ms HACK E8 *............86 B3
Penerley Rd CAT SE6..............164 E1
       RAIN RM13..........................111 K4
Penfold Cl CROY/NA CRO.........211 G1
Penfold La BXLY DA5...............168 E3
Penfold Pl BAY/PAD W2..............8 C1
Penfold Rd ED N9......................37 F3
Penfold St STJWD NW8...............2 B7
Penford Gdns ELTH/MOT SE9...146 C5
Penford St CMBW SE5.............142 C3
Pengarth Rd BXLY DA5............168 E1
Penge La PGE/AN SE20............181 K4
       SNWD SE25........................181 H6
Penhale Cl ORP BR6...............217 G2
Penhall Rd CHARL SE7.............126 C4
Penhill Rd BXLY DA5...............168 D2
Penhurst Rd BARK/HLT IG6......54 B3
Penifather La GFD/PVL UB6......96 D2

WALTH E17............................51 J4
Penrhyn Gdns KUT/HW KT1.....190 E1
Penrhyn Gv WALTH E17............51 J4
Penrhyn Rd KUT/HW KT1.........191 F1
Penrith Cl BECK BR3...............182 E4
       PUT/ROE SW15...................139 H6
Penrith Crs HCH RM12..............93 J5
Penrith Pl WNWD SE27...........162 C4
Penrith Rd BARK/HLT IG6..........55 F2
       NWMAL KT3........................192 A1
       SEVS/STOTM N15.................67 K2
       THHTH CR7.........................180 D5
Penrith St STRHM/NOR SW16...179 H2
Penrose Av OXHEY WD19..........27 J4
Penrose Gv WALW SE17...........122 D5
Penrose Rd ALP/SUD HA0..........79 J3
Penrose St WALW SE17...........122 D5
Penryn St CAMTN NW1...............5 J3
Penry St STHWK SE1.................19 H7
Pensbury Pl VX/NE SW8...........141 H3
Pensbury St VX/NE SW8...........141 H3
Pensford Av RCH/KEW TW9.....137 H3
Penshurst Av BFN/LL DA15......168 B1
Penshurst Gdns EDGW HA8......44 D1
Penshurst Gn HAYES BR2........199 J2
Penshurst Rd BXLYHN DA7......149 G2
       HOM E9................................87 F5
       THHTH CR7.........................196 C2
       TOTM N17............................50 B3
Pensilver Cl EBAR EN4..............21 J5
Penstemon Cl FNCH N3.............46 E2
Pentelow Gdns
       EBED/NFELT TW14..............153 K1
Pentire Rd WALTH E17...............52 B4
Pentland Av EDGW HA8.............30 D4
Pentland Cl ED N9......................36 E4
       GLDGN NW11........................64 C6
Pentland Pl NTHLT UB5..............77 J6
Pentland Rd BUSH WD23...........28 D1
       KIL/WHAMP NW6.................100 D2
Pentlands Cl MTCM CR4............179 G6
Pentlands Dr WAND/EARL SW18...160 B1
Pentlow St PUT/ROE SW15........139 F4
Pentlow Wy BKHH IG9...............39 J2
Pentney Rd BAL SW12..............161 H3
       CHING E4.............................38 B3
       RYNPK SW20........................177 H4
Penton Gv IS N1.........................5 J2
Penton Pl WALW SE17................18 B7
Penton Ri FSBYW WC1X..............5 J4
Penton St IS N1...........................5 J2
Pentonville Rd IS N1...................5 H3
Pentrich Av EN EN1....................24 C1
Pentridge St PECK SE15...........143 G1
Pentyre Av UED N18....................49 K1
Penwerris Av ISLW TW7...........135 H1
Penwith Rd WAND/EARL SW18...160 A4
Penwortham Rd
       STRHM/NOR SW16..............179 G2
Penylan Pl EDGW HA8................44 C3
Penywern Rd ECT SW5.............119 K5
Penzance Pl NTGHL W11..........119 H1
Penzance St NTGHL W11..........119 H1
Peony Gdns SHB W12................118 D1
Peony Pl IS N1.........................198 C5
Peploe Rd KIL/WHAMP NW6....100 A1
Peplow Cl WDR/YW UB7...........112 A1
Pepper Cl EHAM E6..................107 K4
Peppercorn Cl THHTH CR7.......180 E5
Peppermead Sq LEW SE13.......144 D6
Peppermint Cl CROY/NA CRO...195 K4
Peppermint Pl WAN E11.............88 C1
Pepper St POP/IOD E14............124 E3
       STHWK SE1..........................18 C2
Pepys Crs BAR EN5...................20 A6
       CAN/RD E16.........................125 K1
Pepys Est DEPT SE8.................124 B4
Pepys Park Est DEPT SE8........124 C4
Pepys Ri ORP BR6....................202 A4
Pepys Rd NWCR SE14..............144 A3
       RYNPK SW20.......................177 F5
Pepys St TWRH EC3N................13 J5
Perceval Av HAMP NW3.............83 J3
Perch St HACK E8......................86 B2
Percival Ct TOTM N17................50 B3
Percival Gdns CHDH RM6..........73 J3
Percival Rd EN EN1....................24 B5
       FELT TW13..........................153 J4
       MORT/ESHN SW14..............137 K6
       ORP BR6.............................201 G6
Percival St FSBYE EC1V..............6 A6
Percy Av ASHF TW15................152 D6
Percy Bush Rd WDR/YW UB7...112 C3
Percy Gdns PEND EN3...............25 F6
       WPK KT4............................192 A5
       YEAD UB4............................94 C2
Percy Ms FITZ W1T....................10 C2
Percy Rd BXLYHN DA7.............149 F4
       CAN/RD E16.........................106 C4
       GDMY/SEVK IG3....................72 E2
       HPTN TW12.........................173 F3
       ISLW TW7............................136 B5
       MTCM CR4...........................195 F3
       NFNCH/WDSPK N12...............47 G1
       PGE/AN SE20.......................182 A4
       ROMW/RG RM7......................56 D6
       SHB W12.............................118 D2
       SNWD SE25.........................197 G2
       WAN E11...............................88 C2
       WCHMN N21..........................35 G3
       WHTN TW2...........................155 G3
Percy St FITZ W1T....................10 C2
Percy Wy WHTN TW2................155 G3
Peregrine Cl WLSDN NW10........81 F3
Peregrine Ct WELL DA16 *........148 A2
Peregrine Gdns CROY/NA CRO...198 B6
Peregrine Rd BARK/HLT IG6......55 F1
Peregrine Wy WIM/MER SW19...177 F3
Perham Rd WKENS W14............119 H5
Peridot St EHAM E6..................107 J1
Perifield DUL SE21...................162 C3
Perimeade Rd ALP/SUD HA0......97 J1

Periton Rd ELTH/MOT SE9.......146 C5
Perivale Gdns WEA W13............97 H3
Perivale La GFD/PVL UB6..........97 G2
Perivale Village GFD/PVL UB6 *...97 G2
Perkin Cl ALP/SUD HA0..............79 H5
       HSLW TW3..........................135 G5
Perkin's Rents WEST SW1P........16 C4
Perkins Rd BARK/HLT IG6..........72 D2
Perks Cl STHWK SE1..................12 D7
Perks Cl BKHTH/KID SE3..........145 H5
Perpins Rd ELTH/MOT SE9.......167 K1
Perran Rd BRXS/STRHM SW2...162 C4
Perrers Rd HMSMTH W6...........118 E3
Perrin Rd ALP/SUD HA0.............79 H3
Perrins Ct HAMP NW3 *.............83 G2
Perrin's La HAMP NW3...............83 G2
Perrin's Wk HAMP NW3..............83 G2
Perry Av ACT W3........................99 F5
Perry Cl RAIN RM13.................111 F1
Perry Ct SEVS/STOTM N15 *......68 A3
Perryfield Wy CDALE/KGS NW9...63 H4
       RCHPK/HAM TW10...............156 C5
Perry Gdns ED N9......................36 A5
Perry Garth NTHLT UB5..............77 G6
Perry Gv DART DA1...................151 K5
Perry Hall Cl ORP BR6.............202 B4
Perry Hall Rd ORP BR6............202 A4
Perry Hl CAT SE6.....................164 C4
Perry How WPK KT4.................192 C5
Perry Md BUSH WD23................28 C2
       ENC/FH EN2..........................23 H5
Perrymead St FUL/PGN SW6.....139 K2
Perryn Rd ACT W3.....................99 F6
       BERM/RHTH SE16...............123 K3
Perry Ri FSTH SE23..................164 B5
Perry Rd DAGW RM9................110 C4
Perry St CHST BR7...................185 K2
       DART DA1...........................150 B4
Perry V FSTH SE23...................163 K4
Persant Rd CAT SE6.................165 H4
Perseverance Pl BRXN/ST SW9...142 B1
Pershore Cl GNTH/NBYPK IG2...72 C2
Pershore Gv CAR SM5..............194 C3
Pert Cl MUSWH N10...................48 B3
       YEAD UB4.............................95 G3
Perth Av CDALE/KGS NW9.........63 F4
       YEAD UB4.............................95 G3
Perth Cl RYNPK SW20..............177 H4
Perth Rd BARK IG11.................108 D1
       BECK BR3............................183 F5
       FSBYPK N4...........................67 G5
       GNTH/NBYPK IG2..................72 C3
       LEY E10................................69 G5
       PLSTW E13..........................107 F1
       WDGN N22............................49 H4
Perth Ter GNTH/NBYPK IG2.......72 C4
Perwell Av RYLN/HDSTN HA2....59 K5
Petauel Rd TEDD TW11............173 K1
Petavel Rd TEDD TW11............173 K2
Peter Av WLSDN NW10...............81 K5
Peterboat Cl GNWCH SE10.......125 H4
Peterborough Ms
       FUL/PGN SW6....................139 K3
Peterborough Rd CAR SM5.......194 D3
       FUL/PGN SW6....................139 K3
       HRW HA1.............................60 E5
       LEY E10................................70 A2
Peterborough Vls
       FUL/PGN SW6....................140 A2
Petergate BTSEA SW11............140 B5
Peters Cl BCTR RM8..................73 K5
       STAN HA7............................44 A3
       WELL DA16.........................147 K3
Petersfield Cl UED N18...............49 J1
Petersfield Ri PUT/ROE SW15...158 D4
Petersfield Rd ACT W3.............117 K2
Petersham Cl
       RCHPK/HAM TW10...............156 C5
       SUT SM1.............................208 E3
Petersham Dr
       STMC/STPC BR5..................186 A5
Petersham Ms SKENS SW7 *......14 C6
Petersham Pl SKENS SW7..........14 C5
Petersham Rd
       RCHPK/HAM TW10...............156 C5
Peter's HI BLKFR EC4V................12 C5
Peter's La FARR EC1M................12 B1
Peterstone Rd ABYW SE2.........128 C3
Peterstow Cl WIM/MER SW19...159 H4
Peter St SOHO/CST W1F.............10 C5
Peterwood Wy CROY/NA CRO...196 A6
Petherton Rd HBRY N5...............85 J4
Peto Pl CAMTN NW1....................3 K6
Peto St North CAN/RD E16.......106 D6
Petrie Cl CRICK NW2...................82 C4
Petros Gdns KIL/WHAMP NW6 *...83 F3
Petten Cl STMC/STPC BR5.......202 E5
Petten Gv STMC/STPC BR5......202 D5
Pett Cl EMPK RM11....................75 J3
Petticoat La WCHPL E1..............13 H2
Petticoat Sq WCHPL E1..............13 H3
Pettits Bvd ROM RM1.................57 G5
Pettits Cl ROM RM1....................57 G5
Pettits La ROM RM1....................57 G4
Pettits La North ROM RM1.........57 G3
Pettit's Pl DAGE RM10...............92 C3
Pettit's Rd DAGE RM10..............92 C3
Pettiward Cl PUT/ROE SW15....139 F5
Pettley Gdns ROMW/RG RM7......75 F2
Pettman Crs THMD SE28..........127 J3
Pettsgrove Av ALP/SUD HA0......79 J3
Petts HI NTHLT UB5....................78 B3
Petts Wood Rd
       STMC/STPC BR5..................201 K2
Petty France WESTW SW1E........16 B4
Petty Wales MON EC3R..............13 H5
Petworth Cl NTHLT UB5..............77 K5
Petworth Gdns HGDN/ICK UB10...76 A3

RYNPK SW20........................176 E6
Petworth Rd BXLYHS DA6.......149 H6
       NFNCH/WDSPK N12..............47 J1
Petworth St BTSEA SW11.........140 D2
Petworth Wy HCH RM12............93 H2
Petyt Pl CHEL SW5 *..................14 D7
Petyward CHEL SW3..................14 D7
Pevensey Av EN EN1..................24 A3
       FBAR/BDGN N11...................48 D1
Pevensey Cl ISLW TW7.............135 H1
Pevensey Rd FELT TW13...........154 D3
       FSTGT E7.............................88 E2
       TOOT SW17.........................160 C6
Peverel EHAM E6......................108 A5
Peveret Cl FBAR/BDGN N11 *.....48 B2
Peverill Dr TEDD TW11.............173 J1
Pewsey Cl CHING E4...................51 J1
Peyton Pl GNWCH SE10............145 F1
Pharaoh Cl MTCM CR4..............194 E4
Pheasant Cl CAN/RD E16...........107 F5
Phelp St WALW SE17................122 E6
Phelps Wy HYS/HAR UB3.........113 J4
Phene St CHEL SW3..................120 D6
Phil An Wy CRW RM5.................57 F2
Philbeach Gdns ECT SW5.........119 K5
Philchurch Pl WCHPL E1...........104 C5
Philimore
       WOOL/PLUM SE18...............127 K5
Phillip Av BXLY DA5..................169 J4
Philip Gdns CROY/NA CRO.......198 C6
Philip La SEVS/STOTM N15........67 K1
Philippa Gdns ELTH/MOT SE9...146 C6
Philip Rd RAIN RM13.................111 G2
Philip St PLSTW E13.................106 E3
Philip Wk PECK SE15................143 H4
Phillimore Gdns KENS W8.........119 K2
       WLSDN NW10........................82 A6
Phillimore Gardens Cl
       KENS W8.............................119 K3
Phillimore Pl KENS W8..............119 K3
Phillimore Ter KENS W8 *..........119 K3
Phillimore Wk KENS W8.............119 K3
Phillipp St IS N1..........................7 H1
Phillips Cl DART DA1.................170 E1
Philpot La FENCHST EC3M.........13 G5
Philpot St WCHPL E1 *..............104 D5
Phineas Pett Rd
       ELTH/MOT SE9....................146 D4
Phipp's Bridge Rd MTCM CR4...178 C6
Phipps Hatch La ENC/FH EN2.....23 J1
Phipp's Ms BGVA SW1W.............15 K5
Phipp St SDTCH EC2A..................7 G6
Phoebeth Rd LEW SE13............164 D6
Phoenix Cl HACK E8 *..................86 A6
       NTHWD HA6..........................26 D6
       WALTH E17...........................51 H5
       WWKM BR4.........................199 H6
Phoenix Ct BTFD TW8 *............136 D1
       POP/IOD E14.......................124 D4
Phoenix Dr HAYES BR2............215 H2
Phoenix Pk BTFD TW8 *...........116 E5
Phoenix Pl DART DA1...............171 G2
       FSBYW WC1X.........................5 J5
Phoenix Rd CAMTN NW1.............4 C5
       PGE/AN SE20.......................181 K2
Phoenix St LSQ/SEVD WC2H......10 D4
Phoenix Wy HEST TW5.............114 C6
Phoenix Wharf Rd STHWK SE1...19 K3
Physic Pl CHEL SW3..................120 E6
Picardy Manorway BELV DA17...129 J3
Picardy Rd BELV DA17..............129 H5
Picardy St BELV DA17...............129 H3
Piccadilly MYFR/PICC W1J........10 A7
Piccadilly Ar MYFR/PICC W1J......10 A7
Piccadilly Circ REGST W1B........10 C6
Pickard Cl STHGT/OAK N14........34 D3
Pickard St FSBYE EC1V................6 B4
Pickering Av EHAM E6...............108 A2
Pickering Gdns CROY/NA CRO...197 G3
       FBAR/BDGN N11...................48 A2
Pickering Ms BAY/PAD W2........101 F5
Pickering Pl WHALL SW1A *........16 B1
Pickering St IS N1........................85 H6
Pickets Cl BUSH WD23................28 D3
Pickets St BAL SW12.................161 G2
Pickett Cft STAN HA7..................43 K4
Pickett's Lock La ED N9...............36 E4
Pickford Cl BXLYHN DA7...........149 F3
Pickford La BXLYHN DA7...........149 F3
Pickford Rd BXLYHN DA7..........149 F4
Pickfords Whf IS N1 *...................6 C3
Pickhurst Gn HAYES BR2..........199 J4
Pickhurst La WWKM BR4..........199 J4
Pickhurst Md HAYES BR2..........199 J4
Pickhurst Pk HAYES BR2...........199 H3
Pickhurst Ri WWKM BR4...........199 J3
Pickwick Cl HSLWW TW4..........134 D6
Pickwick Ms UED N18..................50 A1
Pickwick Rd DUL SE21...............162 E2
Pickwick St STHWK SE1..............18 C3
Pickwick Wy CHST BR7.............185 H2
Pickworth Cl VX/NE SW8 *.........141 K1
Picton Pl MHST W1U....................9 H4
Picton St CMBW SE5.................142 E1
Pied Bull Yd IS N1 *......................5 K1
Piedmont Rd
       WOOL/PLUM SE18...............127 J5
Pier Head WAP E1W *................123 J1
Piermont Pl BMLY BR1..............184 C5
Piermont Rd EDUL SE22...........143 J4
Pierrepoint Ar IS N1 *...................6 A2
Pierrepoint Rw IS N1 *.................6 A2
Pier Rd CAN/RD E16.................126 D1
       EBED/NFELT TW14..............134 A6
       ERITH DA8..........................130 B6
Pier St POP/IOD E14.................125 F4
Pier Ter WAND/EARL SW18......140 A5
Pigeon La HPTN TW12...............155 F6
Pigott St POP/IOD E14..............105 J5
Pike Cl BMLY BR1.....................184 A1
Pike Rd MLHL NW7.....................31 F6
Pike's End PIN HA5.....................59 F1

Pikestone CI *YEAD* UB4 * 95 J3
Pilgrimage St *STHWK* SE1 .....18 E3
Pilgrim HI *WNWD* SE27 .....162 D6
Pilgrims CI *NTHLT* UB5 .....78 C3
  PLMGR N13 .....35 F6
Pilgrims Ct *DART* DA1 .....151 K6
Pilgrim's La *HAMP* NW3 .....83 H2
Pilgrims Ms *POP/IOD* E14 .....106 E6
Pilgrims PI *ASHF* TW15 * 152 C6
Pilgrim's Ri *EBAR* EN4 .....21 J6
Pilgrim St *BLKFR* EC4V * 12 A4
Pilgrims Wy *ARCH* N19 .....66 D5
  SAND/SEL CR2 .....212 B4
  WBLY HA9 .....80 A1
Pilkington Rd *ORP* BR6 .....216 C1
  PECK SE15 .....143 J3
Pilot CI *DEPT* 124 C6
Pilsden CI *WIM/MER* SW19 * 159 G3
Piltdown Rd *OXHEY* WD19 .....27 H1
Pilton PI *WALW* SE17 .....122 D5
Pimlico Rd *BGVA* SW1W 121 F5
Pinchbeck Rd *ORP* BR6 .....217 F4
Pinchin & Johnsons Yd
  WCHPL E1 * 104 C6
Pinchin St *WCHPL* E1 .....104 C6
Pincott PI *BROCKY* SE4 .....144 A4
Pincott Rd *BXLYHS* DA6 .....149 H6
  WIM/MER SW19 .....178 B4
Pindar St *SDTCH* EC2A 13 G1
Pindock Ms *MV/WKIL* W9 .....101 F3
Pine Apple Ct *WESTW* SW1E * 16 A4
Pine Av *SRTFD* E15 .....88 B3
  WWKM BR4 .....198 E5
Pine CI *LEY* E10 .....69 K6
  PGE/AN SE20 .....181 K4
  STAN HA7 .....29 H6
  STHGT/OAK N14 .....34 C2
Pine Coombe *CROY/NA* CR0 .....213 F2
Pinecrest Gdns *ORP* BR6 .....216 B2
Pinecroft Crs *BAR* EN5 .....20 C5
  WOOL/PLUM SE18 .....148 B1
Pinefield CI *POP/IOD* E14 * 105 J6
Pine Gdns *BRYLDS* KT5 .....191 H4
  RSLP HA4 .....59 F5
Pine Gld *ORP* BR6 .....215 K2
Pine Gv *FSBYPK* N4 .....66 E6
  TRDG/WHET N20 .....32 D3
  WIM/MER SW19 .....177 J1
Pinelands CI *BKHTH/KID* SE3 * 145 J1
Pinelees Ct
  MORT/ESHN SW14 * 137 K5
Pinemartin CI *CRICK* NW2 .....82 A1
Pine Rdg *CAR* SM5 .....210 A6
Pine Rd *CRICK* NW2 .....82 A2
  FBAR/BDGN N11 .....34 A4
Pines CI *NTHWD* HA6 .....40 C2
Pines Rd *BMLY* BR1 .....184 C5
The Pines *NRWD* SE19 * 180 C2
  STHGT/OAK N14 .....22 C6
  WFD IG8 .....38 E5
Pine St *CLKNW* EC1R 5 J6
Pine Tree CI *HEST* TW5 .....134 B1
Pine Wk *BRYLDS* KT5 .....191 H5
Pinewood Av *BFN/LL* DA15 .....167 K3
  PIN HA5 .....42 B2
  RAIN RM13 .....111 K3
Pinewood CI *CROY/NA* CR0 .....213 G1
  NTHWD HA6 .....40 E2
  ORP BR6 .....201 J5
  PIN HA5 .....42 B2
Pinewood Dr *ORP* BR6 .....216 E4
Pinewood Gv *EA* W5 .....97 J6
Pinewood Lodge *BUSH* WD23 * 28 D3
Pinewood Ms
  STWL/WRAY TW19 * 152 A1
Pinewood PI *RDART* DA2 .....170 B4
Pinewood Rd *ABYW* SE2 .....128 E6
  FELT TW13 .....154 A5
  HAYES BR2 .....199 K1
Pinfold Rd *STRHM/NOR* SW16 .....161 K6
Pinglestone CI *WDR/YW* UB7 .....132 B3
Pinkcoat CI *FELT* TW13 .....154 A5
Pinkham Way North Circular
  Rd *NFNCH/WDSPK* N12 .....47 K3
Pinkwell Av *HYS/HAR* UB3 .....113 G4
Pinkwell La *HYS/HAR* UB3 .....113 F4
Pinley Gdns *DAGW* RM9 .....91 H6
Pinnacle HI *BXLYHN* DA7 .....149 J5
Pinnacle HI North
  BXLYHN DA7 .....149 J4
Pinnell Rd *ELTH/MOT* SE9 .....146 C4
Pinner Ct *PIN* HA5 .....60 A1
Pinner Gn *PIN* HA5 .....41 G5
Pinner Gv *PIN* HA5 .....41 J6
Pinner HI *PIN* HA5 .....41 F5
Pinner Hill Rd *PIN* HA5 .....41 G5
Pinner Park Av
  RYLN/HDSTN HA2 .....42 C5
Pinner Park Gdns
  RYLN/HDSTN HA2 .....42 C5
Pinner Rd *HRW* HA1 .....60 B2
  NTHWD HA6 .....40 E4
  OXHEY WD19 .....27 H1
  PIN HA5 .....60 A1
Pinner Vw *RYLN/HDSTN* HA2 .....60 D2
Pinn Wy *RSLP* HA4 .....58 B4
Pintail CI *EHAM* E6 .....107 J4
Pintail Rd *WFD* IG8 .....53 F5
Pintail Wy *YEAD* UB4 .....95 H4
Pinto CI *BORE* WD6 * 31 F1
Pinto Wy *BKHTH/KID* SE3 .....146 A5
Pioneer CI *SHB* W12 .....99 K5
Pioneer St *PECK* SE15 .....143 H2
Pioneer Wy *SHB* W12 .....100 A5
  WATW WD18 .....26 A1
Piper CI *HOLWY* N7 .....85 F3
Piper Rd *KUT/HW* KT1 .....175 H6
Pipers Gdns *CROY/NA* CR0 .....198 B4
Pipers CI *CDALE/KGS* NW9 .....62 E2
Pipers Green La *STAN* HA7 .....30 A5
Piper Wy *IL* IG1 .....72 D5
Pipewell Rd *CAR* SM5 .....194 D3
Pippin CI *CRICK* NW2 .....81 J1
  CROY/NA CR0 .....198 C6
Pippins CI *WDR/YW* UB7 .....112 A3

Piquet Rd *PGE/AN* SE20 .....181 K5
Pirbright Crs *CROY/NA* CR0 .....214 A4
Pirbright Rd
  WAND/EARL SW18 .....159 J3
Pirie St *CAN/RD* E16 .....126 A1
Pitcairn CI *ROMW/RG* RM7 .....74 C1
Pitcairn Rd *MTCM* CR4 .....178 E3
Pitchford St *SRTFD* E15 .....88 B5
Pitfield Crs *THMD* SE28 .....128 B1
Pitfield Est *IS* N1 .....7 F4
  WLSDN NW10 .....80 E4
Pitfold Rd *LEE/GVPK* SE12 .....165 K2
Pitlake *CROY/NA* CR0 .....196 C6
Pitman St *CMBW* SE5 .....142 D1
Pitsea PI *WCHPL* E1 .....105 F5
Pitsea St *WCHPL* E1 .....105 F5
Pitshanger La *EA* W5 .....97 H3
Pitt Crs *WIM/MER* SW19 .....160 A6
Pittman Gdns *IL* IG1 .....90 C5
Pitt Rd *ORP* BR6 .....216 C2
  RYLN/HDSTN HA2 .....60 C6
  THHTH CR7 .....196 D2
Pitts Head Ms *MYFR/PICC* W1J 15 J2
Pittsmead Av *HAYES* BR2 .....199 K4
Pitt St *KENS* W8 .....119 K2
Pittville Gdns *SNWD* SE25 .....181 H6
Pixley St *POP/IOD* E14 .....105 H5
Pixton Wy *CROY/NA* CR0 .....213 H5
Place Farm Av *ORP* BR6 .....201 K5
Plaistow Gv *BMLY* BR1 .....184 A3
  SRTFD E15 .....88 D6
Plaistow La *BMLY* BR1 .....183 K3
Plaistow Park Rd *PLSTW* E13 .....107 F1
Plaistow Rd *PLSTW* E13 .....106 E1
  SRTFD E15 .....88 D6
Plane St *SYD* SE26 .....163 J5
Plane Tree Crs *FELT* TW13 .....154 A5
Plantagenet CI *WPK* KT4 .....207 G2
Plantagenet Gdns *CHDH* RM6 .....73 K4
Plantagenet PI *CHDH* RM6 .....73 K4
Plantagenet Rd *BAR* EN5 .....21 G5
Plantain Gdns *WAN* E11 * 88 B1
Plantain PI *STHWK* SE1 .....18 E2
Plantation Dr *STMC/STPC* BR5 .....202 E6
Plantation La *FENCHST* EC3M 13 G5
Plantation Rd *ERITH* DA8 .....150 D2
The Plantation
  BKHTH/KID SE3 .....145 K3
Plashet Gv *EHAM* E6 .....89 G6
Plashet Rd *PLSTW* E13 .....88 E6
Plassy Rd *CAT* SE6 .....164 E2
Platina St *SDTCH* EC2A 7 F7
Plato Rd *BRXS/STRHM* SW2 .....141 K5
Platt's La *HAMP* NW3 .....82 E1
Platt St *CAMTN* NW1 .....4 C2
Plawsfield Rd *BECK* BR3 .....182 A4
Plaxtol CI *BMLY* BR1 .....184 B4
Plaxtol Rd *ERITH* DA8 .....149 H1
Playfair St *HMSMTH* W6 .....119 F5
Playfield Av *CRW* RM5 .....56 E4
Playfield Crs *EDUL* SE22 .....143 F6
Playfield Rd *EDGW* HA8 .....44 E5
Playford Rd *FSBYPK* N4 .....67 F6
Playgreen Wy *CAT* SE6 .....164 D6
Playground CI *BECK* BR3 .....182 A5
Playhouse Ct *STHWK* SE1 * 18 C2
Playhouse Yd *BLKFR* EC4V * 12 A4
Plaza Pde *ALP/SUD* HA0 * 80 A4
Plaza Wk *CDALE/KGS* NW9 .....44 E6
Pleasance Rd *PUT/ROE* SW15 .....138 E6
  STMC/STPC BR5 .....186 C5
The Pleasance *PUT/ROE* SW15 .....138 E5
Pleasant Gv *CROY/NA* CR0 .....213 H1
Pleasant PI *IS* N1 .....85 H5
  ORP BR6 .....216 C3
Pleasant Vw *ERITH* DA8 .....130 B5
Pleasant Wy *ALP/SUD* HA0 .....97 J1
Plender St *CAMTN* NW1 .....4 A1
Pleshey Rd *ARCH* N19 .....66 C6
Plesman Wy *WLGTN* SM6 .....210 E6
Plevna Crs *SEVS/STOTM* N15 .....68 A3
Plevna Rd *ED* N9 .....36 C5
  HPTN TW12 .....173 G4
Plevna St *POP/IOD* E14 .....125 F3
Pleydell Av *HMSMTH* W6 .....118 C4
  NRWD SE19 .....181 G2
Pleydell Est *FSBYE* EC1V * 6 D5
Pleydell Gdns *NRWD* SE19 * 181 G2
Pleydell St *EMB* EC4Y * 11 K4
Plimsoll CI *POP/IOD* E14 .....105 K5
Plimsoll Rd *FSBYPK* N4 .....85 H1
Plough Farm CI *RSLP* HA4 .....58 B3
Plough La *CROY/NA* CR0 .....210 E2
  EDUL SE22 .....143 G6
  PUR/KEN CR8 .....210 E6
  TEDD TW11 * 174 B1
  WIM/MER SW19 .....178 A1
Plough Lane CI *WLGTN* SM6 .....210 E3
Ploughmans CI *CAMTN* NW1 .....4 B1
Ploughmans End *ISLW* TW7 .....135 J6
Plough PI *FLST/FETLN* EC4A 11 K3
Plough Rd *BTSEA* SW11 .....140 C4
  HOR/WEW KT19 .....207 F5
Plough St *WCHPL* E1 * 13 K3
Plough Ter *BTSEA* SW11 .....140 C5
Plough Wy *BERM/RHTH* SE16 .....124 A4
Plover Wy *BERM/RHTH* SE16 .....124 B3
Powden Buildings
  EMB EC4Y * 11 J5
Plowman CI *UED* N18 .....49 K1
Plowman Wy *BCTR* RM8 .....73 J5
Plumbers Rw *WCHPL* E1 .....104 C5
Plumbridge St *GNWCH* SE10 * 145 F2
Plum CI *FELT* TW13 .....153 K3
Plum Garth *BTFD* TW8 .....116 E4
Plum La *WOOL/PLUM* SE18 .....147 G1
Plumpton Av *HCH* RM12 .....93 K3
Plumpton CI *YEAD* UB4 .....95 H3
Plumpton Wy *CAR* SM5 .....209 J1
Plumstead Common Rd
  WOOL/PLUM SE18 .....127 H6
Plumstead High St
  WOOL/PLUM SE18 .....127 K4

Plumstead Rd
  WOOL/PLUM SE18 .....127 H4
Plumtree CI *DAGE* RM10 .....92 E4
Plumtree Ct *FLST/FETLN* EC4A 11 K3
Plymouth Rd *BMLY* BR1 .....184 A4
  CAN/RD E16 .....106 E5
Plymouth Whf *POP/IOD* E14 .....125 G4
Plympton Av *KIL/WHAMP* NW6 .....82 D5
Plympton CI *BELV* DA17 * 129 F3
Plympton PI *STJWD* NW8 * 2 C7
Plympton Rd *KIL/WHAMP* NW6 .....82 D5
Plympton St *STJWD* NW8 .....2 C7
Pocklington CI *CDALE/KGS* NW9 .....45 G5
Pocock Av *WDR/YW* UB7 .....112 C3
Pocock St *STHWK* SE1 .....18 A2
Podmore Rd
  WAND/EARL SW18 .....140 B5
Poet's Rd *HBRY* N5 .....85 K3
Poets Wy *HRW* HA1 * 60 E1
Pointalls CI *FNCH* N3 .....47 G5
Point CI *GNWCH* SE10 .....145 F2
Pointers CI *POP/IOD* E14 .....124 E5
Point HI *GNWCH* SE10 .....145 F2
Point PI *WBLY* HA9 .....80 D5
Point Pleasant
  WAND/EARL SW18 .....139 K5
Point Wharf La *BTFD* TW8 * 136 E1
Poland St *SOHO/SHAV* W1D 10 B3
Polebrook Rd *BKHTH/KID* SE3 .....146 B4
Polecroft La *CAT* SE6 .....164 C4
Pole Hill Rd *CHING* E4 .....38 A2
  HGDN/ICK UB10 .....76 A3
Polesden Gdns *RYNPK* SW20 .....176 E6
Polesworth Rd *DAGW* RM9 .....110 B1
Polish War Memorial Rbt
  NTHLT UB5 * 77 G4
Pollard CI *CAN/RD* E16 .....106 E6
  CHIG IG7 .....55 C1
  HOLWY N7 .....85 F3
Pollard Rd *MRDN* SM4 .....194 C2
  TRDG/WHET N20 .....33 J4
Pollard St *BETH* E2 .....104 C2
Pollards Crs
  STRHM/NOR SW16 .....179 K6
Pollards HI East
  STRHM/NOR SW16 .....180 A6
Pollards HI North
  STRHM/NOR SW16 .....179 K6
Pollards HI South
  STRHM/NOR SW16 .....179 K6
Pollards HI West
  STRHM/NOR SW16 .....179 K6
Pollard St *CONDST* W1S 9 K4
Pollitt Dr *STJWD* NW8 .....2 A6
Polperro CI *ORP* BR6 .....202 A3
Polperro Ms *LBTH* SE11 .....17 K6
Polsted Rd *CAT* SE6 .....164 C2
Polthorne Gv
  WOOL/PLUM SE18 .....127 J4
Polworth Rd
  STRHM/NOR SW16 .....179 K1
Polygon Rd *CAMTN* NW1 .....4 C3
The Polygon *CLAP* SW4 * 141 H5
Polytechnic St
  WOOL/PLUM SE18 .....127 F4
Pomell Wy *WCHPL* E1 .....13 K3
Pomeroy St *PECK* SE15 .....143 K1
Pomfret Rd *CMBW* SE5 .....142 C4
Pomoja La *ARCH* N19 .....66 E6
Pond CI *BKHTH/KID* SE3 .....145 K3
Ponder St *HOLWY* N7 * 85 F5
Pond Farm Est *CLPT* E5 * 86 E1
Pondfield Rd *DAGE* RM10 .....92 D3
  HAYES BR2 .....199 H5
  ORP BR6 .....216 B1
Pond Gn *RSLP* HA4 .....58 C6
Pond Hill Gdns *CHEAM* SM3 .....208 C4
Pond Lees CI *DAGE* RM10 .....93 F5
Pond Md *DUL* SE21 .....162 E1
Pond Pth *BCTR* RM8 .....92 A3
Pond Rd *BKHTH/KID* SE3 .....145 J4
  SRTFD E15 .....106 C1
Pondside CI *HYS/HAR* UB3 .....133 G1
Pond St *HAMP* NW3 .....83 J3
Pond Wy *TEDD* TW11 .....174 D2
Pondwood Ri *ORP* BR6 .....201 K5
Ponler St *WCHPL* E1 .....104 D5
Ponsard Rd *WLSDN* NW10 .....99 K2
Ponsford St *HOM* E9 .....86 E4
Ponsonby PI *WEST* SW1P 121 J5
Ponsonby Rd *PUT/ROE* SW15 .....158 E2
Ponsonby Ter *WEST* SW1P 121 J5
Pontefract Rd *BMLY* BR1 .....183 J1
Ponton Rd *VX/NE* SW8 .....141 J1
Pont Street Ms *KTBR* SW1X 14 E5
Pont St *KTBR* SW1X 14 E5
Pool CI *BECK* BR3 .....182 D1
Pool Ct *CAT* SE6 .....164 D4
Poole Court Rd *HSLW* TW3 .....134 D3
Poole Rd *HOM* E9 .....87 F4
  HOR/WEW KT19 .....207 F4
Pooles Buildings *FSBYW* WC1X 5 J7
Pooles La *WBPTN* SW10 .....140 B1
Pooles Pk *FSBYPK* N4 .....67 G6
Poole St *IS* N1 .....6 E1
Pooley Dr *MORT/ESHN* SW14 .....137 K4
Poolmans St
  BERM/RHTH SE16 .....124 A2
Pool Rd *E/WMO/HCT* KT8 .....188 E2
  HRW HA1 .....60 D3
Poolsford Rd *CDALE/KGS* NW9 .....45 G3
Poonah St *WCHPL* E1 .....104 E5
Pope CI *EBED/NFELT* TW14 .....153 J3
  WIM/MER SW19 * 178 C2
Pope Rd *HAYES* BR2 .....200 C2
Pope's Av *WHTN* TW2 .....155 K4

Popes Dr *FNCH* N3 .....46 E4
Popes Gv *CROY/NA* CR0 .....213 H1
Pope's La *EA* W5 .....116 E5
Pope's Rd *BRXN/ST* SW9 .....142 B5
Pope St *STHWK* SE1 .....19 H3
Popham CI *FELT* TW13 .....154 D5
Popham Gdns
  RCH/KEW TW9 * 137 J4
Popham Rd *IS* N1 .....85 J6
Popham St *IS* N1 .....85 J6
Popinjays Rw *CHEAM* SM3 * 208 B3
Poplar Av *MTCM* CR4 .....178 E4
  NWDGN UB2 .....115 G3
  ORP BR6 .....201 G6
Poplar Bath St *POP/IOD* E14 .....105 K6
Poplar CI *HOM* E9 .....87 H3
  PIN HA5 .....41 H4
Poplar Court Pde *TWK* TW1 * 156 D1
Poplar Crs *HOR/WEW* KT19 .....206 E4
Poplar Farm CI
  HOR/WEW KT19 .....206 E4
Poplar Gdns *NWMAL* KT3 .....176 A5
Poplar Gv *FBAR/BDGN* N11 .....119 F2
  HMSMTH W6 .....119 F2
  NWMAL KT3 .....176 A6
  WBLY HA9 .....80 E1
Poplar High St *POP/IOD* E14 .....105 K6
Poplar La *BECK* BR3 .....198 E2
Poplar Ms *SHB* W12 .....119 F1
Poplar Mt *BELV* DA17 .....129 J4
Poplar PI *BAY/PAD* W2 .....101 F6
  HYS/HAR UB3 .....113 K1
  THMD SE28 * 109 J6
Poplar Rd *CHEAM* SM3 .....193 J5
  HNHL SE24 .....142 D5
  WIM/MER SW19 .....177 K5
Poplar Rd South
  WIM/MER SW19 .....177 K6
Poplars Rd *WALTH* E17 .....69 K3
The Poplars *STHGT/OAK* N14 .....22 B6
Poplars Rd *ROMW/RG* RM7 .....74 E1
Poplar St *ROMW/RG* RM7 .....74 E1
Poplar Vw *WBLY* HA9 .....61 K6
Poplar Wy *CROY/NA* CR0 .....196 D6
  FELT TW13 .....153 K5
Poplar Wy *BAY/PAD* W2 .....101 G6
  HNHL SE24 .....142 D5
Poppins Ct *FLST/FETLN* EC4A 11 K4
Poppleton Rd *WAN* E11 .....70 C3
Poppy CI *BELV* DA17 .....129 J3
  NTHLT UB5 .....77 J4
  WLGTN SM6 .....195 F5
Porchester Garden Ms
  BAY/PAD W2 .....101 F5
Porchester Gdns *BAY/PAD* W2 .....101 F6
Porchester Ga *BAY/PAD* W2 * 101 G6
Porchester Ms *BECK* BR3 .....182 E2
Porchester PI *BAY/PAD* W2 .....8 D4
Porchester Rd *BAY/PAD* W2 .....101 F5
  KUT/HW KT1 .....175 J5
Porchester Sq *BAY/PAD* W2 .....101 F5
Porchester Square Ms
  BAY/PAD W2 * 101 F5
Porchester Ter *BAY/PAD* W2 .....101 G6
Porch Wy *TRDG/WHET* N20 .....33 K5
Porcupine CI *ELTH/MOT* SE9 .....166 D4
Porden Rd *BRXS/STRHM* SW2 .....142 A5
Porlock Av *RYLN/HDSTN* HA2 .....60 C5
Porlock Rd *EN* EN1 .....36 B2
Porlock St *STHWK* SE1 .....19 F2
Porrington CI *CHST* BR7 .....184 E4
Portal CI *RSLP* HA4 .....58 A6
  WNWD SE27 .....162 B5
Portal Wy *ACT* W3 .....99 F4
Portbury CI *PECK* SE15 .....143 H2
Portchester CI *HNHL* SE24 .....142 D5
Portcullis Lodge Rd *EN* EN1 * 24 A4
Portelet Rd *WCHPL* E1 .....105 F2
Porten Houses *WKENS* W14 * 119 H3
Porten Rd *WKENS* W14 .....119 H3
Porter Av *EHAM* E6 .....107 H1
Porter Rd *EHAM* E6 .....107 K5
Porter Sq *ARCH* N19 .....66 E5
Porter St *MHST* W1U 9 F1
  STHWK SE1 .....12 D7
Porters Wk *WAP* E1W * 104 D6
Porters Wy *WDR/YW* UB7 .....112 C3
Porteus Rd *BAY/PAD* W2 .....101 G4
Portgate CI *MV/WKIL* W9 .....100 D3
Porthallow CI *ORP* BR6 .....217 F2
Porthcawe Rd *SYD* SE26 .....164 B6
Porthkerry Av *WELL* DA16 .....148 B5
Portia Wy *BOW* E3 .....105 H3
The Porticos *CHEL* SW3 * 120 C6
Portinscale Rd *PUT/ROE* SW15 .....139 H6
Portland Av *BFN/LL* DA15 .....168 B1
  NWMAL KT3 .....192 C4
  STNW/STAM N16 .....68 B4
Portland CI *CHDH* RM6 .....74 A2
  WPK KT4 .....192 E4
Portland Cottages
  CROY/NA CR0 * 195 J4
Portland Crs *ELTH/MOT* SE9 .....166 D4
  FELT TW13 .....153 G3
  GFD/PVL UB6 .....96 B4
  STAN HA7 .....43 K3
Portland Dr *ENC/FH* EN2 .....24 A1
Portland Gdns *CHDH* RM6 .....73 K1
  FSBYPK N4 .....67 H3
Portland Gv *VX/NE* SW8 .....142 A2
Portland Ms *SOHO/CST* W1F 10 B4
Portland PI *REGST* W1B * 9 J2
Portland Ri *FSBYPK* N4 .....67 H5
Portland Rd *ASHF* TW15 .....152 B5
  BMLY BR1 .....166 B6
  ELTH/MOT SE9 .....166 D4
  KUT/HW KT1 .....175 F6
  MTCM CR4 .....178 D5
  NTGHL W11 .....119 H1
  NTGHL W11 .....100 C6
  NWDGN UB2 .....114 D3
  SEVS/STOTM N15 .....68 B1
  SNWD SE25 .....197 J1

  YEAD UB4 .....94 C2
Portland Sq *WAP* E1W 123 J1
Portland St *WALW* SE17 .....122 E5
Portland Ter *RCH/KEW* TW9 * 136 E5
Portman Av
  MORT/ESHN SW14 .....138 A4
Portman CI *BXLY* DA5 .....170 B3
  BXLYHS DA6 .....148 E5
  MBLAR W1H 8 E3
Portman Dr *WFD* IG8 .....53 H4
Portman Gdns *CDALE/KGS* NW9 .....45 F6
Portman Ga *CAMTN* NW1 * 2 D7
Portman Ms South *MBLAR* W1H 9 G4
Portman PI *BETH* E2 .....104 E2
Portman Rd *KUT/HW* KT1 .....175 G5
Portman Sq *MBLAR* W1H 9 G4
Portman St *MBLAR* W1H 9 G4
Portman Towers *MBLAR* W1H * 9 F3
Portmeadow Wk *ABYW* SE2 .....128 E2
Portmeers CI *WALTH* E17 * 69 H5
Portmore Gdns *CRW* RM5 .....56 C1
Portnall Rd *MV/WKIL* W9 .....100 D2
Portobello Ct *NTGHL* W11 * 100 D6
Portobello Ms *NTGHL* W11 .....100 E6
Portobello Rd *NKENS* W10 .....100 C4
Portpool La *FSBYW* WC1X 11 J1
Portree St *POP/IOD* E14 .....106 B5
Portsdown Av *GLDGN* NW11 .....64 D3
Portsdown Ms *GLDGN* NW11 .....64 D3
Portsea Ms *BAY/PAD* W2 .....8 D4
Portsea PI *BAY/PAD* W2 * 8 D4
Portslade Rd *VX/NE* SW8 .....141 H3
Portsmouth Av *THDIT* KT7 .....190 B4
Portsmouth Ms *CAN/RD* E16 .....107 F6
Portsmouth Rd
  ESH/CLAY KT10 .....204 A3
  KUT/HW KT1 .....174 E6
  PUT/ROE SW15 .....158 E3
  PUT/ROE SW15 .....159 F2
Portsmouth St *LINN* WC2A 11 G3
Portsoken St *TWRH* EC3N 13 J5
Portugal Gdns *WHTN* TW2 * 155 H4
Portugal St *LINN* WC2A 11 H4
Portway *RAIN* RM13 .....93 J6
  SRTFD E15 .....88 D6
Portway Crs *EW* KT17 .....207 K6
Portway Gdns
  WOOL/PLUM SE18 .....146 C2
Postern Gn *ENC/FH* EN2 .....23 G3
The Postern *BARB* EC2Y * 12 D2
Post La *WHTN* TW2 .....155 J3
Postmill CI *CROY/NA* CR0 .....212 E1
Post Office Ap *FSTGT* E7 .....89 F3
Post Office Wy *VX/NE* SW8 .....141 J1
Post Rd *NWDGN* UB2 .....115 G3
Postway Ms *IL* IG1 * 90 B1
Potier St *STHWK* SE1 .....19 F5
Potter CI *MTCM* CR4 * 179 G5
The Potteries *BAR* EN5 .....20 E6
Potterne CI *WIM/MER* SW19 .....159 G2
Potters CI *CROY/NA* CR0 .....198 B5
  PECK SE15 .....143 F1
Potters Fld *EN* EN1 * 24 A5
Potters Flds *STHWK* SE1 .....19 H1
Potters Gv *NWMAL* KT3 .....191 K1
Potters Heights CI *PIN* HA5 .....41 F3
Potters La *BAR* EN5 .....20 D5
  STRHM/NOR SW16 .....179 J2
Potter's Rd *BAR* EN5 .....21 F5
  FUL/PGN SW6 .....140 B3
Potter St *NTHWD* HA6 .....40 E4
Pottery La *NTGHL* W11 .....119 H1
Pottery Rd *BTFD* TW8 .....117 F6
  BXLY DA5 .....169 K4
Pottery St *BERM/RHTH* SE16 * 123 J2
Pott St *BETH* E2 .....104 D2
Poulett Gdns *TWK* TW1 .....156 B3
Poulett Rd *EHAM* E6 .....107 K1
Poulner Wy *PECK* SE15 * 143 G1
Poulters Wd *HAYES* BR2 .....200 E4
Poulton Av *SUT* SM1 .....209 H1
Poulton CI *HACK* E8 .....86 D4
Poultry *LOTH* EC2R 12 E4
Pound CI *ORP* BR6 .....201 J6
  SURB KT6 .....190 D5
Pound Court Dr *ORP* BR6 .....201 J6
Pound Farm CI
  ESH/CLAY KT10 .....189 J5
Pound La *WLSDN* NW10 .....81 J4
Pound Park Rd *CHARL* SE7 .....126 C5
Pound Pl *ELTH/MOT* SE9 .....167 F6
Pound St *CAR* SM5 .....209 K3
Pountney Rd *BTSEA* SW11 .....141 F4
Poverest Rd *STMC/STPC* BR5 .....202 A2
Powder Mill La *DART* DA1 ...
  WHTN TW2 .....154 E3
Powell CI *EDGW* HA8 .....44 B2
  DAGE RM10 .....92 C2
Powell Rd *BKHH* IG9 .....39 G2
  CLPT E5 .....86 D1
Power Rd *CHSWK* W4 .....117 H4
Powers Ct *TWK* TW1 .....156 E2
Powerscroft Rd *CLPT* E5 .....86 E2
Powis CI *BUSH* WD23 .....28 D3
Powis Gdns *GLDGN* NW11 .....64 D4
  NTGHL W11 .....100 D5
Powis Ms *NTGHL* W11 .....100 D5
Powis PI *BMSBY* WC1N 5 F7
Powis Rd *BOW* E3 .....105 K2
Powis Sq *NTGHL* W11 .....100 D5
Powis St *WOOL/PLUM* SE18 .....127 F3
Powis Ter *NTGHL* W11 .....100 D5
Powlett PI *CAMTN* NW1 .....84 B5
Pownall Gdns *HSLW* TW3 .....135 G5
Pownall Rd *HACK* E8 .....86 B6
  HSLW TW3 .....135 G5
Pownsett Ter *IL* IG1 * 90 C3
Powster Rd *BMLY* BR1 .....183 K1
Powys CI *BXLYHN* DA7 .....148 E6
Powys La *PLMGR* N13 .....48 E1
  STHGT/OAK N14 .....34 E5
Poynders Rd *CLAP* SW4 .....161 H2
Poynings CI *ORP* BR6 .....202 D6
Poynings Rd *ARCH* N19 .....84 C1

Poynings Wy
NFNCH/WDSPK N12 ....46 E1
Poynter Ed EN1 ....24 B6
Poynton Rd STRHM N17 ....50 C5
Poyntz Rd BTSEA SW11 ....140 E3
Poyser St BETH E2 ....104 D1
Praed Ms BAY/PAD W2 ....8 B3
Praed St BAY/PAD W2 ....8 B3
Praget St PLSTW E13 ....107 G1
Pragnell Rd LEE/GVPK SE12 ...166 A4
Prague Pl BRXS/STRHM** SW2 ...141 K6
Prah Rd FSBYPK N4 ....67 G6
Prairie St VX/NE SW8 ....141 F3
Pratt Ms CAMTN NW1 ....4 A1
Pratt St CAMTN NW1 ....4 A1
Pratt Wk LBTH SE11 ....17 K6
Prayle Gv CRICK NW2 ....64 B5
Prebend Gdns HMSMTH W6 ....118 C4
Prebend St IS N1 ....6 C1
Precinct Rd HYS/HAR UB3 ....94 E6
The Precinct IS N1 * 6 C2
Prendergast Rd
BKHTH/KID SE3 ....145 H4
Prentis Rd STRHM/NOR SW16 ...161 K3
Prentiss Ct CHARL SE7 ....126 C4
Presburg Rd NWMAL KT3 ....192 B2
Prescelly Pl EDGW HA8 ....35 K4
Prescot St WCHPL E1 ....13 K5
Prescott Cl EMPK RM11 ....75 K5
Prescott Pl CLAP SW4 ....141 J4
Presentation Ms
BRXS/STRHM SW2 ....162 A4
Presidents Dr WAP E1W 123 J1
President St FSBYE EC1V * 6 C4
Pespa Ct ED N9 ....36 E4
Press Rd WLSDN NW10 ....81 F1
Prestage Wy POP/IOD E14 ....106 A6
Prestbury Rd FSTGT E7 ....89 G5
Prestbury Sq ELTH/MOT SE9 ....166 E6
Prested Rd BTSEA SW11 ....140 D5
Preston Av CHING E4 ....52 A2
Preston Cl STHWK SE1 ....19 G6
Preston Ct BAR EN5 * 21 F5
Preston Dr BXLYHN DA7 ....148 E2
HOR/WEW KT19 ....207 G4
WAN E11 ....71 F2
Preston Gdns IL IG1 ....71 J3
WLSDN NW10 ....81 F4
Preston Hl KTN/HRWW/WS HA3 ..62 A4
Preston Rd
KTN/HRWW/WS HA3 ....62 A4
NRWD SE19 ....180 C2
WAP E1W 70 C3
Preston's Rd POP/IOD E14 ....125 F1
WWKM BR4 ....214 E1
Preston Vis KUT/HW KT1 * 175 G5
Preston Waye
KTN/HRWW/WS HA3 ....62 A4
Prestwich Ter CLAP SW4 * 141 J6
Prestwick Cl NWDGN UB2 ....114 D5
Prestwick Rd OXHEY WD19 ....27 H5
Prestwood Av
KTN/HRWW/WS HA3 ....61 H1
Prestwood Cl
KTN/HRWW/WS HA3 ....61 H1
WOOL/PLUM SE18 ....148 B1
Prestwood Gdns
CROY/NA CRO 196 D4
Prestwood St IS N1 * 6 D3
Pretoria Av WALTH E17 ....69 G1
Pretoria Crs CHING E4 ....38 A3
Pretoria Pde BROCKY SE4 * 144 B3
Pretoria Rd CAR/RD E16 ....106 D2
CHING E4 ....38 A3
IL IG1 ....90 B2
LEY E10 ....69 F6
ROMW/RG RM7 ....74 E1
STRHM/NOR SW16 ....179 G2
TOTM N17 ....50 B2
Pretoria Rd North UED N18 ....50 B2
Prevost Rd FBAR/BDGN N11 .....34 A4
Price Cl MLHL NW7 ....46 C2
TOOT SW17 ....160 E5
Price Rd CROY/NA CRO 211 H3
Price's St STHWK SE1 ....18 B1
Pricklers Hl BAR EN5 ....21 F6
Prickley Wd HAYES BR2 ....199 J5
Priddy's Yd CROY/NA CRO 196 D6
Prideaux Pl ACT W3 ....99 F6
FSBYW WC1X 5 H4
Pridham Rd THHTH CR7 ....196 E1
Priestfield Rd FSTH SE23 ....164 B5
Priestlands Park Rd
BFN/LL DA15 ....168 A5
Priestley Cl STNW/STAM N16 * ..68 B4
Priestley Gdns CHDH RM6 ....73 H5
Priestley Rd MTCM CR4 ....179 F5
Priestley Wy CRICK NW2 ....63 J5
WALTH E17 ....51 F6
Priest Park Av
RYLN/HDSTN HA2 ....60 A6
Priests Av ROM RM1 ....57 F5
Priests Br MORT/ESHN SW14 ...138 B4
Prima Rd BRXN/ST SW9 ....142 B1
Primrose Av ENC/FH EN2 ....23 K2
GDMY/SEVK IG3 ....91 G4
Primrose Cl BOW E3 ....105 J1
CAT SE6 ....183 F1
FNCH N3 ....47 F5
RYLN/HDSTN HA2 ....77 J1
WLGTN SM6 ....195 G6
Primrose Dr WDR/YW UB7 ....112 A4
Primrose Gdns BUSH WD23 ....28 B2
HAMP NW3 ....83 J4
RSLP HA4 ....77 G3
Primrose Hl EMB EC4Y * 11 K4

Primrose Hill Rd HAMP NW3 .....83 K5
Primrose Hill Studios
CAMTN NW1 * 84 A6
Primrose La CROY/NA CRO 197 K5
Primrose Ms CAMTN NW1 * 83 K5
Primrose Pl ISLW TW7 * 136 A3
Primrose Rd LEY E10 ....69 K5
SWFD E18 ....53 F5
Primrose Sq HOM E9 ....86 E5
Primrose St SDTCH EC2A 13 G1
Primrose Wk KUT/HW KT1 * 207 H5
NWCR SE14 ....144 B1
Primula St SHB W12 ....99 J6
Prince Albert Rd CAMTN NW1 * ..3 J2
STJWD NW8 * 2 D3
Prince Arthur Ms HAMP NW3 * ..83 G2
Prince Arthur Rd HAMP NW3 ....83 H2
Prince Charles Dr HDN NW4 ......64 A4
Prince Charles Rd
BKHTH/KID SE3 ....145 J2
Prince Consort Dr CHST BR7 ....185 J4
Prince Consort Rd SKENS SW7 ...14 A4
Princedale Rd NTGHL W11 ....119 H1
Prince Edward Rd HOM E9 ....87 J4
Prince George Av
STHGT/OAK N14 ....22 D6
Prince George Rd
STNW/STAM N16 ....86 A2
Prince George's Av RYNPK
SW20 ....177 F5
Prince Georges Rd
WIM/MER SW19 ....178 C1
Prince Henry Rd CHARL SE7 .....146 C1
Prince Imperial Rd CHST BR7 ...185 G3
WOOL/PLUM SE18 ....146 E2
Prince John Rd ELTH/MOT SE9 ..146 D5
Princelet St WCHPL E1 ....13 K1
Prince of Orange La
GNWCH SE10 * 145 F1
Prince of Wales Cl HDN NW4 * ..63 K1
Prince of Wales Dr
BTSEA SW11 ....140 E2
VX/NE SW8 ....141 J1
Prince of Wales Ga SKENS SW7 ..14 C2
Prince of Wales Pas
CAMTN NW1 * 4 A5
Prince of Wales Rd
BKHTH/KID SE3 ....145 J2
CAN/RD E16 ....107 H5
KTTN NW5 ....84 B4
SUT SM1 ....194 C6
Prince of Wales Ter
CHSWK W4 ....118 B5
KENS W8 ....120 A2
Prince Regent La PLSTW E13 ...107 G3
Prince Regent Ms CAMTN NW1 * ..4 A5
Prince Regent Rd HSLW TW3 ....135 H4
Prince Rupert Rd
ELTH/MOT SE9 ....146 E5
Princes Ar MYFR/PICC W1J 10 B7
Princes Av ACT W3 ....117 H3
CAR SM5 ....209 K5
CDALE/KGS NW9 ....62 C1
FNCH N3 ....47 F4
GFD/PVL UB6 ....96 B5
MUSWH N10 ....48 B6
PLMGR N13 ....49 G1
STMC/STPC BR5 ....201 K2
SURB KT6 ....191 H6
WDGN N22 ....48 D4
WFD IG8 ....39 G2
Princes Cl CDALE/KGS NW9 ....62 C1
EDGW HA8 ....44 B1
FSBYPK N4 ....67 H5
HPTN TW12 ....155 J6
SCUP DA14 ....168 E5
Princes Dr HRW HA1 ....42 E6
Princes Gdns ACT W3 ....98 C5
EA W5 ....97 J3
SKENS SW7 ....14 A4
Princes Ga SKENS SW7 ....14 C3
Princes Gate Ms SKENS SW7 ...14 A4
Princes La MUSWH N10 ....48 A6
Prince's Ms BAY/PAD W2 ....100 E6
HMSMTH W6 * 118 E5
HSLW TW3 ....135 F5
IS N1 * 85 H6
Princes Pde GLDGN NW11 * 64 C3
Princes Pk RAIN RM13 ....93 J5
Princes Park Av GLDGN NW11 ...64 C3
HYS/HAR UB3 ....94 B6
Princes Park Cl HYS/HAR UB3 ...94 B6
Princes Park Ga HYS/HAR UB3 ..94 B6
Princes Park Pde
HYS/HAR UB3 ....94 B6
Princes Pl NTGHL W11 ....119 H1
Prince's Pln HAYES BR2 ....200 D4
Princes Ri LEW SE13 ....145 F2
Princes Riverside Rd
BERM/RHTH SE16 ....124 A1
BKHH IG9 ....39 G4
DART DA1 ....170 E1
FELT TW13 ....153 J5
KUTN/CMB KT2 ....175 H4
MORT/ESHN SW14 ....138 A4
PGE/AN SE20 ....182 A2
RCH/KEW TW9 ....137 G2
RCHPK/HAM TW10 ....137 G3
ROM RM1 ....57 G6
TEDD TW11 ....173 J1
UED N18 ....36 E6
WEA W13 ....116 C1
WIM/MER SW19 ....177 H2
Prince's Ter PLSTW E13 ....89 F6
Princess Alice Wy THMD SE28 ..127 J2
Princess Av WBLY HA9 ....62 A6
Princess Crs FSBYPK N4 ....67 H6
Princesses Pde DART DA1 * 150 C6
Princess La RSLP HA4 ....58 C5

Princess Louise Cl BAY/PAD W2 ...8 B1
Princess May Rd
STNW/STAM N16 ....86 A2
Princess Ms HAMP NW3 * 83 H4
Princess Pde ORP BR6 * 216 A1
Prince's Sq BAY/PAD W2 ....100 E6
Princess Rd CAMTN NW1 ....84 A6
CROY/NA CRO 196 D3
KIL/WHAMP NW6 ....100 E1
Princess St BXLYHN DA7 ....149 G4
STHWK SE1 ....18 B5
Prince's St LOTH EC2R 12 E4
RCH/KEW TW9 ....137 F5
REGST W1B 9 K4
SUT SM1 ....209 H2
TOTM N17 ....50 B3
Prince's Ter PLSTW E13 ....89 F6
Princes St DEPT SE8 ....124 C6
Princes Vw DART DA1 ....171 K3
Princes Wy BKHH IG9 ....39 G4
CROY/NA CRO 211 F3
RSLP HA4 ....77 J2
WIM/MER SW19 ....159 G2
Princes Yd NTGHL W11 * 119 H1
Princethorpe Rd SYD SE26 ......164 A6
Princeton St GINN WC1R 11 H1
Pringle Gdns
STRHM/NOR SW16 ....161 H6
Printers Inn Ct
FLST/FETLN EC4A 11 J3
Printinghouse La
HYS/HAR UB3 ....113 H2
Printing House Yd BETH E2 * 7 H5
Priolo Rd CHARL SE7 ....126 B5
Prior Av BELMT SM2 ....209 J5
Prior Bolton St IS N1 ....85 H4
Prioress Rd WNWD SE27 ....162 C5
Prioress St STHWK SE1 ....19 G5
Priors Cft WALTH E17 ....51 G4
Priors Fld NTHLT UB5 * 78 A4
Priorsford Av STMC/STPC BR5 ..202 B3
Priors Gdns RSLP HA4 ....77 G3
Priors Md EN EN1 ....24 A2
Prior St GNWCH SE10 ....145 F1
Priory Av ALP/SUD HA0 ....79 F2
CEND/HSY/T N8 ....66 D1
CHEAM SM3 ....208 B2
CHING E4 ....37 H5
CHSWK W4 ....118 B3
STMC/STPC BR5 ....201 J3
WALTH E17 ....69 J2
Priory Cl ALP/SUD HA0 ....79 F2
BAR EN5 ....182 B6
BECK BR3 ....182 A6
CHST BR7 ....184 E4
DART DA1 ....151 F6
FNCH N3 ....46 D4
HPTN TW12 ....172 E4
HYS/HAR UB3 ....95 F6
RSLP HA4 ....59 F5
STAN HA7 ....29 F5
STHGT/OAK N14 ....22 B6
SUN TW16 ....172 A3
TRDG/WHET N20 ....32 E2
WIM/MER SW19 ....178 A4
Priory Cottages EA W5 * 98 A4
Priory Ct BLKFR EC4V * 12 A4
E/WMO/HCT KT8 ....189 F1
VX/NE SW8 ....141 J2
WALTH E17 ....51 H6
Priory Crs ALP/SUD HA0 ....79 F1
CHEAM SM3 ....208 B3
NRWD SE19 ....180 D3
Priory Dr ABYW SE2 ....129 F1
STAN HA7 ....28 E4
Priory Field Dr EDGW HA8 ....30 D6
Priory Gdns ALP/SUD HA0 ....79 F2
BARN SW13 ....138 C4
CHSWK W4 ....118 B4
DART DA1 ....171 J4
EFNCH N2 ....47 J6
HPTN TW12 ....172 E4
SNWD SE25 ....197 G1
Priory Green Est IS N1 * 5 G2
Priory Hl ALP/SUD HA0 ....79 F2
DART DA1 ....171 J4
Priory La E/WMO/HCT KT8 ....189 G1
PUT/ROE SW15 ....158 C3
Priory Leas ELTH/MOT SE9 * 166 E4
Priory Market Pl DART DA1 * 171 H2
Priory Ms HCH RM12 ....75 K6
Priory Pk BKHTH/KID SE3 ....145 J4
Priory Park Rd ALP/SUD HA0 .....79 F2
KIL/WHAMP NW6 ....82 D6
Priory Rd BARK IG11 ....90 D5
CEND/HSY/T N8 ....49 F6
CHEAM SM3 ....208 B2
CHSGTN KT9 ....206 A1
CHSWK W4 ....118 A3
DART DA1 ....151 G5
EHAM E6 ....89 H6
HPTN TW12 ....172 E4
HSLW TW3 ....135 J5
MUSWH N10 ....66 C1
RCH/KEW TW9 ....117 H6
Priory St BOW E3 ....105 K2
Priory Ter KIL/WHAMP NW6 ....83 F6
The Priory BKHTH/KID SE3 ....145 J5
Priory Vw BUSH WD23 ....28 E2
Priory Vls FBAR/BDGN N11 * 47 K2
Priory Wk WBPTN SW10 ....120 C5
Priory Wy HYS/HAR UB3 * 113 H6
NWDGN UB2 ....114 C3
RYLN/HDSTN HA2 ....59 J6
WDR/YW UB7 ....112 B6
Pritchard's Rd BETH E2 ....104 C1
Pritchett Rd BERM/RHTH SE16 * ..23 K6
Private Rd EN EN1 ....24 B6
Probert Rd BRXS/STRHM SW2 ..142 B6
Probyn Rd BRXS/STRHM SW2 ...162 C4
Procter St GINN WC1R 11 G2
Procter St MTCM CR4 ....179 F4

Proctors Cl EBED/NFELT TW14 ..153 K3
Progress Wy CROY/NA CRO 196 A6
EN EN1 ....36 C1
WDGN N22 ....49 G5
Promenade Approach Rd
CHSWK W4 ....138 B1
The Promenade CHSWK W4 .....138 B2
EDGW HA8 * 44 C1
Prospect Cl BELV DA17 ....129 H4
HSLW TW3 ....134 E2
RSLP HA4 ....59 H4
SYD SE26 ....163 H6
Prospect Cottages
WAND/EARL SW18 ....139 K5
Prospect Crs WHTN TW2 ....155 H1
Prospect Hl WALTH E17 ....51 K6
Prospect Pl CHSWK W4 ....118 A5
CRICK NW2 ....82 D1
CRW RM5 ....56 C5
EFNCH N2 * 47 H6
HAYES BR2 ....184 A6
RYNPK SW20 ....176 E3
WAP E1W 123 K1
Prospect Rd BARN EN5 ....20 C5
CRICK NW2 ....64 C6
SURB KT6 ....190 D5
WFD IG8 ....39 G6
Prospect St BERM/RHTH SE16 ..123 J2
Prospect V WOOL/PLUM SE18 ..126 D4
Prospero Rd ARCH N19 ....66 C5
Protea Cl CAN/RD E16 ....106 D3
Prothero Gdns HDN NW4 ....63 K2
Prothero Rd FUL/PGN SW6 ....139 H1
Prout Gv WLSDN NW10 ....81 G2
Prout Rd CLPT E5 ....86 D1
Provence St IS N1 * 6 C1
Providence Av
RYLN/HDSTN HA2 ....60 A3
Providence Cl HOM E9 * 87 F6
Providence Ct MYFR/PKLN W1K ..9 H5
Providence La HYS/HAR UB3 .....133 G1
Providence Pl CRW RM5 ....56 B4
IS N1 ....6 B1
Providence Rd WDR/YW UB7 ...112 B1
Providence Row CLERKW EC1M ..5 H4
Providence Sq STHWK SE1 * 19 G2
Providence Yd BETH E2 * 7 K4
Provincial Ter PGE/AN SE20 * ...182 A3
Provost Est IS N1 ....6 E5
Provost Rd HAMP NW3 ....83 K5
Provost St FSBYE EC1V 6 E6
Prowse Av BUSH WD23 ....28 C4
Prowse Pl CAMTN NW1 ....84 C5
Pruden Cl STHGT/OAK N14 * 34 C4
Prusom St WAP E1W 123 J1
Puck La MON EC3R * 13 H5
Pudding La MON EC3R 13 F5
Pudding Mill La SRTFD E15 ....105 K1
Puddle Dock BLKFR EC4V 12 B5
Puffin Cl BARK IG11 ....109 H2
BECK BR3 ....198 A2
Pulborough Rd
WAND/EARL SW18 ....159 J2
Pulborough Wy HSLWW TW4 ...134 A4
Pulford Rd SEVS/STOTM N15 .....67 K3
Pulham Av EFNCH N2 ....65 H1
Pullen's Bldgs WALW SE17 * 18 B7
Pullman Gdns PUT/ROE SW15 ..159 F1
Pullman Ms LEE/GVPK SE12 ....166 D6
Pullross Rd BRXN/ST SW9 ....142 A4
Pulteney Cl BOW E3 ....87 H6
ISLW TW7 ....136 B4
Pulteney Rd SWFD E18 ....53 F5
Pulton Pl FUL/PGN SW6 ....139 K1
Puma Ct WCHPL E1 * 13 J1
Pump Aly BTFD TW8 ....136 E1
Pump Cl NTHLT UB5 * 96 A1
Pump Ct EMB EC4Y * 11 J4
Pump House Cl HAYES BR2 ....183 J5
Pump House Ms WCHPL E1 * 104 C6
Pumping Station Rd
CHSWK W4 ....138 B1
Pump La HYS/HAR UB3 ....113 K2
NWCR SE14 ....143 K1
Punchard Crs PEND EN3 ....25 K1
Punderson's Gdns BETH E2 ......104 D2
Purbeck Av NWMAL KT3 ....192 C3
Purbeck Dr CRICK NW2 ....64 B6
Purbeck Rd EMPK RM11 ....75 J4
Purbrook St STHWK SE1 ....19 J4
Purcell Crs FUL/PGN SW6 ....119 G6
Purcell Crescent FUL/PGN SW6 ..139 H1
Purcell Ms WLSDN NW10 * 81 G5
Purcell Rd GFD/PVL UB6 ....96 B4
Purcell St IS N1 ....7 G2
Purcers Cross Rd
FUL/PGN SW6 ....139 J2
Purchese St CAMTN NW1 * 4 C2
Purdy St BOW E3 ....105 K3
Purelake Ms LEW SE13 * 145 G4
Purfleet Industrial Access Rd
SOCK/AV RM15 ....131 K3
Purkis Cl UX/CGN UB8 ....94 A6
Purland Cl BCTR RM8 ....74 B5
Purland Rd THMD SE28 ....53 J2
Purleigh Av WFD IG8 ....53 H2
Purley Av CRICK NW2 ....64 C1
Purley Cl CLAY IG5 ....54 A5
SAND/SEL CR2 ....211 K5
Purley Pl IS N1 ....85 H5
Purley Rd ED N9 ....35 K4
SAND/SEL CR2 ....211 K6
Purley Wy CROY/NA CRO 196 A5
CROY/NA CRO 211 G2
Purneys Rd ELTH/MOT SE9 ....146 C5
Purrett Rd WOOL/PLUM SE18 ...128 A5
Pursers Cross Rd
FUL/PGN SW6 ....139 J2
Purser's Cross Rd WEA W13 .....116 C1
Pursley Rd MLHL NW7 ....46 A3
Purves Rd WLSDN NW10 ....99 K2
Putney Bridge Ap
FUL/PGN SW6 ....139 H4
Putney Bridge Rd
PUT/ROE SW15 ....139 H5

Putney Common
PUT/ROE SW15 ....139 F4
Putney Ex PUT/ROE SW15 * 139 G5
Putney Gdns CHDH RM6 ....73 H2
Putney Heath PUT/ROE SW15 ..158 E3
Putney Heath La
PUT/ROE SW15 ....159 G1
Putney High St
PUT/ROE SW15 ....139 H5
Putney Hl PUT/ROE SW15 ....159 G2
Putney Park Av
PUT/ROE SW15 ....138 D5
Putney Park La
PUT/ROE SW15 ....138 D5
Puttenham Cl OXHEY WD19 ....27 G5
Pycombe Cnr
NFNCH/WDSPK N12 ....32 D6
Pycroft Wy ED N9 ....36 C5
Pylbrook Rd SUT SM1 ....208 E1
Pylon Wy CROY/NA CRO 195 K5
Pym Cl EBAR EN4 ....21 H6
Pymers Md DUL SE21 ....162 D3
Pymmes Brook Trail EBAR EN4 ..21 J6
EBAR EN4 ....33 K2
ED N9 ....35 K3
PLMGR N13 ....34 C1
STHGT/OAK N14 ....34 B4
Pymmes Cl PLMGR N13 ....49 F1
TOTM N17 ....50 D4
Pymmes Gdns North ED N9 ....36 B5
Pymmes Gdns South ED N9 ......36 B5
Pymmes Green Rd
BAR/BDGN N11 ....34 B6
Pymmes Rd PLMGR N13 ....48 C2
Pymms Brook Dr EBAR EN4 ....21 J5
Pyne Rd SURB KT6 ....191 H5
Pynham Cl ABYW SE2 ....128 B3
Pynnacles Cl STAN HA7 ....43 H1
Pyrland Rd HBRY N5 ....85 K3
RCHPK/HAM TW10 ....157 G1
Pyrmont Gv WNWD SE27 ....162 C5
Pyrmont Rd CHSWK W4 ....117 H6
Pytchley Crs NRWD SE19 ....180 D2
Pytchley Rd EDUL SE22 ....143 F4

Q

The Quadrangle BAY/PAD W2 * ...8 C3
HNHL SE24 * 142 D6
WBPTN SW10 * 140 B6
Quadrant Ar REGST W1B 10 B6
Quadrant Cl HDN NW4 * 63 K2
Quadrant Gv KTTN NW5 ....83 K3
Quadrant Rd RCH/KEW TW9 .....136 E5
THHTH CR7 ....196 C1
The Quadrant BELMT SM2 ....209 G4
BXLYHN DA7 ....148 C2
EDGW HA8 * 44 C1
NKENS W10 ....100 B2
RCH/KEW TW9 ....136 E6
RYLN/HDSTN HA2 * 42 D6
RYNPK SW20 ....177 H4
Quad Rd WBLY HA9 * 61 K3
Quaggy Wk BKHTH/KID SE3 .....145 K5
Quainton St WLSDN NW10 ....81 F1
Quaker La NWDGN UB2 ....115 F3
Quakers Course
CDALE/KGS NW9 ....45 H4
Quakers La ISLW TW7 ....136 B1
Quakers Pl FSTGT E7 ....89 H3
Quaker St WCHPL E1 ....7 J7
Quakers Wk WCHMH N21 ....35 K1
Quality Ct LINN WC2A 11 J3
Quantock Cl HYS/HAR UB3 ....133 G1
Quantock Gdns CRICK NW2 ....64 B6
Quantock Ms PECK SE15 ....143 H3
Quantock Rd BXLYHN DA7 ....150 B5
Quarley Wy PECK SE15 * 143 G1
Quarles Park Rd CHDH RM6 ....73 G3
Quarrendon St FUL/PGN SW6 ..139 K3
Quarr Rd CAR SM5 ....194 C3
Quarry Ms PUR RM19 ....131 K4
Quarry Park Rd SUT SM1 ....208 D4
Quarry Ri SUT SM1 ....208 D4
Quarry Rd WAND/EARL SW18 ...160 B1
Quartermile La LEY E10 ....87 K2
Quatre Ports CHING E4 * 52 B1
**Quay House POP/IOD E14 * 124 D2
Quebec Ms MBLAR W1H 9 F4
Quebec Rd GNTH/NBYPK IG2 * ..72 C3
HYS/HAR UB3 ....95 G6
Quebec Wy
BERM/RHTH SE16 ....124 A2
Quebec Wy
BERM/RHTH SE16 ....124 A2
Queen Adelaide Rd
PGE/AN SE20 ....181 K3
Queen Anne Av HAYES BR2 ......183 K6
Queen Anne Dr
ESH/CLAY KT10 ....204 E5
Queen Anne Rd HOM E9 ....87 F4
Queen Anne Ms CAVSO/HST W1G ..*
Queen Anne Ms WHTN TW2 ......155 J5
Queen Anne's Gdns
CHSWK W4 ....118 B3
EA W5 ....117 F2
EN EN1 ....36 A1
MTCM CR4 ....178 E6
Queen Anne's Ga
STJSPK SW1H 16 C3
BXLYHN DA7 ....148 E4
Queen Anne's Gv CHSWK W4 ...117 F2
EA W5 ....117 F2
EN EN1 ....36 A1
ED N9 ....37 H1
Queen Anne's Pl EN EN1 ....24 B6
Queen Anne St CAVSO/HST W1G ..9 J2
Queen Anne Ter WAP E1W * 104 D6
Queen Borough Gdns
CHST BR7 ....185 J2
Queenborough Gdns
GNTH/NBYPK IG2 ....72 A1
Queen Caroline Est
HMSMTH W6 ....119 F5
Queen Caroline St
HMSMTH W6 ....119 F5

Queen Elizabeth Buildings
EMB EC4Y * 11 J5
Queen Elizabeth College
GNWCH SE10 * 145 K1
Queen Elizabeth Gdns
MRDN SM4 ....193 K1
Queen Elizabeth Rd
KUTN/CMB KT2 ....175 G5
WALTH E17 ....51 G6
Queen Elizabeth's Cl
STNW/STAM N16 ....67 K6
Queen Elizabeth's Dr
STHGT/OAK N14 ....34 E3
Queen Elizabeth St STHWK SE1 ..19 J2
Queen Elizabeth's Wk
STNW/STAM N16 ....67 K6
WLGTN SM6 ....210 D2
Queen Elizabeth Wk
BARN SW13 ....138 E2
Queenhithe BLKFR EC4V * 12 D6
Queen Isabella Wy STBT EC1A ..12 B5
Queen Margaret's Gv IS N1 ....86 A3
Queen Mary Av RYNPK SW20..193 G5
Queen Mary Cl ROM RM1 ....75 K5
SURB KT6 ....206 D6
Queen Mary's Av CAR SM5 ....209 K5
Queen Mother Ga
MYFR/PICC W1 * 15 H1
Queens Acre CHEAM SM3 ....208 B5
Queens Av FELT TW13 ....154 B6
FNCH N3 ....47 G3
GFD/PVL UB6 ....96 B5
KTN/HRWW/WS HA3 ....43 H6
MUSWH N10 ....48 A6
TRDG/WHET N20 ....33 H4
WCHMH N21 ....35 H3
WFD IG8 ....53 F1
Queensberry Ms West
SKENS SW7 * 14 A6
Queensberry Pl MNPK E12 ....89 H5
SKENS SW7 ....14 A6
Queensborough Ms
BAY/PAD W2 * 101 G6
Queensborough Studios
BAY/PAD W2 * 101 F6
Queensborough Ter
BAY/PAD W2 ....101 G6
Queensbridge Pk ISLW TW7..155 K1
Queensbridge Rd HACK E8..........86 A1
CDALE/KGS NW9 ....63 G1
Queensbury St IS N1 ....85 J5
Queens Circ VX/NE SW8..........141 G1
Queen's Cl EDGW HA8..........44 C1
ESH/CLAY KT10 * 204 B2
WLGTN SM6 ....210 B3
Queen's Club Gdns
WKENS W14 * 119 H6
Queens Club Ter
WKENS W14 * 119 J6
Queenscourt WBLY HA9..........80 A2
Queen's Crs KTTN NW5..........84 A4
RCHPK/HAM TW10..........137 G6
Queenscroft Rd
ELTH/MOT SE9 ....166 B1
Queensdale Crs NTGHL W11..119 G1
Queensdale Pl NTGHL W11 ....119 J1
Queensdale Rd NTGHL W11..........119 H1
Queensdale Wk NTGHL W11..........119 H1
Queens Down Rd CLPT E5..........86 D2
Queen's Dr BRYLDS KT5..........191 H4
EA W5 ....98 B5
FSBYPK N4 ....69 H4
LEY E10 ....69 J4
THDIT KT7 ....190 B3
Queen's Elm Sq CHEL SW3..........120 C5
Queen's Gdns BAY/PAD W2 ....101 G6
EA W5 ....97 J4
HDN NW4 ....64 A2
HEST TW5 ....134 D2
RAIN RM13 ....111 F1
Queens Garth FSTH SE23 * ..163 K4
Queen's Ga SKENS SW7 ....120 B2
Queen's Gate Gdns CHST BR7..185 J4
Queensgate Gdns
PUT/ROE SW15 ....138 G2
Queen's Gate Gdns
SKENS SW7 ....120 B3
Queen's Gate Ms SKENS SW7 ..120 B3
Queensgate Pl
KIL/WHAMP NW6 ....82 E5
Queen's Gate Pl SKENS SW7 ..120 B3
Queen's Gate Place Ms
SKENS SW7 ....120 B4
Queen's Gate Ter SKENS SW7..120 B3
Queen's Gv STJWD NW8..........2 L1
Queen's Grove Rd CHING E4 ..38 B3
Queen's Head St IS N1 ....6 B1
Queens Keep TWK TW1 * 156 D1
Queensland Av UED N18..........49 J2
WIM/MER SW19..........178 A4
Queensland Cl WALTH E17..........51 H5
Queensland Pl HOLWY N7..........85 G3
Queens La MUSWH N10..........48 B6
Queens Md EDGW HA8..........44 B2
Queensmead STJWD NW8..........83 H6
Queen's Mead Rd HAYES BR2..183 J5
Queensmere Cl
WIM/MER SW19..........159 G4
Queensmere Rd
WIM/MER SW19..........159 G4
Queensmill Rd FUL/PGN SW6..139 G1
Queens Pde
CEND/HSY/T N8 * 82 H1
EA W5 * 98 B5
FBAR/BDGN N11 * 47 K1
FBAR/BDGN N11 * 48 E3
HDN NW4 * 63 K2
Queens Parade Cl
FBAR/BDGN N11 * 47 K1
Queens Park Gdns FELT TW13 ..153 J5
Queen's Pl MRDN SM4..........193 K1
Queens Prom KUT/HW KT1 ..190 E1
Queen Sq BMSBY WC1N..........5 F7

Queen's Ride BARN SW13 ....138 E4
Queen's Ri RCHPK/HAM TW10..157 G1
Queens Rd BAR EN5..........20 B5
BARK IG11 ....90 C5
BECK BR3 ....182 B5
BKHH IG9 ....39 G4
BMLY BR1 ....183 K5
CHST BR7 ....185 G2
CROY/NA CRO..........196 C3
EA W5 ....98 A5
EN EN1 ....24 A5
ERITH DA8..........130 B6
FBAR/BDGN N11 ....48 A1
FELT TW13 ....154 A5
FNCH N3 ....47 G4
HPTN TW12 ....155 H5
HSLW TW3 ....135 G4
HYS/HAR UB3 ....94 C5
KUTN/CMB KT2 ....175 H5
MORT/ESHN SW14..........138 A4
MRDN SM4 ....193 K1
MTCM CR4 ....178 C6
NWDGN UB2 ....114 D4
NWMAL KT3 ....192 C1
PECK SE15 ....143 K2
PLSTW E13 ....89 F6
RCHPK/HAM TW10 ....157 G1
THHTH CR7 ....196 D1
TEDD TW11 ....174 A2
THDIT KT7 ....190 B2
TWK TW1 ....156 A3
WALTH E17 ....69 H3
WAN E11 ....70 C4
WIM/MER SW19..........177 K2
WELL DA16 ....148 C3
WLGTN SM6 ....210 B4
Queen's West PLSTW E13..........106 E1
Queen's Wk WALW SE17..........122 E6
Queen's Ter ISLW TW7..........136 B5
PLSTW E13..........89 F6
STJWD NW8..........2 A1
THDIT KT7 * 190 B3
WCHPL E1 * 104 E3
Queens Terrace Cottages
HNWL W7 * 115 K2
Queensthorpe Ms SYD SE26*..164 A6
Queensthorpe Rd SYD SE26..164 A6
Queenstown Gdns RAIN RM13..111 H2
Queenstown Rd VX/NE SW8..121 G6
Queen St BXLYHN DA7..........149 G4
CROY/NA CRO..........211 J2
ERITH DA8 * 130 B6
MYFR/PICC W1 ....9 J7
ROMW/RG RM7 ....75 J3
STP EC4M 12 E5
TOTM N17 ....50 A2
Queen Street Pl CANST EC4R..12 D6
Queensville Rd BAL SW12..........162 C2
Queens Wk ASHF TW15..........152 A6
CDALE/KGS NW9 ....62 E6
CHING E4 ....38 B3
EA W5 ....97 J3
RSLP HA4 ....77 G1
Queens Walk Ter RSLP HA4 * ..77 G1
The Queens Wk STHWK SE1 ..13 H7
Queensway BAY/PAD W2 ....101 F6
CROY/NA CRO..........211 F4
Queens Wy FELT TW13 ....154 B6
HDN NW4 ....64 A2
Queensway PEND EN3..........24 E5
STMC/STPC BR5..........201 H2
WWKM BR4 ....214 E2
Queens Well Av
TRDG/WHET N20 ....33 J6
Queens Whf HMSMTH W6 ....119 F5
Queenswood Av HPTN TW12..173 G2
HSLW TW3 ....134 E3
THHTH CR7 ....196 B2
WALTH E17 ....52 A4
WLGTN SM6 ....210 D2
Queenswood Gdns WAN E11..........70 D5
Queenswood Pk FNCH N3..........46 C5
Queenswood Rd
BFN/LL DA15 ....168 A1
FSTH SE23 ....164 B5
Queen's Wood Rd HGT N6..........66 B3
Queen's Yd FITZ W1T * 4 B7
Queen Victoria Av
ALP/SUD HA0 ....79 K5
Queen Victoria St BLKFR EC4V ..12 A5
Queen Victoria Ter
WAP E1W * 104 D6
Queensferd Rd HOLWY N7..........85 F3
Quentin Pl LEW SE13..........145 H4
Quentin Rd LEW SE13..........145 H4
Quernmore Cl BMLY BR1..........183 K2
Quernmore Rd BMLY BR1..........183 K2
FSBYPK N4 ....67 G3
Querrin St FUL/PGN SW6..........140 B3
Questor DART DA1 * 171 J4
Quex Ms KIL/WHAMP NW6..........82 E6
Quex Rd KIL/WHAMP NW6..........82 E6
Quick R:t CHSWK W4..........118 B5
Quicks :d IM/MER SW19..........178 A3
Quick Sc IS N1..........6 H1
Quickswood HAMP NW3..........83 J5
Quiet N)ok HAYES BR2..........215 H1
Quill St EA W5..........98 A2
FSBY'K N4..........85 G2
Quilp St STHWK SE1..........18 C2
Quilter Rd STMC/STPC BR5..202 E5
Quilter : t BETH E2..........104 C2
WOOL/PLUM SE18..........128 C4
Quince Rd LEW SE13..........144 E3
Quinnell Cl WOOL/PLUM SE18..128 E5
Quintin Av RYNPK SW20..........177 H4
Quinton Cl BECK BR3..........183 F6
HEST TW5..........113 K6
WLGTN SM6..........210 B2
Quinton Rd THDIT KT7..........190 B5
Quinton St WAND/EARL SW18..160 B4
Quixley St POP/IOD E14..........106 B6
Quorn Rd EDUL SE22..........143 F5

R

Rabbit Rw KENS W8 *..........119 K1
Rabbits Rd MNPK E12..........89 J2
Rabournmead Dr NTHLT UB5..77 J3
Raby Rd NWMAL KT3..........192 A1
Raby St POP/IOD E14 *..........105 G5
Raccoon Wy HSLWW TW4..134 B3
Rachel Cl BARK/HLT IG6..........72 D1
Rackham Cl WELL DA16..........148 C3
Rackham Ms
STRHM/NOR SW16..........179 H2
Racton Rd FUL/PGN SW6..........119 K6
Radbourne Av EA W5..........116 D4
Radbourne Cl CLPT E5..........87 F2
Radbourne Ct
KTN/HRWW/WS HA3 *..........61 H3
Radbourne Crs WALTH E17..........52 B6
Radbourne Rd BAL SW12..........161 H2
Radcliffe Av ENC/FH EN2..........23 J2
WLSDN NW10..........99 J1
Radcliffe Gdns CAR SM5..........209 J5
Radcliffe Rd CROY/NA CRO..197 G6
KTN/HRWW/WS HA3 *..........43 K5
STHWK SE1..........19 H4
WCHMH N21..........35 H3
Radcliffe Sq PUT/ROE SW15..159 G1
Radcliffe Wy NTHLT UB5..........95 H2
Radcot St LBTH SE11..........122 B5
Raddington Rd NKENS W10..100 C4
Radfield Wy BFN/LL DA15..........167 J2
Radford Est WLSDN NW10 *..........99 G2
Radford Rd LEW SE13..........165 F1
Radford Wy BARK IG11..........109 F2
Radipole Rd FUL/PGN SW6..139 J2
Radius Pk EBED/NFELT TW14 *..133 J5
Radland Rd CAN/RD E16..........106 E5
Radlet Av SYD SE26..........163 K5
Radlett Cl FSTGT E7..........88 D4
Radlett Pl STJWD NW8..........2 C1
Radley Av GDMY/SEVK IG3..........91 F2
Radley Cl EBED/NFELT TW14..153 J3
Radley's Md DAGE RM10..........92 D4
Radley Gdns
KTN/HRWW/WS HA3..........62 A1
Radley Ms KENS W8..........119 K3
Radley Rd TOTM N17..........50 A5
Radley's La SWFD E18..........52 E5
Radley Sq CLPT E5 *..........68 E6
Radlix Rd LEY E10..........69 J5
Radnor Av HRW HA1..........60 E2
WELL DA16..........148 C6
Radnor Cl CHST BR7..........185 K2
MTCM CR4..........195 K2
Radnor Crs REDBR IG4..........71 J2
WOOL/PLUM SE18..........148 B1
Radnor Gdns EN EN1..........24 A2
TWK TW1..........156 A4
Radnor Ms BAY/PAD W2..........8 A4
Radnor Pl BAY/PAD W2..........8 C4
Radnor Rd HRW HA1..........60 D2
KIL/WHAMP NW6..........82 C6
PECK SE15..........143 H1
TWK TW1..........156 A4
Radnor St FSBYE EC1V..........6 D5
Radnor Ter WKENS W14..........119 J4
Radnor Wk CHEL SW3..........120 D5
CROY/NA CRO..........198 B4
Radnor Wy WLSDN NW10..........98 D3
Radstock Av
KTN/HRWW/WS HA3..........43 G6
Radstock Cl FBAR/BDGN N11..48 A1
Radstock St BTSEA SW11 *..........140 D1
Raeburn Av BRYLDS KT5..........191 J3
DART DA1..........150 E6
Raeburn Cl CLDGN NW11..........65 G3
KUT/HW KT1..........174 E5
Raeburn Rd BFN/LL DA15..........167 K1
EDGW HA8..........44 C4
YEAD UB4..........94 B1
Raeburn St BRXS/STRHM SW2..141 K5
Ragate Cl SHAC E9..........87 F3
Raggleswood CHST BR7..........185 F4
Rafford Wy BMLY BR1..........184 A5
Ragged Hall La..
Raglan Cl HSLWW TW4..........134 E6
Raglan Ct SAND/SEL CR2..........211 H3
Raglan Gdns OXHEY WD19..........27 F5
Raglan Rd BELV DA17..........129 H3
EN EN1..........36 B2
HAYES BR2..........200 B1
WALTH E17..........70 A2
WOOL/PLUM SE18..........127 H5
Raglan St KTTN NW5..........84 B4
Raglan Vis WALTH E17 *..........70 A2
Ragian Wy NTHLT UB5..........78 C4
Ragley Cl ACT W3..........117 K2
Raider Cl ROMW/RG RM7..........56 D4
Railey Ms KTTN NW5..........84 C3
Railshead Rd ISLW TW7..........136 C5
Railton Rd HNHL SE24..........142 B6
Railway Ap FSBYPK N4..........67 G3
HRW HA1..........61 F1
STHWK SE1..........13 G7
TWK TW1..........156 B2
WFD IG8..........53 G2
WLGTN SM6..........210 B4
Railway Ar BRXN/ST SW9 *..142 B5
Railway Av BERM/RHTH SE16..123 K2
Railway Cottages
HMSMTH W6 *..........119 F2
SRTFD E15 *..........106 C1
WIM/MER SW19 *..........160 A6
Railway Gv NWCR SE14..........144 C1
Railway Pl BELV DA17..........129 H3
Railway Ri EDUL SE22..........143 F5
Railway Rd TEDD TW11..........155 K6
Railway Side BARN SW13..........138 B4
Railway Station Whf LEY E10 *..69 J3
Railway St BCTR RM8..........73 J5
IS N1..........5 G4
Railway Ter FELT TW13..........153 J3
LEW SE13..........144 E6
WALTH E17..........52 A4
Rainborough Cl WBLY HA9..........80 C4

Rainbow Av POP/IOD E14..........124 E5
Rainbow Ct OXHEY WD19..........27 G1
Rainbow Quay
BERM/RHTH SE16..........124 B3
Rainbow St CMBW SE5..........143 F1
Raine St WAP E1W..........123 J1
Rainham Cl BTSEA SW11..........160 E1
ELTH/MOT SE9..........167 K1
Rainham Rd RAIN RM13..........111 J2
WLSDN NW10..........100 A2
Rainham Rd North DAGE RM10..92 D1
Rainham Rd South DAGE RM10..92 E2
Rainhill Wy BOW E3..........105 J2
Rainsborough Av DEPT SE8..124 B5
Rainsford Cl STAN HA7..........43 J1
Rainsford Rd WLSDN NW10..........98 D2
Rainsford Wy HCH RM12..........75 J5
Rainton Rd CHARL SE7..........125 K5
Rainville Rd HMSMTH W6..........119 F6
Raisins Ho PIN HA5..........41 G6
Raith Av STHGT/OAK N14..........34 D5
Raleigh Av WLGTN SM6..........210 D2
YEAD UB4..........95 G4
Raleigh Cl ERITH DA8..........130 C6
HDN NW4..........64 A2
PIN HA5..........59 H4
RSLP HA4..........58 D6
Raleigh Dr BRYLDS KT5..........191 K5
ESH/CLAY KT10..........204 D3
TRDG/WHET N20..........33 J5
Raleigh Gdns
BRXS/STRHM SW2..........162 A1
MTCM CR4..........178 E6
Raleigh Ms IS N1..........6 B1
ORP BR6..........217 F3
Raleigh Rd CEND/HSY/T N8..........67 G1
ENC/FH EN2..........23 K5
FELT TW13..........153 J5
NWDGN UB2..........114 D5
PGE/AN SE20..........182 A3
RCH/KEW TW9..........137 G4
Raleigh St IS N1..........6 B1
Ralph Perring Ct BECK BR3..........198 D1
Ralston St CHEL SW3..........120 E5
Ralston Wy OXHEY WD19..........27 H4
Rama Cl STRHM/NOR SW16..179 J3
Ramac Wy CHARL SE7..........126 A4
Rama La NRWD SE19..........181 G3
Rambler Cl STRHM/NOR SW16..161 H6
Rame Cl TOOT SW17..........179 F1
Ramillies Cl BRXS/STRHM SW2..162 A1
Ramillies Pl SOHO/CST W1F..........10 A4
Ramillies Rd BFN/LL DA15..........168 C1
CHSWK W4..........118 A3
MLHL NW7..........31 G4
Ramillies St SOHO/SHAV W1D..10 A4
Ramones Ter MTCM CR4 *..........195 H1
Rampart St WCHPL E1..........104 D5
Ram Pas KUT/HW KT1..........174 E5
Rampayne St PIM SW1V..........121 J5
Rampton Cl CHING E4..........37 J5
Ramsay Gdns HARH RM3..........57 K4
Ramsay Rd ACT W3..........117 K3
FSTGT E7..........88 E1
Ramscroft Cl ED N9..........36 A2
Ramsdale Rd TOOT SW17..........179 F1
Ramsden Cl STMC/STPC BR5..202 D5
Ramsden Dr CRW RM5..........56 C3
Ramsden Ga BAL SW12 *..........161 G2
Ramsden Rd BAL SW12..........161 F2
ERITH DA8..........130 A1
FBAR/BDGN N11..........47 K1
ORP BR6..........202 C4
Ramsey Cl CDALE/KGS NW9..63 H3
GFD/PVL UB6..........78 D3
Ramsey Rd THHTH CR7..........196 A3
Ramsey St BETH E2..........104 C3
Ramsey Wy STHGT/OAK N14..34 C2
Ramsgate Cl CAN/RD E16..........126 A1
Ramsgate St HACK E8 *..........86 B4
Ramsgill Ap GNTH/NBYPK IG2..73 F1
Ramsgill Dr GNTH/NBYPK IG2..73 F2
Rams Gv CHDH RM6..........74 A1
Ramulis Dr YEAD UB4..........95 J3
Ramus Wood Av ORP BR6..........216 E3
Rancliffe Gdns ELTH/MOT SE9..166 D1
Rancliffe Rd EHAM E6..........107 J1
Randall Av CRICK NW2..........63 G6
Randall Cl BTSEA SW11..........140 D2
ERITH DA8..........129 K6
Randall Rd LBTH SE11..........121 G4
Randall Rw LBTH SE11..........17 G7
Randell's Rd IS N1..........84 E6
Randisbourne Gdns CAT SE6 *..164 E5
Randle Rd RCHPK/HAM TW10..156 D6
Randlesdown Rd CAT SE6..........164 E5
Randolf Rd HAYES BR2..........200 E5
Randolph Ap CAN/RD E16..........107 G5
Randolph Av MV/WKIL W9..........101 F1
Randolph Cl BXLYHN DA7..........149 K4
KUTN/CMB KT2 *..........175 K1
Randolph Crs MV/WKIL W9..........101 F3
Randolph Gdns
KIL/WHAMP NW6..........101 F1
Randolph Gv CHDH RM6..........73 J2
Randolph Ms MV/WKIL W9..........101 G3
Randolph Rd HAYES BR2..........200 E5
STHL UB1..........114 E2
WALTH E17..........69 K2
Randon Cl RYLN/HDSTN HA2..42 B5
Ranelagh Av BARN SW13..........138 D4
FUL/PGN SW6..........139 J4
Ranelagh Cl EDGW HA8..........30 C6
TWK TW1..........136 C5
Ranelagh Dr EDGW HA8..........30 C6
TWK TW1..........136 C5
Ranelagh Gdns CHSWK W4..........137 J1
FUL/PGN SW6..........139 H4
IL IG1..........71 K5
WAN E11..........71 G2
Ranelagh Gv BCVA SW1W..........121 F5
Ranelagh Pl NWMAL KT3..........192 B2

Ranelagh Rd ALP/SUD HA0..........79 K4
EA W5..........116 E2
EHAM E6..........90 A6
PIM SW1V..........121 H5
SRTFD E15..........88 C1
STHL UB1..........114 C1
TOTM N17..........50 B2
WAN E11..........88 C2
WDGN N22..........49 G4
WLSDN NW10..........99 H1
Ranfurly Rd SUT SM1..........193 K6
Rangefield Rd BMLY BR1..........183 H1
Rangemoor Rd
SEVS/STOTM N15..........68 B3
Rangers Rd BKHH IG9..........38 E2
Rangeworth Pl BFN/LL DA15..168 A5
Rangoon St TWRH EC3N *..........13 J4
Rankin Cl CDALE/KGS NW9..........63 G6
Ranleigh Gdns BXLYHN DA7..149 G1
Ranmere St BAL SW12 *..........161 G3
Ranmoor Cl HRW HA1..........60 D1
Ranmoor Gdns HRW HA1..........60 D1
Ranmore Av CROY/NA CRO..212 B1
Ranmore Pth
STMC/STPC BR5..........202 B1
Ranmore Rd BELMT SM2..........208 B6
Rannoch Cl EDGW HA8..........30 D4
Rannoch Rd HMSMTH W6..........119 F6
Rannock Av CDALE/KGS NW9..63 G4
Ransom Cl OXHEY WD19..........27 G2
Ransom Rd CHARL SE7 *..........126 B5
Ranston St CAMTN NW1..........8 C1
Ranulf Rd CRICK NW2..........82 D2
Ranwell Cl BOW E3 *..........87 H6
Ranworth Cl ERITH DA8..........150 B3
Ranworth Rd ED N9..........36 E4
Ranyard Cl CHSGTN KT9..........206 B1
Raphael Av ROM RM1..........57 H6
Raphael Dr THDIT KT7..........190 A5
Raphael St SKENS SW7..........14 E3
Rapier Cl PUR RM19..........131 J4
Rasper Rd TRDG/WHET N20..33 G4
Rastell Av BRXS/STRHM SW2..161 J4
Ratcliffe Cl LEE/GVPK SE12..165 K2
Ratcliffe Cross St WCHPL E1 *..105 F5
Ratcliffe La POP/IOD E14..........105 G5
Ratcliff Rd FSTGT E7..........89 G3
Rathbone Market
CAN/RD E16 *..........106 D4
Rathbone Pl FITZ W1T..........10 C2
Rathbone Sq CROY/NA CRO *..211 J2
Rathbone St CAN/RD E16..........106 D4
FITZ W1T..........10 B2
Rathcoole Gdns
CEND/HSY/T N8..........67 F2
Rathfern Rd CAT SE6..........164 C3
Rathgar Av WEA W13..........116 C1
Rathgar Cl FNCH N3..........46 D5
Rathgar Rd BRXN/ST SW9..........142 C4
Rathmell Dr CLAP SW4..........161 J1
Rathmore Rd CHARL SE7..........126 A5
Rattray Rd BRXS/STRHM SW2..142 B5
Raul Rd PECK SE15..........143 H2
Raveley St KTTN NW5..........84 C2
Ravencourt Rd ELTH/MOT SE9..166 E5
Ravenet St BTSEA SW11..........141 G2
Ravenfield Rd TOOT SW17..........160 E5
Ravenhill Rd PLSTW E13..........89 G6
Ravenna Rd PUT/ROE SW15..139 G6
Ravenoak Wy CHIG IG7..........54 E1
Ravenor Park Rd GFD/PVL UB6..96 B2
Raven Rd SWFD E18..........53 G5
Raven Rw WCHPL E1..........104 D4
Ravens Ait SURB KT6 *..........190 E2
Ravensbourne Av HAYES BR2..183 G4
STWL/WRAY TW19..........152 C3
Ravensbourne Gdns CLAY IG5..54 A4
WEA W13..........97 H4
Ravensbourne Pk CAT SE6..........164 C2
Ravensbourne Park Crs
CAT SE6..........164 B2
Ravensbourne Pl LEW SE13..144 E3
Ravensbourne Rd BMLY BR1..183 K6
CAT SE6..........164 C2
DART DA1..........151 J4
TWK TW1..........156 D1
Ravensbury Av MRDN SM4..........194 B2
Ravensbury Gv MTCM CR4..........194 C1
Ravensbury La MTCM CR4..........194 C1
Ravensbury Rd
STMC/STPC BR5..........202 A1
WAND/EARL SW18..........160 A4
Ravensbury Ter
WAND/EARL SW18..........160 A4
Ravenscar Rd BMLY BR1..........165 H6
SURB KT6..........191 G6
Ravens Cl CDALE/KGS NW9..........45 H5
EN EN1..........24 A4
HAYES BR2..........183 J5
SURB KT6..........190 E3
Ravenscourt Av HMSMTH W6..118 D4
Ravenscourt Cl DEN/HRF UB9..58 A4
Ravenscourt Gdns
HMSMTH W6..........118 C4
Ravenscourt Pk HMSMTH W6..118 C3
Ravenscourt Pl HMSMTH W6..118 E4
Ravenscourt Rd HMSMTH W6..118 E4
STMC/STPC BR5..........186 B6
Ravenscourt Sq HMSMTH W6..118 D3
Ravenscraig Rd
FBAR/BDGN N11..........34 B1
Ravenscroft Av CLDGN NW11..64 D4
WBLY HA9..........62 A5
Ravenscroft Cl CAN/RD E16..........106 E4
Ravenscroft Cottages
BAR EN5 *..........32 C1
Ravenscroft Pk BAR EN5..........20 B5
Ravenscroft Rd BECK BR3..........181 K5
CAN/RD E16..........106 E4
CHSWK W4..........117 K4
Ravenscroft St BETH E2..........7 K3
Ravensdale Av
NFNCH/WDSPK N12..........33 G6
Ravensdale Gdns NRWD SE19..180 D3
Ravensdale Rd HSLWW TW4..134 D4
STNW/STAM N16..........68 B4

Ravensdon St LBTH SE11 122 B5
Ravensfield DAGW RM9 91 K2
Ravensfield Gdns
HOR/WEW KT19 207 G3
Ravenshaw St
KIL/WHAMP NW6 82 D3
Ravenshill CHST BR7 185 G4
Ravenshurst Av HDN NW4 64 A1
Ravenside Cl UED N18 51 F1
Ravenslea Rd BAL SW12 160 E2
Ravensleigh Gdns BMLY BR1 183 K1
Ravensmead Rd HAYES BR2 183 G3
Ravensmede Wy CHSWK W4 118 C4
Ravens Ms LEE/GVPK SE12 * 145 K6
Ravenstone Rd
CDALE/KGS NW9 * 63 H3
CEND/HSY/T N8 49 F6
Ravenstone St BAL SW12 161 F3
Ravens Wy LEE/GVPK SE12 145 K6
Ravenswood BXLY DA5 169 F3
Ravenswood Av SURB KT6 191 G6
WWKM BR4 199 F5
Ravenswood Cl CRW RM5 56 D1
Ravenswood Ct
KUTN/CMB KT2 175 K2
Ravenswood Crs
RYLN/HDSTN HA2 59 K6
WWKM BR4 199 F5
Ravenswood Gdns ISLW TW7 135 K2
Ravenswood Pk NTHWD HA6 40 E2
Ravenswood Rd BAL SW12 161 G2
CROY/NA CR0 211 H1
WALTH E17 70 A1
Ravensworth Rd
ELTH/MOT SE9 166 E6
WLSDN NW10 * 99 K2
Ravey St SDTCH EC2A 7 G6
Ravine Gv WOOL/PLUM SE18 127 K6
Rav Pinter Cl STNW/STAM N16 68 B4
Rawlings Cl BECK BR3 199 F2
ORP BR6 217 F3
Rawlings Crs WBLY HA9 80 E1
Rawlings St CHEL SW3 14 E6
Rawlins Cl FNCH N3 46 C6
SAND/SEL CR2 213 H5
Rawnsley Av MTCM CR4 194 C2
Rawreth Wk IS N1 * 85 J6
Rawson St BTSEA SW11 141 G2
Rawsthorne Cl CAN/RD E16 126 E1
Rawstorne Pl FSBYE EC1V * 6 A4
Rawstorne St FSBYE EC1V 6 A4
Ray Bell Ct BROCKY SE4 * 144 C3
Raydean Rd BAR EN5 20 E6
Raydons Gdns DAGW RM9 92 A2
Raydons Rd DAGW RM9 92 A3
Raydon St ARCH N19 66 B6
Rayfield Cl HAYES BR2 200 D3
Rayford Av LEE/GVPK SE12 165 J2
Rayford Cl DART DA1 151 F6
Ray Gdns BARK IG11 109 G1
STAN HA7 43 H1
Ray Lamb Wy ERITH DA8 150 E1
Rayleas Cl WOOL/PLUM SE18 147 G2
Rayleigh Av TEDD TW11 173 K2
Rayleigh Cl PLMGR N13 35 K5
Rayleigh Ct KUT/HW KT1 175 H5
Rayleigh Ri SAND/SEL CR2 212 A4
Rayleigh Rd CAN/RD E16 126 A1
PLMGR N13 35 J5
WFD IG8 53 G3
WIM/MER SW19 177 J4
Ray Lodge Rd WFD IG8 53 H2
Raymead Av THHTH CR7 196 B2
Raymere Gdns
WOOL/PLUM SE18 147 K1
Raymond Av SWFD E18 52 D6
WEA W13 116 B3
Raymond Buildings
GINN WC1R * 11 H1
Raymond Cl SYD SE26 181 K1
Raymond Rd BECK BR3 198 B1
GNTH/NBYPK IG2 72 D4
PLSTW E13 89 G5
WIM/MER SW19 177 H2
Raymond Wy ESH/CLAY KT10 * 205 G4
Raymouth Rd
BERM/RHTH SE16 123 K4
Rayne Ct SWFD E18 70 D1
Rayners Cl ALP/SUD HA0 79 K3
Rayners Gdns NTHLT UB5 95 F2
Rayners La PIN HA5 59 K2
RYLN/HDSTN HA2 60 A5
Rayner's Rd PUT/ROE SW15 139 H6
Raynes Av WAN E11 71 G4
Raynes Pk RYNPK SW20 177 F5
Raynham Av UED N18 50 C2
Raynham Rd HMSMTH W6 118 E4
UED N18 50 C1
Raynham Ter UED N18 50 C1
Raynor Cl STHL UB1 114 E1
Raynor Pl IS N1 85 J6
Raynton Cl RYLN/HDSTN HA2 59 J5
YEAD UB4 94 D3
Raynton Dr YEAD UB4 94 C1
YEAD UB4 94 D3
Ray Rd CRW RM5 56 D1
E/WMO/HCT KT8 189 G2
Rays Av UED N18 36 E6
Rays Rd UED N18 36 E6
WWKM BR4 199 F4
Ray St CLKNW EC1R 5 K7
Ray Street Br CLKNW EC1R * 5 K7
Raywood Cl HYS/HAR UB3 133 F1
Reachview Cl CAMTN NW1 84 C5
Read Cl THDIT KT7 190 B4
Reading La HACK E8 86 D4
Reading Rd NTHLT UB5 78 B3
SUT SM1 209 G3
Reading Wy MLHL NW7 46 C1
Reads Cl IL IG1 90 B1
Reapers Cl CAMTN NW1 84 D6
Reapers Wy ISLW TW7 135 J6
Reardon Pth WAP E1W 123 J1
Reardon St WAP E1W 123 J1
Reaston St NWCR SE14 143 K1
Reckitt Rd CHSWK W4 118 B5
Record St PECK SE15 123 K6
Recovery St TOOT SW17 178 D1
Recreation Av ROMW/RG RM7 74 E2
Recreation Rd HAYES BR2 183 J5
NWDGN UB2 114 D4
SYD SE26 164 A6
Recreation Wy MTCM CR4 179 K6
Rectar Pl ARCH N19 66 B6
Rector St IS N1 6 C1
Rectory Cl CHING E4 37 J5
DART DA1 150 B5
FNCH N3 46 D4
RYNPK SW20 177 F5
SCUP DA14 168 C6
STAN HA7 43 H2
SURB KT6 190 D6
Rectory Field Crs CHARL SE7 146 B1
Rectory Gdns BECK BR3 * 182 D4
CEND/HSY/T N8 66 E1
CHST BR7 * 185 H4
NTHLT UB5 77 K6
Rectory Gn BECK BR3 182 C4
Rectory Gv CLAP SW4 141 H4
CROY/NA CR0 196 C6
HPTN TW12 154 E6
Rectory La BUSH WD23 28 A1
EDGW HA8 44 C2
SCUP DA14 168 C6
STAN HA7 43 H1
SURB KT6 190 D5
TOOT SW17 179 F1
WLGTN SM6 210 C2
Rectory Orch WIM/MER SW19 159 H6
Rectory Park Av NTHLT UB5 95 K2
Rectory Pl CHST BR7 * 185 H4
WOOL/PLUM SE18 127 F4
Rectory Rd BARN SW13 138 D3
BECK BR3 182 D4
DAGE RM10 92 C5
HAYES BR2 215 H5
HSLWW TW4 134 A3
HYS/HAR UB3 94 E5
MNPK E12 89 K3
NWDGN UB2 114 E3
STNW/STAM N16 68 B6
SUT SM1 208 E1
WALTH E17 69 K1
Rectory Sq WCHPL E1 105 F4
Reculver Ms UED N18 36 C6
Reculver Rd BERM/RHTH SE16 124 A5
Red Anchor Cl CHEL SW3 120 C6
Redan Pl BAY/PAD W2 * 101 F5
Redan St WKENS W14 119 G3
Redan Ter CMBW SE5 142 C3
Red Barracks Rd
WOOL/PLUM SE18 126 E4
Redberry Gv SYD SE26 163 K5
Redbourne Av FNCH N3 46 E4
Redbourne Dr THMD SE28 109 K5
Redbridge Gdns CMBW SE5 143 F1
Redbridge La East REDBR IG4 71 J2
Redbridge La West WAN E11 71 G3
Redburn St CHEL SW3 120 E6
Redbury Cl RAIN RM13 111 K3
Redcar Cl NTHLT UB5 78 B4
Redcar St CMBW SE5 * 142 D1
Redcastle Cl WAP E1W 104 E6
Red Cedars Rd ORP BR6 201 K4
Redchurch St BETH E2 7 J6
Redcliffe Cl ECT SW5 120 A5
Redcliffe Gdns IL IG1 72 A5
WBPTN SW10 120 A5
Redcliffe Ms WBPTN SW10 120 A5
Redcliffe Pl WBPTN SW10 120 B6
Redcliffe Rd WBPTN SW10 120 B6
Redcliffe Sq WBPTN SW10 120 A5
Redcliffe St WBPTN SW10 * 120 A6
Redclose Av MRDN SM4 193 K2
Redclyffe Rd PLSTW E13 89 G6
Redcroft Rd STHL UB1 96 C6
Redcross Wy STHWK SE1 18 D2
Reddings Cl MLHL NW7 31 H6
The Reddings MLHL NW7 31 H5
Reddington Cl SAND/SEL CR2 211 K6
Reddins Rd PECK SE15 143 H1
Reddons Rd BECK BR3 182 B3
Reddy Rd ERITH DA8 130 C6
Rede Pl BAY/PAD W2 100 E5
Redesdale Gdns ISLW TW7 136 B1
Redesdale St CHEL SW3 120 E6
Redfern Av HSLWW TW4 155 F2
Redfern Rd CAT SE6 165 F2
WLSDN NW10 81 G5
Redfield La ECT SW5 119 K4
Redfield Ms ECT SW5 119 K4
Redford Av THHTH CR7 196 A1
WLGTN SM6 210 E4
Redford Cl FELT TW13 153 J4
Redford Wk IS N1 * 85 H6
Redgate Dr HAYES BR2 200 A6
Redgate Ter PUT/ROE SW15 159 G1
Redgrave Cl CROY/NA CR0 197 G3
Redgrave Rd PUT/ROE SW15 139 G5
Redgrave Ter BETH E2 * 104 C2
Redhall Ter EA W5 * 98 C6
Red Hl CHST BR7 185 F1
Redhill Dr EDGW HA8 44 E5
Redhill St CAMTN NW1 3 K4
Red House La BXLYHS DA6 148 E5
Red House Rd CROY/NA CR0 195 J3
Red House Sq IS N1 85 J5
Redington Gdns HAMP NW3 83 F2
Redington Rd HAMP NW3 83 F1
Redland Gdns
E/WMO/HCT KT8 * 188 E1
Redlands Rd PEND EN3 25 G2
Redlands Wy
BRXS/STRHM SW2 161 K2
Red La ESH/CLAY KT10 205 G4
Redleaf Cl BXLYHN DA7 129 H6
Redlees Cl ISLW TW7 136 B5
Red Lion Cl STMC/STPC BR5 202 D3
WALW SE17 122 E6
Red Lion Ct FLST/FETLN EC4A 11 K3
HSLW TW3 * 135 G4
Red Lion Hl EFNCH N2 47 H5
Red Lion La WOOL/PLUM SE18 147 F2
Red Lion Pde PIN HA5 * 41 J6
Red Lion Pl
WOOL/PLUM SE18 * 147 F2
Red Lion Rd SURB KT6 191 H6
Red Lion Rw CMBW SE5 122 D6
Red Lion Sq GINN WC1R 11 G2
WAND/EARL SW18 * 139 K6
Red Lion St GINN WC1R 11 G2
RCH/KEW TW9 136 E6
Red Lion Yd MYFR/PKLN W1K * 9 H7
Red Lodge Crs BXLY DA5 170 B5
Red Lodge Rd BXLY DA5 170 A5
WWKM BR4 199 F5
Redman Cl NTHLT UB5 95 G1
Redman's Rd WCHPL E1 104 E4
Redmead La WAP E1W 123 H1
Redmead Rd HYS/HAR UB3 113 H4
Redmore Rd HMSMTH W6 * 118 E4
Red Oak Cl ORP BR6 216 B1
Red Pl MYFR/PKLN W1K 9 G5
Redpoll Wy ERITHM DA18 128 E3
Red Post Hl HNHL SE24 142 E6
Redriffe Rd PLSTW E13 106 D1
Redriff Rd BERM/RHTH SE16 124 B3
ROMW/RG RM7 56 D5
Redroofs Cl BECK BR3 182 E4
Redruth Cl WDGN N22 49 F3
Redruth Rd HOM E9 86 E6
Redstart Cl EHAM E6 107 J4
NWCR SE14 * 144 B1
Redston Rd CEND/HSY/T N8 66 D1
Redvers Rd WDGN N22 49 G5
Redvers St IS N1 7 H4
Redwald Rd CLPT E5 87 F2
Redway Dr WHTN TW2 155 H2
Redwing Ct ORP BR6 202 B4
Redwing Ms CMBW SE5 142 D3
Redwing Rd WLGTN SM6 210 E5
Redwood Cl BERM/RHTH SE16 124 B1
BFN/LL DA15 168 B3
BOW E3 105 J1
OXHEY WD19 27 G6
STHGT/OAK N14 34 D2
Redwood Gdns CHIG IG7 55 G1
CHING E4 * 37 K2
Redwood Gv EA W5 116 D3
Redwood Ms VX/NE SW8 141 G4
Redwood Wy BAR EN5 20 B6
Reece Ms SKENS SW7 14 A6
Reed Av ORP BR6 216 E1
Reed Cl CAN/RD E16 106 E4
LEE/GVPK SE12 145 K6
Reede Rd DAGE RM10 92 C4
Reede Wy DAGE RM10 92 D4
Reedham Cl TOTM N17 68 D1
Reedham St PECK SE15 * 143 H3
Reedholm Vls STNW/STAM N16 85 K2
Reed Pl CLAP SW4 141 J5
Reed Pond Wk GPK RM2 57 J5
Reed Rd TOTM N17 50 B6
Reedsfield Cl ASHF TW15 152 E5
Reedsfield Rd ASHF TW15 152 E6
Reed's Pl CAMTN NW1 84 C5
Reedworth St LBTH SE11 17 K7
Reenglass Rd STAN HA7 * 29 K6
Rees Dr STAN HA7 30 A6
Rees Gdns CROY/NA CR0 197 G3
Reesland Cl MNPK E12 90 A4
Rees St IS N1 6 D1
Reets Farm Cl CDALE/KGS NW9 63 G3
Reeves Av CDALE/KGS NW9 63 F4
Reeves Cnr CROY/NA CR0 196 C6
Reeves Ms MYFR/PKLN W1K 9 G6
Reeves Rd BOW E3 105 K3
WOOL/PLUM SE18 127 G6
Reform Rw TOTM N17 50 B5
Reform St BTSEA SW11 140 E3
Regal Cl EA W5 97 K4
WCHPL E1 104 C4
Regal Ct MTCM CR4 178 E6
UED N18 50 B1
Regal Crs WLGTN SM6 210 B1
Regal Dr FBAR/BDGN N11 48 B1
Regal La CAMTN NW1 3 H1
Regal Rw PECK SE15 143 K2
Regal Wy KTN/HRWW/WS HA3 62 A3
Regan Wy IS N1 7 G3
Regarder Rd CHIG IG7 55 H1
Regarth Av ROM RM1 75 G3
Regency Cl CHIG IG7 54 C1
EA W5 98 A5
HPTN TW12 172 E1
Regency Ct EN EN1 23 K6
Regency Crs HDN NW4 46 B5
Regency Dr RSLP HA4 58 C5
Regency Gdns WOT/HER KT12 188 C5
Regency Lawn KTTN NW5 * 84 B1
Regency Ms BECK BR3 183 F4
WLSDN NW10 81 J4
Regency Pde HAMP NW3 * 83 H5
Regency Pl WEST SW1P * 16 C6
Regency St WEST SW1P 16 D7
Regency Ter HGT N6 * 65 K3
SEVS/STOTM N15 68 A2
SKENS SW7 * 120 C5
Regency Wk CROY/NA CR0 198 B3
Regency Wy BXLYHS DA6 148 E4
Regeneration Rd
BERM/RHTH SE16 124 A4
Regent Cl HSLWW TW4 134 A2
KTN/HRWW/WS HA3 62 A3
NFNCH/WDSPK N12 47 G1
Regent Gdns GDMY/SEVK IG3 73 G3
Regent Pde BELMT SM2 * 209 G4
STNW/STAM N16 * 68 B4
Regent Pl CROY/NA CR0 197 G5
WIM/MER SW19 178 B1
Regent Rd BRYLDS KT5 191 G2
HNHL SE24 162 C1
Regents Av PLMGR N13 49 G1
Regents Bridge Gdns
VX/NE SW8 121 K6
Regents Cl SAND/SEL CR2 212 A4
YEAD UB4 94 C4
Regents Dr HAYES BR2 215 H3
WFD IG8 54 A3
Regents Ms STJWD NW8 101 G1
Regent's Park Rd CAMTN NW1 84 A6
FNCH N3 64 D1
Regent's Park Ter CAMTN NW1 84 B6
Regents Pl LOU IG10 39 H2
Regents Plaza
KIL/WHAMP NW6 * 101 F1
Regent Sq BELV DA17 129 J4
BOW E3 105 K2
STPAN WC1H 5 F5
Regent's Rw BETH E2 86 C6
Regent St CHSWK W4 117 H5
REGST W1B 10 A4
WLSDN NW10 100 B2
Regents Whf IS N1 * 5 G2
Regent Whf IS N1 * 5 G2
Reginald Rd DEPT SE8 144 D1
FSTGT E7 88 E5
NTHWD HA6 40 D4
Reginald Sq DEPT SE8 144 D1
Regina Rd FSBYPK N4 67 F5
NWDGN UB2 114 D4
SNWD SE25 181 H6
WEA W13 116 B1
Regina Ter WEA W13 116 B1
Regis Rd KTTN NW5 84 B3
Regnart Buildings CAMTN NW1 4 B5
Reid Cl HYS/HAR UB3 94 C5
PIN HA5 40 E6
Reidhaven Rd
WOOL/PLUM SE18 127 K4
Reigate Av SUT SM1 194 A5
Reigate Rd BMLY BR1 165 K5
GDMY/SEVK IG3 73 F6
Reigate Wy WLGTN SM6 210 E3
Reighton Rd CLPT E5 86 C1
Reinckendorf Av
ELTH/MOT SE9 147 H6
Reizel Cl STNW/STAM N16 68 B5
Relay Rd SHB W12 100 A6
Relf Rd PECK SE15 143 H4
Reliance Ar BRXN/ST SW9 * 142 B5
Reliance Sq SDTCH EC2A 7 H6
Relton Ms SKENS SW7 14 D4
Rembrandt Cl BGVA SW1W * 121 F5
POP/IOD E14 125 G3
Rembrandt Ct HOR/WEW KT19 207 H4
Rembrandt Rd EDGW HA8 * 44 C5
LEW SE13 145 H5
Rembrandt Wy
WOT/HER KT12 188 A6
Remington Rd EHAM E6 107 J5
SEVS/STOTM N15 67 K3
Remington St FSBYE EC1V 6 B3
Remnant St HOL/ALD WC2B 11 G3
Remus Rd BOW E3 87 J5
Rendle Cl CROY/NA CR0 197 G2
Rendlesham Rd CLPT E5 86 C2
ENC/FH EN2 23 H2
Renforth St BERM/RHTH SE16 123 K3
Renfrew Cl EHAM E6 108 A6
Renfrew Rd HSLWW TW4 134 C3
KUTN/CMB KT2 175 K3
LBTH SE11 18 A6
Renmuir St TOOT SW17 178 E2
Rennell St LEW SE13 145 F4
Renness Rd WALTH E17 51 G6
Rennets Cl ELTH/MOT SE9 147 J6
Rennets Wood Rd
ELTH/MOT SE9 147 J6
Rennie Cl ASHF TW15 152 A5
Rennie Est BERM/RHTH SE16 123 J4
Rennie St STHWK SE1 12 A7
Renown Cl CROY/NA CR0 196 C5
ROMW/RG RM7 56 C4
Rensburg Rd WALTH E17 69 F2
Rensburg Vls WALTH E17 * 69 F2
Renshaw Cl BELV DA17 129 G6
Renters Av HDN NW4 64 A3
Renton Cl BRXS/STRHM SW2 * 162 A1
Renton Dr STMC/STPC BR5 202 E4
Renwick Rd BARK IG11 109 H3
Repens Wy YEAD UB4 95 H3
Rephidim St STHWK SE1 19 G5
Replingham Rd
WAND/EARL SW18 159 J3
Reporton Rd FUL/PGN SW6 139 H2
Repository Rd
WOOL/PLUM SE18 126 E6
Repton Av ALP/SUD HA0 79 J2
GPK RM2 57 J6
HYS/HAR UB3 113 G4
Repton Cl CAR SM5 209 J3
Repton Ct BECK BR3 182 E4
Repton Dr GPK RM2 75 J1
Repton Gdns GPK RM2 57 J6
Repton Gv CLAY IG5 53 K4
Repton Rd KTN/HRWW/WS HA3 62 B1
ORP BR6 217 G2
Repton St POP/IOD E14 105 G5
Repulse Cl CRW RM5 56 D4
Reservoir Cl THHTH CR7 180 E6
Reservoir Rd BROCKY SE4 144 B3
RSLP HA4 58 A2
STHGT/OAK N14 22 C6
Resham Cl NWDGN UB2 114 B3
Resolution Wy DEPT SE8 144 D1
Restell Cl BKHTH/KID SE3 125 H6
Restmor Wy CAR SM5 195 F6
Reston Pl KENS W8 120 B2
Restons Crs ELTH/MOT SE9 167 J1
Reston Wy CAN/RD E16 107 H6
Restormel Cl HSLW TW3 135 F6
Retford St BETH E2 7 J4
Retingham Wy CHING E4 37 K4
Retreat Cl KTN/HRWW/WS HA3 61 J2
Retreat Pl HOM E9 86 E4
Retreat Rd RCH/KEW TW9 136 E6
The Retreat BRYLDS KT5 191 G3
CDALE/KGS NW9 63 F2
MORT/ESHN SW14 138 B4
ORP BR6 217 H4
RYLN/HDSTN HA2 60 A4
THHTH CR7 196 E1
WPK KT4 192 E6
Reunion Rw WAP E1W * 104 D6
Reveley Sq BERM/RHTH SE16 124 B2
Revell Ri WOOL/PLUM SE18 128 A6
Revell Rd KUT/HW KT1 175 J5
SUT SM1 208 D4
Revelon Rd BROCKY SE4 144 B5
Revelstoke Rd
WAND/EARL SW18 159 K4
WIM/MER SW19 159 H6
WIM/MER SW19 178 B2
Reventlow Rd ELTH/MOT SE9 167 H3
Reverdy Rd STHWK SE1 123 H4
Reverend Cl RYLN/HDSTN HA2 78 B1
Revere Wy HOR/WEW KT19 207 G6
Revesby Rd CAR SM5 194 D3
Review Rd CRICK NW2 63 H6
DAGE RM10 110 D1
Rewell St FUL/PGN SW6 * 140 B1
Rewley Rd CAR SM5 194 C3
Rex Pl MYFR/PKLN W1K 9 H7
Reydon Av WAN E11 71 G3
Reynard Cl BMLY BR1 184 E6
Reynard Dr NRWD SE19 181 G3
Reynard Pl NWCR SE14 * 124 B6
Reynardson Rd TOTM N17 49 J3
Reynola Gdns CHARL SE7 126 A5
Reynolds Av CHDH RM6 73 J4
CHSGTN KT9 206 A5
MNPK E12 90 A3
Reynolds Cl CAR SM5 194 E5
GLDGN NW11 65 F4
WIM/MER SW19 178 C4
Reynolds Dr EDGW HA8 44 B6
Reynolds Pl BKHTH/KID SE3 146 A1
RCHPK/HAM TW10 157 G1
Reynolds Rd CHSWK W4 117 K3
NWMAL KT3 192 A4
PECK SE15 143 K6
YEAD UB4 95 G3
Reynolds Wy CROY/NA CR0 212 A2
Rheidol Ms IS N1 6 C2
Rheidol Ter IS N1 6 B2
Rheingold Wy WLGTN SM6 210 E6
Rheola Cl TOTM N17 50 B4
Rhoda St BETH E2 7 K6
Rhodes Av WDGN N22 48 C4
Rhodesia Rd BRXN/ST SW9 141 K3
WAN E11 70 B6
Rhodes St HOLWY N7 85 F3
Rhodeswell Rd POP/IOD E14 105 H4
Rhodrons Av CHSGTN KT9 206 A3
Rhondda Gv BOW E3 105 G2
Rhyl Rd GFD/PVL UB6 97 F1
Rhyl St KTTN NW5 84 A4
Rhys Av FBAR/BDGN N11 48 D3
Rialto Rd MTCM CR4 179 F5
Ribble Cl WFD IG8 53 G2
Ribblesdale Av
FBAR/BDGN N11 47 K2
NTHLT UB5 78 B4
Ribblesdale Rd CEND/HSY/T N8 67 F1
STRHM/NOR SW16 179 G1
Ribbon Dance Ms CMBW SE5 142 E2
Ribchester Av GFD/PVL UB6 97 F2
Ribston Cl HAYES BR2 200 E5
Ricardo St POP/IOD E14 105 K5
Ricards Rd WIM/MER SW19 177 J1
Rice Pde STMC/STPC BR5 * 201 J2
Richard Cl WOOL/PLUM SE18 126 D4
Richard House Dr CAN/RD E16 107 H5
Richards Av ROMW/RG RM7 74 E3
Richards Cl BUSH WD23 28 D2
HRW HA1 61 G2
HYS/HAR UB3 113 G6
Richards Cottages CAR SM5 * 209 K3
Richards Fld HOR/WEW KT19 207 F6
Richardson Cl HACK E8 * 86 B6
Richardson Gdns DAGE RM10 92 D4
Richardson Rd SRTFD E15 * 106 C1
Richardson's Ms FITZ W1T 4 A7
Richard's Pl CHEL SW3 14 D6
WALTH E17 51 J6
Richard St WCHPL E1 104 D5
Richbell Pl BMSBY WC1N 11 G1
Richborne Ter VX/NE SW8 142 A1
Richborough Cl
STMC/STPC BR5 202 E1
Richborough Rd CRICK NW2 82 C2
Richens Cl HSLW TW3 135 J3
Riches Rd IL IG1 72 C6
Richfield Rd BUSH WD23 28 D3
Richford Ga HMSMTH W6 * 119 F3
Richford Rd SRTFD E15 88 D6
Richford St HMSMTH W6 119 F2
Richlands Av EW KT17 207 J3
Richmer Rd ERITH DA8 150 D1
Richmond Av CHING E4 52 B1
EBED/NFELT TW14 153 H1
IS N1 85 F6
RYNPK SW20 177 H4
Richmond Br TWK TW1 136 E6
Richmond Buildings
SOHO/SHAV W1D 10 C4
Richmond Cl WALTH E17 69 H3
Richmond Crs CHING E4 52 B1
ED N9 36 C3
IS N1 85 F6
Richmond Dr WFD IG8 54 A3
Richmond Gdns HDN NW4 63 J2
KTN/HRWW/WS HA3 43 F3
Richmond Gn CROY/NA CR0 210 E1
Richmond Gv IS N1 85 H5
Richmond Hl
RCHPK/HAM TW10 157 F1
Richmond Ms SOHO/CST W1F 10 C4
Richmond Pde TWK TW1 * 156 D1
Richmond Park Rd
KUTN/CMB KT2 175 F3
MORT/ESHN SW14 138 A5
Richmond Pl
WOOL/PLUM SE18 127 H4
Richmond Rd BAR EN5 21 G6
CHING E4 * 38 B3
CROY/NA CR0 210 E1
EA W5 117 F2
EFNCH N2 * 47 G5
FBAR/BDGN N11 48 E2
FSTGT E7 89 F3
HACK E8 86 B5
IL IG1 90 C1
ISLW TW7 136 B5

KUTN/CMB KT2 ....174 E1
ROM RM1..........................75 H5
RYNPK SW20.....................176 A4
SEVS/STOTM N15...............68 A5
THHTH CR7 ....196 C1
TWK TW1 ....156 C2
WAN E11 ....70 B6
Richmond St PLSTW E13 ....106 B1
Richmond Ter WHALL SW1A ...17 F2
Richmond Vls WALTH E17 * 51 K4
Richmond Wy SHB W12 ....119 G2
WAN E11 ....70 E6
Richmount Gdns
BKHTH/KID SE14 ....145 K4
Rich St POP/IOD E14..........105 H5
Rickard Cl BRXS/STRHM SW2 ..162 B1
Rickards Cl SURB KT6 ....191 F6
Rickett St FUL/PGN SW6 .....119 K6
Rickman St WCHPL E1..........104 E3
Rickmansworth Rd
NTHWD HA6 ....40 B3
PIN HA5.............................41 F5
Rick Roberts Wy SRTFD E15 ..106 B1
Rickthorne Rd ARCH N19 ......66 E6
Ridding La GFD/PVL UB6.......79 F3
Riddons Rd LEE/GVPK SE12 ...166 B5
Rideout St WOOL/PLUM SE18 126 E4
Rider Cl BFN/LL DA15.........167 K1
The Ride BTFD TW8............116 C5
PEND EN3 ....24 E4
Ridgdale St BOW E3...........105 K1
Ridge Av DART DA1...........170 C1
WCHMH N21........................35 J2
Ridgebrook Rd
BKHTH/KID SE3 ....146 B5
Ridge Cl CDALE/KGS NW9 ......45 H1
HDN NW4 ....46 B5
THMD SE28 ....127 J2
Ridge Crest ENC/FH EN2 ......23 F2
Ridgecroft Cl BXLY DA5........169 K3
Ridge Hl GLDGN NW11 ....64 C5
Ridgemead Cl STHGT/OAK N14 ..34 E4
Ridgemont Gdns EDGW HA8 ....30 E6
Ridgemount Av CROY/NA CRO..198 B6
Ridgemount Gdns ENC/FH EN2 23 F1
Ridge Rd CEND/HSY/T N8.......67 F3
CHEAM SM3 ....193 J5
CRICK NW2 ....82 D1
MTCM CR4........................179 G3
WCHMH N21........................35 K3
Ridges Yd CROY/NA CRO.......211 H1
Ridge Ter WCHMH N21 * 35 J2
The Ridge BAR EN5 * 20 D6
BRYLDS KT5 ....191 H2
BXLY DA5 ....169 F2
ORP BR6 ....201 J6
WHTN TW2 ....155 J2
Ridgeview Cl BAR EN5 ....32 B1
Ridgeview Rd TRDG/WHET N20 ..33 F5
Ridge Wy DART DA1 ....170 C1
FELT TW13 ....154 D5
Ridgeway HAYES BR2...........199 K6
WFD IG8.............................39 G6
Ridgeway Crs ORP BR6 ....216 E1
Ridgeway Crescent Gdns
ORP BR6...........................201 K6
Ridgeway Dr BMLY BR1.........166 A6
Ridgeway East BFN/LL DA15 ..148 A6
Ridgeway Gdns HGT N6.........66 C4
REDBR IG4 ....71 J2
Ridgeway Rd ISLW TW7........135 K1
Ridgeway Rd North ISLW TW7..135 K1
The Ridgeway ACT W3..........117 H3
CDALE/KGS NW9 ....63 F1
CHING E4...........................37 K3
CROY/NA CRO...................211 F1
ENC/FH EN2 ....23 C2
FBAR/BDGN N11 ....33 K6
FNCH N3.............................52 E1
GLDGN NW11 ....64 D5
GPK RM2............................75 J1
KTN/HRWW/WS HA3 ....61 J3
MLHL NW7 ....31 K6
RSLP HA4 ....58 E2
RYLN/HDSTN HA2 ....59 K2
STHGT/OAK N14 ....34 E4
Ridgeway West BFN/LL DA15 ..147 K6
Ridgewell Cl DAGE RM10........92 D6
IS N1.................................5 H5
SYD SE26..........................164 C6
Ridgmount Gdns GWRST WC1E ..10 C1
Ridgmount Rd
WAND/EARL SW18 ....140 A6
Ridgmount St GWRST WC1E ...10 C1
Ridgway RCHPK/HAM TW10 * ..157 F1
WIM/MER SW19..................177 G2
Ridgway Gdns
WIM/MER SW19 ....177 G3
Ridgway Pl WIM/MER SW19 ...177 H2
Ridgway Rd BRXN/ST SW9 .....142 C4
The Ridgway BELMT SM2 ......209 H5
Ridgwell Rd CAN/RD E16.......107 G4
Ridings Av STHGT/OAK N14 .....22 H5
Ridings Cl HGT N6..............66 C4
The Ridings BRYLDS KT5.......191 H2
EA W5.................................98 B3
EBAR EN4 * 33 J2
EW KT17 ....207 H6
The Riding GLDGN NW11.......64 D4
Ridler Rd EN EN1 ....24 A1
Ridley Av WEA W13 ....116 C3
Ridley Cl BARK IG11............91 F5
HARH RM3 ....57 K4
Ridley Rd FSTGT E7 ....89 G2
HACK E8.............................86 B3
HAYES BR2.......................183 J6
WELL DA16.......................148 C2
WIM/MER SW19..................178 A3
WLSDN NW10 ....99 J1
Ridsdale Rd PGE/AN SE20.....181 J4
Riefield Rd ELTH/MOT SE9 ....147 H5

Riesco Dr CROY/NA CRO........212 E4
Riffel Rd CRICK NW2 ....82 A3
Rifle Pl NTGHL W11.............119 G1
Rifle Range La HRW HA1 * 61 F5
Rifle St POP/IOD E14...........105 K4
Rigault Rd FUL/PGN SW6 ......139 J3
Rigby Cl CROY/NA CRO.........211 G1
Rigby La HYS/HAR UB3.........113 G2
Rigby Ms IG IG1..................90 B6
Rigden St POP/IOD E14.........105 K5
Rigeley Rd WLSDN NW10 ....99 J2
Rigg Ap LEY E10 ....69 F5
Rigge Pl CLAP SW4..............141 J5
Riggindale Rd
STRHM/NOR SW16 ....179 J1
Right Side STHGT/OAK N14 * ...34 D5
Riley Rd PEND EN3 ....24 E1
STHWK SE1 ....19 J4
Riley St WBPTN SW10..........140 C1
Rinaldo Rd BAL SW12 ....161 G2
Ring Cl BMLY BR1...............184 A3
Ringcroft St HOLWY N7 ....85 G3
Ringer's Rd BMLY BR1..........183 K6
Ringford Rd
WAND/EARL SW18 ....139 J6
Ringlet Cl CAN/RD E16.........107 F5
Ringlewell Cl EN EN1............24 D3
Ringmer Av FUL/PGN SW6 ......139 H2
Ringmer Pl WCHMH N21 ....35 K1
Ringmer Wy BMLY BR1.........200 E2
Ringmore Ri FSTH SE23........163 J2
Ringshall Rd STMC/STPC BR5..186 B6
Ringslade Rd WDGN N22 ....49 F5
Ringstead Rd CAT SE6 ....164 E2
SUT SM1...........................209 H2
Ring Wy FBAR/BDGN N11 ....48 C2
Ringway NWDGN UB2 ....114 D5
Ringwold Cl BECK BR3.........182 B3
Ringwood Av CROY/NA CRO.....195 K4
ENFCH N2...........................47 K6
Ringwood Cl PIN HA5 * 41 G6
Ringwood Gdns
PUT/ROE SW15 ....158 D4
Ringwood Rd WALTH E17........69 H5
Ringwood Wy HPTN TW12......155 F6
WCHMH N21........................35 H2
Ripley Cl BMLY BR1.............200 E2
CROY/NA CRO...................214 A4
Ripley Gdns MORT/ESHN SW14 ..138 A4
Ripley Ms WAN E11...............70 C3
Ripley Rd BELV DA17...........129 H4
CAN/RD E16.......................107 G5
ENC/FH EN2 ....23 J2
GDMY/SEVK IG3 ....72 E2
HPTN TW12.......................173 F3
Ripley Vis EA W5 * 97 J5
Ripon Cl NTHLT UB5 ....78 A4
Ripon Gdns CHSGTN KT9.......205 K3
IG IG1................................90 A2
Ripon Rd ED N9..................36 D2
TOTM N17 ....67 K1
WOOL/PLUM SE18 ....127 G6
Rippersley Rd WELL DA16......148 B2
Ripple Rd BARK IG11 ....90 C5
BARK IG11.........................90 C5
DAGW RM9........................91 J6
Ripplevale Gv IS N1 ....85 F5
Rippolson Rd
WOOL/PLUM SE18 ....128 A5
Risborough Cl MUSWH N10 * ...48 B6
Risborough Dr WPK KT4 ....192 D4
Risborough St STHWK SE1 ......18 B2
Risdon St BERM/RHTH SE16 ...123 K2
Risebridge Cha ROM RM1......57 H3
Risebridge Rd GPK RM2..........57 H5
Risedale Rd BXLYHN DA7 ......149 J4
Rise Park Gdns ROM RM1 * 57 G5
Rise Park Bvd ROM RM1........57 G4
Rise Park Pde ROM RM1 * 57 G5
The Rise BKHH IG9...............39 H3
BXLY DA5 ....168 D2
DART DA1..........................150 C5
EDGW HA8 ....44 D1
GFD/PVL UB6......................79 G3
MLHL NW7 ....45 H2
PLMGR N13 ....35 G6
SAND/SEL CR2 ....212 E6
WAN E11.............................70 C2
WLSDN NW10 ....81 F3
Rising Hill Cl NTHWD HA6 * 40 A2
Risinghill St IS N1 ....5 J2
Risingholme Cl BUSH WD23....28 B2
KTN/HRWW/WS HA3 ....42 E2
Risinghome Rd
KTN/HRWW/WS HA3 ....42 E5
The Risings WALTH E17 ....70 B1
Risley Av TOTM N17 ....49 J4
Rita Rd VX/NE SW8 ....141 K1
Ritches Rd SEVS/STOTM N15 ..67 J2
Ritchie Rd CROY/NA CRO.......198 B3
Ritchie St IS N1..................5 K2
Ritchings Av WALTH E17.........69 G1
Ritherdon Rd TOOT SW17......161 F4
Ritson Rd HACK E8..............86 C4
Ritter St WOOL/PLUM SE18 ...127 F6
Rivaz Pl HOM E9.................86 E4
Rivenhall Gdns SWFD E18......70 D1
River Av PLMGR N13 ....35 H5
THDIT KT7.........................190 B3
Riverbank E/WMO/HCT KT8...173 K5
River Bank THDIT KT7...........190 A2
WCHMH N21........................35 J2
Riverbank Rd BMLY BR1........165 K5
Riverbank Wy BTFD TW8.......116 D6
River Barge Cl POP/IOD E14 ...125 F2
River Cl NWDGN UB2...........115 H2
RAIN RM13 ....111 K4
RSLP HA4 ....58 D3
WAN E11.............................71 G5
River Ct PUR RM19..............131 J4
Rivercourt Rd HMSMTH W6 ...118 E4
Riverdale Dr
WAND/EARL SW18 ....160 A3
Riverdale Gdns TWK TW1......136 D6
Riverdale Rd BXLY DA5.........169 G2
ERITH DA8........................129 J5

FELT TW13........................154 D6
Felt TW1...........................156 D1
WOOL/PLUM SE18 ....128 A5
Riverdene EDGW HA8............30 E3
Riverdene Rd IL IG1..............90 A1
River Front EN EN1...............23 K4
River Gdns CAR SM5...........195 F6
EBED/NFELT TW14 ....153 K2
River Grove Pk BECK BR3......182 C4
Riverhead Cl WALTH E17.........51 F5
Riverholme Dr
HOR/WEW KT19 ....207 F6
River La RCHPK/HAM TW10....156 D3
Rivermead E/WMO/HCT KT8...173 H6
Rivermead Cl TEDD TW11......174 C1
Rivermead Rd UED N18 * 51 F1
River Meads Av WHTN TW2....155 G5
Rivernook Cl WOT/HER KT12..188 B2
Riverpark Gdns HAYES BR2....183 G5
River Park Rd WDGN N22........49 F5
River Park Vw ORP BR6........202 C4
River Pl IS N1.....................85 J5
River Reach TEDD TW11........174 D2
River Rd BARK IG11.............108 E1
BKHH IG9............................39 J3
Riversdale Rd CRW RM5.........56 D3
HBRY N5.............................85 H1
THDIT KT7.........................190 B2
Riversfield Rd EN EN1............24 A4
Riverside CHARL SE7 ....126 A3
HDN NW4 ....63 K4
RCH/KEW TW9 *..................136 E6
SUN TW16 *.......................172 C5
TWK TW1 * 156 C3
Riverside Av E/WMO/HCT KT8..189 J2
Riverside Cl CLPT E5............68 E5
HNWL W7.........................115 K4
KUT/HW KT1.....................190 E1
STMC/STPC BR5.................186 D5
WLGTN SM6 ....210 B1
Riverside Ct CHING E4 * 37 K1
Riverside Dr CHSWK W4........137 K2
ESH/CLAY KT10..................204 A2
GLDGN NW11 *....................64 C3
MTCM CR4........................194 D2
RCHPK/HAM TW10..............156 B3
Riverside Gdns ALP/SUD HA0...98 A1
ENC/FH EN2 ....23 J3
HMSMTH W6 *....................118 E5
Riverside Ms CROY/NA CRO * ..210 E1
Riverside Pl FBAR/BDGN N11 * ..34 C5
STWL/WRAY TW19 ....152 A1
Riverside Rd IL IG1..............90 B1
OXHEY WD19....................27 H1
SCUP DA14........................169 F5
SEVS/STOTM N15...............68 C2
SRTFD E15 ....105 K1
STWL/WRAY TW19 ....132 A6
TOOT SW17 ....160 A6
The Riverside
E/WMO/HCT KT8 ....173 J6
Riverside Vs SURB KT6 * 190 D5
Riverside Wk ISLW TW7.........135 K4
KUT/HW KT1.....................174 E5
Riverside Wy DART DA1........151 H6
Riverside Yd TOOT SW17 * 160 A5
Riverstone Cl RYLN/HDSTN HA2 ..60 D6
River Ter HMSMTH W6..........119 F5
Riverton Cl MV/WKIL W9 * 100 D2
River View Gdns TWK TW1.....156 A4
Riverview Gv CHSWK W4........117 J6
Riverview Pk CAT SE6...........164 D4
Riverview Rd CHSWK W4........137 J1
HOR/WEW KT19 ....206 E2
River Wk SUN TW16.............172 B5
River Wy GNWCH SE10..........125 J3
HOR/WEW KT19 ....207 F3
WHTN TW2........................155 G4
Riverway PLMGR N13 ....49 G1
Riverwood La CHST BR7.........185 J5
Rivington Av WFD IG8............53 H5
Rivington Crs MLHL NW7.........45 H3
Rivington Pl FSBYE EC1V * 7 H5
Rivington St SDTCH EC2A.........7 H5
Rivington Wk HACK E8............86 C6
Rivulet Rd TOTM N17.............49 J3
Rixon Rd HOLWY N7..............85 G1
Rixsen Rd MNPK E12.............89 J3
Roach Rd BOW E3................87 J5
Roads Pl ARCH N19..............66 E6
Roan St GNWCH SE10..........125 F6
Robarts Cl PIN HA5...............59 F2
Robb Rd STAN HA7................43 G2
Robert Adam St MHST W1U......9 G3
Robert Cl CHIG IG7 * 55 F1
Robert Cl CHIG IG7................55 F1
MV/WKIL W9 *...................101 G3
Robert Dashwood Wy
WALW SE17 ....18 C7
Robert Keen Cl PECK SE15.....143 H2
Robert Lowe Cl NWCR SE14...144 A1
Roberton Dr BMLY BR1..........184 B5
Robertsbridge Rd CAR SM5...194 B4
Roberts Cl CHEAM SM3.........208 B5
DAGE RM10 ....92 C4
ELTH/MOT SE9 ....167 J3
HARH RM3 ....57 K4
STMC/STPC BR5.................202 D2
THHTH CR7 ....180 E6
YEAD UB7 ....112 B1
Roberts Ct CHSGTN KT9........205 K4
PGE/AN SE20 ....181 K4
WLSDN NW10 ....81 G4
Roberts House
WOOL/PLUM SE18 * 146 D1
Roberts Ms KTBR SW1X * 15 G5
Robertson Rd SRTFD E15........88 A6
Robertson St VX/NE SW8........141 G4
Robert's Pl CLKNW EC1R * 5 K6
Robert Sq LEW SE13.............145 F5
Roberts Rd BELV DA17.........129 H5
MLHL NW7 ....46 C1

WALTH E17........................51 K4
Robert St CAMTN NW1............3 K5
CHCR WC2N.......................11 F6
CROY/NA CRO...................211 J1
WOOL/PLUM SE18 ....127 J5
Robeson St BOW E3.............105 H4
Robina Cl BXLYHS DA6..........148 E5
Robin Cl CRW RM5................56 D3
HAMP NW3.........................82 E3
HPTN TW12.......................154 D2
MLHL NW7 ....31 G5
Robin Ct BERM/RHTH SE16 * ..123 H4
WLGTN SM6 ....210 C4
Robin Gv BTFD TW8.............116 D6
HGT N6...............................66 A6
KTN/HRWW/WS HA3 ....62 B3
Robin Hill Dr CHST BR7.........184 D2
Robinhood Cl MTCM CR4.......195 H1
Robin Hood Gdns
POP/IOD E14 * 106 A6
Robin Hood Gn
STMC/STPC BR5.................202 B2
Robin Hood La BXLYHS DA6...148 E6
Robinhood La MTCM CR4.......179 H6
Robin Hood La POP/IOD E14...106 A6
PUT/ROE SW15 ....158 B6
SUT SM1...........................208 E3
Robin Hood Rd
PUT/ROE SW15 ....158 A6
Robin Hood Wy GFD/PVL UB6...79 F4
PUT/ROE SW15 ....158 A6
Robinia Cl BARK/HLT IG6........54 E2
PGE/AN SE20 ....181 H4
Robinia Crs LEY E10..............69 K6
Robin La HDN NW4................46 B6
Robins Gv WWKM BR4.........214 E1
Robinson Cl ENC/FH EN2.........23 J4
HCH RM12 ....93 K5
WAN E11.............................70 C6
Robinson Crs BUSH WD23.......28 C3
Robinson Rd BETH E2...........104 E1
DAGE RM10 ....92 C2
TOOT SW17 ....178 D2
Robins Cl STMC/STPC BR5.....186 C6
Robinson St CHEL SW3..........120 E6
Robinson Wy STMC/STPC BR5 186 C6
Robinwood Pl PUT/ROE SW15..158 A6
Robsart St BRXN/ST SW9.......142 A3
Robson Av WLSDN NW10 ....81 J6
Robson Cl BEAM E6..............107 J5
ENC/FH EN2 ....23 H3
Robson Rd WNWD SE27........162 D5
Rocastle Rd BROCKY SE4.......144 B6
Roch Av EDGW HA8..............44 A5
Rochdale Rd ABYW SE2.........128 C5
WALTH E17..........................69 J4
Rochdale Wy DEPT SE8.........144 D1
Rochelle Cl BTSEA SW11........140 C5
Rochelle St BETH E2...............7 J5
Rochemont Wk HACK E8 * 7 H1
Roche Rd STRHM/NOR SW16..179 K4
Rochester Av BMLY BR1........184 A5
FELT TW13 ....153 J5
PLSTW E13 ....107 H1
Rochester Cl BFN/LL DA15.....168 C1
EN EN1 ....24 A2
STRHM/NOR SW16 * 179 K3
Rochester Dr BXLY DA5........169 H1
PIN HA5.............................59 H2
Rochester Gdns CROY/NA CRO..212 A1
IL IG1................................71 K4
Rochester Ms CAMTN NW1.....84 C5
EA W5...............................116 D4
Rochester Pde FELT TW13 * ...153 K5
Rochester Pl CAMTN NW1......84 C5
Rochester Rd CAMTN NW1......84 C4
CAR SM5 ....209 K2
DART DA1..........................171 K2
HCH RM12 ....93 K4
NTHWD HA6 ....40 D6
Rochester Rw WEST SW1P......16 B6
Rochester Sq CAMTN NW1......84 C5
Rochester St WEST SW1P 16 C5
Rochester Ter CAMTN NW1......84 C4
Rochester Wk STHWK SE1 * 12 E6
Rochester Wy BKHTH/KID SE3 146 A2
BKHTH/KID SE3 *................146 B4
DART DA1..........................170 B2
Rochester Way Relief Rd
ELTH/MOT SE9 ....146 E6
Roche Wk CAR SM5.............194 C5
Rochford Av CHDH RM6...........73 J2
Rochford Cl EHAM E6...........107 H1
HCH RM12 ....93 K4
Rochford Wy CROY/NA CRO....195 K3
Rock Av MORT/ESHN SW14 * ..138 A4
Rockbourne Ms FSTH SE23.....164 A3
Rockbourne Rd FSTH SE23.....164 A3
Rock Cl MTCM CR4...............178 C5
Rockells Pl EDUL SE22..........163 J1
Rockford Av GFD/PVL UB6.......97 H1
Rock Grove Wy
BERM/RHTH SE16 ....123 H4
Rockhall Rd CRICK NW2..........82 B3
Rockhampton Rd
SAND/SEL CR2 ....212 A4
STRHM/NOR SW16..............162 B6
Rock Hl DUL SE21................163 G6
Rock St FSBYPK N4................67 H6
Rockware Av GFD/PVL UB6.......78 E6
Rockways BAR EN5...............31 K3
Rockwell Gdns NRWD SE19....163 F6
Rockwell Rd DAGE RM10.........92 D3
Rocliffe St IS N1....................6 B3

Rocombe Crs FSTH SE23 * 163 K2
Rocque La BKHTH/KID SE3.....145 J4
Roden Gdns CROY/NA CRO.....197 F3
Rodenhurst Rd CLAP SW4.......161 H2
Roden St HOLWY N7..............85 F1
IL IG1................................90 A1
Roderick Rd HAMP NW3..........83 K2
Rodgers Cl BORE WD6............29 G1
Roding Cl ERITH DA8............150 E2
Roding La BKHH IG9...............39 J1
Roding La North WFD IG8.........53 J2
Roding La South REDBR IG4.....71 H2
Roding Ms WAP E1W.............123 H1
Roding Rd CLPT E5................87 F2
EHAM E6............................108 B4
Rodings Rw BAR EN5 * 20 C5
Roding Vw BKHH IG9..............39 H3
Rodmarton St MHST W1U..........9 F2
Rodmell Cl YEAD UB4.............95 J5
Rodmell Slope
NFNCH/WDSPK N12 ....46 D1
Rodmere St GNWCH SE10......125 H5
Rodmill La BRXS/STRHM SW2 161 K2
Rodney Cl CROY/NA CRO.......196 C5
NWMAL KT3 ....192 B2
PIN HA5.............................59 J4
WOT/HER KT12 * 188 B5
Rodney Gdns PIN HA5............58 E2
WWKM BR4.......................214 E2
Rodney Pl STHWK SE1...........18 D6
WALTH E17..........................51 G5
WIM/MER SW19..................178 B4
Rodney Rd MTCM CR4..........178 D5
NWMAL KT3 ....192 B2
WALW SE17 ....18 D7
WAN E11.............................71 F1
WHTN TW2........................155 F2
WOT/HER KT12 ....188 B6
Rodney St IS N1.....................5 H2
Rodway Rd BMLY BR1...........184 A4
PUT/ROE SW15 ....158 D3
Rodwell Cl RSLP HA4 * 59 G5
Rodwell Pl EDGW HA8 * 44 C2
Rodwell Rd EDUL SE22..........163 G1
Roebuck Cl FELT TW15..........154 A6
Roebuck La BKHH IG9............39 G2
Roebuck Rd BARK/HLT IG6......55 G1
CHSGTN KT9......................206 C3
Roedean Av PEND EN3...........24 E2
Roedean Cl ORP BR6...........217 H2
PEND EN3 ....24 E2
Roe Gn CDALE/KGS NW9.........62 E1
Roehampton Cl
PUT/ROE SW15 ....138 D5
Roehampton Dr CHST BR7......185 H2
Roehampton Ga
PUT/ROE SW15 ....158 B1
Roehampton High St
PUT/ROE SW15 ....158 D2
Roehampton La
PUT/ROE SW15 ....138 D6
Roehampton V
PUT/ROE SW15 ....158 B1
Roe La CDALE/KGS NW9.........62 E1
Roe Wy WLGTN SM6............210 E4
Rofant Rd NTHWD HA6............40 C1
Roffey St POP/IOD E14..........125 F2
Rogers Gdns DAGE RM10........92 C3
Rogers Rd CAN/RD E16.........106 D5
DAGE RM10 ....92 C3
TOOT SW17 ....160 C6
Rogers Ruff NTHWD HA6.........40 A4
Roger St BMSBY WC1N............5 H7
Rogers Wk NFNCH/WDSPK N12 ...33 F1
Rojack Rd FSTH SE23............164 A3
Rokeby Gdns WFD IG8............52 E4
Rokeby Pl RYNPK SW20........176 E3
Rokeby Rd BROCKY SE4.........144 C3
Rokeby St SRTFD E15............88 C6
Rokesby Cl WELL DA16..........147 J3
Rokesby Pl ALP/SUD HA0........79 K3
Rokesly Av CEND/HSY/T N8.....66 E2
Roland Gdns SKENS SW7.......120 B5
Roland Ms WCHPL E1............105 F4
Roland Rd WALTH E17.............70 B1
Roland Wy SKENS SW7.........120 B5
WALW SE17 ....19 G7
WPK KT4..........................192 C6
Roles Gv CHDH RM6..............73 K1
Rolfe Cl EBAR EN4................21 J5
Rollesby Rd CHSGTN KT9.......206 C4
Rollesby Wy THMD SE28........109 J6
Rolleston Av STMC/STPC BR5..201 G4
Rolleston Cl STMC/STPC BR5..201 G4
Rolleston Rd SAND/SEL CR2...211 K5
Roll Gdns GNTH/NBYPK IG2....72 B2
Rollins St PECK SE15............123 K6
Rollit Crs HSLW TW3............135 F6
Rollit St HOLWY N7...............85 G3
Rolls Buildings
FLST/FETLN EC4A 11 J3
Rolls Court Av HNHL SE24......142 D6
Rolls Park Av CHING E4...........51 K1
Rolls Park Rd CHING E4..........51 K1
Rolls Rd STHWK SE1.............123 G5
Rolls Royce Cl WLGTN SM6....210 E5
Rolt St NWCR SE14...............124 B6
Rolvenden Gdns BMLY BR1.....184 C4
Rolvenden Pl TOTM N17..........50 C4
Roman Cl ACT W3................117 J2
EBED/NFELT TW14 ....134 A6
RAIN RM13 ....111 F1
Romanfield Rd
BRXS/STRHM SW2 ....162 A2
Romanhurst Av HAYES BR2....199 H1
Romanhurst Gdns BECK BR3 ..199 H1
Roman Rd BORE WD6 * 29 K5
CAR SM5 ....209 K6
Roman Ri NRWD SE19...........180 E2
Roman Rd BETH E2..............105 F1
BOW E3...............................87 K4
CHSWK W4........................118 B4

CRICK NW2 ....82 A1
Rose & Crown Yd STJS SW1Y * ...16 B1
Roseary Cl WDR/YW UB7 ...112 A4
Rose Av MRDN SM4 ...194 B2
MTCM CR4 ...178 E4
SWFD E18 ...53 F5
Rosebank PGE/AN SE20 ...181 J3
Rosebank Av ALP/SUD HA0 ...79 F2
Rose Bank Cl
NFNCH/WDSPK N12 ...47 J1
Rosebank Cl TEDD TW11 ...174 B2
Rosebank Est BOW E3 ...105 H1
Rosebank Gdns ACT W3 * ...99 F5
BOW E3 ...105 H1
Rosebank Gv WALTH E17 ...51 H6
Rosebank Rd HNWL W7 ...115 K2
WALTH E17 ...51 H6
Rosebank Wk CAMTN NW1 * ...84 D5
Rosebank Wy ACT W3 ...99 F5
Roseberry Gdns DART DA1 ...171 F2
FSBYPK N4 ...67 H3
ORP BR6 ...216 E1
Roseberry Pl HACK E8 ...86 B4
Roseberry St
BERM/RHTH SE16 ...123 J4
Rosebery Av BFN/LL DA15 ...167 K2
CLKNW EC1R ...5 J7
MNPK E12 ...89 J4
NWMAL KT3 ...176 C5
RYLN/HDSTN HA2 ...77 J2
THHTH CR7 ...180 D5
TOTM N17 ...50 C5
Rosebery Cl MRDN SM4 ...193 G3
Rosebery Ct CLKNW EC1R * ...5 K7
Rosebery Gdns
CEND/HSY/T N8 * ...66 E2
SUT SM1 ...209 F2
WEA W13 ...97 G5
Rosebery Ms MUSWH N10 ...48 C6
Rosebery Pde EW KT17 * ...207 H5
Rosebery Rd BUSH WD23 ...28 B3
CLAP SW4 ...161 K1
HSLW TW3 ...135 H5
KUT/HW KT1 ...175 K4
MUSWH N10 ...48 C5
SUT SM1 ...208 D4

EHAM E6 ...107 J3
IL IG1 ...90 D4
MUSWH N10 ...9 K6
Roman Sq THMD SE28 ...128 B1
Roman Wy CROY/NA CR0 ...196 C6
DART DA1 ...150 B6
EN EN1 ...24 B6
HOLWY N7 ...85 F4
Romany Gdns CHEAM SM3 ...193 K4
Romany Ri STMC/STPC BR5 ...201 H5
Roma Rd WALTH E17 ...51 G6
Romberg Rd TOOT SW17 ...161 F5
Romborough Gdns LEW SE13 ...145 F6
Romborough V LEW SE13 ...145 F6
Rom Crs ROMW/RG RM7 ...75 G4
Romeland BORE WD6 ...29 K1
Romero Cl BRXN/ST SW9 ...142 A4
Romero Sq BKHTH/KID SE3 ...146 B5
Romeyn Rd STRHM/NOR SW16 ...162 A5
Romford Rd CHIG IG7 ...55 K2
CRW RM5 ...56 B3
MNPK E12 ...90 A1
SRTFD E15 ...88 C5
Romford St WCHPL E1 ...104 C4
Romilly Dr OXHEY WD19 ...27 J3
Romilly Rd FSBYPK N4 ...85 H1
Romilly St SOHO/SHAV W1D ...10 D5
Rommany Cl CHSGTN KT9 ...206 A3
GLDGN NW11 ...65 G5
NWCR SE14 ...143 K1
RYLN/HDSTN HA2 ...60 A4
TOTM N17 ...50 D4
Romney Dr BMLY BR1 ...184 C3
RYLN/HDSTN HA2 ...60 A4
Romney Gdns BXLYHN DA7 ...149 G2
Romney Rd GNWCH SE10 ...125 F6
NWMAL KT3 ...192 A3
WOOL/PLUM SE18 ...127 H3
YEAD UB4 ...94 B1
Romney Rw CRICK NW2 * ...64 B6
Romney St WEST SW1P ...16 D5
Romola Rd HNHL SE24 ...162 C3
Romsey Cl ORP BR6 ...216 C2
Romsey Rd DAGW RM9 ...91 K6
WEA W13 ...97 G6
Romside Pl ROMW/RG RM7 ...75 F1
Rom Valley Wy ROMW/RG RM7 ...75 F3
Ronald Av SRTFD E15 ...106 C2
Ronald Cl BECK BR3 ...198 C2
Ronalds Rd BMLY BR1 ...183 K4
HBRY N5 ...85 H3
Ronaldstone Rd BFN/LL DA15 ...167 K1
Rona Rd HAMP NW3 ...84 A2
Ronart St KTN/HRWW/WS HA3 ...43 F6
Rona Wk IS N1 ...85 K4
Rondu Rd CRICK NW2 ...82 C3
Ronelean Rd SURB KT6 ...206 E1
Roneo Cnr HCH RM12 ...75 H5
Roneo Link HCH RM12 ...75 H5
Ronfearn Av STMC/STPC BR5 ...202 E2
Ron Green Ct ERITH DA8 ...130 A5
Ron Leighton Wy EHAM E6 ...89 J6
Ronnie La BTSEA SW11 ...73 J6
Ronver Rd LEE/GVPK SE12 ...165 K3
Rood La FENCHST EC3M ...13 G5
Rookby Ct WCHMH N21 ...35 H4
Rook Cl RAIN RM13 ...93 J5
WBLY HA9 ...80 C1
Rookeries Cl FELT TW13 ...154 A5
Rookery Dr CHST BR7 ...185 F4
Rookery Gdns STMC/STPC BR5 ...202 D5
Rookery La HAYES BR2 ...200 C5
Rookery Rd CLAP SW4 ...141 H5
The Rookery
STRHM/NOR SW16 * ...180 A2
Rookesley Rd STMC/STPC BR5 ...202 E4
Rookfield Av MUSWH N10 ...66 C1
Rookfield Cl BELMT SM2 ...209 F6
Rooks Ter WDR/YW UB7 * ...112 B2
Rookstone Rd TOOT SW17 ...178 E1
Rookwood Av NWMAL KT3 ...192 D1
WLGTN SM6 ...210 D2
Rookwood Gdns CHING E4 * ...38 D3
Rookwood Rd STNW/STAM N16 ...68 B3
Roosevelt Wy DAGE RM10 ...93 F4
Rootes Dr NKENS W10 ...100 B3
Ropemaker Rd
BERM/RHTH SE16 ...124 B2
Ropemaker's Flds
POP/IOD E14 * ...105 H6
Ropemaker St BARB EC2Y ...12 E1
Ropers La CHING E4 ...52 A1
Ropers Orch CHEL SW3 * ...120 D6
Roper St ELTH/MOT SE9 ...146 E6
Ropers Wy MTCM CR4 ...179 F5
Ropery St BOW E3 ...105 H3
Rope St BERM/RHTH SE16 ...124 B3
Ropewalk Gdns WCHPL E1 ...104 C5
Ropewalk Ms HACK E8 * ...86 B5
Rope Yard Rails
WOOL/PLUM SE18 ...127 G3
Ropley St BETH E2 ...104 C1
Rosa Alba Ms HBRY N5 ...85 J2
Rosa Av ASHF TW15 ...152 D6
Rosary Gdns ASHF TW15 ...134 D3
BUSH WD23 ...28 E2
SKENS SW7 ...120 B4
Rosary Ga BTSEA SW11 ...141 G1
Rosaville Rd FUL/PGN SW6 ...139 J1
Roscoe St STLK EC1Y ...12 E2
Roscoff Cl EDGW HA8 ...44 E4
Roseacre Cl WEA W13 ...97 H4
Roseacre Rd WELL DA16 ...148 C4
Rose Aly LVPST EC2M ...13 H2
STHWK SE1 ...12 D7

Rosebine Av WHTN TW2 ...155 J2
Rosebriars ESH/CLAY KT10 ...204 C3
Rosebury Rd FUL/PGN SW6 ...140 A3
Rosebury Sq WFD IG8 ...54 A3
Rosebury V RSLP HA4 ...58 E6
Rose Ct WCHPL E1 ...13 J2
Rosecourt Rd CROY/NA CR0 ...196 A3
Rosecroft Av HAMP NW3 ...83 F1
Rosecroft Ct STMC/STPC BR5 ...202 D5
Rosecroft Gdns WHTN TW2 ...155 H3
Rosecroft Rd STHL UB1 ...96 A3
Rosecroft Wk ALP/SUD HA0 ...79 K5
PIN HA5 ...59 H2
Rose Dl ORP BR6 ...201 G6
Rosedale Av HYS/HAR UB3 ...94 B4
Rosedale Cl ABYW SE2 ...128 C3
HNWL W7 ...116 A2
STAN HA7 ...43 H2
Rosedale Dr DAGW RM9 ...91 H6
Rosedale Gdns DAGW RM9 ...91 H5
Rosedale Pl CROY/NA CR0 ...198 A4
Rosedale Rd DAGW RM9 ...91 H5
EW KT17 ...207 J3
FSTGT E7 ...89 G3
RCH/KEW TW9 ...137 F5
ROM RM1 ...75 G3
Rosedene CROY/NA CR0 * ...195 K4
GFD/PVL UB6 ...96 A2
MRDN SM4 ...193 K2
STRHM/NOR SW16 ...162 A5
Rosedene Cl DART DA1 ...171 F2
Rosedene Gdns
GNTH/NBYPK IG2 ...72 A1
Rosedene Ter LEY E10 ...69 K6
Rosedew Rd HMSMTH W6 ...119 G6
Rose End WPK KT4 ...193 G5
Rosefield POP/IOD E14 ...105 J6
Rosefield Cl CAR SM5 ...209 J3
Rosefield Gdns POP/IOD E14 ...105 J6
Rose Garden Cl EDGW HA8 ...44 A2
Rose Gdns EA W5 ...116 E3
FELT TW13 ...153 K4
STHL UB1 ...96 B3
STWL/WRAY TW19 ...152 A2
Rose Gln CDALE/KGS NW9 ...63 F1
ROMW/RG RM7 ...75 G5
Roseheart Ms NTGHL W11 ...100 D5
Rosehatch Av CHDH RM6 ...55 K6
Rosehedh Rd HSLWW TW4 ...134 D6
Rosehill ESH/CLAY KT10 ...205 G4
HPTN TW12 ...173 H4
Rose Hi SUT SM1 ...194 A3
Rosehill Av SUT SM1 ...194 B5
Rosehill Court Pde
MRDN SM4 * ...194 A4
Rosehill Gdns GFD/PVL UB6 ...79 F3
SUT SM1 ...194 A3
Rose Hill Pk West SUT SM1 ...194 B4
Rosehill Rd WAND/EARL SW18 ...160 B1
Roseland Cl TOTM N17 ...49 K3
Rose La CHDH RM6 ...74 A1
Rose Lawn BUSH WD23 ...28 C3
Roseleigh Av HBRY N5 ...85 H2
Roseleigh Cl TWK TW1 ...156 E1
Rosemary Av E/WMO/HCT KT8 ...173 F6
ED N9 ...36 D3
ENC/FH EN2 ...23 K2
FNCH N3 ...47 F5
HSLWW TW4 ...134 C3
ROM RM1 ...57 H6
Rosemary Cl CROY/NA CR0 ...195 K4
Rosemary Dr POP/IOD E14 ...106 B5
REDBR IG4 ...71 H2
Rosemary Gdns BCTR RM8 ...74 B5
CHSGTN KT9 ...206 A2
Rosemary La
MORT/ESHN SW14 ...137 K4
Rosemary Rd PECK SE15 ...143 G1
TOOT SW17 ...160 A5

WELL DA16 ...148 A2
Rosemary St IS N1 ...85 K6
Rosemead CDALE/KGS NW9 ...63 H3
Rosemead Av FELT TW13 ...153 J4
MTCM CR4 ...179 H6
WBLY HA9 ...80 A3
Rose Ms USED ENT Av
NFNCH/WDSPK N12 ...47 G2
Rosemont Rd ACT W3 ...98 D6
HAMP NW3 ...83 G4
NWMAL KT3 ...175 K6
RCHPK/HAM TW10 ...156 E1
Rosemont St CHEL SW3 ...14 E7
Rosemount Cl WFD IG8 * ...53 K2
Rosemount Dr BMLY BR1 ...200 E1
Rosemount Rd ALP/SUD HA0 ...80 A6
WEA W13 ...97 G5
Rosenau Crs BTSEA SW11 ...140 E2
Rosenau Rd BTSEA SW11 ...140 D2
Rosendale Rd HNHL SE24 ...162 D2
Roseneath Av WCHMH N21 ...35 H5
Roseneath Pl
STRHM/NOR SW16 ...162 B6
Roseneath Rd BTSEA SW11 ...161 F1
Roseneath Wk EN EN1 ...24 A5
Rosens Cl EDGW HA8 ...30 D5
Rosenthal Rd CAT SE6 ...164 E1
Rosenthorpe Rd PECK SE15 ...144 A6
Rose Park Cl YEAD UB4 ...95 G4
Roserton St POP/IOD E14 ...125 E3
The Rosery CROY/NA CR0 ...198 A3
Rose Sq CHEL SW3 * ...120 C5
The Roses WFD IG8 * ...52 D5
Rose St COVGDN WC2E ...10 E5
Rosethorn Cl BAL SW12 ...161 H2
Rosetta Cl VX/NE SW8 ...141 K1
Roseveare Rd LEE/GVPK SE12 ...166 B6
Roseville Av HSLW TW3 ...135 F6
Roseville Rd HYS/HAR UB3 ...113 K5
Rosevine Rd RYNPK SW20 ...177 F4
Rose Wk BRYLDS KT5 ...191 J4
Rose Wk SURB KT6 ...191 J4
Roseway DUL SE21 ...162 E1
EDGW HA8 ...30 E6
Rose Wy LEE/GVPK SE12 ...145 K6
Rosewell Cl PGE/AN SE20 ...181 J3
Rosewood DART DA2 ...170 B6
Rosewood Av GFD/PVL UB6 ...79 G3
HCH RM12 ...93 J3
Rosewood Cl SCUP DA14 ...168 D5
Rosewood Ct KUTN/CMB KT2 ...175 H4
Rosewood Gv SUT SM1 ...194 B6
Rosewood Ter PGE/AN SE20 * ...181 K3
Rosher Cl SRTFD E15 ...88 B5
Rosina St HOM E9 ...87 F3
Roskell Rd PUT/ROE SW15 ...139 G4
Roslin Rd ACT W3 ...117 J3
Roslin Wy BMLY BR1 ...183 K1
Roslyn Cl MTCM CR4 ...178 C5
Roslyn Gdns GPK RM2 ...57 H5
Roslyn Ms SEVS/STOTM N15 ...68 A2
Roslyn Rd SEVS/STOTM N15 ...67 K2
Rosmead Rd NTGHL W11 ...100 C6
Rosoman Pl CLKNW EC1R ...5 K6
Rosoman St CLKNW EC1R ...5 K5
Rossall Cl EMPK RM11 ...75 J3
Rossall Crs WLSDN NW10 ...98 B2
Ross Av BCTR RM8 ...74 B6
MLHL NW7 ...46 C1
Ross Cl HYS/HAR UB3 ...113 G4
KTN/HRWW/WS HA3 ...42 C3
Rossdale SUT SM1 ...209 J3
Rossdale Dr CDALE/KGS NW9 ...62 E5
ED N9 ...36 E2
Rossdale Rd PUT/ROE SW15 ...139 F5
Rosse Ms BKHTH/KID SE3 ...146 A2
Rossendale St CLPT E5 ...68 D6
Rossendale Wy CAMTN NW1 ...84 C5
Rossetti Rd BERM/RHTH SE16 ...123 J5
Rossignol Gdns CAR SM5 ...195 F6
Rossindel Rd HSLW TW3 ...135 F6
Rossington Cl EN EN1 ...24 D1
Rossington St CLPT E5 ...68 C6
Rossiter Flds BAR EN5 ...32 D1
Rossiter Rd BAL SW12 ...161 G3
Rossland Cl BXLYHS DA6 ...149 H6
Rosslyn Av BARN SW13 ...138 B4
BCTR RM8 ...74 B5
CHING E4 ...38 D4
EBAR EN4 ...33 J1
EBED/NFELT TW14 ...153 K1
Rosslyn Crs HRW HA1 ...61 F1
WBLY HA9 ...80 A1
Rosslyn Hl HAMP NW3 ...83 H3
Rosslyn Park Ms HAMP NW3 ...83 H3
Rosslyn Rd BARK IG11 ...90 D5
TWK TW1 ...156 D1
WALTH E17 ...70 A1
Rossmore Cl CAMTN NW1 * ...2 D7
PEND EN3 ...25 F5
Rossmore Rd CAMTN NW1 ...2 D7
Ross Pde WLGTN SM6 ...210 B4
Ross Rd DART DA1 ...150 C5
SNWD SE25 ...181 F6
WHTN TW2 ...155 H3
WLGTN SM6 ...210 C4
Ross Wy ELTH/MOT SE9 ...146 D4
NTHWD HA6 ...26 D6
Rosswood Gdns WLGTN SM6 ...210 B4
Rostella Rd TOOT SW17 ...160 C6
Rostrevor Av SEVS/STOTM N15 ...68 B3
Rostrevor Gdns NWDGN UB2 ...114 D5
Rostrevor Ms FUL/PGN SW6 ...139 J2

Rotherfield Rd CAR SM5 ...210 A2
Rotherfield St IS N1 ...85 J5
Rotherham Wk STHWK SE1 * ...18 B1
Rotherhill Av
STRHM/NOR SW16 ...179 J2
Rotherhithe New Rd
BERM/RHTH SE16 ...123 J5
Rotherhithe Old Rd
BERM/RHTH SE16 ...124 A4
Rotherhithe St
BERM/RHTH SE16 ...123 K2
BERM/RHTH SE16 ...124 A1
Rotherhithe Tnl
BERM/RHTH SE16 ...123 K2
Rothermere Rd CROY/NA CR0 ...211 F4
Rotherwick Hl EA W5 ...98 B3
Rotherwick Rd GLDGN NW11 ...64 E4
Rotherwood Cl RYNPK SW20 ...177 H4
Rotherwood Rd
PUT/ROE SW15 ...139 G4
Rothery St IS N1 * ...85 H6
Rothery Ter BRXN/ST SW9 * ...142 C1
Rothesay Av GFD/PVL UB6 ...78 D4
RCHPK/HAM TW10 ...137 J5
RYNPK SW20 ...177 H5
Rothesay Rd SNWD SE25 ...196 E1
Rothsay Rd FSTGT E7 ...89 G5
Rothsay St STHWK SE1 ...19 G4
Rothschild Rd CHSWK W4 ...117 K4
Rothschild St WNWD SE27 ...162 C6
Rothwell Gdns DAGW RM9 ...91 J5
Rothwell Rd DAGW RM9 ...91 H6
Rothwell St CAMTN NW1 ...3 H1
Rotterdam Dr POP/IOD E14 ...125 F3
Rouel Rd BERM/RHTH SE16 ...123 H3
Rougemont Av MRDN SM4 ...193 K3
The Roughs NTHWD HA6 ...26 C2
Roundaway Rd CLAY IG5 ...53 K5
Roundel Cl BROCKY SE4 ...144 C5
Round Gv CROY/NA CR0 ...198 A4
Roundhay Cl FSTH SE23 ...164 A4
Roundhedge Wy ENC/FH EN2 ...23 F1
Round Hl SYD SE26 ...163 J4
Roundhill Dr ENC/FH EN2 ...23 F5
Roundlyn Gdns
STMC/STPC BR5 ...202 C1
Roundtable Rd BMLY BR1 ...165 J5
Roundtree Rd ALP/SUD HA0 ...79 H3
Roundways RSLP HA4 ...76 D1
The Roundway
ESH/CLAY KT10 ...205 H2
TOTM N17 ...49 K4
WATW WD18 ...27 J4
Roundwood CHST BR7 ...185 G5
Roundwood Av STKPK UB11 ...113 F2
Roundwood Cl RSLP HA4 ...58 B4
Roundwood Rd WLSDN NW10 ...81 J4
Roundwood Ter
WLSDN NW10 * ...81 J6
Rounton Rd BOW E3 ...105 J3
Roupell Rd BRXS/STRHM SW2 ...162 A3
Roupell St STHWK SE1 ...17 K1
Rousden St CAMTN NW1 ...84 C5
Rouse Gdns DUL SE21 ...163 F6
Rous Rd BKHH IG9 ...39 J3
Routemaster Cl PLSTW E13 ...107 F2
Routh Cl EBED/NFELT TW14 ...153 G3
Routh Rd WAND/EARL SW18 ...160 D3
Routh St EHAM E6 ...107 K4
Rover Av BARK/HLT IG6 ...55 F2
Rowallan Rd FUL/PGN SW6 ...139 H1
Rowan Av CHING E4 ...51 H2
Rowan Cl ALP/SUD HA0 ...79 G1
EA W5 ...117 F2
IL IG1 ...90 D5
NWMAL KT3 ...176 B5
STAN HA7 ...43 F2
Rowan Crs DART DA1 ...171 F5
STRHM/NOR SW16 ...179 H4
Rowan Dr CDALE/KGS NW9 ...45 J6
Rowan Gdns CROY/NA CR0 ...212 B1
Rowan Pl HYS/HAR UB3 ...94 D6
Rowan Rd BTFD TW8 ...136 C1
BXLYHN DA7 ...149 F4
HMSMTH W6 ...119 G4
STRHM/NOR SW16 ...179 H5
WDR/YW UB7 * ...112 A4
The Rowans PLMGR N13 ...35 H2
Rowan Ter PGE/AN SE20 * ...181 H4
WIM/MER SW19 * ...177 H5
Rowantree Cl WCHMH N21 ...35 K3
Rowantree Ms ENC/FH EN2 ...23 H2
Rowantree Rd ENC/FH EN2 ...23 H2
WCHMH N21 ...35 K3
Rowan Wk EFNCH N2 * ...65 G2
HAYES BR2 ...215 K1
NKENS W10 * ...100 C3
Rowanwood Av BFN/LL DA15 ...168 B3
Rowben Cl TRDG/WHET N20 ...33 F3
Rowberry Cl FUL/PGN SW6 ...139 F1
Rowcross St STHWK SE1 ...123 G5
Rowdell Rd NTHLT UB5 ...96 A1
Rowden Pde CHING E4 * ...51 J2
Rowden Pde BECK BR3 ...182 B4
CHING E4 ...51 J2
HOR/WEW KT19 ...206 E2
Rowdon Av WLSDN NW10 ...81 K5
Rowdowns Rd DAGW RM9 ...92 B6
Rowe Gdns BARK IG11 ...109 G1
Rowe La HOM E9 ...86 E3
Rowena Crs BTSEA SW11 ...140 D3
Rowe Wk RYLN/HDSTN HA2 ...78 A1
Rowfant Rd TOOT SW17 ...161 F3
Rowhill Rd CLPT E5 ...86 D2
Rowington Cl BAY/PAD W2 ...101 F4
Rowland Av
KTN/HRWW/WS HA3 ...43 J6
Rowland Gv SYD SE26 ...163 J5
Rowland Hill Av TOTM N17 ...49 J3
Rowland Hill St HAMP NW3 ...83 J3
Rowland Pl NTHWD HA6 ...40 C3

Rowlands Av PIN HA5 ...42 A2
Rowlands Cl HGT N6 * ...66 A3
MLHL NW7 ...46 A3
Rowlands Rd BCTR RM8 ...74 B6
Rowland Wy WIM/MER SW19 ...178 A4
Rowlatt Cl RDART DA2 ...171 F6
Rowley Av BFN/LL DA15 ...168 C2
Rowley Cl ALP/SUD HA0 ...80 B5
OXHEY WD19 ...27 J1
Rowley Cottages
WKENS W14 ...119 J4
Rowley Gdns FSBYPK N4 ...67 J3
Rowley La BAR EN5 ...20 D6
Rowley Rd SEVS/STOTM N15 ...67 J2
Rowley Wy STJWD NW8 ...83 G6
Rowlheys Pl WDR/YW UB7 ...112 B3
Rowlls Rd KUT/HW KT1 ...175 G6
Rowney Gdns DAGW RM9 ...91 J4
Rowney Rd DAGW RM9 ...91 J4
Rowntree Clifford Cl
PLSTW E13 ...107 F3
Rowntree Cl KIL/WHAMP NW6 * ...82 E4
Rowntree Rd WHTN TW2 ...155 K3
Rowse Cl SRTFD E15 ...88 A6
Rowstock Gdns HOLWY N7 ...84 D4
Rowton Rd WOOL/PLUM SE18 ...147 H5
Roxborough Av HRW HA1 ...60 D4
ISLW TW7 ...136 A1
Roxborough Pk HRW HA1 ...60 E3
Roxborough Rd HRW HA1 ...60 C1
Roxbourne Cl NTHLT UB5 ...77 H4
Roxburgh Rd WNWD SE27 ...180 C5
Roxburn Wy RSLP HA4 ...76 D1
Roxby Pl FUL/PGN SW6 ...119 K6
Roxeth Green Av
RYLN/HDSTN HA2 ...60 C6
RYLN/HDSTN HA2 ...78 D1
Roxeth Gv RYLN/HDSTN HA2 ...78 D1
Roxeth Hl RYLN/HDSTN HA2 ...60 D6
Roxley Rd LEW SE13 ...164 E2
Roxton Gdns CROY/NA CR0 ...213 J5
Roxwell Rd BARK IG11 ...109 G1
SHB W12 ...118 D2
Roxwell Wy WFD IG8 ...53 G3
Roxy Av CHDH RM6 ...73 J4
Royal Albert Rd EHAM E6 ...108 A6
Royal Albert Wy CAN/RD E16 ...107 J6
Royal Ar CONDST W1S ...10 A6
Royal Arsenal West
WOOL/PLUM SE18 * ...127 F5
Royal Av CHEL SW3 ...120 E5
WPK KT4 ...192 B6
Royal Botanic Gdns
RCH/KEW TW9 ...137 F1
Royal Circ WNWD SE27 ...162 B5
Royal Cl DEPT SE8 ...124 C6
GDMY/SEVK IG3 ...73 G4
ORP BR6 ...216 B2
STNW/STAM N16 ...68 A5
WIM/MER SW19 * ...159 G4
WPK KT4 ...192 B6
Royal College St CAMTN NW1 ...84 C5
Royal Ct BANK EC3V ...13 F4
ELTH/MOT SE9 * ...166 E5
EN EN1 * ...24 C6
Royal Crs GNTH/NBYPK IG2 ...72 D3
NTGHL W11 ...119 G2
RSLP HA4 ...77 J2
Royal Crescent Ms
NTGHL W11 ...119 G2
Royal Docks Rd EHAM E6 ...108 A4
Royal Dr FBAR/BDGN N11 ...48 A1
Royal Herbert Pavilions
WOOL/PLUM SE18 * ...146 E2
Royal Hl GNWCH SE10 ...145 F1
Royal Hospital Rd CHEL SW3 ...120 E6
Royal Ms BAL SW12 ...161 G2
Royal Mint Ct WCHPL E1 ...13 K5
Royal Mint St WCHPL E1 ...13 K5
Royal Naval Pl NWCR SE14 ...144 C1
Royal Oak Ms TEDD TW11 ...174 B1
Royal Oak Pl EDUL SE22 ...163 J4
Royal Oak Rd BXLYHS DA6 ...149 G6
HACK E8 ...86 D4
Royal Oak Yd STHWK SE1 ...19 G3
Royal Opera Ar STJS SW1Y * ...10 C7
Royal Orchard Cl
WAND/EARL SW18 ...159 H2
Royal Pde BKHTH/KID SE3 ...145 J3
CHST BR7 ...185 H3
FUL/PGN SW6 * ...139 H1
RCH/KEW TW9 * ...137 H1
Royal Quarter
KUTN/CMB KT2 * ...175 F4
Royal Rd CAN/RD E16 ...107 G5
LBTH SE11 ...122 C6
SCUP DA14 ...168 E5
TEDD TW11 ...173 J1
Royal Route WBLY HA9 ...80 B2
Royal St STHWK SE1 ...17 H4
Royal Victor Pl BETH E2 ...105 K1
Roycraft Av BARK IG11 ...109 F1
Roycraft Cl
BRXS/STRHM SW2 * ...162 B3
SWFD E18 ...53 F4
Roydene Rd
WOOL/PLUM SE18 ...127 K6
Roydon Cl LOU IG10 ...39 J2
Roydon Ct WALON/NBYPK IG2 ...72 D3
Roydon St BTSEA SW11 * ...141 G2
Royle Cl GPK RM2 ...57 K2
Royle Crs WEA W13 ...97 G3
Roymount Ct WFD IG8 ...40 D3
Roy Sq POP/IOD E14 ...105 G6
Royston Av CHING E4 ...51 J1
SUT SM1 ...209 H1
WLGTN SM6 ...210 D2
Royston Cl HEST TW5 ...134 B2
Royston Gdns IL IG1 ...71 H3
Royston Gv PIN HA5 ...41 K2
Royston Park Rd PIN HA5 ...41 K3
Royston Rd DART DA1 ...170 C1
PGE/AN SE20 ...182 A4
RCHPK/HAM TW10 ...137 F6
The Roystons BRYLDS KT5 ...191 J2
Royston St BETH E2 ...104 E1
Rozel Rd VX/NE SW8 ...141 H3
Rubastic Rd NWDGN UB2 ...114 A3
Rubens Pl CLAP SW4 ...141 K5

Rubens Rd NTHLT UB5 95 G1
Rubens St CAT SE6 164 C4
Ruby Ms WALTH E17 * 51 J6
Ruby Rd WALTH E17 51 J6
Ruby St PECK SE15 123 J6
WLSDN NW10 80 E5
Ruby Triangle PECK SE15 * 123 J6
Ruckholt Cl LEY E10 87 K1
Ruckholt Rd LEY E10 88 A1
Rucklidge Av WLSDN NW10 99 H1
Rudall Crs HAMP NW3 83 H2
Ruddington Cl CLPT E5 87 G2
Ruddock Cl EDGW HA8 44 E3
Ruddstreet Cl
WOOL/PLUM SE18 127 G4
Rudgwick Ter STJWD NW8 * 2 D1
Rudland Rd BXLYHN DA7 149 J4
Rudloe Rd BAL SW12 161 H2
Rudolf Pl VX/NE SW8 121 K6
Rudolph Rd BUSH WD23 28 A1
KIL/WHAMP NW6 100 E1
PLSTW E13 106 D1
Rudyard Gv EDGW HA8 44 E2
Ruffetts Cl SAND/SEL CR2 212 D5
The Ruffetts SAND/SEL CR2 212 D5
Ruffle Cl WDR/YW UB7 112 B2
Rufford Cl KTN/HRWW/WS HA3 61 G3
Rufford St IS N1 84 E6
Rufford Street Ms IS N1 84 E5
Rufus Cl RSLP HA4 77 H1
Rufus St FSBYE EC1V 7 G5
Rugby Av ALP/SUD HA0 79 J2
ED N9 36 B3
GFD/PVL UB6 78 D4
Rugby Cl HRW HA1 60 E1
Rugby Gdns DAGW RM9 91 J4
Rugby La BELMT SM2 208 B6
Rugby Rd CDALE/KGS NW9 62 C1
CHSWK W4 118 B2
DAGW RM9 91 H5
TWK TW1 155 K1
Rugby St BMSBY WC1N 5 G7
Rugg St POP/IOD E14 105 J6
Ruislip Cl GFD/PVL UB6 96 B3
Ruislip Ct RSLP HA4 * 58 D6
Ruislip Rd GFD/PVL UB6 96 B3
NTHLT UB5 77 G6
Ruislip Rd East GFD/PVL UB6 96 D3
WEA W13 97 G3
Ruislip St TOOT SW17 160 E6
Rumbold Rd FUL/PGN SW6 140 A1
Rum Cl WAP E1W 104 D6
Rumsey Cl HPTN TW12 172 E2
Rumsey Rd BRXN/ST SW9 142 A4
Runbury Cir CDALE/KGS NW9 63 F6
Runcorn Cl TOTM N17 68 D1
Runcorn Pl NTGHL W11 100 C6
Rundell Crs HDN NW4 63 K2
Runes Cl MTCM CR4 194 C1
Runnelfield HRW HA1 78 E1
Runnymede WIM/MER SW19 178 C4
Runnymede Cl WHTN TW2 155 G1
Runnymede Crs
STRHM/NOR SW16 179 J4
Runnymede Gdns
GFD/PVL UB6 96 D1
HSLW TW3 155 G1
Runnymede Rd WHTN TW2 155 G1
The Runway RSLP HA4 77 F3
Rupack St BERM/RHTH SE16 * 123 K2
Rupert Av WBLY HA9 80 A3
Rupert Ct E/WMO/HCT KT8 * 189 F1
SOHO/SHAV W1D 10 C5
Rupert Gdns BRXN/ST SW9 142 C3
Rupert Rd ARCH N19 84 D1
CHSWK W4 118 B3
KIL/WHAMP NW6 100 D1
Rupert St SOHO/SHAV W1D 10 C6
Rural Cl EMPK RM11 75 K5
Rural Wy STRHM/NOR SW16 179 G3
Rusbridge Cl HACK E8 86 C3
Ruscoe Rd CAN/RD E16 106 D5
Ruscombe Wy
EBED/NFELT TW14 153 J2
Rusham Rd BAL SW12 160 E1
Rushbrook Crs WALTH E17 51 H4
Rushbrook Rd ELTH/MOT SE9 167 H4
Rush Common Ms
BRXS/STRHM SW2 162 A2
Rushcroft Rd
BRXS/STRHM SW2 142 B5
CHING E4 51 K3
Rushden Cl NRWD SE19 180 E3
Rushdene ABYW SE2 128 D3
Rushdene Av EBAR EN4 33 J2
Rushdene Cl NTHLT UB5 95 G1
Rushdene Crs NTHLT UB5 95 F1
Rushdene Rd PIN HA5 59 G3
Rushden Gdns CLAY IG5 54 A6
MLHL NW7 46 A2
Rushdon Cl ROM RM1 75 J2
Rushet Rd STMC/STPC BR5 186 B5
Rushett Cl THDIT KT7 190 C5
Rushett Rd THDIT KT7 190 C4
Rushey Cl NWMAL KT3 192 A1
Rushey Gn CAT SE6 164 E2
Rushey Hl ENC/FH EN2 23 F5
Rushey Md BROCKY SE4 144 D6
Rushford Rd BROCKY SE4 164 C1
Rush Green Gdns
ROMW/RG RM7 74 E5
Rush Green Rd ROMW/RG RM7 74 E5
Rushgrove Av CDALE/KGS NW9 63 H1
Rushgrove Pde
CDALE/KGS NW9 * 63 H2
Rushgrove St
WOOL/PLUM SE18 126 E4
Rush Hill Ms BTSEA SW11 141 F4
Rush Hill Rd BTSEA SW11 141 F4
Rushley Cl HAYES BR2 215 H2
Rushmead BETH E2 104 D2
RCHPK/HAM TW10 156 C5
Rushmead Cl CROY/NA CR0 212 B2
Rushmere Ct WPK KT4 192 D6
Rushmere Pl WIM/MER SW19 177 G1
Rushmon Pl CHEAM SM3 * 208 C4
Rushmon Vls NWMAL KT3 * 192 C1
Rushmoor Cl PIN HA5 59 G1
Rushmore Cl BMLY BR1 184 D6
Rushmore Ct WATW WD18 * 26 B1
Rushmore Rd CLPT E5 86 E2
Rusholme Av DAGE RM10 92 C1
Rusholme Gv NRWD SE19 181 F1
Rusholme Rd PUT/ROE SW15 159 G1
Rushout Av
KTN/HRWW/WS HA3 61 H3
Rushton St IS N1 7 F2
Rushworth St STHWK SE1 18 B2
Rushy Meadow La CAR SM5 194 D6
Ruskin Av EBED/NFELT TW14 153 J2
MNPK E12 89 K4
RCH/KEW TW9 137 H1
WELL DA16 148 B4
Ruskin Cl GLDGN NW11 65 F3
Ruskin Dr ORP BR6 216 E1
WELL DA16 148 B4
WPK KT4 192 E6
Ruskin Gdns EA W5 97 K3
HARH RM3 57 K4
KTN/HRWW/WS HA3 62 B2
Ruskin Gv DART DA1 151 K6
WELL DA16 148 B3
Ruskin Rd BELV DA17 129 H4
CAR SM5 210 A3
CROY/NA CR0 196 C6
ISLW TW7 136 A4
STHL UB1 95 J6
TOTM N17 50 B4
Ruskin Wk ED N9 36 C4
HAYES BR2 200 E3
HNHL SE24 142 D6
Ruskin Wy WIM/MER SW19 178 C5
Rusland Av ORP BR6 216 D1
Rusland Park Rd HRW HA1 60 E1
Rusper Cl CRICK NW2 82 A1
STAN HA7 29 J6
Rusper Rd DAGW RM9 91 J4
WDGN N22 49 H5
Russel Cl BECK BR3 182 E6
Russell Av WDGN N22 49 H5
Russell Cl BKHTH/KID SE3 146 B1
BXLYHN DA7 149 H5
CHSWK W4 118 C6
DART DA1 150 D4
NTHWD HA6 40 A1
RSLP HA4 59 G6
WLSDN NW10 80 E5
Russell Ct BAR EN5 * 21 G5
WHALL SW1A 16 B1
Russell Dr STWL/WRAY TW19 152 A1
Russell Gdns GLDGN NW11 64 C3
RCHPK/HAM TW10 156 D4
TRDG/WHET N20 33 J4
WDR/YW UB7 112 D5
WKENS W14 * 119 H3
Russell Gardens Ms
WKENS W14 119 H2
Russell Gv BRXN/ST SW9 142 B2
MLHL NW7 45 G1
Russell Kerr Cl CHSWK W4 * 137 K1
Russell La TRDG/WHET N20 33 K4
Russell Pde GLDGN NW11 * 64 C3
Russell Pl HAMP NW3 83 J3
Russell Rd BKHH IG9 39 G3
CAN/RD E16 106 E5
CDALE/KGS NW9 63 H3
CEND/HSY/T N8 66 D3
CHING E4 37 H6
EN EN1 24 B1
MTCM CR4 178 D6
NTHLT UB5 78 C3
NTHWD HA6 26 A5
SEVS/STOTM N15 68 A3
TRDG/WHET N20 33 J4
WALTH E17 51 H6
WALTH E17 69 K3
WDGN N22 49 F2
WHTN TW2 156 A1
WIM/MER SW19 177 K3
WKENS W14 119 H3
Russell Sq RSQ WC1B 10 E1
Russell St HOL/ALD WC2B 11 G4
Russell Wy OXHEY WD19 27 F2
SUT SM1 209 F3
Russet Cl HGDN/ICK UB10 94 A3
Russet Crs HOLWY N7 * 85 F3
Russet Dr CROY/NA CR0 198 B5
Russets Cl CHING E4 38 B6
Russett Cl ORP BR6 217 H3
Russia Dock Rd
BERM/RHTH SE16 * 124 B1
Russia La BETH E2 104 E1
Russia Rw CITYW EC2V 12 D4
Rusthall Av CHSWK W4 118 A3
Rusthall Cl CROY/NA CR0 197 K3
Rustic Av STRHM/NOR SW16 179 G3
Rustic Pl ALP/SUD HA0 79 K2
Rustington Wk CHEAM SM3 193 J4
Ruston Av BRYLDS KT5 191 J4
Ruston Gdns STHGT/OAK N14 33 J4
Ruston Ms NTGHL W11 * 100 C5
Ruston Rd WOOL/PLUM SE18 126 D3
Ruston St BOW E3 87 H6
Rust Sq CMBW SE5 142 E1
Rutford Rd STRHM/NOR SW16 179 K1
Ruth Cl STAN HA7 62 B1
Rutherford Cl BELMT SM2 209 H4
Rutherford St WEST SW1P 16 C6
Rutherford Wy BUSH WD23 28 E3
WBLY HA9 80 C1
Rutherglen Rd ABYW SE2 128 B6
Rutherwyke Cl EW KT17 207 J4
Ruthin Cl CDALE/KGS NW9 63 G3
Ruthin Rd BKHTH/KID SE3 125 K6
Ruthven St HOM E9 87 F6
Rutland Av BFN/LL DA15 168 B2
Rutland Cl BXLY DA5 168 E3
CHSGTN KT9 206 B4
DART DA1 171 G2
MORT/ESHN SW14 137 J4
WIM/MER SW19 178 D3
Rutland Ct CHST BR7 185 F4
SKENS SW7 14 D3
Rutland Dr MRDN SM4 193 K4
RCHPK/HAM TW10 156 E3
Rutland Gdns BCTR RM8 91 J3
CROY/NA CR0 212 A2
FSBYPK N4 67 H3
SKENS SW7 14 D3
WEA W13 * 97 G4
Rutland Gardens Ms
SKENS SW7 14 D3
Rutland Ga BELV DA17 129 J5
HAYES BR2 199 J1
SKENS SW7 14 C4
Rutland Gate Ms SKENS SW7 * 14 C3
Rutland Gv HMSMTH W6 118 E5
Rutland Ms STJWD NW8 * 83 F6
Rutland Ms South SKENS SW7 * 14 C4
Rutland Pk CAT SE6 164 C4
CRICK NW2 82 A4
Rutland Pl BUSH WD23 * 28 D3
FARR EC1M * 12 B1
Rutland Rd FSTGT E7 89 H5
HOM E9 87 F6
HRW HA1 60 C3
HYS/HAR UB3 113 G4
IL IG1 90 B2
STHL UB1 96 A3
WALTH E17 69 J3
WAN E11 71 F2
WHTN TW2 155 J4
Rutland St SKENS SW7 14 D4
Rutland Wk CAT SE6 164 C4
Rutland Wy STMC/STPC BR5 202 E3
Rutley Cl WALW SE17 122 C6
Rutlish Rd WIM/MER SW19 177 K4
Rutter Gdns MTCM CR4 194 C1
Rutters Cl WDR/YW UB7 112 D2
Rutt's Ter NWCR SE14 144 A2
The Rutts BUSH WD23 28 D3
Ruvigny Gdns PUT/ROE SW15 139 G4
Ruxley Cl HOR/WEW KT19 206 D3
SCUP DA14 186 E2
Ruxley Crs ESH/CLAY KT10 205 H5
Ruxley La HOR/WEW KT19 206 E4
Ruxley Ms HOR/WEW KT19 206 D3
Ruxley Rdg ESH/CLAY KT10 205 G5
Ruxley Towers
ESH/CLAY KT10 * 205 G5
Ryan Cl BKHTH/KID SE3 146 A5
RSLP HA4 59 F5
Ryan Ct OXHEY WD19 * 27 J2
Ryan Dr BTFD TW8 116 B6
Ryarsh Crs ORP BR6 216 E2
Rycroft Wy TOTM N17 * 50 B6
Ryculff Sq BKHTH/KID SE3 145 J3
Rydal Cl HDN NW4 46 C4
Rydal Crs GFD/PVL UB6 97 H2
Rydal Dr BXLYHN DA7 149 H2
WWKM BR4 199 H6
Rydal Gdns CDALE/KGS NW9 63 G2
HSLW TW3 155 G1
PUT/ROE SW15 176 B1
WBLY HA9 61 J5
Rydal Mt HAYES BR2 * 199 J1
Rydal Rd STRHM/NOR SW16 179 J1
Rydal Wy PEND EN3 36 E1
RSLP HA4 77 G2
Rydens Av WOT/HER KT12 188 B6
Rydens Cl WOT/HER KT12 188 B6
Rydens Pk WOT/HER KT12 188 C6
Ryde Pl TWK TW1 156 D1
Ryder Cl BUSH WD23 28 B1
Ryder Dr BERM/RHTH SE16 123 J5
Ryder Gdns RAIN RM13 93 H4
Ryder St STJS SW1Y 10 B7
Ryde Vale Rd BAL SW12 161 G4
Rydon Ms WIM/MER SW19 177 F3
Rydston Cl HOLWY N7 85 F5
Rye Cl BXLY DA5 169 J1
Ryecotes Md DUL SE21 163 F3
Rye Crs STMC/STPC BR5 202 E5
Ryecroft Av CLAY IG5 54 B5
WHTN TW2 155 G3
Ryecroft Rd LEW SE13 145 F6
STMC/STPC BR5 201 J3
STRHM/NOR SW16 180 B2
Ryecroft St FUL/PGN SW6 140 A2
Ryedale EDUL SE22 163 J1
Ryefield Av HGDN/ICK UB10 76 A6
Ryefield Crs PIN HA5 * 40 E5
Ryefield Pde NTHWD HA6 * 40 E5
Ryefield Rd NRWD SE19 180 D2
Rye Hill Pk PECK SE15 143 K5
Ryelands Crs LEE/GVPK SE12 166 B1
Rye La PECK SE15 143 H3
Rye Rd PECK SE15 144 A5
The Rye STHGT/OAK N14 34 C2
Rye Wk PUT/ROE SW15 139 G6
Rye Wy EDGW HA8 44 B2
Ryfold Rd WIM/MER SW19 159 K5
Ryhope Rd FBAR/BDGN N11 34 B6
Ryland Cl FELT TW13 153 J6
Rylandes Rd CRICK NW2 81 J1
SAND/SEL CR2 212 D6
Ryland Rd KTTN NW5 * 84 B4
Rylett Crs SHB W12 118 C3
Rylett Rd SHB W12 118 C2
Rylston Rd FUL/PGN SW6 119 J6
PLMGR N13 35 K5
Rymer Rd CROY/NA CR0 197 F4
Rymer St HNHL SE24 162 C1
Rymill St CAN/RD E16 127 F1
Rysbrack St CHEL SW3 14 E4
Rythe Cl CHSGTN KT9 205 J5
Rythe Ct THDIT KT7 190 B4
Rythe Rd ESH/CLAY KT10 204 D3
Ryves Cottages MTCM CR4 * 179 F5

S

Sabbarton St CAN/RD E16 106 D5
Sabine Rd BTSEA SW11 140 E4
Sable Cl HSLWW TW4 134 B4
Sable St IS N1 85 H5
Sach Rd CLPT E5 68 D6
Sackville Av HAYES BR2 199 K5
Sackville Cl RYLN/HDSTN HA2 78 D1
Sackville Est
STRHM/NOR SW16 161 K5
Sackville Gdns IL IG1 71 K5
Sackville Rd BELMT SM2 208 E5
RDART DA2 171 H5
Sackville St CONDST W1S 10 A6
Saddlers Cl PIN HA5 42 A1
Saddlers Ms KUT/HW KT1 174 D4
Saddlescombe Wy
NFNCH/WDSPK N12 46 E1
Sadler Cl MTCM CR4 178 E5
Sadlers Gate Ms
PUT/ROE SW15 139 F4
Sadlers Ride E/WMO/HCT KT8 173 H5
Saffron Av POP/IOD E14 106 B6
Saffron Cl CROY/NA CR0 195 K3
GLDGN NW11 64 D2
Saffron Hl HCIRC EC1N 11 K2
Saffron Rd CRW RM5 57 F5
Saffron St HCIRC EC1N 11 K1
Saffron Wy SURB KT6 190 E5
Sage Cl EHAM E6 107 K4
Sage Ms EDUL SE22 143 G6
Sage St WCHPL E1 104 E6
Sage Wy FSBYW WC1X 5 G5
Sage Yd SURB KT6 * 191 G5
Saigasso Cl CAN/RD E16 107 H5
Sail St LBTH SE11 17 H6
Sainfoin Rd TOOT SW17 161 F4
Sainsbury Rd NRWD SE19 181 F1
St Agatha's Dr KUTN/CMB KT2 175 G2
St Agatha's Gv CAR SM5 194 E5
St Agnes Cl HOM E9 * 86 E6
St Agnes Pl LBTH SE11 122 C6
St Agnes Well STLK EC1Y 7 F6
St Aidan's Rd EDUL SE22 163 J1
WEA W13 116 C2
St Albans Av CHSWK W4 118 A3
EHAM E6 107 K2
FELT TW13 172 C1
St Albans Crs WDGN N22 49 G4
St Albans Farm
EBED/NFELT TW14 * 134 B6
St Alban's Gdns TEDD TW11 174 B1
St Albans Gv CAR SM5 194 D4
KENS W8 120 A3
St Albans La GLDGN NW11 64 E5
St Alban's Ms BAY/PAD W2 8 B1
St Alban's Pl IS N1 6 A1
St Albans Rd BAR EN5 20 C2
DART DA1 171 J1
GDMY/SEVK IG3 73 F5
KTTN NW5 84 A1
KUTN/CMB KT2 175 F2
SUT SM1 208 D2
WFD IG8 52 E3
WLSDN NW10 81 G6
St Alban's St STJS SW1Y 10 C6
St Albans Ter HMSMTH W6 119 H6
St Alfege Pas GNWCH SE10 125 F6
St Alfege Rd CHARL SE7 126 C6
St Alphage Gdns BARB EC2Y 12 D2
St Alphage Highwalk
BARB EC2Y 12 D2
St Alphage Wk EDGW HA8 * 44 E5
St Alphege Rd ED N9 36 E2
St Alphonsus Rd CLAP SW4 141 H5
St Amunds Cl CAT SE6 164 D6
St Andrews Av ALP/SUD HA0 79 G2
HCH RM12 93 J2
St Andrews Cl
BERM/RHTH SE16 123 J5
CRICK NW2 * 81 K1
ISLW TW7 135 K2
NFNCH/WDSPK N12 * 33 G6
RSLP HA4 59 H6
STAN HA7 * 43 J5
THDIT KT7 190 C5
THMD SE28 109 K5
WIM/MER SW19 178 A2
St Andrew's Ct
WAND/EARL SW18 160 B4
St Andrews Dr STAN HA7 43 J4
STMC/STPC BR5 202 C3
St Andrew's Gv
STNW/STAM N16 67 K5
St Andrew's Hl BLKFR EC4V 12 B5
St Andrews Ms BAL SW12 161 J3
BKHTH/KID SE3 145 K1
STNW/STAM N16 68 A5
St Andrew's Pl CAMTN NW1 3 J6
St Andrew's Rd ACT W3 99 G5
CAR SM5 209 J1
CDALE/KGS NW9 63 F5
CROY/NA CR0 211 J2
ED N9 36 E2
EN EN1 23 K4
GLDGN NW11 64 D3
HNWL W7 115 K2
IL IG1 71 K4
PLSTW E13 107 F2
ROMW/RG RM7 75 F3
SCUP DA14 168 E5
SURB KT6 190 E3
WALTH E17 51 F5
WAN E11 70 C3
WKENS W14 119 H6
WLSDN NW10 81 K4
St Andrew's Sq NTGHL W11 * 100 C5
SURB KT6 190 E3
St Andrews Ter OXHEY WD19 * 41 G1
St Andrew St HCIRC EC1N 11 K2
St Andrews Wy BOW E3 105 K3
St Anna Rd BAR EN5 * 20 B6
St Anne's Av
STWL/WRAY TW19 152 A2
St Anne's Cl HGT N6 84 A1
OXHEY WD19 27 G6
St Annes Ct SOHO/CST W1F 10 C4
St Annes Gdns WLSDN NW10 98 B2
St Anne's Pas POP/IOD E14 * 105 H5
St Anne's Rd ALP/SUD HA0 79 K3
LEY E10 70 B6
St Anne's Rw POP/IOD E14 105 H5
St Anne St POP/IOD E14 105 H5
St Ann's BARK IG11 90 C6
St Anns Ct HDN NW4 * 45 K6
St Ann's Crs WAND/EARL SW18 160 B1
St Anns Gdns KTTN NW5 84 A4
St Ann's Hl WAND/EARL SW18 140 A6
St Ann's Park Rd
WAND/EARL SW18 160 B1
St Ann's Rd BARK IG11 90 C6
BARN SW13 * 138 C3
ED N9 36 B4
HRW HA1 60 E3
NTGHL W11 100 B6
SEVS/STOTM N15 67 K2
St Ann's St WEST SW1P 16 D5
St Ann's Ter STJWD NW8 2 B2
St Ann's Vls NTGHL W11 119 G1
St Ann's Wy CROY/NA CR0 211 H4
St Anselms Rd HYS/HAR UB3 113 J2
St Anthony's Av WFD IG8 53 G3
St Anthonys Cl TOOT SW17 160 D4
WAP E1W * 123 H1
St Anthony's Ct ORP BR6 201 G6
St Anthony's Wy
EBED/NFELT TW14 133 J5
St Antony's Rd FSTGT E7 89 F5
St Arvans Cl CROY/NA CR0 212 A1
St Asaph Rd BROCKY SE4 144 A4
St Aubyn's Av HSLW TW3 135 F6
WIM/MER SW19 177 J1
St Aubyns Cl ORP BR6 217 F1
St Aubyns Gdns ORP BR6 202 A6
St Aubyn's Rd NRWD SE19 181 G2
St Audrey Av BXLYHN DA7 149 H3
St Augustine's Av EA W5 98 A1
HAYES BR2 200 D2
SAND/SEL CR2 211 J5
WBLY HA9 80 A1
St Augustine's Rd BELV DA17 129 G4
CAMTN NW1 84 D5
St Austell Cl EDGW HA8 44 B5
St Austell Rd LEW SE13 145 F3
St Awdry's Rd BARK IG11 90 D6
St Barnabas Cl BECK BR3 183 F5
EDUL SE22 143 F6
St Barnabas' Gdns
E/WMO/HCT KT8 189 F2
St Barnabas Rd MTCM CR4 179 F3
SUT SM1 209 H3
WALTH E17 69 J3
WFD IG8 53 F4
St Barnabas St BGVA SW1W 121 F5
St Barnabas Ter HOM E9 87 F3
St Barnabas Vls VX/NE SW8 141 K2
St Bartholomew's Cl SYD SE26 163 K6
St Bartholomew's Rd
EHAM E6 107 J1
St Benets Cl TOOT SW17 160 D4
St Benet's Gv CAR SM5 194 B4
St Benjamins Dr ORP BR6 217 J6
St Bernards CROY/NA CR0 212 A1
St Bernards Cl WNWD SE27 162 E6
St Bernard's Rd EHAM E6 89 J6
St Blaise Av BMLY BR1 184 A5
St Botolph St TWRH EC3N 13 J3
St Bride's Av EDGW HA8 44 B4
St Brides Cl ERITHM DA18 128 E2
St Bride St FLST/FETLN EC4A 12 A3
St Catherines Cl CHSGTN KT9 205 K4
TOOT SW17 * 160 D4
St Catherines Ct FELT TW13 153 K3
St Catherine's Dr NWCR SE14 144 A3
St Catherines Ms CHEL SW3 14 E6
St Catherines Rd CHING E4 37 J4
RSLP HA4 58 A2
St Chads Cl SURB KT6 190 D4
St Chad's Gdns CHDH RM6 74 A4
St Chad's Pl FSBYW WC1X 5 F4
St Chad's Rd CHDH RM6 74 A3
St Chad's St STPAN WC1H 5 F4
St Charles Pl NKENS W10 100 C4
St Charles Sq NKENS W10 100 C4
St Christopher's Cl ISLW TW7 135 K2
St Christophers Dr
HYS/HAR UB3 95 F6
St Christopher's Ms
WLGTN SM6 210 C3
St Christopher's Pl MHST W1U 9 H4
St Clair Cl CLAY IG5 53 K5
St Clair Dr WPK KT4 207 K2
St Clair Rd PLSTW E13 107 F1
St Clair's Rd CROY/NA CR0 197 F6
St Clare St TWRH EC3N 13 J4
St Clements Ct PUR RM19 131 K4
St Clement's La LINN WC2A 11 H4
St Clements St HOLWY N7 85 G5
St Clements Yd EDUL SE22 * 143 G6
St Cloud Rd WNWD SE27 162 D6
St Crispins Cl HAMP NW3 83 J2
STHL UB1 95 K5
St Cross St HCIRC EC1N 11 K1
St Cuthberts Gdns PIN HA5 * 41 K3
St Cuthberts Rd CRICK NW2 82 D4
PLMGR N13 49 G2
St Cyprian's St TOOT SW17 160 E6
St Davids Cl
BERM/RHTH SE16 * 123 J5
WBLY HA9 80 E1
WWKM BR4 198 E4
St David's Dr EDGW HA8 44 B4
St Davids Ms BOW E3 105 G2
St David's Pl HDN NW4 63 K4
St Davids Sq POP/IOD E14 124 E5
St Denis Rd WNWD SE27 162 E6
St Dionis Rd FUL/PGN SW6 139 J3
St Donatt's Rd NWCR SE14 144 C3
St Dunstan's Av ACT W3 99 F6
St Dunstans Cl HYS/HAR UB3 113 J4
St Dunstans Gdns ACT W3 99 F6
St Dunstan's Hl MON EC3R * 13 G6
SUT SM1 208 C2
St Dunstan's La MON EC3R * 13 G6
St Dunstan's Rd FELT TW13 153 J5
FSTGT E7 89 G4
HMSMTH W6 119 G5
HNWL W7 115 K2
HSLWW TW4 134 B3
SNWD SE25 197 G1
St Edmunds Av RSLP HA4 58 B3

St Edmunds Cl ERITHM DA18.....128 E2
 STJWD NW8.....2 E1
 TOOT SW17.....160 D4
St Edmunds Dr STAN HA7.....43 C4
St Edmunds La WHTN TW2.....155 G2
St Edmunds Rd DART DA1.....151 K5
 ED N9.....36 C2
 IL IG1.....71 K5
St Edmunds Sq BARN SW13.....119 F6
St Edmunds Ter STJWD NW8.....2 D1
St Edward's Cl GLDGN NW11.....64 E3
St Edwards Wy ROM RM1.....75 G1
St Egberts Wy CHING E4.....38 A3
St Elmo Rd SHB W12.....118 C1
St Elmos Rd BERM/RHTH SE16.....124 B2
St Erkenwald Ms BARK IG11.....90 D6
St Erkenwald Rd BARK IG11.....90 D6
St Ervans Rd NKENS W10.....100 C4
St Faith's Cl ENC/FH EN2.....23 J2
St Faith's Rd DUL SE21.....162 C3
St Fidelis' Rd ERITH DA8.....130 A4
St Fillans Rd CAT SE6.....165 F3
St Francis Cl ORP BR6.....217 F5
 OXHEY WD19.....27 F3
St Francis Rd EDUL SE22.....143 F5
St Francis Wy IL IG1.....90 D2
St Gabriel's Cl WAN E11.....71 F5
St Gabriel's Rd CRICK NW2.....82 B3
St George's ED N9.....36 C5
St George's Av CDALE/KGS NW9.....62 E1
 EA W5.....116 E2
 FSTGT E7.....89 F5
 HOLWY N7.....84 E2
 STHL UB1.....95 K6
St George's Circ STHWK SE1.....18 A3
St Georges Cl ALP/SUD HA0.....79 J6
 GLDGN NW11.....64 D3
 THMD SE28.....109 K5
 VX/NE SW8.....141 H2
St George's Ct STP EC4M *.....12 A3
St George's Dr OXHEY WD19.....27 J6
 PIM SW1V.....121 G5
St Georges Flds BAY/PAD W2.....8 D5
St Georges Gdns TOOT SW17.....160 C5
St George's Gv TOOT SW17.....160 C5
St George's Industrial Est
 KUTN/CMB KT2.....174 E1
St George's La MON EC3R *.....13 H5
St George's Ms CAMTN NW1.....83 K5
 CHSWK W4 *.....117 K6
 DEPT SE8.....124 C4
St Georges Pde CAT SE6 *.....164 C4
St George's Rd BECK BR3.....182 E4
 BMLY BR1.....184 D1
 CHSWK W4.....118 A2
 DAGW RM9.....92 A2
 EN EN1.....24 B1
 FELT TW13.....154 D6
 FSTGT E7.....89 F5
 GLDGN NW11.....64 D3
 HNWL W7.....116 A1
 IL IG1.....71 K4
 KUTN/CMB KT2.....175 H3
 LEY E10.....88 A1
 MTCM CR4.....179 G6
 PLMGR N13.....35 F5
 RCH/KEW TW9.....137 G4
 SCUP DA14.....186 E2
 STHWK SE1.....18 A5
 STMC/STPC BR5.....201 J3
 TWK TW1.....156 C6
 WIM/MER SW19.....177 J2
 WLGTN SM6.....210 B3
St Georges Rd West BMLY BR1.....184 D5
St George's Sq FSTGT E7 *.....89 F5
 NWMAL KT3.....176 B6
 PIM SW1V.....121 J5
St George's Square Ms
 PIM SW1V.....121 J5
St Georges Ter CAMTN NW1.....83 K5
 PECK SE15 *.....143 H1
St George St CONDST W1S.....9 K5
St George's Wk CROY/NA CRO.....211 J1
St George's Wy PECK SE15.....123 F6
St Gerards Cl CLAP SW4.....141 H6
St German's Pl BKHTH/KID SE3.....145 K3
St German's Rd FSTH SE23.....164 B3
St Giles Av DAGE RM10.....92 D5
 HGDN/ICK UB10.....76 A2
St Giles Churchyard
 BARB EC2Y *.....12 D2
St Giles Circ SOHO/SHAV W1D.....10 D3
St Giles Cl DAGE RM10.....92 D5
 HEST TW5.....134 D1
 ORP BR6.....216 D3
St Giles Ct LSQ/SEVD WC2H *.....10 D3
St Giles High St
 LSQ/SEVD WC2H.....10 D3
St Giles Pas LSQ/SEVD WC2H.....10 D4
St Giles Rd CMBW SE5.....143 F1
St Gothard Rd WNWD SE27.....162 E6
St Gregory Cl RSLP HA4.....77 F2
St Helena Rd
 BERM/RHTH SE16.....124 A4
St Helena St FSBYW WC1X *.....5 J5
St Helena Ter RCH/KEW TW9 *.....136 E6
St Helens THDIT KT7 *.....189 K4
St Helens Ct ERITH RM13.....111 J3
St Helen's Crs
 STRHM/NOR SW16.....180 A4
St Helens Gdns NKENS W10.....100 B5
St Helens Pl HDTCH EC3A.....13 H3
St Helen's Rd ERITHM DA18.....128 E2
 IL IG1.....71 K4
 STRHM/NOR SW16.....180 A5
 WEA W13.....116 C1
St Helier Av MRDN SM4.....194 B4
St Heliers Av HSLWW TW4.....135 F6
St Helier's Rd LEY E10.....69 K3
St Hildas Cl KIL/WHAMP NW6 *.....82 B6
 TOOT SW17.....160 D4
St Hilda's Rd BARN SW13.....118 E6
St Hughes Cl TOOT SW17 *.....160 D4
St Hugh's Rd PGE/AN SE20.....181 J4
St Ivians Dr GPK RM2.....57 K6
St James Av SUT SM1.....208 E3
 TRDG/WHET N20.....33 J5
 WEA W13.....116 B1
St James Cl EBAR EN4.....21 H4
 NWMAL KT3.....192 C2
 RSLP HA4.....59 G6
 STJWD NW8.....2 E2
 TRDG/WHET N20.....33 J5
St James' Ct WESTW SW1E *.....16 B4
St James' Gdns ALP/SUD HA0.....79 K5
 CHDH RM6.....73 H1
St James Ms POP/IOD E14 *.....125 F3
St James Pl DART DA1.....171 G1
St James Rd CAR SM5.....209 J1
 ED N9.....36 D4
 MTCM CR4.....179 F5
 SRTFD E15.....88 D3
 SURB KT6.....190 E3
 SUT SM1.....208 E4
St James's NWCR SE14.....144 B2
St James's Av BECK BR3.....182 B6
 BETH E2.....104 E1
 HPTN TW12.....173 G1
St James's Chambers
 STJS SW1Y *.....10 B7
St James's Cl TOOT SW17 *.....160 E4
 TOOT SW17 *.....179 F1
 WOOL/PLUM SE18.....127 H5
St James's Cottages
 RCH/KEW TW9 *.....136 E6
St James's Ct KUT/HW KT1 *.....175 F6
 WESTW SW1E.....16 B4
St James's Crs BRXN/ST SW9.....142 B4
St James's Dr BAL SW12.....160 E3
St James's Gdns CAMTN NW1 *.....4 A5
 NTGHL W11.....119 H1
St James's Gv BTSEA SW11.....140 E3
St James's La MUSWH N10.....66 B1
St James's Market STJS SW1Y *.....10 C6
St James's Pk CROY/NA CRO.....196 D4
St James's Pl WHALL SW1A.....16 A1
St James Sq SURB KT6.....190 E3
St James's Rd
 BERM/RHTH SE16.....123 H3
 CROY/NA CRO.....196 D4
 HPTN TW12.....173 G1
 KUT/HW KT1.....175 F5
St James's Rw CHSGTN KT9 *.....205 K4
St James's St STJS SW1Y *.....10 C7
 WALTH E17.....69 G2
St James's Ter STJWD NW8 *.....2 E1
St James's Terrace Ms
 STJWD NW8 *.....2 E1
St James Wk CLKNW EC1R.....6 A7
St Jerome's Gv HYS/HAR UB3.....94 A5
St Joan's Rd ED N9.....36 B4
St John Fil FUL/PGN SW6 *.....139 K1
St John's Av FBAR/BDGN N11 *.....47 K1
 PUT/ROE SW15.....139 G6
 WLSDN NW10.....81 H6
St John's Church Rd HOM E9 *.....86 E3
St John's Cl FUL/PGN SW6 *.....139 K1
 RAIN RM13.....93 J5
 STHGT/OAK N14.....34 C1
 TRDG/WHET N20 *.....33 G5
 WBLY HA9.....80 A3
St Johns Cottages
 PGE/AN SE20 *.....181 K5
St John's Ct BKHH IG9.....39 F5
St John's Crs BRXN/ST SW9.....142 B4
St John's Dr
 WAND/EARL SW18.....160 A5
 WOT/HER KT12.....188 B5
St John's Gdns NTGHL W11.....100 D6
 BARN SW13 *.....138 C3
 RCH/KEW TW9.....136 E6
St John's Hl BTSEA SW11.....140 D5
St John's Hl Gv BTSEA SW11 *.....140 C5
St John's La FARR EC1M.....6 A7
St Johns Pde SCUP DA14 *.....168 C6
 WEA W13 *.....116 C1
St John's Pk BKHTH/KID SE3.....145 K1
St John's Pth FSBYE EC1V *.....6 A7
St John's Rd BARK IG11.....90 E6
 BTSEA SW11.....140 D5
 CAN/RD E16.....106 E5
 CAR SM5.....209 J1
 CHING E4.....37 K6
 CROY/NA CRO.....211 H1
 E/WMO/HCT KT8.....189 J1
 EHAM E6.....107 J6
 ERITH DA8.....130 A5
 FELT TW13.....154 D6
 GLDGN NW11.....64 D4
 GNTH/NBYPK IG2.....72 E3
 HRW HA1.....61 F3
 ISLW TW7.....136 A3
 KUT/HW KT1.....175 G6
 NWDGN UB2.....114 D3
 NWMAL KT3.....175 K6
 PGE/AN SE20.....181 K5
 RCH/KEW TW9.....136 E6
 SCUP DA14.....168 C6
 SEVS/STOTM N15.....68 A3
 STMC/STPC BR5.....201 J3
 SUT SM1.....193 K6
 WALTH E17.....51 K6
 WBLY HA9.....79 K2
 WELL DA16.....148 C4
 WIM/MER SW19.....177 H5
St John's Sq FARR EC1M.....6 A7
St John's Ter FSTGT E7 *.....89 F5
 NKENS W10.....100 C3
 WOOL/PLUM SE18.....127 H6
St John St FSBYE EC1V.....5 K4
St John's V BROCKY SE4.....144 D3
St John's Vls ARCH N19.....66 D6
 KENS W8.....120 A3
St John's Wy ARCH N19.....66 D5
St John's Wood High St
 STJWD NW8.....2 B3
St John's Wood Pk STJWD NW8.....2 B1
St John's Wood Rd STJWD NW8.....2 A4
St John's Wood Ter STJWD NW8.....2 C2
St Josephs Cl NKENS W10.....100 C4
 ORP BR6.....217 F2
St Josephs Dr STHL UB1.....114 C1
St Josephs Gv HDN NW4.....63 K1
St Joseph's Rd ED N9.....36 D2
St Joseph's St VX/NE SW8 *.....141 G2
St Jude's Rd BETH E2.....104 D1
St Jude St STNW/STAM N16.....86 A3
St Julian's Cl
 STRHM/NOR SW16.....162 B6
St Julian's Farm Rd
 WNWD SE27.....162 B6
St Julian's Rd KIL/WHAMP NW6.....82 D5
St Justin Cl STMC/STPC BR5.....186 E5
St Katharine's Prec
 CAMTN NW1 *.....3 J2
St Katharine's Wy WAP E1W.....13 K7
St Katherines Rd
 ERITHM DA18.....128 E2
St Katherines Wk
 NTGHL W11 *.....100 B6
St Keverne Rd ELTH/MOT SE9.....166 D6
St Kilda Rd ORP BR6.....202 A5
 WEA W13.....116 B2
St Kilda's Rd HRW HA1.....60 E3
 STNW/STAM N16.....67 K5
St Kitts Ter NRWD SE19.....181 F1
St Laurence Cl
 KIL/WHAMP NW6.....82 B6
St Lawrence Cottages
 POP/IOD E14 *.....125 F1
St Lawrence Dr PIN HA5.....59 F2
St Lawrence Rd POP/IOD E14.....125 F1
St Lawrence Ter NKENS W10.....100 C4
St Lawrence Wy
 BRXN/ST SW9 *.....142 B3
St Leonard's Av CHING E4.....52 C2
 KTN/HRWW/WS HA3.....61 J2
St Leonard's Gdns HEST TW5.....134 D1
 IL IG1.....90 C3
St Leonards Ri ORP BR6.....216 E2
St Leonard's Rd CROY/NA CRO.....211 H1
St Leonards St BOW E3.....105 K2
St Leonard's Ter CHEL SW3.....120 E6
St Leonards Wk
 STRHM/NOR SW16.....180 A3
St Leonards Wy EMPK RM11.....75 K5
St Loo Av CHEL SW3.....120 D6
St Louis Rd WNWD SE27.....162 E6
St Loy's Rd TOTM N17.....50 B6
St Lucia Dr SRTFD E15.....88 D6
St Luke's Av CLAP SW4.....141 J5
 ENC/FH EN2.....23 K1
 IL IG1.....90 B3
St Luke's Cl SNWD SE25.....197 J3
St Luke's Est FSBYE EC1V *.....6 E6
St Luke's Ms NTGHL W11.....100 D5
St Luke's Pl NTGHL W11.....100 D4
St Lukes's Cl FSBYE EC1V.....6 D6
St Lukes Yd MV/WKIL W9 *.....100 D1
St Malo Av ED N9.....36 E5
St Margarets BARK IG11.....90 D6
St Margarets Av ASHF TW15.....152 E6
 BFN/LL DA15.....167 J3
 CHEAM SM3.....208 C1
 RYLN/HDSTN HA2.....78 C1
 SEVS/STOTM N15.....67 H1
St Margarets Ct
 PUT/ROE SW15 *.....138 E5
St Margarets Crs
 PUT/ROE SW15.....138 E6
St Margaret's Dr TWK TW1.....156 D1
St Margaret's Gv TWK TW1.....156 C1
 WAN E11.....88 D1
 WOOL/PLUM SE18.....127 H6
St Margarets La KENS W8 *.....120 A3
St Margarets Ms
 KUTN/CMB KT2 *.....175 K1
St Margaret's Rd BROCKY SE4.....144 C5
 EDGW HA8.....44 D1
 HNWL W7.....115 K1
 MNPK E12.....71 G6
 RSLP HA4.....58 B5
 TOTM N17.....50 C3
 TWK TW1.....156 C1
 WLSDN NW10.....100 A2
St Margarets Ter
 WOOL/PLUM SE18.....127 H5
St Margaret St WEST SW1P *.....16 E3
St Mark's Cl BAR EN5.....21 F4
 FUL/PGN SW6.....139 K2
St Marks Crs CAMTN NW1 *.....3 K1
St Mark's Ga HOM E9.....87 H5
St Mark's Gv WBPTN SW10.....140 A1
St Mark's Hl SURB KT6.....191 F4
St Mark's Pl NTGHL W11.....100 D5
 WIM/MER SW19 *.....177 H2
St Mark's Ri HACK E8.....86 B3
St Mark's Rd EA W5.....117 F1
 EN EN1.....36 B1
 HAYES BR2.....200 B1
 HNWL W7.....115 K2
 MTCM CR4.....178 E5
 NKENS W10.....100 B5
 SNWD SE25.....197 H1
 TEDD TW11.....174 C3
St Mark's Sq CAMTN NW1.....3 J1
St Mark St WCHPL E1.....13 K4
St Marks Vls FSBYPK N4 *.....67 F6
St Martins NTHWD HA6.....40 B1
St Martins Ap RSLP HA4.....58 C4
St Martin's Av EHAM E6.....107 H1
St Martin's Cl CAMTN NW1.....84 C6
 EN EN1.....24 D2
 ERITHM DA18.....128 E2
 OXHEY WD19.....27 G6
St Martin's Cl CHCR WC2N.....11 J6
 CHCR WC2N.....10 E6
St Martins La BECK BR3.....198 E2
St Martin's-le-Grand STBT EC1A.....12 C3
St Martin's Pl CHCR WC2N.....10 E6
St Martin's Rd BRXN/ST SW9.....142 A3
 DART DA1.....151 J6
 ED N9.....36 D4
St Martin's St LSQ/SEVD WC2H *.....10 D6
St Martin's Wy TOOT SW17.....160 B5
St Mary Abbot's Pl KENS W8 *.....119 J3
St Mary Abbots Ter
 WKENS W14.....119 J3
St Mary At Hl MON EC3R.....13 G6
St Mary Av WLGTN SM6.....210 A1
St Mary Axe HDTCH EC3A.....13 H4
St Marychurch St
 BERM/RHTH SE16.....123 K2
St Mary Graces Ct WCHPL E1 *.....13 K6
St Mary Newington Cl
 WALW SE17 *.....123 F5
St Mary Rd WALTH E17.....69 K1
St Marys BARK IG11.....108 D1
St Marys Ap MNPK E12.....89 K5
St Mary's Av FNCH N3.....46 D5
 HAYES BR2.....199 H1
 NTHWD HA6.....40 C1
 NWDGN UB2.....115 G3
 STWL/WRAY TW19.....152 A2
 TEDD TW11.....174 A2
 WAN E11.....71 F3
St Mary's Cl CHSGTN KT9.....206 B5
 EW KT17.....207 H5
 STMC/STPC BR5.....186 C5
 TOTM N17.....50 C4
St Marys Ct HMSMTH W6.....118 C3
St Mary's Crs HDN NW4.....63 K1
 HYS/HAR UB3.....94 D6
 ISLW TW7.....135 J1
 STWL/WRAY TW19.....152 A2
St Mary's Dr
 EBED/NFELT TW14.....153 F2
St Marys Est
 BERM/RHTH SE16 *.....123 K2
St Mary's Gdns LBTH SE11.....17 K6
St Mary's Ga KENS W8.....120 A3
St Mary's Gn EFNCH N2.....65 G1
St Mary's Gv BARN SW13.....138 E4
 CHSWK W4.....117 J6
 ISLW TW7.....136 B4
 RCH/KEW TW9.....137 G5
St Mary's Man BAY/PAD W2 *.....8 D1
St Mary's Ms KIL/WHAMP NW6 *.....83 F5
St Mary's Pth IS N1 *.....85 H5
 WCHPL E1 *.....104 C4
St Mary's Pl EA W5.....116 E2
 KENS W8.....120 A3
St Mary's Rd BXLY DA5.....169 K3
 CEND/HSY/T N8.....66 E1
 E/WMO/HCT KT8.....189 J2
 EA W5.....116 E2
 EBAR EN4.....33 J2
 ED N9.....36 E3
 GLDGN NW11.....64 C4
 HYS/HAR UB3.....94 D6
 IL IG1.....72 C6
 LEY E10.....70 A3
 PECK SE15.....143 K3
 PLSTW E13.....107 F1
 SNWD SE25.....181 H6
 WAN E11.....88 E1
 WIM/MER SW19.....177 G2
 WLSDN NW10.....81 G6
 WPK KT4.....192 C6
St Mary's Sq BAY/PAD W2 *.....8 A1
 EA W5 *.....116 E2
St Mary St WOOL/PLUM SE18.....127 F4
St Marys Vw
 KTN/HRWW/WS HA3.....61 J2
St Marys Wy CHIG IG7.....54 A1
St Matthew's Av SURB KT6.....191 F5
St Matthews Cl OXHEY WD19.....27 H1
 RAIN RM13.....93 J5
St Matthews Dr BMLY BR1.....184 E6
St Matthew's Rd
 BRXS/STRHM SW2.....142 A5
 EA W5.....116 E1
St Matthew's Rw BETH E2.....104 C2
St Matthew St WEST SW1P.....16 C5
St Matthias Cl CDALE/KGS NW9.....63 H2
St Maur Rd FUL/PGN SW6.....139 J2
St Meddens CHST BR7 *.....185 J3
St Mellion Cl THMD SE28.....109 K5
St Merryn Cl
 WOOL/PLUM SE18.....147 G1
St Michael's Aly BANK EC3V *.....13 G4
St Michaels Av ED N9.....36 E1
St Michaels Cl BMLY BR1.....184 D6
 CAN/RD E16.....107 H4
 ERITHM DA18.....128 E2
 FNCH N3.....46 D5
 NFNCH/WDSPK N12.....47 H1
 WOT/HER KT12.....188 B6
 WPK KT4.....192 C6
St Michaels Crs PIN HA5.....59 J3
St Michael's Gdns NKENS W10.....100 C4
St Michael's Ms BCVA SW1W.....15 G7
St Michaels Ri WELL DA16.....148 C2
St Michael's Rd BRXN/ST SW9.....142 A3
 CRICK NW2.....82 A2
 CROY/NA CRO.....196 D5
 WELL DA16.....148 C4
 WLGTN SM6.....210 C4
St Michael's St BAY/PAD W2.....8 B2
St Michaels Ter HGT N6 *.....66 A5
 WDGN N22.....48 E5
St Mildred's Ct LOTH EC2R *.....12 E4
St Mildreds Rd CAT SE6.....165 H2
St Nicholas Av HCH RM12.....93 J1
St Nicholas Cl BORE WD6.....29 K1
St Nicholas Glebe TOOT SW17.....179 F2
St Nicholas Rd SUT SM1.....209 F3
 THDIT KT7.....190 A3
 WOOL/PLUM SE18.....128 A5
St Nicholas St DEPT SE8.....144 C2
St Nicolas La CHST BR7.....184 C1
St Ninian's Ct TRDG/WHET N20.....33 K5
St Norbert Rd BROCKY SE4.....144 B5
St Olaf's Rd FUL/PGN SW6.....139 H1
St Olave's Rd EHAM E6.....90 A6
St Olave's Wk
 STRHM/NOR SW16.....179 H5
St Onge Pde EN EN1 *.....23 K4
St Oswald's Pl LBTH SE11.....122 A5
St Oswald's Rd
 STRHM/NOR SW16.....180 C4
St Oswulf St WEST SW1P *.....16 D7
St Pancras Gdns CAMTN NW1.....4 D2
St Pancras Wy CAMTN NW1.....84 C5
St Paul's Av
 BERM/RHTH SE16 *.....124 A1
 CRICK NW2.....81 K4
 KTN/HRWW/WS HA3.....62 B2
St Paul's Church Yd STP EC4M.....12 B4
 CHARL SE7.....126 C5
 CHSGTN KT9.....205 K2
 EA W5.....117 G2
 HYS/HAR UB3.....113 G5
St Paul's Cl CAR SM5.....194 D6
 CHSGTN KT9.....205 K2
 EA W5.....117 G2
 HYS/HAR UB3.....113 G5
St Paul's Cray Rd CHST BR7.....185 J4
St Pauls Crs CAMTN NW1.....84 D5
 HDN NW4.....64 A1
St Pauls Dr SRTFD E15.....88 B3
St Paul's Pl IS N1.....85 K4
St Pauls Ri PLMGR N13.....49 H2
St Pauls Rd BARK IG11.....90 C6
 ERITH DA8.....149 K1
 IS N1.....85 J4
 RCH/KEW TW9.....137 G4
 THHTH CR7.....180 D6
St Pauls Ter WALW SE17 *.....122 C6
St Pauls St IS N1.....85 J5
St Paul's Wy FNCH N3.....47 F5
 POP/IOD E14.....105 H4
St Paul's Wood Hl
 STMC/STPC BR5.....185 K5
St Peter's Av BETH E2.....104 C2
 UED N18.....36 C6
 WALTH E17.....70 C1
St Petersburgh Ms
 BAY/PAD W2.....101 F6
St Petersburgh Pl
 BAY/PAD W2.....101 F6
St Peter's Cl BETH E2.....104 C1
 BUSH WD23.....28 D3
 CHST BR7.....185 J3
 CNTH/NBYPK IG2.....72 E1
 RSLP HA4.....59 H6
 TOOT SW17.....160 D4
St Peters Ct BKHTH/KID SE3 *.....145 J6
 E/WMO/HCT KT8.....189 F1
 HDN NW4.....63 K4
St Peters Gdns WNWD SE27.....162 B5
St Peters Gv HMSMTH W6.....118 D4
St Peters Ms FSBYPK N4 *.....67 H2
St Peter's Rd CROY/NA CRO.....211 J3
 E/WMO/HCT KT8.....189 F1
 ED N9.....36 D3
 HMSMTH W6.....118 D5
 KUT/HW KT1.....175 H5
 STHL UB1.....96 A4
St Peter's Sq BETH E2 *.....104 C1
 HMSMTH W6.....118 C5
St Peter's St IS N1.....6 B1
 SAND/SEL CR2.....211 K3
St Peter's Ter FUL/PGN SW6.....139 H1
St Peter's Vis HMSMTH W6.....118 D4
St Peter's Wy ACT W3.....97 K4
 HYS/HAR UB3.....113 G5
St Philip's Av WPK KT4.....192 E6
St Philip Sq VX/NE SW8 *.....141 G3
St Philip St BTSEA SW11.....140 B3
St Philip's Rd HACK E8.....86 C4
 SURB KT6.....190 E3
St Philips Wy IS N1 *.....85 J6
St Quentin Rd WELL DA16.....148 A3
St Quentin Gdns NKENS W10.....100 A4
St Quintin Av NKENS W10.....100 A4
St Raphael's Wy WLSDN NW10.....80 E3
St Regis Cl MUSWH N10.....48 B5
St Ronans Cl EBAR EN4.....21 H1
St Ronans Crs WFD IG8.....52 E3
St Rule St VX/NE SW8.....141 H3
St Saviour's Ct HRW HA1 *.....60 D1
St Saviour's Est STHWK SE1.....19 J4
St Saviour's Rd
 BRXS/STRHM SW2.....142 A6
 CROY/NA CRO.....196 D3
Saints Dr FSTGT E7.....89 H3
St Silas Pl KTTN NW5.....84 A4
St Simon's Av PUT/ROE SW15.....139 F6
St Stephen's Av SHB W12.....118 E2
 WALTH E17.....70 A2

WEA W13....................97 H5
St Stephens CI KTTN NW5 *....83 K3
STHL UB1.....................96 A4
ST JWD NW8...................47 J2
WALTH E17....................69 K2
St Stephen's Crs BAY/PAD W2 ..100 E5
THHTH CR7...................180 B6
St Stephen's Gdns
BAY/PAD W2..................100 E5
TWK TW1......................156 D1
St Stephen's Gv LEW SE13....145 F4
St Stephens Ms BAY/PAD W2 ..100 E4
St Stephens Pde WHALL SW1A..16 E2
St Stephen's Rd BAR EN5.....20 B6
BOW E3......................105 H1
EHAM E6......................89 C5
HSLW TW3....................155 F1
WALTH E17....................69 K2
WDR/YW UB7..................112 A1
WEA W13......................97 H5
St Stephens St VX/NE SW8 *..141 K1
St Swithin's CI MANHO EC4N..12 E5
St Swithun's Rd LEW SE13 *..145 G6
St Theresa's Rd
EBED/NFELT TW14.............133 J5
St Thomas CI SURB KT6.......191 F5
St Thomas' Dr PIN HA5.......41 J4
STMC/STPC BR5...............201 H5
St Thomas Gdns IL IG1.......90 C4
St Thomas Rd BELV DA17......129 K2
CAN/RD E16..................106 E5
CHSWK W4....................137 K1
STHGT/OAK N14................54 D2
St Thomas's Gdns KTTN NW5...84 A4
St Thomas's PI HOM E9.......86 E5
St Thomas's Rd FSBYPK N4....67 G6
WLSDN NW10...................81 G6
St Thomas's Sq HOM E9.......86 D5
St Thomas St STHWK SE1......18 B2
St Thomas's Wy FUL/PGN SW6 .139 J1
St Ursula Gv PIN HA5........59 H2
St Ursula Rd STHL UB1.......96 A5
St Vincent CI WNWD SE27....180 C1
St Vincent Rd WHTN TW2.....155 H1
St Vincents Av DART DA1.....151 K4
St Vincents La MLHL NW7.....46 A1
St Vincents Rd DART DA1.....171 K1
St Vincent St MHST W1U.......9 H2
St Wilfrid's CI EBAR EN4....21 J6
St Wilfrid's Rd EBAR EN4....21 H6
St Winefride's Av MNPK E12..89 K3
St Winifred's CI CHIG IG7...54 E1
St Winifred's Rd TEDD TW11.174 C2
Sakura Dr FBAR/BDGN N11.....48 D4
Saladin Dr PUR RM19........131 K4
Salamanca PI STHWK SE1......17 G7
Salamanca St STHWK SE1......17 G7
Salamander CI KUTN/CMB KT2 .174 D1
Salamander Quay
KUT/HW KT1..................174 E1
Salmons Wy RAIN RM13.......111 G5
Salcombe Dr CHDH RM6........56 A4
MRDW SM4....................193 G5
Salcombe Gdns MLHL NW7......46 A2
Salcombe Rd ASHF TW15......152 B6
STNW/STAM N16...............86 B3
WALTH E17....................69 J3
Salcombe Wy RSLP HA4........58 E6
Salcott Rd BTSEA SW11......140 E6
CROY/NA CR0.................210 E1

Salehurst CI
KTN/HRWW/WS HA3.............62 A2
Salehurst Rd BROCKY SE4....164 C1
Salem PI CROY/NA CR0.......211 J1
Sale PI BAY/PAD W2...........8 C2
Sale St BETH E2.............104 C3
Salford Rd BRXS/STRHM SW2..161 J3
Salhouse CI THMD SE28......109 J5
Salisbury Av BARK IG11......90 E5
FNCH N3......................46 D5
SUT SM1.....................208 D4
Salisbury CI WALW SE17......18 E7
WPK KT4.....................207 H1
Salisbury Ct EMB EC4Y.......11 K4
Salisbury Gdns
WIM/MER SW19 *..............177 H3
Salisbury Pavement
FUL/PGN SW6 *...............139 K1
Salisbury Pl BRXN/ST SW9...142 C1
MBLAR W1H....................8 E1
MHST W1U.....................9 F1
Salisbury Prom
CEND/HSY/T N8 *.............67 H2
Salisbury Rd BAR EN5........20 C4
BXLY DA5....................169 H5
CAR SM5.....................209 K4
CHING E4.....................37 J5
DAGE RM10....................92 D4
FELT TW13...................154 B4
FSBYPK N4....................67 H2
HRW HA1......................60 D2
HSLWW TW4...................134 B4
LEY E10......................70 A6
NWDGN UB2 *.................114 D4
NWMAL KT3...................176 A6
PIN HA5......................58 C1
RCH/KEW TW9.................137 F5
SNWD SE25...................197 H3
WALTH E17....................70 A2
WDGN N22.....................49 H6
WEA W13.....................116 C2
WIM/MER SW19................177 H3
WPK KT4.....................207 F2
Salisbury Sq EMB EC4Y *.....11 K4
Salisbury St ACT W3........117 K2
ST JWD NW8...................2 C7
Salisbury Ter PECK SE15....143 K4
Salisbury Wk ARCH N19.......66 C6
Salix CI SUN TW16..........172 A3
Sally Murray CI MNPK E12....90 A2

Salmen Rd PLSTW E13........106 E1
Salmond CI STAN HA7.........43 G2
Salmon La POP/IOD E14......105 G5
Salmon Ms KIL/WHAMP NW6 *...82 E5
Salmon Rd BELV DA17........129 H5
DART DA1....................151 J4
Salmons Rd CHSGTN KT9......206 A4
ED N9........................36 C5
Salmon St CDALE/KGS NW9.....62 E4
POP/IOD E14 *...............105 H5
Salomons Rd PLSTW E13......107 G4
Salop Rd WALTH E17..........69 F3
Saltash CI SUT SM1.........208 D2
Satash Rd BARK/HLT IG6......54 D3
WELL DA16...................148 D2
Saltcoats Rd CHSWK W4......118 B2
Saltcote CI DART DA1.......170 B1
Saltcroft CI WBLY HA9.......62 D5
Salter CI RYLN/HDSTN HA2....77 K1
Salterford Rd TOOT SW17....179 F2
Salter Rd BERM/RHTH SE16...124 B2
Salters' Hall Ct MANHO EC4N *.12 E5
Salters Rd NKENS W10.......100 B3
WALTH E17....................70 B1
Salters Rw IS N1 *...........85 K4
Salter St POP/IOD E14......105 J6
WLSDN NW10...................99 J2
Salterton Rd HOLWY N7.......84 E1
Saltford CI ERITH DA8......130 B5
Saltley CI EHAM E6..........107 J2
Saltoun Rd BRXS/STRHM SW2..142 B5
Saltram CI SEVS/STOTM N15...68 B1
Saltram Crs MV/WKIL W9.....100 D2
Saltwell St POP/IOD E14....105 J6
Saltwood CI ORP BR6.........217 J2
Saltwood Gv WALW SE17 *....122 E5
Salusbury Rd KIL/WHAMP NW6..82 C6
Salvador TOOT SW17.........178 D1
Salvia Gdns GFD/PVL UB6.....97 G1
Salvin Rd PUT/ROE SW15.....139 G4
Salway CI WFD IG8...........52 E3
Salway Rd SRTFD E15.........88 B4
Samantha CI WALTH E17.......69 H4
Sam Bartram CI CHARL SE7...126 B5
Samels Ct HMSMTH W6........118 D5
Samford St STJWD NW8.........2 C7
Samira CI WALTH E17.........69 H4
Samos Rd PGE/AN SE20.......181 J5
Sampson Av BAR EN5..........20 B6
Sampson CI BELV DA17.......128 E3
Sampson St WAP E1W.........123 H1
Samson St PLSTW E13........107 G1
Samuel CI HACK E8...........86 B6
NWCR SE14...................124 A6
WOOL/PLUM SE18.............126 D4
Samuel Gray Gdns
KUTN/CMB KT2................174 E4
Samuel Lewis Trust Dwellings
CHEL SW3 *..................120 D5
CMBW SE5 *..................142 D2
HACK E8 *....................86 C2
WKENS W14 *.................119 H4
Samuel St WOOL/PLUM SE18...126 E4
Sancroft CI CRICK NW2.......81 K1
Sancroft Rd
KTN/HRWW/WS HA3.............43 F5
Sanctuary CI DART DA1.......171 G1
Sanctuary Ms HACK E8........86 B4
Sanctuary Rd HTHAIR TW6....132 D1
Sanctuary St STHWK SE1......18 D3
The Sanctuary BXLY DA5.....168 E1
WEST SW1P....................16 D4
Sandal CI EA W5..............98 A3
Sandall Rd EA W5.............98 A3
KTTN NW5....................84 C4
Sandal Rd NWMAL KT3........192 B1
UED N18......................50 C1
Sandal St SRTFD E15..........88 C6
Sandalwood CI WCHPL E1.....105 G3
Sandalwood Dr RSLP HA4......58 A4
Sandalwood Rd FELT TW13....154 A5
Sandbach PI
WOOL/PLUM SE18.............127 H5
Sandbourne Av
WIM/MER SW19................178 A6
Sandbourne Rd NWCR SE14....144 B3
Sandbrook CI MLHL NW7.......45 F2
Sandbrook Rd STNW/STAM N16..86 A1
Sandby Gn ELTH/MOT SE9.....146 D4
Sandcliff Rd ERITH DA8.....130 A4
Sandcroft CI PLMGR N13......49 H2
Sandell's Av ASHF TW15.....153 F6
Sanderstead CI BAL SW12....161 H2
Sanders La MLHL NW7.........46 B3
Sanderson CI KTTN NW5 *.....84 B2
Sanders Pde
STRHM/NOR SW16 *...........179 K2
Sanderstead Av GLDGN NW11...64 E4
Sanderstead CI BAL SW12....161 H2
Sanderstead Rd LEY E10......69 G5
SAND/SEL CR2................211 K5
Sandfield Gdns THHTH CR7...180 C6
Sandfield Pl THHTH CR7.....180 D6
Sandfield Rd THHTH CR7.....180 C6
Sandford Av WDGN N22........49 H4
Sandford Rd BXLYHS DA6.....149 F5
EHAM E6......................89 J3
HAYES BR2...................199 K1
Sandford Rw WALW SE17......122 E5
Sandford St FUL/PGN SW6....140 A1
Sandgate CI ROMW/RG RM7.....74 E4
Sandgate La
WAND/EARL SW18.............160 D3
Sandgate Rd WELL DA16......148 D1
Sandgate St PECK SE15......123 J6
Sandhills WLGTN SM6........210 D2
The Sandhills WBPTN SW10 *..120 B5
Sandhurst Av BRYLDS KT5....191 J4
RYLN/HDSTN HA2..............60 A6
Sandhurst CI CDALE/KGS NW9..44 C6
SAND/SEL CR2................212 A6
Sandhurst Dr GDMY/SEVK IG3..91 G2
Sandhurst Pde CAT SE6 *....165 F3

Sandhurst Rd BFN/LL DA15...168 A5
BXLY DA5....................148 E6
CDALE/KGS NW9................44 C6
ED N9........................36 E1
ORP BR6.....................217 G1
Sandhurst Wy SAND/SEL CR2..212 A5
Sandifer Dr CRICK NW2.......82 B1
Sandiford Rd CHEAM SM3.....193 J6
Sandiland Crs HAYES BR2....199 J6
Sandilands CROY/NA CR0.....212 C1
Sandilands Rd FUL/PGN SW6..140 A2
Sandison St PECK SE15......143 G4
Sandland St GINN WC1R.......11 H2
Sandling Ri ELTH/MOT SE9...167 F5
Sandlings CI PECK SE15.....143 J5
The Sandlings WDGN N22......49 H6
Sandmartin Wy WLGTN SM6....195 F5
Sandmere Rd CLAP SW4.......141 K5
Sandon CI ESH/CLAY KT10....189 J5
Sandow Crs HYS/HAR UB3.....113 J5
Sandown Av DAGE RM10........92 E4
ESH/CLAY KT10...............204 C3
Sandown CI HEST TW5........133 K2
Sandown Ct BELMT SM2 *.....209 F5
DAGE RM10....................92 E4
SYD SE26 *..................163 J5
Sandown Ga ESH/CLAY KT10...189 J6
Sandown Rd ESH/CLAY KT10...204 C2
SNWD SE25...................197 J2
Sandown Wy NTHLT UB5........77 H4
Sandpiper CI
BERM/RHTH SE16.............124 C2
WALTH E17....................51 F5
Sandpiper Dr ERITH DA8.....150 E1
Sandpiper Rd SUT SM1.......208 D3
Sandpiper Ter CLAY IG5 *....54 B5
Sandpiper Wy STMC/STPC BR5.202 E1
Sandpit PI CHARL SE7.......126 D5
Sandpit Rd BMLY BR1........183 H1
DART DA1....................151 F5
Sandpits Rd CROY/NA CR0....213 F6
RCHPK/HAM TW10..............156 E4
Sandra CI HSLW TW5.........135 G6
WDGN N22.....................49 J4
Sandridge CI HRW HA1........60 E1
Sandridge St ARCH N19.......66 C6
Sandringham Av RYNPK SW20..177 H4
Sandringham CI EN EN1.......24 A3
WIM/MER SW19................159 G3
Sandringham Crs
RYLN/HDSTN HA2..............78 A1
Sandringham Dr ASHF TW15...152 A6
RDART DA2...................170 B4
WELL DA16...................147 K3
Sandringham Gdns
BARK/HLT IG6................54 C6
E/WMO/HCT KT8..............189 G1
NFNCH/WDSPK N12.............47 H2
HEST TW5....................133 K2
Sandringham Ms EA W5 *......97 K6
Sandringham Rd BARK IG11....91 F4
BMLY BR1....................183 K1
CRICK NW2....................81 K3
CROY/NA CR0.................196 C4
FSTGT E7.....................89 G3
GLDGN NW11...................64 C4
HACK E8......................86 B3
HTHAIR TW6..................132 B6
LEY E10......................70 B4
NTHLT UB5....................78 A5
WDGN N22.....................49 J6
WPK KT4.....................207 J1

Sangley Rd CAT SE6.........164 E2
SNWD SE25...................197 F1
Sangora Rd BTSEA SW11......140 C5
Sankara CI NWMAL/EARL SW18.160 A4
Sansom Rd WAN E11 *.........70 D6
Sansom St CMBW SE5.........142 E1
Sans Wk CLKNW EC1R...........6 A7
Santley St CLAP SW4........141 K5
Santos Rd WAND/EARL SW18...139 K6
Saperton Wk LBTH SE11.......17 H6
Saphora CI ORP BR6.........216 D4
Sapphire CI BCTR RM8........73 J5
Sapphire Rd DEPT SE8.......124 B4
WLSDN NW10...................80 E5
Saracen CI CROY/NA CR0.....196 E3
Saracen's Head Yd
FENCHST EC3M................13 H4
Saracen St POP/IOD E14.....105 J5
Sarah St IS N1...............7 H4
Saratoga Rd CLPT E5.........86 E2
Sardinia St HOL/ALD WC2B....11 G4
Sarita CI KTN/HRWW/WS HA3...42 D5
Sark CI HEST TW5...........135 G1
Sarnesfield Rd ENC/FH EN2 *..23 K5
Sarre Rd CRICK NW2..........82 D3
STMC/STPC BR5...............202 D2
Sarsen Av HSLW TW3.........134 E3
Sarsfeld Rd BAL SW12.......160 E5
Sarsfield Rd GFD/PVL UB6....97 H1
Sartor Rd PECK SE15........144 A5
Sarum Ter BOW E3 *.........105 H3
Satanita CI CAN/RD E16.....107 H5
Satchell Md CDALE/KGS NW9...45 H3
Satchwell Rd BETH E2.......104 C2
Sattar Ms STNW/STAM N16 *...85 K1
Sauls Gn WAN E11............88 C1
Saunders Ness Rd
POP/IOD E14................125 G4
Saunders Rd
WOOL/PLUM SE18.............128 A5
Saunders St LBTH SE11.......17 J6
Saunders Wy DART DA1.......171 J4
THMD SE28...................109 H6
Saunderton Rd ALP/SUD HA0...79 H3
Saunton Av HYS/HAR UB3.....133 J1
Saunton Rd HCH RM12.........75 J3
Savage Gdns EHAM E6........107 K5
TWRH EC3N...................13 H5
Savanah CI PECK SE15 *.....143 G1
Savernake Ct STAN HA7.......43 J2
Savernake Rd ED N9..........36 C1
HAMP NW3....................83 K2
Savery Dr SURB KT6.........190 C4
Savile CI NWMAL KT3........192 B2
THDIT KT7...................190 A5
Savile Gdns CROY/NA CR0....197 G6
Savile Rw CONDST W1S........10 A5
Savile Rd CAN/RD E16.......126 D1
CHDH RM6.....................74 B3
CHSWK W4....................118 A3
TWK TW1.....................156 A3
Savill Gdns RYNPK SW20.....176 D6
Savill Rw WFD IG8...........52 D2
Savona CI WIM/MER SW19.....177 G3
Savona St VX/NE SW8........141 H1
Savoy Av HYS/HAR UB3.......113 H5
Savoy CI EDGW HA8...........44 C2
SRTFD E15....................88 C6
Savoy Ct TPL/STR WC2R *.....11 F6
Savoy Hi TPL/STR WC2R.......11 F6
Savoy Ms BRXN/ST SW9.......141 K4
Savoy Pde EN EN1 *...........24 A4
Savoy Rw TPL/STR WC2R.......11 F5
Savoy Steps TPL/STR WC2R *..11 G6
Savoy St TPL/STR WC2R.......11 G5
Savoy Wy TPL/STR WC2R *.....11 G5
Sawbill CI YEAD UB4.........95 H4
Sawkins CI WIM/MER SW19....159 G4
Sawley Rd SHB W12..........118 C1
Sawtry CI CAR SM5..........194 D4
Sawyer CI ED N9.............36 C4
Sawyers CI DAGE RM10........92 E4
Sawyer's HI RCHPK/HAM TW10.157 G2
Sawyers Lawn WEA W13........97 G5
Sawyer St STHWK SE1........18 C2
Saxby Rd BRXS/STRHM SW2....161 K2
Saxham Rd BARK IG11.........90 E6
Saxlingham Rd CHING E4......38 B5
Saxon Av FELT TW13.........154 E4
Saxonbury Av SUN TW16......172 A6
Saxonbury CI MTCM CR4......178 C6
Saxonbury Gdns SURB KT6....190 D5
Saxon CI SURB KT6..........190 D5
Saxon Dr ACT W3.............98 D5
Saxonfield CI
BRXS/STRHM SW2.............161 J2
Saxon Rd BMLY BR1..........183 J3
EHAM E6......................89 K6
IL IG1.......................90 B4
KUTN/CMB KT2................175 F4
RDART DA2...................171 H5
SHB W12......................99 J5
SNWD SE25...................197 F3
STHL UB1....................114 D1
WBLY HA9.....................80 E1
WDGN N22.....................49 J4
Saxon Wy STHGT/OAK N14......34 D1
Saxony Pde HYS/HAR UB3......94 A3
Saxton CI LEW SE13.........145 G4
Saxville Rd STMC/STPC BR5..186 C6
Sayesbury La UED N18........50 C1
Sayes Court Rd
STMC/STPC BR5..............186 B6
Sayes Court St DEPT SE8....124 C5
Scadbury Gdns
STMC/STPC BR5..............186 D6
Scads Hill CI ORP BR6......202 A3
Scala St FITZ W1T...........10 B1
Scales Rd TOTM N17..........50 B6
Scammell Wy WATW WD18.......26 D1

Scampston Ms NKENS W10.....100 B5
Scampton Rd
STWL/WRAY TW19.............152 C1
Scandrett St WAP E1W *......123 J1
Scarba Wk IS N1 *...........85 K4
Scarborough Rd ED N9........36 E2
FSBYPK N4....................67 H4
HTHAIR TW6 *................153 F1
WAN E11......................70 C5
Scarborough St WCHPL E1.....13 K4
Scarbrook Rd CROY/NA CR0...211 J1
Scarle Rd ALP/SUD HA0.......79 K4
Scarlet CI STMC/STPC BR5...202 C1
Scarlet Rd CAT SE6.........183 H1
Scarsbrook Rd BKHTH/KID SE3.146 C4
Scarsdale PI KENS W8.......120 A3
Scarsdale Rd RYLN/HDSTN HA2.78 C1
Scarsdale Vis KENS W8......119 K3
Scarth Rd BARN SW13........138 C4
Scawen CI CAR SM5..........210 A2
Scawen Rd DEPT SE8.........124 A5
Scawfell St BETH E2..........7 K3
Scaynes Link
NFNCH/WDSPK N12.............32 E6
Sceptre Rd BETH E2.........104 E2
Scholars CI BAR EN5........20 C5
Scholars Rd BAL SW12.......161 H3
CHING E4.....................38 A3
Scholars Wy GPK RM2.........75 K2
Scholefield Rd ARCH N19.....66 D6
Schonfeld Sq STNW/STAM N16..67 K6
Schoolbank Rd GNWCH SE10...125 J4
Schoolbell Ms BOW E3 *.....105 G1
School House La TEDD TW11..174 C3
Schoolhouse La WAP E1W *...105 F6
School La BUSH WD23.........28 D3
KUT/HW KT1..................174 D4
PIN HA5 *....................59 J1
SURB KT6....................191 H5
WELL DA16...................148 C4
School Pas KUT/HW KT1......175 F5
STHL UB1....................114 E1
School Rd CHST BR7.........185 H4
DAGE RM10....................92 C6
E/WMO/HCT KT8...............189 J1
HPTN TW12...................173 H1
HSLW TW3....................135 H4
KUT/HW KT1 *................174 E4
MNPK E12.....................89 K3
WDR/YW UB7..................112 A6
WLSDN NW10...................99 F3
School Road Av HPTN TW12...173 H2
Schooner CI BARK IG11......109 J1
BERM/RHTH SE16.............124 A2
POP/IOD E14.................125 F3
PUT/ROE SW15................139 J6
Sclater St WCHPL E1..........7 J6
Scoble PI STNW/STAM N16.....86 B2
Scoles Crs BRXS/STRHM SW2..162 B3
Scope Wy KUT/HW KT1........191 F1
Scoresby St STHWK SE1.......18 A1
Scorton Av GFD/PVL UB6......97 G1
Scotch Common WEA W13.......97 H4
Scoter CI WFD IG8...........52 E3
Scot Gv PIN HA5.............41 H4
Scotia Rd BRXS/STRHM SW2...162 B2
Scotland Gn TOTM N17........50 B5
Scotland Green Rd PEND EN3..25 F5
Scotland Green Rd North
PEND EN3....................25 G5
Scotland Rd BKHH IG9........39 G3
Scotney CI ORP BR6.........216 A2
Scots CI STWL/WRAY TW19....152 A3
Scotsdale CI CHEAM SM3.....208 C5
STMC/STPC BR5..............185 K1
Scotsdale Rd LEE/GVPK SE12.146 A5
Scotswood CI CLKNW EC1R *....5 K6
Scotswood Wk TOTM N17 *.....50 D3
Scott CI HOR/WEW KT19......206 A4
STRHM/NOR SW16.............180 A4
WDR/YW UB7..................112 C4
Scott Crs ERITH DA8........150 C2
RYLN/HDSTN HA2..............60 B5
Scott Ellis Gdns STJWD NW8..2 A5
Scottes La BCTR RM8........73 K5
Scott Farm CI THDIT KT7....190 C5
Scott Gdns HEST TW5........134 C1
Scott Lidgett Crs
BERM/RHTH SE16.............123 H2
Scott Rd EDGW HA8...........44 D5
Scotts Av HAYES BR2........183 G5
Scotts Dr HPTN TW12........173 G3
Scotts Farm Rd
HOR/WEW KT19...............206 E4
Scott's La HAYES BR2.......183 G6
Scotts Pas WOOL/PLUM SE18 *.127 G4
Scotts Rd BMLY BR1.........183 K3
LEY E10......................69 H6
NWDGN UB2...................114 B3
SHB W12.....................118 E2
Scott St WCHPL E1..........104 D3
Scott's Vd MANHO EC4N......12 E5
Scott Trimmer Wy HSLW TW3..134 D3
Scottwell Dr CDALE/KGS NW9..63 H2
Scoulding Rd CAN/RD E16....106 E5
Scouler St POP/IOD E14.....106 B6
Scout La CLAP SW4..........141 H4
Scout Wy MLHL NW7...........31 F6
Scovell Crs STHWK SE1 *.....18 C3
Scovell Rd STHWK SE1........18 C3
Scrattons Ter BARK IG11....109 K1
Scriven St HACK E8...........86 B6
Scrooby St CAT SE6.........164 E1
Scrubs La WLSDN NW10........99 J2
Scrutton CI BAL SW12.......161 J2
Scrutton St SDTCH EC2A......7 G7
Scutari Rd EDUL SE22 *.....143 J6
Scylla Crs HTHAIR TW6......152 E5
Scylla Rd HTHAIR TW6.......152 E5
PECK SE15...................143 J4
Seabright St BETH E2 *.....104 D2
Seabrook Dr WWKM BR4.......199 H6

Seabrook Gdns ROMW/RG RM7 74 C4
Seabrook Rd BCTR RM8 91 K1
Seaburn Cl RAIN RM13 111 G2
Seacole Cl ACT W3 99 F5
Seacourt Rd ABYW SE2 128 E2
Seacroft Gdns OXHEY WD19 27 H5
Seafield Rd FBAR/BDGN N11 34 D6
Seaford Cl RSLP HA4 58 B6
Seaford Rd EN EN1 24 A5
HTHAIR TW6 132 A6
SEVS/STOTM N15 67 K2
WALTH E17 69 K1
WEA W13 116 C1
Seaford St STPAN WC1H 5 F5
Seaforth Av NWMAL KT3 192 E2
Seaforth Cl ROM RM1 57 G3
Seaforth Crs HBRY N5 85 J3
Seaforth Gdns
HOR/WEW KT19 207 H3
WCHMH N21 35 G3
WFD IG8 53 G1
Seaforth Pl WESTW SW1E 16 B4
Seager Buildings DEPT SE8 * 144 D2
Seager Pl BOW E3 105 H4
Seagrave Cl WCHPL E1 * 105 F4
Seagrave Rd FUL/PGN SW6 119 K6
Seagry Rd WAN E11 70 E3
Seagull La CAN/RD E16 106 E6
Sealand Rd HTHAIR TW6 152 D1
Seal St HACK E8 86 B2
Searles Cl BTSEA SW11 140 D1
Searles Dr EHAM E6 108 B4
Searles Rd STHWK SE1 19 F6
Sears St CMBW SE5 142 E1
Seasprite Cl NTHLT UB5 95 H2
Seaton Av GDMY/SEVK IG3 90 E3
Seaton Cl LBTH SE11 122 C5
PLSTW E13 106 E3
PUT/ROE SW15 158 E3
WHTN TW2 155 J1
Seaton Dr ASHF TW15 152 B4
Seaton Gdns RSLP HA4 76 E1
Seaton Rd ALP/SUD HA0 * 98 A1
DART DA1 170 D2
HYS/HAR UB3 113 G4
MTCM CR4 178 D5
WELL DA16 148 D1
WHTN TW2 155 H1
Seaton St UED N18 50 C1
Sebastian St FSBYE EC1V 6 B5
Sebastopol Rd ED N9 36 C6
Sebbon St IS N1 85 H5
Sebergham Gv MLHL NW7 45 J3
Sebert Rd FSTGT E7 89 G2
Sebright Rd BAR EN5 20 B3
Secker Crs KTN/HRWW/WS HA3 42 C4
Secker St STHWK SE1 17 J1
Second Av ACT W3 118 C1
CHDH RM6 73 J2
DAGE RM10 110 D1
EN EN1 24 B6
HDN NW4 64 B1
HYS/HAR UB3 113 J1
MNPK E12 89 J2
MORT/ESHN SW14 138 B4
NKENS W10 100 C3
PLSTW E13 106 E2
UED N18 36 E6
WALTH E17 69 J2
WBLY HA9 61 K6
WOT/HER KT12 188 A3
Second Cl E/WMO/HCT KT8 189 H1
Second Cross Rd WHTN TW2 155 K4
Second Wy WBLY HA9 80 D2
Sedan Wy WALW SE17 123 F5
Sedcombe Cl SCUP DA14 168 C6
Sedcote Rd PEND EN3 24 E6
Sedding St KTBR SW1X 15 G6
Seddon Rd MRDN SM4 194 C2
Seddon St FSBYW WC1X 5 G5
Sedgebrook Rd
BKHTH/KID SE3 146 C3
Sedgecombe Av
KTN/HRWW/WS HA3 61 J2
Sedgeford Rd SHB W12 118 C1
Sedgehill Rd CAT SE6 182 D1
Sedgemere Av EFNCH N2 47 G6
Sedgemere Rd ABYW SE2 128 D3
Sedgemoor Dr DAGE RM10 92 C2
Sedge Rd TOTM N17 50 E3
Sedgeway CAT SE6 165 J3
Sedgewood Cl HAYES BR2 199 J4
Sedgmoor Pl CMBW SE5 143 F1
Sedgwick Rd LEY E10 70 A6
Sedgwick St HOM E9 87 F3
Sedleigh Rd
WAND/EARL SW18 159 J1
Sedlescombe Rd
FUL/PGN SW6 119 J6
Sedley Cl EN EN1 24 D1
Sedley Pl OXSTW W1C 9 J4
Sednem Ct PECK SE15 143 H3
Sedum Cl CDALE/KGS NW9 62 D2
Seeley Dr DUL SE21 163 F6
Seelig Av CDALE/KGS NW9 63 J4
Seely Rd TOOT SW17 179 F2
Seething La TWRH EC3N 13 H5
Seething Wells La SURB KT6 190 D3
Sefton Av KTN/HRWW/WS HA3 42 D5
MLHL NW7 45 F1
Sefton Cl STMC/STPC BR5 202 A1
Sefton Ct ENC/FH EN2 * 23 H3
Sefton Rd CROY/NA CR0 197 H5
STMC/STPC BR5 202 A1
Sefton St PUT/ROE SW15 139 F3
Sekforde St CLKNW EC1R 6 A7
Sekhon Ter FELT TW13 155 F5
Selah Dr SWLY BR8 187 K4
Selan Gdns YEAD UB4 95 F4
Selbie Av WLSDN NW10 81 H3
Selborne Av BXLY DA5 169 F3
MNPK E12 90 A2
Selborne Gdns GFD/PVL UB6 97 G1
HDN NW4 63 J1
Selborne Rd CMBW SE5 142 E3
CROY/NA CR0 212 A1
IL IG1 72 A6
NWMAL KT3 176 B5
SCUP DA14 168 C6
STHGT/OAK N14 34 E5
WALTH E17 69 H2
WDGN N22 49 F4
Selbourne Av SURB KT6 191 G6
Selby Cha RSLP HA4 59 F6
Selby Cl CHSGTN KT9 206 A5
CHST BR7 185 F2
Selby Gdns STHL UB1 96 A3
Selby Gn CAR SM5 194 D4
Selby Rd CAR SM5 194 D4
EA W5 97 H3
PGE/AN SE20 181 H5
PLSTW E13 107 F4
TOTM N17 50 A2
WAN E11 88 C1
Selby St WCHPL E1 104 C3
Selden Rd PECK SE15 143 K3
Selhurst Cl WIM/MER SW19 159 G3
Selhurst New Rd SNWD SE25 197 F3
Selhurst Pl SNWD SE25 197 F3
Selhurst Rd ED N9 35 K5
SNWD SE25 197 F2
Selinas La BCTR RM8 74 A4
Selkirk Dr ERITH DA8 150 B2
Selkirk Rd TOOT SW17 160 D6
WHTN TW2 155 H4
Sellers Hall Cl FNCH N3 46 E3
Sellincourt Rd TOOT SW17 178 D1
Sellindge Cl BECK BR3 182 C3
Sellons Av WLSDN NW10 81 H6
Sellwood Dr BAR EN5 20 B6
Selsdon Av SAND/SEL CR2 211 K4
Selsdon Cl CRW RM5 56 E4
SURB KT6 191 F2
Selsdon Park Rd
CROY/NA CR0 213 G6
Selsdon Rd CRICK NW2 63 H6
PLSTW E13 89 G6
SAND/SEL CR2 211 K3
SAND/SEL CR2 212 A5
WAN E11 70 E4
WNWD SE27 162 C5
Selsdon Wy POP/IOD E14 124 E3
Selsea Pl STNW/STAM N16 86 A3
Selsey Crs WELL DA16 148 E2
Selsey St BOW E3 105 J4
Selvage La MLHL NW7 45 F1
Selway Cl PIN HA5 59 F1
Selwood Pl SKENS SW7 120 C5
Selwood Rd CHEAM SM3 193 J5
CHSGTN KT9 205 K2
CROY/NA CR0 197 J6
Selwood Ter SKENS SW7 120 C5
Selworthy Cl WAN E11 70 E2
Selworthy Rd CAT SE6 164 C5
Selwyn Av CHING E4 52 A2
GDMY/SEVK IG3 73 F3
RCH/KEW TW9 137 G4
Selwyn Cl HSLWW TW4 134 D5
Selwyn Ct EDGW HA8 44 D3
Selwyn Crs WELL DA16 148 C5
Selwyn Rd BOW E3 105 H1
NWMAL KT3 192 A2
PLSTW E13 89 F6
WLSDN NW10 81 G5
Semley Pl BGVA SW1W 15 H7
STRHM/NOR SW16 180 A5
Semley Rd STRHM/NOR SW16 179 K5
Senate St PECK SE15 143 K3
Seneca Rd THHTH CR7 196 D1
Senga Rd WLGTN SM6 195 F5
Senhouse Rd CHEAM SM3 208 B1
Senior St BAY/PAD W2 101 F4
Senlac Rd LEE/GVPK SE12 166 A3
Sennen Rd EN EN1 36 B2
Senrab St WCHPL E1 105 F5
Sentamu Cl HNHL SE24 162 C3
Sentinel Cl NTHLT UB5 95 J3
September Wy STAN HA7 43 H2
Sequoia Cl BUSH WD23 28 D3
Sequoia Gdns ORP BR6 202 A4
Sequoia Pk PIN HA5 42 B2
Serbin Cl LEY E10 70 A4
Serenaders Rd BRXN/ST SW9 142 B3
Serjeant's Inn EMB EC4Y * 11 K4
Serle St LINN WC2A 11 H3
Sermon Dr SWLY BR8 187 K6
Sermon La BLKFR EC4V 12 C4
Serpentine Rd BAY/PAD W2 15 F1
Service Route No 1 SRTFD E15 88 B5
Service Route No 2 SRTFD E15 88 B5
Service Route No 3 SRTFD E15 88 B4
Serviden Dr BMLY BR1 184 C4
Setchell Est STHWK SE1 19 J6
Setchell Rd STHWK SE1 19 J6
Setchell Wy STHWK SE1 19 J6
Seth St BERM/RHTH SE16 123 K2
Seton Gdns DAGW RM9 91 J5
Settles St WCHPL E1 104 C5
Settrington Rd FUL/PGN SW6 140 A3
Seven Acres CAR SM5 194 D6
NTHWD HA6 40 E2
Seven Dials LSQ/SEVD WC2H 10 E4
Sevenex Pde WBLY HA9 * 80 A3
Seven Kings Rd
GDMY/SEVK IG3 72 E5
Seven Kings Wy
KUTN/CMB KT2 174 E4
Sevenoaks Cl BXLYHN DA7 149 K5
Sevenoaks Rd BROCKY SE4 164 C1
ORP BR6 217 F2
Sevenoaks Wy
STMC/STPC BR5 186 D5
Seven Sisters Rd FSBYPK N4 67 H6
HOLWY N7 85 F1
Seven Stars Yd WCHPL E1 13 K1
Seventh Av HYS/HAR UB3 113 K1
MNPK E12 89 K2
Severnake Cl POP/IOD E14 124 D4
Severn Av GPK RM2 57 K6
NKENS W10 100 C2
Severn Dr EN EN1 24 C1
ESH/CLAY KT10 190 B6
WOT/HER KT12 188 C6
Severn Wy WLSDN NW10 81 H3
Severus Rd BTSEA SW11 140 D5
Seville Ms IS N1 86 A5
Seville St KTBR SW1X 15 F3
Sevington Rd HDN NW4 63 K3
Sevington St MV/WKIL W9 101 F3
Seward Rd BECK BR3 182 A5
HNWL W7 116 B2
Sewardstone Rd BETH E2 104 E1
CHING E4 25 K5
Seward St FSBYE EC1V 6 B6
Sewdley St CLPT E5 87 F1
Sewell Rd ABYW SE2 128 B3
Sewell St PLSTW E13 106 E2
Sextant Av POP/IOD E14 125 G4
Sexton Cl RAIN RM13 93 H6
Seymer Rd ROM RM1 57 F6
Seymour Av EW KT17 207 K6
MRDN SM4 193 G4
TOTM N17 50 C5
Seymour Cl E/WMO/HCT KT8 189 H2
LOU IG10 39 J1
PIN HA5 41 K4
Seymour Dr HAYES BR2 200 E5
Seymour Gdns BROCKY SE4 144 A4
BRYLDS KT5 191 G2
FELT TW13 154 A6
IL IG1 71 K5
RSLP HA4 59 H5
TWK TW1 156 C2
Seymour Ms MBLAR W1H 9 G3
Seymour Pl MBLAR W1H 8 E3
SNWD SE25 197 J1
Seymour Rd CAR SM5 210 A3
CEND/HSY/T N8 67 H2
CHING E4 37 K3
CHSWK W4 117 K4
E/WMO/HCT KT8 189 H2
ED N9 36 D4
EHAM E6 107 H1
FNCH N3 47 F3
HPTN TW12 173 H1
KUT/HW KT1 174 E4
LEY E10 69 H5
MTCM CR4 195 F4
WIM/MER SW19 159 G5
Seymour St BAY/PAD W2 8 E4
MBLAR W1H 9 F4
WOOL/PLUM SE18 127 H4
Seymour Ter PGE/AN SE20 181 J4
Seymour Vls PGE/AN SE20 181 J4
Seymour Wk WBPTN SW10 120 B6
Seyssel St POP/IOD E14 125 F4
Shaa Rd ACT W3 99 F6
Shacklegate La TEDD TW11 155 K6
Shackleton Cl FSTH SE23 163 J4
Shackleton Rd STHL UB1 95 K6
Shacklewell La HACK E8 86 B3
Shacklewell Rd HACK E8 86 B2
Shacklewell Rw HACK E8 86 B2
Shacklewell St BETH E2 7 K6
Shadbolt Av CHING E4 51 G1
Shadbolt Cl WPK KT4 192 C6
Shad Thames STHWK SE1 19 K2
Shadwell Dr NTHLT UB5 95 K2
Shadwell Gdns WCHPL E1 * 104 E6
Shadwell Pierhead WAP E1W 104 E6
Shady Bush Cl BUSH WD23 28 C2
Shaef Wy TEDD TW11 174 B3
Shafter Rd DAGE RM10 92 E4
Shaftesbury Av BAR EN5 21 G5
EBED/NFELT TW14 153 K1
KTN/HRWW/WS HA3 61 K3
NWDGN UB2 115 F4
PEND EN3 25 F3
RYLN/HDSTN HA2 60 C5
SOHO/SHAV W1D 10 C5
Shaftesbury Cir
YLN/HDSTN HA2 * 60 C5
Shaftesbury Gdns
WLSDN NW10 99 G3
Shaftesbury Ms CLAP SW4 141 H6
KENS W8 119 K3
Shaftesbury Pde
RYLN/HDSTN HA2 * 60 C5
Shaftesbury Pl BARB EC2Y * 12 C2
Shaftesbury Rd ARCH N19 66 E5
BECK BR3 182 C5
CAR SM5 194 C4
CHING E4 38 B3
FSTGT E7 89 G5
LEY E10 69 J5
RCH/KEW TW9 137 F5
ROM RM1 75 J3
UED N18 50 A2
WALTH E17 69 K2
The Shaftesburys BARK IG11 108 C1
Shaftesbury St IS N1 6 D3
Shaftesbury Ter
HMSMTH W6 * 118 C4
Shaftesbury Wy WHTN TW2 155 J5
Shaftesbury Waye YEAD UB4 95 F5
Shafteswood Ct TOOT SW17 160 E6
Shafto Ms KTBR SW1X 14 E5
Shafton Ms HOM E9 * 87 F6
Shafton Rd HOM E9 87 F6
Shakespeare Av
EBED/NFELT TW14 153 K1
FBAR/BDGN N11 48 C1
WLSDN NW10 80 E6
YEAD UB4 94 E5
YEAD UB4 95 F3
Shakespeare Crs MNPK E12 89 K5
WLSDN NW10 81 F6
Shakespeare Dr
KTN/HRWW/WS HA3 62 B3
Shakespeare Gdns EFNCH N2 65 K1
Shakespeare Rd ACT W3 117 K1
BXLYHN DA7 149 F2
DART DA1 151 K5
FNCH N3 * 46 E4
HNHL SE24 142 C6
HNWL W7 97 F6
MLHL NW7 31 J6
ROM RM1 75 H3
WALTH E17 51 F5
WLSDN NW10 * 81 F6
Shakespeare Sq BARK/HLT IG6 54 C2
Shakespeare Ter
RCH/KEW TW9 * 137 H4
Shakespeare Wy FELT TW13 154 B6
Shakspeare Ms
STNW/STAM N16 86 A2
Shakspeare Wk
STNW/STAM N16 86 A2
Shalbourne Sq HOM E9 87 H4
Shalcomb St WBPTN SW10 120 B6
Shaldon Dr MRDN SM4 193 H2
RSLP HA4 77 G1
Shaldon Rd EDGW HA8 44 B5
Shalfleet Dr NKENS W10 100 B6
Shalford Cl ORP BR6 216 C2
Shalford Ct IS N1 * 6 A2
Shalimar Gdns ACT W3 98 E6
Shalimar Rd ACT W3 98 E6
Shallons Rd ELTH/MOT SE9 167 G6
Shalstone Rd
MORT/ESHN SW14 137 J4
Shalston Vls SURB KT6 191 G3
Shamrock Rd CROY/NA CR0 196 A3
Shamrock St CLAP SW4 141 J4
Shamrock Wy STHGT/OAK N14 34 B3
Shandon Rd CLAP SW4 161 H1
Shand St STHWK SE1 19 H2
Shandy St WCHPL E1 105 F4
Shanklin Gdns OXHEY WD19 27 G6
Shanklin Rd CEND/HSY/T N8 66 D2
SEVS/STOTM N15 68 C1
Shannon Cl CRICK NW2 82 B1
NWDGN UB2 114 C5
Shannon Gv BRXN/ST SW9 142 A5
Shannon Pl STJWD NW8 2 D2
Shannon Wy BECK BR3 182 E2
Shap Crs CAR SM5 194 E5
Shapland Wy PLMGR N13 49 F1
Shapwick Cl FBAR/BDGN N11 47 K1
Shardcroft Av HNHL SE24 142 C6
Shardeloes Rd BROCKY SE4 * 144 C6
NWCR SE14 144 C3
Shard's Sq PECK SE15 123 H6
Sharland Cl THHTH CR7 196 B3
Sharman Ct SCUP DA14 168 B6
Sharnbrooke Cl WELL DA16 148 D4
Sharon Cl SURB KT6 190 D5
Sharon Gdns HOM E9 86 E6
Sharon Rd CHSWK W4 118 A5
PEND EN3 25 G3
Sharples Hall St CAMTN NW1 83 K5
Sharps La RSLP HA4 58 B5
Sharp Wy DART DA1 151 J5
Sharratt St PECK SE15 123 K6
Sharsted St WALW SE17 122 C5
Sharvel La YEAD UB4 76 E6
Shavers Pl MYFR/PICC W1J 10 C6
Shaw Av BARK IG11 110 A1
Shawbrooke Rd
ELTH/MOT SE9 146 C5
Shawbury Cl CDALE/KGS NW9 45 G5
Shawbury Rd EDUL SE22 143 G6
Shaw Cl BUSH WD23 28 E4
EMPK RM11 75 K5
THMD SE28 128 C1
Shaw Cresent POP/IOD E14 105 G5
Shaw Dr WOT/HER KT12 188 B4
Shawfield Pk BMLY BR1 184 C5
Shawfield St CHEL SW3 120 D5
Shawford Rd HOR/WEW KT19 207 F4
Shaw Gdns BARK IG11 110 A1
Shaw Rd BMLY BR1 165 J5
EDUL SE22 143 F5
PEND EN3 25 F2
Shaw's Cottages FSTH SE23 164 B5
Shaw Sq WALTH E17 51 G4
The Shaw CHST BR7 * 185 H3
Shaw Wy WLGTN SM6 210 E5
Shaxton Crs CROY/NA CR0 214 A6
Sheaf Cottages THDIT KT7 * 189 K5
Shearing Dr CAR SM5 194 B4
Shearling Wy HOLWY N7 84 E4
Shearman Rd BKHTH/KID SE3 145 J5
Shears Cl DART DA1 171 F4
Shearwater Cl BARK IG11 109 G2
Shearwater Rd SUT SM1 208 D3
Shearwater Wy YEAD UB4 95 H5
Shearwood Cresent DART DA1 150 C4
Sheaths Cottages THDIT KT7 * 190 C4
Sheaveshill Av CDALE/KGS NW9 63 G1
Sheaveshill Pde
CDALE/KGS NW9 * 63 G1
Sheen Common Dr
RCHPK/HAM TW10 137 H5
Sheen Court Rd
RCHPK/HAM TW10 137 H5
Sheendale Rd RCH/KEW TW9 137 G5
Sheenewood SYD SE26 181 J1
Sheen Gate Gdns
MORT/ESHN SW14 137 K5
Sheen Gv IS N1 85 G6
Sheen La MORT/ESHN SW14 137 K5
Sheen Pk RCH/KEW TW9 137 G5
Sheen Rd RCH/KEW TW9 137 F5
STMC/STPC BR5 202 A1
Sheen Wy WLGTN SM6 211 F3
Sheen Wd MORT/ESHN SW14 137 K6
Sheepcote Cl HEST TW5 133 K1
Sheepcote La BTSEA SW11 140 E3
STMC/STPC BR5 203 H1
Sheepcote Rd HRW HA1 61 F3
Sheepcotes Rd CHDH RM6 73 K1
Sheephouse Wy NWMAL KT3 192 B4
Sheep La HACK E8 86 D6
Sheep Walk Ms
WIM/MER SW19 177 G2
Sheerwater Rd CAN/RD E16 107 H4
Sheffield Rd HTHAIR TW6 153 F1
Sheffield St LINN WC2A * 11 G4
Sheffield Ter KENS W8 119 K2
Sheffield Wy HTHAIR TW6 133 G6
Shefton Ri NTHWD HA6 40 E3
Sheila Rd CRW RM5 56 D3
Shelbourne Cl PIN HA5 41 K6
Shelbourne Rd TOTM N17 50 D4
Shelburne Dr HSLWW TW4 155 F1
Shelburne Rd HOLWY N7 85 F2
Shelbury Cl SCUP DA14 168 B5
Shelbury Rd EDUL SE22 163 J1
Sheldon Av CLAY IG5 54 B5
HGT N6 65 K4
Sheldon Cl LEE/GVPK SE12 146 A6
PGE/AN SE20 181 J4
Sheldon Pl BETH E2 104 C1
Sheldon Rd BXLYHN DA7 149 G2
CRICK NW2 82 B2
DAGW RM9 92 A5
UED N18 36 A6
Sheldon Sq BAY/PAD W2 101 G4
Sheldon St CROY/NA CR0 211 J1
Sheldrake Cl CAN/RD E16 126 E1
Sheldrake Pl KENS W8 119 J2
Sheldrick Cl MTCM CR4 178 C5
Shelduck Cl SRTFD E15 88 D3
Sheldwich Ter HAYES BR2 * 200 D3
Shelford Pl STNW/STAM N16 85 K1
Shelford Ri NRWD SE19 181 G3
Shelford Rd BAR EN5 32 A1
Shelgate Rd BTSEA SW11 140 E6
Shell Cl HAYES BR2 200 D3
Shellduck Cl CDALE/KGS NW9 45 G5
Shelley Av GFD/PVL UB6 96 D2
HCH RM12 75 H6
MNPK E12 89 J4
Shelley Cl EDGW HA8 30 C6
GFD/PVL UB6 96 D2
NTHWD HA6 40 D1
ORP BR6 216 E1
PECK SE15 143 J3
YEAD UB4 94 E4
Shelley Crs HEST TW5 134 C2
STHL UB1 95 K5
Shelley Dr WELL DA16 147 K2
Shelley Gdns ALP/SUD HA0 61 J6
Shelley Rd WLSDN NW10 81 F6
Shelley Wy WIM/MER SW19 178 C2
Shellgrove Rd
STNW/STAM N16 * 86 A3
Shellness Rd CLPT E5 86 D3
Shell Rd LEW SE13 144 E4
Shellwood Rd BTSEA SW11 140 E3
Shelmerdine Cl BOW E3 105 J4
Shelson Av FELT TW13 153 J6
Shelson Pde FELT TW13 * 153 J5
Shelton Rd WIM/MER SW19 177 K4
Shelton St LSQ/SEVD WC2H * 10 E4
Shenfield Rd WFD IG8 53 F3
Shenfield St IS N1 7 H3
Shenley Av RSLP HA4 58 D6
Shenley Rd CMBW SE5 143 F2
DART DA1 171 K1
HEST TW5 134 D2
Shenstone Cl DART DA1 150 A6
Shepherd Cl FELT TW13 154 D6
Shepherdess Pl FSBYE EC1V 6 D4
Shepherdess Wk IS N1 6 D3
Shepherd Market
MYFR/PICC W1J 15 J1
Shepherd's Bush Gn SHB W12 119 F2
Shepherd's Bush Market
SHB W12 119 F2
Shepherd's Bush Pl SHB W12 * 119 G2
Shepherd's Bush Rd
HMSMTH W6 119 F4
Shepherds Cl CHDH RM6 73 K2
HGT N6 66 B3
ORP BR6 217 F1
STAN HA7 43 G1
Shepherds Gn CHST BR7 185 J3
Shepherd's Hl HGT N6 66 B3
Shepherds La DART DA1 170 D3
HOM E9 87 F3
THMD SE28 127 K1
Shepherd's Leas
ELTH/MOT SE9 * 147 J5
Shepherds Pl MYFR/PKLN W1K 9 G5
Shepherd St MYFR/PICC W1J 15 J1
Shepherds Wk BUSH WD23 28 D4
CRICK NW2 63 J6
HAMP NW3 83 H3
Shepherds Wy SAND/SEL CR2 213 F5
Shepiston La HYS/HAR UB3 112 E4
Shepley Cl CAR SM5 210 A1
Shepley Ms PEND EN3 25 J1
Sheppard Cl EN EN1 24 D1
KUT/HW KT1 191 F1
Sheppard Dr
BERM/RHTH SE16 123 J5
Sheppard St CAN/RD E16 106 D3
Shepperton Rd IS N1 85 K6
STMC/STPC BR5 201 H3
Sheppey Cl ERITH DA8 150 E1
Sheppey Gdns DAGW RM9 91 J5
Sheppey Rd DAGW RM9 91 H5
Sheppey Wk IS N1 * 85 J5
Shepton Houses BETH E2 * 104 E2
Sherard Rd ELTH/MOT SE9 146 D6
Sheraton St SOHO/CST W1F * 10 C4
Sherborne Av NWDGN UB2 115 F4
PEND EN3 24 E3
Sherborne Cl YEAD UB4 95 G5
Sherborne Crs CAR SM5 194 D4
Sherborne Gdns
CDALE/KGS NW9 44 C6
WEA W13 97 H5
Sherborne La MANHO EC4N 12 E5
Sherborne Pl NTHWD HA6 40 B2
Sherborne Rd CHEAM SM3 193 K6
CHSGTN KT9 206 A3
EBED/NFELT TW14 153 G3
STMC/STPC BR5 202 A2
Sherborne St IS N1 85 K6
Sherborne Vls WEA W13 * 97 H4
Sherboro Rd SEVS/STOTM N15 68 B3
Sherbrooke Cl BXLYHN DA7 149 H5
Sherbrooke Rd FUL/PGN SW6 139 J1
Sherbrooke Ter
FUL/PGN SW6 * 139 H1
Sherbrooke Wy WPK KT4 192 E4
Sherbrook Gdns WCHMH N21 35 H2
Shere Cl CHSGTN KT9 205 K3
Sheredan Rd CHING E4 52 B1
Shere Rd GNTH/NBYPK IG2 72 A2
Sherfield Cl NWMAL KT3 191 J1
Sherfield Gdns PUT/ROE SW15 158 C1

Sheridan Cl HARH RM3 .....57 K3
Sheridan Ct DART DA1 .....151 K5
  HSLWW TW4 .....134 D6
Sherlock Crs CHST BR7 .....185 G5
Sheridan Gdns
  KTN/HRWW/WS HA3 .....61 K3
Sheridan Pl BMLY BR1 .....184 C5
  HPTN TW12 .....175 H4
Sheridan Rd BELV DA17 .....129 H4
  BXLYHN DA7 .....149 F4
  FSTGT E7 .....88 D1
  MNPK E12 .....89 J3
  OXHEY WD19 .....27 H2
  RCHPK/HAM TW10 .....156 D4
  WIM/MER SW19 .....177 J4
Sheridan St WCHPL E1 .....104 D5
Sheridan Wk CAR SM5 .....209 K3
  GLDGN NW11 .....64 B4
Sheridan Wy BECK BR3 .....182 C4
Sheringham Av MNPK E12 .....89 K3
  ROMW/RG RM7 .....74 D3
  STHGT/OAK N14 .....34 D1
  WHTN TW2 .....154 E3
Sheringham Dr BARK IG11 .....91 F5
Sheringham Rd HOLWY N7 .....85 G4
  PGE/AN SE20 .....181 K6
Sherington Av PIN HA5 .....42 A3
Sherington Rd BKHTH/KID SE3 .....126 A6
Sherland Rd TWK TW1 .....156 A5
Sherlies Av ORP BR6 .....201 K6
Sherlock Ms MHST W1U 9 G1
Sherman Gdns CHDH RM6 .....73 J5
Sherman Rd BMLY BR1 .....184 D3
Sherrard Rd FSTGT E7 .....89 G4
Sherrards Wy BAR EN5 .....20 E6
Sherrick Green Rd
  WLSDN NW10 .....81 K3
Sherriff Cl ESH/CLAY KT10 .....189 G6
Sherriff Rd KIL/WHAMP NW6 .....82 E4
Sherringham Av FELT TW13 .....153 K5
  TOTM N17 .....50 C5
Sherrock Gdns HDN NW4 .....63 J1
Sherry Ms BARK IG11 .....90 D5
Sherwin Rd NWCR SE14 .....144 A2
Sherwood Av GFD/PVL UB6 .....78 E4
  RSLP HA4 .....58 B5
  STRHM/NOR SW16 .....179 J4
  SWFD E18 .....53 F6
  YEAD UB4 .....95 F3
Sherwood Cl BXLY DA5 .....168 D1
  WALTH E17 .....51 J3
  WEA W13 .....116 C1
Sherwood Ct MBLAR W1H 8 E2
Sherwood Gdns BARK IG11 .....90 D5
  BERM/RHTH SE16 .....123 H5
  POP/IOD E14 .....124 D4
Sherwood House
  RYLN/HDSTN HA2 * 60 C1
Sherwood Park Av
  BFN/LL DA15 .....168 B2
Sherwood Park Rd MTCM CR4 .....195 J1
  SUT SM1 .....208 E3
Sherwood Rd BARK/HLT IG6 .....72 D1
  CROY/NA CR0 .....197 J5
  HDN NW4 .....46 A6
  HPTN TW12 .....173 H1
  RYLN/HDSTN HA2 .....60 C6
  WELL DA16 .....147 K4
  WIM/MER SW19 .....177 J3
Sherwoods Rd OXHEY WD19 .....27 J2
Sherwood St REGST W1B 10 B5
  TRDG/WHET N20 .....33 H5
Sherwood Ter TRDG/WHET N20 .....33 H5
Sherwood Wy WWKM BR4 .....199 F6
Shetland Cl BORE WD6 .....31 F1
Shetland Rd BOW E3 .....105 H1
Shield Dr BTFD TW8 .....116 C6
Shieldhall St ABYW SE2 .....128 D4
Shield Rd ASHF TW15 .....153 F6
Shifford Pth FSTH SE23 .....164 A5
Shillibeer Pl MBLAR W1H 8 D2
Shillingford Cl MLHL NW7 .....46 B3
Shillingford St IS N1 .....85 H6
Shilling Pl HNWL W7 .....116 B1
Shinfield St SHB W12 .....100 A5
Shinglewell Rd ERITH DA8 .....149 H1
Shinners Cl SNWD SE25 .....197 H2
Ship & Mermaid Rw
  STHWK SE1 * 19 G2
Shipka Rd BAL SW12 .....161 G3
Ship La MORT/ESHN SW14 .....137 K4
Shipman Rd CAN/RD E16 .....107 F5
  FSTH SE23 .....164 A4
Ship St DEPT SE8 .....144 D2
Ship Tavern Pas BANK EC3V 13 G5
Shipton Cl BCTR RM8 .....91 K1
Shipton St BETH E2 .....7 K4
Shipwright Rd
  BERM/RHTH SE16 .....124 B2
Shipwright Yd STHWK SE1 * 19 G1
Shirburn Cl FSTH SE23 .....163 K2
Shirbutt St POP/IOD E14 .....105 J6
Shirebrook Rd BKHTH/KID SE3 .....146 C3
Shire Cl EW KT17 .....207 H5
Shirehall Cl HDN NW4 .....64 B3
Shirehall Gdns HDN NW4 .....64 B3
Shirehall La HDN NW4 .....64 B3
Shirehall Pk HDN NW4 .....64 B3
Shire Horse Wy ISLW TW7 .....136 A4
Shire La ORP BR6 .....215 K5
Shire Ms WHTN TW2 .....155 H1
Shire Pl WAND/EARL SW18 .....160 B2
The Shires MV/WKIL W9? 157 F6
Shirland Ms MV/WKIL W9 .....100 E2
Shirland Rd MV/WKIL W9 .....100 E3
Shirley Av BXLY DA5 .....168 E2
  CROY/NA CR0 .....197 K5
  SUT SM1 .....209 J2
Shirley Church Rd
  CROY/NA CR0 .....213 F1
Shirley Cl DART DA1 .....151 K5
  HSLW TW3 .....135 H6
  WALTH E17 * 69 K2
Shirley Crs BECK BR3 .....198 B1

Shirley Dr HSLW TW3 .....135 H6
Shirley Gdns BARK IG11 .....90 E4
  HNWL W7 .....116 A1
Shirley Gv BTSEA SW11 .....141 F4
  ED N9 .....36 E3
Shirley Hills Rd CROY/NA CR0 .....213 F5
Shirley Oaks Rd CROY/NA CR0 .....198 A5
Shirley Park Rd CROY/NA CR0 .....197 J5
Shirley Rd CHSWK W4 .....118 A2
  CROY/NA CR0 .....196 E5
  ENC/FH EN2 .....23 J4
  SCUP DA14 .....167 K5
  SRTFD E15 .....88 C5
  WLGTN SM6 .....210 C6
Shirley Rw SNWD SE25 * 181 H5
Shirley St CAN/RD E16 .....106 D5
Shirley Wy CROY/NA CR0 .....213 H1
Shirlock Rd HAMP NW3 .....83 K2
Shirwell Cl MLHL NW7 .....46 B3
Shobden Rd TOTM N17 .....49 K4
Shobroke Cl CRICK NW2 .....82 A1
Shoebury Rd EHAM E6 .....89 K5
Shoe La FLST/FETLN EC4A 11 K3
  HCIRC EC1N 12 A2
Sholden Gdns STMC/STPC BR5 .....202 D2
Shooters Av
  KTN/HRWW/WS HA3 .....61 J1
Shooters Hill Rd GNWCH SE10 .....145 H2
Shooters Rd ENC/FH EN2 .....23 G1
Shoot-up Hill CRICK NW2 .....82 B5
Shore Cl EBED/NFELT TW14 .....153 K2
  HPTN TW12 .....172 D2
Shoreditch High St WCHPL E1 .....13 H1
Shore Gv FELT TW13 .....155 F4
Shoreham Cl CROY/NA CR0 .....197 J3
  WAND/EARL SW18 .....140 A6
Shoreham Rd (East)
  HTHAIR TW6 .....132 B6
Shoreham Rd (West)
  HTHAIR TW6 .....132 B6
Shoreham Wy HAYES BR2 .....199 K3
Shore Pl HOM E9 .....86 E5
Shore Rd HOM E9 .....86 E5
Shore Wy BRXN/ST SW9 .....142 B3
Shorncliffe Rd STHWK SE1 .....123 G5
Shorndean St CAT SE6 .....165 F3
Shorne Cl BFN/LL DA15 .....168 C1
  STMC/STPC BR5 .....202 E1
Shornefield Cl BMLY BR1 .....185 F6
Shorrolds Rd FUL/PGN SW6 .....139 K1
Shortcroft Rd EW KT17 .....207 H5
Shortcrofts Rd DAGW RM9 .....92 B4
Shorter St TWRH EC3N 13 J5
Shortlands HMSMTH W6 .....119 G4
  HYS/HAR UB3 .....113 G6
Shortlands Cl BELV DA17 .....129 G3
  UED N18 .....35 K6
Shortlands Gdns HAYES BR2 .....183 H5
Shortlands Gv HAYES BR2 .....183 G6
Shortlands Rd HAYES BR2 .....183 G6
  KUTN/CMB KT2 .....175 G3
  LEY E10 .....69 K4
Short La STWL/WRAY TW19 .....152 C2
Short Rd CHSWK W4 .....118 B6
  HTHAIR TW6 .....152 B1
  WAN E11 .....70 C6
Shorts Cft CDALE/KGS NW9 .....62 E1
Shorts Gdns LSQ/SEVD WC2H * 10 E4
Shorts Rd CAR SM5 .....209 J2
Short St HDN NW4 .....64 A1
  STHWK SE1 .....17 K2
Shortway ELTH/MOT SE9 .....166 E5
Short Wy NFNCH/WDSPK N12 .....47 J2
  WHTN TW2 .....155 H2
Shotfield WLGTN SM6 .....210 B4
Shott Cl SUT SM1 .....209 G3
Shottendane Rd
  FUL/PGN SW6 * 139 K2
Shottery Cl ELTH/MOT SE9 .....166 D5
Shottfield Av
  MORT/ESHN SW14 .....138 B5
Shoulder of Mutton Aly
  POP/IOD E14 .....105 G6
Shouldham St MBLAR W1H 8 D2
Showers Wy HYS/HAR UB3 .....113 K1
Shrapnel Cl WOOL/PLUM SE18 .....146 E1
Shrapnel Rd ELTH/MOT SE9 .....146 E4
Shrewsbury Av
  KTN/HRWW/WS HA3 .....62 A1
  MORT/ESHN SW14 .....138 A5
Shrewsbury Cl SURB KT6 .....191 F6
Shrewsbury Crs WLSDN NW10 .....81 F6
Shrewsbury La
  WOOL/PLUM SE18 .....147 G2
Shrewsbury Ms BAY/PAD W2 .....100 E5
Shrewsbury Rd BAY/PAD W2 .....100 E5
  BECK BR3 .....182 B6
  CAR SM5 .....194 D4
  FBAR/BDGN N11 .....48 C2
  FSTGT E7 .....89 H4
  HTHAIR TW6 .....153 F1
  WDGN N22 .....49 F5
Shrewsbury St NKENS W10 .....100 A3
Shrewton Rd TOOT SW17 .....178 E3
Shroffold Rd BMLY BR1 .....165 J6
Shropshire Cl MTCM CR4 .....195 K1
Shropshire Rd WDGN N22 .....49 F3
Shroton St CAMTN NW1 .....8 C1
The Shrubberies CHIG IG7 .....54 C1
  SWFD E18 .....52 E5
Shrubbery Gdns WCHMH N21 .....35 H2
Shrubbery Rd ED N9 .....36 C5
  STRHM/NOR SW16 .....161 K6
The Shrubbery SURB KT6 * 191 F6
Shrubland Cl TRDG/WHET N20 * 33 H4
Shrubland Gv WPK KT4 .....208 A1
Shrubland Rd HACK E8 .....86 C6
  WALTH E17 .....69 J2
Shrublands Av CROY/NA CR0 .....213 J2
Shrublands Cl CHIG IG7 .....54 C2
  SYD SE26 .....163 K5
  TRDG/WHET N20 .....33 H3
Shrubsall Cl ELTH/MOT SE9 .....166 D3
Shubbery Cl IS N1 * 85 H6

Shuna Wk IS N1 * 85 K4
Shurland Av EBAR EN4 .....33 H1
Shurland Gdns PECK SE15 * 143 G1
Shurlock Dr ORP BR6 .....216 C2
Shuters Sq WKENS W14 * 119 J5
Shuttle Cl BFN/LL DA15 .....168 A2
Shuttlemead BXLY DA5 .....169 G2
Shuttle Rd DART DA1 .....150 D4
Shuttle St WCHPL E1 .....104 C3
Shuttleworth Rd BTSEA SW11 .....140 C2
Sibella Rd CLAP SW4 .....141 J3
Sibley Cl BMLY BR1 .....200 D3
  BXLYHS DA6 .....149 F6
Sibley Ct UX/CGN UB8 .....94 A4
Sibley Gv MNPK E12 .....89 J6
Sibthorpe Rd LEE/GVPK SE12 .....166 B2
Sibthorp Rd MTCM CR4 * 178 E5
Sibton Rd CAR SM5 .....194 D4
Sicilian Av NOXST/BSQ WC1A * 11 F2
Sidbury St FUL/PGN SW6 .....139 H2
Sidcup By-Pass Rd SCUP DA14 .....167 K6
Sidcup Hi SCUP DA14 .....186 C1
Sidcup Hill Gdns SCUP DA14 * 186 D1
Sidcup Pl SCUP DA14 .....186 B1
Sidcup Rd ELTH/MOT SE9 .....166 B3
  LEE/GVPK SE12 .....146 A6
Siddeley Dr HSLWW TW4 .....134 D4
Siddons La CAMTN NW1 .....3 F7
Siddons Rd CROY/NA CR0 .....211 G1
  FSTH SE23 .....164 B4
  TOTM N17 .....50 C4
Side Rd WALTH E17 .....69 H2
Sidewood Rd ELTH/MOT SE9 .....167 J3
Sidford Pl STHWK SE1 .....17 J4
Sidings Ms HOLWY N7 .....85 G2
The Sidings LOU IG10 .....39 J1
  WAN E11 .....70 A5
Sidmouth Av ISLW TW7 .....135 K3
Sidmouth Cl OXHEY WD19 .....27 G4
Sidmouth Dr RSLP HA4 .....76 E1
Sidmouth Pde CRICK NW2 * 82 A5
Sidmouth Rd CRICK NW2 .....82 A5
  LEY E10 .....88 A1
  STMC/STPC BR5 .....202 E2
  WELL DA16 .....148 D1
Sidmouth St STPAN WC1H 5 F5
Sidney Av PLMGR N13 .....49 F1
Sidney Elson Wy EHAM E6 .....108 A1
Sidney Gdns BTFD TW8 .....116 D6
Sidney Gv FSBYE EC1V 6 A3
Sidney Rd BECK BR3 .....182 B5
  BRXN/ST SW9 .....142 A3
  FSTGT E7 .....88 E1
  RYLN/HDSTN HA2 .....42 C6
  SNWD SE25 .....197 H2
  TWK TW1 .....156 B1
  WDGN N22 .....49 F3
Sidney Sq WCHPL E1 * 104 E4
Sidney St WCHPL E1 .....104 D4
Sidworth St HACK E8 .....86 D5
Siebert Rd BKHTH/KID SE3 .....125 K6
Siemens Rd WOOL/PLUM SE18 .....126 C3
Sienna Ter CRICK NW2 .....63 J6
Sierra Dr DAGE RM10 .....110 E1
Sigdon Rd HACK E8 .....86 C3
The Sigers PIN HA5 .....59 F3
Signmakers Yd CAMTN NW1 * 3 K1
Sigrist Sq KUTN/CMB KT2 .....175 F4
Silbury Av MTCM CR4 .....178 D4
Silbury St IS N1 * 6 E4
Silecroft Rd BXLYHN DA7 .....149 H2
Silesia Buildings HACK E8 .....86 D5
Silex St STHWK SE1 .....18 B3
Silk Cl LEE/GVPK SE12 .....145 K6
Silkfield Rd CDALE/KGS NW9 .....63 H2
Silk Mill Rd OXHEY WD19 .....27 F2
Silk Mills Pth LEW SE13 .....145 F4
Silkstream Pde EDGW HA8 .....44 E4
Silkstream Rd EDGW HA8 .....44 E4
Silk St BARB EC2Y 12 D1
Silsoe Rd WDGN N22 .....49 F6
Silver Birch Av CHING E4 .....51 H1
Silver Birch Cl CAT SE6 .....164 C5
  FBAR/BDGN N11 .....48 A3
  RDART DA3 .....170 B6
  THMD SE28 .....128 B3
Silver Birch Ms BARK/HLT IG6 .....54 C2
Silverbirch Wk HAMP NW3 * 83 K4
Silvercliffe Gdns EBAR EN4 .....21 J5
Silver Ct KTN/HRWW/WS HA3 .....42 D5
  NWCR SE14 * 144 B1
Silver Crs CHSWK W4 .....117 J4
Silverdale CAMTN NW1 .....4 A3
  ENC/FH EN2 .....22 E5
  SYD SE26 .....163 K6
Silverdale Centre
  ALP/SUD HA0 * 80 B6
Silverdale Cl HNWL W7 .....115 K1
  NTHLT UB5 .....77 K3
  SUT SM1 .....208 D2
Silverdale Dr ELTH/MOT SE9 .....166 D4
  HCH RM12 .....93 K3
  SUN TW16 .....172 A5
Silverdale Gdns HYS/HAR UB3 .....113 K2
Silverdale Rd BXLYHN DA7 .....149 J3
  CHING E4 .....52 A2
  HYS/HAR UB3 .....113 K2
  STMC/STPC BR5 .....186 B6
  STMC/STPC BR5 .....201 K1
Silverdene
  NFNCH/WDSPK N12 * 47 F2
Silver Dene PUT/ROE SW15 * 139 F6
Silvergate HOR/WEW KT19 .....206 E3
Silverhall St ISLW TW7 .....136 B4
Silverholme Cl
  KTN/HRWW/WS HA3 .....62 A4
Silver Jubilee Wy HSLWW TW4 .....134 A3
Silver La WWKM BR4 .....199 G6
Silverleigh Rd THHTH CR7 .....196 A1
Silvermere Av CRW RM5 .....56 D2
Silvermere Dr UED N18 .....51 F1
Silvermere Rd CAT SE6 .....164 D1
Silvermere Rw SNWD SE25 * 181 H5
Silver Pl SOHO/CST W1F 10 B4
Silver Rd LEW SE13 .....144 E4
  NKENS W10 .....100 B6

Silver Spring Cl ERITH DA8 .....129 J6
Silverston Wy STAN HA7 .....43 J2
Silver St EN EN1 .....23 K5
  UED N18 .....35 K6
Silverthorne Rd VX/NE SW8 .....141 G3
Silverthorn Gdns CHING E4 .....37 J4
Silverton Rd HMSMTH W6 .....139 G1
Silvertown Wy CAN/RD E16 .....106 D5
Silvertree La GFD/PVL UB6 .....96 D2
Silver Wk BERM/RHTH SE16 .....124 C1
Silver Wy ROMW/RG RM7 .....56 D6
Silverwood Cl BECK BR3 .....182 D3
  CROY/NA CR0 .....213 H6
  NTHWD HA6 .....40 A4
Silvester Rd EDUL SE22 .....143 G6
Silvester St STHWK SE1 .....18 E3
Silwood Est Regeneration
  Area BERM/RHTH SE16 .....124 A5
Silwood St BERM/RHTH SE16 .....124 A5
Simmil Rd ESH/CLAY KT10 .....204 E3
Simmons Cl TRDG/WHET N20 .....33 J4
Simmons Dr BCTR RM8 .....92 A1
Simmons Gdns EN CLAY KT10 .....204 C3
Simmons La CHING E4 .....38 B4
Simmons Rd
  WOOL/PLUM SE18 .....127 G5
Simms' Wy TRDG/WHET N20 .....33 J4
Simms Cl CAR SM5 .....194 D6
Simms Gdns EFNCH N2 .....47 G5
Simms Rd STHWK SE1 .....123 H4
Simnel Rd LEE/GVPK SE12 .....166 A2
Simon Cl NTGHL W11 .....100 D6
Simonds Rd LEY E10 .....69 J6
Simone Cl BMLY BR1 .....184 C4
Simons Wlk SRTFD E15 .....88 B3
Simpson Cl WCHMH N21 .....23 F6
Simpson Dr ACT W3 .....99 F5
Simpson Rd HSLWW TW4 .....154 E2
  RAIN RM13 .....93 H4
  RCHPK/HAM TW10 .....156 D4
Simpson's Rd HAYES BR2 .....183 K6
  POP/IOD E14 .....105 K6
Simpson St BTSEA SW11 .....140 D3
Simrose Ct WAND/EARL SW18 .....139 K6
Sims Cl ROM RM1 .....75 H1
Sinclair Dr BELMT SM2 .....209 F6
Sinclair Gdns WKENS W14 .....119 G2
Sinclair Gv GLDGN NW11 .....64 A3
Sinclair Rd CHING E4 .....51 H1
  WKENS W14 .....119 H3
Sinclare Cl EN EN1 .....24 B2
Singapore Rd WEA W13 .....116 B1
Singer St FSBYE EC1V 7 F5
Singleton Cl CROY/NA CR0 .....196 D4
  HCH RM12 .....93 H2
  TOOT SW17 .....178 E3
Singleton Scarp
  NFNCH/WDSPK N12 .....46 E1
Sinnott Rd WALTH E17 .....51 F4
Sion Rd TWK TW1 .....156 C3
Sipson Cl WDR/YW UB7 .....112 D6
Sipson La HYS/HAR UB3 .....113 F6
  WDR/YW UB7 .....112 D6
Sipson Rd WDR/YW UB7 .....112 D5
Sipson Wy WDR/YW UB7 .....132 D1
Sir Abraham Dawes Cottages
  PUT/ROE SW15 * 139 H5
Sir Alexander Cl ACT W3 .....118 C1
Sir Cyril Black Wy
  WIM/MER SW19 .....177 K3
Sirdar Rd MTCM CR4 .....179 F2
  NTGHL W11 .....100 B6
  WDGN N22 .....49 J5
Sir John Kirk Cl CMBW SE5 .....142 D1
Sir Thomas More Est
  CHEL SW3 .....120 C6
Sirus Rd NTHWD HA6 .....26 E4
Sise La MANHO EC4N * 12 E4
Sisley Rd BARK IG11 .....90 E6
Sispara Gdns
  WAND/EARL SW18 .....159 J1
Sissinghurst Cl BMLY BR1 .....183 J1
Sissinghurst Rd CROY/NA CR0 .....197 H4
Sister Mabels Wy PECK SE15 .....143 H1
Sisters Av BTSEA SW11 .....140 E5
Sistova Rd BAL SW12 .....161 G3
Sisulu Pl BRXN/ST SW9 .....142 B4
Sittingbourne Av EN EN1 .....35 K1
Sitwell Gv STAN HA7 .....43 F1
Siverst Cl NTHLT UB5 .....78 B4
Siviter Wy DAGE RM10 .....92 D5
Siward Rd HAYES BR2 .....184 A1
  TOOT SW17 .....160 B5
  TOTM N17 .....49 J4
Sixth Av HYS/HAR UB3 .....113 J1
  MNPK E12 .....89 K2
  NKENS W10 .....100 C3
Sixth Cross Rd WHTN TW2 .....155 H5
Skardu Rd CRICK NW2 .....82 C3
Skeena Hl WAND/EARL SW18 .....159 H2
Skeet Hill La STMC/STPC BR5 .....203 G6
Skeffington Rd EHAM E6 .....89 K6
Skeffington St
  WOOL/PLUM SE18 .....127 H3
Skelbrook St
  WAND/EARL SW18 .....160 B4
Skelgill Rd PUT/ROE SW15 .....139 J5
Skelley Rd SRTFD E15 .....88 D5
Skelton Cl HACK E8 * 86 B4
Skelton Rd FSTGT E7 .....88 E4
Skelton's La LEY E10 .....69 K4
Skelwith Rd HMSMTH W6 .....119 F6
Skerne Rd KUTN/CMB KT2 .....174 E4
Sketchley Gdns
  BERM/RHTH SE16 .....124 A5
Sketty Rd EN EN1 .....24 A4
Skiers St SRTFD E15 .....88 C6
Skinner Pl BGVA SW1W * 15 G7
Skinners La BLKFR EC4V 12 D5
  HEST TW5 .....135 G2
Skinner St CLKNW EC1R 6 A6

Skipsey Av EHAM E6 .....107 K2
Skipton Cl FBAR/BDGN N11 .....48 A2
Skipton Dr HYS/HAR UB3 .....113 F3
Skipworth Rd HOM E9 .....86 E6
Skylines Village
  POP/IOD E14 * 125 F2
Sky Peals Rd WFD IG8 .....52 B4
Skyport Dr WDR/YW UB7 .....132 A1
Sladebrook Rd BKHTH/KID SE3 .....146 C4
Sladedale Rd
  WOOL/PLUM SE18 .....127 K5
Slade Gdns ERITH DA8 .....150 C2
Slade Green Rd ERITH DA8 .....150 D2
Slades Cl ENC/FH EN2 .....23 G4
Slades Dr CHST BR7 .....167 H6
Slades Gdns ENC/FH EN2 .....23 G3
Slades Hi ENC/FH EN2 .....23 G3
Slades Ri ENC/FH EN2 .....23 G4
The Slade WOOL/PLUM SE18 .....127 K6
Slade Wk WALW SE17 .....122 C6
Slagrove Pl BROCKY SE4 .....144 A6
Slaidburn St WBPTN SW10 .....120 B6
Slaithwaite Rd LEW SE13 .....145 F5
Slaney Pl HOLWY N7 .....85 G3
Slaney Rd ROM RM1 .....75 G2
Slattery Rd FELT TW13 .....154 C3
Sleaford Gn OXHEY WD19 .....27 H5
Sleaford St VX/NE SW8 .....141 H1
Sledmere Ct
  EBED/NFELT TW14 .....153 H3
Slievemore Cl CLAP SW4 .....141 J4
Slingsby Pl LSQ/SEVD WC2H 10 E5
Slippers Pl BERM/RHTH SE16 .....123 J3
Sloane Av CHEL SW3 .....14 D7
Sloane Ct East CHEL SW3 .....121 F5
Sloane Ct West CHEL SW3 .....121 F5
Sloane Gdns BGVA SW1W 15 G7
  ORP BR6 .....216 C1
Sloane Sq BGVA SW1W 15 C7
Sloane St KTBR SW1X 15 F3
Sloane Ter KTBR SW1X 15 G5
Sloane Wk CROY/NA CR0 .....198 C3
Slocum Cl THMD SE28 .....109 J6
Slough La CDALE/KGS NW9 .....62 E3
Sly St WCHPL E1 * 104 D5
Smaldon Cl WDR/YW UB7 .....112 D3
Smallberry Av ISLW TW7 .....136 A3
Smallbrooke Ms BAY/PAD W2 * 8 A4
Smalley Cl STNW/STAM N16 .....86 B1
Smallwood Rd TOOT SW17 .....160 C6
Smarden Cl BELV DA17 .....129 H5
Smart's Cl HARH RM3 .....57 K4
Smart's Pl NOXST/BSQ WC1A * 11 F3
  UED N18 .....50 C1
Smart St BETH E2 .....105 F2
Smeaton Rd
  WAND/EARL SW18 .....159 K2
  WFD IG8 .....53 K1
Smeaton St WAP E1W 123 J1
Smedley St VX/NE SW8 .....141 J3
Smeed Rd BOW E3 .....87 J5
Smiles Pl LEW SE13 .....145 F3
Smith Cl BERM/RHTH SE16 .....124 A1
Smithfield St STBT EC1A 12 A2
Smithies Rd ABYW SE2 .....128 C4
Smith's Ct SOHO/SHAV W1D * 10 C5
Smithson Rd TOTM N17 .....49 K5
Smith Sq WEST SW1P 16 E5
Smith St BRYLDS KT5 .....191 G3
  CHEL SW3 .....120 E5
Smith Ter CHEL SW3 .....120 E6
Smithwood Cl
  WIM/MER SW19 .....159 H4
Smithy St WCHPL E1 .....104 E4
Smugglers Wy
  WAND/EARL SW18 .....140 A5
Smyrk's Rd WALW SE17 .....123 F5
Smyrna Rd KIL/WHAMP NW6 .....82 E5
Smythe St POP/IOD E14 .....105 K6
Snakes La EBAR EN4 .....22 B4
Snakes La East WFD IG8 .....53 F2
Snakes La West WFD IG8 .....52 E2
Snaresbrook Dr STAN HA7 .....29 K6
Snaresbrook Rd WALTH E17 .....70 C1
Snarsgate St NKENS W10 .....100 A4
Sneath Av GLDGN NW11 .....64 D4
Snell's Pk UED N18 .....50 B2
Sneyd Rd CRICK NW2 .....81 K2
Snowberry Cl BAR EN5 .....32 D1
  WAN E11 .....88 B2
Snowbury Rd FUL/PGN SW6 .....140 A3
Snowden Av HGDN/ICK UB10 .....94 A1
Snowden Dr CDALE/KGS NW9 .....63 G3
Snowden St SDTCH EC2A 7 G7
Snowdon Crs HYS/HAR UB3 .....113 F3
Snowdon Dr CDALE/KGS NW9 .....63 G3
Snowdown Cl PGE/AN SE20 .....181 K4
Snowdrop Cl HPTN TW12 .....173 F2
Snow Hl STBT EC1A 12 A2
Snowsfields STHWK SE1 .....19 F2
Snowshill Rd MNPK E12 .....89 J3
Snowy Fielder Waye
  ISLW TW7 .....136 C3
Soames St PECK SE15 .....143 G4
Soames Wk NWMAL KT3 .....176 B4
Soane Cl EA W5 .....116 E2
Soaphouse La BTFD TW8 .....137 F1
Soho Sq SOHO/SHAV W1D 10 C4
Soho St SOHO/SHAV W1D 10 C4
Sojourner Truth Cl HACK E8 * 86 D4
Solander Gdns WCHPL E1 .....104 D6
Solebay St WCHPL E1 .....105 G3
Solent Ri PLSTW E13 .....106 E2
Solent Rd KIL/WHAMP NW6 .....82 E3
  HTHAIR TW6 .....152 B1
Solna Av PUT/ROE SW15 .....139 F6
Solna Rd WCHMH N21 .....35 K3
Solomon Av UED N18 .....50 C6
Solomon's Pas PECK SE15 .....143 J5
Solon New Rd CLAP SW4 .....141 K5
Solon Rd BRXS/STRHM SW2 .....141 K5
Solway Cl HACK E8 .....86 B4
  HSLWW TW4 .....134 D4
Solway Rd EDUL SE22 .....143 H5
  WDGN N22 .....49 H4
Somaford Gv EBAR EN4 .....33 H1

Somali Rd CRICK NW2......82 D2
Somerby Rd BARK IG11......90 D5
Somercotes Cl EBAR EN4......21 J4
Somerden Rd STMC/STPC BR5...202 E4
Somerfield Rd FSBYPK N4......67 H6
Somerfield St
　BERM/RHTH SE16......124 A5
Somerford Cl PIN HA5......58 E1
Somerford Gv STNW/STAM N16...86 B2
　TOTM N17......50 D4
Somerford St WCHPL E1 *...104 D3
Somerford Wy
　BERM/RHTH SE16......124 B2
Somerhill Av BFN/LL DA15...168 C2
Somerhill Rd WELL DA16......148 C3
Somerleyton Rd BRXN/ST SW9..142 B5
Somers Cl CAMTN NW1......4 C2
Somers Crs BAY/PAD W2......205 K2
　RYNPK SW20......176 E5
　WELL DA16......148 A6
Somerset Cl NWMAL KT3......192 A5
　TOTM N17......49 K5
　WFD IG8......52 E4
Somerset Gdns HGT N6......66 B4
　LEW SE13......144 C3
　STRHM/NOR SW16......180 A6
　TEDD TW11......173 K1
　TOTM N17......50 A3
Somerset Sq WKENS W14 *...119 H3
Somerset Wave HEST TW5...134 D6
Somersham Rd BXLYHN DA7...149 F3
Somers Ms BAY/PAD W2......8 C4
Somers Rd BRXS/STRHM SW2..162 A1
　WALTH E17......69 H1
Somers Wy BUSH WD23......28 C2
Somerton Av RCH/KEW TW9...137 J4
Somerton Rd CRICK NW2......82 B1
　PECK SE15......143 J5
Somertrees Av LEE/GVPK SE12..166 A5
Somervell Rd RYLN/HDSTN HA2..77 K3
Somerville Av BARN SW13...119 H6
Somerville Rd CHDH RM6......73 J2
　DART DA1......171 J1
　PGE/AN SE20......182 A3
Sonderburg Rd HOLWY N7......67 F6
Sondes St WALW SE17......122 E6
Songhurst Cl CROY/NA CRO...196 A4
Sonia Cl OXHEY WD19......27 G2
Sonia Gdns NFNCH/WDSPK N12..135 F1
　WLSDN NW10......81 H2
Sonning Gdns HPTN TW12...172 D2
Sonning Rd SNWD SE25......197 H3
Soper Cl CHING E4......51 H1
　FSTH SE23......164 A3
Soper Ms PEND EN3......25 J1
Sophia Cl HOLWY N7......85 F4
Sophia Rd CAN/RD E16......107 F5
　LEY E10......69 K5
Sophia St POPL/IOD E14 *...105 G6
Sopwith Av CHSGTN KT9......206 A3
Sopwith Cl KUTN/CMB KT2...175 H1
Sopwith Rd HEST TW5......134 B1
Sopwith Wy KUTN/CMB KT2..175 F4
　VX/NE SW8......141 G1
Sorrel Bank CROY/NA CRO *..213 G6
Sorrel Cl THMD SE28......128 A1
Sorrel Gdns EHAM E6......107 J4
Sorrel La POP/IOD E14......106 B5
Sorrell Cl BRXN/ST SW9 *...142 B3
　NWCR SE14......144 B1
Sorrel Wk ROM RM1......56 F6
Sorrento Rd SUT SM1......209 F1
Sotheby Rd HBRY N5......85 J2
Sotheran Cl HACK E8......86 C6
Soudan Rd BTSEA SW11......140 E2
Souldern Rd WKENS W14 *...119 G3
Sounds Ldg SWLY BR8......203 K3
South Access Rd LEY E10......69 G3
South Africa Rd SHB W12......99 K6
Southall La NWDGN UB2......114 A6
Southall St STHWK SE1......18 E3
Southampton Buildings
　LINN WC2A......11 J2
Southampton Gdns
　MTCM CR4......195 K2
Southampton Ms CAN/RD E16..126 A1
Southampton Pl
　NOXST/BSQ WC1A......11 F2
Southampton Rd HAMP NW3...83 K3
　HTHAIR TW6......152 C1
Southampton Rw
　NOXST/BSQ WC1A......11 F1
　RSQ WC1B......10 E1
Southampton St
　COVGDN WC2E......11 F5
Southampton Wy CMBW SE5..142 E1
Southam St NKENS W10......100 C3
South Ap NTHWD HA6......26 B5
South Audley St
　MYFR/PKLN W1K......9 H1
South Av CAR SM5......210 A5
　CHING E4......37 K2
　RCH/KEW TW9 *......137 H3
　STHL UB1......95 K6
South Avenue Gdns STHL UB1...95 K6
South Bank STHWK SE1......11 K6
　SURB KT6......191 F3

Southbank THDIT KT7......190 C4
South Bank Ter SURB KT6 *..191 F3
South Birkbeck Rd WAN E11...88 B1
South Black Lion La
　HMSMTH W6......118 D5
South Bolton Gdns
　WBPTN SW10......120 A5
Southborough Cl SURB KT6...190 E5
Southborough La HAYES BR2..200 D2
Southborough Rd BMLY BR1..184 D6
　HOM E9......86 E6
　SURB KT6......191 F5
Southborough Rd (The Lane)
　SURB KT6 *......191 F5
Southbourne HAYES BR2......199 K4
Southbourne Av
　CDALE/KGS NW9......44 E5
Southbourne Cl PIN HA5......59 J4
Southbourne Crs HDN NW4...64 C1
Southbourne Gdns IL IG1......90 C5
　LEE/GVPK SE12......146 A6
　RSLP HA4......59 F5
Southbridge Pl CROY/NA CRO..211 J2
Southbridge Rd CROY/NA CRO..211 J2
Southbridge Wy NWDGN UB2..114 D2
Southbrook Rd
　LEE/GVPK SE12......165 H1
　STRHM/NOR SW16......179 K4
Southbury Av EN EN1......24 A5
Southbury Rd EN EN1......111 K4
　RAIN RM13......111 J4
South Carriage Dr KTBR SW1X...15 F2
　SKENS SW7......15 F4
Southchurch Rd EHAM E6......107 K1
South Cl BAR EN5......20 D4
　BXLYHS DA6......148 E5
　DAGE RM10......92 C6
　HGT N6......66 B3
　PIN HA5......59 K6
　WDR/YW UB7......112 D3
　WIM/MER SW19......159 F5
The South Colonnade
　POP/IOD E14......124 D1
Southcombe St WKENS W14...119 H4
Southcote Av BRYLDS KT5......191 J4
　FELT TW13......153 K4
Southcote Ri RSLP HA4......58 B4
Southcote Rd ARCH N19......66 C2
　SNWD SE25......197 J2
　WALTH E17......51 F6
South Countess Rd WALTH E17..51 H4
South Crs CAN/RD E16......106 B4
Southcroft Av WELL DA16......147 H4
　WWKM BR4......199 F6
Southcroft Rd ORP BR6......216 C1
　STRHM/NOR SW16......179 G2
South Cross Rd BARK/HLT IG6..72 C2
South Croxted Rd DUL SE21..162 E6
South Dagenham Rd
　CHIG IG7......54 D2
Southdean Gdns
　WIM/MER SW19......159 J4
Southdown Av HNWL W7......116 B3
Southdown Crs
　CNTH/NBYPK IG2......72 E2
　RYLN/HDSTN HA2......60 C5
Southdown Dr RYNPK SW20..177 H6
Southdown Rd CAR SM5......210 A6
　EMPK RM11......75 K4
　RYNPK SW20......177 G6
Southdown Vls
　SEVS/STOTM N15 *......67 H2
South Dr ORP BR6......216 E4
　RSLP HA4......58 C5
South Ealing Rd EA W5......116 E2
South Eastern Av ED N9......36 B5
South Eaton Pl BGVA SW1W...15 H6
South Eden Park Rd BECK BR3..198 E4
South Edwardes Sq KENS W8..119 J3
Southend Cl ELTH/MOT SE9...167 G1
Southend Crs ELTH/MOT SE9..167 F1
Southend La CAT SE6......164 C4
Southend Rd BECK BR3......182 D4
　CLAY IG5......53 J6
　EHAM E6......89 K3
South End Rd HAMP NW3......83 J2
　RAIN RM13......93 J6
Southend Rd (North Circular)
　WALTH E17 *......52 B4
Southend Rd (North Circular
　Rd) SWFD E18......52 E5
South End Rw KENS W8......120 A3
Southern Av
　EBED/NFELT TW14......153 K3
　SNWD SE25......181 G6
Southern Down FELT TW13 *...154 B1
Southern Dr LOU IG10......39 K1
Southerngate Wy NWCR SE14..144 B1
Southern Perimeter Rd
　HTHAIR TW6......152 C1
Southern Rd EFNCH N2......65 K1
　PLSTW E13......107 F1
Southern Rw NKENS W10......100 B3
Southern St IS N1......5 H2
Southern Wy GNWCH SE10...125 J4
　ROMW/RG RM7......74 C3
Southerton Rd HMSMTH W6 *..119 F4
South Esk Rd FSTGT E7......89 G4
Southey Rd BRXN/ST SW9......142 B2
　SEVS/STOTM N15......68 A2
　WIM/MER SW19......177 K3
Southey St PGE/AN SE20......182 A3
Southfield BAR EN5......32 A1
Southfield Gdns TWK TW1......156 A6
Southfield Pk RYLN/HDSTN HA2..60 B1
Southfield Rd CHST BR7......186 A6
　CHSWK W4......118 A3
　PEND EN3......36 D1
Southfields E/WMO/HCT KT8..189 K3
　HDN NW4......45 K6
Southfields Ms
　WAND/EARL SW18 *......159 K1
Southfields Rd
　WAND/EARL SW18......159 K1

Southfleet Rd ORP BR6......216 E1
South Gdns WBLY HA9 *......62 C6
South Gv HGT N6......66 A6
　SEVS/STOTM N15......67 K4
South Gate Av FELT TW13......153 C6
Southgate Gv IS N1......85 K5
Southgate Rd IS N1......85 K6
South Gipsy Rd WELL DA16..148 E4
South Hall Dr RAIN RM13......111 K5
South Hl CHST BR7......184 D2
South Hill Av HRW HA2......78 C4
South Hill Gv HRW HA1......78 E1
South Hill Pk HAMP NW3......83 J2
South Hill Park Gdns
　HAMP NW3......83 J2
South Hill Rd HAYES BR2......199 H1
Southholme Cl NRWD SE19..181 F4
Southill La PIN HA5......58 E1
Southill St POP/IOD E14......105 K5
South Island Pl BRXN/ST SW9..142 A1
South Kensington Station Ar
　SKENS SW7......120 B3
South Lambeth Pl VX/NE SW8..122 A6
South Lambeth Rd
　VX/NE SW8......141 K1
Southland Rd
　WOOL/PLUM SE18......128 B6
　WOOL/PLUM SE18......148 A1
Southlands Dr
　WIM/MER SW19......159 G4
Southlands Gv BMLY BR1......199 J1
Southlands Rd HAYES BR2......200 J6
South La KUT/HW KT1......175 J6
　NWMAL KT3......192 A1
South La West NWMAL KT3..192 A1
South Lodge Av MTCM CR4..195 K4
South Lodge Crs ENC/FH EN2...22 D6
South Lodge Dr
　STHGT/OAK N14......22 E6
South Md CDALE/KGS NW9......45 H4
　HOR/WEW KT19......207 H5
Southmead Rd
　WIM/MER SW19......159 H5
South Molton La
　MYFR/PKLN W1K......9 J4
South Molton Rd CAN/RD E16..106 D5
South Molton St
　MYFR/PKLN W1K......9 J4
Southmont Rd ESH/CLAY KT10..189 K6
Southmoor Wy HOM E9......87 H4
South Mt TRDG/WHET N20 *..33 G4
South Norwood Hl
　SNWD SE25......181 F4
South Oak Rd
　STRHM/NOR SW16......162 A6
Southold Ri ELTH/MOT SE9...166 E5
Southolm St BTSEA SW11......141 G2
South Ordnance Rd PEND EN3..25 J1
Southover BMLY BR1......183 K1
　NFNCH/WDSPK N12......32 E6
South Pde CHEL SW3......120 C5
　CHSWK W4......118 A4
　EDGW HA8......44 C5
　WLGTN SM6......210 C4
South Park Crs CAT SE6......165 J3
　IL IG1......90 D1
South Park Dr GDMY/SEVK IG3..90 E1
South Park Gv NWMAL KT3..191 K1
South Park Hill Rd
　SAND/SEL CR2......211 K3
South Park Ms FUL/PGN SW6..140 A4
South Park Rd IL IG1......90 D2
South Park Ter IL IG1......90 D1
South Park Wy RSLP HA4......77 G4
South Pl BRYLDS KT5......191 G4
　LVPST EC2M......13 F2
　PEND EN3......24 E6
South Place Ms LVPST EC2M...13 F2
Southport Rd
　WOOL/PLUM SE18......127 J4
Southridge Pl RYNPK SW20..177 G3
South Ri BAY/PAD W2 *......8 D5
　CAR SM5......209 J6
South Rd CHDH RM6......73 K3
　EA W5......116 E4
　ED N9......36 C3
　EDGW HA8......44 C4
　ERITH DA8......150 C1
　FELT TW13......172 C5
　FSTH SE23......164 A4
　HPTN TW12......172 D2
　STHL UB1......114 E1
　WDR/YW UB7......112 C5
　WHTN TW2......155 J3
　WIM/MER SW19......178 B2
South Rw BKHTH/KID SE3......145 K3
Southsea Rd KUT/HW KT1......191 F1
South Sea St
　BERM/RHTH SE16......124 C3
South Side HMSMTH W6......118 C3
　SEVS/STOTM N15 *......68 B1
Southside Common
　WIM/MER SW19......177 G2
South Sq GINN WC1R......11 J2
　GLDGN NW11......64 E3
South St BMLY BR1......183 K5
　ISLW TW7......136 B4
　MYFR/PKLN W1K......9 H1
　PEND EN3......25 K1
　RAIN RM13......110 D1
　ROM RM1......75 G3
Spa Rd BERM/RHTH SE16......19 J3
Sparrow Cl HPTN TW12......172 D2
Sparrow Dr STMC/STPC BR5..201 H5
Sparrow Farm Dr
　EBED/NFELT TW14......154 C2
Sparrow Farm Rd EW KT17..207 K3
Sparrow Gn DAGE RM10......92 D1
Sparrows Herne BUSH WD23...28 B2
Sparrows La ELTH/MOT SE9..167 H5

South Vale Rd SURB KT6......191 F6
South Vw BMLY BR1......184 A5
South Vw Cl BXLY DA5......169 G1
South View Ct NRWD SE19 *..180 D3
Southview Cl TOOT SW17......179 F1
　WIM/MER SW19......178 B3
Southview Gdns WLGTN SM6..210 C5
South Vw Rd CEND/HSY/T N8..48 C6
　LOU IG10......39 K1
　PIN HA5......41 F3
　RDART DA2......171 K6
Southviews SAND/SEL CR2......213 F6
South Vw Wk CAMTN NW1 *...84 D4
South Vl/NE SW8......141 K2
Southville Cl
　EBED/NFELT TW14......153 H3
　HOR/WEW KT19......207 F6
Southville Crs
　EBED/NFELT TW14......153 H3
Southville Rd
　EBED/NFELT TW14......153 H3
　THDIT KT7......190 B4
South Wk WWKM BR4......214 C1
Southwark Br STHWK SE1......12 D6
Southwark Bridge Rd
　STHWK SE1......12 D7
Southwark Park Est
　BERM/RHTH SE16 *......123 J4
Southwark Park Rd
　BERM/RHTH SE16......19 K6
Southwark Pl BMLY BR1......184 E6
Southwark St STHWK SE1......12 B7
Southwater Cl BECK BR3......182 E3
　POP/IOD E14......105 H5
South Wy CROY/NA CRO......213 G1
　FBAR/BDGN N11......48 C2
Southway GLDGN NW11......65 F3
　HAYES BR2......199 K4
South Wy RYLN/HDSTN HA2...60 A1
　RYNPK SW20......193 G1
South Wy WBLY HA9......80 C3
Southway WLGTN SM6......210 C2
Southway Cl SHB W12 *......118 E2
Southwell Av NTHLT UB5......78 A4
Southwell Gdns SKENS SW7...120 B4
Southwell Grove Rd WAN E11..70 C6
Southwell Rd CMBW SE5......142 D4
　CROY/NA CRO......196 C3
　KTN/HRWW/WS HA3......61 K3
South Western Rd TWK TW1...156 B1
Southwest Rd WAN E11......70 B5
Southwick Ms BAY/PAD W2......8 B3
Southwick Pl BAY/PAD W2......8 C4
Southwick St BAY/PAD W2......8 C3
Southwick Yd BAY/PAD W2 *...8 C4
Southwold Dr BARK IG11......91 G3
Southwold Rd BXLY DA5......169 J1
　CLPT E5......68 D6
Southwood Av HGT N6......66 B4
　KUTN/CMB KT2......175 K4
Southwood Cl BMLY BR1......200 E1
　WPK KT4......193 G5
Southwood Dr BRYLDS KT5..191 K4
Southwood Gdns
　ESH/CLAY KT10......205 G2
　CNTH/NBYPK IG2......72 B1
Southwood Lawn Rd HGT N6...66 B4
Southwood Rd HGT N6 *......66 B4
　ELTH/MOT SE9......167 G4
　THMD SE28......128 C1
South Worple Wy
　MORT/ESHN SW14......138 A4
Southy Ms CAN/RD E16......125 K1
Sovereign Cl EA W5......97 J4
　WAP E1W......104 D6
Sovereign Crs
　BERM/RHTH SE16......105 H6
Sovereign Gv ALP/SUD HA0...79 K1
Sovereign Ms BETH E2 *......7 J2
　EBAR EN4......21 K4
Sovereign Pk POP/IOD E14..124 B3
Sovereign Pl HRW HA1......61 F2
Sovereign Rd BARK IG11......109 J2
Sowerby Cl ELTH/MOT SE9..166 E1
Sowrey Av RAIN RM13......93 H4
Space Waye
　EBED/NFELT TW14......134 A6
Spafield St CLKNW EC1R......5 J5
Spa Green Est CLKNW EC1R *...5 J4
Spa Hi NRWD SE19......180 E4
Spalding Cl EDGW HA8......45 G3
Spalding Rd HDN NW4......64 A3
　TOOT SW17......179 G1
Spaniards Cl GLDGN NW11......65 G5
Spaniards End HAMP NW3......65 G4
Spaniards Rd HAMP NW3......65 G6
Spanish Pl MHST W1U *......9 H3
Spanish Rd WAND/EARL SW18..140 B6
Sparkbridge Rd HRW HA1......60 E1
Sparkes Cl HAYES BR2......200 A1
Sparke Ter CAN/RD E16 *......106 D5
Sparkford Gdns
　FBAR/BDGN N11 *......48 A1
Sparks Cl ACT W3......99 F5
　BCTR RM8......73 K6
　HPTN TW12......172 D2

Sparrows Wy BUSH WD23......28 C3
Sparrows Wick BUSH WD23 *...28 C3
Sparshott Rd ARCH N19......67 F5
　BARK IG11......90 D5
Spartan Cl WLGTN SM6......210 E5
Sparta St GNWCH SE10......145 F2
Speakers Ct CROY/NA CRO *..196 E5
Spearman St
　WOOL/PLUM SE18 *......127 F6
Spear Ms ECT SW5......119 K4
Spears Rd ARCH N19......66 E5
Speart La HEST TW5......134 D1
Spectrum Pl WALW SE17 *......122 E5
Spedan Cl HAMP NW3......83 F1
Speedwell St DEPT SE8......144 D1
Speedy Pl STPAN WC1H......4 E4
Speer Rd THDIT KT7......190 A3
Speirs Cl NWMAL KT3......192 C3
Spekehill ELTH/MOT SE9......166 E5
Speke Rd THHTH CR7......180 E5
Speldhurst Cl HAYES BR2......199 J2
Speldhurst Rd CHSWK W4......118 A3
　HOM E9......87 F5
Spellbrook Wk IS N1 *......85 J6
Spelman St WCHPL E1......104 C4
Spence Cl BERM/RHTH SE16..124 C2
Spencer Av CFNCH N3......49 F2
　HYS/HAR UB3......94 C5
Spencer Cl E/FNCH N3......201 K6
　ORP BR6......201 K6
　WFD IG8......53 G1
　WLSDN NW10......98 B2
Spencer Gdns
　MORT/ESHN SW14......137 K6
Spencer Hill WIM/MER SW19 *..177 H2
Spencer Hill Rd
　WIM/MER SW19......177 H3
Spencer House CLAP SW4 *...141 K2
Spencer Ms CLAP SW4......141 K2
　HMSMTH W6......119 H6
Spencer Pk WAND/EARL SW18..140 C6
Spencer Pas BETH E2......104 D1
Spencer Pl CROY/NA CRO......196 E4
　IS N1......85 H5
Spencer Ri KTTN NW5......84 B2
Spencer Rd ACT W3......117 K1
　ALP/SUD HA0......79 J5
　BMLY BR1......183 J3
　BTSEA SW11......140 C5
　CEND/HSY/T N8......67 F2
　CHSWK W4......137 K1
　E/WMO/HCT KT8......189 H1
　EHAM E6......89 H1
　FBAR/BDGN N11......34 B6
　GDMY/SEVK IG3......73 F5
　ISLW TW7......135 K2
　KTN/HRWW/WS HA3......42 E5
　MTCM CR4......194 E1
　RAIN RM13......111 F2
　RYNPK SW20......176 E5
　TOTM N17......50 C4
　WALTH E17......52 A1
　WHTN TW2......155 K5
Spencer St FSBYE EC1V......6 A5
　NWDGN UB2......114 C2
Spenser Gv
　STNW/STAM N16......86 A2
Spenser Ms DUL SE21......162 E3
Spenser Rd HNHL SE24......142 C6
Spenser St WESTW SW1E......16 B4
Spensley Wk STNW/STAM N16..85 K1
Speranza St WOOL/PLUM SE18..128 A5
Sperling Rd TOTM N17......50 B5
Spert St POP/IOD E14......105 G6
Speyside STHGT/OAK N14......34 C1
Spey St POP/IOD E14......106 A4
Spey Wy ROM RM1......57 G3
Spezia Rd WLSDN NW10......99 J1
Spicer Cl BRXN/ST SW9......142 C3
　WOT/HER KT12......188 B3
Spices Yd CROY/NA CRO......211 J2
Spielman Rd DART DA1......151 J5
Spigurnell Rd TOTM N17......49 K4
Spikes Bridge Rd STHL UB1......95 J5
Spindle Cl WOOL/PLUM SE18..126 E3
Spindlewood Gdns
　CROY/NA CRO......212 A2
Spindrift Av POP/IOD E14......124 D4
Spinel Cl WOOL/PLUM SE18..128 A5
Spinnaker Cl BARK IG11......109 H2
Spinnells Rd RYLN/HDSTN HA2..59 J6
Spinney Cl BECK BR3......198 E1
　NWMAL KT3......192 B2
　RAIN RM13......111 J1
Spinney Dr EBED/NFELT TW14..153 F2
Spinney Gdns DAGW RM9......92 A3
　NRWD SE19......181 G1
Spinney Oak BMLY BR1......184 D5
The Spinneys BMLY BR1......184 E5
The Spinney ALP/SUD HA0......79 G1
　BAR EN5......20 E3
　BARN SW13......118 E5
　CHEAM SM3......208 A2
　NFNCH/WDSPK N12 *......47 G3
　SCUP DA14......187 F1
　STAN HA7......44 A1
　STRHM/NOR SW16......161 H5
　WCHMH N21......35 G2
The Spires DART DA1......171 G4
Spirit Quay WAP E1W......123 H1
Spital Sq WCHPL E1......13 H1
Spital St DART DA1......171 G1
　WCHPL E1......104 C4
Spital Yd WCHPL E1 *......13 H1
Spitfire Est HEST TW5 *......114 B5
Spitfire House
　WOOL/PLUM SE18 *......146 D1
Spitfire Rd WLGTN SM6......211 F5
Spitfire Wy HEST TW5 *......114 C5
Spode Wk KIL/WHAMP NW6 *...83 F3
Spondon Rd SEVS/STOTM N15..68 C1
Spoonbill Wy YEAD UB4......95 H4
Spooner Wk WLGTN SM6......210 D3

Sportsbank St *CAT* SE6 ....165 F2
Sportsman Pl *BETH* E2 ....86 C6
Spottons Gv *TOTM* N17 ....49 J4
Spout Hl *CROY/NA* CR0 ....213 J3
Spratt Hall Rd *WAN* E11 ....70 E3
Spray St *WOOL/PLUM* SE18 ...127 G4
Spreighton Rd
E/WMO/HCT KT8 ....189 G1
Sprimont Pl *CHEL* SW3 ....120 E5
Springall St *PECK* SE15 ....143 J1
Springbank *WCHMH* N21 ....35 F1
Springbank Rd *LEW* SE13 ....165 H1
Springbank Wk *CAMTN* NW1 ....5 J2
Springbourne Ct *BECK* BR3 ......183 F4
Spring Bridge Rd *EA* W5 ....97 K6
Spring Cl *BAR* EN5 ....20 B6
BCTR RM8 ....73 K5
Springclose La *CHEAM* SM3 ....208 C4
Spring Cnr *FELT* TW13 * 153 K5
Spring Cottages *SURB* KT6 * ...190 E2
Spring Court Rd *ENC/FH* EN2 .....23 G1
Springcroft Av *EFNCH* N2 ....47 K6
Springdale Rd *STNW/STAM* N16 .85 K2
Spring Dr *PIN* HA5 ....58 E3
Springfield *BUSH* WD23 ....28 D3
CLPT E5 ....68 D5
Springfield Av *HPTN* TW12 ....173 G2
MUSWH N10 ....48 C6
RYNPK SW20 ....177 J6
Springfield Cl
NFNCH/WDSPK N12 ....47 F1
STAN HA7 ....35 G3
Springfield Cnr *HOLWY* N7 * 85 G2
Springfield Gdns *BMLY* BR1 .....200 E1
Springfield Gdns *BMLY* BR1 .....200 E1
CDALE/KGS NW9 ....63 F2
CLPT E5 ....68 D5
RSLP HA4 ....59 F5
WFD IG8 ....53 G3
WWKM BR4 ....198 E6
Springfield Gv *CHARL* SE7 ....126 B6
Springfield La *KIL/WHAMP* NW6 ..83 F6
Springfield Mt *CDALE/KGS* NW9 .63 G2
Springfield Parade Ms
PLMGR N13 ....35 G6
Springfield Pl *NWMAL* KT3 ....191 K1
Springfield Ri *SYD* SE26 ....163 J6
Springfield Rd *BMLY* BR1 ....200 E1
BXLYHN DA7 ....149 J4
CHING E4 ....38 C3
EHAM E6 ....89 K5
FBAR/BDGN N11 ....48 C1
HNWL W7 ....115 K1
HRW HA1 ....60 D4
KUT/HW KT1 ....191 F1
SEVS/STOTM N15 ....68 C1
SRTFD E15 * 106 C2
STJWD NW8 ....83 G6
SYD SE26 ....182 D2
TEDD TW11 ....174 B1
THHTH CR7 ....180 D4
WALTH E17 ....69 H5
WELL DA16 ....148 C4
WHTN TW2 ....155 F3
WIM/MER SW19 ....177 J1
WLGTN SM6 ....210 B3
YEAD UB4 ....114 B1
Springfield Wk
KIL/WHAMP NW6 ....83 F6
Spring Gdns
E/WMO/HCT KT8 ....189 H2
HBRY N5 ....85 J3
HCH RM12 ....93 K2
ORP BR6 ....217 H4
ROMW/RG RM7 ....74 D3
WFD IG8 ....53 G3
WHALL SW1A 10 E7
WLGTN SM6 ....210 C3
Spring Gv *CHSWK* W4 ....117 G6
HPTN TW12 ....173 G4
LOU IG10 ....39 H1
MTCM CR4 ....179 F4
Spring Grove Crs *HSLW* TW3 ....135 H4
Spring Grove Rd *HSLW* TW3 .....135 H4
ISLW TW7 ....135 G4
RCHPK/HAM TW10 ....137 G6
Springhead Rd *ERITH* DA8 ....130 C6
Spring Hl *CLPT* E5 ....68 C4
SYD SE26 ....163 K6
Spring Lake *STAN* HA7 ....29 H6
Spring La *CLPT* E5 ....68 D5
EFNCH N2 ....48 A6
SNWD SE25 ....197 J3
Spring Ms *MHST* W1U * 9 G1
Spring Park Av *CROY/NA* CR0 ...198 A6
Springpark Dr *BECK* BR3 ....183 F6
FSBYPK N4 ....67 J5
Spring Park Pth *CROY/NA* CR0 ..198 A6
Spring Pl *KTTN* NW5 ....84 A3
Springpond Rd *DAGW* RM9 ....92 A3
Springrice Rd *LEW* SE13 ....165 G1
Spring Rd *FELT* TW13 ....153 J5
Spring Shaw Rd
STMC/STPC BR5 ....186 B4
Spring St *BAY/PAD* W2 ....8 A4
EW KT17 ....207 H6
Spring Tide Cl *PECK* SE15 * 143 H2
Spring V *BXLYHN* DA7 ....149 J5
Springvale Av *BTFD* TW8 ....116 E5
Spring V North *DART* DA1 ....171 G2
Spring V South *DART* DA1 ....171 G2
Springvale Ter *WKENS* W14 .....119 G3
Springvale Wy
STMC/STPC BR5 ....186 C6
Spring Villa Rd *EDGW* HA8 ....44 C3
Spring Vis *WEA* W13 * 116 C1
Spring Wk *WCHPL* E1 ....104 C4
Springwater Cl
WOOL/PLUM SE18 ....147 F2
Springwell Av *WLSDN* NW10 .....81 H6
Springwell Rd *HEST* TW5 ....134 C2
STRHM/NOR SW16 ....162 B6
Springwood Cl *BOW* E3 ....105 J1
Springwood Crs *EDGW* HA8 ....30 E4
Springwood Wy *ROM* RM1 ....75 J2
Sprowston Ms *FSTGT* E7 ....88 E4
Sprowston Rd *FSTGT* E7 ....88 E3

Sprucedale Gdns
CROY/NA CR0 ....213 G2
WLGTN SM6 ....210 E6
Spruce Hills Rd *WALTH* E17 ....51 K5
Sprules Rd *BROCKY* SE4 ....144 B3
Spurfield *E/WMO/HCT* KT8 ....173 G6
Spurgeon Av *NRWD* SE19 ....180 E4
Spurgeon Rd *NRWD* SE19 ....180 E4
Spurgeon St *STHWK* SE1 ....18 E5
Spurling Rd *DAGW* RM9 ....92 B4
EDUL SE22 * 143 G5
Spurrell Av *BXLY* DA5 ....170 A6
Spur Rd *BARK* IG11 ....108 C2
EBED/NFELT TW14 ....134 A6
EDGW HA8 ....30 B6
ISLW TW7 ....136 B1
ORP BR6 ....202 B6
SEVS/STOTM N15 * 67 K3
STHWK SE1 ....17 J2
WHALL SW1A 16 A3
Spurstowe Rd *HACK* E8 ....86 D4
Spurstowe Ter *HACK* E8 ....86 C3
The Square *CAR* SM5 ....209 K4
HMSMTH W6 ....119 F5
IL IG1 ....72 A4
RCH/KEW TW9 ....137 F6
STRPK UB11 ....113 C1
WFD IG8 ....53 F1
Squarey St *TOOT* SW17 ....160 B5
Squire Gdns *STJWD* NW8 ....2 A5
Squires Ct *WIM/MER* SW19 ......159 K6
Squires La *FNCH* N3 ....47 G4
Squire's Mt *HAMP* NW3 * 83 H1
Squires Wy *RDART* DA2 ....170 A6
Squires Wood Dr *CHST* BR7 * ...184 E3
Squirrel Cl *HSLWW* TW4 ....134 B4
Squirrel Ms *WEA* W13 * 97 G6
Squirrels Cl *NFNCH/WDSPK* N12 .33 G6
Squirrels Gn *WPK* KT4 ....192 C6
Squirrel's Heath Av *GPK* RM2 ....57 K6
The Squirrels *BUSH* WD23 ....28 D1
LEE/GVPK SE12 * 145 K5
PIN HA5 * 47 J5
Squirries St *BETH* E2 ....104 C2
Stable Cl *KUTN/CMB* KT2 ....175 G2
NTHLT UB5 ....96 A1
Stable Ms *TWK* TW1 * 156 A3
WNWD SE27 ....162 D1
Stables End *ORP* BR6 ....216 C1
The Stables Market
CAMTN NW1 * 84 B5
Stables Wy *LBTH* SE11 ....122 B5
Stable Wk *EFNCH* N2 * 47 H4
Stable Wy *NKENS* W10 ....100 A5
Stable Yard Rd *WHALL* SW1A 16 B2
Stacey Av *UED* N18 ....36 E6
Stacey Cl *LEY* E10 ....70 B2
Stacey St *HOLWY* N7 ....85 G1
LSQ/SEVD WC2H 10 D4
Stackhouse St *KTBR* SW1X 14 E4
Stacy Pth *CMBW* SE5 * 143 F1
Staddon Cl *BECK* BR3 ....198 B1
Staddon Ct *BECK* BR3 ....198 B1
Stadium Rd *HDN* NW4 ....63 K4
WOOL/PLUM SE18 ....146 E1
Stadium Rd East *HDN* NW4 ....63 K4
Stadium Wy *DART* DA1 ....151 H5
WBLY HA9 ....80 B2
Staffa Rd *LEY* E10 ....69 G5
Stafford Cl *CHEAM* SM3 ....208 C4
KIL/WHAMP NW6 ....100 E2
STHGT/OAK N14 ....22 C5
WALTH E17 ....69 H1
Stafford Cross *CROY/NA* CR0 ...211 F3
Stafford Gdns *CROY/NA* CR0 ....211 F3
Stafford Pl *RCHPK/HAM* TW10 .157 G2
WESTW SW1E 16 A5
Stafford Rd *BOW* E3 ....105 H1
CROY/NA CR0 ....211 G2
FSTGT E7 ....89 G5
KIL/WHAMP NW6 ....100 E2
KTN/HRWW/WS HA3 ....42 C3
NWMAL KT3 ....175 K6
RSLP HA4 ....76 D2
SCUP DA14 ....167 K6
WLGTN SM6 ....210 C4
Staffordshire St *PECK* SE15 .....143 H2
Stafford St *CONDST* W1S 10 A7
Stafford Ter *KENS* W8 ....119 K3
Stag Cl *EDGW* HA8 ....44 D5
Staggart Gn *CHIG* IG7 ....55 F1
Stag La *BKHH* IG9 ....39 F4
CDALE/KGS NW9 ....44 E6
PUT/ROE SW15 ....158 C5
Stag Pl *WESTW* SW1E 16 A4
Stags Wy *ISLW* TW7 ....116 A6
Stainbank Rd *MTCM* CR4 ....179 G6
Stainby Cl *WDR/YW* UB7 ....112 B3
Stainby Rd *TOTM* N17 ....50 C4
Stainer St *STHWK* SE1 ....19 F1
Staines Av *CHEAM* SM3 ....193 G6
Staines Rd *EBED/NFELT* TW14 .134 C6
EBED/NFELT TW14 ....152 E3
IL IG1 ....90 D2
WHTN TW2 ....155 H5
Staines Rd East *SUN* TW16 ......172 C4
Stainforth Rd *CNTH/NBYPK* IG2 .72 D4
WALTH E17 ....69 J1
Staining La *CITYW* EC2V 12 D3
Stainmore Cl *CHST* BR7 ....185 J4
Stainsbury St *BETH* E2 ....104 E1
Stainsby Rd *POP/IOD* E14 ....105 J5
Stainton Rd *CAT* SE6 ....145 H5
PEND EN3 ....24 E2
Stalbridge St *CAMTN* NW1 ....8 D1
Stalham St *BERM/RHTH* SE16 ..123 J3
Stalham Wy *BARK/HLT* IG6 ....54 B4
Stambourne Woodland Wk
NRWD SE19 ....181 F3
Stamford Brook Av
HMSMTH W6 ....118 C3
Stamford Brook Gdns
HMSMTH W6 ....118 C3

Stamford Brook Rd
HMSMTH W6 ....118 C3
Stamford Cl *HAMP* NW3 * 83 G1
KTN/HRWW/WS HA3 ....42 E3
SEVS/STOTM N15 ....68 C1
STHL UB1 ....96 A6
Stamford Cottages
WBPTN SW10 * 140 A1
Stamford Dr *HAYES* BR2 ....199 J1
Stamford Gdns *DAGW* RM9 ....91 J3
Stamford Gv East
STNW/STAM N16 ....68 C5
Stamford Gv West
STNW/STAM N16 ....68 C5
Stamford Hl *STNW/STAM* N16 ....68 B5
Stamford Rd *DAGW* RM9 ....91 H5
EHAM E6 ....89 J6
IS N1 ....86 A5
SEVS/STOTM N15 ....68 C2
Stamford St *STHWK* SE1 ....11 J7
Stamp Pl *BETH* E2 ....7 J3
Stanborough Cl *HPTN* TW12 ....172 E2
Stanborough Pas *HACK* E8 ....86 B4
Stanborough Rd *HSLW* TW3 .....135 J4
Stanbridge Pl *WCHMH* N21 ....35 H4
Stanbridge Rd *PUT/ROE* SW15 .139 F4
Stanbrook Rd *ABYW* SE2 ....128 C2
Stanbury Ct *HAMP* NW3 ....83 K4
Stanbury Rd *PECK* SE15 ....143 K3
Stancroft *CDALE/KGS* NW9 ....63 G1
Standale Gv *RSLP* HA4 ....58 A2
Standard Pl *SDTCH* EC2A 7 H5
Standard Rd *BELV* DA17 ....129 H5
BXLYHS DA6 ....149 F5
HSLWW TW4 ....134 D4
PEND EN3 ....25 G1
WLSDN NW10 ....98 E3
Standen Rd *WAND/EARL* SW18 .159 K2
Standfield Rd *DAGE* RM10 ....92 C3
Standish Rd *HMSMTH* W6 ....118 D4
Stane Cl *WIM/MER* SW19 ....178 A3
Stane Gv *VX/NE* SW8 ....141 J3
Stane Wy *WOOL/PLUM* SE18 ...146 C1
Stanford Cl *HPTN* TW12 ....172 E2
ROMW/RG RM7 ....74 D3
RSLP HA4 ....58 A3
WFD IG8 ....53 J2
Stanford Pl *WALW* SE17 ....53 J2
Stanford Rd *FBAR/BDGN* N11 .....47 K1
SKENS SW7 ....120 A3
STRHM/NOR SW16 ....179 K5
Stanford St *PIM* SW1V 16 C7
Stanford Wy
STRHM/NOR SW16 ....179 J5
Stangate Gdns *STAN* HA7 ....29 H6
Stanger Rd *SNWD* SE25 ....197 H1
Stanham Pl *DART* DA1 ....151 H5
Stanham Rd *DART* DA1 ....151 J6
Stanhope Av *FNCH* N3 ....46 D6
HAYES BR2 ....199 K5
KTN/HRWW/WS HA3 ....42 D4
Stanhope Cl
BERM/RHTH SE16 * 124 A2
Stanhope Gdns *BCTR* RM8 ....92 B1
FSBYPK N4 ....67 H3
HGT N6 ....66 C3
IL IG1 ....71 K5
MLHL NW7 ....45 H1
SKENS SW7 ....120 B4
Stanhope Ga *BAY/PAD* W2 ....8 C1
MYFR/PKLN W1K 9 H1
Stanhope Gv *BECK* BR3 ....198 C2
Stanhope Ms East *SKENS* SW7 .120 B4
Stanhope Ms South
SKENS SW7 ....120 A4
Stanhope Ms West *SKENS* SW7 .120 A4
Stanhope Pde *CAMTN* NW1 * 3 K4
Stanhope Park Rd
GFD/PVL UB6 ....96 C3
Stanhope Pl *BAY/PAD* W2 ....8 E4
Stanhope Rd *BAR* EN5 ....32 B1
BCTR RM8 ....74 B6
BFN/LL DA15 ....168 B6
BXLYHN DA7 ....149 F5
CAR SM5 ....210 A5
CROY/NA CR0 ....212 A1
GFD/PVL UB6 ....96 C4
HGT N6 ....66 C3
NFNCH/WDSPK N12 ....47 G1
RAIN RM13 ....111 J1
WALTH E17 ....70 A2
Stanhope Rw *MYFR/PICC* W1J * .15 J1
Stanhope St *CAMTN* NW1 ....4 A4
Stanhope Ter *BAY/PAD* W2 ....8 B5
WHTN TW2 ....156 A2
Stanier Cl *WKENS* W14 ....119 J5
Stanlake Rd *SHB* W12 ....119 F1
Stanlake Vis *SHB* W12 ....119 F1
Stanley Av *ALP/SUD* HA0 ....80 A5
BARK IG11 ....109 F2
BCTR RM8 ....74 B5
BECK BR3 ....183 F6
GFD/PVL UB6 ....96 B2
NWMAL KT3 ....192 D2
Stanley Cl *ALP/SUD* HA0 ....80 A5
ELTH/MOT SE9 ....167 H3
GPK RM2 ....75 J1
VX/NE SW8 ....122 A6
Stanley Crs *NTGHL* W11 ....100 D6
Stanleycroft Cl *ISLW* TW7 ....135 K2
Stanley Gdns *ACT* W3 ....118 B2
CRICK NW2 ....82 A3
MTCM CR4 * 179 F2
NTGHL W11 ....100 D6
WLGTN SM6 ....210 C4
Stanley Gardens Rd
TEDD TW11 ....173 K1
Stanley Gv *CROY/NA* CR0 ....196 B3
VX/NE SW8 ....141 F3
Stanley Park Dr *ALP/SUD* HA0 ...80 B5
Stanley Park Rd *CAR* SM5 ....209 K6
WLGTN SM6 ....210 B5
Stanley Pas *CAMTN* NW1 ....4 E3
Stanley Rd *ACT* W3 ....117 J3
BELMT SM2 ....209 F4
CAR SM5 ....209 K6

Star & Garter Hl
RCHPK/HAM TW10 ....157 F3
Starboard Wy *POP/IOD* E14 .....124 D3
Starbuck Cl *ELTH/MOT* SE9 .....167 F6
Starch House La *BARK/HLT* IG6 ..54 E2
Star Cl *PEND* EN3 ....36 E1
Starcross St *CAMTN* NW1 ....4 B5
Starfield Rd *SHB* W12 ....118 D2
Star Hl *DART* DA1 ....170 E2
Star La *CAN/RD* E16 ....106 C3
STMC/STPC BR5 ....202 E1

Star & Garter Hl continued...

Starling Cl *BKHH* IG9 ....38 E3
PIN HA5 ....41 G6
Starling Rd *CROY/NA* CR0 ....198 B3
Starmans Cl *DAGW* RM9 ....92 A6
Star Pl *WAP* E1W * 13 K6
Star Rd *HGDN/ICK* UB10 ....94 A3
ISLW TW7 ....135 J3
WKENS W14 ....119 J6
Star St *BAY/PAD* W2 ....8 C3
Starts Cl *ORP* BR6 ....216 A1
Starts Hill Av *ORP* BR6 ....216 B2
Starts Hill Rd *ORP* BR6 ....216 A1
Starveall Cl *WDR/YW* UB7 ....112 C3
Star Yd *LINN* WC2A 11 J3
State Farm Av *ORP* BR6 ....216 B2
Staten Gdns *TWK* TW1 ....156 A3
Statham Gv *STNW/STAM* N16 ....85 K1
UED N18 ....50 A1
Station Ap *ALP/SUD* HA0 ....79 H4
BAR EN5 ....21 G5
BECK BR3 ....182 B4
BELMT SM2 ....208 C5
BKHH IG9 * 39 H6
BXHTH/KID SE3 ....146 A3
BXLYHN DA7 ....149 F3
BXLYHN DA7 ....149 F3
CAMTN NW1 * 3 G7
CHING E4 ....38 C6
CHST BR7 ....184 D2
CHST BR7 ....185 F4
CROY/NA CR0 * 196 E6
DART DA1 ....171 H5
ESH/CLAY KT10 ....205 F1
FBAR/BDGN N11 ....48 B1
FSTGT E7 ....88 E2
FUL/PGN SW6 * 139 H4
GFD/PVL UB6 ....96 C2
GLDGN NW11 * 64 D4
HAYES BR2 ....199 K5
HOR/WEW KT19 ....207 F4
HPTN TW12 ....173 F4
HYS/HAR UB3 ....113 J1
KIL/WHAMP NW6 * 82 E6
KUT/HW KT1 ....175 H5
NFNCH/WDSPK N12 ....33 F6
NTHWD HA6 ....40 C6
ORP BR6 ....202 A6
ORP BR6 ....217 H5
OXHEY WD19 ....27 J2
PIN HA5 ....41 J6
RCH/KEW TW9 ....137 G2
RSLP HA4 ....58 C5
RYLN/HDSTN HA2 * 60 D6
SAND/SEL CR2 ....211 K6
STMC/STPC BR5 ....202 C1
STRHM/NOR SW16 ....179 J1
SURB KT6 ....190 E5
SWFD E18 * 52 E6
SYD SE26 ....182 C1
WALTH E17 ....69 J2
WAN E11 ....70 E2
WAN E11 * 71 F4
WDR/YW UB7 ....112 B1
WELL DA16 ....148 B2
WFD IG8 ....53 G2
WLSDN NW10 ....99 H1
Station Approach Rd
CHSWK W4 ....137 K1
Station Ar *GTPST* W1W * 3 K7
Station Av *HOR/WEW* KT19 ......207 G6
NWMAL KT3 ....176 B2
RCH/KEW TW9 ....137 H2
Station Buildings *HAYES* BR2 * .199 K5
Station Chambers *EA* W5 * 98 A5
Station Cl *HPTN* TW12 ....173 G4
Station Cottages *WDGN* N22 * ...48 E5
Station Crs *ALP/SUD* HA0 ....79 H4
ASHF TW15 ....152 B5
BKHTH/KID SE3 ....125 K5
SEVS/STOTM N15 ....67 K1
Stationers Hall Ct *STP* EC4M * 12 B4
Station Est *BECK* BR3 ....198 A1
Station Estate Rd
EBED/NFELT TW14 ....154 A3
Station Garage Ms
STRHM/NOR SW16 * 179 J2
Station Gdns *CHSWK* W4 ....137 K1
Station Gv *ALP/SUD* HA0 ....80 A4
Station HI *HAYES* BR2 ....199 K6
Station House Ms *ED* N9 ....36 C6
Station Pde *ACT* W3 * 98 B5
BAL SW12 * 161 F3
BARK IG11 ....90 C6
BELMT SM2 * 209 G4
BMLY BR1 * 183 K4
BXLYHN DA7 * 149 F3
CHSWK W4 ....117 K1
CLPT E5 * 86 E1
CRICK NW2 ....82 A4
EA W5 * 117 G1
EBAR EN4 * 33 J1
EBED/NFELT TW14 ....154 A2
EDGW HA8 ....44 B3
EHAM E6 * 89 J5
HCH RM12 ....93 K2
KTN/HRWW/WS HA3 ....78 A5
NTHLT UB5 ....78 B4
PIN HA5 ....59 H2
PLSTW E13 * 89 G6
RCH/KEW TW9 ....137 H2
ROM RM1 * 58 A6
RSLP HA4 ....76 A2
RYLN/HDSTN HA2 * 78 B2
SAND/SEL CR2 * 211 J4
Station Pas *PECK* SE15 ....143 K2
SWFD E18 * 53 F5
Station Pl *FSBYPK* N4 * 67 G6
Station Ri *WNWD* SE27 ....162 C4
Station Rd *ASHF* TW15 ....152 C6
BAR EN5 ....21 G6
BARK/HLT IG6 ....54 D6
BARN SW13 ....138 C3
BCTR RM8 ....91 K1
BELV DA17 ....129 H3
BMLY BR1 ....183 K4

BXLYHN DA7 ....149 F4
CAR SM5 ....209 K2
CHDH RM6 ....73 K4
CHINC E4 ....38 B3
CHSGTN KT9 ....206 A3
CROY/NA CR0 ....196 D5
DART DA1 ....170 C1
EA W5 ....98 B5
EDGW HA8 ....44 C2
ESH/CLAY KT10 ....189 J6
ESH/CLAY KT10 ....204 D5
FBAR/BDGN N11 ....48 B1
FNCH N3 ....46 E4
GPK RM2 ....75 K1
HAYES BR2 ....183 H5
HDN NW4 ....63 J3
HNWL W7 ....115 K1
HOLWY N7 ....84 C1
HPTN TW12 ....173 C4
HRW HA1 ....60 B2
HRW HA1 ....61 F1
HSLW TW3 ....135 G5
HYS/HAR UB3 ....113 J5
IL IG1 ....72 B6
IL IG1 ....90 B1
KUT/HW KT1 ....174 E1
KUTN/CMB KT2 ....175 H4
LEW SE13 ....92 C4
MLHL NW7 ....45 G2
MNPK E12 ....89 H2
NWMAL KT3 ....192 E2
ORP BR6 ....202 A6
PGE/AN SE20 ....181 K2
RYLN/HDSTN HA2 ......60 B3
SCUP DA14 ....168 B5
STMC/STPC BR5 ....197 G1
TEDD TW11 ....174 B2
THDIT KT7 ....190 A4
TOTM N17 ....156 A3
TWK TW1 ....156 A5
WALTH E17 ....69 G3
WCHMH N21 ....35 H3
WDGN N22 ....48 E5
WDGN N22 ....48 E5
WDR/YW UB7 ....112 B2
WIM/MER SW19 ....178 B4
WLSDN NW10 ....81 J5
WWKM BR4 ....199 F6
Station Rd North BELV DA17 ..129 J3
Station Sq STMC/STPC BR5 ...201 H2
Station St SRTFD E15 ....88 B5
Station Ter CMBW SE5 ....142 D2
  WLSDN NW10 ....100 B1
Station Vw GFD/PVL UB6 .....78 D6
  HBRY N5 ....85 H2
Station Wy BKHH IG9 ....39 H6
  CHEAM SM3 ....208 C4
  ESH/CLAY KT10 ....204 C4
Station Yd ASHF TW15 ....152 C6
  RSLP HA4 * 58 B6
  STHL UB1 * 114 E2
Staunton Rd KUTN/CMB KT2 ..175 G3
Staunton St DEPT SE8 ....124 C6
Staveley Cl HOLWY N7 * 84 E2
  PECK SE15 ....143 K2
Staveley Gdns CHSWK W4 ....138 A2
Staveley Rd CHSWK W4 ......117 K6
Staverton Rd CRICK NW2 ....82 A6
Stave Yard Rd
  BERM/RHTH SE16 ....124 B1
Stavordale Rd CAR SM5 .....194 B4
  HBRY N5 ....85 H2
Stayner's Rd WCHPL E1 .....105 F3
Stayton Rd SUT SM1 ....208 E1
Steadfast Rd KUT/HW KT1 ...174 E4
Stead St WALW SE17 ....18 C7
Steam Farm La
  EBED/NFELT TW14 ....133 J5
Stean St HACK E8 ....86 B6
Stebbing Wy BARK IG11 .....109 G1
Stebondale St POP/IOD E14 ..125 F5
Stedly SCUP DA14 ....168 B6
Stedman Cl BXLY DA5 ....170 B5
Steed Cl EMPK RM11 ....75 K6
Steedman St WALW SE17 .....18 C7
Steeds Rd MUSWH N10 ....47 K4
Steele Ap BARK IG11 ....109 H1
Steele Rd CHSWK W4 ....117 K3
  ISLW TW7 ....136 B5
  TOTM N17 ....50 A6
  WAN E11 ....88 C1
  WLSDN NW10 ....98 E1
Steele's Ms North HAMP NW3 *..83 K4
Steele's Ms South HAMP NW3 *..83 K4
Steele's Rd HAMP NW3 ......83 K4
Steeles Studios HAMP NW5 *..83 K4
Steel's La WCHPL E1 ....104 E5
Steep Cl ORP BR6 ....217 F4
Steep Hl CROY/NA CR0 ......212 A2
  STRHM/NOR SW16 ....161 J3
Steeplands BUSH WD23 ......28 B2
Steeple Cl FUL/PGN SW6 ....139 H4
  WIM/MER SW19 ....177 H1
Steeple Wk IS N1 * 6 C1
Steerforth St
  WAND/EARL SW18 ....160 A4
Steering Cl ED N9 ....36 E3
Steers Md MTCM CR4 ....178 E4
Steers Wy BERM/RHTH SE16 ..124 B2
Stella Rd TOOT SW17 ....178 E2
Stelling Rd ERITH DA8 .....150 A1
Stellman Cl CLPT E5 ....86 C1
Stembridge Rd PGE/AN SE20 ..181 J5
Stephan Cl HACK E8 ....86 C6
Stephen Av RAIN RM13 ......93 J4
Stephen Cl ORP BR6 ....217 F1
Stephendale Rd
  FUL/PGN SW6 ....140 A4
Stephen Ms FITZ W1T * 10 C2
Stephen Pl CLAP SW4 * 141 H4
Stephen Rd BXLYHN DA7 .....149 K4
Stephenson Cl WELL DA16 ...148 A3
Stephenson Rd HNWL W7 .....97 F5
  WALTH E17 ....69 G2

WHTN TW2 ....155 F2
Stephenson St CAN/RD E16 ..106 C4
  WLSDN NW10 ....99 G2
Stephenson's Rd CAMTN NW1 ..4 B1
Stephen's Rd SRTFD E15 ...88 C6
Stephen St FITZ W1T 10 C2
Stepney Cswy WCHPL E1 ....105 F5
Stepney Gn WCHPL E1 ......104 E4
Stepney High St WCHPL E1 ..105 F4
Stepney Wy MTCM 179 F4
  WCHPL E1 ....104 E4
Sterling Av EDGW HA8 ......30 B6
Sterling Cl WLSDN NW10 ....81 J5
Sterling Gdns NWCR SE14 ..124 B6
Sterling Pl EA W5 ....117 F4
Sterling Rd ENC/FH EN2 ....23 K2
Sterling St SKENS SW7 .....14 D4
Sterling Wy (North Circular)
  UED N18 ....49 K1
Stern Cl BARK IG11 ....109 J1
Sterndale Rd DART DA1 ....171 J2
  WKENS W14 ....119 G3
Sterne St SHB W12 ....119 G2
Sternhall La PECK SE15 ...143 H4
Sternhold Av
  BRXS/STRHM SW2 ....161 K4
Sterry Crs DAGE RM10 .....92 C3
Sterry Dr HOR/WEW KT19 ...207 G2
  THDIT KT7 ....189 K3
Sterry Gdns DAGE RM10 ....92 C4
Sterry Rd BARK IG11 ......91 F6
  DAGE RM10 ....92 B2
Sterry St STHWK SE1 ......18 E3
Steucers La FSTH SE23 ....164 B3
Steve Biko La CAT SE6 ....164 D6
Steve Biko Rd HOLWY N7 ...85 G1
Steve Biko Wy HSLW TW3 ...135 F4
Stevedale Rd WELL DA16 ...148 D3
Stevedore St WAP E1W 123 J1
Stevenage Rd EHAM E6 .....90 A4
  FUL/PGN SW6 ....139 G2
Stevens Av HOM E9 ....86 E4
Stevens Cl BECK BR3 ......182 D2
  BXLY DA5 ....170 A6
  HPTN TW12 ....172 E2
  PIN HA5 ....59 G2
Stevens Gn BUSH WD23 .....28 C3
Stevens' La ESH/CLAY KT10 .205 G5
Stevenson Cl BAR EN5 .....33 H1
  ERITH DA8 ....150 E1
Stevenson Crs
  BERM/RHTH SE16 ....123 H5
Stevens Rd BCTR RM8 ......73 H6
Stevens St STHWK SE1 .....19 H3
Steventon Rd SHB W12 .....118 D1
Stewart Cl CDALE/KGS NW9 ..62 E3
  CHST BR7 ....185 G2
  HPTN TW12 ....172 E2
Stewart Rd SRTFD E15 .....88 B2
Stewartsby Cl UED N18 ....49 J1
Stewart's Gv CHEL SW3 ....120 C5
Stewart's La VX/NE SW8 ...141 G1
Stewart's Rd VX/NE SW8 ...141 H2
Stewart St POP/IOD E14 ...124 E2
Stew La BLKFR EC4V 12 C5
Steyne Rd ACT W3 ....117 K1
Steyning Gv ELTH/MOT SE9 .166 E6
Steynings Wy
  NFNCH/WDSPK N12 ....46 E1
Steyning Wy HSLWW TW4 ...134 B5
Steynton Av BXLY DA5 ....169 F4
Stickland Rd BELV DA17 ...129 H4
Stickleton Cl GFD/PVL UB6 .96 B2
Stilecroft Gdns ALP/SUD HA0 .79 H1
Stile Hall Gdns CHSWK W4 .117 H5
Stiles Cl ERITH DA8 ......129 J5
  HAYES BR2 ....200 D3
Stillingfleet Rd BARN SW13 .118 D6
Stillington St WEST SW1P ..16 B6
Stillness Rd FSTH SE23 ...164 B1
Stipularis Dr YEAD UB4 ...95 H3
Stirling Av PIN HA5 ......59 H4
  WLGTN SM6 ....210 E5
Stirling Cl RAIN RM13 ....111 K2
  SCUP DA14 ....167 K6
  STRHM/NOR SW16 ....179 H3
Stirling Dr ORP BR6 ......217 H3
Stirling Gv HSLW TW3 .....135 H3
Stirling Rd ACT W3 ....137 H1
  BRXN/ST SW9 ....141 K4
  HYS/HAR UB3 ....95 F5
  KTN/HRWW/WS HA3 ....42 E6
  PLSTW E13 ....107 F1
  TOTM N17 ....50 C4
  WALTH E17 ....51 G5
  WDGN N22 ....49 H4
  WHTN TW2 ....155 F2
Stirling Wk BRYLDS KT5 ...191 J4
Stirling Wy BORE WD6 .....31 F1
  CROY/NA CR0 ....195 K4
Stiven Crs RYLN/HDSTN HA2 .77 K1
St John's Est IS N1 ......7 F3
St Martin-in-the-fields
  CHCR WC2N * 10 E6
Stockbury Rd CROY/NA CR0 .197 K3
Stockdale Rd BCTR RM8 ....74 B6
Stockfield Rd ESH/CLAY KT10 .204 E3
  STRHM/NOR SW16 ....162 A5
Stockford Av MLHL NW7 ....46 C3
Stockholm Rd
  BERM/RHTH SE16 ....123 K5
Stockholm Wy WAP E1W * ...123 H1
Stockhurst Cl PUT/ROE SW15 .139 F3
Stockingswater La PEND EN3 .25 G3
Stockland Rd ROMW/RG RM7 .75 F3
Stock La RDART DA2 ....171 F6
Stockley Farm Rd
  WDR/YW UB7 ....112 E3
Stockley Rd WDR/YW UB7 ...112 E3
Stock Orchard Crs HOLWY N7 .85 F3
Stock Orchard St HOLWY N7 .85 F3
Stockport Rd
  STRHM/NOR SW16 ....179 J4

Stocksfield Rd WALTH E17 *..52 A6
Stocks Pl POP/IOD E14 ....105 H6
Stock St PLSTW E13 ....106 E1
Stockton Cl BAR EN5 ......21 G5
Stockton Gdns MLHL NW7 ...31 H5
  TOTM N17 ....49 J3
Stockton Rd TOTM N17 .....49 J3
  UED N18 ....50 C2
Stockwell Av BRXN/ST SW9 .142 A4
Stockwell Cl BMLY BR1 ....184 A5
Stockwell Gdns BRXN/ST SW9 ..142 A3
Stockwell La BRXN/ST SW9 .142 A3
Stockwell Park Crs
  BRXN/ST SW9 ....142 A3
Stockwell Park Rd
  BRXN/ST SW9 ....142 A3
Stockwell Park Wk
  BRXN/ST SW9 ....142 A4
Stockwell Rd BRXN/ST SW9 .142 A3
Stockwell St GNWCH SE10 ..125 F6
Stockwell Ter BRXN/ST SW9 ..142 A2
Stoddart Rd PGE/AN SE20 ..181 J4
Stofield Gdns ELTH/MOT SE9 ..166 C4
Stoford Cl WIM/MER SW19 .159 H3
Stoke Av BARK/HLT IG6 ....55 G2
Stokenchurch St
  FUL/PGN SW6 ....140 A2
Stoke Newington Church St
  STNW/STAM N16 ....85 K1
Stoke Newington Common
  STNW/STAM N16 ....86 B1
Stoke Newington High St
  STNW/STAM N16 ....86 B1
Stoke Newington Rd
  STNW/STAM N16 ....86 B3
Stoke Pl WLSDN NW10 ......99 H2
Stoke Rd KUTN/CMB KT2 ...175 K5
  VX/NE SW8 ....142 A2
Stokesby Rd CHSGTN KT9 ..206 B4
Stokesley St SHB W12 .....99 H5
Stokes Rd CROY/NA CR0 ...198 A3
  EHAM E6 ....107 K4
Stoll Cl CRICK NW2 ....82 A1
Stonard Rd BCTR RM8 .....91 H3
  PLMGR N13 ....35 G1
Stonards Hl LOU IG10 .....39 K1
Stondon Pk FSTH SE23 ....164 B1
Stonebridge Pk WLSDN NW10 ..81 F5
Stonebridge Rd
  SEVS/STOTM N15 ....68 B2
Stonebridge Wy WBLY HA9 .80 E4
Stone Buildings LINN WC2A ..11 H2
Stonechat Sq EHAM E6 ....107 J4
Stone Cl BCTR RM8 ....92 B1
  CLAP SW4 ....141 H3
  WDR/YW UB7 ....112 C1
Stonecot Cl CHEAM SM3 ...193 H5
Stonecot Hl CHEAM SM3 ...193 H5
Stone Crs EBED/NFELT TW14 ..153 J2
Stonecroft Rd ERITH DA8 .149 K1
Stonecroft Wy CROY/NA CR0 ..195 K4
Stonecutter St
  FLST/FETLN EC4A 12 A3
Stonefield Cl BXLYHN DA7 .149 H4
  RSLP HA4 ....77 J5
Stonefield St IS N1 .....85 G6
Stonegate Cl STMC/STPC BR5 ..186 D6
Stone Gv EDGW HA8 ....30 A6
Stonegrove Gdns EDGW HA8 ..44 B1
Stonehall Av IL IG1 .....71 J3
Stone Hall Gdns KENS W8 *..120 A3
Stone Hall Pl KENS W8 ....120 A3
Stoneham Rd FBAR/BDGN N11 ..48 C1
Stonehill Cl MORT/ESHN SW14 ..138 A6
Stonehill Rd CHSWK W4 ...117 H5
  MORT/ESHN SW14 ....137 K6
Stonehills Ct DUL SE21 ..163 F5
Stonehill Woods Pk
  SCUP DA14 * 187 J2
Stonehorse Rd PEND EN3 ..24 E6
Stone House Ct LVPST EC2M ..13 H1
Stonehouse La RSEV TN14 .217 K6
Stonehouse Rd RSEV TN14 .217 K6
Stoneleigh Av EN EN1 ....24 D1
  WPK KT4 ....207 J1
Stoneleigh Broadway
  EW KT17 ....207 J3
Stoneleigh Crs
  HOR/WEW KT19 ....207 H3
Stoneleigh Park Av
  CROY/NA CR0 ....198 A3
Stoneleigh Park Rd
  HOR/WEW KT19 ....207 H4
Stoneleigh Pl NTGHL W11 .100 B6
Stoneleigh Rd BMLY BR1 ..185 G6
  CAR SM5 ....194 D4
  CLAY IG5 ....53 K6
  TOTM N17 ....50 B5
Stoneleigh St NTGHL W11 .100 B6
Stoneleigh Ter ARCH N19 .66 B6
Stonell's Rd TOOT SW17 ..160 E5
Stonemasons Cl
  SEVS/STOTM N15 ....67 K1
Stonenest St FSBYPK N4 ..67 F5
Stone Park Av BECK BR3 ..198 E1
Stone Pl WPK KT4 ....192 D6
Stone Rd HAYES BR2 ......199 J4
Stones Cross Rd SWLY BR8 .203 K2
Stones End St STHWK SE1 .18 C3
Stonewall EHAM E6 ....108 A4
Stonewood Rd ERITH DA8 .130 B5
Stoney Aly WOOL/PLUM SE18 ..147 F2
Stoneyard La POP/IOD E14 .105 K6
Stoneycroft Cl LEE/GVPK SE12 ..165 J2
Stoneycroft Rd WFD IG8 ..53 J2
Stoneydown Av WALTH E17 .51 G1
Stoneyfields Gdns EDGW HA8 ..30 E6
Stoneyfields La EDGW HA8 .44 E1
Stoney La HDTCH EC3A 13 H3
Stoney St STHWK SE1 .....12 E7
Stonhouse St CLAP SW4 ...141 J4

Stonnell's Rd BTSEA SW11 .140 E6
Stonor Rd WKENS W14 .....119 J4
Stonycroft Cl PEND EN3 ..25 G3
Stopes St PECK SE15 .....143 G1
Stopford Rd PLSTW E13 ...88 E6
  WALW SE17 ....122 C5
Store Rd CAN/RD E16 .....127 F2
Storers Quay POP/IOD E14 .125 G4
Store St GWRST WC1E 10 C2
  SRTFD E15 ....88 B3
Storey Rd HGT N6 ....65 K3
  WALTH E17 ....69 H1
Storey's Ga STJSPK SW1H .16 D3
Stories Ms CMBW SE5 * ...143 F3
Stories Rd CMBW SE5 .....143 F3
Stork Rd FSTGT E7 ....88 D4
Storksmead Rd EDGW HA8 ..45 G3
Storks Rd BERM/RHTH SE16 ..123 H3
Stormont Rd BTSEA SW11 .141 F5
  HGT N6 ....65 K4
Stormont Wy CHSGTN KT9 .205 J3
Stormount Dr HYS/HAR UB3 ..113 F2
Storrington Rd CROY/NA CR0 ..197 G5
Story St IS N1 ....85 F5
Stothard Pl SDTCH EC2A *..13 H1
Stothard St WCHPL E1 ....104 E3
Stott Cl WAND/EARL SW18 .160 C1
Stoughton Av CHEAM SM3 .208 B3
Stoughton Cl LBTH SE11 .17 H7
  PUT/ROE SW15 ....158 D3
Stour Av NWDGN UB2 ......115 F3
Stourcliffe St MBLAR W1H .8 E4
Stourhead Cl WIM/MER SW19 ..159 G2
Stourhead Gdns RYNPK SW20 ..176 D6
Stour Rd BOW E3 ....87 J5
  DAGE RM10 ....74 C6
  DART DA1 ....150 D4
Stourton Av FELT TW13 ...154 E6
Stowage DEPT SE8 ....124 E6
The Stowage DEPT SE8 ....124 E6
Stow Crs WALTH E17 ......51 G4
Stowe Gdns ED N9 ....36 B3
Stowe Pl SEVS/STOTM N15 .50 A6
Stowe Rd ORP BR6 ....217 H2
  SHB W12 ....118 E2
Stowting Rd ORP BR6 .....216 E2
Stox Md KTN/HRWW/WS HA3 .42 D4
Stracey Rd WLSDN NW10 ...81 F6
Strachan Pl RYNPK SW20 *..177 F2
Stradbroke Dr CHIG IG7 ..54 B1
Stradbroke Gv BKHH IG9 ..39 H5
  CLAY IG5 ....53 J6
Stradbroke Pk CHIG IG7 ..54 B2
Stradbroke Rd HBRY N5 ...85 J2
Stradbrook Cl
  RYLN/HDSTN HA2 ....77 K1
Stradella Rd HNHL SE24 ..162 D1
Strafford Av CLAY IG5 ...53 K5
Strafford Rd ACT W3 .....117 K2
  BAR EN5 ....20 C4
  HSLW TW3 ....134 E4
  TWK TW1 ....156 C1
Strafford St POP/IOD E14 .124 D2
Strahan Rd BOW E3 ....105 G2
Straight Rd HARH RM3 ....57 K1
Straightsmouth GNWCH SE10 ..145 F1
The Straight NWDGN UB2 ..114 C2
Strait Rd EHAM E6 ....107 K6
Straker's Rd EDUL SE22 ..143 J5
Strand CHCR WC2N 11 F6
Strand Dr RCH/KEW TW9 ...137 J1
Strandfield Cl
  WOOL/PLUM SE18 ....127 K5
Strand-on-the-Green
  CHSWK W4 ....117 H6
Strand Pl UED N18 ....36 A6
Strangways Ter WKENS W14 ..119 J3
Stranraer Wy IS N1 ......84 E6
Strasburg Rd BTSEA SW11 .141 F2
Stratfield Park Cl WCHMH N21 ..35 H2
Stratford Cl BARK IG11 ..91 G5
  DAGE RM10 ....92 E3
Stratford Gv PUT/ROE SW15 ..139 G5
Stratford House Av BMLY BR1 ..184 D6
Stratford Pl OXSTW W1C ..9 J4
Stratford Rd HTHAIR TW6 .152 E1
  KENS W8 ....119 K4
  NWDGN UB2 ....114 D4
  PLSTW E13 ....106 D1
  THHTH CR7 ....196 B1
  YEAD UB4 ....95 F3
Stratford Studios KENS W8 ..119 K4
Stratford Vis CAMTN NW1 ..84 C5
Strattan Cl WAND/EARL SW18 ..159 K1
Strathaven Rd
  LEE/GVPK SE12 ....166 A1
Strathblaine Rd BTSEA SW11 ..140 C6
Strathbrook Rd
  STRHM/NOR SW16 ....162 A6
Strathcona Rd WBLY HA9 ..61 K4
Strathdale STRHM/NOR SW16 ..180 A1
Strathdon Dr TOOT SW17 ..160 C5
Strathearn Av HYS/HAR UB3 ..133 J1
  WHTN TW2 ....155 H3
Strathearn Cottages
  TRDG/WHET N20 * 32 C5
Strathearn Pl BAY/PAD W2 .8 C5
Strathearn Rd SUT SM1 ...208 E3
  WIM/MER SW19 ....177 J1
Stratheden Rd BKHTH/KID SE3 ..145 K2
Strathfield Gdns BARK IG11 ..90 D4
Strathleven Rd
  BRXS/STRHM SW2 ....141 K6
Strathmore Gdns EDGW HA8 ..44 D5
  FNCH N3 ....47 F4
  HCH RM12 ....93 J2
  KENS W8 ....119 K1
Strathmore Rd CROY/NA CR0 ..196 D4
  TEDD TW11 ....155 K6
  WIM/MER SW19 ....159 K5
Strathnairn St
  BERM/RHTH SE16 * 123 H4
Strathray Gdns HAMP NW3 .83 J4
Strath Ter BTSEA SW11 ...140 D5
Strathville Rd
  WAND/EARL SW18 ....159 K4

Strathyre Av
  STRHM/NOR SW16 ....180 B6
Stratton Av WLGTN SM6 ...210 D6
Stratton Cl BXLYHN DA7 ..149 F4
  EDGW HA8 ....44 B2
  HSLW TW3 ....134 E2
  WIM/MER SW19 ....193 K1
  WOT/HER KT12 ....188 B5
Stratton Ct PIN HA5 .....40 E5
Strattondale St POP/IOD E14 ..125 F3
Stratton Dr BARK IG11 ...90 E3
Stratton Gdns STHL UB1 ..95 K5
Stratton Rd BXLYHN DA7 ..149 F4
  WIM/MER SW19 ....193 K1
  WOT/HER KT12 ....177 K5
Strauss Rd CHSWK W4 * ...118 A2
Strawberry Flds ORP BR6 .216 D3
Strawberry Hill Rd TWK TW1 ..156 A5
Strawberry La CAR SM5 ...209 K1
Strawberry Ter MUSWH N10 *..47 K4
Strawberry V EFNCH N2 ...47 H4
  TWK TW1 ....156 A5
Streakes Field Rd CRICK NW2 ..63 J6
Streamdale ABYW SE2 .....128 C6
Stream La EDGW HA8 ......44 D2
Streamline Ms EDUL SE22 .163 J3
Streamside Cl ED N9 .....36 B3
  HAYES BR2 ....199 K2
Stream Wy BELV DA17 .....129 H6
Streatfeild Av EHAM E6 ..89 K6
Streatfield Rd
  KTN/HRWW/WS HA3 ......43 J6
Streatham Cl
  STRHM/NOR SW16 ....161 K4
Streatham Common North
  STRHM/NOR SW16 ....179 J3
Streatham Common South
  STRHM/NOR SW16 ....179 K2
Streatham Ct
  STRHM/NOR SW16 ....161 K5
Streatham Gn
  STRHM/NOR SW16 * 161 K5
Streatham High Rd
  STRHM/NOR SW16 ....161 K6
Streatham Hi
  BRXS/STRHM SW2 ....161 K5
Streatham Pl
  BRXS/STRHM SW2 ....161 K1
Streatham St NOXST/BSQ WC1A ..10 E3
Streatham V
  STRHM/NOR SW16 ....161 K5
Streathbourne Rd TOOT SW17 ..161 F4
Streatleigh Pde
  STRHM/NOR SW16 * 161 K4
Streatley Pl HAMP NW3 ...83 H2
Streatley Rd KIL/WHAMP NW6 ..82 D5
Streeters La WLGTN SM6 ..210 D1
Streetfield Ms BKHTH/KID SE3 ..145 K3
Streimer Rd SRTFD E15 ...106 A1
Strelley Wy ACT W3 ......99 G6
Stretton Rd CROY/NA CR0 .197 F4
  RCHPK/HAM TW10 ....156 B4
Strickland Rw
  WAND/EARL SW18 ....160 C2
Strickland St DEPT SE8 ..144 D3
Strickland Wy ORP BR6 ...217 F2
Stride Rd PLSTW E13 .....106 D1
Strimon Cl ED N9 ....36 E4
Stripling Wy WATW WD18 ..26 E1
Strode Cl MUSWH N10 .....48 A3
Strode Rd FSTGT E7 ......88 E2
  FUL/PGN SW6 ....139 G1
  TOTM N17 ....50 A5
  WLSDN NW10 ....81 K4
Strone Rd FSTGT E7 ......89 G4
Strone Wy YEAD UB4 ......95 J3
Strongbow Crs ELTH/MOT SE9 ..146 E6
Strongbow Rd ELTH/MOT SE9 ..146 E6
Strongbridge Cl
  RYLN/HDSTN HA2 ....59 K6
Stronsa Rd SHB W12 .....118 C2
Strood Av ROMW/RG RM7 ..75 F5
Stroud Crs PUT/ROE SW15 .158 C5
Stroudes Cl WPK KT4 .....192 C4
Stroud Fld NTHLT UB5 ....77 J4
Stroud Ga RYLN/HDSTN HA2 ..78 B2
Stroud Green Rd FSBYPK N4 ..67 F5
Stroud Green Wy
  CROY/NA CR0 ....197 K4
Stroud Rd SNWD SE25 .....197 H3
  WIM/MER SW19 ....159 K5
Strouds Cl CHDH RM6 .....73 H2
Strout's Pl BETH E2 .....7 H4
Strutton Gd STJSPK SW1H .16 C4
Strype St WCHPL E1 ......13 J2
Stuart Av CDALE/KGS NW9 .63 H4
  EA W5 ....117 G2
  HAYES BR2 ....199 K5
  RYLN/HDSTN HA2 ....77 K1
  WOT/HER KT12 ....188 B5
Stuart Crs CROY/NA CR0 ..213 H1
  HYS/HAR UB3 ....94 A5
  WDGN N22 ....49 F4
Stuart Evans Cl WELL DA16 ..148 D4
Stuart Gv TEDD TW11 .....173 K1
Stuart Mantle Wy ERITH DA8 ..150 A1
Stuart Pl MTCM CR4 ......178 E4
Stuart Rd ACT W3 ....117 K1
  BARK IG11 ....91 F6
  EBAR EN4 ....33 J2
  KIL/WHAMP NW6 ....100 E3
  KTN/HRWW/WS HA3 ......43 F4
  PECK SE15 ....143 K5
  RCHPK/HAM TW10 ....156 C4
  THHTH CR7 ....196 D1
  WALTH E17 ....51 G5
  WIM/MER SW19 ....159 K5
Stubbs Cl CDALE/KGS NW9 .62 E2

Stubbs Dr BERM/RHTH SE16...123 J5
Stubbs Wy WIM/MER SW19...178 C4
Stucley Pl CAMTN NW1...84 B5
Stucley St HEST TW5...135 H4
Studdridge St FUL/PGN SW6...139 K3
Studd St IS N1...85 H6
Studholme Ct HAMP NW3 *...82 E2
Studholme St PECK SE15...143 J1
Studio Ms HDN NW4...45 A6
Studio Pl KTBR SW1X...15 F3
The Studios BUSH WD23...28 A1
Studland Cl BFN/LL DA15...168 A5
Studland Rd HNWL W7...96 D5
  KUTN/CMB KT2...182 A1
  SYD SE26...182 A1
Studland St HMSMTH W6...118 E4
Studley Av CHING E4...52 B3
Studley Cl CLPT E5...87 G3
Studley Ct SCUP DA14...186 C1
Studley Dr REDBR IG4...71 H3
Studley Grange Rd HNWL W7...115 K3
Studley Rd CLAP SW4...141 K2
  DAGW RM9...91 K6
  FSTGT E7...89 F4
Stukeley Rd FSTGT E7...89 F5
Stukeley St HOL/ALD WC2B...11 F3
Stumps Hill La BECK BR3...182 D2
Sturdy Rd PECK SE15...143 J3
Sturge Av WALTH E17...51 K4
Sturgeon Rd WALW SE17...122 D5
Sturges Fld CHST BR7...185 J3
Sturgess Av HDN NW4...63 K4
Sturge St STHWK SE1...18 C3
Sturmer Wy HOLWY N7...85 F3
Sturminster Ct YEAD UB4...95 G5
Sturrock Cl SEVS/STOTM N15...67 K1
Sturry St POP/IOD E14...105 K5
Sturt St IS N1...6 D3
Stutfield St WCHPL E1...104 C5
Styles Gdns BRXN/ST SW9...142 C4
Styles Wy BECK BR3...199 F1

Sudbourne Rd
  BRXS/STRHM SW2...141 K6
Sudbrooke Rd BAL SW12...160 E1
Sudbrook Gdns
  RCHPK/HAM TW10...157 F5
Sudbrook La
  RCHPK/HAM TW10...157 F3
Sudbury EHAM E6...108 A1
Sudbury Av ALP/SUD HA0...79 J1
Sudbury Court Dr HRW HA1...79 J4
Sudbury Court Rd HRW HA1...79 J4
Sudbury Crs ALP/SUD HA0...79 H3
  BMLY BR1...183 J1
Sudbury Cft ALP/SUD HA0...79 F2
Sudbury Gdns CROY/NA CRO...212 A2
Sudbury Heights Av
  GFD/PVL UB6...79 G3
Sudbury Hl HRW HA1...78 E2
Sudbury Hill Cl ALP/SUD HA0...79 F2
Sudbury Rd BARK IG11...91 F3
Sudeley St IS N1...6 B3
Sudlow Rd WAND/EARL SW18...139 K5
Sudrey St STHWK SE1...18 C3
Suez Av GFD/PVL UB6...97 F1
Suez Rd PEND EN3...25 G5
Suffield Rd CHING E4...37 K6
  PGE/AN SE20...181 K5
  SEVS/STOTM N15...68 B2
Suffolk La CANST EC4R...12 E5
Suffolk Park Rd WALTH E17...69 G1
Suffolk Rd BARK IG11...90 D5
  BARN SW13...138 C1
  DAGE RM10...92 D3
  DART DA1...171 H1
  GDMY/SEVK IG3...72 E3
  PEND EN3...24 D6
  PLSTW E13...106 D2
  RYLN/HDSTN HA2...59 K3
  SCUP DA14...186 D3
  SEVS/STOTM N15...67 K3
  SNWD SE25...197 G1
  WLSDN NW10...81 G5
  WPK KT4...192 C6
Suffolk St FSTGT E7...88 E3
  STJS SW1Y...10 D7

Sugar House La SRTFD E15...106 A1
Sugar Loaf Wk BETH E2 *...104 E2
Sugden Rd BTSEA SW11...141 F4
  THDIT KT7...190 B5
Sugden Wy BARK IG11...91 F1
Sulgrave Gdns HMSMTH W6...119 F2
Sulgrave Rd HMSMTH W6...119 F2
Sulina Rd BRXS/STRHM SW2...161 K2
Sulivan Ct FUL/PGN SW6...139 K3
Sulivan Rd FUL/PGN SW6...139 K4
Sullivan Av CAN/RD E16...107 H4
Sullivan Cl BTSEA SW11...140 D4
  DART DA1...171 J1
  E/WMO/HCT KT8...173 F6
  YEAD UB4...95 G4
Sullivan Rd LBTH SE11...17 K6
Sullivan Wy BORE WD6...29 J1
Sultan Rd WAN E11...71 F1
Sultan St BECK BR3...182 A5
  CMBW SE5...142 D1
Sumatra Rd KIL/WHAMP NW6...82 E4
Sumburgh Rd BAL SW12...141 F6
Summer Av E/WMO/HCT KT8...189 K2
Summercourt Rd WCHPL E1...104 E5
Summer Crossing THDIT KT7...190 A2
Summerene Cl
  STRHM/NOR SW16...179 H3
Summerfield Av
  KIL/WHAMP NW6...100 C1
  NFNCH/WDSPK N12...47 J2
Summerfield La SURB KT6...190 E6
Summerfield Rd EA W5...97 H3
  LOU IG10...39 H1
Summerfield St
  LEE/GVPK SE12...165 J2
Summer Gdns
  E/WMO/HCT KT8...189 K2
Summer Gv BORE WD6...29 K1
Summer Hl CHST BR7...185 F5

Summerhill Cl ORP BR6...216 E2
Summerhill Gv EN EN1...36 A1
Summerhill Rd DART DA1...171 G2
  SEVS/STOTM N15...67 K1
Summerhill Wy MTCM CR4...179 F4
Summerhouse La
  WDR/YW UB7...112 A6
Summerhouse Rd
  STNW/STAM N16...68 A6
Summerland Gdns
  MUSWH N10...48 B6
Summerlands Av ACT W3...98 E6
Summerlee Av EFNCH N2...65 K1
Summerlee Gdns EFNCH N2...65 K1
Summerley St
  WAND/EARL SW18...160 A4
Summer Pl WATW WD18 *...26 D1
Summer Rd E/WMO/HCT KT8...189 J2
  THDIT KT7...189 H3
Summersby Rd HGT N6...66 B3
Summerskill Cl ED N9...36 D5
Summers La
  NFNCH/WDSPK N12...47 H3
Summers Rw
  NFNCH/WDSPK N12...47 J2
Summers St CLKNW EC1R...5 J7
Summerstown TOOT SW17...160 B5
Summerton Wy THMD SE28...109 K6
Summer Trees SUN TW16...172 A4
Summerville Gdns SUT SM1...208 D4
Summerwood Rd ISLW TW7...156 A1
Summit Av CDALE/KGS NW9...63 F2
Summit Cl CDALE/KGS NW9...63 F2
  EDGW HA8...44 C3
  STHGT/OAK N14...34 C3
Summit Dr WFD IG8...53 H5
Summit Est STNW/STAM N16 *...68 C4
Summit Rd NTHLT UB5...78 A5
  WALTH E17...69 K1
Summit Wy NRWD SE19...181 F3
  STHGT/OAK N14...34 B4
Sumner Av PECK SE15...143 G2
Sumner Cl ORP BR6...216 C2
Sumner Gdns CROY/NA CRO...196 C5
Sumner Pl CHEL SW3...120 C5
  SKENS SW7 *...14 B7
Sumner Place Ms SKENS SW7...14 B7
Sumner Rd CROY/NA CRO...196 C5
  HRW HA1...60 C4
  PECK SE15...143 G2
Sumner Rd South
  CROY/NA CRO...196 B5
Sumner St STHWK SE1...12 C7
Sumpter Cl HAMP NW3...83 G4
Sunbeam Crs NKENS W10...100 A3
Sunbeam Rd WLSDN NW10...99 F3
Sunbury Av MLHL NW7...45 F2
  MORT/ESHN SW14...138 A5
Sunbury Ct BAR EN5 *...20 C5
  SUN TW16...172 C5
Sunbury Gdns MLHL NW7...45 F2
Sunbury La BTSEA SW11...140 C2
Sunbury Rd CHEAM SM3...208 B1
  FELT TW13...153 K4
Sunbury St WOOL/PLUM SE18...126 E3
Sunbury Wy FELT TW13...172 E1
Sun Ct ERITH DA8...150 C5
Suncroft Pl SYD SE26...163 K5
Sunderland Mt FSTH SE23 *...164 A4
Sunderland Rd EA W5...116 E3
  FSTH SE23...164 A4
Sunderland Ter BAY/PAD W2 *...101 F5
Sundew Av SHB W12...99 J6
Sundew Ct ALP/SUD HA0 *...98 A1
Sundial Av SNWD SE25...181 G6
Sundorne Rd CHARL SE7...126 A5
Sundra Wk WCHPL E1 *...105 F3
Sundridge Av BMLY BR1...184 A3
  CHST BR7...184 C3
  WELL DA16...147 H2
Sundridge Cl DART DA1...171 K1
Sundridge Ho BMLY BR1 *...184 B3
Sundridge Pde BMLY BR1 *...184 C3
Sundridge Pl CROY/NA CRO...197 J5
Sundridge Rd CROY/NA CRO...197 H5
  WELL DA16...147 J4
Sun in Sands Rbt
  BKHTH/KID SE3...146 A1
Sunkist Wy WLGTN SM6...210 E6
Sunland Av BXLYHS DA6...149 F5
Sun La BKHTH/KID SE3...146 A1
Sunleigh Rd ALP/SUD HA0...80 A6
Sunley Gdns GFD/PVL UB6...97 G1
Sunlight Cl WIM/MER SW19...178 B2
Sunlight Sq BETH E2 *...104 D2
Sunna Gdns SUN TW16...172 A5
Sunningdale STHGT/OAK N14...34 B7
Sunningdale Av ACT W3...99 G6
  BARK IG11...90 E6
  FELT TW13...154 D4
  RAIN RM13...93 J5
  RSLP HA4...59 G1
Sunningdale Cl BERM/RHTH SE16 *...123 J5
  STAN HA7...43 G3
  SURB KT6...191 F6
  THMD SE28...110 A5
Sunningdale Gdns
  CDALE/KGS NW9...62 E2
  KENS W8 *...119 K3
Sunningdale Ldg EDGW HA8 *...44 B1
Sunningdale Rd BMLY BR1...200 D1
  RAIN RM13...93 J5
  SUT SM1...208 D2
Sunningfields Crs HDN NW4...45 K5
Sunningfields Rd HDN NW4...45 K6
Sunninghill Ct ACT W3 *...117 K2
Sunninghill Rd LEW SE13...144 E3
Sunny Bank SNWD SE25...181 H6
Sunny Crs WLSDN NW10...80 E5
Sunnycroft Rd HSLW TW3...135 G3
  SNWD SE25...197 H1
  STHL UB1...96 A4
Sunnydale ORP BR6...201 F6

Sunnydale Gdns MLHL NW7...45 F2
Sunnydale Rd LEE/GVPK SE12...146 A6
Sunnydene Av CHING E4...52 B1
  RSLP HA4...58 E5
Sunnydene Gdns ALP/SUD HA0...79 J4
Sunnydene St SYD SE26...164 B6
Sunnyfield MLHL NW7...31 H6
Sunny Gardens Rd HDN NW4...46 A6
Sunny Hl HDN NW4...45 K6
Sunnyhill Cl CLPT E5...87 G2
Sunnyhill Rd
  STRHM/NOR SW16...161 K6
Sunnyhurst Cl SUT SM1...208 E1
Sunnymead Av MTCM CR4...179 J6
Sunnymead Rd
  CDALE/KGS NW9...63 F4
  PUT/ROE SW15...138 E6
Sunnymede Av
  HOR/WEW KT19...207 G6
Sunnymede Dr BARK/HLT IG6...72 B1
Sunny Ms CRW RM5...56 C3
Sunny Nook Gdns
  SAND/SEL CR2...211 K4
Sunny Pl HDN NW4...64 A1
The Sunny Rd PEND EN3...25 F1
Sunnyside CAT SE6 *...164 C2
  CRICK NW2...82 D1
  WOT/HER KT12...188 B2
Sunnyside Dr CHING E4...38 A2
Sunnyside Pl WIM/MER SW19 *...177 H2
Sunnyside Rd ARCH N19...66 D4
  EA W5...116 E1
  IL IG1...90 C1
  LEY E10...69 J5
  TEDD TW11...155 J6
Sunnyside Rd East ED N9...36 C5
Sunnyside Rd North ED N9...36 B5
Sunnyside Rd South ED N9...36 B5
Sunny Vw CDALE/KGS NW9...63 F2
Sunny Wy NFNCH/WDSPK N12...47 J3
Sun Pas BERM/RHTH SE16 *...123 H3
Sunray Av BRYLDS KT5...191 J6
  HAYES BR2...200 D3
  HNHL SE24...142 E6
  WDR/YW UB7...112 A2
Sunrise Cl FELT TW13...154 E5
Sun Rd WKENS W14...119 J5
Sunset Av CHING E4...37 K3
  WFD IG8...38 D6
Sunset Cl ERITH DA8...150 E1
Sunset Ct ABR/ST RM4...57 K1
Sunset Gdns SNWD SE25...181 F5
Sunset Rd HNHL SE24...142 D5
  WOOL/PLUM SE18...128 B2
Sunset Vw BAR EN5...20 C3
Sunshine Wy MTCM CR4...178 E5
Sun St LVPST EC2M...13 G1
Sun Street Pas LVPST EC2M...13 G2
Superior Dr ORP BR6...217 J6
Surbiton Ct SURB KT6...190 D3
Surbiton Court Ms SURB KT6 *...190 E5
Surbiton Hall Cl KUT/HW KT1...191 F1
Surbiton Hill Pk BRYLDS KT5...191 G3
Surbiton Hill Rd SURB KT6...191 F2
Surbiton Rd KUT/HW KT1...190 E1
Surlingham Cl THMD SE28...109 K6
Surma Cl WCHPL E1...104 C3
Surmans Cl DAGW RM9...91 J6
Surrendale Pl MV/WKIL W9...100 E3
Surrey Canal Rd PECK SE15...123 K6
Surrey Crs CHSWK W4...117 H5
Surrey Gv SUT SM1...209 H1
  WALW SE17...123 F5
Surrey La BTSEA SW11...140 D2
Surrey La Est BTSEA SW11 *...140 D2
Surrey Ms WNWD SE27...163 F6
Surrey Quays Rd
  BERM/RHTH SE16...124 A3
Surrey Rd BARK IG11...90 E5
  DAGE RM10...92 E3
  HRW HA1...60 C3
  PECK SE15...144 A6
  WWKM BR4...198 E5
Surrey Rw STHWK SE1...18 A2
Surrey Sq WALW SE17...123 F5
Surrey St CROY/NA CRO...211 J1
  PLSTW E13...107 F2
  TPL/STR WC2R...11 H5
Surrey Ter WALW SE17...19 H7
Surrey Water Rd
  BERM/RHTH SE16...124 A1
Surridge Gdns NRWD SE19...180 E2
Surr St HOLWY N7...84 E3
Sury Basin KUTN/CMB KT2...175 F4
Susan Cl ROMW/RG RM7...56 E6
Susannah St POP/IOD E14...105 K5
Susan Rd BKHTH/KID SE3...146 A3
Susan Wd CHST BR7...185 F4
Sussex Av ISLW TW7...135 K4
Sussex Cl ARCH N19 *...66 E6
  NWMAL KT3...192 B1
  REDBR IG4...71 K3
  TWK TW1...156 C2
Sussex Gdns BAY/PAD W2...8 B5
  CHSGTN KT9...205 K4
  FSBYPK N4...67 J2
Sussex Ms East BAY/PAD W2 *...8 B5
Sussex Ms West BAY/PAD W2...8 B5
Sussex Pl BAY/PAD W2...8 B5
  ERITH DA8...149 J1
  HMSMTH W6...119 F5
  NWMAL KT3...192 B1
Sussex Ring
  NFNCH/WDSPK N12...46 E1
Sussex Rd CAR SM5...209 K4
  DART DA1...171 K2
  EHAM E6...108 A1
  ERITH DA8...149 J1
  HGDN/ICK UB10...76 A2
  HRW HA1...60 C2

  MTCM CR4...195 K2
  NWDGN UB2...114 C3
  NWMAL KT3...192 B1
  SAND/SEL CR2...211 K4
  SCUP DA14...186 D1
  STMC/STPC BR5...202 D5
  WWKM BR4...198 E5
Sussex Sq BAY/PAD W2...8 B5
Sussex St PIM SW1V...121 G5
  PLSTW E13...107 F2
Sussex Wy ARCH N19...66 E6
  EBAR EN4...22 B6
  STMC/STPC BR5...186 B6
  WALTH E17...51 G4
Swandon Wy WAND/EARL SW18...140 B5
Swan Dr CDALE/KGS NW9...45 G5
Swanfield St BETH E2...7 J5
Swan Island TWK TW1 *...156 B5
Swan La CANST EC4R...12 E6
  DART DA1...170 C2
  LOU IG10...39 G2
  TRDG/WHET N20...33 G4
Swanley Rd WELL DA16...148 D2
Swan Md STHWK SE1...19 G5
Swan Ms BRXN/ST SW9...142 A3
Swan Pas WCHPL E1 *...13 K6
Swan Pl BARN SW13...138 C2
Swan Rd BERM/RHTH SE16...123 K2
  FELT TW13...172 E1
  STHL UB1...96 B5
  WDR/YW UB7...112 A2
  WOOL/PLUM SE18...126 C3
Swanscombe Rd CHSWK W4...118 A5
  NTGHL W11...119 G1
Swansea Rd
  EBED/NFELT TW14...153 F1
  PEND EN3...24 E5
Swanston Pth OXHEY WD19...27 G5
Swan St ISLW TW7...136 C4
  STHWK SE1...18 D3
Swanton Gdns
  WIM/MER SW19...159 G3
Swanton Rd ERITH DA8...149 H1
Swan Wk CHEL SW3...120 E6
Swanwick Cl PUT/ROE SW15...158 C2
Swan Yd IS N1 *...85 H4
Sward Rd STMC/STPC BR5...202 B3
Swaton Rd BOW E3...105 J3
Swaylands Rd BELV DA17...129 H6
Swaythling Cl UED N18...36 D6
Swedenbourg Gdns
  WCHPL E1...104 C6
Sweden Ga BERM/RHTH SE16...124 B4
Sweeney Crs STHWK SE1...19 K3
Sweeps La STMC/STPC BR5...202 E2
Sweet Briar Gv ED N9...36 B5
Sweet Briar Rd ED N9...36 B5
Sweet Briar Wk UED N18...36 B5
Sweetmans Av PIN HA5...41 H6
Sweets Wy TRDG/WHET N20...33 H4
Swete St PLSTW E13...106 E1
Sweyn Pl BKHTH/KID SE3...145 K3
Swift Cl HYS/HAR UB3...94 D5
  RYLN/HDSTN HA2...60 A1
  THMD SE28...109 H6
  WALTH E17...51 G3
Swift Rd FELT TW13...154 D6
  NWDGN UB2...114 E3
Swiftsden Wy BMLY BR1...183 H1
Swift St FUL/PGN SW6...139 H2
Swinbrook Rd NKENS W10...100 C4
Swinburne Crs CROY/NA CRO...197 K4
Swinburne Rd PUT/ROE SW15...138 D5
Swinderby Rd ALP/SUD HA0...80 A4
Swindon Cl GDMY/SEVK IG3...72 E6
Swindon St SHB W12...118 E1
Swinfield Cl FELT TW13...154 D6
Swinford Gdns BRXN/ST SW9...142 C4
Swingate La
  WOOL/PLUM SE18...147 K1
Swinnerton St HOM E9...87 G3
Swinton Cl WBLY HA9...62 D5
Swinton Pl FSBYW WC1X...5 G4
Swinton St FSBYW WC1X...5 G4
Swires Shaw HAYES BR2...215 G2
Swithland Gdns
  ELTH/MOT SE9...166 E6
Swyncombe Av EA W5...116 C4
Swynford Gdns HDN NW4...63 J1
Sybil Ms FSBYPK N4 *...67 H4
Sybil Phoenix Cl DEPT SE8...124 B5
Sybourn St WALTH E17...69 H4
Sycamore Av BFN/LL DA15...168 A1
  BOW E3...87 H6
  EA W5...116 E3
  HYS/HAR UB3...94 C6
Sycamore Cl ACT W3...118 B1
  CAN/RD E16...106 C3
  CAR SM5...209 K2
  EBAR EN4...33 K1
  ED N9...48 C1
  EDGW HA8...44 E1
  FELT TW13...153 K5
  NTHLT UB5...77 J6
  SAND/SEL CR2...212 A3
Sycamore Gdns MTCM CR4...178 C5
  SHB W12...118 E3
Sycamore Gv CAT SE6...165 F1
  CDALE/KGS NW9...62 E4
  GPK RM2...75 J5
  NWMAL KT3...192 A1
  PGE/AN SE20...181 H4
Sycamore Hl FBAR/BDGN N11...48 A2
Sycamore Ms CLAP SW4...141 H4
Sycamore Rd ERITH DA8...130 A5
  WIM/MER SW19...177 F2
Sycamore St FSBYE EC1V...6 C7
Sycamore Wk NKENS W10...100 C3
Sycamore Wy TEDD TW11...174 D2
Sydcote DUL SE21 *...162 D4
Sydenham Av SYD SE26...181 J1
  WCHMH N21...35 H1
Sydenham Cottages
  LEE/GVPK SE12...166 B4
Sydenham Hl FSTH SE23...163 K5
Sydenham Pk SYD SE26...163 K5
Sydenham Park Rd SYD SE26...163 K5
Sydenham Ri FSTH SE23...163 J4
Sydenham Rd CROY/NA CRO...196 D5
  SYD SE26...163 K6
Sydenham Station Ap
  SYD SE26...163 K6
Sydmons Ct FSTH SE23...163 K2
Sydner Rd STNW/STAM N16...86 B2
Sydney Cl SKENS SW7...14 B7

Sydney Gv HDN NW4 64 A2
Sydney Ms CHEL SW3 14 B7
Sydney Pl SKENS SW7 14 B7
Sydney Rd ABYW SE2 128 E3
BARK/HLT IG6 54 C5
BXLYHS DA6 148 E5
CEND/HSY/T N8 67 G1
EBED/NFELT TW14 153 K3
ENC/FH EN2 23 K5
MUSWH N10 48 B4
RCH/KEW TW9 137 F5
RYNPK SW20 177 G5
SCUP DA14 167 K6
SUT SM1 208 E2
TEDD TW11 174 A1
WAN E11 71 F3
WEA W13 116 B1
WFD IG8 52 E1
Sydney St CHEL SW3 120 D5
Sydney Ter ESH/CLAY KT10 * 205 F4
Sylvan Av CHDH RM6 74 B3
MLHL NW7 45 G2
WDGN N22 49 G3
Sylvan Gdns SURB KT6 190 E4
Sylvan Gv CRICK NW2 82 B2
PECK SE15 123 J6
Sylvan Hl NRWD SE19 181 G4
Sylvan Rd FSTGT E7 88 E4
IL IG1 72 C6
NRWD SE19 181 G4
WALTH E17 * 69 J2
WAN E11 70 E2
Sylvan Ter PECK SE15 * 143 J1
Sylvan Wk BMLY BR1 184 E6
Sylvan Wy BCTR RM8 91 H1
WWKM BR4 214 C2
Sylverdale Rd CROY/NA CR0 211 H1
Sylvester Av CHST BR7 184 E2
Sylvester Pth HACK E8 * 86 D4
Sylvester Rd ALP/SUD HA0 79 J3
EFNCH N2 47 G5
HACK E8 * 86 D4
WALTH E17 * 69 H4
Sylvia Av PIN HA5 41 K2
Sylvia Gdns WBLY HA9 80 D5
Symes Ms CAMTN NW1 4 A2
Symington Ms HOM E9 87 F3
Symister Ms IS N1 * 7 G5
Symons Cl PECK SE15 143 K4
Symons St CHEL SW3 15 F7
Symphony Cl EDGW HA8 44 D3
Symphony Ms NKENS W10 100 C2
Syon Gate Wy BTFD TW8 136 C1
Syon La ISLW TW7 116 A6
ISLW TW7 136 C1
Syon Pk ISLW TW7 * 136 C4
Syon Park Gdns ISLW TW7 136 A1

T

Tabard Garden Est STHWK SE1 18 E2
Tabard St STHWK SE1 18 E4
Tabernacle Av PLSTW E13 106 E3
Tabernacle St SDTCH EC2A 7 F7
Tableer Av CLAP SW4 141 H6
Tabley Rd HOLWY N7 84 E2
Tabor Gdns CHEAM SM3 208 D4
Tabor Gv WIM/MER SW19 177 H3
Tabor Rd HMSMTH W6 118 E3
Tachbrook Rd
EBED/NFELT TW14 153 J2
NWDGN UB2 114 C4
Tachbrook St PIM SW1V 16 B7
Tack Ms BROCKY SE4 144 D4
Tadema Rd WBPTN SW10 140 B1
Tadmor St SHB W12 119 G1
Tadworth Av NWMAL KT3 192 C1
Tadworth Pde HCH RM12 93 K2
Tadworth Rd CRICK NW2 63 J6
Taeping St POP/IOD E14 124 E4
Taffy's How MTCM CR4 178 D6
Tait Rd CROY/NA CR0 197 F4
Takeley Cl CRW RM5 57 F5
Talacre Rd KTTN NW5 84 A4
Talbot Av EFNCH N2 47 H6
OXHEY WD19 27 J2
Talbot Cl SEVS/STOTM N15 68 B1
Talbot Ct BANK EC3V 13 F5
Talbot Crs HDN NW4 63 J2
Talbot Gdns GDMY/SEVK IG3 73 G6
Talbot Pl BKHTH/KID SE3 145 H3
Talbot Rd ALP/SUD HA0 79 K3
CAR SM5 210 A3
DAGW RM9 92 B5
EDUL SE22 143 F5
EHAM E6 108 A1
FSTGT E7 88 E2
HGT N6 66 A3
ISLW TW7 136 B5
KTN/HRWW/WS HA3 43 F5
NTGHL W11 100 D5
NWDGN UB2 114 D4
SEVS/STOTM N15 68 B1
THHTH CR7 196 E1
WDGN N22 48 C5
WEA W13 * 97 G6
WHTN TW2 155 K3
Talbot Sq BAY/PAD W2 8 A4
Talbot Wk NTGHL W11 100 C5
WLSDN NW10 * 81 G4
Talbot Yd STHWK SE1 18 E1
Talcott Pth
BRXS/STRHM SW2 * 162 B3
Talfourd Pl PECK SE15 143 G2
Talfourd Rd PECK SE15 143 G2
Talgarth Rd WKENS W14 119 H5
Talgarth Wk CDALE/KGS NW9 63 G2
Talisman Cl GDMY/SEVK IG3 73 H5
Talisman Sq SYD SE26 163 H6
Talisman Wy WBLY HA9 80 B1
Tallack Cl KTN/HRWW/WS HA3 42 E3
Tallack Rd LEY E10 69 H5
Tall Elms Cl HAYES BR2 199 J2
Tallis Cl CAN/RD E16 107 F5
Tallis Gv CHARL SE7 126 A6
Tallis St EMB EC4Y 11 K5
Tallis Vw WLSDN NW10 81 F4
Tallow Rd BTFD TW8 116 D6
Tall Trees STRHM/NOR SW16 180 A6
Talma Gdns WHTN TW2 155 K2
Talmage Cl FSTH SE23 163 K2
Talman Gv STAN HA7 43 K2
Talma Rd BRXS/STRHM SW2 142 B5
Talwin St BOW E3 105 K2
Tamar Cl BOW E3 * 87 H6
Tamarind Yd WAP E1W 123 H1
Tamarisk Sq SHB W12 99 H6
Tamar St CHARL SE7 126 D4
Tamesis Gdns WPK KT4 192 B6
Tamian Wy HSLWW TW4 134 B5
Tamworth Av WFD IG8 52 C2
Tamworth La MTCM CR4 179 G6
Tamworth Pk MTCM CR4 195 G1
Tamworth Pl CROY/NA CR0 * 196 D6
Tamworth Rd CROY/NA CR0 196 D6
Tamworth St FUL/PGN SW6 119 K6
Tancred Rd FSBYPK N4 67 H3
Tandridge Dr ORP BR6 201 J5
Tanfield Av CRICK NW2 81 H2
Tanfield Rd CROY/NA CR0 211 J2
Tangier Rd RCHPK/HAM TW10 137 J4
Tangleberry Cl BMLY BR1 200 E1
Tangle Tree Cl FNCH N3 47 F5
Tanglewood Cl CROY/NA CR0 212 E1
STAN HA7 28 E5
Tanglewood Wy FELT TW13 154 A5
Tangley Gv PUT/ROE SW15 158 C2
Tangley Park Rd HPTN TW12 * 172 E1
Tangmere Crs HCH RM12 93 K4
Tangmere Gdns NTHLT UB5 95 G1
Tangmere Gv KUTN/CMB KT2 174 E1
Tangmere Wy CDALE/KGS NW9 45 G5
Tanhouse Fld KTTN NW5 * 84 D3
Tankerton Houses
STPAN WC1H * 5 F5
Tankerton Rd SURB KT6 191 G6
Tankerton St STPAN WC1H 5 F5
Tankerton Ter CROY/NA CR0 * 196 A4
Tankerville Rd
STRHM/NOR SW16 179 J3
Tank Hill Rd PUR RM19 131 K4
Tankridge Rd CRICK NW2 63 K6
The Tanneries WCHPL E1 * 104 E3
Tanners Cl WOT/HER KT12 188 A3
Tanners End La UED N18 36 A6
Tanner's Hl DEPT SE8 144 D2
Tanners La BARK/HLT IG6 54 C6
Tanners Ms DEPT SE8 144 C2
Tanner St BARK IG11 90 C4
STHWK SE1 19 J3
Tannery Cl CROY/NA CR0 198 A2
DAGE RM10 92 D1
Tannington Ter HBRY N5 85 G1
Tannsfeld Rd SYD SE26 182 A1
Tansley Cl HOLWY N7 84 D3
Tanswell St STHWK SE1 * 17 J3
Tansy Cl EHAM E6 108 A5
Tantallon Rd BAL SW12 161 F3
Tant Av CAN/RD E16 106 D5
Tantony Gv CHDH RM6 55 K6
Tanworth Cl NTHWD HA6 40 A2
Tanworth Gdns PIN HA5 41 F5
Tan Yard La BXLY DA5 * 169 H2
Tanza Rd HAMP NW3 83 K2
Tapestry Cl BELMT SM2 209 F5
Taplow Ct MTCM CR4 194 D1
Taplow Rd PLMGR N13 35 J6
Taplow St IS N1 6 D3
Tappesfield Rd PECK SE15 143 K4
Tapping Cl KUTN/CMB KT2 * 175 H3
Tapp St WCHPL E1 104 D3
Tapster St BAR EN5 20 D4
Taransay Wk IS N1 85 K4
Tara Ter BROCKY SE4 * 144 B4
Tarbert Rd EDUL SE22 143 F6
Tarbert Wk WCHPL E1 104 E6
Target Cl EBED/NFELT TW14 153 H1
Tariff Rd UED N18 50 C2
Tarleton Gdns FSTH SE23 163 J3
Tarling Cl SCUP DA14 168 C5
Tarling Rd CAN/RD E16 106 D5
EFNCH N2 47 G5
Tarling St WCHPL E1 104 D5
Tarnbank ENC/FH EN2 22 E6
Tarn St STHWK SE1 18 C5
Tarnwood Pk ELTH/MOT SE9 166 E3
Tarragon Cl NWCR SE14 * 144 B1
Tarragon Gv SYD SE26 182 A2
Tarrant Pl MBLAR W1H 8 E2
Tarriff Crs DEPT SE8 124 C4
Tarrington Cl
STRHM/NOR SW16 * 161 J6
Tarver Rd WALW SE17 122 C5
Tarves Wy GNWCH SE10 144 E1
Tash Pl FBAR/BDGN N11 * 48 B1
Tasker Cl HYS/HAR UB3 133 F1
Tasker Rd HAMP NW3 83 K3
Tasmania Ter UED N18 49 J2
Tasman Rd BRXN/ST SW9 141 K4
Tasso Rd HMSMTH W6 119 H6
Tate Gdns BUSH WD23 28 E2
Tate Rd CAN/RD E16 126 E1
SUT SM1 208 E3
Tatham Pl STJWD NW8 2 B2
Tatnell Rd FSTH SE23 164 B1
Tattersall Cl ELTH/MOT SE9 146 D6
Tatton Crs CLPT E5 68 B4
Tatum Rd WLSDN NW10 80 E5
Tatum St WALW SE17 19 F7
Tauheed Cl FSBYPK N4 67 J6
Taunton Av HSLW TW3 135 H3
RYNPK SW20 176 E5
Taunton Cl BARK/HLT IG6 55 F2
BXLYHN DA7 150 A4
CHEAM SM3 193 K5
Taunton Dr EFNCH N2 47 G5
ENC/FH EN2 23 G4
Taunton Ms CAMTN NW1 2 E7
Taunton Pl CAMTN NW1 2 E6
Taunton Rd GFD/PVL UB6 78 B5
LEE/GVPK SE12 145 H6
Taunton Wy STAN HA7 44 A6
Tavern Cl CAR SM5 194 D4
Taverners Cl NTGHL W11 119 H1
Taverner Sq HBRY N5 * 85 J2
Taverners Wy CHING E4 38 C3
Tavistock Av GFD/PVL UB6 97 G1
MLHL NW7 46 B3
WALTH E17 51 F6
Tavistock Cl STNW/STAM N16 * 86 A3
Tavistock Ct COVGDN WC2E * 11 F5
Tavistock Crs MTCM CR4 195 K1
NTGHL W11 100 D5
Tavistock Gdns GDMY/SEVK IG3 90 E2
Tavistock Gv CROY/NA CR0 196 E4
Tavistock Ms NTGHL W11 * 100 D5
Tavistock Pl STHGT/OAK N14 * 34 B1
STPAN WC1H 5 F6
Tavistock Rd CAR SM5 194 C5
CROY/NA CR0 196 E5
EDGW HA8 44 B4
FSBYPK N4 67 K3
HAYES BR2 199 K1
HGDN/ICK UB10 76 B3
NTGHL W11 100 D5
SWFD E18 52 E6
WAN E11 88 D2
WDR/YW UB7 112 A1
WELL DA16 148 D2
WLSDN NW10 99 H1
Tavistock Sq STPAN WC1H 4 D6
Tavistock St COVGDN WC2E 11 F5
Tavistock Ter ARCH N19 84 E1
Taviton St STPAN WC1H 4 C6
Tavy Br ABYW SE2 128 D2
Tavy Cl LBTH SE11 122 B5
Tawney Rd THMD SE28 109 H6
Tawny Cl FELT TW13 153 K5
WEA W13 116 C1
Tawny Wy BERM/RHTH SE16 124 A4
Tayben Av WHTN TW2 155 K1
Taybridge Rd BTSEA SW11 141 F4
Tayburn Cl POP/IOD E14 106 A5
Tayfield Cl HGDN/ICK UB10 76 B1
Taylor Av RCH/KEW TW9 137 J3
Taylor Cl CRW RM5 56 C3
DEPT SE8 124 C6
HPTN TW12 173 H1
HSLW TW3 135 H2
ORP BR6 217 F2
TOTM N17 50 C3
Taylor Rd MTCM CR4 178 D3
WLGTN SM6 210 B3
Taylor Rw RDART DA2 171 F5
Taylor's Buildings
WOOL/PLUM SE18 127 G4
Taylors Cl SCUP DA14 168 A6
Taylors Ct FELT TW13 153 K4
Taylor's Gn ACT W3 * 99 G5
Taylor's La BAR EN5 20 D2
SYD SE26 163 J6
WLSDN NW10 81 G5
Taylors Md MLHL NW7 * 45 J1
Taymount Ri FSTH SE23 163 K4
Tayport Cl IS N1 85 F5
Tayside Dr EDGW HA8 30 D5
Tay Wy ROM RM1 57 H4
Taywood Rd NTHLT UB5 95 J3
STHL UB1 95 K2
Teak Cl BERM/RHTH SE16 124 B1
Teal Av STMC/STPC BR5 202 E1
Teal Cl CAN/RD E16 107 H4
Teal Dr NTHWD HA6 40 A3
Teale St BETH E2 104 C1
Tealing Dr HOR/WEW KT19 207 F2
Teal Pl SUT SM1 208 D3
Teasel Cl CROY/NA CR0 198 A5
Teasel Crs THMD SE28 127 K1
Teasel Wy SRTFD E15 106 C2
Teather St CMBW SE5 143 F1
Tebworth Rd TOTM N17 50 B3
Technology Pk
CDALE/KGS NW9 * 45 F6
Teck Cl ISLW TW7 136 B3
Tedder Cl CHSGTN KT9 205 J3
RSLP HA4 76 E3
Tedder Rd SAND/SEL CR2 213 F5
Teddington Pk TEDD TW11 174 A1
Teddington Park Rd
TEDD TW11 156 B6
Tedworth Gdns CHEL SW3 120 E5
Tedworth Sq CHEL SW3 * 120 E5
Tees Av GFD/PVL UB6 96 E1
Teesdale Av ISLW TW7 136 B2
Teesdale Cl BETH E2 104 C1
Teesdale Gdns ISLW TW7 136 B2
SNWD SE25 181 F5
Teesdale Rd WAN E11 70 D3
Teesdale St BETH E2 104 D2
Teesdale Yd BETH E2 * 104 D1
The Tee ACT W3 99 G5
Teevan Cl CROY/NA CR0 197 H4
Teevan Rd CROY/NA CR0 197 H4
Teign Ms ELTH/MOT SE9 166 D4
Teignmouth Cl CLAP SW4 141 J5
EDGW HA8 44 B5
Teignmouth Gdns
GFD/PVL UB6 97 G1
Teignmouth Rd CRICK NW2 82 B3
WELL DA16 148 D3
Telcote Wy RSLP HA4 * 59 G4
Telegraph Hl HAMP NW3 83 F1
Telegraph La ESH/CLAY KT10 205 F2
Telegraph Ms GDMY/SEVK IG3 73 F5
Telegraph Pas
BRXS/STRHM SW2 161 K2
Telegraph Pl POP/IOD E14 124 E4
Telegraph Rd PUT/ROE SW15 158 E2
Telegraph St LOTH EC2R 12 E3
Telephone Pl WKENS W14 * 119 J6
Telferscot Rd BAL SW12 161 J3
Telford Av BRXS/STRHM SW2 161 K3
Telford Cl NRWD SE19 181 G2
WALTH E17 69 G4
Telford Dr WOT/HER KT12 188 B4
Telford Rd CDALE/KGS NW9 63 J4
ELTH/MOT SE9 167 J4
NKENS W10 100 C4
STHL UB1 96 B6
WHTN TW2 155 F2
Telford Rd North Circular Rd
FBAR/BDGN N11 48 C2
Telfords Yd WAP E1W * 104 C6
Telford Ter PIM SW1V * 121 H6
Telford Wy ACT W3 99 G4
YEAD UB4 95 J4
Telham Rd EHAM E6 108 A1
Tell Gv EDUL SE22 143 G5
Tellisford ESH/CLAY KT10 204 B2
Tellson Av WOOL/PLUM SE18 146 D2
Telscombe Cl ORP BR6 201 K6
Temeraire Pl BTFD TW8 117 G5
Temeraire St
BERM/RHTH SE16 123 K2
Tempelhof Av HDN NW4 64 A4
Temperley Rd BAL SW12 161 F2
Tempest Wy RAIN RM13 93 J4
Templar Dr THMD SE28 109 K5
Templar Pl HPTN TW12 173 F3
Templars Av GLDGN NW11 64 D3
Templars Ct DART DA1 * 151 K6
Templars Crs FNCH N3 46 E5
Templars Dr
KTN/HRWW/WS HA3 * 42 D2
Templar St CMBW SE5 142 C3
Temple Av BCTR RM8 74 C5
CROY/NA CR0 213 H1
EMB EC4Y 11 K5
TRDG/WHET N20 33 H2
Temple Cl FNCH N3 46 D5
THMD SE28 127 H3
WAN E11 70 C4
Templecombe Rd HOM E9 86 E6
Templecombe Wy MRDN SM4 193 H2
Temple Dwellings BETH E2 * 104 D1
Temple Fortune Hl
GLDGN NW11 64 E2
Temple Fortune La
GLDGN NW11 64 E3
Temple Gdns BCTR RM8 91 K1
EMB EC4Y * 11 J5
GLDGN NW11 64 D3
WCHMH N21 * 35 H4
Temple Gv ENC/FH EN2 23 H4
GLDGN NW11 64 E3
Temple Hl DART DA1 151 J6
Temple Hill Sq DART DA1 151 J6
Temple La EMB EC4Y 11 K4
Templeman Rd HNWL W7 97 F4
Templemead Cl ACT W3 99 G5
Temple Mead Cl STAN HA7 43 H2
Temple Mills La LEY E10 87 K2
SRTFD E15 88 A3
Temple Pde BAR EN5 * 33 H2
Temple Pl TPL/STR WC2R 11 H5
Temple Rd CEND/HSY/T N8 67 F1
CHSWK W4 117 K3
CRICK NW2 82 A2
CROY/NA CR0 211 K1
EA W5 116 E3
EHAM E6 89 J6
HSLW TW3 135 H5
RCH/KEW TW9 137 G3
Temple Sheen Rd
MORT/ESHN SW14 137 K5
Temple St BETH E2 104 D1
Temple Ter WDGN N22 * 49 G5
Templeton Av CHING E4 37 J6
Templeton Cl NRWD SE19 180 E4
STNW/STAM N16 * 86 A3
Templeton Pl ECT SW5 119 K4
Templeton Rd FSBYPK N4 67 K3
Temple Wy SUT SM1 209 H1
Templewood WEA W13 97 H4
Templewood Av HAMP NW3 83 F1
Templewood Gdns HAMP NW3 83 F1
Temple Yd BETH E2 104 C2
Tempsford Cl ENC/FH EN2 23 J4
Temsford Cl RYLN/HDSTN HA2 42 C5
Tenbury Cl FSTGT E7 89 H3
Tenbury Ct BAL SW12 161 J3
Tenby Av KTN/HRWW/WS HA3 43 H5
Tenby Cl CHDH RM6 74 A3
Tenby Gdns NTHLT UB5 78 A4
Tenby Rd CHDH RM6 74 A3
EDGW HA8 44 B4
PEND EN3 24 E4
WALTH E17 69 G2
WELL DA16 148 E2
Tench St WAP E1W * 123 J1
Tenda Rd STHWK SE1 123 J4
Tendring Wy CHDH RM6 73 J2
Tenham Av BRXS/STRHM SW2 161 J4
Tenison Wy STHWK SE1 17 J1
Tenniel Cl BAY/PAD W2 101 G5
Tennison Rd SNWD SE25 197 G1
Tennis St STHWK SE1 18 E2
Tenniswood Rd EN EN1 24 B2
Tennyson Av CDALE/KGS NW9 44 E6
MNPK E12 89 J5
NWMAL KT3 192 E2
TWK TW1 156 A3
WAN E11 70 E4
Tennyson Cl
EBED/NFELT TW14 153 K1
PEND EN3 25 F6
WELL DA16 147 K2
Tennyson Rd DART DA1 151 K6
HNWL W7 97 F6
HSLW TW3 135 H3
KIL/WHAMP NW6 82 D6
LEY E10 69 K5
MLHL NW7 45 J1
PGE/AN SE20 182 A3
SRTFD E15 88 C5
WALTH E17 69 H3
WIM/MER SW19 178 B2
Tennyson St VX/NE SW8 141 G3
Tennyson Wy HCH RM12 75 H5
Tensing Rd NWDGN UB2 115 F3
Tentelow La NWDGN UB2 115 G3
Tenterden Cl ELTH/MOT SE9 166 E6
HDN NW4 46 B6
Tenterden Dr HDN NW4 46 B6
Tenterden Gdns CROY/NA CR0 197 H4
HDN NW4 46 B6
Tenterden Gv HDN NW4 64 A1
Tenterden Rd BCTR RM8 74 B6
CROY/NA CR0 197 J4
TOTM N17 50 B3
Tenterden St CONDST W1S 9 K4
Tenter Gnd WCHPL E1 13 J2
Tent Peg La STMC/STPC BR5 201 H2
Tent St WCHPL E1 104 D3
Teredo St LEW SE13 144 E3
Terling Cl WAN E11 88 D1
Terling Rd BCTR RM8 74 C6
Terling Wk IS N1 * 85 J6
Terminus Pl BGVA SW1W 15 K5
Terrace Gdns BARN SW13 138 C3
Terrace La RCHPK/HAM TW10 157 F1
Terrace Rd HOM E9 87 F5
PLSTW E13 88 E6
WOT/HER KT12 188 A4
The Terrace BARN SW13 138 B3
BETH E2 * 104 E2
CHING E4 * 38 C5
DEPT SE8 * 124 C4
EFNCH N2 * 66 A1
FNCH N3 * 46 D5
FSTH SE23 * 164 B2
KIL/WHAMP NW6 82 E6
Terrace Vls HMSMTH W6 * 118 D5
Terrace Wk DAGW RM9 92 A3
Terrac St RCH/KEW TW9 137 G5
Terrapin Rd TOOT SW17 161 G5
Terretts Pl IS N1 85 H5
Terrick Rd WDGN N22 48 E4
Terrick St SHB W12 99 K5
Terrilands PIN HA5 41 K6
Terront Rd SEVS/STOTM N15 67 J2
Tessa Sanderson Wy
GFD/PVL UB6 78 D3
Testerton Rd NTGHL W11 * 100 B6
Testerton Wk NTGHL W11 * 100 B6
Tetbury Pl IS N1 6 A1
Tetcott Rd WBPTN SW10 140 B1
Tetherdown MUSWH N10 48 A6
Tetty Wy BMLY BR1 183 K5
Teversham La VX/NE SW8 141 K2
Teviot Cl WELL DA16 148 C2
Teviot St POP/IOD E14 106 A4
Tewkesbury Av FSTH SE23 163 J3
PIN HA5 59 J3
Tewkesbury Cl LOU IG10 39 J1
Tewkesbury Gdns
CDALE/KGS NW9 44 D6
Tewkesbury Rd CAR SM5 194 C5
SEVS/STOTM N15 67 K4
WEA W13 116 B1
Tewkesbury Ter
FBAR/BDGN N11 48 C2
Tewson Rd WOOL/PLUM SE18 127 K5
Teynham Av EN EN1 35 K1
Teynham Gn HAYES BR2 199 K2
Teynton Ter TOTM N17 49 J4
Thackeray Av TOTM N17 50 C5
Thackeray Cl ISLW TW7 136 B3
WIM/MER SW19 177 G3
Thackeray Dr CHDH RM6 73 H4
Thackeray Ms HACK E8 86 C4
Thackeray Rd EHAM E6 107 H1
VX/NE SW8 141 G3
Thackeray St KENS W8 120 A3
Thakeham Cl SYD SE26 181 J1
Thalia Cl GNWCH SE10 125 G6
Thame Rd BERM/RHTH SE16 124 A2
Thames Av DAGW RM9 110 E2
GFD/PVL UB6 97 F1
WBPTN SW10 140 B2
Thames Bank
MORT/ESHN SW14 137 K3
Thamesbank Pl THMD SE28 109 J5
Thames Cir POP/IOD E14 124 D4
Thames Cl HPTN TW12 173 G5
RAIN RM13 111 K5
Thames Down Link
BRYLDS KT5 191 K2
HOR/WEW KT19 206 E2
NWMAL KT3 192 A5
WPK KT4 207 F1
Thames Dr RSLP HA4 58 A3
Thames Eyot TWK TW1 * 156 B4
Thames Ga DART DA1 151 K6
Thamesgate Cl
RCHPK/HAM TW10 156 C6
Thameside TEDD TW11 174 E3
Thames Meadow
E/WMO/HCT KT8 173 F6
Thamesmere Dr THMD SE28 109 G6
Thames Pth BARN SW13 138 C2
BTFD TW8 137 F1
CLPT E5 87 F1
GNWCH SE10 125 F6
ISLW TW7 136 D3
POP/IOD E14 124 D3
SRTFD E15 106 A1
STHWK SE1 121 K5
SUN TW16 172 B6
TWRH EC3N 13 H7
WEST SW1P 17 F5
Thames Pl PUT/ROE SW15 139 G4
Thamespoint TEDD TW11 * 174 E3
Thames Quay WBPTN SW10 * 140 B2
Thames Reach KUT/HW KT1 * 174 E4
Thames Rd BARK IG11 109 G2
CAN/RD E16 126 C1
CHSWK W4 117 J6
DART DA1 150 D4
Thames Side KUT/HW KT1 174 E4
THDIT KT7 190 C3
Thames St GNWCH SE10 124 E6
HPTN TW12 173 G5
KUT/HW KT1 174 E5
SUN TW16 172 A6
Thamesvale Cl HSLW TW3 135 F3
Thames Village CHSWK W4 137 K2
Thamley PUR RM19 131 K4
Thanescroft Gdns
CROY/NA CR0 212 A1
Thanet Dr HAYES BR2 215 H1
Thanet Pl CROY/NA CR0 211 J2

Thanet Rd BXLY DA5...169 H2
ERITH DA8...150 B3
Thanet St STPAN WC1H...4 E1
Thane Vs HOLWY N7...85 F1
Thant Cl LEY E10...51 J1
Tharp Rd WLGTN SM6...210 D3
Thatcham Gdns
TRDG/WHET N20...33 G2
Thatcher Cl WDR/YW UB7...112 B2
Thatchers Wy ISLW TW7...135 J6
Thatches Gv CHDH RM6...74 A1
Thavies Inn FLST/FETLN EC4A...11 K3
Thaxted Pl RYNPK SW20...177 G3
Thaxted Rd BKHH IG9...39 H2
ELTH/MOT SE9...167 H4
Thaxton Rd FUL/PGN SW6...119 J6
Thayers Farm Rd BECK BR3...182 B4
Thayer St MHST W1U...9 H3
Theatre Sq SRTFD E15...88 B4
Theatre St BTSEA SW11...140 E4
The Beverly MRDN SM4...193 G3
The Courtyard HAYES BR2...215 J4
Theed St STHWK SE1...17 J1
Thelma Gv TEDD TW11...174 B2
Theobald Crs
KTN/HRWW/WS HA3...42 C4
Theobald Rd CROY/NA CR0...196 C6
WALTH E17...
Theobald's Rd STHWK SE1...18 E5
Theodora Wy PIN HA5...40 D6
Theodore Rd LEW SE13...165 G1
Therapia La CROY/NA CR0...195 K4
Therapia Rd EDUL SE22...163 K1
Theresa Rd HMSMTH W6...118 D4
Theresa's Wk SAND/SEL CR2...211 K6
Thermopylae Ga POP/IOD E14...124 D4
Theseus Wk IS N1...6
Thesiger Rd PGE/AN SE20...182 A3
Thessaly Rd VX/NE SW8...141 J2
Thetford Cl PLMGR N13...49 H2
Thetford Gdns RAIN RM13...
DAGW RM9...91 K5
NWMAL KT3...192 B2
Theydon Gdns RAIN RM13...93 J3
Theydon Gv IGFD IG8...53 G2
Theydon Rd CLPT E5...68 E6
Theydon St WALTH E17...69 H4
Thicket Crs SUT SM1...209 G2
Thicket Gv DAGW RM9...91 J4
PGE/AN SE20...181 H3
Thicket Rd PGE/AN SE20...181 H3
SUT SM1...209 G2
Thicket Ter PGE/AN SE20 *...181 H3
Third Av ACT W3...118 C1
CHDH RM6...73 J3
DAGE RM10...92 D6
EN EN1...24 B6
HYS/HAR UB3...113 J1
MNPK E12...89 J2
NKENS W10...100 C2
PLSTW E13...106 E2
WALTH E17...69 J3
WBLY HA9...61 K5
Third Cl E/WMO/HCT KT8...189 G1
Third Cross Rd WHTN TW2...155 J4
Thirleby Rd EDGW HA8...45 F1
WEST SW1P...16 B5
Thirlmere Av GFD/PVL UB6...97 J2
Thirlmere Gdns WBLY HA9...61 J5
Thirlmere Ri BMLY BR1...183 J2
Thirlmere Rd BXLYHN DA7...149 K3
MUSWH N10...48 B4
STRHM/NOR SW16...161 J6
Thirsk Cl NTHLT UB5...78 A4
Thirsk Rd BTSEA SW11...141 F4
MTCM CR4...179 F3
SNWD SE25...196 E1
Thirza Rd DART DA1...171 K1
Thisilefield Cl BAR EN5...168 E3
Thistlebrook ABYW SE2...128 D3
Thistlecroft Gdns STAN HA7...43 K4
Thistledene THDIT KT7...189 K3
Thistledene Av CRW RM5...56 D1
RSLP HA4...76 A2
Thistle Gv WBPTN SW10 *...120 B5
Thistlemead CHST BR7...185 G2
Thistlewaite Rd CLPT E5...86 D1
Thistlewood Cl HOLWY N7...67 F6
Thistleworth Cl ISLW TW7...114 C6
Thistley Cl NFNCH/WDSPK N12...47 J2
Thomas à Beckett Cl HRW HA1...79 F2
Thomas Baines Rd
BTSEA SW11...140 C4
Thomas Cribb Ms EHAM E6...107 K5
Thomas Dean Rd SYD SE26 *...164 C6
Thomas Dinwiddy Rd
LEE/GVPK SE12...166 A4
Thomas Doyle St STHWK SE1...18 A4
Thomas' La CAT SE6...164 D2
Thomas Moore St WAP E1W...104 C6
Thomas Moore Wy EFNCH N2...47 G6
Thomas More St WAP E1W *...104 C6
Thomas North Ter
CAN/RD E16...106 D4
Thomas Pl KENS W8...120 A3
Thomas Rd POP/IOD E14...105 H5
Thomas St WOOL/PLUM SE18...127 F4
Thomas Wall Cl SUT SM1...209 F3
Thompson Av CMBW SE5...142 D1
RCH/KEW TW9...137 J4
Thompson Cl CHEAM SM3...193 K5
IL IG1...72 C6
Thompson Rd DAGW RM9...92 B1
EDUL SE22...163 G1
HSLW TW3...135 G5
Thompson's Av CMBW SE5 *...142 D1
Thomson Crs CROY/NA CR0...196 B5
Thomson Rd
KTN/HRWW/WS HA3...42 E6
Thoresby St IS N1...6 E4
Thoresby Rd ...
Thorkhill Gdns THDIT KT7...190 B5

Thorkhill Rd THDIT KT7...190 C5
Thornaby Gdns UED N18...50 D2
Thorn Av BUSH WD23...28 C3
Thornbury Av ISLW TW7...135 J1
Thornbury Cl STNW/STAM N16...86 A1
Thornbury Ct STNW/STAM N16...86 A1
Thornbury Rd CLAP SW4...161 K1
ISLW TW7...135 J1
Thornbury Sq HGT N6...66 C5
Thorncliffe Rd CLPT E5...86 E1
Thorncliffe Rd CLAP SW4...161 K1
NWDGN UB2...114 E5
Thorn Cl HAYES BR2...201 F3
NTHLT UB5...95 K2
Thorncombe Rd EDUL SE22...143 F6
Thorn Ct BELMT SM2 *...209 F5
Thorncroft EMPK RM11...75 K5
Thorncroft Rd SUT SM1...209 F2
Thorncroft St VX/NE SW8...141 K1
Thorndean St
WAND/EARL SW18...160 B4
Thorndene Av TRDG/WHET N20...33 K3
Thorndike Av NTHLT UB5...77 H6
Thorndike Cl WBPTN SW10...140 B1
Thorndike Rd IS N1...85 K4
Thorndike St PIM SW1V *...16 C7
Thorndon Cl STMC/STPC BR5...186 A5
Thorndon Gdns
HOR/WEW KT19...207 G2
Thorndon Rd STMC/STPC BR5...186 A5
Thorndyke Ct PIN HA5...41 K3
Thorne Cl CAN/RD E16...106 E5
ERITH DA8...149 K1
ESH/CLAY KT10...205 G5
WAN E11...88 C2
Thornel Gdns CROY/NA CR0...211 K4
Thorne Rd VX/NE SW8...141 K1
Thorne's Cl BECK BR3...183 F6
Thorne St BARN SW13...138 B4
Thornet Wood Rd BMLY BR1...201 F1
Thorney Crs BTSEA SW11...140 D1
Thorneycroft Cl
WOT/HER KT12...188 B3
Thorneycroft Dr PEND EN3...25 J1
Thorney Hedge Rd CHSWK W4...117 J4
Thornfield Av MLHL NW7 *...46 C4
Thornfield Pde MLHL NW7 *...46 C4
Thornfield Rd SHB W12...118 E2
Thornford Rd LEW SE13...145 F6
Thorngate Rd MV/WKIL W9...100 E3
Thorngrove Rd PLSTW E13...89 F6
Thornham Gv SRTFD E15...88 B3
Thornham St GNWCH SE10...124 E6
Thornhaugh St STPAN WC1H...4 D7
Thornhill Av SURB KT6...191 G6
WOOL/PLUM SE18...147 K1
Thornhill Bridge Whf IS N1...5 F1
Thornhill Gdns BARK IG11...90 E6
LEY E10...87 K1
Thornhill Gv IS N1...85 F5
Thornhill Rd CROY/NA CR0...196 D4
IS N1...85 F5
LEY E10...87 K1
NTHWD HA6...40 A4
SURB KT6...191 F6
Thornhill Sq IS N1...85 F5
Thornlaw Rd WNWD SE27...162 B6
Thornley Cl TOTM N17...50 C3
Thornley Dr RYLN/HDSTN HA2...60 B6
Thornsbeach Rd CAT SE6...165 F3
Thornsett Pl PGE/AN SE20...181 J5
Thornsett Rd PGE/AN SE20...181 J5
WAND/EARL SW18...160 A4
Thornsett Ter PGE/AN SE20 *...181 J5
Thornton Av
BRXS/STRHM SW2...161 J4
CHSWK W4...118 B4
CROY/NA CR0...195 K4
WDR/YW UB7...112 C3
Thornton Cl WDR/YW UB7...112 C3
Thornton Dene BECK BR3...182 D5
Thornton Gdns BAL SW12...161 J3
Thornton Gv PIN HA5...42 A2
Thornton Hl WIM/MER SW19...177 H3
Thornton Pl MBLAR W1H...8 E1
Thornton Rd BAL SW12...161 J2
BAR EN5...20 C4
BELV DA17 *...129 J4
BMLY BR1...183 K1
CAR SM5...194 C6
IL IG1...90 B3
MORT/ESHN SW14...138 A5
THHTH CR7...196 A5
UED N18...36 E5
WAN E11...88 B1
WIM/MER SW19...177 G2
Thornton Rw THHTH CR7...196 B2
Thorntons Farm Av
ROMW/RG RM7...74 E6
Thornton St BRXN/ST SW9...142 B3
Thornton Wy GLDGN NW11...65 F2
Thorntree Rd CHARL SE7...126 C5
Thornville Gv MTCM CR4...178 C5
Thornville St DEPT SE8...144 D2
Thornwood Cl SWFD E18...53 F1
Thornwood Rd LEW SE13...145 H6
Thorogood Gdns SRTFD E15...88 C3
Thorogood Wy RAIN RM13...93 G6
Thorold Rd IL IG1...72 B6
NFNCH/WDSPK N12...33 F6
Thorparch Rd VX/NE SW8...141 J2
Thorpebank Rd SHB W12...118 D1
Thorpe Cl NKENS W10...100 C5
ORP BR6...217 F2
SYD SE26 *...164 A6
Thorpe Crs OXHEY WD19...27 F2
Thorpe Hall Rd WALTH E17...52 A4
Thorpe Rd BARK IG11...90 D5
EHAM E6...89 K6

FSTGT E7...88 E1
KUTN/CMB KT2...175 F5
SEVS/STOTM N15...68 A3
WALTH E17 *...51 H5
Thorpewood Av FNCH N3...64 D1
Thorpland Av HGDN/ICK UB10...76 A1
Thorsden Wy NRWD SE19 *...181 F1
Thorverton Rd CRICK NW2...82 C1
Thoydon Rd BOW E3...105 G1
Thrale Rd STRHM/NOR SW16...179 H1
Thrale St STHWK SE1...18 D1
Thrasher Cl HACK E8 *...86 B6
Thrawl St WCHPL E1...13 K2
Threadneedle St LOTH EC2R...13 F4
Three Colts La BETH E2...104 D3
Three Colt St POP/IOD E14 *...105 H6
Three Corners BXLYHN DA7...149 J3
Three Kings Yd MYFR/PKLN W1K...9 J5
Three Meadows Ms
KTN/HRWW/WS HA3...43 F4
Three Mill La BOW E3...106 A2
Three Oak La STHWK SE1...19 J2
Threshers Pl NTGHL W11...100 C6
Thriffwood SYD SE26...163 K5
Thrigby Rd CHSGTN KT9...206 B4
Throckmorton Rd
CAN/RD E16...107 F5
Throgmorton Av OBST EC2N...13 F3
Throgmorton St OBST EC2N...13 F3
Throwley Cl ABYW SE2...128 D3
Throwley Rd SUT SM1...209 F3
Throwley Wy SUT SM1...209 F2
Thrupp Cl MTCM CR4...179 G5
Thrush Gn RYLN/HDSTN HA2...60 A1
Thrush St WALW SE17...122 D5
Thunderer Rd DAGW RM9...110 E2
Thurbarn Rd CAT SE6...182 E1
Thurland Rd BERM/RHTH SE16...123 H3
Thurlby Cl WFD IG8...53 K1
Thurlby Rd ALP/SUD HA0...79 H4
WNWD SE27...162 B6
Thurleigh Av BAL SW12...161 F1
Thurleigh Rd BAL SW12...160 E1
Thurleston Av MRDN SM4...193 H2
Thurlestone Av GDMY/SEVK IG3...91 F2
NFNCH/WDSPK N12...47 K2
Thurloe Cl SKENS SW7...14 C6
Thurloe Gdns ROM RM1...75 J3
Thurloe Pl SKENS SW7...14 B6
Thurloe Place Ms SKENS SW7 *...14 B6
Thurloe Sq SKENS SW7...14 C6
Thurloe St SKENS SW7...14 B6
Thurlow Cl CHING E4...52 A1
Thurlow Gdns ALP/SUD HA0...79 K3
BARK/HLT IG6...54 C2
Thurlow Hl DUL SE21...162 D3
Thurlow Park Rd DUL SE21...162 D4
Thurlow Rd HAMP NW3...83 H3
HNWL W7...116 B2
Thurlow St WALW SE17...123 F5
Thurlow Ter KTTN NW5...83 K3
Thursland Rd SCUP DA14...187 F2
Thursley Crs CROY/NA CR0...214 B5
Thursley Gdns
WIM/MER SW19...159 F4
Thursley Rd ELTH/MOT SE9...166 E5
Thurso St TOOT SW17...160 B1
Thurstan Rd RYNPK SW20...176 E3
Thurston Rd DEPT SE8...144 E3
STHL UB1...95 K5
Thurtle Rd BETH E2...7 K1
Thwaite Cl ERITH DA8...129 J6
Thyer Cl ORP BR6...216 C2
Thyra Gv NFNCH/WDSPK N12...47 F2
Tibbats's Rd BOW E3...105 K3
Tibbenham Pl CAT SE6...164 E3
Tibberton Sq IS N1...85 J5
Tibbets Cl WIM/MER SW19...159 G3
Tibbet's Ride PUT/ROE SW15...159 G2
Tiber Cl BOW E3...87 J6
Tiber Gdns IS N1...5 F1
Ticehurst Cl STMC/STPC BR5...186 B6
Ticehurst Rd FSTH SE23...164 B4
Tickford Cl ABYW SE2...128 D2
Tidal Basin Rd CAN/RD E16...106 D6
Tidenham Gdns CROY/NA CR0...212 A1
Tideswell Rd CROY/NA CR0...213 J1
Tideway Cl RCHPK/HAM TW10...156 C6
Tideway Wk VX/NE SW8 *...121 H6
Tidey St BOW E3...105 J4
Tidford Rd WELL DA16...148 A3
Tidworth Rd BOW E3...105 J3
Tiepigs La WWKM BR4...199 H6
Tierney Rd BRXS/STRHM SW2...161 K3
Tierney Ter
BRXS/STRHM SW2 *...161 K3
Tiger La HAYES BR2...200 A1
Tiger Wy CLPT E5...86 D2
Tigres Cl ED N9...36 E4
Tilbrook Rd BKHTH/KID SE3...146 A4
Tilbury Cl PECK SE15...143 G1
STMC/STPC BR5...186 C5
Tilbury Rd EHAM E6...89 K6
LEY E10...70 A4
Tideseley Rd PUT/ROE SW15...159 F1
Tile Farm Rd ORP BR6...216 D1
Tilehurst Rd CHEAM SM3...208 C3
WAND/EARL SW18...160 C3
Tile Kiln La BXLY DA5...169 K4
HGT N6 *...66 C5
PLMGR N13...49 J1
Tileyard Rd HOLWY N7...84 E5
Tilford Av CROY/NA CR0...214 A5
Tilford Gdns WIM/MER SW19...159 G3
Tilia Cl SUT SM1...208 D3
Tilia Rd CLPT E5...86 D2
Tiller Rd POP/IOD E14...124 D3
Tillett Cl WLSDN NW10...80 E4
Tillett Wy BETH E2...7 K4
Tilley Rd FELT TW13...153 K3
Tillingbourne Gdns FNCH N3...46 D6
Tillingbourne Gn
STMC/STPC BR5...202 B2

Tillingbourne Wy FNCH N3...64 D1
Tillingham Wy
NFNCH/WDSPK N12...32 E6
Tilling Rd CRICK NW2...63 K5
Tilling Wy WBLY HA9...79 K1
Tillman St WCHPL E1...104 D5
Tilloch St IS N1...85 F5
Tillotson Rd ED N9...36 B4
IL IG1...72 A4
KTN/HRWW/WS HA3...42 B5
Tilney Gdns IS N1...85 K4
Tilney Rd DAGW RM9...92 B4
NWDGN UB2...114 B4
Tilney St MYFR/PKLN W1K...9 H7
Tilson Cl CMBW SE5 *...143 F1
Tilson Gdns BRXS/STRHM SW2...161 K2
Tilson Rd TOTM N17...50 C4
Tilston Cl WAN E11...88 D1
Tilt Yard Ap ELTH/MOT SE9...166 E1
Timber Cl CHST BR7...185 F5
Timbercroft HOR/WEW KT19...207 G2
Timbercroft La
WOOL/PLUM SE18...127 K6
Timberdene Av BARK/HLT IG6...54 C4
Timberland Cl PECK SE15 *...143 H1
Timberland Rd WCHPL E1...104 D5
Timber Pond Rd
BERM/RHTH SE16...124 A2
Timberslip Dr WLGTN SM6...210 D6
The Timbers CHEAM SM5 *...208 C4
Timber St FSBYE EC1V *...6 C6
Timberwharf Rd
SEVS/STOTM N15...68 C3
Time Sq HACK E8 *...86 B3
Times Sq SUT SM1...209 F3
Timothy Cl BXLYHS DA6...149 F6
Timothy Cl BRXN/ST SW9...142 C2
Tindal St BRXN/ST SW9...142 C2
Tine Rd CHIG IG7...55 F5
Tinniswood Cl HBRY N5...85 G3
Tinsley Cl SNWD SE25...181 J6
Tinsley Rd WCHPL E1...104 E4
Tintagel Crs EDUL SE22...143 G5
Tintagel Dr STAN HA7...43 K1
Tintagel Rd ORP BR6...202 D6
Tintern Av CDALE/KGS NW9...62 E1
Tintern Cl PUT/ROE SW15...139 H6
WIM/MER SW19...178 B3
Tintern Gdns STHGT/OAK N14...34 E2
Tintern Rd CAR SM5...194 C5
WDGN N22...49 J4
Tintern St CLAP SW4...141 K5
Tinto Rd CAN/RD E16...106 E4
Tinworth St STHWK SE1...121 K5
Tippetts Cl ENC/FH EN2...23 H2
Tipthorpe Rd BTSEA SW11...141 F4
Tipton Dr CROY/NA CR0...212 A2
Tiptree Cl CHING E4...38 A5
Tiptree Crs CLAY IG5...54 A6
Tiptree Dr ENC/FH EN2...23 K5
Tiptree Rd RSLP HA4...77 F3
Tirlemont Rd SAND/SEL CR2...211 J5
Tirrell Rd CROY/NA CR0...196 D3
Tisbury Rd STRHM/NOR SW16...179 K5
Tisdall Pl WALW SE17...19 F7
Titan Ct BTFD TW8...117 G5
Titchborne Rw BAY/PAD W2...8 C4
Titchfield Rd CAR SM5...194 C5
STJWD NW8...2 D2
Titchfield Wk CAR SM5...194 C4
Titchwell Rd
WAND/EARL SW18...160 C3
Tite St CHEL SW3...120 E6
Tithe Barn Cl KUTN/CMB KT2...175 G4
Tithe Barn Wy NTHLT UB5...95 F1
Tithe Cl MLHL NW7...45 J4
WOT/HER KT12...188 A3
YEAD UB4...95 F2
The Tithe HDN NW4 *...45 J4
Tithe Farm Av
RYLN/HDSTN HA2...78 A1
Tithe Farm Cl RYLN/HDSTN HA2...78 A1
Tithe Wk MLHL NW7...45 J4
Titian Av BUSH WD23...28 E2
Titley Cl CHING E4...51 J1
Titmus Cl UX/CGN UB8...94 A5
Titmuss Av THMD SE28...109 H6
Titmuss St SHB W12 *...118 E2
Tiverton Av CLAY IG5...54 A6
Tiverton Cl CROY/NA CR0...197 G4
Tiverton Rd ALP/SUD HA0...98 A1
EDGW HA8...44 B5
HSLW TW3...135 G3
RSLP HA4...76 E1
SEVS/STOTM N15...68 A3
UED N18...50 A1
WLSDN NW10...82 A6
Tiverton St STHWK SE1...18 C5
Tiverton Wy CHSGTN KT9...205 J3
MLHL NW7...46 B3
Tivoli Gdns WOOL/PLUM SE18...126 D4
Tivoli Rd CEND/HSY/T N8...66 D2
HSLW TW4...134 D5
WNWD SE27...180 D1
Toad La HSLW TW4...134 E4
Tobago St POP/IOD E14...124 D2
Tobin Cl HAMP NW3...83 J5
Toby La WCHPL E1...105 G3
Toby Wy SURB KT6...191 K2
Tokenhouse Yd LOTH EC2R...12 E3
Tokyngton Av WBLY HA9...80 C4
Toland Sq PUT/ROE SW15...138 D6
Tolcarne Dr PIN HA5...40 E5
Toley Av KTN/HRWW/WS HA3...42 A2
Tollbridge Cl NKENS W10...100 C3
Tollesbury Gdns BARK/HLT IG6...54 D5
Tollet St WCHPL E1...105 F3
Tollgate Dr DUL SE21...163 F4
YEAD UB4...95 H5
Tollgate Gdns
KIL/WHAMP NW6 *...100 E1
Tollgate Rd EHAM E6...107 J4
Tollhouse La WLGTN SM6...210 C6

Tollhouse Wy ARCH N19...66 C6
Tollington Pk FSBYPK N4...67 F6
Tollington Pl FSBYPK N4...67 F6
Tollington Rd HOLWY N7...85 F2
Tollington Wy HOLWY N7...84 E1
Tolmer's Sq CAMTN NW1...4 B6
Tolpits La WATW WD18...26 B2
Tolpuddle Av PLSTW E13...89 G6
Tolpuddle St IS N1...5 K2
Tolsford Rd CLPT E5...86 D3
Tolson Rd ISLW TW7...136 B4
Tolverne Rd RYNPK SW20...177 F4
Tolworth Broadway SURB KT6...191 H5
Tolworth Cl SURB KT6...191 K5
Tolworth Gdns CHDH RM6...73 K2
Tolworth Park Rd SURB KT6...191 G6
Tolworth Ri North
BRYLDS KT5...191 K4
Tolworth Ri South
BRYLDS KT5...191 K5
NWMAL KT3...192 A4
Tolworth Rd SURB KT6...191 G6
Tolworth U/P (Kingston
By-Pass) SURB KT6...206 C1
Tom Coombs Cl ELTH/MOT SE9...146 D5
Tom Groves Cl SRTFD E15...88 B3
Tom Hood Cl SRTFD E15...88 B3
Tom Jenkinson Rd
CAN/RD E16...125 K1
Tomlin's Gv BOW E3...105 J2
Tomlinson Cl BETH E2...7 K5
CHSWK W4...117 J5
Tomlins Orch BARK IG11...90 C6
Tomlins Ter POP/IOD E14...105 G4
Tom Mann Cl BARK IG11...90 E6
Tom Nolan Cl SRTFD E15...106 C1
Tompion St FSBYE EC1V...6 A5
Tom Smith Cl GNWCH SE10 *...125 H6
Tomswood Hl BARK/HLT IG6...54 C4
Tomswood Rd CHIG IG7...54 A2
Tonbridge Crs
KTN/HRWW/WS HA3...62 A1
Tonbridge Rd
E/WMO/HCT KT8...188 C1
Tonbridge St STPAN WC1H...4 E5
Tonfield Rd CHEAM SM3...193 J5
Tonge Cl BECK BR3...198 D2
Tonsley Hl WAND/EARL SW18...140 A6
Tonsley Pl WAND/EARL SW18...140 A6
Tonsley Rd WAND/EARL SW18...140 A6
Tonsley St WAND/EARL SW18...140 A6
Tonstall Rd MTCM CR4...179 F5
Tony Cannell Ms BOW E3 *...105 H2
Tooke Cl PIN HA5...41 J4
Tookey Cl KTN/HRWW/WS HA3...62 A4
Took's Ct FLST/FETLN EC4A...11 J3
Tooley St STHWK SE1...19 G1
Toorack Rd
KTN/HRWW/WS HA3...42 D5
Tooting Bec Gdns
STRHM/NOR SW16...161 J6
Tooting Bec Rd TOOT SW17...161 F5
Tooting Gv TOOT SW17...178 D1
Tooting High St TOOT SW17...178 D2
Tootswood Rd HAYES BR2...199 H2
Topcliffe Dr ORP BR6...216 D2
Topham Sq TOTM N17...49 J4
Topham St CLKNW EC1R *...5 J6
Top House Ri CHING E4...38 A2
Topiary Sq RCH/KEW TW9...137 G4
Topley St ELTH/MOT SE9...146 B5
Topmast Point POP/IOD E14 *...124 D2
Top Pk BECK BR3...199 H2
Topsfield Cl CEND/HSY/T N8...66 D2
Topsfield Pde
CEND/HSY/T N8 *...66 E2
Topsfield Rd CEND/HSY/T N8...66 E2
Topsham Rd TOOT SW17...160 E5
Torbay Rd KIL/WHAMP NW6...82 D5
RYLN/HDSTN HA2...59 J6
Torbay St CAMTN NW1 *...84 B5
Torbitt Wy GNTH/NBYPK IG2...73 F2
Torbridge Cl EDGW HA8...44 A3
Torcross Dr FSTH SE23...163 K4
Torcross Rd RSLP HA4...77 F1
Tor Gdns KENS W8...119 K2
Tor Gv THMD SE28...127 K1
Tormead Cl SUT SM1...208 E4
Tormount Rd
WOOL/PLUM SE18...127 K6
Toronto Av MNPK E12...89 K2
Toronto Rd IL IG1...72 B5
Torquay Gdns REDBR IG4...71 H1
Torquay St BAY/PAD W2...101 F4
Torrens Rd BRXS/STRHM SW2...142 A6
SRTFD E15...88 D4
Torrens Sq SRTFD E15...88 D4
Torrens St FSBYE EC1V...6 A3
Torres Sq POP/IOD E14...124 D5
Torre Wk CAR SM5...194 D1
Torriano Av KTTN NW5...84 D3
Torriano Cottages KTTN NW5 *...84 C3
Torriano Ms KTTN NW5...84 C3
Torridge Gdns PECK SE15...143 K5
Torridge Rd THHTH CR7...196 C2
Torridon Cl SRTFD E15...88 B4
Torridon Rd CAT SE6...165 G3
Torrington Av
NFNCH/WDSPK N12...47 H1
Torrington Cl ESH/CLAY KT10...204 A4
Torrington Dr
RYLN/HDSTN HA2...78 B1
Torrington Gdns
FBAR/BDGN N11...48 C2
GFD/PVL UB6...79 J6
Torrington Gv
NFNCH/WDSPK N12...33 H6
Torrington Pk
NFNCH/WDSPK N12...47 J1
Torrington Pl FITZ W1T...10 B1
CWRST WC1E...4 C7
WAP E1W *...123 H1
Torrington Rd BCTR RM8...74 B5
ESH/CLAY KT10...204 A4
GFD/PVL UB6...79 J6
RSLP HA4...58 E6
Torrington Sq CROY/NA CR0 *...196 E4

STPAN WC1H...4 D7
Torrington Wy MRDN SM4...193 K4
Tor Rd WELL DA16...148 D2
Torr Rd PGE/AN SE20...182 A3
Torver Rd HRW HA1...60 E1
Torver Wy ORP BR6...216 D1
Torwood Rd PUT/ROE SW15...138 D6
Tothill St STJSPK SW1H...16 C3
Totnes Rd WELL DA16...148 C1
Totnes Vls FBAR/BDGN N11 *...48 C1
Totnes Wk EFNCH N2...65 H1
Tottan Ter WCHPL E1 *...105 F5
Tottenhall Rd PLMGR N13...49 G2
Tottenham Court Rd FITZ W1T...4 B7
Tottenham Gn East
SEVS/STOTM N15...68 B1
Tottenham Gn East South Side
SEVS/STOTM N15...68 B1
Tottenham La CEND/HSY/T N8...66 E3
Tottenham Ms FITZ W1T *...10 B1
Tottenham Rd IS N1...86 A4
Tottenham St FITZ W1T...10 B2
Totterdown St TOOT SW17...160 E6
Totteridge Common
TRDG/WHET N20...31 K4
Totteridge La TRDG/WHET N20...32 E4
Totteridge Village
TRDG/WHET N20...32 D3
Totternhoe Cl
KTN/HRWW/WS HA3...61 J2
Totton Rd THHTH CR7...180 B6
Toulmin St STHWK SE1...18 C3
Toulon St CMBW SE5...142 D1
Tournay Rd FUL/PGN SW6...139 K1
Toussaint Wk
BERM/RHTH SE16...123 H3
Tovil Cl PGE/AN SE20...181 H5
Towcester Rd BOW E3...105 K3
Tower Br WAP E1W...13 J7
Tower Bridge Ap TWRH EC3N...13 J7
Tower Bridge Ms ALP/SUD HA0...79 F2
Tower Bridge Rd STHWK SE1...19 H4
Tower Buildings WAP E1W *...123 J1
Tower Cl BARK/HLT IG6...54 B2
HAMP NW3...83 H3
ORP BR6...202 A6
PGE/AN SE20...181 J3
Tower Ct LSQ/SEVD WC2H *...10 E4
Tower Gdns ESH/CLAY KT10...205 H5
Tower Gardens Rd TOTM N17...49 J4
Tower Hamlets Rd FSTGT E7...88 D2
WALTH E17...69 J1
Tower Hl TWRH EC3N...13 H6
Tower Hill Ter MON EC3R...13 J6
Tower La WBLY HA9 *...79 K1
Tower Ms CLPT E5...87 G3
WALTH E17...69 J1
Tower Mill Rd CMBW SE5 *...143 F1
Tower Park Rd DART DA1...150 C6
Tower Pl MON EC3R...13 H6
Tower Ri RCH/KEW TW9...137 F4
Tower Rd BELV DA17...129 K4
BXLYHN DA7...149 J5
DART DA1...171 F2
ORP BR6...202 A6
TWK TW1...156 A5
WLSDN NW10...81 J5
Tower Royal MANHO EC4N *...12 D5
Towers Av HGDN/ICK UB10...94 A2
Towers Ct HGDN/ICK UB10 *...94 A2
Towers Pl RCH/KEW TW9...137 F6
Towers Rd PIN HA5...41 J4
STHL UB1...96 A3
Tower St LSQ/SEVD WC2H...10 E4
Tower Ter WDGN N22...49 F5
Tower Vw CROY/NA CR0...198 B5
Towfield Rd FELT TW13...154 E4
Towncourt Crs
STMC/STPC BR5...201 H2
Towncourt La STMC/STPC BR5...201 J3
Towncourt Pth FSBYPK N4...67 J5
Town End Pde KUT/HW KT1 *...174 E6
Towney Md NTHLT UB5...95 K1
Town Farm Wy
STWL/WRAY TW19 *...152 A2
Townfield Rd HYS/HAR UB3...113 K1
Townfield Sq HYS/HAR UB3...113 J1
Town Field Wy ISLW TW7...136 B3
Town Hall Approach Rd
SEVS/STOTM N15...68 B1
Townhall Av CHSWK W4...118 A5
Town Hall Pde
BRXS/STRHM SW2 *...142 A5
Town Hall Rd BTSEA SW11...140 E4
Townholm Crs HNWL W7...116 A3
Town La STWL/WRAY TW19...152 A2
Townley Ct SRTFD E15...88 D4
Townley Rd BXLYHS DA6...149 H5
EDUL SE22...143 F6
Townley St WALW SE17...122 E5
Town Meadow BTFD TW8...136 E1
Townmead Rd FUL/PGN SW6...140 B3
RCH/KEW TW9...137 J3
Town Quay BARK IG11...90 C6
Town Rd ED N9...36 D4
Townsend Av STHGT/OAK N14...34 D6
Townsend La CDALE/KGS NW9...63 F4
Townsend Ms
WAND/EARL SW18...160 B4
Townsend Rd SEVS/STOTM N15...68 B2
STHL UB1...114 D1
STJWD NW8...2 D2
WOOL/PLUM SE18...127 G3
Townsend St STHWK SE1...19 G6
Townsend Wy NTHWD HA6...40 D3
Townsend Yd HGT N6...66 A5
Townshend Cl SCUP DA14...186 D3
Townshend Est STJWD NW8...2 C2
Townshend Rd CHST BR7...185 G1
RCH/KEW TW9...137 G5
STJWD NW8...2 C1
Townshend Ter RCH/KEW TW9...137 G5
Townson Av NTHLT UB5...95 F1
Townson Wy NTHLT UB5...94 E1
Town Whf ISLW TW7 *...136 C4
Towpath WOT/HER KT12 *...188 A1
Towpath Rd UED N18...51 F2
Towpath Wy CROY/NA CR0...197 G3
Towton Rd WNWD SE27...162 D4
Toynbec Cl CHST BR7...167 G6
Toynbee Rd RYNPK SW20...177 H4
Toynbee St WCHPL E1...13 J2
Toyne Wy HGT N6...65 K3
Tracey Av CRICK NW2 *...82 A3
Trade Cl PLMGR N13...35 G6
Trader Rd EHAM E6...108 B6
Tradescant Rd VX/NE SW8...141 K1
Trading Estate Rd
WLSDN NW10 *...98 E3
Trafalgar Av PECK SE15...123 G6
TOTM N17...50 A2
WPK KT4...193 G5
Trafalgar Chambers
CHEL SW3 *...120 C5
Trafalgar Gdns KENS W8 *...120 A3
WCHPL E1...105 F4
Trafalgar Gv GNWCH SE10...125 G6
Trafalgar Ms HOM E9 *...87 H4
Trafalgar Pl UED N18...50 C1
WAN E11...70 E1
Trafalgar Rd DART DA1...171 H4
GNWCH SE10...125 H5
RAIN RM13...111 H1
WHTN TW2...155 J4
WIM/MER SW19...178 A3
Trafalgar Sq STJS SW1Y *...10 D7
Trafalgar St WALW SE17...122 E5
Trafalgar Wy CROY/NA CR0...196 B6
POP/IOD E14...125 F1
Trafford Cl BARK/HLT IG6...55 F2
SRTFD E15...87 K3
Trafford Rd THHTH CR7...196 A2
Trahorn Cl WCHPL E1...104 C3
Tramway Av ED N9...36 D2
SRTFD E15...88 B5
Tramway Cl PGE/AN SE20...181 K4
Tramway Pth MTCM CR4...194 D1
Tranby Ms HOM E9...87 F3
Tranley Ms HAMP NW3 *...83 J2
Tranmere Rd ED N9...36 B2
WAND/EARL SW18...160 B4
WHTN TW2...155 G2
Tranquil Pas BKHTH/KID SE3 *...145 J3
Tranquil Ri ERITH DA8...130 B5
Tranquil V BKHTH/KID SE3...145 J3
Transept St CAMTN NW1...8 D2
Transmere Rd STMC/STPC BR5...201 H3
Transom Cl BERM/RHTH SE16...124 B4
Transom Sq POP/IOD E14...124 E5
Transport Av BTFD TW8...116 C6
Tranton Rd BERM/RHTH SE16...123 J3
Traps La NWMAL KT3...176 B5
Travellers Site CHING E4 *...51 H3
Travellers Wy HEST TW5...134 B3
Travers Cl WALTH E17...51 F4
Travers Rd HOLWY N7...85 G1
Treacy Cl BUSH WD23...28 C4
Treadgold St NTGHL W11...100 B6
Treadway St BETH E2...104 D1
Treaty Centre HSLW TW3 *...135 G4
Treaty St IS N1...5 G1
Trebeck St MYFR/PICC W1J...9 J7
Trebovir Rd ECT SW5...119 K5
Treby St BOW E3...105 H3
Trecastle Wy HOLWY N7...84 D2
Tredegar Rd BOW E3...105 H1
FBAR/BDGN N11...48 D3
RDART DA2...170 D5
Tredegar Sq BOW E3...105 H2
Trederwen Rd HACK E8...86 C6
Tredown Rd SYD SE26...181 K1
Tredwell Cl BRXS/STRHM SW2...162 A4
HAYES BR2...200 C1
Tredwell Rd WNWD SE27...162 C6
Tree Cl RCHPK/HAM TW10...156 E3
Treen Av BARN SW13...138 C4
Tree Rd CAN/RD E16...107 G5
Treeside Cl WDR/YW UB7...112 A4
Tree Top Ms DAGE RM10...93 F4
Treetops Cl ABYW SE2...129 F5
NTHWD HA6...40 B1
Treetops Vw LOU IG10...39 H1
Tree View Cl NRWD SE19...181 F4
Treewall Gdns BMLY BR1...166 A6
Trefgarne Rd DAGE RM10...74 C6
Trefoil Rd WAND/EARL SW18...140 B6
Tregaron Av CEND/HSY/T N8...66 E4
Tregaron Gdns NWMAL KT3...192 B1
Tregarvon Rd BTSEA SW11...141 F5
Tregenna Av RYLN/HDSTN HA2...78 A2
Tregenna Cl STHGT/OAK N14...22 C6
Tregony Rd ORP BR6...217 F2
Trego Rd HOM E9...87 J5
Tregothnan Rd BRXN/ST SW9...141 K4
Tregunter Rd WBPTN SW10...120 B6
Trehearn Rd BARK/HLT IG6...54 D3
Treherne Ct BRXN/ST SW9 *...142 C2
Trehern Rd MORT/ESHN SW14...138 A4
Trehurst St CLPT E5...87 G3
Trelawney Est HOM E9 *...86 E4
Trelawney Rd BARK/HLT IG6...54 D3
Trelawn Rd BRXS/STRHM SW2...142 B6
LEY E10...88 A1
Trelawny Cl WALTH E17...69 K1
Trellis Sq BOW E3...105 H2
Treloar Gdns NRWD SE19...180 E2
Trelwney Est HOM E9 *...86 E4
Tremadoc Rd CLAP SW4...141 J5
Tremaine Cl BROCKY SE4...144 D3
Tremaine Rd PGE/AN SE20...181 J5
Trematon Pl TEDD TW11...174 D3
Tremlett Gv ARCH N19...84 C1
Tremlett Ms ARCH N19 *...84 C1
Trenance Gdns GDMY/SEVK IG3...91 G1
Trenchard Av RSLP HA4...77 F3
Trenchard Cl CDALE/KGS NW9...45 G4
STAN HA7...43 H2
Trenchard St GNWCH SE10...125 G5
Trenchold St VX/NE SW8 *...121 K6
Trenear Cl ORP BR6...217 G2
Trenholme Rd PGE/AN SE20...181 J3
Trenholme Ter PGE/AN SE20...181 J3
Trenmar Gdns WLSDN NW10...99 K2
Trent Av EA W5...116 D3
Trentbridge Cl BARK/HLT IG6...55 F2
Trent Ct WAN E11...70 E2
Trent Gdns STHGT/OAK N14...34 B1
Trentham Dr STMC/STPC BR5...202 B1
Trentham St
WAND/EARL SW18...159 K3
Trent Pk EBAR EN4 *...22 C3
Trent Rd BKHH IG9...39 F3
BRXS/STRHM SW2...142 A6
Trent Wy WPK KT4...208 A1
YEAD UB4...94 C2
Trentwood Side ENC/FH EN2...23 F4
Treport St WAND/EARL SW18...160 A2
Tresco Cl BMLY BR1...183 H2
Trescoe Gdns CRW RM5...56 E1
RYLN/HDSTN HA2...59 J4
Tresco Gdns GDMY/SEVK IG3...73 F6
Tresco Rd PECK SE15...143 J5
Tresham Crs STJWD NW8...2 C6
Tresham Rd BARK IG11...91 F5
Tresilian Av WCHMH N21...23 F6
Tressell Cl IS N1...85 H5
Tressillian Crs BROCKY SE4...144 D4
Tressillian Rd BROCKY SE4...144 D4
Trestis Cl YEAD UB4...95 H3
Treswell Rd DAGW RM9...92 A6
Tretawn Gdns MLHL NW7...31 G6
Tretawn Pk MLHL NW7...31 G6
Trevanion Rd WKENS W14 *...119 H5
Treve Av HRW HA1...60 C4
Trevelyan Av MNPK E12...89 K3
Trevelyan Cl DART DA1...151 J5
Trevelyan Crs
KTN/HRWW/WS HA3...61 K4
Trevelyan Gdns WLSDN NW10 *...82 A6
Trevelyan Rd SRTFD E15...88 D2
TOOT SW17...178 E2
Treveris St STHWK SE1...18 B1
Treverton St NKENS W10...100 B3
Treves Cl WCHMH N21...23 F6
Treville St PUT/ROE SW15...158 E2
Treviso Rd FSTH SE23...164 A4
Trevithick Cl
EBED/NFELT TW14...153 J3
Trevithick Dr DART DA1...151 J5
Trevithick St DEPT SE8...124 D6
Trevone Gdns PIN HA5...59 J3
Trevor Cl EBAR EN4...33 H1
HAYES BR2...199 K4
ISLW TW7...136 A6
KTN/HRWW/WS HA3...43 F3
NTHLT UB5...95 G1
Trevor Crs RSLP HA4...76 D2
Trevor Gdns EDGW HA8...45 F4
Trevor Pl SKENS SW7...14 D3
Trevor Rd EDGW HA8...45 F4
HYS/HAR UB3...113 H2
WFD IG8...52 E3
WIM/MER SW19...177 H3
Trevor Sq SKENS SW7...14 D3
Trevor St SKENS SW7...14 D3
Trevose Rd WALTH E17...52 B4
Trevose Wy OXHEY WD19...27 G5
Trewenna Dr CHSGTN KT9...205 K3
Trewince Rd RYNPK SW20...177 F4
Trewint St WAND/EARL SW18...160 B4
Trewsbury Rd SYD SE26...182 A1
Triandra Wy YEAD UB4...95 H4
Triangle Est LBTH SE11 *...122 A5
Triangle Pas EBAR EN4 *...21 G5
Triangle Pl CLAP SW4...141 J5
Triangle Rd HACK E8...86 D6
The Triangle BFN/LL DA15 *...168 B2
HACK E8...86 D6
KUT/HW KT1...175 K5
Triangle Wy ACT W3...117 H3
Trident Pl CHEL SW3 *...120 C6
Trident St BERM/RHTH SE16...124 A4
Trident Wy NWDGN UB2...114 A3
Trig La BLKFR EC4V...12 C5
Trigon Rd VX/NE SW8...142 A1
Trilby Rd FSTH SE23...164 A4
Trim St NWCR SE14...124 C6
Trinder Rd ARCH N19...66 E5
BAR EN5...20 A6
Tring Av ACT W3...117 G2
STHL UB1...95 K5
WBLY HA9...80 C4
Tring Cl GNTH/NBYPK IG2...72 D2
Trinidad Gdns DAGE RM10...93 F5
Trinidad St POP/IOD E14...105 H6
Trinity Av EFNCH N2...47 H6
EN EN1...36 B1
Trinity Buoy Whf
POP/IOD E14 *...106 B4
Trinity Church Rd BARN SW13...118 E6
Trinity Church Sq STHWK SE1...18 D4
Trinity Cl CLAP SW4 *...141 H5
HACK E8 *...86 B4
HAYES BR2...200 D5
HSLWW TW4...134 E5
LEW SE13...145 G5
NTHWD HA6...40 C2
SAND/SEL CR2...212 A6
WAN E11...70 C6
Trinity Ct ELTH/MOT SE9...167 G1
Trinity Crs TOOT SW17...160 E4
Trinity Dr UX/CGN UB8...94 A5
Trinity Est DEPT SE8...124 C5
Trinity Gdns BRXN/ST SW9...142 A5
CAN/RD E16...106 D4
DART DA1...171 G1
Trinity Gn WCHPL E1 *...104 E4
Trinity Gv GNWCH SE10...145 F2
Trinity Ms PGE/AN SE20...181 K4
Trinity Pde HSLW TW3 *...135 G4
Trinity Pk CHING E4 *...51 H2
Trinity Pl BXLYHS DA6...149 G5
TWRH EC3N...13 J5
Trinity Ri BRXS/STRHM SW2...162 C2
Trinity Rd BARK/HLT IG6...54 C6
EFNCH N2...47 H6
RCH/KEW TW9 *...137 G4
STHL UB1...114 D1
WAND/EARL SW18...160 C1
WDGN N22...48 E3
WIM/MER SW19...177 K2
Trinity Sq TWRH EC3N...13 H6
Trinity St CAN/RD E16...106 D4
ENC/FH EN2...23 J3
STHWK SE1...18 D3
Trinity Wy ACT W3...99 G6
CHING E4...51 H2
Trio Pl STHWK SE1...18 D3
Tristan Sq BKHTH/KID SE3...145 H4
Tristram Cl WALTH E17...52 B6
Tristram Dr ED N9...36 B5
Tristram Rd BMLY BR1...165 J6
Triton Sq CAMTN NW1...4 A6
Tritton Av CROY/NA CR0...210 E2
Tritton Rd DUL SE21...162 E5
Triumph Cl HYS/HAR UB3...133 F2
Triumph Rd EHAM E6...107 K5
Trojan Wy CROY/NA CR0...211 F1
Troon Cl BERM/RHTH SE16...123 J5
THMD SE28...109 K5
Troon St WCHPL E1...105 G5
Trosley Rd BELV DA17...129 H6
Trossachs Rd EDUL SE22...143 F6
Trothy Rd STHWK SE1...123 H4
Trott Rd MUSWH N10...48 A3
Trott St BTSEA SW11...140 C2
Trotwood CHIG IG7...54 D2
Troughton Rd CHARL SE7...126 A5
Troutbeck Rd NWCR SE14...144 B2
Trout Rd WDR/YW UB7...112 A1
Trouville Rd CLAP SW4...161 H1
Trowbridge Rd HOM E9...87 H4
Trowlock Av TEDD TW11...174 D2
Trowlock Wy TEDD TW11...174 D2
Troy Ct KENS W8...119 K3
Troy Rd NRWD SE19...180 E2
Troy Town PECK SE15...143 H4
Trubshaw Rd NWDGN UB2...115 G3
Trueman Cl EDGW HA8 *...44 D3
Trulock Rd TOTM N17...50 C3
Truman's Rd STNW/STAM N16...86 A3
Trumpers Wy HNWL W7...116 A3
Trumpington Rd FSTGT E7...88 D2
Trump St CITYW EC2V...12 D4
Trundlers Wy BUSH WD23...28 E3
Trundle St STHWK SE1...18 C2
Trundleys Rd DEPT SE8...124 B6
Trundley's Ter DEPT SE8...124 A4
Truro Gdns IL IG1...71 J4
Truro Rd WALTH E17...69 H1
WDGN N22...48 E3
Truro St KTTN NW5...84 A4
Truro Wy YEAD UB4...94 C2
Trusedale Rd EHAM E6...107 K5
Truslove Rd WNWD SE27...180 B1
Trussley Rd HMSMTH W6...119 F3
Trustons Gdns EMPK RM11...75 J4
Tryfan Cl REDBR IG4...71 H2
Tryon Crs HOM E9...86 E6
Tryon St CHEL SW3...120 E5
Trystings Cl ESH/CLAY KT10...205 G4
Tuam Rd WOOL/PLUM SE18...127 J6
Tubbenden Cl ORP BR6...216 E1
Tubbenden Dr ORP BR6...216 D2
Tubbenden La ORP BR6...216 D2
Tubbenden La South ORP BR6...216 D3
Tubbs Rd WLSDN NW10...99 H1
Tuck Rd RAIN RM13...93 J4
Tudor Av GPK RM2...57 J6
HPTN TW12...173 F2
WPK KT4...207 K1
Tudor Cl ASHF TW15...152 B6
BRXS/STRHM SW2 *...162 A1
CDALE/KGS NW9...62 E6
CHEAM SM3...208 B3
CHSGTN KT9...206 A3
CHST BR7...184 E4
DART DA1...170 E1
HAMP NW3...83 J3
HGT N6...66 C4
HPTN TW12...173 H1
MLHL NW7...45 J2
PIN HA5...58 E2
WFD IG8...53 F1
WLGTN SM6...210 C5
Tudor Ct ELTH/MOT SE9 *...146 D5
SWLY BR8...203 K4
WALTH E17...69 H4
Tudor Ct North WBLY HA9...80 C3
Tudor Ct South WBLY HA9...80 D3
Tudor Crs BARK/HLT IG6...54 C2
ENC/FH EN2...23 J2
Tudor Dr GPK RM2...75 J1
KUTN/CMB KT2...175 F1
MRDN SM4...193 G3
WOT/HER KT12...188 C5
Tudor Enterprise Pk
KTN/HRWW/WS HA3 *...42 D6
Tudor Est WLSDN NW10 *...98 D1
Tudor Gdns ACT W3...98 C5
BARN SW13...138 B4
CDALE/KGS NW9...62 E6
GPK RM2...75 J1
TWK TW1...156 A3
WWKM BR4...214 A1
Tudor Gv HOM E9...86 E5
Tudor Ms WLSDN NW10...81 J4
Tudor Pde ELTH/MOT SE9 *...146 D5
Tudor Pl MTCM CR4...178 D3
NRWD SE19 *...181 G3
Tudor Rd BAR EN5...20 E4
BARK IG11...91 F5
BECK BR3...183 F6
CHING E4...51 K2
ED N9...36 D2
HACK E8...86 D6
HPTN TW12...173 F3
HSLW TW3...135 J5
HYS/HAR UB3...94 B5
KTN/HRWW/WS HA3...42 D5
KUTN/CMB KT2...175 H3
NRWD SE19...181 G3
PIN HA5...41 G5
PLSTW E13...89 G6
SNWD SE25...197 J2
STHL UB1...95 J6
Tudor Sq HYS/HAR UB3...94 B4
Tudor St EMB EC4Y...11 K5
Tudor Wy ACT W3...117 H2
STHGT/OAK N14...34 D3
STMC/STPC BR5...201 J3
Tudor Well Cl STAN HA7...43 H1
Tudway Rd BKHTH/KID SE3...146 B5
Tufnail Rd DART DA1...171 J1
Tufnell Park Rd HOLWY N7...84 D2
Tufter Rd CHIG IG7...55 F1
Tufton Gdns E/WMO/HCT KT8...173 G5
Tufton Rd CHING E4...37 J6
Tufton St WEST SW1P...16 E5
Tugboat St THMD SE28...127 K2
Tugela Rd CROY/NA CR0...196 E3
Tugela St CAT SE6...164 C4
Tugmutton Cl ORP BR6...216 B2
Tulip Cl CROY/NA CR0...198 A5
EHAM E6...107 J4
HPTN TW12...172 E2
NWDGN UB2...115 H2
Tulip Gdns CHING E4...38 B5
IL IG1...90 B4
Tulip Wy WDR/YW UB7...112 A4
Tull St CAR SM5...194 E4
Tulse Cl BECK BR3...183 F6
Tulse Hl BRXS/STRHM SW2...162 B2
Tulsemere Rd WNWD SE27...162 D4
Tummons Gdns SNWD SE25...181 F5
Tuncombe Rd UED N18...36 A6
Tunis Rd SHB W12...119 F1
Tunley Gn POP/IOD E14...105 H4
Tunley Rd TOOT SW17...161 F4
WLSDN NW10...81 G6
Tunmarsh La PLSTW E13...107 G2
Tunnan Leys EHAM E6...108 A5
Tunnel Av GNWCH SE10...125 H3
Tunnel Gdns FBAR/BDGN N11...48 C3
Tunnel Link Rd HTHAIR TW6...132 D6
Tunnel Rd BERM/RHTH SE16...123 K2
Tunnel Rd East WDR/YW UB7...132 E1
Tunnel Rd West WDR/YW UB7...132 D2
Tunstall Av BARK/HLT IG6...55 G2
Tunstall Cl ORP BR6...216 E2
Tunstall Rd BRXN/ST SW9...142 A5
CROY/NA CR0...197 F5
Tunstock Wy BELV DA17...129 G3
Tunworth Cl CDALE/KGS NW9...62 E3
Tunworth Crs PUT/ROE SW15...158 C1
Tupelo Rd LEY E10...69 K6
Tuppy St THMD SE28...127 H3
Turene Cl WAND/EARL SW18...140 B5
Turin Rd ED N9...36 E2
Turin St BETH E2...104 C2
Turkey Oak Cl NRWD SE19...181 F4
Turks Rw CHEL SW3...121 F5
Turle Rd FSBYPK N4 *...67 F6
STRHM/NOR SW16...179 K5
Turlewray Cl FSBYPK N4...67 F5
Turley Cl SRTFD E15...88 C6
Turnagain La
FLST/FETLN EC4A *...12 A3
Turnage Rd BCTR RM8...74 A5
Turnant Rd TOTM N17...49 J4
Turnberry Cl
BERM/RHTH SE16...123 J5
HDN NW4...46 B5
Turnberry Ct OXHEY WD19 *...27 G5
Turnberry Wy ORP BR6...201 J5
Turnbury Cl THMD SE28...109 K5
Turnchapel Ms CLAP SW4...141 G4
Turner Av MTCM CR4...178 E4
SEVS/STOTM N15...68 A1
WHTN TW2...155 H5
Turner Cl ALP/SUD HA0...79 K4
BRXN/ST SW9...142 C2
GLDGN NW11...65 F3
Turner Ct CMBW SE5 *...142 E5
DART DA1...151 F6
Turner Dr GLDGN NW11...65 F3
Turner Ms BELMT SM2...209 F5
Turner Rd EDGW HA8...44 A5
NWMAL KT3...192 A4
WALTH E17...70 A1
Turners Cl TRDG/WHET N20...33 K5
Turners Meadow Wy
BECK BR3...182 C4
Turner's Rd BOW E3...105 H4
Turner St CAN/RD E16...106 D5
WCHPL E1...104 D4
Turners Wy CROY/NA CR0...196 B6
Turner's Wd GLDGN NW11...65 G5
Turneville Rd WKENS W14...119 J6
Turney Rd DUL SE21...162 D2
Turnham Green Ter
CHSWK W4...118 B4
Turnham Rd BROCKY SE4...144 B6
Turnmill St FARR EC1M...5 K7
Turnpike Cl DEPT SE8...144 C1
Turnpike Dr ORP BR6...217 J6
Turnpike La CEND/HSY/T N8...67 G1
SUT SM1...209 G3
Turnpike Link CROY/NA CR0...197 F6
Turnpike Ms CEND/HSY/T N8 *...49 G6
Turnpike Pde
SEVS/STOTM N15 *...49 H6
Turnpike Wy ISLW TW7...136 B2
Turnstone Cl CDALE/KGS NW9 *...45 G5
PLSTW E13...106 E2
Turnstone Ter WEA W13 *...97 F3
Turpentine La PIM SW1V...121 G5
Turpin Av CRW RM5...56 C3
Turpin Cl WAP E1W...105 F6
Turpington Cl HAYES BR2...200 D3
Turpington La HAYES BR2...200 D2
Turpin La ERITH DA8...130 D6
Turpin Rd EBED/NFELT TW14...153 J1
Turpin's La WFD IG8...53 K1
Turpins Yd CRICK NW2 *...63 K6
GNWCH SE10...145 F1
Turpin Wy WLGTN SM6...210 B5
Turquand St WALW SE17...18 D7
Turret Gv CLAP SW4...141 H4
Turton Rd ALP/SUD HA0...80 A3
Turville St BETH E2...7 J6
Tuscan Rd WOOL/PLUM SE18...127 J5
Tuskar St GNWCH SE10...125 H5
Tweeddale Gv HGDN/ICK UB10...76 A1
Tweeddale Rd CAR SM5...194 C5

Tweedmouth Rd PLSTW E13....107 F1
Tweed Wy ROM RM1....57 F3
Tweedy Rd BMLY BR1....183 K4
Twelvetrees Crs BOW E3....106 E5
Twentyman Cl WFD IG8....52 E1
Twickenham Br TWK TW1....136 E6
Twickenham Cl CROY/NA CRO....211 F1
Twickenham Gdns
 GFD/PVL UB6....79 G3
 KTN/HRWW/WS HA3....42 C5
Twickenham Rd FELT TW13....154 E5
 TEST TW11....155 F5
 ISLW TW7....136 A4
 RCH/KEW TW9....136 D6
 TEDD TW11....174 B1
 WAN E11....70 B6
Twig Folly Cl BETH E2....105 F1
Twig Folly Whf BETH E2 *....105 F1
Twigg Cl ERITH DA8....150 B1
Twilley St WAND/EARL SW18....160 A2
Twine Cl BARK IG11....109 H2
Twine Ct WHCPL E1....104 E6
Twineham Gn
 NFNCH/WDSPK N12....32 E6
Twine Ter BOW E3 *....105 H3
Twining Av WHTN TW2....155 H5
Twinn Rd MLHL NW7....46 C2
Twin Tumps Wy THMD SE28....109 G6
Twisden Rd KTTN NW5....84 B2
Twisleton Ct DART DA1....171 J3
Twybridge Wy WLSDN NW10....80 E5
Twycross Ms SDNCH SE10....125 H5
Twyford Abbey Rd
 WLSDN NW10....98 B2
Twyford Av ACT W3....98 C6
 EFNCH N2....47 K6
Twyford Crs ACT W3....117 H1
Twyford Rd CAR SM5....194 C5
 IL IG1....78 B3
 RYLN/HDSTN HA2....60 B4
Twyford St IS N1....85 F6
Tyas Rd CAN/RD E16....106 D6
Tybenham Rd WIM/MER SW19....177 K6
Tyberry Rd PEND EN3....24 D4
Tyburn La HRW HA1....61 F5
Tyburn Wy MBLAR W1H....9 F5
Tye La ORP BR6....216 C3
Tyers Ga STHWK SE1....19 G3
Tyers St LBTH SE11....122 A5
Tyers Ter LBTH SE11....122 A5
Tyeshurst Cl ABYW SE2....129 F5
Tylecroft Rd
 STRHM/NOR SW16....179 K5
Tylehurst Gdns IL IG1....90 C5
Tyler Cl BETH E2....7 J2
Tyler Rd CAMTN NW1....149 J1
Tylers Ga KTN/HRWW/WS HA3....62 A3
Tylers Green Rd SWLY BR8....203 K4
Tyler St GNWCH SE10....125 H5
 FSTGT E7....89 C2
Tylney Av NRWD SE19....181 G1
Tylney Rd BMLY BR1....184 C5
 FSTGT E7....89 C2
Tynan Cl EBED/NFELT TW14....153 K3
Tyndale La IS N1....85 H5
Tyndale Ter IS N1....85 H5
Tyndall Rd LEY E10....70 A6
 WELL DA16....148 A4
Tyneham Cl BTSEA SW11....141 F4
Tyneham Rd BTSEA SW11....141 F3
Tynemouth Cl EHAM E6....108 B5
Tynemouth Dr EN EN1....24 C1
Tynemouth Rd MTCM CR4....179 F3
 SEVS/STOTM N15....
 WOOL/PLUM SE18....127 H5
Tynemouth St FUL/PGN SW6....140 B3
Tynemouth Ter
 SEVS/STOTM N15 *....68 B1
Tyne St WCHPL E1....13 L4
Tynsdale Rd WLSDN NW10....81 G5
Type St BETH E2....105 F1
Tyrawley Rd FUL/PGN SW6....140 A2
Tyre La CDALE/KGS NW9 *....63 G1
Tyrell Cl HRW HA1....
Tyrone Rd EHAM E6....107 K1
Tyron Wy SCUP DA14....167 K6
Tyrrell Av WELL DA16....148 B6
Tyrrell Rd EDUL SE22....143 H5
Tyrrel Wy CDALE/KGS NW9 *....63 H4
Tyrwhitt Rd BROCKY SE4....144 D4
Tysoe St CLKNW EC1R....
Tyson Gdns FSTH SE23 *....163 K2
Tyson Rd FSTH SE23....163 K2
Tyssen Rd STNW/STAM N16 *....86 B1
Tyssen St HACK E8....
 IS N1....7 H2
Tytherton Rd ARCH N19....84 D1

U

Uamvar St POP/IOD E14....105 K4
Uckfield Gv MTCM CR4....179 F4
Udall Gdns CRW RM5....56 C2
Udall St WEST SW1P....16 E7
Udney Park Rd TEDD TW11....174 B2
Uffington Rd WLSDN NW10....81 J6
 WNWD SE27....
Ufford Cl KTN/HRWW/WS HA3....42 B3
Ufford Rd KTN/HRWW/WS HA3....42 B3
Ufford St STHWK SE1....18 A2
Ufton Rd IS N1....86 A5
Uhura Sq STNW/STAM N16 *....86 A1
Ullathorne Rd
 STRHM/NOR SW16....161 H4
Ulleswater Rd STHGT/OAK N14....34 E6
Ullin St POP/IOD E14....106 A4
Ullswater Cl BMLY BR1....183 H2
 PUT/ROE SW15 *....
 YEAD UB4....94 C1
Ullswater Cl
 RYLN/HDSTN HA2....60 A4
Ullswater Crs PUT/ROE SW15....158 A4
Ullswater Rd BARN SW13....138 D1

WNWD SE27....162 C4
Ullswater Wy HCH RM12....93 J3
Ulster Gdns PLMGR N13....35 J6
Ulster Pl CAMTN NW1....10 D1
Ulundi Rd BKHTH/KID SE3....125 H6
Ulva Rd PUT/ROE SW15....139 G5
Ulverscroft Rd EDUL SE22....143 G6
Ulverston Rd WALTH E17....52 B5
Ulysses Rd KIL/WHAMP NW6....82 D3
Umberston St WCHPL E1 *....104 C5
Umbria St PUT/ROE SW15....158 D1
Umfreville Rd FSBYPK N4....67 H3
Undercliff Rd LEW SE13....144 E4
Underhill BAR EN5....20 E6
Underhill Ct BAR EN5 *....20 E6
Underhill Rd EDUL SE22....143 H6
Underhill St CAMTN NW1....3 K1
Underne Av STHGT/OAK N14....34 B4
Undershaft HDTCH EC3A....13 J5
Undershaw Rd BMLY BR1....165 H5
Underwood CROY/NA CRO....214 A4
Underwood Rd CHING E4....51 K1
 WCHPL E1....104 C3
 WFD IG8....53 H5
Underwood Rw IS N1....6 D4
Underwood St IS N1....6 D4
The Underwood
 ELTH/MOT SE9....166 E4
Undine Cl ROM/PIOD E14....124 E4
Undine St TOOT SW17....178 E1
Uneeda Dr GFD/PVL UB6....78 D4
Union Cl WAN E11....88 B2
Union Ct CLAP SW4....141 K3
 OBST EC2N....
Union Dr WCHPL E1 *....105 G3
Union Gv VX/NE SW8....141 J3
Union Ms BRXN/ST SW9....141 K3
Union Pk GNWCH SE10....125 J5
Union Rd ALP/SUD HA0....80 A4
 CROY/NA CRO....196 D4
 FBAR/BDGN N11....48 D2
 HAYES BR2....200 C2
 NTHLT UB5....96 A2
 VX/NE SW8....141 J3
Union Sq IS N1....6 C1
Union St BAR EN5....20 C5
 KUT/HW KT1....174 E5
 SRTFD E15....88 B6
 STHWK SE1....11 J8
Union Wk BETH E2....7 J4
Unity Cl CROY/NA CRO....213 K6
 NRWD SE19....180 D1
 WLSDN NW10....81 J4
Unity Ms CAMTN NW1....4 E7
University Cl MLHL NW7....45 H3
University Gdns BXLY DA5....169 G2
University Pl ERITH DA8....149 J1
University Rd WIM/MER SW19....178 C2
University St FITZ W1T....4 F9
University Wy CAN/RD E16....108 A4
 DART DA1....151 K5
Unwin Av EBED/NFELT TW14....133 G6
Unwin Cl PECK SE15....123 H6
Unwin Rd ISLW TW7....135 K4
 SKENS SW7....14 B4
Upbrook Ms BAY/PAD W2....101 G5
Upcerne Rd WBPTN SW10....140 B6
Upcroft Av EDGW HA8....44 E1
Updale Rd SCUP DA14....168 A6
Upfield CROY/NA CRO....212 D1
Upfield Rd HNWL W7....97 F3
Uphall Rd IL IG1....90 B3
Upham Park Rd CHSWK W4....118 B4
Uphill Dr CDALE/KGS NW9....62 E2
 MLHL NW7....45 G1
Uphill Gv MLHL NW7....31 G6
Uphill Rd MLHL NW7....31 G6
Upland Ms EDUL SE22....143 H6
Upland Rd BELMT SM2....209 H5
 BXLYHN DA7....149 G4
 EDUL SE22....143 H6
 PLSTW E13....106 E3
 SAND/SEL CR2....211 K3
Uplands BECK BR3....182 D5
Uplands Cl MORT/ESHN SW14....137 J6
Uplands Park Rd ENC/FH EN2....23 G3
Uplands Rd CEND/HSY/T N8....67 F2
 CHDH RM6....73 K1
 EBAR EN4....33 J2
 ORP BR6....202 C5
 WFD IG8....53 J3
The Uplands RSLP HA4....58 E5
Uplands Wy WCHMH N21....23 G4
Upminster Rd South....111 J3
Upney La BARK IG11....91 F5
Upnor Wy WALW SE17....19 K7
Uppark Dr GNTH/NBYPK IG2....72 C3
Upper Abbey Rd BELV DA17....129 G4
Upper Addison Gdns
 WKENS W14....119 H2
Upper Bank St POP/IOD E14....124 E1
Upper Bardsey Wk IS N1 *....85 J4
Upper Belgrave St KTBR SW1X....15 H4
Upper Berenger Wk
 WBPTN SW10 *....140 C1
Upper Berkeley St MBLAR W1H....9 F4
Upper Beulah HI NRWD SE19....181 F4
Upper Blantyre Wk
 WBPTN SW10 *....140 C1
Upper Brighton Rd SURB KT6....190 E4
Upper Brockley Rd
 BROCKY SE4....144 C3
Upper Brook St
 MYFR/PKLN W1K....9 G6
Upper Butts BTFD TW8....116 D6
Upper Caldy Wk IS N1 *....85 J4
Upper Camelford Wk
 NTGHL W11 *....100 C5
Upper Cavendish Av FNCH N3....46 E6
Upper Cheyne Rw CHEL SW3....120 D6
Upper Clapton Rd CLPT E5....68 D5
Upper Clarendon Wk
 NTGHL W11 *....100 C5
Upper Dartrey Wk
 WBPTN SW10 *....140 C1
Upper Dengie Wk IS N1 *....85 J6

Upper Elmers End Rd
 BECK BR3....198 B2
Upper Farm Rd
 E/WMO/HCT KT8....188 C1
Upper Gn East MTCM CR4....178 E5
Upper Gn West MTCM CR4....178 E6
Upper Grosvenor St
 MYFR/PKLN W1K....9 G6
Upper Grotto Rd TWK TW1....156 A4
Upper Gnd STHWK SE1....11 J7
Upper Gv SNWD SE25....197 F1
Upper Grove Rd BELV DA17....129 G6
Upper Gulland Wk IS N1 *....85 J4
Upper Ham Rd
 KUT/HW KT1....156 E6
Upper Handa Wk IS N1 *....85 K4
Upper Harley St CAMTN NW1....3 H6
Upper Hawkwell Wk IS N1 *....85 J6
Upper Hitch OXHEY WD19....27 J1
Upper Holly Hill Rd BELV DA17....129 J5
Upper John St SOHO/CST W1F....10 F5
Upper Lismore Wk IS N1 *....85 J4
Upper Ldg KENS W8 *....120 A1
Upper Ml HMSMTH W6....119 E4
Upper Marsh STHWK SE1....17 H4
Upper Montagu St MBLAR W1H....9 F2
Upper Mulgrave Rd
 BELMT SM2....208 C5
Upper North St POP/IOD E14....105 K5
Upper Paddock Rd
 OXHEY WD19....27 J1
Upper Park Rd BELV DA17....129 J4
 BMLY BR1....184 A4
 FBAR/BDGN N11....48 B1
 HAMP NW3....83 K4
 KUTN/CMB KT2....175 H2
Upper Phillimore Gdns
 KENS W8....119 K2
Upper Rainham Rd HCH RM12....93 H2
Upper Ramsey Wk IS N1 *....85 K4
Upper Rawreth Wk IS N1 *....85 J5
Upper Richmond Rd
 PUT/ROE SW15....138 E5
Upper Richmond Rd West
 RCHPK/HAM TW10....137 H5
Upper Rd PLSTW E13....106 E2
 WLGTN SM6....210 E3
Upper St Martin's La
 LSQ/SEVD WC2H....10 L4
Upper Selsdon Rd
 SAND/SEL CR2....212 C6
Upper Sheppey Wk IS N1 *....85 J4
Upper Sheridan Rd BELV DA17....129 H4
Upper Shirley Rd
 CROY/NA CRO....212 E1
Upper Sq ISLW TW7....136 B4
Upper St IS N1....5 K2
Upper Sunbury Rd
 HPTN TW12....172 E4
Upper Sutton La HEST TW5....135 F1
Upper Tachbrook St PIM SW1V....16 E6
Upper Tail OXHEY WD19....27 J1
Upper Talbot Wk NTGHL W11 *....100 C5
Upper Teddington Rd
 KUT/HW KT1....174 D4
Upper Ter HAMP NW3....83 G1
Upper Thames St BLKFR EC4V....12 C6
Upper Tollington Pk
 FSBYPK N4....67 G5
Upper Tooting Pk TOOT SW17....160 E4
Upperton Rd SCUP DA14....168 B6
Upperton Rd East PLSTW E13....107 G2
Upperton Rd West PLSTW E13....107 G2
Upper Tooting Rd TOOT SW17....160 E6
Upper Town Rd STHL UB1....96 B3
Upper Tulse HI
 BRXS/STRHM SW2....162 A2
Upper Vernon Rd SUT SM1....209 H3
Upper Walthamstow Rd
 WALTH E17....70 B1
Upper Whistler Wk
 WBPTN SW10 *....140 B1
Upper Wickham La
 WELL DA16....148 C3
Upper Wimpole St
 CAVSQ/HST W1G....9 H1
Upper Woburn Pl CAMTN NW1....4 D5
Uppingham Av STAN HA7....43 J6
Upsall Dr PLMGR N13....35 J1
Upstall St CMBW SE5....142 C2
Upton Av FSTGT E7....88 E5
Upton Cl BXLY DA5....169 G1
 CRICK NW2....82 C1
Upton Dene BELMT SM2....209 F5
Upton Gdns
 KTN/HRWW/WS HA3....61 J3
Upton La FSTGT E7....89 F4
Upton Lodge Cl BUSH WD23....28 C2
Upton Park Rd FSTGT E7....89 F5
Upton Rd BXLYHS DA6....149 F5
 HSLW TW3....135 F4
 THHTH CR7....180 E5
 UED N18....50 C1
 WOOL/PLUM SE18....127 H6
Upton Rd South BXLY DA5....169 G1
Upway NFNCH/WDSPK N12....47 J3
Upwood Rd LEE/GVPK SE12....165 K1
 STRHM/NOR SW16....179 K4
Urban Ms FSBYPK N4....67 H4
Urlwin St CMBW SE5....122 D6
Urlwin Wk BRXN/ST SW9....142 B2
Urmston Dr WIM/MER SW19....159 H3
Ursula Ms FSBYPK N4....67 H5
Ursula St BTSEA SW11....140 D2
Urswick Gdns DAGW RM9....92 A5
Urswick Rd CLPT E5....86 D2
 DAGW RM9....91 K5
Usborne Ms VX/NE SW8....142 A1
Usher Rd BOW E3....87 H6
Usk Rd BTSEA SW11....140 B5
Usk St BETH E2....105 F2
Uvedale Rd DAGE RM10....74 C6
 ENC/FH EN2....23 K6
Uverdale Rd WBPTN SW10....140 B1
Uxbridge Rd HCH RM12....93 H6
 FELT TW13....154 C4
 HGDN/ICK UB10....94 A3

 HPTN TW12....155 H6
 HPTN TW12....173 C1
 KUT/HW KT1....190 E1
 SHB W12....118 D1
 STHL UB1....115 F1
 WEA W13....116 C1
Uxbridge Rd (Harrow Weald)
 KTN/HRWW/WS HA3....42 C3
Uxbridge Rd (Hatch End)
 PIN HA5....41 J4
Uxbridge Road High St
 STHL UB1....114 E1
Uxbridge Rd (Pinner) PIN HA5....41 J4
Uxbridge Rd (Stanmore)
 STAN HA7....43 F2
Uxbridge Rd The Broadway
 YEAD UB4....95 H6
Uxbridge St KENS W8....119 K1
Uxendon Crs WBLY HA9....62 A5
Uxendon HI WBLY HA9....62 B5

V

Valance Av CHING E4....38 D3
Valan Leas HAYES BR2....183 H6
Vale Cl EFNCH N2....47 K6
 MV/WKIL W9....101 G2
 ORP BR6....216 A2
 TWK TW1....156 B5
Vale Cottages
 PUT/ROE SW15 *....158 B5
Vale Ct ACT W3 *....118 C1
Vale Crs PUT/ROE SW15....158 B6
Vale Cft ESH/CLAY KT10....205 F5
Vale Dr BAR EN5....20 D5
Vale End EDUL SE22....143 G5
Vale Gv ACT W3....118 A1
 FSBYPK N4....67 J4
Vale La ACT W3....98 C4
Valence Av BCTR RM8....73 K5
Valence Circ BCTR RM8....91 K1
Valence Wood Rd BCTR RM8....91 K1
Valencia Rd STAN HA7....29 J6
Valency Cl NTHWD HA6....26 D6
Valentia Pl BRXN/ST SW9....142 B5
Valentine Av BXLY DA5....169 F4
Valentine Rd HOM E9 *....87 F4
 RYLN/HDSTN HA2....78 B1
Valentines Rd IL IG1....72 C5
Valentines Wy ROMW/RG RM7....75 G6
Vale of Health HAMP NW3....83 G1
Valerian Wy SRTFD E15....106 C2
Vale Ri GLDGN NW11....64 D5
Vale Rd BMLY BR1....185 F5
 DART DA1....170 E3
 ESH/CLAY KT10....204 E6
 FSBYPK N4....67 J4
 FSTGT E7....89 F4
 MTCM CR4....179 J6
 SUT SM1....209 F2
 WPK KT4....207 H1
Vale Rd North SURB KT6....191 F6
Vale Rd South SURB KT6....191 F6
Vale Rw HBRY N5....85 H1
Vale Royal HOLWY N7....84 E5
Vale St DUL SE21....162 E5
Valeswood Rd BMLY BR1....183 J1
Vale Ter FSBYPK N4....67 J3
The Vale ACT W3....118 A1
 CHEL SW3....120 D6
 CROY/NA CRO....198 A6
 EBED/NFELT TW14....154 A1
 GLDGN NW11....64 B4
 HEST TW5....114 D6
 MUSWH N10....48 B4
 RSLP HA4....77 G2
 STHGT/OAK N14....34 E2
 SUN TW16....172 A3
Valetta Gv PLSTW E13....106 E1
Valetta Rd ACT W3....118 C2
Valette St HACK E8....86 C4
Valiant Cl NTHLT UB5....95 H2
 ROMW/RG RM7....56 C5
Valiant Wy EHAM E6....107 K4
Vallance Rd WALTH E17....70 A1
Valley Av NFNCH/WDSPK N12....33 H4
Valley Cl DART DA1....170 C1
 LOU IG10....39 K1
 PIN HA5....41 F5
Valley Dr CDALE/KGS NW9....62 D2
Valleyfield Rd
 STRHM/NOR SW16....180 A1
Valley Fields Crs ENC/FH EN2....23 G3
Valley Gdns ALP/SUD HA0....80 B5
 WIM/MER SW19....178 C3
Valley Gv CHARL SE7....126 B5
Valley HI LOU IG10....39 K1
Valley Pk WATW WD18....26 A2
Valley Rd BELV DA17....129 J4
 ERITH DA8....129 K4
 HAYES BR2....183 H5
 STMC/STPC BR5....186 C4
 STRHM/NOR SW16....162 A6
Valley Side CHING E4....37 J5
Valley Vw BAR EN5....32 C1
Valley Vw CROY/NA CRO....197 K6
Valliere Rd WLSDN NW10....99 J2
Valliers Wood Rd BFN/LL DA15....167 K3
Vallis Wy CHSGTN KT9....205 K2
 WEA W13....97 G5
Valmar Rd CMBW SE5....142 D2
Val McKenzie Av HOLWY N7....85 G1
Valnay St TOOT SW17....178 E1
Valognes Av WALTH E17....51 G4
Valonia Gdns
 WAND/EARL SW18....159 J1
Vambery Rd
 WOOL/PLUM SE18....127 H6
Vanbrough Crs NTHLT UB5....95 G1
Vanbrugh Dr WOT/HER KT12....188 B4
Vanbrugh Flds BKHTH/KID SE3....125 J6

Vanbrugh Pk GNWCH SE10....125 J5
Vanbrugh Pk BKHTH/KID SE3....125 J1
Vanbrugh Park Rd
 BKHTH/KID SE3....145 J1
Vanbrugh Park Rd West
 BKHTH/KID SE3....145 J1
Vanbrugh Rd CHSWK W4....118 A3
Vanbrugh Ter BKHTH/KID SE3....145 K1
Vanburgh Cl CAN/RD E16....107 H4
 ORP BR6....201 K5
Vancouver Cl ORP BR6....217 G3
Vancouver Man EDGW HA8....44 D4
Vancouver Rd EDGW HA8....44 D4
 FSTH SE23....164 B4
 RCHPK/HAM TW10....156 C5
 YEAD UB4....95 F3
Vanderbilt Rd
 WAND/EARL SW18....160 B3
Vanderville Gdns EFNCH N2....47 C5
Vandome Cl CAN/RD E16....107 F5
Vandon St STJSPK SW1H....16 E4
Van Dyck Av NWMAL KT3....192 A4
Vandyke Cl PUT/ROE SW15....159 G1
Vandyke Cross ELTH/MOT SE9....146 D6
Vandy St SDTCH EC2A....7 G7
Vane Cl HAMP NW3....83 H3
 KTN/HRWW/WS HA3....62 B3
Vanessa Cl BELV DA17....129 H5
Vanessa Wy BXLY DA5....170 B5
Van Gogh Cl ISLW TW7....136 B4
Vanguard Cl CDALE/KGS NW9 *....45 E6
 CAN/RD E16....106 E4
 CROY/NA CRO....196 C5
 ROMW/RG RM7....56 D5
Vanguard St DEPT SE8....144 D2
Vanguard Wy CROY/NA CRO....212 B2
 WLGTN SM6....210 E5
Vanneck Sq PUT/ROE SW15 *....138 D6
Vanoc Gdns BMLY BR1....165 K6
Vansittart Rd FSTGT E7....88 C2
Vansittart St NWCR SE14....144 B1
Vanston Pl FUL/PGN SW6....139 K1
Vantage Pl KENS W8....119 K3
Vant Rd TOOT SW17....178 E1
Varcoe Rd BERM/RHTH SE16....123 J5
Vardens Rd BTSEA SW11....140 C5
Varden St WCHPL E1....104 D5
Vardon Cl ACT W3....99 F5
Varley Dr TWK TW1....136 C5
Varley Rd CAN/RD E16....107 F5
Varley Wy MTCM CR4....178 C5
Varna Rd FUL/PGN SW6....139 H1
 HPTN TW12....173 G4
Varndell St CAMTN NW1....4 A4
Varsity Dr TWK TW1....135 K5
Varsity Rw MORT/ESHN SW14....137 K3
Vartry Rd SEVS/STOTM N15....68 A3
Vassall Rd BRXN/ST SW9....142 B1
Vauban Br BERM/RHTH SE16....19 K5
Vauban St BERM/RHTH SE16....19 L5
Vaughan Av HDN NW4....63 H2
 HMSMTH W6....118 C4
Vaughan Est BETH E2 *....7 J4
Vaughan Gdns IL IG1....71 K4
Vaughan Rd CMBW SE5....142 D4
 HRW HA1....60 C4
 SRTFD E15....88 D4
 THDIT KT7....190 C4
 WELL DA16....148 A3
Vaughan St BERM/RHTH SE16....124 C2
Vaughan Wy WAP E1W....104 C6
Vaughan Williams Cl DEPT SE8....144 D1
Vauxhall Br VX/NE SW8....121 K5
Vauxhall Bridge Rd PIM SW1V....16 B7
Vauxhall Gdns SAND/SEL CR2....211 J6
Vauxhall Gv VX/NE SW8....122 A5
Vauxhall Pl DART DA1....171 H2
Vauxhall St LBTH SE11....122 A5
Vauxhall Wk LBTH SE11....122 A5
Vawdrey Cl WCHPL E1....104 E3
Veals Md MTCM CR4....178 D4
Vectis Gdns TOOT SW17....179 G2
Vectis Rd TOOT SW17....179 G2
Veda Rd LEW SE13....144 D5
Vega Crs NTHWD HA6....40 D1
Vega Rd BUSH WD23....28 C2
Veldene Wy RYLN/HDSTN HA2....77 K1
Vellum Dr CAR SM5....210 A1
Venables Cl DAGE RM10....92 D2
Venables St BAY/PAD W2....8 B1
Vencourt Pl HMSMTH W6....118 D5
Venetian Rd CMBW SE5....142 D3
Venetia Rd EA W5....116 E2
 FSBYPK N4....67 H3
Venner Rd SYD SE26....181 K2
Venners Cl BXLYHN DA7....150 B3
Venn St CLAP SW4....141 H5
Ventnor Av STAN HA7....43 H4
Ventnor Dr TRDG/WHET N20....33 F5
Ventnor Gdns BARK IG11....90 E5
Ventnor Rd BELMT SM2....209 F5
 NWCR SE14....144 A1
Ventnor Ter SEVS/STOTM N15 *....68 C1
Venture Cl BXLY DA5....169 F2
Venus Ms MTCM CR4....178 D6
Venus Rd WOOL/PLUM SE18....126 E3
Vera Av WCHMH N21....23 G6
Vera Ct OXHEY WD19....27 H2
Vera Lynn Cl FSTGT E7....88 E2
Vera Rd FUL/PGN SW6....139 H2
Verbena Cl CAN/RD E16....106 D3
Verbena Gdns HMSMTH W6....118 D5
Verdant La CAT SE6....165 H3
Verdayne Av CROY/NA CRO....198 A1
Verderers Rd CHIG IG7....55 G1
Verdun Rd BARN SW13....138 D1
 WOOL/PLUM SE18....128 D6
Vereker Rd WKENS W14....119 H5
Vere St CAVSQ/HST W1G....9 J4
Vermont Cl ENC/FH EN2....23 H5
Vermont Rd NRWD SE19....180 E2

SUT SM1 ....209 F1
WAND/EARL SW18 ....160 A1
Verney Gdns DAGW RM9 ....92 A2
Verney St BERM/RHTH SE16 ....123 J5
DAGW RM9 ....92 A3
Verney Wy WLSDN NW10 ....81 F1
Verney Wy BERM/RHTH SE16 ...123 J5
Vernham Rd
  WOOL/PLUM SE18 ....127 H6
Vernon Av MNPK E12 ....89 K2
  RYNPK SW20 ....177 G5
  WFD IG8 ....53 F3
Vernon Cl HOR/WEW KT19 ....206 E4
  STMC/STPC BR5 ....186 C6
  STWL/WRAY TW19 ....152 B3
Vernon Crs EBAR EN4 ....34 A1
Vernon Dr STAN HA7 ....43 G4
Vernon Pl FSBYW WC1X 11 F2
Vernon Ri FSBYW WC1X 11 G7
Vernon Rd BOW E3 ....105 H1
  CRW RM5 ....56 E1
  FELT TW13 ....153 J4
  GDMY/SEVK IG3 ....73 F5
  MORT/ESHN SW14 ....138 A4
  SRTFD E15 ....88 C5
  SUT SM1 ....209 G3
  WALTH E17 ....69 K1
  WAN E11 ....70 C5
Vernon Sq FSBYW WC1X 5 H4
Vernon St WKENS W14 ....119 H4
Vernon Yd NTGHL W11 ....100 D6
Veroan Rd BXLYHN DA7 ....149 F3
Verona Ct CHSWK W4 ....118 B5
Verona Dr SURB KT6 ....191 F6
Veronica Gdns
  STRHM/NOR SW16 ....179 H4
Veronica Rd TOOT SW17 ....161 G5
Verran Rd BAL SW12 * 161 G2
Versailles Rd PGE/AN SE20 ....181 H3
Verulam Av WALTH E17 ....69 H4
Verulam Ct CDALE/KGS NW9 * 63 J4
Verulam Rd GFD/PVL UB6 ....96 A3
Verulam St FSBYW WC1X 11 J1
Verwood Dr EBAR EN4 ....21 K4
Verwood Rd RYLN/HDSTN HA2 ....42 C5
Veryan Cl STMC/STPC BR5 ....202 D1
Vespan Rd SHB W12 ....118 D2
Vesta Rd BROCKY SE4 ....144 B3
Vestry Rd FSTH SE23 ....164 A3
Vestry Ms CMBW SE5 ....143 F2
Vestry Rd CMBW SE5 ....143 F2
  WALTH E17 ....69 K2
Vestry St IS N1 ....6 E3
Vevey St CAT SE6 ....164 C4
Viaduct Pl BETH E2 ....104 D2
Viaduct St BETH E2 ....104 D2
The Viaduct MUSWH N10 * 66 B1
  SWFD E18 ....52 E5
Vian St LEW SE13 ....144 E4
Vibart Gdns BRXS/STRHM SW2 ...162 A2
Vibart Wk IS N1 * 5 J1
Vibia Cl STWL/WRAY TW19 ....152 A2
Vicarage Cl ERITH DA8 ....129 K6
  NTHLT UB5 ....77 K1
  RSLP HA4 ....58 C4
  WPK KT4 ....192 D5
Vicarage Ct BECK BR3 * 182 B6
Vicarage Crs BTSEA SW11 ....140 C2
BECK BR3 ....182 D4
MORT/ESHN SW14 ....138 A6
Vicarage Dr BARK IG11 ....90 C5
Vicarage Farm Rd HEST TW5 .....134 D2
Vicarage Flds WOT/HER KT12 .....188 B3
Vicarage Gdns MTCM CR4 ....178 D6
Vicarage Ga KENS W8 ....120 A2
Vicarage Gv CMBW SE5 ....142 E2
Vicarage La EHAM E6 ....107 K2
  IL IG1 ....72 D5
  SRTFD E15 ....88 C4
Vicarage Pde
  SEVS/STOTM N15 * 67 J1
Vicarage Pk WOOL/PLUM SE18 ..127 H5
Vicarage Rd BXLY DA5 ....169 J3
  CROY/NA CR0 ....211 G1
  DAGE RM10 ....92 D5
  HCH RM12 ....75 J5
  HDN NW4 ....63 K2
  KUT/HW KT1 ....174 E5
  LEY E10 ....69 K4
  MORT/ESHN SW14 ....137 K6
  SRTFD E15 ....88 C4
  SUT SM1 ....208 E2
  TEDD TW11 ....174 B1
  TOTM N17 ....50 C3
  WATW WD18 ....26 E2
  WHTN TW2 ....155 H1
  WHTN TW2 ....155 K4
  WOOL/PLUM SE18 ....127 H5
Vicarage Wk BTSEA SW11 * 140 C2
Vicarage Wy RYLN/HDSTN HA2 ...60 A3
  WLSDN NW10 ....81 F2
Vicars Bridge Cl ALP/SUD HA0 ....98 A1
Vicar's Cl IS N1 ....6 A1
  HOM E9 ....86 E6
  SRTFD E15 ....88 E6
Vicars Hill LEW SE13 ....144 E5
Vicars Oak Rd NRWD SE19 ....181 F2
Vicar's Rd KTTN NW5 ....84 A3
Viceroy Cl EFNCH N2 * 65 J1
Viceroy Pde EFNCH N2 * 65 J1
Viceroy Rd VX/NE SW8 ....141 K2
Vickers Cl WLGTN SM6 ....211 F5
Vickers Rd ERITH DA8 ....130 A5
Victor Ap ALP/SUD HA0 ....80 A5
Victoria Av WESTW SW1E 15 J5
Victoria Av CRW RM5 ....56 D2
  E/WMO/HCT KT8 ....173 G6
  EHAM E6 ....89 H6
  FNCH N3 ....46 D4
  HSLW TW3 ....135 H4
  SURB KT6 ....190 E4

WBLY HA9 ....80 D4
WLGTN SM6 ....210 A1
Victoria Cl E/WMO/HCT KT8 .....173 F6
  EBAR EN4 ....21 H6
  HRW HA1 * 61 F3
  HYS/HAR UB3 ....94 B5
Victoria Cottages
  RCH/KEW TW9 ....137 G2
  WCHPL E1 * 104 C4
Victoria Crs NRWD SE19 ....181 F2
  SEVS/STOTM N15 ....68 A2
  WIM/MER SW19 * 177 J3
Victoria Dr WIM/MER SW19 ....159 G2
Victoria Emb TPL/STR WC2E 11 J6
  WHALL SW1A 17 F3
Victoria Embankment Gdns
  CHCR WC2N * 11 F7
Victoria Gdns HEST TW5 ....134 D2
  NTGHL W11 ....119 K1
Victoria Ga BAY/PAD W2 ....8 B1
Victoria Gv KENS W8 ....120 B3
  NFNCH/WDSPK N12 ....47 H1
Victoria Grove Ms
  BAY/PAD W2 * 101 F6
Victoria La BAR EN5 ....20 D5
  HYS/HAR UB3 ....113 G5
Victoria Ms KIL/WHAMP NW6 ....82 E6
  WAND/EARL SW18 ....160 B3
Victorian Gv STNW/STAM N16 ......86 A1
Victorian Rd STNW/STAM N16 ....86 A1
Victoria Pde RCH/KEW TW9 * 137 H2
Victoria Park Rd HOM E9 ....86 E6
Victoria Park Sq BETH E2 ....104 E2
Victoria Pk Studios HOM E9 * 86 E4
Victoria Pl RCH/KEW TW9 ....136 E6
Victoria Ri CLAP SW4 ....141 G4
Victoria Rd ACT W3 ....99 F4
  BARK IG11 ....90 B4
  BFN/LL DA15 ....168 A5
  BXLYHS DA6 ....39 H4
  BUSH WD23 ....28 B3
  BXLYHS DA6 ....149 H6
  CHING E4 ....38 C3
  CHST BR7 ....185 F1
  DAGE RM10 ....92 E4
  DART DA1 ....151 G6
  EA W5 ....97 H4
  EBAR EN4 ....21 H5
  ERITH DA8 ....130 B6
  FELT TW13 ....154 A4
  FSBYPK N4 ....67 F4
  HAYES BR2 ....200 C2
  HDN NW4 ....64 A1
  KENS W8 ....120 B3
  KIL/WHAMP NW6 ....100 D1
  KUT/HW KT1 ....175 G5
  MLHL NW7 ....45 H1
  MORT/ESHN SW14 ....138 A4
  MTCM CR4 ....178 D3
  NWDGN UB2 ....114 E3
  PLSTW E13 ....106 E1
  ROM RM1 ....75 H2
  RSLP HA4 ....58 E6
  SEVS/STOTM N15 * 68 B1
  SURB KT6 ....190 E3
  SUT SM1 ....209 H5
  SWFD E18 ....53 F6
  TEDD TW11 ....174 B1
  TWK TW1 ....156 C1
  UED N18 ....36 B3
  WALTH E17 ....51 J5
  WAN E11 ....70 B6
  WDGN N22 ....48 D4
Victoria Sq BGVA SW1W 15 K4
Victoria St BELV DA17 ....129 G4
  SRTFD E15 ....88 C5
  WESTW SW1E 15 J5
Victoria Ter EA W5 * 116 E1
  FSBYPK N4 ....67 H1
  HRW HA1 ....61 F4
Victoria Vls RCH/KEW TW9 ....137 G4
Victoria Yd WCHPL E1 * 104 C5
Victor Rd PGE/AN SE20 ....182 A3
  RYLN/HDSTN HA2 ....42 C5
  TEDD TW11 ....173 K1
  WLSDN NW10 ....99 K2
Victors Dr HPTN TW12 * 172 D2
Victors Wy BAR EN5 ....20 D4
Victory Av MRDN SM4 ....194 B2
Victory Pk WBLY HA9 * 79 K1
Victory Pl NRWD SE19 ....181 F2
  WALW SE17 ....18 E6
Victory Rd RAIN RM13 ....111 J1
  WAN E11 ....70 E1
  WIM/MER SW19 ....178 B3
Victory Road Ms
  WIM/MER SW19 ....178 B3
Victory Wy BERM/RHTH SE16 ....124 B2
  HEST TW5 ....114 B5
  ROMW/RG RM7 ....56 D5
Vienna Cl WFD IG8 ....52 B1
View Cl CHIG IG7 ....54 D1
  HGT N6 ....65 K4
  HRW HA1 ....60 D1
View Crs CEND/HSY/T N8 ....66 D2
Viewfield Cl
  KTN/HRWW/WS HA3 ....62 A4
Viewfield Rd BFN/LL DA15 ....168 D3
  WAND/EARL SW18 ....159 J1
Viewland
  WOOL/PLUM SE18 ....128 A5
View Rd HGT N6 ....65 K4
The View ABYW SE2 ....129 F5
Viga Rd WCHMH N21 ....35 G1
Vigilant Cl SYD SE26 ....163 H6
Vignoles Rd ROMW/RG RM7 ......74 C4
Vigo St CONDST W1S 10 B6
Viking Cl BOW E3 ....105 G1
Viking Gdns EHAM E6 ....107 J4
Viking Pl LEY E10 ....69 H6
Viking Wy ERITH DA8 ....130 C3

Villacourt Rd
  WOOL/PLUM SE18 ....148 B1
Village Ar CHING E4 ....38 B1
Village Cl CHING E4 ....38 B1
  HAMP NW3 * 83 H3
Village Green Rd DART DA1 ....150 B4
Village Ms CDALE/KGS NW9 * 63 F6
Village Park Cl EN EN1 ....35 K1
Village Rd EN EN1 ....35 K1
  FNCH N3 ....46 C5
Village Rw BELMT SM2 ....208 E5
The Village CHARL SE7 ....126 C6
Village Wy ASHF TW15 ....152 C6
  BARK/HLT IG6 ....54 D3
  BECK BR3 ....198 D1
  DUL SE21 ....162 E1
  PIN HA5 ....59 J4
  WLSDN NW10 ....81 F2
Village Wy East PIN HA5 ....59 H4
  RYLN/HDSTN HA2 ....60 A4
Villa Rd BRXN/ST SW9 ....142 B4
Villas Rd WOOL/PLUM SE18 ......127 H4
Villa St WALW SE17 ....122 E5
Villiers Av BRYLDS KT5 ....191 G2
  WHTN TW2 ....154 E3
Villiers Cl BRYLDS KT5 ....191 G1
  LEY E10 ....69 J6
Villiers Gv BELMT SM2 ....208 B6
Villiers Rd BECK BR3 ....182 A5
  CRICK NW2 ....81 J4
  ISLW TW7 ....135 K3
  KUT/HW KT1 ....175 G6
  OXHEY WD19 ....27 H2
  STHL UB1 ....114 E1
Villiers St CHCR WC2N 11 F7
Vincam Cl WHTN TW2 ....155 C2
Vincennes Est WNWD SE27 * 162 E6
Vincent Av BRYLDS KT5 ....191 J6
Vincent Cl BAR EN5 ....20 E4
  BARK/HLT IG6 ....54 D2
  BFN/LL DA15 ....167 K3
  ESH/CLAY KT10 ....204 B3
  HAYES BR2 ....200 A1
  WDR/YW UB7 ....112 D6
Vincent Gdns CRICK NW2 ....81 H1
Vincent Rd FSBYPK N4 * 68 C5
Vincent Rd ACT W3 ....117 K3
  ALP/SUD HA0 ....80 B5
  CHING E4 ....52 B2
  CROY/NA CR0 ....197 F4
  DACW RM9 ....92 A4
  HSLWW TW4 ....134 C4
  ISLW TW7 ....135 J2
  KUT/HW KT1 ....175 H6
  SEVS/STOTM N15 * 67 J1
  WDGN N22 ....49 G5
  WOOL/PLUM SE18 ....126 E4
Vincent Rw HPTN TW12 ....173 H2
Vincents Cl BERM/RHTH SE16 ...124 B2
Vincent Sq WDGN N22 * 49 G5
  WEST SW1P 16 C6
Vincent St CAN/RD E16 ....106 E4
  WEST SW1P 16 C6
Vincent Ter IS N1 ....6 A2
Vince Vls SEVS/STOTM N15 * 67 J1
Vine Cl BRYLDS KT5 ....191 G3
  SUT SM1 ....209 F2
  WDR/YW UB7 ....112 D4
Vine Cottages HNWL W7 * 115 K1
  WCHPL E1 * 104 E5
Vine Ct KTN/HRWW/WS HA3 ....62 A3
  WCHPL E1 * 104 C5
Vine Gdns IL IG1 ....90 C3
Vinegar Aly WALTH E17 ....51 K5
Vinegar Yd STHWK SE1 ....19 G2
Vine Hi CLKNW EC1R 5 J7
Vine La STHWK SE1 * 19 H1
Vine Pl HSLW TW3 ....135 G5
Vineries Cl WDR/YW UB7 ....112 D6
The Vineries CAT SE6 * 164 D3
  EN EN1 ....24 A4
  STHGT/OAK N14 ....34 C1
Vine Rd BARN SW13 ....138 C4
  E/WMO/HCT KT8 ....189 H1
  ORP BR6 ....217 F4
  SRTFD E15 ....88 D5
Vine Rw RCHPK/HAM TW10 * 137 F6
Viners Cl WOT/HER KT12 ....188 B5
Vines Av FNCH N3 ....47 F4
Vine Sq WKENS W14 * 119 J5
Vine St MYFR/PICC W1J 10 A6
  ROM RM7 ....74 E2
  TWRH EC3N 13 J4
Vine Street Br FARR EC1M 5 K7
Vine Yd STHWK SE1 ....18 D2
Vineyard Av MLHL NW7 ....46 C3
Vineyard Cl CAT SE6 ....164 D3
  KUT/HW KT1 ....175 G6
Vineyard Gv FNCH N3 ....47 F4
Vineyard Hill Rd
  WIM/MER SW19 ....159 K6
Vineyard Pth
  MORT/ESHN SW14 ....138 A4
Vineyard Rd FELT TW13 ....153 K5
Vineyard Rw KUT/HW KT1 ....174 D4
The Vineyard
  RCHPK/HAM TW10 ....136 E6

Violet Gdns CROY/NA CR0 ....211 H3
Violet Hl STJWD NW8 ....101 G1
Violet La SAND/SEL CR2 ....211 H5
Violet Rd BOW E3 ....105 K3
  SWFD E18 ....53 F6
  WALTH E17 ....69 J3
Violet St BETH E2 ....104 D3
Virgil St STHWK SE1 ....17 H4
Virginia Cl BRYLDS KT5 ....190 E4
  NWMAL KT3 ....191 K1
Virginia Gdns BARK/HLT IG6 ....54 D3
Virginia Rd BETH E2 ....7 J5
  THHTH CR7 ....180 D4
Virginia St WCHPL E1 * 104 C6
Viscount Cl FBAR/BDGN N11 ....48 B1
Viscount Dr EHAM E6 ....107 K4
Viscount Gv NTHLT UB5 ....95 H2
Viscount Rd
  STWL/WRAY TW19 ....152 A2
Viscount St BARB EC2Y 6 C7
Viscount Wy HTHAIR TW6 ....133 H5
Vista Av PEND EN3 ....25 F3
Vista Dr REDBR IG4 ....71 H2
The Vista CHING E4 ....38 A2
  ELTH/MOT SE9 ....166 D2
Vista Wy KTN/HRWW/WS HA3 ......62 A3
Viveash Cl HYS/HAR UB3 ....113 J3
Vivian Av HDN NW4 ....63 K2
  WBLY HA9 ....80 C4
Vivian Cl OXHEY WD19 ....26 E6
Vivian Gdns OXHEY WD19 ....26 E5
  WBLY HA9 ....80 C3
Vivian Rd BOW E3 ....105 G1
Vivian Sq PECK SE15 ....143 J4
Vivian Wy EFNCH N2 ....65 J2
Vivien Cl CHSGTN KT9 ....206 A5
Vivienne Cl TWK TW1 ....156 E1
Vixen Ms HACK E8 * 86 B6
Voce Rd WOOL/PLUM SE18 ....147 J1
Voewood Cl NWMAL KT3 ....192 C3
Voltaire Rd CLAP SW4 ....141 J4
Volt Av WLSDN NW10 ....99 G2
Volta Wy CROY/NA CR0 ....196 A5
Voluntary Pl WAN E11 ....70 E3
Vorley Rd ARCH N19 ....66 C6
Voss Ct STRHM/NOR SW16 ....179 K2
Voss St BETH E2 ....104 C2
Voyagers Cl THMD SE28 ....109 J5
Vulcan Cl EHAM E6 ....108 A5
Vulcan Ga ENC/FH EN2 ....23 G3
Vulcan Rd BROCKY SE4 ....144 C3
Vulcan Ter BROCKY SE4 ....144 C3
Vulcan Wy HOLWY N7 ....85 F4
  WLGTN SM6 ....210 F6
Vyner Rd ACT W3 ....99 F6
Vyner St BETH E2 ....104 D1
The Vyne BXLYHN DA7 ....149 J4
Vyse Cl BAR EN5 ....20 A5

W

Wadbrook St KUT/HW KT1 ....174 E5
Wadding St WALW SE17 ....18 E7
Waddington Cl EN EN1 ....24 A5
Waddington Rd SRTFD E15 ....88 B3
Waddington St SRTFD E15 ....88 B4
Waddington Wy NRWD SE19 ......180 D4
Waddon Cl CROY/NA CR0 ....211 G2
Waddon Court Rd
  CROY/NA CR0 ....211 G2
Waddon Marsh Wy
  CROY/NA CR0 ....196 A5
Waddon New Rd
  CROY/NA CR0 ....211 H1
Waddon Park Av
  CROY/NA CR0 ....211 G2
Waddon Rd CROY/NA CR0 ....211 G2
Waddon Wy CROY/NA CR0 ....211 G4
Wade Av STMC/STPC BR5 ....202 E4
Wade House STHWK SE1 * 123 H2
Wade Rd CAN/RD E16 ....107 G5
Wades Gv WCHMH N21 ....35 G1
Wade's Hl WCHMH N21 ....35 G1
Wade's La TEDD TW11 ....174 B1
Wadeson St BETH E2 ....104 D1
Wade's Pl POP/IOD E14 ....105 K6
Wadeville Av CHDH RM6 ....74 A3
Wadeville Cl BELV DA17 ....129 H5
Wadham Av WALTH E17 ....51 K3
Wadham Gdns GFD/PVL UB6 ....78 D4
  HAMP NW3 ....83 J6
Wadham Rd CHING E4 ....51 J3
  PUT/ROE SW15 ....139 H5
Wadhurst Cl PGE/AN SE20 ....181 J5
Wadhurst Rd CHSWK W4 ....118 A3
Wadley Rd WAN E11 ....70 C4
Wadsworth Cl GFD/PVL UB6 ....97 J1
  PEND EN3 ....25 F6
Wadsworth Rd GFD/PVL UB6 ....97 H1
Wager St BOW E3 ....105 H3
Waghorn Rd
  KTN/HRWW/WS HA3 ....43 K6
  PLSTW E13 ....89 G6
Waghorn St PECK SE15 ....143 H4
Wagner St PECK SE15 ....143 K1
Wagstaff Gdns DAGW RM9 ....91 J5
Wagtail Cl CDALE/KGS NW9 ....45 G5
  SL UB1 ....95 F5
Wagtail Wk BECK BR3 ....199 F2
Wagtail Wy STMC/STPC BR5 ......202 E1
Waid Cl DART DA1 ....171 J1
Waights Ct KUTN/CMB KT2 ....175 F4
Wainfleet Av CRW RM5 ....56 E5
Wainford Cl
  WIM/MER SW19 ....159 G3
Wainwright Gv ISLW TW7 ....135 J5
Waite Davies Rd
  LEE/GVPK SE12 ....165 J2
Waite St CMBW SE5 ....123 G6
Wakefield Gdns IL IG1 ....71 J3
  NRWD SE19 ....181 F3
Wakefield Ms STPAN WC1H * 5 F4
Wakefield Rd FBAR/BDGN N11 ....48 D1
  RCHPK/HAM TW10 ....136 E6

SEVS/STOTM N15 ....68 B2
Wakefield St EHAM E6 ....89 J6
  STPAN WC1H 5 F4
  UED N18 ....50 C1
Wakehams Hl PIN HA5 ....41 K6
Wakeham St IS N1 ....85 K4
Wakehurst Rd BTSEA SW11 ....140 E6
Wakeling La ALP/SUD HA0 ....79 H1
Wakeling Rd WEA W7 ....97 F4
Wakeling St WCHPL E1 * 105 G5
Wakelin Rd SRTFD E15 ....106 C1
Wakeman Rd WLSDN NW10 ....100 A3
Wakemans Hill Av
  CDALE/KGS NW9 ....63 F2
Wakering Rd BARK IG11 ....90 C5
Wakerly Cl EHAM E6 ....107 K5
Wakley St FSBYE EC1V 6 A4
Walberswick St VX/NE SW8 ....141 K1
Walbrook MANHO EC4N 12 E5
Walburgh St WCHPL E1 ....104 D5
Walcorde Av WALW SE17 ....18 D7
Walcot Rd PEND EN3 ....25 H3
Walcot Sq LBTH SE11 ....17 K6
Walcott St WEST SW1P 16 B7
Waldeck Gv WNWD SE27 * 16 F2
Waldeck Rd CHSWK W4 ....117 H6
  DART DA1 ....171 J2
  MORT/ESHN SW14 ....137 K4
  SEVS/STOTM N15 ....67 H1
  WEA W7 ....116 B2
Waldegrave Gdns TWK TW1 * 156 A5
Waldegrave Pk TWK TW1 ....156 A6
Waldegrave Rd BCTR RM8 ....73 J6
  BMLY BR1 ....200 D2
  CEND/HSY/T N8 * 49 G2
  EA W5 ....98 B6
  NRWD SE19 ....181 G3
  TWK TW1 ....156 A6
Waldegrove CROY/NA CR0 ....212 B1
Waldemar Av FUL/PGN SW6 ....139 H2
  WEA W7 ....116 B1
Waldemar Rd WIM/MER SW19 ...177 K1
Walden Av CHST BR7 ....166 E6
  PLMGR N13 ....35 J6
  RAIN RM13 ....93 H5
Walden Cl BELV DA17 ....129 G5
Walden Gdns THHTH CR7 ....196 A1
Waldenhurst Rd
  STMC/STPC BR5 ....202 E4
Walden Pde CHST BR7 * 184 E2
Walden Rd CHST BR7 ....184 E2
  TOTM N17 ....49 K4
Waldens Cl STMC/STPC BR5 .....202 E4
Waldenshaw Rd FSTH SE23 ....163 K3
Waldens Rd STMC/STPC BR5 ....203 F5
Walden St WCHPL E1 ....104 D5
Walden Wy BARK/HLT IG6 ....54 D3
  MLHL NW7 ....46 B2
The Waldrons CROY/NA CR0 ......211 J2
Waldron's Yd RYLN/HDSTN HA2 ..60 D6
Waldstock Rd THMD SE28 ....108 G6
Waleran Cl STAN HA7 ....43 F2
Walerand Rd LEW SE13 ....145 F3
Wales Av CAR SM5 ....209 K3
Wales Cl PECK SE15 ....143 J1
Wales Farm Rd ACT W3 ....99 F4
Waleton Acres WLGTN SM6 * 210 C4
Waley St WCHPL E1 * 105 F4
Walfield Av TRDG/WHET N20 ....33 F2
Walford Rd STNW/STAM N16 ....86 A2
Walfrey Gdns DAGW RM9 ....92 A5
Walham Green Ct
  FUL/PGN SW6 * 140 A1
Walham Gv FUL/PGN SW6 ....139 K1
Walham Ri WIM/MER SW19 ....177 H2
Walham Yd FUL/PGN SW6 * 139 K1
Walkden Rd CHST BR7 ....167 F6
Walker Cl DART DA1 ....150 E5
  EBED/NFELT TW14 ....153 J2
  FBAR/BDGN N11 ....34 C6
  HNWL W7 ....115 K1
  HPTN TW12 ....172 E2
  WOOL/PLUM SE18 ....127 H4
Walker's Ct SOHO/CST W1F 10 C5
Walkerscroft Md CAT SE6 ....164 E4
  DUL SE21 ....162 E5
Walker's Pl PUT/ROE SW15 ....139 H5
The Walks EFNCH N2 ....47 H6
The Walk PLMGR N13 * 35 G5
Wallace Cl THMD SE28 ....109 K6
Wallace Crs CAR SM5 ....209 K3
Wallace Rd IS N1 ....85 J4
Wallace Wy ARCH N19 * 66 D6
Wallbutton Rd BROCKY SE4 ....144 B3
Wallcote Av CRICK NW2 ....64 B5
Wall End Rd EHAM E6 ....90 A5
Wallenger Av GPK RM2 ....57 K6
Waller Dr NTHWD HA6 ....40 E5
Waller Rd NWCR SE14 ....144 A3
Wallers Cl DAGW RM9 ....92 A6
  WFD IG8 ....53 K2
Wallers Hoppit LOU IG10 ....39 J1
Wallflower St SHB W12 ....118 C6
Wallgrave Rd ECT SW5 ....120 A4
Wallhouse Rd ERITH DA8 ....151 F1
Wallingford Av NKENS W10 ....100 B4
Wallington Cl RSLP HA4 ....58 A3
Wallington Cnr WLGTN SM6 * 210 B2
Wallis Cl BTSEA SW11 ....140 C4
  EMPK RM11 ....75 K5
Wallis Rd HOM E9 ....87 H4
  STHL UB1 ....96 B6

Wallorton Gdns
MORT/ESHN SW14 138 A5
Wallside BARB EC2Y * 12 D2
Wall St IS N1 85 K4
Wallwood Rd WAN E11 70 B4
Wallwood St POP/IOD E14 105 H4
Walmar Cl EBAR EN4 21 H2
Walmer Cl CHING E4 37 K4
ORP BR6 216 D2
ROMW/RG RM7 56 D5
Walmer Gdns WEA W13 116 B2
Walmer Rd NTGHL W11 100 C6
Walmer Ter WOOL/PLUM SE18 127 H4
Walmgate Rd GFD/PVL UB6 79 H6
Walmington Fold
NFNCH/WDSPK N12 46 E2
Walm La CRICK NW2 82 B4
Walney Wk IS N1 * 85 J4
Walnut Av WDR/YW UB7 112 D3
Walnut Cl BARK/HLT IG6 72 D1
CAR SM5 209 K3
DEPT SE8 124 C6
HYS/HAR UB3 94 C6
Walnut Ct EA W5 * 117 F2
Walnut Gdns SRTFD E15 88 C3
Walnut Gv EN EN1 23 K6
Walnut Ms BELMT SM2 209 G5
Walnut Rd LEY E10 69 J6
Walnuts Rd ORP BR6 202 B5
Walnut Tree Av DART DA1 171 H4
MTCM CR4 * 178 D6
Walnut Tree Cl BARN SW13 138 C2
CHST BR7 185 H4
Walnut Tree Rd BCTR RM8 73 K6
BTFD TW8 117 F6
ERITH DA8 130 B5
GNWCH SE10 * 125 H5
HEST TW5 114 E6
Walnut Tree Wk LBTH SE11 17 J6
Walnut Wy BKHH IG9 39 H5
RSLP HA4 77 G4
Walpole Av RCH/KEW TW9 137 G3
Walpole Cl PIN HA5 42 A2
WEA W13 116 D2
Walpole Crs TEDD TW11 174 A1
Walpole Gdns CHSWK W4 117 K5
WHTN TW2 155 K4
Walpole Ms STJWD NW8 2 A1
Walpole Pl TEDD TW11 174 A1
Walpole Rd CROY/NA CR0 196 E6
EHAM E6 89 G5
HAYES BR2 200 C2
SURB KT6 191 F4
SWFD E18 52 D4
TEDD TW11 174 A1
TOTM N17 49 J5
WALTH E17 69 G1
WHTN TW2 155 K4
WIM/MER SW19 178 C2
Walpole St CHEL SW3 120 E5
Walrond Av WBLY HA9 80 A3
Walsham Cl STNW/STAM N16 68 C5
THMD SE28 109 K6
Walsham Rd
EBED/NFELT TW14 154 A2
NWCR SE14 144 A3
Walsingham Gdns
HOR/WEW KT19 207 G2
Walsingham Pk CHST BR7 185 J5
Walsingham Rd CLAP SW4 161 F1
CLPT E5 86 C1
ENC/FH EN2 23 K6
MTCM CR4 194 E2
STMC/STPC BR5 186 C4
WEA W13 * 116 B1
Walsingham Wk BELV DA17 129 H6
Walter Rodney Cl MNPK E12 89 K4
Walters Cl HYS/HAR UB3 113 J2
Walters Rd PEND EN3 24 E6
SNWD SE25 197 F1
Walter St BETH E2 105 F2
KUTN/CMB KT2 * 175 F4
Walters Wy FSTH SE23 164 A1
Walters Yd BMLY BR1 183 K5
Walter Ter WCHPL E1 105 F5
Walterton Rd MV/WKIL W9 100 D3
Walter Wk EDGW HA8 44 E2
Waltham Av CDALE/KGS NW9 62 C3
HYS/HAR UB3 113 F3
Waltham Cl DART DA1 170 D1
STMC/STPC BR5 202 E5
Waltham Dr EDGW HA8 44 C5
Waltham Pk WALTH E17 51 J3
Waltham Park Wy CHING E4 * 51 J3
Waltham Rd CAR SM5 194 C5
NWDGN UB2 114 D3
WFD IG8 53 J2
Walthamstow Av CHING E4 51 J3
Walthamstow Av (North
Circular) CHING E4 51 G1
Waltham Wy CHING E4 37 H5
Waltheof Av TOTM N17 49 K4
Waltheof Gdns TOTM N17 49 K4
Walton Av CHEAM SM3 208 D1
NWMAL KT3 192 C1
RYLN/HDSTN HA2 77 K3
WBLY HA9 80 D1
Walton Cl CRICK NW2 63 K6
HRW HA1 60 D1
VX/NE SW8 141 K1
Walton Dr HRW HA1 60 D1
WLSDN NW10 81 F4
Walton Gdns ACT W3 98 D4
FELT TW13 153 J6
WBLY HA9 62 A6
Walton Gn CROY/NA CR0 213 K6
Walton Pk WOT/HER KT12 188 C6
Walton Park La
WOT/HER KT12 188 D6
Walton Pl CHEL SW3 14 E4
Walton Rd CRW RM5 56 B3
HRW HA1 60 D1
MNPK E12 90 A2
PLSTW E13 107 G1
SCUP DA14 168 C5
SEVS/STOTM N15 * 68 B1
WOT/HER KT12 188 C2
Walton St CHEL SW3 14 D6
ENC/FH EN2 23 K2
Walton Vls IS N1 * 86 A5
Walton Wy ACT W3 98 D4
MTCM CR4 195 H1
Walt Whitman Cl HNHL SE24 * 142 C5
Walverns Cl OXHEY WD19 27 G1
Walworth Pl WALW SE17 122 D5
Walworth Rd STHWK SE1 18 C6
Walwyn Av BMLY BR1 200 C1
Wanborough Dr
PUT/ROE SW15 158 E3
Wanderer Dr BARK IG11 109 J2
Wandle Bank CROY/NA CR0 210 E1
WIM/MER SW19 178 C2
Wandle Ct HOR/WEW KT19 206 E2
Wandle Court Gdns
CROY/NA CR0 210 E1
Wandle Rd CROY/NA CR0 210 E1
CROY/NA CR0 211 J1
MRDN SM4 194 C2
TOOT SW17 160 D4
WLGTN SM6 195 G6
Wandle Side CROY/NA CR0 211 F1
WLGTN SM6 210 B1
Wandle Wy MTCM CR4 194 E2
WAND/EARL SW18 160 A3
Wandsworth Br
WAND/EARL SW18 140 B4
Wandsworth Bridge Rd
FUL/PGN SW6 140 A2
Wandsworth Common West
Side WAND/EARL SW18 140 B6
Wandsworth High St
WAND/EARL SW18 139 K6
Wandsworth Rd VX/NE SW8 141 G4
Wangey Rd CHDH RM6 73 K4
Wanless Rd HNHL SE24 142 D4
Wanley Rd CMBW SE5 142 E5
Wanlip Rd PLSTW E13 107 F3
Wannock Gdns BARK/HLT IG6 54 B3
Wansbeck Rd HOM E9 87 H5
Wansdown Pl FUL/PGN SW6 140 A1
Wansey St WALW SE17 18 D7
Wansford Rd WFD IG8 53 G4
Wanstead Cl BMLY BR1 184 B5
Wanstead La IL IG1 71 J3
Wanstead Park Av MNPK E12 71 H6
Wanstead Park Rd IL IG1 71 J5
Wanstead Pl WAN E11 70 E3
Wanstead Rd BMLY BR1 184 B5
Wansunt Rd BXLY DA5 169 K3
Wantage Rd LEE/GVPK SE12 145 J6
Wantz La RAIN RM13 111 K3
Wantz Rd DAGE RM10 92 D2
Wapping Dock St WAP E1W * 123 J1
Wapping High St WAP E1W 123 H1
Wapping La WAP E1W 104 D6
Wapping Wall WAP E1W 123 K1
Warbank La KUTN/CMB KT2 176 C3
Warbeck Rd SHB W12 118 E1
Warberry Rd WDGN N22 49 F5
Warboys Ap KUTN/CMB KT2 175 J2
Warboys Crs CHING E4 52 A1
Warboys Rd KUTN/CMB KT2 175 J2
Warburton Cl IS N1 86 A4
KTN/HRWW/WS HA3 42 D2
Warburton Rd HACK E8 86 D6
WHTN TW2 155 G3
Warburton St HACK E8 86 D6
Warburton Ter WALTH E17 51 K5
Wardalls Gv NWCR SE14 * 143 K1
Ward Cl ERITH DA8 130 A6
SAND/SEL CR2 212 A3
Wardell Cl EDGW HA8 45 G3
Warden Av CRW RM5 56 E1
RYLN/HDSTN HA2 59 J5
Warden Rd KTTN NW5 84 A4
Wardens Gv STHWK SE1 18 C1
Wardle St HOM E9 87 F3
Wardley St WAND/EARL SW18 160 A2
Wardo Av FUL/PGN SW6 139 H2
Wardour Ms SOHO/CST W1F 10 B4
Wardour St SOHO/CST W1F 10 B3
Ward Rd ARCH N19 84 C2
SRTFD E15 * 88 B6
Wardrobe Pl BLKFR EC4V * 12 B4
The Wardrobe
RCH/KEW TW9 * 136 E6
Wards Rd GNTH/NBYPK IG2 72 D4
Wards Wharf Ap CAN/RD E16 126 C2
Wareham Cl HSLW TW3 135 G5
Waremead Rd
GNTH/NBYPK IG2 72 B2
Warepoint Dr THMD SE28 127 J2
Warfield Rd
EBED/NFELT TW14 153 H2
HPTN TW12 173 G4
WLSDN NW10 100 B2
Warfield Yd WLSDN NW10 * 100 B2
Wargrave Av SEVS/STOTM N15 68 B3
Wargrave Rd RYLN/HDSTN HA2 78 C1
Warham Rd FSBYPK N4 67 G2
KTN/HRWW/WS HA3 43 F6
SAND/SEL CR2 211 J3
Warham St CMBW SE5 142 C1
Waring Cl ORP BR6 217 F4
Waring Dr ORP BR6 217 F4
Waring Rd SCUP DA14 186 D2
Waring St WNWD SE27 162 D6
Warkworth Gdns ISLW TW7 136 B1
Warkworth Rd TOTM N17 49 K3
Warland Rd WOOL/PLUM SE18 147 J1
Warley Av BCTR RM8 74 B4
YEAD UB4 94 E4
Warley Rd CLAY IG5 54 A4
ED N9 36 E4
WFD IG8 53 F3
YEAD UB4 94 E5
Warley St BETH E2 105 F2
Warlingham Rd THHTH CR7 196 C1
Warlock Rd MV/WKIL W9 100 D3
Warlters Cl HOLWY N7 * 84 E2
Warlters Rd HOLWY N7 84 E2
Warltersville Rd ARCH N19 66 E4
Warming Cl CLPT E5 * 87 F1
Warmington Rd HNHL SE24 162 D1
Warmington St PLSTW E13 106 E3
Warminster Rd SNWD SE25 181 H5
Warminster Sq SNWD SE25 181 H5
Warminster Wy MTCM CR4 179 G4
Warmwell Av CDALE/KGS NW9 45 G4
Warndon St BERM/RHTH SE16 123 K4
Warneford Pl OXHEY WD19 27 J1
Warneford Rd
KTN/HRWW/WS HA3 43 K6
Warneford St HOM E9 86 D6
Warne Pl BFN/LL DA15 168 C1
Warner Av CHEAM SM3 193 H6
Warner Cl CDALE/KGS NW9 63 H4
HPTN TW12 172 E1
HYS/HAR UB3 133 G1
SRTFD E15 88 C3
Warner Pl BETH E2 104 C1
Warner Rd BMLY BR1 183 J3
CEND/HSY/T N8 66 D1
CMBW SE5 142 D2
WALTH E17 69 G1
Warner St CLKNW EC1R 5 J7
Warner Ter POP/IOD E14 * 105 J4
Warner Yd CLKNW EC1R 5 J7
Warnford Rd ORP BR6 217 F3
Warnham Court Rd CAR SM5 209 K5
Warnham Rd
NFNCH/WDSPK N12 47 J1
Warple Ms ACT W3 * 118 B2
Warple Wy ACT W3 118 B2
Warren Av BMLY BR1 183 H3
ORP BR6 217 F3
RCHPK/HAM TW10 137 J5
SAND/SEL CR2 213 F5
WAN E11 * 88 B1
Warren Cl BXLYHS DA6 149 H6
ED N9 37 F2
ESH/CLAY KT10 204 C2
WBLY HA9 61 K6
YEAD UB4 95 G4
Warren Ct CHARL SE7 126 B5
Warren Crs ED N9 36 B2
Warren Cutting
KUTN/CMB KT2 176 A3
Warrender Rd ARCH N19 84 C1
Warrender Wy RSLP HA4 58 E4
Warren Dr GFD/PVL UB6 96 B3
HCH RM12 93 J1
ORP BR6 217 H3
RSLP HA4 59 H4
Warren Dr North BRYLDS KT5 191 J5
Warren Dr South BRYLDS KT5 191 K5
The Warren Dr WAN E11 71 G4
Warren Flds STAN HA7 * 29 J6
Warren Gdns ORP BR6 217 G3
Warren La STAN HA7 29 G4
WOOL/PLUM SE18 127 G3
Warren Ms FITZ W1T 4 A7
Warren Pk KUTN/CMB KT2 175 K2
Warren Park Rd SUT SM1 209 H4
Warren Pond Rd CHING E4 38 D3
Warren Ri KUTN/CMB KT2 176 A4
Warren Rd BARK/HLT IG6 72 D2
BUSH WD23 28 C3
BXLYHS DA6 149 H6
CHING E4 38 A4
CRICK NW2 63 H6
CROY/NA CR0 197 F5
DART DA1 171 H5
HAYES BR2 199 K6
KUTN/CMB KT2 176 A3
LEY E10 88 A1
ORP BR6 217 F3
SCUP DA14 168 D5
WAN E11 71 G3
WHTN TW2 155 J1
WIM/MER SW19 178 D2
Warrens Shawe La EDGW HA8 30 D4
Warren St FITZ W1T 4 A7
The Warren BELMT SM2 209 H6
HEST TW5 134 E1
MNPK E12 89 J2
WPK KT4 207 F2
YEAD UB4 94 E5
Warren Wy MLHL NW7 46 C2
Warren Wood Cl HAYES BR2 199 K6
Warriner Dr ED N9 36 C5
Warriner Gdns BTSEA SW11 140 E2
Warrington Crs MV/WKIL W9 101 G3
Warrington Gdns
MV/WKIL W9 101 G3
Warrington Pl POP/IOD E14 * 125 F1
Warrington Rd BCTR RM8 73 K6
CROY/NA CR0 211 H1
HRW HA1 60 E2
RCHPK/HAM TW10 136 E6
Warrington Sq BCTR RM8 73 K6
Warrior Sq MNPK E12 90 A2
Warsaw Cl RSLP HA4 77 F4
Warspite Rd
WOOL/PLUM SE18 126 D3
Warton Rd SRTFD E15 88 A6
Warwall EHAM E6 108 B5
Warwick Av EDGW HA8 30 D5
MV/WKIL W9 101 G4
RYLN/HDSTN HA2 77 K2
Warwick Chambers
KENS W8 * 119 K3
Warwick Cl BUSH WD23 28 E2
BXLY DA5 169 H2
EBAR EN4 21 H6
HPTN TW12 173 H3
ORP BR6 217 G1
Warwick Ct HHOL WC1V 11 H2
SURB KT6 191 F6
Warwick Crs BAY/PAD W2 101 G4
YEAD UB4 94 D3
Warwick Dene EA W5 117 F1
Warwick Dr PUT/ROE SW15 138 E5
Warwick Gdns FSBYPK N4 67 J2
IL IG1 72 B5
THDIT KT7 189 K2
THHTH CR7 * 196 B1
WKENS W14 119 J3
Warwick Gv BRYLDS KT5 191 G4
CLPT E5 68 D5
Warwick House St STJS SW1Y 10 C7
Warwick La STP EC4M 12 B4
Warwick Pde
KTN/HRWW/WS HA3 * 43 H5
Warwick Pl EA W5 116 E2
MV/WKIL W9 101 G4
THDIT KT7 * 190 B3
Warwick Pl North PIM SW1V * 16 A7
Warwick Rd BAR EN5 21 F5
CHING E4 51 J1
EA W5 117 F1
FBAR/BDGN N11 48 D2
HSLWW TW4 134 A4
KUT/HW KT1 174 D4
MNPK E12 89 J3
NWDGN UB2 114 E3
NWMAL KT3 175 K6
PGE/AN SE20 181 J6
SCUP DA14 186 C1
SRTFD E15 88 D4
SUT SM1 209 G3
THDIT KT7 190 A2
THHTH CR7 180 B6
UED N18 36 B6
WALTH E17 51 H4
WAN E11 71 F2
WDR/YW UB7 112 B1
WELL DA16 148 D4
WHTN TW2 155 K3
WKENS W14 119 J4
Warwick Rw WESTW SW1E 16 A4
Warwickshire Pth DEPT SE8 144 C1
Warwick Sq PIM SW1V 16 A7
STP EC4M * 12 B3
Warwick Square Ms PIM SW1V 16 A7
Warwick St REGST W1B 10 B5
Warwick Ter WALTH E17 * 70 B2
WOOL/PLUM SE18 127 J6
Warwick Wy DART DA1 171 H4
PIM SW1V 121 G5
Warwick Yd STLK EC1Y * 6 D7
Washington Av MNPK E12 89 J3
Washington Cl BOW E3 105 K2
Washington Rd BARN SW13 138 D1
EHAM E6 89 G5
KUT/HW KT1 175 H5
SWFD E18 52 D5
WPK KT4 192 E6
Wastdale Rd FSTH SE23 164 A3
Watchfield Ct CHSWK W4 * 117 K5
The Watch
NFNCH/WDSPK N12 * 33 G6
Watcombe Rd SNWD SE25 197 J2
Waterbank Rd CAT SE6 164 E5
Waterbeach Rd DAGW RM9 91 J4
Water Brook La HDN NW4 64 A2
Watercress Pl IS N1 86 A5
Waterdale Rd ABYW SE2 128 B6
Waterden Crs SRTFD E15 87 J3
Waterden Rd SRTFD E15 87 J3
Waterer Ri WLGTN SM6 210 D4
Waterfall Cottages
WIM/MER SW19 178 C2
Waterfall Rd FBAR/BDGN N11 34 B6
WIM/MER SW19 178 C2
Waterfall Ter TOOT SW17 178 D2
Waterfield Cl BELV DA17 129 H3
THMD SE28 128 C1
Waterfield Cottages
MORT/ESHN SW14 * 137 J5
Waterfield Gdns SNWD SE25 197 F1
Waterford Rd FUL/PGN SW6 140 A2
Waterford Wy WLSDN NW10 81 K3
The Waterfront BORE WD6 * 29 H1
Water Gdns STAN HA7 43 H2
The Water Gdns BAY/PAD W2 8 C3
Watergate EMB EC4Y 12 A5
Watergate St DEPT SE8 124 D6
The Watergate OXHEY WD19 27 H4
Waterhall Av CHING E4 38 C6
Waterhall Cl WALTH E17 51 F4
Waterhead Cl ERITH DA8 150 B1
Waterhouse Cl HAMP NW3 83 H3
Wateridge Cl POP/IOD E14 124 D3
Wateringbury Cl
STMC/STPC BR5 186 C6
Water La CAMTN NW1 84 B5
ED N9 36 D3
GDMY/SEVK IG3 91 F1
KUT/HW KT1 174 E4
MON EC3R 13 H6
NWCR SE14 143 K1
PUR RM19 131 K4
SCUP DA14 169 G5
SRTFD E15 88 C4
TWK TW1 156 B3
Water Lily Cl NWDGN UB2 115 H2
Waterloo Br STHWK SE1 11 H6
Waterloo Cl EBED/NFELT TW14 153 J3
HOM E9 86 E3
Waterloo Gdns BETH E2 104 E1
ROMW/RG RM7 75 F3
Waterloo Pl CAR SM5 * 209 K1
RCH/KEW TW9 117 H6
STJS SW1Y 10 C7
Waterloo Rd BARK/HLT IG6 54 C5
CRICK NW2 63 J6
EHAM E6 89 G5
FSTGT E7 88 D3
LEY E10 69 J4
ROMW/RG RM7 75 F2
STHWK SE1 17 J1
SUT SM1 209 H3
Waterloo Ter IS N1 85 H5
Waterlow Rd ARCH N19 66 C5
Waterman Cl OXHEY WD19 27 F1
Watermans Cl
KUTN/CMB KT2 * 175 F3
Watermans Ms EA W5 * 98 A6
Waterman Sq PGE/AN SE20 181 K3
Waterman St PUT/ROE SW15 139 G4
Waterman Wy WAP E1W 123 J1
Watermead
EBED/NFELT TW14 153 H3
Watermead La CAR SM5 194 E3
Watermeadow Cl ERITH DA8 150 E1
Watermeadow La
FUL/PGN SW6 140 B3
Watermead Rd CAT SE6 165 F6
Watermead Wy TOTM N17 50 E3
Watermens Sq PGE/AN SE20 * 181 K3
Water Ms PECK SE15 143 K5
Watermill Cl
RCHPK/HAM TW10 156 D5
Watermill La UED N18 50 A1
Water Mill Wy FELT TW13 154 E4
Watermill Wy WIM/MER SW19 178 B4
Watermint Cl STMC/STPC BR5 202 E1
Watermint Quay CLPT E5 68 C4
Water Rd ALP/SUD HA0 80 B6
Water's Edge FUL/PGN SW6 * 139 G2
Watersedge HOR/WEW KT19 206 E2
Watersfield Wy EDGW HA8 43 K3
Waterside DART DA1 150 B6
WALTH E17 68 E3
Waterside Av BECK BR3 198 E2
Waterside Cl BARK IG11 91 G2
BERM/RHTH SE16 123 H2
BOW E3 87 H6
NTHLT UB5 95 K2
SURB KT6 191 F6
THMD SE28 128 A1
Waterside Ct LEW SE13 * 145 G5
Waterside Dr WOT/HER KT12 188 A2
Waterside Rd NWDGN UB2 115 F3
Waterside Wy TOOT SW17 160 B6
Watersmeet Wy THMD SE28 109 K5
Waterson St BETH E2 7 J4
Watersplash Cl KUT/HW KT1 175 F6
Watersplash La HEST TW5 114 A5
HYS/HAR UB3 113 K4
Waters Rd CAT SE6 165 H5
KUT/HW KT1 175 J5
Waters Sq KUT/HW KT1 175 J6
Water St TPL/STR WC2R 11 J5
Water Tower Hl CROY/NA CR0 211 K2
Water Tower Pl IS N1 5 K1
Waterworks La CLPT E5 69 F6
Waterworks Rd
BRXS/STRHM SW2 161 K1
Watery La HYS/HAR UB3 113 G5
NTHLT UB5 95 G1
RYNPK SW20 177 J5
STMC/STPC BR5 186 C2
Wates Wy MTCM CR4 194 E3
Wateville Rd TOTM N17 49 J4
Watford Cl BTSEA SW11 140 D2
Watford Heath OXHEY WD19 27 H2
Watford Heath Farm
OXHEY WD19 * 27 H2
Watford Rd BORE WD6 29 J1
CAN/RD E16 106 E4
HRW HA1 79 G1
NTHWD HA6 40 E2
Watford Wy HDN NW4 63 J1
MLHL NW7 31 F6
Watford Wy (Barnet By-Pass)
MLHL NW7 45 G1
Watkin Rd WBLY HA9 80 D1
Watkinson Rd HOLWY N7 85 F4
Watling Av EDGW HA8 44 E4
Watling Ct STP EC4M 12 D4
Watlings Cl CROY/NA CR0 198 B3
Watling St BXLYHS DA6 149 K6
PECK SE15 123 F6
STP EC4M 12 C4
Watlington Gv SYD SE26 182 B1
Watney Market WCHPL E1 104 D5
Watney Rd MORT/ESHN SW14 137 K4
Watneys Rd CROY/NA CR0 195 J2
Watney St WCHPL E1 104 D5
Watson Av CHEAM SM3 193 H6
EHAM E6 90 A5
Watson Cl STNW/STAM N16 85 K3
WIM/MER SW19 178 D2
Watson's Ms CAMTN NW1 8 D2
Watsons Rd WDGN N22 49 F5
Watson's St DEPT SE8 144 D1
Wattisfield Rd CLPT E5 86 E1
Watts Cl SEVS/STOTM N15 68 A2
Wattsdown Cl PLSTW E13 88 E6
Watts Gv BOW E3 105 J4
Watt's La CHST BR7 185 G4
TEDD TW11 174 B1
Watts Rd THDIT KT7 190 B4
Watts St PECK SE15 143 G2
WAP E1W 123 J1
Wat Tyler Rd GNWCH SE10 145 F3
Wauthier Cl PLMGR N13 49 H1
Wavell Dr BFN/LL DA15 167 K1
Wavel Ms KIL/WHAMP NW6 83 F5
Wavel Pl SYD SE26 163 G6
Wavendon Av CHSWK W4 118 A5
Waveney Av PECK SE15 143 J5
Waveney Cl WAP E1W 123 H1
Waverley Av BRYLDS KT5 191 J3
CHING E4 37 H6
SUT SM1 194 A6
WALTH E17 52 B6
WBLY HA9 80 B3
WHTN TW2 154 E3
Waverley Cl E/WMO/HCT KT8 189 F2
HAYES BR2 200 C2
HYS/HAR UB3 113 G4
Waverley Crs
WOOL/PLUM SE18 127 J6
Waverley Gdns BARK IG11 108 E1
BARK/HLT IG6 54 C5
EHAM E6 107 J4
NTHWD HA6 40 E4
Waverley Gv FNCH N3 46 B6
Waverley Pl FSBYPK N4 * 67 H5
STJWD NW8 2 A2
Waverley Rd CEND/HSY/T N8 66 D3
ENC/FH EN2 23 H5
EW KT17 207 K3
RAIN RM13 111 K2
RYLN/HDSTN HA2 59 J4
SNWD SE25 197 J1
STHL UB1 96 A6
SWFD E18 53 G4
TOTM N17 50 D3
WALTH E17 52 A6
WOOL/PLUM SE18 127 H5
Waverley Wy CAR SM5 209 J4

Waverton Rd
WAND/EARL SW18 ....160 B2
Waverton St *MYFR/PICC* W1J 9 J7
Wavertree Rd
BRXS/STRHM SW2 ....162 A3
SWFD E18 ....52 E5
Waxlow Crs *STHL* UB1 ....96 A5
Waxlow Rd *WLSDN* NW10 ....98 D1
Waxlow Wy *NTHLT* UB5 ....95 K3
Waxwell La *PIN* HA5 ....41 H6
Wayborne Gv *RSLP* HA4 ....58 A3
Waye Av *HEST* TW5 ....133 K2
Wayfarer Rd *NTHLT* UB5 ....95 H3
Wayford St *BTSEA* SW11 ....140 D3
Wayland Av *HACK* E8 ....86 C3
Waylands *HYS/HAR* UB3 ....94 B4
Waylett Pl *ALP/SUD* HA0 * 79 K2
WNWD SE27 ....162 C5
Wayne Cl *ORP* BR6 ....217 F1
Wayneflete Tower Av
ESH/CLAY KT10 ....204 A1
Wayside Av *CROY/NA* CR0 ....211 H1
Wayneflete Sq *NKENS* W10 ....100 B6
Wayneflete St
WAND/EARL SW18 ....160 B2
Wayside *CROY/NA* CR0 * 213 K4
GLDGN NW11 * 64 C5
MORT/ESHN SW14 ....137 K5
Wayside Av *MUSWH* W23 ....28 D1
Wayside Cl *ROM* RM1 ....57 H6
STHGT/OAK N14 ....34 C1
Wayside Ct *TWK* TW1 ....156 D1
Wayside Gdns *DAGE* RM10 ....92 C3
Wayside Gv *ELTH/MOT* SE9 ....166 E6
Wayside Ms *GNTH/NBYPK* IG2 ....72 A3
Weald Cl *BERM/RHTH* SE16 ....123 J5
HAYES BR2 ....200 D6
Weald La *KTN/HRWW/WS* HA3 ....42 D5
Weald Ri *KTN/HRWW/WS* HA3 ....43 F3
Weald Sq *CLPT* E5 * 68 D6
Wealdstone Rd *CHEAM* SM3 ....193 J6
The Weald *CHST* BR7 ....184 C2
Weald Wy *ROMW/RG* RM7 ....74 D4
YEAD UB4 ....94 C2
Wealdwood Gdns *PIN* HA5 ....42 B2
Weale Rd *CHING* E4 ....38 B5
Wealdon Gdns *ENC/FH* EN2 ....23 K2
Weardale Rd *LEW* SE13 ....145 G5
Wear Pl *BETH* E2 ....104 D2
Wearside Rd *LEW* SE13 ....144 E5
Weatherley Cl *BOW* E3 ....105 H4
Weaver Cl *CROY/NA* CR0 ....212 B2
EHAM E6 ....108 B6
Weavers Cl *ISLW* TW7 ....135 K5
Weavers La *STHWK* SE1 ....19 H1
Weavers Ter *FUL/PGN* SW6 *..119 K6
Weavers St *NKENS* W10 ....104 C3
Weavers Wy *CAMTN* NW1 ....84 C6
Weaver Wk *WNWD* SE27 ....162 C6
Webb Cl *NKENS* W10 ....100 A3
Webber Cl *BORE* WD6 ....29 K1
ERITH DA8 ....150 E1
Webber Rw *STHWK* SE1 ....17 J3
Webber St *STHWK* SE1 ....17 K2
Webb Est *CLPT* E5 * 68 C4
Webb Pl *WLSDN* NW10 ....99 H2
Webb Rd *BKHTH/KID* SE3 ....125 J6
Webbscroft Rd *DAGE* RM10 ....92 D2
Webb's Rd *BTSEA* SW11 ....140 E6
YEAD UB4 ....94 E2
Webb St *STHWK* SE1 ....19 G5
Webster Gdns *EA* W5 ....116 E1
Webster Rd *BERM/RHTH* SE16 ..123 H3
WAN E11 ....88 A1
Wedderburn Rd *BARK* IG11 ....90 E6
HAMP NW3 ....83 H3
Wedgewood Cl *NTHWD* HA6 * 40 A3
Wedgwood Wk
KIL/WHAMP NW6 * 83 F3
Wedgewood Wy *NRWD* SE19 ..180 D3
Wedlake St *NKENS* W10 ....100 C3
Wedmore Av *CLAY* IG5 ....54 A4
Wedmore Gdns *ARCH* N19 ....66 E6
Wedmore Ms *ARCH* N19 ....84 D1
Wedmore Rd *GFD/PVL* UB6 ....96 D2
Wedmore St *ARCH* N19 ....84 D1
Weech Rd *KIL/WHAMP* NW6 ....82 E2
Weedington Rd *KTTN* NW5 ....84 A3
Weekley Sq *BTSEA* SW11 * 140 C4
Weigall Rd *LEE/GVPK* SE12 ....145 K5
Weighhouse St *MYFR/PKLN* W1K ..9 H4
Weighton Rd
KTN/HRWW/WS HA3 ....42 D4
PGE/AN SE20 ....181 J5
Weimar St *PUT/ROE* SW15 ....139 H4
Weirdale Av *TRDG/WHET* N20 ..33 K4
Weir Hall Av *UED* N18 ....49 K2
Weir Hall Gdns *UED* N18 ....49 K1
Weir Hall Rd *UED* N18 ....49 K2
Weir Rd *BAL* SW12 ....161 H3
BXLY DA5 ....169 J2
WIM/MER SW19 ....160 A6
Weirside Gdns *WDR/YW* UB7 ..112 A1
Weirs Pas *CAMTN* NW1 ....4 D4
Weiss Rd *PUT/ROE* SW15 ....139 G4
Welbeck Av *BFN/LL* DA15 ....168 B3
BMLY BR1 ....165 K6
YEAD UB4 ....95 F3
Welbeck Cl *EW* KT17 ....207 J5
NWMAL KT3 ....192 C2
Welbeck Rd *EBAR* EN4 ....33 H1
EHAM E6 ....107 H2
RYLN/HDSTN HA2 ....60 B5
SUT SM1 ....194 B6
Welbeck St *CAVSQ/HST* W1G 9 J3
Welbeck Vls *WCHMH* N21 * 35 J3
Welbeck Wy *CAVSQ/HST* W1G 9 J3
Welby St *PLSTW* E13 ....107 G3
Welch Pl *PIN* HA5 ....41 G4
Weldon Cl *RSLP* HA4 ....77 F4
Weldon Dr *E/WMO/HCT* KT8 ..188 E1
Well Pl *FBAR/BDGN* N11 ....48 B1
Welfare Rd *SRTFD* E15 ....88 D6
Welford Cl *CLPT* E5 * 87 F1
Welford Pl *WIM/MER* SW19 ..159 H6

Welham Rd *TOOT* SW17 ....179 F1
Welhouse Rd *CAR* SM5 ....194 D6
Wellacre Rd
KTN/HRWW/WS HA3 ....61 H5
Wellan Cl *BFN/LL* DA15 ....148 C6
Welland Gdns *GFD/PVL* UB6 ..97 F1
Welland Ms *WAP* E1W 123 H1
Wellands Cl *BMLY* BR1 ....184 E5
Welland St *GNWCH* SE10 ....125 F6
Well Ap *BAR* EN5 ....20 A6
Wellbrook Rd *ORP* BR6 ....216 A2
Wellby Cl *ED* N9 ....36 D5
Well Cl *RSLP* HA4 ....77 J1
STRHM/NOR SW16 ....162 A6
Well Ct *STP* EC4M 12 D4
Wellclose Sq *WCHPL* E1 ....104 C6
Wellclose St *WCHPL* E1 ....104 C6
Well Cottage Cl *WAN* E11 ....71 G4
Well Ct *STP* EC4M 12 D4
Welldon Crs *HRW* HA1 ....60 E3
Weller St *STHWK* SE1 ....18 C2
Wellesley Av *HMSMTH* W6 ....118 E3
NTHWD HA6 ....40 C1
Wellesley Cl *CHARL* SE7 * 126 B5
Wellesley Ct *MV/WKIL* W9 ....101 G2
Wellesley Court Rd
CROY/NA CR0 ....196 E6
Wellesley Crs *WHTN* TW2 ....155 K4
Wellesley Gv *CROY/NA* CR0 ..196 E6
Wellesley Pde *WHTN* TW2 * ..155 K5
Wellesley Park Ms *ENC/FH* EN2 ..23 H3
Wellesley Pl *CAMTN* NW1 * 4 C5
KTTN NW5 ....84 A3
Wellesley Rd *BELMT* SM2 ....209 G4
CHSWK W4 ....117 H5
CROY/NA CR0 ....196 D5
HRW HA1 ....60 E2
IL IG1 ....72 B6
KTTN NW5 ....84 A3
WALTH E17 ....69 J3
WAN E11 ....70 C2
WHTN TW2 ....155 K5
Wellesley St *WCHPL* E1 ....105 F4
Wellesley Ter *IS* N1 ....6 D4
Wellfield Av *MUSWH* N10 ....48 B6
Wellfield Gdns *CAR* SM5 ....209 J6
Wellfield Rd
STRHM/NOR SW16 ....161 K6
Wellfit St *HNHL* SE24 ....142 C4
Wellgarth *GFD/PVL* UB6 ....79 H4
Wellgarth Rd *GLDGN* NW11 ....65 F5
Well Gv *TRDG/WHET* N20 ....33 G3
Well Hall Pde *ELTH/MOT* SE9 ..146 E5
Well Hall Rd *ELTH/MOT* SE9 ..146 E5
Wellhouse La *BAR* EN5 ....20 A5
Wellhouse Rd *BECK* BR3 ....198 C1
Wellhurst Cl *ORP* BR6 ....217 F5
Welling High St *WELL* DA16 ..148 C4
Wellington Av *BFN/LL* DA15 ..168 B1
CHING E4 ....37 J4
ED N9 ....36 D5
HSLW TW3 ....135 F6
PIN HA5 ....41 K4
SEVS/STOTM N15 ....68 C3
WPK KT4 ....208 A1
Wellington Cl *DAGE* RM10 ....92 E5
NTGHL W11 ....100 E5
NWCR SE14 * 144 A2
OXHEY WD19 ....27 J5
Wellington Crs *NWMAL* KT3 ..175 J6
Wellington Dr *DAGE* RM10 ....92 E5
Wellington Gdns *CHARL* SE7 ..126 B5
EDUL SE22 ....143 H5
HOLWY N7 ....85 F4
STRHM/NOR SW16 ....161 K6
Wellington Pde *BFN/LL* DA15 *..148 B6
Wellington Park Est
CRICK NW2 * 63 J6
Wellington Pas *WAN* E11 * 70 E2
Wellington Pl *EFNCH* N2 * 65 J2
STJWD NW8 ....2 C5
Wellington Rd *BELV* DA17 ....129 G5
BXLY DA5 ....168 E1
CROY/NA CR0 ....196 C4
DART DA1 ....171 F1
EBED/NFELT TW14 ....116 D4
EHAM E6 ....107 K1
EN EN1 ....24 A6
FSTGT E7 ....88 D2
HAYES BR2 ....200 B3
HPTN TW12 ....155 J6
KTN/HRWW/WS HA3 ....42 E6
LEY E10 ....69 G5
NKENS W10 * 100 B2
PIN HA5 ....41 K4
RAIN RM13 ....111 K2
STMC/STPC BR5 ....202 C3
WALTH E17 ....51 G6
WAN E11 ....71 F2
WIM/MER SW19 ....159 K4
Wellington Rd North
HSLW TW4 ....134 E4
Wellington Rd South
HSLW TW4 ....134 E6
Wellington Rw *BETH* E2 ....7 K4
Wellington Sq *CHEL* SW3 ....120 E5
Wellington St *COVGDN* WC2E ..11 F5
WOOL/PLUM SE18 ....127 F4
Wellington Ter *BAY/PAD* W2 *..100 E6
CEND/HSY/T N8 ....49 G6
HRW HA1 ....60 D1
WAP E1W 123 J1
Wellington Wy *BOW* E3 ....105 J3
Welling Wy *ELTH/MOT* SE9 ..147 K4
Well La *MORT/ESHN* SW14 ..137 K6
Wellmeadow Rd *HNWL* W7 ..116 B4
LEW SE13 ....145 H6
Well Rd *BAR* EN5 ....20 A6
HAMP NW3 ....83 H1
Wells Cl *NTHLT* UB5 ....95 G2
SAND/SEL CR2 ....212 A3
Wells Dr *CDALE/KGS* NW9 ....63 F5
Wells Gdns *IL* IG1 ....71 J4

RAIN RM13 ....93 H4
Wells House Rd *WLSDN* NW10 ..99 G4
Wellside Rd *EBAR* EN5 ....20 C5
Wellside Gdns
MORT/ESHN SW14 ....137 K5
Wells Ms *FITZ* W1T * 10 B2
Wellsmoor Gdns *BMLY* BR1 ..185 F6
Wells Park Rd *SYD* SE26 ....163 H5
Wells Pl *CMBW* SE5 ....143 F1
WAND/EARL SW18 ....160 B2
Wellspring Crs *WBLY* HA9 ....62 D6
Wells Ri *STJWD* NW8 ....2 E1
Wells Rd *BMLY* BR1 ....184 E5
SHB W12 ....119 F2
Wells Sq *FSBYW* WC1X 5 G5
Wells St *GTPST* W1W 10 A2
Wellstead Av *ED* N9 ....36 E2
Wellstead Rd *EHAM* E6 ....108 A1
Wells Ter *FSBYPK* N4 ....67 G6
The Wells *STHGT/OAK* N14 ....34 D5
Well St *HOM* E9 ....86 E5
SRTFD E15 ....88 C4
Wellwood Rd *GDMY/SEVK* IG3 ..73 G5
Welsford St *STHWK* SE1 ....123 H5
Welsh Cl *PLSTW* E13 ....106 E2
Welshpool St *HACK* E8 * 86 C6
Welshside Rd *CDALE/KGS* NW9 ..63 G2
Welstead Wy *CHSWK* W4 ....118 C4
Weltje Rd *HMSMTH* W6 ....118 D5
Welton Rd *WOOL/PLUM* SE18 ..147 K1
Welwyn Av *EBED/NFELT* TW14 ..153 J1
Welwyn St *BETH* E2 ....104 E2
Welwyn Wy *YEAD* UB4 ....94 C3
Wembley Hill Rd *WBLY* HA9 ..80 B3
Wembley Park Dr *WBLY* HA9 ..80 B2
Wembley Rd *HPTN* TW12 ....173 F4
Wembley Wy *WBLY* HA9 ....80 D4
Wemborough Rd *STAN* HA7 ....35 J5
Wembury Ms *HGT* N6 ....66 C4
Wembury Rd *HGT* N6 ....66 A4
Wemyss Rd *BKHTH/KID* SE3 ..145 J3
Wendela Ct *HRW* HA1 ....78 E1
Wendell Rd *SHB* W12 ....118 C2
Wendling Rd *SUT* SM1 ....194 C5
Wendon St *BOW* E3 ....87 H6
Wendover Cl *YEAD* UB4 ....95 H3
Wendover Dr *NWMAL* KT3 ....192 C3
Wendover Rd *ELTH/MOT* SE9 ..146 D4
HAYES BR2 ....200 A1
WLSDN NW10 ....99 H1
Wendover Wy *BUSH* WD23 ....28 D1
ORP BR6 ....202 B3
WELL DA16 ....148 B6
Wendy Cl *EN* EN1 ....36 B1
Wendy Wy *ALP/SUD* HA0 ....80 A6
Wenlock Gdns *NFNCH/WDSPK* N12 * ..47 F1
Wenlock Rd *EDGW* HA8 ....44 D4
IS N1 ....6 C3
Wenlock St *IS* N1 ....6 D3
Wennington Rd *BOW* E3 ....105 F1
RAIN RM13 ....111 K4
Wensley Av *WFD* IG8 ....52 E3
Wensley Cl *CRW* RM5 ....56 C1
ELTH/MOT SE9 ....166 E1
FBAR/BDGN N11 ....47 K5
Wensleydale Av *CLAY* IG5 ....53 J5
Wensleydale Gdns *HPTN* TW12 ..173 G3
Wensleydale Rd *HPTN* TW12 ..173 F4
Wensley Rd *UED* N18 ....50 D2
Wentland Cl *CAT* SE6 ....165 G4
Wentland Rd *CAT* SE6 ....165 H4
Wentworth Av *FNCH* N3 ....46 E3
Wentworth Cl *ASHF* TW15 ....152 E6
FNCH N3 ....47 F3
HAYES BR2 ....199 K6
MRDN SM4 ....193 K4
ORP BR6 ....216 E3
SURB KT6 ....190 E6
THMD SE28 ....109 K5
Wentworth Dr *DART* DA1 ....170 D2
PIN HA5 ....58 E2
Wentworth Gdns *PLMGR* N13 ..35 H5
Wentworth Hl *WBLY* HA9 ....62 B5
Wentworth Ms *BOW* E3 ....105 H3
Wentworth Pk *FNCH* N3 ....47 F3
Wentworth Pl *STAN* HA7 * 43 H2
Wentworth Rd *BAR* EN5 ....20 B3
CROY/NA CR0 ....196 B4
GLDGN NW11 ....64 D3
MNPK E12 ....89 H3
Wentworth St *WCHPL* E1 ....13 K2
Wentworth Wy *PIN* HA5 ....59 J1
RAIN RM13 ....111 K2
Wenvoe Av *BXLYHN* DA7 ....149 J3
Wepham Cl *YEAD* UB4 ....95 H4
Wernbrook St
WOOL/PLUM SE18 ....127 H6
Werndee Rd *SNWD* SE25 ....197 H1
Werneth Hall Rd *CLAY* IG5 ....53 K6
Werrington St *CAMTN* NW1 ....4 B3
Werter Rd *PUT/ROE* SW15 ....139 H5
Wesleyan Pl *KTTN* NW5 ....84 B2
Wesley Av *CAN/RD* E16 ....125 K1
HSLW TW3 ....134 D3
WLSDN NW10 ....99 F2
Wesley Cl *HOLWY* N7 ....67 F6
LBTH SE11 ....122 C5
RYLN/HDSTN HA2 ....60 C5
STMC/STPC BR5 ....186 D6
Wesley Rd *HYS/HAR* UB3 ....94 E6
LEY E10 ....70 A4
WLSDN NW10 ....80 E6
Wesley Sq *NTGHL* W11 ....100 B5
Wesley St *CAVSQ/HST* W1G 9 H2
Wessex Av *WIM/MER* SW19 ..177 K5
Wessex Cl *CDMY/SEVK* IG3 ....73 F5
KUT/HW KT1 ....175 J4
THDIT KT7 ....190 A6
Wessex Ct *BECK* BR3 * 182 B4
Wessex Dr *ERITH* DA8 ....150 B3

PIN HA5 ....41 J3
Wessex Gdns *GLDGN* NW11 ....64 C5
Wessex La *GFD/PVL* UB6 ....96 D1
Wessex Rd *HTHAIR* TW6 ....132 B4
Wessex St *BETH* E2 ....104 E2
Wessex Ter *MTCM* CR4 * 194 D2
Wesson Md *CMBW* SE5 * 142 D1
Westacott *YEAD* UB4 ....94 C4
Westacott Cl *ARCH* N19 ....66 D5
West Ap *STMC/STPC* BR5 ....201 H2
West Arbour St *WCHPL* E1 ....105 F5
West Av *FNCH* N3 ....46 E6
HDN NW4 ....64 B2
HYS/HAR UB3 ....94 D1
PIN HA5 ....59 K4
STHL UB1 ....95 K6
WALTH E17 ....69 K2
WLGTN SM6 ....210 E3
West Avenue Rd *WALTH* E17 ..69 J1
West Bank *BARK* IG11 ....90 B6
ENC/FH EN2 ....23 J4
STNW/STAM N16 ....68 A4
Westbank Rd *HPTN* TW12 ....173 H2
West Barnes La *NWMAL* KT3 ..192 E3
RYNPK SW20 ....176 E6
Westbeech Rd *WDGN* N22 ....49 G6
Westbere Dr *STAN* HA7 ....43 K1
Westbere Rd *CRICK* NW2 ....82 C2
Westbourne Av *ACT* W3 ....99 F5
CHEAM SM3 ....193 H6
Westbourne Cl *YEAD* UB4 ....95 G3
Westbourne Crs *BAY/PAD* W2 ..8 A5
Westbourne Crescent Ms
BAY/PAD W2 * 8 A5
Westbourne Dr *FSTH* SE23 ..164 A4
Westbourne Gdns
BAY/PAD W2 ....101 F5
Westbourne Ga *BAY/PAD* W2 ....8 B5
Westbourne Gv *BAY/PAD* W2 ..100 E5
Westbourne Grove Ms
NTGHL W11 * 100 E5
Westbourne Grove Ter
BAY/PAD W2 ....101 F5
Westbourne Park Rd
BAY/PAD W2 ....100 E5
Westbourne Pl *ED* N9 ....36 D5
Westbourne Rd *BXLYHN* DA7 ..148 E1
CROY/NA CR0 ....197 G3
FELT TW13 ....153 J5
HOLWY N7 ....85 F4
SYD SE26 ....182 A2
Westbourne St *BAY/PAD* W2 ..8 A4
Westbourne Ter *BAY/PAD* W2 ..8 A4
Westbourne Terrace Ms
BAY/PAD W2 ....101 G5
Westbourne Terrace Rd
BAY/PAD W2 ....100 E5
Westbridge Cl *SHB* W12 ....118 D1
Westbridge Rd *BTSEA* SW11 ..140 C2
Westbrook Av *HPTN* TW12 ....172 E3
Westbrook Cl *EBAR* EN4 ....21 H4
Westbrook Crs *EBAR* EN4 ....21 H4
Westbrook Dr *STMC/STPC* BR5 ..202 E5
Westbrooke Crs *WELL* DA16 ..148 D4
Westbrooke Rd *BFN/LL* DA15 ..167 J4
WELL DA16 ....148 C3
Westbrook Rd *BKHTH/KID* SE3 ..146 A1
HEST TW5 ....134 E1
THHTH CR7 ....180 E4
Westbury Av *WDGN* N22 * 49 H6
ESH/CLAY KT10 ....205 F4
STHL UB1 ....96 A4
WDGN N22 ....49 H6
Westbury Cl *RSLP* HA4 ....58 E4
Westbury Gv
NFNCH/WDSPK N12 ....46 E2
Westbury La *BKHH* IG9 ....39 H4
Westbury Lodge Cl *PIN* HA5 ..41 H6
Westbury Pl *BTFD* TW8 ....116 E6
Westbury Rd *ALP/SUD* HA0 ....80 A4
BARK IG11 ....90 D6
BECK BR3 ....182 B6
BKHH IG9 ....39 G3
BMLY BR1 ....184 C4
CROY/NA CR0 ....196 E4
EA W5 ....98 A5
FBAR/BDGN N11 ....48 D2
FELT TW13 ....154 C3
FSTGT E7 ....88 E4
IL IG1 ....72 A6
NFNCH/WDSPK N12 ....46 E2
NTHWD HA6 ....40 C1
NWMAL KT3 ....176 A6
PGE/AN SE20 ....182 A4
WALTH E17 ....51 J4
Westbury Ter *FSTGT* E7 ....89 F4
West Carriage Dr *BAY/PAD* W2 ..14 D2
West Central St
LSQ/SEVD WC2H 10 E3
West Chantry
KTN/HRWW/WS HA3 ....42 A4
Westchester Dr *HDN* NW4 ....46 B6
Westcliffe Vis *KUT/HW* KT1 * ..175 G5
West Cl *ASHF* TW15 ....152 B6
EBAR EN4 ....22 A6
ED N9 ....36 B5
GFD/PVL UB6 ....96 C1
HPTN TW12 ....172 E2
WBLY HA9 ....80 D1
Westcombe Av *CROY/NA* CR0 ..195 K3
Westcombe Dr *BAR* EN5 ....20 E6
Westcombe Hl *BKHTH/KID* SE3 ..125 K6
Westcombe Lodge Dr
YEAD UB4 ....94 B4
Westcombe Park Rd
BKHTH/KID SE3 ....145 K1
West Common Rd *HAYES* BR2 ..215 G2
Westcombe Av *RYNPK* SW20 ..176 C4
Westcote Ri *RSLP* HA4 ....58 A3
Westcote Rd
STRHM/NOR SW16 ....179 H1
Westcott Cl *BMLY* BR1 ....200 D2
CROY/NA CR0 ....213 K6
SEVS/STOTM N15 * 68 B3

Westcott Crs *HNWL* W7 ....96 E4
Westcott House
POP/IOD E14 * 105 J6
Westcott Rd *WALW* SE17 ....122 C6
West Ct *ALP/SUD* HA0 ....79 J1
Westcroft Cl *CRICK* NW2 ....82 C2
PEND EN3 ....24 E1
Westcroft Gdns *MRDN* SM4 ..177 J3
Westcroft Rd *CAR* SM5 ....210 A2
Westcroft Sq *HMSMTH* W6 * ..118 D4
Westcroft Wy *CRICK* NW2 ....82 C2
West Cromwell Rd *ECT* SW5 ..119 K4
West Cross Route *SHB* W12 ..100 B6
West Cross Wy *BTFD* TW8 ....116 C6
Westdale Rd
WOOL/PLUM SE18 ....127 G6
Westdean Av *LEE/GVPK* SE12 ..166 A3
Westdean Cl
WAND/EARL SW18 ....160 A1
Westdown Rd *CAT* SE6 ....164 D2
SRTFD E15 ....88 A2
West Drayton Park Av
WDR/YW UB7 ....112 A3
West Drayton Rd *UX/CGN* UB8 ..94 A4
West Dr *BELMT* SM2 ....208 B6
KTN/HRWW/WS HA3 ....42 D2
STRHM/NOR SW16 ....161 H5
West Drive Gdns
KTN/HRWW/WS HA3 ....42 D2
West Eaton Pl *BCVA* SW1W 15 G6
West Eaton Place Ms
KTBR SW1X 15 G6
West Ella Rd *WLSDN* NW10 ....81 G6
West End Av *LEY* E10 ....70 A2
PIN HA5 ....59 H1
West End Cl *WLSDN* NW10 ....80 E5
West End La *BAR* EN5 ....20 A5
ESH/CLAY KT10 ....204 A3
HYS/HAR UB3 ....133 G1
KIL/WHAMP NW6 ....82 E5
PIN HA5 ....41 H6
West End Rd *RSLP* HA4 ....76 E2
RSLP HA4 ....77 J3
STHL UB1 ....114 D1
Westerdale Rd *GNWCH* SE10 ..125 K5
Westergate Rd *ABYW* SE2 ....129 F6
Westerham Av *ED* N9 ....35 K5
Westerham Dr *BFN/LL* DA15 ..168 C1
Westerham Rd *HAYES* BR2 ....215 H4
LEY E10 ....69 K3
Westerley Crs *SYD* SE26 * 182 C1
Western Av *DAGE* RM10 ....92 E4
EA W5 ....98 A5
GFD/PVL UB6 ....97 F2
GLDGN NW11 ....64 B4
RSLP HA4 ....77 G5
Western Ct *FNCH* N3 * 46 E2
Western Gdns *EA* W5 ....98 D6
Western Gtwy *CAN/RD* E16 ..106 E6
Western La *BAL* SW12 ....161 F2
Western Man *BAR* EN5 * 20 E5
Western Ms *MV/WKIL* W9 ....100 D3
Western Pde *BAR* EN5 ....20 E6
BAR EN5 ....21 F6
Western Pl *BERM/RHTH* SE16 ..123 K2
Western Rd *BRXN/ST* SW9 ....142 B4
EA W5 ....97 K6
EFNCH N2 ....47 K2
MTCM CR4 ....178 D4
NWDGN UB2 ....114 D3
PLSTW E13 ....89 G6
ROM RM1 ....75 H2
SUT SM1 ....208 E3
WALTH E17 ....70 A2
WDGN N22 ....48 E5
WLSDN NW10 ....99 F2
Western Ter *HMSMTH* W6 * ..118 D5
Western Vw *HYS/HAR* UB3 ..113 J2
Westernville Gdns
GNTH/NBYPK IG2 ....72 C4
Western Wy *BAR* EN5 ....32 C1
THMD SE28 ....127 K3
Westferry Circ *POP/IOD* E14 ..124 E1
Westferry Rd *POP/IOD* E14 ..105 J6
Westfield Cl *CDALE/KGS* NW9 ....44 E6
FUL/PGN SW6 ....140 B1
PEND EN3 ....25 G4
SUT SM1 ....208 D2
WBPTN SW10 ....140 B3
Westfield Dr
KTN/HRWW/WS HA3 ....61 K1
Westfield Gdns *CHDH* RM6 ....73 J3
KTN/HRWW/WS HA3 ....61 K1
Westfield La
KTN/HRWW/WS HA3 ....61 K1
Westfield Pk *PIN* HA5 ....41 K3
Westfield Park Dr *WFD* IG8 ..53 J2
Westfield Rd *BECK* BR3 ....182 C5
BXLYHN DA7 ....149 K4
CROY/NA CR0 ....196 C6
DAGW RM9 ....92 A2
MLHL NW7 ....44 E6
MTCM CR4 ....178 D5
SURB KT6 ....190 E2
SUT SM1 ....208 D2
WEA W13 ....116 C2
WOT/HER KT12 ....188 B4
Westfields *BARN* SW13 ....138 C4
Westfields Av *BARN* SW13 ..138 B4
Westfields Rd *ACT* W3 ....98 D4
Westfield St
WOOL/PLUM SE18 ....126 C3
Westfield Wy *RSLP* HA4 ....76 D1
WCHPL E1 ....105 G2
West Garden Pl *BAY/PAD* W2 ..8 D4
West Gdns *TOOT* SW17 ....178 D2
WAP E1W 104 D6
West Ga *EA* W5 ....98 A2
Westgate Est
EBED/NFELT TW14 * 152 E3
Westgate Rd *BECK* BR3 ....183 F4
DART DA1 ....171 J3

SNWD SE25 .....197 J1
Westgate St HACK E8 .....86 D6
Westgate Ter WBPTN SW10 .....120 A5
Westgade Ct
  KTN/HRWW/WS HA3 .....61 K2
West Green Rd GFD/PVL UB6 .....78 D6
West Green Rd
  SEVS/STOTM N15 .....67 K1
West Gv GNWCH SE10 .....145 F2
WFD IG8 .....53 G2
Westgrove La GNWCH SE10 .....145 F2
West Halkin St KTBR SW1X 15 G4
West Hallowes ELTH/MOT SE9 .....166 C5
West Ham La SRTFD E15 .....88 C6
West Hampstead Ms
  KIL/WHAMP NW6 .....83 F4
West Harding St
  FLST/FETLN EC4A * 11 K3
West Hatch Mnr RSLP HA4 .....58 D5
Westhay Gdns
  MORT/ESHN SW14 .....137 J6
West Heath Av GLDGN NW11 .....64 E5
West Heath Cl DART DA1 .....170 C1
  HAMP NW3 .....82 E1
West Heath Dr GLDGN NW11 .....64 E5
West Heath Gdns HAMP NW3 .....82 E1
West Heath Rd ABYW SE2 .....128 E6
  DART DA1 .....170 C1
  HAMP NW3 .....82 E1
West Hl DART DA1 .....171 G1
  RYLN/HDSTN HA2 .....60 E6
  SAND/SEL CR2 .....212 A6
  WAND/EARL SW18 .....139 K6
  WBLY HA9 .....62 B5
  WIM/MER SW19 .....158 E2
West Hill Dr DART DA1 .....171 F1
West Hill Pk HGT N6 .....65 K6
West Hill Ri DART DA1 .....171 G1
West Hill Rd WAND/EARL SW18..159 K1
West Hill Wy TRDG/WHET N20..33 G2
Westholm GLDGN NW11 .....65 F4
West Holme ERITH DA8 .....149 K2
Westholme ORP BR6 .....201 K4
Westholme Gdns RSLP HA4 .....58 E5
Westhorne Av ELTH/MOT SE9 .....166 C1
Westhorpe Gdns HDN NW4 .....46 A6
Westhorpe Rd PUT/ROE SW15..139 F4
West House Cl
  WIM/MER SW19 .....159 H3
Westhurst Dr CHST BR7 .....185 G1
West India Av POP/IOD E14 .....124 D1
West India Dock Rd
  POP/IOD E14 .....105 J6
Westlake Cl PLMGR N13 .....35 G5
  YEAD UB4 .....95 J3
Westland Cl
  STWL/WRAY TW19 * 152 B1
Westland Dr HAYES BR2 .....199 J6
Westland Pl FSBYE EC1V 6 E4
Westlands Cl HYS/HAR UB3..113 K4
Westlands Ter BAL SW12 .....161 H1
West La BERM/RHTH SE16 .....123 J2
Westlea Rd HNWL W7 .....116 B3
Westleigh Av PUT/ROE SW15..139 F6
Westleigh Dr BMLY BR1 .....184 C5
Westleigh Gdns EDGW HA8 .....44 C4
West Links ALP/SUD HA0 .....97 K2
Westlinton Cl MLHL NW7 .....46 C2
West Lodge Av ACT W3 .....117 H1
West Lodge Ct ACT W3 * 117 H1
Westmacott Dr
  EBED/NFELT TW14 .....153 K3
West Ml KENS W8 .....119 K1
West Malling Wy HCH RM12 .....93 K3
West Md HOR/WEW KT19 .....207 G4
Westmead PUT/ROE SW15 .....158 E2
West Md RSLP HA4 .....77 G2
Westmead RSLP HA4 .....77 G2
Westmead Rd SUT SM1 .....209 H2
Westmede Dr WFD IG8 * 52 E4
Westmere Dr MLHL NW7 .....31 F6
Westmere Dr CAN/RD E16..106 A4
West Ms PIM SW1V 15 K7
  TOTM N17 * 50 E3
Westminster Av THHTH CR7..180 C5
Westminster Br WHALL SW1A..17 F3
Westminster Bridge Rd
  WHALL SW1A 17 J3
Westminster Cl
  EBED/NFELT TW14 .....153 K3
  TEDD TW11 .....174 B1
Westminster Dr PLMGR N13..34 E1
Westminster Gdns BARK IG11..108 E1
  BARK/HLT IG6 .....54 C2
  CHING E4 .....38 C1
Westminster Rd ED N9 .....36 D3
  HNWL W7 .....115 K1
  SUT SM1 .....194 C6
Westmoat Cl BECK BR3 .....183 F4
Westmoor Gdns ENF EN3..25 F3
Westmoor Rd PEND EN3 .....25 F3
Westmoor St CHARL SE7..126 C4
Westmoreland Av WELL DA16..147 K5
Westmoreland Dr BELMT SM2..209 F6
Westmoreland Pl BMLY BR1 *..183 K6
  EA W5 .....97 K3
  PIM SW1V * 121 G5
Westmoreland Rd BARN SW13..138 D2
  KTN/HRWW/WS HA3 .....42 C3
  WALW SE17 .....122 E6
  WWKM BR4 .....199 H2
Westmoreland St
  CAVSQ/HST W1G 9 H2
Westmoreland Ter
  PGE/AN SE20 * 181 J3
  PIM SW1V 121 G5
Westmorland Cl MNPK E12..71 H6
  TWK TW1 * 156 C1
Westmorland Rd HRW HA1..60 B2
  WALTH E17 .....69 J3
West Oak BECK BR3 .....183 G4
Westoe Rd ED N9 .....36 D4
Weston Av E/WMO/HCT KT8..188 D1
  THDIT KT7 .....189 K4

Weston Dr STAN HA7 .....43 H4
Weston Gdns ISLW TW7 .....135 J2
Weston Gn DAGW RM9 .....92 A2
Weston Green Rd
  ESH/CLAY KT10 .....189 J5
Weston Gv BMLY BR1 .....183 J4
Weston Pk CEND/HSY/T N8..66 E3
  KUT/HW KT1 .....175 F5
  THDIT KT7 .....189 K5
Weston Ri CLKNW WC1X * 5 H1
Weston Rd BMLY BR1 .....183 J4
  CHSWK W4 .....117 K3
  DAGW RM9 .....92 A2
  ENF/FH EN2 .....23 K3
  THDIT KT7 .....189 K5
Weston St STHWK SE1 .....19 G2
Weston Wk HACK E8 * 86 D5
Westover Cl BELMT SM2 .....209 F6
Westover Hl HAMP NW3 .....64 E6
Westover Rd
  WAND/EARL SW18 .....160 B1
Westow Hl NRWD SE19 .....181 F2
Westow St NRWD SE19 .....181 F2
West Pk ELTH/MOT SE9 .....166 D4
West Park Av RCH/KEW TW9..137 J2
West Park Cl CHDH RM6 .....73 K2
  MLHL NW7 * 115 H6
West Park Rd NWDGN UB2..115 J1
  RCH/KEW TW9 .....137 H2
West Parkside GNWCH SE10..125 H2
West Pl NWDGN UB2 * 115 G4
  WIM/MER SW19 * 177 F1
Westpole Av EBAR EN4 .....22 B5
Westport Rd PLSTW E13 .....107 F3
Westport St WCHPL E1 .....105 F5
West Poultry Av FARR EC1M..12 A2
West Quarters SHB W12 .....99 J5
West Quay Dr YEAD UB4 .....95 J4
West Rp HTHAIR TW6 .....132 D2
West Ridge Gdns GFD/PVL UB6..96 C1
West Ri BAY/PAD W2 * 8 B5
West Rd CHDH RM6 .....74 A3
  CHEL SW3 .....120 E5
  CLAP SW4 .....141 J6
  EA W5 .....98 A4
  EBAR EN4 .....33 K2
  EBED/NFELT TW14 .....153 G2
  KUTN/CMB KT2 .....175 K4
  ROMW/RG RM7 .....75 F4
  SRTFD E15 .....88 D6
  TOTM N17 .....50 D2
  WDR/YW UB7 * 112 C3
West Wrn NKENS W10 .....100 A1
Westrow Dr BARK IG11 .....91 G5
Westrow Gdns GDMY/SEVK IG3..73 F2
West Sheen V RCH/KEW TW9..137 G5
West Side BMLY BR1 * 44 K5
West Side Common
  WIM/MER SW19 .....177 F2
West Smithfield STBT EC1A..12 A2
West Sq LBTH SE11 .....18 A5
West St BETH E2 .....86 D1
  BMLY BR1 .....183 K4
  BROMLY DA7 .....149 G5
  CAR SM5 .....209 K2
  CROY/NA CR0 .....211 J2
  ERITH DA8 .....130 A4
  HRW HA1 .....60 C6
  LSO/SEVD WC2H 10 D4
  SUT SM1 .....209 F3
  WALTH E17 .....69 K2
  WAN E11 * 88 B1
West Street La CAR SM5 .....209 K2
West Street Pl CROY/NA CR0 *..211 J2
West Temple Sheen
  MORT/ESHN SW14 .....137 J6
West Tenter St WCHPL E1..13 K4
West Towers PIN HA5 .....59 H5
West Vw EBED/NFELT TW14..153 F3
Westview HNWL W7 * 96 E5
Westview Ct NKENS W10 .....100 A5
Westview Ct BORE WD6 .....29 K1
Westview Crs ED N9 .....36 A2
Westview Dr WFD IG8 .....53 H5
West View Gdns BORE WD6..29 K1
West View Rd DART DA1..171 J1
Westville Rd SHB W12 .....118 D5
  THDIT KT7 .....190 B4
West Wk EBAR EN4 .....34 A3
  HYS/HAR UB3 .....113 K1
West Warwick Pl PIM SW1V *..16 A7
West Wy CROY/NA CR0 .....198 A6
  EDGW HA8 .....44 D2
  HEST TW5 * 134 C2
Westway NKENS W10 .....100 D4
West Wy PIN HA5 .....59 H1
  RSLP HA4 .....58 D5
Westway RYNPK SW20 .....192 E1
  SHB W12 .....99 J6
West Wy STMC/STPC BR5 .....202 C1
  UED N18 .....35 K6
  WLSDN NW10 .....81 F2
Westway Cl RYNPK SW20 .....176 E6
West Way Gdns CROY/NA CR0..198 A6
Westways HOR/WEW KT19..207 H2
Westwell Cl STMC/STPC BR5..202 E5
Westwell Rd
  STRHM/NOR SW16 .....179 K2
Westwell Road Ap
  STRHM/NOR SW16 .....179 K2
Westwick Gdns HMSMTH W6..119 G2
  HSLWW TW4 .....134 A3
Westwood Av NRWD SE19..180 D4
  RYLN/HDSTN HA2 .....78 A2
Westwood Cl BMLY BR1 .....184 C6
  ESH/CLAY KT10 .....204 C1
Westwood Gdns BARN SW13..138 C4
Westwood Hl SYD SE26 .....181 H4
Westwood La WELL DA16..148 B5

Westwood Pk FSTH SE23 .....163 J2
Westwood Pl SYD SE26 * 181 H1
Wetheral Dr STAN HA7 .....43 H4
Wetherby Cl NTHLT UB5 .....78 B4
Wetherby Gdns ECT SW5 .....120 B5
Wetherby Ms ECT SW5 .....120 A5
Wetherby Pl ECT SW5 .....120 B4
Wetherby Rd ENC/FH EN2 .....23 J2
Wetherby Wy CHSGTN KT9..206 A5
Wetherden St WALTH E17 .....69 H4
Wetherell Rd HOM E9 .....87 F6
Wetherill Rd MUSWH N10 .....48 A4
Wexford Rd BAL SW12 .....160 E2
Weybourne St
  WAND/EARL SW18 .....160 B4
Weybridge Ct
  BERM/RHTH SE16 * 123 J5
Weybridge Rd THHTH CR7..196 B1
Wey Ct HOR/WEW KT19 .....206 E2
Weydown Cl WIM/MER SW19..159 H5
Weyhill Rd WCHPL E1 * 104 C5
Weyland Rd BCTR RM8 .....92 B1
Weyman Rd BKHTH/KID SE3..146 B2
Weymouth Av EA W5 .....116 D3
  MLHL NW7 .....45 F1
Weymouth Cl EHAM E6 .....108 B5
Weymouth Ct BELMT SM2..209 F5
Weymouth Ms CAVSQ/HST W1G..9 J1
Weymouth Ms CAVSQ/HST W1C..9 H1
Weymouth St CAVSQ/HST W1G..9 H1
Weymouth Ter BETH E2 .....7 J2
Weymouth Vls FSBYPK N4 *..67 F6
Weymouth Wk STAN HA7 .....43 G2
Whadcoat St FSBYPK N4 .....67 G6
Whalebone Av CHDH RM6 .....74 B3
Whalebone Gv CHDH RM6 .....74 B3
Whalebone La North
  CHDH RM6 .....74 A1
  CRW RM5 .....56 A3
Whalebone La South
  BCTR RM8 .....74 B5
Whales Yd SRTFD E15 * 88 C5
Wharfdale Cl FBAR/BDGN N11..48 A2
Wharfdale Rd IS N1 .....5 F2
Wharfedale Gdns THHTH CR7..196 A1
Wharfedale St WBPTN SW10..120 A5
Wharf La POP/IOD E14 .....105 H5
  TWK TW1 * 156 B3
Wharf Pl BETH E2 .....86 D6
Wharf Rd IS N1 .....6 C3
  PEND EN3 .....37 G1
  SRTFD E15 .....88 B6
Wharfside Cl ERITH DA8 .....130 C5
Wharfside Rd POP/IOD E14..106 C4
Wharf St CAN/RD E16 .....106 C4
Wharf Ter PUT/ROE SW15..139 H5
Wharncliffe Dr STHL UB1..115 J1
Wharncliffe Gdns SNWD SE25..181 F5
Wharncliffe Rd SNWD SE25..180 E5
Wharton Cl WLSDN NW10 .....81 G4
Wharton Cottages
  FSBYW WC1X * 5 H5
Wharton Rd BMLY BR1 .....184 A4
Wharton St FSBYW WC1X 5 H5
Whateley Rd EDUL SE22 .....143 G6
  PGE/AN SE20 .....182 A3
Whatley Av RYNPK SW20..177 G6
Whatman Rd FSTH SE23 .....164 A2
Wheastone Rd NKENS W10..100 C4
Wheatfields PEND EN3 .....25 G2
Wheatfield Wy KUT/HW KT1..175 F5
Wheathill Rd PGE/AN SE20..181 J5
Wheatlands HEST TW5 .....115 F6
Wheatlands Rd TOOT SW17..161 F5
Wheatley Cl HDN NW4 .....45 J2
Wheatley Crs HYS/HAR UB3..94 E6
Wheatley Gdns ED N9 .....36 A4
Wheatley Rd ISLW TW7 .....136 A4
Wheatley St CAVSQ/HST W1G..9 H2
Wheatley Terrace Rd
  ERITH DA8 .....130 C6
Wheatsheaf Cl NTHLT UB5 .....77 H4
Wheatsheaf La FUL/PGN SW6..139 F1
  VX/NE SW8 .....141 K1
Wheatsheaf Ter
  FUL/PGN SW6 * 139 J1
Wheatstone Cl
  WIM/MER SW19 .....178 C4
Wheatstone Rd NKENS W10..100 C4
Wheeler Gdns IS N1 * 84 E6
Wheeler La WCHPL E1 .....13 J1
Wheeler Pl HAYES BR2 .....200 A1
Wheelers Cross BARK IG11..108 D1
Wheelers Dr RSLP HA4 * 58 A3
Wheel Farm Dr DAGE RM10..92 E1
Wheelock Cl ERITH DA8 .....149 J1
Wheelright St HOLWY N7 .....85 F5
Whelan Wy WLGTN SM6 .....210 D1
Whellock Rd CHSWK W4 .....118 B3
Whenman Av BXLY DA5 .....169 K4
Whetstone Cl NFNCH/WDSPK N12..47 H1
Whetstone Pk LINN WC2A..11 G3
Whetstone Rd BKHTH/KID SE3..146 B3
Whewell Rd ARCH N19 .....66 E6
Whidborne Cl DEPT SE8 .....144 D3
Whidborne St STPAN WC1H..5 F5
Whimbrel Wy YEAD UB4 .....95 H5
Whinchat Rd THMD SE28 .....127 J3
Whinfell Cl STRHM/NOR SW16..179 J1
Whinyates Rd ELTH/MOT SE9..146 D4
Whippendell Cl
  STMC/STPC BR5 .....186 C5
Whippendell Wy
  STMC/STPC BR5 .....186 C5
Whipps Cross Rd WAN E11..70 C5
Whiskin St CLKNW EC1R 6 A5
Whistler Gdns EDGW HA8 .....44 B5
Whistlers Av BTSEA SW11 *..140 C6

Whistler St HBRY N5 .....85 H3
Whistler Wk WBPTN SW10 *..140 B1
Whiston Rd BETH E2 .....7 J2
Whitbread Cl TOTM N17 .....50 C4
Whitbread Rd BROCKY SE4..144 B5
Whitburn Rd LEW SE13 .....144 E6
Whitby Av WLSDN NW10 .....98 D2
Whitby Gdns CDALE/KGS NW9..44 D6
  SUT SM1 .....194 D6
Whitby Pde RSLP HA4 * 59 G6
Whitby Rd RSLP HA4 .....58 E1
  RYLN/HDSTN HA2 .....60 B6
  SUT SM1 .....194 D6
  WOOL/PLUM SE18 .....126 E4
Whitby St WCHPL E1 .....7 J6
Whitcher Cl NWCR SE14 .....124 B6
Whitcher Pl CAMTN NW1 .....84 C5
Whitchurch Av EDGW HA8 .....44 B3
Whitchurch Cl EDGW HA8 .....44 B2
Whitchurch Gdns EDGW HA8..44 B3
Whitchurch La EDGW HA8 .....43 J3
Whitchurch Pde EDGW HA8 *..44 C3
Whitchurch Rd NKENS W10..100 B5
Whitcomb St SOHO/SHAV W1D..10 C5
Whitcome Ms RCH/KEW TW9..137 J2
Whiteadder Wy POP/IOD E14..124 E4
Whitear Wk SRTFD E15 .....88 B4
Whitebarn La DAGE RM10..110 C1
Whitebeam Av HAYES BR2..201 F4
Whitebeam Cl VX/NE SW8 *..142 A1
White Bear Pl HAMP NW3 *..83 H2
White Bear Yd CLKNW EC1R *..5 J7
White Bridge Cl
  EBED/NFELT TW14 .....153 J1
White Butts Rd RSLP HA4..77 H1
Whitechapel High St
  WCHPL E1 * 13 K3
Whitechapel Rd WCHPL E1..104 C5
White Church La WCHPL E1..104 C5
White City Cl SHB W12 .....100 A6
White City Rd SHB W12 .....100 A6
White Conduit St IS N1 .....5 K2
Whitecote Rd STHL UB1 .....96 C5
White Craig Cl PIN HA5 .....42 A1
Whitecroft Cl BECK BR3 .....199 F1
Whitecroft Wy BECK BR3 .....199 F2
Whitecross St STLK EC1Y 6 D6
Whitefield Av CRICK NW2 .....64 A5
Whitefield Cl PUT/ROE SW15..159 H1
  STMC/STPC BR5 .....186 D6
Whitefoot La BMLY BR1 .....165 F5
Whitefoot Ter BMLY BR1 .....165 J5
Whitefriars Av
  KTN/HRWW/WS HA3 .....42 E3
Whitefriars Dr
  KTN/HRWW/WS HA3 .....42 E3
Whitefriars St EMB EC4Y 11 K4
White Gdns DAGE RM10 .....92 C4
White Gate Gdns
  KTN/HRWW/WS HA3 .....42 E3
Whitehall Cl WHALL SW1A..16 E1
Whitehall Crs CHSGTN KT9..205 K3
Whitehall Gdns ACT W3 .....117 H1
  CHING E4 .....38 C4
  CHSWK W4 .....117 J6
  WHALL SW1A * 16 E1
Whitehall La BKHH IG9 .....39 F4
  ERITH DA8 .....150 C3
Whitehall Pk ARCH N19 .....66 C5
Whitehall Park Rd CHSWK W4..117 J6
Whitehall Pl WHALL SW1A..16 E1
  WLGTN SM6 * 210 B2
Whitehall Rd CHING E4 .....38 C3
  HARW HA1 .....61 F3
  HAYES BR2 .....200 C3
  HNWL W7 .....116 B2
  THHTH CR7 .....196 B2
Whitehall St TOTM N17 .....50 B3
White Hart Av THMD SE28..128 A3
White Hart La BARN SW13..138 C4
  ROMW/RG RM7 .....56 D5
  WDGN N22 .....49 H5
White Hart Rd ORP BR6 .....202 B4
  WOOL/PLUM SE18 .....127 K4
White Hart Slip BMLY BR1 *..183 K5
White Hart St LBTH SE11..122 B5
White Hart Ter TOTM N17 *..50 B3
White Hart Vd STHWK SE1 *..18 E1
White Hart Yd BAR EN5 * 199 F6
Whitehaven Cl HAYES BR2..199 K1
Whitehaven St STJWD NW8..2 C7
Whitehead Cl RDART DA2..171 H1
  UED N18 .....49 K1
  WAND/EARL SW18 .....160 B2
Whitehead's Gv CHEL SW3 .....14 E7
Whiteheath Av RSLP HA4 .....58 B4
White Heron Ms TEDD TW11 *..174 A2
Whitehill Rd DART DA1 .....150 E5
Whitehorn Pl WDR/YW UB7..112 C1
Whitehorse La SNWD SE25..197 F1
White Horse La WCHPL E1..105 F4
White Horse Ms STHWK SE1..17 K4
White Horse Rd CROY/NA CR0..196 D6
White Horse Rd EHAM E6..107 K2
White Horse Rd WCHPL E1..105 G5
Whitehorse Rd CROY/NA CR0..196 D4
  WCHPL E1 * 105 H4
White Horse St MYFR/PICC W1J..15 K1
White Horse Yd LOTH EC2R..13 F3
White House Dr STAN HA7..29 J6
Whitehouse Wy
  STHGT/OAK N14 .....34 B4
Whitehurst Dr UED N18 .....51 F1
White Kennett St HDTCH EC3A..13 H3
White Ledges WEA W13 .....97 J5
Whiteley Rd NRWD SE19..180 E1
Whiteley Rd NRWD SE19..155 F5
White Lion Ct LOTH EC2R *..13 G4
Whiteledge CROY/NA CR0 .....198 B6
  PECK SE15 * 123 K6
White Lion Hl BLKFR EC4V..12 B5
White Lion St IS N1 .....5 J3
White Ldg NRWD SE19..180 C3
White Lodge Cl BELMT SM2..209 G5

EFNCH N2 .....65 J3
ISLW TW7 * 136 B3
The White Ldg BAR EN5 *..20 C4
White Lyon Ct STBT EC1A..12 C1
White Oak Dr BECK BR3..183 F5
White Oak Gdns BFN/LL DA15..168 A1
Whiteoaks La GFD/PVL UB6..96 D1
White Orchards STAN HA7..43 G2
  TRDG/WHET N20 .....32 D3
White Post St NWCR SE14..143 K1
White Post Rd BOW E3 .....87 K2
White Rd SRTFD E15 .....88 C5
Whites Av GNTH/NBYPK IG2..72 E3
White's Grounds STHWK SE1..19 H2
White's Grounds Est STHWK SE1..19 H2
Whites Meadow BMLY BR1 *..201 F1
White's Rw WCHPL E1 .....13 J2
White's Sq CLAP SW4 .....141 J5
Whitestile Rd BTFD TW8 .....116 D5
Whitestone La HAMP NW3..83 G1
Whitestone Wk HAMP NW3..83 G1
White Twr Wy WCHPL E1..105 G4
Whitethorn Gdns
  CROY/NA CR0 .....197 G6
  ENC/FH EN2 .....23 K6
Whitethorn St BOW E3 .....105 J4
Whitewebbs Wy
  STMC/STPC BR5 .....186 A4
Whitfield Ct RYNPK SW20..177 G5
Whitfield Pl FITZ W1T * 4 A7
Whitfield Rd BXLYHN DA7..149 G1
  EHAM E6 .....89 G5
  GNWCH SE10 .....145 G2
Whitfield St FITZ W1T * 10 B1
Whitford Gdns MTCM CR4..178 E6
Whitgift Av SAND/SEL CR2..211 H4
Whitgift St CROY/NA CR0..211 J2
  STHWK SE1 * 17 G6
Whitings Rd BAR EN5 .....20 A6
Whitings Wy EHAM E6 .....108 A4
Whitland Rd CAR SM5 .....194 C5
Whitley Cl STWL/WRAY TW19..152 B1
Whitley Rd TOTM N17 .....50 A5
Whitlock Dr WIM/MER SW19..159 H3
Whitman Rd WCHPL E1 .....105 G5
Whitmead Cl SAND/SEL CR2..211 K4
Whitmore Cl FBAR/BDGN N11..48 B1
Whitmore Est IS N1 * 7 H1
Whitmore Gdns WLSDN NW10..100 A1
Whitmore Rd BECK BR3 .....182 C6
  HRW HA1 .....60 D3
  IS N1 .....7 G1
Whitnell Wy PUT/ROE SW15 *..139 F6
Whitney Av REDBR IG4 .....71 H1
Whitney Rd LEY E10 .....69 J4
Whitney Wk SCUP DA14 .....187 F2
Whitstable Cl BECK BR3 .....182 C4
Whitstone La BECK BR3 .....199 F1
Whittaker Av RCH/KEW TW9 *..136 E6
Whittaker Rd CHEAM SM3..208 D1
  EHAM E6 .....89 G5
Whittaker St BCVA SW1W..15 G7
Whitta Rd MNPK E12 .....89 H2
Whittell Gdns SYD SE26 .....163 K5
Whittingstall Rd
  FUL/PGN SW6 .....139 J2
Whittington Av BANK EC3V..13 G4
  YEAD UB4 .....94 D4
Whittington Ms
  NFNCH/WDSPK N12 .....33 G6
Whittington Rd WDGN N22..48 E3
Whittington Wy PIN HA5 .....59 J2
Whittlebury Cl CAR SM5 .....209 K5
Whittle Cl STHL UB1 .....96 B5
  WALTH E17 .....69 G3
Whittle Rd HEST TW5 .....134 B1
  NWDGN UB2 .....115 J2
Whittlesea Rd
  KTN/HRWW/WS HA3 .....42 C3
Whittlesey St STHWK SE1..17 K1
Whitton Av East GFD/PVL UB6..78 E3
Whitton Av West GFD/PVL UB6..78 C3
Whitton Cl GFD/PVL UB6 .....79 H4
Whitton Dene HSLW TW3..135 G6
  WHTN TW2 .....155 J1
Whitton Dr GFD/PVL UB6 .....79 H4
Whitton Manor Rd WHTN TW2..155 H1
Whitton Rd HSLW TW3 .....135 G5
  WHTN TW2 * 155 K1
Whitton Waye HSLW TW3..155 F1
Whitwell Rd PLSTW E13 .....106 E2
Whitworth Rd SNWD SE25..181 F6
  WOOL/PLUM SE18 .....147 F1
Whitworth St GNWCH SE10..125 H5
Whorlton Rd PECK SE15 .....143 H4
Whybridge Cl RAIN RM13 .....93 H5
Whymark Av WDGN N22 .....49 G6
Whytecroft HEST TW5 .....134 C1
Whyteville Rd FSTGT E7 .....89 F4
Wichling Cl STMC/STPC BR5..202 E5
Wickersley Rd BTSEA SW11..141 F3
Wickers Oake NRWD SE19 *..163 G6
Wicket Rd GFD/PVL UB6 .....97 G2
The Wickets ASHF TW15..152 B6
The Wicket CROY/NA CR0..213 J5
Wickford St WCHPL E1 .....104 E3
Wickford Wy WALTH E17 *..68 E1
Wickham Av CHEAM SM3..208 A3
  CROY/NA CR0 .....198 B6
Wickham Cha WWKM BR4..199 G4
Wickham Cl ENF EN3 .....25 F4
  NWMAL KT3 .....192 B2
Wickham Court Rd
  WWKM BR4 .....199 F6
Wickham Crs WWKM BR4..199 G6
Wickham Gdns BROCKY SE4..144 C4
Wickham La ABYW SE2 .....128 B6
Wickham Ms BROCKY SE4..144 C3
Wickham Rd BECK BR3 .....182 E6
  BROCKY SE4 * 144 C4
  CHING E4 .....52 A3
  CROY/NA CR0 .....198 B6

KTN/HRWW/WS HA3 ....42 D5
Wickham St *LBTH* SE11 ....122 A5
WELL DA16 ....147 K3
Wickham Wy *BECK* BR3 ....199 F1
Wick La *BOW* E3 ....87 J6
Wickliffe Av *NFNCH* N3 ....46 C5
Wickliffe Gdns *WBLY* HA9 ....62 D6
Wicklow St *FSBYW* WC1X 5 L7
Wick Rd *HOM* E9 ....87 G4
TEDD TW11 ....174 C3
Wick St *ELTH/MOT* SE9 ....166 C6
Wicksteed Cl *BXLY* DA5 ....170 A5
Wickwood St *CMBW* SE5 ....142 C5
Widdenham Rd *HOLWY* N7 ....85 F2
Widdecombe Av
RYLN/HDSTN HA2 ....59 J6
Widdin St *SRTFD* E15 ....88 C5
Widecombe Gdns *REDBR* IG4 ....71 J1
Widecombe Rd *ELTH/MOT* SE9 ....166 D5
Widecombe Wy *EFNCH* N2 ....65 H2
Widegate St *WCHPL* E1 ....13 H2
Widenham Cl *PIN* HA5 ....59 G1
Wide Wy *MTCM* SW4 ....179 J6
Widgeon Cl *CAN/RD* E16 ....107 F5
Widgeon Rd *ERITH* DA8 ....150 E1
Widley Rd *MV/WKIL* W9 ....100 E3
Widmore Lodge Rd *BMLY* BR1 ....184 C5
Widmore Rd *BMLY* BR1 ....184 A5
Wieland Rd *NTHWD* HA6 ....40 E3
Wigeon Wy *YEAD* UB4 ....95 H5
Wiggins La *RCHPK/HAM* TW10 ....156 D5
Wiggins Md *CDALE/KGS* NW9 ....45 H3
Wigginton Av *WBLY* HA9 ....80 E5
Wightman Rd *CEND/HSY/T* N8 ....67 F3
Wigley Rd *FELT* TW13 ....154 C4
Wigmore Rd *MHST* W1U 9 J5
Wigmore Rd *CAR* SM5 ....194 C6
Wigmore St *MHST* W1U 9 H5
Wigram Rd *WAN* E11 ....71 G3
Wigram Sq *WALTH* E17 ....52 A6
Wigston Cl *UED* N18 ....50 A1
Wigston Rd *PLSTW* E13 ....107 F3
Wigton Gdns *STAN* HA7 ....44 A4
Wigton Pl *LBTH* SE11 ....122 B5
Wigton Rd *WALTH* E17 ....51 H4
Wilberforce Ms *CLAP* SW4 ....141 J5
Wilberforce Rd
CDALE/KGS NW9 ....63 J3
FSBYPK N4 ....85 H1
Wilberforce Wy
WIM/MER SW19 ....177 G2
Wilbraham Pl *KTBR* SW1X 15 G6
Wilbury Wy *UED* N18 ....49 K1
Wilby Ms *NTGHL* W11 ....119 J1
Wilcot Av *OXHEY* WD19 ....27 J2
Wilcot Cl *OXHEY* WD19 ....27 J2
Wilcox Cl *VX/NE* SW8 ....141 K1
Wilcox Rd *SUT* SM1 ....209 F2
TEDD TW11 ....155 J6
VX/NE SW8 ....141 K1
Wildcares *NTHWD* HA6 ....26 D6
Wild Ct *HOL/ALD* WC2B 11 J4
Wildcroft Gdns *STAN* HA7 ....43 K2
Wildcroft Rd *PUT/ROE* SW15 ....159 F2
Wilde Cl *HACK* E8 ....86 C6
Wilde Pl *PLMGR* N13 ....49 H2
Wilderness Rd *BUSH* WD23 ....160 C2
Wilder Cl *RSLP* HA4 ....59 F5
Wilderness Ms *CLAP* SW4 ....141 G5
Wilderness Rd *CHST* BR7 ....185 G3
The Wilderness
E/WMO/HCT KT8 ....189 H2
HPTN TW12 * 155 G6
Wilde Rd *ERITH* DA8 ....149 J2
Wilderton Rd *STNW/STAM* N16 ....68 A4
Wildfell Rd *CAT* SE6 ....164 E2
Wild Goose Dr *NWCR* SE14 ....143 K2
Wild Hatch *GLDGN* NW11 ....64 E3
Wild Oaks Cl *NTHWD* HA6 ....40 D2
Wild's Rents *STHWK* SE1 ....19 G4
Wild St *HOL/ALD* WC2B 11 F4
Wildwood *NTHWD* HA6 ....40 B2
Wildwood Cl *LEE/GVPK* SE12 ....165 J2
Wildwood Gv *HAMP* NW3 ....65 G5
Wildwood Ri *GLDGN* NW11 ....65 G5
Wildwood Rd *GLDGN* NW11 ....65 G5
Wildwood Ter *GLDGN* NW11 ....65 G5
Wilford Cl *ENC/FH* EN2 * 23 K4
NTHWD HA6 ....40 B3
Wilfred Av *RAIN* RM13 ....111 J4
Wilfred Owen Cl
WIM/MER SW19 ....178 B2
Wilfrid Gdns *ACT* W3 ....98 E4
Wilkes Rd *BTFD* TW8 ....117 F6
Wilkes St *WCHPL* E1 ....13 K1
Wilkie Cl *HYS/HAR* UB3 ....113 J5
MTCM CR4 ....178 D6
Wilkins Cl *MTCM* CR4 ....178 D3
Wilkinson Gdns *SNWD* SE25 ....181 F4
Wilkinson Rd *CAN/RD* E16 ....107 G5
Wilkinson St *VX/NE* SW8 ....142 A1
Wilkinson Wy *CHSWK* W4 ....118 A2
Wilks Gdns *CROY/NA* CR0 ....198 B5
Wilks Av *DART* DA1 ....171 J4
Wilks Pl *IS* N1 ....7 H3
Willan Rd *TOTM* N17 ....49 K5
Willan Wall *CAN/RD* E16 ....106 D6
Willard St *VX/NE* SW8 ....141 G4
Willcocks Cl *CHSGTN* KT9 ....206 A1
Willcott Rd *ACT* W3 ....117 J1
Will Crooks Gdns
ELTH/MOT SE9 ....146 C5
Willenfield Rd *WLSDN* NW10 ....98 E1
Willenhall Av *BAR* EN5 ....33 G1
Willenhall Dr *HYS/HAR* UB3 ....94 C6
Willenhall Rd
WOOL/PLUM SE18 ....127 G5
Willersley Av *BFN/LL* DA15 ....168 A3
ORP BR6 ....216 D1
Willersley Cl *BFN/LL* DA15 ....168 A3
Willesden La *KIL/WHAMP* NW6 ....82 B4
Willes Rd *KTTN* NW5 ....84 B4
Willett Cl *NTHLT* UB5 ....95 C2
STMC/STPC BR5 ....201 K3

Willett Rd *THHTH* CR7 ....196 B2
Willett Wy *STMC/STPC* BR5 ....201 J2
William Ash Cl *DAGW* RM9 ....91 H4
William Barefoot Dr
ELTH/MOT SE9 ....167 F6
William Booth Rd
PGE/AN SE20 ....181 H4
William Carey Wy *HRW* HA1 ....60 E3
William Cl *CRW* RM5 ....56 E4
EFNCH N2 ....47 H5
LEW SE13 ....145 F4
NWDGN UB2 * 115 H2
William Covell Cl *ENC/FH* EN2 * 23 F1
William Dr *STAN* HA7 ....43 G2
William Ellis Wy
BERM/RHTH SE16 * 123 H3
William Foster La *WELL* DA16 ....148 B3
William Gdns *PUT/ROE* SW15 ....138 E6
William Guy Gdns *BOW* E3 ....105 K2
William Iv St *CHCR* WC2N 10 E6
William Margrie Cl
PECK SE15 * 143 H3
William Ms *KTBR* SW1X 15 F3
William Morley Cl *EHAM* E6 ....89 H6
William Morris Cl *WALTH* E17 ....51 H6
William Morris Wy
FUL/PGN SW6 ....140 B4
William Petty Wy
STMC/STPC BR5 ....202 D5
William Rd *CAMTN* NW1 ....4 A5
SUT SM1 ....209 G3
WIM/MER SW19 ....177 H3
Williams Av *WALTH* E17 ....51 H4
William's Buildings
WCHPL E1 * 104 E3
Williams Cl *CEND/HSY/T* N8 * 66 D3
FUL/PGN SW6 ....139 H1
Williams Dr *HSLW* TW3 ....135 F5
Williams Gv *SURB* KT6 ....190 D3
WDGN N22 ....49 G4
Williams La *MORT/ESHN* SW14 ....137 K4
MRDN SM4 ....194 B3
Williamson Cl *GNWCH* SE10 ....125 J5
Williamson Rd *FSBYPK* N4 ....67 H5
Williamson St *HOLWY* N7 * 84 E2
Williamson Wy *MLHL* NW7 ....46 C2
Williams Rd *NWDGN* UB2 ....114 D4
WEA W13 * 116 B1
William St *BARK* IG11 ....90 C5
CAR SM5 ....209 J1
KTBR SW1X 15 F3
LEY E10 ....69 K3
TOTM N17 ....50 B3
Williams Wy *RDART* DA2 ....170 A4
Willifield Wy *GLDGN* NW11 ....64 E2
Willingale Cl *WFD* IG8 * 53 H2
Willingdon Rd *WDGN* N22 ....49 H5
Willingham Cl *KTTN* NW5 ....84 C3
Willingham Ter *KTTN* NW5 ....84 C3
Willingham Wy *KUT/HW* KT1 ....175 H5
Willington Rd *BRXN/ST* SW9 ....141 K4
Willis Av *BELMT* SM2 ....209 J4
Willis Rd *CROY/NA* CR0 ....196 D4
ERITH DA8 ....129 K4
SRTFD E15 ....88 D6
Willis St *POP/IOD* E14 ....105 K5
Willmore End *WIM/MER* SW19 ....178 A4
Willoughby Av *CROY/NA* CR0 ....211 F2
Willoughby Dr *RAIN* RM13 ....93 G5
Willoughby Gv *TOTM* N17 ....50 D3
Willoughby La *TOTM* N17 ....50 D3
Willoughby Ms *TOTM* N17 * 50 D3
Willoughby Park Rd *TOTM* N17 ....50 D3
Willoughby Rd *CEND/HSY/T* N8 ....49 G6
HAMP NW3 ....83 H2
KUTN/CMB KT2 ....175 G4
TWK TW1 * 136 D6
Willoughby Wy *CHARL* SE7 ....126 A4
Willow Av *BARN* SW13 ....138 C3
BFN/LL DA15 ....168 B1
Willow Bank
RCHPK/HAM TW10 ....156 C5
Willowbay Cl *BAR* EN5 ....32 B1
Willow Bridge Rd *IS* N1 ....85 J5
Willowbrook *HPTN* TW12 ....173 G1
Willowbrook Est *PECK* SE15 * 143 G1
Willowbrook Rd *NWDGN* UB2 ....114 E3
PECK SE15 ....143 G1
STWL/WRAY TW19 ....152 B3
The Willow Centre *MTCM* CR4 ....194 E6
Willow Cl *BKHH* IG9 ....39 H5
BTFD TW8 ....116 D6
BXLY DA5 ....169 G1
CAT SE6 ....165 J3
HAYES BR2 ....200 D2
HCH RM12 ....93 K1
STMC/STPC BR5 ....202 C3
Willow Ct *STAN* HA7 * 43 K3
Willowcourt Av
KTN/HRWW/WS HA3 ....61 H2
Willow Dean *PIN* HA5 * 41 H5
Willow Dene *BUSH* WD23 * 28 E1
Willowdene *HGT* N6 * 65 K4
Willow Dene *PIN* HA5 ....41 H5
Willowdene Cl *WHTN* TW2 ....155 H2
Willow Dr *BAR* EN5 ....20 C5
Willow End *NTHWD* HA6 ....40 E2
SURB KT6 ....191 F5
TRDG/WHET N20 ....32 E4
Willowfields Cl
WOOL/PLUM SE18 ....127 K5
Willow Gdns *HSLW* TW3 ....135 F2
RSLP HA4 ....76 D1
Willow Gv *CHST* BR7 ....185 F2
Willowhayne Dr
WOT/HER KT12 ....188 A4
Willowhayne Gdns *WPK* KT4 ....208 A2
Willowherb Wk *CRW* RM5 ....56 E4
Willow La *MTCM* CR4 ....194 D2
WOOL/PLUM SE18 ....126 E4
Willowmead Cl *EA* W5 ....97 K4
Willowmere *ESH/CLAY* KT10 ....204 C2
Willow Mt *CROY/NA* CR0 ....212 A2
Willow Pl *WEST* SW1P 16 B6
Willow Rd *CHDH* RM6 ....74 A3
DART DA1 ....171 F5

EA W5 ....117 F2
EN EN1 ....24 B2
ERITH DA8 ....150 B2
HAMP NW3 ....83 H2
NWMAL KT3 ....191 K1
WLGTN SM6 ....210 B5
Willows Av *MRDN* SM4 ....194 A2
Willows Cl *PIN* HA5 ....41 G5
Willows Ter *WLSDN* NW10 * 99 H1
The Willows *BECK* BR3 * 182 D4
EBAR EN4 ....33 J1
ESH/CLAY KT10 ....204 E4
Willow St *CHING* E4 ....38 B5
ROMW/RG RM7 ....74 E1
SDTCH EC2A 7 G6
Willow Ter *PGE/AN* SE20 * 181 J4
Willow Tree Cl *BOW* E3 ....87 G6
Willowtree Cl *HGDN/ICK* UB10 ....76 A1
Willow Tree Cl *NTHLT* UB5 ....77 K4
WAND/EARL SW18 ....160 B3
YEAD UB4 ....95 G3
Willow Tree La *YEAD* UB4 ....95 H3
Willow Tree Rd *YEAD* UB4 ....94 E4
Willow Tree Wk *BMLY* BR1 ....184 A4
Willowtree Wy *THHTH* CR7 ....180 B4
Willow V *CHST* BR7 ....185 F2
SHB W12 * 99 K6
Willow Wk *WIM/MER* SW19 * 178 C4
Willow Wd Crs *SNWD* SE25 ....197 F3
Willow Wren Wnf
NWDGN UB2 * 114 A4
Will Rd *KTTN* NW5 ....84 B4
Willrose Crs *ABYW* SE2 ....128 D5
Willsbridge Ct *CAT* SE6 * 164 C6
Wills Crs *HSLW* TW3 ....155 G1
Wills Gv *MLHL* NW7 ....45 J1
Wilman Gv *HACK* E8 ....86 C5
Wilmar Cl *YEAD* UB4 ....94 B3
Wilmar Gdns *WWKM* BR4 ....198 E5
Wilmcote Cl *FUL/PGN* SW6 ....119 K6
Wilmer Cl *KUTN/CMB* KT2 ....175 G1
Wilmer Crs *KUTN/CMB* KT2 ....175 G1
Wilmer Gdns *IS* N1 ....7 H1
Wilmer Lea Cl *SRTFD* E15 ....88 B6
Wilmer Pl *STNW/STAM* N16 ....68 B6
Wilmer Wy *FBAR/BDGN* N11 ....48 B6
Wilmington Av *CHSWK* W4 ....138 A1
ORP BR6 ....217 H3
Wilmington Court Rd
RDART DA2 ....170 D5
Wilmington Gdns *BARK* IG11 ....90 D5
Wilmington Sq *FSBYW* WC1X 5 K6
Wilmington St *FSBYW* WC1X 5 J6
Wilmot Cl *PECK* SE15 ....143 H1
Wilmot Pl *CAMTN* NW1 ....84 C5
WEA W13 ....116 C2
Wilmot Rd *CAR* SM5 ....209 K3
DART DA1 ....150 C6
LEY E10 ....69 K6
TOTM N17 ....49 K6
Wilmount St
WOOL/PLUM SE18 ....127 G4
Wilna Rd *WAND/EARL* SW18 ....160 B2
Wilsham St *NTGHL* W11 ....119 G1
Wilshaw Cl *HDN* NW4 ....45 J6
Wilshaw St *NWCR* SE14 ....144 D2
Wilsmere Dr
KTN/HRWW/WS HA3 ....42 E3
NTHLT UB5 ....77 H4
Wilson Av *MTCM* CR4 ....178 D3
Wilson Cl *SAND/SEL* CR2 ....211 K3
WBLY HA9 ....62 B3
Wilson Dr *WBLY* HA9 ....62 B3
Wilson Gdns *HRW* HA1 ....60 C4
Wilson Gv *BERM/RHTH* SE16 ....123 J2
Wilson Rd *CHSGTN* KT9 ....206 B4
CMBW SE5 ....143 F2
IL IG1 ....71 K4
PLSTW E13 ....107 H2
Wilson's Av *TOTM* N17 ....50 B5
Wilson's Pl *POP/IOD* E14 ....105 H5
Wilson's Rd *HMSMTH* W6 ....119 G5
Wilson St *LVPST* EC2M 13 F1
WALTH E17 ....70 A2
WCHMN N21 ....35 G2
Wilson Wk *CHSWK* W4 * 118 C4
Wilstone Cl *YEAD* UB4 ....95 J3
Wilthorne Gdns *DAGE* RM10 ....92 C5
Wilton Av *CHSWK* W4 ....118 B5
Wilton Cl *WDR/YW* UB7 ....112 A6
Wilton Crs *KTBR* SW1X 15 G3
WIM/MER SW19 ....177 J4
Wilton Dr *CRW* RM5 ....56 E3
Wilton Est *HACK* E8 * 86 C4
Wilton Gdns *E/WMO/HCT* KT8 ....173 F6
EBED/NFELT TW14 ....153 H3
WOT/HER KT12 ....188 C5
Wilton Gv *NWMAL* KT3 ....192 C3
WIM/MER SW19 ....177 J4
Wilton Ms *HACK* E8 * 86 D4
KTBR SW1X 15 H4
Wilton Pl *KTBR* SW1X 15 G3
Wilton Rd *ABYW* SE2 ....128 D3
EBAR EN4 ....33 K4
HSLWW TW4 ....134 C4
MUSWH N10 ....48 A4
PIM SW1V 16 A5
WIM/MER SW19 ....178 C3
WIM/MER SW19 ....15 J5
Wilton Sq *IS* N1 ....85 K6
Wilton St *KTBR* SW1X 15 J4
Wilton Ter *KTBR* SW1X 15 G4
Wilton Vis *IS* N1 ....85 K6
Wilton Wy *FELT* TW13 ....154 A4
Wilton Wy *HACK* E8 ....86 C4

Wiltshire Cl *CHEL* SW3 ....14 D7
MLHL NW7 * 45 H1
Wiltshire Gdns *FSBYPK* N4 ....67 J3
WHTN TW2 ....155 H3
Wiltshire La *PIN* HA5 ....40 D6
ORP BR6 ....202 B4
Wiltshire Rd *BRXN/ST* SW9 ....142 B4
THHTH CR7 ....180 B6
Wiltshire Rw *IS* N1 ....6 E1
Wilverley Crs *NWMAL* KT3 ....192 B3
Wimbart Rd
BRXS/STRHM SW2 * 162 A2
Wimbledon Park Side
PUT/ROE SW19 ....158 E2
Wimbledon Br
WIM/MER SW19 ....177 J2
Wimbledon Hill Rd
WIM/MER SW19 ....177 H2
Wimbledon Park Rd
WIM/MER SW19 ....159 H5
Wimbledon Park Side
WIM/MER SW19 ....159 G4
Wimbledon Rd *TOOT* SW17 ....160 B6
Wimbolt St *BETH* E2 ....104 C2
Wimborne Av *NWDGN* UB2 ....115 F4
STMC/STPC BR5 ....186 A6
YEAD UB4 ....95 F5
Wimborne Cl *BKHH* IG9 ....39 G4
LEE/GVPK SE12 ....145 J6
WPK KT4 ....193 F5
Wimborne Dr *CDALE/KGS* NW9 ....44 C6
PIN HA5 ....59 H4
Wimborne Gdns *WEA* W13 ....97 H5
Wimborne Rd *ED* N9 ....36 C4
TOTM N17 ....50 A5
Wimborne Wy *BECK* BR3 ....198 A1
Wimbourne St *IS* N1 ....6 E2
Wimpole Cl *HAYES* BR2 ....200 B1
KUT/HW KT1 ....175 G5
Wimpole Ms *CAVSQ/HST* W1G 9 J1
Wimpole Rd *WDR/YW* UB7 ....112 A1
Wimpole St *CAVSQ/HST* W1G 9 J3
Wimshurst Cl *CROY/NA* CR0 ....195 K5
Wincanton Crs *NTHLT* UB5 ....78 A3
Wincanton Gdns *BARK/HLT* IG6 ....54 B3
Wincanton Rd
WAND/EARL SW18 ....159 J2
RDART DA2 ....170 C1 (Wincanton Rd *BXLYHN* DA7 ....149 K5)
Wincanton Rd
WAND/EARL SW18 ....159 J2
Winchcombe Rd *CAR* SM5 ....194 C4
Winchcomb Gdns
ELTH/MOT SE9 ....146 C4
Winchelsea Av *BXLYHN* DA7 ....149 G1
Winchelsea Cl *PUT/ROE* SW15 ....139 G6
Winchelsea Rd *FSTGT* E7 ....88 E2
TOTM N17 ....50 A5
WLSDN NW10 ....81 F6
Winchelsey Ri *SAND/SEL* CR2 ....212 B4
Winchendon Rd *FUL/PGN* SW6 ....139 J2
TEDD TW11 ....155 J6
Winchester Av *CDALE/KGS* NW9 ....44 B6
HEST TW5 ....114 E6
KIL/WHAMP NW6 ....82 C6
Winchester Cl *EN* EN1 * 36 A1
ESH/CLAY KT10 ....204 A3
HAYES BR2 ....183 J6
KUTN/CMB KT2 ....175 J3
LBTH SE11 ....18 B7
Winchester Ct *PIN* HA5 * 41 H6
STHGT/OAK N14 ....34 C2
Winchester Crs *RYLN/HDSTN* HA2 ....78 A2
Winchester Dr *PIN* HA5 ....59 H3
Winchester Ms *WPK* KT4 ....193 G6
Winchester Pk *HAYES* BR2 ....183 J6
Winchester Pl *HACK* E8 * 86 B3
HGT N6 ....66 B5
Winchester Rd *BXLYHN* DA7 ....148 E3
CHING E4 ....52 A3
ED N9 ....36 B3
FELT * TW13 ....154 E5
HAMP NW3 ....83 H5
HAYES BR2 ....183 J6
HGT N6 ....66 B5
HYS/HAR UB3 ....133 H1
IL IG1 ....72 C2
KTN/HRWW/WS HA3 ....62 A1
ORP BR6 ....217 J2
TWK TW1 ....156 C1
Winchester St *STHWK* SE1 ....12 E7
Winchester St *ACT* W3 ....117 K1
PIM SW1V 16 A7
Winchester Wk *STHWK* SE1 ....12 E7
Winchet Wy *ENC/FH* EN2 ....23 H2
Winchfield Cl
KTN/HRWW/WS HA3 ....61 J3
Winchfield Rd *SYD* SE26 ....182 B1
Winchilsea Crs
E/WMO/HCT KT8 ....173 H5
Winchmore Hill Rd
STHGT/OAK N14 ....34 C2
Winchmore Vis *WCHMH* N21 * 35 F2
Winckley Cl
KTN/HRWW/WS HA3 ....62 B2
Wincott St *LBTH* SE11 ....17 K6
Wincrofts Dr *ELTH/MOT* SE9 ....147 J5
Windall Cl *NRWD* SE19 ....181 H4
Windborough Rd *CAR* SM5 ....210 A5
Windermere Av *FNCH* N3 ....46 E6
HCH RM12 ....93 J3
KIL/WHAMP NW6 ....82 C6
RSLP HA4 ....59 G4
WBLY HA9 ....43 H6
WIM/MER SW19 ....178 A6
Windermere Cl *DART* DA1 ....170 D4
EBED/NFELT TW14 ....153 H3
ORP BR6 ....216 B1
STWL/WRAY TW19 ....152 A3
Windermere Gdns *REDBR* IG4 ....71 J2
Windermere Gv *WBLY* HA9 ....61 J3
Windermere Hall *EDGW* HA8 * 44 B1
Windermere Rd *ARCH* N19 ....66 C6
BXLYHN DA7 ....149 K3
CROY/NA CR0 ....197 G5
EA W5 ....116 D3
MUSWH N10 ....48 B4
PLMGR N13 ....35 G5
STRHM/NOR SW16 ....179 H4
WIM/MER SW19 ....177 J5
WWKM BR4 ....199 H6
Winders Rd *BTSEA* SW11 ....140 D3

Windfield Cl *SYD* SE26 ....164 A6
Windham Rd *RCH/KEW* TW9 ....137 G4
Winding Wy *BCTR* RM8 ....91 J1
Windlass Pl *DEPT* SE8 ....124 B4
Windlesham Gv
WIM/MER SW19 ....159 G3
Windley Cl *FSTH* SE23 ....163 K4
Windmill Cl *LEW* SE13 ....145 F3
STHWK SE1 * 123 H4
SURB KT6 ....190 D6
Windmill Dr *CLAP* SW4 ....141 G6
CRICK NW2 ....82 C1
Windmill Gdns *ENC/FH* EN2 ....23 G4
Windmill Gv *CROY/NA* CR0 ....196 D4
Windmill Hl *ENC/FH* EN2 ....23 H4
HAMP NW3 * 83 G1
RSLP HA4 ....58 D5
Windmill La *BAR* EN5 ....31 H1
BUSH WD23 ....28 E3
EA W5 ....96 C4
GFD/PVL UB6 ....96 C4
HAYES BR2 ....215 G2
NWDGN UB2 ....115 H2
SRTFD E15 ....88 B5
SURB KT6 ....190 C4
Windmill Pas *CHSWK* W4 * 118 B4
Windmill Ri *KUTN/CMB* KT2 ....175 J3
Windmill Rd *CHSWK* W4 ....118 B4
CROY/NA CR0 ....196 D4
EA W5 ....116 D4
HPTN TW12 ....173 G1
MTCM CR4 ....195 G1
UED N18 ....35 K6
WAND/EARL SW18 ....160 C1
WIM/MER SW19 ....159 H5
Windmill Rw *LBTH* SE11 ....122 B5
Windmill St *BUSH* WD23 ....28 E3
FITZ W1T 10 C2
Windmill Wk *STHWK* SE1 * 18 A1
Windmill Wy *RSLP* HA4 ....58 D5
Windrose Cl *BERM/RHTH* SE16 ....124 A2
Windrush *NWMAL* KT3 ....191 J1
Windrush Cl *BTSEA* SW11 * 140 C5
CHSWK W4 * 137 K1
Windrush La *FSTH* SE23 ....164 A5
Windrush Rd *WLSDN* NW10 ....81 F6
Windsor Av *CHEAM* SM3 ....208 C1
E/WMO/HCT KT8 ....173 F6
EDGW HA8 ....30 D4
NWMAL KT3 ....191 K2
WALTH E17 ....51 F5
WIM/MER SW19 ....178 B4
Windsor Cl *CHST* BR7 ....185 G1
FNCH N3 ....46 C5
NTHWD HA6 ....40 E6
RYLN/HDSTN HA2 ....77 K1
WNWD SE27 ....162 D6
Windsor Ct *PIN* HA5 * 41 H6
STHGT/OAK N14 ....34 C1
Windsor Crs *RYLN/HDSTN* HA2 ....78 A2
WBLY HA9 ....62 D1
Windsor Dr *ASHF* TW15 ....152 A6
DART DA1 ....170 D1
EBAR EN4 ....33 K1
ORP BR6 ....217 G4
Windsor Gdns *CROY/NA* CR0 ....210 E1
HYS/HAR UB3 ....113 G3
MV/WKIL W9 ....100 E4
Windsor Ms *CAT* SE6 ....165 F3
Windsor Park Rd
HYS/HAR UB3 ....133 J1
Windsor Rd *BAR* EN5 ....32 B1
BCTR RM8 ....73 K6
BXLYHS DA6 ....149 F5
CHING E4 ....37 K6
CRICK NW2 ....81 K4
EA W5 ....98 A6
FNCH N3 ....46 C5
FSTGT E7 ....89 F3
HOLWY N7 ....84 E1
HSLWW TW4 ....134 A2
IL IG1 ....90 C2
KTN/HRWW/WS HA3 ....42 C4
LEY E10 ....69 K6
NWDGN UB2 ....114 D3
PLMGR N13 ....35 G5
RCH/KEW TW9 ....137 G3
TEDD TW11 ....173 J1
THHTH CR7 ....180 C5
TOTM N17 ....50 C5
WAN E11 ....70 E5
WPK KT4 ....192 D6
The Windsors *BKHH* IG9 ....39 J4
Windsor St *IS* N1 ....85 H6
Windsor Ter *IS* N1 ....6 E5
Windsor Wk *CMBW* SE5 ....142 E3
Windsor Wy *WKENS* W14 ....119 G4
Windspoint Dr *PECK* SE15 ....123 J6
Windstock Cl
BERM/RHTH SE16 ....124 C3
Windus Rd *STNW/STAM* N16 ....68 B3
Windy Rdg *BMLY* BR1 ....184 D4
Windy Ridge Cl
WIM/MER SW19 ....177 G1
Wine Cl *WAP* E1W 104 E6
Wine Office Ct
FLST/FETLN EC4A 11 K3
Winery La *KUT/HW* KT1 ....175 G6
Winey Cl *CHSGTN* KT9 ....205 J5
Winforton St *GNWCH* SE10 ....145 F2
Winfrith Rd *WAND/EARL* SW18 ....160 B2
Wingate Crs *CROY/NA* CR0 ....195 K3
Wingate Rd *IL* IG1 ....90 B3
HMSMTH W6 ....118 E3
SCUP DA14 ....186 D1
SHB W12 ....118 E3
Wingfield Ms *PECK* SE15 * 143 H4
Wingfield Rd *KUTN/CMB* KT2 ....175 G2
SRTFD E15 ....88 C3
WALTH E17 ....69 K2
Wingfield St *PECK* SE15 ....143 H4
Wingfield Wy *RSLP* HA4 ....77 F4
Wingford Rd
BRXS/STRHM SW2 ....161 K1
Wingmore Rd *HNHL* SE24 ....142 D4
Wingrave Rd *HMSMTH* W6 ....119 F6

Wingrove Rd CAT SE6.............165 H4
Wings Cl SUT SM1.............208 E2
Winifred Cl BAR EN5.............31 H1
Winifred Pl NFNCH/WDSPK N12...47 G1
Winifred Rd BCTR RM8.............91 K6
  DART DA1.............150 E6
  ERITH.............130 B5
  HPTN TW12.............155 F6
  WIM/MER SW19.............177 K4
Winifred St CAN/RD E16.............126 E1
Winifred Ter EN EN1.............36 B2
  PLSTW E13.............106 E1
Winkfield Rd WDGN N22.............49 G4
Winkley St BETH E2.............104 D1
Winkworth Cottages
  WCHPL E1 *.............104 E3
Winlaton Rd BMLY BR1.............165 G6
Winmill Rd BCTR RM8.............92 B1
Winn Common Rd
  WOOL/PLUM SE18.............127 K6
Winnett St SOHO/SHAV W1D...10 C5
Winnington Cl EFNCH N2.............65 H3
Winnington Rd EFNCH N2.............65 H4
  PEND EN3.............24 E1
Winnipeg Dr ORP BR6.............217 H4
Winn La WDR/YW UB7.............112 A4
Winn Rd LEE/GVPK SE12.............165 K3
Winns Av WALTH E17.............51 H6
Winns Ms SEVS/STOTM N15...68 A1
Winns Ter WALTH E17.............51 J5
Winsbeach WALTH E17.............51 J5
Winscombe Crs EA W5.............97 K3
Winscombe St KTTN NW5.............84 B1
Winscombe Wy STAN HA7.............43 G1
Winsford Rd CAT SE6.............164 C5
Winsford Ter UED N18 *.............49 J1
Winsham Gv BTSEA SW11.....141 F6
Winslade Rd
  BRXS/STRHM SW2.............141 K6
Winsland Ms BAY/PAD W2.....8 A3
Winsland St BAY/PAD W2.....8 A3
Winsley St GTPST W1W.............10 A3
Winslow Cl PIN HA5.............59 F3
  WLSDN NW10.............81 G1
Winslow Gv CHING E4.............38 C4
Winslow Rd HMSMTH W6.....119 F6
Winslow Wy FELT TW13.............154 D5
Winsor Ter EHAM E6.............108 B4
Winstanley Rd BTSEA SW11....140 C4
Winstead Gdns DAGE RM10....92 E5
Winston Av CDALE/KGS NW9..63 G4
Winston Cl KTN/HRWW/WS HA3..43 F2
  ROMW/RG RM7.............74 D1
Winston Ct
  KTN/HRWW/WS HA3.............42 B4
Winston House SURB KT6 *..191 F2
Winston Rd STNW/STAM N16...85 K2
Winston Wy IL IG1.............90 B1
Winter Av EHAM E6.............89 J6
Winterbourne Rd BCTR RM8..91 J1
  CAT SE6.............164 C3
  THHTH CR7.............196 B1
Winter Box Wk
  RCHPK/HAM TW10.............137 G6
Winterbrook Rd HNHL SE24..142 D1
Winterburn Cl FBAR/BDGN N11..48 A2
Winterfold Cl WIM/MER SW19..159 H4
Winters Rd THDIT KT7.............190 C4
Winterstoke Rd CAT SE6.............164 C3
Winterwell Rd
  BRXS/STRHM SW2.............141 K6
Winthorpe Rd PUT/ROE SW15..139 H5
Winthrop St WCHPL E1.............104 D4
Winthrop St WCHPL E1 *.............104 E4
Winton Av FBAR/BDGN N11....48 C3
Winton Cl ED N9.............37 F2
Winton Gdns EDGW HA8.............44 B3
Winton Rd ORP BR6.............216 D2
The Wintons BUSH WD23 *........28 C4
Wirral Wood Cl CHST BR7.....185 F2
Wisbeach Rd CROY/NA CR0....196 E2
Wisborough Rd SAND/SEL CR2..212 B6
Wisdons Cl DAGE RM10.............74 D5
Wise La MLHL NW7.............45 J2
  WDR/YW UB7.............112 A4
Wiseman Rd LEY E10 *.............69 J6
Wise Rd SRTFD E15.............88 A6
Wiseton Rd TOOT SW17.............160 D3
Wishart Rd BKHTH/KID SE3..146 C3
Wishaw Wk FBAR/BDGN N11...48 E2
Wisley Rd BTSEA SW11.............140 E6
  STMC/STPC BR5.............186 B5
Wistaria Cl ORP BR6.............217 F3
Wisteria Cl IL IG1.............90 B3
  MLHL NW7.............45 H2
Wisteria Rd LEW SE13.............145 G5
Witanhurst La HGT N6.............66 A5
Witan St BETH E2.............104 D2
Witham Cl LOU IG10.............39 J1
Witham Rd DAGE RM10.............92 C3
  GPK RM2.............75 K2
  ISLW TW7.............135 J2
  PGE/AN SE20.............181 K6
  WEA W13.............116 B1
Withens Cl STMC/STPC BR5 *..202 D1
Witherby Cl CROY/NA CR0.....212 A3
Witherington Rd HBRY N5 *....85 G3
Withers Md CDALE/KGS NW9...45 H4
Witherston Rd
  WIM/MER SW19.............159 G2
Withy La RSLP HA4.............58 A2
Withy Md CHING E4.............38 C4
Witley Crs CROY/NA CR0.....214 A4
Witley Gdns NWDGN UB2.....114 E4
Witley Rd ARCH N19.............66 D6
Witney Cl PIN HA5.............41 K2
Witney Pth FSTH SE23.............164 A5
Wittenham Wy CHING E4.............38 B4
Wittering Cl KUTN/CMB KT2..174 E1
Wittersham Rd BMLY BR1.....183 J1
Wivenhoe Cl PECK SE15.............143 J4
Wivenhoe Ct HSLW TW3.............134 E5
Wivenhoe Rd BARK IG11.............109 G1

Wiverton Rd SYD SE26.............181 K2
Wix Dr DAGW RM9.............91 K6
Wix's La CLAP SW4.............141 G5
Woburn Av WIS *.............97 H4
Woburn Av HCH RM12.............93 J2
Woburn Cl BUSH WD23.............28 C1
  THMD SE28.............109 H5
  WIM/MER SW19.............178 B2
Woburn Pl STPAN WC1H.............4 D7
Woburn Rd CAR SM5.............194 D5
  CROY/NA CR0.............196 D5
Woburn Sq STPAN WC1H.............4 D7
Woburn Wk STPAN WC1H.............4 E7
Wodeham Gdns WCHPL E1....104 C4
Wodehouse Av CMBW SE5....143 G2
Wodehouse Rd DART DA1.....151 K5
Woffington Cl KUT/HW KT1...174 D4
Woking Cl PUT/ROE SW15.....138 C5
Woldham Pl HAYES BR2.............200 B1
Woldham Rd HAYES BR2.............200 B1
Wolds Dr ORP BR6.............216 A2
Wolfe Cl HAYES BR2.............199 K3
  YEAD UB4.............95 F2
Wolfe Crs CHARL SE7.............126 C5
Wolferton Rd MNPK E12.............89 K2
Wolffington Rd WNWD SE27..162 C6
Wolfram Cl LEW SE13.............145 H6
Wolftencroft Cl BTSEA SW11..140 D4
Wollaston Cl STHWK SE1.............18 B6
Wolmer Cl EDGW HA8.............30 C5
Wolmer Gdns EDGW HA8.............30 B3
Wolseley Av WAND/EARL SW18..159 K4
Wolseley Gdns CHSWK W4....117 J6
Wolseley Rd CEND/HSY/T N8..66 D3
  CHSWK W4.............117 K4
  FSTGT E7.............89 F5
  KTN/HRWW/WS HA3.............42 E6
  MTCM CR4.............195 F4
  ROMW/RG RM7.............75 F4
  WDGN N22.............49 F4
Wolseley St STHWK SE1.............19 K3
Wolsey Av EHAM E6.............108 A2
  THDIT KT7.............190 A2
  WALTH E17.............51 H6
Wolsey Cl HSLW TW3.............135 H5
  KUTN/CMB KT2.............175 J4
  NWDGN UB2.............115 H3
  RYNPK SW20.............176 E3
  WPK KT4.............207 J2
Wolsey Crs ELTH/MOT SE9 *..166 E1
Wolsey Crs CROY/NA CR0.....214 A6
  MRDN SM4.............193 J4
Wolsey Dr KUTN/CMB KT2....175 F1
  WOT/HER KT12.............188 C5
Wolsey Gdns BARK/HLT IG6...54 B1
Wolsey Gv EDGW HA8.............45 F3
  ESH/CLAY KT10.............204 B2
Wolsey Ms KTTN NW5.............84 C4
  ORP BR6.............217 F3
Wolsey Rd ASHF TW15.............152 B6
  E/WMO/HCT KT8.............189 J1
  EN EN1.............24 D1
  ESH/CLAY KT10.............204 B2
  HPTN TW12.............173 H2
  IS N1.............85 J3
  NTHWD HA6.............26 A4
Wolsey St WCHPL E1.............104 E4
Wolsey Wy CHSGTN KT9.............206 C3
Wolsley Cl DART DA1.............150 B6
Wolstonbury
  NFNCH/WDSPK N12 *.............46 E1
Wolvercote Rd ABYW SE2.....128 E2
Wolverley St BETH E2 *.............104 D2
Wolverton Av KUTN/CMB KT2..175 H4
Wolverton Gdns EA W5.............98 B6
  HMSMTH W6.............119 G4
Wolverton Rd STAN HA7.............43 H2
Wolverton Wy STHGT/OAK N14..22 C6
Wolves La WDGN N22.............49 G3
Womersley Rd CEND/HSY/T N8..67 F3
Wonersh Wy BELMT SM2.....208 B6
Wonford Cl KUTN/CMB KT2...176 B4
Wontner Cl IS N1.............85 J5
Wontner Rd BAL SW12.............160 E4
Woodall Cl CHSGTN KT9.............205 J5
Woodall Rd PEND EN3.............37 F1
Woodbank Rd BMLY BR1.....165 J5
Woodbastwick Rd SYD SE26..182 A2
Woodberry Av
  RYLN/HDSTN HA2.............60 C1
  WCHMH N21.............35 G2
Woodberry Cl MLHL NW7.............46 B3
Woodberry Crs MUSWH N10..66 B1
Woodberry Down FSBYPK N4..67 J4
Woodberry Gdns
  NFNCH/WDSPK N12.............47 G2
Woodberry Gv BXLY DA5.............170 A5
  FSBYPK N4.............67 J4
  NFNCH/WDSPK N12.............47 G2
Woodbine Cl WHTN TW2.............155 J4
Woodbine Gv ENC/FH EN2....23 K1
  PGE/AN SE20.............181 J3
Woodbine La WPK KT4.............207 K1
Woodbine Pl WAN E11.............71 F2
Woodbine Rd BFN/LL DA15...167 K3
Woodbines Av KUT/HW KT1...174 E6
Woodbine Ter HOM E9.............86 E4
Woodborough Rd
  PUT/ROE SW15.............138 E5
Woodbourne Av
  STRHM/NOR SW16.............161 J5
Woodbourne Dr
  ESH/CLAY KT10.............205 F4
Woodbourne Gdns
  WLGTN SM6.............210 B5
Woodbridge Cl HOLWY N7.....67 F6
Woodbridge St BARK IG11.....91 F5
Woodbridge St CLKNW EC1R..6 A6
Woodbrook Rd ABYW SE2.....128 B6
Woodburn Cl HDN NW4.............64 B2
Woodbury Cl CROY/NA CR0...197 G6
  WAN E11.............71 F1
Woodbury Gdns
  LEE/GVPK SE12.............166 A6
Woodbury Park Rd WEA W13..97 H3

Woodbury St TOOT SW17.....178 D1
Woodchester Sq BAY/PAD W2..101 F4
Woodchurch Cl SCUP DA14...167 F5
Woodchurch Dr BMLY BR1....184 C3
Woodchurch Rd
  KIL/WHAMP NW6.............82 E5
Wood Cl BETH E2.............104 C3
  BXLY DA5.............170 E5
  CDALE/KGS NW9.............63 F4
  HRW HA1.............60 D4
Woodclyffe Dr CHST BR7.....185 F5
Woodcock Dell Av
  KTN/HRWW/WS HA3.............61 J4
Woodcock Hl
  KTN/HRWW/WS HA3.............61 H4
Woodcocks CAN/RD E16.............107 G4
Woodcombe Crs FSTH SE23..163 K3
Woodcote Av EN EN1.............36 E1
Woodcote Av HCH RM12.............93 J2
  MLHL NW7.............46 A2
  THHTH CR7.............196 C1
  WLGTN SM6.............210 B6
Woodcote Dr ORP BR6.............201 J4
Woodcote Gn WLGTN SM6....210 C6
Woodcote Ms LOU IG10.............39 H2
  WLGTN SM6.............210 B4
Woodcote Pl WNWD SE27 *...180 C1
Woodcote Rd WAN E11.............71 F4
Wood Crest BELMT SM2 *.....209 G5
Woodcroft ELTH/MOT SE9.....166 E5
  GFD/PVL UB6.............79 G4
  WCHMH N21.............35 F3
Woodcroft Av MLHL NW7.............45 G3
  STAN HA7.............43 G4
Woodcroft Ms DEPT SE8.............124 A4
Woodcroft Rd THHTH CR7....196 C2
Wood Dene PECK SE15 *.............143 J2
Wood Dr CHST BR7.............184 D2
Woodedge Cl CHING E4.............38 D3
Wooden Bridge Ter
  WNWD SE27 *.............162 C5
Wood End HYS/HAR UB3.............94 C5
  SWLY BR8.............203 K1
Wood End Av RYLN/HDSTN HA2..78 C2
Wood End Cl NTHLT UB5.............78 D3
Woodend Gdns ENC/FH EN2..22 E5
Wood End Gdns NTHLT UB5..78 C3
Wood End La NTHLT UB5.............78 C3
Wood End Rd HRW HA1.............78 D2
Wood End Green Rd
  HYS/HAR UB3.............94 B4
The Wood End WLGTN SM6....210 B6
Wood End Wy NTHLT UB5.............78 C3
Wooder Gdns FSTGT E7.............88 E2
Wooderson Cl SNWD SE25....197 F1
Woodfall Av BAR EN5.............20 C6
Woodfall Dr DART DA1.............150 C5
Woodfall Rd FSBYPK N4.............67 G6
Woodfall St CHEL SW3.............120 E5
Woodfarrs CMBW SE5.............142 E5
Wood Fld HAMP NW3 *.............83 K4
Woodfield Av ALP/SUD HA0...79 J1
  CAR SM5.............210 A4
  EA W5.............97 J3
  NTHWD HA6.............26 C2
  STRHM/NOR SW16.............161 J5
Woodfield Cl EN EN1.............24 A5
  NRWD SE19.............180 D3
Woodfield Crs EA W5.............97 K3
Woodfield Dr EBAR EN4.............34 A1
  GPK RM2.............75 J1
Woodfield Gv
  STRHM/NOR SW16.............161 J5
Woodfield La
  STRHM/NOR SW16.............161 J5
  ESH/CLAY KT10.............189 H6
Woodfield Pl MV/WKIL W9.....100 D3
Woodfield Rd BUSH WD23.....28 D3
  EA W5.............97 J3
  HSLWW TW4.............134 A3
  MV/WKIL W9.............100 D4
  THDIT KT7.............190 A6
Woodfield Wy
  FBAR/BDGN N11.............48 D3
Woodford Av GNTH/NBYPK IG2..71 K2
Woodford Bridge Rd
  REDBR IG4.............71 J1
Woodford Crs PIN HA5.............41 F5
Woodford New Rd WALTH E17..70 D1
Woodford Pl WBLY HA9.............62 A5
Woodford Rd FSTGT E7.............89 F2
  SWFD E18.............70 E1
Woodgate Av CHSGTN KT9....205 K3
Woodgate Crs NTHWD HA6....40 E2
Woodgate Dr
  STRHM/NOR SW16.............179 J3
Woodger Rd SHB W12.............119 F2
Woodget Cl EHAM E6.............107 J5
Woodgrange Av EA W5.............117 G1
  EN EN1.............36 C5
  KTN/HRWW/WS HA3.............61 K2
  NFNCH/WDSPK N12.............47 H2
Woodgrange Cl
  KTN/HRWW/WS HA3.............61 K2
Woodgrange Gdns EN EN1....36 C5
Woodgrange Rd FSTGT E7.....88 E3
Woodgrange Ter EN EN1 *.....36 C5
Woodhall Av DUL SE21.............163 G5
  PIN HA5.............41 J4
Woodhall Dr DUL SE21.............163 G5
  PIN HA5.............41 J3
Woodhall Ga PIN HA5.............41 H3
Woodhall La OXHEY WD19.....27 H3
Woodham Ct SWFD E18.............70 D1
Woodham Rd CAT SE6.............165 F5
Woodhatch Cl EHAM E6.............107 J4
Woodhaven Gdns
  BARK/HLT IG6.............72 C1

Woodhayes Rd
  WIM/MER SW19.............177 F3
Woodhead Dr ORP BR6.............216 E1
Woodheyes Rd WLSDN NW10..81 G3
Woodhill WOOL/PLUM SE18..126 D4
Woodhill Crs
  KTN/HRWW/WS HA3.............61 K5
Woodhouse Av GFD/PVL UB6..97 F1
Woodhouse Cl EDUL SE22.....143 H5
  GFD/PVL UB6.............97 F1
  HYS/HAR UB3.............113 H4
Woodhouse Eaves NTHWD HA6..40 E1
Woodhouse Gv FSTGT E7.....89 J4
Woodhouse Rd
  NFNCH/WDSPK N12.............47 G2
  WAN E11.............88 D1
Woodhurst Av
  STMC/STPC BR5.............201 H3
Woodhurst Rd ABYW SE2.....128 C5
  ACT W3.............117 K1
Woodington Cl ELTH/MOT SE9..167 F1
Woodknoll Dr CHST BR7.............184 E4
Woodland Ap GFD/PVL UB6...79 G4
Woodland Cl CDALE/KGS NW9..62 E4
  HOR/WEW KT19 *.............207 G3
  NRWD SE19.............181 E5
  WFD IG8.............39 F5
Woodland Ct GLDGN NW11 *..64 D2
Woodland Crs
  BERM/RHTH SE16.............124 A2
  GNWCH SE10.............125 H6
Woodland Gdns ISLW TW7.....135 K4
  MUSWH N10.............66 B1
Woodland Gv CROY/NA CR0..211 G5
  GNWCH SE10.............125 H5
Woodland Hl NRWD SE19.....181 F2
Woodland Ms
  STRHM/NOR SW16.............161 K5
Woodland Ri GFD/PVL UB6....79 G4
  MUSWH N10.............66 B1
Woodland Rd CHING E4.............38 A3
  FBAR/BDGN N11.............48 B3
  NRWD SE19.............181 F1
  THHTH CR7.............196 B1
Woodlands BXLYHS DA6.............149 J6
  GLDGN NW11.............64 C3
  RYLN/HDSTN HA2.............60 A1
  WBLY HA9.............62 B1
Woodlands Av ACT W3.............117 J1
  BFN/LL DA15.............167 K3
  CHDH RM6.............73 K3
  FNCH N3.............47 G3
  NWMAL KT3.............175 J5
  RSLP HA4.............59 G5
  WAN E11.............71 F5
  WPK KT4.............192 C6
Woodlands Cl BMLY BR1.....184 E5
  CHDH RM6.............73 K3
  ESH/CLAY KT10.............205 F5
  GLDGN NW11.............64 C2
Woodlands Dr STAN HA7.............43 F2
  SUN TW16.............172 B5
Woodlands Gdns WALTH E17..70 C1
Woodlands Gv ISLW TW7.....135 K3
Woodlands Pk BXLY DA5.....169 K6
Woodlands Park Rd
  GNWCH SE10.............125 J6
  SEVS/STOTM N15.............67 J2
Woodlands Rd BARN SW13...138 C4
  BMLY BR1.............184 E5
  BXLYHN DA7.............149 F4
  ENC/FH EN2.............23 K1
  HRW HA1.............61 F3
  IL IG1.............90 C1
  ISLW TW7.............135 K4
  ORP BR6.............217 G4
  ROM RM1.............57 H6
  STHL UB1.............95 H6
  SURB KT6.............190 E5
  WALTH E17.............52 A6
  WAN E11.............70 C6
Woodlands St LEW SE13.....165 G2
Woodlands Ter SWLY BR8 *...203 K3
The Woodlands
  BRXN/ST SW9 *.............142 C1
  ESH/CLAY KT10.............189 H6
  HRW HA1.............60 E2
  ISLW TW7.............136 A3
  LEW SE13.............165 G2
  ORP BR6.............217 H4
  STAN HA7 *.............43 H1
  STHGT/OAK N14.............34 B3
  WLGTN SM6.............210 B6
Woodlands Wy
  PUT/ROE SW15.............139 J6
Woodland Ter CHARL SE7.....126 D4
Woodland Wk HAMP NW3.....83 J3
  HOR/WEW KT19.............206 C4
Woodland Wy ABYW SE2.....128 E4
  BRYLDS KT5.............191 J6
  CROY/NA CR0.............198 B5
  MLHL NW7.............45 H2
  MRDN SM4.............193 J1
  STMC/STPC BR5.............201 H1
  WCHMH N21.............35 G4
  WFD IG8.............39 F5

Woodleigh Av
  NFNCH/WDSPK N12.............47 J2
Woodleigh Gdns
  STRHM/NOR SW16.............161 K5
Woodley Cl TOOT SW17.............178 E3
Woodley La SUT SM1.............208 C2
Woodley Rd ORP BR6.............202 D6
Wood Lodge Gdns BMLY BR1..184 D3
Wood Lodge La WWKM BR4..214 A1
Woodman Ms RCH/KEW TW9..137 J2
Woodman Pth BARK/HLT IG6..54 E2
Woodman Rd BARK/HLT IG6...55 F1
  CHIG IG7.............55 F1
Woodmans Gv WLSDN NW10..81 H3
Woodmansterne La CAR SM5..209 J6
Woodmansterne Rd
  STRHM/NOR SW16.............179 J2
Wood Md TOTM N17 *.............50 C2
Woodmere ELTH/MOT SE9....166 E3
Woodmere Av CROY/NA CR0..198 B4
Woodmere Cl BTSEA SW11...141 F4
  CROY/NA CR0.............198 A4
Woodmere Gdns
  CROY/NA CR0.............198 A4
Woodmere Wy BECK BR3.....199 G2
Woodnook Rd
  STRHM/NOR SW16.............161 G1
Woodpecker Cl BUSH WD23...28 C3
  ED N9.............24 E6
  KTN/HRWW/WS HA3.............43 H5
Woodpecker Ms LEW SE13...145 G5
Woodpecker Mt CROY/NA CR0..213 G6
Woodpecker Rd NWCR SE14..124 B6
  THMD SE28.............109 J5
Woodquest Av HNHL SE24....142 D6
Wood Ride EBAR EN4.............21 H2
  STMC/STPC BR5.............201 J1
Woodridge Cl ENC/FH EN2 *..23 G2
Woodridge Wy NTHWD HA6...40 C2
Woodriding Av PIN HA5.............41 K4
Woodridings Cl PIN HA5.............41 K3
Woodriffe Rd WAN E11.............70 B4
Wood Ri PIN HA5.............58 E2
Wood Rd WLSDN NW10.............80 E5
Woodrow WOOL/PLUM SE18..126 D4
Woodrow Av YEAD UB4.............94 D4
Woodrow Cl GFD/PVL UB6....79 H5
Woodrow Ct TOTM N17 *.............50 D3
Woodrush Cl NWCR SE14.....144 B1
Woodrush Wy CHDH RM6.....73 K1
Woodseer St WCHPL E1.............13 K1
Woodsford Sq WKENS W14...119 H1
Woodside BKHH IG9.............39 G4
  GLDGN NW11.............64 E2
  ORP BR6.............217 G3
  WIM/MER SW19.............177 J1
Woodside Av ALP/SUD HA0...80 A6
  CHST BR7.............185 H1
  ESH/CLAY KT10.............189 K4
  HGT N6.............65 K2
  NFNCH/WDSPK N12.............33 G2
  SNWD SE25.............197 J3
Woodside Cl ALP/SUD HA0...80 A6
  BRYLDS KT5.............191 K4
  BXLYHN DA7.............150 B3
  RSLP HA4.............58 B3
  STAN HA7.............43 H1
Woodside Ct EA W5 *.............117 F1
Woodside Court Rd
  CROY/NA CR0.............197 H4
Woodside Crs BFN/LL DA15..167 K5
Woodside Dr RDART DA2.............170 B6
Woodside End ALP/SUD HA0..80 A6
Woodside Gdns CHING E4.....51 K1
  TOTM N17.............50 A6
Woodside Grange Rd
  NFNCH/WDSPK N12.............33 F6
Woodside Gn SNWD SE25....197 J3
Woodside Gv
  NFNCH/WDSPK N12.............33 G5
Woodside La BXLY DA5.............168 E5
  TRDG/WHET N20.............33 G2
Woodside Pde BFN/LL DA15 *..167 K5
Woodside Park Av WALTH E17..70 D3
Woodside Park Rd
  NFNCH/WDSPK N12.............33 F6
Woodside Pl ALP/SUD HA0....80 A6
Woodside Rd BFN/LL DA15...167 K5
  BMLY BR1.............200 D2
  BXLYHN DA7.............150 A3
  KUTN/CMB KT2.............175 F3
  NRWD SE19.............181 F3
  NWMAL KT3.............176 A5
  PLSTW E13.............107 G3
  SNWD SE25.............197 J3
  SUT SM1.............209 G1
  WDGN N22.............49 F3
  WFD IG8.............38 E6
Woods Ms MYFR/PKLN W1K....9 F5
Woodsome Rd KTTN NW5.....84 A1
Woods Pl STHWK SE1.............19 H5
Woodspring Rd
  WIM/MER SW19.............159 H4
Woods Rd PECK SE15.............143 J2
Woodstead Gv EDGW HA8.....44 A2
The Woods NTHWD HA6.............26 E4
Woodstock Av CHEAM SM3...193 J4
  GLDGN NW11.............64 C4
  ISLW TW7.............136 B6
  STHL UB1.............95 K2
  WEA W13.............116 B3
Woodstock Cl BXLY DA5.............169 G3
  STAN HA7.............44 A5
Woodstock Gdns BECK BR3..182 E4
  IL IG3.............73 G6
  YEAD UB4.............94 D4
Woodstock Gra EA W5 *.............117 F1
Woodstock Gv SHB W12.............119 G2
Woodstock La North
  SURB KT6.............190 D6
Woodstock La South
  CHSGTN KT9.............205 J2

Woodstock Ms *CAVSQ/HST* W1G......9 H2
Woodstock Ri *CHEAM* SM3....193 J5
Woodstock Rd *ALP/SUD* HA0....80 B5
  BUSH WD23....28 E2
  CAR SM5....210 A3
  CHSWK W4....118 B4
  CROY/NA CR0....211 K1
  FSBYPK N4....67 G5
  FSTGT E7 *....88 D4
  GLDGN NW11....64 D4
  WALTH E17....52 A6
Woodstock St *CAN/RD* E16....106 D5
  OXSTW W1C....9 J4
Woodstock Ter *POP/IOD* E14....105 K6
Woodstone Av *EW* KT17....207 J3
Wood St *BAR* EN5....20 A5
  CAN/RD E16....107 F6
  CHSWK W4....118 B5
  CITYW EC2V....12 D3
  KUT/HW KT1....174 E5
  MTCM CR4....195 F4
  WALTH E17 *....52 A6
Woodsyre *SYD* SE26....163 G6
Wood Ter *CRICK* NW2 *....63 H6
Woodthorpe Rd
  PUT/ROE SW15....138 E5
Woodtree Cl *HDN* NW4....46 B5
Wood V *FSTH* SE23....163 J5
  MUSWH N10....66 C2
Woodvale Av *SNWD* SE25....181 G6
Woodview Av *CHING* E4....38 A6
Woodview Cl *ORP* BR6....201 H6
  PUT/ROE SW15....158 A6
Woodview Rd *SWLY* BR8....187 K5
Woodville Cl *LEE/GVPK* SE12....145 K6
  TEDD TW11 *....156 A1
Woodville Gdns *BARK/HLT* IG6....54 B5
  EA W5....98 A5
  RSLP HA4....58 A4
  SURB KT6 *....190 E6
Woodville Rd *BAR* EN5....21 F4
  EA W5....98 A5
  GLDGN NW11....64 C4
  KIL/WHAMP NW6 *....100 D1
  MRDN SM4....193 K1
  RCHPK/HAM TW10....156 C5
  STNW/STAM N16....86 A3
  SWFD E18....53 F5
  THHTH CR7....180 E6
  WALTH E17....69 G1
  WAN E11....70 D5
Woodville St
  WOOL/PLUM SE18....126 D4
Woodward Av *HDN* NW4....63 J2
Woodward Cl *ESH/CLAY* KT10....205 F4
Woodwarde Rd *EDUL* SE22....163 F1
Woodward Gdns *DAGW* RM9....91 J5
  STAN HA7 *....43 F3
Woodward Rd *DAGW* RM9....91 H5
Wood Wy *ORP* BR6....201 F6
Woodway Crs *HRW* HA1....61 G3
Woodwaye *OXHEY* WD19....27 G2
Woodwell St
  WAND/EARL SW18....140 B6
Wood Wf *CNWCH* SE10....124 E6
Woodyard Cl *KTTN* NW5....84 A3
Woodyard La *DUL* SE21....163 F2
Woodyates Rd *LEE/GVPK* SE12....165 K1
Woolacombe Rd
  BKHTH/KID SE3....146 B3
Woolacombe Wy
  HYS/HAR UB3....113 H4
Woolbrook Rd *DART* DA1....170 B1
Wooler St *WALW* SE17....122 E5
Woolf Cl *THMD* SE28....128 C1
Woolf Ms *STPAN* WC1H....4 E6
Woollaston Rd *FSBYPK* N4....67 H3
Woollett Cl *DART* DA1....150 D5
Woolmead Av *CDALE/KGS* NW9....63 J4
Woolmer Gdns *UED* N18....50 C1
Woolmer Rd *UED* N18....50 C1
Woolmore St *POP/IOD* E14....106 A6
Woolneigh St *FUL/PGN* SW6....140 A4
Woolridge Wy *HOM* E9 *....86 E5
Wool Rd *RYNPK* SW20....176 E3
Woolstaplers Wy
  BERM/RHTH SE16....123 H3
Woolston Cl *WALTH* E17....51 F5
Woolstone Rd *FSTH* SE23....164 B4
Woolwich Church St
  CHARL SE7....126 D4
Woolwich Common
  WOOL/PLUM SE18....127 F6
Woolwich Foot Tnl
  CAN/RD E16....127 F2
Woolwich High St
  WOOL/PLUM SE18....127 F3
Woolwich Manor Wy
  CAN/RD E16....127 G1
Woolwich Manorway
  CAN/RD E16....127 G2
Woolwich Manor Wy
  EHAM E6....107 K3
Woolwich New Rd
  WOOL/PLUM SE18....127 G5
  BXLYHN DA7....149 H4
  CHARL SE7....146 A1
  CNWCH SE10....125 K5
Wooster Gdns *POP/IOD* E14....106 B5
Wootton Gv *FNCH* N3....46 E4
Wootton St *STHWK* SE1 *....17 K2
Worbeck Rd *PGE/AN* SE20....181 H1
Worcester Av *TOTM* N17....50 C3
Worcester Cl *CRICK* NW2....81 J1
  CROY/NA CR0....198 C4
  MTCM CR4....179 F5
Worcester Ct *WOT/HER* KT12....188 B6
Worcester Crs *MLHL* NW7....31 G5
  WFD IG8....38 E4
Worcester Dr *CHSWK* W4....118 B3
Worcester Gdns *GFD/PVL* UB6....78 C4
  IL IG1....71 J4
  WPK KT4....207 G1

Worcester Ms
  KIL/WHAMP NW6 *....83 F4
Worcester Park Rd *WPK* KT4....206 E1
Worcester Rd *BELMT* SM2....208 E5
  MNPK E12....89 K1
  WALTH E17....51 F5
  WIM/MER SW19....177 J2
Worcesters Av *EN* EN1....24 C1
Wordsworth Av *GFD/PVL* UB6....96 D1
  MNPK E12....89 J5
  SWFD E18....52 D6
Wordsworth Dr *CHEAM* SM3....208 A2
Wordsworth Pde
  CEND/HSY/T N8 *....67 H1
Wordsworth Pl *HAMP* NW3....83 K3
Wordsworth Rd *HPTN* TW12....154 E4
  PGE/AN SE20....182 A3
  STHWK SE1....19 J7
  STNW/STAM N16....86 A2
  WELL DA16....147 K2
  WLGTN SM6....210 C4
Wordsworth Wk *GLDGN* NW11....64 E1
Wordsworth Wy *DART* DA1....151 K5
  WDR/YW UB7....112 B4
Worfield St *BTSEA* SW11....140 D1
Worgan St *BERM/RHTH* SE16....124 A3
  LBTH SE11....122 A5
Worland Rd *SRTFD* E15....88 C5
Worlds End Est
  WBPTN SW10 *....140 C1
Worlds End La *ORP* BR6....217 G5
  WCHMH N21....23 F6
Worlds End Pas
  WBPTN SW10 *....140 C1
Worleys Dr *ORP* BR6....216 D2
Worlidge St *HMSMTH* W6....119 F5
Worlingham Rd *EDUL* SE22....143 G5
Wormholt Rd *SHB* W12....118 D1
Wormholt Ter *SHB* W12 *....118 D1
Wormwood St *OBST* EC2N....13 G3
Wornington Rd *NKENS* W10....100 C4
Woronzow Rd *STJWD* NW8....2 B1
Worple Av *ISLW* TW7....136 B6
  WIM/MER SW19....177 F3
Worple Cl *RYLN/HDSTN* HA2....59 K5
Worple Rd *ISLW* TW7....136 B5
  RYNPK SW20....177 G4
Worple Road Ms
  WIM/MER SW19....177 J2
Worple St *MORT/ESHN* SW14....138 A4
Worple Wy *RCHPK/HAM* TW10....137 G2
  RYLN/HDSTN HA2....59 K5
Worslade Rd *TOOT* SW17....160 C6
Worsley Bridge Rd *SYD* SE26....182 C1
Worsley Gv *CLPT* E5....86 C2
Worsley Rd *WAN* E11....88 C2
Worsopp Dr *CLAP* SW4....141 H6
Worth Cl *ORP* BR6....216 E2
Worthfield Cl *HOR/WEW* KT19....207 F5
Worth Gv *WALW* SE17 *....122 E5
Worthing Cl *SRTFD* E15....88 C6
Worthing Rd *HEST* TW5....114 E6
Worthington Cl *MTCM* CR4....195 G1
Worthington Rd *SURB* KT6....191 G5
Wortley Rd *CROY/NA* CR0....196 B4
  EHAM E6....89 H6
Worton Gdns *ISLW* TW7....135 J3
Worton Hall *ISLW* TW7....136 A4
Worton Wy *ISLW* TW7....135 J3
Wotton Gn *STMC/STPC* BR5....202 E1
Wotton Rd *CRICK* NW2....82 A2
  DEPT SE8....124 C6
Wouldham Rd *CAN/RD* E16....106 D5
Wouldham Ter
  STMC/STPC BR5 *....186 C6
Wragby Rd *WAN* E11 *....88 C1
Wrampling Pl *ED* N9....36 C3
Wray Av *CLAY* IG5....54 A6
Wray Crs *FSBYPK* N4....66 E6
Wrayfield Rd *CHEAM* SM3....208 B1
Wray Rd *BELMT* SM2....208 D6
Wraysbury Cl *HSLWW* TW4....134 D6
Wrays Wy *YEAD* UB4....94 C4
Wrekin Rd *WOOL/PLUM* SE18....147 H1
Wren Av *CRICK* NW2....82 A3
  NWDGN UB2....114 E4
Wren Cl *CAN/RD* E16....106 D5
  ED N9....37 F3
  STMC/STPC BR5....186 E6
Wren Crs *BUSH* WD23....28 C3
Wren Dr *WDR/YW* UB7....112 A3
Wren Gdns *DAGW* RM9....91 K3
  HCH RM12....75 H5
Wren Ms *LEW* SE13 *....145 H5
Wren Rd *CMBW* SE5....142 E2
  DAGW RM9....91 K3
  SCUP DA14....168 D6
Wren St *FSBYW* WC1X....5 H6
Wrentham Av *WLSDN* NW10....100 B1
Wrenthorpe Rd *BMLY* BR1....165 H6
Wrenwood Wy *PIN* HA5....59 F1
Wrexham Rd *BOW* E3....105 J1
Wricklemarsh Rd
  BKHTH/KID SE3....146 B2
Wrigglesworth St *NWCR* SE14....144 A1
Wright Cl *LEW* SE13....145 G5
Wright Rd *HEST* TW5....114 A6
Wrights Aly *WIM/MER* SW19....177 F2
Wrights Cl *DAGE* RM10....92 D2
Wrights La *KENS* W8....119 K3
Wrights Rd *BOW* E3 *....105 H1
  SNWD SE25....181 F6
Wright's Rw *WLGTN* SM6....210 B2
Wrigley Cl *CHING* E4....52 B1
Wrottesley Rd *WLSDN* NW10....99 K1
  WOOL/PLUM SE18....127 H6
Wroughton Rd *BTSEA* SW11....160 E1
Wroughton Ter *HDN* NW4 *....63 K1
Wroxall Rd *DAGW* RM9....91 J4
Wroxham Gdns
  FBAR/BDGN N11....48 C3

Wroxham Rd *THMD* SE28....109 K6
Wroxham Wy *BARK/HLT* IG6....54 B4
Wroxton Rd *PECK* SE15....143 K3
Wrythe Gn *CAR* SM5....209 K1
Wrythe Green Rd *CAR* SM5....209 K1
Wrythe La *CAR* SM5....194 C5
Wulfstan St *SHB* W12....99 H5
Wyatt Cl *BERM/RHTH* SE16....124 C2
  BUSH WD23....28 E2
  FELT TW13....154 C3
  YEAD UB4....95 G3
Wyatt Dr *BARN* SW13....118 E6
Wyatt Park Rd
  BRXS/STRHM SW2....162 A4
Wyatt Rd *DART* DA1....150 C4
  FSTGT E7....88 E4
  HBRY N5....85 J1
Wyatt's La *WALTH* E17....52 A6
Wybert St *CAMTN* NW1 *....3 K6
Wyborne Wy *WLSDN* NW10....80 E5
Wyburn Av *BAR* EN5....20 D4
Wychcombe Studios
  HAMP NW3 *....83 K4
Wycherley Cl *BKHTH/KID* SE3....145 J1
Wycherley Crs *BAR* EN5....33 F1
Wychwood Av *EDGW* HA8....43 K2
  THHTH CR7....180 D6
Wychwood Cl *EDGW* HA8....43 K2
  SUN TW16....172 A5
Wychwood End *HGT* N6....66 C4
Wychwood Gdns *CLAY* IG5....71 K1
Wychwood Wy *NTHWD* HA6....40 D3
Wycliffe Cl *WELL* DA16....148 A2
Wycliffe Rd *BTSEA* SW11....141 F3
  WIM/MER SW19....178 A2
Wyclif St *FSBYE* EC1V....6 A5
Wycombe Gdns *GLDGN* NW11....64 E6
Wycombe Pl
  WAND/EARL SW18....160 B1
Wycombe Rd *ALP/SUD* HA0....80 C6
  GNTH/NBYPK IG2....71 K2
  TOTM N17....50 C4
Wydell Cl *MRDN* SM4....193 G3
Wydenhurst Rd *CROY/NA* CR0....197 H4
Wydeville Manor Rd
  LEE/GVPK SE12....166 A6
Wye Cl *ASHF* TW15....152 E6
  ORP BR6....202 A4
Wyemead Crs *CHING* E4....38 C4
Wye St *BTSEA* SW11....140 C4
Wyevale Cl *NTHWD* HA6....40 A6
Wyfields *CLAY* IG5....54 B4
Wyfold Rd *FUL/PGN* SW6....139 G1
Wyke Cl *ISLW* TW7....116 A6
Wyke Gdns *HNWL* W7....116 A3
Wykeham Av *DAGW* RM9....91 J4
Wykeham Cl *WDR/YW* UB7....112 D6
Wykeham Gn *DAGW* RM9....91 J4
Wykeham Hl *WBLY* HA9....62 B5
Wykeham Ri *TRDG/WHET* N20....32 C5
Wykeham Rd *HDN* NW4....64 A2
  KTN/HRWW/WS HA3....61 H1
Wyke Rd *BOW* E3....87 J5
  RYNPK SW20....177 F5
Wylchin Cl *PIN* HA5....58 D1
Wyldes Cl *GLDGN* NW11....65 G5
Wyldfield Gdns *ED* N9....36 B4
Wyld Wy *WBLY* HA9....80 D4
Wyleu St *FSTH* SE23....164 B2
Wylie Rd *NWDGN* UB2....115 F3
Wyllen Cl *WCHPL* E1....104 E3
Wylo Dr *BAR* EN5....31 J1
Wymark Cl *RAIN* RM13....111 H1
Wymering Rd *MV/WKIL* W9....100 E2
Wymond St *PUT/ROE* SW15....139 F4
Wynan Rd *POP/IOD* E14....124 D5
Wynaud Ct *WDGN* N22....49 F2
Wyncham Av *BFN/LL* DA15....167 K3
Wynchgate
  KTN/HRWW/WS HA3....42 E3
  STHGT/OAK N14....34 E2
Wyncroft Cl *BMLY* BR1....184 E6
Wyndale Av *CDALE/KGS* NW9....62 C3
Wyndcliff Rd *CHARL* SE7....126 A6
Wyndcroft Cl *ENC/FH* EN2....23 H4
Wyndham Cl *BELMT* SM2....208 E5
  ORP BR6....201 H1
Wyndham Crs *HSLWW* TW4....154 E1
  KTTN NW5....84 A4
Wyndham Est *CMBW* SE5....142 D1
Wyndham Ms *MBLAR* W1H....8 E2
Wyndham Pl *MBLAR* W1H....8 E2
Wyndham Rd *CMBW* SE5....142 D1
  EBAR EN4....33 K3
  EHAM E6....89 H6
  KUTN/CMB KT2....175 G3
  WEA W13....116 C3
Wyndham St *CAMTN* NW1....8 E1
  KTTN NW5 *....8 E2
Wyndham Yd *MBLAR* W1H....8 E2
Wyneham Rd *HNHL* SE24....142 E6
Wynell Rd *FSTH* SE23....164 A5
Wynford Gv *STMC/STPC* BR5....186 C6
Wynford Pl *BELV* DA17....129 H6
Wynford Rd *IS* N1....5 H1
Wynford Wy *ELTH/MOT* SE9....166 E5
Wynlie Gdns *PIN* HA5....41 F5
Wynn Bridge Cl *WFD* IG8....53 H4
Wynndale Rd *SWFD* E18....53 F4
Wynne Rd *BRXN/ST* SW9....142 B3
Wynn's Av *BFN/LL* DA15....148 B6
Wynnstay Gdns *KENS* W8 *....119 K3
Wynter St *BTSEA* SW11....140 B5
Wynton Gdns *SNWD* SE25....197 G2
Wynton Pl *ACT* W3....98 D5
Wynyard Ter *LBTH* SE11 *....122 A5
Wynyatt St *FSBYE* EC1V....6 A4
Wyre Gv *EDGW* HA8....30 E5
  HYS/HAR UB3....113 K4
Wyresdale Crs *GFD/PVL* UB6....97 F2
Wytelcaf Cl *RSLP* HA4....58 D4
Wythburn Pl *MBLAR* W1H....8 E4
Wythenshawe Rd *DAGE* RM10....92 C1
Wythes Cl *BMLY* BR1....184 E5
Wythes Rd *CAN/RD* E16....126 D1
Wythfield Rd *ELTH/MOT* SE9....166 E1

Wyvenhoe Rd
  RYLN/HDSTN HA2....78 C1
Wyvern Cl *DART* DA1....171 F2
  ORP BR6....217 H1
Wyvern Est *NWMAL* KT3 *....176 D6
Wyvil Rd *VX/NE* SW8....141 K1
Wyvis St *POP/IOD* E14....105 K4

Y

Yabsley St *POP/IOD* E14....125 F1
Yalding Gv *STMC/STPC* BR5....202 E1
Yalding Rd *BERM/RHTH* SE16....123 H3
Yale Cl *HSLWW* TW4....134 K6
Yale Wy *HCH* RM12....93 J2
Yarborough Rd
  WIM/MER SW19....178 C4
Yardley Cl *CHING* E4....25 K6
Yardley La *CHING* E4....25 K6
Yardley St *FSBYW* WC1X....5 J6
Yarmouth Crs *TOTM* N17....68 D2
Yarmouth Pl *MYFR/PICC* W1J....15 J1
Yarnton Wy *ABYW* SE2....128 D3
  ERITHM DA18....129 G3
Yarrow Crs *EHAM* E6....107 J4
Yateley St *WOOL/PLUM* SE18....126 C5
Yeading Av *RYLN/HDSTN* HA2....59 J6
Yeading Fk *YEAD* UB4....95 F4
Yeading Gdns *YEAD* UB4....94 D5
Yeading La *YEAD* UB4....95 F5
Yeames Cl *WEA* W13....97 G5
Yeate St *IS* N1....85 K5
Yeatman Rd *HGT* N6....65 K5
Yeats Cl *LEW* SE13 *....145 G3
  WLSDN NW10....81 G4
Ye Cnr *OXHEY* WD19....27 H1
Yeend Cl *E/WMO/HCT* KT8....189 F1
Yeldham Rd *HMSMTH* W6....119 F5
Yeldham Vls *HMSMTH* W6 *....119 G5
Yelverton Rd *BTSEA* SW11....140 C3
Yenston Cl *MRDN* SM4....193 K3
Yeoman Cl *WNWD* SE27....162 C5
Yeoman Dr *STWL/WRAY* TW19....152 B3
Yeoman Rd *NTHLT* UB5....77 J5
Yeomans Acre *RSLP* HA4....58 E3
Yeoman's Rw *CHEL* SW3....14 D5
Yeoman St *BERM/RHTH* SE16....124 B4
Yeomans Wy *ENF* EN3 *....24 D5
Yeomans Yd *WCHPL* E1....13 K5
Yeoman Wy *BARK/HLT* IG6....54 C5
Yeo St *BOW* E3....105 K4
Yeovil Cl *ORP* BR6....201 K5
Yeovilton Pl *KUTN/CMB* KT2....174 D6
Yerbury Rd *ARCH* N19....84 D1
Yester Dr *CHST* BR7....184 D3
Yester Pk *CHST* BR7....184 E3
Yester Rd *CHST* BR7....184 E3
Yew Cl *BKHH* IG9....39 J4
Yewdale Cl *BMLY* BR1....183 H2
Yewfield Rd *WLSDN* NW10....81 H5
Yew Gv *CRICK* NW2....82 B2
Yews AV *SHF* TW15 *....152 E6
Yew Tree Cl *LEW* SE13....145 F4
Yewtree Cl *MUSWH* N10....48 A4
  RYLN/HDSTN HA2....60 B1
Yew Tree Cl *WCHMH* N21....35 G2
  WELL DA16....148 B1
  WPK KT4....192 D5
Yew Tree Ct *BORE* WD6....29 K1
Yew Tree Gdns *CHDH* RM6....74 A2
  ROMW/RG RM7....75 F2
Yew Tree Rd *BECK* BR3....182 C6
  SHB W12....99 H6
Yew Tree Wk *HSLWW* TW4....134 E6
Yew Wk *HRW* HA1....60 E5
Yoakley Rd *STNW/STAM* N16....68 A6
Yoke Cl *HOLWY* N7....84 E4
Yolande Gdns *ELTH/MOT* SE9....146 D6
Yonge Pk *HOLWY* N7....85 F4
York Av *BFN/LL* DA15....167 K4
  HNWL W7....115 K1
  HYS/HAR UB3....94 A5
  MORT/ESHN SW14....137 K6
  STAN HA7 *....43 H4
York Br *CAMTN* NW1....3 G6
York Buildings *CHCR* WC2N....11 F6
York Cl *CMBW* SE5....142 D5
  EHAM E6....107 K5
  HNWL W7....115 K1
  MRDN SM4....194 A1
York Gdns *WOT/HER* KT12....188 C6
York Ga *CAMTN* NW1 *....3 H7
  STHGT/OAK N14....34 E2
York Gv *PECK* SE15....143 K2
York Hl *WNWD* SE27....162 C5
York House Pl *KENS* W8....120 A2
Yorkland Av *WELL* DA16....148 A3
York Ms *IL* IG1....90 A1
  KTTN NW5....84 B3
York Pde *BTFD* TW8 *....116 E5
York Pl *BTSEA* SW11....140 B4
  CDALE/KGS NW9....63 J3
  IL IG1....72 A6
York Ri *KTTN* NW5....84 B1
  ORP BR6....201 K6
York Rd *ACT* W3....98 E5
  BAR EN5....21 G6
  BELMT SM2....208 E4
  BTFD TW8....116 E5
  BTSEA SW11....140 C3
  CHING E4....51 J1
  CROY/NA CR0....196 B4
  DART DA1....171 J2
  EA W5....116 D3
  FBAR/BDGN N11....48 D2
  FSTGT E7....88 E4
  HSLW TW3....135 G4
  IL IG1....90 A1
  KTN/HRWW/WS HA3....61 F2
  LEY E10....88 A1
  NTHWD HA6....40 E5
  RAIN RM13....93 H5
  RCHPK/HAM TW10....137 G6
  STHWK SE1....17 H2

  TEDD TW11....155 K6
  UED N18....50 D1
  WALTH E17....69 F2
  WCHMH N21....35 K2
  WIM/MER SW19....178 A2
Yorkshire Cl *STNW/STAM* N16....86 A1
Yorkshire Gdns *UED* N18....50 D1
Yorkshire Grey Yd *GINN* WC1R *....11 G2
Yorkshire Rd *MTCM* CR4....195 K2
  POP/IOD E14....105 G5
York Sq *POP/IOD* E14....105 G5
York St *MBLAR* W1H....8 E2
  MHST W1U....9 G1
  MTCM CR4....195 F4
York Street Chambers
  MHST W1U *....9 F1
York Ter *ENC/FH* EN2....23 J1
  ERITH DA8....149 K2
York Ter East *CAMTN* NW1....3 H7
York Ter West *CAMTN* NW1....3 G7
Yorkton St *BETH* E2....104 C1
York Wy *CHSGTN* KT9....205 K5
  FELT TW13....154 E5
  IS N1....5 F2
  TRDG/WHET N20....33 K5
York Way Ct *IS* N1 *....5 F1
York Way Est *HOLWY* N7....84 E4
Youngmans Cl *ENC/FH* EN2....23 J2
Youngs Rd *GNTH/NBYPK* IG2....72 D2
Young St *KENS* W8....120 A2
Yoxley Ap *GNTH/NBYPK* IG2....72 C5
Yoxley Dr *GNTH/NBYPK* IG2....72 C5
Yukon Rd *BAL* SW12....161 G2
Yunus Khan Cl *WALTH* E17....69 J5

Z

Zambezie Dr *ED* N9....36 E5
Zampa Rd *BERM/RHTH* SE16....123 K5
Zander Ct *BETH* E2....104 C2
Zangwill Rd *BKHTH/KID* SE3....146 C2
Zealand Av *WDR/YW* UB7....132 A1
Zealand Rd *BOW* E3....105 G1
Zelah Rd *STMC/STPC* BR5....202 C4
Zennor Rd *BAL* SW12....161 H5
Zenoria St *EDUL* SE22....143 G5
Zermatt Rd *THHTH* CR7....196 D2
Zetland St *POP/IOD* E14....106 A4
Zion Pl *THHTH* CR7....196 E1
Zion Rd *THHTH* CR7....196 E1
Zoar St *STHWK* SE1....12 C7
Zoffany St *ARCH* N19....66 D6

2 Willow Road
HAMP NW3 ....83 J2
22 Jermyn Street Hotel
STJS SW1Y 10 B6
51 Buckingham Gate Hotel
WESTW SW1E 16 B4
AAIS
DART DA1 ....171 H2
Aacrotya Medical Centre
SEVS/STOTM N15 ....67 J1
Abbey Business Centre
VX/NE SW8 ....141 H2
The Abbey Clinic
BELV DA17 ....129 G5
Abbey Christian School for
the English Language
STJWD NW8 ....101 G1
Abbey College London
BAY/PAD W2 ....100 E5
The Abbey Court Townhouse
Hotel
BAY/PAD W2 ....100 E6
Abbey Industrial Estate
ALP/SUD HA0 ....80 B6
MTCM CR4 ....194 E2
Abbey Lane Commercial
Estate
SRTFD E15 ....106 B1
Abbey Medical Centre
STJWD NW8 ....83 F6
Abbey Mills
WIM/MER SW19 ....178 B4
Abbey Park Industrial
Estate
BARK IG11 ....108 B1
Abbey Primary School
ABYW SE2 ....128 D3
MRDN SM4 ....193 K4
Abbey Road Health Centre
SRTFD E15 ....88 C6
Abbey Road Studios
STJWD NW8 ....101 G1
Abbey Sports Centre
BARK IG11 ....90 C6
Abbey Trading Estate
SYD SE26 ....182 B1
Abbey Wharf Industrial
Estate
BARK IG11 ....108 D2
Abbey Wood School
ABYW SE2 ....128 B3
Abbotsbury Primary School
MRDN SM4 ....193 K2
ABC Cinema
HAMP NW3 ....83 J3
PUT/ROE SW15 ....139 H4
Abercorn School
MBLAR W1H 8 E2
STJWD NW8 ....101 G1
Aberdeen Wharf
WAP E1W 123 J1
Aberglen Industrial Estate
HYS/HAR UB3 ....113 G2
Abingdon House School
KENS W8 ....119 K3
Abney Park Cemetery
STNW/STAM N16 ....68 A6
Acacia Business Centre
WAN E11 ....88 C1
The Academy at Peckham
PECK SE15 ....143 G2
The Academy School
HAMP NW3 ....83 H2
Acland Burghley School
KTTN NW5 ....84 B2
Acorn Industrial Park
DART DA1 ....150 D6
Acorn Medical Centre
TWK TW1 ....156 B3
Acre Road Health Clinic
KUTN/CMB KT2 ....175 G3
Acton Business Centre
WLSDN NW10 ....99 F3
Acton Central Industrial
Estate
ACT W3 ....98 D6
Acton Health Centre
ACT W3 ....117 K1
Acton High School
ACT W3 ....117 H2
Acton Hospital
ACT W3 ....117 H2
Acton Lane Commercial
Centre
CHSWK W4 ....117 K2
Acton Park Industrial Estate
ACT W3 ....118 A2
ACT W3 ....118 C1
Acton Superbowl
ACT W3 ....98 C4
Acton Swimming Baths
ACT W3 ....117 K1
Acumen (Anglo School)
NRWD SE19 ....181 K4
Adams Bridge Business
Centre
WBLY HA9 ....80 D3
Adamsrill Primary School
SYD SE26 ....164 B5
Adath Yisroel Cemetery
EN EN1 ....24 B2
Addey & Stanhope School
NWCR SE14 ....144 C2
Addington Court Golf Club
CROY/NA CR0 ....213 H6
Addington Golf Club
CROY/NA CR0 ....213 H2
Addington Palace Golf Club
CROY/NA CR0 ....213 G4
Addiscombe CC
CROY/NA CR0 ....212 C1
Addison Primary School
WKENS W14 ....119 G3
Adelphi Theatre
COVGDN WC2E 11 F6
Adler Industrial Estate
HYS/HAR UB3 ....113 G2

Admiral Hyson Industrial
Estate
STHWK SE1 ....123 J4
Admiralty Arch
STJS SW1Y 10 D7
ADT College
PUT/ROE SW15 ....139 J6
The Adult College of Barking
& Dagenham
BARK IG11 ....90 E4
Adult Education Centre
DART DA1 ....171 J2
POP/IOD E14 ....125 F3
Aerodrome Hotel
CROY/NA CR0 ....211 G4
Africa Centre
COVGDN WC2E 11 F5
Agency of Jewish Education
HDN NW4 ....64 B1
Agnew's
CONDST W1S 10 A7
Agora Shopping Centre
PECK SE15 ....143 H3
Ainslie Wood Primary School
CHING E4 ....51 K1
Airbase Unity Elementary
School
RSLP HA4 ....58 A6
Airbus Coach Station
HTHAIR TW6 ....132 C4
Air Call Business Centre
CDALE/KGS NW9 ....45 F6
Airedale Physiotherapy
Clinic
CHSWK W4 ....118 C5
Airlinks Golf Club
NWDGN UB2 ....114 B4
Air Links Industrial Estate
HEST TW5 ....114 B5
Airport Gate Business Centre
WDR/YW UB7 ....132 C1
Aksaray Sports Club
STNW/STAM N16 ....85 K2
The Alan D School of
Hairdressing
GTPST W1W 10 B3
Albany Centre & Theatre
DEPT SE8 ....144 C1
Albany Clinic
BFN/LL DA15 ....168 B6
WIM/MER SW19 ....178 A3
The Albany College
HDN NW4 ....63 K2
Albany Park Canoe &
Sailing Club
KUTN/CMB KT2 ....174 E2
Albany School
(Grant Maintained)
PEND EN3 ....25 F1
The Albany School
HCH RM12 ....75 K6
Albemarle Primary School
WIM/MER SW19 ....159 H4
Albert Memorial
SKENS SW7 ....14 A2
Albion Health Centre
WCHPL E1 ....104 D4
Albion J & I School
BERM/RHTH SE16 ....123 K2
Albion Street Health
Centre
BERM/RHTH SE16 ....123 K2
Albright Industrial Estate
RAIN RM13 ....111 H4
The Alchemy Gallery
CLKNW EC1R 5 J6
Alderbrook Primary School
BAL SW12 ....161 G2
Aldersbrook County
Secondary School
MNPK E12 ....71 G5
Aldersbrook Primary School
MNPK E12 ....71 F5
Alderwood Primary School
ELTH/MOT SE9 ....167 J1
Aldgate Bus Station
HDTCH EC3A 13 J3
Aldwych Theatre
HOL/ALD WC2B 11 G4
Alexander McLeod Primary
School
ABYW SE2 ....128 C5
Alexandra Avenue Clinic
RYLN/HDSTN HA2 ....59 K6
Alexandra Business Centre
PEND EN3 ....25 F5
Alexandra Infant School
KUTN/CMB KT2 ....175 H5
PGE/AN SE20 ....182 A3
Alexandra Junior School
HSLW TW3 ....135 G3
SYD SE26 ....182 A2
Alexandra Palace
(Historic House)
WDGN N22 ....48 D6
Alexandra Palace Ice Rink
WDGN N22 ....48 D5
Alexandra Park School
FBAR/BDGN N11 ....48 C3
Alexandra Road Clinic
WDGN N22 ....49 F5
Alexandra School
RYLN/HDSTN HA2 ....59 K6
Al Falah Boys School
CLPT E5 ....86 D1
Alfred Salter Primary School
BERM/RHTH SE16 ....124 A2
Alfreds Way Industrial Estate
BARK IG11 ....91 G6
Allenby Primary School
STHL UB1 ....96 A5
Allen Edwards Primary
School
CLAP SW4 ....141 K2
The All England Lawn Tennis
& Croquet Club
WIM/MER SW19 ....159 G5

Allergy Clinic
CAVSQ/HST W1G 9 J2
Allsyns Junior School
EDUL SE22 ....143 F6
Allfarthing JMI School
WAND/EARL SW18 ....160 B1
All Saints Benhilton CE
Primary School
SUT SM1 ....209 F1
All Saints Catholic School &
Technology College
BCTR RM8 ....74 C5
All Saints CE Junior School
NRWD SE19 ....181 F4
All Saints CE Primary School
BKHTH/KID SE3 ....145 H3
CAR SM5 ....210 A3
CRICK NW2 ....82 D1
FUL/PGN SW6 ....139 H5
PUT/ROE SW15 ....139 F4
TRDG/WHET N20 ....33 H4
WIM/MER SW19 ....178 B3
All Souls CE Primary School
GTPST W1W 10 A2
Ailum Medical Centre
WAN E11 ....70 B4
Alma Primary School
BERM/RHTH SE16 ....123 H4
PEND EN3 ....25 F6
Almeida Theatre
IS N1 ....85 H5
Al-Noor Primary School
GDMY/SEVK IG3 ....73 H5
Alperton Cemetery
ALP/SUD HA0 ....79 K6
Alperton Community School
ALP/SUD HA0 ....80 A5
Alperton High School
ALP/SUD HA0 ....79 K6
Alperton Sports Ground
ALP/SUD HA0 ....97 K1
Alpha Business Centre
WALTH E17 ....69 H2
Alpha Preparatory School
HRW HA1 ....60 E2
Alpine Business Centre
EHAM E6 ....108 A4
Al Sadiq High School for Boys
& Al-Zahra Girls School
KIL/WHAMP NW6 ....82 C6
Alscot Road Industrial Estate
STHWK SE1 ....19 K6
Altmore Infant School
EHAM E6 ....89 K5
The Alton School
PUT/ROE SW15 ....158 C2
Ambler Primary School
FSBYPK N4 ....85 H1
Ambleside Junior School
WOT/HER KT12 ....188 B5
AMC Business Centre
WLSDN NW10 ....98 D2
American Intercontinental
University
MHST W1U 9 H2
The American School in
London
STJWD NW8 ....83 G6
AMF Bowling
LEW SE13 ....145 F4
Amida Golf
FELT TW13 ....155 F5
Ampthill Square Medical
Centre
CAMTN NW1 ....4 B3
Anchorage Point Industrial
Estate
CHARL SE7 ....126 B3
Anchor Bay Industrial Estate
ERITH DA8 ....150 C1
Anchor Retail Park
WCHPL E1 ....104 E3
Andover Medical Centre
HOLWY N7 ....85 F1
The Andrew Ewing Primary
School
HEST TW5 ....134 E1
Anerley School
NRWD SE19 ....181 H4
Angel Centre
DART DA1 ....171 H1
Angerstein Business Park
GNWCH SE10 ....125 K4
Anglian Industrial Estate
BARK IG11 ....109 F3
Animal Cemetery
REDBR IG4 ....53 H6
Annemount School
EFNCH N2 ....65 G3
Annunciation RC Infant School
EDGW HA8 ....45 F4
The Annunciation RC Junior
School
MLHL NW7 ....45 F2
Anson Primary School
CRICK NW2 ....82 B3
Ante Natal Clinic
EFNCH N2 ....48 A6
Antonys RC Primary School
WFD IG8 ....38 E6
Apex Hotel
MON EC3R 13 H5
Apex Industrial Estate
WLSDN NW10 ....99 H3
Apex Retail Park
FELT TW13 ....154 E5
Apollo Theatre
SOHO/SHAV W1D 10 C5
Apollo Victoria Theatre
PIM SW1V 16 A5
Apostolic Nuncio
WIM/MER SW19 ....159 F5
Applegarth Primary School
CROY/NA CR0 ....213 K4
Apsley House, The Wellington
Museum
KTBR SW1X 15 G2

Aquarius Business Park
CRICK NW2 ....63 J5
Aquarius Golf Club
EDUL SE22 ....143 K6
Aragon Primary School
MRDN SM4 ....193 H4
Arcadia Shopping Centre
EA W5 ....97 K6
Arcadia University
BAY/PAD W2 ....101 F6
The Archbishop Lanfranc
School
CROY/NA CR0 ....195 K3
Archbishop Michael Ramsey
Technology College
CMBW SE5 ....142 C1
Archbishop Sumners CE
Primary School
LBTH SE11 ....17 K7
Archbishop Tenisons CE
School
CROY/NA CR0 ....212 B1
Archbishop Tenison's School
VX/NE SW8 ....122 A6
Archdale Business Centre
RYLN/HDSTN HA2 ....60 C6
Archdeacon Cambridge's CE
Primary School
WHTN TW2 ....155 K4
Arches Business Centre
NWDGN UB2 ....114 E2
Arches Leisure Centre
GNWCH SE10 ....125 G6
Archgate Business Centre
NFNCH/WDSPK N12 ....33 G6
Architecture Association
School of Architecture
RSQ WC1B 10 C2
Archway Business Centre
ARCH N19 ....84 D1
Archway Leisure Centre
ARCH N19 ....66 C6
Arena Estate
FSBYPK N4 ....67 H3
Argyle Primary School
STPAN WC1H 5 F5
Arklow Trading Estate
NWCR SE14 ....124 B6
Armourers & Braziers' Hall
LOTH EC2R 12 E3
Arndale Health Centre
WAND/EARL SW18 ....159 K1
Arnhem Wharf Primary
School
POP/IOD E14 ....124 C3
Arnold House School
STJWD NW8 ....2 A2
Arnos Pool
FBAR/BDGN N11 ....48 D1
Arsenal FC
(Emirates Stadium)
HOLWY N7 ....85 G2
Art School
BECK BR3 ....198 B2
Artsdepot
NFNCH/WDSPK N12 ....47 G1
The Arts Educational School
CHSWK W4 ....118 B4
Arts Theatre
LSQ/SEVD WC2H 10 D5
Ashbourne College
KENS W8 ....120 A2
Ashburnham Primary School
WBPTN SW10 ....140 C1
Ashburton Community
School
CROY/NA CR0 ....197 J4
Ashburton Primary School
CROY/NA CR0 ....197 J3
Ashby Mill School
CLAP SW4 ....141 K6
Ashfield Junior School
BUSH WD23 ....28 B2
Ashford Clinic
ASHF TW15 ....152 B5
Ashford High School
ASHF TW15 ....152 B5
Ashford Industrial Estate
ASHF TW15 ....153 F6
The Ashford & St Peters
Hospital
STWL/WRAY TW19 ....152 B4
Ashford Sports Club
STWL/WRAY TW19 ....152 A6
STWL/WRAY TW19 ....152 C5
Ashgrove College
WALTH E17 ....51 J6
Ashgrove Trading Estate
BMLY BR1 ....183 G2
Ashleigh Commercial Estate
CHARL SE7 ....126 B4
Ashmead Primary School
BROCKY SE4 ....144 D3
Ashmole Centre
STHGT/OAK N14 ....34 C3
Ashmole Primary School
VX/NE SW8 ....122 A6
Ashmole School
STHGT/OAK N14 ....34 C3
Ashmount Primary School
ARCH N19 ....66 D4
Ashton House School
ISLW TW7 ....135 J2
Ashton Playing Fields Track
WFD IG8 ....53 J2
Aspen House School
LBTH SE11 ....122 C6
Aspen House Secondary &
Primary School
BRXS/STRHM SW2 ....161 K3
Asquith Court School
HPTN TW12 ....173 G4
KTN/HRWW/WS HA3 ....61 H3
Asquith School
PEND EN3 ....24 E5
Assembly Rooms
SURB KT6 ....191 F1

Associated Newspapers
BERM/RHTH SE16 ....124 A3
Aston Clinic
NWMAL KT3 ....192 B1
Aston House School
EA W5 ....97 K5
Asylum Medical Centre
CEND/HSY/T N8 ....49 G6
Athelney Primary School
CAT SE6 ....164 D5
Athelstan House School
HPTN TW12 ....173 F4
Athenaeum Hotel
MYFR/PICC W1J 15 J1
Athena House School
CLPT E5 ....86 E2
Atherton Leisure Centre
SRTFD E15 ....88 D4
Athlone House Hospital
HGT N6 ....65 K5
Athlon Industrial Estate
ALP/SUD HA0 ....97 K1
Atkinson Morley Hospital
RYNPK SW20 ....176 E3
Atlantic House (Richmond
American International
University) *KENS* W8 ....120 A3
Atlas Business Centre
CRICK NW2 ....63 K6
Atlas Transport Estate
BTSEA SW11 ....140 B3
Attlee Youth & Community
Centre
WCHPL E1 ....13 K2
Auriol Junior School
HOR/WEW KT19 ....207 H2
Australia House
HOL/ALD WC2B 11 H4
Aveling Park School
WALTH E17 ....51 J5
Avenue House Museum
FNCH N3 ....46 D5
Avenue Pre School
WEA W13 ....97 H5
Avenue Industrial Estate
CHING E4 ....51 H2
Avenue Primary School
KIL/WHAMP NW6 ....82 C5
MNPK E12 ....71 J2
Avondale Park Primary
School
NTGHL W11 ....100 B6
Avon House School
WFD IG8 ....38 E6
Avon Trading Estate
WKENS W14 ....119 J4
Axis Business Centre
SRTFD E15 ....87 K3
The Aylesham Centre
PECK SE15 ....143 H2
Ayloff Primary School
HCH RM12 ....93 K2
Aylward First & Middle
Schools
STAN HA7 ....43 K1
Aylward School
UED N18 ....35 K6
Aylwin Secondary School
STHWK SE1 ....19 K6
BAA Heathrow Visitor Centre
HTHAIR TW6 ....132 E2
Babington House School
CHST BR7 ....184 E2
Back Care Clinic
WPK KT4 ....192 D5
Bacon's College
BERM/RHTH SE16 ....124 B1
Baden Powell House
SKENS SW7 ....120 B4
Baglioni Hotel
KENS W8 ....120 B2
Bakers Hall
MON EC3R 13 H5
Balaam Leisure Centre
PLSTW E13 ....106 E3
Bales College
NKENS W10 ....100 B2
Balfour Business Centre
NWDGN UB2 ....114 C3
Balgowan Primary School
BECK BR3 ....182 B5
Balham Boys Preparatory
Secondary School
BAL SW12 ....161 G2
Balham Girls Preparatory
Secondary School
TOOT SW17 ....160 E5
Balham Health Centre
BAL SW12 ....161 G4
Balham Leisure Centre
TOOT SW17 ....161 F4
Balmoral Trading Estate
BARK IG11 ....109 F3
Baltic Exchange
HDTCH EC3A 13 H3
Bancrofts School
WFD IG8 ....38 E5
Bandon Hill Cemetery
WLGTN SM6 ....210 D3
Bandon Hill Primary School
WLGTN SM6 ....210 D4
Bangabandhu Primary
School
BETH E2 ....104 E2
Bank of England Extension
CITYW EC2V 12 C4
Bank of England (& Museum)
LOTH EC2R 12 E4
Bankside Gallery
STHWK SE1 ....12 B6
Bankside Jetty
STHWK SE1 ....12 C6
Bankside Park Industrial
Estate
BARK IG11 ....109 G3
Bannister Stadium
KTN/HRWW/WS HA3 ....42 C2

Bannockburn Primary School
  WOOL/PLUM SE18 ....**128** A4
Banqueting House Whitehall
  WHALL SW1A **16** E1
Barbara Speake Theatre
School
  ACT W3 ....**99** G6
Barber Surgeons' Hall
  BARB EC2Y **12** D2
Barbican Cinema
  BARB EC2Y **12** C1
The Barbican
  BARB EC2Y **12** C1
Barbican Theatre
  BARB EC2Y **12** D1
Barclay J & I School
  LEY E10 ....**70** B3
Barham Primary School
  ALP/SUD HA0 ....**79** J4
Baring Primary School
  LEE/GVPK SE12 ....**165** K2
Baring Road Medical Centre
  BMLY BR1 ....**165** K4
Barkantine Clinic
  POP/IOD E14 ....**124** C2
Barking Abbey
Comprehensive School
(Lower) *IL* IG1 ....**90** D3
Barking Abbey
Comprehensive School
(Upper) *BARK* IG11 ....**91** F4
Barking Abbey Industrial
Estate
  BARK IG11 ....**90** B6
Barking Abbey Leisure Centre
  BARK IG11 ....**91** G4
Barking Abbey School
  BARK IG11 ....**91** F4
Barking College
  ROMW/RG RM7 ....**75** F6
Barking Football Club
  BCTR RM8 ....**91** H3
Barking Hospital
  BARK IG11 ....**91** F5
Barking Industrial Park
  BARK IG11 ....**91** F6
Barking RUFC
  DAGW RM9 ....**91** K6
Barkingside Cemetery
  BARK/HLT IG6 ....**54** B6
Barkingside FC
  BARK/HLT IG6 ....**72** D1
Barlby Primary School
  NKENS W10 ....**100** B3
Barley Lane Primary School
  GDMY/SEVK IG3 ....**73** C4
Barnabas Medical Centre
  NTHLT UB5 ....**78** C4
Barn Croft Primary School
  WALTH E17 ....**69** G3
Barnehurst Primary School
  ERITH DA8 ....**149** K2
Barnehurst Public Golf Club
  BXLYHN DA7 ....**150** A4
Barn Elms Athletics Track
  BARN SW13 ....**138** E3
Barn Elms Water Sports
Centre
  PUT/ROE SW15 ....**139** F3
Barnes Cray Primary School
  DART DA1 ....**150** D5
Barnes Hospital
  MORT/ESHN SW14 ....**138** A4
Barnes Primary School
  BARN SW13 ....**138** B4
Barnes Sports Club
  BARN SW13 ....**138** C2
Barnet College
  BAR EN5 ....**20** D5
  CDALE/KGS NW9 ....**45** H4
  EBAR EN4 ....**33** K3
  FBAR/BDGN N11 ....**33** K5
  HDN NW4 ....**63** J3
  NFNCH/WDSPK N12 ....**47** G1
Barnet Copthall Pool
  HDN NW4 ....**45** K3
Barnet Copthall Stadium
  HDN NW4 ....**46** A4
Barnet County Court
  BAR EN5 ....**21** G5
  FNCH N3 ....**46** E4
Barnet FC (Underhill)
  BAR EN5 ....**20** D5
Barnet General Hospital
  BAR EN5 ....**20** B5
Barnet Health Centre
  BAR EN5 ....**20** D5
Barnet Hill JMI School
  BAR EN5 ....**20** D6
Barnet Hospital Chest Clinic
  BAR EN5 ....**20** B5
Barnet Magistrates Court
  BAR EN5 ....**20** C5
Barnet Museum
  BAR EN5 ....**20** C5
Barnet Trading Estate
  BAR EN5 ....**20** D4
Barnfield Primary School
  EDGW HA8 ....**44** A4
Barnhill Community High
School
  YEAD UB4 ....**95** F2
Barn Hotel
  RSLP HA4 ....**58** C6
Barnsbury Complex
  HOLWY N7 ....**85** G5
Barnsbury School for Girls
  IS N1 ....**85** G4
Barons Court Theatre
  WKENS W14 ....**119** H5
Barratt Industrial Park
  BOW E3 ....**106** A3
Barrett Industrial Park
  STHL UB1 ....**115** F1
Barrett Way Industrial
Estate
  KTN/HRWW/WS HA3 ....**42** D6

Barrington Primary School
  WELL DA16 ....**148** E3
Barrow Hedges Primary
School
  CAR SM5 ....**209** J5
Barrow Hill Junior School
  STJWD NW8 ....**2** C3
Barton House Health Centre
  STNW/STAM N16 ....**85** K1
Barwell Business Park
  CHSGTN KT9 ....**205** K5
Bassett House School
  NKENS W10 ....**100** D5
Baston School
  HAYES BR2 ....**200** A6
Bath Factory Estate
  HNHL SE24 ....**162** D1
Battersea Arts Centre (BAC)
  BTSEA SW11 ....**140** E4
Battersea Business Centre
  BTSEA SW11 ....**141** F4
Battersea Dogs' Home
  VX/NE SW8 ....**141** G1
Battersea Sports Centre
  BTSEA SW11 ....**140** C4
Battersea Technology College
  BTSEA SW11 ....**140** E2
Battersea Tutorial College
  TOOT SW17 ....**161** F4
BBC Broadcasting House
  REGST W1B **9** K2
BBC Media Village
  SHB W12 ....**100** A3
BBC Studios
  MV/WKIL W9 ....**101** F3
BBC Television Centre
  SHB W12 ....**100** A6
BBC Worldwide
  SHB W12 ....**100** A5
Beal High School
  REDBR IG4 ....**53** J6
Beam Primary School
  DAGE RM10 ....**110** E1
Beatrice Tate School
  BETH E2 ....**104** D2
Beatrix Potter Primary School
  WAND/EARL SW18 ....**160** B3
Beauclerc Infant School
  SUN TW16 ....**172** B6
The Beaufort Hotel
  CHEL SW5 ....**14** E5
Beaumont Primary School
  LEY E10 ....**69** K4
Beaver College
  BAY/PAD W2 ....**100** E6
The Beavers Community
Primary School
  HSLWW TW4 ....**134** B4
Beaverwood School for Girls
  CHST BR7 ....**185** K2
Beckenham Business Park
  BECK BR3 ....**182** B2
Beckenham CC
  BECK BR3 ....**182** B3
Beckenham Crematorium
  BECK BR3 ....**181** K6
Beckenham Hospital
  BECK BR3 ....**182** C5
Beckenham Leisure Centre
  BECK BR3 ....**182** B4
Beckenham Place Park
Golf Course
  BECK BR3 ....**182** C2
Beckenham RFC
  BECK BR3 ....**198** B1
Beckenham Town FC
  BECK BR3 ....**198** D2
Becket Sports Centre
  DART DA1 ....**171** F1
Beckford Primary School
  KIL/WHAMP NW6 ....**82** D3
Beckmead School
  BECK BR3 ....**198** D5
The Beck Theatre
  HYS/HAR UB3 ....**94** D5
Beckton Ski Centre
  EHAM E6 ....**108** A3
Beckton Special School
  CAN/RD E16 ....**107** H4
Beckton Triangle Retail
Park
  EHAM E6 ....**108** B2
Becontree Day Hospital
  BCTR RM8 ....**74** A6
Becontree Primary School
  BCTR RM8 ....**91** H1
Bective House Clinic
  PUT/ROE SW15 ....**139** G3
Beddington Infants School
  WLGTN SM6 ....**210** C1
Beddington Medical Centre
  CROY/NA CR0 ....**210** E2
Beddington Park Primary
School
  CROY/NA CR0 ....**210** D1
Beddington Trading Estate
  CROY/NA CR0 ....**195** K5
Bedelsford School
  KUT/HW KT1 ....**175** F6
Bedenfield Clinic
  SCUP DA14 ....**187** F1
Bedfont Health Clinic
  EBED/NFELT TW14 ....**153** H2
Bedfont Industrial Park
  ASHF TW15 ....**153** G5
Bedfont J & I School
  EBED/NFELT TW14 ....**153** H1
Bedfont Lakes Country Park
  EBED/NFELT TW14 ....**153** F4
Bedfont Lakes Office Park
  EBED/NFELT TW14 ....**153** F3
Bedford Hotel
  RSQ WC1B **11** F1
Bedington Infant School
  WLGTN SM6 ....**210** C2
Bedonwell Clinic
  ABYW SE2 ....**129** F3

Bedonwell Medical Centre
  BELV DA17 ....**129** G5
Bedonwell Primary School
  BXLYHN DA7 ....**129** F6
Beecholme Primary School
  MTCM CR4 ....**179** G4
Beechwood School
  STRHM/NOR SW16 ....**161** K5
Beehive Preparatory School
  REDBR IG4 ....**71** K1
The Beehive School
  ARCH N19 ....**66** D4
Beis Hamedrash Elyon
  GLDGN NW11 ....**64** C4
Beis Malka Girls School
  STNW/STAM N16 ....**68** B5
Beis Rochel D'Satmar Girls
School
  STNW/STAM N16 ....**68** A4
Beis Trana Girls School
  STNW/STAM N16 ....**68** A4
Beis Yaakov Primary School
  CDALE/KGS NW9 ....**45** F6
Bellamy's Wharf
  BERM/RHTH SE16 ....**124** A1
Bellenden Primary School
  PECK SE15 ....**143** H4
Bellenden Road Business
Centre
  PECK SE15 ....**143** G3
Bellenden Road Retail Park
  PECK SE15 ....**143** G2
Bellerbys College
  DEPT SE8 ....**124** E6
Belleville Primary School
  BTSEA SW11 ....**140** E6
Belle Vue Cinema
  WLSDN NW10 ....**81** K5
Bell Industrial Estate
  CHSWK W4 ....**117** K4
Bellingham Trading Estate
  CAT SE6 ....**164** E5
Bell Lane JMI School
  HDN NW4 ....**64** B1
Belmont First & Middle School
  KTN/HRWW/WS HA3 ....**43** F5
Belmont J & I School
  WDGN N22 ....**49** J6
Belmont (Mill Hill Preparatory
School)
  MLHL NW7 ....**31** J5
Belmont Park School
  LEY E10 ....**70** A3
Belmont Primary School
  CHSWK W4 ....**118** A4
  ERITH DA8 ....**149** H1
Belmore Primary School
  YEAD UB4 ....**95** F2
Belvedere Day Hospital
  WLSDN NW10 ....**81** J6
Belvedere Industrial Estate
  BELV DA17 ....**130** A1
Belvedere Link Business Park
  ERITH DA8 ....**129** K3
Belvedere Primary School
  BELV DA17 ....**129** J4
Belvue Business Centre
  NTHLT UB5 ....**78** B5
Belvue School
  NTHLT UB5 ....**78** A6
Benedict House Preparatory
School
  BFN/LL DA15 ....**168** A6
Benedict Primary School
  MTCM CR4 ....**178** C6
Benhurst JMI School
  RAIN RM12 ....**93** K1
Ben Jonson Primary School
  WCHPL E1 ....**105** G3
Bensham Manor School
  THHTH CR7 ....**196** D2
Benson Primary School
  CROY/NA CR0 ....**213** G1
Bentalls Shopping Centre
  KUT/HW KT1 ....**174** E5
Benthal Primary School
  STNW/STAM N16 ....**86** D1
The Bentley Kempinski Hotel
  SKENS SW7 ....**120** B4
Bentley Wood Girls School
  STAN HA7 ....**43** F1
Bentworth Primary School
  SHB W12 ....**99** K5
Ben Uri Gallery, London Jewish
Museum of Art
  STJWD NW8 ....**83** H6
Beormund School
  STHWK SE1 ....**18** E3
Berger Primary School
  HOM E9 ....**87** F4
The Berkeley Hotel
  KTBR SW1X **15** G2
Berkeley Primary School
  HEST TW5 ....**114** C6
Berlitz Schools of Languages
  HHOL WC1V **11** H2
Bermondsey Town Hall
  STHWK SE1 ....**19** J5
Bermondsey Trading Estate
  BERM/RHTH SE16 ....**123** K4
Berrymede Infant School
  ACT W3 ....**117** J2
Berrymede Junior School
  ACT W3 ....**117** J2
Bertram House School
  TOOT SW17 ....**161** F4
Bessemer Grange J & I School
  HNHL SE24 ....**142** E6
Bessemer Park Industrial
Estate
  BRXN/ST SW9 ....**142** C5
Best Western Bromley Court
Hotel
  BMLY BR1 ....**183** H2
Best Western Cumberland
Hotel
  HRW HA1 ....**61** F3

Best Western Hotel
  HAMP NW3 ....**83** H5
Best Western Lodge Hotel
  PUT/ROE SW15 ....**139** J6
Best Western Master Robert
Hotel
  HEST TW5 ....**134** E2
Best Western Mostyn Hotel
  MBLAR W1H **9** F4
Beth Jacob Grammar School
  HDN NW4 ....**64** A1
Bethlem Royal Hospital
  BECK BR3 ....**198** D4
Bethnal Green Technology
College
  BETH E2 ....**7** G1
Beths Grammar School
for Boys
  BXLY DA5 ....**169** H1
Beulah Infant School
  THHTH CR7 ....**180** D5
Beverley School
  NWMAL KT3 ....**192** D2
Beverley Trading Estate
  MRDN SM4 ....**193** G4
Bevington Primary School
  NKENS W10 ....**100** C4
Bexley CC
  BXLY DA5 ....**169** G5
Bexley College
  BXLY DA5 ....**169** K4
Bexley Grammar School
  WELL DA16 ....**148** C5
Bexleyheath Centre
  BXLYHS DA6 ....**149** F5
Bexleyheath Golf Club
  BXLYHS DA6 ....**149** F6
Bexleyheath Marriott Hotel
  BXLYHS DA6 ....**149** G6
Bexleyheath School
  BXLYHN DA7 ....**149** G5
Bexley RFC
  BXLY DA5 ....**169** H2
BFI London IMAX Cinema
  STHWK SE1 ....**17** H1
Bickley Park CC
  BMLY BR1 ....**184** D5
Bickley Park Preparatory
School
  BMLY BR1 ....**184** C6
Bickley Park School
  BMLY BR1 ....**184** D5
Big Ben
  WHALL SW1A **17** F3
Bigland Green Primary School
  WCHPL E1 ....**104** D5
Billingsgate Fish Market
  POP/IOD E14 ....**124** E1
Bingham Hotel
  TWK TW1 ....**156** E1
Birchmere Business Park
  THMD SE28 ....**128** C2
Birchwood Park Golf Club
  RDART DA2 ....**187** K3
Bird College
  SCUP DA14 ....**168** B5
Birkbeck College
  GWRST WC1E **4** D7
  RSQ WC1B **10** D2
Birkbeck Primary School
  SCUP DA14 ....**168** C5
Bishop Challoner Catholic
Collegiate School
  WCHPL E1 ....**104** E6
Bishop Challoner Girls
School
  WCHPL E1 ....**104** C6
Bishop Challoner School
  HAYES BR2 ....**183** C5
Bishop Douglas RC School
  EFNCH N2 ....**47** G5
Bishop Gilpin Primary School
  WIM/MER SW19 ....**177** J1
Bishop John Robinson CE
Primary School
  THMD SE28 ....**109** J6
Bishop Justus CE (Secondary)
School
  HAYES BR2 ....**200** D4
Bishop Perrin CE Primary
School
  WHTN TW2 ....**155** G2
Bishop Ramsey CE School
  RSLP HA4 ....**58** D4
Bishop Ramsey CE School
(Upper)
  RSLP HA4 ....**58** E4
Bishopsgate Institute
  LVPST EC2M **13** H2
Bishop Stopfords School
  EN EN1 ....**24** C3
Bishop Thomas Grant School
  STRHM/NOR SW16 ....**180** A1
Bishop Winnington Ingram
CE Primary School
  RSLP HA4 ....**58** B4
Bittacy Business Centre
  MLHL NW7 ....**46** C2
Blackburn Trading Estate
  STWL/WRAY TW19 ....**152** C1
Blackfen Medical Centre
  BFN/LL DA15 ....**148** A6
Blackfen School for Girls
  BFN/LL DA15 ....**168** C1
Blackfriars Millennium Pier
  EMB EC4Y **11** K5
Blackfriars Pier
  BLKFR EC4V **12** B5
Blackheath Bluecoat CE
School
  BKHTH/KID SE3 ....**146** A1
Blackheath Business Estate
  BKHTH/KID SE3 ....**145** F2
The Blackheath Clinic
  BKHTH/KID SE3 ....**145** K5
Blackheath High School GDST
  BKHTH/KID SE3 ....**145** J3

Blackheath High Senior
School
  BKHTH/KID SE3 ....**145** K1
Blackheath Hospital
  BKHTH/KID SE3 ....**145** J4
Blackheath Preparatory
School
  BKHTH/KID SE3 ....**145** K2
Blackheath RFC
  (the Rectory Field)
  BKHTH/KID SE3 ....**146** A1
Blackwall Trading Estate
  POP/IOD E14 ....**106** B4
Blair Peach Primary School
  STHL UB1 ....**114** C1
Blake College
  GTPST W1W **10** A1
Blanche Nevile School
  MUSWH N10 ....**48** A6
Blenheim Business Centre
  MTCM CR4 ....**178** E4
Blenheim Primary School
  ORP BR6 ....**202** E6
Blenheim Shopping Centre
  PGE/AN SE20 ....**181** K3
Blessed Dominic RC Primary
School
  CDALE/KGS NW9 ....**45** G5
Blessed Sacrament RC
Primary School
  IS N1 ....**5** F1
Blood Transfusion Centre
  EDGW HA8 ....**44** D3
Bloomfield Clinic Guys
  STHWK SE1 ....**19** F2
Bloomsbury College
  FUL/PGN SW6 ....**139** K1
Bloomsbury Theatre
  GWRST WC1E **4** C6
Blossom House School
  RYNPK SW20 ....**177** F3
Blossoms Inn Medical
Centre
  BLKFR EC4V **12** D5
Blue Gate Fields Primary
School
  WCHPL E1 ....**104** E6
The Blue School
  ISLW TW7 ....**136** B4
Blyth's Wharf
  POP/IOD E14 ....**105** G6
BMI Medical Centre
  CAVSQ/HST W1G **9** H2
Bnois Jerusalem School
  STNW/STAM N16 ....**67** K4
The Bob Hope Theatre
  ELTH/MOT SE9 ....**166** E1
Bodywise Natural Health
Centre
  BETH E2 ....**104** E2
Bolem Cinema
  EHAM E6 ....**107** H1
Bolingbroke Hospital
  BTSEA SW11 ....**140** D6
Bolingbroke Primary School
  BTSEA SW11 ....**140** C4
Bond First School
  MTCM CR4 ....**178** E5
Bond Primary School
  MTCM CR4 ....**178** E5
Bonner Primary School
  BETH E2 ....**105** F1
Bonneville Primary School
  CLAP SW4 ....**161** H1
Bonnington Hotel
  RSQ WC1B **11** F1
Bonus Pastor Roman Catholic
School
  BMLY BR1 ....**165** G6
Boomes Industrial Estate
  RAIN RM13 ....**111** H3
Booster Cushion Theatre
  WDGN N22 ....**49** F5
Borough Market
  STHWK SE1 ....**12** E7
Boston Business Park
  HNWL W7 ....**115** K3
Boston University
  HYS/HAR UB3 ....**94** D3
Botwell RC Primary School
  HYS/HAR UB3 ....**113** J2
Boundary Business Centre
  MTCM CR4 ....**178** C5
Bounds Green Health Centre
  FBAR/BDGN N11 ....**48** D3
Bounds Green Industrial
Estate
  FBAR/BDGN N11 ....**48** B2
Bounds Green Primary
School
  FBAR/BDGN N11 ....**48** E3
Bourne CP School
  RSLP HA4 ....**77** G3
Bourne Hall Health Centre
  EW KT17 ....**207** H6
Bourne Hall Museum
  EW KT17 ....**207** H6
Bourne Road Industrial Park
  DART DA1 ....**150** A6
Bourneside Sports Club
  STHGT/OAK N14 ....**34** E3
Bousfield Primary School
  WBPTN SW10 ....**120** B5
Boutcher CE Primary School
  STHWK SE1 ....**19** J5
Bowater House
  SKENS SW7 ....**14** E3
Bow County Court
  SRTFD E15 ....**88** C4
Bowden House Clinic
  HRW HA1 ....**60** E6
Bower Park School
  ROM RM1 ....**57** G2
Bowes Primary School
  FBAR/BDGN N11 ....**48** D1
Bowes Road Clinic
  FBAR/BDGN N11 ....**48** C1

Bow Industrial Park
SRTFD E15 ....87 J5
Bowling Club
EA W5 ....97 J6
Bowls Club
PUT/ROE SW15 ....139 F3
STRHM/NOR SW16 ....161 K4
Bowman Trading Estate
CDALE/KGS NW9 ....44 C6
Bow Secondary School
BOW E3 ....105 J1
Bow Triangle Business Centre
BOW E3 ....105 J3
Boxgrove Primary School
ABYW SE2 ....128 D3
Boys' Club
EDGW HA8 ....44 C3
BPP Law School
HHOL WC1V 11 G2
Brackenbury Health Centre
HMSMTH W6 ....118 E3
Brackenbury Primary School
HMSMTH W6 ....118 E3
Bracken Industrial Estate
BARK/HLT IG6 ....55 F3
Bracton Centre
RDART DA2 ....170 C4
Brady Recreation Centre
WCHPL E1 ....104 C4
Braeside Senior School
BKHH IG9 ....39 F3
Braincroft Primary School
CRICK NW2 ....81 H1
Braintree Road Industrial
Estate
RSLP HA4 ....77 K2
Bramah's Tea & Coffee
Museum
STHWK SE1 ....18 D1
Brampton College
HDN NW4 ....64 A1
Brampton Manor School
EHAM E6 ....107 H3
Brampton Primary School
BXLYHN DA7 ....148 E3
EHAM E6 ....107 J2
Brandlehow Primary School
PUT/ROE SW15 ....139 J5
Brandlys Health Centre
PLSTW E13 ....106 E3
Breakspear Crematorium
RSLP HA4 ....58 A2
Breaside Preparatory
School
BMLY BR1 ....184 B4
Brecknock Primary School
HOLWY N7 ....84 D4
Bredinghurst School
PECK SE15 ....143 K5
Brent Adult College
WLSDN NW10 ....81 F6
Brent Arts Council
CRICK NW2 ....81 J1
Brent Child & Family Clinic
WLSDN NW10 ....81 H3
Brent Cross Shopping Centre
HDN NW4 ....64 A4
Brentfield Medical Centre
WLSDN NW10 ....81 F4
Brentfield Primary School
WLSDN NW10 ....81 F4
Brentford Business Centre
BTFD TW8 ....136 D1
Brentford County Court
BTFD TW8 ....136 E1
Brentford FC London Broncos
RLFC (Griffin Park)
BTFD TW8 ....116 E6
Brentford Fountain Leisure
Centre
BTFD TW8 ....117 G5
Brentford Health Centre
BTFD TW8 ....116 D6
Brentford School for Girls
BTFD TW8 ....116 E6
Brent Knoll School
FSTH SE23 ....164 A5
Brent Magistrates Court
House
WLSDN NW10 ....81 G4
Brent Park Industrial Estate
NWDGN UB2 ....114 A3
Brentside First School
HNWL W7 ....96 E3
Brentside High School
HNWL W7 ....96 E3
Brentside Primary School
HNWL W7 ....96 E3
Brent Trading Estate
WLSDN NW10 ....81 G3
Brent Valley Golf Club
HNWL W7 ....96 E6
Brentwaters Business Park
BTFD TW8 ....136 D1
Brewers' Hall
CITYW EC2V 12 D2
Brewery Industrial Estate
IS N1 ....6 C3
Brewery Mews Business
Centre
ISLW TW7 ....136 A4
The Brewery
ROMW/RG RM7 ....75 G3
Brick Lane Music Hall
CAN/RD E16 ....126 C1
FSBYE EC1V 7 H5
Brick Lane Music House
WCHPL E1 ....7 K7
Bricklayer Arms Industrial
Estate
STHWK SE1 ....19 J7
The Bridewell Theatre
EMB EC4Y 12 A4
The Bridge Business Centre
NWDGN UB2 ....115 F2
Bridge Lane Theatre
BTSEA SW11 ....140 D2

The Bridge Leisure Centre
SYD SE26 ....182 C1
Bridge Park Business &
Leisure Centre
WLSDN NW10 ....80 D5
The Bridge School
ARCH N19 ....66 C6
CLKNW EC1R 6 A1
HOLWY N7 ....84 D4
Brigham Young University
BAY/PAD W2 ....100 E6
Bright Sparks Montessori
School
WKENS W14 ....119 G2
Brigstock Medical Centre
THHTH CR7 ....196 C2
Brimsdown Industrial
Estate
PEND EN3 ....24 E3
Brimsdown Primary School
PEND EN3 ....25 F4
Brindishe Primary School
LEE/GVPK SE12 ....145 J6
Britain & London Visitor
Centre
STJS SW1Y 10 C7
Britannia Business Centre
CRICK NW2 ....82 B2
Britannia Leisure Centre
IS N1 ....7 F1
Britannia Sports Ground
WALTH E17 ....51 J3
Britannia Village Primary
School
CAN/RD E16 ....126 A1
British Cartoon Centre
BMSBY WC1N 5 F7
British College of Osteopathy
HAMP NW3 ....83 G4
British Dental Association
CAVSQ/HST W1G 9 J2
The British Hernia Centre
HDN NW4 ....63 K2
British Library
CAMTN NW1 ....4 D4
British Library Newspaper
Library
CDALE/KGS NW9 ....45 G6
British Medical Association
STPAN WC1H 4 D6
British Museum
RSQ WC1B 10 E2
British Telecom Tower
GTPST W1W 10 A1
BRIT School for
Performing Arts
CROY/NA CR0 ....196 E3
Brittons Technology
College
RAIN RM13 ....93 H5
Brixton Academy
BRXN/ST SW9 ....142 B4
Brixton Recreation Centre
BRXN/ST SW9 ....142 B4
Broadfields Primary School
EDGW HA8 ....30 C4
Broadgate
LVPST EC2M 13 F1
Broadgate Ice Arena
LVPST EC2M 13 F2
Broadhurst School
KIL/WHAMP NW6 ....83 G5
Broadmead J & I School
CROY/NA CR0 ....196 E3
Broadwalk Shopping Centre
EDGW HA8 ....44 C2
Broadwater Farm Primary
School
TOTM N17 ....49 K5
Broadwater Primary School
TOOT SW17 ....160 E6
Broadway Clinic
EDGW HA8 ....44 D4
Broadway Retail Park
CRICK NW2 ....82 B2
Broadway Shopping Centre
BXLYHS DA6 ....149 H5
HMSMTH W6 ....119 F5
Broadway Square Shopping
Centre
BXLYHS DA6 ....149 H5
Broadway Squash & Fitness
Centre
HMSMTH W6 ....119 G4
Brocklebank Health Centre
WAND/EARL SW18 ....160 A2
Brocklebank Industrial Estate
GNWCH SE10 ....125 K4
Brockley Cross Business
Centre
BROCKY SE4 ....144 B4
Brockley Primary School
BROCKY SE4 ....144 C6
Brockwell Lido
HNHL SE24 ....162 C1
Bromet Primary School
OXHEY WD19 ....27 H2
Bromley Cemetery
BMLY BR1 ....183 J3
Bromley College of Further
& Higher Education
HAYES BR2 ....200 C5
BMLY BR1 ....183 J4
Bromley County Court
BMLY BR1 ....183 K4
Bromley FC
HAYES BR2 ....200 A2
Bromley Golf Club
HAYES BR2 ....200 D4
Bromley High School GDST
BMLY BR1 ....201 F1
Bromley Industrial Centre
BMLY BR1 ....184 C6
Bromley Mall Indoor Market
BMLY BR1 ....183 K5
Bromley Museum
ORP BR6 ....202 C4

Bromley Road Infant School
BECK BR3 ....182 E4
Bromley Road Retail Park
CAT SE6 ....164 E4
Bromley Ski Centre
STMC/STPC BR5 ....186 E4
Bromley Tennis Centre
ORP BR6 ....216 D1
Brompton Cemetery
WBPTN SW10 ....120 A6
Brompton Medical Centre
ECT SW5 ....120 A5
Brompton Oratory
SKENS SW7 ....14 C5
Bromyard Leisure Centre
ACT W3 ....118 B1
Brondesbury College for Boys
KIL/WHAMP NW6 ....82 B5
Brook Community Primary
School
HACK E8 ....86 C3
Brook Trading Estate
ROM RM1 ....75 H4
Brookfield Primary School
CHEAM SM3 ....193 H5
HGT N6 ....66 B6
Brook House FC
YEAD UB4 ....94 D2
Brook Industrial Estate
YEAD UB4 ....114 C1
Brook Industrial Park
STMC/STPC BR5 ....202 D1
Brookland Primary School
GLDGN NW11 ....65 F1
Brooklands Primary School
BKHTH/KID SE3 ....145 K4
Brook Lane Business Centre
BTFD TW8 ....116 E5
Brookmarsh Trading Estate
DEPT SE8 ....144 E1
Brookmead Industrial Estate
CROY/NA CR0 ....195 H3
Brookside Primary School
YEAD UB4 ....95 G2
Broomfield House School
RCH/KEW TW9 ....137 G2
Broomfield School
FBAR/BDGN N11 ....48 D1
Broomsleigh Business Park
SYD SE26 ....182 C1
Broomwood Hall Lower
School
BAL SW12 ....160 E1
STRHM/NOR SW16 ....161 J1
Brothwick Wharf
DEPT SE8 ....124 D5
Brownlow Medical Centre
FBAR/BDGN N11 ....48 E1
Brown's Hotel
MYFR/PICC W1J 9 K6
Bruce Castle Museum
TOTM N17 ....50 A4
Bruce Grove Primary School
TOTM N17 ....50 B5
Brunei Gallery
STPAN WC1H 4 D7
Brunel Engine House
BERM/RHTH SE16 ....123 K2
Brunel University
GLDGN NW11 ....64 B3
ISLW TW7 ....135 K1
TWK TW1 ....156 C5
Brunel University
(Osterley Campus) Track
ISLW TW7 ....135 K1
Brunswick Health Centre
FBAR/BDGN N11 ....34 A4
Brunswick Housing &
Shopping Centre
BMSBY WC1N 5 F6
Brunswick Industrial Park
FBAR/BDGN N11 ....34 B6
Brunswick Medical Centre
BMSBY WC1N 4 E6
Brunswick Park JMI School
STHGT/OAK N14 ....34 A3
Brunswick Park Primary
School
CMBW SE5 ....142 E1
BT Centre
STBT EC1A 12 C3
Buckhurst Hill FC
BKHH IG9 ....39 J3
Buckhurst Hill Primary School
BKHH IG9 ....39 J4
Buckingham College
Preparatory School
PIN HA5 ....59 K3
Buckingham College School
HRW HA1 ....60 E2
Buckingham Palace
WHALL SW1A 15 K3
Buckingham Primary School
HPTN TW12 ....172 E1
Buckingham Road Cemetery
IL IG1 ....72 D6
Buckland Infant School
CHSGTN KT9 ....206 B3
Building Centre
GWRST WC1E 10 C2
Builders Crafts College
SRTFD E15 ....88 A5
Builders Wood School
FSTGT E7 ....184 A4
Bullsbridge Industrial Estate
NWDGN UB2 ....114 A4
The Bull Theatre
BAR EN5 ....20 D5
BUPA Roding Hospital
REDBR IG4 ....53 H6
Burbage School
IS N1 ....7 G1
Burdett Coutts CE Primary
School
WEST SW1P 16 C5
Burgess Business Park
CMBW SE5 ....142 E1

Burgess Park Tennis Centre
CMBW SE5 ....122 D6
Burlington Danes School
SHB W12 ....99 K5
Burlington Infant School
NWMAL KT3 ....192 C1
Burnham Trading Estate
DART DA1 ....151 G3
Burnhill Business Centre
BECK BR3 ....182 D5
Burnley Road Clinic
WLSDN NW10 ....81 J3
Burnside Industrial Estate
BARK/HLT IG6 ....55 H1
Burnt Ash Primary School
BMLY BR1 ....183 K1
Burnt Oak Junior School
BFN/LL DA15 ....168 B3
Burntwood School
TOOT SW17 ....160 C4
Bursted Wood Primary
School
BXLYHN DA7 ....149 J3
Burwell Industrial Estate
LEY E10 ....69 G5
Burwood School
ORP BR6 ....202 E6
Bushey Golf & Country Club
BUSH WD23 ....28 A3
Bushey Hall School
BUSH WD23 ....27 K1
Bushey Health Centre
BUSH WD23 ....27 K1
Bushey Heath Primary School
BUSH WD23 ....28 D3
Bushey Museum & Art Gallery
BUSH WD23 ....28 A1
Bush Hill Park Golf Club
WCHMH N21 ....23 J6
Bush Hill Park Medical Centre
EN EN1 ....36 B1
Bush Hill Park Primary School
EN EN1 ....24 C6
Bush House (BBC)
HOL/ALD WC2B 11 G4
Bush Industrial Estate
ARCH N19 ....84 C1
WLSDN NW10 ....99 F3
The Business Academy Bexley
ERITHM DA18 ....129 F2
The Business Design Centre
IS N1 ....5 K1
Business Training & Solutions
CDALE/KGS NW9 ....45 H4
Bute House Preparatory
School for Girls
HMSMTH W6 ....119 F4
Butlers Wharf
STHWK SE1 ....19 K1
Butler's Wharf Business
Centre
STHWK SE1 ....19 K2
Butler's Wharf Pier
STHWK SE1 ....19 K2
Butterfly House
ISLW TW7 ....136 C2
Butterfly Sports Club
ELTH/MOT SE9 ....167 G1
Buxlow Preparatory School
WBLY HA9 ....80 A1
Buzzard Creek Industrial
Estate
BARK IG11 ....109 F2
BARK IG11 ....109 F4
Byam Shaw School of Art
ARCH N19 ....66 C6
Byfleet Industrial Estate
WATW WD18 ....26 A3
Bygrove Primary School
POP/IOD E14 ....105 K5
Byron Court Primary School
ALP/SUD HA0 ....61 J2
Cabot Place
POP/IOD E14 ....124 D1
Cadogan Pier
CHEL SW3 ....120 D6
Caledonian Market
STHWK SE1 ....19 H4
Cally Pool
IS N1 ....85 F6
Calverton Primary School
CAN/RD E16 ....107 H5
Cambell Primary School
DAGW RM9 ....91 K5
Camberwell Business Centre
CMBW SE5 ....142 E1
Camberwell College of Arts
CMBW SE5 ....143 F2
Camberwell Leisure Centre
CMBW SE5 ....142 E2
Camberwell New Cemetery
PECK SE15 ....164 A1
Camberwell Trading Estate
CMBW SE5 ....142 C3
Cambridge Park Bowling
& Sports Club
TWK TW1 ....156 D1
Cambridge School
HMSMTH W6 ....118 E4
Cambridge Theatre
LSQ/SEVD WC2H 10 E4
Camden Arts Centre
HAMP NW3 ....83 F3
Camden House Clinic
BKHTH/KID SE3 ....145 H3
Camden Junior School
CAR SM5 ....209 K2
Camden Market
CAMTN NW1 ....84 A5
Camden Mews Day Hospital
CAMTN NW1 ....84 C4
Camden People's Theatre
CAMTN NW1 ....4 A5
Camden School for Girls
KTTN NW5 ....84 C4
Camden Theatre
CAMTN NW1 ....4 A2

Camden Town Hall &
St Pancras Library
CAMTN NW1 ....4 E4
Camelot Primary School
PECK SE15 ....143 J1
Cameron House School
CHEL SW3 ....120 C6
Camperdown House
WCHPL E1 ....13 K4
Campion House College
ISLW TW7 ....135 J1
Campsbourne J & I School
CEND/HSY/T N8 ....48 E6
Canada House
STJS SW1Y 10 D7
Canada House Business
Centre
RSLP HA4 ....59 G5
Canada Place
POP/IOD E14 ....124 D1
Canada Square
POP/IOD E14 ....124 E1
Canada Water Retail Park
BERM/RHTH SE16 ....124 A3
Canada Wharf Museum
BERM/RHTH SE16 ....124 C1
Canal Cafe Theatre
BAY/PAD W2 ....101 G4
Canary Riverside
BERM/RHTH SE16 ....124 C1
Canary Wharf Pier
POP/IOD E14 ....124 C1
Canberra Primary School
SHB W12 ....99 K6
Canbury Business Centre
KUTN/CMB KT2 ....175 F4
Canbury 2000 Business Park
KUTN/CMB KT2 ....175 F4
Canbury Medical Centre
KUTN/CMB KT2 ....175 J2
Canbury School
KUTN/CMB KT2 ....175 J2
Cann Hall Primary School
WAN E11 ....88 D1
Cannizaro House Hotel
WIM/MER SW19 ....177 F2
Cannon Hill Clinic
STHGT/OAK N14 ....34 E5
Cannon Lane Primary School
PIN HA5 ....59 H3
Cannon Sports Club
CANST EC4R 12 D5
Cannon Trading Estate
WBLY HA9 ....80 D2
Cannon Wharf Business
Centre
DEPT SE8 ....124 B4
Cannon Workshops
POP/IOD E14 ....105 J6
Canon Barnett Primary
School
WCHPL E1 ....13 K3
Canonbury Business Centre
IS N1 ....85 J6
Canonbury Primary School
IS N1 ....85 H4
Canon Palmer RC High School
IL IG1 ....72 E5
Canons High School
EDGW HA8 ....44 B5
The Canons Leisure Centre
MTCM CR4 ....194 E1
Canterbury Industrial
Estate
NWCR SE14 ....124 A6
Cantium Retail Park
STHWK SE1 ....123 H6
Capital Business Centre
ALP/SUD HA0 ....97 K1
MTCM CR4 ....194 E2
SAND/SEL CR2 ....211 K4
Capital City Academy
WLSDN NW10 ....81 K6
The Capital Hotel
CHEL SW3 ....14 E3
Capital Industrial Estate
BELV DA17 ....129 J4
BELV DA17 ....129 K1
Capital Radio
LSQ/SEVD WC2H 10 D6
Capital Wharf
WAP E1W 123 H1
Capitol Industrial Park
CDALE/KGS NW9 ....44 B6
Caplan Estate
MTCM CR4 ....179 H4
Cardiff Road Industrial Estate
WATW WD18 ....27 F1
Cardinal Hinsley High School
WLSDN NW10 ....81 J6
Cardinal Pole RC School
HOM E9 ....87 G4
Cardinal Pole RC Secondary
Lower School
HOM E9 ....87 F5
Cardinal Road Infant School
FELT TW13 ....154 A3
The Cardinal Vaughan
Memorial School
WKENS W14 ....119 H2
Cardinal Wiseman RC School
Technology and Art College
GFD/PVL UB6 ....96 C4
Cardwell Primary School
WOOL/PLUM SE18 ....126 E4
Carew Manor School
WLGTN SM6 ....210 D1
Carlisle Infant School
HPTN TW12 ....173 G2
Carlton House
STJS SW1Y 16 C1
The Carlton Mitre Hotel
E/WMO/HCT KT8 ....173 K6
Carlton Primary School
KTTN NW5 ....84 A3
Carlton Vale Infant School
MV/WKIL W9 ....100 D2

Carlyle's House (NT)
CHEL SW3 ....120 D6
Carnwath Road Industrial Estate
FUL/PGN SW6 ....140 A4
Carpenters Park Cemetery
OXHEY WD19 ....27 K6
Carpenters Business Park
SRTFD E15 ....87 J4
Carpenters' Hall
OBST EC2N 13 F2
Carpenters Primary School
SRTFD E15 ....88 A6
Carshalton AFC
SUT SM1 ....209 J1
Carshalton College of Further Education
CAR SM5 ....209 K1
Carshalton High School for Boys
CAR SM5 ....194 C6
Carshalton High School for Girls
CAR SM5 ....209 J1
Carshalton War Memorial Hospital
CAR SM5 ....209 K3
Carternhatch Primary School
EN EN1 ....24 D2
Caryl Thomas Clinic
HRW HA1 ....60 E1
The Cassel Hospital
RCHPK/HAM TW10 ....156 E6
Cassidy Medical Centre
FUL/PGN SW6 ....139 K1
Castilion Primary School
THMD SE28 ....109 J5
Castlebar Special School
WEA W13 ....97 G4
Castlecombe Primary School
ELTH/MOT SE9 ....184 D1
Castle Hill Primary School
CROY/NA CR0 ....214 A4
Castle Industrial Estate
WALW SE17 ....18 C6
Casualty Plus' Clinic
BTFD TW8 ....116 D5
Caterham High School
CLAY IG5 ....53 K5
Catford Cricket & Sports Club
CAT SE6 ....164 E3
Catford Cyphers CC
CAT SE6 ....164 C4
Catford Girls School
CAT SE6 ....165 G5
Catford Trading Estate
CAT SE6 ....164 E4
Catford Wanderers Sports Club
CAT SE6 ....165 F6
Cathall Leisure Centre
WAN E11 ....88 B1
Cathedral School of St Saviour & St Mary Overie
STHWK SE1 ....18 D1
Cator Park School for Girls
BECK BR3 ....182 B3
Cavendish College
FITZ W1T 10 C1
Cavendish Hotel
STJS SW1Y 10 B7
Cavendish Primary School
CHSWK W4 ....138 B1
Cavendish School
BERM/RHTH SE16 ....123 K4
The Cavendish School
CAMTN NW1 ....84 B6
Cavendish Special School
HNWL W7 ....97 F5
Caxton Hall
STJSPK SW1H 16 C4
Caxton Trading Estate
HYS/HAR UB3 ....113 H2
Cayley Primary School
WCHPL E1 ....105 G4
Cecil Park Clinic
PIN HA5 ....59 J1
The Cedar School
FSTGT E7 ....89 G4
Cedars First & Middle School
KTN/HRWW/WS HA3 ....42 C4
The Cedars Primary School
HEST TW5 ....133 K1
Cedar Way Industrial Estate
CAMTN NW1 ....84 D5
Cenotaph
WHALL SW1A 16 E2
Centaurs Business Centre
ISLW TW7 ....116 B6
Centaurs RFC
ISLW TW7 ....116 A6
Central Business Centre
WLSDN NW10 ....81 G3
Central Criminal Court
STP EC4M 12 A3
Centrale Shopping Centre
CROY/NA CR0 ....196 D6
Central Foundation Boys School
SDTCH EC2A 7 F6
Central Foundation Girls School (Lower)
BOW E3 ....105 G2
Central Foundation Girls School (Upper)
BOW E3 ....105 H2
Central Hall
STJSPK SW1H 16 D3
Central Hendon Clinic
HDN NW4 ....63 K1
Central London County Court
CAVSQ/HST W1 ....3 J7
Central London Golf Club
TOOT SW17 ....160 C4
Central London Markets
STBT EC1A 12 A2

Central Medical Centre
MRDN SM4 ....194 B1
Central Middlesex Hospital
WLSDN NW10 ....98 E2
Central Park Arena
DART DA1 ....171 H3
Central Park Primary School
EHAM E6 ....107 H1
Central St Martins College of Art & Design
RSQ WC1B 11 G2
Central School of Ballet
CLKNW EC1R 5 K7
Central School of Fashion
GTPST W1W 10 C3
Central School of Speech & Drama
HAMP NW3 ....83 H5
Central Square Shopping Centre
WBLY HA9 ....80 A4
Centre Court Shopping Centre
WIM/MER SW19 ....177 J2
Centre Point
LSQ/SEVD WC2H 10 D3
Chace Community School
EN EN1 ....24 A2
The Chadwell Heath Foundation School
CHDH RM6 ....73 H3
Chadwell Heath Industrial Park
BCTR RM8 ....74 A3
Chadwell Heath Leisure Centre
CHDH RM6 ....73 K3
Chadwell Infant & Primary School
CHDH RM6 ....73 J4
Chaffinch Business Park
BECK BR3 ....182 A6
Chailey Industrial Estate
HYS/HAR UB3 ....113 K2
Chalcot School
CAMTN NW1 ....84 B4
Chalgrove Primary School
FNCH N3 ....46 C6
Chalkhill Primary School
WBLY HA9 ....80 D1
The Chamberlain Hotel
TWRH EC3N 13 J5
Chambers Business Park
WDR/YW UB7 ....112 D6
Chambers Wharf
BERM/RHTH SE16 ....123 H2
Chandlers Field Primary School
E/WMO/HCT KT8 ....189 F2
Chandos Business Centre
WLGTN SM6 ....210 C4
Channelsea Business Centre
SRTFD E15 ....106 B1
Channing School
HGT N6 ....66 B5
Chapel End Infant School
WALTH E17 ....51 K4
Chapel End Junior School
WALTH E17 ....51 K4
Chapman Park Industrial Estate
WLSDN NW10 ....81 H4
Charing Cross Hospital
HMSMTH W6 ....119 G6
The Charles Dickens Museum
BMSBY WC1N 5 G7
Charles Dickens Primary School
STHWK SE1 ....18 C3
Charles Edward Brooke School (Lower School)
CMBW SE5 ....142 C2
Charles Edward Brooke School (Upper School)
BRXN/ST SW9 ....142 C2
Charlotte Sharman Primary School
LBTH SE11 ....18 A4
Charlotte Turner Primary School
DEPT SE8 ....124 D6
Charlton Athletic FC (The Valley)
CHARL SE7 ....126 B5
Charlton Health & Fitness Centre
CHARL SE7 ....126 B5
Charlton House
CHARL SE7 ....126 C6
Charlton Manor Junior School
CHARL SE7 ....146 C1
Charlton RFC
ELTH/MOT SE9 ....167 G2
Charlton School
CHARL SE7 ....126 D6
Charrington Bowl
SURB KT6 ....191 J6
Charville Primary School
YEAD UB4 ....94 C1
Charter Clinic
CHEL SW3 ....120 E5
Charterhouse
CLKNW EC1R 6 A7
Charteris Road Sports Centre
KIL/WHAMP NW6 ....82 D6
Charter Nightingale Hospital & Counselling Centre
CAMTN NW1 ....8 D1
The Charter School
HNHL SE24 ....142 E6
Chartfield School
PUT/ROE SW15 ....138 E6
Chartwell Business Centre
BMLY BR1 ....184 C6
Chase Bridge Primary School
WHTN TW2 ....155 K1

Chase Farm Hospital
ENC/FH EN2 ....23 G1
Chase Lane J & I School
ENC/FH EN2 ....37 H6
Chase Lane Primary School
CHING E4 ....37 K6
Chase Road Trading Estate
WLSDN NW10 ....99 F3
Chase Side Primary School
ENC/FH EN2 ....23 J5
Chaseville Clinic
WCHMH N21 ....35 F1
Chatsworth Infant School
BFN/LL DA15 ....168 B3
Chatsworth J & I School
HSLW TW3 ....135 H5
Chaucer Clinic
NWDGN UB2 ....115 J2
Cheam Common J & I School
WPK KT4 ....192 E6
Cheam Fields Primary School
CHEAM SM3 ....208 C3
Cheam High School
CHEAM SM3 ....208 C2
Cheam Leisure Centre
CHEAM SM3 ....208 B2
Cheam Park Farm Junior School
CHEAM SM3 ....208 C1
Cheam Sports Club
CHEAM SM3 ....208 C5
Chelsea Barracks
BGVA SW1W 121 F5
Chelsea Bridge Business Centre
VX/NE SW8 ....141 G1
Chelsea Centre & Theatre
WBPTN SW10 ....140 B1
Chelsea Cinema
CHEL SW3 ....120 D5
The Chelsea Club Leisure Centre
FUL/PGN SW6 ....120 A6
Chelsea College of Art & Design
CHEL SW3 ....120 D5
SHB W12 ....118 E2
WEST SW1P 121 K5
Chelsea FC (Stamford Bridge)
FUL/PGN SW6 ....140 A1
Chelsea Fields Industrial Estate
WIM/MER SW19 ....178 C4
Chelsea Leisure Centre
CHEL SW3 ....120 D5
Chelsea Old Town Hall
CHEL SW3 ....120 D5
Chelsea Physic Garden
CHEL SW3 ....120 E6
Chelsea & Westminster Hospital
WBPTN SW10 ....120 B6
Chelsea Wharf
WBPTN SW10 ....140 C1
Chennestone Community School
SUN TW16 ....172 A5
Cherington House Health Centre
HNWL W7 ....116 A1
Cherry Garden Pier
BERM/RHTH SE16 ....123 J2
Cherry Garden School
BERM/RHTH SE16 ....123 H4
Cherry Lane Primary School
WDR/YW UB7 ....112 C4
Cherry Orchard Primary School
CHARL SE7 ....146 B1
Chessington CC
CHSGTN KT9 ....205 J5
Chessington Community College & Sports Centre
CHSGTN KT9 ....205 K5
Chessington Golf Club
CHSGTN KT9 ....205 K5
The Chesterfield Mayfair Hotel
MYFR/PICC W1J 9 J7
Chesterton Primary School
BTSEA SW11 ....141 F2
Chestnut Grove School
BAL SW12 ....161 F3
Chestnuts Primary School
SEVS/STOTM N15 ....67 J2
Cheyne Centre
CHEL SW3 ....120 D6
Chicken Shed Theatre
STHGT/OAK N14 ....22 A6
Chigwell Golf Club
CHIG IG7 ....54 A1
Childeric Primary School
NWCR SE14 ....144 B1
Childs Hill Clinic
CRICK NW2 ....64 D6
Childs Hill Primary School
CRICK NW2 ....82 C1
Childs Welfare Clinic
BCTR RM8 ....91 J3
Chiltonian Industrial Estate
LEE/GVPK SE12 ....165 J1
Chimnocks Wharf
POP/IOD E14 ....105 G6
Chingford CE Infant School
CHING E4 ....38 B5
Chingford CE Junior School
CHING E4 ....38 B3
Chingford Foundation School
CHING E4 ....37 K3
Chingford Hall Primary School
CHING E4 ....51 H2
Chingford Health Centre
CHING E4 ....37 H6
Chingford Industrial Centre
CHING E4 ....51 G1

Chingford RFC
CHING E4 ....37 J3
Chisenhale Primary School
BOW E3 ....105 G1
Chislehurst Caves
CHST BR7 ....185 F4
Chislehurst Cemetery
CHST BR7 ....185 K1
Chislehurst Golf Club
CHST BR7 ....185 G3
Chislehurst Natural Health Centre
CHST BR7 ....185 G2
Chislehurst & Sidcup Grammar School
BFN/LL DA15 ....168 C4
Chiswick & Bedford Park Preparatory School
CHSWK W4 ....118 B4
Chiswick Business Park
CHSWK W4 ....117 J4
Chiswick Community School
CHSWK W4 ....138 A1
Chiswick House
CHSWK W4 ....118 A6
Chrisp Street Health Centre
POP/IOD E14 ....105 K5
Christ Church Bentinck CE Primary School
CAMTN NW1 ....8 C1
Christ Church Brondesbury CE J & I School
KIL/WHAMP NW6 ....82 D6
Christ Church CE Infant School
NWMAL KT3 ....176 B6
Christ Church CE Junior School
NWMAL KT3 ....176 A6
Christ Church CE Primary School
BAR EN5 ....20 B3
BRXN/ST SW9 ....142 B2
BRXS/STRHM SW2 ....162 A3
BRYLDS KT5 ....191 H5
BTSEA SW11 ....140 C6
CHEL SW3 ....120 C6
FSTH SE23 ....164 A4
WOOL/PLUM SE18 ....147 F2
Christchurch CE Primary School
HAMP NW3 ....83 H1
WCHPL E1 ....13 K2
Christ Church CE Middle School
EA W5 ....97 K6
Christchurch Industrial Centre
STHWK SE1 ....12 A1
Christ Church Primary School
ERITH DA8 ....130 A4
Christchurch Primary School
IL IG1 ....72 B5
Christ Church School
CAMTN NW1 ....3 K3
Christian Meeting Hall
BARK IG11 ....182 D4
Christopher Hatton Primary School
FSBYW WC1X 5 J7
Christ's College Finchley
FNCH N3 ....47 F6
Christs College School
EFNCH N2 ....47 F6
Christs School
RCHPK/HAM TW10 ....137 G6
Christ the King RC First School
STWL/WRAY TW19 ....152 A1
Christ the King RC Primary School
FSBYPK N4 ....67 F5
Christ the King Sixth Form College
LEW SE13 ....145 G4
Chrysalis Theatre
BAL SW12 ....161 F3
Chrysanthemum Clinic
CHSWK W4 ....137 K1
Chrysolyte Independent Christian School
STHWK SE1 ....19 G4
Church Down Adult School
LEE/GVPK SE12 ....165 K4
Church End Medical Centre
WLSDN NW10 ....81 G4
Church Farm House Museum
HDN NW4 ....45 K6
Church Farm Swimming Pool
EBAR EN4 ....33 K3
Churchfield Primary School
ED N9 ....36 B3
Churchfield School
WOOL/PLUM SE18 ....128 A4
Churchfields J & I School
SWFD E18 ....52 E4
Churchfields Primary School
BECK BR3 ....182 A6
Church Hill Primary School
EBAR EN4 ....33 K2
Church House
WEST SW1P 16 D4
Churchill Clinic
STHWK SE1 ....17 K4
Churchill College
RYNPK SW20 ....177 G5
Churchill Gardens Primary School
PIM SW1V 121 H5
Churchill Museum & Cabinet War Rooms
STJSPK SW1H 16 D2
Churchill Theatre
BMLY BR1 ....183 K5
Church Mead Infant School
LEY E10 ....69 J5
Church Mead Junior School
LEY E10 ....69 J5

Church Stairs
BERM/RHTH SE16 ....123 J2
Church Trading Estate
ERITH DA8 ....150 D1
Cineworld Cinema
BXLYHS DA6 ....149 G5
FELT TW13 ....154 A4
WDGN N22 ....49 G5
Citigroup Tower
POP/IOD E14 ....124 E1
City Business Centre
BERM/RHTH SE16 ....123 K2
City Business College
FSBYE EC1V 6 C5
City Central Estate
FSBYE EC1V 6 C5
City College of Higher Education
IS N1 ....7 F4
City & Guilds of London Art School
LBTH SE11 ....122 B5
City Health Centre
FSBYE EC1V 6 E4
City & Islington College
FSBYE EC1V 6 A4
FSBYE EC1V 6 D5
FSBYPK N4 ....67 H6
HBRY N5 ....85 G4
HOLWY N7 ....84 E2
IS N1 ....85 J6
STLK EC1Y 6 E7
City & Islington Sixth Form College
FSBYE EC1V 6 A3
City Literary College
HHOL WC1V 11 F3
City of East London College
WCHPL E1 ....104 C5
The City of London Academy
STHWK SE1 ....123 H5
The City of London Academy
EDUL SE22 ....143 H6
City of London Business College
SEVS/STOTM N15 ....68 A2
SEVS/STOTM N15 ....68 C2
City of London Cemetery
MNPK E12 ....71 J6
City of London Club
OBST EC2N 13 G3
City of London College
WCHPL E1 ....104 C5
City of London Crematorium
MNPK E12 ....89 H1
City of London Magistrates Court
LOTH EC2R 12 E4
City of London School
BLKFR EC4V 12 B5
City of London School for Girls
BARB EC2Y 12 C1
City of London School Sports Ground
LEE/GVPK SE12 ....166 B4
City of Westminster Cemetery
HNWL W7 ....116 A1
City of Westminster College
BAY/PAD W2 ....8 A1
MV/WKIL W9 ....100 D2
MV/WKIL W9 ....101 F3
City of Westminster Vehicle Pound
MYFR/PKLN W1K 9 F2
City University
FSBYE EC1V 6 A4
FSBYE EC1V 6 B6
IS N1 ....6 C3
STBT EC1A 12 C2
WCHPL E1 ....104 C1
City University Business School
BARB EC2Y 12 D1
Civic Centre & Bromley Palace
BMLY BR1 ....184 A5
Civic Medical Centre
HRW HA1 ....60 E2
Civil Service Recreation Centre
WEST SW1P 16 D5
Civil Service Sports Ground
LEE/GVPK SE12 ....166 B1
Clapham Common Clinic
CLAP SW4 ....141 J5
Clapham Manor Primary School
CLAP SW4 ....141 H4
Clapham Manor Street Public Baths
CLAP SW4 ....141 J4
Clapham North Business Centre
CLAP SW4 ....141 J4
Clapham Picture House
CLAP SW4 ....141 J4
Clapton Girls Technology College
CLPT E5 ....86 E2
Clapton Jewish Boys School
CLPT E5 ....68 B4
Clara Grant Primary School
BOW E3 ....105 J3
Clare House Primary School
BECK BR3 ....183 F5
Claremont Clinic
FSTGT E7 ....89 G3
Claremont Fan Court School
ESH/CLAY KT10 ....204 B4
Claremont High School
KTN/HRWW/WS HA3 ....62 A2
Claremont Landscape Garden (NT)
ESH/CLAY KT10 ....204 A5

Claremont Way Industrial Estate
CRICK NW2 ....64 A5
Clarence House
WHALL SW1A 16 B2
Clarendon Primary School
ASHF TW15 ....152 C5
Clarendon Special School
HPTN TW12 ....173 G2
Claridge's Hotel
MYFR/PKLN W1K 9 J1
Claverings Industrial Estate
ED N9 ....36 E4
Claygate Primary School
ESH/CLAY KT10 ....204 E5
Clayhall Clinic
CLAY IG5 ....53 J6
Clayponds Hospital
BTFD TW8 ....117 F4
Cleeve Park School
SCUP DA14 ....168 D5
Clementine Churchill Hospital
HRW HA1 ....78 E1
Cleopatra's Needle
CHCR WC2N 11 G7
Clerkenwell County Court
IS N1 ....6 A2
Clerkenwell Heritage Centre
FARR EC1M 6 A7
Clerkenwell Parochial CE Primary School
CLKNW EC1R 5 J5
Cleveland Primary School
IL IG1 ....90 B2
Cleves Primary School
EHAM E6 ....89 H6
C & L Golf & Country Club
NTHLT UB5 ....77 F5
Clifton Lodge School
EA W5 ....97 J6
Clifton Primary School
NWDGN UB2 ....114 D4
Clink Exhibition
STHWK SE1 ....12 E7
Clissold Leisure Centre
STNW/STAM N16 ....85 K1
Clissold Park Natural Health Centre
STNW/STAM N16 ....68 A6
Clitterhouse Primary School
CRICK NW2 ....64 B6
C & L Leisure Centre
RSLP HA4 ....77 F5
Clockhouse Industrial Estate
EBED/NFELT TW14 ....152 E3
Clockhouse Primary School
CRW RM5 ....56 D2
Clock Museum
CITYW EC2V 12 D3
Cloisters Business Centre
VX/NE SW8 ....141 G1
Clore Gallery
WEST SW1P 16 E1
Clore Tikva School
BARK/HLT IG6 ....54 C5
Clothworkers' Hall
FENCHST EC3M 13 H5
Clouster's Green
IWAP E1W 123 H1
Cobbold Estate
WLSDN NW10 ....81 H4
Cobourg Primary School
CMBW SE5 ....123 G6
Cochrane Theatre
GINN WC1R 11 G2
Cockfosters Sports Ground
EBAR EN4 ....21 K4
The Cockpit Theatre
STJWD NW8 ....2 C7
Coldharbour Industrial Estate
CMBW SE5 ....142 D3
Coldharbour Leisure Centre
ELTH/MOT SE9 ....166 E4
Coldharbour Sports Ground
ELTH/MOT SE9 ....167 F4
Colebrooke Primary School
IS N1 ....6 A2
Colegrave School
SRTFD E15 ....88 B3
Coleraine Park Primary School
TOTM N17 ....50 D4
Coleridge Primary School
HGT N6 ....66 D4
Colet Court
BARN SW13 ....118 D5
Colfe's Preparatory School
LEE/GVPK SE12 ....165 K1
Colfe's Senior School
LEE/GVPK SE12 ....165 K1
Colindale Business Park
CDALE/KGS NW9 ....44 E6
Colindale Hospital
CDALE/KGS NW9 ....45 G6
Colindale Primary School
CDALE/KGS NW9 ....63 H1
Coliseum Theatre
CHCR WC2N 10 E6
College Fields Business Centre
WIM/MER SW19 ....178 D4
College of Arms
BLKFR EC4V 12 C4
College of Central London
SOTCH EC2A 7 G6
College of Fuel Technology
HGT N6 ....66 A3
The College of Law
FITZ W1T 10 C2
LINN WC2A 11 J3
College of North East London
CEND/HSY/T N8 ....68 D1
SEVS/STOTM N15 ....68 B1
WDGN N22 ....48 C4
College of North West London
KIL/WHAMP NW6 ....82 E6
WBLY HA9 ....80 C1
WLSDN NW10 ....81 H3

College of Organists
FLST/FETLN EC4A 11 K2
College Park School
BAY/PAD W2 ....101 F5
Collier Row Clinic
CRW RM5 ....56 D4
Collier Row FC
CRW RM5 ....56 B4
Collingwood Business Centre
ARCH N19 ....84 E1
Collingwood Preparatory School
WLGTN SM6 ....210 B3
Collins Method School
CRICK NW2 ....82 A4
Collis Primary School
TEDD TW11 ....174 C2
Colnbrook School
OXHEY WD19 ....27 G4
Coloma Convent Girls School
CROY/NA CR0 ....213 F1
Colonnades Leisure Park
CROY/NA CR0 ....211 G4
The Colonnades Shopping Centre
BGVA SW1W 15 J6
Colours Sports Club
SUT SM1 ....209 G3
Columbia Primary School
BETH E2 ....7 K4
Colvestone Primary School
HACK E8 ....86 B3
Colville Primary School
NTGHL W11 ....100 D5
Colyers Lane Medical Centre
ERITH DA8 ....150 A2
Colyers Primary School
ERITH DA8 ....150 A2
Comber Grove Primary School
CMBW SE5 ....142 D1
Comedy Theatre
STJS SW1Y 10 C6
Comelle House Trading Estate
DEPT SE8 ....124 B5
Comfort Hotel
ENC/FH EN2 ....23 H3
Comfort Inn
ECT SW5 ....119 K4
HYS/HAR UB3 ....113 H5
Commonwealth Institute
WKENS W14 ....119 J3
Community Arts Centre
ENC/FH EN2 ....144 E1
Community Care Centre
ENC/FH EN2 ....23 K2
Community Centre (Island History Trust)
POP/IOD E14 ....125 F4
Community College and School
GNWCH SE10 ....145 F1
The Community College
HACK E8 ....86 D6
Compass Theatre
HGDN/ICK UB10 ....76 A1
Complementary Health Centre
LEE/GVPK SE12 ....165 K1
Compton Leisure Centre
NTHLT UB5 ....77 J6
The Compton School
NFNCH/WDSPK N12 ....47 J2
Compton Sports Centre
NFNCH/WDSPK N12 ....47 J2
Concord Business Centre
ACT W3 ....98 D4
Conductive Education Centre
MUSWH N10 ....48 C6
Conduit House
GNWCH SE10 ....145 G1
Coney Hill School
HAYES BR2 ....199 J6
Connaught Business Centre
CDALE/KGS NW9 ....63 H2
CROY/NA CR0 ....211 F4
MTCM CR4 ....194 E2
The Connaught Hotel
MYFR/PKLN W1K 9 H6
Connaught House School
BAY/PAD W2 ....8 E4
Connaught School for Girls
WAN E11 ....70 C5
Conrad Hotel
WBPTN SW10 ....140 B2
Consort Clinic
PECK SE15 ....143 J4
Consulate General of Monaco
SKENS SW7 ....14 A6
Consulate of Burkina Faso
BTSEA SW11 ....140 B4
Consulate of Chile
CAVSQ/HST W1G 3 J7
Consulate of Colombia
GTPST W1W 10 A3
Consulate of Eritrea
IS N1 ....5 K2
Consulate of Guinea
MYFR/PKLN W1K 9 G6
Consulate of Panama
MYFR/PICC W1J 15 J1
Convent of Jesus & Mary Infant School
CRICK NW2 ....82 A4
Convent of Jesus & Mary Language College
WLSDN NW10 ....81 H6
Conway Hall
FSBYW WC1X 11 G1
Conway Medical Centre
WOOL/PLUM SE18 ....127 J5
Conway Primary School
WOOL/PLUM SE18 ....127 K4
Coombe Girls School
NWMAL KT3 ....176 A5
Coombe Hill Golf Club
KUTN/CMB KT2 ....176 A3

Coombe Hill J & I School
NWMAL KT3 ....176 A4
Coombe Wood Golf Club
KUTN/CMB KT2 ....175 J3
Coopers' Hall
LVPST EC2M 13 H2
Coopers Lane Primary School
LEE/GVPK SE12 ....165 K4
Coopers Technology College
CHST BR7 ....185 H4
Copenhagen Primary School
IS N1 ....5 F1
Copland Specialist Science College
WBLY HA9 ....80 B3
Coppermill Primary School
WALTH E17 ....69 F2
Coppetts Wood Hospital
MUSWH N10 ....47 K4
Coppetts Wood Primary School
MUSWH N10 ....48 A4
Coppice Primary School
CHIG IG7 ....55 G1
Copthall School
MLHL NW7 ....45 K3
Copthorne Tara Hotel
KENS W8 ....120 A3
Cordwainers College
HACK E8 ....86 E5
Corinthian Casuals FC
SURB KT6 ....206 C1
Coronet Cinema
KENS W8 ....119 K1
SEVS/STOTM N15 ....49 H6
Corpus Christi RC Primary School
BRXS/STRHM SW2 ....142 A6
Corus Hotel
BAY/PAD W2 ....8 A5
BORE WD6 ....30 A2
Cosmopolitan College
IS N1 ....5 G3
Coston Secondary Modern Girls School
GFD/PVL UB6 ....96 C1
Coteford Infant School
PIN HA5 ....58 E2
Courtauld Institute Gallery
TPL/STR WC2R 11 G5
Courtauld Institute of Art
TPL/STR WC2R 11 H6
Court Farm Industrial Estate
STWL/WRAY TW19 ....152 C1
Courtfield Medical Centre
ECT SW5 ....120 A4
Courtland JMI School
MLHL NW7 ....31 G4
Covent Garden Flower Market
VX/NE SW8 ....121 J6
Covent Garden Medical Centre
LSQ/SEVD WC2H 10 E4
CPFC Soccer & Sports Centre
BRXN/ST SW9 ....142 A4
Crafts Council
IS N1 ....5 K3
Crampton Primary School
WALW SE17 ....18 B7
Cranbrook College
IL IG1 ....72 A6
Cranford Community College
HEST TW5 ....114 A6
Cranford Infant School
HSLWW TW4 ....133 K3
Cranford Junior School
HSLWW TW4 ....134 A3
Cranford Park Junior School
HYS/HAR UB3 ....113 J4
Cranford Park Primary School
HYS/HAR UB3 ....113 J2
Cranleigh Gardens Industrial Estate
STHL UB1 ....95 K4
Cranmer Primary School
MTCM CR4 ....194 E1
The Craven Clinic
HMSMTH W6 ....118 E4
Craven Park Health Centre
WLSDN NW10 ....81 F6
Craven Park Medical Centre
WLSDN NW10 ....81 F6
Crawford Primary School
CMBW SE5 ....142 D2
Crayfield Industrial Park
STMC/STPC BR5 ....186 D5
Crayfields Business Park
STMC/STPC BR5 ....186 D4
Crayford Commercial Centre
DART DA1 ....150 B6
Crayford Industrial Estate
DART DA1 ....150 C6
Crayford Leisure Centre & Greyhound Stadium
DART DA1 ....170 B1
Crayford Medical Centre
DART DA1 ....150 C6
Crayside Industrial Estate
DART DA1 ....150 D4
Cray Valley Golf Club
STMC/STPC BR5 ....187 F4
Creekmouth Industrial Estate
BARK IG11 ....109 F3
Creek Road Health Centre
DEPT SE8 ....124 D6
Creek Road Industrial Estate
DEPT SE8 ....124 E6
Cremer Business Centre
BETH E2 ....7 J3
Crewe House
MYFR/PICC W1J 9 J7
Cricket Green School
MTCM CR4 ....178 D6
Cricket Pavilion
WEST SW1P 16 C6

Cricklefield Stadium
IL IG1 ....72 E6
Cricklewood Trading Estate
CRICK NW2 ....82 C1
Crispin Industrial Centre
UED N18 ....50 E1
Criterion Theatre
MYFR/PICC W1J 10 B6
Crockenhill Primary School
SWLY BR8 ....203 K3
Crofton Leisure Centre
BROCKY SE4 ....164 D1
Crofton School
BROCKY SE4 ....164 D1
Croham Hurst Golf Club
SAND/SEL CR2 ....212 B4
Cromer Road Primary School
BAR EN5 ....21 F4
Cromwell Business Centre
BARK IG11 ....108 E2
Cromwell Hospital
KENS W8 ....120 A4
Crook Log Primary School
BXLYHS DA6 ....148 E5
Crook Log Sports Centre
WELL DA16 ....148 E4
Crossways Academy
BROCKY SE4 ....144 B3
Crouch End Art School
CEND/HSY/T N8 ....66 E2
Crouch End Health Centre
CEND/HSY/T N8 ....66 E2
Crouch Hill Recreation Centre
CEND/HSY/T N8 ....66 E2
Crowland Primary School
SEVS/STOTM N15 ....68 C2
Crowlands Primary School
ROMW/RG RM7 ....74 E3
Crown Business Centre
WDR/YW UB7 ....112 C1
Crown Close Business Centre
BOW E3 ....87 J6
Crown Court
ISLW TW7 ....135 K2
Crown Court at the Borough
STHWK SE1 ....18 B2
Crowndale Health Centre
CAMTN NW1 ....4 B2
Crowne Plaza Hotel
WDR/YW UB7 ....112 D4
Crownfield Primary School
ROMW/RG RM7 ....56 C5
Crown Lane Clinic
STHGT/OAK N14 ....34 C3
Crown Lane Primary School
WNWD SE27 ....162 D6
Crown Moran Hotel
CRICK NW2 ....82 B2
Crown Trading Centre
HYS/HAR UB3 ....113 H2
Crown Woods School
ELTH/MOT SE9 ....147 H6
Croydon Airport Industrial Estate
CROY/NA CR0 ....211 G5
Croydon Bowling Club
SAND/SEL CR2 ....211 J3
Croydon Cemetery
CROY/NA CR0 ....196 A2
Croydon Clocktower Cinema
CROY/NA CR0 ....211 J1
Croydon College
CROY/NA CR0 ....211 K1
Croydon Crematorium
THHTH CR7 ....195 K2
Croydon Fairfield Halls Cinema
CROY/NA CR0 ....211 K1
Croydon FC
SNWD SE25 ....197 K2
Croydon Road Industrial Estate
BECK BR3 ....197 K1
Croydon Sports Arena
SNWD SE25 ....197 K2
Crusader Industrial Estate
FSBYPK N4 ....67 J3
Crusoe House School
IS N1 ....6 E4
Crystal Palace FC (Selhurst Park)
SNWD SE25 ....197 F1
Crystal Palace Museum
NRWD SE19 ....181 G2
Cuaco Sports Ground
BECK BR3 ....182 D2
Cubitt Town Primary School
POP/IOD E14 ....125 F3
Cuddington Cemetery
WPK KT4 ....192 E6
Cuddington CP School
WPK KT4 ....207 H1
Cuddington Croft Primary School
BELMT SM2 ....208 B6
Culloden Primary School
POP/IOD E14 ....106 B5
Culvers House Primary School
MTCM CR4 ....195 F4
Cumberland Business Park
WLSDN NW10 ....98 D2
The Cumberland Hotel
OXSTW W1C 9 F4
Cumberland Park Industrial Estate
WLSDN NW10 ....99 J2
The Cumming Museum
WALW SE17 ....18 C7
Cumnor House School
SAND/SEL CR2 ....211 H6
Curwen Primary School
PLSTW E13 ....106 E1
Curzon Mayfair Cinema
MYFR/PICC W1J 15 J1
Curzon Soho Cinema
SOHO/SHAV W1D 10 D5

Custom House
MON EC3R 13 G6
Cutlers' Hall
STP EC4M 12 B3
Cutty Sark Clipper Ship
GNWCH SE10 ....125 F6
Cygnet Clinic Beckton
EHAM E6 ....108 B4
Cygnus Business Centre
WLSDN NW10 ....81 H3
Cypress Infant School
SNWD SE25 ....181 F5
Cypress Junior School
SNWD SE25 ....181 F5
Cyprus College of Art
WNWD SE27 ....162 C6
Cyril Jackson Primary School
POP/IOD E14 ....105 H6
Dagenham Chest Clinic
BCTR RM8 ....92 B1
Dagenham Priory Comprehensive School & Performing Arts College
DAGE RM10 ....92 D5
Dagenham & Redbridge FC
DAGE RM10 ....92 D3
Dagenham Superbowl
DAGE RM10 ....110 D1
Dagenham Swimming Pool
DAGE RM10 ....74 C6
Daiglen School
BKHH IG9 ....39 G3
Daily Telegraph
POP/IOD E14 ....124 D3
Dairy Meadow Primary School
NWDGN UB2 ....114 E3
D'Albiac House
HTHAIR TW6 ....132 D3
Dali Universe
STHWK SE1 ....17 G2
Dallington School
FSBYE EC1V 6 B6
Dalmain Primary School
FSTH SE23 ....164 B3
Damilola Taylor Centre
PECK SE15 ....143 G1
Danegrove Primary School
EBAR EN4 ....33 J1
Danesfield Manor School
WOT/HER KT12 ....188 A6
Danetree School
HOR/WEW KT19 ....206 E5
Danson Mansion
BXLYHS DA6 ....148 D5
Danson Primary School
BXLYHS DA6 ....148 C5
Danson Watersports Centre
BXLYHS DA6 ....148 D5
Darell Primary School
RCH/KEW TW9 ....137 H4
Darent Industrial Park
ERITH DA8 ....131 G5
Darrick Wood Primary School
ORP BR6 ....216 B2
Darrick Wood School
ORP BR6 ....216 B1
Darrick Wood Sports Centre
ORP BR6 ....216 C1
Darrick Wood Swimming Pool
ORP BR6 ....216 B1
Dartford Adult Education Centre
DART DA1 ....171 F2
Dartford County Court
DART DA1 ....171 H1
Dartford Golf Club
DART DA1 ....170 E4
Dartford Grammar School for Boys
DART DA1 ....171 F1
Dartford Grammar School for Girls
DART DA1 ....171 F2
Dartford Magistrates Court
DART DA1 ....171 G1
Dartford Museum & Library
DART DA1 ....171 H2
Dartford Natural Health Centre
DART DA1 ....171 H2
Dartford Technology College
DART DA1 ....171 F2
Dartford West Health Centre
DART DA1 ....171 F1
Darwin Centre
SKENS SW7 ....14 A5
Dashmesh Darbar Sikh Temple
MNPK E12 ....89 K4
Datapoint Business Centre
BOW E3 ....106 A3
Daubeney Primary School
CLPT E5 ....87 G2
The David Beckham Academy
GNWCH SE10 ....125 J2
David Livingstone Primary School
THHTH CR7 ....180 D4
David Lloyd Leisure Centre
KENS W8 ....120 A4
NFNCH/WDSPK N12 ....47 H3
David Lloyd Sports Centre
EN EN1 ....24 C3
David Lloyd Tennis Centre
SCUP DA14 ....186 D1
Davidson Primary School
CROY/NA CR0 ....197 G4
Davies Lane Primary School
WAN E11 ....70 D6
Davies College
STHWK SE1 ....18 E2
Dawlish Primary School
LEY E10 ....70 A6
Days Hotel
MLHL NW7 ....30 D4

STHWK SE1 ....17 J5
Days Hotel London South Ruislip
RSLP HA4 ....77 G2
Days Inn
PIM SW1V 121 H5
Days Lane Primary School
BFN/LL DA15 ....168 A1
Dean College of London
HOLWY N7 ....85 F1
Deanesfield Primary School
RSLP HA4 ....77 H2
Deansbrook Primary School
MLHL NW7 ....44 D2
Deansfield Primary School
ELTH/MOT SE9 ....147 F4
De Bohun Primary School
STHGT/OAK N14 ....22 B6
Delta Wharf
GNWCH SE10 ....125 G2
Denmead School
HPTN TW12 ....173 F3
Denvale Trade Centre
STMC/STPC BR5 ....202 C2
Denver Industrial Estate
RAIN RM13 ....111 H4
Department for Environment, Food and Rural Affairs
CHCR WC2N 10 E7
Department for Transport
WEST SW1P 16 D6
Department of Art & Design (London Metropolitan University) WCHPL E1 ....13 K3
Department of Economics (London Metropolitan University) TWRH EC3N 13 J4
Department of Education
STJSPK SW1H 16 D3
Department of Health
WHALL SW1A 16 E2
Department of Sociology & Anthropology (Goldsmiths University of London)
NWCR SE14 ....144 B2
Department of Trade & Industry
STJSPK SW1H 16 D4
Deptford Business Centre
NWCR SE14 ....124 A5
Deptford Green School
NWCR SE14 ....144 C1
Deptford Park Business Centre
DEPT SE8 ....124 B5
Deptford Park Primary School
DEPT SE8 ....124 B5
Deptford Trading Estate
DEPT SE8 ....124 B5
Dersingham Infant School
MNPK E12 ....89 K3
Derwentwater Primary School
ACT W3 ....117 K1
Design Museum
STHWK SE1 ....19 K1
Deutsche Schule
RCHPK/HAM TW10 ....156 E3
Devonshire Hospital
MHST W1U 9 H1
Devonshire House Preparatory School
HAMP NW3 ....83 H3
Devonshire House School
HAMP NW3 ....83 G3
Devonshire Primary School
BELMT SM2 ....209 G5
Diamond College
OXHO/SHAV W1D 10 D3
Diana Fountain
E/WMO/HCT KT8 ....174 A5
Diana Princess of Wales Fountain
BAY/PAD W2 ....14 B1
Diane Matthews Clinic
ROMW/RG RM7 ....75 F1
Dilloway Industrial Estate
NWDGN UB2 ....114 D2
Discovery Business Park
BERM/RHTH SE16 ....123 H3
Docklands Medical Centre
POP/IOD E14 ....124 D4
Docklands Sailing Centre
POP/IOD E14 ....124 D3
Docklands Sailing & Watersports Centre
BERM/RHTH SE16 ....124 C3
Dockmaster's House
POP/IOD E14 ....105 J6
Dockwell's Industrial Estate
EBED/NFELT TW14 ....134 A6
Dockyard Industrial Estate
WOOL/PLUM SE18 ....126 D3
Dog Kennel Hill Primary School
EDUL SE22 ....143 F4
Dokal Industrial Estate
NWDGN UB2 ....114 D2
Dollis Infant School
MLHL NW7 ....46 A3
Dollis Junior School
MLHL NW7 ....46 A3
The Dolphin Leisure Centre
ROM RM1 ....75 H1
The Dolphin School
BTSEA SW11 ....140 D6
The Dominie
BTSEA SW11 ....140 E2
Dominion Business Park
ED N9 ....37 F4
Dominion Theatre
RSQ WC1B 10 D3
Donhead (Wimbledon College Preparatory School)
WIM/MER SW19 ....177 G3
Donmar Warehouse Theatre
LSQ/SEVD WC2H 10 E4

Donnington Primary School
WLSDN NW10 ....81 K5
The Dorchester Hotel
MYFR/PKLN W1K 9 H7
Dorchester Primary School
WPK KT4 ....193 H5
Dorma Trading Park
LEY E10 ....69 F5
Dormers Wells High School
STHL UB1 ....96 A5
Dormers Wells Leisure Centre
STHL UB1 ....96 B5
Dormers Wells Medical Centre
STHL UB1 ....96 A5
Dormers Wells Primary School
STHL UB1 ....96 B6
Dorothy Barley Primary School
BCTR RM8 ....91 H3
Dorset Road Infant School
ELTH/MOT SE9 ....166 D4
Dorset Square Hotel
CAMTN NW1 ....8 E1
Douglas Bader Foundation
PUT/ROE SW15 ....158 D1
Dovers Corner Industrial Estate
RAIN RM13 ....111 H2
Downderry Primary School
BMLY BR1 ....165 H5
Downe Manor Primary School
NTHLT UB5 ....95 F2
Downham Health Centre
BMLY BR1 ....165 H6
Downhills Primary School
TOTM N17 ....67 K1
Downsell Primary School
SRTFD E15 ....88 B2
Downshall Primary School
GNTH/NBYPK IG2 ....72 E4
Downsview Primary School
NRWD SE19 ....180 D3
Downsview School
CLPT E5 ....86 D2
Drapers Hall
LOTH EC2R 13 F3
Drapers Sports Ground
SRTFD E15 ....88 A2
The Draycott Hotel
CHEL SW3 ....15 F6
Drayton Green Primary School
WEA W13 ....97 G6
Drayton Manor High School
HNWL W7 ....97 F6
Drayton Park Primary School
HBRY N5 ....85 G3
DRCA Business Centre
BTSEA SW11 ....141 F2
Drew Primary School
CAN/RD E16 ....126 D1
Driving School & Road Safety Centre
KTN/HRWW/WS HA3 ....43 G5
The Drizen School
EDGW HA8 ....44 C3
Dr Johnson's House
FLST/FETLN EC4A 11 K3
Dr Triplett's CE J & I School
HYS/HAR UB3 ....94 D5
Drury Way Industrial Estate
WLSDN NW10 ....81 F2
Duchess Theatre
COVGDN WC2E 11 G5
Ducks Infants School
DUL SE21 ....163 G5
Duff Miller College
SKENS SW7 ....120 B3
Duke of York Column
STJS SW1Y 16 D1
Duke of York Theatre
CHCR WC2N 10 E6
Dulverton Primary School
ELTH/MOT SE9 ....167 J4
Dulwich College
DUL SE21 ....163 F3
Dulwich College Preparatory School
DUL SE21 ....163 G5
Dulwich College Track
DUL SE21 ....163 F4
Dulwich Hamlet FC
EDUL SE22 ....143 F4
Dulwich Hamlet Junior School
HNHL SE24 ....162 E1
Dulwich Hospital
EDUL SE22 ....143 F4
Dulwich Leisure Centre
EDUL SE22 ....143 H5
Dulwich Medical Centre
EDUL SE22 ....143 H6
Dulwich Picture Gallery
DUL SE21 ....162 E2
Dulwich & Sydenham Hill Golf Club
DUL SE21 ....163 H4
Dulwich Village CE Infant School
DUL SE21 ....163 F1
Dunbar Wharf
POP/IOD E14 ....105 H6
Duncombe Primary School
ARCH N19 ....66 E5
Dundee Wharf
POP/IOD E14 ....105 H6
Dunningford Primary School
WIM/MER SW19 ....177 J3
Dunningford Primary School
HCH RM12 ....93 H3
Dunraven School & Upper School
STRHM/NOR SW16 ....162 A5
Duppas Junior School
CROY/NA CR0 ....211 H3
Durand Primary School
BRXN/ST SW9 ....142 A2
Durands Wharf
BERM/RHTH SE16 ....124 C2

Durants School
PEND EN3 ....24 E2
Durdans Park Primary School
STHL UB1 ....95 K4
Durston House School
EA W5 ....97 K5
Dysart School
KUTN/CMB KT2 ....156 E6
SURB KT6 ....191 F4
Dyslexia Teaching Centre
ECT W5 ....120 A5
Eaglesfield School
WOOL/PLUM SE18 ....147 F2
Eagle Trading Estate
MTCM CR4 ....194 E3
Ealdham Primary School
ELTH/MOT SE9 ....146 B5
Ealing Abbey
EA W5 ....97 J5
Ealing Abbey Scriptorium
WEA W13 ....97 J5
The Ealing Broadway Centre
EA W5 ....97 K6
Ealing Central Sports Ground
GFD/PVL UB6 ....97 G1
Ealing College Upper School
WEA W13 ....97 G5
Ealing CC
EA W5 ....98 A5
Ealing Film Studios
EA W5 ....116 D1
Ealing Golf Club
GFD/PVL UB6 ....97 H2
Ealing, Hammersmith & West London College
ACT W5 ....117 J1
WKENS W14 ....119 G4
Ealing Hospital
NWDGN UB2 ....115 J2
Ealing Independent College
EA W5 ....97 J6
Ealing Northern Sports Centre
GFD/PVL UB6 ....78 D2
Ealing Park Health Centre
EA W5 ....116 E4
Ealing Road Trading Estate
BTFD TW8 ....116 E5
Ealing Sports Club
EA W5 ....98 A6
Ealing Tutorial College
EA W5 ....97 K6
Ealing & West London College
EA W5 ....97 K6
Eardley Primary School
STRHM/NOR SW16 ....179 H2
Earlham J & I School
WDGN N22 ....49 G3
Earlham Primary School
FSTGT E7 ....88 D3
Earl's Court Exhibition Centre
FUL/PGN SW6 ....119 K5
Earlsfield Primary School
WAND/EARL SW18 ....160 B3
Earlsmead First & Middle School
RYLN/HDSTN HA2 ....77 K2
Earlsmead Primary School
SEVS/STOTM N15 ....68 B1
Earth Galleries
SKENS SW7 ....14 B5
East Acton Primary School
ACT W3 ....99 G6
East Barking Centre
BCTR RM8 ....91 J3
East Barnet Health Centre
EBAR EN4 ....21 H6
East Barnet School
EBAR EN4 ....21 H4
East Beckton District Centre
EHAM E6 ....107 K4
Eastbrook Comprehensive School
DAGE RM10 ....92 E2
Eastbrook End Cemetery
ROMW/RG RM7 ....93 G1
Eastbrookend Country Park
ROMW/RG RM7 ....93 F2
Eastbury Comprehensive School
BARK IG11 ....91 H6
Eastbury Farm JMI School
NTHWD HA6 ....26 D6
Eastbury Infant School
BARK IG11 ....91 H5
Eastcote CC
PIN HA5 ....59 F2
Eastcote Health Centre
PIN HA5 ....59 G4
Eastcote Industrial Estate
RSLP HA4 ....59 G2
Eastcote Lane Cemetery
RYLN/HDSTN HA2 ....78 B1
Eastcote Primary School
WELL DA16 ....147 J4
Eastcourt Independent School
CDMY/SEVK IG3 ....73 G5
East End Computing & Business College
WCHPL E1 ....104 D5
Eastern Business Park
HTHAIR TW6 ....133 J3
Eastfield Primary School
PEND EN3 ....25 F1
East Finchley Cemetery
EFNCH N2 ....47 F6
East Finchley Medical Centre
EFNCH N2 ....65 J1
East Finchley School of English
EFNCH N2 ....47 J1
Eastgate Business Park
LEY E10 ....69 G5
East Greenwich Christ Church CE Primary School
GNWCH SE10 ....125 H4

East Ham Industrial Estate
EHAM E6 ....107 H5
East Ham Jewish Cemetery
EHAM E6 ....107 J2
East Ham Leisure Centre
EHAM E6 ....89 K6
East Ham Memorial Hospital
EHAM E6 ....89 K5
East Ham Nature Reserve
EHAM E6 ....107 K3
East Lane Business Park
WBLY HA9 ....79 K1
Eastlea Community Centre
CAN/RD E16 ....106 D3
Eastlea Community School
CAN/RD E16 ....106 C3
East London Business College
WAN E11 ....70 C5
East London Cemetery
PLSTW E13 ....106 D2
East London Crematorium
SRTFD E15 ....106 D2
East London RFC
EHAM E6 ....107 K4
East London RUFC
SRTFD E15 ....106 D1
Eastman Dental Hospital
FSBYW WC1X 5 G6
East Molesey CC
E/WMO/HCT KT8 ....173 H6
East Sheen Cemetery
RCHPK/HAM TW10 ....137 H6
East Sheen Primary School
MORT/ESHN SW14 ....138 B3
East Thamesmead Business Park
ERITHM DA18 ....129 G2
East Wickham Primary School
WELL DA16 ....148 A3
Eaton Manor RFC
WAN E11 ....71 G2
Eaton Square Preparatory School
BGVA SW1W 15 J6
Eaton Square School
PIM SW1V 16 A7
Ecclesbourne Primary School
THHTH CR7 ....196 D2
Eckerd College
GWRST WC1E 10 C1
Ecole de Mime Corporel Dramatique & Theatre de l'Ange Fou ARCH N19 ....66 E5
Eden College
STHWK SE1 ....18 B4
Edenham High School
CROY/NA CR0 ....198 B4
Eden High School
FUL/PGN SW6 ....139 J2
Eden Medical Centre
WKENS W14 ....119 J4
Edenvale Child Health Clinic
MTCM CR4 ....179 F3
Eden Walk Shopping Centre
KUT/HW KT1 ....175 F5
Edes Business Park
WLGTN SM6 ....195 F6
Edgebury Primary School
CHST BR7 ....167 H6
Edge Business Centre
CRICK NW2 ....63 K6
Edgebarrow Cemetery
WLGTN SM6 ....30 C4
Edgware Clinic
EDGW HA8 ....44 C2
Edgware College
KIL/WHAMP NW6 ....83 G4
Edgware Community Hospital
EDGW HA8 ....44 D3
Edgware FC & Wealdstone FC
EDGW HA8 ....44 C3
Edgware Infant School
EDGW HA8 ....44 C2
Edgware Junior School
EDGW HA8 ....44 C2
Edinburgh Primary School
WALTH E17 ....69 H2
Edith Neville Primary School
CAMTN NW1 ....4 C3
Edmonton Cemetery
WCHMH N21 ....35 K4
Edmonton County Court
UED N18 ....50 C1
Edmonton Green Shopping Centre
ED N9 ....36 D4
Edmonton Leisure Centre
ED N9 ....36 C5
Edmonton Upper School
EN N11 ....36 B2
Edmund Waller Primary School
NWCR SE14 ....144 A3
Education Centre
WOOL/PLUM SE18 ....127 G5
Edward Betham CE Primary School
GFD/PVL UB6 ....96 D2
Edward Pauling School
FELT TW13 ....153 H4
Edward Wilson Primary School
BAY/PAD W2 ....101 K4
Edwin Lambert School
EMPK RM11 ....75 J2
Effra Road Retail Park
BRXS/STRHM SW2 ....142 B6
Effra Site (St George Wharf) under development
VX/NE SW8 ....121 K5
The Egerton House Hotel
CHEL SW3 ....14 D5
Eglinton Junior School
WOOL/PLUM SE18 ....127 F6
Eglinton Primary School
WOOL/PLUM SE18 ....147 F1

Elbourne Trading Estate
BELV DA17 ....129 J3
Eldenwall Industrial Estate
BCTR RM8 ....74 A5
Eldon JMI School
ED N9 ....36 D3
Eleanor Palmer Primary School
KTTN NW5 ....84 C2
Eleanor Smith Special School
PLSTW E13 ....106 E1
Electrical Trades Union College
ESH/CLAY KT10 ....204 A2
Electric Cinema
NTGHL W11 ....100 D5
Electron Trade Centre
STMC/STPC BR5 ....202 C1
Elephant & Castle Leisure Centre
LBTH SE11 ....18 B6
Elephant & Castle Shopping Centre
STHWK SE1 ....18 B5
Elers Clinic
HYS/HAR UB3 ....113 G4
Elfrida Primary School
CAT SE6 ....164 E6
Eliot Bank Primary School
FSTH SE23 ....163 J4
Elizabeth Garrett Anderson Hospital
CAMTN NW1 ....4 D5
Elizabeth Selby Infant School
BETH E2 ....104 C2
Elizabeth Trading Estate
NWCR SE14 ....124 A6
Ellen Wilkinson Primary School
CAN/RD E16 ....107 H4
Ellen Wilkinson School for Girls
ACT W3 ....98 B5
Ellerslie Square Industrial Estate
BRXS/STRHM SW2 ....141 K5
Ellingham Primary School
CHSGTN KT9 ....205 K3
Elliott School
PUT/ROE SW15 ....159 F1
Elmbridge Leisure Centre
WOT/HER KT12 ....188 C3
Elm Court School
WNWD SE27 ....162 C4
Elmgrove First & Middle School
KTN/HRWW/WS HA3 ....61 G3
Elmhurst Primary School
FSTGT E7 ....89 F7
Elmhurst School
SAND/SEL CR2 ....211 K3
Elm Lea Trading Estate
TOTM N17 ....50 C3
Elmwood Junior School
CROY/NA CR0 ....196 C4
Elm Wood Primary School
DUL SE21 ....162 E5
Elsdale Street Health Centre
HOM E9 ....86 E5
Elsley Primary School
WBLY HA9 ....80 B4
Elsley School
BTSEA SW11 ....141 F4
Eltham Bus Station
ELTH/MOT SE9 ....146 E6
Eltham CE Primary School
ELTH/MOT SE9 ....146 E6
Eltham College Junior School
ELTH/MOT SE9 ....166 C3
Eltham College Senior School
ELTH/MOT SE9 ....166 C4
Eltham Crematorium
ELTH/MOT SE9 ....147 J3
Eltham Green School
ELTH/MOT SE9 ....166 C1
Eltham Health Clinic
ELTH/MOT SE9 ....146 D6
Eltham Health & Fitness Centre
ELTH/MOT SE9 ....167 F1
Eltham Hill Technology College
ELTH/MOT SE9 ....166 D1
Eltham Palace
ELTH/MOT SE9 ....166 D2
Eltham Pools
ELTH/MOT SE9 ....146 D6
Eltham Warren Golf Club
ELTH/MOT SE9 ....147 G6
Elthorne Park High School
HNWL W7 ....116 A3
Elthorne Sports Centre
HNWL W7 ....116 A3
Elysian Business Centre
YEAD UB4 ....95 G4
Emanuel School
BTSEA SW11 ....140 C6
Embankment Pier
CHCR WC2N 11 F7
Embassy of Afghanistan
SKENS SW7 ....15 K3
Embassy of Albania
BGVA SW1W 15 K5
Embassy of Algeria
NTGHL W11 ....119 H1
Embassy of Angola
MYFR/PKLN W1K 9 G5
Embassy of Argentina
MYFR/PKLN W1K 9 J5
Embassy of Armenia
KENS W8 ....120 A3
Embassy of Austria
KTBR SW1X 15 G4
Embassy of Bahrain
SKENS SW7 ....120 B3
Embassy of Belarus
KENS W8 ....120 A2

Embassy of Belgium
KTBR SW1X 15 H5
Embassy of Bolivia
BCVA SW1W 15 H5
Embassy of Bosnia-Herzegovina
CAVSQ/HST W1G 9 K3
Embassy of Brazil
MYFR/PKLN W1K 9 G5
Embassy of Bulgaria
SKENS SW7 ....120 B3
Embassy of Cameroon
NTGHL W11 ....119 H1
Embassy of China
CAVSQ/HST W1G 9 J1
Embassy of Costa Rica
BAY/PAD W2 ....101 G6
Embassy of Cote D'Ivoire
KTBR SW1X 15 H4
Embassy of Croatia
GTPST W1W 3 K7
Embassy of Cuba
LSQ/SEVD WC2H 10 E3
Embassy of Democratic Republic of The Congo
KTBR SW1X 15 F5
Embassy of Denmark
KTBR SW1X 14 E4
Embassy of Dominican Republic
BAY/PAD W2 ....101 F5
Embassy of Ecuador
KTBR SW1X 14 E4
Embassy of Egypt
MYFR/PICC W1J 9 J7
Embassy of Estonia
SKENS SW7 ....120 B2
Embassy of Ethiopia
SKENS SW7 ....14 B3
Embassy of Finland
KTBR SW1X 15 G4
Embassy of France
KTBR SW1X 15 F2
Embassy of Georgia
KENS W8 ....120 A2
Embassy of Germany
KTBR SW1X 15 G4
Embassy of Ghana
HGT N6 ....66 B5
Embassy of Greece
NTGHL W11 ....119 J1
Embassy of Guatemala
WBPTN SW10 ....120 A6
Embassy of Honduras
MBLAR W1H 9 F1
Embassy of Hungary
KTBR SW1X 15 H5
Embassy of Iceland
KTBR SW1X 15 C6
Embassy of Indonesia
MYFR/PKLN W1K 9 H6
Embassy of Iran
SKENS SW7 ....14 B3
Embassy of Iraq
SKENS SW7 ....120 B3
Embassy of Ireland
KTBR SW1X 15 J5
Embassy of Israel
KENS W8 ....120 A2
Embassy of Italy
MYFR/PKLN W1K 9
Embassy of Japan
MYFR/PICC W1J 15 K1
Embassy of Jordan
KENS W8 ....119 G2
Embassy of Korea
WESTW SW1E 16 B4
Embassy of Krygyzstan
MBLAR W1H 8 E2
Embassy of Kuwait
KTBR SW1X 15 J3
Embassy of Latvia
CAMTN NW1 ....3 G7
Embassy of Lebanon
·*KENS* W8 ....120 A1
Embassy of Liberia
BAY/PAD W2 ....100 E6
Embassy of Lithuania
MBLAR W1H 8 E2
Embassy of Luxembourg
KTBR SW1X 15 G3
Embassy of Mexico
MYFR/PICC W1J 15 J1
Embassy of Mongolia
KENS W8 ....120 A2
Embassy of Morocco
SKENS SW7 ....120 B4
Embassy of Mozambique
FITZ W1T 4 A7
Embassy of Myanmar
MYFR/PICC W1J 9 J7
Embassy of Nepal
KENS W8 ....120 A1
Embassy of Netherlands
SKENS SW7 ....120 B2
Embassy of Norway
KTBR SW1X 15 H4
Embassy of Paraguay
SKENS SW7 ....120 A3
Embassy of Peru
KTBR SW1X 15 F4
Embassy of Philippines
KENS W8 ....120 A1
Embassy of Poland
CAVSQ/HST W1G 9 J1
Embassy of Portugal
KTBR SW1X 15 G3
Embassy of Qatar
MYFR/PKLN W1K 15 H1
Embassy of Romania
KENS W8 ....120 A2
Embassy of Russian Federation
KENS W8 ....120 A1
Embassy of Saudi Arabia
MYFR/PICC W1J 9 J7

Embassy of Senegal
CRICK NW2 ....82 A5
Embassy of Slovak Republic
KENS W8 ....120 A1
Embassy of Slovenia
MRCH W1U 9 J5
Embassy of Spain
KTBR SW1X 15 H4
Embassy of Sudan
WHALL SW1A 16 A1
Embassy of Sweden
MBLAR W1H 8 E2
Embassy of Switzerland
MBLAR W1H 8 E2
Embassy of Syria
KTBR SW1X 15 G3
Embassy of Thailand
SKENS SW7 ....120 B3
Embassy of the Holy See
WIM/MER SW19 ....159 F5
Embassy of the Republic of Gabon
SKENS SW7 ....120 B3
Embassy of Tunisia
SKENS SW7 ....14 B3
Embassy of Turkey
KTBR SW1X 15 H3
Embassy of Turkmenistan
FITZ W1T 10 B2
Embassy of Ukraine
NTGHL W11 ....119 H1
Embassy of United Arab Emirates
BAY/PAD W2 ....14 B2
Embassy of Uruguay
SKENS SW7 ....14 D4
Embassy of USA
MYFR/PKLN W1K 9 G5
Embassy of Uzbekistan
NTGHL W11 ....119 J1
Embassy of Venezuela
SKENS SW7 ....14 B5
Embassy of Yemen
SKENS SW7 ....14 A6
Emberhurst School
ESH/CLAY KT10 ....189 J4
Ember Sports Club
ESH/CLAY KT10 ....189 H5
Embroidery World Business Centre
WFD IG8 ....53 H5
EMD Walthamstow Cinema
WALTH E17 ....69 J1
Emery Theatre
POP/IOD E14 ....105 K5
Emmanuel CE Primary School
KIL/WHAMP NW6 ....82 E3
Empire Cinema
LSQ/SEVD WC2H 10 D5
Endsleigh Industrial Estate
NWDGN UB2 ....114 D4
Enfield Business Centre
PEND EN3 ....24 E3
Enfield Chace Lower School
ENC/FH EN2 ....24 A1
Enfield College
PEND EN5 ....24 E4
Enfield County School
ENC/FH EN2 ....23 K4
Enfield CC
EN EN1 ....24 A5
Enfield Golf Club
ED N9 ....36 E4
Enfield Grammar School (Upper)
ENC/FH EN2 ....23 K4
English Martyrs RC Primary School
WALW SE17 ....18 E7
WCHPL E1 ....13 K4
English National Ballet School
WBPTN SW10 ....140 B1
Ensham Secondary School
TOOT SW17 ....178 E1
Enterprise Business Park
POP/IOD E14 ....124 E2
Enterprise Industrial Estate
BERM/RHTH SE16 ....123 K5
Epsom & Ewell High School
HOR/WEW KT19 ....206 E4
Eric Liddell Sports Centre
ELTH/MOT SE9 ....166 C4
Eridge House Preparatory School
FUL/PGN SW6 ....139 J3
Erith & District Hospital
ERITH DA8 ....130 A6
Erith Health Centre
ERITH DA8 ....130 B6
Erith Library & Museum
ERITH DA8 ....130 B5
Erith Playhouse
ERITH DA8 ....130 C5
Erith School
ERITH DA8 ....149 K1
Erith School Community Sports Centre
ERITH DA8 ....149 K1
Erith Small Business Centre
ERITH DA8 ....130 C6
Erith Sports Centre
ERITH DA8 ....130 B6
Erith Stadium
ERITH DA8 ....130 B6
Ernest Bevin College
TOOT SW17 ....160 D5
Eros
MYFR/PICC W1J 10 C6
Esher CE High School
ESH/CLAY KT10 ....204 A1
Esher Church Primary School
ESH/CLAY KT10 ....204 C4
Esher College
THDIT KT7 ....189 K4

Esher RFC
WOT/HER KT12 ....188 D6
Essendine Primary School
KIL/WHAMP NW6 ....100 E2
Essex Primary School
MNPK E12 ....89 J4
Ethelburga GM School
BTSEA SW11 ....140 D2
Ethel Davis School
CHDH RM6 ....73 H2
Euro Business Centre
SRTFD E15 ....88 D6
Eurolink Business Centre
BRXS/STRHM SW2 ....142 B5
Europa Trading Estate
ERITH DA8 ....130 A5
European Business Centre
CDALE/KGS NW9 ....45 F6
European Business School London
CAMTN NW1 ....3 F6
European College of Business Management
SDTCH EC2A 7 G6
European School of Economics
KTBR SW1X 15 H3
European Vocational College
HDTCH EC3A 13 H4
Euro Way School
CEND/HSY/T N8 ....49 G6
Euro Way School London
FSBYPK N4 ....67 H4
Euston Centre University of Westminster
CAMTN NW1 ....4 A6
Euston Tower
CAMTN NW1 ....4 A6
Evans Business Centre
CRICK NW2 ....81 J1
Eveline Lowe Primary School
PECK SE15 ....123 G5
Evendine College
SOHO/SHAV W1D 10 C3
Eversley Medical Centre
CROY/NA CR0 ....196 B3
Eversley Primary School
WCHMH N21 ....22 E6
Everyman Cinema
HAMP NW3 ....83 G2
Evolution House
RCH/KEW TW9 ....137 F3
Ewell Athletics Track
HOR/WEW KT19 ....207 H4
Ewell Castle Junior School
EW KT17 ....207 H6
Ewell Castle School
EW KT17 ....207 J6
Ewell Grove Infant School
EW KT17 ....207 H6
ExCeL Exhibition Centre
CAN/RD E16 ....107 F6
Exchange Square
SDTCH EC2A 13 G1
The Exchange
IL IG1 ....72 B6
Exhibition Halls
BARB EC2Y 12 D1
WBLY HA9 ....80 C2
Eye Clinic
NOXST/BSQ WC1A 10 D3
Faculty of Engineering & Science (University of Westminster)
FITZ W1T 10 B1
Fairchann Trading Estate
DEPT SE8 ....144 E1
IS N1 ....6 C2
The Faircross Complementary Medical Centre
BARK IG11 ....90 E4
Fairfield Clinic
BKHH IG9 ....39 F3
Fairfield Pool & Leisure Centre
DART DA1 ....171 H2
Fairfield Trade Park
KUT/HW KT1 ....175 G6
Fairholme Primary School
EBED/NFELT TW14 ....153 G3
Fairlawn Primary School
FSTH SE23 ....163 K2
Fairley House School
PIM SW1V 16 C7
Fairlop Primary School
BARK/HLT IG6 ....54 C4
Fairview Industrial Centre
RAIN RM13 ....111 F5
Fairview Industrial Estate
HYS/HAR UB3 ....113 J2
Fairview Medical Centre
STRHM/NOR SW16 ....179 K4
Fairway Primary School
MLHL NW7 ....31 F4
Fairways Business Park
LEY E10 ....69 G6
Falconbrook Primary School
BTSEA SW11 ....140 C3
Falcon Business Centre
BTSEA SW11 ....140 D5
Falcon Park Industrial Estate
WLSDN NW10 ....81 G3
The Falcon School for Girls
EA W5 ....117 G1
Falkner House School
SKENS SW7 ....120 B5
Family Records Centre
FSBYW WC1X 5 J5
Fanmakers' Hall
LVPST EC2M 13 G2
Fan Museum
GNWCH SE10 ....145 F1
Faraday Building
BLKFR EC4V 12 B4
Farm Lane Trading Estate
FUL/PGN SW6 ....119 K6

Farnborough Primary School
ORP BR6 ....216 D3
Farnell House Medical Centre
HSLW TW3 ....135 G2
Farnham Green Primary School
GDMY/SEVK IG3 ....73 G3
Farrington & Stratford House School
CHST BR7 ....185 J3
Fashion & Textile Design Museum
STHWK SE1 ....19 H5
Featherstone High School
NWDGN UB2 ....114 C4
Featherstone Industrial Estate
NWDGN UB2 ....114 D2
Featherstone Road Health Clinic
NWDGN UB2 ....114 D3
Felnex Trading Estate
WLGTN SM6 ....195 F6
Feltham Airparcs Leisure Centre
FELT TW13 ....154 C4
Feltham Athletics Arena
EBED/NFELT TW14 ....153 K2
Felthambrook Industrial Estate
FELT TW13 ....154 A5
Feltham Community College
FELT TW13 ....154 B4
Feltham Hill Infant School
FELT TW13 ....153 J5
Feltham Hill Junior School
FELT TW13 ....153 J5
Feltham & Hounslow Borough FC
EBED/NFELT TW14 ....153 K2
Feltham Superbowl
FELT TW13 ....154 A4
Fenstanton J & I School
BRXS/STRHM SW2 ....162 B3
Fenton House
HAMP NW3 ....83 G1
Ferrier Industrial Estate
WAND/EARL SW18 ....140 A5
Ferry Island Retail Park
TOTM N17 ....50 B6
Ferry Lane Industrial Estate
RAIN RM13 ....111 J4
WALTH E17 ....50 E6
Ferry Lane Primary School
TOTM N17 ....68 D1
Festival Pier
STHWK SE1 ....11 H7
Field End Primary School
RSLP HA4 ....77 H1
Fielding Primary School
WEA W13 ....116 C3
Film House Cinema
RCH/KEW TW9 ....136 E6
Financial Times
POP/IOD E14 ....106 A5
STHWK SE1 ....12 D7
Finchley Campus of St Marys CE School
NFNCH/WDSPK N12 ....47 H2
Finchley Catholic High School
NFNCH/WDSPK N12 ....33 G5
Finchley CC
FNCH N3 ....47 F5
Finchley Golf Club
MLHL NW7 ....46 D2
Finchley Industrial Centre
NFNCH/WDSPK N12 ....33 G6
Finchley Lido
NFNCH/WDSPK N12 ....47 H3
Finchley Memorial Hospital
NFNCH/WDSPK N12 ....47 G3
Finchley Youth Theatre
EFNCH N2 ....47 J6
Finsbury Circus Medical Centre
LVPST EC2M 13 F2
Finsbury Health Centre
CLKNW EC1R 5 J6
Finsbury Leisure Centre
FSBYE EC1V 6 D5
Finsbury Park Track
FSBYPK N4 ....67 H4
Finton House School
TOOT SW17 ....160 E4
Fircroft Primary School
TOOT SW17 ....160 E4
Fire Brigade Museum
STHWK SE1 ....18 C2
Firepower (Museum of Artillery)
WOOL/PLUM SE18 ....127 G3
Firs Farm Primary School
PLMGR N13 ....35 K5
Fisher Athletic FC
BERM/RHTH SE16 ....124 A1
Fishmonger's Hall
CANST EC4R 12 E6
Fitness Unlimited Leisure Centre
BOW E3 ....105 J1
Fitzjohns Primary School
HAMP NW3 ....83 H3
Fitzrovia Medical Centre
FITZ W1T 4 A7
Fitzroy Nuffield Hospital
MBLAR W1H 8 E3
Five Bridges
LBTH SE11 ....122 A5
Five Elms Primary School
DAGW RM9 ....92 B1
Five Ways Business Centre
FELT TW13 ....154 A5
Flamsteed House Museum
GNWCH SE10 ....145 G1
Flaxman Sports Centre
CMBW SE5 ....142 D3
Fleecefield Primary School
ED N9 ....36 C6

Fleet Primary School
HAMP NW3 ....83 K3
Fleetway Business Park
GFD/PVL UB6 ....97 H1
Fleming Lab Museum
BAY/PAD W2 ....8 B3
Flora Gardens Primary School
HMSMTH W6 ....118 E4
Florence Nightingale Museum
STHWK SE1 ....17 G3
Flutters Leisure Centre
FUL/PGN SW6 ....139 K1
FOB School
CLPT E5 ....68 C4
Follys End Christian High School
SNWD SE25 ....197 F3
The Foot Clinic
WIM/MER SW19 ....177 H2
Fordbridge Medical Centre
ASHF TW15 ....152 C6
The Ford College
CONDST W1S 9 K4
Fordgate Business Park
BELV DA17 ....129 K2
Ford Industrial Park
DAGW RM9 ....110 D2
Fordview Industrial Estate
RAIN RM13 ....111 F2
Foreign & Commonwealth Office
WHALL SW1A 16 D2
Foreland Medical Centre
NTGHL W11 ....100 C6
Forest Business Park
LEY E10 ....69 F4
Forestdale Primary School
CROY/NA CR0 ....213 G6
Foresters Primary School
WLGTN SM6 ....210 D4
Forest Gate Community School
FSTGT E7 ....88 E3
Forest Hill Business Centre
FSTH SE23 ....163 K4
Forest Hill Industrial Estate
FSTH SE23 ....163 K4
Forest Hill Pools
SYD SE26 ....163 K4
Forest Hill School
FSTH SE23 ....164 A5
Forest House Business Centre
WAN E11 ....70 D4
Forest Industrial Park
BARK/HLT IG6 ....54 E3
Forest Park Cemetery & Crematorium
BARK/HLT IG6 ....55 J1
Forest Road Medical Centre
WALTH E17 ....51 H6
Forest School
WALTH E17 ....70 C1
Forest Trading Estate
WALTH E17 ....51 F6
Forge Close Clinic
HAYES BR2 ....199 K5
Forge Lane Primary School
FELT TW15 ....172 D2
The Former Health Centre
CHARL SE7 ....126 C4
Forster Park Primary School
CAT SE6 ....165 H5
Fortismere School
EFNCH N2 ....47 K5
Fortune Theatre
HOL/ALD WC2B 11 F4
The Forum
EDGW HA8 ....44 C2
Fossdene Primary School
CHARL SE7 ....126 A5
Foster's Primary School
WELL DA16 ....148 D4
Foulds School
BAR EN5 ....20 B4
The Foundling Museum
BMSBY WC1N 5 F6
Fountayne Business Centre
SEVS/STOTM N15 ....68 C2
Fountayne Road Health Centre
STNW/STAM N16 ....68 C6
Four Seasons Hotel
BERM/RHTH SE16 ....124 C1
MYFR/PKLN W1K 15 J2
Foxfield Primary School
WOOL/PLUM SE18 ....127 H5
Fox Primary School
KENS W8 ....119 K1
Frances Bardsley School for Girls
ROM RM1 ....75 J2
Franciscan Primary School
TOOT SW17 ....161 F6
Francis Holland School
BGVA SW1W 15 H7
CAMTN NW1 ....2 E7
Frank Barnes Primary School
STJWD NW8 ....2 A5
Franklin Industrial Estate
PGE/AN SE20 ....181 K4
Freehold Industrial Centre
HSLWW TW4 ....134 B6
Free Trade Wharf
WAP E1W 105 F6
Freightliners City Farm
HOLWY N7 ....85 F4
Fresh Wharf Estate
BARK IG11 ....90 B6
Freuchen Medical Centre
WLSDN NW10 ....99 H1
Freud Museum
HAMP NW3 ....83 H4
Friars Primary Foundation School
STHWK SE1 ....18 A2
Friends House
CAMTN NW1 ....4 C5

Friern Barnet School
 FBAR/BDGN N11 ....47 K1
Friern Bridge Retail Park
 FBAR/BDGN N11 ....48 B2
Frithwood Primary School
 NTHWD HA6 ....40 D2
Frogmore Industrial Estate
 HBRY N5 ....85 J2
 HYS/HAR UB3 ....113 H2
 WLSDN NW10 ....98 E2
Fryent Country Park
 KTN/HRWW/WS HA3 ....62 C4
Fryent Medical Centre
 CDALE/KGS NW9 ....62 K4
Fryent Primary School
 CDALE/KGS NW9 ....62 K4
Fulham Cemetery
 FUL/PGN SW6 ....139 G1
Fulham Clinic
 FUL/PGN SW6 ....119 H6
Fulham Cross Secondary
 School
 FUL/PGN SW6 ....139 G1
Fulham FC (Craven Cottage)
 PUT/ROE SW15 ....139 F2
Fulham Medical Centre
 FUL/PGN SW6 ....140 A1
Fulham Palace
 FUL/PGN SW6 ....139 G3
Fulham Pools
 FUL/PGN SW6 ....119 H6
Fulham Preparatory School
 WKENS W14 ....119 H6
Fulham Pre-Preparatory
 School
 FUL/PGN SW6 ....139 H3
Fulham Primary School
 FUL/PGN SW6 ....119 K6
Fuller Smith & Turner
 Sports Club
 CHSWK W4 ....138 B2
Fullwell Cross Health Centre
 BARK/HLT IG6 ....54 C5
Fullwell Cross Swimming Pool
 & Recreation Centre
 BARK/HLT IG6 ....54 C5
Fullwood Primary School
 BARK/HLT IG6 ....72 C1
Fulwell Golf Club
 HPTN TW12 ....155 J6
Furness Primary School
 WLSDN NW10 ....99 J1
Furzedown Primary School
 TOOT SW17 ....179 G2
Furze Infant School
 CHDH RM6 ....74 A3
Future Business College
 CONDST W1S 9 K4
Gainsborough Clinic
 PLMGR N13 ....35 F6
Gainsborough Primary School
 HOM E9 ....87 H4
 SRTFD E15 ....106 C2
Galleywall Primary School
 BERM/RHTH SE16 ....123 J4
Galliard Primary School
 ED N9 ....36 C1
Gallions Mount Primary
 School
 WOOL/PLUM SE18 ....128 A5
Gallions Primary School
 EHAM E6 ....108 B5
Gallions Reach Shopping Park
 EHAM E6 ....108 B4
Gants Hill Medical Centre
 GNTH/NBYPK IG2 ....72 A3
Gardener Industrial Estate
 SYD SE26 ....182 B1
Garden House School
 BGVA SW1W 121 F5
Garden Primary School
 MTCM CR4 ....179 J6
Garden Suburb Primary
 School
 GLDGN NW11 ....64 D2
Garfield Primary School
 FBAR/BDGN N11 ....48 B1
 WIM/MER SW19 ....178 B2
Garratt Park Secondary
 Special School
 WAND/EARL SW18 ....160 A5
Garrick Industrial Centre
 CDALE/KGS NW9 ....63 H2
Garrick Theatre
 LSO/SEVD WC2H 10 E1
Garth Primary School
 MRDN SM4 ....194 C2
The Garth Road Industrial
 Centre
 MRDN SM4 ....193 F4
Gascoigne Primary School
 BARK IG11 ....90 C6
Gate Cinema
 KENS W8 ....119 K1
Gatehouse School
 BETH E2 ....105 F1
The Gatehouse Theatre
 HGT N6 ....66 A4
Gate Theatre
 NTGHL W11 ....119 K1
Gateway Business Centre
 SYD SE26 ....182 B2
 WOOL/PLUM SE18 ....127 H3
Gateway Industrial Estate
 WLSDN NW10 ....99 H2
Gatton School
 TOOT SW17 ....160 D6
Gayhurst Primary School
 HACK E8 ....86 C5
Gearies Infant School
 GNTH/NBYPK IG2 ....72 A2
Gearies Junior School
 GNTH/NBYPK IG2 ....72 B2
Geffrye Museum
 BETH E2 ....7 H3
Gemini Business Estate
 NWCR SE14 ....124 A5

General Medical Clinics
 WCHPL E1 ....13 J1
Genesis Cinema
 WCHPL E1 ....104 E3
Geoffrey Chaucer
 Technology College
 STHWK SE1 ....18 E5
The Geoffrey Lloyd Foulkes
 Clinic
 IL IG1 ....72 A6
Geoffrey Whitworth Theatre
 DART DA1 ....150 D5
George Eliot J & I School
 STJWD NW8 ....83 G6
George Greens School
 POP/IOD E14 ....125 F5
George Mitchell School
 LEY E10 ....69 K5
George Spicer Primary School
 EN EN1 ....24 B4
George Tomlinson Primary
 School
 WAN E11 ....70 C5
Germal College
 FSBYPK N4 ....67 G5
Gibbs Green Special School
 WKENS W14 ....119 J5
Gibson Business Centre
 TOTM N17 ....50 B2
The Gibson Business Centre
 TOTM N17 ....50 B2
Gidea Park College
 GPK RM2 ....57 J6
Gidea Park Primary School
 GPK RM2 ....75 H1
The Gielgud Theatre
 SOHO/CST W1F 10 C5
Giffin Business Centre
 DEPT SE8 ....144 D1
Gifford Primary School
 NTHLT UB5 ....95 K1
Gilbert Collection
 TPL/STR WC2R 11 G5
Gilbert Colvin Primary School
 CLAY IG5 ....54 A4
Gilbert Scott Primary School
 SAND/SEL CR2 ....213 G5
Gillespie Primary School
 HBRY N5 ....85 H1
Girdlers' Hall
 CITYW EC2V 12 D2
Glade Primary School
 CLAY IG5 ....53 K4
*The Glades Shopping Centre
 BMLY BR1 ....183 K5
Gladstone Medical Centre
 CRICK NW2 ....81 H2
Gladstone Park Primary School
 WLSDN NW10 ....81 J3
Glaziers/Scientific Instrument
 Makers Hall
 STHWK SE1 ....12 E7
Glebe First & Middle School
 KTN/HRWW/WS HA3 ....61 K1
Glebe Primary School
 HGDN/ICK UB10 ....76 B2
Glebe School
 WWKM BR4 ....199 G5
Gleen Lecky Health Centre
 PUT/ROE SW15 ....139 G5
Glenbrook Primary School
 CLAP SW4 ....161 J1
Glencairn Sports Club
 FBAR/BDGN N11 ....48 C3
Glendower Preparatory
 School
 SKENS SW7 ....120 B4
Glenham College
 IL IG1 ....72 B6
Glenlyn Medical Centre
 E/WMO/HCT KT8 ....189 H2
Glenthorne High School
 CHEAM SM3 ....193 K5
Globe Primary School
 BETH E2 ....104 E2
Globe Wharf
 BERM/RHTH SE16 ....105 F6
Gloucester Primary School
 PECK SE15 ....143 F1
Godolphin & Latymer School
 HMSMTH W6 ....118 E4
Godwin Junior School
 FSTGT E7 ....89 F2
Godwin Primary School
 DAGW RM9 ....92 A5
Goethe Institute
 SKENS SW7 ....14 B4
Golborne Medical Centre
 NKENS W10 ....100 D3
Goldbeaters Primary School
 EDGW HA8 ....45 F4
Golden Hinde Educational
 Trust
 STHWK SE1 ....12 E6
Golders Green Crematorium
 GLDGN NW11 ....64 E4
Golders Green Health Centre
 GLDGN NW11 ....65 F5
Golders Hill Health Centre
 GLDGN NW11 ....65 G5
Golders Hill School
 GLDGN NW11 ....64 E4
Goldhawk Industrial Estate
 SHB W12 ....118 E3
Goldsmiths College
 BROCKY SE4 ....144 C4
 DEPT SE8 ....124 D6
 LEW SE13 ....145 H5
Goldsmiths College Sports
 Ground
 SCUP DA14 ....169 G5
Goldsmiths Hall
 STBT EC1A 12 C3
Gonville Primary School
 THHTH CR7 ....196 A2
Gooding Health Centre
 HOLWY N7 ....84 E4

Goodmayes Retail Park
 CHDH RM6 ....73 H4
Goodrich J & I School
 EDUL SE22 ....163 H1
Good Shepherd RC Primary
 School
 BMLY BR1 ....165 J6
 CROY/NA CR0 ....213 K5
The Good Shepherd RC
 Primary School
 SHB W12 ....118 C2
Goodwyn School
 MLHL NW7 ....45 J1
Goose Green Primary School
 EDUL SE22 ....143 G5
Goose Green Trading Estate
 EDUL SE22 ....143 H5
Gordonbrook Primary School
 BROCKY SE4 ....144 D6
Gordon Hospital
 WEST SW1P 16 C7
Gordon House Health Centre
 WEA W13 ....116 C1
Gordon Infant School
 IL IG1 ....90 D1
Gordon Primary School
 ELTH/MOT SE9 ....146 E5
Goresbrook Leisure Centre
 DAGW RM9 ....91 K6
Goresbrook Sports Centre
 DAGW RM9 ....91 K6
The Goring Hotel
 BGVA SW1W 15 K4
Corringe Park Primary School
 MTCM CR4 ....179 F4
Gosai Cinema
 WEA W13 ....116 C1
Gosbury Hill Health Centre
 CHSGTN KT9 ....206 A2
Gosford Primary School
 REDBR IG4 ....71 K2
Gospel Oak Primary School
 HAMP NW3 ....84 A2
Gove Farm Retail Park
 CHDH RM6 ....73 J4
Gower House School
 CDALE/KGS NW9 ....62 E6
Grace Business Centre
 MTCM CR4 ....194 E3
Grace Theatre at the
 Latchmere
 BTSEA SW11 ....140 E3
Graduate School of
 Management
 TOTM N17 ....50 B4
Grafton Primary School
 BCTR RM8 ....74 A6
 HOLWY N7 ....84 E1
Grahame Park Health Centre
 CDALE/KGS NW9 ....45 G4
Grahame Park J & I School
 CDALE/KGS NW9 ....45 G4
Granard Business Centre
 MLHL NW7 ....45 G2
Granard Primary School
 PUT/ROE SW15 ....158 E1
Granby Sports Club
 CHST BR7 ....184 D1
Grand Avenue Primary School
 BRYLDS KT5 ....191 K4
Grande Vitesse Industrial
 Centre
 STHWK SE1 ....18 B1
Grand Union Industrial
 Estate
 WLSDN NW10 ....98 D1
Grange Blooms Hotel
 RSQ WC1B 10 E1
The Grange City Hotel
 TWRH EC3N 13 J5
Grange First & Middle School
 RYLN/HDSTN HA2 ....60 B5
Grange Fitzrovia Hotel
 GTPST W1W 9 K1
Grange Holborn Hotel
 NOXST/BSQ WC1A 11 F2
Grange Langham Court Hotel
 GTPST W1W 9 K2
The Grange Museum
 CRICK NW2 ....81 H2
Grange Park Clinic
 YEAD UB4 ....94 D3
Grange Park Preparatory
 School
 WCHMH N21 ....35 H1
Grange Park Primary School
 WCHMH N21 ....23 G5
 YEAD UB4 ....94 D3
Grange Primary School
 CAN/RD E16 ....106 D3
 EA W5 ....116 E2
 STHWK SE1 ....19 G5
Grange Rochester Hotel
 WEST SW1P 16 C6
Grange Strathmore Hotel
 SKENS SW7 ....120 B3
Grange Whitehall Hotel
 RSQ WC1B 10 E2
Grangewood Independent
 School
 FSTGT E7 ....89 H1
Grangewood School
 PIN HA5 ....58 E2
Granton Primary School
 STRHM/NOR SW16 ....179 H3
Granville Road Industrial
 Estate
 CRICK NW2 ....64 D6
Grasmere Primary School
 STNW/STAM N16 ....85 K2
Grasshoppers RFC
 ISLW TW7 ....116 A6
Grassroots School
 HPTN TW12 ....173 F4
Grasvenor Avenue Infant
 School
 BAR EN5 ....32 E1

Gravel Hill Primary School
 BXLYHS DA6 ....149 J6
Graveney School
 TOOT SW17 ....179 G2
Graves Yard Industrial Estate
 WELL DA16 ....148 B3
Grays Farm Primary School
 STMC/STPC BR5 ....186 A6
Grazebrook Primary School
 STNW/STAM N16 ....68 A2
Great Cambridge Industrial
 Estate
 EN EN1 ....24 D1
Great Chapel Street Medical
 Centre
 SOHO/SHAV W1D 10 C3
Great Eastern Hotel
 LVPST EC2M 13 G2
Greater London Authority
 Headquarters (City Hall)
 STHWK SE1 ....19 H1
Great Jubilee Wharf
 WAP E1W 123 J1
Great Scotland Yard
 WHALL SW1A 10 D7
Great Western Industrial Park
 NWDGN UB2 ....115 G2
Great West Trading Estate
 BTFD TW8 ....116 C6
Greenacres Primary School
 ELTH/MOT SE9 ....167 F4
The Green CE Primary School
 TOTM N17 ....50 B6
Green Dragon Primary School
 BTFD TW8 ....117 F5
Greenfield Medical Centre
 CRICK NW2 ....82 C1
Greenfield Primary School
 OXHEY WD19 ....41 G1
Greenfields Junior School
 SAND/SEL CR2 ....211 K6
Greenfields Special School
 MUSWH N10 ....47 K4
Greenford Avenue Medical
 Centre
 HNWL W7 ....96 E4
Greenford Green Clinic
 GFD/PVL UB6 ....78 E3
Greenford High School
 STHL UB1 ....96 A2
Greenford Industrial Estate
 GFD/PVL UB6 ....78 B6
Greenford Park Cemetery
 GFD/PVL UB6 ....96 B4
Greenford Road Medical
 Centre
 GFD/PVL UB6 ....96 D1
Greenford Sports Centre
 STHL UB1 ....96 A2
Greengate Medical Centre
 PLSTW E13 ....107 F2
Greengrove College
 STHGT/OAK N14 ....34 C4
Greenheath Business Centre
 BETH E2 ....104 C2
Greenhill College
 HRW HA1 ....61 F2
Greenhill Park Medical Centre
 WLSDN NW10 ....81 G6
Greenland Pier
 BERM/RHTH SE16 ....124 C3
Green Lane Business Park
 ELTH/MOT SE9 ....167 F4
Green Lane Primary School
 WPK KT4 ....192 E4
Greenleaf Primary School
 WALTH E17 ....51 H6
Greenmead Primary School
 PUT/ROE SW15 ....138 E6
The Green School for Girls
 ISLW TW7 ....136 B1
Greenshaw High School
 SUT SM1 ....194 B6
Greenshields Industrial Estate
 CAN/RD E16 ....125 K1
Greenside Primary School
 SHB W12 ....118 D2
Greenslade Primary School
 WOOL/PLUM SE18 ....127 J6
Green Street Green Primary
 School
 ORP BR6 ....217 F4
Greenvale School
 FSTH SE23 ....164 B5
Greenwich Centre Business
 Park
 DEPT SE8 ....144 E1
Greenwich Cinema
 GNWCH SE10 ....145 F1
Greenwich Community
 College
 WOOL/PLUM SE18 ....127 G4
 WOOL/PLUM SE18 ....127 J6
Greenwich Industrial Estate
 CHARL SE7 ....126 A4
 GNWCH SE10 ....144 E1
Greenwich Natural Health
 Centre
 GNWCH SE10 ....145 F1
Greenwich Pier
 GNWCH SE10 ....125 F5
Greenwich School of
 Management
 GNWCH SE10 ....145 F1
Greenwich Theatre &
 Art Gallery
 GNWCH SE10 ....145 G1
Greenwood Primary School
 NTHLT UB5 ....78 C3
Greenwood Theatre
 STHWK SE1 ....19 F1
Green Wrythe Primary School
 CAR SM5 ....194 C5
Greig City Academy
 CEND/HSY/T N8 ....67 F1
Gresham College
 HCIRC EC1N 11 J2

Gresham Way Industrial
 Estate
 WIM/MER SW19 ....160 A5
Grey Coat Hospital CE School
 for Girls
 WEST SW1P 16 C5
The Greycoat Hospital
 WEST SW1P 16 C7
Grey Court School
 RCHPK/HAM TW10 ....156 E5
Griffen Manor School
 WOOL/PLUM SE18 ....147 K2
Grimsdyke First & Middle
 School
 PIN HA5 ....41 K2
Grims Dyke Golf Club
 PIN HA5 ....42 A1
Grim's Dyke Hotel
 KTN/HRWW/WS HA3 ....42 D1
Grinling Gibbons Primary
 School
 DEPT SE8 ....124 C6
Grist Memorial Sports Club
 E/WMO/HCT KT8 ....189 K2
Grocers' Hall
 CITYW EC2V 12 E4
Grosvenor House Hotel
 MYFR/PKLN W1K 9 G6
The Grove Health Centre
 SHB W12 ....118 C2
Grove House (Froebel College)
 PUT/ROE SW15 ....158 C1
Grove House Primary School
 for Deaf Children
 WNWD SE27 ....162 C4
Grovelands Priory Hospital
 STHGT/OAK N14 ....34 C3
Grovelands School
 WOT/HER KT12 ....188 A3
Grove Medical Centre
 DEPT SE8 ....124 B4
The Grove Medical Centre
 ARCH N19 ....66 D6
Grove Park Industrial Estate
 CDALE/KGS NW9 ....63 F1
Grove Park Primary School
 CHSWK W4 ....117 K6
Grove Park School
 CDALE/KGS NW9 ....62 E1
Grove Primary School
 CHDH RM6 ....73 H2
Grove Road Primary School
 HSLW TW3 ....135 F5
The Groves Medical Centre
 NWMAL KT3 ....176 B6
Grove Village Medical Centre
 EBED/NFELT TW14 ....153 J3
Guardian Angels RC Primary
 School
 BOW E3 ....105 G3
Guardian Newspapers
 POP/IOD E14 ....124 E2
Guards' Chapel and Museum
 STJSPK SW1H 16 C3
Guildhall Annex
 KUT/HW KT1 ....174 E6
Guildhall Art Gallery
 CITYW EC2V 12 D3
Guildhall School of Music
 and Drama
 BARB EC2Y 12 D1
 STLK EC1Y 6 D7
Gumley House Convent
 School
 ISLW TW7 ....136 B4
Gunnersbury Catholic
 School
 BTFD TW8 ....116 D5
Gunnersbury Park Museum
 ACT W3 ....117 H3
Gurnell Leisure Centre
 WEA W13 ....97 F2
Guru Gobind Singh Khalsa
 College
 CHIG IG7 ....39 G3
Guru Nanak Medical Centre
 STHL UB1 ....114 C1
Guy's Hospital
 STHWK SE1 ....19 F1
Guys Kings and Thomas
 Medical School (Kings
 College London)
 STHWK SE1 ....12 C7
Gwyn Jones Primary School
 WAN E11 ....70 B4
GX Superbowl
 EHAM E6 ....108 A4
Gypsy Moth IV
 GNWCH SE10 ....125 F6
Haberdashers Askes
 Hatcham College
 NWCR SE14 ....144 A3
Haberdashers' Hall
 STBT EC1A 12 A2
Hackbridge Primary School
 WLGTN SM6 ....195 F5
Hackney Business Centre
 HACK E8 ....86 D4
Hackney City Farm
 BETH E2 ....104 C1
Hackney Community College
 IS N1 ....7 G3
Hackney Empire Variety
 Theatre
 HACK E8 ....86 D4
Hackney Free & Parochial CE
 School
 HOM E9 ....86 E4
The Hackney Museum
 HACK E8 ....86 D4
Hackney Sports Centre
 HOM E9 ....87 J2
Hadley Wood Golf Club
 EBAR EN4 ....21 J2
Hadley Wood Primary
 School
 EBAR EN4 ....21 J1

The Haelan Clinic
CEND/HSY/T N8 ....66 E3
Haggerston School
BETH E2 ....7 K2
Haggerston Swimming Pool
BETH E2 ....7 K1
Hague Primary School
BETH E2 ....104 D3
Hailey Road Business Park
ERITHM DA18 ....129 H2
Haimo Primary School
ELTH/MOT SE9 ....146 C6
Hainault Business Park
BARK/HLT IG6 ....55 J1
Hainault Forest Golf Club
CHIG IG7 ....55 K2
Hainault Forest High School
& the Learning Centre
BARK/HLT IG6 ....55 G1
Hakim Qureshi Clinic
NWDGN UB2 ....114 D3
The Hale Clinic
CAMTN NW1 ....3 K7
Half Moon Theatre
WCHPL E1 ....105 F3
Haling Manor High School
SAND/SEL CR2 ....211 H5
The Halkin Hotel
KTBR SW1X 15 H3
Halley Primary School
POP/IOD E14 ....105 G4
Halifield Clinic
BAY/PAD W2 ....101 G5
Halifield Primary School
BAY/PAD W2 ....101 G5
The Hall Junior School
HAMP NW3 ....83 H4
Hallmark Trading Estate
WBLY HA9 ....80 E2
Hall Place
BXLY DA5 ....169 K1
Halls Business Centre
HYS/HAR UB3 ....113 K3
The Hall School
HAMP NW3 ....83 H4
Hall School Wimbledon
RYNPK SW20 ....177 G4
Hall School Wimbledon
Junior Dept
PUT/ROE SW15 ....158 D5
Hallsville Primary School
CAN/RD E16 ....106 E5
Halstow Primary School
GNWCH SE10 ....125 J5
Hambrough Primary School
STHL UB1 ....114 D1
Hamer Indoor Market
BOW E3 ....105 H1
Ham Health Clinic
RCHPK/HAM TW10 ....156 D5
Ham House (NT)
RCHPK/HAM TW10 ....156 D3
Hamilton Road Industrial
Estate
WNWD SE27 ....162 E6
Hamlet International
Industrial Estate
ERITH DA8 ....130 A5
Hammersmith Apollo
HMSMTH W6 ....119 F5
Hammersmith Cemetery
HMSMTH W6 ....119 G5
Hammersmith Hospital
SHB W12 ....99 J5
Hammersmith Industrial
Estate
HMSMTH W6 ....119 F6
Hammersmith New
Cemetery
RCH/KEW TW9 ....137 J3
Hammersmith Palais
HMSMTH W6 ....119 F4
Hammersmith Physio &
Sports Injury Clinic
HMSMTH W6 ....119 F4
Hammersmith & West
London College
WKENS W14 ....119 H4
Hampden Gurney School
MBLAR W1H 8 D3
Ham & Petersham CC
RCHPK/HAM TW10 ....156 E6
The Hampshire School
BAY/PAD W2 ....101 F6
SKENS SW7 ....14 C3
Hampstead College of
Fine Art
HAMP NW3 ....83 J4
Hampstead CC
KIL/WHAMP NW6 ....83 F3
Hampstead Golf Club
CLDGN NW11 ....65 G4
Hampstead Medical Centre
HAMP NW3 ....83 G2
Hampstead Parochial CE
School
HAMP NW3 ....83 G2
Hampstead School
CRICK NW2 ....82 C2
The Hampstead School of Art
HAMP NW3 ....82 E2
Hampstead School of English
KIL/WHAMP NW6 ....82 E2
Hampstead Theatre
HAMP NW3 ....83 H5
Hampton Cemetery
HPTN TW12 ....173 F3
Hampton Community
College
HPTN TW12 ....173 F1
Hampton Court House School
E/WMO/HCT KT8 ....173 K5
Hampton Court Palace
E/WMO/HCT KT8 ....174 A6
Hampton Court Palace
Golf Club
SURB KT6 ....190 D2

Hampton Farm Industrial
Estate
FELT TW13 ....154 D5
Hampton FC
HPTN TW12 ....173 G4
Hampton Hill Junior School
HPTN TW12 ....173 H1
Hampton Infant School
HPTN TW12 ....172 D3
Hampton Junior School
HPTN TW12 ....173 F4
The Hampton Medical Centre
HPTN TW12 ....173 F3
Hampton Open Air Pool
HPTN TW12 ....173 H3
Hampton Road Industrial
Park
CROY/NA CR0 ....196 D5
Hampton School
HPTN TW12 ....173 F1
Hampton Wick Infant School
TEDD TW11 ....174 D3
Handel's House
MYFR/PKLN W1K 9 J5
Handsworth Health Clinic
CHING E4 ....52 B2
Handsworth Primary School
CHING E4 ....52 B2
Hanover Primary School
IS N1 ....6 B2
Hanover Trading Estate
HOLWY N7 ....84 E3
Hanover West Industrial
Estate
WLSDN NW10 ....98 E2
Hanworth Trading Estate
FELT TW13 ....154 D5
Harbinger Primary School
POP/IOD E14 ....124 D4
Harborough School
ARCH N19 ....66 D6
Harenc School
SCUP DA14 ....186 D1
Hargrave Park Primary
School
ARCH N19 ....66 C6
Haringey Arts Council
ED N9 ....36 C4
Haringey Community Health
Clinic
SEVS/STOTM N15 ....68 B1
Haringey Magistrates Court
HGT N6 ....66 A3
Harlesden Primary School
WLSDN NW10 ....99 G1
Harley Medical Centre
CAVSQ/HST W1G 9 K3
The Harley Medical Centre
CANST EC4R 12 C5
Harley Street Clinic
CAVSQ/HST W1G 9 J2
The Harley Street Clinic
CAVSQ/HST W1G 9 J1
Harlington Community
School
HYS/HAR UB3 ....113 G4
Harlyn Primary School
PIN HA5 ....41 F6
The Harold Macmillan
Medical Centre
HRW HA1 ....60 D4
Harp Business Centre
CRICK NW2 ....63 J6
Harpley School
WCHPL E1 ....104 E3
Harrington Hill Primary
School
CLPT E5 ....68 D5
Harris City Technology College
NRWD SE19 ....181 G4
Harrodian School
BARN SW13 ....138 C1
Harrods Store
CHEL SW5 ....14 E4
Harrovian Business Village
HRW HA1 ....60 D4
Harrow Arts Centre
PIN HA5 ....42 A3
Harrow Borough FC
RYLN/HDSTN HA2 ....78 A2
Harrow College
HRW HA1 ....60 E4
KTN/HRWW/WS HA3 ....42 E2
Harrow CC
HRW HA1 ....78 E2
Harrow Crown Courts
HRW HA1 ....42 D6
Harrow Heritage Museum
RYLN/HDSTN HA2 ....42 C6
Harrow High School
HRW HA1 ....61 G3
Harrow Leisure Centre
KTN/HRWW/WS HA3 ....43 F6
Harrow Magistrates Court
HRW HA1 ....61 F1
Harrow RFC
STAN HA7 ....27 K5
Harrow Road Health Centre
MV/WKIL W9 ....100 E4
Harrow School
HRW HA1 ....60 E4
RYLN/HDSTN HA2 ....60 E6
Harrow Town CC
RYLN/HDSTN HA2 ....60 A5
Harrow Weald Cemetery
KTN/HRWW/WS HA3 ....42 E2
Harry Gosling Primary School
WCHPL E1 ....104 C5
Hartley Primary School
EHAM E6 ....89 J6
Hartsbourne Golf &
Country Club
BUSH WD23 ....28 C4
Hartsbourne Primary School
BUSH WD23 ....28 D4
Harvington School
EA W5 ....97 J5

Haseltine Primary School
SYD SE26 ....164 C6
Haslemere Business Centre
EN EN1 ....24 D5
Haslemere Industrial Estate
EBED/NFELT TW14 ....133 K6
WAND/EARL SW18 ....160 A4
Haslemere Primary School
MTCM CR4 ....178 C5
Hasmonean High School
Boys Site
HDN NW4 ....46 B5
Hasmonean High School
Girls Site
MLHL NW7 ....45 J4
Hasmonean Primary School
HDN NW4 ....64 B2
Haste Hill Golf Club
NTHWD HA6 ....40 C5
Hastings Clinic
BRXS/STRHM SW2 ....142 A6
Hastingwood Trading Estate
UED N18 ....51 G2
Hatcham Mews Business
Centre
NWCR SE14 ....144 A1
Hatch End High School
KTN/HRWW/WS HA3 ....42 B3
Hatch End Swimming Pool
PIN HA5 ....42 A3
Hatfield Primary School
MRDN SM4 ....193 H3
Hathaway Primary School
HNWL W7 ....97 F4
Hatton School
WFD IG8 ....53 H6
Havelock Primary School
NWDGN UB2 ....114 E3
Haven Green Clinic
EA W5 ....97 K5
Havering College of Further
& Higher Education
EMPK RM11 ....75 K4
Havering Magistrates Court
ROM RM1 ....75 G1
Haverstock School
HAMP NW3 ....84 A4
Hawes Down Clinic
WWKM BR4 ....199 G6
Hawes Down Primary School
WWKM BR4 ....199 G5
The Hawker Centre
KUTN/CMB KT2 ....174 E1
Hawkesdown House School
KENS W8 ....119 K1
Hawkins Clinic
PUT/ROE SW15 ....139 G5
RYNPK SW20 ....176 C4
Hawksmoor Primary School
THMD SE28 ....109 H6
Hawley Infant School
CAMTN NW1 ....84 B5
Haydon School
PIN HA5 ....40 D6
Hayes Bridge Middle School
STHL UB1 ....114 D2
Hayes Bridge Retail Park
YEAD UB4 ....95 G6
Hayes CC
HYS/HAR UB3 ....94 D5
Hayes FC
HYS/HAR UB3 ....94 D6
Hayes Grove Priory Hospital
HAYES BR2 ....199 K6
The Hayes Manor School
HYS/HAR UB3 ....94 B5
Hayes Park J & I School
YEAD UB4 ....94 D3
Hayes Pool
HYS/HAR UB3 ....113 J1
Hayes Primary School
HAYES BR2 ....200 A6
Hayes School
HAYES BR2 ....200 A6
Hayes Social and Sports Club
HYS/HAR UB3 ....94 D6
Hayes Stadium Sports Centre
HYS/HAR UB3 ....94 B5
Hay Lane School
CDALE/KGS NW9 ....62 E1
Haymerle School
PECK SE15 ....123 H6
Hays Galleria
STHWK SE1 ....13 G7
Hayward Gallery
STHWK SE1 ....17 H1
Hazelbury Infants School
ED N9 ....36 A5
Hazeldene Medical Centre
WBLY HA9 ....80 D4
Hazelwood Infant School
PLMGR N13 ....35 H6
Hazelwood Junior School
PLMGR N13 ....35 G6
Headstart Montessori School
TOOT SW17 ....160 B5
The Health Clinic
SKENS SW7 ....14 B6
Healy Medical Centre
CLPT E5 ....68 D5
The Heart Hospital
CAVSQ/HST W1G 9 H2
Heathbrook Primary School
VX/NE SW8 ....141 H3
Heath Business Centre
HSLW TW3 ....135 H5
Heathcote Secondary School
CHING E4 ....38 C4
Heathfield College
HAYES BR2 ....215 G4
Heathfield Primary School
WHTN TW2 ....155 F3
Heathfield School
PIN HA5 ....59 H4
Heath House Preparatory
School
BKHTH/KID SE3 ....145 J3

The Heathland School
HSLWW TW4 ....154 E1
Heathmere Primary School
PUT/ROE SW15 ....158 D3
Heathpark Golf Club
WDR/YW UB7 ....112 D3
Heathrow Airport
HTHAIR TW6 ....132 E3
Heathrow Airport Central
Bus & Coach Station
HTHAIR TW6 ....132 D4
Heathrow International
Trading Estate
HSLWW TW4 ....134 A4
Heathrow Medical Centre
HYS/HAR UB3 ....113 G5
Heathrow Primary School
WDR/YW UB7 ....112 C6
Heathrow World Cargo
Centre
HTHAIR TW6 ....132 C6
Heathside Preparatory
School
HAMP NW3 ....83 G2
Heathway Industrial Estate
DAGE RM10 ....92 D2
Heathway Medical Centre
DAGW RM9 ....92 B2
Heavers Farm Primary School
SNWD SE25 ....197 G2
Heber Primary School
EDUL SE22 ....163 G1
Heckford Street Business
Centre
WAP E1W 105 F6
Hedges & Butler Estate
SRTFD E15 ....106 A1
Hedgewood School
YEAD UB4 ....94 C2
Helena Road Clinic
WLSDN NW10 ....81 K2
Heliport Industrial Estate
BTSEA SW11 ....140 C3
Hellenic College of London
KTBR SW1X 14 E5
Helston Court Business
Centre
WIM/MER SW19 ....176 E1
Henderson Hospital
BELMT SM2 ....208 E6
Hendon Cemetery
MLHL NW7 ....46 B4
Hendon Crematorium
MLHL NW7 ....46 B3
Hendon FC
CRICK NW2 ....64 B6
Hendon Golf Club
MLHL NW7 ....46 A3
Hendon Preparatory School
HDN NW4 ....46 B6
Hendon School
HDN NW4 ....64 B2
Hendon Secretarial College
HDN NW4 ....63 K2
Hendon Youth Sports
Centre
CRICK NW2 ....64 B4
Henrietta Barnett School
GLDGN NW11 ....65 F2
Henry Cavendish Primary
School
BAL SW12 ....161 H3
Henry Compton School
FUL/PGN SW6 ....139 G2
Henry Fawcett Primary
School
LBTH SE11 ....122 B6
Henry Green Primary School
BCTR RM8 ....73 K5
Henry Maynard J & I School
WALTH E17 ....70 A2
Henwick Primary School
ELTH/MOT SE9 ....146 C4
Herbert Morrison Primary
School
VX/NE SW8 ....141 K1
Hereward House School
HAMP NW3 ....83 J4
Her Majesty's Theatre
STJS SW1Y 10 D7
Hermitage Primary School
WAP E1W 123 H1
Herne Hill School
HNHL SE24 ....142 D6
Herne Hill Stadium
(Cycle Centre)
HNHL SE24 ....162 E1
Heron Industrial Estate
SRTFD E15 ....105 K1
Heronsgate Primary School
THMD SE28 ....127 J3
Heron Trading Estate
ACT W3 ....98 D4
Hersham Trading Estate
WOT/HER KT12 ....188 D6
Heston Community School
HEST TW5 ....135 F1
Heston Community Sports
Hall
HEST TW5 ....135 F1
Heston Industrial Mall
HEST TW5 ....135 F1
Heston Infant School
HEST TW5 ....135 F1
Heston Junior School
HEST TW5 ....135 F1
Heston Park CC
HEST TW5 ....114 E6
Heston Swimming Baths
HEST TW5 ....114 E6
Higgs Industrial Estate
HNHL SE24 ....142 C4
Highams Lodge Business
Centre
WALTH E17 ....51 F2
Highams Park School
CHING E4 ....52 B2

Highbury Corner Magistrates
Court
HOLWY N7 ....85 G4
Highbury Fields School
HBRY N5 ....85 H2
Highbury Grove School
HBRY N5 ....85 J3
Highbury Park Clinic
HBRY N5 ....85 H1
Highbury Pool
HBRY N5 ....85 H4
Highbury Quadrant Primary
School
HBRY N5 ....85 J2
Highbury Square
Development
HBRY N5 ....85 H1
High Commission of Angola
MHST W1U 9 F2
High Commission of Antigua &
Barbuda
MHST W1U 9 G3
High Commission of Bahamas
MYFR/PICC W1J 9 H7
High Commission of
Bangladesh
SKENS SW7 ....120 B3
High Commission of
Barbados
FITZ W1T 10 C3
High Commission of Belize
CAVSQ/HST W1G 9 K3
High Commission of
Botswana
OXSTW W1C 9 J4
High Commission of Brunei
KTBR SW1X 15 G4
High Commission of Canada
MYFR/PKLN W1K 9 H5
High Commission of Cyprus
MYFR/PKLN W1K 9 G5
High Commission of
Dominica
ECT SW5 ....120 A4
High Commission of Fiji
SKENS SW7 ....120 B2
High Commission of Grenada
ECT SW5 ....120 A4
High Commission of Guyana
BAY/PAD W2 ....101 F6
High Commission of Jamaica
SKENS SW7 ....14 A3
High Commission of Kenya
CAVSQ/HST W1G 9 J1
High Commission of Lesotho
KTBR SW1X 15 G4
High Commission of Malawi
MYFR/PKLN W1K 9 J5
High Commission of Malaysia
KTBR SW1X 15 H3
High Commission of Maldives
MHST W1U 9 G1
High Commission of Malta
CONDST W1S 10 B6
High Commission of Namibia
CAVSQ/HST W1G 9 K2
High Commission of
New Zealand
STJS SW1Y 10 C7
High Commission of Nigeria
CHCR WC2N 10 E7
EMB EC4Y 11 K4
High Commission of Pakistan
KTBR SW1X 15 F4
High Commission of
Papua New Guinea
STJS SW1Y 10 B7
High Commission of St Lucia
KENS W8 ....120 A2
High Commission of
Seychelles
MHST W1U 9 F1
High Commission of
Sierra Leone
REGST W1B 10 A3
High Commission of Singapore
KTBR SW1X 15 F3
High Commission of
South Africa
CHCR WC2N 10 E7
High Commission of Sri Lanka
BAY/PAD W2 ....8 B5
High Commission of Swaziland
HNHL SE24 ....16 A4
High Commission of
the Gambia
KENS W8 ....120 A2
High Commission of Tonga
MBLAR W1H 8 D2
High Commission of Trinidad
& Tobago
KTBR SW1X 15 G4
High Commission of Uganda
WHALL SW1A 10 D7
High Commission of Zambia
SKENS SW7 ....120 B2
High Commission
of Zimbabwe
CHCR WC2N 10 E6
High Cross Centre
SEVS/STOTM N15 ....68 C1
High Elms Country Park
ORP BR6 ....216 C5
High Elms Golf Club
ORP BR6 ....216 C5
Highfield Infant School
HAYES BR2 ....199 J1
Highfield Junior School
HAYES BR2 ....199 H1
Highfield Primary School
WCHMH N21 ....35 H3
Highfield School
WAND/EARL SW18 ....160 D2
Highgate Cemetery
HGT N6 ....66 B5
Highgate Golf Club
EFNCH N2 ....65 J3

Highgate Junior School
HGT N6 ....65 K4
Highgate Montessori School
BAR EN5 ....20 C4
Highgate Primary School
HGT N6 ....65 K3
Highgate Private Hospital
HGT N6 ....65 K3
Highgate School
HGT N6 ....65 K4
Highgate Wood School
MUSWH N10 ....66 C2
Highgrove Pool
RSLP HA4 ....58 E4
Highlands J & I School
IL IG1 ....71 K5
Highlands Primary School
IL IG1 ....71 K5
Highshore School
PECK SE15 ....143 G2
High View Primary School
BTSEA SW11 ....140 C5
Highview Primary School
WLGTN SM6 ....210 E3
The Highway Primary School
ORP BR6 ....217 J3
The Highway Trading Centre
WAP E1W 105 F6
Hillbrook Primary School
TOOT SW17 ....160 E6
Hillcroft College
SURB KT6 ....191 F3
Hillcross Primary School
MRDN SM4 ....193 J1
Hillgate Hill Murugan Temple
HGT N6 ....66 B4
Hill House Preparatory School
CHEL SW3 ....120 D6
Hill House School
KTBR SW1X 14 E5
Hill Mead Infant School
BRXN/ST SW9 ....142 C5
Hillmead Primary School
BRXN/ST SW9 ....142 C5
Hills Grove Primary School
WELL DA16 ....148 D1
Hillside Primary School
NTHWD HA6 ....40 E3
STMC/STPC BR5 ....202 D4
Hillyfield Primary School
WALTH E17 ....51 G6
Hilly Fields Medical Centre
BROCKY SE4 ....144 D6
Hilton Docklands Pier
BERM/RHTH SE16 ....124 C1
The Hiltongrove Business
Centre
WALTH E17 ....69 J1
Hinchley Wood Primary
School
ESH/CLAY KT10 ....190 B6
Hinchley Wood School &
Sixth Form Centre
ESH/CLAY KT10 ....190 B6
Hinley Clinic
LBTH SE11 ....17 K7
Hispaniola
WHALL SW1A 17 F1
Hitherfield Primary School
STRHM/NOR SW16 ....162 B4
Hither Green Cemetery
LEW SE13 ....165 J4
Hither Green Primary
School
LEW SE13 ....165 G1
HM Customs
HTHAIR TW6 ....132 E2
HM Prison
BRXS/STRHM SW2 ....161 K1
HOLWY N7 ....84 E2
HOLWY N7 ....85 F4
SHB W12 ....99 J5
THMD SE28 ....127 K3
WAND/EARL SW18 ....160 C2
HMS Belfast
STHWK SE1 ....13 H7
HMS President
EMB EC4Y 11 K5
HM Young Offender
Institution
FELT TW13 ....153 G5
Hobbayne First & Middle
School
HNWL W7 ....97 F5
Hobbayne Primary School
HNWL W7 ....96 E5
Hogarth Business Park
CHSWK W4 ....118 B6
Hogarth Industrial Estate
WLSDN NW10 ....99 J3
Hogarth's House
CHSWK W4 ....118 A6
Holbeach Primary School
CAT SE6 ....164 D2
Holborn College
WOOL/PLUM SE18 ....126 C4
Holborn College Independent
School
HMSMTH W6 ....119 F5
Holborn Medical Centre
BMSBY WC1N 5 G7
Holborn Town Hall
HHOL WC1V 11 F3
Holiday Inn
CAMTN NW1 ....4 B5
FSBYW WC1X 5 H5
Holland House
WKENS W14 ....119 J2
Holland House School
EDGW HA8 ....30 C6
Holland Park Pre-Preparatory
School
WKENS W14 ....119 J3
Holland Park School
KENS W8 ....119 J2
Holland Park Theatre
WKENS W14 ....119 J2

Holland Street Clinic
KENS W8 ....119 K2
Hollickwood JMI School
MBAR N10 ....48 B3
Holloway School
HOLWY N7 ....84 D3
Holndale Primary School
PECK SE15 ....143 H3
The Hollyfield School
SURB KT6 ....191 F2
Holly House Private Hospital
BKHH IG9 ....39 F4
Hollymount Primary School
RYNPK SW20 ....177 F4
Holly Park JMI School
FBAR/BDGN N11 ....48 A1
Hollywood Bowl
BERM/RHTH SE16 ....124 A3
The Holme
CAMTN NW1 ....3 F5
Holmleigh Primary School
STNW/STAM N16 ....68 B5
Holy Cross Preparatory
School
KUTN/CMB KT2 ....175 K3
Holy Cross Primary School
FUL/PGN SW6 ....139 K2
Holy Cross RC Convent School
NWMAL KT3 ....192 A1
Holy Cross RC Primary School
CAT SE6 ....165 F3
Holy Family RC Primary
School
BKHTH/KID SE3 ....146 A5
POP/IOD E14 ....105 J6
Holy Family Technology
College
WALTH E17 ....69 K1
Holy Ghost RC Primary School
BAL SW12 ....160 E2
Holy Innocents Catholic
Primary School
ORP BR6 ....217 F1
Holy Trinity CE Junior School
WLGTN SM6 ....210 C2
Holy Trinity CE Primary School
BRXS/STRHM SW2 ....162 A2
DART DA1 ....151 F6
EFNCH N2 ....47 H6
KIL/WHAMP NW6 ....83 G4
KTBR SW1X 15 G6
NTHWD HA6 ....40 A2
RCHPK/HAM TW10 ....137 H5
SYD SE26 ....163 K4
Holy Trinity College
BMLY BR1 ....184 B4
Holy Trinity in St Silas
CAMTN NW1 ....84 B5
Holy Trinity Primary School
HACK E8 ....86 B4
WIM/MER SW19 ....177 K2
Holy Trinity School
BFN/LL DA15 ....168 A3
CHEL SW3 ....15 F6
Holywell School
WATW WD18 ....26 D1
Homefield Preparatory
School
SUT SM1 ....208 E3
Home Office
STJSPK SW1H 16 B3
Homerton College of
Technology
HOM E9 ....86 E3
Homerton University Hospital
HOM E9 ....87 F3
Homoeopathic Health Centre
PLSTW E13 ....106 E3
The Homoeopathic Health
Centre
MLHL NW7 ....45 H1
Honeypot Business Centre
STAN HA7 ....44 A4
Honeypot Lane Centre
STAN HA7 ....43 K4
Honeypot Medical Centre
STAN HA7 ....44 A5
Honeywell Primary School
BTSEA SW11 ....160 E1
Honor Oak Crematorium
FSTH SE23 ....144 A6
Honor Oak Gallery
FSTH SE23 ....164 A1
Honor Oak Health Centre
BROCKY SE4 ....144 B5
Honourable Artillery
Company HQ
FSBYE EC1V 6 E7
Hook Lane Primary School
WELL DA16 ....148 B4
Hook Rise South Industrial
Park
CHSGTN KT9 ....206 B1
Hope Primary School
CMBW SE5 ....143 F1
Horizon Business Centre
ED N9 ....37 F4
Horizon Industrial Estate
PECK SE15 ....123 H6
Horizon School
STNW/STAM N16 ....86 A2
The Horniman Museum &
Gardens
FSTH SE23 ....163 J5
Horniman Primary School
FSTH SE23 ....163 J5
Horn Park Primary School
LEE/GVPK SE12 ....166 A2
Hornsby House School
BAL SW12 ....161 F3
Hornsey Central Hospital
CEND/HSY/T N8 ....66 D2
Hornsey Rise Health Centre
ARCH N19 ....66 D4
Hornsey Secondary School
for Girls
CEND/HSY/T N8 ....67 F2

Horn Stairs
BERM/RHTH SE16 ....124 C1
Horseferry Road Magistrates
Court
WEST SW1P 16 D5
Horse Guards Parade
WHALL SW1A 16 D1
Horsenden Hill Golf Club
GFD/PVL UB6 ....79 H4
Horsenden Primary School
GFD/PVL UB6 ....78 E4
Horton Country Park
HOR/WEW KT19 ....206 C6
Horton Industrial Park
WDR/YW UB7 ....112 C1
Horton Park Golf & Country
Club
HOR/WEW KT19 ....206 E5
Hortus Cemetery
NWDGN UB2 ....114 E2
Hospital of St John &
St Elizabeth
STJWD NW8 ....2 A3
The Hotel at Chelsea
FUL/PGN SW6 ....140 A1
Hotel Ibis
CAMTN NW1 ....4 B5
CAN/RD E16 ....107 F5
FUL/PGN SW6 ....119 K6
GNWCH SE10 ....125 J1
HGN/HAR UB3 ....133 H2
POP/IOD E14 ....106 A6
SRTFD E15 ....88 C4
WBLY HA9 ....80 C3
The Hotel Russell
RSQ WC1B 4 E7
Hotham Primary School
PUT/ROE SW15 ....139 G5
Hotspur Industrial Estate
TOTM N17 ....50 D2
Houndsfield Primary School
ED N9 ....36 C2
Hounslow Business Park
HSLW TW3 ....135 F5
Hounslow CC
HSLW TW3 ....134 E3
Hounslow Cemetery
HSLWW TW4 ....154 C2
Hounslow College
Independent School
FELT TW13 ....154 C6
Hounslow Heath Golf Club
HSLWW TW4 ....134 C6
Hounslow Heath Infant
School
HSLWW TW4 ....134 D4
Hounslow Heath Junior
School
HSLWW TW4 ....134 D4
Hounslow Manor School
HSLW TW3 ....135 G4
Hounslow Manor Sports Hall
HSLW TW3 ....135 G4
Hounslow Town Primary
School
HSLW TW3 ....135 H4
House of Detention
CLKNW EC1R 5 K6
House of St Barnabus
SOHO/SHAV W1D 10 C4
Houses of Parliament
WHALL SW1A 17 F3
Houston Business Park
YEAD UB4 ....114 B1
Howard Primary School
SAND/SEL CR2 ....211 J2
Howbury Centre
ERITH DA8 ....150 D1
Howland Quay
BERM/RHTH SE16 ....124 A3
Hoxton Hall Community
Theatre
IS N1 ....7 G2
HQS Wellington
(Master Mariners)
TPL/STR WC2R 11 J6
HSBC Sports Club
BECK BR3 ....182 B2
HSBC Tower
POP/IOD E14 ....124 E1
Hubbinet Industrial Estate
ROMW/RG RM7 ....56 E6
Hugh Myddelton Primary
School
CLKNW EC1R 5 K5
The Humana Wellington
Hospital
STJWD NW8 ....2 B4
Humber Trading Estate
CRICK NW2 ....63 K6
Hunterian Museum
LINN WC2A 11 H3
Hunters Hall Primary School
DAGE RM10 ....92 D3
Hunter Street Health Centre
STPAN WC1H 4 E6
Huntsman Sports Club
BKHTH/KID SE3 ....145 K5
Hurlingham Business Park
FUL/PGN SW6 ....139 K4
Hurlingham & Chelsea
Secondary School
FUL/PGN SW6 ....139 K4
Hurlingham House
FUL/PGN SW6 ....139 J4
Hurlingham Private School
PUT/ROE SW15 ....139 J5
Huron University
RSQ WC1B 10 E1
Hurricane Trading Centre
CDALE/KGS NW9 ....45 H4
Hurstmere School
BFN/LL DA15 ....168 C3
Hurst Park Primary School
E/WMO/HCT KT8 ....173 F6
Hurst Primary School
BXLY DA5 ....168 E3

Hyatt Carlton Tower Hotel
KTBR SW1X 15 F5
Hyatt Regency-The Churchill
MBLAR W1H 9 F3
The Hyde Industrial Estate
CDALE/KGS NW9 ....63 H2
The Hyde School
CDALE/KGS NW9 ....63 H2
Hyland House School
WALTH E17 ....52 B5
Hyleford Leavers Unit School
BARK/HLT IG6 ....54 D5
Hyleford School
IL IG1 ....90 E3
Hythe Road Industrial Estate
WLSDN NW10 ....99 J3
Ian Mikardo High School
BOW E3 ....105 K2
Ibstock Place School
PUT/ROE SW15 ....158 B1
ICA Cinema
STJS SW1Y 10 D7
ICA Centre
CLPT E5 ....86 D1
Ickburgh School
CLPT E5 ....86 D1
Ickenham Clinic
HGDN/ICK UB10 ....76 A1
Ihlara Sport FC
HBRY N5 ....85 J2
IKEA Store Brent Park
WLSDN NW10 ....81 F3
IKEA Store Croydon
CROY/NA CR0 ....196 A5
IKEA Store Edmonton
TOTM N17 ....50 E2
Ilderton Primary School
PECK SE15 ....123 K6
Ilford County High School
BARK/HLT IG6 ....54 C5
Ilford Golf Club
IL IG1 ....71 K5
Ilford Jewish Primary School
BARK/HLT IG6 ....54 D6
Ilford Medical Centre
IL IG1 ....90 B1
Ilford Preparatory School
GDMY/SEVK IG3 ....73 F5
Ilford Retail Park
IL IG1 ....72 C6
Ilford Swimming Pool
IL IG1 ....72 D6
Ilford Ursuline High School
IL IG1 ....72 B6
Iman Zakaria Academy
FSTGT E7 ....89 J3
Imber Court Trading Estate
E/WMO/HCT KT8 ....189 J3
Immanuel CE Primary
School
STRHM/NOR SW16 ....179 K2
Immanuel College
BUSH WD23 ....28 E2
Immanuel School
ROM RM1 ....57 G2
Imperial College
PUT/ROE SW15 ....139 G3
SKENS SW7 ....14 A4
Imperial College Athletic
Ground
HYS/HAR UB3 ....113 F6
Imperial College of Science
SKENS SW7 ....14 A3
Imperial College of Science &
Technology
SKENS SW7 ....14 B3
Imperial College School of
Medicine
PIM SW1V 16 C7
Imperial War Museum
STHWK SE1 ....17 K5
Imperial War Museum Annexe
LBTH SE11 ....17 K5
Inchbald School of Design
BGVA SW1W 15 H5
Independent Industrial
Estate
WDR/YW UB7 ....112 C1
Independent Jewish School
HDN NW4 ....64 B2
India House
HOL/ALD WC2B 11 G5
Infant College
IL IG1 ....72 A6
Innellan House School
PIN HA5 ....41 H4
Inner London Sessions House
(Crown Court)
STHWK SE1 ....18 C3
Innholders Hall
CANST EC4R 12 D5
Innkeeper's Lodge
BECK BR3 ....198 D3
CHEAM SM3 ....208 A5
MTHLT UB5 ....78 A4
SAND/SEL CR2 ....212 A6
STHGT/OAK N14 ....34 E5
WAN E11 ....70 E1
WFD IG8 ....53 K2
Inns of Court & Chancery
TPL/STR WC2R 11 J4
Inns of Court Law School
GINN WC1R 11 H1
Institute of Education
GWST WC1E 4 D7
Institute of Education
University of London
RSQ WC1B 4 D7
Intercontinental Hotel
MYFR/PICC W1J 15 H1
International Community
School
CAMTN NW1 ....3 G3
International School of
Havana
STJS SW1Y 10 D7
International School of
London
ACT W3 ....117 H4

International Trading Estate
NWDGN UB2 ....114 A3
Invicta Industrial Estate
SRTFD E15 ....106 A2
Invicta Primary School
BKHTH/KID SE3 ....125 K6
Invicta Sports Club
DART DA1 ....151 G6
Inwood Business Centre
HSLW TW3 ....135 G5
IORA Independent School
BRXN/ST SW9 ....142 B4
Ironmonger Row Baths
FSBYE EC1V 6 C5
Ironmongers Hall
STBT EC1A 12 C2
Islamia Girls School
KIL/WHAMP NW6 ....82 C6
Islamic College for Advanced
Study
WLSDN NW10 ....81 K5
The Islamic Grammar School
WAND/EARL SW18 ....159 J2
Island Clinic
POP/IOD E14 ....125 F2
Isleworth Cemetery
ISLW TW7 ....136 B3
Isleworth Recreation Centre
ISLW TW7 ....136 A5
Isleworth & Syon School
for Boys
ISLW TW7 ....135 K1
Isleworth Town Primary
School
ISLW TW7 ....136 A3
Islington Arts & Media School
FSBYPK N4 ....67 F5
Islington Business Centre
IS N1 ....85 J6
Islington Crematorium
MUSWH N10 ....47 K4
Islington Green Medical
Centre
IS N1 ....85 H6
Islington Green School
IS N1 ....6 B1
Islington Tennis Centre
HOLWY N7 ....84 E4
Islington Town Hall
IS N1 ....85 H5
Ismaili Centre
SKENS SW7 ....14 B6
Italia Conti Academy of
Theatre Arts
BRXN/ST SW9 ....141 K4
Italian Hospital
PIM SW1V 16 A6
Ithaca College
SKENS SW7 ....120 B4
Ivybridge Primary School
TWK TW1 ....156 A1
Ivybridge Retail Park
ISLW TW7 ....136 A2
Ivydale Primary School
PECK SE15 ....144 A5
Jack & Jill School
HPTN TW12 ....173 F2
WHTN TW2 ....155 K4
Jack Taylor School
STJWD NW8 ....83 G6
Jack Tizard School
FUL/PGN SW6 ....139 G2
SHB W12 ....100 A6
Jacques Prevert School
HMSMTH W6 ....119 G4
Jamahiriya School
CHEL SW3 ....120 D6
James Allens Preparatory
Girls School
HNHL SE24 ....142 E6
James Dixon Primary School
PGE/AN SE20 ....181 H4
Jamestown Mental Health
Centre
HAMP NW3 ....83 K5
James Wolfe Primary School
GNWCH SE10 ....144 E1
Jamiatul Ummah School
WCHPL E1 ....104 D5
Janet Adegoke Leisure Centre
SHB W12 ....99 J6
The Japanese School
ACT W3 ....98 C6
Japan Green Medical Centre
ACT W3 ....117 J1
Jenner Health Centre
FSTH SE23 ....164 B3
Jenny Hammond Primary
School
WAN E11 ....88 C2
Jermyn Street Theatre
MYFR/PICC W1J 10 B6
Jessop Primary School
HNHL SE24 ....142 C5
Jewel Tower
WEST SW1P 16 E4
Jewish Cemetery
GLDGN NW11 ....64 E3
Jewish Community Theatre
HNHL SE24 ....142 E6
Jewish Free School
KTN/HRWW/WS HA3 ....62 B3
HNHL SE24 ....184 D4
The Jewish Museum
CAMTN NW1 ....3 J1
FNCH N3 ....46 E5
Johanna Primary School
STHWK SE1 ....17 J3
John Ball Primary School
BKHTH/KID SE3 ....145 K1
John Betts Primary School
HMSMTH W6 ....118 D3
John Bramston Primary
School
BARK/HLT IG6 ....55 C2
John Burns Primary School
BTSEA SW11 ....141 F3

John Chilton School
NTHLT UB5 ....**77** J5
John Dixon Clinic
BERM/RHTH SE16 ....**123** J3
John Donne Primary School
PECK SE15 ....**143** J2
John F Kennedy Special School
SRTFD E15 ....**88** B6
John Keble CE Primary School
WLSDN NW10 ....**99** H1
John Kelly Boys & Girls Technology College
CRICK NW2 ....**81** H1
The John Loughborough School
TOTM N17 ....**50** B5
John Lyon School
RYLN/HDSTN HA2 ....**60** D5
John Nightingale School
E/WMO/HCT KT8 ....**172** E6
John Orwell Sports Centre
WAP E1W **123** H1
John Paul II RC School
WIM/MER SW19 ....**159** G2
John Perryn Primary School
ACT W3 ....**99** G5
John Perry Primary School
DAGE RM10 ....**93** F4
John Roan Lower School
BKHTH/KID SE3 ....**145** J1
John Roan School
BKHTH/KID SE3 ....**145** H1
John Ruskin College
SAND/SEL CR2 ....**213** G5
John Ruskin Primary School
WALW SE17 ....**122** D6
John Scott Health Centre
FSBYPK N4 ....**67** J5
John Scurr Primary School
WCHPL E1 ....**104** C3
John Smith House
WALW SE17 ....**18** C7
Johnsons Industrial Estate
HYS/HAR UB3 ....**113** K3
John Stainer Primary School
BROCKY SE4 ....**144** B4
The Jo Richardson Community School
DAGW RM9 ....**91** K6
Joseph Clarke Special School
CHING E4 ....**52** B2
Joseph Hood Primary School
RYNPK SW20 ....**177** H5
Joseph Lancaster Primary School
STHWK SE1 ....**18** D5
Joydens Wood Infant School
RDART DA2 ....**170** B6
Joydens Wood Junior School
BXLY DA5 ....**170** B6
Jubilee Country Park
BMLY BR1 ....**201** G1
Jubilee Market
COVGDN WC2E **11** F5
Jubilee Primary School
BRXS/STRHM SW2 ......**162** B1
THMD SE28 ....**109** J6
Jubilee Sports Ground
CHING E4 ....**38** B6
Julians Primary School
STRHM/NOR SW16 ......**162** B6
Jumeirah Carlton Tower Hotel
KTBR SW1X **15** F4
Junior & Youth Centre
BOW E3 ....**105** H4
Juno Way Industrial Estate
NWCR SE14 ....**124** A6
Jurys Clifton-Ford Hotel
MHST W1U **9** H2
Jurys Great Russell Street
RSQ WC1B **10** D3
Jurys Inn
CROY/NA CRO **196** D6
Jurys Inn Chelsea
FUL/PGN SW6 ....**140** B2
Jurys Inn Hotel
HTHAIR TW6 ....**133** J4
Jurys Inn Islington
IS N1 ....**5** J5
Jurys Kensington Hotel
SKENS SW7 ....**14** A7
JVC Business Park
CRICK NW2 ....**63** J5
Kaizen Primary School
PLSTW E15 ....**107** F3
Kangley Business Centre
SYD SE26 ....**182** C1
Katella Trading Estate
BARK IG11 ....**108** E2
Katherine Road Medical Centre
FSTGT E7 ....**89** G4
Keats House Museum
HAMP NW3 ....**83** H2
Keble Preparatory School
WCHMH N21 ....**35** G2
Keen Students Supplementary School
WCHPL E1 ....**104** C4
Keir Hardie Primary School
CAN/RD E16 ....**106** E4
Keith Davis Cue Sports Club
DAGW RM9 ....**91** K5
Kelmscott Community Centre
WALTH E17 ....**69** H3
Kelmscott Leisure Centre
WALTH E17 ....**69** H3
Kelmscott School
WALTH E17 ....**69** H3
Kelsey Park School
BECK BR3 ....**182** D6
Kelvin Industrial Estate
GFD/PVL UB6 ....**78** B6
GFD/PVL UB6 ....**96** D2
Kemnal Technology College
STMC/STPC BR5 ....**186** C3

Kempton Park Racecourse
SUN TW16 ....**172** A3
Ken Barrington Centre
LBTH SE11 ....**122** A6
Kender Primary School
NWCR SE14 ....**143** K2
Kenmont Primary School
WLSDN NW10 ....**99** J2
Kenmore Park Middle School
KTN/HRWW/WS HA3 ......**43** K6
Kenneth More Theatre
IL IG1 ....**90** C1
Kensal Green Cemetery
WLSDN NW10 ....**99** K2
Kensal Rise Primary School
KIL/WHAMP NW6 ....**100** B3
Kensington and Chelsea College
NKENS W10 ....**100** C3
Kensington Avenue Primary School
THHTH CR7 ....**180** B5
Kensington Business Centre
SKENS SW7 ....**14** C1
Kensington & Chelsea College
NTGHL W11 ....**119** J2
Kensington & Chelsea Town Hall
KENS W8 ....**119** K2
The Kensington Dyslexia Teaching Centre
KENS W8 ....**120** A3
The Kensington Gardens School
BAY/PAD W2 ....**101** F6
Kensington Leisure Centre
NTGHL W11 ....**100** B6
Kensington Market
KENS W8 ....**120** A2
Kensington Palace
KENS W8 ....**120** A1
Kensington Park School
REGST W1B **9** K1
Kensington Preparatory School
FUL/PGN SW6 ....**139** J2
Kensington Primary School
MNPK E12 ....**89** K4
Kensington School of Business
HCIRC EC1N **11** K1
Kensington Temple Institute of Education
EA W5 ....**98** A2
Kensington Wharf
WBPTN SW10 ....**140** C1
Kensit Memorial College
FNCH N3 ....**46** C5
Kentish Town CE Primary School
KTTN NW5 ....**84** C3
Kentish Town Health Centre
KTTN NW5 ....**84** C4
Kentish Town Industrial Estate
KTTN NW5 ....**84** B3
Kentish Town Sports Centre
KTTN NW5 ....**84** A4
Kenton Clinic
KTN/HRWW/WS HA3 ......**62** A2
Kenton CC
KTN/HRWW/WS HA3 ......**61** J1
Kent Park Industrial Estate
PECK SE15 ....**123** J6
Kenwood House
HAMP NW3 ....**65** J5
The Keren School
FNCH N3 ....**65** H2
Keston CE Primary School
HAYES BR2 ....**215** H3
Kew Bridge Steam Museum
BTFD TW8 ....**117** G5
Kew College
RCH/KEW TW9 ....**137** H1
Kew Palace
RCH/KEW TW9 ....**137** F1
Kew Retail Park
RCH/KEW TW9 ....**137** J2
Kew Riverside Primary School
RCH/KEW TW9 ....**137** J3
Keyplan & Roxburghe College
FITZ W1T **4** B7
Keyworth Primary School
WALW SE17 ....**122** C5
Khalsa College London
HRW HA1 ....**61** F3
Kidbrooke Park Primary School
BKHTH/KID SE3 ....**146** B3
Kidbrooke School
BKHTH/KID SE3 ....**146** C3
Kilburn Park Junior School
KIL/WHAMP NW6 ....**100** D2
Killick Street Medical Centre
IS N1 ....**5** C2
Kilmorie Primary School
FSTH SE23 ....**164** B4
Kimberley Industrial Estate
WALTH E17 ....**51** H3
Kimpton Industrial Estate
CHEAM SM3 ....**193** J6
King Alfred School
GLDGN NW11 ....**65** F5
King Athelstan Primary School
KUT/HW KT1 ....**175** G6
King Edwards Road Clinic
RSLP HA4 ....**58** B5
King Edward VII Hospital for Officers
MHST W1U **9** H1
King Fahad Academy (Girls Upper School)
EA W5 ....**116** D4

The Kingfisher Medical Centre
DEPT SE8 ....**124** C6
The Kingfisher Sports Centre
KUT/HW KT1 ....**175** F5
King George Hospital
GDMY/SEVK IG3 ....**73** G2
Kingham Industrial Estate
WLSDN NW10 ....**99** F2
King & Queen Wharf
BERM/RHTH SE16 ....**105** F6
Kings Avenue Medical Centre
STHL UB1 ....**96** C5
Kings Avenue School
CLAP SW4 ....**141** K6
Kingsbury Green Primary School
CDALE/KGS NW9 ....**62** D2
Kingsbury High School (Lower School)
CDALE/KGS NW9 ....**62** E1
Kingsbury High School (Upper School)
CDALE/KGS NW9 ....**62** D1
Kingsbury Hospital
CDALE/KGS NW9 ....**62** C1
Kingsbury Tamil School
CDALE/KGS NW9 ....**44** D6
Kingsbury Trading Estate
CDALE/KGS NW9 ....**62** E3
King's College (Hampstead Campus)
HAMP NW3 ....**82** E2
King's College Hospital
CMBW SE5 ....**142** D4
Kings College London
CMBW SE5 ....**142** E3
HOL/ALD WC2B **11** F4
STHWK SE1 ....**12** A7
STHWK SE1 ....**18** D1
WEST SW1P **16** B6
Kings College London - Law
TPL/STR WC2R **11** H5
Kings College London (Waterloo Campus)
STHWK SE1 ....**17** J1
Kings College London SW19
WIM/MER SW19 ....**177** F2
Kings College London School of Medicine & Dentistry
CMBW SE5 ....**142** E3
DUL SE21 ....**162** E1
Kings College Sports Ground
RSLP HA4 ....**58** C3
Kings College London - Humanities
TPL/STR WC2R **11** G5
Kingsdale School
DUL SE21 ....**163** F5
Kings Estate
HCH RM12 ....**93** J2
Kingsford Community School
PLSTW E13 ....**107** G3
Kingsgate Business Centre
KUTN/CMB KT2 ....**175** F4
Kingsgate Primary School
KIL/WHAMP NW6 ....**82** E5
Kings Hall Leisure Centre
CLPT E5 ....**86** E3
Kings Head Theatre
IS N1 ....**85** G6
Kings House School
RCHPK/HAM TW10 ......**137** G6
Kingsland College of Business Studies
SRTFD E15 ....**106** B1
Kingsland Health Centre
HACK E8 ....**86** B5
Kingsland Shopping Centre
HACK E8 ....**86** B4
Kingsley Primary School
CROY/NA CRO **196** A5
Kings Mall Shopping Centre
HMSMTH W6 ....**119** F4
Kingsmeadow Athletics Centre
KUT/HW KT1 ....**175** H6
Kingsmead Primary School
CLPT E5 ....**87** G2
Kingsmead School
EN N1 ....**24** C5
The Kings Oak Private Hospital
ENC/FH EN2 ....**23** G1
King Solomon High School
BARK/HLT IG6 ....**54** D5
Kings Private Clinic
GDMY/SEVK IG3 ....**73** F5
MHST W1U **9** G1
Kings School of English
BECK BR3 ....**182** C5
Kings Stairs
BERM/RHTH SE16 ....**123** J2
Kingston Business Centre
CHSGTN KT9 ....**206** A1
Kingston College of Further Education
KUT/HW KT1 ....**175** F6
Kingston College Theatre
KUT/HW KT1 ....**174** E6
Kingston Crematorium
KUT/HW KT1 ....**175** H6
Kingston Crown Court
KUT/HW KT1 ....**174** E6
Kingston Grammar School
KUT/HW KT1 ....**175** G5
Kingston Hospital
KUTN/CMB KT2 ....**175** H4
Kingstonian FC
NWMAL KT3 ....**175** J6
Kingston University
BRYLDS KT5 ....**191** H2
KUT/HW KT1 ....**175** F6
KUT/HW KT1 ....**174** C7
KUTN/CMB KT2 ....**176** A3
PUT/ROE SW15 ....**158** C4
King Street College
HMSMTH W6 ....**119** F4

Kingsway Business Park
HPTN TW12 ....**172** E4
Kingsway College
CAMTN NW1 ....**4** A6
FSBYW WC1X **5** H5
KTTN NW5 ....**84** B4
STPAN WC1H **4** C5
Kingswood Primary School
WNWD SE27 ....**162** E6
Kisharon School
GLDGN NW11 ....**64** D3
K+K Hotel George
ECT SW5 ....**119** K4
KLC School of Design
WBPTN SW10 ....**140** B2
Knightsbridge Barracks
SKENS SW7 ....**14** D3
Knightsbridge Medical Centre
KTBR SW1X **15** F4
The Knightsbridge Under School
SKENS SW7 ....**120** B4
Knollmead Primary School
BRYLDS KT5 ....**191** K6
Knowledge Point School
HOLWY N7 ....**85** F4
Kobi Nazrul Primary School
WCHPL E1 ....**104** C5
KP Estate
RAIN RM13 ....**111** G6
Kubrick Business Estate
FSTGT E7 ....**89** F2
Laban Centre for Movement & Dance
DEPT SE8 ....**144** E1
Laburnum Health Centre
DAGE RM10 ....**74** C6
Lady Bankes Primary School
RSLP HA4 ....**58** E5
The Lady Eleanor Holles School
HPTN TW12 ....**173** G1
Lady Margaret Primary School
STHL UB1 ....**95** K4
Lady Margaret School
FUL/PGN SW6 ....**139** K2
Ladywell Arena
LEW SE13 ....**164** E1
Ladywell Cemetery
BROCKY SE4 ....**144** C6
Ladywell Leisure Centre
LEW SE13 ....**145** F6
Lake Business Centre
TOTM N17 ....**50** C2
Laker Industrial Estate
BECK BR3 ....**182** C1
Lambeth Academy
CLAP SW4 ....**141** H6
Lambeth Cemetery
TOOT SW17 ....**178** B1
Lambeth College
BRXS/STRHM SW2 ......**142** A6
CLAP SW4 ....**141** H6
STHWK SE1 ....**19** H1
STRHM/NOR SW16 ......**161** K4
VX/NE SW8 ....**141** J2
Lambeth County Court
LBTH SE11 ....**122** B5
Lambeth Crematorium
TOOT SW17 ....**160** B6
Lambeth Hospital
BRXN/ST SW9 ....**141** K4
Lambeth Palace
STHWK SE1 ....**17** G5
Lambs Court
POP/IOD E14 ....**105** G6
Lamont Business Centre
CROY/NA CRO **195** K4
Lamorbey Swimming Centre
BFN/LL DA15 ....**168** B4
Lampton School
HSLW TW3 ....**135** F2
The Lanark Medical Centre
MV/WKIL W9 ....**101** F2
Lancaster House
WHALL SW1A **16** A2
Lancasterian Primary School
TOTM N17 ....**50** A4
Lancaster Road Industrial Estate
EBAR EN4 ....**21** H6
Lancelot Medical Centre
ALP/SUD HA0 ....**79** K3
The Landmark Hotel
CAMTN NW1 ....**8** E1
The Lanesborough Hotel
KTBR SW1X **15** G2
Lanford Obesity Clinic
ED N9 ....**36** D2
Langbourne Primary School
DUL SE21 ....**163** F5
Langdon Down Centre
TEDD TW11 ....**174** D3
Langdon Park School
POP/IOD E14 ....**105** K5
Langdon School
EHAM E6 ....**108** B1
Langford Primary School
FUL/PGN SW6 ....**140** A3
Langham Hotel
CAVSQ/HST W1G **9** K3
The Langham School
SEVS/STOTM N15 ....**67** J1
Langhedge Lane Industrial Estate
UED N18 ....**50** B2
Langley Park Girls School & Sports Centre
BECK BR3 ....**198** E2
Langley Park Golf Club
BECK BR3 ....**199** G3
Langley Park School for Boys
BECK BR3 ....**198** E3
Langthorne Health Centre
WAN E11 ....**88** B1
Langthorne Hospital
WAN E11 ....**88** B2

Lansbury Lawrence Primary School
POP/IOD E14 ....**105** K5
Lansdowne College
BAY/PAD W2 ....**101** F6
Lansdowne School
BRXN/ST SW9 ....**142** A4
La Retraite RC Girls School
BAL SW12 ....**161** H2
Lark Hall Primary School
CLAP SW4 ....**141** J3
Larkshall Business Centre
CHING E4 ....**38** B4
Larmenier Infant School
HMSMTH W6 ....**119** G4
La Sainte Union Convent School
KTTN NW5 ....**84** A1
La Salette RC Primary School
RAIN RM13 ....**111** J2
Latchmere J & I School
KUTN/CMB KT2 ....**175** G2
Latchmere Leisure Centre
BTSEA SW11 ....**140** E3
Lathom Junior School
EHAM E6 ....**89** J5
Latymer All Saints CE Primary School
ED N9 ....**36** B4
The Latymer Preparatory School
HMSMTH W6 ....**118** D5
The Latymer School
ED N9 ....**36** A4
Latymer Upper School
HMSMTH W6 ....**118** D4
Launcelot Primary School
BMLY BR1 ....**165** K6
Laurance Haines School
WATW WD18 ....**26** E1
Laurel Clinic
EA W5 ....**116** D4
Lauriston Primary School
HOM E9 ....**87** F6
Lavender Primary School
ENC/FH EN2 ....**23** K1
Lawdale Junior School
BETH E2 ....**104** C2
Lawrence Trading Estate
GNWCH SE10 ....**125** H4
Lawrence Wharf
BERM/RHTH SE16 ....**124** C1
Laycock Primary School
IS N1 ....**85** G4
Lazards Sports Club
SUN TW16 ....**172** A4
Leadenhall Market
BANK EC3V **13** G4
Lea Park Trading Estate
LEY E10 ....**69** H4
Leaside Business Centre
PEND EN3 ....**25** H3
Leathermarket Gardens
STHWK SE1 ....**19** G3
Leathersellers Sports Ground
LEE/GVPK SE12 ....**166** B2
Leathers Hall
HDTCH EC3A **13** G3
Lea Valley Primary School
TOTM N17 ....**50** C3
Lea Valley Trading Estate
UED N18 ....**36** E6
UED N18 ....**51** F2
L'Ecoles Des Petits School
FUL/PGN SW6 ....**140** A3
Lee Manor Primary School
LEW SE13 ....**165** H1
Leeside Court
BERM/RHTH SE16 ....**124** A1
Leeside Trading Estate
TOTM N17 ....**50** E3
Leesons Primary School
STMC/STPC BR5 ....**186** B6
Lee Valley Campsite
CHING E4 ....**25** K3
Lee Valley Ice Centre
LEY E10 ....**69** F6
Lee Valley Camping & Caravan Park
ED N9 ....**37** F3
Lee Valley Leisure Complex & Golf Club
ED N9 ....**37** G2
Lee Valley Watersports Centre
CHING E4 ....**51** G2
The Leigh City Technology College
DART DA1 ....**171** K3
The Leigh City Technology College (West Campus)
DART DA1 ....**171** K3
Leigh Close Industrial Estate
NWMAL KT3 ....**192** A1
Leighton House Museum
WKENS W14 ....**119** J3
Lemuel Findlay Supplementary School
SEVS/STOTM N15 ....**68** B1
Lena Gardens Primary School
HMSMTH W6 ....**119** F3
Leo Baeck College Centre for Jewish Education
FNCH N3 ....**46** E5
Leopold Primary School
WLSDN NW10 ....**81** H5
Leopold Street Clinic
BOW E3 ....**105** H4
Lesnes Abbey
BELV DA17 ....**128** E4
Lesnes Abbey (remains of)
ABYW SE2 ....**128** C6
Lessness Heath Primary School
BELV DA17 ....**129** H5

Lewin Mead Community
Mental Health Centre
STRHM/NOR SW16 ......179 J2
Lewis Clinic
CAR SM5 ......210 A2
Lewisham Bridge Primary
School
LEW SE13 ......144 A4
Lewisham Business Centre
NWCR SE14 ......124 A6
Lewisham Centre
LEW SE13 ......145 F4
Lewisham College
DEPT SE8 ......144 D2
Lewisham Coroners Office
LEW SE13 ......144 E6
Lewisham Crematorium
CAT SE6 ......165 J4
Lewisham Lions Centre
BERM/RHTH SE16 ......123 K5
Lewisham Police Station
LEW SE13 ......145 F4
The Leys Primary School
DAGE RM10 ......92 E5
Leyton Business Centre
LEY E10 ......69 H6
Leyton Cross
RDART DA2 ......170 D4
Leyton FC
LEY E10 ......69 H5
Leyton Industrial Village
LEY E10 ......69 F4
Leyton Leisure Centre
LEY E10 ......69 K4
Leyton Orient FC
(Matchroom Stadium)
LEY E10 ......87 K1
Leytonstone School
WAN E11 ......70 C3
Leyton VI Form College
LEY E10 ......70 B3
Leyton Youth Sports Ground
LEY E10 ......69 K5
The Liberty City Clinic
SDTCH EC2A 7 G6
Liberty II Centre
ROM RM1 ......75 G1
Liberty Middle School
MTCM CR4 ......178 D5
The Liberty
ROM RM1 ......75 G2
Library & Community
Centre
BTSEA SW11 ......140 C4
Lilian Baylis Technology
School
LBTH SE11 ......122 A5
Lilian Baylis School
LBTH SE11 ......17 H7
VX/NE SW8 ......121 K6
Lilian Baylis Theatre
CLKNW EC1R 6 A4
Lilian Bishop School of
English
SKENS SW7 ......14 A6
Limehouse Hole Stairs
BERM/RHTH SE16 ......124 C1
Limes Farm Primary School
CHIG IG7 ......54 D2
Lime Trees Park Golf Club
NTHLT UB5 ......77 G6
Lincoln Road Clinic
EN EN1 ......24 C6
Lincoln's Inn
LINN WC2A 11 H3
Linden Bridge School
WPK KT4 ......207 G1
Linden Lodge School
WIM/MER SW19 ......159 H3
Lindon Bennett School
FELT TW13 ......172 C1
Linford Christie Stadium
SHB W12 ......99 J4
The Link Day Primary School
CROY/NA CR0 ......210 E2
The Link Secondary School
CROY/NA CR0 ......211 F2
Links Primary School
TOOT SW17 ......179 F2
Linley House School
BRYLDS KT5 ......191 G5
Linley Sambourne House
WKENS W14 ......119 J2
Linnet House Clinic
STJWD NW8 ......2 C3
Linton Mead Primary
School
THMD SE28 ......109 H6
Lionel Road Primary School
BTFD TW8 ......117 F4
Liongate Hotel
E/WMO/HCT KT8 ......174 A6
Lion House School
PUT/ROE SW15 ......139 G5
Lismarrine Industrial Park
BORE WD6 ......29 H1
Lisson Grove Health Centre
STJWD NW8 ......2 C6
Lister Community School
PLSTW E13 ......107 F1
The Lister Hospital
BGVA SW1W 121 G5
Lister House Clinic
CAVSQ/HST W1G 9 J3
Little Danson Welfare Clinic
WELL DA16 ......148 B5
Little Eden & Eden High
School
FELT TW13 ......154 C6
Little Hands Theatre
HDN NW4 ......64 A1
Little Heath School
CHDH RM6 ......73 H1
Little Ilford School
MNPK E12 ......89 K3
Little St Helens School
NTHWD HA6 ......40 C2

Little Stanmore First &
Middle School
EDGW HA8 ......44 A4
Little Wandsworth School
TOOT SW17 ......161 F4
Livesey Museum for Children
PECK SE15 ......123 J6
Livingstone Hospital
DART DA1 ......171 J2
Livingstone Primary School
EBAR EN4 ......21 H4
The Livity School
BRXS/STRHM SW2 ......141 K6
Lloyd Park Centre
WALTH E17 ......51 J5
Lloyd's
FENCHST EC3M 13 G4
Lloyds Register CC
DUL SE21 ......162 E3
Locks View Court
POP/IOD E14 ......105 G6
Lockwood Industrial Park
TOTM N17 ......50 D6
Lombard Business Centre
SYD SE26 ......140 C3
Lombard Business Park
WAND/EARL SW18 ......196 A4
WIM/MER SW19 ......160 C1
Lombard Trading Estate
CHARL SE7 ......178 B5
Lombardy Retail Park
HYS/HAR UB3 ......126 A4
London Academy
EDGW HA8 ......95 F5
London Academy of Music
& Dramatic Art
KENS W8 ......30 B6
London Aquarium
WHALL SW1A 119 K4
London Area Terminal
Control Centre
WDR/YW UB7 ......112 C2
London Arena
POP/IOD E14 ......124 E5
London Bridge City Pier
STHWK SE1 ......13 G1
London Bridge Hospital
STHWK SE1 ......13 F7
London Bridge Hotel
STHWK SE1 ......18 E1
London Bridge Sports Centre
CANST EC4R 12 E6
London Business School
CAMTN NW1 ......2 E6
The London Canal Museum
IS N1 ......5 F2
London Capital College
CAMTN NW1 ......4 E7
London Chest Hospital
BETH E2 ......104 E1
London City Airport
CAN/RD E16 ......126 D1
London City College (English
Language Institute) &
Schiller International
University STHWK SE1 ......17 H1
London City Mission
STHWK SE1 ......19 H2
The London Clinic
CAVSQ/HST W1G 3 H7
London College of Business
& Computer Services
CLAP SW4 ......141 J5
London College of Business
& Computing
BETH E2 ......104 D1
London College of
Communication
LBTH SE11 ......18 B5
London College of Fashion
CAVSQ/HST W1G 9 K3
MYFR/PKLN W1K 9 H3
SDTCH EC2A 7 H6
London College of Further
Education
LBTH SE11 ......18 A7
London College of Higher
Education
CLAP SW4 ......141 G4
London College of
International Business
Studies HHOL WC1V 11 F2
The London College
KENS W8 ......119 K1
London Commodity Exchange
WAP E1W 13 K6
London Cornish RFC
PUT/ROE SW15 ......158 C5
London Dungeon
STHWK SE1 ......13 F7
London Electronics College
ECT SW5 ......119 K5
London Esthetique
CAVSQ/HST W1G 9 K3
London Eye
STHWK SE1 ......17 G2
London Eye Clinic
CAVSQ/HST W1G 9 J2
London Fields Primary School
HACK E8 ......86 D6
London Foot Hospital
FITZ W1T 4 A7
London Gender Clinic
HDN NW4 ......63 K3
London Glass Blowing
Workshop
STHWK SE1 ......19 G3
London Group Business Park
CRICK NW2 ......63 H5
London Guildhall University
TWRH EC3N 13 J5
London Guildhall University
Sports Ground
LEE/GVPK SE12 ......166 B4
London Heart Clinic
CAVSQ/HST W1G 9 J2

The London Industrial Estate
EHAM E6 ......108 A4
London Industrial Park
EHAM E6 ......108 B4
London International Film
School
LSQ/SEVD WC2H 10 E4
The London Irish Youth
Theatre
HGT N6 ......66 B5
London Islamic School /
Madrasah
WCHPL E1 ......104 D5
London IT College
GNTH/NBYPK IG2 ......72 A3
London Jewish Girls High
School
HDN NW4 ......64 A2
London Ladies & Girls FC
CAT SE6 ......182 E1
London Lane Clinic
BMLY BR1 ......183 J3
London Lighthouse
NTGHL W11 ......100 C5
London Living Theatre
SYD SE26 ......164 A6
London Marriott Hotel
HAMP NW3 ......83 J5
MYFR/PKLN W1K 9 H5
STHWK SE1 ......17 G2
London Marriott Hotel
Park Lane
OXSTW W1C 9 G3
London Marriott West India
Quay Hotel
POP/IOD E14 ......105 J6
London Metropolitan
University
HBRY N5 ......85 J3
HOLWY N7 ......85 F2
HOLWY N7 ......85 F2
LVPST EC2M 13 J2
WCHPL E1 ......13 J3
WCHPL E1 ......104 C5
London Nautical School
STHWK SE1 ......11 K7
London Open College
FSBYE EC1V 6 B4
London Oratory School
FUL/PGN SW6 ......139 K1
London Road Medical Centre
CROY/NA CR0 ......196 B3
London School of Economics
CLKNW EC1R 5 K5
HHOL WC1V 10 E3
HOL/ALD WC2B 11 G4
STHWK SE1 ......12 C7
London School of Hygiene &
Tropical Medicine
GWRST WC1E 10 D1
London School of Theology
NTHWD HA6 ......40 B2
London Scottish Golf Club
WIM/MER SW19 ......158 E5
London Silver Vaults
LINN WC2A 11 J2
The London Television Centre
(LWT)
STHWK SE1 ......11 J7
London Tourist Board &
Convention Centre
BGVA SW1W 15 J4
London Toy & Model Museum
BAY/PAD W2 ......101 G6
London Transport Bus Depot
BXLYHN DA7 ......149 J4
London Underwriting Centre
MON EC3R 13 G5
London Weather Centre
HCIRC EC1N 11 J1
The London Welbeck Hospital
CAVSQ/HST W1G 9 H2
London Welsh FC
RCH/KEW TW9 ......137 F4
London Welsh School
CRICK NW2 ......82 A4
London West Crematorium
WLSDN NW10 ......99 K3
London Wetland Centre
BARN SW13 ......138 E2
London Zoo
CAMTN NW1 ......3 G2
Lonesome Primary School
MTCM CR4 ......179 G5
Long Ditton County Infant
School
SURB KT6 ......190 D5
Longfield Primary School
RYLN/HDSTN HA2 ......60 A3
Longford Community School
EBED/NFELT TW14 ......153 J2
Longford Industrial Estate
HPTN TW12 ......173 G2
Longlands Primary School
BFN/LL DA15 ......167 K5
Long Lane AFC
BKHTH/KID SE3 ......146 B3
Longmead Primary School
WDR/YW UB7 ......112 A4
Longshaw Primary School
CHING E4 ......38 B5
Lord Chancellors Department
WEST SW1P 16 D5
Lord Lister Health Centre
FSTGT E7 ......88 E2
Lordship Lane Clinic
TOTM N17 ......50 A5
Lordship Lane Primary
School
WDGN N22 ......49 J4
Lord's Tour & MCC Museum
STJWD NW8 ......2 A5
Lorimar Business Centre
RAIN RM13 ......111 G5
Loughborough Primary
School
CMBW SE5 ......142 D2

Lovelace Primary School
CHSGTN KT9 ......205 J3
Lovell's Wharf
GNWCH SE10 ......125 G5
Lower Clapton Health
Centre
CLPT E5 ......86 E2
Lower Place Business Centre
WLSDN NW10 ......98 E1
Lower Sydenham Industrial
Estate
SYD SE26 ......182 C1
Lowfield Medical Centre
DART DA1 ......171 H2
Lowther Primary School
LEY E10 ......69 F5
Lowther Primary School
BARN SW13 ......118 D6
Loxford School of Science &
Technology
IL IG1 ......90 D3
Loyola Preparatory School
BKHH IG9 ......39 G3
LPR Sports Club
BARK/HLT IG6 ......55 F4
LSE Sports Club
NWMAL KT3 ......192 A3
LT Lost Property Office
CAMTN NW1 ......3 F7
Lubavitch House School
(Senior Girls)
STNW/STAM N16 ......68 B3
Lucas Vale Primary School
DEPT SE8 ......144 D2
Lutomer House Business
Centre
POP/IOD E14 ......124 E1
Lux Cinema
IS N1 ......7 G3
Lycee Francais
SKENS SW7 ......14 A6
Lycee Francais
Charles De Gaulle
BTSEA SW11 ......141 G5
The Lyceum Theatre
COVGDN WC2E 11 G5
Lyndean Industrial Estate
ABYW SE2 ......128 D3
Lyndhurst House Preparatory
School
HAMP NW3 ......83 H3
Lyndhurst Primary School
CMBW SE5 ......142 E3
Lyon Business Park
BARK IG11 ......108 E1
Lyon Park J & I School
ALP/SUD HA0 ......80 B5
Lyonsdown School
BAR EN5 ......21 G6
Lyric Theatre
SOHO/SHAV W1D 10 C5
Lyric Theatre Hammersmith
HMSMTH W6 ......119 F4
Mabwin Supplementary
School
ED N9 ......36 D4
Macaulay CE Primary School
CLAP SW4 ......141 G5
Madame Tussauds & The
London Auditorium
CAMTN NW1 ......3 F7
Madeira Grove Clinic
WFD IG8 ......53 F1
Madison Bowl
NTHWD HA6 ......40 C3
Madni Girls School
WCHPL E1 ......104 D5
Madrasah-E-Darul Qirat
Majidiah School
WCHPL E1 ......104 D6
Mahatma Gandhi Industrial
Estate
BRXN/ST SW9 ......142 C4
Maida Vale Medical Centre
MV/WKIL W9 ......101 F2
Malcolm Primary School
PGE/AN SE20 ......181 K3
The Malden Centre
NWMAL KT3 ......192 C4
Malden Golf Club
NWMAL KT3 ......176 B5
Malden Manor Primary
School
NWMAL KT3 ......192 B4
Malden Parochial Primary
School
WPK KT4 ......192 B5
Malden Road Baths
CHEAM SM3 ......208 B2
Malham Road Industrial
Estate
FSTH SE23 ......164 A3
Mall Galleries
STJS SW1Y 10 D7
The Mall School
WHTN TW2 ......155 J5
Malmaison Charterhouse
Square Hotel
FARR EC1M 12 B1
Malmesbury Primary School
MRDN SM4 ......194 B4
Malorees J & I School
KIL/WHAMP NW6 ......82 B5
Malory School
BMLY BR1 ......165 K6
Mandarin Oriental Hotel
KTBR SW1X 15 G2
The Mandeville Hotel
MHST W1U 9 H3
Mandeville Primary School
CLPT E5 ......87 G1
Mandeville Special School
NTHLT UB5 ......77 K4
Manford Industrial Estate
ERITH DA8 ......130 E6
Manford Way Health Centre
BARK/HLT IG6 ......55 G2

Manor Brook Medical Centre
BKHTH/KID SE3 ......146 A3
Manor Drive Health Centre
WPK KT4 ......192 C5
Manorfield Primary School
POP/IOD E14 ......105 K4
Manor Infant School
BARK IG11 ......91 F4
Manor Oak Primary School
STMC/STPC BR5 ......202 E2
Manor Park Cemetery
FSTGT E7 ......89 H2
Manor Park Crematorium
MNPK E12 ......89 J2
Manor Park Methodist School
SUT SM1 ......209 G3
Manor Primary School
SRTFD E15 ......106 C1
The Manor Primary School
ROM RM7 ......75 H2
Manorside Primary School
FNCH N3 ......47 F4
Manor Special School
WLSDN NW10 ......100 B1
Manor Way Business Centre
RAIN RM13 ......111 F4
Mansion House
MANHO EC4N 12 E4
Mapledown School
CRICK NW2 ......64 B4
Maple Grove Business Centre
HSLWW TW4 ......134 B5
Maple House School
MNPK E12 ......89 J2
Maple Industrial Estate
FELT TW13 ......153 K4
Maple Infant School
SURB KT6 ......190 E2
Maples Business Centre
IS N1 ......85 G5
Marble Arch
MBLAR W1H 9 F5
Marble Hill House
TWK TW1 ......156 D2
Maria Fidelis Convent
Lower School
CAMTN NW1 ......4 B5
Maria Fidelis Convent
Upper School
CAMTN NW1 ......4 C4
Maria Montessori Childrens
House
HAMP NW3 ......83 H3
Mariner Business Centre
CROY/NA CR0 ......211 F3
Marion Richardson Primary
School
WCHPL E1 ......105 F5
Marion Vian Primary School
BECK BR3 ......198 A2
Maritime Greenwich College
DEPT SE8 ......144 D1
Maritime Industrial Estate
CHARL SE7 ......126 A4
Maritime Museum
GNWCH SE10 ......125 H4
Marjorie McClure School
CHST BR7 ......185 H4
The Marjory Kinnon School
EBED/NFELT TW14 ......133 H6
Market Trading Estate
NWDGN UB2 ......114 A4
Marks Gate Junior School
CHDH RM6 ......56 A6
Marlborough CC
DUL SE21 ......163 H5
Marlborough Day Hospital
STJWD NW8 ......101 G2
Marlborough First & Middle
School
HRW HA1 ......60 D1
Marlborough House
STJS SW1Y 16 B1
Marlborough Primary School
CHEL SW3 ......14 D7
ISLW TW7 ......136 B2
Marlborough Trading Estate
BFN/LL DA15 ......168 B3
RCH/KEW TW9 ......137 J2
Marlowe Business Centre
NWCR SE14 ......144 B1
Marner Primary School
BOW E3 ......105 K3
Marriott Hotel
ECT SW5 ......120 A4
KIL/WHAMP NW6 ......101 F1
HYS/HAR UB3 ......133 G2
MBLAR W1H 8 D3
Marshalls Park School
ROM RM1 ......57 G5
Marshall Street Leisure Centre
SOHO/CST W1F 10 B4
Marsh Gate Business Centre
SRTFD E15 ......106 A1
Marshgate Primary School
RCHPK/HAM TW10 ......137 G6
Marshgate Trading Estate
SRTFD E15 ......87 K5
Marsh Green School
DAGW RM9 ......110 C1
Martan College
HOL/ALD WC2B 11 F3
Martinbridge Industrial Estate
EN EN1 ......24 C6
Martindale Industrial Estate
EN EN1 ......24 A6
Martin Infant School
EFNCH N2 ......47 J6
Marvels Lane Primary School
LEE/GVPK SE12 ......166 B6
Mary Boone School
WKENS W14 ......119 H4
Maryland Industrial Estate
SRTFD E15 ......88 C3

Maryland Primary School
SRTFD E15 ....88 C3
Marylebone Health Centre
CAMTN NW1 ....3 H7
Marylebone Magistrates Court
CAMTN NW1 ....8 D1
Marymount International
School
KUTN/CMB KT2 ....175 K3
Mary Wallace Theatre
TWK TW1 ....156 B3
Maswell Business Centre
HSLW TW3 ....135 H6
Matilda Marks Kennedy
Primary
MLHL NW7 ....45 H1
Matrix Business Centre
DART DA1 ....151 K6
Maudlin's Green
WAP E1W 13 K7
The Maudsley Hospital
CMBW SE5 ....142 E3
Maughan Library
Kings College)
LINN WC2A 11 J3
Mawbrey Brough Health
Centre
VX/NE SW8 ....141 K1
The Mawney School
ROMW/RG RM7 ....75 F2
Mayday University
Hospital
THHTH CR7 ....196 C3
Mayesbrook Park Arena
BARK IG11 ....91 G5
Mayespark Primary School
GDMY/SEVK IG3 ....91 G1
Mayfield Primary School
HNWL W7 ....96 D5
Mayfield School
PIN HA5 ....41 J6
Mayflower Primary School
POP/IOD E14 ....105 K3
Mayplace Primary School
BXLYHN DA7 ....150 A5
Maypole Primary School
RDART DA2 ....170 B5
Maytime School
IL IG1 ....90 A1
Mayville J & P School
WAN E11 ....88 C1
McEntee School
WALTH E17 ....51 H4
McKay Trading Estate
NKENS W10 ....100 C3
McMillan Clinic
HYS/HAR UB3 ....94 A6
The Mead Infant School
WPK KT4 ....207 H1
Meadlands Primary School
RCHPK/HAM TW10 ....156 D6
Meadowgate School
BROCKY SE4 ....144 A4
Meadowside Leisure Centre
BKHTH/KID SE3 ....146 B5
The Meadow Special
School
STMC/STPC BR5 ....186 B5
Mead Road Infant School
CHST BR7 ....185 H2
The Medical Centre
WAND/EARL SW18 ....160 A1
Medical Express Clinic
CAVSQ/HST W1G 9 J1
Mednurs Clinic
SEVS/STOTM N15 ....67 K3
Megabowl
KUTN/CMB KT2 ....175 F5
Melcombe Primary School
HMSMTH W6 ....119 G6
Meli-white House Hotel
CAMTN NW1 ....3 K6
Mellish Industrial Estate
WOOL/PLUM SE18 ....126 C3
Mellow Lane School
HGDN/ICK UB10 ....94 A3
Melrose Special School
MTCM CR4 ....178 D6
Memorial Hospital
WOOL/PLUM SE18 ....147 F3
The Menorah Foundation
School
EDGW HA8 ....44 E3
Menorah Grammar School
GLDGN NW11 ....64 C4
Menorah Primary School
GLDGN NW11 ....64 C4
Mercers' Hall
CITYW EC2Y 12 D4
The Merchant Taylors Hall
BANK EC3V 13 F4
Merchant Taylors School
NTHWD HA6 ....26 C3
Mercure London City
Bankside Hotel
STHWK SE1 ....18 C1
Meridian Clinic
BRXN/ST SW9 ....142 A4
Meridian Locality Mental
Health Centre
CHARL SE7 ....126 B6
Meridian Primary School
GNWCH SE10 ....125 G5
Meridian Sports Club
CHARL SE7 ....146 D1
Merlin Primary School
BMLY BR1 ....165 K5
Merlin School
PUT/ROE SW15 ....139 G6
Mermaid Theatre
BLKFR EC4V 12 B5
Merrielands Retail Park
DAGW RM9 ....92 B6
Merry Hill Infant School
BUSH WD23 ....28 B2

Merryhills Clinic
ENC/FH EN2 ....23 F4
Merryhills Primary School
ENC/FH EN2 ....23 F5
Merton Abbey Primary
School
WIM/MER SW19 ....178 A4
Merton Adult College
RYNPK SW20 ....177 H6
Merton College
MRDN SM4 ....193 J3
Merton Court Preparatory
School
SCUP DA14 ....168 D6
Merton Industrial Park
WIM/MER SW19 ....178 B4
Merton Park Primary School
WIM/MER SW19 ....177 J5
Merton Road Industrial
Estate
WAND/EARL SW18 ....159 K2
Metro Business Centre
SYD SE26 ....182 C2
The Metro Golf Centre
HDN NW4 ....46 A4
Metro Industrial Centre
ISLW TW7 ....135 K3
Metropolitan Business Centre
IS N1 ....86 A5
Metropolitan Hospital
STHWK SE1 ....17 K4
The Metropolitan Hotel
MYFR/PKLN W1K 15 J1
Metropolitan Police Hayes
Sports Club
HAYES BR2 ....199 J6
Metropolitan Police Training
School; Hendon
CDALE/KGS NW9 ....45 H6
Metropolitan Tabernacle
STHWK SE1 ....18 B6
Metro Trading Centre
WBLY HA9 ....80 D2
Michael Faraday Primary
School
WALW SE17 ....122 E5
Michael Manley Industrial
Estate
VX/NE SW8 ....141 H2
Michael Sobell Sinai School
KTN/HRWW/WS HA3 ......62 C3
The Michael Tippett School
LBTH SE11 ....17 K7
Midas Business Centre
DAGE RM10 ....92 C2
Midas Industrial Estate
DAGE RM10 ....92 C2
Middle Park Primary School
ELTH/MOT SE9 ....166 C2
Middle Row Primary School
NKENS W10 ....100 C3
Middlesex Business Centre
NWDGN UB2 ....115 F2
Middlesex CCC
(Lord's Cricket Ground)
STJWD NW8 ....2 B4
Middlesex Guildhall
STJSPK SW1H 16 D3
Middlesex Hospital Medical
School
FITZ W1T 10 B1
Middlesex Hospital Nurses
Home
GTPST W1W 10 A1
Middlesex Hospital School of
Physiotherapy
FITZ W1T 10 B1
Middlesex Hospital Sports
Ground
CHST BR7 ....186 A1
Middlesex School of
Complementary Medicine
STAN HA7 ....44 A4
Middlesex University
ARCH N19 ....66 C5
EBAR EN4 ....34 A1
GLDGN NW11 ....65 F5
HDN NW4 ....63 K1
PEND EN3 ....25 F6
STNGT/OAK N14 ....22 C5
WDGN N22 ....48 E5
Middlesex University
(Enfield Campus)
PEND EN3 ....24 D6
Middlesex University
Museum
EBAR EN4 ....22 A6
Middlesex University
(Trent Park Campus)
EBAR EN4 ....22 C3
Midfield Primary School
STMC/STPC BR5 ....186 B3
Midway Mission Hospital
BETH E2 ....7 J5
Milbourne Lodge Junior
School
ESH/CLAY KT10 ....204 C3
Milbourne Lodge School
ESH/CLAY KT10 ....204 D4
Mile End & Bow Business
Centre
WCHPL E1 ....104 D4
Mile End Hospital
WCHPL E1 ....105 F2
Mile End Stadium
POP/IOD E14 ....105 H4
Milehams Industrial Estate
PUR RM19 ....131 K3
Miles Coverdale Primary
School
SHB W12 ....119 F2
Milestone Hotel
KENS W8 ....120 A2
Millbank Millennium Pier
WEST SW1P 16 E7
Millbank Primary School
WEST SW1P 16 D7

Millbank Tower
WEST SW1P 16 E7
Millennium Arena
BTSEA SW11 ....141 F1
Millennium Bailey's Hotel
SKENS SW7 ....120 B4
Millennium Balloon
STHWK SE1 ....19 H1
Millennium Gloucester Hotel
ECT SW5 ....120 A4
Millennium Harbour
POP/IOD E14 ....124 C2
Millennium Hotel
KTBR SW1X 15 F3
Millennium Hotel London
Mayfair
MYFR/PKLN W1K 9 H6
The Millennium Primary
School
GNWCH SE10 ....125 J3
Millennium Quay
DEPT SE8 ....124 E6
Millennium Wharf
POP/IOD E14 ....124 C3
Mill Farm Business Park
HSLWW TW4 ....154 D2
Millfields J & I School
CLPT E5 ....86 E2
Millfield Theatre
UED N18 ....35 K6
Mill Green Business Park
MTCM CR4 ....194 E4
Mill Hill Cemetery
MLHL NW7 ....46 A2
Mill Hill County High
School
MLHL NW7 ....31 G4
The Mill Hill CC
MLHL NW7 ....32 A5
Mill Hill Golf Club
MLHL NW7 ....31 G4
Mill Hill Industrial Estate
MLHL NW7 ....45 H2
Mill Hill School
MLHL NW7 ....31 K6
Mill Lane Medical Centre
KIL/WHAMP NW6 ....82 E3
Mill Lane Trading Estate
CROY/NA CRO 211 F1
Mill River Trading Estate
PEND EN3 ....25 G5
Millside Industrial Estate
DART DA1 ....151 G5
Mill Street Clinic
STHWK SE1 ....19 K2
Mill Trading Estate
WLSDN NW10 ....98 D1
The Mill Trading Estate
WLSDN NW10 ....98 E2
Millwall FC (The New Den)
BERM/RHTH SE16 ....123 K5
Milmead Industrial Centre
TOTM N17 ....50 D5
Milton Natural Health Centre
HGT N6 ....66 C4
Minet Clinic
HYS/HAR UB3 ....113 K1
Minet J & I School
HYS/HAR UB3 ....114 A1
Ministry of Defence
WHALL SW1A 16 E1
Mint Business Park
CAN/RD E16 ....106 E4
Mirravale Trading Estate
CHDH RM6 ....74 A4
Mission Grove Primary
School
WALTH E17 ....69 H2
Mitcham CC
MTCM CR4 ....194 D1
Mitcham Golf Club
MTCM CR4 ....195 F2
Mitcham Industrial Estate
MTCM CR4 ....179 F4
Mitcham Vale High School
MTCM CR4 ....179 G5
Mitchell Brook Primary
School
WLSDN NW10 ....81 F4
Mitre Bridge Industrial Park
NKENS W10 ....99 K3
Mitre House Hotel
BAY/PAD W2 ....8 A1
Moatbridge School
ELTH/MOT SE9 ....166 C1
The Moat School
FUL/PGN SW6 ....139 H3
Moberly Sports & Education
Centre
WLSDN NW10 ....100 B2
Molesey Hospital
E/WMO/HCT KT8 ....189 F2
Mollison Drive Health Centre
WLGTN SM6 ....210 E5
Monega Primary School
MNPK E12 ....89 H5
Monken Hadley CE Primary
School
BAR EN5 ....20 E2
Monkfrith Primary School
EBAR EN4 ....34 A2
Monks Hill Sports Centre
SAND/SEL CR2 ....213 G5
Monks Orchard Primary
School
CROY/NA CRO 198 A2
Monson Primary School
NWCR SE14 ....144 A1
The Montague on the
Gardens Hotel
RSQ WC1B 10 E1
Montbelle Primary School
ELTH/MOT SE9 ....167 F6
Montcalm-Hotel Nikko
MBLAR W1H 9 F4
Monteagle Primary School
DAGW RM9 ....91 H6

Montem Primary School
HOLWY N7 ....85 F1
Montpelier Primary School
EA W5 ....97 K4
The Monument
CANST EC4R 13 F5
Moore Place Golf Club
ESH/CLAY KT10 ....204 A3
Moorfields Eye Hospital
FSBYE EC1V 6 E5
Moor Lane Junior School
CHSGTN KT9 ....206 B3
Moor Park Industrial Estate
WATW WD18 ....26 A2
Mora Primary School
CRICK NW2 ....82 A2
Morden Cemetery
MRDN SM4 ....193 F3
Morden College Homes
BKHTH/KID SE3 ....145 K3
Morden First School
MRDN SM4 ....193 J4
Morden Hall Medical
Centre
WIM/MER SW19 ....178 A6
Morden Hall Park (NT)
MRDN SM4 ....194 A1
Morden Mount Primary
School
LEW SE13 ....144 E3
Morden Park Pool
MRDN SM4 ....193 J2
Morden Road Clinic
WIM/MER SW19 ....178 A6
More House School
KTBR SW1X 15 F5
Moreland Primary School
FSBYE EC1V 6 B4
Moriah Jewish Day School
MLHL NW7 ....59 J5
Morley College
STHWK SE1 ....17 K4
Morningside Primary School
HOM E9 ....86 E4
Mornington Sports &
Fitness Centre
CAMTN NW1 ....84 B6
Morpeth School
BETH E2 ....104 E2
Mortimer Road Clinic
WLSDN NW10 ....100 A2
Mortimer School
STRHM/NOR SW16 ....161 J4
Mortlake Cemetery
MORT/ESHN SW14 ....138 B4
Mortlake Crematorium
RCH/KEW TW9 ....137 J3
Moselle School
TOTM N17 ....50 A5
Mosian Foundation
Supplementary School
STNW/STAM N16 ....68 A3
Mossbourne Community
Academy
HACK E8 ....86 C2
Mossford Green Primary
School
BARK/HLT IG6 ....54 C5
Moss Hall Primary School
FNCH N3 ....47 F2
The Mother & Baby Clinic
HOM E9 ....86 E2
Mottingham Community
Health Clinic
ELTH/MOT SE9 ....166 D6
Mottingham Primary School
ELTH/MOT SE9 ....166 C5
Mount Carmel RC Primary
School
EA W5 ....116 D3
Mount Carmel RC Technology
College for Girls
ARCH N19 ....66 D5
The Mount Infant School
NWMAL KT3 ....175 J6
Mount Medical Centre
FELT TW13 ....154 D2
Mount School
MLHL NW7 ....45 K1
Mount Stewart Primary School
KTN/HRWW/WS HA3 ......61 K3
Mowlem Primary School
BETH E2 ....104 E1
Mowlem Trading Estate
TOTM N17 ....50 E3
MPR Eurotots School
KIL/WHAMP NW6 ....82 B5
MS Business Centre
PIN HA5 ....41 H6
MSP Business Centre
WBLY HA9 ....80 D2
Muchute City Farm
POP/IOD E14 ....125 F4
Mudlands Estate
RAIN RM13 ....111 G2
Mulberry Business Centre
BERM/RHTH SE16 ....124 A2
Mulberry House School
CRICK NW2 ....82 C3
Mulberry Primary School
TOTM N17 ....50 D5
Mulberry School for Girls
WCHPL E1 ....104 D5
Mulgrave Primary School
WOOL/PLUM SE18 ....127 F4
Munroe Centre
STHWK SE1 ....19 J2
Murky Puddle Theatre
NWMAL KT3 ....176 C6
Murray Business Centre
STMC/STPC BR5 ....186 C6
Muschamp Primary School
CAR SM5 ....194 D6
Museum in Docklands
POP/IOD E14 ....105 J6
Museum of Fulham Palace
FUL/PGN SW6 ....139 G3

Museum of Garden History
STHWK SE1 ....17 F5
Museum of London
BARB EC2Y 12 C2
Museum of London
(Archaeological Research
Centre) IS N1 ....6 D1
Museum of Richmond
TWK TW1 ....136 E6
Museum of Rugby &
Twickenham Stadium
Tours WHTN TW2 ....155 K1
Museum of the Artillery in
the Rotunda
CHARL SE7 ....126 D5
Museum of the Order of
St John
FARR EC1M 6 B7
Musical Museum
BTFD TW8 ....117 F6
Muswell Hill Bowling Club
MUSWH N10 ....48 A6
Muswell Hill Golf Club
MUSWH N10 ....48 B4
Muswell Hill Primary
School
MUSWH N10 ....48 B6
Myatt Garden Primary
School
BROCKY SE4 ....144 C3
Myatts Field Clinic
BRXN/ST SW9 ....142 C3
N1 Shopping Centre
IS N1 ....5 K2
Nagi Business Centre
ALP/SUD HA0 ....97 K1
Nags Head Shopping Centre
HOLWY N7 ....84 E1
Naima Jewish Preparatory
School
KIL/WHAMP NW6 ....101 F1
Nash College of Further
Education
WWKM BR4 ....214 D1
The National Archives
RCH/KEW TW9 ....137 J1
National Army Museum
CHEL SW3 ....120 E6
National Film Theatre
IS N1 ....11 H7
National Gallery
LSQ/SEVD WC2H 10 D6
National Hospital for
Neurology & Neurosurgery
RSQ WC1B 4 E7
National Hospital for Sick
Children (Great Ormond
Street) BMSBY WC1N 5 F7
National Maritime Museum
GNWCH SE10 ....125 G6
National Physical
Laboratory
TEDD TW11 ....173 K2
National Portrait Gallery
LSQ/SEVD WC2H 10 D6
National Sports Centre
NRWD SE19 ....181 H2
National Temperance
Hospital
CAMTN NW1 ....4 A4
National Youth Theatre of
Great Britain
HOLWY N7 ....84 E1
Natural History Museum
SKENS SW7 ....14 A5
Natural Therapy Clinic
TOOT SW17 ....179 G1
Natwest Sports Club
BECK BR3 ....182 C2
Navigation College
CANST EC4R 12 D5
NEC Harlequins RFC
(Twickenham Stoop
Stadium) WHTN TW2 .....155 K2
Negus Sixth Form Centre
WOOL/PLUM SE18 ....127 J6
Nelson Dock Museum
BERM/RHTH SE16 ....124 C1
Nelson Hospital
RYNPK SW20 ....177 J5
Nelson Primary School
EHAM E6 ....108 A1
WHTN TW2 ....155 C1
Nelson's Column
STJS SW1Y 10 D7
Nelson Trading Estate
WIM/MER SW19 ....178 A4
Neo Clinic
PIM SW1V 16 A6
The New Ambassadors
Theatre
LSQ/SEVD WC2H 10 D4
New Atlas Wharf
POP/IOD E14 ....124 C3
The New Aylesbury Medical
Centre
WALW SE17 ....122 E5
New Brentford Cemetery
HSLW TW3 ....134 C3
Newbury Park Health Centre
GNTH/NBYPK IG2 ....72 D3
The New Business Centre
WLSDN NW10 ....99 H2
New Caledonian Wharf
BERM/RHTH SE16 ....124 C3
New Chiswick Pool
CHSWK W4 ....138 C1
New City Primary School
PLSTW E13 ....107 G2
New Connaught Rooms
HOL/ALD WC2B 11 F3
New Covent Garden Market
VX/NE SW8 ....141 J1
New Crane Wharf
WAP E1W 123 K1
New Cross Sports Arena
NWCR SE14 ....144 B1

New End Primary School
HAMP NW3 ....83 C2
New End Theatre
HAMP NW3 ....83 G1
New England Industrial Estate
BARK IC11 ....108 C1
Newfield Primary School
WLSDN NW10 ....81 H5
Newham College of Further Education
EHAM E6 ....107 K1
SRTFD E15 ....88 C5
Newham General Hospital
PLSTW E13 ....107 G1
Newham Leisure Centre
PLSTW E13 ....107 G4
Newham Medical Centre
PLSTW E13 ....107 G1
Newham Sixth Form College
PLSTW E13 ....107 H5
Newham Training & Education Centre
SRTFD E15 ....88 C4
New Health Centre
TOTM N17 ....50 A4
Newington Court Business Centre
STHWK SE1 ....18 C5
Newington Green Primary School
STNW/STAM N16 ....86 A3
Newington Industrial Estate
WALW SE17 ....18 B7
New Kings Primary School
FUL/PGN SW6 ....139 J3
Newland House School
TWK TW1 ....156 A6
New London Theatre
LSQ/SEVD WC2 ....11 F3
Newnham J & I School
RSLP HA4 ....59 G5
New North Community School
IS N1 ....85 J5
Newport J & I School
LEY E10 ....70 A6
New River Sports Centre
WDGN N22 ....49 H3
New River Village
CEND/HSY/T N8 ....49 F6
New Rush Hall School
IL IG1 ....72 C6
New School
FUL/PGN SW6 ....139 J2
New Scotland Yard
STJSPK SW1H 16 C4
News International
WAP E1W 104 D6
New Southgate Cemetery
FBAR/BDGN N11 ....34 B5
New Southgate Crematorium
FBAR/BDGN N11 ....34 B5
New Southgate Industrial Estate
FBAR/BDGN N11 ....48 C1
New Southgate Pain Clinic & Medical Centre
FBAR/BDGN N11 ....48 C1
New Spitalfields Market
LEY E10 ....87 J2
Newstead Wood School for Girls
ORP BR6 ....216 D1
Newton Farm First & Middle School
RYLN/HDSTN HA2 ....59 K6
Newton Industrial Estate
CHDH RM6 ....73 K1
Newton Medical Centre
BAY/PAD W2 ....101 F5
Newton Preparatory School
VX/NE SW8 ....141 G1
Newtons Primary School
RAIN RM13 ....111 F1
New Victoria Hospital
KUTN/CMB KT2 ....176 B4
New Woodlands School
BMLY BR1 ....165 H6
Nightingale Clinic
PLSTW E13 ....107 G1
Nightingale Primary School
CLPT E5 ....86 C1
SWFD E18 ....71 G1
WDGN N22 ....49 F5
WOOL/PLUM SE18 ....127 G6
Nightingale School
TOOT SW17 ....160 D4
The Nightingale School
STHWK SE1 ....17 G3
Noam Primary School
NFNCH/WDSPK N12 ....47 F1
Noel Coward
CHCR WC2N 10 E5
Noel Park Primary School
WDGN N22 ....49 H5
No 41 Hotel
WESTW SW1E 15 K4
Nonsuch High School for Girls
CHEAM SM3 ....208 B5
Nonsuch House Hotel
EW KT17 ....208 A3
Nonsuch Primary School
EW KT17 ....207 K3
Noor Ul Islam School
LEY E10 ....70 A6
Norbury Complementary Therapy Clinic
STRHM/NOR SW16 ....180 A4
Norbury First & Middle School
HRW HA1 ....60 E2
Norbury Health Centre
STRHM/NOR SW16 ....180 A5
Norbury Manor Primary School
STRHM/NOR SW16 ....179 K4

Norbury Manor Secondary Girls School
STRHM/NOR SW16 ....180 B4
Norbury Trading Estate
STRHM/NOR SW16 ....180 A5
Norfolk House School
MUSWH N10 ....48 B5
Norland Place School
NTGHL W11 ....119 H1
Norlington School
LEY E10 ....70 B5
Normand Croft Community School
WKENS W14 ....119 J6
Normandy Primary School
BXLYHN DA7 ....150 A2
Normanhurst School
CHING E4 ....38 B2
Norman Park Athletics Track
HAYES BR2 ....200 A3
Norman Shaw Building (MP's Offices)
WHALL SW1A 16 E2
North Acton Business Park
ACT W3 ....99 F5
North Beckton Primary School
EHAM E6 ....107 K3
North Bridge House
HAMP NW3 ....83 G4
North Bridge House School
HAMP NW3 ....83 H4
North Bridge House Senior School
CAMTN NW1 ....3 J1
Northbrook CE School
LEE/GVPK SE12 ....145 H6
Northbury Primary School
BARK IG11 ....90 B4
North Clinic
BMLY BR1 ....183 K4
Northcote Lodge School
BTSEA SW11 ....160 D1
North Croydon Medical Centre
THHTH CR7 ....196 C3
North Ealing Primary School
WEA W13 ....97 H3
North East Surrey Crematorium
NWMAL KT3 ....193 F3
Northend Primary School
ERITH DA8 ....150 C2
North End Trading Estate
ERITH DA8 ....150 B1
North Feltham Trading Estate
EBED/NFELT TW14 ....134 A5
Northfields Industrial Estate
ALP/SUD HA0 ....80 C6
Northfields Prospect Business Centre
PUT/ROE SW15 ....139 J5
Northgate Business Centre
EN EN1 ....24 D4
Northgate Clinic
CDALE/KGS NW9 ....63 G3
Northgate Industrial Park
CRW RM5 ....56 B5
North Harringay Primary School
CEND/HSY/T N8 ....67 G1
North Havering College of Adult Education
ROM RM1 ....75 G1
North Kensington Video-Drama Project
NKENS W10 ....100 C5
North London Collegiate School
EDGW HA8 ....44 A2
The North London Hospice
NFNCH/WDSPK N12 ....33 F5
North London School of Physiotherapy
ARCH N19 ....66 C5
North London Tutorial College
HDN NW4 ....64 A3
North Middlesex Golf Club
NFNCH/WDSPK N12 ....33 H5
North Middlesex Hospital
UED N18 ....50 A1
Northolt Aerodrome
RSLP HA4 ....76 E4
Northolt High School
NTHLT UB5 ....77 K4
Northolt Primary School
NTHLT UB5 ....77 H5
Northolt Road Clinic
RYLN/HDSTN HA2 ....78 C1
Northolt Swimarama
NTHLT UB5 ....78 A4
North Pole Depot
WLSDN NW10 ....99 H3
North Primary School
STHL UB1 ....95 K6
Northside Primary School
NFNCH/WDSPK N12 ....47 G1
The North Street Health Centre
CLAP SW4 ....141 H4
Northumberland Heath Medical Centre
ERITH DA8 ....150 A1
Northumberland Heath Primary School
ERITH DA8 ....149 J2
Northumberland Park Community School
TOTM N17 ....50 C3
Northumberland Park Industrial Estate
TOTM N17 ....50 D2
Northview Primary School
WLSDN NW10 ....81 C2
Northway School
MLHL NW7 ....30 E5
North West Kent College
RDART DA2 ....170 E4

North West London Jewish Primary School
CRICK NW2 ....82 C5
North West London Medical Centre
MV/WKIL W9 ....101 G2
North Westminster Community School
BAY/PAD W2 ....8 A2
North Westminster Community Secondary School
MV/WKIL W9 ....100 E3
North Weylands Industrial Estate
WOT/HER KT12 ....188 D6
Northwick Park Hospital & Clinical Research Centre
HRW HA1 ....61 H4
Northwold Primary School
CLPT E5 ....68 C6
Northwood Cemetery
NTHWD HA6 ....40 D5
Northwood College
NTHWD HA6 ....40 D5
Northwood Football Club
NTHWD HA6 ....40 B3
Northwood Golf Club
NTHWD HA6 ....40 B3
Northwood & Pinner Community Hospital
NTHWD HA6 ....40 E4
Northwood Preparatory School
RKW/CH/CXG WD3 ....26 A4
Northwood Primary School
ERITH DA18 ....129 F3
Northwood Sports Centre
NTHWD HA6 ....41 F4
Norwegian/British Monument
BAY/PAD W2 ....8 C7
The Norwegian School
WIM/MER SW19 ....177 F3
Norwood Green Infant School
NWDGN UB2 ....114 D5
Norwood Green Junior School
NWDGN UB2 ....114 D5
Norwood Heights Shopping Centre
NRWD SE19 ....181 F2
Norwood School
NRWD SE19 ....180 D1
Notre Dame RC Girls School
STHWK SE1 ....18 A4
Notre Dame RC Primary School
WOOL/PLUM SE18 ....127 G6
Notre Dame University
LSQ/SEVD WC2H 10 D4
Notting Hill & Ealing High School Senior Department
WEA W13 ....97 H4
Novello Theatre
HOL/ALD WC2B 11 G5
Novotel
CAMTN NW1 ....4 D4
CAN/RD E16 ....107 F6
GNWCH SE10 ....148 E1
STHWK SE1 ....13 H5
TWRH EC3N 13 H5
WDR/YW UB7 ....112 D4
Novotel London Waterloo
STHWK SE1 ....17 G6
Novotel London West
HMSMTH W6 ....119 G5
Nower Hill High School
PIN HA5 ....60 A1
NTGB Sports Ground
EHAM E6 ....90 A4
Nuffield Hospital
ENC/FH EN2 ....23 G3
Nugent Shopping Park
STMC/STPC BR5 ....202 C1
Number 10 Bowling
ROM RM1 ....75 G2
Nutrition Clinic
MHST W1U 9 G1
The O2
POP/IOD E14 ....125 G1
O2 Centre
HAMP NW3 ....83 G4
Oakdale Infant School
SWFD E18 ....53 F5
Oakdale Junior School
SWFD E18 ....53 G5
Oakfield Preparatory School
DUL SE21 ....162 E4
Oakfield Primary School
DART DA1 ....171 G4
Oakfield Road Industrial Estate
PGE/AN SE20 ....181 J3
Oak Hill Health Centre
SURB KT6 ....191 F3
Oakhill Primary School
WFD IG8 ....52 C2
Oakington Manor School
WBLY HA9 ....80 D3
Oakland CP School
EBAR EN4 ....33 K1
Oaklands Primary School
HNWL W7 ....116 A2
Oaklands School
ISLW TW7 ....135 J4
Oaklands Secondary School
BETH E2 ....104 C2
Oak Lane Cemetery
TWK TW1 ....156 B2
Oak Lane Medical Centre
TWK TW1 ....156 C2
Oakleigh School
TRDG/WHET N20 ....33 J5

Oak Lodge JMI School
WWKM BR4 ....198 E4
Oak Lodge Medical Centre
EDGW HA8 ....44 D3
Oak Lodge School
BAL SW12 ....160 E2
FNCH N3 ....47 G6
Oakthorpe Primary School
UED N18 ....49 J1
Oak Tree Medical Centre
GDMY/SEVK IG3 ....72 E6
Oakwood Business Park
WLSDN NW10 ....99 F2
Oakwood Medical Centre
STHGT/OAK N14 ....22 C4
Oakwood School
BXLYHN DA7 ....150 A5
Oasis Sports Centre
LSQ/SEVD WC2H 10 E3
Obstetrics Hospital
GWRST WC1E 4 B7
Occupational Health Centre
CROY/NA CR0 ....211 K1
Odeon Cinema
BAR EN5 ....20 E6
BAY/PAD W2 ....2 E6
BECK BR3 ....182 C5
BERM/RHTH SE16 ....124 A3
CAMTN NW1 ....84 B6
ELTH/MOT SE9 ....146 D5
ESH/CLAY KT10 ....204 B2
FITZ W1T 10 A1
HAMP NW3 ....83 H5
HAYES BR2 ....183 K5
HOLWY N7 ....84 E1
KENS W8 ....119 K3
KUT/HW KT1 ....175 F5
MUSWH N10 ....66 A1
RCH/KEW TW9 ....136 E6
ROM RM1 ....75 H2
STJS SW1Y 10 C6
STRHM/NOR SW16 ....161 K5
WIM/MER SW19 ....177 K3
Odeon Covent Gardens Cinema
LSQ/SEVD WC2H 10 D4
Odeon Wardour Street Cinema
SOHO/SHAV W1D 10 C5
Odessa Infant School
FSTGT E7 ....88 E3
Odyssey Business Park
RSLP HA4 ....77 F3
Old Actonians Sports Club
EA W5 ....117 G2
Old Admiralty
STJS SW1Y 16 D1
Old Bancroftians FC
BKHH IG9 ....39 H6
Old Barnes Cemetery
BARN SW13 ....138 E3
Old Beckenhamian RFC
WWKM BR4 ....214 B1
Old Bellgate Wharf
POP/IOD E14 ....124 C3
Old Bexley Business Park
BXLY DA5 ....169 J2
Old Bexley CE Primary School
BXLY DA5 ....169 G3
Old Brockleians Sports Ground
LEE/GVPK SE12 ....166 B1
Old Bromlians CC
HAYES BR2 ....200 A3
Old Cemetery
EDUL SE22 ....163 J1
Old Colfeian Sports Club
LEE/GVPK SE12 ....145 K6
Old Curiosity Shop
LINN WC2A 11 G3
Old Elthamians Sports Club
CHST BR7 ....185 K2
Oldfield House Special School
HPTN TW12 ....172 E4
Oldfield Primary School
GFD/PVL UB6 ....96 D1
Oldfields Trading Estate
SUT SM1 ....208 E1
Old Fold Manor Golf Club
BAR EN5 ....20 C2
Old Ford Primary School
BOW E3 ....105 H1
Oldhill Medical Centre
STNW/STAM N16 ....68 B5
Old Jamaica Business Estate
BERM/RHTH SE16 ....19 K4
Old Lyonian Sports Ground
RYLN/HDSTN HA2 ....60 C2
Old Millhillians Sports Ground
RYLN/HDSTN HA2 ....42 A4
Old Oak Primary School
SHB W12 ....99 H5
Old Operating Theatre & Herb Garret Museum
STHWK SE1 ....18 E1
Old Owens Sports Ground
TRDG/WHET N20 ....33 H3
Old Palace Primary School
BOW E3 ....105 K2
Old Palace School
CROY/NA CR0 ....211 H1
Old Royal Naval College
GNWCH SE10 ....125 G5
Old Royal Observatory Greenwich
GNWCH SE10 ....145 G1
Old Spitalfields Market Hall
WCHPL E1 ....13 J1
Old Station Museum
CAN/RD E16 ....127 F2
Old Sun Wharf
POP/IOD E14 ....105 G6
Old Tiffinians Sports Ground
E/WMO/HCT KT8 ....189 K2

Old Treasury
WHALL SW1A 16 E2
Old Vicarage School
RCHPK/HAM TW10 ....157 F1
Old Vic Theatre
STHWK SE1 ....17 K2
Old War Office
WHALL SW1A 16 E1
Old Wilsonians Sports Club
WWKM BR4 ....199 H5
Olga Primary School
BOW E3 ....105 G1
Oliver Business Park
WLSDN NW10 ....98 E1
Oliver Goldsmith Primary School
CDALE/KGS NW9 ....63 F2
CMBW SE5 ....143 G2
Oliver House Preparatory School
CLAP SW4 ....161 G1
Olympia
WKENS W14 ....119 H3
Olympia Industrial Estate
WDGN N22 ....49 F5
Olympic Industrial Estate
WBLY HA9 ....80 C2
Olympic Retail Park
WBLY HA9 ....80 C2
Olympic Trading Estate
WBLY HA9 ....80 D2
One Aldwych Hotel
COVGDN WC2E 11 G5
The One Stanley Medical Centre
ALP/SUD HA0 ....80 A5
On Sai Clinic
ECT SW5 ....120 A4
Open Air Theatre
CAMTN NW1 ....3 G1
The Open University
FSBYW WC1X 5 G4
HAMP NW3 ....82 E2
Ophaboom Theatre
WLSDN NW10 ....99 K1
Optimax Laser Eye Clinic
HAMP NW3 ....83 G4
Orange Tree Theatre
RCH/KEW TW9 ....137 F5
Orchard Business Centre
BECK BR3 ....182 C1
The Orchard Health Centre
BARK IG11 ....108 C1
Orchard Hill College
WLGTN SM6 ....210 B4
Orchard House School
CHSWK W4 ....118 A4
Orchard J & I School
HOM E9 ....86 E5
The Orchard Junior School
HSLWW TW4 ....135 F5
Orchard Primary School
SCUP DA14 ....186 C1
The Orchard School
E/WMO/HCT KT8 ....189 J2
Orchard Shopping Centre
DART DA1 ....171 G1
The Orchard Theatre
DART DA1 ....171 H1
Orchard Way Primary School
CROY/NA CR0 ....198 B4
Oriel Primary School
FELT TW13 ....154 D5
Orient Industrial Park
LEY E10 ....69 J6
Orion Business Centre
NWCR SE14 ....124 A5
Orleans House Gallery
TWK TW1 ....156 C3
Orleans Infant School
TWK TW1 ....156 C2
Orley Farm School
HRW HA1 ....78 D1
Orpington College of Further Education
ORP BR6 ....202 B6
The Orpington Halls
ORP BR6 ....202 B6
Orpington Hospital
ORP BR6 ....217 F2
Orpington Mental Health Centre
ORP BR6 ....217 F1
Orpington Retail Park
STMC/STPC BR5 ....202 D1
Orpington Superbowl
ORP BR6 ....202 B5
Orpington Trade Centre
STMC/STPC BR5 ....186 C6
Osidge JMI School
STHGT/OAK N14 ....34 C3
Osier Industrial Estate
WAND/EARL SW18 ....139 K5
Osmani Primary School
WCHPL E1 ....104 C4
Osteopathic Clinic
HOR/WEW KT19 ....207 F3
Osterley Park & House (NT)
ISLW TW7 ....115 H6
Osterley RFC
NWDGN UB2 ....115 G3
Our Lady Immaculate RC Primary School
BRYLDS KT5 ....191 J5
Our Lady of Dolours RC Primary School
BAY/PAD W2 ....101 F4
Our Lady of Grace RC Junior School
CRICK NW2 ....81 K1
Our Lady of Grace RC Primary School
CHARL SE7 ....126 A6
Our Lady of Lourdes RC Primary School
BKHTH/KID SE3 ....145 G2
FBAR/BDGN N11 ....48 B1

WAN E11 ....70 D3
WLSDN NW10 ....80 K6
Our Lady of Muswell RC
Primary School
MUSWH N10 ....48 A5
Our Lady of the Rosary RC
School
ELTH/MOT SE9 ....167 K1
Our Lady of the Sacred Heart
School
HOLWY N7 ....85 F3
Our Lady of the Visitation RC
Combined Primary School
GFD/PVL UB6 ....96 C3
Our Lady of Victories RC
Primary School
SKENS SW7 ....120 B4
Our Lady of Victorys RC
Primary School
PUT/ROE SW15 ....139 G5
Our Lady Queen of Heaven
RC Primary School
WIM/MER SW19 ....159 G2
Our Lady RC Primary School
POP/IOD E14 ....105 H5
Our Lady & St Johns RC
Primary School
BTFD TW8 ....116 D5
Our Lady & St Joseph Primary
School
IS N1 ....86 A4
Our Lady & St Philip Neri RC
Infant School
FSTH SE23 ....164 A5
Our Lady & St Phillip Neri RC
Primary School
SYD SE26 ....164 B6
Our Ladys Catholic Primary
School
DART DA1 ....171 G1
Our Ladys RC Primary School
CAMTN NW1 ....84 C6
Oval Business Centre
LBTH SE11 ....122 A5
Oval House Theatre
LBTH SE11 ....122 B6
Oval Primary School
CROY/NA CRO 197 F5
Overton Grange School
BELMT SM2 ....209 F6
Oxford Gardens Primary
School
NKENS W10 ....100 B5
Oxford House College
SOHO/SHAV W1D 10 C3
Oxhey Infant School
OXHEY WD19 ....27 J1
Oxhey Park Golf Centre
OXHEY WD19 ....27 H3
Oxhey Wood Primary School
OXHEY WD19 ....27 G6
Oxo Tower Wharf
STHWK SE1 ....11 K6
Paddington Bowling &
Sports Club
MV/WKIL W9 ....101 F3
Paddington Green Primary
School
BAY/PAD W2 ....2 A7
Paddington Recreation
Ground Athletics Track
MV/WKIL NW6 ....100 E2
Paddock School
PUT/ROE SW15 ....138 C5
Pain Relief Clinic
HDN NW4 ....63 K3
Paint Pots Montessori School
WBPTN SW10 ....120 B6
Pakeman Primary School
HOLWY N7 ....85 F1
Palace Gardens Shopping
Centre
ENC/FH EN2 ....23 K4
Palace of Westminster
WHALL SW1A 17 F3
Palace Theatre
SOHO/SHAV W1D 10 D5
Palladium Theatre
SOHO/CST W1F 10 A4
Palmers Green High School
WCHMH N21 ....35 G4
Palmerston Business Centre
SUT SM1 ....209 G3
Palm House
RCH/KEW TW9 ....137 G2
Panorama Pier
STHWK SE1 ....12 B6
Paradise Swimming Pools
MLHL NW7 ....45 G1
Paray House School
FUL/PGN SW6 ....139 J3
Parayhouse School
WBPTN SW10 ....140 B1
Parchmore Medical Centre
THHTH CR7 ....180 D6
Pardes House & Beis Yaakov
School
FNCH N3 ....46 D5
Parent Infant Clinic
HAMP NW3 ....83 G3
Parish CE Primary School
BMLY BR1 ....183 K3
Parish Church CE Primary
School
CROY/NA CRO 211 H1
Park Business Centre
KIL/WHAMP NW6 ....100 E2
Parkes Townhouse Hotel
CHEL SW3 ....14 D4
Parkfield Industrial Estate
BTSEA SW11 ....141 F3
Parkfield JMI School
HDN NW4 ....63 K4
Parkgate House School
CLAP SW4 ....141 F5
Park Hall Trading Estate
WNWD SE27 ....162 D5

Park High School
STAN HA7 ....43 K5
Park Hill Junior School
CROY/NA CRO 211 K1
Parkhill Primary School
CLAY IG5 ....53 K6
Park Hill School
KUTN/CMB KT2 ....175 H3
Park House Medical Centre
KIL/WHAMP NW6 ....100 C1
Park House RFC
HRW HA1 ....200 B6
The Park Inn Heathrow
WDR/YW UB7 ....132 E1
Parklands Primary School
RDM RM1 ....57 F6
Park Lane Primary School
WBLY HA9 ....80 A2
Park Medical Centre
BERM/RHTH SE16 ....124 A4
Park Mews Small Business
Centre
HNHL SE24 ....162 D1
Park Road Clinic
CEND/HSY/T N8 ....66 D2
Park Road Swimming
Centre
CEND/HSY/T N8 ....66 D2
Park Royal Business Centre
WLSDN NW10 ....99 F3
Park School for Girls
IL IG1 ....72 A6
Parkside Business Estate
DEPT SE8 ....124 C6
Parkside Clinic
NTCHL W11 ....100 C5
Parkside Health
NTCHL W11 ....100 C5
Parkside Hospital
WIM/MER SW19 ....159 G5
Park Walk Primary School
WBPTN SW10 ....120 C6
Parkway Primary School
ERITHM DA18 ....129 F3
Parkway Trading Estate
HEST TW5 ....114 B6
Parkwood Primary School
FSBYPK N4 ....67 H6
Parliament Hill Fields
Athletics Track
HAMP NW3 ....83 K2
Parliament Hill Lido
HAMP NW3 ....84 A2
Parliament Hill School
KTTN NW5 ....84 A2
Parmiter Industrial Estate
BETH E2 ....104 D1
Parnells Sports Ground
KTN/HRWW/WS HA3 ....62 B3
Parsloes Primary School
DAGW RM9 ....92 B4
Parsons Green Health Clinic
FUL/PGN SW6 ....139 K2
Passport Language Schools
BMLY BR1 ....184 A4
Patent Office
FLST/FETLN EC4A 11 J2
The Patrick Doody Clinic &
Health Centre
WIM/MER SW19 ....177 K3
Pattinson Clinic
RCH/KEW TW9 ....136 E6
The Paul Robeson Theatre
HSLW TW3 ....135 G4
Pavilion Barclays Sports
Ground
EA W5 ....98 A4
The Pavilion Leisure Centre
BMLY BR1 ....183 K5
Pavilion Restaurant
RCH/KEW TW9 ....137 F3
Paxton Primary School
NRWD SE19 ....181 G2
PDSA Hospital
REDBR IG4 ....53 H6
Peace Pagoda
CHEL SW3 ....140 E1
Peacock Estate
TOTM N17 ....50 B2
Peacock Industrial Estate
TOTM N17 ....50 B5
The Peacock Theatre
HOL/ALD WC2B 11 G4
Peall Road Industrial Estate
CROY/NA CRO 196 A3
Peckham Park Primary
School
PECK SE15 ....143 H1
The Peckham Pulse Health
& Leisure Centre
PECK SE15 ....143 H2
Pelham Primary School
BXLYHN DA7 ....149 H4
WIM/MER SW19 ....177 K3
Pembridge Hall
BAY/PAD W2 ....100 E6
Pendragon Secondary School
BMLY BR1 ....165 K5
Pentavia Retail Park
MLHL NW7 ....45 H3
Penwortham Primary School
STRHM/NOR SW16 ....179 G2
Percival David Foundation of
Chinese Art
STPAN WC1H 4 D6
Perivale Industrial Park
GFD/PVL UB6 ....97 G1
Perivale New Business Centre
GFD/PVL UB6 ....97 J1
Perivale Park Athletics Track
GFD/PVL UB6 ....96 E2
Perivale Park Golf Course
GFD/PVL UB6 ....96 E2
Perivale Primary School
GFD/PVL UB6 ....97 J1
Perrin Road Clinic
ALP/SUD HA0 ....79 H2

Perry Hall Primary School
ORP BR6 ....202 A3
Perrymount Primary School
FSTH SE23 ....164 A4
Petchy Academy
CLPT E5 ....86 C2
Peterborough Primary
School
FUL/PGN SW6 ....139 K3
Peterborough & St Margarets
High School
STAN HA7 ....28 E5
Peter Hills School
BERM/RHTH SE16 ....124 A1
Peter James Business
Centre
HYS/HAR UB3 ....113 K2
Peterley Business Centre
BETH E2 ....104 D1
Peter Pan Statue
BAY/PAD W2 ....8 A7
The Petersham Hotel
RCHPK/HAM TW10 ....157 F2
Petric Museum of Egyptia
Archaeology
GWRST WC1E 4 C7
Petts Hill Primary School
NTHLT UB5 ....78 B3
Pewterers' Hall
CITYW EC2V 12 D2
Phoenix Business Centre
POP/IOD E14 ....105 J4
Phoenix Cinema
EFNCH N2 ....65 J1
Phoenix College
MRDN SM4 ....194 A2
Phoenix High School
SHB W12 ....99 J6
Phoenix Industrial Estate
HRW HA1 ....61 F1
Phoenix Leisure Centre
CAT SE6 ....164 E2
Phoenix School
HAMP NW3 ....83 H4
Phoenix Secondary &
Primary School
BOW E3 ....105 H2
Phoenix Theatre
LSQ/SEVD WC2H 10 D4
Phoenix Trading Estate
GFD/PVL UB6 ....79 J6
Physical Energy Statue
BAY/PAD W2 ....14 A1
Piccadilly Theatre
SOHO/SHAV W1D 10 C5
Pickford Lane Medical Centre
BXLYHN DA7 ....149 F2
Pickhurst Infant School
WWKM BR4 ....199 H5
Pickhurst Junior School
WWKM BR4 ....199 J5
Picture House Cinema
SRTFD E15 ....88 B4
Pilgrims Way J & I School
PECK SE15 ....123 K6
Pilot Industrial Centre
WLSDN NW10 ....99 G3
Pilton Estate
CROY/NA CRO 196 C6
Pimlico School
PIM SW1V 121 H5
Pinewood Primary School
CRW RM5 ....56 D1
Pinkwell Primary School
HYS/HAR UB3 ....113 F4
Pinnacles Cricket & Squash
Club
SUT SM1 ....208 E4
Pinner Hill Golf Club
PIN HA5 ....41 F2
Pinner Medical Centre
PIN HA5 ....59 J1
Pinner Park Primary School
PIN HA5 ....42 B6
Pinner View Medical Centre
HRW HA1 ....60 C2
Pinner Wood Primary School
PIN HA5 ....41 G4
Pioneers Industrial Park
CROY/NA CRO 195 K5
Pippins School
ASHF TW15 ....152 C6
Pitshanger Manor Museum
EA W5 ....116 D1
Plaisterers Hall
STBT EC1A 12 C2
Plaistow Hospital
PLSTW E13 ....107 F1
Plaistow Primary School
PLSTW E13 ....89 G6
Plantation House Medical
Centre
LOTH EC2R 13 F3
Plashet Jewish Cemetery
MNPK E12 ....89 H4
Plashet Road Medical Centre
FSTGT E7 ....89 F5
Plashet School
EHAM E6 ....89 J5
Players Theatre
CHCR WC2N 11 F7
The Playhouse
CHCR WC2N 11 F7
Plaza Business Centre
PEND EN3 ....25 H3
Pleasance Theatre
HOLWY N7 ....84 E4
Plumcroft Primary School
WOOL/PLUM SE18 ....127 H6
Plumstead Leisure Centre
WOOL/PLUM SE18 ....128 A5
Plumstead Manor School
WOOL/PLUM SE18 ....127 J5
The Pointer School
BKHTH/KID SE3 ....145 K2
Police Cadet School
WAN E11 ....70 E5

The Polish Institute &
Sikorski Museum
SKENS SW7 ....14 B3
Polish War Memorial
RSLP HA4 ....77 F4
Polka Theatre for Children
WIM/MER SW19 ....178 A2
Ponders End Industrial
Estate
PEND EN3 ....25 H5
Pooles Park Primary School
FSBYPK N4 ....67 F6
Pools in the Park
RCH/KEW TW9 ....136 E5
Pope John Primary School
SHB W12 ....99 K6
Pop in Business Centre
WBLY HA9 ....80 D3
Poplar Business Park
POP/IOD E14 ....106 A6
Poplar Primary School
WIM/MER SW19 ....177 K6
Pop Up Theatre
CLKNW EC1R 5 K3
Porchester Leisure Centre
BAY/PAD W2 ....101 G5
Portcullis House
WHALL SW1A 17 F3
Portico City Learning
Centre
CLPT E5 ....86 E2
The Portland Hospital
REGST W1B 3 K7
Portland House Medical
Centre
GFD/PVL UB6 ....95 B3
Portland Medical Centre
SNWD SE25 ....197 J2
Portland Place School
REGST W1B 9 K1
The Portman Clinic
HAMP NW3 ....83 H4
Portobello Market
NKENS W10 ....100 C4
Portobello Medical Centre
NTCHL W11 ....100 C5
Portway Primary School
SRTFD E15 ....88 E6
Pound Park Nursery School
CHARL SE7 ....126 C5
The Pountney Clinic
HSLW TW3 ....135 F4
Poverest Primary School
STMC/STPC BR5 ....202 B2
Powergate Business Park
WLSDN NW10 ....99 F2
Power industrial Estate
ERITH DA8 ....150 C2
The Power Station London
(under re-development)
VX/NE SW8 ....141 G1
Premier Cinema
PECK SE15 ....143 H3
Premier Travel Inn
BARK IG11 ....90 B6
BTFD TW8 ....117 F6
CAN/RD E16 ....107 H6
CHDH RM6 ....74 A2
CROY/NA CRO 211 G4
CROY/NA CRO 212 C5
EBED/NFELT TW14 ....153 H3
EE/WMO/HCT KT8 ....189 H1
EDGW HA8 ....44 C3
EHAM E6 ....108 A4
FUL/PGN SW6 ....139 H4
GFD/PVL UB6 ....97 G2
HOR/WEW KT19 ....207 G5
HTHAIR TW6 ....133 H2
HYS/HAR UB3 ....112 E4
IS N1 ....6 C2
KTN/HRWW/WS HA3 ....61 H3
PUR RM19 ....131 J5
REDBR IG4 ....71 H2
STHWK SE1 ....12 D7
STHWK SE1 ....17 G2
STHWK SE1 ....19 H3
STPAN WC1H 4 C5
WBLY HA9 ....80 C1
WHTN TW2 ....155 H5
WIM/MER SW19 ....178 B4
YEAD UB4 ....95 F5
Prendergast School
BROCKY SE4 ....144 D5
Preston Manor School
WBLY HA9 ....62 B6
Preston Medical Centre
WBLY HA9 ....80 A1
Preston Park Primary School
WBLY HA9 ....61 K5
Priestmead First & Middle
Schools
KTN/HRWW/WS HA3 ....43 H6
Primary School
CHEL SW3 ....120 D5
Primrose Hill School
CAMTN NW1 ....84 A6
Primrose Montessori School
HBRY N5 ....85 J1
Prince Charles Cinema
LSQ/SEVD WC2H 10 D5
Prince Edward Theatre
SOHO/SHAV W1D 10 C4
Prince of Wales Theatre
SOHO/SHAV W1D 10 C6
Princes College
NOXST/BSQ WC1A 10 E3
Princes Court Business
Centre
WAP E1W 104 D6
Princes Park Stadium
DART DA1 ....171 K3
Princes Plain Primary School
HAYES BR2 ....200 D4
Princess Avenue School
MUSWH N10 ....48 B6
Princess Frederica CE J & I
School
WLSDN NW10 ....99 K1

Princess Grace Hospital
MHST W1U 3 C7
Princess Louise Hospital
NKENS W10 ....100 A4
Princess May Primary School
STNW/STAM N16 ....86 A3
Princess of Wales
Conservatory
RCH/KEW TW9 ....137 C1
The Princess Royal
Distribution Centre
WLSDN NW10 ....80 D6
Princess Royal
University Hospital
ORP BR6 ....216 A1
Prior Weston Primary School
STLK EC1Y 6 D7
Priory CE Primary School
WIM/MER SW19 ....178 A1
The Priory Leisure Centre
STMC/STPC BR5 ....202 D5
Priory Retail Park
WIM/MER SW19 ....178 C3
Priory School
STMC/STPC BR5 ....202 D5
Priory Shopping Centre
DART DA1 ....171 G1
Priory Special School
SNWD SE25 ....197 G1
The Priory
ORP BR6 ....202 C4
Privy Council
STJS SW1Y 16 C1
Privy Council Office
WHALL SW1A 16 E1
Progress Business Park
CROY/NA CRO 196 A6
Pronto Trading Estate
YEAD UB4 ....94 C4
Prospect House School
PUT/ROE SW15 ....159 G2
Proteus School
KIL/WHAMP NW6 ....83 F5
Proud Gallery
CHCR WC2N 10 E6
Providence Road School
WDR/YW UB7 ....112 B1
Provident Industrial Estate
HYS/HAR UB3 ....113 K2
PS Tattershall Castle
WHALL SW1A 17 F1
Pump House
BERM/RHTH SE16 ....124 B1
Pump Lane Industrial Estate
HYS/HAR UB3 ....114 A2
The Purcell School
HRW HA1 ....78 D1
Purdy Hicks Gallery
STHWK SE1 ....12 A7
Purfleet Industrial Park
SOCK/AV RM15 ....131 J1
Purfleet Primary School
PUR RM19 ....131 K4
Purley Oaks Primary School
SAND/SEL CR2 ....211 K5
Pursuit Centre
WAP E1W 104 E6
Putney Animal Hospital
PUT/ROE SW15 ....139 G5
Putney Arts Theatre
PUT/ROE SW15 ....139 G5
Putney Exchange Shopping
Centre
PUT/ROE SW15 ....139 G5
Putney High School
PUT/ROE SW15 ....139 G6
Putney Leisure Centre
PUT/ROE SW15 ....139 F5
Putney Lower Common
Cemetery
BARN SW13 ....138 E3
Putneymead Medical Centre
PUT/ROE SW15 ....139 F5
Putney Park School
PUT/ROE SW15 ....138 E5
Putney School of Art
PUT/ROE SW15 ....139 H5
Putney Vale Cemetery
PUT/ROE SW15 ....158 D4
Putney Vale Crematorium
PUT/ROE SW15 ....158 D4
Pylon Trading Estate
CAN/RD E16 ....106 B3
Quadrant Business Park
KIL/WHAMP NW6 ....82 C6
Quality Hotel
HRW HA1 ....60 D3
PIM SW1V 15 K7
WBLY HA9 ....80 C2
Quebec Industrial Estate
BERM/RHTH SE16 ....124 B2
Queen Charlotte's & Chelsea
Hospital
SHB W12 ....99 K5
Queen Charlotte's Cottage
RCH/KEW TW9 ....136 E3
Queen Elizabeth Centre
WEST SW1P 16 D3
Queen Elizabeth Conference
Centre
WEST SW1P 16 D3
Queen Elizabeth Hall
STHWK SE1 ....11 G7
Queen Elizabeth Hospital
WOOL/PLUM SE18 ....126 E6
Queen Elizabeth II School
MV/WKIL W9 ....100 D3
Queen Elizabeth Museum
CHING E4 ....38 D2
Queen Elizabeths Boys School
BAR EN5 ....20 B4
Queen Elizabeths Girls School
BAR EN5 ....20 C4
Queen Elizabeth Stadium
EN EN1 ....24 B3
Queenhithe Stairs
BLKFR EC4V 12 C6

Queen Mary College University of London
WCHPL E1 ....105 F3
Queen Mary's Hospital
HAMP NW3 ....83 G1
Queen Marys Hospital
SCUP DA14 ....186 B1
Queen Mary's Hospital for Children
SUT SM1 ....194 B1
Queen Mary's University Hospital
PUT/ROE SW15 ....158 D1
Queen Mary & Westfield College
SWFD E18 ....52 E4
Queen Mother Sports Centre
PIM SW1V 16 A6
Queensbridge Primary School
HACK E8 ....86 B5
Queensbridge Sports Centre
HACK E8 ....86 B5
Queen's Building
HTHAIR TW6 ....132 E4
The Queens CE Primary School
RCH/KEW TW9 ....137 G1
Queen's Club
WKENS W14 ....119 H5
Queens College London
CAVSQ/HST W1G 9 J2
Queen's Gallery
BGVA SW1W 15 K3
Queens Gate School
SKENS SW7 ....120 B4
Queens Hospital
ROMW/RG RM7 ....75 G4
The Queens House
GNWCH SE10 ....125 G6
Queens Manor Primary School
FUL/PGN SW6 ....139 F1
Queensmead School
RSLP HA4 ....77 H2
Queensmead Sports Centre
RSLP HA4 ....77 H3
Queens Medical Centre
RCHPK/HAM TW10 ....137 G6
Queensmill School
FUL/PGN SW6 ....139 K3
Queens Park Community School
WLSDN NW10 ....82 A6
Queens Park Health Centre
NKENS W10 ....100 C2
Queens Park Primary School
NKENS W10 ....100 C2
Queens Park Rangers FC (Loftus Road Stadium)
SHB W12 ....118 E1
Queen's Road Cemetery
CROY/NA CRO 196 D3
Queens Theatre
SOHO/SHAV W1D 10 C5
Queensway Business Centre
PEND EN3 ....24 E5
Queenswell Infant School
TRDG/WHET N20 ....33 H4
Queen Victoria Memorial
WHALL SW1A 16 A3
The Questors Theatre
EA W5 ....97 J6
Quwwat Ul Islam Girl's School
FSTGT E7 ....88 E4
Radcliffe College
SOHO/SHAV W1D 10 A4
Radisson Edwardian Berkshire Hotel
OXSTW W1C 9 J4
Radisson Edwardian Grafton Hotel
CAMTN NW1 ....4 A6
Radisson Edwardian Hampshire Hotel
LSQ/SEVD WC2H 10 D6
Radisson Edwardian Hotel
HYS/HAR UB3 ....133 F1
Radisson Edwardian Kenilworth Hotel
RSQ WC1B 10 D2
Radisson Edwardian Marlborough Hotel
RSQ WC1B 10 D2
Radisson Edwardian Mayfair Hotel
MYFR/PICC W1J 9 K6
Radisson Edwardian Mountbatten Hotel
LSQ/SEVD WC2H 10 E4
Radisson Edwardian Vanderbilt Hotel
SKENS SW7 ....120 B4
Radisson SAS Portman Hotel
MBLAR W1H 9 F3
Raglan Infant School
EN EN1 ....36 A1
Raglan Junior School
EN EN1 ....36 A2
Raglan Primary School
HAYES BR2 ....200 B1
Railton Road Clinic
HNHL SE24 ....142 C6
Rainbow Industrial Estate
RYNPK SW20 ....176 E5
Rainbow Montessori School
KIL/WHAMP NW6 ....83 F5
Rainbow Quay
BERM/RHTH SE16 ....124 B3
Raines Foundation School
BETH E2 ....104 D2
Rainham Hall (NT)
RAIN RM13 ....111 J3
Rainham Trading Estate
RAIN RM13 ....111 G2
Rainham Village Primary School
RAIN RM13 ....111 J3

Ramac Industrial Estate
CHARL SE7 ....125 K5
Ramada Encore Hotel
ACT W3 ....99 F4
Ramada Hotel
BAY/PAD W2 ....101 F6
EA W5 ....98 B6
Randal Cremer Primary School
BETH E2 ....7 J2
Ranelagh Gardens (Site of Chelsea Flower Show)
CHEL SW3 ....121 F5
Ranelagh Primary School
SRTFD E15 ....106 C1
Rangefield Primary School
BMLY BR1 ....183 H1
Ransomes Dock Business Centre
BTSEA SW11 ....140 D1
Raphael Independent School
EMPK RM11 ....75 J3
The Rathbone Education Centre
CAN/RD E16 ....106 D4
Rathbow Clinic
BAY/PAD W2 ....2 B7
Rathfern Primary School
FSTH SE23 ....164 C3
Ravenor Primary School
GFD/PVL UB6 ....96 A2
The Ravensbourne College of Design & Communication
CHST BR7 ....185 F1
The Ravensbourne School
HAYES BR2 ....200 A1
Ravenscourt Park Preparatory School
HMSMTH W6 ....118 D4
Ravenscourt Medical Centre
GLDGN NW11 ....64 D4
Ravenscroft Primary School
CAN/RD E16 ....106 E3
Ravenscroft School
TRDG/WHET N20 ....32 D2
Ravenside Retail Park
UED N18 ....51 F2
Ravensquay Business Centre
STMC/STPC BR5 ....202 C2
Ravenstone Primary School
BAL SW12 ....161 F3
Ravenswood Industrial Estate
WALTH E17 ....70 A1
Ravens Wood School
HAYES BR2 ....215 H1
Ray Cochrane Beauty School
CAMTN NW1 ....9 F1
Ray Lodge Primary School
WFD IG8 ....53 H2
Raynes Park High School
RYNPK SW20 ....176 E6
Rayne Park Sports Ground
RYNPK SW20 ....176 D5
Raynes Park Vale FC
RYNPK SW20 ....193 G2
Raynham Primary School
UED N18 ....50 C1
RCA
SKENS SW7 ....120 B3
RCA Sculpture School
BTSEA SW11 ....140 D1
Reay Primary School
BRXN/ST SW9 ....142 B1
Records Office
CLKNW EC1R 5 K6
Rectory Business Centre
SCUP DA14 ....168 C4
Rectory Paddock School
STMC/STPC BR5 ....186 D5
Redbridge College
CHDH RM6 ....73 H2
Redbridge Drama Centre
SWFD E18 ....52 E4
Redbridge Museum
IL IG1 ....90 B1
Redbridge Primary School
REDBR IG4 ....71 J2
Redbridge Sports Centre
BARK/HLT IG6 ....54 D4
Redbridge Tuition Service
GNTH/NBYPK IG2 ....72 D3
Redburn Industrial Estate
PEND EN3 ....37 F1
Reddiford School
PIN HA5 ....59 J1
Redford Lodge Psychiatric Hospital
ED N9 ....36 C4
Red Gates School
CROY/NA CRO 211 G3
Redhill Junior School
CHST BR7 ....185 G1
Red House (NT)
BXLYHS DA6 ....149 F5
Redlands Primary School
WCHPL E1 ....104 E4
Red Lion Business Park
SURB KT6 ....191 G6
Redriff Primary School
BERM/RHTH SE16 ....124 B2
Red Rose Trading Estate
EBAR EN4 ....21 H6
Regal International College
ALP/SUD HA0 ....80 A3
Regent Business Centre
HYS/HAR UB3 ....114 E2
Regent Clinic
CAVSQ/HST W1G 9 J2
Regent College London
PIN HA5 ....59 K4
Regent's Park Barracks
CAMTN NW1 ....3 J5
Regents Park Clinic
CAMTN NW1 ....2 E6

Regents Park Medical Centre
CAMTN NW1 ....3 K4
Regent's Park Track
CAMTN NW1 ....2 E2
Regina Coeli RC Primary School
SAND/SEL CR2 ....211 H5
Renaissance Chancery Court Hotel
HHOL WC1V 11 G2
The Renaissance Hotel
HTHAIR TW6 ....133 F2
Renoir Cinema
BMSBY WC1N 5 F6
Renwick Industrial Estate
BARK IG11 ....109 H1
Rewards Centre
HSLW TW3 ....135 H4
Reynard Mills Trading Estate
BTFD TW8 ....116 D5
Reynolds Performing Arts
RDART DA2 ....170 B4
Reynolds Sports Centre
ACT W3 ....117 H2
Rhodes Avenue Primary School
WDGN N22 ....48 C4
Rhodes Farm Clinic
MLHL NW7 ....32 A6
Rhyl Primary School
KTTN NW5 ....84 A4
RIBA Library Drawings & Manuscript Collection
MBLAR W1H 9 F3
Ricards Lodge High School
WIM/MER SW19 ....159 J6
Richard Alibon Primary School
DAGE RM10 ....92 C3
Richard Atkins Primary School
BRXS/STRHM SW2 ....161 K2
Richard Cloudesley School
STLK EC1Y 6 C7
Richard Cobden Primary School
CAMTN NW1 ....4 B1
Richdales Istitute
ALP/SUD HA0 ....79 K6
Rich Industrial Estate
PECK SE15 ....123 J6
STHWK SE1 ....19 H5
Richmond Adult & Community College
RCH/KEW TW9 ....136 E5
Richmond American International University
RCHPK/HAM TW10 ....157 F1
The Richmond Clinic
RCH/KEW TW9 ....137 G5
Richmond Community College
TWK TW1 ....156 A3
Richmond FC
RCH/KEW TW9 ....136 E5
Richmond Gate Hotel
RCHPK/HAM TW10 ....157 F2
The Richmond Golf Club
RCHPK/HAM TW10 ....157 F4
The Richmond Green Medical Centre
RCH/KEW TW9 ....136 E6
Richmond Hill Hotel
RCHPK/HAM TW10 ....157 F2
Richmond House School
HPTN TW12 ....172 E1
Richmond Magistrates Court
RCH/KEW TW9 ....136 E5
Richmond Park Golf Club
PUT/ROE SW15 ....158 B2
Richmond Park National Nature Reserve
RCHPK/HAM TW10 ....158 B4
Richmond Road Medical Centre
KUTN/CMB KT2 ....175 F3
Richmond Theatre
RCH/KEW TW9 ....136 E5
Richmond upon Thames College
WHTN TW2 ....155 K2
Ridge House Clinic
WCHMH N21 ....35 K2
Ridgeway Hotel
CHING E4 ....37 K4
Ridgeway Primary School
SAND/SEL CR2 ....212 A6
Rio Cinema
BARK E8 ....86 B3
Ripley Arts Centre
BMLY BR1 ....184 C4
Ripple Infant School
BARK IG11 ....90 E6
Risebridge Golf Club
ROM RM1 ....57 H3
Rise Park Primary School
ROM RM1 ....57 F4
Risley Avenue Primary School
TOTM N17 ....50 A4
The Ritz Hotel
WHALL SW1A 10 A7
Ritzy Cinema
BRXN/ST SW9 ....142 B5
Riverbank Park Plaza Hotel
STHWK SE1 ....17 G7
River Brent Business Park
HNWL W7 ....115 H3
River Gardens Business Centre
EBED/NFELT TW14 ....134 A5
River House Montessori School
POP/IOD E14 ....124 D1
River Mole Business Park
ESH/CLAY KT10 ....189 F5

River Place Health Centre
IS N1 ....85 J5
River Road Business Park
BARK IG11 ....108 E2
Riversdale Primary School
WAND/EARL SW18 ....159 K3
Riverside Business Park
WAND/EARL SW18 ....160 A3
Riverside Business Park
WIM/MER SW19 ....178 B4
Riverside Community Health Care
WKENS W14 ....119 G3
Riverside Golf Club
THMD SE28 ....110 A5
Riverside Industrial Estate
BARK IG11 ....109 G2
DART DA1 ....151 H6
Riverside Primary School
BERM/RHTH SE16 ....123 H2
Riverside Quarter
WAND/EARL SW18 ....139 K5
Riverside Studios Cinema
HMSMTH W6 ....118 E5
Riverside Swimming Centre
ERITH DA8 ....130 B5
Riverside Wandle Trading Estate
MTCM CR4 ....194 A4
Riverston School
LEE/GVPK SE12 ....145 K6
Riverview CE Primary School
HOR/WEW KT19 ....206 E2
The RJ Mitchell Primary School
HCH RM12 ....93 K4
RNLI Lifeboat Station
TWRH EC3N 13 H7
Roan Industrial Estate
MTCM CR4 ....178 D4
Robert Blair Primary School
HOLWY N7 ....84 E4
Robert Browning Primary School
WALW SE17 ....122 E5
Robin Hood Infant School
SUT SM1 ....208 E3
Robin Hood Junior School
SUT SM1 ....209 F3
Robin Hood Lane Health Centre
SUT SM1 ....208 E3
Robin Hood Primary School
KUTN/CMB KT2 ....176 A1
Robinsfield Infant School
STJWD NW8 ....2 B2
The Roche School
WAND/EARL SW18 ....139 K6
Rockliffe Manor Primary School
WOOL/PLUM SE18 ....128 A6
Rockmount Primary School
NRWD SE19 ....180 D2
Rockware Business Centre
GFD/PVL UB6 ....78 D6
Roding Primary School
BCTR RM8 ....91 J2
WFD IG8 ....53 J3
Roebuck Road Trading Estate
BARK/HLT IG6 ....55 H2
Roe Green J & I School
CDALE/KGS NW9 ....62 D1
Roehampton Church School
PUT/ROE SW15 ....158 E2
The Roehampton Priory Hospital
PUT/ROE SW15 ....138 C5
Roehampton Recreation Centre
PUT/ROE SW15 ....138 E4
Roehampton University
PUT/ROE SW15 ....159 H1
Roehampton University (Digby Stuart College)
PUT/ROE SW15 ....138 C6
Roehampton University (Froebel College)
PUT/ROE SW15 ....158 C1
Roehampton University (Southlands College)
PUT/ROE SW15 ....138 D5
Roger Ascham Primary School
WALTH E17 ....51 H4
Roger Bannister Sports Ground
KTN/HRWW/WS HA3 ....42 C2
Rokeby School
KUTN/CMB KT2 ....175 K3
SRTFD E15 ....88 B5
Rokesly Primary School
CEND/HSY/T N8 ....66 E2
Roman Bath
TPL/STR WC2R 11 H5
Roman Industrial Estate
CROY/NA CRO 197 F4
Roman Road Primary School
EHAM E6 ....107 H3
Roman Wall Remains
BARB EC2Y 12 C2
Romford Cemetery
ROMW/RG RM7 ....74 E4
Romford Clinic
ROM RM1 ....75 H1
Romford County Court
ROM RM1 ....75 H1
Romford Golf Club
GPK RM2 ....57 J6
Romford Ice Arena
ROM RM1 ....75 G4
Romford IT Learning Centre
ROM RM1 ....75 G2
Romford Shopping Hall
ROM RM1 ....75 G1
Ronald Rose Primary School
PUT/ROE SW15 ....159 G2

Rood Lane Medical Centre
FENCHST EC3M 13 G5
Rooks Heath High School
RYLN/HDSTN HA2 ....78 A1
Roosevelt Memorial
MYFR/PKLN W1K 9 H5
Ropery Business Park
CHARL SE7 ....126 B4
Rosary Priory High School
BUSH WD23 ....28 E1
Rosary RC Infant School
HAMP NW3 ....114 E6
Rosary RC Primary School
HAMP NW3 ....83 J3
Rosebery Industrial Park
TOTM N17 ....50 D5
Rose Bruford College
BECK BR3 ....168 C3
Roselands Clinic
NWMAL KT3 ....191 K1
Rose McAndrew Clinic
BRXN/ST SW9 ....142 A3
Rosemead Preparatory School
DUL SE21 ....162 D4
Rosendale Primary School
DUL SE21 ....162 D2
Rose of Kingston (Kingston Theatre)
KUT/HW KT1 ....174 E5
Rose Theatre Exhibition
STHWK SE1 ....12 C7
Rosetta Primary School
CAN/RD E16 ....107 F4
Rosewood Medical Centre
HCH RM12 ....93 K3
Rosh Pinah Primary School
EDGW HA8 ....30 D4
Rosslyn Park RFC
PUT/ROE SW15 ....138 C5
Rotherfield Primary School
IS N1 ....85 J6
Rotherhithe Primary School
BERM/RHTH SE16 ....123 K4
The Rotunda
KUT/HW KT1 ....175 F5
The Roundhouse Theatre
CAMTN NW1 ....84 A5
Roundshaw J & I School
WLGTN SM6 ....210 E6
Rowan Preparatory School
ESH/CLAY KT10 ....205 F5
Rowans School
RYNPK SW20 ....176 D3
Rowhill School
RDART DA2 ....171 F6
Rowley Industrial Park
ACT W3 ....117 J3
Roxbourne Medical Centre
RYLN/HDSTN HA2 ....60 B6
Roxbourne Middle School
RYLN/HDSTN HA2 ....59 H6
Roxeth First & Middle School
RYLN/HDSTN HA2 ....60 C6
Roxeth Manor First School
RYLN/HDSTN HA2 ....78 A1
Roxeth Mead School
RYLN/HDSTN HA2 ....60 D6
Roxwell Trading Park
LEY E10 ....69 G4
Royal Academy of Arts
MYFR/PICC W1J 10 A6
Royal Academy of Dance
BTSEA SW11 ....140 D2
Royal Academy of Dramatic Art
GWRST WC1E 10 C1
Royal Academy of Music
CAMTN NW1 ....3 H7
Royal Air Force Museum
CDALE/KGS NW9 ....45 J5
Royal Albert Hall
SKENS SW7 ....14 A3
Royal Arsenal
WOOL/PLUM SE18 ....127 G3
Royal Ballet School
COVGDN WC2E 11 F4
The Royal Ballet School
RCHPK/HAM TW10 ....158 A3
Royal Blackheath Golf Club
ELTH/MOT SE9 ....166 C2
Royal Botanic Gardens Kew School
RCH/KEW TW9 ....137 G3
Royal Brompton & National Heart Hospitals
CHEL SW3 ....120 C5
Royal Chace Hotel
ENC/FH EN2 ....23 F1
Royal College of Anaesthetists
RSQ WC1B 10 E1
Royal College of Art
SKENS SW7 ....120 B2
Royal College of Music
SHB W12 ....118 D5
SKENS SW7 ....14 A4
Royal College of Nursing
CAMTN NW1 ....4 B6
IS N1 ....6 A1
Royal College of Obstetricians & Gynaecologists
CAMTN NW1 ....2 E6
Royal College of Ophthalmologists
CAMTN NW1 ....3 G3
Royal College of Paediatrics & Child Health
GTPST W1W 9 K1
The Royal College of Pathology
STJS SW1Y 16 C1
Royal College of Physicians
CAMTN NW1 ....3 J6
Royal College of Surgeons
LINN WC2A 11 H3

Royal College of Veterinary Surgeons
WEST SW1P 16 E6
Royal Courts of Justice
LINN WC2A 11 H4
Royal Court Theatre
BGVA SW1W 15 G7
The Royal Court Young Peoples Theatre
NKENS W10 .....100 C1
The Royal Dock Community School
CAN/RD E16 .....107 G5
Royal Docks Medical Centre
EHAM E6 .....108 A5
Royal Epping Forest Golf Club
CHING E4 .....38 C2
Royal Exchange
BANK EC3V 13 F4
Royal Festival Hall
STHWK SE1 .....17 G1
Royal Free Hospital School of Medicine
HAMP NW3 .....83 J3
Royal Garden Hotel
KENS W8 .....120 A2
Royal Geographical Society
SKENS SW7 .....14 A3
The Royal Horseguards Hotel
WHALL SW1A 17 F1
Royal Horticultural Society New Hall
WEST SW1P 16 C5
Royal Horticultural Society Old Hall
WEST SW1P 16 C6
Royal Hospital
RCH/KEW TW9 .....137 F6
Royal Hospital Chelsea
CHEL SW3 .....120 E5
Royal Hospital for Neuro-Disability
PUT/ROE SW15 .....159 H1
Royal Hospital & Home
PUT/ROE SW15 .....158 E2
Royal Hospital Museum
CHEL SW3 .....121 F5
Royal Institute of British Architects
REGST W1B 9 K1
Royal Institution's Faraday Museum
MYFR/PICC W1J 9 K6
Royal Lancaster Hotel
BAY/PAD W2 .....8 B6
The Royal London Estate
TOTM N17 .....50 D3
Royal London Homeopathic Hospital
BMSBY WC1N 11 F1
The Royal London Hospital
WCHPL E1 .....104 D4
Royal Marsden Hospital
CHEL SW3 .....120 C5
The Royal Mews
BGVA SW1W 15 H4
Royal Mid-Surrey Golf Club
RCH/KEW TW9 .....136 E4
Royal Military School of Music
WHTN TW2 .....155 J1
Royal Mint Court
TWRH EC3N 13 K6
Royal National Orthopaedic Hospital
GTPST W1W 3 K7
STAN HA7 .....29 H3
Royal National Theatre
CMBW SE5 .....142 D1
STHWK SE1 .....11 J7
Royal National Throat, Nose & Ear Hospital
FSBYW WC1X 5 G4
Royal Opera House
COVGDN WC2E 11 F4
Royal Park Primary School
SCUP DA14 .....169 F5
Royal Russell School
CROY/NA CR0 .....212 D4
Royal Society of Arts
CHCR WC2N 11 F6
Royal Society of Medicine
CAVSQ/HST W1G 9 J3
Royal Veterinary College
CAMTN NW1 .....4 C1
Royal Victoria Docks Watersports Centre
CAN/RD E16 .....106 E6
Royal Wimbledon Golf Club
WIM/MER SW19 .....176 E1
Royston Primary School
PGE/AN SE20 .....182 A4
RSPCA Animal Hospital
FSBYPK N4 .....67 F6
The Rubens at the Palace Hotel
BGVA SW1W 15 K4
Rudolph Steiner Hall
CAMTN NW1 .....2 E6
Rufus Business Centre
WIM/MER SW19 .....160 A4
Ruislip Gardens Primary School
RSLP HA4 .....76 C2
Ruislip Golf Club
HGDN/ICK UB10 .....58 A6
Ruislip Manor FC
RSLP HA4 .....58 D6
Ruislip RFC
RSLP HA4 .....58 C6
Ruislip Woods National Nature Reserve
NTHWD HA6 .....40 A6

RSLP HA4 .....58 C2
Rush Croft School
CHING E4 .....51 K3
Rushey Green Primary School
CAT SE6 .....164 E3
Rush Green Primary School
ROMW/RG RM7 .....75 F5
Rushmore Junior School
CLPT E5 .....86 E2
Ruskin House School
HNHL SE24 .....142 D6
The Russell JMI School
RCHPK/HAM TW10 .....156 E4
The Russell School
RCHPK/HAM TW10 .....156 E3
Russet House School
EN1 N1 .....24 D2
Rutlish School
RYNPK SW20 .....177 J5
Ruxley Corner Industrial Estate
SCUP DA14 .....186 E2
Ruxley Park Golf Centre
STMC/STPC BR5 .....186 E4
Ryefield Primary School
HGDN/ICK UB10 .....76 B6
Ryelands Primary School
SNWD SE25 .....197 J2
Rye Oak Primary School
PECK SE15 .....143 J4
Sacred Heart Catholic Primary School
PUT/ROE SW15 .....138 D6
Sacred Heart High School
HMSMTH W6 .....119 F4
Sacred Heart Junior School
HMSMTH W6 .....119 G4
Sacred Heart Language College
KTN/HRWW/WS HA3 .....42 E5
Sacred Heart RC Infant School
BTSEA SW11 .....140 D3
Sacred Heart RC Primary School
NWMAL KT3 .....192 D1
OXHEY WD19 .....27 K1
RSLP HA4 .....58 C6
TEDD TW11 .....174 C5
TRDG/WHET N20 .....33 J4
Sacred Heart RC School
CMBW SE5 .....142 D2
Sacred Heart School
HOLWY N7 .....85 F5
Saddlers Hall
CITYW EC2V 12 D3
Sadler's Wells Theatre
CLKNW EC1R 5 K4
SAE Institute
HOLWY N7 .....84 E3
Safari Cinema
CROY/NA CR0 .....196 C5
Safari Cinema & Bingo
HRW HA1 .....61 F2
Sai Medical Centre
POP/IOD E14 .....106 A6
St Agathas RC Primary School
KUTN/CMB KT2 .....175 G2
St Agnes RC Primary School
BOW E3 .....105 J2
CRICK NW2 .....82 C1
St Aidans Primary School
FSBYPK N4 .....67 G4
St Aidans RC Primary School
IL IG1 .....72 D5
St Albans CE Primary School
HCIRC EC1N 11 J1
St Albans Health Clinic
HGT N6 .....84 A1
St Albans RC Aided Primary School
E/WMO/HCT KT8 .....189 G2
St Albans CE Church & School Presbytery
HCH RM12 .....93 J3
St Albans RC JMI School
HCH RM12 .....93 K5
St Albans Road Infant School
DART DA1 .....171 J1
St Alfege with St Peter CE Primary School
GNWCH SE10 .....125 F6
St Aloysius College
HGT N6 .....66 C5
St Aloysius RC Infant School
CAMTN NW1 .....4 C4
St Aloysius RC Junior School
CAMTN NW1 .....4 B3
St Andrew & St Francis CE JMI School
CRICK NW2 .....81 J4
St Andrews CE JMI School
TRDG/WHET N20 .....32 D4
St Andrews CE Primary School
EN EN1 .....23 K3
STHGT/OAK N14 .....34 C2
St Andrews CE School
CROY/NA CR0 .....211 H2
St Andrews Greek School
CAMTN NW1 .....84 B4
St Andrews Hospital
BOW E3 .....105 K3
St Andrews Primary School
BRXN/ST SW9 .....142 A3
IS N1 .....85 H5
St Andrews School
RYLN/HDSTN HA2 .....60 B2
WLSDN NW10 .....81 K5
St Angelas Ursuline Convent School
FSTGT E7 .....89 F4
St Annes Catholic High School for Girls
ENC/FH EN2 .....23 K5
PLMGR N13 .....35 G6

St Annes CE Primary School
WAND/EARL SW18 .....140 A6
St Annes CP School
STWL/WRAY TW19 .....152 B2
St Annes CE Primary School
LBTH SE11 .....122 A6
St Anne's Special School
MRDN SM4 .....193 K2
St Anne's Trading Estate
POP/IOD E14 .....105 H5
St Anns CE Primary School
SEVS/STOTM N15 .....67 K2
St Ann's General Hospital
FSBYPK N4 .....67 J2
St Anns School
HNWL W7 .....115 K1
St Ann's Shopping Centre
HRW HA1 .....60 E3
St Anselms RC Primary School
DART DA1 .....151 J6
HRW HA1 .....60 E4
NWDGN UB2 .....114 E3
St Anselms RC Primary School
TOOT SW17 .....161 F5
St Anthonys Hospital
WPK KT4 .....193 G5
St Anthonys RC Primary School
EDUL SE22 .....163 H1
PGE/AN SE20 .....181 J4
St Anthony's School (Junior House)
HAMP NW3 .....83 H3
St Anthony's School (Senior House)
HAMP NW3 .....83 G3
St Antonys RC Primary School
FSTGT E7 .....88 E5
St Aubyns School
WFD IG8 .....52 D5
St Augustines CE High School
KIL/WHAMP NW6 .....100 E1
St Augustines Primary School
BELV DA17 .....129 G3
KIL/WHAMP NW6 .....101 F1
St Augustines Priory School
EA W5 .....98 A4
St Augustines RC Infant School
GNTH/NBYPK IG2 .....72 B2
St Augustines RC Primary School
CAT SE6 .....182 E1
GNTH/NBYPK IG2 .....72 B2
HMSMTH W6 .....119 H6
St Barnabas & St Philip's CE Primary School
KENS W8 .....119 K3
St Bartholomews CE Primary School
SYD SE26 .....163 K6
St Bartholomews Hospital
STBT EC1A 12 B2
St Bartholomews Medical School
FARR EC1M 6 B7
St Bartholomews & Royal London School of Medicine
FARR EC1M 12 C1
St Bartholomew's the Great
STBT EC1A 12 B2
St Barts Hospital Sports Ground
CHST BR7 .....185 J2
St Bedes RC Infant School
BAL SW12 .....161 J3
St Bedes RC Primary School
CHDH RM6 .....73 J2
St Benedicts Junior School
EA W5 .....97 J4
St Benedicts School
EA W5 .....97 K4
St Bernadette Catholic Junior School
BAL SW12 .....161 H2
St Bernadettes RC First and Middle School
KTN/HRWW/WS HA3 .....62 A1
St Bonaventures School
FSTGT E7 .....88 E5
St Boniface RC Primary School
TOOT SW17 .....178 E1
St Catherines RC Girls School
BXLYHS DA6 .....149 J6
St Catherines RC J & I School
WDR/YW UB7 .....112 A2
St Catherines RC School
BAR EN5 .....20 D5
St Catherines School
TWK TW1 .....156 A4
St Cecilia's CE Primary School
WAND/EARL SW18 .....159 H2
St Cecilias RC Primary School
WPK KT4 .....193 G6
St Chads RC Primary School
SNWD SE25 .....197 F2
St Charles Hospital
NKENS W10 .....100 B4
St Charles RC Primary School
NKENS W10 .....100 B4
St Christinas Preparatory School
STJWD NW8 .....2 D2
St Christophers School
BECK BR3 .....183 F5
HAMP NW3 .....83 H3
WBLY HA9 .....80 B1
St Clare Business Park
HPTN TW12 .....173 H2
St Clement Danes CE Primary School
HOL/ALD WC2B 11 G4
St Clement & St James CE Primary School
NTGHL W11 .....119 H1

St Clements Hospital
BOW E3 .....105 H2
St Clements Primary School
EW KT17 .....207 H6
St Columbas RC Boys School
BXLYHS DA6 .....149 J6
St Cuthbert With St Matthias CE Primary School
ECT SW5 .....120 A5
St Cyprians Greek Orthodox Primary School
THHTH CR7 .....180 D5
St Davids College
WWKM BR4 .....198 E4
St Davids Health Centre
STWL/WRAY TW19 .....152 A2
St Davids School
ASHF TW15 .....152 C5
St Dominics RC Primary School
HAMP NW3 .....83 K3
St Dominics Sixth Form College
HRW HA1 .....60 E6
St Dunstans CE Primary School
CHEAM SM3 .....208 C4
St Dunstans College
CAT SE6 .....164 C3
St Ebba's Hospital
HOR/WEW KT19 .....206 E6
St Edmunds RC Primary School
ED N9 .....36 D3
POP/IOD E14 .....124 D4
WHTN TW2 .....155 G2
St Edwards CE Comprehensive School
CHDH RM6 .....74 C3
St Edwards CE Primary School
ROM RM1 .....75 F1
St Edwards RC JMI School
STJWD NW8 .....2 C7
St Elizabeths RC Primary School
RCHPK/HAM TW10 .....157 G1
St Elpheges RC Primary School
WLGTN SM6 .....210 E4
St Eugene de Mazenod RC Primary School
KIL/WHAMP NW6 .....82 E5
St Faiths CE School
WAND/EARL SW18 .....140 A6
St Fidelis Catholic Primary School
ERITH DA8 .....129 K6
St Francesca Cabrini Primary School
FSTH SE23 .....163 K1
St Francis de Sales RC Junior & Infant School
TOTM N17 .....50 A3
St Francis of Assisi Primary School
NKENS W10 .....100 B6
St Francis RC Primary School
PECK SE15 .....123 H6
SRTFD E15 .....88 C3
St Francis Xavier College
BAL SW12 .....161 G1
St Gabriels CE Primary School
PIM SW1V 121 H5
St George's Cathedral
STHWK SE1 .....17 K4
St Georges CE Primary School
BMLY BR1 .....184 B5
CMBW SE5 .....143 F1
VX/NE SW8 .....141 H2
St Georges College
HOLWY N7 .....85 G1
St Georges Elizabethan Theatre
HOLWY N7 .....84 D2
St Georges Hanover Square CE Primary School
MYFR/PKLN W1K 9 H6
St Georges Hospital
TOOT SW17 .....178 D1
St Georges Industrial Estate
KUTN/CMB KT2 .....174 E5
PLMGR N13 .....49 H3
St Georges Medical Centre
HDN NW4 .....45 K6
St Georges RC Primary School
ENC/FH EN2 .....23 K3
HRW HA1 .....79 F1
St Georges RC School
MV/WKIL W9 .....101 F1
St Georges Shopping Centre & Cinema
HRW HA1 .....60 D3
St George the Martyr CE Primary School
BMSBY WC1N 5 G7
St Gildas RC Junior School
CEND/HSY/T N8 .....66 E4
St Giles College London Central
RSQ WC1B 11 F1
St Giles School
SAND/SEL CR2 .....211 H4
St Gregorys High School
KTN/HRWW/WS HA3 .....61 K2
St Gregorys RC Primary School
EA W5 .....97 J3
St Helens Catholic Infant School
WALTH E17 .....70 A2
St Helens RC Primary School
BRXN/ST SW9 .....142 B4
CAN/RD E16 .....106 D3
St Helens School
NTHWD HA6 .....40 C2
St Helier Hospital
CAR SM5 .....194 B5

St Hildas School
BUSH WD23 .....28 B2
St Ignatius RC Primary School
SEVS/STOTM N15 .....68 A3
St James CE J & I School
BERM/RHTH SE16 .....123 H3
St James CE Primary School
MUSWH N10 .....66 A1
NWCR SE14 .....144 B2
PEND EN3 .....24 E3
St James CE Junior School
FSTGT E7 .....88 D3
St James Independent School for Senior Boys
TWK TW1 .....156 B4
St James Independent School for Senior Girls
WKENS W14 .....119 H4
St James Independent Schools For Junior Boys & Girls *WKENS* W14 .....119 H4
St James Medical Centre
CROY/NA CR0 .....196 E4
St James RC Primary School
HAYES BR2 .....201 G2
WHTN TW2 .....155 K5
St James & St Michaels CE Primary School
BAY/PAD W2 .....101 G6
St James's Health Centre
WALTH E17 .....69 G2
St James's Palace
WHALL SW1A 16 B1
St James the Great RC Primary School
PECK SE15 .....143 G2
THHTH CR7 .....180 C5
St Joachims RC Primary School
CAN/RD E16 .....107 C5
St Joan of Arc RC Primary School
HBRY N5 .....85 H2
St John Fisher RC First & Middle School
PIN HA5 .....60 A1
St John Fisher RC Primary School
ERITH DA18 .....129 F3
GFD/PVL UB6 .....97 J2
RYNPK SW20 .....193 F2
St John of Jerusalem CE Primary School
HOM E9 .....86 E5
St Johns and St James CE School
UED N18 .....50 B1
St Johns Angell Town CE Primary School
BRXN/ST SW9 .....142 C3
St Johns CE First School
STAN HA7 .....29 G6
St Johns CE Middle School
STAN HA7 .....29 G6
St Johns CE Primary School
BETH E2 .....104 E1
BKHH IG9 .....39 F3
CROY/NA CR0 .....213 F1
FBAR/BDGN N11 .....33 K6
KUT/HW KT1 .....175 F6
PGE/AN SE20 .....181 K3
TRDG/WHET N20 .....33 G4
St Johns CE School
CDALE/KGS NW9 .....63 G2
St John CE Walham Green School
FUL/PGN SW6 .....139 H2
St John's Concert Hall
WEST SW1P 16 E5
St Johns Highbury Vale CE Primary School
HBRY N5 .....85 H2
St John's Hospital Day Centre
BTSEA SW11 .....140 C5
St John's Lodge
CAMTN NW1 .....3 G4
St Johns Preparatory & Senior School
ENC/FH EN2 .....23 G2
St Johns Primary School
WEA W13 .....97 G6
St Johns RC Primary School
BERM/RHTH SE16 .....124 B2
St Johns RC Special School
WFD IG8 .....54 A1
St Johns & St Clements CE J & I School
PECK SE15 .....143 H4
St Johns School
NTHWD HA6 .....41 F2
St Johns Upper Holloway CE Primary School
ARCH N19 .....84 D1
St Johns Walworth CE Primary School
WALW SE17 .....18 C7
St Johns Way Medical Centre
ARCH N19 .....66 D5
St Johns Wood Preparatory School
STJWD NW8 .....2 C4
St John the Baptist CE Junior School
KUT/HW KT1 .....174 E3
St John the Baptist CE Primary School
BMLY BR1 .....165 F6
IS N1 .....7 G3
St John the Divine CE Primary School
CMBW SE5 .....142 C1
St John the Evangelist RC Primary School
IS N1 .....6 A2
St John Vianney RC Primary School
SEVS/STOTM N15 .....67 H1

St Josephs Academic RC School
BKHTH/KID SE3 ....145 H4
St Joseph's Annexe
ABYW SE2 ....128 D6
St Josephs Catholic Infant School
LEY E10 ....69 H5
St Josephs Catholic Junior School
CMBW SE5 ....142 D1
St Josephs Catholic Primary School
BMLY BR1 ....184 B3
St Josephs College
STRHM/NOR SW16 ....180 C2
St Josephs Convent School
WAN E11 ....70 E3
St Josephs Primary School
HDN NW4 ....63 K1
WAND/EARL SW18 ....139 K6
St Josephs RC College
MLHL NW7 ....31 H6
St Josephs RC First & Middle School
KTN/HRWW/WS HA3 ....43 G5
St Josephs RC Infant School
NRWD SE19 ....180 D2
St Josephs RC Junior School
LEY E10 ....69 J5
NRWD SE19 ....180 D2
WBLY HA9 ....80 B3
St Josephs RC Primary School
ARCH N19 ....66 B5
BARK IG11 ....90 C6
BERM/RHTH SE16 ....123 K3
CHEL SW3 ....14 E7
DAGW RM9 ....92 B5
DART DA1 ....150 A5
DEPT SE8 ....144 D1
GNWCH SE10 ....125 H5
HNWL W7 ....115 K1
HOL/ALD WC2B 11 F5
KUT/HW KT1 ....175 F5
OXHEY WD19 ....27 F5
STHWK SE1 ....18 D2
STHWK SE1 ....123 H2
WLSDN NW10 ....81 G5
St Judes CE Primary School
HNHL SE24 ....162 C1
STHWK SE1 ....18 A5
St Judes & St Pauls CE Primary School
IS N1 ....86 A3
St Katharine Pier
WAP E1W 13 K7
St Katherine
TPL/STR WC2R 11 H6
St Lawrence Business Centre
FELT TW13 ....154 A4
St Lawrence Catholic School
FELT TW13 ....154 A4
St Lawrence Junior School
E/WMO/HCT KT8 ....173 J6
St Lawrence University
BMSBY WC1N 5 H7
St Leonards CE Primary School
STRHM/NOR SW16 ....179 J1
St Leonards Hospital
IS N1 ....7 H2
St Luke's Catholic Sixth Form College
SCUP DA14 ....186 B1
St Lukes CE Primary School
CAN/RD E16 ....106 D5
FSBYE EC1V 6 D5
KUTN/CMB KT2 ....175 G4
MV/WKIL W9 ....100 D1
POP/IOD E14 ....125 G4
WNWD SE27 ....180 D1
St Luke's Health Centre
CAN/RD E16 ....106 D5
St Luke's Hospital for the Clergy
FITZ W1T 4 A7
St Lukes School
THHTH CR7 ....196 B1
St Lukes Woodside Hospital
MUSWH N10 ....66 A1
St Margaret Clitherow RC Primary
THMD SE28 ....128 C1
St Margaret Lee CE Primary School
LEW SE13 ....145 H5
St Margarets Business Centre
TWK TW1 ....156 B2
St Margarets Clitherow RC Primary School
WOOL/PLUM SE18 ....127 H6
St Margarets Primary School
WBLY HA9 ....80 E1
St Margarets Primary School
BARK IG11 ....90 B6
St Margarets School
BUSH WD23 ....28 A2
HAMP NW3 ....83 F2
St Marks Catholic School
HSLW TW3 ....134 E4
St Marks CE Primary School
ARCH N19 ....66 A4
HAYES BR2 ....183 K6
LBTH SE11 ....122 A6
SNWD SE25 ....197 H1
St Marks Industrial Estate
CAN/RD E16 ....126 C1
St Marks Primary School
HNWL W7 ....115 K4
MTCM CR4 ....178 E5
St Marthas Senior School
EBAR EN4 ....20 E2
St Martin-in-the-Fields
CHCR WC2N 10 E6
St Martin in the Fields High School
BRXS/STRHM SW2 ....162 C3

St Martin of Porres Primary School
FBAR/BDGN N11 ....48 C2
St Martins Hospital
MYFR/PKLN W1K 9 G5
St Martins Medical Centre
RSLP HA4 ....58 C4
St Martins School
MLHL NW7 ....45 G1
St Martins School of Art
SOHO/SHAV W1D 10 C4
St Martins Theatre
LSQ/SEVD WC2H 10 D5
St Mary Abbots CE Primary School
KENS W8 ....120 A2
St Mary at St Pancras CE Primary School
CAMTN NW1 ....4 C3
The St Marylebone CE School
MHST W1U 9 H1
St Marylebone Crematorium
FNCH N3 ....47 F6
St Mary Magdalene CE Primary School
MV/WKIL W9 ....101 F4
WOOL/PLUM SE18 ....126 E4
St Mary Magdalene Primary School
HOLWY N7 ....85 G4
St Mary Magdalen RC Junior School
CRICK NW2 ....81 K4
St Mary Magdalens Catholic Primary School
BROCKY SE4 ....144 B5
MORT/ESHN SW14 ....158 A4
St Mary of the Angels RC Primary School
NTGHL W11 ....100 D1
St Marys Abbey
MLHL NW7 ....31 J5
St Mary & St Joseph Catholic School
SCUP DA14 ....186 A1
St Mary & St Michael RC Primary School
WCHPL E1 ....104 E5
St Mary & St Peters CE Primary School
TEDD TW11 ....173 K1
St Marys Bryanston Square CE Primary School
MBLAR W1H 8 D1
St Marys Catholic Primary School
CHING E4 ....38 B3
HCH RM12 ....75 J5
St Marys CE Junior School
CEND/HSY/T N8 ....66 E1
STWL/WRAY TW19 ....152 B1
THDIT KT7 ....190 C5
St Mary's Cemetery
BTSEA SW11 ....140 D6
St Marys CE Primary School
CHSGTN KT9 ....206 A4
EBAR EN4 ....33 J1
FNCH N3 ....46 D4
IS N1 ....85 H5
LEW SE13 ....144 E6
St Mary's CE Primary School
PUT/ROE SW15 ....139 G4
St Marys CE Primary School
STNW/STAM N16 ....67 K6
TWK TW1 ....156 B2
WALTH E17 ....69 K1
WLSDN NW10 ....81 G4
St Marys Greek Cathedral
WDGN N22 ....49 F4
St Marys High School
CROY/NA CR0 ....196 D5
St Marys Hospital
BAY/PAD W2 ....8 B3
St Marys Hospital Medical School
BAY/PAD W2 ....8 B3
St Marys Infant School
CAR SM5 ....209 J2
St Mary's Junior School
TWK TW1 ....156 C2
St Marys Kilburn Primary School
KIL/WHAMP NW6 ....82 E6
St Marys Primary School
WKENS W14 ....119 G3
St Marys RC Infant School
CAR SM5 ....209 K3
St Marys RC J & I School
WALTH E17 ....52 A6
St Marys RC Junior School
WALTH E17 ....52 A6
St Mary's RC Primary School
BECK BR3 ....183 F3
St Mary's RC Primary School
CHSWK W4 ....118 B5
St Marys RC Primary School
CLAP SW4 ....141 H6
ELTH/MOT SE9 ....147 F6
St Marys RC Primary School
FSBYPK N4 ....67 K2
St Marys RC Primary School
ISLW TW7 ....136 B4
KIL/WHAMP NW6 ....100 E1
NKENS W10 ....100 C3
PEND EN3 ....25 F5
VX/NE SW8 ....141 G2
WIM/MER SW19 ....177 K3
St Marys CE & St Johns CE Primary School
HDN NW4 ....63 K2
St Marys School
CEND/HSY/T N8 ....67 F2
HAMP NW3 ....83 G3
St Marys University College Twickenham
TWK TW1 ....156 A5

St Matthews CE Primary School
PEND EN3 ....24 E6
RYNPK SW20 ....176 D4
SURB KT6 ....191 F4
WDR/YW UB7 ....112 B1
St Mattrias CE Primary School
BETH E2 ....7 K6
STNW/STAM N16 ....86 A3
St Meryl RC School
OXHEY WD19 ....27 J5
St Michael at Bowes CE Junior School
PLMGR N13 ....49 G2
St Michaels and St Martins RC Primary School
HSLWW TW4 ....134 E4
St Michaels Catholic Grammar School
NFNCH/WDSPK N12 ....47 F1
St Michaels CE Primary School
ENC/FH EN2 ....23 J2
HGT N6 ....66 A4
WAND/EARL SW18 ....159 J2
WDGN N22 ....49 F4
St Michaels CE Aided Primary School Hall
WELL DA16 ....148 D2
St Michaels RC Primary School
EHAM E6 ....107 K1
St Michaels RC Secondary School
BERM/RHTH SE16 ....123 H2
St Michaels Sydenham CE Primary School
SYD SE26 ....164 B6
The St Michael Steiner School
WAND/EARL SW18 ....139 K6
St Monicas RC Primary School
IS N1 ....7 G4
St Monica's RC Primary School
IS N1 ....7 G4
St Monicas RC Primary School
STHGT/OAK N14 ....34 E5
St Nicholas Centre
SUT SM1 ....209 F3
St Nicholas Preparatory School
CDALE/KGS NW9 ....62 E6
SKENS SW7 ....14 B3
St Nicholas School
BORE WD6 ....30 A1
CHST BR7 ....185 H3
St Olaves Grammar School
ORP BR6 ....217 H1
St Olaves Preparatory School
ELTH/MOT SE9 ....167 G4
St Pancras Hospital
CAMTN NW1 ....4 C1
St Pancras International Youth Hostel
CAMTN NW1 ....4 D1
St Pancras & Islington Cemetery
EFNCH N2 ....47 J4
St Patricks Church School
STHWK SE1 ....17 J1
St Patricks Infants School
WAP E1W 123 J1
St Patricks International School
SOHO/SHAV W1D 10 B3
St Patricks Primary School
KTTN NW5 ....84 B4
St Patricks RC JMI School
ROMW/RG RM7 ....56 D4
St Patricks RC Primary School
WALTH E17 ....69 G1
WOOL/PLUM SE18 ....127 J4
St Paulinus CE Primary School
DART DA1 ....150 B5
St Pauls & All Hallows CE Infant School
TOTM N17 ....50 C3
St Pauls & All Hallows CE Junior School
TOTM N17 ....50 C3
St Paul's Cathedral
STP EC4M 12 C4
St Paul's Cathedral School
STP EC4M 12 C4
St Pauls CE Primary School
BTFD TW8 ....116 E6
CHSGTN KT9 ....206 A2
FBAR/BDGN N11 ....48 A1
HAMP NW3 ....83 J5
MLHL NW7 ....31 K6
WALW SE17 ....122 C5
WCHMH N21 ....35 H2
WCHPL E1 ....104 C5
St Pauls CE Junior School
KUTN/CMB KT2 ....175 H3
St Pauls Cray CE Primary School
STMC/STPC BR5 ....186 D6
St Pauls Cray Health Clinic
STMC/STPC BR5 ....186 B5
St Pauls Girls School
HMSMTH W6 ....119 G4
St Paul's Primary School
HMSMTH W6 ....119 F5
St Pauls RC Primary School
THDIT KT7 ....190 C5
WDGN N22 ....49 F5
St Pauls RC School
ABYW SE2 ....128 B6
St Pauls Road Medical Centre
IS N1 ....85 H4
St Pauls School
BARN SW13 ....118 C5
St Pauls Steiner School
IS N1 ....85 K4
St Pauls Way Community School
BOW E3 ....105 J4

St Pauls with St Lukes CE Primary School
BOW E3 ....105 H4
St Paul's with St Michael's CE Primary School
HACK E8 ....86 C6
St Peter Chanel RC Primary School
SCUP DA14 ....186 D1
St Peter & Paul RC Primary School
STMC/STPC BR5 ....185 K5
St Peter & St Pauls Primary School
FSBYE EC1V 6 A6
St Peters Catholic School
ROM RM1 ....57 F6
St Peters CE Primary School
HMSMTH W6 ....118 D5
MV/WKIL W9 ....100 D3
WALW SE17 ....122 E5
WAP E1W 123 K1
St Peters Eaton Square CE Primary School
BGVA SW1W 15 J5
St Peter's Hospital
COVGDN WC2E 11 F5
St Peters Primary School
SAND/SEL CR2 ....211 K4
St Peter RC Primary School
DAGW RM9 ....92 B6
WOOL/PLUM SE18 ....127 G5
St Philips School
CHSGTN KT9 ....205 K4
SKENS SW7 ....120 B4
St Phillips Infant School
SKENS SW7 ....163 J6
St Philomenas Catholic High School
CAR SM5 ....209 J3
St Philomenas RC Primary School
STMC/STPC BR5 ....202 D4
St Quintins Health Centre
NKENS W10 ....100 A4
St Raphaels Hospice
WPK KT4 ....193 G6
St Raphaels RC Primary School
NTHLT UB5 ....95 F1
St Raphaels Way Medical Centre
WLSDN NW10 ....80 E3
St Richards with St Andrews CE Primary School
RCHPK/HAM TW10 ....156 C5
St Robert Southwell RC Primary School
CDALE/KGS NW9 ....62 D3
St Saviour & St Olaves School
STHWK SE1 ....19 F5
St Saviours CE Primary School
HNHL SE24 ....142 D4
MV/WKIL W9 ....101 F5
POP/IOD E14 ....105 K4
WALTH E17 ....51 H6
St Saviours CE Infant School
EA W5 ....116 E1
St Saviours RC Primary School
LEW SE13 ....145 K5
St Scholasticas RC Primary School
CLPT E5 ....86 C1
St Stephens CE Junior School
TWK TW1 ....156 B1
St Stephens CE Primary School
BAY/PAD W2 ....100 E4
DEPT SE8 ....144 D5
SHB W12 ....119 F1
St Stephens CE School
VX/NE SW8 ....141 K1
St Stephens Primary School
EHAM E6 ....89 G1
St Stephens RC Primary School
WELL DA16 ....148 B4
St Swithun Wells RC Primary School
RSLP HA4 ....77 G1
St Teresa RC Primary School
BCTR RM8 ....91 J2
St Teresas RC Primary School
KTN/HRWW/WS HA3 ....42 C4
St Theresas RC Primary School
FNCH N3 ....46 E6
St Thomas a' Becket RC Primary School
ABYW SE2 ....128 B3
St Thomas Becket RC Primary School
SNWD SE25 ....197 H3
St Thomas CE Primary School
NKENS W10 ....88 C4
St Thomas' Hospital
STHWK SE1 ....17 G4
St Thomas More RC Primary School
BXLYHN DA7 ....149 G3
ELTH/MOT SE9 ....146 D4
St Thomas More RC School
CHEL SW3 ....14 E6
ELTH/MOT SE9 ....167 F1
WDGN N22 ....49 F3
St Thomas of Canterbury Primary School
MTCM CR4 ....179 F6
St Thomas of Canterbury RC Primary School
FUL/PGN SW6 ....139 J1
St Thomas the Apostle College
PECK SE15 ....143 K2

St Ursulas Catholic Infant School
HARH RM5 ....57 K2
St Ursulas Convent School
GNWCH SE10 ....145 G1
St Vincent De Paul RC Primary School
WEST SW1P 16 A5
St Vincents Catholic Primary School
ELTH/MOT SE9 ....166 D6
St Vincents Hospital
PIN HA5 ....40 C6
St Vincents RC Primary School
ACT W3 ....98 D6
BCTR RM8 ....73 J6
St Vincent's RC Primary School
MHST W1U 9 G2
St Vincents RC Primary School
MLHL NW7 ....31 K6
St Walter & St John Sports Ground
TOOT SW17 ....160 D3
St William of York Primary School
FSTH SE23 ....164 B2
St Winefrides Catholic Primary School
MNPK E12 ....89 K3
St Winifreds Catholic Junior School
LEE/GVPK SE12 ....165 J1
St Winifreds RC Infant School
LEW SE13 ....145 K6
SS Angelas & Bonaventures Sixth Form Centre
FSTGT E7 ....89 F4
SS Peter & Paul RC Primary School
MTCM CR4 ....194 E1
SS Peter & Pauls Catholic Primary School
IL IG1 ....90 D1
Salcombe Preparatory School (Infants)
STHGT/OAK N14 ....34 B1
Salcombe Preparatory School (Juniors)
STHGT/OAK N14 ....34 B2
Salisbury Primary School
MNPK E12 ....89 H3
Salisbury School
ED N9 ....36 E2
Salters' Hall
BARB EC2Y 12 D2
Salusbury Primary School
KIL/WHAMP NW6 ....82 C6
Salvatorian College
KTN/HRWW/WS HA3 ....42 D5
Samaritan & Western Ophthalmic Hospital
MBLAR W1H 8 E1
Samuel Jones Industrial Estate
PECK SE15 ....143 F1
Samuel Rhodes School
IS N1 ....85 G6
Sanderstead Junior School
SAND/SEL CR2 ....211 K6
Sandgate Trading Estate
BERM/RHTH SE16 ....123 J5
Sandhurst Primary School
CAT SE6 ....165 H2
Sandown Golf Centre
ESH/CLAY KT10 ....204 B1
Sandown Grandstand & Exhibition Centre
ESH/CLAY KT10 ....204 B1
Sandown Industrial Park
ESH/CLAY KT10 ....189 F6
Sandown Park Racecourse
ESH/CLAY KT10 ....204 B1
Sandown Sports Club & Dry Ski Slope
ESH/CLAY KT10 ....204 B1
Sandringham Primary School
FSTGT E7 ....89 F4
Sandy Lodge Golf Club
NTHWD HA6 ....26 B4
Sapcote Trading Centre
WLSDN NW10 ....81 H3
Sarah Bonnell School
SRTFD E15 ....88 C4
Sarum Hall School
HAMP NW3 ....83 J5
Sattmer Trust School
STNW/STAM N16 ....68 C6
Savoy Pier
TPL/STR WC2R 11 G6
Savoy Theatre
TPL/STR WC2R 11 G6
Saxon Business Centre
WIM/MER SW19 ....178 B5
Sayer Clinic
CROY/NA CR0 ....211 F2
Sayer Clinics
MBLAR W1H 9 F4
Schomberg House
STJS SW1Y 16 B1
School of English
GLDGN NW11 ....64 E5
School of Oriental & African Studies
GWRST WC1E 4 D7
The School of Pharmacy
BMSBY WC1N 5 H7
The School of St David & St Katharine
CEND/HSY/T N8 ....66 E1
Science Museum
SKENS SW7 ....14 B5
Science Museum IMAX Cinema
SKENS SW7 ....14 A5

The Science Museum Library
SKENS SW7 ....14 A4
Scotts Park Primary School
BMLY BR1 ....184 B4
Scott Wilkie Primary School
CAN/RD E16 ....107 G5
Screen on Baker Street
Cinema
MHST W1U 9 F1
Screen on the Green Cinema
IS N1 ....6 A1
Screen on the Hill Cinema
HAMP NW3 ....83 J3
Sebright Primary School
BETH E2 ....104 C1
Secombe Centre
SUT SM1 ....209 F4
Sedgehill School
CAT SE6 ....182 E1
Sedgewick Centre
WCHPL E1 ....13 K3
Selborne Primary School
GFD/PVL UB6 ....97 F1
The Selfridge Hotel
MBLAR W1H 9 H4
Selhurst High School for Boys
CROY/NA CRO 196 E3
The Selhurst Medical Centre
SNWD SE25 ....197 F3
Sellincourt School
TOOT SW17 ....178 D2
Selsdon High School
SAND/SEL CR2 ....213 F5
Selsdon Primary School
SAND/SEL CR2 ....212 E6
Selsdon Road Industrial
Estate
SAND/SEL CR2 ....211 K5
Selwyn Primary School
CHING E4 ....52 A2
PLSTW E13 ....88 E6
Sergeant Industrial Estate
WAND/EARL SW18 ....160 A1
Serpentine Gallery
BAY/PAD W2 ....14 B1
Servite RC Primary School
WBPTN SW10 ....120 B6
Seven Islands Leisure Centre
BERM/RHTH SE16 ....123 K3
Seven Kings Health Centre
GDMY/SEVK IG3 ....72 E5
Seven Kings High School
GNTH/NBYPK IG2 ....72 D4
Seven Mills Primary School
POP/IOD E14 ....124 D2
Sevenoaks Way Industrial
Estate
STMC/STPC BR5 ....186 D6
Seven Sisters Primary School
SEVS/STOTM N15 ....67 K2
Seymour Gardens Medical
Centre
IL IG1 ....71 K5
Seymour Leisure Centre
MBLAR W1H 8 E2
Shaare Zedek Medical Centre
GLDGN NW11 ....64 D3
Shacklewell Primary School
HACK E8 ....86 B2
Shadwell Dock Stairs
WAP E1W 105 F6
Shaftesbury High School
KTN/HRWW/WS HA3 ....42 B4
Shaftesbury Hospital
LSQ/SEVD WC2H 10 E4
Shaftesbury Medical Centre
RYLN/HDSTN HA2 ....60 C5
Shaftesbury Park Primary
School
BTSEA SW11 ....141 F4
Shaftesbury Primary School
FSTGT E7 ....89 G5
Shaftesbury Theatre
LSQ/SEVD WC2H 10 E3
Shahjalal Medical Centre
WCHPL E1 ....104 C5
Shakespeare Business Centre
BRXN/ST SW9 ....142 C4
Shakespeare's Globe
Exhibition & Theatre
STHWK SE1 ....12 B6
The Shamrock Sports Club
ACT W3 ....98 E5
Shannon Corner Retail Park
NWMAL KT3 ....192 D1
Shapla J & I School
WCHPL E1 ....104 C6
Sharp Sports Centre
EDGW HA8 ....44 C2
Shawcroft School
STMC/STPC BR5 ....203 F2
Sheen International School
MORT/ESHN SW14 ....138 B5
Sheen Lane Health Centre
MORT/ESHN SW14 ....137 K4
Sheen Lawn Tennis & Squash
Club
MORT/ESHN SW14 ....137 K6
Sheen Mount Primary
School
RCHPK/HAM TW10 ....137 J6
Sheen Sports Centre
MORT/ESHN SW14 ....138 B5
Shell Centre
STHWK SE1 ....17 H1
Shelley School
CLAP SW4 ....141 H4
Shenstone School
DART DA1 ....150 A6
Shepherd's Bush CC
ACT W3 ....99 G6
Shepherd's Bush Empire
SHB W12 ....119 F2
Sheraton Belgravia Hotel
KTBR SW1X 15 G5
Sheraton Business Centre
GFD/PVL UB6 ....97 J1

Sheraton Park Tower Hotel
KTBR SW1X 15 F2
Sheraton Skyline Hotel
HYS/HAR UB3 ....133 G1
Sheringdale Primary School
WAND/EARL SW18 ....159 J3
Sheringham Junior School
MNPK E12 ....89 K2
Sherington Primary School
CHARL SE7 ....126 A6
Sherlock Holmes Hotel
MHST W1U 9 F1
Sherlock Holmes Museum
CAMTN NW1 ....3 F7
Sherwood Park Primary
School
BFN/LL DA15 ....168 C1
Sherwood Park School
WLGTN SM6 ....210 D1
Sherwood School
MTCM CR4 ....195 H1
Shirley Clinic
CROY/NA CRO 197 K5
Shirley High School
CROY/NA CRO 213 F1
Shirley Oaks Hospital
CROY/NA CRO 197 K4
Shirley Park Golf Club
CROY/NA CRO 197 J6
Shirley Wanderers RFC
CROY/NA CRO 214 A2
Shooters Hill Golf Club
WOOL/PLUM SE18 ....147 H2
Shooters Hill Post 16 Campus
WOOL/PLUM SE18 ....147 F1
Shooting Star House
(Childrens Hospice)
HPTN TW12 ....172 E2
Shopping City
WDGN N22 ....49 F5
The Shopping Hall
EHAM E6 ....89 J6
Shore Business Centre
HOM E9 ....86 E5
Shoreditch Comprehensive
School
IS N1 ....7 H3
Shoreditch County Court
STLK EC1Y 7 F6
Shortlands Golf Club
HAYES BR2 ....183 H4
Shotfield Health Clinic
WLGTN SM6 ....210 B4
Showcase Cinema
WDGN N22 ....49 G5
Showcase Newham Cinema
BARK IG11 ....108 C2
Shrewsbury House School
SURB KT6 ....190 E6
Shrewsbury Road Health
Centre
FSTGT E7 ....89 H5
Sidcup Cemetery
BXLY DA5 ....168 E4
Sidcup Golf Club
BFN/LL DA15 ....168 B4
Sidcup Health Centre
SCUP DA14 ....168 B5
Sidcup Sports Club
SCUP DA14 ....168 A6
Sidney Russell School
DAGW RM9 ....92 A2
Silicon Business Centre
GFD/PVL UB6 ....97 J1
Silverdale Industrial Estate
HYS/HAR UB3 ....113 K1
Silver Industrial Estate
TOTM N17 ....50 B5
Silver Street Medical Centre
UED N18 ....36 A6
Silver Wing Industrial Estate
CROY/NA CRO 211 F4
Simon Marks Jewish Primary
School
STNW/STAM N16 ....68 B5
Singlegate Primary School
WIM/MER SW19 ....178 C3
Sion College
EMB EC4Y 11 K5
Sion Manning RC Girls School
NKENS W10 ....100 B4
Sir Francis Drake Primary
School
DEPT SE8 ....124 B5
Sir George Monoux College
WALTH E17 ....51 K5
Sir James Altham Swimming
Pool
OXHEY WD19 ....41 J1
Sir James Barrie School
VX/NE SW8 ....141 H2
Sir John Cass Foundation &
Redcoat CE Secondary
School WCHPL E1 ....105 F4
Sir John Cass Foundation
School
HDTCH EC3A 13 H4
Sir John Lillie Primary
School
HMSMTH W6 ....119 H6
Sir John Soane's Museum
LINN WC2A 11 G3
Sir Thomas Abney Primary
School
STNW/STAM N16 ....67 K4
Sir Thomas Lipton Memorial
Hospital
STHGT/OAK N14 ....34 B2
Sir William Burrough Primary
School
POP/IOD E14 ....105 G5
Site of Greenwich Hospital
GNWCH SE10 ....125 J5
Six Bridges Trading Estate
STHWK SE1 ....123 H5
The Sixth Form College
CLPT E5 ....86 D1

Skillion Business Park
BARK IG11 ....109 F2
Skinners Companys Lower
Girls School
CLPT E5 ....68 D5
Skinners Companys School
for Girls
STNW/STAM N16 ....68 A4
Slade Green FC
ERITH DA8 ....150 E2
Slade Green Primary School
ERITH DA8 ....150 D1
Slade School of Fine Art
STPAN WC1H 4 C5
Sleaford Industrial Estate
VX/NE SW8 ....141 H1
Sloane Hospital
BECK BR3 ....183 G4
Smallberry Green Primary
School
ISLW TW7 ....136 B3
Smallwood Primary School
TOOT SW17 ....160 C6
SMA Medical Centre
LEY E10 ....69 K4
Smithy Street School
WCHPL E1 ....104 E4
Snaresbrook College
Preparatory School
SWFD E18 ....52 E5
Snaresbrook Crown Court
WAN E11 ....70 D2
Snaresbrook Primary
School
SWFD E18 ....70 E1
Snooker Club
WEA W13 ....116 C3
Snowsfields Primary School
STHWK SE1 ....19 G2
Sobell Leisure Centre
HOLWY N7 ....85 F1
Sobell Medical Centre
HOLWY N7 ....85 G2
Sofitel St James Hotel
STJS SW1Y 10 C7
Soho Parish CE Primary
School
SOHO/CST W1F 10 C5
Solent Road Health Centre
KIL/WHAMP NW6 ....82 E4
Somerset House
COVGDN WC2E 11 G5
Somers Town Community
Sports Centre
CAMTN NW1 ....4 B3
Sorsby Health Centre
CLPT E5 ....87 F2
Southall & West London
College
STHL UB1 ....114 D2
South Bank Business Centre
VX/NE SW8 ....121 J6
Southbank International
School Hampstead
HAMP NW3 ....83 G4
Southbank International
School Kensington
NTGHL W11 ....100 D6
South Bank University
STHWK SE1 ....18 A3
STHWK SE1 ....18 C4
Southborough Primary
School
HAYES BR2 ....201 F2
Southborough School
SURB KT6 ....206 A1
Southbury Primary School
PEND EN3 ....24 D5
South Camden Community
School
CAMTN NW1 ....4 B2
South Chelsea College
BRXN/ST SW9 ....142 A5
South Croydon Medical Centre
SAND/SEL CR2 ....211 J5
South Croydon Sports Club
CROY/NA CRO 212 A3
South Eastern University
HOLWY N7 ....85 F1
Southern Road Primary
School
PLSTW E13 ....107 F1
Southfield First & Middle
School
CHSWK W4 ....118 B2
Southfield Medical Centre
CHSWK W4 ....118 A2
The Southfields Clinic
WAND/EARL SW18 ....159 K1
Southfields Community
College
WAND/EARL SW18 ....159 K3
Southgate Cemetery
STHGT/OAK N14 ....34 C4
Southgate College
STHGT/OAK N14 ....34 C4
Southgate Compton CC
STHGT/OAK N14 ....21 K5
Southgate Leisure Centre
STHGT/OAK N14 ....34 D2
Southgate Road Medical
Centre
IS N1 ....85 K5
Southgate School
EBAR EN4 ....22 B6
South Grove Primary School
WALTH E17 ....69 G3
South Hampstead CC
WALTH E17 ....69 G3
South Hampstead High School
HAMP NW3 ....83 H4
South Haringay Infant School
FSBYPK N4 ....67 H5
South Herts Golf Club
TRDG/WHET N20 ....32 E3
Southlake Primary School
ABYW SE2 ....128 E2

South Lewisham Health
Centre
CAT SE6 ....165 F6
South London Crematorium
MTCM CR4 ....179 H5
South London Gallery
CMBW SE5 ....143 F2
The South London Natural
Health Centre
CLAP SW4 ....141 H5
South London Tamil School
CROY/NA CRO 196 D4
Southmead Primary
School
WIM/MER SW19 ....159 H3
South Norwood Country
Park
SNWD SE25 ....197 K1
South Norwood Hill Medical
Centre
SNWD SE25 ....181 F5
South Norwood Medical
Centre
SNWD SE25 ....197 F1
South Norwood Pools &
Fitness Centre
SNWD SE25 ....197 H2
South Norwood Primary
School
SNWD SE25 ....197 H2
South Park Business Centre
IL IG1 ....72 E6
South Park Clinic
IL IG1 ....90 E2
South Park Hotel
SAND/SEL CR2 ....212 A2
South Park Primary School
GDMY/SEVK IG3 ....90 E1
South Quay Plaza
POP/IOD E14 ....124 E2
South Rise Primary School
WOOL/PLUM SE18 ....127 J5
Southside Industrial Estate
VX/NE SW8 ....141 H1
Southside Shopping Centre
WAND/EARL SW18 ....160 A1
South Thames College
PUT/ROE SW15 ....139 G6
PUT/ROE SW15 ....158 C1
TOOT SW17 ....178 D1
WAND/EARL SW18 ....140 A6
Southville Infant School
EBED/NFELT TW14 ....153 J3
Southwark Bridge Business
Centre
STHWK SE1 ....18 D1
Southwark Bridge Stairs
BLKFR EC4V 12 C6
Southwark Cathedral
STHWK SE1 ....12 E7
Southwark College
BERM/RHTH SE16 ....123 J3
CMBW SE5 ....143 F1
STHWK SE1 ....17 K2
STHWK SE1 ....19 H4
Southwark Crown Court
STHWK SE1 ....13 G7
Southwark Park Primary
School
BERM/RHTH SE16 ....123 J3
Southwark Park Sports
Centre
BERM/RHTH SE16 ....123 K4
Southwark Sports Ground
DUL SE21 ....163 G3
South West Middlesex
Crematorium
FELT TW13 ....154 D3
Southwood Primary School
CLPT E5 ....68 E6
South Woodford Health
Centre
SWFD E18 ....52 E4
Southwood Hospital
HGT N6 ....66 A4
Southwood Primary School
DAGW RM9 ....92 A2
Sovereign Business Centre
PEND EN3 ....25 H4
The Space Arts Centre Cinema
DEPT SE8 ....124 C4
Sparrow Farm Community
Junior School
EW KT17 ....207 K3
Sparrow Farm Infant School
EBED/NFELT TW14 ....154 B2
Sparrow Farm Junior School
EBED/NFELT TW14 ....154 B2
Spa School
STHWK SE1 ....123 H4
Speakers Corner
BAY/PAD W2 ....9 F5
The Speech & Language
Hearing Centre
CAMTN NW1 ....4 D4
Speedway Industrial Estate
HYS/HAR UB3 ....113 G2
Speke's Monument
BAY/PAD W2 ....120 D1
Spelthorne Sixth Form
College
ASHF TW15 ....152 C6
Spencer House
WHALL SW1A 16 A1
The Spires Shopping Centre
BAR EN5 ....20 C4
Spiritualist Temple
CRICK NW2 ....82 A5
Spitalfields Community Farm
WCHPL E1 ....104 C3
Spitalfields Health Centre
WCHPL E1 ....13 K1
Spitfire Business Park
CROY/NA CRO 211 G4
Splashworld Swimming
Centre
BXLYHS DA6 ....148 E5

Springfield Christian School
CAT SE6 ....164 C5
Springfield Community
Primary School
SEVS/STOTM N15 ....68 C3
Springfield Hospital
TOOT SW17 ....160 D5
Springfield Primary School
VX/NE SW8 ....141 J1
Spring Grove Primary School
ISLW TW7 ....135 J3
Springhallow School
HNWL W7 ....97 F5
Spring Park Primary School
CROY/NA CRO 213 J1
Springvale Retail Park
STMC/STPC BR5 ....186 D6
Springwell Infant School
HEST TW5 ....134 D1
Springwell Junior School
HEST TW5 ....134 D1
Spurgeon's College
SNWD SE25 ....181 F5
Squirrels Heath Junior School
GPK RM2 ....75 K2
Squirrels Trading Estate
HYS/HAR UB3 ....113 J3
Sri Saddhatissa International
Buddhist Temple
CDALE/KGS NW9 ....62 E2
The Stables Gallery &
Art Centre
CRICK NW2 ....81 J2
Stadium Business Centre
WBLY HA9 ....80 D1
Stadium Industrial Estate
WBLY HA9 ....80 D3
Stadium Retail Park
WBLY HA9 ....80 C1
Stafford Cross Business Park
CROY/NA CRO 211 F3
The Stafford Hotel
WHALL SW1A 16 A1
Stag Lane Industrial Estate
CDALE/KGS NW9 ....44 E6
Stag Lane Primary School
EDGW HA8 ....44 C5
Stamford Clinic
HMSMTH W6 ....118 D4
Stamford Hill Primary School
SEVS/STOTM N15 ....67 K3
Stanburn Middle School
STAN HA7 ....43 J3
Standard Industrial Estate
CAN/RD E16 ....126 C2
CAN/RD E16 ....126 C2
Stanford Primary School
STRHM/NOR SW16 ....179 J4
Stanhope Primary School
GFD/PVL UB6 ....96 C3
Stanley J & I School
TEDD TW11 ....155 K6
Stanley Park High School
CAR SM5 ....210 A4
Stanley Park Primary School
CAR SM5 ....209 K5
Stanley Technical High
School
SNWD SE25 ....181 G6
Stanmore College
STAN HA7 ....43 H2
Stanmore Golf Club
STAN HA7 ....43 H3
Stanton School of English
BAY/PAD W2 ....101 F5
Stanton Square Industrial
Estate
SYD SE26 ....164 C6
Staple Inn Buildings
HHOL WC1V 11 J2
Staples Corner Business
Park
CRICK NW2 ....63 J5
Star Business Centre
RAIN RM13 ....111 F4
Starksfield Primary School
ED N9 ....36 A3
Star Primary School
CAN/RD E16 ....106 C3
The Space Arts Centre Cinema
STP EC4M 12 B4
Stationery Office
HOL/ALD WC2B 11 G3
Stebon Primary School
POP/IOD E14 ....105 H4
Stephen Hawking Primary
Special School
POP/IOD E14 ....105 G5
Stepney Day Hospital
WCHPL E1 ....104 E5
Stepney Greencoat CE
Primary School
POP/IOD E14 ....105 H5
Stepney Green College
WCHPL E1 ....105 F4
Sterling Industrial Estate
DAGE RM10 ....92 D2
Sterling Way Clinic
UED N18 ....50 B1
Stewart Fleming Primary
School
PGE/AN SE20 ....181 K6
Stewart Headlam Primary
School
WCHPL E1 ....104 D3
Stillness Primary School
FSTH SE23 ....164 B1
Stirling Retail Park
BORE WD6 ....31 F1
Stirling Way Industrial
Estates
CROY/NA CRO 195 K4
Stock Exchange
STBT EC1A 12 B3
Stockley Park Business
Centre
STKPK UB11 ....113 F1

Stockley Park Golf Club
  STKPK UB11 ....94 A6
Stockwell Park School
  BRXN/ST SW9 ....142 A2
Stockwell Primary School
  BRXN/ST SW9 ....142 A4
Stoke Newington School
  STNW/STAM N16 ....85 K1
The Stonebridge Primary
  School
  WLSDN NW10 ....80 E6
Stonebridge Shopping
  Centre
  WLSDN NW10 ....81 F6
Stonehill Business Centre
  UED N18 ....51 F2
Stonehill Business Park
  UED N18 ....51 F1
Stone Lake Retail Park
  CHARL SE7 ....126 B4
Stoneleigh First School
  EW KT17 ....207 K2
Stoneydown Park Primary
  School
  WALTH E17 ....69 G1
Stowford College
  BELMT SM2 ....209 G5
Strand on the Green J & I
  School
  CHSWK W4 ....117 H6
Strand Palace Hotel
  COVGDN WC2E 11 F5
Stratford College
  SRTFD E15 ....88 C5
Stratford Magistrates Court
  SRTFD E15 ....88 B5
Stratford School
  FSTGT E7 ....88 E3
Stratford Shopping Centre
  SRTFD E15 ....88 B5
Strathmore School
  RCHPK/HAM TW10 ....156 E3
Strawberry Fields School
  NTGHL W11 ....100 E6
Strawberry Hill Golf Club
  WHTN TW2 ....155 K5
Streatham Cemetery
  TOOT SW17 ....160 D5
Streatham & Clapham High
  School Junior Department
  BRXS/STRHM SW2 ....162 A3
Streatham & Clapham High
  School Senior Department
  STRHM/NOR SW16 ....161 H5
Streatham & Croydon RFC
  THHTH CR7 ....196 B2
Streatham Ice Rink
  STRHM/NOR SW16 ....179 K1
Streatham Leisure Centre
  STRHM/NOR SW16 ....161 K4
Streatham Modern School
  STRHM/NOR SW16 ....179 K2
Streatham Park Cemetery
  MTCM CR4 ....179 H5
Streatham Swimming Pool
  STRHM/NOR SW16 ....179 K1
Streatham Vale Sports Club
  STRHM/NOR SW16 ....179 H3
Streatham Wells Primary
  School
  BRXS/STRHM SW2 ....162 A4
Stroud Green Primary
  School
  FSBYPK N4 ....67 G5
Studholme Medical Centre
  ASHF TW15 ....152 C6
The Study Preparatory School
  WIM/MER SW19 ....177 G1
The Study School
  NWMAL KT3 ....192 B2
Sudbourne Primary School
  BRXS/STRHM SW2 ....142 A6
Sudbury Court Sports Club
  ALP/SUD HA0 ....79 J1
Sudbury Golf Club
  GFD/PVL UB6 ....79 J4
Sudbury Primary School
  ALP/SUD HA0 ....79 H2
Suffolks Primary School
  EN EN1 ....24 D3
Sulivan Primary School
  FUL/PGN SW6 ....139 K3
Summerside JMI School
  NFNCH/WDSPK N12 ....47 H2
Sunbury Court
  SUN TW16 ....172 C5
Sundridge Park Golf Club
  BMLY BR1 ....184 B2
Sun Life Trading Estate
  EBED/NFELT TW14 ....133 K4
Sunnyfields Primary School
  HDN NW4 ....45 K4
Sunnyhill Primary School
  STRHM/NOR SW16 ....162 A6
Sunshine House School
  NTHWD HA6 ....40 B2
Super Bowl
  BXLYHS DA6 ....149 G5
Surbiton Business Centre
  SURB KT6 ....190 E3
Surbiton Cemetery
  KUT/HW KT1 ....191 H1
Surbiton Golf Club
  CHSGTN KT9 ....205 H2
Surbiton High School
  SURB KT6 ....191 F1
Surbiton Hospital
  SURB KT6 ....191 F3
Surbiton Natural Health
  Centre
  SURB KT6 ....191 F3
Surrey CCC (The Oval)
  LBTH SE11 ....122 A6
Surrey Docks Farm
  BERM/RHTH SE16 ....124 C2
Surrey Docks Health Centre
  BERM/RHTH SE16 ....124 B2

Surrey Docks Watersports
  Centre
  BERM/RHTH SE16 ....124 B3
Surrey Quays Leisure Park
  BERM/RHTH SE16 ....124 A3
Surrey Quays Shopping
  Centre
  BERM/RHTH SE16 ....124 A3
Surrey Square Primary
  School
  WALW SE17 ....123 F5
Susi Earnshaw Theatre
  School
  BAR EN5 ....20 D5
Sussex House School
  KTBR SW1X 14 E6
Sutcliffe Park Athletics Track
  LEE/GVPK SE12 ....146 A6
Sutton Alternative Health
  Centre
  SUT SM1 ....209 F3
Sutton Arena
  CAR SM5 ....194 C4
Sutton Bowling Club
  BELMT SM2 ....208 E6
Sutton Cemetery
  CHEAM SM3 ....193 J6
Sutton College of Learning
  for Adults
  SUT SM1 ....209 F3
Sutton Grammar School
  for Boys
  SUT SM1 ....209 G3
Sutton High Junior School
  SUT SM1 ....209 F4
Sutton High School
  for Girls GDST
  SUT SM1 ....208 E4
Sutton House
  HACK E8 ....86 E3
Suttons Business Park
  RAIN RM13 ....111 F2
Sutton Superbowl
  SUT SM1 ....209 F3
Sutton United FC
  SUT SM1 ....208 E2
Sutton West Centre
  SUT SM1 ....208 E3
Swaffield Primary School
  WAND/EARL SW18 ....160 B1
Swakeleys School
  HGDN/ICK UB10 ....94 A1
Swaminarayan School
  WLSDN NW10 ....81 F4
Swan Business Centre
  CHSWK W4 ....118 A4
Swan Business Park
  DART DA1 ....151 G5
Swan Lane Pier
  CANST EC4R 12 E6
Swanlea School
  WCHPL E1 ....104 D3
Swanscombe School
  WOT/HER KT12 ....188 B5
Swedish School
  BARN SW13 ....118 D6
Swiss Cottage Leisure
  Centre
  HAMP NW3 ....83 H5
Swiss Cottage School
  STJWD NW8 ....83 H4
Swissôtel the Howard
  TPL/STR WC2R 11 H5
Swiss Re-insurance Tower
  HDTCH EC3A 13 H4
Sybil Elgar School
  EA W5 ....98 A6
  NWDGN UB2 ....114 E3
Sybourn Infant School
  LEY E10 ....69 G6
The Sybourn Junior School
  WALTH E17 ....69 H4
Sydenham Girls School
  SYD SE26 ....163 J5
Sydenham High Junior
  School
  SYD SE26 ....163 J6
Sydenham High School
  Sports Ground
  CAT SE6 ....182 D1
Sydenham High Senior
  School
  SYD SE26 ....181 J1
The Sydney Russell School
  DAGW RM9 ....91 K3
Syon House
  BTFD TW8 ....136 D2
Syon Park
  BTFD TW8 ....136 D3
Syon Park School
  ISLW TW7 ....136 C2
Syracuse University
  NTGHL W11 ....100 D6
Tabard Theatre
  CHSWK W4 ....118 B4
Taberner House
  CROY/NA CR0 ....211 J1
TA Centre
  EDGW HA8 ....44 D3
  HRW HA1 ....61 F2
  NFNCH/WDSPK N12 ....47 H4
Tait Road Industrial Estate
  CROY/NA CR0 ....197 F3
Talmud Torah School
  STNW/STAM N16 ....67 K4
Tamian Industrial Estate
  HSLWW TW4 ....134 B5
Tamworth Manor High School
  STRHM/NOR SW16 ....179 J6
Tandem Centre
  WIM/MER SW19 ....178 C4
Tate Britain
  WEST SW1P 16 E7
Tate Modern
  STHWK SE1 ....12 B7
Tavistock Clinic
  HAMP NW3 ....83 H4

TAVR Centre
  KUT/HW KT1 ....190 E1
Tavy Clinic
  ABYW SE2 ....128 D2
Tawhid Boys School
  STNW/STAM N16 ....68 B6
Teddington Business Park
  TEDD TW11 ....174 A1
Teddington Cemetery
  TEDD TW11 ....155 K6
Teddington Clinic
  TEDD TW11 ....173 K2
Teddington Memorial
  Hospital
  TEDD TW11 ....173 K2
Teddington Pool & Fitness
  Centre
  TEDD TW11 ....174 D1
Teddington School
  TEDD TW11 ....174 D1
The Teddington Theatre
  Club Ltd
  E/WMO/HCT KT8 ....189 J2
Telferscot Primary School
  BAL SW12 ....161 H3
Temperate House
  RCH/KEW TW9 ....137 G3
Temple Hill Primary School
  DART DA1 ....151 K6
Tenby Road Clinic
  EDGW HA8 ....44 B5
Tennis and Squash Club
  FNCH N3 ....46 C4
Tenterden Sports Ground
  KTN/HRWW/WS HA3 ....62 A4
Terence McMillan Stadium
  PLSTW E13 ....107 G3
Tetherdown Primary School
  MUSWH N10 ....66 A1
Thames Barrier
  VX/NE SW8 ....126 C2
Thames Barrier Information
  & Learning Centre
  CHARL SE7 ....126 C3
Thames Ditton & Esher
  Golf Club
  ESH/CLAY KT10 ....189 J6
Thames Ditton Infant School
  THDIT KT7 ....190 A3
Thames Dittop Junior School
  THDIT KT7 ....190 A4
Thames House
  WEST SW1P 16 E4
Thameside Industrial Estate
  CAN/RD E16 ....126 C1
Thames Magistrates Court
  BOW E3 ....105 J2
Thamesmead Leisure Centre
  THMD SE28 ....109 G6
Thamesmead Shopping
  Centre
  THMD SE28 ....109 G6
Thames Valley University
  EA W5 ....97 J6
  EA W5 ....116 E1
Thamesview Business Centre
  RAIN RM13 ....111 G4
Thames View Clinic
  BARK IG11 ....109 F1
Thames View J & I School
  BARK IG11 ....109 G1
Thames Water Tower
  NTGHL W11 ....119 G2
Thatched House Hotel
  SUT SM1 ....208 D4
Theatre Centre
  BECK BR3 ....182 E5
Theatre for Mankind
  FSBYPK N4 ....67 F5
Theatre Museum Library &
  Archive
  COVGDN WC2E 11 F5
Theatre of the Dispossessed
  WIM/MER SW19 ....159 G3
Theatre Royal
  HOL/ALD WC2B 11 F4
  SRTFD E15 ....88 B4
Theatre Royal Haymarket
  STJS SW1Y 10 D6
Theodore McLeary Primary
  School
  EDUL SE22 ....143 G5
Therapia Trading Estate
  CROY/NA CR0 ....195 J4
Thistlebrook Industrial Estate
  ABYW SE2 ....128 D3
Thistle Hotel
  CAMTN NW1 ....4 B5
  CHCR WC2N 10 E6
  FSBYE EC1V 6 C5
  KENS W8 ....120 B2
Thistle Hyde Park Hotel
  BAY/PAD W2 ....101 G6
Thistle Kensington Gardens
  Hotel
  BAY/PAD W2 ....101 G6
Thistle Marble Arch Hotel
  MBLAR W1H 9 F4
Thistle Piccadilly Hotel
  SOHO/SHAV W1D 10 D6
Thistle Tower Hotel
  WAP E1W 13 J7
Thistle Westminster Hotel
  WESTW SW1E 15 K5
Thomas Arnold Primary School
  DAGW RM9 ....92 B5
Thomas Buxton Primary
  School
  WCHPL E1 ....104 C3
Thomas Fairchild Primary
  School
  IS N1 ....6 E2
Thomas Francis Academy
  BRXN/ST SW9 ....142 C5
Thomas Gamuel Primary
  School
  WALTH E17 ....69 J3

Thomas Jones Primary School
  NTGHL W11 ....100 C5
Thomas London Independent
  Day School
  KENS W8 ....120 A3
Thomas Road Industrial
  Estate
  POP/IOD E14 ....105 J4
Thomas's Preparatory School
  BTSEA SW11 ....140 C5
  BTSEA SW11 ....140 E6
Thomas Tallis School
  BKHTH/KID SE3 ....146 A4
Thornhill Primary School
  IS N1 ....85 G5
Thornton Heath Health
  Centre
  THHTH CR7 ....196 D1
Thornton Heath Pools &
  Fitness Centre
  THHTH CR7 ....196 D1
Thornton Road Industrial
  Estate
  CROY/NA CR0 ....195 K3
Thorntree Primary School
  CHARL SE7 ....126 C5
Thorpe Hall Primary School
  WALTH E17 ....52 A4
Three Bridges Business
  Centre
  NWDGN UB2 ....115 H2
Three Bridges Primary School
  NWDGN UB2 ....115 G3
Three Mills Heritage Centre
  BOW E3 ....106 A2
Thurston Industrial Estate
  LEW SE13 ....144 E4
Tidemill Primary School
  DEPT SE8 ....144 D1
Tideway Industrial Estate
  VX/NE SW8 ....121 H6
Tiffin Girls School
  KUTN/CMB KT2 ....175 F2
Tiffin School & Sports Centre
  KUTN/CMB KT2 ....175 G5
Tiller Centre
  (Swimming Baths)
  POP/IOD E14 ....124 D3
Tiller Leisure Centre
  POP/IOD E14 ....124 D3
Timbercroft Primary School
  WOOL/PLUM SE18 ....147 K1
Timbers Clinic
  KTN/HRWW/WS HA3 ....42 D2
Times Square Shopping
  Centre
  SUT SM1 ....209 F3
Tiverton Primary School
  SEVS/STOTM N15 ....68 A3
Tobacco Dock
  WAP E1W 104 D6
Tokyngton Community
  Centre
  WBLY HA9 ....80 D3
Toldos School
  STNW/STAM N16 ....67 K5
Tollgate Primary School
  CROY/NA CR0 ....197 K3
  PLSTW E13 ....107 G3
Tolworth CP School
  SURB KT6 ....191 G5
Tolworth Girls School
  SURB KT6 ....206 B1
Tolworth Recreation Centre
  SURB KT6 ....206 B1
Tom Hood School
  WAN E11 ....88 D1
Tooting Bec Athletics Track
  TOOT SW17 ....161 G6
Tooting Bec Lido
  STRHM/NOR SW16 ....161 H5
Tooting Leisure Centre
  TOOT SW17 ....160 C6
Tooting & Mitcham United
  Football Club
  MTCM CR4 ....179 K4
Torah Temimah Primary
  School
  CRICK NW2 ....81 K2
Torah Vodaas
  GLDGN NW11 ....64 D6
Torriano Primary School
  KTTN NW5 ....84 C3
Torridon Primary School
  CAT SE6 ....165 G4
Torrington Clinic
  NFNCH/WDSPK N12 ....47 G1
Torrington Park Health
  Centre
  NFNCH/WDSPK N12 ....33 G6
Total Health Clinic
  SHB W12 ....118 E2
Tottenham Green Leisure
  Centre
  SEVS/STOTM N15 ....68 A2
Tottenham Hale Retail Park
  SEVS/STOTM N15 ....68 C1
Tottenham Hotspur FC
  (White Hart Lane)
  TOTM N17 ....50 B3
Tottenham Park Cemetery
  ED N9 ....36 D5
Tottenham Sports Centre
  TOTM N17 ....50 B2
Totteridge CC
  TRDG/WHET N20 ....32 E4
Tower 42
  OBST EC2N 13 G3
The Tower Bridge Exhibition
  STHWK SE1 ....19 J1
Tower Bridge Primary School
  STHWK SE1 ....19 J1
Tower Bridge Wharf
  WAP E1W 13 J7
Tower Hamlets College
  POP/IOD E14 ....105 K6
  WCHPL E1 ....104 D4

Tower House School
  MORT/ESHN SW14 ....137 K5
Tower Industrial Estate
  SNWD SE25 ....197 H1
Tower Medical Centre
  WCHPL E1 ....104 C5
Tower Millennium Pier
  TWRH EC3N 13 H7
Tower of London
  TWRH EC3N 13 J6
Tower Retail Park
  DART DA1 ....150 C6
Towers Business Park
  WBLY HA9 ....80 D2
Tower Stairs
  MON EC3R 13 G6
Town Farm Primary School
  STWL/WRAY TW19 ....152 A2
Townley Grammar School
  for Girls
  BXLYHS DA6 ....169 G1
Townmead Business
  Centre
  FUL/PGN SW6 ....140 B3
Townsend Industrial Estate
  WLSDN NW10 ....80 E6
Townsend Primary School
  WALW SE17 ....19 G6
Toynbee Hall & Curtain Theatre
  WCHPL E1 ....13 J2
Trade Union Congress
  NOXST/BSQ WC1A 10 D3
Trafalgar Business Centre
  BARK IG11 ....109 F3
Trafalgar Primary & Infant
  School
  WHTN TW2 ....155 J4
Trafalgar Square
  STJS SW1Y 10 D7
Trafalgar Trading Estate
  PEND EN3 ....25 H5
Tramshed Theatre
  WOOL/PLUM SE18 ....127 G4
Trans Atlantic College
  BETH E2 ....7 J2
Transport House
  WEST SW1P 16 E5
Travelodge
  ACT W3 ....98 C3
  BTFD TW8 ....117 H6
  BTSEA SW11 ....140 D4
  CAMTN NW1 ....B D1
  CAR/RD E16 ....126 C1
  FSBYW WC1X 5 H4
  HEST TW5 ....114 B6
  IL IG1 ....90 B1
  KUTN/CMB KT2 ....175 F5
  LSQ/SEVD WC2H 10 C1
  POP/IOD E14 ....106 B5
  REDBR IG4 ....71 K3
  STPAN WC1H 5 F3
  SURB KT6 ....191 J5
  WCHPL E1 ....13 J3
  WLSDN NW10 ....98 C3
Treasury
  WHALL SW1A 16 E3
The Treaty Centre
  HSLW TW3 ....135 G4
Treehouse School
  MUSWH N10 ....66 A1
The Treehouse School
  BMSBY WC1N 5 G6
Trent CE Primary School
  EBAR EN4 ....21 K5
Trent Country Park
  EBAR EN4 ....22 A3
Trent Park Cemetery
  EBAR EN4 ....22 A4
Trent Park Golf Club
  STHGT/OAK N14 ....22 C5
Trevor Roberts School
  HAMP NW3 ....83 H5
Tricycle Theatre
  KIL/WHAMP NW6 ....82 D5
Trident Business Centre
  TOOT SW17 ....178 E1
Trinity Business Centre
  BERM/RHTH SE16 ....124 C2
Trinity Catholic Lower High
  School
  WFD IG8 ....38 E6
Trinity College Centre
  PECK SE15 ....143 F1
Trinity College London
  STHWK SE1 ....121 K5
Trinity College of Music
  GNWCH SE10 ....125 F6
  MHST W1U 9 H2
Trinity Hospital
  GNWCH SE10 ....125 G5
Trinity House
  TWRH EC3N 13 H5
Trinity RC High School (Upper)
  WFD IG8 ....38 E6
Trinity St Marys Primary
  School
  BAL SW12 ....161 F3
Trinity School
  CROY/NA CR0 ....197 K6
  DAGE RM10 ....92 C1
Trinity School Belvedere
  BELV DA17 ....129 K4
Trinity Trading Estate
  HYS/HAR UB3 ....113 K3
Tripcock Point Development
  Site
  THMD SE28 ....109 F6
Triumph Trading Estate
  TOTM N17 ....50 C2
Trocadero
  SOHO/SHAV W1D 10 C6
Trojan Business Centre
  WLSDN NW10 ....81 H4
Troy Industrial Estate
  HRW HA1 ....61 F2
True Buddha School
  IS N1 ....5 G4

TS Queen Mary
TPL/STR WC2R 11 G6
Tubbenden J & I Schools
ORP BR6 ....216 D2
Tudor Lodge Health Centre
WIM/MER SW19 ....159 G3
Tudor Lodge Hotel
PIN HA5 ....59 F3
Tudor Primary School
NFNCH/WDSPK N12 ....47 G3
STHL UB1 ....95 J6
Tufnell Park Primary School
HOLWY N7 ....84 D2
Tuke School
PECK SE15 ....143 J2
Tulloch Clinic
SHB W12 ....119 G1
Tunnel Avenue Trading
Estate
GNWCH SE10 ....125 G2
Turney School
DUL SE21 ....162 D2
Turnham Primary School
BROCKY SE4 ....144 B5
Turtle Key Arts Centre
FUL/PGN SW6 ....119 K6
Tutorial College of West
London
STHL UB1 ....115 F1
TV Studios
WBLY HA9 ....80 C1
Tweeddale Primary School
CAR SM5 ....194 C4
Twickenham Cemetery
WHTN TW2 ....155 G3
Twickenham Park Health
Centre
TWK TW1 ....156 D1
Twickenham Preparatory
School
HPTN TW12 ....173 G4
Twickenham Stadium
ISLW TW7 ....155 K1
Twickenham Trading
Estate
TWK TW1 ....156 A1
Two Bridges Business Park
SAND/SEL CR2 ....211 K4
Twyford CE High School
ACT W3 ....117 H1
Twyford Sports Centre
ACT W3 ....117 J1
Tyburn Infant School
STJWD NW8 ....2 B6
Tynemouth Road Health
Centre
SEVS/STOTM N15 ....68 B1
The Type Museum
BRXN/ST SW9 ....142 A2
Tyssen Primary School
STNW/STAM N16 ....68 C5
UCG Cinema
CRICK NW2 ....63 K5
UCI Cinema
ED N9 ....37 F2
SUT SM1 ....209 F3
UCI Empire Cinema
LSQ/SEVD WC2H 10 D6
UCI Filmworks Cinema
GNWCH SE10 ....125 J4
UGC Cinema
EA W5 ....97 K6
EN EN1 ....24 C5
HMSMTH W6 ....118 E4
SOHO/SHAV W1D 10 C5
WBPTN SW10 ....120 C5
UK Passport Office
PIM SW1V 15 K6
Underhill J & I School
BAR EN5 ....20 C6
Unicorn Primary School
BECK BR3 ....198 E2
Unicorn School
RCH/KEW TW9 ....137 G2
Unicorn Theatre
STHWK SE1 ....19 H2
United Medical & Dental
Schools
STHWK SE1 ....17 G4
United Services Sports
Ground
CHSWK W4 ....138 B2
Unity Trading Estate
KTTN NW5 ....84 B2
Unity Trading Estate
WFD IG8 ....53 H6
University Church of Christ
the King
STPAN WC1H 4 C7
University College Hospital
CAMTN NW1 ....4 B6
HAMP NW3 ....83 H4
University College Junior
School
HAMP NW3 ....83 G2
University College London
FITZ W1T 10 B1
STPAN WC1H 4 C6
University College London,
Astor College
FITZ W1T 10 B1
University College London
Medical School
FITZ W1T 10 A1
University College School
HAMP NW3 ....83 G3
University Hospital Lewisham
LEW SE13 ....144 E6
University of California
WHALL SW1A 16 A1
University of East London
BARK IG11 ....91 G2
CAN/RD E16 ....108 A6
PLSTW E13 ....107 F2
SRTFD E15 ....88 A6
SRTFD E15 ....88 C4
SRTFD E15 ....106 D1

University of Greenwich
DART DA1 ....171 J4
ELTH/MOT SE9 ....167 J1
GNWCH SE10 ....125 C5
WOOL/PLUM SE18 ....127 F3
University of Greenwich
(Mansion Site)
ELTH/MOT SE9 ....167 H1
University of Greenwich
Sports Ground
ELTH/MOT SE9 ....146 D5
ELTH/MOT SE9 ....167 H2
University of London
BAY/PAD W2 ....8 A4
BMSBY WC1N 5 F7
CLKNW EC1R 5 K6
FITZ W1T 10 C5
GWRST WC1E 10 D1
MBLAR W1H 8 D3
STPAN WC1H 4 D6
University of London
Athletics Ground
NWMAL KT3 ....192 D2
University of the Arts
London
MYFR/PKLN W1K 9 J4
University of Westminster
CAMTN NW1 ....4 A6
CAVSQ/HST W1G 9 K5
CHSWK W4 ....137 K2
FITZ W1T 10 A3
GTPST W1W 9 J1
HGT N6 ....65 J5
HRW HA1 ....61 G4
MHST W1U 9 G1
Uphall Primary School
IL IG1 ....90 B3
Upland Primary School
BXLYHN DA7 ....149 G4
Uplands Business Park
WALTH E17 ....51 F5
Upper Montagu Street Clinic
CAMTN NW1 ....8 E1
Upper Tooting Independent
High School
TOOT SW17 ....160 D4
Upton Cross Primary School
PLSTW E13 ....89 F6
Upton Day Hospital
BXLYHS DA6 ....149 F5
Upton Lane Medical Centre
FSTGT E7 ....89 F4
Upton Primary School
BXLY DA5 ....149 F6
Upton Road School
BXLYHS DA6 ....149 F6
The Urdang Academy
LSQ/SEVD WC2H 10 E4
Ursuline High School
RYNPK SW20 ....177 G3
Ursuline Preparatory School
RYNPK SW20 ....177 G3
Uxbridge College
HYS/HAR UB3 ....94 E6
Uxbridge County Court
HYS/HAR UB3 ....94 C4
Uxendon Manor JMI School
KTN/HRWW/WS HA3 ....62 A2
Vale Farm Sports Centre
ALP/SUD HA0 ....79 H2
Vale Industrial Estate
WATW WD18 ....26 A3
The Vale Medical Centre
FSTH SE23 ....164 B4
Valence House Museum &
Library
BCTR RM8 ....73 K6
Valence Junior School
BCTR RM8 ....73 K6
Valentine High School
CNTH/NBYPK IG2 ....72 A3
Valentines High Lower School
CNTH/NBYPK IG2 ....72 B2
Vale Park Industrial
ACT W3 ....118 D2
The Vale School
SKENS SW7 ....120 B3
Valley Link Business centre
PEND EN3 ....37 G1
Valley Link Business Estate
PEND EN3 ....37 G1
Valley Primary School
HAYES BR2 ....183 J5
Valmar Trading Estate
CMBW SE5 ....142 D2
V & A Museum of Childhood
BETH E2 ....104 E2
Vanbrugh Theatre
GWRST WC1E 4 C7
Vanguard Trading Estate
SRTFD E15 ....88 A6
Vaudeville Theatre
COVGDN WC2E 11 F5
Vaughan First & Middle School
RYLN/HDSTN HA2 ....60 C3
Vauxhall Primary School
LBTH SE11 ....122 A5
Vernon House Special
School
WLSDN NW10 ....80 E3
Vestry Hall
MTCM CR4 ....178 E6
Vestry House Museum
WALTH E17 ....69 K1
Vicarage Fields Health Clinic
BARK IG11 ....90 C5
The Vicarage Field Shopping
Centre
BARK IG11 ....90 C5
Vicarage Primary School
EHAM E6 ....107 K2
Vicars Green Primary School
GFD/PVL UB6 ....97 J1
VI Components Industrial
Park
ERITH DA8 ....130 B5
Victoria & Albert Museum
SKENS SW7 ....14 B5

Victoria Business Centre
WELL DA16 ....148 B3
Victoria Bus Station
PIM SW1V 15 K5
Victoria Chiropractic Clinic
SKENS SW7 ....14 E3
Victoria Coach Station
BGVA SW1W 15 J7
Victoria Hall
FNCH N3 ....46 D4
Victoria Industrial Estate
ACT W3 ....99 F4
Victoria Industrial Park
DART DA1 ....151 G6
Victoria Junior School
FELT TW13 ....154 A3
Victoria Medical Centre
PIM SW1V 16 B7
Victoria Palace Theatre
BGVA SW1W 15 K5
Victoria Park Industrial
Centre
HOM E9 ....87 H5
Victoria Park Plaza Hotel
PIM SW1V 16 A6
Victoria Place Shopping
Centre
BGVA SW1W 15 K6
Victoria Rail/air Terminal
PIM SW1V 15 K6
Victoria Retail Park
RSLP HA4 ....77 H3
Victoria Wharf
POP/IOD E14 ....105 G6
Victoria Wharf Industrial
Estate
DEPT SE8 ....124 B5
Victor Seymour Infant
School
CAR SM5 ....209 K1
Victory Business Centre
ISLW TW7 ....136 A5
Victory Day School
BTSEA SW11 ....140 E2
Victory Primary School
WALW SE17 ....18 D6
Viking Business Centre
ROMW/RG RM7 ....74 E4
Viking Primary School
NTHLT UB5 ....95 H2
Village Infant School
DAGE RM10 ....92 C5
The Village School
HAMP NW3 ....83 K4
Villiers High School
STHL UB1 ....115 F1
The Vine Clinic
KUTN/CMB KT2 ....175 F2
Vine Medical Centre
E/WMO/HCT KT8 ....173 H6
The Vines School
BTSEA SW11 ....141 F5
The Vineyard Primary School
RCHPK/HAM TW10 ....157 F1
Vinopolis, City of Wine
STHWK SE1 ....12 D6
Vinters' Hall
BLKFR EC4V 12 D5
VIP Trading Estate
CHARL SE7 ....126 B4
Virginia Primary School
BETH E2 ....7 J5
Virgo Fidelis Convent Schools
NRWD SE19 ....180 D2
Vision College of Technology
HOM E9 ....87 J4
Vita et Pax School
STHGT/OAK N14 ....22 B6
Vittoria Primary School
IS N1 ....5 H1
Voyager Business Estate
BERM/RHTH SE16 ....123 H3
VUE Cinema
ACT W3 ....98 C5
CROY/NA CR0 ....196 A6
DAGW RM9 ....92 A6
FUL/PGN SW6 ....139 K1
HAMP NW5 ....83 G4
HRW HA1 ....60 E3
LSQ/SEVD WC2H 10 D5
NFNCH/WDSPK N12 ....47 H3
ROMW/RG RM7 ....75 G2
SHB W12 ....119 G2
Vulcan Business Centre
CROY/NA CR0 ....214 C6
Waddon Clinic
CROY/NA CR0 ....211 G3
Waddon Infant School
CROY/NA CR0 ....211 G3
Wadham Lodge Sports
Centre
WALTH E17 ....51 K4
Wadsworth Business Centre
GFD/PVL UB6 ....97 J1
The Waldegrave Clinic
TEDD TW11 ....174 A1
Waldegrave Girls School
WHTN TW2 ....155 J5
Waldo Industrial Estate
BMLY BR1 ....184 B6
Waldorf School of
SW London
BAL SW12 ....161 H4
Waldron Health Centre &
Surgery
NWCR SE14 ....144 C1
Walker Primary School
STHGT/OAK N14 ....34 D4
The Wallace Centre
DEPT SE8 ....124 E6
The Wallace Collection
MHST W1U 9 G3
Wallbrook Business Centre
HSLWW TW4 ....134 A4
Wallington County Grammar
School
WLGTN SM6 ....210 B1

Wallington High School
for Girls
WLGTN SM6 ....210 B6
Walmer Road Clinic
NTGHL W11 ....100 C6
Walm Lane Clinic
CRICK NW2 ....82 B3
Walnuts Leisure Centre
ORP BR6 ....202 B5
Walnuts Shopping Centre
ORP BR6 ....202 B5
Walnut Tree Walk Primary
School
LBTH SE11 ....17 J0
Waltham Forest College
WALTH E17 ....50 E6
WALTH E17 ....51 K6
Waltham Forest Magistrates
Court
WALTH E17 ....51 K5
Waltham Forest Pool & Track
WALTH E17 ....51 K5
Waltham Forest Theatre
WALTH E17 ....51 H6
Walthamstow Business
Centre
WALTH E17 ....52 A5
Walthamstow Greyhound
Stadium
WALTH E17 ....51 K3
Walthamstow School
for Girls
WALTH E17 ....69 K1
Walton Business Centre
WOT/HER KT12 ....188 A4
Walton Casuals FC
WOT/HER KT12 ....188 A2
Walton Community
Hospital
WOT/HER KT12 ....188 A6
Walton Swimming Pool
WALW SE17 ....188 A5
Walworth Lower School
WALW SE17 ....122 C5
Walworth Town Hall
WALW SE17 ....18 C7
Walworth Upper School
STHWK SE1 ....123 F5
Wandle Recreation Centre
WAND/EARL SW18 ....160 A1
Wandle Trading Estate
MTCM CR4 ....194 E4
Wandle Valley School
CAR SM5 ....194 D4
Wandsworth Adult College
BTSEA SW11 ....141 F2
TOOT SW17 ....160 D4
Wandsworth Cemetery
WAND/EARL SW18 ....160 B3
Wandsworth County Court
PUT/ROE SW15 ....139 H6
Wandsworth Trading Estate
WAND/EARL SW18 ....160 A2
Wanstead CC
WAN E11 ....71 F4
Wanstead CE Primary School
WAN E11 ....70 E2
Wanstead Golf Club
WAN E11 ....71 F4
Wanstead High School
WAN E11 ....71 G3
Wanstead Hospital
WAN E11 ....71 F1
Wanstead Leisure Centre
WAN E11 ....71 G3
Wapping Wharf
WAP E1W 123 K1
Warehouse Theatre
CROY/NA CR0 ....196 E6
War Memorial Sports Ground
SUT SM1 ....209 J2
Warnford Industrial Estate
HYS/HAR UB3 ....113 H2
Warren Comprehensive
School
CHDH RM6 ....74 B2
Warren Dell Primary School
OXHEY WD19 ....27 C5
Warrender School
RSLP HA4 ....58 D4
Warren Junior School
CHDH RM6 ....74 B2
The Warren Medical Centre
YEAD UB4 ....95 F1
Warren Road Primary School
ORP BR6 ....217 F2
Warren Sports Centre
CHDH RM6 ....74 B2
Warwick Dubbing Theatre
SOHO/CST W1F 10 C4
Warwick Estate
BAY/PAD W2 ....101 F4
Warwick Leadlay Gallery
GNWCH SE10 ....125 F6
Warwick School for Boys
WALTH E17 ....70 A1
The Washington Mayfair
Hotel
MYFR/PICC W1J 9 K7
Waterfront Leisure Centre
WOOL/PLUM SE18 ....127 F3
Watergate School
CAT SE6 ....182 E1
LEW SE13 ....144 E5
Waterloo Health Centre
STHWK SE1 ....17 J3
Watermans Arts, Cinema &
Theatre Centre
BTFD TW8 ....117 F6
The Watermans Hall
MON EC3R 13 G6
Watermeads High School
MRDN SM4 ....194 C3
Watermill Business Centre
PEND EN3 ....25 H3
Water Rats Theatre
STPAN WC1H 5 F5

Waterside Business Centre
ISLW TW7 ....136 C5
Waterside Primary School
WOOL/PLUM SE18 ....127 J5
The Waterside Trading
Centre
HNWL W7 ....115 K3
Watersports Centre
FSBYPK N4 ....67 J3
Waterways Business Centre
PEND EN3 ....25 H1
Watling Clinic
EDGW HA8 ....45 F3
Watling Medical Centre
EDGW HA8 ....44 E4
Wavelengths Leisure Pool &
Library
DEPT SE8 ....144 D1
Waverley Industrial Estate
HRW HA1 ....42 D6
Waverley Lower Secondary
School
EDUL SE22 ....143 J6
Waverley School
EDUL SE22 ....143 K6
PEND EN3 ....24 E5
Waxchandlers' Hall
CITYW EC2V 12 D3
Weald First & Middle School
KTN/HRWW/WS HA3 ....43 F3
Webster Graduate Studies
Center
CAMTN NW1 ....3 F6
Welbeck Clinic
CRICK NW2 ....82 E1
Welbourne Primary School
SEVS/STOTM N15 ....68 C1
Wellcome Institute
CAMTN NW1 ....4 C6
Welldon Park Middle School
RYLN/HDSTN HA2 ....78 C2
The Welling Clinic
WELL DA16 ....148 B3
Welling Medical Centre
WELL DA16 ....148 A5
Welling School
WELL DA16 ....148 C2
Wellington Arch
MYFR/PICC W1J 15 H2
Wellington Barracks
WESTW SW1E 16 B5
Wellington Primary School
BOW E3 ....105 J2
HSLW TW3 ....134 E3
Welling United FC
WELL DA16 ....148 C5
Wells Primary School
WFD IG8 ....39 F6
Wembley Arena
WBLY HA9 ....80 C2
Wembley Commercial Centre
WBLY HA9 ....61 K6
Wembley Conference Centre
WBLY HA9 ....80 B2
Wembley FC
ALP/SUD HA0 ....79 H2
Wembley High Technology
College
ALP/SUD HA0 ....79 J1
Wembley Hospital
ALP/SUD HA0 ....79 K4
Wembley Manor Primary
School
WBLY HA9 ....80 A1
Wembley Park Business
Centre
WBLY HA9 ....80 D1
Wembley Stadium
WBLY HA9 ....80 C2
Wembley Stadium Industrial
Estate
WBLY HA9 ....80 C1
WBLY HA9 ....80 E1
Wendell Park Primary School
SHB W12 ....118 C2
Wentworth Tutorial College
GLDGN NW11 ....64 B3
The Wernher Collection at
Ranger's House
GNWCH SE10 ....145 G2
Wesley's Chapel, House &
Museum
STLK EC1Y 6 E6
Wessex Gardens Primary
School
GLDGN NW11 ....64 C5
West Acton Primary School
ACT W3 ....98 D5
West Beckton Health
Centre
CAN/RD E16 ....107 G4
Westbourne Green Sports
Complex
BAY/PAD W2 ....100 E4
Westbourne Primary School
SUT SM1 ....208 D1
Westbridge College
BTSEA SW11 ....140 D2
Westbrooke School
WELL DA16 ....148 E4
The Westbury Hotel
CONDST W1S 9 K5
Westbury Medical Centre
WDGN N22 ....49 J5
Westcroft Leisure Centre
CAR SM5 ....210 C1
West Drayton Primary
School
WDR/YW UB7 ....112 B2
West Ealing Business Centre
WEA W13 ....97 G6
Western Avenue Business
Park
ACT W3 ....98 D3
Western International
Market
NWDGN UB2 ....114 A4

Western Trading Estate
  WLSDN NW10 ....98 E3
West Ewell Infant School
  HOR/WEW KT19 ....207 F3
Westfields Primary School
  BARN SW13 ....138 C3
Westgate Business Centre
  NKENS W10 ....100 C3
Westgate Primary School
  DART DA1 ....171 G2
West Green Primary School
  SEVS/STOTM N15 ....67 J1
West Grove Primary School
  STHGT/OAK N14 ....34 D2
West Ham Church Primary
  School
  SRTFD E15 ....88 D6
West Ham Lane Clinic
  SRTFD E15 ....88 C6
West Hampstead Clinic
  KIL/WHAMP NW6 ....82 E5
West Ham United FC
  (Upton Park)
  PLSTW E13 ....107 H1
West Hatch High School
  WFD IG8 ....53 K1
West Hendon Clinic
  CDALE/KGS NW9 ....63 H3
West Hill Primary School
  DART DA1 ....171 F1
  WAND/EARL SW18 ....139 K6
West India Pier
  POP/IOD E14 ....124 C2
West India Shopping
  Centre
  POP/IOD E14 ....124 D1
Westland Heliport
  BTSEA SW11 ....140 C4
West Lea School
  ED N9 ....36 A5
West Lodge Park Hotel
  EBAR EN4 ....21 K1
West Lodge Preparatory
  School
  BFN/LL DA15 ....168 A5
West Lodge Primary School
  PIN HA5 ....59 H1
West London Academy
  NTHLT UB5 ....77 H6
West London Academy
  Primary
  NTHLT UB5 ....77 H5
West London County Court
  WKENS W14 ....119 H4
West London Magistrates
  Court
  HMSMTH W6 ....119 G5
West London Tamil School
  WLSDN NW10 ....99 H1
West Mead Clinic
  RSLP HA4 ....77 G1
West Middlesex Golf Club
  STHL UB1 ....96 C6
West Middlesex University
  Hospital
  ISLW TW7 ....136 B3
Westminster Abbey
  WEST SW1P 16 E4
Westminster Abbey Choir
  School
  WEST SW1P 16 D4
Westminster Business Square
  LBTH SE11 ....122 A5
Westminster Cathedral
  WESTW SW1E 16 A5
Westminster Cathedral Choir
  School
  WEST SW1P 16 B5
Westminster Cathedral RC
  Primary School
  PIM SW1V 121 J5
Westminster City Hall
  WESTW SW1E 16 B4
Westminster City School
  WESTW SW1E 16 B4
Westminster College
  SOHO/CST W1F 10 B5
Westminster Hall
  WHALL SW1A 17 F3
Westminster Industrial Estate
  WOOL/PLUM SE18 ....126 C3
Westminster Kingsway
  College
  CAMTN NW1 ....4 A5
  WEST SW1P 16 B6
Westminster Natural Health
  Centre
  PIM SW1V 16 A7
Westminster Pier
  WHALL SW1A 17 F3
Westminster School
  WEST SW1P 16 E4
Westminster Theatre
  WESTW SW1E 16 A4
Westminster Under School
  WEST SW1P 16 C7
Westmoor Community Clinic
  PUT/ROE SW15 ....158 D2
West Norwood Clinic
  WNWD SE27 ....162 D4
West Norwood Crematorium
  WNWD SE27 ....162 D5
West One Shopping Centre
  MYFR/PKLN W1K 9 H4
Weston Green School
  THDIT KT7 ....189 K5
Weston Park Clinic
  CEND/HSY/T N8 ....66 E2
Weston Park Primary School
  CEND/HSY/T N8 ....67 F2
Westpoint Trading Estate
  ACT W3 ....98 D4
West Ramp Coach Park
  HTHAIR TW6 ....132 D2
West Ruislip Elementary
  School
  HGDN/ICK UB10 ....76 A1

West 12 Shopping & Leisure
  Centre
  SHB W12 ....119 G2
West Thames College
  ISLW TW7 ....135 K2
West Thamesmead Business
  Park
  THMD SE28 ....128 A3
West Thornton Primary
  School
  CROY/NA CRO 196 A4
West Twyford Primary School
  WLSDN NW10 ....98 C1
Westward Preparatory
  School
  WOT/HER KT12 ....188 A6
Westway Business Centre
  BAY/PAD W2 ....101 F4
Westway Sports Centre
  NKENS W10 ....100 B5
West Wickham Swimming
  Baths
  WWKM BR4 ....199 F5
West Wimbledon Primary
  School
  RYNPK SW20 ....176 E6
Westwood College
  WELL DA16 ....147 J5
Westwood Language College
  for Girls
  NRWD SE19 ....180 D3
Westwood Primary School
  WELL DA16 ....147 K5
Westwood School
  BUSH WD23 ....28 D4
Wetherby Preparatory
  School
  NTGHL W11 ....100 E6
Wetherby Pre-Preparatory
  School
  BAY/PAD W2 ....100 E6
Whaddon House Clinic
  CMBW SE5 ....143 F1
Whipps Cross Hospital
  WAN E11 ....70 E3
White Bridge Primary School
  LOU IG10 ....39 J2
Whitechapel Art Gallery
  WCHPL E1 ....13 K3
Whitechapel Sports Centre
  WCHPL E1 ....104 C4
Whitefield School
  CRICK NW2 ....64 D1
Whitefield School & Leisure
  Centre
  WALTH E17 ....52 B4
Whitefriars First & Middle
  School
  KTN/HRWW/WS HA3 ....42 E5
Whitefriars Trading Estate
  KTN/HRWW/WS HA3 ....42 D5
Whitehall Primary School
  CHING E4 ....38 C4
Whitehall Theatre
  WHALL SW1A 10 D7
White Hart Lane School
  WDGN N22 ....49 H3
Whiteheath Junior School
  RSLP HA4 ....58 A3
Whitehorse Manor Primary
  School
  THHTH CR7 ....196 E2
The White House Preparatory
  School
  BAL SW12 ....161 J3
Whitelands College
  PUT/ROE SW15 ....158 C2
Whiteleys Shopping Centre
  BAY/PAD W2 ....101 F5
Whiterose Trading Estate
  EBAR EN4 ....33 J2
Whitgift Almshouses
  CROY/NA CRO 196 D6
Whitgift School
  SAND/SEL CR2 ....211 J3
Whitgift Shopping Centre
  CROY/NA CRO 196 D6
Whitings Hill Primary
  School
  BAR EN5 ....20 A6
Whitmore High School
  RYLN/HDSTN HA2 ....60 C5
Whitmore Primary School
  IS N1 ....7 F2
Whittingham Community
  Primary School
  WALTH E17 ....51 G4
Whittington Hospital
  ARCH N19 ....66 B6
Whitton Health Centre
  WHTN TW2 ....155 H3
Whitton Health Clinic
  WHTN TW2 ....155 G3
Whitton School
  WHTN TW2 ....155 H3
Whitton Sports & Fitness
  Centre
  WHTN TW2 ....155 G4
Whybridge Infant School
  RAIN RM13 ....93 J6
Whybridge Junior School
  RAIN RM13 ....93 H6
Wickham Court School
  WWKM BR4 ....214 B2
Wickham Theatre
  WWKM BR4 ....214 B1
Wide Way Health Clinic
  MTCM CR4 ....179 J6
Widmore Centre
  BMLY BR1 ....184 B5
Wigmore Hall
  CAVSQ/HST W1G 9 J3
Wigram House (University of
  Westminster)
  WEST SW1P 16 C5
Wilberforce Primary School
  NKENS W10 ....100 A1

Wilbury Primary School
  UED N18 ....49 K1
Willesden Centre for Health
  & Care
  WLSDN NW10 ....81 J5
Willesden County Court
  WLSDN NW10 ....99 G1
Willesden Medical Centre
  CRICK NW2 ....81 K4
Willesden Sports Centre
  WLSDN NW10 ....81 K6
Willesden Sports Stadium
  WLSDN NW10 ....81 K6
William Bellamy J & I School
  DAGE RM10 ....74 C6
William Byrd School
  HYS/HAR UB3 ....113 F6
William C Harvey Special
  School
  TOTM N17 ....49 K6
William Davies Primary
  School
  FSTGT E7 ....89 H4
William Ellis School
  KTTN NW5 ....84 A1
William Ellis Sports Ground
  EDGW HA8 ....44 C4
William Ford CE Junior School
  DAGE RM10 ....92 C5
William Hogarth School
  CHSWK W4 ....118 B6
William Morris Academy
  HMSMTH W6 ....119 G5
William Morris Gallery
  WALTH E17 ....51 J6
William Morris Primary
  School
  MTCM CR4 ....179 J6
William Morris School
  WALTH E17 ....51 G4
William Patten Primary
  School
  STNW/STAM N16 ....68 B6
William Torbitt J & I School
  GNTH/NBYPK IG2 ....72 E2
William Tyndale Primary
  School
  IS N1 ....85 H5
Willington School
  WIM/MER SW19 ....177 J2
Willow Business Centre
  MTCM CR4 ....194 E2
Willow Business Park
  SYD SE26 ....163 K5
Willowfield Adult Education
  Centre
  WALTH E17 ....51 F6
Willowfield School
  HNHL SE24 ....142 D5
  WALTH E17 ....51 G6
The Willows Clinic
  CHST BR7 ....185 F2
The Willows School
  YEAD UB4 ....95 H3
Willow Tree Primary School
  NTHLT UB5 ....77 J4
Wilmington Boys Grammar
  School
  RDART DA2 ....170 E5
Wilmington Grammar School
  for Girls
  RDART DA2 ....170 E4
Wilmington Hall School
  RDART DA2 ....170 D5
Wilmington Primary School
  RDART DA2 ....170 E5
Wilson's School
  WLGTN SM6 ....210 E4
Wimbledon Chase Primary
  School
  RYNPK SW20 ....177 H4
Wimbledon Common
  Golf Club
  WIM/MER SW19 ....176 E1
Wimbledon Common
  Pre-Preparatory School
  WIM/MER SW19 ....177 F2
Wimbledon (Gap Road)
  Cemetery
  WIM/MER SW19 ....160 A6
Wimbledon High School
  WIM/MER SW19 ....177 H2
Wimbledon House School
  WIM/MER SW19 ....177 J4
Wimbledon Lawn Tennis
  Museum
  WIM/MER SW19 ....159 H5
Wimbledon Magistrates
  Court
  WIM/MER SW19 ....177 K2
Wimbledon Park Athletics
  Track
  WIM/MER SW19 ....159 J4
Wimbledon Park Golf Club
  WIM/MER SW19 ....159 J5
Wimbledon Park Primary
  School
  WIM/MER SW19 ....159 K4
Wimbledon Recreation
  Centre
  WIM/MER SW19 ....178 A2
Wimbledon RFC
  RYNPK SW20 ....176 C3
Wimbledon School of Art
  WIM/MER SW19 ....177 H4
  WIM/MER SW19 ....177 J4
Wimbledon Stadium
  WIM/MER SW19 ....160 A6
Wimbledon Stadium Business
  Centre
  WIM/MER SW19 ....160 A5
Wimbledon Theatre
  WIM/MER SW19 ....177 J3
Winchcombe Business Centre
  PECK SE15 ....123 F6
Winchmore Hill Clinic
  WCHMH N21 ....35 H3

Winchmore Hill CC
  WCHMH N21 ....35 J5
Winchmore School
  WCHMH N21 ....35 J4
Windmill Business Centre
  NWDGN UB2 ....115 H1
Windmill School
  BRXS/STRHM SW2 ....161 K1
Windmill Trading Estate
  MTCM CR4 ....195 H6
Windrush Primary School
  THMD SE28 ....128 C1
Winfield House
  CAMTN NW1 ....2 C3
Wingate & Finchley FC
  NFNCH/WDSPK N12 ....47 H3
Wingate Trading Estate
  TOTM N17 ....50 B3
Wingfield Primary School
  BKHTH/KID SE3 ....145 K4
Winns Primary School
  WALTH E17 ....51 H5
Winsor Primary School
  EHAM E6 ....108 A5
Winston Churchill's Britain
  at War Experience
  STHWK SE1 ....19 F1
Winterbourne Infant School
  THHTH CR7 ....196 B1
Winton Primary School
  IS N1 ....5 H2
Witley Industrial Estate
  NWDGN UB2 ....114 E4
Wolf Fields Primary School
  NWDGN UB2 ....114 E4
Wolfson Hillel Primary
  School
  STHGT/OAK N14 ....34 D1
Wolfson Medical Centre
  RYNPK SW20 ....176 D3
Wolsey Business Park
  WATW WD18 ....26 B2
Wolsey Junior School
  CROY/NA CRO 214 B5
The Women's Library
  WCHPL E1 ....13 J3
The Woodberry Clinic
  MUSWH N10 ....48 B6
Woodbridge High School &
  Language College
  WFD IG8 ....53 F3
Woodbrook School
  BECK BR3 ....182 A6
Woodbury Down Primary
  School
  FSBYPK N4 ....67 J4
Woodcroft Primary School
  EDGW HA8 ....45 F3
Wood End J & I Schools
  GFD/PVL UB6 ....78 D3
Wood End Park Junior
  School
  UX/CGN UB8 ....94 A6
Woodfield School
  CDALE/KGS NW9 ....63 G5
Woodford County High
  School for Girls
  WFD IG8 ....52 D2
Woodford Golf Club
  WFD IG8 ....52 D1
Woodford Green Preparatory
  School
  WFD IG8 ....52 E2
Woodford Green Primary
  School
  WFD IG8 ....52 D1
Woodford Trading Estate
  WFD IG8 ....53 C5
Woodgrange Infant School
  FSTGT E7 ....89 F2
Woodgrange Park
  Cemetery
  MNPK E12 ....89 H3
Wood Green Crown Court
  WDGN N22 ....49 G4
Wood Green Health Centre
  WDGN N22 ....49 F4
Wood Green Old Boys FC
  WDGN N22 ....49 G5
Woodhall School
  OXHEY WD19 ....27 J6
Woodhill Primary School
  CHARL SE7 ....126 D4
Woodhouse College
  NFNCH/WDSPK N12 ....47 H2
Woodlands F & M School
  KTN/HRWW/WS HA3 ....42 C3
Woodlands J & I School
  IL IG1 ....90 D2
Woodlands Medical Centre
  LEW SE13 ....165 G1
Wood Lane Medical Centre
  RSLP HA4 ....58 C5
Wood Lane School
  FUL/PGN SW6 ....140 B2
Wood Lane Sports Centre
  BCTR RM8 ....74 D5
Woodmansterne Primary
  School
  STRHM/NOR SW16 ....179 J4
Woodridge Primary
  School
  NFNCH/WDSPK N12 ....32 E5
Woodside Health Centre
  SNWD SE25 ....197 J2
Woodside Infant School
  CROY/NA CRO 197 H4
Woodside Junior School
  WALTH E17 ....52 A6
Woodside Park Golf Club
  NFNCH/WDSPK N12 ....32 E6
Woodside Park International
  School
  FBAR/BDGN N11 ....47 K1
  NFNCH/WDSPK N12 ....33 F6
Woodside School
  BELV DA17 ....129 J4

Wood Wharf
  POP/IOD E14 ....124 E1
Wood Wharf Business Park
  POP/IOD E14 ....125 F2
Woolmore Primary School
  POP/IOD E14 ....106 A6
Woolwich County Court
  WOOL/PLUM SE18 ....127 F3
Woolwich Crown Court
  THMD SE28 ....127 K2
Woolwich Polytechnic
  School
  THMD SE28 ....128 B1
Worcesters Primary School
  ENC/FH EN2 ....24 B1
World Business Centre
  Heathrow
  HTHAIR TW6 ....133 F2
Worlds End Place
  WBPTN SW10 ....140 B1
World Spiritual University
  WLSDN NW10 ....81 J5
World University Service
  STLK EC1Y 6 E7
Wormholt Park Primary
  School
  SHB W12 ....99 J6
Worple Primary School
  ISLW TW7 ....136 B5
Worsley Bridge Junior
  School
  BECK BR3 ....182 D3
Worton Hall Industrial Estate
  ISLW TW7 ....135 K5
Wrencote
  CROY/NA CRO 211 J1
Wyborne Primary School
  ELTH/MOT SE9 ....167 G3
Wyke Green Golf Club
  ISLW TW7 ....116 A6
Wykeham Primary School
  KCH RM12 ....75 J5
  WLSDN NW10 ....81 F1
Wyndhams Theatre
  CHCR WC2N 10 D5
Wyvil Primary School
  VX/NE SW8 ....141 K1
Yale University Press
  HAMP NW3 ....83 J2
Yardley Primary School
  CHING E4 ....37 K1
Yeading FC
  YEAD UB4 ....114 B1
Yeading Medical Centre
  NTHLT UB5 ....95 G2
Yeading Primary School
  YEAD UB4 ....95 G4
Yerbury Primary School
  ARCH N19 ....84 D1
Yeshivo Horomo Talmudical
  College
  STNW/STAM N16 ....67 K5
Yesodey Hatorah Jewish
  School
  STNW/STAM N16 ....68 A4
Yesodey Hatorah Senior
  Girls School
  STNW/STAM N16 ....68 B4
Yetev Lev Day School
  for Boys
  STNW/STAM N16 ....68 C5
Yiewsley Health Centre
  WDR/YW UB7 ....112 B1
YMCA Leisure Centre
  RSQ WC1B 10 D3
York Clinic
  STHWK SE1 ....18 E1
York Hall
  BETH E2 ....104 D1
York Rd Junior School &
  Language Unit
  DART DA1 ....171 J2
York Water Gate
  CHCR WC2N 11 F7
Young Actors Theatre
  IS N1 ....5 J1
Young Vic Theatre
  STHWK SE1 ....17 K2
Zennor Road Industrial
  Estate
  BAL SW12 ....161 H3
Zephyr Business Centre
  SEVS/STOTM N15 ....68 A1
Ziam Trading Estate
  CLPT E5 ....68 E5

Schools address data provided by Education Direct

Petrol station information supplied by Johnsons

One-way street data provided by © Tele Atlas N.V. Tele Atlas

Garden centre information provided by

Garden Centre Association Britains best garden centres

Wyevale Garden Centres

The boundary of the London congestion charging zone supplied by
Transport for London

The statement on the front cover of this atlas is sourced, selected and quoted
from a reader comment and feedback form received in 2004

How do I find the perfect place?

AA | **Street by Street** QUESTIONNAIRE

Dear Atlas User
Your comments, opinions and recommendations are very important to us.
So please help us to improve our street atlases by taking a few minutes
to complete this simple questionnaire.

You do not need a stamp (unless posted outside the UK). If you do not want to remove
this page from your street atlas, then photocopy it or write your answers on a plain sheet
of paper.

Send to: Marketing Assistant, AA Publishing, 14th Floor Fanum House,
FREEPOST SCE 4598, Basingstoke RG21 4GY

ABOUT THE ATLAS...

Please state which city / town / county street atlas you bought:

_____
_____

Where did you buy the atlas? (City, Town, County)

_____

For what purpose? (please tick all applicable)

To use in your own local area ☐   **To use on business or at work** ☐

Visiting a strange place ☐   **In the car** ☐   **On foot** ☐

Other (please state)

_____

Have you ever used any street atlases other than AA Street by Street?

Yes ☐   **No** ☐

If so, which ones?

_____

Is there any aspect of our street atlases that could be improved?
(Please continue on a separate sheet if necessary)

_____
_____
_____
_____

ML038w

continued overleaf

Please list the features you found most useful:

_____
_____
_____
_____

Please list the features you found least useful:

_____
_____
_____
_____

LOCAL KNOWLEDGE...

Local knowledge is invaluable. Whilst every attempt has been made to make the information contained in this atlas as accurate as possible, should you notice any inaccuracies, please detail them below (if necessary, use a blank piece of paper) or e-mail us at _streetbystreet@theAA.com_

_____
_____
_____

ABOUT YOU...

Name (Mr/Mrs/Ms) _____

Address _____

Postcode _____

Daytime tel no _____

E-mail address _____

Which age group are you in?

Under 25 ☐   **25-34** ☐   **35-44** ☐   **45-54** ☐   **55-64** ☐   **65+** ☐

Are you an AA member?   Yes ☐   No ☐

Do you have Internet access?   Yes ☐   No ☐

Thank you for taking the time to complete this questionnaire. Please send it to us as soon as possible, and remember, you do not need a stamp (unless posted outside the UK).

We may use information we hold about you to write to, telephone or email you about other products and services offered by the AA, we do NOT disclose this information to third parties.

Please tick here if you do not wish to hear about products and services from the AA. ☐